T&T Clark Companion to Atonement

Forthcoming titles in this series include:

T&T Clark Companion to Christian Prayer, edited by Ashley Cocksworth and John C. McDowell
T&T Clark Companion to Colin Gunton, edited by Myk Habets and Andrew Picard
T&T Clark Companion to de Lubac, edited by Jordan Hillebert
T&T Clark Companion to Pneumatology, edited by Daniel Castelo and Kenneth M. Loyer
T&T Clark Companion to Political Theology, edited by Ruben Rosario Rodriguez
T&T Clark Companion to Schillebeeckx, edited by Stephan van Erp
T&T Clark Companion to Thomas. F. Torrance, edited by Paul D. Molnar and Myk Habets
T&T Clark Companion to the Theology of Kierkegaard, edited by David J. Gouwens and Aaron Edwards

Titles already published include:
T&T Clark Companion to Atonement, edited by Adam J. Johnson
T&T Clark Companion to Augustine and Modern Theology, edited by C.C. Pecknold and Tarmo Toom
T&T Clark Companion to the Doctrine of Sin, edited by Keith L. Johnson and David Lauber
T&T Clark Companion Liturgy, edited by Alcuin Reid
T&T Clark Companion to Methodism, edited by Charles Yrigoyen Jr
T&T Clark Companion to Nonconformity, edited by Robert Pope
T&T Clark Companion to Reformation Theology, edited by David M, Whitford
T&T Clark Companion to the Septuagint, edited by James K. Aitken

T&T Clark Companion to Atonement

Edited by
Adam J. Johnson

t&tclark

LONDON • NEW YORK • OXFORD • NEW DELHI • SYDNEY

T&T CLARK
Bloomsbury Publishing Plc
50 Bedford Square, London, WC1B 3DP, UK
1385 Broadway, New York, NY 10018, USA
29 Earlsfort Terrace, Dublin 2, Ireland

BLOOMSBURY, T&T CLARK and the T&T Clark logo
are trademarks of Bloomsbury Publishing Plc

First published in Great Britain 2017
Paperback edition first published 2021

Copyright © Adam J. Johnson, 2017

Adam J. Johnson has asserted his right under the Copyright,
Designs and Patents Act, 1988, to be identified as Author of this work.

For legal purposes the Acknowledgements on p. xiii constitute
an extension of this copyright page.

Cover image © yamix / Shutterstock

All rights reserved. No part of this publication may be reproduced or
transmitted in any form or by any means, electronic or mechanical,
including photocopying, recording, or any information storage or retrieval
system, without prior permission in writing from the publishers.

Bloomsbury Publishing Plc does not have any control over, or responsibility for,
any third-party websites referred to or in this book. All internet addresses given
in this book were correct at the time of going to press. The author and publisher
regret any inconvenience caused if addresses have changed or sites have
ceased to exist, but can accept no responsibility for any such changes.

A catalogue record for this book is available from the British Library.

Library of Congress Cataloging-in-Publication Data
Names: Johnson, Adam J., editor.
Title: T & T Clark companion to atonement / edited by Adam J. Johnson.
Other titles: T and T Clark companion to atonement |
Companion to atonement Description: New York: Bloomsbury T&T Clark, 2017. |
Series: Bloomsbury companions; 5 |
Includes bibliographical references.
Identifiers: LCCN 2016053295 | ISBN 9780567565532 (hardback) |
ISBN 9780567677297 (epub)
Subjects: LCSH: Atonement. | BISAC: RELIGION / Theology. |
RELIGION / Christian Theology / Ecclesiology.
Classification: LCC BT265.3.T62 2017 | DDC 232/.3–dc23
LC record available at https://lccn.loc.gov/2016053295

ISBN: HB: 978-0-5675-6553-2
PB: 978-0-5677-0111-4
ePDF: 978-0-5676-7728-0
eBook: 978-0-5676-7729-7

Typeset by Newgen Knowledge Works Pvt Ltd., Chennai, India

To find out more about our authors and books visit
www.bloomsbury.com and sign up for our newsletters.

We dedicate this book to the contributors of this volume who went to be with the Lord prior to its completion. While more qualified than ever as saints and theologians, they lack (for the time being) the ability to share with us the fruits of their vision.
Ralph Del Colle
I. Howard Marshall
Edward T. Oakes
John Webster

Contents

Preface		xii
Acknowledgments		xiii
1	Atonement: The Shape and State of the Doctrine *Adam J. Johnson*	1
2	These Three Atone: Trinity and Atonement *Fred Sanders*	19
3	Atonement and Incarnation *Ivor J. Davidson*	35
4	Resurrection and Atonement in the Theology of Thomas F. Torrance *Paul D. Molnar*	57
5	The Atonement and the Holy Spirit *Christopher R. J. Holmes*	77
6	God's Reconciling Work: Atonement in the Old Testament *Stephen B. Chapman*	95
7	Theologies of the Atonement in the New Testament *Joel B. Green*	115
8	Athanasius's Incarnational Soteriology *Thomas G. Weinandy*	135
9	St. Gregory of Nyssa on the Dynamics of Salvation *John A. McGuckin*	155
10	Anselmian Atonement *Katherine Sonderegger*	175
11	Thomas Aquinas's Pauline Theology of the Atonement *Charles Raith II*	195
12	The Fury of Love: Calvin on the Atonement *Paul Dafydd Jones*	213
13	Karl Barth *Shannon Nicole Smythe*	237
14	Christ's Descent into Hell *Rodney Howsare*	257
15	The Persistence of the Ransom Theory of the Atonement *Adam Kotsko*	277
16	Penal Substitution *Stephen R. Holmes*	295

17 Methodological Issues in Approaching the Atonement *Oliver D. Crisp* 315

18 Crucified—So What? Feminist Rereadings of the
    Cross-Event *Arnfríður Guðmundsdóttir* 335

Essays 355

19 Peter Abelard *Adam J. Johnson* 357

20 Acts (Book of) *I. Howard Marshall* 361

21 Angels *Adam J. Johnson* 365

22 The Apostolic Fathers *Harry O. Maier* 371

23 Ascension *Andrew Burgess* 377

24 Augustine *David Vincent Meconi* 381

25 Gustaf Aulén *Roland Spjuth* 389

26 Baptism *W. Travis McMaken* 393

27 Bernard of Clairvaux *Anthony N. S. Lane* 399

28 Blood *Eugene F. Rogers, Jr.* 403

29 Bonaventure *Andrew B. Salzmann* 407

30 Book of the Twelve *Don Collett* 411

31 Rudolf Bultmann *David W. Congdon* 417

32 John McLeod Campbell *Peter K. Stevenson* 421

33 Catherine of Siena *Adam Eitel* 427

34 Covenant *Jeremy R. Treat* 431

35 Thomas Cranmer *Scott Harrower* 437

36 Creation and Animals *David L. Clough* 441

37 Creeds *Ashley Cocksworth* 447

38 Culture *Paul Louis Metzger* 451

39 Cyril of Alexandria *Donald Fairbairn* 457

40	Ecclesiology *Joseph Mangina*	461
41	Jonathan Edwards *Garry J. Williams*	467
42	Eschatology *Graham A. Cole*	473
43	Eucharist *Scott Harrower*	479
44	Exemplarism *Adam Kotsko*	485
45	Expiation/Propitiation *Graham A. Cole*	489
46	Forgiveness *Cynthia L. Rigby*	493
47	P. T. Forsyth *Jason A. Goroncy*	499
48	René Girard *Adam J. Johnson*	505
49	Global Theology *Mark D. Baker*	509
50	Gospel of John *Edward W. Klink III*	515
51	Hugo Grotius *Gert van den Brink*	523
52	Colin Gunton *Andrew C. Picard*	527
53	Hebrews *David M. Moffitt*	533
54	Hegel and Baur *Peter C. Hodgson*	537
55	The Historical Books *Richard S. Briggs*	543
56	Ignatius of Antioch *Harry O. Maier*	547
57	Imagination *Trevor A. Hart*	551
58	*Imago Dei* *Ryan S. Peterson*	557
59	Impassibility (Divine) *Daniel Castelo*	563
60	Irenaeus of Lyons *John Behr*	569
61	Letter of James *Robert W. Wall*	577
62	John's Letters *Matthew D. Jensen*	581
63	Justification *Alan Spence*	585
64	Kant *Nathan A. Jacobs*	591

65	Kierkegaard *Murray Rae*	597
66	Kingdom of God *Cynthia L. Rigby*	601
67	Liberation Theology *Jules A. Martinez Olivieri*	605
68	Peter Lombard *G. R. Evans*	609
69	Martin Luther *Robert A. Kolb*	613
70	Major Prophets *Mark S. Gignilliat*	623
71	Matthew and Mark *Jonathan T. Pennington*	631
72	Ministry *Andrew Root*	639
73	The Missions of the Divine Persons *Adonis Vidu*	645
74	Jürgen Moltmann *Matthias Grebe*	651
75	*Munus Triplex* *Adam J. Johnson*	655
76	John Owen *Kelly M. Kapic*	659
77	Wolfhart Pannenberg *Kent Eilers*	665
78	The Apostle Paul *Timothy G. Gombis*	669
79	Pentateuch *T. Desmond Alexander*	677
80	1–2 Peter *David R. Nienhuis*	685
81	Politics *Peter J. Leithart*	689
82	Post-Reformation Dogmatics *Brannon Ellis*	693
83	Prayer *Ashley Cocksworth*	701
84	The Problem of Evil *Matthias Grebe*	707
85	Reconciliation *Thomas Andrew Bennett*	713
86	Revelation (Book of) *Joseph Mangina*	719
87	Albrecht Ritschl *Matthew J. Aragon Bruce*	723
88	Salvation in Christ Alone *Veli-Matti Kärkkäinen*	729
89	Sanctification *Ben Rhodes*	733

90 Friedrich Schleiermacher *Justin Stratis*	739
91 John Duns Scotus *Thomas M. Ward*	743
92 Sin *Adam Neder*	749
93 Socinus *Alan W. Gomes*	753
94 Hugh of St. Victor *G. R. Evans*	759
95 Substitution and Representation *Jeannine Michele Graham*	763
96 Supra/infralapsarianism *Edwin Chr. van Driel*	769
97 Theological Interpretation of Scripture *Scott R. Swain*	775
98 Union with Christ *Mark A. Garcia*	781
99 Universalism *Tom Greggs*	787
100 Violence *Adam J. Johnson*	791
101 Wesleyan Theologies *Thomas H. McCall*	797
102 Wisdom Books (Old Testament) *Craig G. Bartholomew*	801
103 Wrath *Jeremy J. Wynne*	807
List of Contributors	813
Author/Person Index	821
Scripture Index	831
Subject Index	847

Preface

This *Companion* seeks to contribute to the renewal and development of the doctrine of the atonement. Negatively, it seeks to move beyond commonly held assumptions about the mutually exclusive nature of theories of the atonement and simplistic views of the history of the doctrine (in which there were three main types of theories throughout the history of the church). Positively, it seeks to offer an expansive view of the doctrine, rooted in and contributing to further developments in doctrinal, biblical, and historical studies. If there is an emphasis within the volume, it lies in paying particular attention to the doctrinal intersections so vital to a full understanding of the atonement.

Given this aim, the various chapters seek to model future work on the doctrine, equipping the reader for this work. While the various authors do not all agree, and their positions will at times be at odds, the underlying vision for a more biblically, historically, and theologically expansive understanding of the work of Christ is largely shared, as is the desire to provide the reader with those resources necessary for this task. For this reason, the contributors have been asked to equip, more than summarize. Space constraints and the scope of the vision make it nearly impossible for any of the following essays to offer a complete overview of their respective topics.

Likewise, space constraints prohibit the inclusion of a wide variety of topics and figures relevant to the atonement.[1] The goal is to provide an example through the selection of key topics and figures, giving the reader those concepts, definitions, context, and sources (primary or secondary) which will be most helpful in contributing to further research, either in the topics covered in this book, or others which by necessity or oversight have been omitted.

In short, the contributors to this volume hope that this book will furnish the church with the tools and example it needs to join us in this ongoing task. While there is a time and place for definitive and binding statements, comprehensive summaries, and decisive conclusions, this book aims rather to reinvigorate and redirect studies within this doctrine, for the sake of its growth and development in the years to come.

---

1 So many of the mystic theologians (such as Julian of Norwich and John of the Cross), poets (particularly those of the Anglican tradition, such as Herbert and Donne), post-Reformation Lutherans and Catholics, non-Western Christian traditions (Arab Christians such as Theodore Abūl Qurrah, or Indian Christians), biblical scholars of the past few centuries... the list of omissions is vast as to be discouraging.

Acknowledgments

Acknowledging those who played a formative role in the making of this volume would include the reduplication of the list of contributors—for the contributors of this volume have been a constant source of assistance for which I am very grateful. My goal in editing this volume was to have such a resource on my shelf, and I am exceptionally thankful for the work the contributors have done to make this possible.

A handful of friends and colleagues lent a particularly helpful hand, making key recommendations for entries and contributors, without which the volume would have been significantly impoverished. Among these are Michael Allen, Scott Harrower, Matt Jenson, Ryan Peterson, Ben Rhodes, Fred Sanders, and Ben Sutton.

This volume in particular calls for the acknowledgment of Thomas Kraft and Anna Turton, who trusted me with this project. I never would have pursued such a daunting task without their trust and wisdom. I remember with great fondness my conversation with Thomas in a Starbucks in San Francisco as we first discussed this project. As I walked away from that meeting, I felt as though the keys to the kingdom had been handed to me, laughing out loud as I sauntered down the street—what better place for such behavior than San Francisco?

Biola University and the Torrey Honors Institute have helped me greatly to bring this project to completion through course releases and, above all, their support of my research assistant, Rachael Smith, who is as efficient as a small and well-trained army of editors. Additional thanks go to Daniel Chrosniak, Garrett Eaglin, Hannah Grady and Micah Hogan, who stepped in at the eleventh hour to help complete the biblical index.

As with all my work, I did not do this alone: my time is my family's time, and my labor is theirs. I thank my wife, Katrina, and our sons, Reuben, Nathan, and Simeon, for the opportunity and motivation to work on this book.

1

Atonement: The Shape and State of the Doctrine

Adam J. Johnson

The doctrine of the atonement is the church's act of worship, an act of faith seeking to understand and expound the manifold ways in which the whole life, death and resurrection of Jesus Christ, the incarnate Son of God and Messiah of Israel, was the chosen and effective means of the triune God to bring about the reconciliation and fulfillment of all things which God had made (in heaven, earth and below the earth) through a restored relation to himself, veiled now and made fully manifest in the Eschaton.

The goal of this doctrine is to understand and expound: the sanctified intellect's joyful act of worship,[1] as the church and its members seek to understand the God who revealed himself in his saving act, by means of God's chosen witness to that act, Holy Scripture.[2] Developing this doctrine is thus first and foremost an act of submission, of learning, recognizing, and understanding the witness we have received, for its origin lies in the decision and act of God, who does not merely seek to save his creatures, but to be known and worshipped by them as he is, as the Savior.

Only in a secondary and derivative way does the doctrine of the atonement dwell upon and respond to the challenges and heresies of its day. Biblical, theological, philosophical, religious, ethical, and other critiques have their vital role to play in the development and formation of doctrine (not least in holding it accountable to its true vocation). But as the church's calling and freedom to

---

[1] John Webster, *Holiness* (London: SCM, 2003), 8–12.
[2] Ibid., 17–21.

develop doctrine stems from the being and act of God, such critiques and questions play at most a significant ministerial role in holding the church accountable to its primary calling: joyful and rigorous reflection upon and development of the scriptural testimony to the saving work of the Lord Jesus. This is all the more true, given that the church's primary end endures beyond all conflict and error, joining the angels in their never-ending privilege of worship, singing "blessed is the lamb who was slain" (Rev. 5:12) in ever new stanzas and choruses (Ps. 96:1).

But this call to worship is a great and demanding task, for Christ's work is a complex and multidimensional act by an equally complex agent[3]—the work of the triune God in the incarnate Son, Jesus Christ, the promised Messiah of Israel. In this most central event in the history of creation, Father, Son, and Holy Spirit employ the ever-abundant resources of the divine life for our sakes, each divine person of the one Godhead fully active in this life and work of the eternal Son born of Jewish flesh.[4] Above all it is the presence and activity of this God which gives the life and work of the man Jesus its abundant meaning, for by making himself the means of our salvation, God has enacted the simple yet abundant riches of the divine life for our salvation,[5] such that it is the meaning and significance of the divine life itself which is the source, means, and end of salvation.[6] God, who is the source, means, and end of creation, is likewise the one from whom, by whom, and for whom our salvation derives (Col. 1:16–20;

---

[3] Appreciation of this complexity, while common prior to Enlightenment, has waxed and waned in the centuries since. It has been fairly commonplace in the previous century to assume three main views of the atonement (*Christus victor*, satisfaction/penal substitution, and exemplarism), in part due to the influence of Gustaf Aulén, *Christus Victor: An Historical Study of the Three Main Types of the Idea of Atonement*, trans. A. G. Hebert (New York: Macmillan, 1951). The movement in recent years has been toward a more expansive understanding of the work of Christ, for biblical, theological, and historical reasons. Cf. John McIntyre, *The Shape of Soteriology: Studies in the Doctrine of the Death of Christ* (Edinburgh: T & T Clark, 1992); Scot McKnight, *A Community Called Atonement* (Nashville, TN: Abingdon Press, 2007); Adam Johnson, *Atonement: A Guide for the Perplexed* (New York: T & T Clark, 2015).

[4] Cf. Robert Sherman, *King, Priest and Prophet: A Trinitarian Theology of Atonement* (Edinburgh: T & T Clark, 2004); Thomas H. McCall, *Forsaken: The Trinity and the Cross, and Why It Matters* (Downers Grove, IL: IVP Academic, 2012); Johnson, *Atonement: A Guide for the Perplexed*; Bruce L. McCormack, "The Ontological Presuppositions of Barth's Doctrine of the Atonement," in *The Glory of the Atonement: Biblical, Historical and Practical Perspectives*, ed. Roger J. Nicole, Charles E. Hill, and Frank A. James (Downers Grove, IL: InterVarsity Press, 2004).

[5] Cf. Johnson, *Atonement: A Guide for the Perplexed*; Stephen R. Holmes, "A Simple Salvation? Soteriology and the Perfections of God," in *God of Salvation*, ed. Ivor J. Davidson and Murray A. Rae (Burlington, VT: Ashgate, 2011).

[6] McCall, *Forsaken*; John Webster, "'It Was the Will of the Lord to Bruise Him': Soteriology and the Doctrine of God," in *God of Salvation*, ed. Ivor J. Davidson and Murray A. Rae (Burlington, VT: Ashgate, 2011); Holmes, "A Simple Salvation? Soteriology and the Perfections of God"; Adonis Vidu, *Atonement, Law, and Justice: The Cross in Historical and Cultural Contexts* (Grand Rapids, MI: Baker Academic, 2014); Johnson, *Atonement: A Guide for the Perplexed*; McCormack, "Ontological Presuppositions"; Keith Johnson, "Penal Substitution as an Undivided Work of the Triune God," *Trinity Journal* 36 (2015).

Heb. 2:10). At every point Christ's work derives its nature and character from the heart and will of the triune God, particularly the doctrines of the Trinity, divine attributes, and election.

But at the same time this act of God takes up within it the significance with which God has freely endowed his creation, particularly his covenantal partners, humankind. As an Israelite, Jesus lives both a fully human life and a specifically Jewish one, participating in the history of God and his chosen people as the Messiah of his people and the rightful heir of the garden temple that was to be humankind's from the beginning.[7] Everything that it means for God to be God, and everything that it means for humankind to be God's unique and image-bearing creature in covenantal fellowship,[8] is at play in informing the complex event that is the life and work of Jesus Christ.[9]

This complexity on the part of the primary agent (both theologically and anthropologically) is fitted to the task at hand. The mission of Jesus involves overcoming the reality and consequences of sin while simultaneously bringing to completion God's creative purposes: a cosmic work of redemption, restoration, and fulfillment that includes individual guilt but far transcends it. The disarray of the heavenly powers (Eph. 6:12), and the groaning of the earth (Rom. 8:22), our burden of shame (Jer. 3:25), guilt (Is. 53:10), ignorance (Acts 17:30), and death (Rom. 5:12), the disastrous consequences of our misdirected worship (Rom. 1:18–32), the personal and social realities and consequences of our treason against God's kingdom (Amos 2:6–12), all these and more come to a head in the work of Christ, in whom God deals with them once and for all. But this negative dimension, which overcomes sin by bearing and doing away with it, is but the first movement of a far greater plan, wherein Christ recapitulates, or sums up and fulfills in himself the plan of God for his treasured creation.[10] It is in Christ that we find life as it was meant to be, properly ordered toward God and his purposes. It is in him that the Old Testament covenants and promises are fulfilled, that the plan for creation disdained by Adam and Eve is brought to

---

[7] G. K. Beale, *The Temple and the Church's Mission: A Biblical Theology of the Dwelling Place of God* (Downers Grove, IL: InterVarsity Press, 2004), 81–122, 313–334.
[8] Emphasis on the atonement as a covenantal reality is receiving renewed attention. R. Larry Shelton, *Cross and Covenant: Interpreting the Atonement for 21st Century Mission* (Tyrone, GA: Paternoster, 2006); Michael J. Gorman, *The Death of the Messiah and the Birth of the New Covenant: A (Not So) New Model of the Atonement* (Eugene: Cascade Books, 2014). See also the earlier work of Torrance and Barth in this regard, particularly the latter's *CD* IV/1.
[9] The life of Christ, according to the Bible, extends all the way back to the election of God to create (Col. 1:16), and all the way forward to future of Jesus's reign. While the focus is upon the life, death, and resurrection, the larger scope of the life of Jesus should not be ignored.
[10] Recapitulation, a hermeneutic approach to the work of Christ via the relation between the Old and New Testaments by Irenaeus, has gained increasing popularity in recent years.

its proper end. It is in and through him that creation is reordered, restored, and made "very good" (Gen. 1:31) once more, never again to be threatened.

A work of such proportions includes all the horror of the cross, while extending beyond it to the resurrection—the reestablishment of Christ (and in him, all creation) within the life and fellowship of God, seated at God's right hand (Acts 2:33). And from this central movement (from cross to the empty tomb) the work of Christ reaches out to encompass the whole life, ascension, and second coming of Christ.[11] For it is only by means of this whole life, willed and accomplished by the one God, Father, incarnate Son, and Holy Spirit,[12] that the fullness of sin could be overcome, and more importantly, that the whole of God's plan for creation could be completed by the same one who made it in the first place.[13] This is, after all, a work of at-one-ment: of making creation one with God, a oneness in the intimacy of relationship, in the fulfillment of God's purposes for his creatures, and a oneness impermeable to the threat of sin and death.[14] Nothing less than the whole work of Christ, centering on the death and resurrection, but extending far beyond it, could bring about such a comprehensive and multifaceted work of one-making.

The doctrine of the atonement aims at giving a complete and balanced account of the work of Christ, for it is within the context of the Creator making himself the means in Jesus Christ to realizing his sweeping creative purposes in the face of sin that more specific questions, controversies, and doctrinal development find their place. The alternative is disastrous, wherein near-sighted and myopic contemporary trends dictate the terms for theological discussion. As in building the soaring cathedrals of days gone by, only a proper foundation, structure, balance, and proportion within the doctrine will provide the architectural qualities necessary to accommodate the pressing concerns of the day,

---

[11] The following works have contributed greatly to our understanding of the ascension in the work of Christ: Douglas Farrow, *Ascension Theology* (London: T & T Clark, 2011); Andrew R. Burgess, *The Ascension in Karl Barth* (Burlington, VT: Ashgate, 2004); David M. Moffitt, *Atonement and the Logic of Resurrection in the Epistle to the Hebrews* (Boston: Brill, 2011).

[12] Whether the Father willed the death of Jesus is a subject of considerable debate in contemporary thought. For a recent contribution to this discussion, cf. Nicholas E. Lombardo, *The Father's Will: Christ's Crucifixion and the Goodness of God* (New York: Oxford, 2013).

[13] This relation between the creator and the recreator is one of the fundamental premises in: Athanasius, *On the Incarnation*, trans. John Behr (Yonkers, NY: St Vladimir's Seminary Press, 2011).

[14] This expansive view of the "one-ness" in at-one-ment is rooted in the oneness of unity of the divine life, which also characterizes the unity of God's purposes for his creatures. A view of at-one-ment focused simply on one-ness with God or neighbor is insufficient, regardless of its strengths. Another way of making this point is to put it in terms of satisfaction. The whole point of the doctrine of satisfaction is to satisfy God—but what satisfies him? Balanced accounts? Zero net gain in his creative enterprise? Not in the least—nothing but the fulfillment of God's purposes satisfies the creator God.

while making room for ongoing thought and worship in the years to come. While questions such as those regarding divine violence,[15] the role of metaphor,[16] the extent of the atonement,[17] and the viability of competing theories of the atonement are significant and warrant sustained reflection, it is only as we attend to the shape and trajectory of the whole of the doctrine of Christ's reconciling work that we are equipped to tap into the deepest resources for answering, reframing, or rejecting these questions.

Of course, we can think of doctrine in terms of a set of (formal or informal) topics under which we have a variety of relevant questions and answers.[18] Much better, however, to think of doctrine in terms of a structural entity. To build on the image of a cathedral, doctrine has its foundational features that support the whole edifice. Built upon this foundation are the walls and buttresses, which define the shape of the whole, sometimes apparently standing on their own, and in other instances working only in tension and harmony with other elements, as when the arches, columns, and domes work together to constitute the whole. But structure alone is insufficient, for it is the delightful sense of harmony and proportion that distinguishes a functional space from an architectural wonder fit to cultivate worship for centuries.

Polemic theology has its place, but at best it is a vital though limited and ultimately passing task of the church. Much more important is the emphasis upon the foundation, parts, relations, and proportions of the doctrine, which constitute the essential and proper task of theology: the work of the church knowing and worship its beginning and end, the triune God. It is precisely this emphasis upon the shape and structure of the atonement that provides that depth and

---

[15] Brad Jersak and Michael Hardin, eds., *Stricken by God? Nonviolent Identification and the Victory of Christ* (Grand Rapids, MI: Eerdmans, 2007); Marit Trelstad, "Introduction: The Cross in Context," in *Cross Examinations: Readings on the Meaning of the Cross Today*, ed. Marit Trelstad (Minneapolis: Fortress, 2006); J. Denny Weaver, *The Nonviolent Atonement* (Grand Rapids, MI: Eerdmans, 2001).

[16] Janet Martin Soskice, *The Kindness of God: Metaphor, Gender, and Religious Language* (Oxford: Oxford University Press, 2007); Hans Boersma, *Violence, Hospitality, and the Cross: Reappropriating the Atonement Tradition* (Grand Rapids, MI: Baker Academic, 2004); Colin E. Gunton, *The Actuality of Atonement: A Study of Metaphor, Rationality, and the Christian Tradition* (Grand Rapids, MI: Eerdmans, 1989); Mark D. Baker and Joel B. Green, *Recovering the Scandal of the Cross: Atonement in New Testament and Contemporary Contexts*, 2nd ed. (Downers Grove, IL: InterVarsity Press, 2003).

[17] Adam J. Johnson, ed., *5 Views on the Extent of the Atonement* (Grand Rapids, MI: Zondervan, 2018); David Gibson and Jonathan Gibson, eds., *From Heaven He Came and Sought Her: Definite Atonement in Historical, Biblical, Theological, and Pastoral Perspective* (Wheaton: Crossway, 2013).

[18] Such, for instance, is the scholastic approach of Thomas Aquinas in the *Summa Theologica*, following the pattern set by Lombard's *Sentences*. This method is perfectly acceptable, assuming that one has (like Thomas) a comprehensive understanding of the whole of the doctrine and its constituent parts, informing the selection and ordering of the questions one asks.

perspective which sustains the doctrine in the long run, while strengthening and honing its polemic fronts, whatever those may be at present and in the years to come.

The Shape of the Doctrine

What then is the shape of the doctrine of the atonement? How do we reach a sufficiently broad and rich understanding of this work? The first and basic move is to recognize that the atonement receives its shape first and foremost from the fact that the being, life, and will of God are constitutive for every element of the doctrine. It is the triune God, the maker of heaven and earth, who is active in Jesus Christ, and it his will and character which determines every step of the way, whether directly, as he himself is active in this work, or indirectly, as he is the source of all creation, and that which all creation either conforms to or rebels against. Atonement doctrine derives its shape, meaning, and significance from the prior and greater reality of the eternal life of God, revealed and enacted decisively in the life of Jesus Christ.

The internal dynamics of the life of the Father, Son, and Holy Spirit (such as the divine origins and *perichoresis*), the divine attributes (such as the divine love, patience, long-suffering, holiness, goodness, and righteousness), the history of God's self-involvement with creation and the people of Israel in terms of his laws, covenants, promises, self-giving, and self-naming, at every step it is the person and work of the triune God which implicitly and explicitly constitutes the essential premises, elements, and purposes of any explanation of Christ's work—for this is his work: his action, his creation, his purposes. Because it is *God's* work of reclaiming *God's* creation by means of *God's* own life and act, for the accomplishment of *God's* purposes, the shape of the doctrine of the atonement is essentially Trinitarian, marked off at every point by the being and act of the one God: Father, Son, and Holy Spirit.

Among God's works, the life of Christ—particularly his death and resurrection—is the central locus of divine self-revelation, which marks the great transition from promise to fulfillment, from the Abrahamic and Davidic Covenants to the New Covenant, with all the changes (and continuity) implicit therein. Far more than an event, or even an event in the divine life, this particular work stretches back into the eternity of the divine life, as the subject and object of divine election, and forward into eternity.[19] In thinking about the life

---

[19] Karl Barth's grasp of this, as seen in *CD* II/2, is unparalleled.

and work of Christ, we are delving into the heart of God and his concern for his creative enterprise, for there is no such thing as creation apart from the will and purposes of its maker, Jesus Christ (John 1:3; Col. 1:16–17). It is at this point, on this ground, that the "cathedral" of atonement doctrine is built—the work of Christ. So while the Trinity shapes every element, the life, death, resurrection, and ascension of Jesus is where that shaping occurs, with special emphasis upon the death and resurrection.

Five Key Elements

While the divine life and will unconditionally shape every aspect of the atonement, and the edifice of the doctrine rises from the ground charted by the life of Christ, there are five main components to any theory of the atonement which together, in their many interrelations, provide the basic features of this building. First are the *characters in this history*, this relationship. The triune God made man in Jesus Christ through the incarnation of the Son takes center stage, but along with him the whole of humanity (Jew and Gentile alike),[20] the angelic and demonic hosts,[21] and the full spectrum of the animal kingdom[22] all play their respective roles. Creation is the stage for covenant, for God's binding of himself in relationship to his creatures that he might share the divine life with them.[23] Accordingly, the creatures with whom God is in relationship provide the basic building blocks of this building—it is with them that the triune God is concerned.

How the relationships between these characters is construed, or how these building blocks are connected and related within the structure, is largely a matter of the second main component of any theory: *the divine attribute(s) it emphasizes*. Athanasius's incorruption, Anselm's honor, Barth's justice, Campbell's love, Forsyth's holiness, Schleiermacher's impassibility, each of these theologians emphasize a unique attribute of God (in the midst of a host of other attributes to which they might refer), to give character and definition to their account of the

---

[20] The former elected in him before the foundation of the world (Eph. 1:3–6), and the latter being incorporated through hearing and responding to the word of truth (Eph. 1:13–14). Cf. the similar argument concerning election and predestination in Paul's Epistle to the Romans.
[21] Adam Johnson, "Where Demons Fear to Tread: Venturing into an Obscure Corner of the Doctrine of the Atonement Concerning the Un-Fallen Angels," *Journal of Reformed Theology* 9, no. 1 (2015).
[22] David L. Clough, *On Animals: Volume 1: Systematic Theology* (London: T & T Clark, 2012).
[23] See Barth's development of creation as the external basis of the covenant and vice versa in *CD* III/1.

works of Christ. Theories of the atonement, in order to limit the scope of their work and focus the energy of their treatment, emphasize one divine attribute to develop the relationships between the characters in this drama—for while all the attributes are present and active in Christ, highlighting one or the other casts the whole scene in a very different light, drawing our attention to different aspects of our salvation in Christ.[24] Just as a building is formed not simply by its parts but by their relations, it is precisely the divine attributes that provide the resources for speaking of this range of relations.

The third component hinges upon the second, accounting for *the problem of sin* Christ overcomes in terms of the perversion of this attribute, guiding us into a deeper understanding of the reality and implications of a particular dimension of our rebellion against God's character and will. The tension supporting an arch likewise tears it apart—for the power of goodness, lacking the bounds which keeps it in check, is precisely the power that is so destructive and evil. That is, the same relations that explain the strength of the building account for its demise, when those relations are perverted either through lack of proportion, changing circumstances, or misuse. And the consequences, of course, are disastrous, whether in architecture, human relations, or doctrine. Just as our salvation is manifold, so is our dilemma, and one responsibility of the doctrine of the atonement is to honor the nature of this manifold dilemma, bringing such diverse issues as guilt, shame, demonic oppression, environmental crises, and systemic poverty under the scope of its inquiry. The work of Christ, after all, reconciles *all things*, all sin, all things currently opposing the will and purpose of God.

The final two dimensions consider how the work of Christ *saves us from* this reality of sin (primarily through his death), and how he *saves us for* a creaturely participation in the reality of the divine life (primarily through his resurrection). Christ came not merely to free us from bondage, or remove our sin and ignorance, but to clothe us in righteousness, and build us up into a holy temple (1 Pet. 2:5). Both elements are vital. On the one hand, there is the matrix of realities and consequences from which we are saved by the work of Christ. But just as we don't restore a building merely to remove rubble and hazardous conditions, so Christ came that he might bring this building to completion, to perfection. The work of Christ is fundamentally positive, constructive, and life-giving, though it contains within it an essentially negative, destructive, and deadly element.

---

[24] Johnson, *Atonement: A Guide for the Perplexed*.

Above all, Christ came that he might extend to the creature participation in the life and character of God, thereby restoring all relations, overcoming all sin, and bringing about our full salvation.

These five components ultimately entail the whole of Christian doctrine. I put them in this abbreviated form to give clarity and definition to our speech. While such abbreviation has its place, it must always serve the higher end of theology outlined already, encouraging reflection into the whole set of relations between the various Christian doctrines (creation, pneumatology, ecclesiology etc.) and their subtopics within the doctrine of the atonement. For the shape of the doctrine of the atonement is determined by the life of God and is ordered to the life of God—a doctrine that contains within itself the whole sweep of theology, as God takes up his creation by means of his own self-involvement, bringing it to fulfillment in and through himself. While these five components play an important heuristic role in thinking about the basic shape of the work of Christ, ultimately theology, like the God it serves, is one, and this unity must play itself out in sustained attention to the whole set of doctrinal interrelationships. Nowhere is this truer than the atonement, which every doctrine looks toward or builds from. When put this way, these five main parts of any atonement theory must be a vehicle toward a fuller understanding and exposition of this event, rather than a rigid construct hampering further exploration.

Theories of the Atonement

This brings us to how we are to understand the phrase "theory of atonement" in the first place—a phrase largely unique to the past two hundred years. Prior to that, theologians sought to explain the efficacy of the work of Christ by exploring the manifold reasons making Jesus's death and resurrection necessary or fitting.[25] Multiple explanations were a matter of course, given the complexity of the problem(s) to be overcome—more a matter of "let me count the ways" than boiling things down to one primary view. As part of the Enlightenment's influence, however, particularly in attempts to summarize and classify the history of doctrine, theories often came to be seen as unique and mutually exclusive explanations held by individual theologians and the churches or schools that

---

[25] See, for instance, the many explanations for Christ's death and resurrection in Athanasius's *On the Incarnation*, or Thomas's *ST* III.46–49.

followed them.²⁶ While this is not the place to offer a full critique of this unfortunate turn of events, it bears noting that this understanding of "theory" is (1) a late development in the history of doctrine, (2) subject to considerable criticism (and outright rejection), and (3) one that should not be presupposed without due theological warrant.

It is far more advisable to interpret theories as largely complementary expositions of the work of Christ. The key lies in the explanation of their diversity. If this is a matter of the cultural husk that came to surround (or contaminate) the gospel, or competing definitions of key concepts, then the differences will remain, and theories continue to vie for supremacy. If the diversity lies deeper still, however, if it lies in the different aspects of the divine character enacted for our salvation, the different dimensions of the plight of sin from which we are saved, and the complex nature of the life for which we are saved, then an altogether different understanding emerges. Different theories may be mutually complementary accounts of the work of Christ, exploring how his life, death, and resurrection were effective for us by means of emphasizing the role of different divine attributes in the work of Christ, the characters and forces involved, the sin they overcome, and the salvation they bring.²⁷ A diversity of theories is thus inherent in the saving action of the living God who in and of himself is diverse in the fullness of the divine attributes. While historical differences between theories remain, and biblical and theological disagreements remain, the diversity proper to the life of God as it is active in Christ demands a corresponding diversity in our explanations of how this work was effective.

The Future of the Doctrine

This vision of the doctrine calls for constructive theological work, furnished by biblical and historical retrieval.²⁸ That is to say, it calls for a move beyond the standard questions of the day, into fuller and richer explorations of the ways

---

[26] A case in point is the thought of Abelard, which the Enlightenment turned into an exemplarist theory, largely to serve its own purposes. Cf. Alister E. McGrath, "The Moral Theory of the Atonement: An Historical and Theological Critique," *Scottish Journal of Theology* 38, no. 2 (1985).

[27] While many theories in the course of the history of the church do in fact conflict with each other, this is a function of their respective development of different aspects of the work of Christ, and not ingredient in the simple fact that they are different theories.

[28] John B. Webster, "Theologies of Retrieval," in *The Oxford Handbook of Systematic Theology* (New York: Oxford, 2007).

that the atonement relates to the whole of Christian doctrine and its constituent parts, bringing new life and worship to the field. And while this is an inherently constructive project, the best tool for accomplishing it is biblical and historical retrieval. Biblical study is vital, for it is God's self-revelation through Scripture that is the basis for the theological task. Apart from this anchor and guide, there is little to distinguish theology from idle (though hopefully benevolent) speculation. At the same time, historical study is likewise vital, for it is the record of the church's interpretation of Scripture, providing us with nearly endless categories and possibilities that energize and rejuvenate the work of biblical studies. One of the best antidotes to the limitations of our culturally laden questions, concepts, and presuppositions is sustained interaction with equally limited questions, concepts, and presuppositions of other cultures, past and present.[29] Struggling to delve into our varied Christian heritage offers one of the most profitable sources for self-critique on the one hand, and new and creative avenues for exploration on the other, for these theologians' reading of Scripture (and the history of theology preceding them) is just as biased as our own, but biased in different ways.[30]

While some might caution that studying the works of others may encumber true genius with a spirit of subservience, the greatness of the church is of a lively submissive sort, steeped in the thought of others, and ultimately in the thought of God. It is no less great, noble, and creative for the fact that it is properly submissive to its Lord and the theological mothers and fathers that preceded it, for its goal is not novelty but deepened, enriched, and invigorated understanding of the ever-rich God. And just as our theological heritage consists of a fluid interplay of dogmatic, biblical, philosophical, historical, pastoral, and contemplative categories and methods, it is likewise the reintegration of these fields which will contribute to the rejuvenation of the doctrine of the atonement in the present day—an effort which will equip the church to address the polemic charges leveled against it, by means of its attention to the far greater task of worshipping the triune God who in Jesus Christ became man for our sake and for our salvation.

---

[29] A glaring weakness of this volume is the intentional omission of essays and chapters from current non-Western perspectives. A single chapter or essay on this topic, or even essays on "African" and "South American" perspectives, would be of little use—as though there is one "African" perspective on the matter! The present project is a theology of retrieval, which I hope to complement with an international project drawing on the insights of different contemporary cultures.

[30] This is essentially the argument of C. S. Lewis, in his introduction to Athanasius, *On the Incarnation*.

Constructive Developments

The good news is that such work is well under way. First, in terms of historical awareness within studies of the doctrine, there are good signs that Aulén's legacy is rapidly diminishing,[31] as increasing momentum builds toward the appreciation of the multiplicity of theories held throughout the history of the church. While one still finds many works that presuppose the "three main views of the atonement,"[32] this is becoming less and less common.[33] Historical accuracy is in and of itself sufficient reason to debunk this artificial categorization and limitation of atonement theories, but the bigger concern is that such a framework for interpreting the history of the doctrine hampers our appreciation of both the immense diversity and simultaneous homogeneity of views which are of significant value in their own right, and an invaluable resource toward renewed interpretation of Scripture.

Second, responsible historical work is impacting introductory or general works on the atonement. Irenaeus is perhaps at the forefront of the movement, as his thought has significantly influenced a number of contemporary works.[34] Significant work on Anselm[35] is on the cusp of reshaping the tiresome abuse of this thought in popular books. This is likewise true of Abelard, who is widely (and falsely) reputed to be the father of "exemplarist" theories of the atonement.[36] One

---

[31] The work of Aulén was necessary and helpful in his own context, but harmful to the doctrine in its impact on wider circles of thought.

[32] Cf. Thomas F. Torrance, *Atonement: The Person and Work of Christ* (Downers Grove, IL: InterVarsity Press, 2009); Sherman, *King, Priest and Prophet*; Daniel L. Migliore, *Faith Seeking Understanding: An Introduction to Christian Theology* (Grand Rapids, MI: Eerdmans, 2004); Gordon Graham, "Atonement," in *The Cambridge Companion to Christian Philosophical Theology*, ed. Charles Taliaferro and Chad V. Meister (New York: Cambridge University Press, 2010).

[33] Cf. McIntyre, *Soteriology*; Baker and Green, *Recovering*; Michael Horton, *The Christian Faith: A Systematic Theology for Pilgrims on the Way* (Grand Rapids, MI: Zondervan, 2011); McKnight, *Community*.

[34] Cf. Boersma, *Violence*; Adam Kotsko, *The Politics of Redemption: The Social Logic of Salvation* (New York: T&T Clark, 2010); McKnight, *Community*.

[35] Cf. Daniel Deme, *The Christology of Anselm of Canterbury* (Aldershot: Ashgate, 2003); Katherine Sonderegger, "Anselm, Defensor Fidei," *International Journal of Systematic Theology* 9, no. 3 (2007); David S. Hogg, *Anselm of Canterbury: The Beauty of Theology* (Burlington, VT: Ashgate, 2004).

[36] Recent scholarship has debunked this view, and it is only a matter of time before a substantial retelling of the history of exemplarism sets matters straight. Kotsko, *Politics*; Richard E. Weingart, *The Logic of Divine Love: A Critical Analysis of the Soteriology of Peter Abailard* (London: Clarendon, 1970); Thomas Williams, "Sin, Grace, and Redemption," in *The Cambridge Companion to Abelard*, ed. Jeffrey E. Brower and Kevin Guilfoy (New York: Cambridge University Press, 2004); Philip Quinn, "Abelard on Atonement: Nothing Unintelligible, Arbitrary, Illogical, or Immoral About It," in *Reasoned Faith: Essays in Philosophical Theology in Honor of Norman Kretzmann*, ed. Eleonore Stump and Norman Kretzmann (Ithaca, NY: Cornell University Press, 1993). This will no doubt be facilitated by the recent translation of Abelard's full commentary: Peter Abelard, *Commentary on the Epistle to the Romans*, trans. Steven R. Cartwright (Washington, DC: Catholic University of America Press, 2011).

final example of this retrieval work is John McLeod Campbell, whose thought is undergoing a small but significant renaissance.[37]

Third, the history of an entire doctrine is likewise under rehabilitation in broad and sometimes quite divergent circles, as a number of traditions and figures are seeking to explore, popularize, and modify a range of theories known variously as *theōsis*, divinization, and participation (in Christ and/or God).[38] These theories, particularly influential in the history of Eastern Christianity, explore the work of Christ in terms of his bringing humankind into a creaturely union with God. This vein of thought is simultaneously the locus of careful historical work and contemporary innovation (with some of the latter being highly polemical and irresponsible), and is particularly promising for the ways it draws upon the history of doctrine to interweave the character of God, power of the resurrection, and the role of the Holy Spirit into the doctrine of the atonement.

On the other side of the supposed biblical/theological divide, similarly excellent work is likewise strengthening and diversifying atonement studies. David Moffitt's work on the role of the resurrection and ascension in Hebrews is a wonderful example of biblical studies retrieving a whole spectrum of the work of Christ typically minimized within historical, biblical, and dogmatic work on the subject.[39] Similarly important (and ultimately related) work on the Pentateuch develops the unique significance of the sacrificial system as distinct from penal categories, focused on cleansing.[40] Such works build up accounts of sin, atonement, and salvation in a manner distinct from judicial categories, dealing primarily (though not exclusively) with the notion of (im)purity, dovetailing beautifully with the theology of Hebrews. A third example of such biblical study is recent work on the relation between covenant and atonement.[41] A noteworthy

---

[37] Deryck W. Lovegrove, "So Rich a Soil: John Mcleod Campbell, on Christian Atonement," *Scottish Journal of Theology* 42, no. 3 (1989); T. F. Torrance, "John Mcleod Campbell (1800–1872)," in *Scottish Theology: From John Knox to John Mcleod Campbell* (Edinburgh: T & T Clark, 1996); Leanne Van Dyk, *The Desire of Divine Love: John Mcleod Campbell's Doctrine of the Atonement* (New York: P. Lang, 1995).

[38] Stephen Finlan and Vladimir Kharlamov, *Theōsis: Deification in Christian Theology* (Eugene, OR: Pickwick, 2006); Vladimir Kharlamov, *Theōsis: Deification in Christian Theology*, vol. 2 (Eugene, OR: Pickwick Publications, 2011); Michael J. Christensen and Jeffery A. Wittung, *Partakers of the Divine Nature: The History and Development of Deificiation in the Christian Traditions* (Grand Rapids, MI: Baker Academic, 2007).

[39] Cf. Moffitt, *Atonement and the Logic of Resurrection in the Epistle to the Hebrews*; Farrow, *Ascension Theology*; Burgess, *The Ascension in Karl Barth*.

[40] Jay Sklar, *Sin, Impurity, Sacrifice, Atonement: The Priestly Conceptions* (Sheffield: Sheffield Phoenix, 2005); Frances M. Young, *Sacrifice and the Death of Christ* (London: SPCK, 1975).

[41] Cf. Gorman, *The Death of the Messiah and the Birth of the New Covenant: A (Not So) New Model of the Atonement*; Trelstad, "Lavish Love: A Covenantal Ontology," in *Cross Examinations: Readings on the Meaning of the Cross Today*, ed. Marit Trelstad (Minneapolis: Fortress, 2006); Michael Scott Horton, *Covenant and Salvation: Union with Christ* (Louisville, KY: WJK, 2007).

feature of many of these biblical studies is that they are increasingly in dialog with theological studies, both historical and contemporary. The results of this cross-pollination, or more aptly, the gradual overcoming of this artificial and disastrous rupture, promise to be of great benefit for everyone involved.

Such developments have their counterparts within constructive dogmatic work on the atonement, which in recent years has aggressively developed the doctrinal interrelations with regard to the atonement. This is most true of the doctrine of the Trinity, motivated in part by feminist, womanist, and nonviolent critiques of traditional views.[42] Even apart from polemic concerns, however, this stands as a vibrant and dynamic field, building off of the significant attention given to the doctrine of the Trinity in recent decades on the one hand, and attention to Christ's descent into hell on the other.[43] Recent studies have also drawn attention to the relationship between atonement and the doctrines of election,[44] the divine attributes,[45] and ecclesiology.[46] Perhaps the two most outstanding loci for development in this regard are creation and pneumatology. While the Holy Spirit is often said to apply the work of Christ, or communicate the benefits of Christ's work to the believer, scant reflection has been offered on the role of the Holy Spirit in the atoning work itself—in the death, resurrection, and ascension of Jesus Christ. Similarly, the resources within the doctrine of creation have been relatively untapped in studies of Christ's work, though new interest in environmental/ecological issues on the one hand, and Irenaeus, Athanasius, and other patristic theologians on the other may bring about a shift in this regard.

Alongside these historical, biblical, and doctrinal developments, it is worth noting an increased interest in broadening the scope of material relevant for

---

[42] McCormack, "Ontological Presuppositions"; McCall, *Forsaken*; Johnson, *Atonement: A Guide for the Perplexed*; Webster, "It Was the Will"; Sherman, *King, Priest and Prophet*.

[43] This line of thought builds on the trajectory established by the Church Fathers and beyond, arguably takes some inspiration from Hegel, and was developed in large part by Hans Urs von Balthasar (along with popes John Paul II and Benedict XVI) and Karl Barth, and popularized by Jürgen Moltmann and Alan Lewis. Cf. Hans Urs von Balthasar, *Mysterium Paschale: The Mystery of Easter*, trans. Aidan Nichols (San Francisco: Ignatius Press, 1990); Alan E. Lewis, *Between Cross and Resurrection: A Theology of Holy Saturday* (Grand Rapids, MI: Eerdmans, 2001); Alyssa Lyra Pitstick, *Christ's Descent into Hell: John Paul II, Joseph Ratzinger, and Hans Urs Von Balthasar on the Theology of Holy Saturday* (Grand Rapids, MI: Eerdmans, 2016); David Lauber, *Barth on the Descent into Hell: God, Atonement and the Christian Life* (Burlington, VT: Ashgate, 2004).

[44] Cf. McCormack, "Ontological Presuppositions"; Gibson and Gibson, *From Heaven He Came and Sought Her: Definite Atonement in Historical, Biblical, Theological, and Pastoral Perspective*. See also the ecumenically oriented discussion of this topic in the forthcoming: Johnson, *5 Views on the Extent of the Atonement*.

[45] Cf. Holmes, "A Simple Salvation? Soteriology and the Perfections of God"; Johnson, *Atonement: A Guide for the Perplexed*.

[46] Cf. Peter Schmiechen, *Saving Power: Theories of Atonement and Forms of the Church* (Grand Rapids, MI: Eerdmans, 2005).

equipping and advancing studies of the atonement. Frances M. Young, for instance, has recently published a delightful book drawing not only upon Patristic sources, but ancient art, liturgy, and other theologically rich subject areas, to enrich her understanding of Christ's atonement.[47] The incorporation of such a diverse and rich body of reflection from the history of the church promises to invigorate an already burgeoning field.[48]

Critique and Polemic Fronts

While the emphasis in this chapter is undoubtedly upon the constructive nature of the theological task, theology does not happen in a vacuum, and it is often the case that polemic leads to doctrinal growth. The single greatest challenge to theories of the atonement that are in any way rooted in the theological tradition(s) of the church can be summed up in terms of nonviolent critiques and alternatives. The gist of this position is that interpretations of Christ's work which posit the crucifixion and death of Christ as an event willed or in some sense executed by the Father are intolerable, for they posit an intolerable violence within the character and life of God.[49] Constructive alternatives vary widely, but the conviction that God is nonviolent in all his interactions, and especially the cross, is a widely shared, deeply held, and revolutionary thesis for the doctrine.[50]

---

[47] Frances M. Young, *Construing the Cross: Type, Sign, Symbol, Word, Action* (Eugene, OR: Cascade Books, 2015). See also: Richard Viladesau's trilogy of books on the Passion of Christ in the theology and the arts, from the catacombs to the Baroque period, and O. Larry Yarbrough, *Engaging the Passion: Perspectives on the Death of Jesus* (Minneapolis: Fortress, 2015).

[48] A burgeoning field deserving attention is that of analytic theology. Analytic theologians and philosophers of religion are demonstrating a growing interest in the doctrine of the atonement. Cf. Oliver Crisp, "Non-Penal Substitution," *IJST* 9, no. 4 (2007); Eric T. Yang and Stephen T. Davis, "Atonement and the Wrath of God," in *Locating Atonement: Explorations in Constructive Dogmatics*, ed. Oliver Crisp and Fred Sanders (Grand Rapids, MI: Zondervan, 2015); Oliver Crisp, "Original Sin and Atonement," in *The Oxford Handbook of Philosophical Theology*, ed. Thomas P. Flint and Michael C. Rea (New York: Oxford University Press, 2009); Ronald Jay Feenstra and Cornelius Plantinga, *Trinity, Incarnation, and Atonement: Philosophical and Theological Essays* (Notre Dame, IN: University of Notre Dame Press, 1989); Paul Moser, "Sin and Salvation," in *The Cambridge Companion to Christian Philosophical Theology*, ed. Charles Taliaferro and Chad V. Meister (New York: Cambridge University Press, 2010); Eleonore Stump, "Atonement and Justification," in *Trinity, Incarnation, and Atonement: Philosophical and Theological Essays*, ed. Ronald Jay Feenstra and Cornelius Plantinga (Notre Dame, IN: University of Notre Dame Press, 1989); Marilyn McCord Adams, *Christ and Horrors: The Coherence of Christology* (Cambridge: Cambridge University Press, 2006).

[49] Darrin W. Snyder Belousek, *Atonement, Justice, and Peace: The Message of the Cross and the Mission of the Church* (Grand Rapids, MI: William B. Eerdmans, 2012); Darby Kathleen Ray, *Deceiving the Devil: Atonement, Abuse, and Ransom* (Cleveland: Pilgrim Press, 1998); Weaver, *The Nonviolent Atonement*.

[50] Kathryn Tanner, *Christ the Key* (Cambridge: Cambridge University Press, 2010); Kotsko, *Politics*; S. Mark Heim, *Saved from Sacrifice: A Theology of the Cross* (Grand Rapids, MI: Eerdmans, 2006).

This critique, in many ways a variant of problems raised against traditional views of the atonement for centuries,[51] is partly responsible for another major polemic front of the doctrine: the orthodoxy and relative significance of penal substitution. Though aspects of this doctrine were widely held in the early church, it began to emerge more clearly in Thomas Aquinas's development of Anselm, and came into its own in the Reformers and post-Reformation theologians.[52] Increasing attacks have contributed to a new dynamic for some groups, in which penal substitution has become *the theory* rather than *one of several theories* of the atonement.[53] This entrenchment leads to a dangerous lack of proportion and perspective. Fortunately, not all proponents of penal substitution are making this move, such that its entrenchment on the one hand, and creative and multi-aspectual development on the other are happening concurrently. Several factors are at play in this discussion: (1) the question of the role of penal substitution vis-à-vis other theories of the atonement, (2) the nature of divine violence, inasmuch as this is an indirect way of approaching those questions and topics, and (3) most importantly, the role of the doctrine of the Trinity and of the divine attributes (particularly justice, righteousness, and wrath).[54]

For an increasing number of theologians, the vacuum created by the critique of penal substitution has been filled with variants of the *Christus victor* theory—a long-standing train of reflection exploring the work of Christ as depriving Satan of his (real or usurped) power or rights over creation and humankind. This family of theories is exceptionally diverse, ranging from revitalizations of traditional positions[55] to demythologized accounts which employ categories of "victory,"

---

[51] Cf. Faustus Socinus, *De Iesu Christo Servatore: Hoc Est Cur & Qua Ratione Iesus Christus Noster Seruator Fit* (Radaeus: Ordinum Aegidius Typographus, 1611); Immanuel Kant, *Religion within the Boundaries of Mere Reason*, trans. Allen W. Wood and George Di Giovanni (New York: Cambridge University Press, 1998); Ludwig Feuerbach, *The Essence of Christianity*, trans. George Eliot (Amherst, NY: Prometheus Books, 1989).

[52] ST III 46–49; John Calvin, *Institutes of the Christian Religion* (Philadelphia: Westminster Press, 1960); François Turrettini, *Institutes of Elenctic Theology*, vol. 2 (Phillipsburg: P & R Publishing, 1992); Charles Hodge, *Systematic Theology* (Grand Rapids, MI: Eerdmans, 1986); James I. Packer, "What Did the Cross Achieve: The Logic of Penal Substitution," *Tyndale Bulletin* 25 (1974).

[53] Stephen R. Holmes, "Ransomed, Healed, Restored, Forgiven: Evangelical Accounts of the Atonement," in *The Atonement Debate: Papers from the London Symposium on the Theology of Atonement*, ed. Derek Tidball, David Hilborn, and Justin Thacker (Grand Rapids, MI: Zondervan, 2008).

[54] Derek Tidball, David Hilborn, and Justin Thacker, eds., *The Atonement Debate: Papers from the London Symposium on the Theology of Atonement* (Grand Rapids, MI: Zondervan, 2008); Charles E. Hill and Frank A. James, eds., *The Glory of the Atonement: Biblical, Historical and Practical Perspectives* (Downers Grove, IL: InterVarsity Press, 2004); McCall, *Forsaken*; Boersma, *Violence*; Vidu, *Atonement, Law, and Justice: The Cross in Historical and Cultural Contexts*.

[55] Gregory A. Boyd, "Christus Victor View," in *The Nature of the Atonement: Four Views*, ed. James K. Beilby and Paul R. Eddy (Downers Grove, IL: IVP Academic, 2006); Lombardo, *The Father's Will: Christ's Crucifixion and the Goodness of God*.

"ransom," and "Satan" by filling them with new meaning, often tied to views of evil as a societal force.[56]

Summary

The doctrine of the atonement is no simple matter. To plumb its depths is to delve into the whole of the Bible, and the history of Christian reflection upon this book in biblical, theological, liturgical, and artistic reflection. No simple set of questions and answers, distinctions, and catch phrases will do justice to the complexity of the saving work of Jesus Christ—for this is the center of Christian doctrine, that to which and from which all other doctrinal reflection flows. And if this is to remain a stream of thought which waters and nourishes the church, we must learn to reinvigorate the old questions, and move on to ask new ones, for we are as likely as any other group in the history of the church to fall into ruts and stale patterns of thinking.

How best to do this? By playing at the boundaries—at the boundaries between doctrines, allowing the insights and developments in other doctrines to bear fruit and implications within the doctrine of the atonement; at the boundaries of cultures, lending an attentive ear to other cultures, past and present, and the questions and perspectives alien to our own which can and should open our eyes to see things anew; at the boundaries of disciplines, dwelling on the possibilities and challenges raised by other theological subdisciplines than those in which we are trained, or other disciplines altogether, such as those of philosophy, sociology, history, and literature; at social and ecclesial boundaries, seeking to listen, honor, and embrace those whose experiences and views differ wildly from our own. But underlying this zest for an expansive understanding of the doctrine lies the core commitment unifying it all: the atoning work of Jesus Christ is the work of the triune God, receiving from him its distinctive meaning and significance. Every field, every insight, plays at best a ministerial role, witnessing to this central insight.

---

[56] Ray, *Deceiving the Devil: Atonement, Abuse, and Ransom*; Weaver, *The Nonviolent Atonement*; Aulén, *Christus Victor*; René Girard, *I See Satan Fall Like Lightning* (Maryknoll, NY: Orbis, 2001).

2

These Three Atone: Trinity and Atonement

Fred Sanders

It is hard to delineate the boundary between the doctrines of Trinity and atonement because each doctrine, taken at its most expansive, makes such heavy requisitions from the other. Unless material from each field is featured prominently in the other, neither doctrine can be developed properly. Not even in the darkest ages of modernism did the situation ever quite degenerate into Trinity *versus* atonement; rather the two doctrines have tended to thrive or wilt in unison. These are not two hostile doctrines that stand in need of reconciliation to each other (to use language from atonement doctrine), nor are they simply the same subject matter subsisting distinctly in relation, or indwelling each other perichoretically (to use language from Trinitarian doctrine). Calibrating them to each other is a major task for any systematic theological vision, and expounding them in due proportion is a true test of any theologian's sagacity.

Trinity and Atonement: Doctrinal Obligations

The obligation of the doctrine of the Trinity is to be a doctrine about God, which certainly ought to give Trinitarian theology more than enough work to keep it occupied. In fact, it is incumbent on Trinitarian theology to be a doctrine concerning God's eternal, essential being in a way that distinguishes itself from doctrines about God's outward actions: it concerns who God is rather than what God does. There must be something of a *sola* in Trinitarian doctrine, a protest that preserves this doctrine from being reduced and relativized. After we have said all we must say (and there is much) about the doctrine as a mystery of salvation, a map of our participation in the divine life, the structuring grammar of an ecclesial encounter with God, the pattern of God's ways in the world, and so on, we must recall that the triune God has a self-sufficient life of its own, which is occupied with more than just being the transcendental referent of that mapping, structuring, and patterning. In the doctrine of the Trinity we are at all times speaking of a God who would already have been fully actualized even if he had never undertaken those actions which constitute him as the three-personed mystery of a contingent salvation.[1] To omit this note of distinction is to expose all the other content of Trinitarian doctrine to the risk of being merely a congeries of observations about what happens in the course of human events. A god entangled in world process by bands of necessity is a god dissolved and lost into world process.

Yet Trinitarian theology necessarily canvases a broader theological field, drawing at least from Christology and pneumatology if it is to have anything at all Trinitarian to say about God. It does not just add the doctrines of an eternal Son and an eternal Spirit to a doctrine of God, but fetches what it knows of their identities from the incarnate, crucified, risen Savior and his outpoured Spirit. That is, Trinitarian theology is an interpretation of the work of atonement. It takes up all the material of salvation history together as a whole and places it against the horizon of God's eternal being, in order to specify the Christian God by describing the connection between God and the economy of salvation. All the other work of the doctrine of the Trinity flows from this source in the economy. It speaks about the eternal, triune being of God on the basis of that God's self-revealing works and words in the world.

The obligation of the doctrine of atonement is to be a doctrine about salvation, which certainly ought to give atonement theology more than enough to keep it occupied. Minimally, the doctrine of atonement must analyze a problem and explain its resolution: the problem of sin resolved by forgiveness, the problem of vice resolved by the power to be virtuous, the problem of mortality resolved by eternal life, the problem of oppression resolved by powerful deliverance, and so on. But the doctrine of atonement always outstrips this tidy problem-solution schema because it gathers its material from a wider range of truths. It cannot speak of a problem without describing the normative background situation, which the problem (conceptually if not chronologically) disturbs, and it cannot describe that background without describing its transcendent source. In this

---

[1] Robert Sokolowski, *The God of Faith and Reason: Foundations of Christian Theology* (Washington, DC: The Catholic University of America Press, 1995), 21–30.

way the doctrine of atonement implicates and presupposes doctrines of creation and God, respectively.

Developed with appropriate amplitude, the doctrine of atonement can scarcely be contained or delimited within the terrain of Christian doctrine. As Adam Johnson argues, "We must keep firmly in mind the synthetic nature of the doctrine of the atonement, comprised as it is of the doctrines of the Trinity, divine attributes, Christology, hamartiology and eschatology (especially the doctrine of heaven/salvation)."[2] As a consummately comprehensive and synthetic doctrine (for what other message can Christian theology reflect on than the gospel message?), the doctrine of the atonement sometimes seems to be the unified field within which all the other doctrinal fields are comprehended. Johnson's list of the contents of atonement theology, for example, includes the doctrine of God: both the Trinity and the divine attributes. What he has in mind is not the possibility of atonement outflanking and surrounding Trinity, but atonement doctrine drawing its form and content from the form and content of the doctrine of God. Thus "it is the business of the doctrine of the atonement to unpack the reality of God's triune life as basis for God's saving activity in Christ."[3] As the doctrine of the atonement carries out that task, it too connects the economy of salvation to the eternal being of God.

Johnson's account of atonement is illuminating in this regard because, without distorting the doctrine of God, it presses the doctrine of God into service to the doctrine of atonement. The exposition of atonement theology has often suffered under the burden of arguments about its central idea or main point. Johnson argues that along with a certain kind of focus and unity, the doctrine of the atonement also has a "unique diversity proper to" the divine act of atoning. That diversity, he says, is

> the diversity proper to the triune God whose act this was, in the fullness of his divine attributes. "God was in Christ," accomplishing the work of reconciling "all things" (1 Cor 5:19). God: Father, Son and Holy Spirit; the God of Abraham, Isaac and Jacob; the God who is merciful, gracious, patient, loving, good, kind, righteous, faithful, constant, wrathful, holy, omniscient … This God, in the fullness his character, was in Christ, reconciling all things to himself. And by means of this work 'all things' are taken up and reconciled to God by means of God

---

[2] Adam J. Johnson, *Atonement: A Guide for the Perplexed* (London: Bloomsbury T & T Clark, 2015), 180.
[3] Ibid., 67.

himself, by means of the diversity and richness proper to God's own being and life.[4]

Atonement, on this maximizing view, rises to the level of a mega-doctrine. In fact there seem to be only two such complex mega-doctrines at work in the Christian theological system: Trinity and atonement. These are thick descriptions of who God is on one hand, and what God does on the other. The being and act of God seem to practically exhaust the scope of Christian doctrine between them, without remainder and without any definite boundary between them.

This view of Trinity and atonement as the mega-doctrines of systematic theology is neither self-evident nor uncontroversial. Even when it is affirmed, it is not without its attendant dangers. We might describe two basic options available for relating the two complexes. First we will consider the schema of placing the Trinity within the atonement; and second the schema of placing the atonement within the Trinity. Gleaning the strengths from each schema while seeking to be instructed by the errors they have sometimes led to, we conclude with a constructive proposal designed to provide balance: the clue to keep the doctrines of Trinity and atonement rightly related is to coordinate them both within the doxological context which is their origin and goal.[5]

Trinity in Atonement

To place the Trinity in the atonement is generally an epistemological move. It begins with the premise, already noted, that anything we know about the triunity of God we know from what was revealed to us in the saving work of Christ. In classical idiom, this is because the temporal missions of the Son and the Holy Spirit are the gracious manifestations to us of the eternal processions of the Son and the Spirit within the divine being. By meeting the Son and the Spirit in the economy of salvation, we gain true knowledge of them as eternal Son and eternal Spirit, which they would have been without the economy of salvation. All of this is true, and the venerable doctrine of temporal missions as enactments, extensions, or prolongations of the eternal processions constitutes a classic

---

[4] Ibid., 23.
[5] For a doxological framing of the doctrine of the Trinity with special reference to the doctrine of revelation and recommendations for a program of exegesis, see Fred Sanders, *The Triune God* (Grand Rapids, MI: Zondervan, 2016).

theologoumenon with irreplaceable explanatory power. Yet care must be taken in its use. To speak of the Son's mission may unduly direct attention to the act of incarnation rather than to the passion, death, and resurrection of Christ. And it is the latter with which we have to do. An incarnation of the Son of God, which was not ordered to the passion, would be at best a speculative counterfactual possibility; the incarnation we actually know is one that is always "ordered to the passion."[6] So "the mission of the Son" refers to the entire scope of the life, death, and resurrection of Jesus Christ, rather than just to the fact or the moment of his enfleshment.

The epistemological point is sometimes made more drastically, depending on how worried a theologian is about the dangers of abstraction. Fearing that incarnation and Trinity can function as mere conceptual principles rather than as the conclusions of exegetical insight and spiritual perception, John Behr rejects any formulation that would describe Christian theology as being constructed on the axes of Trinity and incarnation. He laments a modern situation in which the doctrines about God and Christ have already been received as established facts, and the story of the Bible is then fitted within those parameters:

> Trinitarian theology is made into a realm unto itself, requiring subsequent reflection on "the Incarnation" of one of the three divine persons: Triadology followed by Christology. In this perspective, the Trinity and the Incarnation are taken as being the linchpins of Christian theology—Christian faith is "Trinitarian" and "incarnational." This has become an unquestioned premise for most twentieth-century theology.[7]

It is an odd complaint, considering that a theologian like Behr affirms the tri-unity of God and the incarnation of the Son. What he objects to, however, is the tendency of these doctrines to float free of their origin and take on an unwarranted appearance of stability in the form of what he calls "familiar shorthand formulae."[8] Trinity and incarnation, he insists, are not conceptual axes within which to understand the story of Jesus Christ's death and resurrection. The doctrines of the Trinity and incarnation were and are nothing but an exegetical interpretation of the death and resurrection of Christ.

---

[6] Hans Urs von Balthasar, *Mysterium Paschale: The Mystery of Easter* (Grand Rapids, MI: Eerdmans, 1993), 12–13. An author who does justice to the speculative alternative case is Edwin Chr. van Driel, *Incarnation Anyway: Arguments for Supralapsarian Christology* (Oxford: Oxford University Press, 2008).
[7] John Behr, "The Paschal Foundation of Christian Theology," *St Vladimir's Theological Quarterly* 45, no. 2 (2001), 116.
[8] Ibid., 115.

Behr seems to be taking a step further than the epistemological claim that we only know about the Trinity through the passion, in that he is commending a more thorough revision of methodological assumptions. He argues for "the paschal foundation of Christian theology" in a stronger sense, in opposition to Christian theology "construed in terms of the gradual development of a dogmatic edifice," in which patristic thought can be divorced "from the given revelation of God in Christ, and ... made to retell that revelation in a different manner, so that the Word of God is no longer the locus of God's self-expression."[9] Christian doctrine as a whole, Behr argues,

> quite simply is not based upon the supposed two axes of Trinity and Incarnation ... Rather, theological reflection, beginning with the original apostles and continuing with all those who follow in their tradition, develops as a response to the marvelous work of God in Jesus Christ, the crucified and exalted Lord.[10]

In our terms, Behr is contending for a doctrine of the Trinity that is configured interior to the doctrine of the atonement (or, as Behr would say, "the pascha") in such a way that the latter governs the former. "Christian theology is a response to the Passion of the Savior, and reflects on the work of God through this prism"; this reveals "the unity of all theology in the paschal faith."[11]

The argument has much to commend it, and certainly functions well as a corrective to the abstractness of some recent theology. But it is open to objections of at least a cautionary sort on two fronts. First, it risks being so cross-centered that it has to pretend that the character of God is not yet disclosed until the passion of Christ. But the character of the God of Jesus Christ is already established in the Old Testament before it opens up to display a wealth of inner riches in the passion of Christ. As Behr himself points out, even our narratives of the death and resurrection of Christ are already themselves exegetical and interpretive moves performed on key texts of the Old Testament: Psalm 110, Psalm 22, Isaiah 53. Unless we admit that God is already truly known through the history of his interactions with Israel, we cannot make sense, Trinitarian or otherwise, out of the paschal events. Pushed to extremes, Behr's "paschal foundation" reads as almost an Eastern Orthodox inflection of a Barthian protest, or at least an idea from the apocalyptic school of recent biblical studies.

In some theological proposals, the "Trinity in atonement" schema expands beyond its epistemological and methodological starting point and takes on

---

[9] Ibid., 119.
[10] Ibid., 120.
[11] Ibid.

ontological seriousness. Robert Jenson's drastic version of Trinitarianism is a case in point. Committed to the proposition that "the primal systematic function of Trinitarian teaching is to identify the theos in 'theology,'"[12] Jenson offers a revisionist metaphysic on its basis. Identity is a thing narrated in a history with meaningful coherence, and this applies to God above all: "Since the biblical God can truly be identified by narrative, his hypostatic being, his self-identity, is constituted in dramatic coherence."[13] Scott Swain has pointed out that in Jenson's work, God is not only identified *by* his historical actions in Israel and Christ, but is actually identified *with* them in a strong, ontological sense. Identifying God *by* the atonement is just good biblical theology.[14] Identifying God *with* the atonement requires, as Jenson consistently asserts, a complete rethinking of metaphysics, and a willingness to call God an event that takes place between Jesus and his Father. Here Trinity is inside of atonement because there simply is no outside of atonement.[15]

The most expansive critique of all these tendencies emerged in the late work of John Webster. Without deviating from a commitment to God's self-revelation in the saving economy, Webster began to be concerned that configuring the doctrine of the Trinity too nearly internal to the atonement inevitably distorted the shape of a systematic theology by failing to attend programmatically to the creator-creature distinction. As his attention increasingly shifted to the doctrine of creation, Webster began to valorize not the two mega-doctrines we have been discussing, but rather "two distributed doctrines" which make themselves felt pervasively throughout the entire theological system. The first distributed doctrine is the Trinity, "of which all other articles of Christian teaching are an amplification or application, and which therefore permeates theological

---

[12] Robert Jenson, *Systematic Theology* volume I: The Triune God (NY: Oxford University Press, 1997), 60.
[13] Ibid., I:64.
[14] Scott R. Swain, *The God the Gospel: Robert Jenson's Trinitarian Theology* (Downers Grove, IL: IVP Academic, 2013), 86.
[15] The conclusion is pervasive in Jenson, in some of his most arresting formulations. See, for instance, his claim "that the Spirit rests upon the Son is not a phenomenon merely of the economic Trinity—there are in any case no such phenomena." Jenson, *Systematic Theology* I:143. On the other hand, in the preface to Volume II, Jenson made an interesting confession. Having put the entirety of Christology and pneumatology inside of the doctrine of God (in the first volume), he seriously considered including all of soteriology, ecclesiology, and eschatology there as well, in order to make the point that these so-called external works are truly taken into the God's lordly identity. "But organizing the work on the plausible principle that finally *all* [emphasis in the original] Christian teaching in one way or another tells God's own story would of course have obliterated the point." (Jenson, *Systematic Theology volume II: The Works of God* (New York: Oxford University Press, 1999), v. Any systematic theology that stuck to Jenson's first principle would have to exhaust itself in a first volume, without remainder. And if everything is the doctrine of God, what is the doctrine of God?

affirmations about every matter." But instead of naming atonement (or salvation, or the economy) as the second such doctrine, Webster displaces it with creation. "The doctrine of creation," he says, "is ubiquitous ... It is not restricted to one particular point in the sequence of Christian doctrine, but provides orientation and a measure of governance to all that theology has to say about all things in relation to God."[16] The doctrine of creation "brackets and qualifies everything that is said about the nature and course of all that is not God," and therefore must already be in place before statements about soteriology can be deployed fittingly.[17]

Without an operative doctrine of creation in place to govern statements about God's saving action, "the existence and history of created things may be assumed as a given, quasi-necessary, reality, rather than a wholly surprising effect of divine goodness, astonishment at which pervades all Christian teaching."

> Exposition of the history of grace as the final cause of creation ... results in ... presenting the relation of God and creatures as one between divine and human persons and agents who, for all their differences, are strangely commensurable, engaging one another in the same space, deciding, acting, and interacting in the world as a commonly inhabited field of reality.[18]

What beguiles theologians into this disordered exposition is often "the sheer prominence and human intensity of the central subject and episode of redemption history." In short, the attention given to Jesus Christ the Savior leaves theology so enraptured with the story and the drama of the economy of salvation that it becomes very difficult to get the necessary perspective, "the setting of the work of grace in the work of nature."[19] The result is disastrous:

> Such an arrangement of Christian doctrine raises an expectation that what needs to be said about the natures of God and the creatures of God, and therefore of their relation, may be determined almost exhaustively by attending to the economy of salvation—the history of election and reconciliation in the missions of the Son and the Holy Spirit. Accordingly, if God and creatures are chiefly conceived as dramatis personae in an enacted sequence of lost and regained fellowship, talk of the non-reciprocity of their relation seems theologically and religiously unbecoming.[20]

---

[16] John Webster, "Non ex aequo: God's Relation to Creatures," in *God without Measure: Working Papers in Christian Theology, Vol. I: God and the Works of God* (Edinburgh: T&T Clark, 2016), 117.
[17] Ibid., 117.
[18] Ibid., 118.
[19] Ibid.
[20] Ibid., 118–119.

At the end of his career, Webster was just beginning to deploy the doctrine of creation as one of the tools that could keep the doctrine of the Trinity from being distorted by absorption into the doctrine of atonement. Perhaps there are other theological tools that could serve equally well, and other ways of approaching this set of issues without making Webster's move of promoting the doctrine of creation to the status of the second distributed doctrine alongside the doctrine of the Trinity. In his earlier work, Webster himself was more tentative about letting the doctrine of creation relativize the doctrine of salvation, directing attention to "the scope of the *opera Dei exeuntia*," which is "wider than that of the single theme of salvation, however widely ramified that theme may be."[21] Webster's Trinity-creation duo fits well with the Reformed Thomist grammar he developed, in which the task of Christian theology was to confess God, and then all things in relation to God. Even for those who cannot accept Webster's prescription, it stands as an instructive warning about the dangers of the controlling power of the Trinity-atonement duo, and a helpful vantage point on the entire Trinity-in-atonement schema.

Atonement in Trinity

Alongside the schema of locating Trinity in atonement, a number of recent theological projects can be described as locating atonement in the Trinity. That is, they confess the eternal being of God as Father, Son, and Holy Spirit, and then confess the greatness of what this God has accomplished in the economy of salvation, and finally ask about the transcendental ground of what they have seen in salvation history. Generally these theologies are characterized by wonder and astonishment at the greatness of what God has done in the atonement. It is this high view of redemption accomplished that leads them to turn back to God and ask, what is there in God that forms the basis of this great salvation? Or, to put the question in more modern Trinitarian idiom, what is the immanent Trinitarian analogate of economic atonement?

Certain answers suggest themselves immediately and must be immediately rejected. Since the atonement requires the Son to suffer in his human nature on our behalf, an influential tradition of modern theology has affirmed that there

---

[21] John Webster, "Rector et Iudex Super Omnia Genera Doctrinarum? The Place of the Doctrine of Justification," in *God without Measure Vol. I*, 163. This essay was originally published in 2009; "Non ex aequo" in 2014.

must be something like suffering in the divine essence. And since the atonement requires the Father to give his Son over, some theologians conclude that there must be the transcendental possibility of divine self-abandonment in eternity, perhaps as a breach or gap between the Father and the Son. Jürgen Moltmann has been the most significant advocate of rejecting the classical doctrine of divine impassibility in favor of a radically cross-centered, radically Trinitarian doctrine of divine suffering, "the pathos of God." Moltmann asserted that "the theology of the cross must be the doctrine of the Trinity and the doctrine of the Trinity must be the theology of the cross."[22] He even described the cross as the event of God's self-abandonment in history. If this is not an entirely Hegelian doctrine of God, it is at least a fairly thoroughly historicized one, and Moltmann was intentional about this: "The doctrine of the Trinity is the conceptual framework that is necessary if we are to understand this history of Christ as being the history of God."[23] He puts the atonement into the heart of the Trinity, eternally and essentially. "If a person once feels the infinite passion of God's love," he argues, "then he understands the mystery of the triune God. God suffers with us—God suffers from us—God suffers for us."[24] For Moltmann, the doctrine of the Trinity itself is not a statement about the being of God in itself, but always already a doctrine of the redemptive suffering of God for us.

The fortunes of full-blown theopaschism have risen and fallen over the past forty years. While the affirmation that God suffers seems to arise spontaneously from considering the depth of God's commitment to redeeming fallen sinners, very few theologians are willing to follow through with a complete rejection of the venerable tradition that teaches divine impassibility. Impassibility is just too tightly integrated with a number of other divine perfections to be excised without doing permanent damage to the doctrine of God. The suffering of Jesus Christ is an essential element of our redemption, but there must be something else present in the Trinity that forms the ground and possibility for the Son to appropriate the suffering of our nature and take it to himself.

Some more cautious answers have included Nicholas Wolterstorff's discussion of justice in the Trinity.[25] He nimbly considers whether the justice that God

---

[22] Jürgen Moltmann, *The Crucified God* (New York: Harper & Row, 1974), 241.
[23] Jürgen Moltmann, "The Trinitarian History of God," in *The Future of Creation* (Philadelphia: Fortress Press, 1979), 81.
[24] Jürgen Moltmann, *The Trinity and the Kingdom* (New York: Harper & Row, 1981), 4.
[25] Nicholas Wolterstorff, "Is There Justice in the Trinity?" in *God's Life in Trinity*, ed. Miroslav Volf and Michael Welker (Minneapolis: Fortress Press, 2006), 177–187.

brings about on earth has a transcendental ground in the being of the Trinity, and makes some crucial distinctions on his way to answering. "If the whole of justice involves the rendering of judgment, then there is no justice within the Trinity." However, justice as judgment is derivative from what Wolterstorff calls "primary justice," which "consists of treating persons with due respect for their worth."[26] This sounds like something that does obtain between Father and Son in the Spirit; in fact, it sounds like something that is merely a redescription of interpersonal love. Wolterstorff's approach to the question of what there is in the Trinity that manifests itself as justice or atonement among us is exemplary in several ways. Edward T. Oakes has attempted something similar when handling the question of whether there is distance in the Trinity, or an interval or gap between the persons.[27] As an interpreter of Balthasar, Oakes is concerned to provide some necessary groundwork for some of Balthasar's more daring speculative moves. Confronted with instances of diastasis and distance in the theology of redemption, Balthasar famously attempted to find room for those distances within the distinction between the Father and the Son. Creation seems to require a metaphysical distance from God. While the Son is certainly not metaphysically distant from, even different from, the Father, Balthasar argued that the principle of uncreated personal distinction in the Trinity is what makes possible the principle of creation's distinction from the creator. Even the interval of alienation in hell is not a distance that outflanks the distinction between Father and Son. If Balthasar's more venturesome formulations are hard to affirm, Oakes carefully navigates what is and is not acceptable here: "distinction (diakrasis) yes, distance (diastasis) no."[28] Similar caution should be urged on any number of contemporary projects that seek to find in the Trinity the primal origin of what is manifest in the economy. Hospitality, for instance, may be a form of grace in salvation history, and may be unpacked as a kind of generosity that makes room and lets others be. But any attempt to locate hospitality in the being of God will shipwreck on the etymology of *philoxenia*: love for aliens. Whatever we can say about the Father, Son, and Spirit making room for each other, we can never describe them as overcoming estrangement, pacifying hostility, compensating for unworthiness, breaking down barriers, bridging a gap, transversing a distance to come to each other, or solving interpersonal problems. It simply won't do. Atonement is not in the Trinity in that way.

---

[26] Ibid., 177.
[27] Edward T. Oakes, S.J., "Diastasis in the Trinity," in *A Man of the Church: Honoring the Theology, Life, and Witness of Ralph Del Colle*, ed. Michel Rene Barnes (Eugene, OR: Pickwick, 2012), 125–147.
[28] Ibid., 125.

Atonement and the Praise of Triune Glory

For systematic theology, there is a perennial question of how to handle the doctrine of the Trinity and the doctrine of the atonement together in a way that adequately displays their overlap and differentiation. None of the approaches that we have considered here are without their merits, and each of them provides something that should not be omitted from a satisfactory treatment of the complex theme. In particular, the question of correlating the eternal Trinity with the historical atonement is a vexed one. The waves of historicism are always threatening to capsize the theological boats, yet history must have its proper place in this doctrine. How shall we keep our wits about us, surrounded by such outsized themes and exposed to such dangers of error? When all the options have been considered, the best way to coordinate these two mega-doctrines is to look back to the origin of both doctrines, and forward their goals. Fortunately, the origin and goal are identical. Trinitarian theology and atonement theology arise from, and terminate in, the same response to God: praise. Doxology summons us to say what God has done, and who he is. Any elaboration of the doctrines of Trinity and atonement must move within this doxological sphere, and any attempt to coordinate their obligations with each other must take its bearings from its orienting task: to praise God in both conceptual profusion and reverent restraint.

A relatively minor and certainly neglected theologian from the Methodist tradition may offer the clearest example of a well-digested solution to using praise to solve the problem of relating Trinity and atonement as major loci in a system. William Burt Pope's three-volume *Compendium of Systematic Theology*[29] faces the problem squarely. The doctrine of God must come very early in a theological system; almost first, depending on how much methodological groundwork is necessary. But for a theologian committed to a maximal development of the atonement, the content of the doctrine of God must be derived from its most conspicuous display in the course of salvation history. Indeed, Pope is committed to the proposition that "the gradual unfolding of the mystery of redemption is also the gradual unfolding of the mystery of the Triune God."[30] This being the case, an early doctrine of God will have to smuggle in material from a later doctrine of atonement. Alternatively, a theologian could provide a sketchy initial

---

[29] William Burt Pope, *A Compendium of Christian Theology: Being Analytical Outlines of a Course of Theological Study, Biblical, Dogmatic, Historical* (London: Wesleyan Conference Office, 1879).

[30] Ibid., II:101.

doctrine of God and then wait until after the discussion of the atonement to describe more fully what has been learned about the divine Trinity and perfections from "the gradual unfolding of the mystery of the Triune God."

What Pope does is split the difference and double the doctrine of God. In the early chapters of his *Compendium*, he provides a solid treatment of God's tri-unity, perfections, and glory. The discussion is solid, orderly, and well proportioned. After these sections, he moves on to the doctrines of creation, humanity, then sin, Christology, and salvation. He wraps up an excellent and lengthy discussion of salvation with a section on "The Finished Atonement." It's at the end of this section that Pope makes his crucial move. Though he already discussed the Name of God, the Attributes of God, and the Trinity, Pope now sets aside several pages to take these doctrines up again. Why? Because

> in the finished work of Christ, the Name, Attributes and Government of God are most fully exhibited and glorified. The triune Name is made known; the Love and Righteousness of God have their highest and best manifestation, as the expression of the Divine will, and the Moral Government of the Supreme is supremely vindicated.[31]

In his characteristic style, Pope summarizes vast stretches of biblical teaching with a suggestive quotation from Scripture: "The Son, addressing the Father a prayer which regards the Atonement as accomplished, declares: I have manifested Thy name unto the men which Thou gavest me out of the world" (John 17:6).[32] Pope unpacks this "manifestation of God's name" as the revelation of the name "Father" which was brought to us by the Son and completed in the Spirit. He goes on to explain the principle of revelation behind this:

> The name of the Triune God is especially made known and therefore glorified in the meditation of the Incarnate Redeemer. The revelation of the Trinity is bound up with the revelation of redemption; the development of one was the development of the other, and both were perfected together.[33]

The doctrine of the Trinity, in Pope's presentation of it, is not a bit of esoteric information about God, but a fact made known when God put salvation into effect: when the Son and Spirit entered human history decisively, the Trinity was revealed. "Our Lord pronounced The Name of the Father, and of the Son, and

---

[31] Ibid., II:276.
[32] Ibid.
[33] Ibid.

of the Holy Ghost only after His resurrection. The mystery of His perfect love unfolded the mystery of His perfect essence."[34]

Although the glorification of the eternal Trinity is the main point Pope wants to make, he goes on to ponder the way the finished atonement glorifies God's name in other ways: "that Name is not only the Triune Name, but the assemblage of the Divine perfections." Again Pope is torn in two directions: On the one hand, he has already discussed the Divine perfections in the doctrine of God in volume 1, but on the other hand, he cannot bypass their revelation in the finished work of the atonement:

> In the New Testament it is obvious that with scarcely an exception every reference to the combined or individual perfections of God refers to their exhibition in the work of Christ. At least, all other allusions lead up to this. Not to repeat what has already been made prominent under the Divine Attributes, it may suffice to mention the new and perfect revelation of the holiness and love of God as disclosed in the Atonement.[35]

What Pope is up to here is undercutting the inadequate notion that Christian theology can start by defining the characters of its story ("in this corner, God; in that corner, man") and then go on to describe the actions they undertake. In the case of God, the only way Christian theology can get started is to admit that God has most definitively revealed himself in Christ the redeemer, so we have to describe the saving work of Christ as the beginning of our theology. If the doctrine of God started on page one, the doctrine of redemption had to have been on page zero, or perhaps in a long and all-determining preface. In other words, by treating the Name, Triunity, and Attributes of God in the middle of volume two, Pope underlines the fact that Christian thought has been presupposing the finished atonement all along. Volume one, page one, of Pope's *Compendium* was already normed and formed by the work of Christ:

> There is nothing that belongs to our conception of the Divine nature which is not manifested in His Son, Who both in His active and in His passive righteousness reveals all that is in the Father. Man, in fact, knows God only as a God of redemption; nor will He ever by man be otherwise known. Throughout the Scriptures of truth we have a gradual revelation of the Divine Being which is not finished until it is finished in Christ; God also, as well as man, is *en auto*

---

[34] Ibid., II:277.
[35] Ibid., II:278.

pepleromenos, COMPLETE IN HIM. It is not enough to say that the Trinity Whom Christians adore is made known in Jesus, and that this or the other attribute which theology ascribes to Him is illustrated in His work. God Himself, with every idea we form of His nature, is given to us by the revelation of Christ. The gracious and awful Being Who is presented in the Christian Scriptures is not in all respects such a Deity as human reason would devise or tolerate when presented. But to us there is but ONE GOD; and we must receive Him as He is made known to us through the mystery of the Atoning Mediation of His Son. His Name is proclaimed only in the Cross; there we have His Divine and only Benediction; and every Doxology in Revelation derives its strength and fervour from the Atonement.[36]

Doxology is no excuse for imprecise thinking or careless expressions. The rigor of systematic theology ought to be kept in place even as we acknowledge that praise is the medium in which the problem of balancing Trinity and atonement can be resolved graciously. Theology is in fact best offered as praise to the God of salvation when it comes forth in the form of appropriately measured description of the being and act of the atoning Trinity.

One of the central idioms of late-twentieth-century Trinitarian theologizing was the terminology of economic and immanent Trinity, largely in response to Karl Rahner's celebrated *Grundaxiom*, "the economic Trinity is the immanent Trinity, and vice versa."[37] Translated into these terms, the two schemas we have considered in this chapter would run as follows: Locating the Trinity inside the doctrine of the atonement would mean that the economic or atoning Trinity is the immanent Trinity, or that the three-personed God we meet in salvation history simply is the three-personed God of his own eternal identity. This is an attempt to recognize the earnestness and intimacy of the divine self-giving that constitutes Christian salvation. That first half of Rahner's Rule is, to that extent, true and necessary to affirm, within certain limitations that ought to be obvious. What must be simultaneously maintained is that the conditions of the economy of salvation, or of the work of atonement, bring with them a host of considerations. To say that in the atonement we are dealing with the immanent Trinity is to say, "the economic Trinity is the immanent Trinity under the conditions of the economy." But to the extent that God is giving himself to us under the conditions

---

[36] Ibid., II:279.
[37] I surveyed its origin and influence in Fred Sanders, *The Image of the Immanent Trinity: Rahner's Rule and the Theological Interpretation of Scripture* (New York: Peter Lang, 2004). More recently I have argued that the terminology itself has a distorting bias and ought to be used much more circumspectly, in Sanders, *Triune God*, 147–156.

of the economy, God is not alienated from his aseity or failing to be free in the very act of intervening.

Locating the atonement inside the Trinity would bring us into alignment with the more controversial second half of Rahner's Rule, "the immanent Trinity is the economic Trinity." Rahner's "vice versa" has always run the risk of collapsing God's identity into the process of redemption, and translation into our present terms would make that danger even more evident. What would it mean to take that further step of saying that the eternal God simply is the atoning God? Such a locution could easily mean that God is nothing but what he is for us and our salvation. That must not be affirmed or implied. As Karl Barth asked, "What would 'God for us' mean if it were not said against the background of 'God in Himself?'"[38] But if we said such a thing with an intent to praise the God of our salvation, we might mean, with William Burt Pope, that "the revelation of the Trinity is bound up with the revelation of redemption; the development of one was the development of the other, and both were perfected together."[39] In this way, the doxological setting of these two mega-doctrines helps keep their claims within the proper bounds, keep the two doctrines rightly related to each other, and ensure that the obligations of each are faithfully carried out.

---

[38] Karl Barth, *Church Dogmatics* I/1, 171. See also Hans Joachim Iwand, "Wider den Mißbrauch des 'pro me' als methodisches Prinzip in der Theologie," *Evangelische Theologie* 14 (1954), 120–124.

[39] Pope, *Compendium* II:276.

3

Atonement and Incarnation

Ivor J. Davidson

The theology of the atonement is, or ought to be, inseparable from the theology of the incarnation. If atonement speaks of the means by which estranged creatures are in mercy set "at one" with their creator and he with them, at the core of its doctrinal confession lies faith's claim concerning the essential context of that matter: "the Word became flesh, and made his dwelling among us" (John 1:14). In the enfleshment of this Word or Son of God and all that it entails, creaturely salvation is definitively worked out. The climax of the enfleshed One's worldly existence, his violent death on a Roman cross, is—literally—"crucial" to the achievement, but the significance of his death depends entirely upon the identity of its subject. If we ask *how* his action is atoning, we are immediately directed to the first defining feature in the "great mystery" of proper relation to God: "he was manifested in flesh" (1 Tim. 3:16). The phrase speaks not of advent only, the conception and birth of a Jewish infant in Bethlehem, but the totality of a journey: childhood and maturity, relationships and calling, sufferings and sorrows, ministry and teaching, temptations and trials, passion and cross. There is the burial of a broken body, the silence of a borrowed tomb. Gloriously, there is more: bodily resurrection from the grave, bodily ascension into heaven, enthronement, and ministry at God's right hand. What takes place along that whole path, and chiefly at its end, makes all the difference in the world. In this flesh and no other, death is abolished, life and immortality are brought to light. All this happens, the gospel says, in "the appearing of our Savior Christ Jesus" (2 Tim. 1:10).

Person and Work

Western Christian teaching has long seen fit to differentiate the person and work of Christ, treating these as formally distinct themes—one concerned with who he is, the other with what he does. The distinction is valid, but requires care. It is certainly inappropriate to reduce Christology to an expressionist sketch of the ways in which the Savior benefits us personally, or to render his essential status only as summary of his functions in the economy of salvation. To impulses of that kind modern theology has been quite prone, though the anxiety which underlies them—that interest in the person of Christ in analytic terms tends toward a formal or speculative theology, detached from the history of Jesus, remote from the redemptive experience of his followers—is largely misplaced. What we say about the work of Christ does not exhaust what we say about its agent, nor does the articulation of a metaphysical Christology necessarily abstract the character of the Savior from its density in time, or risk the collapse of his salvific significance into an abstruse conceptual formula.

Nevertheless, as Christian faith has from earliest times recognized, there can be no sharp dichotomy between person and work. The mission of Jesus the Savior (Mt. 1:21) is the locus of his self-identification; his person in our midst is already the enactment of a saving embassy in time, the effects of which are bound entirely to his incomparable dignity. In real-world history, this one figure in the human story has worked a redemption that is a comprehensively wonderful—deliverance *from* sin, death, alienation, and judgment; freedom *for* life, for fellowship, for flourishing, for our ultimate fulfillment as creatures. The achievement is what it is because it is he who has done it, in all the singularity of his credentials. Divine Son, coequal with God, he is also the "human Christ Jesus," one enfleshed subject: the "one mediator between God and humans" (1 Tim. 2:5). To know the mediator's work is not to appropriate something known independently of his person, or to be credited with benefits secured by Christ but transferred to us only nominally or in abstraction: it is to receive *him*, and all things in and with him. The value of his saving action, in all its transformative effect, is available no other way; he himself *is* our peace (Eph. 2:14).

If the work of Christ is so connected with his person, those who in faith seek understanding of how his work atones face a task demanding but delightful: the contemplation of what it means that he, the Lord, should take flesh and dwell among us, for us and for our salvation. Such contemplation is response to the wonder of liberation; it is undertaken in relation to a living subject, not an inert or abstract theme. In this sphere, theology is not cast upon its own resources, for it operates in the self-communicative presence of the One it confesses. Raised and exalted, fleshly still, this Lord is pleased to afford us, in the power of his Spirit, true knowledge of his saving splendor—of what it is that he has wrought in reconciling us to God, and what it means that he appears now in the presence of God for us (Heb. 9:24). His acts in history, concrete and determinate, are not restricted to an elusive past, or to some notional transaction that has occurred over our heads: they are of decisive personal consequence. Alive, active, vocal, he is present as human at God's right hand, and his life there is directed toward our interests: "he is able to save for all time those who come to God through him, for he always lives to make intercession for them" (Heb. 7:25). Raised "with" him (Eph. 2:6; Col. 2:12; 3:1), and secure in that status, we remain as yet, in our present bodily state, "away from" him (2 Cor. 5:6); yet here too, in this world, he binds himself to us in astonishing intimacy. We are "in" him, he "in" us. These are the staggering lengths to which the mediator's graciousness toward us has gone, this the reach to which it does and will yet extend.

The calling of atonement theology is thus entirely privileged—to offer wondering testimony to that which this One gives, for our infinite blessing, in the giving of himself. Normed by the gospel set forth in Holy Scripture, inspired and sanctified instrument of his living authority over his own, soteriology listens for his voice, and aims in the strength of his Spirit to render its response—provisional, inadequate, human—as a faithful echo of his self-announcement. A dogmatic of the incarnate Savior's atonement is only an attentive repetition of what is presented to us there, an attempt to set out the testimony of Scripture's gospel in summary form.

What Kind of Incarnation?

In talking of the incarnation, I refer to the church's doctrine of *ontological* incarnation, as classically confessed in the creeds of the fourth to the seventh centuries. I do not mean an account of divine incarnation as "symbol," "myth," or "metaphor," as variously proposed in revisionist theologies. There are many reasons why proposals along those lines are problematic. The most elementary objection is that, whatever their motivations or idiom, they do violence to the most basic logic of Christian faith. According to that logic, it simply makes no sense to speak of the saving identity of Jesus as something other than the actual presence of the God of Israel *as* the self-same being as this figure of human history.

Early Christian texts present various accounts of Jesus and his actions, an array of Christological images and titles; the language of incarnation is not on the surface of quite a number of these, and the discourse of ontology as it came to be deploys idiom unknown to the first worshippers of Jesus as risen. What that language seeks to *identify*, however—the unique relation between this Jesus and the one true God from whom alone salvation can come—is intellectually basic to the worship in which the followers of Jesus engaged from very early on. It cannot be dismissed as a late development, nor can it be transposed into nominalist or symbolic terms without essential loss.

Nonliteral understandings of incarnation as option (or alleged necessity) in Christian theology face plenty of challenges; it would be otiose to rehearse them here. In the area of soteriology they are quickly swamped by moralism, emerging as heavily subjective or culturally conservative. Against such domestications, ontology stands as enduringly necessary corrective: the matter of the incarnation is more radical than that. However attractive the proposed ideals may be, their center of gravity is wrong. Jesus is Savior, not cipher; his saving identity has to do with who he *is*, indissolubly, as God humanly in our midst: as such, he does more than urge us to reach higher in our quests to be good.

What Kind of Atonement?

Ontological incarnation is indispensable. But our sense of what it means for a theology of salvation can be a bit narrow. In popular thinking, "incarnation" is generally associated with the start of Jesus's life on earth, "atonement" more or less entirely with its end. The associations are understandable, but when they loom large it is easy for each term to be diminished in its reach. If incarnation and atonement are cordoned off from each other, or if incarnation is viewed only as a logical presupposition for atonement that is largely available for treatment on its own, the theology of salvation tends to be treated in isolation from its deep background in the doctrine of the God whose desire it is to share his life with us. Without attention to that background, the details of saving action tend to be blurred, their ends misrepresented: the life of Jesus may appear of limited significance; atonement by means of a violent death may seem mere mechanism, a grim remedial measure for a creaturely problem or an instrument by which a somehow constrained creator resolves a dilemma imposed upon him by abstract obligations.[1] In turn, its benefits may emerge as formal or extrinsic, a transaction over our heads rather than the personal relation of which the gospel speaks.

As check on these dangers, it is sometimes suggested that the theology of the atonement ought frankly to focus less on the death of Jesus and more on the significance of his life-act as a whole.[2] What matters, it is argued, is not so much (or not only) that he suffers and dies in our place as that God takes flesh and dwells among us. In that, a new situation is established for humanity as such: in the Word's assumption of flesh, humanity itself is healed, transformed, and restored. Whatever else may be said about this approach, it remains vitally important that atonement is not so directly identified with the person of the incarnate Christ that the specific course of his personal history suffers eclipse. Person and office must be taken together, but if we say in an unqualified way that the person of the mediator just *is* his atoning work, or imply that everything that really matters is accomplished in the Word's taking of flesh per se, we evacuate his temporal path—not least its climax—of its determinate content. The entire reality of his life-act is saving, but much more is going on in atonement than some metaphysical alchemy in Mary's womb, or anything that is completed short of the events that take place at the end of the mediator's earthly course. The action occurs— atonement is *made*—not merely as through the Spirit's work God the Son *comes* as human, but as he is *present* as human, and definitively as he *goes* as human, via the specific path of cross and grave, to the place from which he came, at the Father's side.[3]

If we are to phrase the relationship of incarnation and atonement with due care, we must keep in mind that both speak of what it means that there should be this One mediator whose mediation occurs in a specific set of events in time

---

[1] It should however be noted that the language of dilemma as famously deployed by Athanasius in *On the Incarnation* has little to do with abstract obligations, focusing much more on the creator's desire that his creatures should know him. I also do not think that medieval treatments of the necessity and/or fittingness of the incarnation, such as Anselm's approach in *Cur Deus Homo*, trade in abstract principles half as much as their critics have sometimes supposed.

[2] See, for example, Thomas F. Torrance, *The Mediation of Christ*, rev. ed. (Edinburgh: T&T Clark, 1992); *Incarnation: The Person and Life of Christ*, ed. Robert T. Walker and Milton Keynes (Paternoster/Colorado Springs, CO: IVP Academic, 2008); *Atonement: The Person and Work of Christ*, ed. Robert T. Walker and Milton Keynes (Paternoster/Colorado Springs, CO: IVP Academic, 2009. For some other accents, see Kathryn Tanner, *Christ the Key* (Cambridge: Cambridge University Press, 2010), 247–273.

[3] The history of divine exile and humiliation—human homecoming and exaltation as the actualization in time of God's determination to have his being for and with us—is Karl Barth's way of presenting the theology of reconciliation in *Church Dogmatics* [*CD*] (Edinburgh: T&T Clark, 1956–75), IV/1–3. For Barth, the Reformed doctrine of the two states of humiliation and exaltation is pursued in nonsequential terms, though not consistently so, and for good reasons.

and space. If there is a certain sense in which it may be said that "Jesus Christ is the atonement,"[4] he is so only as the One who in his *actual* living, dying, rising, and ascending maintains, accomplishes, and fulfills the covenant; atonement is effected *there*, not simply (if it may be so said) in the fact of his existence. The ontology of the incarnation is crucial throughout, but the metaphysics of the divine assumption of flesh do not subsume the concrete realities of the history in which the mediator carries out his personal office.[5] Atonement is wrought *in* this drama.

Behind the whole occurrence, without detriment to its historical density but its sovereign cause at every point, lies God's self-determination to enact his triune being so, in reiteration of his own holy majesty, for the blessing of his creatures. Ahead of it all, the intended outcome or *telos*, lies the wondrous reality that these creatures—estranged from him and under his judgment as they otherwise are—should by this means come to have fellowship with him in his holiness even so, that he should have joy in being their God. In essentially correlative but not just identical ways, incarnation and atonement speak of what takes place in the personal outworking of that resolute purpose, and as the personal means to that most glorious of ends. They talk with differing content on a common theme: on what comes to pass in the particular set of happenings of which it is said: "God ... in Christ ... reconciling" (2 Cor. 5:19).

What, at minimum, must be said about the identity of the mediator in this movement, and what does this entail for our attempts to set forth his saving work?

The God Who Atones: Divine "Becoming"

The incarnation, *the* atonement: according to the gospel, the event of God's redemptive presence in the person of his Son incarnate is unqualified in its uniqueness, categorically different from all other realities in the world's story. Theology has not always grasped the point, but the incarnation brooks no analogical predication; it is *sui generis*, an instance of itself, without parallel, extension or approximation. It is not an intensification of a general creaturely possibility, or a moment of exceptional commitment on the part of an independently

---

[4] Ibid., IV/1, 34.
[5] For a robust endeavor to integrate person and office in a way that does justice to both, see Michael S. Horton, *Lord and Saviour: A Covenant Christology* (Louisville, KY: Westminster John Knox Press, 2005).

existing human being, specially inspired or called to a unique degree of intimacy with God. The subject of the action is antecedently different from any creaturely agent: the only-begotten Son, begotten of his Father before all worlds, his origins are eternally divine, without beginning in time, a reiteration in God's own life; coequal with his Father, he is "of the same substance" with him: "light of light," "very God of very God."

Primordially this divine Son, the Christ in whose fleshly history atonement is wrought is as such "the one Lord" already, personally subsistent second mode of being of the only Lord there is. Nothing he does in the world *makes* him Lord; it is *as* Lord that he acts, and so confirms his glory. The chief attestation of that reality in time, his resurrection from the dead, is of immense significance soteriologically—a divine act that confirms what has been achieved in his dying, and secures his fleshly continuity as prolepsis of our own. But the verdict is only a declaration "in power" (Rom. 1:4) of who he in fact is in the events that precede it; it does not place him ontologically anywhere he was not before.

Contrary to various readings of the matter, the divine Son does not scale himself down in becoming human, or leave aspects of his essential deity behind, or become hemmed in by finitude. The path he takes involves voluntary humiliation, his being "for a little time made lower" in respect to creatures (Heb. 2:9); but in taking "a servant's form," "humbling" himself and becoming "obedient to death, even death on a cross" (Phil. 2:7–8), he does not contradict his divinity—he reiterates it. The condescension lies entirely within the possibilities of the sufficiency from which it derives. The Son who belongs antecedently with the Father and the Spirit "becomes" human: he remains as divine as ever he was in the process.

"Becoming" is a sovereign act, unilateral and irreversible, a movement *from* God *to* us. It takes place, as do all God's "outward" works, in triune form, repeating the essential relations in which the one God eternally subsists *ad intra*, ineffably self-communicative in his innermost being. It *repeats* these relations: it does not amplify them, for they are perfect already; God is already utterly realized, in need of no outward turn to expand his identity. The incarnation occurs in free majesty, no matter of divine enhancement. Yet, free—and so indeed "new"—as the action is in time, it is in all its aspects anticipated by the nature of God's eternally triune being. Each of the persons of the Godhead is engaged in his own distinct manner in the incarnational economy, but the movement in its totality is the work of the God in whom there is—essentially—harmony of purpose and oneness in strategy. The Son, not the Father or the Spirit, takes on flesh.

But his doing so is purposed by the Father and enabled by the Spirit. The whole occurrence involves the "togetherness" of the Three whose relational fellowship *is* God's eternal essence, the abundance of life in himself.

The incarnation tells us that this is where a theology of atonement needs to *start*: with the doctrine of God. The authenticity of the Son's *fleshly* identity is vital to his saving work, and to this we shall come. But we must linger here first. The whole business of atoning action has, without qualification, its source in God. A more expansive treatment of the economy would require to show how God's immanent life is the essential and necessary basis of all that is ultimately happening; consideration of the divine perfections provides a vital check upon many misconstruals of atonement, such as those which suppose God's love and God's justice to be in tension in the matter, or those which suggest that God in himself is somehow changed or even completed in what is done. The immediate point is this: in his antecedent plenitude, his limitless adequacy, goodness, and blessedness in himself, the triune God is infinitely qualified to be our Savior.[6] As the incarnation is the personal initiative of *this* God, the salvation it brings has its whole basis in his generosity—his immeasurably loving will to live his life not just in the perfection of his own completeness but also in fellowship with others. It is no part of the incarnate Son's action to render God gracious to creatures for the first time, or to turn an otherwise unloving God into one who is only henceforth well disposed toward them. The incarnate Son makes peace (Col. 1:20), but he does not make God love us. Behind his mission lies already the unfathomable depth of the triune God's commitment to himself in his commitment to the world.

Theology has expended a good deal of energy historically on whether the incarnation should be said to be "necessary" for creaturely salvation, and if so in what sense, and on the relationship between what might be said to be necessary and what might be said to be "fitting" for God. However such matters are tackled, what is going on in the great act of divine becoming brings about a purpose on which God has been set since before the foundation of the world, and to which he has bound himself. The completion of this purpose is foreshadowed extensively in time, in God's covenantal history with his creatures. Though his creatures in perversity turn from him and repudiate the intimacy for which they were made, God pledges himself to them in free and sovereign

---

[6] See John Webster, "'It was the Will of the Lord to Bruise Him': Soteriology and the Doctrine of God," in *God of Salvation: Soteriology in Theological Perspective*, ed. Ivor J. Davidson and Murray A. Rae (Farnham and Burlington, VT: Ashgate, 2011), 15–34.

mercy. He chooses the most unlikely and vexatious of beneficiaries: the patriarchs and Israel. These subjects evince no native merit or potential to qualify them for his favor, yet God consecrates himself for relationship with them, promises that not only they but one day, along with them, all the earth will know his blessing. And he remains faithful: in spite of their ingratitude and infidelity, he bears patiently with them, honors his gracious promises; Israel's God goes on dealing with his people amid chaos, bondage, wandering, exile—judging them, yes, but caring for them still, reaffirming his will to bless them, extending his mercy again and again through the prophetic, priestly, and royal ministers of his purposes. In all this, the history says, the creator is demonstrating how deeply he has chosen to vest himself in relationship with his creatures. Their rebellions incur his righteous anger, but *because* the covenanting God is eternally the High and Holy One, not *despite* that fact, he is jealous concerning the commitments into which he has entered, and upon which he has staked the honor of his name. There is dark plight for God's erring and exiled ones, but in his loving holiness he is and will yet be their Redeemer, the Lord who does not carry out his fierce anger upon them with terminal effects. Through them he will bring to fulfillment his ancient pledge that they will know the One for whom they were made.

The incarnation says that here, at the fullness of time (Gal. 4:4), God displays the immensity of his commitment to himself in his commitment to the undeserving. He comes in *person*, in One who is "Son," the ultimate Elect Servant; not just a special delegate or even an angelic emissary, but the very "radiance of his glory and exact representation of his being" (Heb. 1:2–3). This One makes God known (Jn. 1:18; cf. Mt. 11:27) like none before him, as he alone is qualified to do; here, God enacts as never before his ancient pledge: "I will be God for you." *This* mercy does not merely address the bondage and exile of old: it deals with creaturely evil and its just deserts on another scale entirely. Behind it stands a vast back-history, reaching far beyond all the mighty acts that have anticipated it, achieving what they never could. Here an *eternal* covenant is fulfilled; here a "mystery hidden for ages in God" (Eph. 3:9) is brought to light.

Incarnate Atonement: Taking Flesh

The divine Son "takes" or "assumes" flesh (*sarx*). That it is *human* flesh is hardly insignificant: he comes as the true Image of God, the Last Adam, the "real" man. As we shall see, his fleshliness has consequence for creation and creatures of all kinds, but its human form remains of central importance: here is the divine Image as it is meant to be, the particular covenant-partner God intends, the human creature in right relation to its creator.

The flesh that is taken comes to be as a specific act of divine creation: it has no reality independently of that which it is given in the act of its assumption. There is no annexation of a freestanding human entity. What is established is, however, utterly real; as Chalcedon has it, the Son is not only "consubstantial" (*homoousios*) with the Father in his divinity, he is also consubstantial *with us* in his humanity. In genuine human flesh (1 Jn. 4:2; 2 Jn. 7) he comes, "born of woman" (Gal. 4:4). *Pace* every form of Docetism, this flesh is fully material. There is affirmation, not disdain, for the physical and all that it involves: chemical structures, biological processes, vulnerability, and dependence. In him, we are told, "all things" in the physical universe cohere (Col. 1:17); yet all the divine fullness of the agent and sustainer of everything is present here— "*bodily*" (Col. 2:9). He is "seen" with human eyes, "looked upon," "touched" (1 John 1:1–2). Located in time and space, his body at times does things most bodies do not, it is clear that the Word is not restricted by the flesh he assumes.[7] His human "form" (Phil. 2:8) evinces no special glory; there is, as the tradition has variously pictured it, a hiddenness to his revealing work, a veiling as well as a disclosure of majesty in accommodation of finitude—or perhaps the definitive reminder that God's Godness may be radically counterintuitive for us, its presence an apocalypse *sub contrario*. Yet there is no attrition of deity in any of it: this is what God qua God is, how God qua God is able to be.

The Son is not only embodied: in Chalcedonian language, he has a "rational soul," what we might perhaps collectively describe as genuine intellectual, psychological, and spiritual characteristics: human mental gifts, human emotions, a human will.[8] He thinks and makes choices with a human mind, faces temptations "in every respect" as we do (Heb. 4:15), utters "loud cries and tears" (Heb. 5:7). The completeness of his humanity, mental and spiritual as well as physical, is soteriologically vital. The mediator is unable to represent us if he is not one with us. If some essential aspect of our humanity is missing in him, that aspect remains outside the scope of his redemptive action: in the famous contention of

---

[7] The claim has its critics, but remains, I believe, important: see Andrew M. McGinnis, *The Son of God beyond the Flesh: A Historical and Theological Study of the* Extra Calvinisticum (London and New York: Bloomsbury T&T Clark, 2014).

[8] The elaboration of a theology of his human willing is a product of Christology after Chalcedon, formally acknowledged at the Council of Constantinople in 680/1. On the essential contribution of Maximus the Confessor, see Demetrios Bathrellos, *The Byzantine Christ: Person, Nature, and Will in the Christology of St. Maximus the Confessor* (Oxford: Oxford University Press, 2004).

Gregory of Nazianzus, "that which is not assumed is not healed."[9] The flesh of the mediator is—holistically, psychosomatically—true human flesh, "of one stock" with whatever it is that makes us all that we essentially are as human (Heb. 2:11).

His flesh is particular. It has a certain gender, ethnicity, size, and appearance. The incarnate One speaks a certain human language, belongs in a specific economic and cultural situation, has a specific set of relations definitive of who he is. He is a son of Israel, of David's and Abraham's lineage. Conceived of Mary, he is firstborn in Joseph the carpenter's family, brought forth in Bethlehem, child refugee in Egypt, reared in Nazareth, worshipper in Jerusalem, baptized by John, itinerant teacher in Galilee and Judaea. He has disciples and friends of varying degrees of intimacy; he also has enemies, who find reasons to repudiate all that he is about; and he has those who will kill him, life's Author, in the end (Acts 3:14–15). The particular features of the mediator's humanity are contingent in the sense that divine incarnation could presumably have occurred otherwise,[10] but their particularity attests his authenticity as an individual human being, and his place as Israel's Servant, not least the Servant who suffers. The Son does not simply become human: he becomes *a* man, Jesus of Nazareth.

In its particularity, his fleshly reality is of universal consequence. This is true at several levels. In the divine taking of human flesh, all human flesh is affirmed as immeasurably precious to God: in all its stages and conditions, in its most vulnerable and marginal of forms, in a mother's womb, in a silent tomb. True Image of God, the incarnate One confirms how much the image matters: its original great goodness in God's sight, its enduring value, notwithstanding all that sin has done to its representation. He sanctifies anew all that is involved in being human as God intends: embodiment, psychology, creativity, relationship, environment, and interdependence with other creatures. He is unashamed to call us his brothers and sisters (Heb. 2:11), to exist as participant within as well as maker of the creaturely realm. His humanity cannot be duplicated by moral imitation, but the beneficiaries of his atoning work are saved "into" the human identity enacted in him, established anew as agents in correspondence to the pattern he makes known: his human being, in proper fellowship with God and with the rest of creation, is what our being human will yet be.

What occurs in his life-act is not merely illustrative: it is re-determinative of the plight in which human beings exist in estrangement from God. There are

---

[9] Gregory of Nazianzus, *Epistle* 101.5, in Gregory of Nazianzus, *On God and Christ: The Five Theological Orations and Two Letters to Cledonius*, trans. Frederick Williams and Lionel R. Wickham (Crestwood, NY: St Vladimir's Seminary Press, 2002).

[10] Thus it is impossible to treat the maleness of Jesus, for example, as ontologically essential.

two elements to this. First, he identifies with us as we are. He participates in a world afflicted by the Fall, with all its privation, disease, injustice, alienation, and conflict, and comes himself "in the likeness of sinful flesh" (Rom. 8:3). Second, there is, for all that, a vital difference between him and us: in our nature, he is "without sin" (Heb. 4:15); he knows no sin (2 Cor. 5:21); "in him is no sin" (1 Jn. 3:5); he is "holy, blameless, unstained, separated from sinners" (Heb. 7:26–7). One with us, he is what we are not, does what we do not do.

Christology has struggled over how to express this: the Son takes flesh in a broken world, yet is sinless. The latter is vital: it is *because* he is without sin that he is able to redeem; were he sinner himself, he too would need redemption. At the same time, the redemptive consequences of his being human without sin depend entirely upon his community of nature with our own; were he not one with us, he could not act for us in the ways Scripture insists he does. What does this imply about the status of his flesh? At the very least, it is clear that sinfulness, or indeed even the possibility of sinning, is not of the essence of human nature as such: he is properly human *as* the One who knows no sin. Is it possible to say more? According to much of the Western tradition, it has been necessary to say that the flesh of the mediator is true and complete, but not "fallen" in itself. In the past two centuries this has been heavily challenged, with substantial appeal to Greek patristic thought.[11] The flesh that is taken in the incarnation is indeed "fallen," it is argued, and vitally so, for only by entering into the actual conditions of our human state in its estrangement from God does the mediator save. He heals our fallen nature by descending into the depths of its diseased state and making it new from the inside; it is not some "perfect" flesh that needs to be saved, after all, but flesh as it is for those who have broken covenant with their maker. This does not, however, mean that he is himself a sinner: he takes "fallen" flesh, yet crucially indeed he does not sin; he effects change for us as he lives differently within the same fleshly conditions.

Critics of the "unfallen" flesh position argue that it effectively idealizes the flesh of Christ, and in practice undermines the genuineness of his participation in the human situation in need of redemption. If it is *not* "fallen" flesh that is assumed, there is no healing for *that* flesh; it is not the healthy who need a physician, but the sick. It is also sometimes said that the fleshly path of the mediator is wholly unlike ours if we posit, as Western theology often has, that, as bearer of

---

[11] For an enthusiastic rendition of some of the patristic and later material, noting the obvious modern examples of Edward Irving and Karl Barth, see Thomas G. Weinandy, *In the Likeness of Sinful Flesh: An Essay on the Humanity of Christ* (Edinburgh: T&T Clark, 1993).

an "unfallen" human nature, he is not only sinless in practice but "impeccable" by nature—literally "unable" to sin. The arguments for "fallen" flesh, on the other hand, are said to be unable to explain how it is that the Savior is not himself a sinner, and thus unable to save, if he has a "fallen" human nature. It may also be argued that the notion of "fallen" flesh renders his saving work all too vulnerable. If formally the mediator is "peccable"—able in principle to sin since his human nature is sinful, even if he does not sin in practice (either on his own strength or as enabled by the Holy Spirit)—this leaves open at least the theoretical possibility that his saving action is capable of failure; that surely severs it from its proper anchorage in his status as sent One.

Much of the debate inevitably turns upon understandings of original sin and its consequences, and upon how Christ's "natures" may be said to relate. The discussion has frequently lacked clarity on what might be meant by "fallen" or "sinful" flesh, and the historical resources have frequently not been well deployed.[12] It is absolutely clear that the incarnate Son is sinless in his person, and necessarily so. It is equally clear that his sinlessness has nothing to do with moral idealism, or to the potential isolation of his human nature as abstractly perfect.[13] As the gospels present it, there is no archetypal perfection about his fleshly identity, no stained-glass sanctity. Holy and Righteous One, he overturns conventions as to what is clean and unclean; full of grace and truth, he yet gets angry, curses fig trees, speaks fiercely to and of opponents, pronounces woes on communities who reject his message, stages a shocking demonstration in the courts of Israel's most sacred space. Notorious "friend" of sinners, he seems to many of his contemporaries an appalling flouter of Torah: a libertarian, demon-possessed, a blasphemer.

The mediator's fleshly path is a site of intense moral drama. He is tempted in every way as we are (Heb. 4:15); his human career involves "loud cries and tears," the *learning* of obedience through what he suffers (Heb. 5:7–10). He delights in God's will (Heb. 10:5–10), always does what pleases his Father (John 8:29), but there is no sense in which his humanity is calmly steered through the world by divine autopilot, no serene constancy of insight into what lies around the corner. He has human decisions to make about what it means to do his Father's will, and

---

[12] See, for example, Kelly M. Kapic, "The Son's Assumption of a Human Nature: A Call for Clarity," *IJST* 3 (2001), 154–166; also Oliver D. Crisp, *Divinity and Humanity: The Incarnation Reconsidered* (Cambridge: Cambridge University Press, 2007), 90–117; Ian A. McFarland, "Fallen or Unfallen? Christ's Human Nature and the Ontology of Human Sinfulness," *IJST* 4 (2008), 399–415.

[13] See Ivor J. Davidson, "Pondering the Sinlessness of Jesus Christ: Moral Christologies and the Witness of Scripture," *IJST* 4 (2008), 372–398.

human intimacy with the Father does not—*pace* Thomas—mean perpetual beatific vision or an easy road; his life is characterized by prayer, heard for his "reverent submission," but the hearing does not save him from death (Heb. 5:7).[14] He walks by human faith, without which it is impossible humanly to please God; he is assaulted by trials of ferocious intensity, almost overwhelmed at the last by what they entail. His human nature in itself offers him no shield from trouble: enacted before us, it only intensifies it. *Judged* by his way of being human, "Away with him!" the sinners cry (John 19:15).

He comes in the likeness of sinful flesh, and evinces neither unarguable moral perfection of a conventional sort nor obvious insulation from the pressures and temptations which are the lot of flesh in a fallen world. More than that: his human path involves specific and persistent assault upon his very raison d'être; for him to yield would in principle mean the dissolution of his saving office. Obedience for him is not generalized virtue, but faithfulness to the One who appointed him (Heb. 3:2). Yet his human nature surely cannot be described as "fallen" or "sinful" without immediate qualification. Though "of" Mary, his flesh is created and sanctified uniquely as *his* flesh, taken for the specific, and in no sense haphazard, role that is his. As he fulfills that role, his humanity is the same as ours but different from the start, for its entire reality is found in the person of the Son who in the Spirit's power takes it and makes it his own.[15]

The directedness of his history, its movement toward a decisive bearing of the world's sin, not his own, involves his steadfast human obedience with a human mind and a human will; yet as we appraise that history it is inconceivable that it should fail, or that its outcome should ever be in jeopardy, for it repeats the Son's eternally harmonious relation to his Father in the Spirit. He is one with the Father and at one with the Father's will before ever he comes, and as he is among us in his obedience so he essentially is. If we are to speak of impeccability, as surely we must, we must acknowledge that there is no immediately obvious divine hegemony at work in the Son's human refusal of sin, and for him no evasion of anguish or, to his human mind, the possibility of failure and all its responsibility. But it is by the same Spirit who binds him to the Father essentially that he is of necessity upheld. His flesh is of universal consequence for sinners

---

[14] For a constructive contribution to a much-discussed theme, see R. Michael Allen, *The Christ's Faith: A Dogmatic Account* (London and New York: T&T Clark, 2009).

[15] The *enhypostasia* is, I think, enriched by attention to the role of the Spirit in creating, sanctifying, and sustaining the flesh that is personalized in the Son. It should be noted that the role of the Spirit in his conception does not, however, "explain" his sinlessness in biological or genetic terms: it signals only that his flesh does not come to be as other flesh does. His flesh is nonetheless authentic and complete for that.

because in the person of the mediator human flesh is indeed human flesh actualized in practice as it ought to be; from its earliest origins, this is flesh in unbroken intimacy with God, created and sanctified definitively by the Spirit's work for a path of human fellowship with God. Fellowship in the world means no abstract steady state, however, a detached representation of some perfect form; it means active and passive obedience, and that unto death: a life of overcoming of increasing intensity, advance toward destiny at escalating cost, the cutting of a way toward the cross. And so it is that this man's faithfulness puts right from the human side the consequences of all our disobedience (Rom. 5:12–21); he is able to offer himself "without blemish" to God (Heb. 9:14), a spotless Lamb (1 Pet. 1:19): in *his* flesh, unlike in ours, sin is condemned (Rom. 8:3).

Every stage of the mediator's divine-human existence is of salvific density: "from the time when he took on the form of a servant, he began to pay the price of liberation in order to redeem us."[16] The divinity and humanity that "concur" in his person do so, Chalcedon insists, "without confusion, without change, without division, without separation." Different traditions have found reasons to prefer the first pair of negatives over the second, and vice versa, and have talked in their own ways about how the respective features of divinity and humanity relate. However we phrase the matter, the fundamental point is that the mediator's work is a fully human as well as a fully divine business, and that as the One incarnate subject he acts according to both natures.[17] Stating the vicariousness of his saving action thus involves attention to the totality of his human obedience in identification with us—in baptism, prayer, repudiation of sin, commitment to vocation—and to the pattern of his compassion, his care for others, his enactment of kingdom life as different from anything else on offer along the paths of human righteousness.

How the narrative is depicted in conceptual terms may vary. One powerful image in patristic theology is that of *recapitulation*: the Savior passes through each stage of the human journey, perfectly fulfilling the broken covenant; this way, he reorders the human situation—Adam's story of fall, Israel's story of exile—by reenacting it, restoring not only the human creature but creation itself to God. The theme (which picks up on Eph. 1:10) is famously developed in the later second century by Irenaeus,[18] but it also predates him, and later patristic

---

[16] John Calvin, *Institutes of the Christian Religion*, ed. John T. McNeill, trans. Ford Lewis Battles, 2 vols (Philadelphia: Westminster Press, 1960) [Calvin, *Inst.*], II.xvi.5 (vol. 1, 507).

[17] I am unlikely to surprise if I confirm, with as little offense as I can, that I consider a Reformed Christology may do a better job of upholding the point than a Lutheran one.

[18] See, for example, Eric Osborn, *Irenaeus of Lyons* (Cambridge: Cambridge University Press, 2001), pt. III.

writers richly develop it as well, not least in the seventh century by Maximus the Confessor, as an account of cosmic salvation.[19] Other language speaks in *therapeutic* or *medicinal* terms: the Savior's action serves to heal us of the disease and disfigurement of sin, and so he not only enacts the Image of God as it truly is but *restores* it in us from its state of damage or loss. In both cases, there may be frequent links to the semantics of *victory*: as he overcomes sin and temptation himself, the Savior is able decisively to free us from our bondage, delivering us from captivity to the demons or malign forces that deceive and enslave us. In Reformed theology, there has been great emphasis on the mediator's fulfillment of his work as execution of a *threefold office*, an idea clearly discernible in Old Testament images of God's anointed deliverer: he is the ultimate prophet, priest, and king.[20] Accounts of his *covenantal* righteousness, *sacrificial* obedience, or *satisfaction* of the requirements of God's honor may well be connected with such concepts, as of course may be the vital biblical theme that Christ is not only a representative of but also a *substitute* for others. Other imagery again speaks of the incarnation in overtly *participatory* terms, focusing on the "wondrous exchange" in which, "out of his measureless benevolence," the Son of God becomes Son of Man with us so as to make us sons and daughters of God with him.[21] As a theology of *theosis* envisages this, he becomes human so that humans might become divine[22]—the end of his saving work is that we become "partakers of the divine nature" (2 Pet. 1:4).[23]

Some theological expansions of participatory language are better anchored biblically than others, and the concept requires careful treatment if it is not to be deployed in ways that a biblical doctrine of God and God's dealings with creatures will not support. Atonement is no abstract divinization of human essence, nor is it some especially inspiring concentration of a general *methexis* of all creaturely reality in God. Certain ways of construing so-called vicarious humanity,[24] or the upshot for us of Christ's participation in flesh, invite quite serious

---

[19] See, for example, Paul M. Blowers and Robert L. Wilken, *On the Cosmic Mystery of Christ: Selected Writings from St Maximus the Confessor* (Crestwood, NY: St Vladimir's Seminary Press, 2003).

[20] See, for example, Robert Sherman, *King, Priest, and Prophet: A Trinitarian Theology of Atonement* (New York and London: T&T Clark International, 2004). On Calvin as exemplar, see Stephen Edmondson, *Calvin's Christology* (Cambridge: Cambridge University Press, 2004).

[21] Calvin, *Inst.* 4.17.2 (vol. 2, 1362).

[22] Cf., for example, Irenaeus, *Against Heresies* 3.19.1; Athanasius, *On the Incarnation* 54.3; *Against the Arians* 1.38, 48; 2.61.

[23] On the patristic background, see Norman Russell, *The Doctrine of Deification in the Greek Patristic Tradition* (Oxford: Oxford University Press, 2004).

[24] For an oft-cited short statement, see James B. Torrance, "The Vicarious Humanity of Christ," in *The Incarnation: Ecumenical Studies in the Nicene-Constantinopolitan Creed, AD 381*, ed. Thomas F. Torrance (Edinburgh: Handsel Press, 1981), 127–147.

criticisms,[25] particularly where they also trade upon questionable readings of historical theology that exaggerate alleged problems of "extrinsicism," "nominalism," or "contractualism" in Western traditions.[26] But the human as well as divine aspects of the mediator's action must certainly be set forth, and that will involve among other things attention to his human as well as divine *willing* of salvation as he acts on our behalf and in our place. Images of his mediatorial work as fleshly readily overlap or complement one another, and are not mutually exclusive. As is often remarked, the considerable range of the biblical language points to the immensity of what is done; some syntheses are considerably more important than others, but the church has, with reason, avoided the isolation of a single account as exclusive.

Flesh and its Destiny

The Son's fleshly presence in time does not atone but for its finale. The life that leads to the cross is indeed saving, but the proportions of the story told by the gospel-writers are overwhelmingly governed by the destiny to which the divine "must" drives the subject forward. The Son who comes to serve comes to give his life (Mark 10:45). His final passion is not where suffering for him begins, nor is it the point at which his suffering starts to matter in salvific terms, but it takes him to a place of darkness beyond anything that precedes it: to the dereliction of Calvary's cry to heaven's Sender: "Why have you forsaken me?" This, definitively, is the Son's "hour," and in its depths scarcely filial, it seems, does he feel; here, in a finally decisive way, he takes covenant cursedness to himself, and "becomes" a curse for us (Gal. 3:13). The narrative of his saving achievement in flesh involves, non-negotiably, the story of his *death* (1 Cor. 1:18, 23; 15:3): without that, no

---

[25] For one example, see John McLeod Campbell, *The Nature of the Atonement* (orig. 1856, new edn., intr. James B. Torrance, Eugene, OR: Wipf & Stock, 1996): the atoning action of Christ consists in his vicarious confession of sins on our behalf: in uttering a perfect "Amen" in humanity to God's judgment upon human sin, he offers the one true human response of penitence or repentance before God on our behalf. As alternative to classical accounts of what is wrought in Christ's suffering for us, the notion is, I believe, decidedly problematic, though it continues to find enthusiasts.

[26] *Theosis* in particular has become a heavily abused and often ill-defined concept in contemporary theology, with far too little differentiation between the various *kinds* of participatory language found in the traditions of East and West, and glib assumptions as to what to make of alleged points of commonality or distinction. The constructive intentions in some of this are no doubt commendable, but it remains vital to treat texts and authors on their own terms and in their own contexts. For some of the issues, see, for example, J. Todd Billings, *Calvin, Participation and the Gift: The Activity of Believers in Union with Christ* (Oxford: Oxford University Press, 2007); Grant Macaskill, *Union with Christ in the New Testament* (Oxford: Oxford University Press, 2013), chapter 2–3.

atonement. Human agents, Jew and Gentile, are responsible for what takes place, but there is, as always, a whole other dimension, especially here: "the definite plan and foreknowledge of God" (Acts 2:23). The Son is "handed over" (Rom. 8:32) by his Father, and not spared; the Servant is bruised, smitten, and afflicted in execution of divine purpose (Isa. 53:4–10). Voluntary sharer in that purpose, no one takes his life from him, either (John 10:17–18): he "gives" himself (John 6:50–1; Gal. 2:20; Eph. 5:2, 25; 1 Tim. 2:6). The descent begun in the Virgin's womb leads to the descent into hell. Only here is there a "finishing" of what he comes to do (John 19:30).

The physicality of it all belongs not to some "model" of atonement but to the reality of the history as Scripture tells it. It is in the mediator's body that our sins are borne (1 Pet. 2:24); in the offering of his body that we are sanctified (Heb. 10:10); it is "in the body of his flesh through death" that he reconciles us (Col. 1:22). The shedding of his blood on the cross is vital to what he does in making peace (Col. 1:20), in cleansing the defiled (1 Jn. 1:7), in ransoming the captives (Rev. 5:9; cf. 1 Pet. 1:18–19), in bringing the estranged into covenant fellowship (Eph. 2:13), and to his own capacity to enter into heaven as the ultimate high priest (Heb. 9).

Nonviolent construals of atonement, which variously seek to reassess what it might mean to speak of the death of Jesus as a sacrifice to end all sacrifices—in some sense an "anti-sacrifice"—risk the downgrading of the reality. This death is more than a symbol, or even an ultimate divine repudiation of creaturely violence: in all its darkness and horror, it is, we are told, what God's love takes him to in order to vindicate his name and address his creatures' need. The social and political circumstances are no doubt fundamental, and the final potency of the occurrence in moral terms for us is indeed crucial; but there is no going past its primary constitutive rationale: this fleshly death occurs for our *sins* (1 Cor. 15:3; cf. Rom. 4:25; Gal. 1:4), for *us* (1 Thess. 5:10; cf. 1 Pet. 3:18), and for a *sin-offering* (Rom. 8:3). The motivation is, unreservedly, divine love, but the matter is also the action of the God who is and must be just in justifying, and who "puts forward" this One in realization of that (Rom. 3:25–26). In this fleshly sacrifice, the blood that is of necessity spilt is divine (Acts 20:28); in this death, God provides the Lamb; in this death, the sins of a whole world and their entailments for God as well as the world are divinely addressed, as they must be. The edges of what all this involves must be traced elsewhere in this volume. But there is no divine abuse of a human victim; there is the triune God's bearing of the cost of what it means that he should love sinners. The incarnation requires us to identify all the essential perfections of God's triune being in what occurs at this site;

for this God, mercy, tenderness, and compassion exist in no tension with holiness, wrath, and justice, and need no reconciliation *through* the action: they are expressed at once *as* he acts.

The cross completes a work not done beforehand, yet the business of fleshly salvation does not end there either. Physically raised, the mediator takes his human body, glorified yet still marked by wounds (cf. Rev. 5:6), into heaven, and makes presentation of his once-for-all sacrifice. Enthroned, given a name above every name, he is human still: he intercedes in flesh for those who suffer, remembering his own struggles, we might say, as though they were yesterday. In his enduring humanity, he prays for them and represents them, the only mediator and advocate they could possibly require at the throne of God. He leads them into the presence of his Father, and by his Spirit enables them to participate in heaven's worship. Human still, he will return, and every eye shall see him; as human, he will judge: "No mean assurance, this—that we shall be brought before no other judgment seat than that of our Redeemer, to whom we must look for our salvation!"[27]

In New Testament perspective, what is wrought in this flesh is cosmic in its scope. *All* creation is "for" the One who takes flesh; through his action "all things" are ultimately reconciled to God, "whether things on earth or things in heaven" (Col. 1:16, 19). At the last, "all things in heaven and on earth" are to be "summed up" under him as their head (Eph. 1:10). Meantime, nonhuman creation remains in "frustration" and in "bondage to decay," "groaning ... right up to the present time"; but it is promised its liberation also in due course: it too waits "in eager expectation," it too will share in "the glorious freedom of the children of God" (Rom. 8:19–22). Animals feature prominently in visions of God's peaceable kingdom, and not merely as ancillaries to humanity's ends[28]; plants, other life-forms, angels and spirits, and inanimate objects are all ingredient in a created realm renewed and set free for fellowship with its maker. Whatever we are to make of the biblical pictures of creation's fulfillment, and the necessary place within those of the final judgment of God upon evil and its agents, the eschatological depiction of salvation's reach is unimaginably rich in its splendor. The perfecting of God's purposes for his human image is, we are told, of fundamental significance for the scene, not least insofar as it is *as* human specifically that God redeems and restores, but creaturely reality as a whole, in all its complexity, is

---

[27] Calvin, *Inst.* 2.16.18 (vol. 1, 526).
[28] See further, for example, David L. Clough, *On Animals*, vol. 1: *Systematic Theology* (London and New York: T&T Clark International, 2012), pt. 2.

brought to its *telos* in consequence of what is done by the humanly enfleshed Savior.[29]

One way of gaining (tiny) purchase on this is to say that the *materiality* of incarnate atonement is of eternal consequence. There is, the gospel declares, no gnostic salvation: in taking flesh to save, the Word unites himself irrevocably to matter, and so to the dust and atoms of the universe. Whatever it means to speak of our glorification in a "spiritual body," of the putting on of "imperishability" in place of transience and mortality (1 Cor. 15:42–50), the resurrection of *his* body bears sure promise that other bodies will be raised, and that there will at the last be a glorified material order, "a new heaven and a new earth, the home of righteousness" (2 Pet. 3:14). Atonement does not provide a mechanism for the transportation of human life to some purely spiritual realm, nor any means by which creation in general is ever released from participation in material form: such form is fundamental to its perfected dignity. An entire ethics, politics, aesthetics, and science of our present human situation derives from taking all this seriously: if the whole future of the physical universe is bound up with what is done in the incarnate Christ, and with the final manifestation of his glory, atonement in flesh requires us to think in terms that are as big as it gets.

The Primacy of Christ

If the ultimate in the triune God's commitment to his creation is the presence of Jesus Christ, incarnation and atonement are no second best, a mere contingency measure for a world gone wrong. For some, it has been appropriate to speak of the Fall itself—notwithstanding all that it has meant in terms of evil, injustice, and suffering—as a *felix culpa,* for awful as it has been it has been met by the coming of Immanuel.[30] Such reasoning stretches moral sensibilities to the limits, and is difficult to sustain exegetically. Yet it is clear that the salvation wrought in Christ cannot be presented as a remedial act on the part of a disappointed or puzzled creator: it brings about a state of affairs which this creator has in his loving freedom intended from the first.

---

[29] For one provocative approach to the territory, see Paul J. Griffiths, *Decreation: The Last Things of All Creatures* (Waco, TX: Baylor University Press, 2014).

[30] *Felix culpa* has roots in Augustine; the most famous expression is in the *Exultet*, from the Latin liturgy for Holy Saturday: *O felix culpa, quae talem ac tantum meruit habere redemptorem!* (O happy fault, that merited the possession of such and so great a Redeemer!).

For important strands within the Christian tradition, this means that we must take with full seriousness the possibility that God might well have become incarnate regardless of whether or not his creatures had disobeyed him—such is his desire to have intimacy with us. On that reckoning, atonement by the incarnate One's action sets right a broken relation, but it is no patch-up job: it is the outworking of a primal commitment that God always would take what is ours in order that we might come to participate in him.[31] The logic takes a range of forms, and makes different kinds of claims about why it might be "natural" or desirable for God, while remaining free, so to commit himself. Some ways of thinking about these matters are clearly speculative. In contemporary theology, however, it has been argued, following the lead of Barth, that it is precisely the concrete—*non*speculative—history of the mediator that requires us to think anew about the essence of the God who takes flesh. If God is truly made known in Jesus Christ, the *Logos asarkos* is already the *Logos incarnandus*, the Word who is to take flesh in time.[32]

As the modern debate has made clear, to press such reasoning hard may be to end up so historicizing the being of God as to risk collapsing the freedom and plenitude of God's life in himself regardless of any world. We ought not so to historicize divine ontology as to risk equation of God's eternal being *simpliciter* with his free and majestic *reiteration* of his being in time, nor should we speak, by a different metaphysical route, of historical events as locus of God's coherence in himself, such that atonement itself becomes a matter of "reconciliation in God."[33] Salvation is indeed worked out in this world; there can be no notion that everything occurs in an eternal decree of which historical happenings are mere shadow. Incarnation and atonement save in time. But they do so because they derive from the infinite depth of God's triune life, and because they bring to pass in history his resolve to share that life, in all its antecedent perfection, with us.[34]

---

[31] The issue can be traced in various ways in Greek and Byzantine theology; in Western tradition, it first began to receive serious attention in the eleventh century, and became a subject of great debate between Scotist and Thomist theologians from the thirteenth, in consequence particularly of Duns Scotus's influential efforts to demonstrate divine free choice, rather than any necessity imposed upon God by sin, as the basis of God's determination to become incarnate. On modern variants which deploy differing strategies toward some similar ends, see Edwin Chr. van Driel, *Incarnation Anyway: Arguments for Supralapsarian Christology* (New York: Oxford University Press, 2008).

[32] For some of the building blocks of the argument, see Bruce L. McCormack, *Orthodox and Modern: Studies in the Theology of Karl Barth* (Grand Rapids, MI: Baker Academic, 2008), pt. 3.

[33] Robert Jenson, "Reconciliation in God," in *The Theology of Reconciliation*, ed. Colin E. Gunton (London and New York: T&T Clark, 2003), 159–166.

[34] On a number of the critical issues, see Michael T. Dempsey, ed., *Trinity and Election in Contemporary Theology* (Grand Rapids, MI: Eerdmans, 2011); see also now Paul Molnar, *Faith, Freedom and the Spirit: The Economic Trinity in Barth, Torrance and Contemporary Theology* (Downers Grove, IL: IVP Academic, 2015).

Nevertheless, if incarnation and atonement are grounded in this God's free and loving consecration of himself to be God with us, and if their saving work reaches all the way back into God's very purposes in creating, they certainly express the immensity of the love with which God chooses to bind himself to that which is contingent. The atoning action of God in flesh confirms that nothing blocks the triune creator's loving will for fellowship; that, however terrible sin and evil are, they are not an insuperable problem for him; and that he is committed to going to these lengths that we might know him. The God who elects himself for incarnation is the God whose Son is indeed the Lamb slain from the foundation of the world (Rev. 13:8). That is how precious we are to him.

The gospel of atonement by God incarnate remains the best news in the world. It declares the divine good pleasure *actually* to save us (1 Cor. 1:21), the determinate power and wisdom of God (1 Cor. 1:24) for the reconciliation, redemption, and perfection of the lost. Just as such, it announces the lifting of our load, the overcoming of our alienation, the breaking of our captivity. Just as such, it sets us up as agents, privileged to spend our energies in wondering testimony to the incarnate One, to whom we are in faith united and in whose transformative presence we think and speak. In his manifestation in flesh, we are afforded knowledge and enjoyment of our creator; for his fleshly appearance once more, in glory not in shame, we wait. Seeing him then, as he really is, we shall, we are told, be like him, and all manner of things shall in him be new. Yet in him and with him already, his inheritance as Son is ours; brought near, complete, in him our fleshly brother, we too are God's children *now* (1 John 3:2). What it finally means that creation itself should know the peace he has secured, all the evil that despoils it definitively banished in consequence of his atoning work, is a mystery that does not yet appear. The present anticipation of that mystery in the Spirit's power is, however, a glimpse already of all the fulfillment that creatures as such can ever conceivably desire.

4

Resurrection and Atonement in the Theology of Thomas F. Torrance

Paul D. Molnar

In his view of the incarnation T. F. Torrance insisted that we "cannot earn knowledge of Christ, we cannot achieve, or build up to it"[1] because when we know him, the very actuality of that knowledge and thus its possibility come to us as he discloses himself to us "by his own power and agency, by his Holy Spirit."[2] What he declares to us is the simple but profoundly important fact that this man Jesus is "God without reserve, man without reserve, the eternal truth in time, the Word of God made flesh."[3] For Torrance one cannot understand who Christ is or what he has done and is doing for us unless we allow the object of faith, namely, Jesus Christ in his uniqueness as God become man for us and for our salvation to be the sole factor shaping what we think and say about these matters. When it comes to thinking about the person and work of Jesus Christ, our thinking must be scientific in that "it must be faithful to the whole fact of the mystery of Christ."[4] We can never simply focus on one aspect of the mystery such as the historical, eschatological, or transcendental because the mystery of Jesus concerns the fact (inaccessible to historical investigation and to any transcendental investigation per se) that in his particular history we are "confronted by the eternal in union with time. Here in our human flesh in Jesus Christ we are confronted with the eternal Word of God which has assumed our human nature and existence into oneness with God."[5] Torrance insists that there really is "no

---

[1] Thomas F. Torrance, *Incarnation: The Person and Life of Christ*, ed. Robert T. Walker (Downers Grove, IL: InterVarsity Press, 2008), 2.
[2] Ibid.
[3] Ibid., 3.
[4] Ibid., 7.
[5] Ibid., 8.

knowledge of God, no real experience of God's help and redemption" apart from that historical act of God within history—the act of "*God in time, God as man, God active in history*."[6]

Torrance began his thinking about atonement in much the same way, insisting that we cannot explain the meaning of Christ's death for us, of our reconciliation with God enacted and accomplished in his life, death, and resurrection from any point outside of him and of his action in the Holy Spirit enabling us to know its true meaning. Hence, "*we cannot think our way into the death of Christ because the continuity of our thinking and striving has been interrupted by it, but we may think our way from it* if we follow the new and living way opened to us in the crucifixion."[7] This means that we cannot attempt to "fit the death of Jesus into our life and our own preconceptions or notions" because, confronted with this unique person and work as the reconciler and revealer which always must be held together, we encounter God acting *as* man, from both the divine and human side, for us. Thus, we must "be conformed to his death. We can understand the cross only by *metanoia*, repentance and a change of mind, which is correlative on our part to the 'wonderful exchange' ... on Christ's part when he who was rich was made poor for our sakes that we might become rich."[8] The atonement itself reveals to us "the very fact that God himself had to descend into our bottomless pit of evil and guilt in order to construct continuity between us and God."[9]

This means that there is no continuity between us and God that can be found apart from Christ.[10] All our statements therefore about the meaning of atonement must be "based upon the inherent synthesis to be found in the person of the mediator and not in any logical or rational presuppositions which we bring to interpret what he has done for us."[11] This means that if Jesus is seen or understood simply as a man dying on the cross, then Christianity itself would be immoral:

> What Christ did and suffered for us God himself did and suffers as the Father of the Son ... only God can bear the wrath of God, and if the Atonement really

---

[6] Ibid.
[7] Thomas F. Torrance, *Atonement: The Person and Work of Christ*, ed. Robert T. Walker (Downers Grove, IL: InterVarsity Press, 2009), 3.
[8] Ibid.
[9] Ibid., 4.
[10] Ibid. Continuity is found in the fact that God himself achieved and made this a reality "through his atoning *act* and the intervention of his own *being* ... the cross provides a wisdom that 'the Greeks' or humankind in general know nothing of" (emphases in the original).
[11] Ibid.

means anything at all it must mean that it is God who suffers there in Jesus Christ—if the divinity of Christ is denied the Christian doctrine of atonement becomes immoral—that is why spurious ideas of atonement go along with weak faith in the Deity of Christ.[12]

The Christian doctrine of atonement becomes immoral when the mystery of Christ's deity is disregarded or discounted because no human being can stand in for another before God and God does not demand some sort of appeasement by means of a human act of placating him *before* he loves us; rather what happened in the death of Jesus Christ was that God himself entered into the human situation marked by sin and death precisely in order to forgive our sins by becoming himself the Judge judged in our place.

This is where the resurrection must be seen to connect with the doctrines of atonement and incarnation. Hence, "the resurrection was not just an event that happened to Christ, for it corresponded to the kind of Person he was in his own Being."[13] There is, in other words, complete consistency between "the resurrection event and the essence of the resurrected One." While we may attempt to approach and understand Christ in his humanity,

> as soon as we confront him in the power of his resurrection our understanding of his humanity must be set within the fact of *the whole Christ*, as God manifest in the flesh, the Creator in our midst as human creature, come to effect the recreation of human nature from within its existence in space and time.[14]

Thus, the very relation of the resurrection to Christ's person reveals to us "that it is *the whole Jesus Christ who is the content of the resurrection*, for all of his life from birth to resurrection forms an indissoluble unity."[15] And that unity is forged and maintained between God and us sinners who are justified and sanctified in Christ himself, quite apart from anything we can do or think we must do in order to save or reconcile ourselves to God. This is why Torrance insists that the meaning of the crucifixion can only be discerned from the perspective of the resurrection; this because Jesus himself is "the great Passover from death to life, from man-in-death to man-in-the life-of-God, from damnation to salvation."[16] In light of this, one could never just focus on the cross because it was

---

[12] Thomas F. Torrance, *The Doctrine of Jesus Christ* (Eugene, OR: Wipf and Stock, 2002), 146–147.
[13] Thomas F. Torrance, *Space, Time and Resurrection* (hereafter *STR*) (Edinburgh: T&T Clark, 1998), 60.
[14] Ibid.; emphasis in the original.
[15] Ibid.; emphasis in the original.
[16] Ibid., 42.

the crucified Jesus who rose from the dead and is as such our atonement who is now active as the ascended and coming Lord. In what follows, I will attempt to explain how and why the resurrection makes an enormous difference in one's explanation of atonement by considering the relation between resurrection and justification, reconciliation and redemption.

Resurrection and Justification

Torrance is well known for insisting that justification by faith (grace) must not be restricted merely to the forensic aspect by implying that it only means the non-imputation of our sins. It also means our "positive sharing in his divine-human righteousness." The strength of his position rests in his positive emphasis on Christ's bodily resurrection. This emphasis forcefully connects God's merciful act of forgiveness, which reinstates us "before God as though we had not sinned,"[17] with the fact that this righteousness is enacted in us through the power of the resurrection by the action of the Holy Spirit uniting us to Christ himself.[18] Such righteousness thus does not simply hover over us. It is an act that recreates sinners by "blotting out what is past."[19] The resurrection reveals that God, as the one who forgives, "bears the cost and burden of forgiveness." God was directly at work in Jesus, "making himself responsible for our condition,"[20] and bore the cost of our forgiveness in himself. Torrance repeats Karl Barth's assertion that Jesus Christ was the Judge judged in our place. Here we get a glimpse of why Torrance will not accept a merely forensic view of justification—we share in Christ's righteousness through the power of his resurrection—a power that disclosed the fact that forgiveness was "translated into our existence by crucifixion and resurrection, by judgment and recreation." Forgiveness thus means that the status of the sinner as a sinner has been rejected and sinners are freely given the status of being "pure and holy before God."[21]

To illustrate the connection between forgiveness and resurrection, Torrance relies on the account of the cure of the paralytic in Mark 2:1–12 and Luke

---

[17] Ibid., 61.
[18] See Thomas F. Torrance, *Kingdom and Church: A Study in the Theology of the Reformation* (Eugene, OR: Wipf and Stock, 1996), 100ff. See also Torrance, "Justification: Its Radical Nature and Place in Reformed Doctrine and Life," in *Theology in Reconstruction* (London: SCM Press Ltd, 1965), 150–168, at 150–151.
[19] Torrance, *STR*, 61.
[20] Ibid.
[21] Ibid.

5:17–26. Jesus cured the man after saying that he did that "in order that you may know that the Son of Man has power on earth to forgive sins."[22] Torrance notes that the Greek term for resurrection, *egeiro*, is used there, which suggests that the early church understood the incident as "falling within the sphere of the power of the resurrection."[23] Indeed, the early church understood the relation of forgiveness and resurrection as the demonstration of divine power in Jesus's word of healing: "forgiveness reached its full reality in the healing and creative work of God upon the whole man."[24] This underscores Torrance's claim that if Christ's bodily resurrection is in any way undercut, then so too would our reconciliation with God (our justification and sanctification) be damaged.[25] In opposition to any such thinking Torrance insists that St. Paul would not have been "mocked in Athens (Acts 17:32)" and would not have been considered mad by Festus (Acts 26:25) "when he spoke of the resurrection of Jesus, had he not meant the resurrection of the whole man leaving behind an empty grave."[26] It is in Christ's resurrection from the dead that whatever God and Jesus had to say about forgiveness "became actualized in the same sphere of reality as that to which we belong. The word of pardon was fully enacted in our existence."[27] That indeed, is the meaning of St. Paul's claim that if Jesus has not been raised from the dead then we are still in our sins.

In this event, God's "no" to sin and "yes" to us become one so that the resurrection can be considered the fulfilment of our justification. Our righteousness as children of God is not simply declared; it is established. Just as the physical event of healing the paralytic demonstrated that his sins really were forgiven according to Jesus's word of forgiveness, so too "the resurrection tells us that when God declares a man just, that man *is* just."[28]

For Torrance any Protestant view of justification that refuses to acknowledge that "to justify is to make righteous," in the sense just described, does so because it circumvents the resurrection. Thinking of justification only in light of the cross, as a non-imputation of sins because of what Christ did for us displays a serious misunderstanding just because the resurrection is in reality the fulfilment of our justification. Even though Torrance admits that on

---

[22] Ibid., 62.
[23] Ibid.
[24] Ibid.
[25] Ibid., 65. Contemporary reiterations of this problematic view can be found in such works as: Roger Haight, S.J., *Jesus, Symbol of God* (Maryknoll, NY: Orbis Books, 1999), 125, 145–146.
[26] Torrance, *STR*, 65.
[27] Ibid., 62.
[28] Ibid., 63.

such a view one could alleviate some of the difficulty here by relating the cross to Christ's incarnate life and to his active obedience and thus to "his positive divine-human righteousness," yet he maintains "that would still be empty and unreal, merely a judicial transaction, unless the doctrine of justification bears in its heart a relation of real union with Christ."[29] Unless such a union with Christ takes place through the power of the Spirit, "Christ would remain, as it were, inert or idle."[30] But that is the point of the resurrection: we actively and truly share in Christ's righteousness through the power of the resurrection so that justification must be seen as "a creative event in which our regeneration or renewal is already included within it."[31] Since the resurrection "is an actual event in the raising of Jesus Christ in the fullness of his humanity from corruption and death, then justification must correspondingly be a creative, regenerating event."[32] Justification and resurrection thus are intimately connected so that if one is distorted then so is the other. Torrance's main point then is that justification must be understood as "a continuing act in Christ, in whom we are continuously being cleansed, forgiven, sanctified, renewed, and made righteous."[33]

Torrance goes further in questioning the Protestant view of justification, wondering whether or not its insistence that justification cannot mean "a making righteous" does not imply "a Marcionite dichotomy between redemption and creation."[34] In Jesus Christ, God's "no" to sin and evil and "yes" to creation come together and for that reason redemption and creation must be held together. Because Christ's resurrection takes place in our created space and time, redemption of our created existence cannot be pushed totally into the future or detached from God's actions in history. Torrance thus maintains that those who do not expound Christ's bodily resurrection as an objective event in time and space are really exhibiting what he calls "concealed forms of deism" or

---

[29] Ibid.
[30] Ibid. Importantly, Torrance adds, following Calvin, that sanctification is not our human response "that must be added to justification, but the continual renewing and re-enacting in the believer of a justification that is made once and for all" (*Kingdom and Church*, 101). Hence we are incorporated into Christ through baptism, continually nourished as his body through the Eucharist, thus deepening our union with Christ so that "sanctification is the continual unfolding and maintaining of our justification" (ibid., 101). Union with Christ through faith means "an actual participation in his death and resurrection ... His resurrection is the 'substance and pledge' ... of ours" (ibid., 102). We are also "sharers in His ascension," so that faith merges with hope for eternal life as we await Christ's return.
[31] Ibid.
[32] Ibid.
[33] Ibid., 64.
[34] Ibid.

"deistic dualism."[35] Such deistic views present God as detached from creation because they fail to acknowledge that God was and is active in creation precisely in a uniquely creative way in a this-worldly event (Christ's resurrection from the dead).

All of this must be understood within an eschatological perspective, of course, because there is a "time-lag" between Christ's resurrection and ascension and our resurrection. But we cannot relegate "the fulfilment of the last things wholly into the future" since, through the Spirit, we already are in union with the risen Christ now and thus "taste already the power of the age to come"; hence "we cannot forget the fact of Pentecost when the power of the risen Christ was poured out upon the Church and indeed upon 'all flesh.'"[36] This "*realized justification* through the power of the resurrection" is "mediated to us in the Sacraments." For this reason, "every kind of deistic dualism between God and our world is rejected by the resurrection of Christ."[37] Torrance does not stop here but insists that a proper view of the resurrection is so vital that it shapes our doctrine of God and indeed our view of the universe. For if Christ has not been raised, then, as St. Paul said, our faith is in vain and "we are even found to be misrepresenting God" (1 Cor. 15: 14–15). Put another way, if Jesus's story ends with the cross, then his life was "an unmitigated tragedy" and it can be understood only as "the supreme proof of the irrationality of the universe in which we live."[38]

In clear opposition to Bultmann's reduction of the Easter event to the Easter faith of the disciples, Torrance insists that "belief in the resurrection as a real happening in our human existence, as objective act of God, within the space and time of our world, is once again the great dividing line between Christians in our own day" because our redemption is truly at stake here. Take away Christ's bodily resurrection and you take away our actual redemption from sin and death and any possible union with Christ through the Spirit. Take away the "empty tomb" and you take away the "the *wholeness* of our redemption in a *whole* Christ"[39]—an issue as pressing in our own day as in the last quarter of the twentieth century.[40]

---

[35] Ibid., 65.
[36] Ibid.
[37] Ibid.; emphasis in the original.
[38] Ibid., 65–66.
[39] Ibid., 66; emphases in the original.
[40] For examples, see Paul D. Molnar, *Incarnation and Resurrection: Toward a Contemporary Understanding* (Grand Rapids, MI: Eerdmans, 2007) and Roger Haight's position noted above.

The Resurrection and Reconciliation

Torrance explicates the connection between reconciliation and resurrection in the context of Romans 8:32ff., where St. Paul powerfully asserts that nothing can separate us from the love of God demonstrated in Christ's death and resurrection. The union between God and us that began with the birth of Jesus and extended throughout his incarnate life was "fully and finally achieved on man's side and on God's side in the crucifixion and resurrection of Jesus Christ."[41] Echoing Romans 8, Torrance maintains that God's love has now been inserted into our existence in Christ and that because it has survived death and judgment in Christ's resurrection, "it remains final and complete" and "nothing in heaven or earth can or will undo" it. This means that the resurrection is the completed and creative act of God's righteous mercy overcoming all contradiction between God and creatures, as we have just seen in connection with the doctrine of justification. His main point in this context is that in his resurrection from the dead, Jesus Christ completed the union between God and creatures in such a way that "there is now no longer any barrier between God and man—enmity is utterly abolished." Consequently, any idea of atonement without the resurrection would not really be reconciliation between God and creatures. Without reconciliation, atonement would not have reached its final and proper goal which is "union with the Father, in peace. It is thus the resurrection of our human nature in Christ into communion with the life of God that is the end and goal of atonement."[42]

Torrance explains that God's steadfast love achieved its goal—it has triumphed "over all the contradiction and separation of evil and their judgment by the holy love of God."[43] But this means that, in the midst of death and hell,

> the steadfastness of the Son of Man is such that it held on its way in utter obedience to the Father in the spirit of holiness … so that he raised himself up from the dead in perfect Amen to the Father's Will, acquiescing in his verdict upon our sin but responding in complete trust and love to the Father.[44]

In this light, the resurrection is the goal of the "obedience of the Son of Man in answer to the steadfast love of the Father."[45] This is Christ's active obedience which, for Torrance, must be seen together with his passive obedience, that is,

---

[41] Torrance, *STR*, 66.
[42] Ibid., 67.
[43] Ibid.
[44] Ibid., 67–68.
[45] Ibid., 68.

his submission to the Father's will in experiencing powerlessness and death vicariously for us.[46] In this connection he was raised by a "sheer act of Almighty God."[47]

Further, if Jesus had been allowed to see corruption, then on the one hand, "God would not have been true to himself" and on the other, "Jesus would not have been true to God" since he would have failed in his holiness by not rising above judgment, which in Torrance's understanding means rising from the grave "in complete agreement with the Father."[48] Furthermore, Jesus did not simply resign himself to the Father's will on the cross; that "Amen" was "positive and affirmative fulfilment" while the resurrection was "the complete Amen of the Son to the Father as of the Father to the Son."[49] What all of this means is that without the resurrection of Jesus from the dead, "reconciliation would prove a hollow fiasco" since the separation between God and us created by sin would remain. Christ's "substitutionary and representative obedience unto death" therefore was "perfectly efficacious and sufficient, both from the side of God and from the side of man."[50] Therefore, any thought of conditional salvation or self-justification is completely set aside in Jesus's substitutionary and representative life of perfect obedience. Not only was our justification by grace costly to God in the form of Christ's suffering and death, but it is also costly to us in that we must take up our cross and follow Christ alone in all things.[51]

Important here is the fact that in John 11:25, Jesus is reported to have said, "I am the resurrection and the life" so that "in this *I am* of the risen Lord the atonement becomes abiding and enduring fact, and reconciliation becomes eternally valid and eternally living reality between God and man."[52] The resurrection discloses that in Jesus, atonement "is identical with his Person in action" so that reconciliation must be seen "as the living and everlasting union of God and man in Christ."[53] In the sense of the Apocalypse of John, he is the one who, though

---

[46] Torrance thus thinks a proper view of satisfaction would see this as the Father's satisfaction "in the Son who has fulfilled the Father's good pleasure in making righteous atonement" (ibid., 54), rather than in a legalistic vision that equates satisfaction with meeting "the demands of justice" (ibid., 52).
[47] Ibid., 51.
[48] Ibid., 68.
[49] Ibid.
[50] Ibid.
[51] See Paul D. Molnar, *Thomas F. Torrance: Theologian of the Trinity* (Farnham: Ashgate, 2009), 168–186.
[52] Torrance, *STR*, 68; emphasis in the original.
[53] Ibid., 69. Here we see "the essentially dynamic nature of God's unchangeableness or constancy" which is the "antithesis of all inertial immutability or immobility" such as we find in death, Thomas F. Torrance, *The Christian Doctrine of God, One Being Three Persons* (Edinburgh: T&T Clark, 1996), 242–243.

he was dead, now lives so that "reconciliation is identical with the living and personal Being of the Mediator and as such marches through the ages and is present in the midst of all world affairs."[54] In all he did throughout his incarnate life as it culminated in his death and resurrection, Jesus Christ himself "is the living Atonement or Reconciliation in the form of personal Being and Reality in God."[55]

Several key implications must be noted here. First, we are adopted into sonship in Christ himself so that in faith and in a "lively" hope engendered by Christ's resurrection from the dead (1 Pet. 1:3f.), we may pray to God as our Father since we are now "joint heirs with Christ, who is the first-born among many brethren" (Rom. 8:14–17, 29).[56] Second, "our human nature is now set within the Father-Son relationship of Christ. Through faith in Christ and union with him we share brotherhood with him and so share with him the Fatherhood of God, and in and through him we share in the one Spirit of the living God."[57] As suggested also in John 17, we "share in the union of the Son with the Father."[58] To understand properly what it means to say that we partake of the divine nature (2 Pet. 1:4), Torrance maintains that we must hold together our understanding of the resurrection and ascension because in him human nature "is exalted to the right hand of God."[59] While Jesus's relation to God is utterly unique "since he is God the Son in the unity of the Holy Trinity," the fact that our human nature in him has been raised from the dead "implies a reconciliation or oneness with God which is not identity, yet a real sharing not only in his human nature but in the life and love of God embodied in him."[60] By grace, we receive this from him as the incarnate fullness of God who dwells in him bodily. Finally, Torrance links together three crucial patristic insights to clarify his understanding of our union and communion with God here: (1) there is the "*consubstantial* union" of the Father and Son "*in the Holy Spirit* who is Love, the Love that God is"; (2) there is the "*hypostatic union* between the divine and human natures in the one Person of Christ" which takes place through the Holy Spirit "who is the Love of God"; and (3) there is the *communion* or *koinonia* of the Spirit mediated to us from the Father through the Son, "who is the Love of God poured into our hearts." It is thus through the Holy

---

[54] Torrance, *STR*.
[55] Ibid.
[56] Ibid.
[57] Ibid.
[58] Ibid., 70.
[59] Ibid.
[60] Ibid.

Spirit who is the Love of God that we are united with Christ and made to be "partakers of the divine nature."[61]

Resurrection and the Knowledge of God

The resurrection enables our understanding that Jesus Christ himself is "the Truth" (John 14:6). Because of the hypostatic union, Jesus is and remains "uncreated Truth and created truth in one."[62] He is not just the eternal Word of God, but the Word who became flesh. Hence he is not just God's Word addressed to us but the "answering word of man addressed to God in the unity of his one Person."[63] Because of the incarnation and the hypostatic union, there is a genuine "actualization of the Truth of God among us" such that this "creates its own counterpart in us to itself."[64] Torrance often speaks of thinking from a center in God and not from a center in ourselves in order to know God and ourselves accurately. It is here, in his understanding of the resurrection in relation to the incarnation and thus to the hypostatic union, that the possibility of that thinking finds its basis. We cannot and do not have to leave the sphere of history and of space and time in order to know the transcendent God with our creaturely concepts; what we learn here is that through our views and concepts in all their limitation, we are enabled to speak objectively and consequently accurately of God only because of the resurrection and only through the power of the resurrection, as the Spirit unites us with Christ and thus with the Father. Here is where true, accurate, and objective knowledge of the "ultimate Being and Reality" of God is empowered. Torrance insists that without the resurrection, not only would there be a lasting disconnection between God's Word and Act, but there also would be "a final disjunction between our acts of knowing and the reality of God himself, or between our statements about God and their objective referent in God."[65]

This is an enormous claim. Torrance never ascribes true knowledge of God to us, that is, to any sort of obediential potency in our experiences of faith, hope, or love or of our knowledge per se, because in his view our thinking needs to be healed or reconciled to God before we are able to speak accurately about God himself. This is the place where one might say that our reconciliation with God

---

[61] Ibid. See also Thomas F. Torrance, *The Trinitarian Faith: The Evangelical Theology of the Ancient Catholic Church* (Edinburgh: T&T Clark, 1988), 140; and *The Christian Doctrine of God*, 95, for more on how Torrance understands 2 Peter 1:4.
[62] Ibid., 71.
[63] Ibid.
[64] Ibid.
[65] Ibid.

is most intimately and decisively connected with the resurrection via the incarnation. Thus, knowledge of God can never be considered a possibility resident in our human conceptuality which is marked by sin and death and needs to be united with the humanity of Christ and thus to the healing grace of atonement actualized in him vicariously for our benefit. That this takes place at all in us is an act of the Holy Spirit and can only be recognized in faith.[66] But what is it that is actually recognized here?

The answer is to be found in the connection between atonement and the resurrection once again. Torrance believes that evangelical theology tended to work with what he called "unbaptised reason" since it failed to think through completely "the transformation of human reason in light of the Word made flesh in Jesus Christ."[67] What he meant by this is that the mind of both church and society needed to be "inwardly formed by the gospel" and hence to be evangelized. For the New Testament "the mind of man is alienated at its very root" so that it "is in the human mind that sin is entrenched, and so it is right there, the gospel tells us, that we require to be cleansed by the blood of Christ and to be healed and reconciled to God."[68] Torrance is not thinking dualistically here by separating our minds from our bodies. On the contrary: our mental being is real and is created out of nothing just as is our body; and the human person is "the body of the soul and the soul of their body, or the body of their mind and the mind of their body, a unitary whole"[69]; the entire human person needs redemption. With this in view, Torrance insists (with the Greek fathers) that the mind governs all our human behavior, though modern people tend to think of the will as the determining factor in human behavior. This did not mean the Greek fathers were not interested in the will or freedom of the will as modern people are. Rather, they recognized what many modern people seem to misunderstand, namely, that although we have free will, "we are not at all free to escape from our self-will,"[70] the "twisted state of affairs in the depths of the human mind."[71] Since it is precisely our mental activity which controls our behavior, thinking, and culture, it is there that "we have become estranged from the truth and hostile to God. And it is

---

[66] For a discussion of the relationship between atonement and the Trinity, see Torrance, The Mediation of Christ (Colorado Springs: Helmers & Howard, 1992), chapter 5.
[67] Torrance, *Atonement*, 438.
[68] Ibid.
[69] Ibid.
[70] Ibid., 439. See also Torrance, *The Mediation of Christ*, 85–86. Our only way out of this predicament is by sharing in Christ's conversion of our will back to God in our place through faith.
[71] Ibid.

there in the ontological depths of the human mind that we desperately need to be redeemed and healed."[72]

That is one of the key reasons Torrance consistently opposed all forms of Apollinarianism—any notion that in the incarnation "the human mind was displaced by the divine mind." Any such displacement of the human mind in its twisted condition by the divine act of incarnation would have to mean that the doctrine of reconciliation or atonement had been detached from the incarnation and that God did not assume the sinful human nature which we all share. Our minds and hearts would remain untouched by the incarnation and atonement, and in a very real way the full meaning of the resurrection, as the enabling power of God healing our minds so that we may know God truly out of himself, would have been circumvented.[73] It is in Christ himself that our fallen, "enslaved human nature, our twisted, distorted, bent mind" is assumed and converted, healed and sanctified throughout his entire life. That is what is completed and disclosed fully in the risen Lord himself. The Son of God not only took upon himself our actual sins, but original sin and guilt "in order to heal, convert, and sanctify the human mind in himself and reconcile it to God."[74] Here Torrance forcefully maintains that both Protestant and Catholic theologians need to engage in "repentant rethinking of everything before the face of Jesus Christ ... you cannot separate evangelical theology from that profound experience of the radical changing and transforming of your mind that comes through dying and rising with Christ."[75] This is why Torrance held that "divine revelation conflicts sharply with the structure of our natural reason, with the secular patterns of thought that have already become established in our minds through the twist of our ingrained mental alienation from God."[76] That is what needs transformation and that is what must occur in and through our union with Christ, through the power of the resurrection, by means of the love of God poured into our hearts by the Holy Spirit. That is what it means to have the mind of Christ in the Pauline sense.

At this point Torrance notes that Athanasius insisted that we had to learn "to think strictly 'in accordance with the nature' (*kata physin*) of God the Father as he is made known to us through the Son and in the Holy Spirit, that is, in an

---

[72] Ibid.
[73] See Torrance's explanation of how the atonement relates to our knowledge of the Trinity in *The Mediation of Christ*, 109ff.
[74] Torrance, *Atonement*, 440.
[75] Ibid., 443.
[76] Ibid.

essentially godly way."⁷⁷ To think like that "from a centre in God himself, is, he claimed, what *theologia* strictly is."⁷⁸ Thinking from a center in our unregenerated human reason and thus from a center in ourselves would end in mythology and projection instead of theological understanding of the truth.

> Either you think from out of a mind centred in God through union with the mind of the Lord Jesus, or you think from out of a mind centred in yourself, alienated from God and inwardly hostile to the truth incarnate in the Lord Jesus, that is, in a way that is finally governed by the unregenerate and unbaptised reason.⁷⁹

All of this suggests that because God has united our humanity in its totality with himself in the incarnation "that in and through Jesus Christ we may yet know God in his reality beyond ourselves. The whole epistemic function of the incarnation thus comes to complete fruition in the resurrection of Christ in the fullness of his humanity."⁸⁰

To make his point even clearer, Torrance contrasts his view with gnostic and docetic thinking which refuses to acknowledge the fact that Christ rose bodily from the dead. Consequently, they separated God from the world and thus from human forms of thought. As a result they argued that one could only speak symbolically here since "God in himself is beyond our knowledge."⁸¹ So the Gnostic Basileides held, "We do not know what [God] is but only what he is not."⁸² Hence, our statements about God "do not terminate upon his reality" because our knowledge "does not rest upon any objective ground in God" but rather are understood as "expressions in the realm of myth and ritual."⁸³ Conceived in this context, the resurrection is merely a symbol "which does not correspond with reality" and only expresses our human self-understanding and self-expression.⁸⁴ Opposing this approach Torrance insists that the resurrection, as understood in the New Testament and in the early church, meant that in Jesus Christ the reality of God and our human reality "intersect and overlap" such that "we in Jesus Christ may actually and truly know God and have communion with him without having to take leave of the realm of our own this-worldly existence. The

---

⁷⁷ Ibid., 445.
⁷⁸ Ibid.
⁷⁹ Ibid., 446.
⁸⁰ Torrance, *STR*, 71–72.
⁸¹ Ibid., 72.
⁸² Ibid. See also *Trinitarian Faith*, 50.
⁸³ Ibid.
⁸⁴ Ibid.

resurrection is therefore our pledge that statements about God in Jesus Christ have an objective reference in God, and are not just projections out of the human heart and imagination."[85] The slightest weakening of the fact of Christ's bodily resurrection means that statements about God become merely mythological projections out of the human heart and imagination marked by sin (self-will). In that way, "we fashion a God in terms of the creaturely content of our own ideas."[86] This sinful predicament is what is overcome in the resurrection because it is this that finally establishes the bridge between God and us on both sides of "the chasm that divides them."[87] Here Torrance agrees with Barth that the resurrection is the starting point for a "scientific theology."[88] It is what he calls "*the primal datum of theology from which there can be no abstracting*, and the normative presupposition for every valid dogmatic judgment and for the meaningful construction of a Christian theology."[89] Importantly, the resurrection "is not derivable from empirical reflection, and is established beyond any religious *a priori*"[90] because it is an act of God in the person of Christ enabling a knowledge that can only come through God as a revelation, as grace through faith.

The Resurrection and Redemption

The final aspect that will help explain how Torrance conceives the relation between resurrection and atonement concerns the relationship between resurrection and redemption. First, redemption must be understood to mean the redemption of the whole person from nothingness and death: "the deliverance of man out of all darkness, death and destruction, into light, life and being."[91] Redemption means the restoration of our human existence in its fullness and integrity, including our bodily existence. This was achieved in Jesus's own bodily resurrection from the dead. It is precisely in that new humanity or new creation that redemption has already occurred; our perishable existence has been redeemed. Hence, the risen Lord himself is the source and heart of our redemption from the grave. He experienced the grave for us and for our salvation. Torrance stresses, with Athanasius, that the meaning of Jesus's

---

[85] Ibid., 72–73; emphasis mine.
[86] Ibid., 73.
[87] Ibid.
[88] Ibid.
[89] Ibid., 74; emphasis in the original.
[90] Ibid.
[91] Ibid.

own resurrection "must be understood in accordance with the nature and work of Christ" which means "in accordance with the nature of the One who rose from the dead."[92] This important point suggests that no true understanding of redemption is possible apart from Jesus himself, the redeemer, and thus apart from his bodily resurrection from the grave. For Torrance the "'rose again' must be understood as determined by the nature of the Subject of that event, Christ himself."[93] Misconstruing this "who" would immediately lead to a misunderstanding of both resurrection and redemption.

Jesus was the creative Word of God through whom the world was created. He was made flesh and was and is therefore "creative life within our fallen and corrupt existence."[94] His life is "recreative" life. Because his bodily resurrection cannot for an instant be separated from this incarnate existence, his resurrection must be understood as resurrection "out of our mortal and corrupt humanity, where we are dead in trespasses and sins."[95] His history is thus "sheer miracle." His entire human life, as sinless and in its perfection, "is itself resurrection." In that sense it is "the passing of the old into the new."[96] This resurrection of Jesus from the grave after his death on the cross is "the same event as the human and historical life of Jesus but now taking place out of the depth of our corruption where corruption is finalized and fixed in death." So while some contemporary theologians are unable to conceptualize an actual existence in our history of the risen Lord after his death, Torrance asserts that his resurrection must have the same historical palpability as his entire life history, including his death on the cross. What Jesus himself did by allowing himself to die for us vicariously was to "invade the last stronghold of evil" in its ultimate reality in the form of death.[97] In that way he personally broke out of death, destroying it for us.

Torrance rejects the idea that Christ's resurrection is an "infringement of natural law" because that idea cuts the connection between the nature of "the resurrected One" and the resurrection itself.[98] Torrance explains that in the New Testament the reaction of people to Jesus's miracles was one of astonishment because in Jesus his person and deed "corresponded perfectly with one

---

[92] Ibid., 75.
[93] Ibid.
[94] Ibid.
[95] Ibid.
[96] Ibid.
[97] Ibid.
[98] If it were an infringement of the natural law then one could explain it by observation and one would separate resurrection as an interruption of what is natural from the fact that it is natural to the unique person and work of Jesus. But since Jesus is the resurrection and the life, the resurrection can only be explained from him and not from nature as an interruption of the natural order.

another."⁹⁹ Who he was indeed was manifested in what he did since his person and acts were entirely one. His resurrection thus "was recognized to be in entire accordance with his nature and person."¹⁰⁰ That is precisely the astounding thing about Jesus—this was not simply a miracle, but in all its wonder, it was "not a whit different from the essential nature of the risen one in himself."¹⁰¹ It corresponded to Jesus's own claim to be the resurrection and the life and the truth itself. In other words, Jesus himself is "the reality of the resurrection and the new life that breaks out of death through it."¹⁰² This connection between the event of resurrection and the "essence of the resurrected One" led to the understanding that Jesus's whole life "together with his resurrection" was indeed the "manifestation among men and on earth and in time of the ultimate and original and final creative activity of God."¹⁰³ With this in mind one cannot consider the resurrection an interruption of the laws of nature because it is a creative act within nature. And while it is a creative act within nature it is not a *creatio ex nihilo*, but a "new creation out of the old order."¹⁰⁴ It cannot be observed any more than the original act of creation could be observed. So instead of claiming that the resurrection is an interruption of the laws of nature, Torrance maintains that just as "creation is the manifestation of the creative source of created reality and its immanent order" so the resurrection is a "creative activity itself breaking through and manifesting itself within the events of the created world."¹⁰⁵

That is "why the resurrection is so baffling to thought and observation."¹⁰⁶ While we may observe created reality, we cannot observe "the creative processes."¹⁰⁷ Similarly, we cannot "observe the resurrecting processes, but we may (or will be able to) observe the actuality of Jesus Christ—for here too we are concerned with creation, although it is new creation."¹⁰⁸ Since we have a new creation in Jesus, we also have a creative happening that cannot be observed: "By its very nature it is no more observable than creation as such, yet it is just as factual and real as creation."¹⁰⁹ There is, however, a further complication here. Since the resurrection is a "new creation" it simply cannot be observed within

---

[99] Ibid., 76.
[100] Ibid.
[101] Ibid.
[102] Ibid.
[103] Ibid., 77.
[104] Ibid., 78.
[105] Ibid.
[106] Ibid., 77.
[107] Ibid., 78.
[108] Ibid.
[109] Ibid.

the "frame of the old order" because it is not continuous with the old order and is thus not "comparable to it, and apprehensible entirely within the connections of the old order."[110] Here we see the fruit of Torrance's scientific theology, which operates on the assumption that to know something as it truly is requires that we must allow the unique nature of the object of reflection to determine what we say about it. In this case, he says, "It stands to reason that it [the resurrection] must be known in accordance with its own nature, out of itself."[111] This also means that we must think through the relation of the resurrection to space and time within the continuing existence of the world. And that insight takes him into the realm of the ascension, eschatology, and Christ's advent relations with us in the history between his first and second coming through the Spirit. That, however, is a subject for another time.

Here it is important to recall that as the resurrection is intimately connected with atonement, so it is also closely related to redemption or the final restoration of creaturely life. In the resurrection of Jesus, God has made good his sinful creatures, overcome the contradiction between creator and creature, and since Jesus was "raised for our justification" we know that "God's Yes is finalized in and through the No of his resistance to all corruption, evil and death."[112]

> It is in the resurrection, then, that the ultimate content and purpose of the atonement and reconciliation come to fruition and to view—in the recreation of man in communion with God. This involves the restoration of true creaturehood to man, the affirmation of man in the fullness of his human existence and reality. *This is the ontological side of redemption, the healing and restoring of being in relation to the creative Source of all being.*[113]

Torrance draws several crucial conclusions from this. Because our creaturely existence is once and for all established in Jesus beyond all nothingness and death, we have in Jesus the "humanizing" of "dehumanized man."[114] Following Athenagoras who believed that "apart from the resurrection, and its link with creation, man could not survive as man"[115] Torrance holds that "if there is no resurrection, human nature is no longer genuinely human."[116] This explains why Torrance is adamant that resurrection means resurrection of the body:

[110] Ibid.
[111] Ibid.
[112] Ibid., 78–79.
[113] Ibid., 79; emphasis in the original.
[114] Ibid.
[115] Ibid.
[116] Ibid., 82.

"any 'resurrection' that is not bodily is surely a contradiction in terms."[117] Take away the bodily resurrection of Jesus and the inner connection between resurrection and redemption is broken, as is the connection between resurrection and atonement. That explains why Torrance so persistently opposed spiritualizing interpretations of the resurrection, especially Bultmann's reduction of the Easter event to the rise of faith on the part of the disciples. In such a perspective, not only is the meaning of the resurrection missed, by being reduced to a subjective reaction to the "story" of Jesus, but so also is the true meaning of what it means to be human. This is the case because the true meaning of human nature can only be seen in its recreation in the new humanity of Jesus, the risen Lord. And it can only be seen in the power of his Spirit and in faith now since he has ascended into heaven and has yet to return to complete the redemption of all creation.

> If the resurrection of Jesus is not actual and historical reality, then the powers of sin and death and non-being remain unconquered and unbroken and we are still in the bondage of death. That is not an idea that could have been anticipated, but once the resurrection took place it yielded as part of its intelligible reality a circle of ideas within which the empirical event of the resurrection was understood and appropriated.[118]

In light of this Torrance insisted that there were empirical correlates of the resurrection as a recreative act of God within history so that the entire Gospel "now regarded in the light of Easter, was seen to pivot finally upon the *empty tomb*."[119] Take this away and you also remove from view the fact that Jesus now lives "in the fullness and integrity of his human nature" and as such is no longer subject to the "corroding forces of corruption" since, through the Spirit, he is no longer subject to death. Thus, there was indeed a second history of Jesus after his death where he physically interacted with the disciples "in such a way that he could be touched and seen to be no apparition, but above all it was the *personal self-identification of the familiar Jesus* that was the paramount factor."[120] While some contemporary theologians have great difficulty with this idea, mainly because they tend to spiritualize the resurrection by allowing it to be defined in abstraction from the historical Jesus who rose from the grave and now interacts with us as the ascended and advent Lord, Torrance thinks any such abstraction is an

---

[117] Ibid.
[118] Ibid., 83.
[119] Ibid.; emphasis in the original.
[120] Ibid.; emphasis in the original.

indication of a dualist view of our human relations with God. And there are consequences to that: any refusal to accept Christ's bodily resurrection misses the comforting truth of the Gospel, namely, that nothing really can separate us from the love of God revealed and active in the God who has reconciled humanity to himself in the death and resurrection of Jesus Christ.[121]

---

[121] For further study on this topic, I commend to the reader the following works: Molnar, *Thomas F. Torrance*; Kye Won Lee, *Living in Union with Christ: The Practical Theology of Thomas F. Torrance* (New York: Peter Lang, 2003); Dick O. Eugenio, *Communion with the Triune God: The Trinitarian Soteriology of T. F. Torrance* (Eugene, OR: Pickwick Publications, 2014); Elmer M. Colyer, *How to Read T. F. Torrance: His Trinitarian & Scientific Theology* (Downers Grove, IL: InterVarsity Press, 2001).

5

The Atonement and the Holy Spirit

Christopher R. J. Holmes

Introduction

The atonement is a Trinitarian act: the three persons of the Holy Trinity are involved in its achievement. The act of atonement comes from somewhere, and that source is the life of the three; it is the being of the Trinity that is atonement's presupposition. In this chapter, I discuss the person and work of the third of the three, the Holy Spirit, in relationship to the atonement. My primary conversation partner in this is Karl Barth, as I consider how the Spirit's acts in God are revealed in the Spirit's work among us in relationship to the atonement. How the Spirit originates in God, the Spirit's procession from the Father through the Son, provides, I argue, important resources for contemplating the pneumatological dimension of the atonement.

Some might think it odd that I take Karl Barth as my primary interlocutor for thinking through the Spirit's role in the atonement. Among certain Anglo-American voices in Protestant divinity, Barth is thought to have a weak pneumatology. I think Barth is important to talk about in a chapter on the atonement and the Holy Spirit because of his insistence that God remains God in all that God does for us and for our salvation. The Spirit acts as and always remains God in giving us the life of God's Son. Barth presses God's provenience, because the atonement, as an act of the Trinity, has its source in the utterly prevenient life of the Trinity. I advance this point in terms of God's life as the ground and principle of intelligibility for the atonement. The atonement is a matter of the Son and Spirit of God in divine mission to us.

In this chapter, I discuss three points. I consider whom and how the Spirit is in the life of the Trinity. Second, I discuss the pneumatological dimension of the atonement: what does the Spirit do in relationship to Christ's atoning for sin in his person on the cross, and how does this activity of the Spirit express the Spirit's procession from the Father and the Son? Third and last, I explore why the mission of the Spirit among us cannot be untethered from the mission of the Son. Atonement provides us with an excellent doctrinal reference for appreciating the Spirit's mission as revealing the Spirit's procession from the Father through the Son.

The Who and the How of the Holy Spirit

In Barth's programmatic treatment of the Spirit's divinity in §12.2 of *CD* I/1 (*The Eternal Spirit*), he describes who the Spirit is in God and how the Spirit originates in God. The Spirit is "of the essence of God Himself."[1] The Spirit "is antecedently in God Himself."[2] Who is the Spirit? The Spirit is God, for in God is unity of being between Father, Son, and Spirit. The Spirit, Barth argues, is "no less and no other than God Himself, distinct from Him whom Jesus calls His Father, distinct also from Jesus Himself, yet no less than the Father, and no less than Jesus, God Himself, altogether God."[3] When we talk about the Spirit, we are talking about God; when we contemplate what the Spirit does, we are contemplating the works of God.

In order to unfold the character of the Spirit's divinity, Barth turns to the Nicene-Constantinopolitan Creed of 381. The Spirit "is the common factor in the mode of being of God the Father and that of God the Son. He is what is common to them, not in so far as they are one God, but in so far as they are the Father and the Son."[4] Accordingly, what distinguishes the Spirit from the first and second modes (or persons) is that the Spirit is their "common factor."[5] The Spirit arises in relation to Father and Son; they do not arise in relation to the Spirit. The Spirit originates in relation to Father and Son as the "togetherness or communion," or better, "the fellowship, the act of communion, of the Father and

---

[1] Karl Barth, *Church Dogmatics*, 4 vols. (Edinburgh: T&T Clark, 1956–1975),
[2] Ibid.
[3] Ibid., 467. It is worth noting that Barth says this in the first part (*God as Redeemer*, §12.I) after having described the work of the Spirit as consisting "in freedom, freedom to have a Lord, this Lord, God, as Lord." See Barth, *CD* I/1, 457.
[4] Ibid., 469.
[5] Ibid.

the Son."⁶ This is Barth's description of the Spirit's procession, of how the Spirit proceeds as God from the Father and Son. The how of the Spirit is equivalent to an originating relation. The Spirit "is the bond of peace" between the Father and Son.⁷ This is what Scripture allows us to say regarding how the Spirit comes to be in relation to the other two. The Spirit is who the Spirit is only "in his relation to the other divine modes of being."⁸

The Spirit acts among us as the Spirit acts in God. The Spirit, together with Father and Son, is "pure act."⁹ What the Spirit does among us is repeat or reiterate the Spirit's acts within the eternal life of God. A key quotation runs, "In this work of His on us He [the Spirit] simply does in time what He does eternally in God."¹⁰ What the Spirit accomplishes among us repeats what the Spirit does in God. What the Spirit does in God is unite Father and Son to one another. The Spirit in so doing is neither prior nor posterior to them, but is love proceeding, the love of the Father for the Son and the Son for the Father. On the basis of New Testament texts including Galatians 4:6 and Romans 8:9, Barth argues that there must be a "*relatio originis*"—a causal relation—between the Son and Spirit. New Testament patterns of speech demonstrate, on the one hand, that the Spirit is from the Father and the Son, and, on the other hand, that the Father and Son are not from the Spirit. Barth affirms: "If the rule holds good that God in His eternity is none other than the One who discloses Himself to us in His revelation, then in the one case as in the other the Holy Spirit is the Spirit of the love of the Father and the Son, and so *procedens ex Patre Filioque*."¹¹ This is what Barth calls the "*immanent Filioque*."¹²

Such a sketch of the metaphysics of the Spirit is necessary if we are to understand why the acts of the Spirit in relation to the Father and Son go all the way down in God and why the Spirit acts as the Spirit does. Barth secures two points. First, the Spirit, who is God, is the "full consubstantial fellowship between Father and Son."¹³ Second, the Spirit is God as "the love of the Father and the Son."¹⁴

---

[6] Ibid., 469–470.
[7] Ibid., 481, 470.
[8] Ibid., 470.
[9] Karl Barth, *Erklärung des Johannes-Evangeliums (Kapitel 1-8): Vorlesung Münster Wintersemester 1925/1926, wiederholt in Bonn, Sommersemester 1933*, ed. Walther Fürst (Zürich: Theologischer Verlag, 1999), 249.
[10] Barth, *CD* I/1, 471. Cf. IV/3.2, 760, wherein Barth writes, "Just as the Holy Spirit, as Himself an eternal divine 'person' or mode of being, as the Spirit of the Father and the Son (*qui ex Patre Filioque procedit*), is the bond of peace between the two, so in the historical work of reconciliation he is the One who constitutes and guarantees the unity of the *totus Christus*."
[11] *CD* I/1, 483.
[12] Ibid., 481.
[13] Ibid., 481–482.
[14] Ibid., 483.

That is how the Spirit originates in God. Such a glimpse into the life of God is key if we are to appreciate the relation between the atonement of Christ and the Holy Spirit. We shall see in the next section that the mission of the Spirit reveals his procession from the Father and Son. Without clarity regarding whom the Spirit is and how the Spirit is God, we cannot understand the Spirit's acts.

The Atonement in Pneumatological Perspective

The atonement is an event, a happening in history. It has to do with a particular historical person, Jesus of Nazareth. This historical person is unlike any other person, however, for unlike us, he is God. The Son of God "does not give up being God in becoming a creature, in becoming man."[15] The Son of God reveals himself among us as he has always been in relation to the Father and the Spirit. That there is such a history that is atonement is because there is a God whose deity is so secure that he, in the person of the Son and by the power of the Holy Spirit, does not lose himself in "His way into the far country."[16] "God is always God even in His humiliation," insists Barth.[17]

What allows Barth to say "God is always God even in His humiliation," that "the Godhead of the man Jesus remains intact and unaltered?"[18] The answer is "true Godhead."[19] The way of the Son into the far country to stand "in the place and under the accusation of a sinner with other sinners" is the way of one "who is free in His love, and therefore not His own prisoner."[20] The anterior condition or presupposition of the atonement is Jesus's "true Godhead."[21] In greater detail, "True Godhead in the New Testament is being in the absolute freedom of love, and therefore the being of the Most High who is high and almighty and eternal and righteous and glorious not also but precisely in His lowliness."[22] "Godhead" describes God's being. God loves out of the freedom intrinsic to God's very being. That is "the presupposition of our reconciliation."[23] What the Son does in

---

[15] *CD* IV/1, 185.
[16] Ibid.
[17] Ibid., 179.
[18] Ibid.
[19] Ibid., 191.
[20] Ibid., 176, 187.
[21] Ibid., 191.
[22] Ibid.
[23] Ibid., 195.

reconciling cannot be considered apart from his Godhead and thus the Father and the Spirit in God's life.

The begotten nature of the Son has temporal form inasmuch as his mission attests his origin—his being (eternally) begotten—from the Father. The Father sends, the Son is sent. The Father is superior—in the sense of order and not of being—insofar as he begets and sends, but the Father is only the Father in relation to the one begotten by him. The eternal generation of the Son from the being of the Father indicates a unity of being between them that includes, as we have seen, the Spirit. In the inner life of God, one begets and another is begotten and the third proceeds—is breathed. The processions of the Son from the Father and the Spirit from the Father and Son as their unity and love ground and structure their missions.

The Father begets the Son in the fellowship and love of another, which is the Holy Spirit. Their inner or immanent life is demonstrated in the work of atonement, and supplies the rationale for the atonement's shape. When Barth describes Jesus's obedience unto death as "an obedience of the one true God Himself in His proper being," he assumes the Son's begottenness from the Father in the Spirit as the condition of possibility for his obedience unto death.[24] Why does Barth press this point? He wants us to recognize that "we are in fact dealing with an overflowing" of the holy Trinity.[25] In the outward works of God, we encounter God as God truly is inwardly, from eternity. As Barth notes, "The true and living God is the One whose Godhead consists in this [Jesus's] history."[26] Although such a statement suggests a conflation of God with his works, Barth's dialectical wheels keep spinning, and so he goes on to say that the basis of what Jesus does is "His own being, ... His own inner life," a life that can never be abstracted from the Father and Spirit.[27] Accordingly, there is not any gap between the one nature of the Trinity of persons and what the Trinity does for us and for our salvation. The Godhead of God "consists in this [Jesus's] history" inasmuch as it is *God*'s history, God's work "*ad extra*, in the world. He is in and for the world what He is in and for Himself."[28] God has his life *in se*, independent of his saving history. The life of God, Father, Son, and Holy Spirit is utterly prevenient. The atonement is a work in the world of what God is in and for himself: Father, Son, and Holy

---

[24] *CD* IV/1, 200.
[25] Ibid., 201.
[26] Ibid., 203.
[27] Ibid.
[28] Ibid., 203, 204.

Spirit. God's work has a source, and that source is the utter plenitude of God's being.

The reason why God's being cannot be derived from God's act in Barth's mind has to do with the aseity of the three in the eternal life of the Trinity. The Spirit acts as the Spirit does precisely because the Spirit is from eternity "the love with which you [i.e., the Father] have loved me [i.e., your Son]."[29] Apart from and prior to the created order, the Spirit is this love. In other words, God the Father, God the Son, and God the Spirit do not need anyone or anything outside of one another in order to be: God has being with respect to himself. God's being is as a result of the originating relations of begetting, being begotten, and proceeding, and is as such eternally self-posited being. In a crucial statement Barth unfolds via the language of originating relations who God is in and for himself, the necessary fellowship of the three.

> The Father is not the Father and the Son is not the Son without a mutual affirmation and love in the Holy Spirit ... The eternity of the fatherly begetting and of the being begotten of the Son, which is the basis of their relationship, their free but also necessary fellowship and love in the activity of the Holy Spirit as the third divine mode of being of the same kind.[30]

This is who and how God is in and for himself, the very condition of possibility for incarnation and atonement. The reason why one cannot untether talk of the atonement of Jesus Christ from the Spirit (as well as the Father) is because the Spirit is eternally the mutual affirmation and love of the Father and the Son. The Son is not the Son without the Father and without the Spirit in whom the Son loves the Father and the Father loves the Son. The Son affirms the Father and the Father affirms the Son in the Spirit, as has been the case from eternity. As we contemplate the atonement, we see one God who is incomprehensibly three at work for us and for our salvation, whose inner life is the motor as it were for his words toward the outside.

To recap so far, anything that the Son does refers us to the Father who begets him and the Spirit who is their love. Atonement, as with incarnation, has to do with *God*. In the saving work of Jesus we "take part in the history of the inner life of His Godhead, in the movement in which from and to all eternity He is Father, Son and Holy Spirit, and therefore the one true God."[31] The inner life of God as pure act and plenitude of being is revealed in a series of temporal acts, the acts

---

[29] John 17:26.
[30] CD IV/1, 209.
[31] Ibid., 215.

of the Son and Spirit in mission to us. God has life apart from us, and a history with us, and that history has its center in what the Son in the Spirit effects: atonement. Jesus Christ's faithfulness as true God and true man, and simultaneously his receiving and his breathing forth of the Spirit at Pentecost, the Holy Spirit of the Father, "the love with which you have loved me," are nothing less than the conversion of the world to God. Jesus Christ is the new creation come. He is "the evangel"; in him are we "liberated," those "whose sin is cancelled and forgiven" and filled with his promised Spirit.[32] The consummation of his passion in the cross is "the great day of atonement, the day of the dawn of a new heaven and a new earth, the birthday of a new man." The great day of atonement is the day in which he gives up his Spirit to Jews and Gentiles, enemies and friends alike.[33] It is the day of the new birth.

What of the first principles of "the great day of atonement?"[34] In what sense does the great day rest on God's complete and perfect life? The great day assumes a Trinitarian reference. The Son is God together with the Father and the Spirit. The costly obedience of the Son demonstrates his unity with the Spirit who gives him the strength to fulfill his mission. As Barth maintains, "God's own activity and being ... is the truth and power of that which takes place here."[35] The cross is the new humanity's birthday—he kills "our sin in his own death"—because it is the cross of the "eternal God [together] with the Father and the Holy Spirit."[36] Put again, the cross is intelligible only as a Trinitarian reality. The Father loves the crucified Christ in the Spirit and Christ, in turn, loves the Father in the Spirit even unto death. The obedience of the Son to the will of the Father even unto death is a fruit of the Spirit who sustains him in fidelity to his Father's purposes, though it cost him his life.

In section §59.3 (*The Verdict of the Father*), the pneumatological dimension of the atonement is clearest. Barth cannot describe the nature of the relationship between Jesus Christ and us without reference to the Holy Spirit. Barth calls this a "real and spiritual problem."[37] The Holy Spirit aligns us to who Christ is for us. As the act of communion of the Father and Son, the Spirit extends their communion in such a way among us that through Christ's cross are we able to share in it. This reveals the significance of the Spirit for the atonement understood as

---

[32] Ibid., 225, 242.
[33] Ibid., 259.
[34] Ibid.
[35] *CD* IV/1, 273, 280.
[36] Ibid., 280.
[37] Ibid., 293. By "spiritual," Barth means, as does Paul, a problem that would have us do with the Holy Spirit.

a triune act or event. The Spirit does not take the fruit of Christ's high priestly work and appropriate it to us. No, to argue such is to occlude the full force of the identity of the one resurrected—"*Christus pro nobis praesens.*"[38] Accordingly, the Spirit neither renders Christ present nor the atonement effective. Atonement is effective; and it has its reality and expansive force because Jesus Christ is God, together with the Father and the Spirit. Atonement's cosmic reach has to do with the nature of Jesus Christ as the Son of God, true God and true man, one God, together with the Father and Spirit. The atonement's efficacy and reach are therefore a function of his oneness in being with the Father and the Spirit. He lives, dies, and is raised in the Spirit who exalts him to the right hand of the Father, even as he, the exalted one, is present and comes to us in the Word and Spirit.

From eternity does the Son come from the Father and the Spirit from them. The atonement of Jesus Christ continues to come to us in the Spirit because Jesus is never without the Spirit. Indeed, Jesus breathes the Spirit upon us, continuing to encounter us in the Spirit.[39] Herein we glimpse something of how things are in God. Jesus breathes upon us the Spirit he receives from the Father from eternity. The resurrected and glorified Jesus lives in the Spirit, as he has from eternity. This is how he is present for us. He is present in the Spirit with whom he is one. His presence to us reveals his identity as the one who receives the Spirit as the Father's only begotten. The Father loves the Son in the Spirit, and the Son the Father in that same Spirit. It is their holy fellowship that is the presupposition of and also what is expressed in their saving work among us.

T. F. Torrance is helpful here for understanding Barth's treatment. The Spirit redeems us into the life of God, the blood of Christ having redeemed us from guilt. We die with Christ in our baptism, and are raised with him by his Spirit to newness of life. Just as the Spirit raised Christ, so are we, by virtue of our baptism in him, raised in the Spirit. Torrance describes the work of the Spirit thus: "atonement actualising itself."[40] That is to say, "through [Christ's] Spirit we are incorporated into him."[41] Why? Following the logic of the Johannine Pentecost, the Spirit incorporates into Christ because Jesus Christ breathes the Spirit.[42] The Spirit is given by Christ "without measure," only to return us to him and thus to the Father.

---

[38] Ibid., 291.
[39] See John 20:19–23.
[40] Thomas F. Torrance, *Atonement: The Person and Work of Christ*, ed. Robert T. Walker (Downers Grove, IL: IVP Academic, 2009), 189.
[41] Ibid.
[42] See John 20:22.

The Christ-event is itself from somewhere, namely, "the grace of the Father."[43] It is to the Father that we return through the incarnation and atonement of the Son in the Spirit. Again, we must ask: why? Indeed, why does God work in this way? Why does the Spirit and not the Son actualize atonement? This reason has to do with how things are in God. As with Torrance, Barth argues, "the Holy Spirit—who is also the *kurios* according to 2 Corinthians 3:17—is within the Trinity: God Himself maintaining His unity as Father and Son, God in the love which unites Him as Father with the Son, and as Son with the Father."[44] In the Spirit is the love of the Father for the Son and the Son for the Father poured out. The luminous character of the atonement has to do with the divine life, specifically its expression among us in the mission of the Son and Spirit whose work of reconciling (the Son) and revealing (the Spirit) expresses an immanent reality. That Jesus's atonement actualizes itself among us in the Spirit reveals the inner life of the Trinity. The Holy Spirit is the love of the Father for the Son and the Son for the Father proceeding.

When Barth thinks about the dimension of the atonement that most intensively refers us to the Holy Spirit, it is the resurrection. In the resurrected Christ is the human situation decisively altered, "the situation of Christians and of all men."[45] The resurrection is a matter of "the force and authority of the verdict of the Holy Spirit."[46] Why does the Spirit raise Jesus, following Romans 8, wherein the Father is also said to have raised him? Because the three cannot cease to be what they have always been. The Son, "who in His person allowed our judgment to be visited on Himself, who in that way accomplished our reconciliation with God," *is* the Father's Son through whom the Spirit proceeds.[47] The incarnate Son's assumption of sin and death does not destroy his unity with the Father and the Spirit. The Spirit in raising Jesus unites him to his Father, as the Spirit has from eternity. The Spirit unites the Son to the Father and the Father to the Son, and now does so again in raising Jesus. That is what the Spirit does, precisely because the Spirit is "love proceeding" in God and therefore among us.[48] The Spirit raises the Son, reuniting him with his Father, and the Father thereby vindicates the Son as his beloved in the Spirit. The Spirit's mission is to reveal the Spirit's origin as the love of the Father for the Son and the Son for the Father.[49]

---

[43] John 3:34; *CD* IV/1, 308.
[44] *CD* IV/1, 308.
[45] Ibid., 317.
[46] Ibid., 320.
[47] *CD* IV/1, 343.
[48] This is Thomas's language. See *ST* I, q. 37, a. 1, ad 4. See *Basic Writings of Saint Thomas Aquinas*, Vol. I, ed. Anton C. Pegis (Indianapolis: Hackett, 1997).
[49] See John 17:26.

The atonement as a Christological doctrine has to do with Jesus, "the Judge judged and the Priest sacrificed."[50] But who is Jesus but God's Son, God together with the Father and the Spirit? The Spirit's raising of the Son is a demonstration of what is true, antecedently speaking, in God: the Spirit as the bond of the unity between Father and Son. We know that the Spirit unites Father and Son in God's life because we have watched in faith the events of Easter. The Spirit's acts among us—principally, in the raising of Jesus—derive from the Spirit's acts in God. The Spirit unites Father to Son and Son to Father in God and therefore among us.

The work of the Father and of the Spirit in the raising of Jesus is unintelligible apart from recourse to God's inner life. Barth writes, "He [the Father] willed to give to the inner and secret radiance of His glory an outward radiance in the sphere of creation and its history. He willed to give to His eternal life space and time. And that is what He did when He called Jesus Christ to life from the dead."[51] The resurrection of the crucified has as its anterior condition the Father's glory, "his eternal life."[52] This life has "space and time" precisely in the raising of the crucified.[53] Barth's insight regarding the Father can be pneumatologically extended. We see the Spirit's "eternal life" on display in the Spirit's raising of Jesus. The Spirit does not cease to be the Spirit of the Father and the Son, the Son's crucifixion notwithstanding. Even our "No" to Jesus and his Father's purposes cannot overcome their determination to be our God and have us as their people. All the moments of the economy of salvation are a function of a life that is complete in it. In the raising of Jesus, we receive in faith a glimpse of the perfection of that life, including that of the Spirit.

The atonement is thus a derivative doctrine, that is to say, it is located downstream of the doctrine of God and of the Trinity. The anterior condition of atonement and its principle of intelligibility is the ontologically self-sufficient life of the one God and the Trinity of persons. These three who have life in relation to their common and indivisible essence are free to order us to the life they are and have from and to eternity. Thus the Father sends the Son in the Spirit in the "fullness of time" (Gal. 4:4). The Father is the necessary preceding condition of the Son's sending, the Spirit the ongoing reality in which the Son is sent and the one in whom he (the Son) comes again.[54] The basic presupposition of the sending of the Son is his being begotten of the Father, and Pentecost's presupposition

---

[50] *CD* IV/1, 349.
[51] Ibid., 308.
[52] Ibid., 349.
[53] Ibid.
[54] See John 14:18: "I will not leave you orphaned; I am coming to you."

is the Spirit's proceeding from the Father through his beloved Son. The origin of the atoning economy of God is the perfect being of the one God whose inner life includes distinction—Father, Son, and Holy Spirit. Jesus's mission is to give us his Spirit, and his Spirit's mission is to declare him from whom he originates, together with the Father.

The testimony of John's (5:26) Gospel to the Son is that he "has life in Himself." What is the source of the Son's life? It is the Spirit. The life that the Son pours out in his own life and death is the life of the Spirit. Jesus lives in the Spirit, among us and from eternity. The atonement is a spiritual event insofar as it takes place in the Spirit and lives and is born by the Spirit. Barth writes, "Where this community lives by the Holy Spirit, Jesus Christ Himself lives on earth, in the world and in history."[55] The resurrected Jesus lives by the verdict of the Father and by the Holy Spirit insofar as he can be said to live on earth wherein people live by him. Jesus lives, and he lives by the Spirit. Indeed, "the doctrine of reconciliation cannot stop at that of the person and work of Jesus Christ."[56] Its source and ground is the Father and its liveliness—its contemporaneity—is the Holy Spirit, for it is in the Spirit that an "inclusive Christology" has its force.[57] Raised in the Spirit, Jesus ever lives and intercedes in the Spirit on behalf of the saints. The atonement is indeed exclusively Christological insofar as its form is concerned—"the Judge judged and the Priest sacrificed," Jesus Christ the Son.[58] However, the atonement in its totality assumes a Trinitarian foundation and reference. The life that the Son has in himself and gives us through his ministry, cross, and glorious resurrection is the life that is common to the three. The life we receive in Christ is the life of the Father and the Spirit: the Son as "the exact imprint" of the Father and the Spirit as "the Spirit of Christ" (Heb. 1:3; Rom. 8:9). The oneness of being between the three grounds the indivisibility of their work, for example, the giving and perfecting of life.

To sum up this section, the Father is atonement's presupposition, the Spirit its ongoing actuality. "It [the Yes of God] was and is His [the Father's] Yes to the Son whom He elected and loved from all eternity."[59] The Father loves the Son whom he elected from all eternity in the Spirit, and in the Spirit is the beloved Son raised to eternity. The works of God derive from the acts of the three in God; the faithfulness of God among us has a source, God's triune life. In describing the

---

[55] *CD* IV/1, 353.
[56] Ibid., 354.
[57] Ibid.
[58] *CD* IV/1, 349.
[59] Ibid., 356.

atonement, I think we must liberally deploy the Trinitarian referent, not only as the atonement's presupposition, but also as its ongoing principle of intelligibility. When it comes to the Spirit, the Spirit's acts in God are revealed in the Spirit's raising the Son. The Spirit is intrinsic to the Son: just as the Son is perpetually born by the Father, so does the Spirit perpetually proceed from the Father through his only begotten Son, from and to all eternity. The risen, ascended, and glorified Jesus bestows his presence through the Spirit who is the very love with which the Father loves him and he the Father. In the Spirit, therefore, we by faith share in the Father's love of the Son and the Son's love for the Father. The pneumatological dimension of the atonement emphasizes just this. Christ died and was raised so that "the love with which you have loved me may be in them, and I in them" (John 17:26).

The Mission and Origin of the Spirit

In this last major section, I use atonement doctrine as a test case to explore why the mission of the Spirit cannot be untethered from the Spirit's originating relations with respect to Father and Son. Barth helps us to understand this when he writes that the Spirit is "God Himself maintaining His unity as Father and Son, God in the love which unites Him as Father with the Son, and as Son with the Father."[60] The resurrection of the crucified Jesus, the verdict that the Father declares in raising him, reveals the immanent unity of Father and Son in the Spirit. The death of Jesus cannot rend asunder the holy fellowship of the three who are one: The Father raises him in the Spirit, the Spirit raises him, and, astonishingly, he raises himself—"Destroy this temple, and in three days I will raise it up" (John 2:19). God maintains his unity over and against death "in the love [i.e., the Spirit] which unites."[61] The Spirit who alone guarantees the work of the Son of God does so as the Spirit who from eternity unites Father and Son to one another and us to them. Accordingly, what takes place in the economy of salvation repeats and reveals what is true in God. The Spirit is the love who proceeds from them.

The relationship between the Spirit poured out as "the promise of the Father" (Acts 1:4) and the Spirit as "God Himself maintaining His unity" has to be developed in an account of the atonement.[62] God's life toward the inside and

---

[60] *CD* IV/1, 348.
[61] Ibid.
[62] Ibid.

God's life toward the outside correspond. Of this, George Hunsinger writes, "The relationship between who and what the triune God is in himself and who and what he is in relation to the creation is one of *correspondence* ... the former (the eternal Trinity) is specified as the ground of the latter (the economic Trinity)."[63] Why does the Spirit come from the Father, following John 15:26? The answer has to do with the procession of the Spirit from the Father in God, that is, in the eternal Trinity. The Spirit is "*the being spirited from the Father through the Son.*"[64] Such talk, however "bent and twisted as the language is," does something important.[65] Namely, it reminds us that the order of the three in God is repeated among us. That is why the three act as they do. That is why the Spirit is, in a logical but not temporal sense, *after* the Father and Son. The Spirit does not declare the Spirit's self, following John 16:14, as the Spirit is sent by the Son from the Father so as to declare the Son. The order in which the three relate to one another in the economy corresponds to their order from eternity.

Talk of order in God also prevents us from talking, as Barth does at certain points, of "a pure obedience [in God], subordination and subjection."[66] The mission of the Son reveals his origin from the Father as does the mission of the Spirit his origin from Father and Son. The Spirit unites Father to Son and Son to Father in God and among us. Instead of there being "subordination and subjection" in God, as Barth suggests, I think it better to speak of order in God. In the case of the Spirit, the Spirit is ordered to the Father and the Son from whom the Spirit proceeds. However, what happens among us expresses what is antecedently true. That the Spirit acts as the Spirit does among us has to do with how things are in God; the Spirit's acts are expressive of an eternal order.

Why is the Spirit sent? To reveal the love of the Father for the Son and the Son for the Father, which is precisely what the Spirit does in raising Jesus. This helps us to understand why the Son and not the Spirit became flesh. The Spirit in God and among us is "love proceeding."[67] This is not love of the Spirit for the Spirit's self but the love of the Father and Son proceeding. By the Spirit do we share in the filial love of the Father for the Son and the Son for the Father,

---

[63] George Hunsinger, *Reading Barth with Charity: A Hermeneutical Proposal* (Grand Rapids, MI: Baker Academic, 2015), 19–20; emphasis in the original.

[64] Denys Turner, *Thomas Aquinas: A Portrait* (New Haven, CT: Yale University Press, 2013), 126; emphasis in the original.

[65] Ibid.

[66] *CD* IV/1, 304. For a trenchant account of the shortcomings of such language and of T. F. Torrance's distancing of himself from it in favor of a more salutary manner of expression, see Paul D. Molnar, *Faith, Freedom and the Spirit: The Economic Trinity in Barth, Torrance and Contemporary Theology* (Downers Grove, IL: IVP Academic, 2015), 335ff.

[67] *ST* I, q. 37, a. 1, ad 4.

and that sharing is our beatitude. The Spirit does not unite us to the Spirit's self through Jesus's death and resurrection. Rather, the Spirit unites us to him and to his Father. The source of the acts of the three is their life. God determines from eternity that we will share as creatures in the life that has always been.

The work of the Spirit in raising Jesus from the dead is intelligible only in relation to the procession of the Spirit in the inner life of God. The work of the Spirit comes from somewhere. Reflection on the atonement deepens our sense of where the Spirit comes from. The movement of God to the creature is the movement of Word and Spirit. The atonement's form is exclusively Christological, yes, but to describe it in terms of "the Judge judged and the Priest sacrificed" as we must is not to describe a work of the Son per se to which an act of the Spirit is then added.[68] The reason for this has to do with the shape of the divine life itself. If Son and Spirit truly co-inhere, if the Son's begottenness from the Father is simultaneous with the proceeding of the Spirit from the Father, then we have to see "the Judge judged and the Priest sacrificed" in the Spirit. The work of the Son and Spirit in atonement is what their mission (understood as the temporal expression of their procession from the Father, the Son in an immediate sense, the Spirit in a mediate sense as the one who proceeds from the Father through the Son) accomplishes. The Son is the Father's only begotten in the Spirit; the Father *is* the begetting of the Son in the Spirit; and Jesus is our judge and priest in the Spirit. Therefore, the Spirit is not simply the liveliness of what Jesus accomplishes, the principle of his incarnation's and atonement's contemporaneity. Far more than that, the Spirit throughout his ministry, passion, and death enables Jesus to be who he is, the Son of the Father. By the Spirit he enacts his filial relation to the Father, even unto death.

The act of atonement in Jesus Christ lives by the Spirit insofar as the Spirit "take[s] what is mine and declares it to you" (John 16:14). The Spirit takes what is *the* fruit of Christ's mission—namely, reconciliation—and declares it to us. The incarnate Son's passion and death, his raising by the grace of the Father, these are guaranteed by the Spirit. Christ's breathing of the Spirit in John 20:22 and his Father's pouring out of the Spirit in Acts 2 witness a single movement that arises from the life of the Trinity itself. The Spirit's other-directed, that is, Christ-directed, and work is sourced in the causal relation of the Son to Spirit in God's life. The Son (eternally) causes the Spirit as does the Father, the Son secondarily and the Father primarily.

---

[68] CD IV/1, 349.

Because the Spirit is united in being with Father and Son, the Spirit is not after in an ontological sense. That is why we cannot conceive of the Spirit's awakening work as subsequent to Jesus. The Spirit is not extrinsic to the Son but (again) intrinsic to him, in like manner to the Son as one intrinsic to the Father. The Son is united from eternity to the Father in the Spirit, is the Son of the Father in the Spirit as the love that unites them. If such is the case, then, the form of atonement is indeed Christological, but its ground is the triune life.

Contemplation of the atonement encourages understanding of its source. What I have sought to do in this section is think through how God's life supplies us with a rationale as to why the three act as they do. Contemplation of the inner life of God, Father, Son, and Spirit helps us to see what qualifies the Son to be our judge and priest and the Spirit's taking of what is his and declaring it to us.

Conclusion

Jesus would have us believe that he is from the Father. Jesus's works throughout John's Gospel attest his origin. That said, many do not believe Jesus's own testimony. "Yet we know where this man [Jesus] comes from; but when the Messiah comes, no one will know where he is from" (John 7:27). Jesus's interlocutors think that he speaks falsely of his origin. By living and dying in the Spirit, Jesus seeks to convince them otherwise. I mention the Johannine witness at the conclusion because it supplies us with a key image for tethering the Spirit to Christ and the atonement he makes in his person. That image is testimony: the Spirit testifies on Jesus's behalf as the love with which the Father loves him and he the Father.[69] In all that the Son does, he expresses his generation from the Father. The Son's sending from the Father is the term that his generation has in the world—"so that they may believe that you sent me" (John 11:42). In all that the Spirit does, the Spirit expresses his origin from the Father and the Son as "love proceeding."[70] The Spirit's origin supplies us with the rationale as to why the Spirit acts as the Spirit does. The Spirit testifies to the Father through the Son because the Spirit is from the Father through the Son.

The Spirit's testimony is an other-directed enterprise. The Spirit does not bear witness to the Spirit's self but instead to Christ. With reference to the atonement, the Spirit takes the atonement that is the history of Jesus Christ

---

[69] See John 15:26.
[70] *ST* I, q. 37, a. 1, ad 4.

and declares it in such a way that Jesus is said to live by the Spirit's declaration of him. While not collapsing them, there is nonetheless a profound parallelism between the risen Jesus and the Spirit, especially in the Fourth Gospel and Paul. The "I am coming to you" of John 17:13 and "The Lord is the Spirit" of 2 Corinthians 3:17 attest this. Christ has ascended, and he is present as the ascended one by the Spirit. Jesus's ascended presence is as intensive as his earthly presence because of the Spirit's testimony and indwelling on Christ's behalf and in his name.

A well-proportioned account of the atonement faithful to the biblical witness is metaphysically motivated. It wants to inquire after and account for the immanent rationale for why the persons act as they do. Indeed, it understands such an inquiry to be material in nature. The Spirit's activity and presence is a function of the Spirit's identity in God.

Karl Barth, to his great credit and with outstanding cogency, helps us to see that God—Father, Son, and Spirit—remains God in all that God does. God does not lose himself in the determination to be our God and have us as his people. Atonement is God the Son's great achievement, together with the Father and Spirit. It is the fruit that his proclamation and enactment of the Kingdom brings about; similarly, his overcoming of our disobedience and death and his making expiation for our sin in his very person on the cross. Because the Son is God in the love that unites him with the Father, the Son is not God without the Spirit. Barth's rich insight about God's Lordship, God's sovereignty with respect to all God does, rests upon an account of how the three originate in God. Such talk involves, as we have noted, originating relations. That Christ is present for us as the one who suffered, died, and was raised is because he exists from eternity in the Spirit whom he receives and breathes upon us from the Father.

The Spirit's immanent reality as the love that unites is on display in the resurrected Jesus's living by him. Jesus lives—as he always has—from the love that binds him to his Father and his Father to him. Barth is a most useful resource for thinking through the relationship between the Holy Spirit and the atonement. He appreciates that the atonement's ground is the shared divinity of the Father, Son, and Spirit. Specifically, Barth helps us to see that the Spirit's acts among us correspond to the Spirit's acts in God. The Spirit unites in God and therefore among us. Throughout Jesus's ministry, its culmination in his cross, and in his glorious resurrection and ascension, the Spirit enables Jesus to be who he is from eternity: the Father's beloved Son. The Father continues to pour out the Spirit through Jesus, the Spirit who unites in time the one who sends and the one sent as the Spirit has from eternity.[71] The atonement that is the history of Jesus Christ lives by the Spirit; the Spirit continues—as the Spirit always has—to be "love proceeding."[72] Rightly relating atonement doctrine to the doctrine of the Spirit is a matter of significant import. Its principle of intelligibility lies with the Father who begets and sends, the only begotten Son who is sent, and the Spirit who is breathed by the Father through the Son, binding Father to Son and Son to Father in order that their love might have "a term" among and for us.[73]

---

[71] See Romans 8: 9–11.
[72] *ST* I, q. 37, a. 1, ad 4.
[73] Yves Congar, *I Believe in the Holy Spirit*, trans. David Smith, vol. 2, "*He Is Lord and Giver of Life*" (New York: Crossroad, 1997), 44.

6

God's Reconciling Work: Atonement in the Old Testament

Stephen B. Chapman

Care must be taken with the phrase "atonement in the Old Testament," which can over-determine the scope of inquiry in advance, foreclose certain possibilities prematurely, and prevent adequate consideration of the Old Testament's full witness regarding sin and salvation. There are at least five ways in which such misunderstanding occurs: (1) when the *idea* of atonement supplants the Bible's wider vision of reconciliation between God and all creation; (2) when the *nature* of atonement is primarily conceived in terms of "propitiation" and "penal substitution," that is, as the appeasement of God's anger and the satisfaction of divine punishment through the provision of a replacement victim; (3) when the *mode* of atonement is understood as a single transaction between humanity and God, usually involving blood sacrifice; (4) when the *scope* of atonement is thought to include only human beings; (5) when *models* of atonement operate with a notion of divine agency that is too juridical and too blunt, neglecting the cosmic dimension of both sin and salvation. In this chapter, I will take up each of these pitfalls in turn and use them to sketch the contours of an alternate approach.

Misconception 1: "Atonement" is Synonymous with Divine Reconciliation

Treatments of "atonement in the Old Testament" tend to focus on the terminology and procedures of the priestly sacrifices as well as the image of the suffering servant in Isaiah 53.¹ However, "reconciliation" in the Old Testament involves a much larger frame of reference entailing the entirety of the Old Testament's story and theological thrust. At its broadest level, the Old Testament depicts the creation of a world by God, the introduction of brokenness into that world, and God's subsequent efforts to heal the breach. *Everything* in the Old Testament is about God's persistent efforts on behalf of reconciliation—God's choice of Noah and his family, God's election of Abraham and the people of Israel, God's establishment of a covenant and a nation, that nation's exile and return to the land, and a future consummation of God's plan in which the people of Israel, by virtue of their faithful example and God's persistent mercy, will finally succeed in regaining the nations for God. This vast theological vision would need to be explored and detailed in order to offer a fully adequate treatment of reconciliation within the Old Testament, yet summaries of "atonement" hardly ever address such an expansive horizon.²

It proves helpful to envision two circles of concern within the Old Testament, an outer circle in which the issue is God's ultimate redemption of all things, and an inner circle in which God's forgiveness of sin is at stake.³ The outer circle is increasingly recognized as the realm of creation theology, which not only understands the world as having been made by God but also as damaged by sin and waiting upon God's final act of deliverance.⁴ This cosmic dimension to atonement can be designated "reconciliation," but then it should also be stressed how (from a biblical standpoint) such reconciliation is still a matter of atonement, with atonement just more broadly construed.⁵ Even more importantly, "atonement" in the narrower sense has to be recognized as part and parcel of this

---

[1] This phenomenon appears true of Jewish as well as Christian treatments; for example, Jacob Milgrom, "Atonement in the OT," in *The Interpreter's Dictionary of the Bible: Supplemental Volume*, ed. Keith Crim et al. (Nashville: Abingdon, 1976), 78–82.

[2] Christopher J. H. Wright, "Atonement in the Old Testament," in *The Atonement Debate: Papers from the London Symposium on the Theology of Atonement*, ed. Derek Tidball, David Hilborn, and Justin Thacker (Grand Rapids, MI: Zondervan, 2008), 69–82, comes close by framing atonement as how the Old Testament describes and addresses "the human predicament." Language about "the human predicament" can also be found in Paul Fiddes, *Past Event and Present Salvation: The Christian Idea of Atonement* (Louisville, KY: Westminster John Knox, 1989), 3–13.

[3] Similarly, Otto J. Baab, "The God of Redeeming Grace: Atonement in the Old Testament" *Interpretation* 10 (1956), 142–143.

[4] See further Terence E. Fretheim, *God and World in the Old Testament: A Relational Theology of Creation* (Nashville, TN: Abingdon, 2005).

[5] Gerald O'Collins, "Redemption: Some Crucial Issues," in *The Redemption: An Interdisciplinary Symposium on Christ as Redeemer*, ed. Stephen T. Davis, Daniel Kendall, and Gerald O'Collins (Oxford: Oxford University Press, 2004), 5 n. 4, attempts to relate the two by describing atonement as "the means of redemption or salvation." As O'Collins rightly notes, Christian discourse allows references to a "coming" redemption but not a "coming" atonement. However, Daniel 9:24 does use √kpr with reference to the future.

larger sphere of reconciliation. It is illegitimate to decouple the two, as if they are somehow different in kind.

The inner circle lies largely, although not entirely, within the province of sacrificial theology in the Old Testament. The word "atonement" is usually used for it, but this circle in fact stretches beyond the performance of sacrifice to embrace, for instance, the role of nonliturgical prayer and personal repentance as well (e.g., Ps. 51). How best to understand the theology of sacrifice in ancient Israel continues to be debated, but atonement in this narrower sphere of concern certainly refers to the repair of relationships, both among fellow Israelites and between the Israelites and God.[6] However, using the language of "atonement" only for this inner circle threatens to sever the essential link between the two related spheres of God's reconciling work, resulting in an overemphasis on atonement's sacrificial aspect.

Misconception 2: Atonement is Properly about "Propitiation" and "Penal Substitution"

The question of whether atonement means *propitiation* (appeasement or pacification) has dominated the scholarly literature for the past eighty years, ever since the publication of C. H. Dodd's *The Bible and the Greeks* in 1935.[7] Dodd contended that the various Hellenistic Greek terms used for "atonement" are better understood as "sanctify," "purify," or "purge," a range of meaning for which Dodd employed the word *expiation*. A central point in Dodd's discussion had to do with the grammatical objects of the Greek verbs under consideration. The meaning of propitiation would call for a personal object (i.e., one "propitiates" God), whereas the sense of expiation better suits an impersonal object (i.e., one "expiates" an altar or worship place). Dodd was unable to locate any examples within the Greek Old Testament in which a form of *hiláskesthai* (atone) was used in a religious context with God as the grammatical object.[8]

---

[6] Although it may be Israel's covenant that basically divides these two spheres, it goes too far to restrict atonement and sacrificial theology to Israel alone. Other peoples also offer sacrifices in the Old Testament (e.g., the Philistines offer an *'āšām* of golden tumors [?] and mice in 1 Sam. 6:4), and the expectations of Israel's God for holiness and justice extend beyond Israel. The problem of sin is universal (e.g., Eccl. 7:20; cf. 1 Kgs. 8:46; Prov. 20:9).

[7] C. H. Dodd, *The Bible and the Greeks* (London: Hodder & Stoughton, 1935).

[8] Ibid., 92. He did identify two examples in which the meaning "propitiate" seemed correct to him, but in these examples (Gen. 32:20; Prov. 16:14) the context was not religious and the object of the verb was not God. For early evangelical critiques of Dodd's position, see Roger R. Nicole, "C. H. Dodd and the Doctrine of Propitiation," *Westminster Theological Journal* 17 (1954–55), 117–157; Leon Morris, *The Apostolic Preaching of the Cross* (Grand Rapids, MI: Eerdmans, 1960), 136–156.

Dodd's proposal provoked strong defenses of "propitiation" as the more appropriate translation. Two aspects of propitiation were sometimes lumped together and confused in the ensuing discussion. One was the term's implication of God's wrath. The other was the representative or vicarious nature of the sacrificial offering. Both aspects were intentionally affirmed in the slogan "penal substitution," which hardened into the main counter-position to Dodd's and became an evangelical rallying cry.[9] In this phrase "substitution" insists on the nature of propitiation as the sacrifice of a replacement victim, while "penal" refers to a punishment that requires satisfaction, thus also connoting God's righteous judgment and displeasure at sin.

Expiation in Leviticus

Dodd's position, which had been framed as an investigation of Greek linguistic usage and Hellenistic Judaism, eventually received considerable support from Jacob Milgrom's lifelong exploration of Israel's sacrificial system and the book of Leviticus.[10] In analyzing the details of Hebrew *kipper* (= atone?) Milgrom insisted just as strongly as Dodd on identifying the predominant rationale for Israelite sacrifice as the purification of the altar and the sanctuary, and he viewed the *ḥaṭṭā't* (one of the main offerings detailed in Leviticus) as exclusively a "purification offering" rather than a "sin offering" (the traditional translation).

In the *ḥaṭṭā't*, the worshiper would present the required animal or animal substitute at the entrance to the tent of meeting. If presenting an animal, the worshiper would lay one hand upon the animal's head and kill it. The priest would collect the animal's blood and toss it seven times before the curtain that separated off the tent's inner sanctum. He would smear more blood on the horns of the incense altar and pour out the remainder of the blood at the base of the sacrificial altar. Then he would burn portions of the animal's entrails (i.e., fat, kidneys, and part of the liver) on that same altar, afterward transporting the animal's remains outside the camp for disposal. Noteworthy in this procedure is how the killing itself is not the focus of the rite (i.e., the animal's death is not the main part of the sacrifice, only a means to an end; the animal is not killed by the priest but by the worshiper; the animal is not killed on the

---

[9] See the influential statement of J. I. Packer, "What Did the Cross Achieve? The Logic of Penal Substitution," *Tyndale Bulletin* 25 (1974), 3–46.

[10] Above all, in Jacob Milgrom, *Leviticus: A New Translation with Introduction and Commentary* (Anchor Bible 3; 3 vols.; New York: Doubleday, 1991–2001).

altar but at the tent's entrance).[11] Indeed, because the required sacrificial gift was graduated according to economic need, in some cases (i.e., for the poor) a grain offering was substituted for the animal and no blood at all was shed (e.g., Lev. 5:11–13).[12]

The rationale for this offering is disputed. According to Milgrom it lay in rinsing away the impurities that infiltrated the worship place. Those impurities had to be cleansed by sacrificial blood, which functioned as a kind of "ritual detergent."[13] Once again, Milgrom pointed to verbal patterns in the description of the sacrifice. The subject of *kipper* (Piel) is usually the priest, he observed, but the direct object of *kipper* is never God or a person.[14] A person can only be an indirect object of *kipper* (as signaled by accompanying use of the Hebrew prepositions *'al* or *ba'ad*). According to Milgrom, this syntactical pattern reflects what was enacted in the ritual: *ḥaṭṭā't* blood is only applied to the sanctuary, not the person.[15]

Even so, most scholars have been somewhat suspicious of Milgrom's sharp distinctions and programmatic preference for expiation over propitiation,[16] preferring to conclude that Israelite sacrifices had differing nuances of expiation and propitiation, depending on their various contexts.[17] Somehow God was genuinely affected by what transpired.[18] Somehow "forgiveness" (√*slḥ* Niph.), and not only purification, occurred by the conclusion of the *ḥaṭṭā't* (Lev. 4:20, 26, 31, 35; 5:10, 13).[19] Nevertheless, there remains the expiatory character of *kipper* language and the forcefulness of Milgrom's comprehensive interpretation, which has been widely influential.[20]

---

[11] See further Christian A. Eberhart, *Studien zur Bedeutung der Opfer im Alten Testament: die Signifikanz von Blut- und Verbrennungsriten im kultischen Rahmen* (WMANT 94; Neukirchen-Vluyn: Neukirchener, 2002), 187–221.

[12] In other words, the *ḥaṭṭā't* does not absolutely require blood manipulation. For an affirmation of this point (often merely explained away as an "exception"), see William K. Gilders, *Blood Ritual in the Hebrew Bible: Meaning and Power* (Baltimore, MD: Johns Hopkins University Press, 2004), 138.

[13] Jacob Milgrom, *Studies in Cultic Theology and Terminology* (Studies in Judaism in Late Antiquity 36; Leiden: Brill, 1983), 77.

[14] Milgrom, "Atonement," 81; *Studies*, 76.

[15] See Milgrom, "Atonement," 78; cf. idem, *Studies*, 76. Blood is applied to a person in the *ḥaṭṭā't* rituals for the leper and priestly ordination, but this blood comes from sacrifices other than the *ḥaṭṭā't*.

[16] See John H. Hayes, "Atonement in the Book of Leviticus," *Interpretation* 52 (1998), 10; Bernd Janowski, *Sühne als Heilsgeschehen: traditions- und religionsgeschichtliche Studien zur Sühnetheologie der Priesterschrift* (WMANT 55; Neukirchen-Vluyn: Neukirchener, 2000); N. Kiuchi, *The Purification Offering in the Priestly Literature: Its Meaning and Function* (JSOTSup 56; Sheffield: Sheffield Academic, 1987).

[17] See, for example, Roy E. Gane, *Cult and Character: Purification Offerings, Day of Atonement, and Theodicy* (Winona Lake, IN: Eisenbrauns, 2005), 106–143, 267–284; Gilders, *Blood Ritual*, 29–32.

[18] Wright, "Atonement," 77.

[19] Gary Anderson, "Sacrifice and Sacrificial Offerings," in *Anchor Bible Dictionary*, ed. David Noel Freedman; 6 vols (New York: Doubleday, 1992), 5:880; Gilders, *Blood Ritual*, 137.

[20] Milgrom later apparently modified his theory somewhat by explaining expiation as having occurred not only by blood manipulation but also through the ingestion of sacrificial meat by the priest; see his *Leviticus*, 1:624–25.

The Semitic etymology of *kipper* continues to be uncertain and debated. The term may have once meant "cover," "wipe clean," or possibly "ransom."[21] However, "expiation" does seem to be the better translation of the word within the present text of Leviticus.[22] In his *Old Testament Theology*, John Goldingay echoes Milgrom and Dodd by stressing the way the term is used, particularly with regard to its grammatical object: "The object of *kipper* is the offense that a person has committed, not the one they have offended. Thus sacrifices do not propitiate God, as if they presuppose that God was angry."[23] Many Old Testament scholars would presently agree that sacrificial "expiation" was the fundamental aspect of what occurred in ancient Israelite worship. The open question is whether sometimes such worship might have also had a propitiatory dimension.

For instance, Leviticus 17:11 provides an exception to the expiation model by describing atonement as somehow for the "lives" (*něpāšôt*) of the worshipers rather than for the altar.[24] What is difficult to know is just how much of an exception it is. The same Hebrew phrase (*kipper* + "for your lives") appears in Exodus 30:16, but with reference to money rather than blood. Implied is a view of atonement as redemption or ransom. Historical-critical scholars have thus tended to view Leviticus 17:11 as a later broadening of the atonement idea, with the intention of accommodating a ransom model—not least because of the usual identification of Leviticus 17 as the beginning of the (later?) Holiness Code.[25]

---

[21] The parallel with √*mḥh* ("blot out") in Jeremiah 18:23 provides strong evidence for the meaning "wipe out, wipe clean." However, the replacement of √*kpr* with √*ksh* (Piel, "cover") in the apparent quotation of Jeremiah 18:23 in Nehemiah 4:5 [Heb. 3:37] seems then to point in the opposite direction. See F. Maas, "*kpr*," *Theological Lexicon of the Old Testament*, ed. Ernst Jenni and Claus Westermann, trans. Mark E. Biddle; 3 vols (Peabody, MA: Hendrickson, 1997), 2:625.

[22] Some scholars now argue that sacrifice had a basically propitiatory sense in the prehistory and early stages of the biblical tradition, but that this understanding of sacrifice gradually modulated into expiation. See Yitzhaq Feder, *Blood Expiation in Hittite and Biblical Ritual: Origins, Context, and Meaning* (SBLWAWSup 2; Atlanta: Society of Biblical Literature, 2011), 167–173; Janowski, *Sühne*, 177. Blood rites were routinely associated in antiquity with "bloodthirsty" inhabitants of the underworld; see Feder, *Expiation*, 209–210.

[23] John Goldingay, *Old Testament Theology, Volume 3: Israel's Life* (Downers Grove, IL: IVP Academic, 2009), 145.

[24] Jacob Milgrom, "A Prolegomenon to Leviticus 17:11," *JBL* 90 (1971), 149–156, did attempt to incorporate this verse into his expiatory interpretation of sacrifice, but his effort has been roundly rebuffed. He argued that Leviticus 17:11 only applied to the fellowship offering and addressed a need to atone for the animal's blood used in that ritual. For criticism, see Notker Füglister, "Sühne durch Blut—Zur Bedeutung von Leviticus 17,11," in *Studien zum Pentateuch: Walter Kornfeld zum 60. Geburtstag*, ed. Georg Braulik (Vienna: Herder, 1977), 143–164; Kiuchi, *Purification Offering*, 102–103; Rolf Rendtorff, "Another Prolegomenon to Leviticus 17:11," in *Pomegranates and Golden Bells: Studies in Biblical, Jewish, and Near Eastern Ritual, Law, and Literature in Honor of Jacob Milgrom*, ed. David P. Wright, David Noel Wright, and Avi Hurvitz (Winona Lake, IN: Eisenbrauns, 1995), 23–28.

[25] Gilders, *Blood Ritual*, 185.

However, evangelical scholars have frequently reconstructed the ransom idea as the root meaning of *kipper* (perhaps in combination with its purifying sense), in hope of providing support for the penal substitution position.[26] Questions regarding the translation of *kipper* and the proper understanding of ancient Israel's sacrificial rituals are made all the more challenging because the received form of Leviticus likely reflects a process of religious development and editorial revision. It cannot be assumed that every aspect of Leviticus as it currently stands is part of a unified, consistent conception of sacrifice, as it once existed at a single moment in time.[27]

Expiation as Representative and Participatory

The criticism that the expiation model fails by not capturing the "substitutionary" dimension of sacrifice is unpersuasive. True, if animals were sacrificed primarily in order to cleanse the altar, rather than to substitute for a human sin or a life, then such sacrifice does not appear to be "substitutionary" to the same degree. But in the expiation model, the altar is still being cleansed *for the sake of* the worshiper and the worshiping community.[28] In other words, expiation does not rule out the possibility that purification sacrifices were understood as in some sense representative or even vicarious.[29] A religious object, such as an animal's blood, was still being used in order to achieve reconciliation between the worshiper and God. Yet some interpreters, particularly in the evangelical tradition, use the terms "substitutionary" and "vicarious" as if they are exact synonyms.[30]

---

[26] For example, Morris, *Apostolic Preaching*, 148; Emile Nicole, "Atonement in the Pentateuch," in *The Glory of the Atonement: Biblical, Historical and Practical Perspectives; Essays in Honor of Roger Nicole*, ed. Charles E. Hill and Frank A. James III (Downers Grove, IL: InterVarsity, 2004), 35–50; David Peterson, "Atonement in the Old Testament," in *Where Wrath and Mercy Meet: Proclaiming the Atonement Today*, ed. David Peterson (Waynesboro, GA: Paternoster, 2001), 1–25.

[27] This realization also pinpoints a basic problem in Milgrom's approach; see further Brevard S. Childs, *Old Testament Theology in a Canonical Context* (Philadelphia: Fortress, 1985), 169–170.

[28] A number of scholars would hold out for the "purgation" of the worshiper as well as the worship place in Leviticus; see John G. Gammie, *Holiness in Israel* (Overtures to Biblical Theology; Minneapolis: Augsburg Fortress, 1989), 38–40; Baruch A. Levine, *In the Presence of the Lord: A Study of Cult and Some Cultic Terms in Ancient Israel* (Studies in Judaism in Late Antiquity 5; Leiden: Brill, 1974), 101–114. Crucial to this discussion is use of the Hebrew preposition *min*, which sometimes appears to indicate (e.g., Lev. 4:26; 5:6) that sacrifice does cleanse the worshiper "from" (NRSV: "for") his sin.

[29] This is, after all, how Hebrew 9:13–14 understands purificatory sacrifice.

[30] See, for example, Gordon J. Wenham, "The Theology of Old Testament Sacrifice," in *Sacrifice in the Bible*, ed. Roger T. Beckwith and Martin J. Selman (Grand Rapids, MI: Baker, 1995), 79–80.

A major alternative has been provided by Hartmut Gese,[31] who proposed that a process of participatory "identification" rather than "substitution" lay at the heart of Israelite sacrifice, symbolized above all by the laying of the worshiper's hand upon the head of the sacrificial animal prior to killing it.[32] On this view, a sacrifice could be interpreted as "on behalf of" or "for" the worshiper without necessarily being made "instead of" the worshiper's own death.[33] Indeed, for Gese the purpose of the *ḥaṭṭāʾt* was participatory without being substitutionary—to bring the worshiper, through the medium of shed blood, "into contact with the holy."[34] In this way Gese's reconstruction articulates and preserves an ultimate goal of reconciliation. His view is therefore able to affirm that in Israel's worship life sins really were forgiven and broken relationships in fact restored. One of the chief problems with the penal substitution view is that it has all too often been employed to undermine or negate the efficacy of Old Testament sacrifice altogether, with some Christian theologians insisting that in and of itself Israel's worship life was only a sham.[35] Yet to take the Old Testament

---

[31] Hartmut Gese, "The Atonement," in idem, *Essays on Biblical Theology*, trans. Keith Crim (Minneapolis: Augsburg, 1981), 93–116. If I have understood Gese correctly, then the tendency to treat "substitutionary" and "vicarious" as synonyms has apparently also affected the English version of his essay. Although Gese has been translated as arguing for "substitution," what he in fact supports is a view of "inclusive *Stellvertretung*," or "a *Stellvertretung* that includes the one bringing the sacrifice," *as opposed to* "a transfer of sins with the subsequent execution of the one bearing the sins, the sacrificial animal" ("Atonement," 106). However, "substitution" has misleadingly been used to translate the German term *Stellvertretung*, which should instead be rendered in English as "representation." In German a *Stellverterter* is a "representative" or a "deputy" rather than a "substitute."

[32] Wenham, "Theology," 79, notes that the Hebrew verb used in conjunction with the hand-laying is actually "press" ($\sqrt{smk}$) rather than "place" or "lay" ($\sqrt{śym}$), perhaps a further indication of the action's significance. Wenham proceeds to reject an interpretation in which the hand gesture is understood as transferring sin from the worshiper to the animal, although others argue along such lines, particularly with regard to the Day of Atonement ritual (cf. Lev. 16:21). However, in the Day of Atonement ritual the priest uses two hands instead of the more usual one-handed gesture. Gese ("Atonement," 105–106) interestingly suggests that the "giving" of sins to the scapegoat is explicitly specified precisely because the hand gesture itself does not imply it. Also, Wenham quite sensibly notes that if sin was indeed transferred to the animal then it would be difficult to see how that animal could still be used in the sacrifice or how its blood could cleanse the sanctuary. On the single-hand gesture as connoting identification rather than transference, see further David P. Wright, "The Gesture of Hand Placement in the Hebrew Bible and in Hittite Literature," *Journal of the American Oriental Society* 106 (1986), 433–446.

[33] For this distinction and use of language, see Brad Jersak, "Nonviolent Identification and the Victory of Christ," in *Stricken by God? Nonviolent Identification and the Victory of Christ*, ed. Brad Jersak and Michael Hardin (Grand Rapids, MI: Eerdmans, 2007), 42.

[34] Gese, "Atonement," 110; cf. 106.

[35] For example, John Calvin, *Institutes of the Christian Religion*, ed. John T. McNeill; trans. Ford Lewis Battles; 2 vols (Philadelphia: Westminster, 1960), 1:349, "For what is more vain or absurd than for men to offer a loathsome stench from the fat of cattle in order to reconcile themselves to God? . . . The whole cultus of the law, taken literally and not as shadows and figures corresponding to the truth, will be utterly ridiculous." Cf. Heb. 10:4.

with full seriousness is to recognize how Israel already knew "atonement" as a reality prior to God's action in Christ.

The Day of Atonement ritual (Lev. 16) is also frequently cited as a warrant for a substitutionary view of sacrifice. However, the text of Leviticus makes clear that atonement is completed before the scapegoat rite begins (Lev. 16:20; "When he has finished atoning [√*kpr*] the holy place and the tent of meeting and the altar, he shall present the live goat").[36] There is indeed a representative aspect to what the scapegoat does (Lev. 16:22; "The goat shall carry on itself all their iniquities to an isolated region"), but the goat is neither killed nor sacrificed.[37] The procedure is therefore better interpreted as an elimination rite, analogous to Leviticus 14:1–32 and Zechariah 5:5–11.[38] Although the ritual for a person with a skin condition, as detailed in Leviticus 14:1–32, does include blood sacrifice, here again the text explicitly frames the ritual as not actually effecting the healing of the person, which it assumes has already taken place, but rather facilitating his or her subsequent reintroduction into the community (Lev. 14:3; "If the priest sees that the leper has been healed, then . . .").

So there is little basis for interpreting Old Testament sacrifice as "substitutionary."[39] However, expiation can still be understood as participatory, representative, and vicarious. Another reason for viewing expiation as having a vicarious aspect is that the major sacrifices in Leviticus appear to have been performed in a customary sequence: purification offering (*ḥaṭṭā't*), burnt offering (*'ōlâ*), and fellowship offering (*šĕlāmîm*).[40] Thus, expiation or purification may have been only the first step of a sacrificial process that went on to include even more powerfully vicarious symbols and procedures. The "atoning" aspect of the *'ōlâ* is likewise disputed, and may have changed over time, but some texts do relate its purpose to the forgiveness of sins (Lev. 1:4; 16:24; cf. Gen. 8:20–21; Job 1:5).[41]

---

[36] Biblical translations in this chapter are my own unless otherwise indicated.
[37] Fiddes, *Past Event*, 73; Milgrom, *Leviticus*, 1:1021. Contra Peterson, "Atonement," 15. Simon Gathercole, *Defending Substitution: An Essay on Atonement* (Grand Rapids, MI: Baker Academic, 2015), 37–38, neglects to explain how this ceremony can be considered an act of "substitution" if the scapegoat is neither killed nor sacrificed.
[38] Maas, "*kpr*," 629–630. In the received form of the biblical text, the scapegoat rite has likely been expanded to include an expiatory function; see Milgrom, *Leviticus*, 1:1082–1083.
[39] Even Gathercole, *Defending Substitution*, 37 n. 34, seems largely to agree: "A substitutionary function of the slaughtered offerings is by no means clear."
[40] Anson F. Rainey, "The Order of Sacrifices in Old Testament Ritual Texts," *Biblica* 51 (1970), 485–498.
[41] For further discussion, see Jenson, "Sacrificial System," 28–29.

Expiation as Objective and Necessary

The criticism that the expiation model fails by inadequately acknowledging God's righteousness and wrath has perhaps more justification—and points to a theological anxiety that does seem to motivate some "liberal" advocates of the expiation model.[42] There is no getting around the very real wrath of God toward sin throughout the Old Testament or God's stern, insistent demand for justice and holiness. For this reason advocates of "penal" atonement initially score a compelling point. Sometimes divine wrath *is* averted by the death of the guilty (e.g., Num. 25:1–5; Josh. 7:22–26); occasionally √*kpr* does appear in conjunction with divine anger (e.g., Ps. 78:38; Jer. 18:23; both, however, with God as subject rather than object of √*kpr*). The vicarious nature of sacrifice as well as its role in averting divine anger also seem evident in the later Jewish tradition of the martyred seven brothers, who "bring to an end the wrath of the Almighty" (2 Macc. 7:38, NRSV) by providing "a ransom [*antípsychon*] for the sin of our nation ... as an atoning sacrifice [*hilastērion*]" (4 Macc. 17:21–22, NRSV).[43] This last example is particularly telling because it acknowledges a vicarious dimension to a loss of *innocent* human life, a view that has sometimes been considered foreign to early (Palestinian) Judaism.[44]

Yet in Leviticus, as we have seen, the language of *kipper* is not used in a propitiatory manner, and it is striking to realize how little appeal there is to divine anger throughout the book.[45] A reference to divine anger has sometimes been seen in the repeated motif of the "pleasant odor" (NRSV; Heb. *rēyaḥ-nîḥōaḥ*) that rises from certain burnt sacrifices (Lev. 1:9, 13, 17; 2:2, 9, 12; 3:5, 16; 4:31; 23:13; 26:31; cf. Gen. 8:21).[46] The implication of the phrase is certainly that God

---

[42] For example, C. H. Dodd, *The Epistle of Paul to the Romans* (New York: Harper, 1932), 20–21, called the wrath of God "a thoroughly archaic idea." This was not the case, however, with Milgrom; see, for example, his "Atonement," 80.

[43] Cf. 4 Macc. 1:11; 6:29; 18:4. These passages were neglected by Dodd; see Nicole, "Dodd," 132–133. However, the view they present is arguably still not one of penal substitution. See David A. Brondos, *Paul on the Cross: Reconstructing the Apostle's Story of Redemption* (Minneapolis: Fortress, 2006), 27–31. The substantive *antípsychon* (literally, a "for-life") appears in fact to have been coined on the basis of Leviticus 17:11; see David A. deSilva, *4 Maccabees: Introduction and Commentary on the Greek Text in Codex Sinaiticus* (Septuagint Commentary Series; Leiden: Brill, 2006), 249–252. In this way the same uncertainties about sacrificial logic in Leviticus merely transfer to Maccabees.

[44] Milgrom, "Atonement" 82, rules out this kind of belief as "an explicit OT doctrine," although he concedes that it may be implicit in Isaiah 53. However, significant evidence for this belief in the Hellenistic period is provided by Martin Hengel, *The Atonement: The Origins of the Doctrine in the New Testament* (Philadelphia: Fortress, 1981), 60–61.

[45] The use of √*qṣp* in Leviticus 10:6 and *baḥămat-qerî* in Leviticus 26:28 are exceptions that prove the rule. Frank S. Thielman, "The Atonement," in *Central Themes in Biblical Theology: Mapping Unity in Diversity*, ed. Scott J. Hafemann and Paul R. House (Grand Rapids, MI: Baker Academic, 2007), 107, openly reads God's wrath into Leviticus 17:11, although the text itself makes no reference to it.

[46] Wenham, "Atonement," 81.

is affected by burnt sacrifice, which therefore does accomplish something in objective terms.[47] But it will not do to smuggle in a view of propitiation by glossing the phrase as "soothing aroma" and then suggesting that the scent from the fire appeases God's wrath.[48] The phrase provides too little support for such a far-reaching conclusion. Actually, the phrase is finally more conspicuous for its difference from the rest of the presentation in Leviticus than for its compatibility with it. The phrase is more likely a "frozen" linguistic element from the past, which has survived and retained a place in Israel's discourse of sacrifice, even though it is arguably out of step with the rest of the description.[49]

Yes, there are other biblical passages that depict atonement as a means of avoiding God's displeasure. One thinks in particular of Numbers 16:46-48 (cf. Heb. 17:11-13), in which incense is used to effect *kipper* and avert a divinely imposed plague (cf. 2 Sam. 24:21). But a striking phenomenon within the Old Testament literature is in fact how rarely sacrifice is described or enjoined as a response to divine wrath. However, it also goes too far to gloss expiation as merely "showing you are sorry" and to dismiss it as a species of "subjective atonement." Expiation in Milgrom's description is a deadly serious business that objectively purges the sanctum of contamination, which is physically real though invisible to the eye.[50] Purgation thus effects a true change in the worshiper's status before God. It does not describe something only internal to the human heart.

Still, the term "penal" properly refers not just to judgment but to *punishment*, and it is here that a significant problem arises. The fundamental issue is not whether God becomes angry at sin—God does—but whether God demands retribution in the form of a legal penalty. In the biblical thought-world "sin" is not identical with "crime,"[51] although one can certainly point to cases in which the two categories appear to overlap (e.g., capital crimes must be "purged" as well as punished; Deut. 17:12). "Sin" is likewise not always a moral failing but sometimes a matter of impurity. Indeed, the *ḥaṭṭā't* in particular is *not* presented as a cultic response to a crime for which the penalty of death applies but to a minor and *unintentional* sin.[52] "High-handed" or intentional sin cannot be atoned by

---

[47] Wright, "Atonement," 76-77.
[48] As in Wenham, "Atonement," 80-81; Wright, "Atonement," 76-77.
[49] Klaus Seybold, "Reconciliation/Atonement: II. Old Testament," in *Religion in the Past and Present: Encyclopedia of Theology and Religion,* ed. Hans Dieter Betz et al. (Boston: Brill, 2007-13), 10:664-665. Seybold also calls attention to the phrase "making [God's] face pleasant" (e.g., Exod. 32:11, etc.).
[50] Milgrom, "Atonement," 79, famously describes sin as "a miasma that, wherever committed, is attracted magnet-like to the sanctuary"; idem, *Studies,* 77.
[51] Moshe Greenberg, "Crimes and Punishment," in *Interpreter's Dictionary of the Bible,* ed. George Arthur Buttrick; 4 vols (Nashville: Abingdon, 1962), 1:733-734.
[52] Füglister, "Sühne," 146.

ordinary sacrifice (Num. 15:30–31) but only in a special ritual on the Day of Atonement (Lev. 16:16). Moreover, sometimes the *ḥaṭṭāʾt* appears in contexts in which no sin has even been committed (e.g., the dedication of an altar, Lev. 8:14–15; childbirth, Lev. 12:6–8).[53]

Accounts of atonement as "satisfaction" are also generally difficult to evaluate, in part because the term "satisfaction" has been invoked in quite diverse ways. Like the language of "atonement" generally, "satisfaction" has often taken on connotations of propitiation, substitution, and punishment.[54] In Old Testament sacrifice there is indeed something that "needs" to be done in order to make things right, and once it is done the urgency of the necessity has certainly been "satisfied." But how does one understand the nature of that necessity? Might it not turn on the need for holiness before God rather than legal obedience? Might it not arise out of the solemn, life-or-death promise made as part of the covenantal pact between God and Israel? Could it even be lodged mysteriously within the fabric of creation itself? Affirmative responses to these questions are also not mutually exclusive.

Misconception 3: Atonement Involves a Single Mode of Reconciliation

Although sacrificial offerings, particularly those employing blood, tend to predominate in the theological discussion, the Old Testament describes multiple means of atonement.[55] There were offerings and ceremonies that did not necessarily entail the shedding of any blood, or were at least not focused primarily on blood, and yet achieved reconciliation for the worshiper: for example, grain offerings (1 Sam. 3:14; 26:17–20; Lev. 2:1–16; 5:11–13; 6:14–23; 14:20), applications of oil (Lev. 14:18, 26–29) or water (Lev. 15:5–12; 1 Sam. 7:6) or wine (Exod. 29:40–41), the bird ritual (Lev. 14:1–9), the scapegoat ritual (Lev. 16:10, 16–20), the ransom for a military census (Exod. 30:16), incense offerings (Num. 16:46; Isa 6:6–7?), and the ritual of the heifer with the broken neck (Deut. 21:1–9).[56]

---

[53] Hayes, "Atonement," 7.
[54] See the admirably clear, if brief, account of how such connotations were somewhat foreign even to Anselm's view of atonement in O'Collins, "Redemption," 9–10.
[55] *Contra* Fisher Humphreys, *The Death of Christ* (Nashville, TN: Broadman, 1978), 26: "Like the Jewish priests themselves, [the author of Hebrews] believed that forgiveness was possible only when sacrificial blood had been shed (Heb. 9:22)."
[56] For an unconvincing defense of the implicit importance of blood in all Israelite sacrifice, see Nicole, "Atonement," 41–46. He characterizes Leviticus 5:11–13 as "an exception among exceptions" (45).

These practices kept the worshiper "right" before God, although not all featured blood manipulation or even involved the killing of an animal.[57]

Especially because of the persistent stress on blood sacrifice in the Christian theological tradition, it is important to emphasize again that even in the sacrifices that did involve blood manipulation, it was the manipulation itself that was ritually significant, rather than the killing of the animal per se.[58] The killing of the animal is noticeably de-emphasized in sacrificial texts by not being described or even mentioned, and the priest did not perform it. The worshiper killed the animal as a preparatory act rather than as the centerpiece of the atoning event.[59] Both the variety and character of the atoning rituals argue against a penal substitution model.[60]

Mention can further be made of the *'āšām*, the "reparation offering" (Lev. 5:14–6:7), whose rationale is also still somewhat obscure. As part of this ritual, the sacrificial animal was apparently only sometimes killed (Lev. 7:1–6) and without any blood manipulation.[61] The animal's value might be converted into a monetary amount instead. Either way, the offerer, someone who had misappropriated or misused the property of a neighbor (or of God), was then required to provide full restitution plus an additional 20 percent. So in this case, the desired reconciliation was achieved as much by repayment as by sacrifice.

Finally, the Old Testament describes atonement as *more* than sacrifice: "Sacrifice and offering you have not desired; you have dug out my ears. Burnt offering and purification offering you have not requested" (Ps. 40:6 [Heb. 7]); "The sacrifices of God are a broken spirit; a broken and crushed heart, O God, you will not despise" (Ps. 51:17 [Heb. 19]). Both prophetic Scripture and the Psalms testify to a dimension of atonement that extends beyond literal sacrifice and at points even exists in significant tension with sacrificial practice (e.g., 1 Sam. 15:22; Hos. 6:6; Mic. 6:6–8). In part this aspect of the Old Testament's witness highlights the need for personal repentance if forgiveness is to be achieved.[62] Such testimony indicates the biblical tradition's resistance to the sort

---

[57] See further Frank H. Gorman, "Sacrifices and Offerings," in *The New Interpreter's Dictionary of the Bible*, ed. Katharine Doob Sakenfeld; 5 vols (Nashville: Abingdon, 2009), 5:2–32.
[58] It is thus a mistake to take Heb. 9:22 ("without the shedding of blood there is no forgiveness of sins") and impose it on Leviticus as the hermeneutical key to an understanding of Old Testament sacrifice. "Shedding" might also be translated "pouring"; see David M. Moffitt, *Atonement and the Logic of Resurrection in the Epistle to the Hebrews* (NTSup 141; Leiden: Brill, 2011), 291–292 n. 157.
[59] *Contra* Wenham, "Atonement," 82: "The animal is a substitute for the worshipper. Its death makes atonement for the worshipper."
[60] Cf. J. S. Whale, *Victor and Victim: The Christian Doctrine of Redemption* (Cambridge: Cambridge University Press, 1960), 53: "You cannot punish a cupful of barley."
[61] Hayes, "Atonement," 11.
[62] Childs, *Old Testament Theology*, 170–173. See further Bruce K. Waltke, "Atonement in Psalm 51: 'My Sacrifice, O God, Is a Broken Spirit,'" in *The Glory of the Atonement: Biblical, Theological and*

of magical thinking that imagines rites and rituals as functioning successfully without repentance and a corresponding commitment to subsequent "amendment of life." It remains impressive that ancient Israel had such a keen apprehension of how the practice of religion could itself compound, even generate sin (e.g., Is. 1:10–17; Jer. 7:9–11; Amos 4:4–5).

Misconception 4: Atonement Pertains Only to People

Ecclesiastes 3:19–21 suggests that humans and animals share a *common* predicament: "For the fate of humans and animals is the same; as the one dies, so dies the other. They all have the same breath/spirit [Heb. *rûaḥ*], and humans have no advantage over the animals." Atonement should therefore not be conceived as a response to the "human condition" alone, as if human beings were somehow separate and of sole value, but as relating to a larger range of concerns touching all living things and indeed the created world itself. In the biblical portrayal, animals are depicted as loving objects of divine compassion: "For every creature of the forest is mine, the cattle on a thousand hills. I know every bird of the mountains, and whatever moves in the field is in my care" (Ps. 50:10–11). They have their own dignity before God ("Look at Behemoth, which I made just as I made you," Job 40:15), and they praise God on their own (Ps. 148:7–10).

Along with Israel, God rescued animals from Egypt (Exod. 12:37–38). They are God's covenant partners alongside human beings (Gen. 9:8–17; Hos. 2:20 [Heb. 18]), and as such they have certain legal rights (Exod. 20:10; 23:11–12; Lev. 25:6–7; Deut. 5:14; 22:1–4, 6–7; 23:15–16) and responsibilities (Exod. 13:11–16; 20:10; Deut. 5:14). Animals can apparently sin (Gen. 3:14–15) and be punished (Gen. 9:5; Exod. 21:28–32). In cases of sexual activity between animals and humans, bloodguilt attaches to both (Lev. 20:15–16). God's anger extends to human beings and animals, even plants: "my wrath shall be poured out on this place, on human beings and animals, on the trees of the field and the fruit of the ground" (Jer. 7:20; cf. Exod. 9:9 and passim). Animals can also repent (Jon. 3:5–8), and God exhibits mercy to all creatures (Ps. 145:8–16). Even "salvation" is not for human beings alone: "you save [√*yš'* Hiph.] humans and animals, O Lord" (Ps. 36:6 [Heb. 7]).

Practical Perspectives, ed. Charles E. Hill and Frank A. James III (Downers Grove, IL: InterVarsity, 2004), 51–60.

In light of this pronounced and yet still underappreciated scriptural emphasis, the notion that there is a special mode of reconciliation called "atonement," which applies only to human beings, misrepresents the biblical witness. To the contrary, the God who created all creatures can be trusted to put all creatures right in the end, as the Old Testament's inspiring visions of eschatological peace depict (e.g., Is. 2:1–4; 11:6–9; 65:25; cf. Rom. 8:19–22; Col. 1:15–20; Eph. 1:10). More poignantly, this perspective casts the practice of sacrifice in a new light. Who are the real offerers within the ancient sacrificial system, and by means of whose blood is human reconciliation with God achieved? The sacrificial nonhuman animals are in fact the ones making the actual sacrifice, and their innocence arguably ennobles them even above human faithfulness.[63] Precisely by this logic is Jesus remembered as the Lamb of God as well as the Good Shepherd. The full cost of human reconciliation with God is paid not only by the repentance of human worshipers, but also by the blood of their animal deputies. Perhaps ironically, animal sacrifice therefore reflects the high religious value of animals in Israel's worldview rather than being an act of neglect, denigration, or abuse.[64] Nevertheless, atonement theories typically proceed as if only human well-being was of ultimate divine concern.[65]

Misconception 5: Divine Agency is Exclusively Forensic and Not Also Cosmic

God's justice should not be conceived as a disconnected series of discrete verdicts: Israel's understanding of divine action was more coherent and differentiated. "Righteousness" (*ṣedeq/ṣĕdāqâ*) is a fundamentally relational term in

---

[63] Jonathan Morgan, "Sacrifice in Leviticus: Eco-Friendly Ritual or Unholy Waste?" in *Ecological Hermeneutics: Biblical, Historical and Theological Perspectives* (ed. David G. Horrell et al. (New York: T&T Clark, 2010), 42.
[64] Cf. Oded Borowski, "Animals in the Religions of Syria-Palestine," in *A History of the Animal World in the Ancient Near East*, ed. Billie Jean Collins; Handbook of Oriental Studies 64 (Leiden: Brill, 2002), 424. Cf. Stephen Bigger, "Symbol and Metaphor in the Hebrew Bible," in *Creating the Old Testament: The Emergence of the Hebrew Bible*, ed. Stephen Bigger (Oxford: Blackwell, 1989), 60: "the secularization of killing for food has diminished our view of animal life." A related misconception about atonement is that Jesus' sacrifice brought an end to all animal sacrifice within the Christian tradition. However, as detailed in David Grumett and Rachel Muers, *Theology on the Menu: Asceticism, Meat and Christian Diet* (New York: Routledge, 2010), 107–127, some Christians have continued to practice animal sacrifice, especially in Eastern Orthodoxy (e.g., in the *matal* or *madagh* ritual of the Armenian church).
[65] For a stimulating theological corrective, see David L. Clough, *On Animals: Volume 1, Systematic Theology* (New York: T&T Clark, 2012). I have drawn on Clough's work in drafting this section.

the Old Testament, with a strong creational dimension (e.g., Ps. 72:3; Is. 45:8; 48:18; 61:11; Amos 5:24; Joel 2:23), often amounting to a conception of world order.[66]

Divine agency must accordingly be understood in a more nuanced manner than is often recognized. Although there are certainly instances of God in the role of judge, sovereignly imposing direct consequences (e.g., 1 Sam. 25:38; Prov. 15:25), there are also numerous cases in which God works indirectly behind the scenes or *through* people, events, and the natural world.[67] God can use harmful human intentions to bring about the good (Gen. 50:20), harness "a strong east wind" to deliver Israel from Egypt (Exod. 14:21), and employ the Assyrians to execute judgment upon Israel (Is. 10:5–6). Particularly noteworthy is the act-consequence model of causation found throughout the various Old Testament traditions. As described by Klaus Koch in a classic essay,[68] this model attributes the consequences of harmful actions partly to the nature of those actions themselves.

There is thus a creational logic to blessing and curse, which possess an intrinsic relation to the character of the actions that have preceded them. Revealing examples are found in Proverbs, such as "Whoever digs a pit will fall into it, and a stone will come back on the one who starts it rolling" (Prov. 26:27; cf. Prov. 28:10; Ps. 7:14–16; Hos. 10:12–13). This relationship between act and consequence is neither mechanical nor foolproof. But it does amount to a presumptive expectation, and it cannot be relegated to the mythological world behind the text, but rather constitutes one fundamental aspect of the Old Testament's manifold theological witness.[69] Nor is this aspect of the biblical witness limited to the Old Testament (cf. Mt. 7:1–2; 26:52; 2 Cor. 5:10; Gal. 6:7–8).[70]

As much as God sometimes appears in the role of sovereign judge, sometimes God is perceived more as ratifying or suspending the presumptive creational

---

[66] Hans Heinrich Schmid, *Gerechtigkeit als Weltordnung: Hintergrund und Geschichte des alttestamentlichen Gerechtigkeitsbegriffes* (Beiträge zur historischen Theologie 40; Tübingen: Mohr Siebeck, 1968).

[67] See further Gerhard von Rad, "The Beginning of Historical Writing in Ancient Israel," in *The Problem of the Hexateuch and Other Essays*, trans. E. W. Trueman Dicken (New York: McGraw-Hill, 1966), 166–204.

[68] Klaus Koch, "Is There a Doctrine of Retribution in the Old Testament?" in *Theodicy in the Old Testament,* ed. James L. Crenshaw; Issues in Religion and Theology 4 (Philadelphia: Fortress, 1983), 57–87.

[69] Stephen B. Chapman, "Reading the Bible as Witness: Divine Retribution in the Old Testament," *Perspectives in Religious Studies* 31 (2004), 171–190.

[70] For further discussion, Stephen H. Travis, *Christ and the Judgement of God: The Limits of Divine Retribution in New Testament Thought*, 2d ed. (Peabody, MA: Hendrickson, 2008).

logic already attaching to acts and their consequences (e.g., 2 Sam. 3:39; 1 Kgs. 8:31–32; Prov. 25:21–22). This indirect view of divine retribution applies even to the shedding of non-sacrificial blood (both human [Gen. 9:5–6; 2 Sam. 16:7–8; 21:1] and animal [Lev. 17:3–4]) and the resultant bloodguilt, which is envisioned as "returning on the head" of the slayer (e.g., Josh. 2:19; 2 Sam. 1:16; 1 Kgs. 2:31–33, 36–37; Ezek. 33:4; cf. Obad. 1:15).[71] Other sins, especially sexual sins and heterodox religious practices, can also be viewed as eliciting bloodguilt (Lev. 20:9, 11–12, 16, 27; Ezek. 18:10–13). Shed blood pollutes the land as well as the sanctuary (Num. 35:33), and the land itself demands expiation (Gen. 4:10). Folk wisdom even today knows that "blood will out."

God cannot altogether dispense with retribution because in this fashion the operation of justice is woven into the very fabric of creation (cf. Gen. 18:25).[72] In creating the world, God has in effect agreed to honor creation's structures and natural processes. God expects human beings to live in accordance with creation's "structural justice,"[73] and God feels pain when humans are irresponsible with their moral stewardship. The "requirement" for atoning blood is thus not within God, but within the world that God has made. This insight opens up the possibility of construing the need for atonement as more creational, more in line with the pain and suffering existing within the natural world, even within the process of evolution itself.[74] Sacrifice is enjoined because of the brokenness of creation, which results in a self-perpetuating cycle of violence (e.g., Hos. 4:1–3). In Israel's understanding, repentance and sacrifice break that cycle by surrendering violence to God (Deut. 32:34–43; cf. Rom. 12:19). In this way Old Testament sacrifice can be viewed as staging and redirecting creational violence, rather than enacting the violence of God.[75]

---

[71] See further Henning Graf Reventlow, "Sein Blut komme über sein Haupt," *Vetus Testamentum* 10 (1960), 211–227 and Klaus Koch, "Der Spruch 'sein Blut bleibe auf seinem Haupt' und die israelitische Auffassung vom vergossenen Blut," *Vetus Testamentum* 12 (1962), 396–416 = 412–431 and 432–456 (respectively) in *Das Prinzip der Vergeltung in Religion und Recht des Alten Testaments*, ed. Klaus Koch (Wege der Forschung 125; Darmstadt: Wissenschaftliche Buchgesellschaft, 1972).

[72] Terence J. Kleven, "Old Testament Teaching on Necessity in Creation and Its Implication for the Doctrine of Atonement," in *Divine Creation in Ancient, Medieval, and Early Modern Thought: Essays Presented to the Rev'd Dr Robert D. Crouse*, ed. Michael Treschow, Willemien Otten, and Walter Hannam (Leiden: Brill, 2007), 23–44.

[73] Fiddes, *Past Event*, 10, 92. He apparently takes this phrase from Paul Tillich, *Systematic Theology* 3 vols (Chicago: University of Chicago Press, 1967), 2:201.

[74] For further discussion of this theological trajectory, see Christopher Southgate, *The Groaning of Creation: God, Evolution, and the Problem of Evil* (Louisville: Westminster John Knox, 2008).

[75] Cf. Frank H. Gorman, Jr., *The Ideology of Ritual: Time and Status in the Priestly Theology* (Sheffield: JSOT Press, 1990), 9: "the Priestly ritual system is best understood as the meaningful enactment of world in the context of Priestly creation theology."

Christian Appropriation

For far too long Christian theologians have taken one interpretation of Paul as their starting point for reflection on atonement, and then read Paul into Hebrews and Hebrews into Leviticus.[76] More careful consideration of the Old Testament witnesses reveals the vast, cosmic sweep of God's reconciling work and usefully corrects reductive interpretations of atonement sometimes made on the basis of New Testament scripture. The New Testament everywhere relies upon the language, imagery, and conceptions of the Old Testament in order to present the person and work of Christ. A crucial aspect of the New Testament's witness to Jesus is not just that Jesus died, but that for some mysterious reason Jesus "had" to die (Mt. 16:21; cf. Mark 8:31; Luke 9:22). Something made his death necessary, even for God (Luke 22:41–42).[77]

What Christian "atonement theory" attempts to do, at its most basic level, is to articulate this sense of necessity on the basis of the biblical witnesses, from the Old Testament as well as the New. One of the main ways that the Bible explains it is to gesture toward the long-reaching plan of God to redeem all of creation (e.g., Is. 46:8–11; Jer. 29:11; Acts 2:23; 3:18). Many of the specifics within this plan remain a mystery, although its broad contours can be traced throughout the Bible and beyond. From this vantage point, it is not only clear that Jesus's death was designed by God to achieve a purpose within that plan, but that a crucial part of God's overriding purpose lay in opening up the rights and responsibilities of Israel's covenantal life to the other peoples of the world.[78]

The New Testament knows this divine plan, both its prior history and its future scope, from the Old Testament. It takes a special interest in the Old Testament's sacrificial tradition as a prime reservoir of metaphor, allusion, and logic to employ in understanding Jesus's teachings and death. Within this ancient tradition, sacrifice is viewed as primarily about reconciliation with God, but it is also expiatory, representative, and vicarious in nature.[79] On analogy with

---

[76] For an interpretation of Hebrews that instead aligns with Leviticus, see Moffitt, *Atonement*, 215–296.

[77] *Contra* Brondos, *Paul*, 30: "there is no type of necessity to which Israel's God is subject" (original in italics). On the New Testament material, see Charles H. Cosgrove, "The Divine *dei* in Luke-Acts: Investigations into the Lukan Understanding of God's Providence," *Novum Testamentum* 26 (1984), 168–190; Joel B. Green, "Jesus on the Mount of Olives (Luke 22:39–46): Tradition and Theology," *Journal for the Study of the New Testament* 26 (1986), 29–48; John T. Squires, *The Plan of God in Luke-Acts* (SNTSMS 76; Cambridge: Cambridge University Press, 1993).

[78] See further Michael J. Gorman, *The Death of the Messiah and the Birth of the New Covenant: A (Not So) New Model of the Atonement* (Eugene, OR: Cascade, 2014).

[79] Gese's work in particular suggests that the origins of Paul's "participatory soteriology" can be located squarely in Israel's sacrificial tradition. Cf. 1 Cor. 10:16. It is often overlooked that even

Israel's tradition of sacrifice, it should not be said that God punished Jesus for human sin. Instead it should be confessed that Jesus completely identified with *creaturely* life and experienced the full extent of creation's *estrangement* from God: "It is both true and important to say that he 'was judged in our place'— that he experienced divine judgment on sin in the sense that he endured the God-ordained consequences of human sinfulness. But this is not the same as to say that he bore our punishment."[80] In becoming humanity's sacrifice, the Lamb of God decisively broke the cycle of creational violence and thereby demonstrated how it could continue to be broken,[81] by abjuring self-defense (Mt. 26:52) and vengeance (1 Pet. 2:23–24), and by embodying forgiveness (Luke 23:34; Acts 7:60) and self-sacrifice (Phil. 2:5–11).

Morris, *Apostolic Preaching*, 279–280, concluded his treatment with an appeal for an "inclusive" view of substitution.

[80] Stephen H. Travis, "Christ as Bearer of Divine Judgment in Paul's Thought about the Atonement," in *Jesus of Nazareth: Lord and Christ; Essays on the Historical Jesus and New Testament Christology*, ed. Joel B. Green and Max Turner (Grand Rapids, MI: Eerdmans, 1994), 345.

[81] See further Christopher D. Marshall, "Atonement, Violence and the Will of God: A Sympathetic Response to J. Denny Weaver's *The Nonviolent Atonement*," *Mennonite Quarterly Review* 77 (2003), 91–92.

7

Theologies of the Atonement in the New Testament

Joel B. Green

We need not suppose that throughout the primitive Church the same beliefs were everywhere emphasized in the same way; on the contrary, it is rather to be expected that at some centres [sic] certain aspects were appreciated more than others, and in consequence, received greater emphasis, just as in later times and indeed down to the present day. Variety rather than uniformity, and simplicity of statement rather than elaborate argument, are likely to have been characteristic of the earliest period.[1]

New Testament scholar Vincent Taylor penned these words three-quarters of a century ago in his classic study, *The Atonement in New Testament Teaching*. They refer particularly to what he called the church's "doctrine" of the atonement, and especially to that doctrine in the first thirty years after Jesus's execution on a Roman cross. Taylor goes on to explore the variety of atonement beliefs among New Testament writers. Interested as he is in finding unity among these diverse views, it is nonetheless telling that he is able to speak only in general terms of a constellation of sacrificial ideas at the root of the New Testament witness to reconciliation,[2] and to identity such common concerns as the reality of sin as barrier to reconciliation and the importance of God's initiative in Christ in effecting reconciliation for all. In this modern classic articulation of the atonement in

---

[1] Vincent Taylor, *The Atonement in New Testament Teaching* (London: Epworth, 1940), 11.
[2] Even so, he admits that no category, not even the sacrificial, is fully inclusive of the New Testament's teaching on the atonement. See further, Vincent Taylor, *Jesus and His Sacrifice: A Study of the Passion-Sayings in the Gospels* (London: Macmillan, 1937).

the New Testament, then, Taylor documented the peril awaiting any who might attempt to represent New Testament teaching on the atonement in narrow, one-dimensional terms, or to find in the New Testament a historical or theological foundation for doing the same today.[3]

This chapter extends the lines Taylor and others have drawn by exploring diverse ways in which New Testament writers represent the cross's saving significance. My point of departure is the theological claim that Jesus's crucifixion marks a fundamental change in relations between God and God's people, for the whole of humanity, and indeed for the cosmos. Taylor regarded the process of articulating this claim as a dynamic one, illumined by the Holy Spirit, and enriched by the experiences and perceptions of people within the life of a worshipping community.[4] This is doubtlessly true, though I will want to broaden the contexts within which atonement theologies took shape by allowing for influences beyond the borders of worshipping communities, including the early Christian mission and the day-to-day contexts within which that mission was practiced. Along the way, I will also have occasion to warn against too narrow a focus on the cross of Christ, a focus that should never be allowed to separate Jesus's life from the manner of his death, or Jesus's death from his resurrection and exaltation.

Jesus and the Gospels: An Overview

What did Jesus think of his own death? We have no documents from the hand of Jesus of Nazareth, but we do have in the New Testament four Gospels, each of which purports to represent his life and ministry in theological-biographical terms. With the inelegant expression "theological-biographical," I mean only to admit that the Gospels make no claim to portray "Jesus as he really was" but rather provide us with narratives that are themselves the results of inescapable choices about what is significant and that intractably locate events in webs of significance; accordingly, they are theologically determined narrative

---

[3] For more recent arguments against this kind of reductionism, see, for example, Mark D. Baker and Joel B. Green, *Recovering the Scandal of the Cross: Atonement in New Testament and Contemporary Contexts*, 2nd ed. (Downers Gove, IL: IVP Academic, 2011); John Driver, *Understanding the Atonement for the Mission of the Church* (Scottdale, PA: Herald, 1986); Scot McKnight, *A Community Called Atonement* (Nashville, TN: Abingdon, 2007).

[4] Taylor, *Atonement*, 49.

representations of historical events.⁵ Each of these four Gospels embed Jesus's death deeply in the narrative of his life and in the divine purpose he serves.

Jesus's death casts its shadow across almost every page of the Gospels. This is due in part to the opposition he attracted, opposition that leads to scenes of conflict as well as plots against his life (e.g., Mark 3:1-6). Moreover, according to the Gospels, Jesus anticipated his death, tying it into the overarching purpose of God (e.g., Mark 8:31; 9:31; 10:33-34). As Taylor recognized, "Jesus undoubtedly believed that His sufferings were not due to chance or human violence alone, but were events lying deep in the Providence of God."⁶ Remarkably, though, he seldom spoke of his death as in some sense salvific.

According to the synoptic Gospels, Jesus articulates some form of atonement theology at only two points: (1) the so-called ransom saying—"The Son of Man came not to be served but to serve, and to give his life a ransom for many" (Mark 10:45; see Mt. 20:28); and (2) the saying at the Last Supper—"This is my blood of the covenant, which is poured out for many" (Mark 14:24; see the parallels in Mt. 26:26-29; Luke 22:19-20; 1 Cor. 11:23-25).⁷

The narrative settings of these two sayings are important in two primary respects. First, the points at which a theology of the atonement is most transparent in the gospel tradition are intimately related to scenes where concerns with power and status-seeking characteristic of the Roman Empire are on display among Jesus's followers. On the one hand, these scenes indicate how the struggle for power and quest for status infiltrated even the inner circle of Jesus's disciples. On the other hand, this correlation of atonement theology and scenes displaying deep-rooted dispositions toward acquiring and maintaining relative status and power evidences the depth of Jesus's unwavering posture over against those dispositions throughout his ministry and ethical teaching. The necessity of understanding Jesus's death in relation to the entirety of his life and ministry could hardly be more apparent.

Second, the atonement theology to which Jesus bears witness in these two sayings is deeply rooted in Israel's own story. "Ransom," or "means of release" (λύτρον), belongs to the semantic domain of "deliverance" or "salvation." Jesus's counsel to his quarreling disciples that they comport themselves as slaves rather

---

⁵ See Joel B. Green, "Rethinking 'History' for Theological Interpretation," *Journal of Theological Interpretation* 5, no. 2 (2011), 159-174; more broadly, Albert Cook, *History/Writing: The Theory and Practice of History in Antiquity and in Modern Times* (Cambridge: Cambridge University Press, 1988). This section is adapted from Joel B. Green, "The Death of Jesus and the Ways of God: Jesus and the Gospels on Messianic Status and Shameful Suffering," *Interpretation* 52 (1998), 24-37.
⁶ Taylor, *Atonement*, 13-14.
⁷ Unless otherwise noted, all translations of biblical texts follow the NRSV.

than despotic rulers brings to mind the Roman slave trade, where a ransom might serve as the price of emancipation. It also recalls that great act of deliverance that lies at the foundation of Israel's peoplehood, when God ransomed Israel from Egyptian slavery. As the Lord told Moses, "Go! Tell the sons of Israel, saying, 'I am the Lord, and I will bring you out from the domination of the Egyptians, and I will deliver (λυτρόομαι) you from slavery, and I will redeem you by a raised arm and great judgment'" (Exod. 6:6, NETS). God ransoms Israel not by "paying someone off" but by delivering them from Egyptian slavery (e.g., Exod. 6:6; 16:13). These two images, the slave trade and Israel's exodus, remind us that metaphors like "ransom" can have more than one sense, not all of which are realized in a given context. Methodologically, one must differentiate between possible or virtual properties and actual ones.[8] In Jesus's message, we hear nothing about an exchange of payment. Conceptually, then, the portrait he provides is tied to exodus and new exodus, and reminiscent of the Isaianic servant whose death is efficacious for the salvation of many.

Regarding the Last Supper tradition, we should not overlook how Luke portrays the disciples at the table, again squabbling over relative greatness, or how Paul presents the Last Supper tradition within his argument against Corinthian factionalism (1 Cor. 11:17–34). Again, Jesus's representation of the atoning significance of his impending death is set in a context in which it provides a stark alternative to the world system to which his followers fall prey. Pressing further, we see how at the Last Supper Jesus embraced Israel's expectations for deliverance, intimating that the new exodus, God's decisive act of deliverance, was coming to fruition now, in his death. Moreover, he developed the meaning of his death in terms borrowed from the constitution of Israel as God's covenant people (Exod. 24:8), the end of exile (see Zech. 9:9–11), and the hope of covenant renewal (Jer. 31:31–33).

In short, in both the ransom saying and at the Last Supper, Jesus forged a view of himself as the one through whose suffering Israel, and through Israel the nations, would experience divine redemption. Indeed, Jesus's mission as this is known to us in the Gospels is directed toward revitalizing Israel as God's people. Pursuing this aim compelled him to proclaim and embody an ethic grounded in Israel's Scriptures and brought him into conflict with the conveyers of alternative religious and political life-worlds and practices. Everything—his interpretation of Israel's Scriptures, his practices of prayer and worship, his astounding choice

---

[8] See Umberto Eco, *Semiotics and the Philosophy of Language*, Advances in Semiotics (Bloomington: Indiana University Press, 1984), 97–129.

of table companions, his engagement with children, his miracles of healing and exorcism—leads to the cross. Calling twelve disciples as representative of restored Israel, weaving the hopes of new exodus and the eschatological era into his ministries of word and deed, speaking of the fulfillment of God's promises to Israel, his prophetic action at the temple in anticipation of a temple not made by human hands—through such actions, Jesus countered the present world order, maintained that God was at work in his person and mission, and chose a path that would lead to his death. Atonement theology may center on the cross of Christ, then, but the cross is never separated from Jesus's life.

In other words, a model of the atonement with a solid claim to being biblical cannot represent the death of Jesus in terms that do not interpret profoundly the reality of his crucifixion as the consequence of a life in the service of God's purpose and in opposition to all manner of competing social, political, and religious agenda. Nor can atonement theology, understood in this light, be reduced to the relationship of the individual to God, to an objective moment in the past when Jesus paid the price for our sins, or, indeed, to notions of salvation divorced from holiness of life in the world.

The Gospel of Luke and the Acts of the Apostles

In addition to reflecting on a composite portrait of the saving significance of Jesus's death in the Gospels, we can focus on the particular atonement theologies of each of the Gospels.[9] I have chosen, first, to examine Luke-Acts because of its peculiar way of approaching the relationship of salvation and atonement.[10] I will then turn to John's Gospel and the Johannine writings.

Salvation and Exaltation

In Lukan theology, forgiveness of sins and the outpouring and reception of the Holy Spirit serve as synecdoches for salvation itself. This is consonant

---

[9] Cf. George C. Heider, "Atonement and the Gospels," *Journal of Theological Interpretation* 2 (2008), 259–273. For this section, I have adapted material from Joel B. Green, "'Was It Not Necessary for the Messiah to Suffer These Things and Enter into His Glory?': The Significance of Jesus' Death for Luke's Soteriology," in *The Spirit and Christ in the New Testament and Christian Theology: Essays in Honour of Max Turner*, ed. I. Howard Marshall, Volker Rabens, and Cornelis Bennema (Grand Rapids, MI: Eerdmans, 2012), 71–85.

[10] See the survey in Timothy W. Reardon, "Recent Trajectories and Themes in Lukan Soteriology," *Currents in Biblical Research* 12, no. 1 (2013), 77–95.

with Second Temple Jewish literature, in which these two, forgiveness of sins and the outpouring of the Spirit, signify Israel's restoration. Accordingly, for Luke-Acts, salvation is grounded in God's gracious visitation in Christ to restore God's people, which has as its sequelae the multiethnic community of Christ-followers known for economic sharing and hospitality, prayer, witness, and mission.

What is the means by which this salvation is actualized? Three texts in the book of Acts clearly identify Jesus's resurrection and ascension—that is, Jesus's exaltation—as the means by which Jesus gives salvation. The first is the Pentecost speech in Acts 2. Luke (2:1–13) portrays the outpouring of the Holy Spirit, leading eventually to the question, "What does this mean?". Peter replies in terms of the expected era of salvation sketched in Joel 2:28–32, which he interprets in relation to Psalms 16 and 110. First, he insists that what has happened on this day of Pentecost is nothing less than the fresh work of the Holy Spirit, poured out in fulfillment of Joel's promise of restoration. Second, he urges that the Pentecostal phenomena testify, together with the Psalms and Jesus's followers, that Jesus has divine prerogatives so that he is able to dispense the blessings of salvation, the gift of the Holy Spirit being chief among these. Finally, Peter claims, these events comprise the onset of "the last days," which are marked by the universal offer of salvation and threat of judgment, so that all are called to conversion. Raised up, the Lord Jesus now serves as God's coregent and in this capacity administers the Father's promise, the gift of the Spirit.

We find a second affirmation of the saving significance of Jesus's exaltation in Peter's speech to the Jerusalem council in Acts 5:31: "God exalted him at his right hand as Leader and Savior that he might give repentance to Israel and forgiveness of sins." This is a straightforward assertion that Jesus's exaltation confirms his status as Savior and his capacity as Savior to "give" repentance and forgiveness of sins. As the gift of the Holy Spirit represented the whole of salvation in Acts 2, so here repentance and forgiveness of sins do the same.

Finally, in the midst of his preaching at Cornelius's residence, Peter (10:43) proclaims, "All the prophets testify about him that everyone who believes in him receives forgiveness of sins through his name." Again, forgiveness of sins is a synecdoche for salvation. The logic of Peter's claim depends on our recognizing the ramifications of Jesus's resurrection and ascension. The prophets (like the Old Testament as a whole) do proclaim the forgiveness of sins but identify the Lord, Israel's God, as the one who offers pardon. According to Luke, Jesus, who is Lord on account of his exaltation, now possesses the divine prerogative to administer the benefits of salvation, here represented as forgiveness of sins.

Jesus's Atoning Death

These three texts ground Luke's soteriology in Jesus's exaltation rather than in his death as such. Two other texts point to Luke's awareness of an interpretation of Jesus's death in soteriological terms, suggesting that Luke has placed "his stamp of approval"[11] on a more traditional atonement theology. First, Jesus's words at the Last Supper speak to the atoning significance of his death: "This is my body, which is given for you," and "This cup that is poured out for you is the new covenant in my blood" (Luke 22:19-20).[12] As we saw in the previous section, here is evidence in Luke's Gospel of an interpretation of Jesus's death in terms of Israel's hope of covenant renewal (Jer. 31:31-33).

Jesus's atoning death is also witnessed in Acts 20:28. As a comparison of different translations illustrates, the sense of this text is not straightforward.[13] Does Paul refer to "the church of the Lord" or "the church of God"? Is the church purchased with "his own blood" or with "the blood of his own"? If "the blood of his own," then is this a reference to Jesus? To martyrs? The difficulty here is that a plain reading of the text would have Paul claiming that God purchased the church with *God's* own blood—a theological infelicity addressed by ancient scribes and contemporary translators alike. Stated in this way, this claim would be without precedent or analogy in any other biblical text. In the end, the sense of this text in Acts is probably like the rendering we find in the NRSV: "shepherd the church of God that he obtained with the blood of his own Son." Although Acts 20:28 uses a term not otherwise used in this sense in the NT, περιποιέω, we do find references elsewhere to God's acquiring (e.g., Eph. 1:14; 1 Pet. 2:9-10) or "purchasing" (1 Cor. 6:20; 7:23; cf. 2 Pet. 2:1) a people. Atonement in Acts 20:28

---

[11] This phrase is borrowed from Reginald H. Fuller, "Luke and the Theologia Crucis," in *Sin, Salvation and the Spirit: Commemorating the Fiftieth Year of the Liturgical Press*, ed. Daniel Durken (Collegeville, MN: Liturgical Press, 1979), 214-220 (219).

[12] In the past, some scholars discounted the significance of these words as non-Lukan; cf., for example, Joachim Jeremias, *The Eucharistic Words of Jesus* (Philadelphia: Fortress, 1966), 154-155; G. D. Kilpatrick, *The Eucharist in Bible and Liturgy*, The Moorhouse Lectures 1975 (Cambridge: Cambridge University Press, 1983), 31-32.

[13] See the helpful discussion of variant renderings and this text's stylistic/theological ambiguity in Steve Walton, *Leadership and Lifestyle: The Portrait of Paul in the Miletus Speech and 1 Thessalonians*, Society of New Testament Studies Monograph Series 108 (Cambridge: Cambridge University Press, 2000), 94-98.

thus turns on the metaphor of an economic exchange rooted in Jesus's sacrificial death.

Jesus and Isaiah's Servant

By way of portraying the significance of Jesus's death, another strand of evidence may be of even more interest. I refer to the importance of Luke's dependence on Isaiah's portrait of the Servant of the Lord in developing his Christology. The interweaving of Jesus's life, death, and exaltation supports for Luke a robust soteriology—and Luke interprets Jesus's career thus imagined in Isaianic terms.

It is easy to urge that, for Luke, the character of Jesus's death must be grasped in relation to the character of his life. Jesus's mission "to bring good news to the poor" (Luke 4:18) led to these charges against him: "We found this man perverting our nation, forbidding us to pay taxes to the emperor, and saying that he himself is the Messiah, a king" (Luke 23:2; see also 23:5, 14). Such allegations, and especially the claim that Jesus "perverts our nation/the people" (vv. 2, 14), dovetail well with the argument that Jesus had to be eliminated as a religious deceiver and false prophet. Reference to "perverting" would draw the attention of a Roman proconsul concerned with keeping the peace and identify Jesus as a false prophet (Deut. 13, 17).[14] The claim that Jesus's exaltation is integrated theologically into Luke's portrayal of the significance of Jesus's death is also easily observed. Jesus's words on the Emmaus road locate the Messiah's suffering and death together with the Messiah's entering into his glory under the heading of divine necessity: "Was it not necessary that the Messiah should suffer these things and then enter into his glory?" (Luke 24:26).

Luke's soteriology thus shares the stage with the shape of Jesus's career, from humiliation to exaltation, and both of these are bound together with Luke's interest in Isaiah's Servant. Let me document briefly this last interest.[15] First, Luke recalls Isaiah's Servant as he sketches the universal ramifications of Jesus's mission (Luke 2:32; Isa. 49:6). Second, at Jesus's death he is declared the Righteous

---

[14] So Graham N. Stanton, "Jesus of Nazareth: A Magician and a False Prophet Who Deceived God's People?" in *Jesus of Nazareth: Lord and Christ: Essays on the Historical Jesus and New Testament Christology*, ed. Joel B. Green and Max Turner (Grand Rapids, MI: Eerdmans, 1995), 164–180; August Strobel, *Die Stunde der Wahrheit: Untersuchungen zum Strafverfahren gegen Jesus*, Wissenschaftliche Untersuchungen zum Neuen Testament 21 (Tübingen: Mohr Siebeck, 1980).

[15] More fully, cf. Joel B. Green, "The Death of Jesus, God's Servant," in *Reimaging the Death of the Lukan Jesus*, ed. Dennis D. Sylva, Athenaums Monografien: Theologie, Bonner Biblische Beiträge 73 (Frankfurt-am-Main: Anton Hain, 1990), 1–28, 170–173.

One (Luke 23:47)—an allusion to Isaiah 53:11.[16] Third, in his Jerusalem speech (Acts 3:13–14), Peter depicts Jesus using terms from Isaiah 52:13–53:12. Fourth, Luke identifies Jesus in his passion with the Suffering Servant; thus, Jesus cites Isaiah 53:12 with reference to his suffering and death (Luke 22:37), he refuses to speak in his own defense (Luke 23:9; cf. Isa. 53:7), and he is mocked in the language of Isaiah 42:1: "the Chosen One" (Luke 23:35). Finally, we find other references to the Servant in Luke-Acts, not least in the citation of Isaiah 53:7–8 in Acts 8:32–33.

These elements allow us to speak of Luke's interest in the salvation-historical necessity of the cross at the same time that we highlight Jesus's exaltation as the grounds of the offer of salvation. The Isaianic portrait of the Suffering Servant holds in tandem these two motifs, suffering and vindication. We read this particularly in Isaiah 53:11 where, following his death, "my righteous servant will justify many." Taking this interpretive path, Luke shows the necessity of Jesus's death as the Servant of the Lord who, through his being raised up, brings salvation—and he demonstrates this without depending on an interpretation of the Servant's or Jesus's suffering as a substitutionary sacrifice. In his fidelity to his mission, Jesus, by embracing the career of the Servant, both exemplifies the way of salvation for those who would come after him and opens the way of repentance, forgiveness, and Spirit-endowed life and mission. Though anointed by God, and righteous before him, he is rejected by people. Rejected by people, he is raised up by God—and with him those who occupy society's margins are also raised up. Accordingly, Jesus's life, death, and resurrection, read together, are exemplary and effective.

The Writings of John

Traditionally, five New Testament books are associated with John: the Gospel of John, three letters of John, and the book of Revelation.

The Fourth Gospel

According to John's Gospel, Jesus came from the Father to give life, and he gives life by giving up his own life (see John 3:16–17). John draws on Israel's Scriptures

---

[16] Cf. Robert J. Karris, "Luke 23:47 and the Lucan View of Jesus' Death," *Journal of Biblical Literature* 105 (1986), 65–74.

to make this clear. For example, we may hear in the background of claims concerning the "giving" of God's Son echoes of the "binding of Isaac" in Genesis 22 (see John 1:29; 3:16; 19:17). Other texts point in this general direction as well, such as John's (10:11–18) portrait of Jesus as the Good Shepherd who lays down his life on behalf of the sheep. Reminiscences of Passover and exodus abound: John the Baptist speaks of Jesus as the lamb of God who brings forgiveness of sins (John 1:29, 36), Jesus's death coincides with the time of the Passover sacrifice (John 18:28; 19:14), the hyssop and basin are present at the cross (John 19:29; cf. Exod. 12:22), witnesses see the blood flow from Jesus's side (John 19:35; cf. Exod. 12:13), and the soldiers do not break Jesus's legs (John 19:31–37; cf. Exod. 12:46). Echoes of Exodus continue in John 6, where in an extended discourse Jesus compares himself to the "bread from heaven" that fed Israel; now, however, those who ingest his life will have life.

Another, distinctive feature of John's presentation of Jesus's death is his focus on the motif of "raising up." This image appears first in 3:14–15: "Just as Moses lifted up the snake in the wilderness, so the Son of Man must be lifted up, that everyone who believes in him may have eternal life" (see John 8:28; 12:32–33). John's Gospel makes clear that this "lifting up" expresses John's theology of the Son's glory and identifies the means by which Jesus will be executed, namely, by being "lifted up" on a cross (see John 12:33; 18:32). From early on, though, the purpose of that lifting up is clear enough; it is salvific, life-giving for believers.

A further image of salvation in John's Gospel is light, or revelation. Terms like believing, understanding, seeing, and knowing signify much more than cognitive exercises, but refer to the transformation of people as God's children, a transformation effected through the revelation of God in Jesus (see John 9). In Jesus we see the Father (John 14:1–11), and in the cross the fullness of his love is disclosed. For John's Gospel, these two perspectives—the cross as atoning sacrifice and as redemptive revelation—are complementary.[17]

1 John

The motif of revelation is continued in the opening of 1 John, where it appears together with an unambiguous reference to the cleansing effect of Jesus's death

---

[17] See Max Turner, "Atonement and the Death of Jesus in John: Some Questions to Bultmann and Forestell," *Evangelical Quarterly* 62 (1990), 99–122; also, George L. Carey, "The Lamb of God and Atonement Theories," *Tyndale Bulletin* 32 (1981), 97–122; Bruce H. Grigsby, "The Cross as an Expiatory Sacrifice in the Fourth Gospel," *Journal for the Study of the New Testament* 15 (1982), 51–80.

(1:5–2:2; cf. 5:6–8). Here the author is on the offensive, countering claims of sinlessness, claims that fail to take sin's power seriously enough. To the contrary, he asserts the reality of sin and affirms the greater power of Jesus's death to cleanse us from sin. The image he employs, "atoning sacrifice" (1 John 2:2), is drawn from Israel's history—the sin offering (Lev. 25:9) and especially the Day of Atonement (Lev. 16:16).

The importance of the connection of this text with the Day of Atonement is suggested by the relationship between impurity and sin, addressed in Leviticus 16. Sin results in impurity in the temple, so the ritual prescribed for the Day of Atonement calls for purification of the sanctuary/temple and the use of a scapegoat. Immediately following the purgation of the sanctuary, the high priest places his hands on the goat's head, confesses over it Israel's sins, and sends the goat into the wilderness, effectively banishing the people's sins. In this rite, the scapegoat is not butchered and presented as a sacrificial offering, and there is no attempt (or necessity) to appease God. The problem is sin, which defiles people. Jesus's death thus cleanses and readies people for renewed fellowship with God.

The Book of Revelation

The central Christological image in the book of Revelation is the Lamb, and this portrait is centered in chapter 5. Here, John narrates a dramatic scene, initially tragic in its attempt to locate the one authorized to break the seal and open the scroll held in God's right hand. The only one who is qualified is "the Lion of the tribe of Judah, the Root of David," the triumphant, militaristic Messiah of God (Rev. 5:5). When Rev. (5:9) trains his eyes on the Lion, however, what he sees is a slaughtered Lamb, whose worthiness to open the scroll is tied to his death:

> You are worthy to take the scroll and to open its seals,
> for you were slaughtered and by your blood you ransomed for God
> saints from every tribe and language and people and nation.

Jesus is the conquering Messiah, and the manner of his victory is his slaughter. Jesus's death is evil's defeat.

John develops the significance of Jesus's death through various images. It liberates from sin and, like a covenant sacrifice, creates a people for God (Rev. 1:5; 5:9–10). In 5:9–10, the central image is borrowed from the marketplace: Jesus "purchased" a people for God. To whom did Jesus "pay" the price of his own blood? This aspect of the metaphor is not developed, and we should probably understand it as a way of underscoring the seriousness (or costliness) of rebellion against God and his purposes. In 7:9–17, the death of Jesus is portrayed as a cleansing or sanctifying agent.

Additionally, Jesus's death defeats evil. Revelation places the drama of salvation on the cosmic stage, so that the Lamb's slaughter wins a cosmic victory. The munitions of this warfare go unidentified, for we are told little of how the cross overcomes evil. What is clear is that the faithfulness of Jesus in his life-giving death is faithfulness to God's eternal will. Jesus's death shows how God measures fidelity and triumph and, because God is the uncontested sovereign of the universe, Jesus's faithfulness in his death repeals all other powers and agendas.

Paul

Ernst Käsemann, one of the twentieth century's leading Pauline scholars, observed that, for Paul, the cross is "the signature" of the resurrected Christ.[18] Emphatically put: no cross, no gospel. How this is so for Paul invites reflection on a constellation of images. This suggests the importance of interpreting Pauline texts in relation to the larger story he is telling, without trying too quickly to fit his atonement thought into a neat presentation. Paul's gospel sets the cross of Christ within the larger story in which God's agenda to save God's people and, indeed, the entire cosmos is unveiled. The cross is the means by which God reveals his own covenant faithfulness, through which the whole world becomes the beneficiary of God's restorative justice. And this gospel cannot be summed up in a single atonement image or model or theory.

A Sample Text: Romans 3:21–26

Within the letter of Romans, 3:21–26 is a central text for understanding Paul's view of the atonement. This short paragraph is tightly packed and how we understand it depends on how we make sense of its place in the argument Paul has been making.

Romans 3:21–26 is the heading for a subsection of the letter (3:21–4:25) wherein Paul returns to the theme broached in 1:16–17: the gospel "is the power of God for salvation to everyone who has faith, to the Jew first and also to the

---

[18] Ernst Käsemann, "The Saving Significance of Jesus' Death," in *Perspectives on Paul* (Philadelphia: Fortress, 1971), 32–59 (56).

Greek. For in it the righteousness of God is revealed through faith for faith." Here the apostle recalls his earlier emphases on *all* (whether Jew or Gentile), the response of faith, and the disclosure of God's righteousness. In preparation for this new section, 3:21–23 summarizes the argument in 1:18–3:20 ("all have sinned and fallen short of God's glory") and signals an epochal shift (3:21: "but now"; see 3:26: "at the present time").

What is this epochal shift? *In the past,* human sin—defined in 1:18–23 as idolatry that suppresses the truth about God—led to God's revelation of his righteousness in terms of his wrath, as God handed people over to the consequences of their idolatry. *But now,* God has revealed his righteousness "apart from the law" (3:21), underscoring again the common lot of Jew and Gentile in God's plan. In this new time, God reveals his righteousness not by means of his wrath but by means of the faithfulness of Jesus Christ, which culminates in his death and its effects, the benefits of which are available to those who believe.

One problem over which readers of Romans have struggled is how to make sense of Paul's use in 3:25 of the term ἱλαστήριον, which the NRSV translates as "sacrifice of atonement." The term refers to the means by which the goodwill of a god is recovered. What stands in the way of right relations with God? One possibility is that Jesus's death was needed in order to overcome God's wrath. Taking note of Paul's references to divine anger in 1:18; 2:5 (twice); 3:5, this view urges that Paul needed to show how God's anger against human sin was addressed. In this view, Christ's "sacrifice of atonement" was Christ's taking upon himself the penalty due the human race on account of their sin. Some of Paul's first-century readers could have understood his language in just this way. Among the Romans, for instance, it was not uncommon to appease deities through worship and sacrifice. However, this would be a strange way to portray Israel's God.

Unlike the portrait of the ancient gods we find in Greek and Roman literature, Israel's Scriptures depict a God whose anger is neither whimsical nor irrational. Far from capricious, God's wrath is kindled by idolatry and injustice. God's wrath is typically a response to Israel's idolatry—as in the account of the golden calf (Exod. 32:9–10). Due to Moses's mediation, God "changed his mind about the disaster that he planned to bring on his people" (Exod. 32:14). God's "personality," so to speak, is not one quickly or impulsively given to anger or retribution. Instead, we repeatedly read that God is "slow to anger, and abounding in steadfast love" (e.g., Exod. 34:6; Num. 14:18). God's wrath is relationally based, not retributively motivated—it seeks to restore and protect God's people. God might avert his wrath in response to repentance, prayer, or mediation, but even this is a result of God's own, gracious change of mind. Never do we read in Israel's Scriptures that Israel's sacrificial system served as a means of averting or assuaging God's wrath.[19]

In short, it is unlikely that Jesus's atoning sacrifice in Romans 3 assuages divine wrath. Rather than to Greco-Roman notions of sacrifice, we turn instead to patterns of sacrifice in the Scriptures. Among these, the most important for our purposes is the purification offering (e.g., Lev. 4:1–6:7; 6:24–7:10; see Lev. 16), the focus of which is on the cleansing effect of sin. These sacrifices had to do with "expiation" (the means by which God frees and cleanses people from the onus and blemish of sin) rather than "propitiation" (a means of averting God's wrath). Sin has resulted in an estranged relationship between the sinner and God, and it is this separation that must be addressed. Serving as mediator, the priest resolves the broken relationship through sacrifice, wherein the shedding of blood signifies the offering of the lives of those for whom the sacrifice is made. In the end, "sin" pollutes, stains, and spoils; sacrifice wipes away sin and its effects.

In fact, Paul speaks of Jesus's sacrificial death in various ways. For example, his reference to Jesus as "Passover lamb" in 1 Corinthians 5:7 calls to mind the Passover, which, celebrated annually, memorialized and reappropriated God's election and great act of deliverance. Read in relation to Paul's directive regarding the presence of an immoral person within the church ("Drive out the wicked person from among you," 1 Cor. 5:1–13), this allusion to Passover marks the Corinthian believers as a community of persons set apart from the bondage of sin as the distinctive people of God. The apostle speaks of Jesus's death as a "sin offering" in several Pauline texts (Rom. 3:25; 5:9; 8:3; 2 Cor. 5:21; Eph. 1:7; 2:13; Col. 1:20). In these instances, Paul speaks to the effectiveness of sacrifice in terms of exchange and representation: sin and death transferred to the sacrificial victim, its purity and life to those who receive the benefits of the sacrifice. Jesus's death wipes away sin and its effects.

In Romans 3:21–26, then, the problem to be overcome is the human assault on God's righteousness sketched in 1:18–3:20 and summarized in 3:23, that all have sinned. For Paul, human unfaithfulness is now addressed through the faithfulness of Jesus Christ, which Paul understands as the revelation of God's own covenant faithfulness. God's own initiative comes to the fore: by his grace, as a gift, through a divine act of liberation (a term that reminds us of God's mighty act of

---

[19] On these points, see Mark J. Boda, *A Severe Mercy: Sin and Its Remedy in the Old Testament*, Siphrut: Literature and Theology of the Hebrew Scriptures 1 (Winona Lake, IN: Eisenbrauns, 2009).

delivering Israel from Egyptian slavery) in Christ. For Paul, then, God's righteousness is revealed for all (Jew and Gentile) who believe through the faithfulness of Jesus Christ, whose faithfulness unto death wipes away all human hostility toward God, thereby underscoring that Jew and Gentile are on the same footing.

Atonement Metaphors in Paul

Casting about more broadly, we find in Paul's letters a virtual cornucopia of atonement images. For example, *reconciliation* may stand at the center of the apostle's presentation of the effects of Jesus's death in 2 Corinthians 5:14–6:2, but other motifs are mentioned too: *substitution* ("for us," 5:14, 15), *representation* or *interchange* (5:14, 21),[20] *sacrifice* (5:21), *justification* (implicitly, 5:19, 21), *forgiveness* (5:19), and *new creation* (5:16–17). Moreover, the *cross and resurrection* of Christ appear together as salvific events (5:15). Paul's argument and choice of terminology center on reconciliation because he needs to counter the boasting of his opponents at Corinth and to bridge the distance that has opened up between himself and his Corinth audience. Rooting the message of reconciliation in Jesus's sacrificial death and asserting that reconciliation entails living no longer for oneself but for Christ (and thus for others), he addresses his first aim. His impassioned appeal to the Corinthians to be reconciled to God (5:20; 6:1–2), followed by an affirmation of his own open-handedness to the Corinthians (6:11–13; 7:2), deals with the second.

A second text, Galatians 3:10–14, also bears witness to the myriad ways Paul expounds the saving character of the cross of Christ: Christ as the *representative* of Israel in whose death the *covenant* reaches its climax;[21] *justification* (3:11); *redemption* (3:13), evoking exodus and exilic themes (cf. the corollary of *adoption* in 3:26–29); *substitution* ("for us," 3:13); *sacrifice* (3:13); *promise of the Spirit* (3:14); and *triumph over the powers*. As before, Paul has chosen his categories carefully, for in this case he needs to demonstrate how anyone, Jew or Gentile, can participate in the blessings of Abraham. The answer for Paul is the cross, through which believers share in the benefits of the new creation and are counted as God's people because of their inclusion in the salvific work of

---

[20] See Morna D. Hooker, "Interchange and Atonement," *Bulletin of the John Rylands University Library of Manchester* 60 (1978), 462–481; "Interchange in Christ," *Journal of Theological Studies* 22 (1974), 349–361; and more recently, *Not Ashamed of the Gospel: New Testament Interpretations of the Death of Christ* (Grand Rapids, MI: Eerdmans, 1994), 20–46.

[21] See N. T. Wright, *The Climax of the Covenant: Christ and the Law in Pauline Theology* (Minneapolis, MN: Fortress, 1991), 137–156.

Christ. Christ's death marks the new aeon in which Gentiles may be embraced, in Christ, as children of Abraham.

In Paul's writings, as in the New Testament more generally, the saving significance of Jesus's death is represented chiefly (though not exclusively) by means of five image patterns. These refer to central spheres of public life in the larger Greco-Roman world: the law court (e.g., justification), commercial dealings (e.g., redemption), social relationships (e.g., reconciliation), worship (e.g., sacrifice), and warfare (e.g., triumph over evil). Each opens a window into a cluster of terms and concepts that relate to that particular sphere of public life. For example, without using the actual term *sacrifice*, Paul can refer to Jesus as the "Passover Lamb" (1 Cor. 5:7) and as "first fruits" (1 Cor. 15:20, 23; cf. Lev. 23; Deut. 16), and he can refer to the handing over of Jesus in ways that recall the binding of Isaac (Rom. 8:32; cf. Gen. 22). Similarly, "reconciliation" can be represented by the term itself (Rom. 5:10–11; 11:15; 1 Cor. 7:11; 2 Cor. 5:18–20; Eph. 2:16; Col. 1:20, 22), but also by the language of peace (Eph. 2:14–18) and the many reconciling practices (e.g., Rom. 16:16), pleas (e.g., Philemon), and testimonies (e.g., Gal. 3:26–29) that pervade the Pauline corpus.

Why are there so many images? First, language for the atonement is metaphorical. Calling our language metaphorical does not detract from the concreteness of that language or the actions and experiences to which that language refers. It means rather that we conceive of the saving significance of Jesus's death in multiple ways through implicit comparison with real-world institutions and experiences. Second, language for the atonement is pastoral. The language by which Paul portrays the effectiveness of Jesus's death depends in part on the needs he hopes to address. If people are oppressed by hostile powers, they need to be delivered. If they exist in a state of enmity, they need to be reconciled. And so on. Paul draws on different images in relation to his understanding of a local congregation's particular needs. Third, we have to account for wider cultural considerations. The reach of the cross may be universal, but the message of the cross must be articulated in context-specific ways. Not surprisingly, then, Paul draws atonement images from both Israel's own Scriptures and religious life and the wider public discourse of Roman antiquity.

General Epistles

We turn now from an overview of Paul's approach to the atonement to consider perspectives from two general epistles, Hebrews and 1 Peter.

Hebrews

Reflection on Jesus's death pervades Hebrews,[22] with Jesus's sacrificial death developed in three ways. First, Jesus's death draws attention to his obedience, even to the point of pouring out his life in a noble death. His obedience is representative of the obedience of all and is accepted by God as a perfect sacrifice—and, so, it calls people to follow Jesus, leader and pioneer, in the journey of obedience to God.[23] Second, Jesus's death ratifies the (new) covenant between God and his people, itself providing the measure of faithful behavior for God's covenant partners.[24] Third, Hebrews develops Jesus's sacrificial death in relation to the Day of Atonement, even if the author is selective in his choice of regulations related to the annual ceremony in Leviticus 16. Our author thus bypasses material related to the scapegoat in favor of the sacrificial goat—a decision that highlights the identification of Jesus as the sinless, sacrificial victim who cleanses the sin that is an affront to God in order to lead people into God's own presence.[25]

If, from the perspective of Israel's Scriptures, sin rendered people unclean and excluded them from God's presence, the institution of sacrifice was largely concerned with the removal of this impediment. What Hebrews describes, then, is the action of God to initiate covenant relations with humanity. Christ is the forerunner who through his suffering and death not only enters God's presence ahead of us but also wipes away all barriers so that humanity might enter with him. In doing so, Jesus is both sacrificial offering and high priest. Unlike priests who carried on their work in the Jerusalem temple, however, Jesus is without sin and has no need to offer a sacrifice for himself. Yet, as one who stands in solidarity with humanity, he is able to embody the mediatorial role of a priest. As the perfect priest and the perfect sacrifice, his death obviates the need for additional sacrificial offerings (see Heb. 9:25–28; 10:10, 12–14).

If the perfection of Jesus as a high priest untainted by sin and as an unblemished sacrificial victim are central to Hebrews, room is left in the author's reflection on Jesus's death for a second image. In Hebrews 2:14–15 Jesus's death is also positioned over against the life-threatening powers of evil. Jesus's death, that is, declares the power of the devil null and void.

---

[22] See Hooker, *Not Ashamed of the Gospel*, 112–124.
[23] See John Dunnill, *Covenant and Sacrifice in the Letter to the Hebrews*, Society of New Testament Studies Monograph Series 75 (Cambridge: Cambridge University Press, 1992).
[24] Compare Hebrews 9:19–21 with Exodus 24:1–8.
[25] Cf. Barnabas Lindars, *The Theology of the Letter to the Hebrews*, New Testament Theology (Cambridge: Cambridge University Press, 1991), 84–101.

1 Peter

Christ's suffering is crucial for Peter's message since his audience's faithfulness has resulted in their own suffering in the world. Accordingly, the suffering of Christ permeates the whole of this brief letter, accented particularly in 1 Peter 1:2, 19; 2:21–25; 3:18–22; 4:1; 5:1. The author sketches the significance of Christ's suffering under three headings. First, *Christ exemplifies innocent suffering* (2:19–20; 3:16–17; 4:1–2, 13–16). Christ modeled faithfulness due to the undeserved character of his suffering and in his refusal to retaliate against those who caused his suffering. Second, *Christ exemplifies effective suffering*. His suffering is the basis of liberation (1:2, 19; 3:18). By way of analogy, the suffering of Christ's followers is a form of witness with the potential of turning disbelievers to God (2:12, 15; 3:1–2). Moreover, their suffering is a participation in his, and particularly a participation in the messianic woes by which the age of salvation is realized (4:12–19). Finally, *Christ exemplifies the vindication of the suffering righteous* (1:11; 2:20; 4:13–14; 5:1, 10). The career of Christ demonstrates that suffering is a precursor to glory, with the path to vindication passing through suffering.

With regard to the saving significance of Christ's death, the collection of images in 1:18–19 is especially interesting: "knowing that you were liberated from the emptiness of your inherited way of life—not by such perishable things as gold or silver, but by the precious blood of Christ, like that of a lamb without blemish or defect" (my translation). Here, Peter's atonement theology conflates three Old Testament images: "liberation" or "ransom," "lamb," and the combination of "blood" and "[a lamb] without blemish or defect." The author thus weaves an atonement theology out of the yarn of God's liberating Israel from Egyptian enslavement (e.g., Exod. 6:6; 15:13; Deut. 7:8; Isa. 43:1); the tradition of the Passover sacrifice (Exod. 12) and its appropriation within early Christianity (e.g., John 1:29, 36; 1 Cor. 5:7); and Israel's economy of sacrifice, particularly, the "purification offering" (e.g., Lev. 4:1–6:7; 6:24–7:10; see Lev. 16). He portrays Jesus's honorable death as effective in wiping away sin and its effects. In doing so, however, Peter (1:18) makes clear that believers are liberated not from divine wrath, but from "the emptiness of your inherited way of life" (my translation). "Liberation" belongs to the larger semantic domain of salvation understood in terms of war, a reality that coheres well with texts like this one in which an "inherited way of life" and its "desires" present themselves as forces against which God has undertaken battle.

Peter represents the effect of Jesus's atoning death with two images. First, through Jesus's death, "we have died to sins," so we "live to righteousness" (2:24), a movement paralleled in imagery taken from Isaiah: "you were straying like sheep, but now have been turned to the shepherd and guardian of your lives" (2:25). This way of putting things emphasizes again that Christ's suffering was not deserved (see already 2:22-23); rather, the sin (and straying) was symptomatic of the situation of those for whom he died. Here, atonement is not something that happens outside of the person, but is a cleansing from sin that opens up new life. Thus, Jesus's suffering can rightly be described as an event of "sanctifying atonement," since Christ's death takes the place of others in such a way that affects their very being, that opens to them "a new life-reality."[26] Second, drawing on the words of Isaiah, Peter announces that atonement effects healing. Were we to adopt a view of disease at home in the world of 1 Peter, we would recognize that the two images—movement from death to life, and healing—speak to the same reality: cleansing for holiness. Healing refers to human recovery, to the restoration of health in all its respects, and, then, to patterns of health in which we are fully alive. Peter's concern, then, is with the conformation of his audience into Christ-likeness.

A Diversity of Images

To say that Jesus's death is "for us" is to remind ourselves that his execution on a Roman cross displayed the character of God's saving mercy. These two—the ancient Mediterranean world within which Jesus was executed and God's eternal purpose—anchor efforts at articulating the significance of Jesus's death and resurrection. Even accounting for these two points, though, much remains to be said regarding *how* this event could accomplish and signal the salvation of God's people. At the intersection of the particularity of Jesus's crucifixion and the eternal character of God's mission we find not one but many models of the atonement.

We should not imagine that this variety is merely an index of the interests of different writers. Paul can write of substitution, representation, sacrifice, justification, forgiveness, reconciliation, triumph over the powers, redemption, and more. John can speak of illumination as well as sacrifice. Luke weaves atonement into the fabric of Jesus's entire career. Hebrews presents Jesus as both the perfect

---

[26] Otfried Hofius, "The Fourth Servant Song in the New Testament Letters," in *The Suffering Servant: Isaiah 53 in Jewish and Christian Sources*, ed. Bernd Janowski and Peter Stuhlmacher (Grand Rapids, MI: Eerdmans, 2004), 163–188.

high priest and the perfect sacrificial victim. 1 Peter speaks of Jesus's death as a ransom and sacrifice, while the Book of Revelation presents Jesus's death in terms of military triumph and redemption. This variety might appropriately lead us to the conclusion that the significance of Jesus's death could not be represented without remainder by any one concept or theory or metaphor. This is due to the profundity of Jesus's death as saving event, but also to the variety of contexts within which Jesus's death requires explication and the variety of ways in which the human situation can be understood.

As with Vincent Taylor's study, so too we can discern within this variety some common threads. (1) Each image of the atonement presumes a portrait of the human situation. How one articulates the saving significance of Jesus's death is tied to different conceptualizations of human need. People who are blind need illumination. Slaves need liberation. (2) The message of atonement is all-encompassing, and cannot be reduced to one group of people, to one individual, nor to some aspect of the human person. What happened on the cross had universal significance: for Jew and Gentile, for slave and free, for male and female; and has the whole universe as its object, giving rise to images of new creation (2 Cor. 5:17) and cosmic reconciliation (Col. 1:15–20). The cross opens the way for salvation as a call to reflect in day-to-day life the quality of life, oriented to the other, on exhibition in Jesus's death on behalf of others. Atonement is divine gift, but it summons and enables human response. (3) In the restoration of broken relationships, God's initiative is paramount. Paul is representative in his affirmation that God's love has the upper hand in divine-human relations, and that God was at work in Christ to bring the world back to God (Rom. 5:1–11; 2 Cor. 5:19).

8

Athanasius's Incarnational Soteriology

Thomas G. Weinandy

The biblical narrative is Athanasius's soteriological template, beginning with the act of creation and concluding with Jesus's glorious Second Coming at the end of time. The Father's eternal plan was to bring humankind into an everlasting living communion with him through his Word in the love of the Holy Spirit. This chapter will examine the biblical soteriology that governed the whole of Athanasius's theological writings and is divided into four parts. The first two sections will examine his two-part work—*Contra Gentes* and *De Incarnatione*. The third will study his anti-Arian/pro-Nicene writings, and the fourth will assess his later *Letters to Serapion* concerning the Holy Spirit.

Contra Gentes: A Soteriological Prolegomena

Contra Gentes and *De Incarnatione* are Athanasius's introduction to the Christian faith, "the knowledge of our religion" (1.1).[1] As the title, *Contra Gentes*, suggests, Athanasius first presents an apologetic defense on behalf of the Christian faith while simultaneously demonstrating that it is superior to idolatrous paganism and erroneous philosophies. He realizes that the Gentiles "scoff at, and laugh loudly at us" because of the cross of Christ. They should instead know that Jesus

---

[1] All quotations cited in this section are from *Contra Gentes*. Unless otherwise noted all translations of Athanasius's works are based upon the *Nicene and Post-Nicene Fathers*, Second Series, Vol. 4, St. Athanasius, ed. A. Robertson (Edinburgh: T&T Clark, reprinted 1987). However, they have frequently been altered, sometimes significantly, in order to conform more closely to the Greek and so ensure accuracy and clarity. Also, unless otherwise noted, where available the following Greek texts were employed: *Athanasius Werke*, ed. M. Tetz and H.-G. Opitz (Berlin: de Gruyter, 1935–2000). Also used: B. Montfaucon, *S.P.N. Athanasii archiepiscopi Alexandrini opera omnia quae exstant*, J.P. Mingne, *Patrologia Graeca* 25–26 (Paris: 1857).

is the Savior because by his cross he has conquered demons, makes known the Father, and daily wins many to faith. Jesus triumphs because he who "ascended the Cross is Word of God and Saviour of the World" (1.3–5). To enlighten the pagans, Athanasius addresses their central philosophical tenets: the nature of God and his relation to the world and humankind, and the nature of man and the origin of evil. This serves as a prolegomenon to his fuller explanation of the salvific work of Jesus as the Son of God incarnate in *De Incarnatione*.

Being Created in the image of the Word

Athanasius's biblical soteriological concerns are immediately evident. He first asserted that "from the beginning wickedness did not exist" (2.1). The one good God created everything good and humankind was created in God's image.

> For God, the fashioner and king of all, who subsists beyond all essence and human conception, inasmuch as he is good and exceedingly noble, made the human race after his own image through his own Word, our Saviour Jesus Christ. Through this likeness to himself, he constituted man able to see and to know essential realities, giving him also a conception and knowledge of his own eternity, in order that, preserving his nature intact, he might never depart from his idea of God, nor recoil from the communion of the saints, but having the grace of [God] who gave it, and possessing also the power proper to the Word of the Father, he might rejoice and have fellowship with the deity, living an immortal life, unhindered and blessed. For, having nothing to hinder his knowledge of the divinity, he ever beholds, by his purity, the image of the Father, God the Word, after whose image he was made. He is filled with awe in contemplating that providence which through him [the Word], [extends] to the universe. (2.2)

This passage contains Athanasius's foundational understanding of the Father's original salvific plan. Two points must be noted here. First, the act of creation ontologically distinguishes God from all else: as the "Maker" and "King" of all, God transcends all that is created. He exists in a manner that differs in kind from all else. This transcendent otherness of God makes him incomprehensible to the finite human mind. This otherness, however, is the source of the goodness and nobility that compels him to create humankind in his own image through his very own Word.

Second, since the Father creates through the Word, the Word is the ontological and epistemological bond between the Father and humankind. The Word is ontologically the perfect divine image of the Father and for human beings to be made in God's image is to be made in the ontological image of that Word and so in the likeness of the Father as well. Having been ontologically created through the Word and so in his own image, human beings are naturally empowered to share in the Word's ability to know the Father. Thanks to this likeness to the Word, man is able to rejoice in fellowship with God for he beholds "the Image of the Father, God the Word, after whose image he was made." In contemplating the Word, humankind "sees in him also the Father of the Word." Thus, humankind possesses the "purity of soul" that is in itself "sufficient to reflect God" and so come to know him (2.3).

The Nature of Sin and Its Consequences

While human beings were created in the image of the Word and were able to live through him, in contemplative communion with the Father, they "began to seek in preference things nearer to themselves" (3.1). Instead of pondering the heights of God, they "fell into lust of themselves preferring what was their own to the contemplation of divine realities" (3.2). Sinful human beings turned away from God and turned toward their earthly bodily life with all its sensual pleasures. Because human beings focused exclusively on this life, that is a life apart from God, they anxiously feared death.

Contrary to the Gnostics and the Manicheans, who place the source of evil in the some malevolent god who created foul matter, Athanasius, in keeping with Scripture, recognizes that sin and evil spring from the misuse of human freedom: instead of choosing what is good—God—human beings choose what is evil. Evil is not ontologically constitutive of the created order but stems from the free moral depravity of human beings. Athanasius concludes "that evil is not from God, nor is it in God, nor has it existed from the beginning, nor is it of any substantive existence; but men, in departing from the contemplation of the good, devise and imagine that which is not, according to their desires" (7.3).

The Centrality of the Divine Word

At this juncture, Athanasius returns to his major theme—the salvific centrality of the Word both in his relationship to humankind and to the Father. Because the Father creates everything through his Word, he also governs all through his Word.

> He [the Father] made all things by his own eternal Word, and granted substantive existence to creation, not leaving it to be troubled and tossed about in its own nature, lest it risk returning to non-being; but, since he is good, he governs and settles the whole creation by his own Word, who himself is also God. (41.3)

When the Father creates everything through his Word, he establishes an unbreakable providential bond with the whole of creation through the governance of his Word. Because the Word is distinct from the Father and yet one with the Father in sharing his divine being and attributes, he is able to make present the salvific presence of the Father.

> For, as he is the Word and Wisdom of the Father, thus he condescended to created things and, that he may impart the knowledge of him who begat him, he became himself life, and door, and shepherd, and way, and king, and guide, and above all Saviour, life-giver, light and providence over all. (47.1)

All of the titles attributed to the Son make the Father present to human beings (Word, Wisdom, Brightness, Light, and Life) and in so doing, the Son is the means by which the Father leads human beings to himself (Door, Shepherd, Way, King, Guide, and Savior). Because the Son possesses these divine "fatherly" attributes, the Father does not hide the Son from creatures but reveals him and in so doing the Father "reveals himself also" (47.2).

In all of the above, the Son holds the central place. The Son, as the Father's Word, is the creator and providential mediator who establishes an immediate mutual relationship of life, knowledge, and love between the Father and humankind. In the aftermath of sin, the Father will salvifically act through his Son, so as to reestablish this communal bond of fellowship.

De Incarnatione: Jesus, the Incarnate Savior

Not surprisingly, the Word of the Father is the bond between *Conte Gentes* and *De Incarnatione*. Athanasius writes:

> It is, then, proper for us to begin the treatment of this subject by speaking of the creation of the universe, and of God its Artificer, so that it may be duly perceived that the renewal of creation has been the work of the self-same Word that made it at the beginning. For it will appear not inconsonant for the Father to have wrought its salvation in him by whose means he made it. (1.4)[2]

---

[2] All quotations in this section are taken from *De Incarnatione*.

Significantly, Athanasius, following the biblical narrative, insightfully perceives that the Son of God, as the Father's Word and Wisdom, inextricably conjoins protology and soteriology and, ultimately, eschatology.

The Father's Dilemma

The incarnation can only be fully appreciated if one recognizes that sin has thrown into jeopardy the Father's plan that humankind was created to share in his incorruptible nature and so live in communion with him.

> God had made man, and willed that he should abide in incorruption; but men, having despised and rejected the contemplation of God, and devised and contrived evil for themselves ... received the condemnation of death with which they had been threatened; and from thenceforth no longer remained as they were made, but were being corrupted according to their devises; and death had the mastery over them as king. For transgression of the commandment was turning them back to their natural state, so just as they had their being out of nothing, so also, as might be expected, they might look for corruption into nothing in the course of time. (4.4)

In the light of sin's devastation, the breaking of humankind's incorruptible communion with God, Athanasius pointedly asks: "What was God in his goodness to do" (6.7)? In the face of sin God was confronted with a number of dilemmas, not least of which was his own good name.

Death and corruption are "at once monstrous and unseemly," but God had to remain true to his word: "For God would not be true, if when he had said we should die, man died not" (6.3). Yet, it is equally unseemly that human beings "once made rational, and having partaken of the Word, should go to ruin and turn again toward non-existence by the way of corruption" (6.4–6). There is no profit in man's ruin.

> Far better were they not made, than once made, left to neglect and ruin. For neglect reveals weakness and not goodness on God's part—if, that is, he allows his own work to be ruined when once he had made it—more so than if he had never made man at all. (6.7–8)

Having created human beings, not only could they accuse God of weakness in indifferently observing and feebly agonizing over their demise, but, worst of all, God would stand accused in his very own eyes. "It was, then, out of the question to leave men to the current of corruption; because this would be unseemly, and unworthy of God's goodness" (6.10).

The sinful situation is such that it can only be resolved through the Word becoming man and within his humanity achieve humankind's salvation. Athanasius offers a number of arguments.

The Incarnation: The Restoration of Incorruptibility

First, Athanasius once again conjoins protology and soteriology. As it was through the Word that human beings were first created in his image, so:

> His it was once more both to bring the corruptible to incorruption, and to maintain intact the just claim of the Father, and above all, he alone of natural fitness was both able to recreate everything, and worthy to suffer on behalf of all and to be ambassador for all with the Father. (7.5, see also 10.3)

Since human beings were created in the Word's image, there is a "natural fitness" that the Word, as their ambassador, recreates them in his image through his salvific suffering. Second, the Word has an inherent responsibility for humankind's well-being and so willingly comes to dwell in their midst. The motivation for such condescending love is in the Word's taking pity on the human race lest "his Father's handiwork in men be spent for nought" and so "he takes unto himself a body, and that of no different sort from ours" (8.1–2).

Here we see the role of sin within Athanasius's thought and the calamitous consequences of death and corruption that are sin's penalty. Yet, the Word of God willingly assumed his responsibility out of love for humankind and his Father. He does not want the work, which the Father first achieved through him, to come to naught—the demise of humankind and so the humiliation of his Father. In order to address all of these intertwined issues adequately, the Word of God, who is incorporeal, incorruptible, and immortal, must assume what is corporeal, corruptible, and mortal: namely, become man.

Third, Athanasius articulates a very significant twofold soteriological principle. On the one hand, the Word "takes a body of our own kind" or "one of like nature because all were under the penalty of the corruption of death" (8.3–4, see also 8.2, 10.4, and 37.2). The Word assumed a humanity taken from the sinful race of Adam, humanity "under the penalty of the corruption of death," for only then could he recreate it.[3] On the other hand, this sin-scarred humanity was "from a spotless and stainless virgin, knowing not a man, a body

---

[3] For a further discussion of this issue, see T. Weinandy, *In the Likeness of Sinful Flesh: An Essay on the Humanity of Christ* (Edinburgh: T&T Clark, 1993).

clean and in very truth pure from intercourse of men" (8.3, see also 20.4). Athanasius may appear to be contradicting himself in that he wants the Word's assumed humanity to be both of the sinful stock of Adam and from a spotless Virgin. However, Athanasius is establishing that the Word of God must assume a nature like our own if it is to be our nature that he recreates and that he must do so as one who is himself not a sinner. Only in so doing he is able to offer an efficacious sacrifice to his Father. As a member of our fallen race he offers himself *in our stead* and yet, being holy and pure, he offers himself *on our behalf*. Assuming a humanity from the flesh of the Virgin Mary assures, for Athanasius, both that his humanity bears the scars of sinful corruptibility and equally that it be hallowed so as to allow the Son of God to obtain humankind's salvation through it.

Fourth, employing his twofold soteriological principle, Athanasius focuses upon the salvific nature of Jesus's death and resurrection.

> And thus taking from our bodies one of like nature, because all were under penalty of the corruption of death he gave it over to death in the stead of all, and offered it to the Father—doing this, moreover, of his loving-kindness, to the end that, firstly, all being held to have died in him, the law involving the ruin of men might be undone (inasmuch as its power was fully spent in the Lord's body, and had no longer holding-ground against men, his peers), and that, secondly, he might turn them again toward incorruption, and quicken them from death by the appropriation of his body and by the grace of the resurrection, banishing death from them like straw from the fire. (8.4)

Athanasius's argument is ultimately quite clear: the Word assumed our humanity and so assumed our corruption and death. Because he was one of us, he could stand in our stead and offer his sinless humanity as a loving sacrifice to the Father, accomplishing two goals. First, being one with our sin-marred humanity, the Word and all human beings are conjoined and so, reminiscent of Paul, all have died in union with him, and the law by which all were condemned to die was fulfilled in him. Second, having died on our behalf and so reconciling us to the Father, Christ is now able to share with them his incorruptible resurrection, uniting them to himself through grace.

Fifth, Athanasius further elaborates on the causal logic of Christ's redemptive work.

> [The Word] takes to himself a body capable of death, that it, by partaking of the Word who is above all, might be worthy to die in the stead of all, and might because of the Word which was come to dwell in it, remain incorruptible, and

> that thenceforth corruption might be stayed from all by the grace of the resurrection. (9.1)

While the Word takes a corruptible body like our own, this body is worthy to die on our behalf for it shares in the holiness of the Word. Moreover, the body of the Word truly dies, but then it rises incorruptible since it is the body of the incorruptible Word. As a result incorruptibility is shared with humankind through the grace of the resurrection.

The reason that the Word incarnate procures for human beings the incorruptible life of the resurrection is that he offers

> unto death the body he himself had taken, as an offering and sacrifice free from stain, straightway he put away death from all his peers by the offering of an equivalent. For being over all, the Word of God naturally by offering his own temple and corporeal instrument for the life of all satisfied the debt by his death. (9.1-2, see also 20.2, 5–6)

Because the Word, having assumed our very nature, offers his pure and stainless human life as a sacrifice in our stead and our behalf, he contravenes and offsets the debt of death incurred and so owed by sin. Here, we unmistakably perceive the centrality of the cross within Athanasius's soteriology. The cross is salvific precisely because the Son assumed our sinful nature and so the penalty of death, but in so doing his death was a pure, holy, and loving sacrifice to the Father though which we were reconciled to him. Having been reconciled to the Father through the cross, we are now united to him through the risen Lord Jesus. "The incorruptible Son of God, being conjoined with all by a like nature, naturally clothed all with incorruption by the promise of the resurrection" (9.2, see also 20.2 and 21.1). Christ's bodily sacrificial death and bodily glorious resurrection is the culmination of the Gospel's soteriological narrative, for reconciled human beings are only able to acquire once more incorruptibility by sharing in the incorruptible humanity of the risen Christ. As the first-fruit, Christ's risen incorruptible humanity establishes and so becomes the exemplar of what will be the eschatological end of all faithful Christians—the fullness of incorruptible divine life as risen human beings.

Finally, Athanasius articulates a second soteriological reason for the incarnation, that is, recreating humankind once more in the image of God. Since sin marred humankind's divine image thus depriving it of divine knowledge, Athanasius again asks: "What then was God to do? Or what was to be done save the renewing of that which was in God's image, so that by it men might once more be able to know him" (13.7)? The only way this could be done is by the presence of the very Image of God, our Lord Jesus Christ ... Whence the Word of God came in his own person, that, as he was the Image of the Father, he might be able to create afresh the man after the image ... None other then was sufficient for this need, save the Image of the Father. (13.7 and 9)

Athanasius emphasizes that the incarnate Word revealing the truth of the Father accomplishes this renewal

What the Word does bodily is of the utmost significance since it is through these bodily deeds that human beings through their own bodily senses perceive that such deeds were done by God. In perceiving his bodily deeds, the Word persuades human beings that "he is not man only, but also God, and the Word and Wisdom of the true God" (16.1). But if death was wound closely to the body and was ruling over it as though united to it, it was required that life also should be wound closely to the body, that so the body, by putting on life in its stead, should cast off corruption ... For this cause the Savior reasonably put on him a body, in order that the body, becoming wound closely to the Life, should no longer, as mortal, abide in death, but, as having put on immortality, should thenceforth rise again and remain immortal ... Therefore he put on a body, that he might find death in the body, and blot it out (44.5–6, see also 20.4).

Athanasius does not mean that salvation is accomplished in the single act of the incarnation. Rather, the incarnation initiates the salvific work of Christ that finds its completion and summation in the cross, and so culminates in the ensuing resurrection. Having wound the body of death closely to himself in the incarnation, the Word of life transforms it into his incorruptible divine life through his death and resurrection, whereby his risen humanity is now wound closely to himself. Christians are now wound closely to the risen Christ and so are renewed in his risen likeness.

The Christian's Soteriological Testimony to the Cross and Resurrection

While Athanasius takes up various arguments proffered by Jews and Greeks against the cross and resurrection, the real proof for the salvific efficacy of the cross and resurrection is the testimony of Jesus's followers—Christians no longer cower in the face of death, for they know that "Christ tread it down as dead" (27.1). Where in the past even holy men and women wept for the dead, now they know that death, in the light of Christ's resurrection, is the beginning of life for they become "incorruptible through the resurrection" (27.2). Not only do

Christians have contempt for death but, when persecuted, they eagerly embrace it as "witnesses of the resurrection" (27.3). This is true not only of men, but also of the young, and even of women (see 27.3 and 29.4–5). Not only is the devil held up to mockery and scorn, but also:

> Death having been conquered and exposed by the Saviour on the cross, and bound hand and foot, all they who are in Christ, as they pass by, trample on him, and witnessing to Christ scoff at death, jesting at him, and saying what has been written against him of old "O death, where is thy victory? O grave, where is thy sting?"' (27.4, see also 29)

In a flurry of rhetorical questions Athanasius drives his point home that only in the name of Christ and by the sign of his Cross are the lives of sinful men and women transformed into lives of virtue, even to the extent that the young commit themselves to a life of virginity (see 50.4–53).

With enthusiasm and confidence (maybe overconfidence), Athanasius perceives all evil and sin diminishing and the Gospel spreading everywhere to all men and women, thus testifying to the triumph of Jesus Christ and his cross and resurrection (see 55). Athanasius's consistent concluding refrain, in the midst of this triumphal soteriological narrative, is: "Now this is at once a proof of the divinity of the Saviour" (52.4). It is clear "to all eyes" that "he who abides is God, and the true Son of God, his only-begotten Word" (55.6). For Athanasius the soteriological benefits of Christ are irrefutably manifested for all to see if they have but the eyes and the will to perceive them.

Athanasius concludes by professing (in probably his most memorable statement), "he (the Son) was made man that we might be made God; and he manifested himself by a body that we might receive the idea of the unseen Father; and he endured the insolence of men that we might inherit immortality" (54.3). Here Athanasius summarizes his entire soteriology. The incarnation of the Word and his subsequent salvific actions, most especially his death on the cross and his resulting glorious resurrection, procure for humankind a proper knowledge of Father and the divinizing benefits of incorruptibility.

Athanasius also highlights that all he has stated is in conformity with Sacred Scripture. There we learn what concerns the Son's first coming in the flesh, but also

> his second glorious and truly divine appearing to us, when no longer in lowliness but in his own glory—no longer in humble guise, but in his own magnificence—he is to come, no more to suffer, but thenceforth to render to all the fruit of

his own cross, that is, the resurrection and incorruption; and not longer to be judged, but to judge all by which each has done in the body, whether good or evil; where there is laid up for the good the kingdom of heaven, but for them that have done evil everlasting fire and outer darkness. (56.3)

The work of the Word began within the act of creation when human beings were first created in his image. It then comes to its final completion when he comes at the end of time and human beings share fully in his glorious and incorruptible life having been transformed into his full likeness of his Sonship, thereby sharing, in union with him, in the everlasting divine life and love of the Father. For Athanasius, protology, soteriology, and eschatology find their unity in the one Word.

Athanasius's Incarnational Soteriology— Anti-Arian/Pro-Nicene Works

Athanasius is most remembered as a staunch defender of the Son's full divinity and his passionate endorsement of the Council of Nicea's dogmatic proclamation that the Son is *homoousion* (consubstantial or one in being) with the Father. What is frequently overlooked is that his zealous defense of and fervent advocacy for the Son's divinity was founded upon his incarnational soteriology. This soteriological concern, for Athanasius, was at the heart of the Arian crisis. In this section, we will first examine Athanasius's understanding of the incarnation since it is fundamental to his soteriology and then give a summary of his soteriology that flows from the incarnation.

Defining the Incarnational-Soteriological "Becoming"

The following exemplifies and summarizes the whole of Athanasius's incarnational soteriology.

> For man, if joined to a creature, was not deified, unless the Son were truly God; nor was man brought into the Father's presence unless he had been his natural and true Word who had put on the body. And as we would not have been delivered from sin and the curse, unless it had been human flesh by nature that the Word put on (for there should be nothing common to us with what is foreign), so also the man would not have been deified unless the Word who became flesh had been by nature from the Father and true and proper to him. Therefore

> the union was of this kind, that he might unite what is man by nature to him who is of the nature of the Godhead, and his salvation and deification might be sure. Therefore let those who deny that the Son is from the Father by nature and proper to his *ousia*, deny also that he took true human flesh from the ever-virgin Mary; for in neither case would it have been of profit to us men, whether the Word were not true and naturally Son of God, or the flesh not true which he assumed. (*Contra Arianos*, 2.70; see also 2.69)

In this passage, Athanasius asserts the three prerequisite incarnational truths necessary for salvation. First, we could not come into the Father's presence and truly know him if the Son were not himself God. Our deification is predicated upon his full divinity as the Father's Son. Second, only if it were our own genuine tangible flesh, and not something foreign to us, that the Son of God took on, could we be truly deified. Third, in order for the divine Son to save and deify our humanity, the coming together—the incarnational "becoming"—must be such as actually to unite "what is man by nature to him who is of the nature of the Godhead." The divine Son must actually and *truly be* man.

Athanasius recognizes that to possess a proper understanding of the incarnation, one must properly conceive and clearly articulate the nature of the incarnational "become." First, "become" does not mean that the Son of God came to dwell within an already existing man.

> He became man, and did not come into man; for this is necessary to know, lest these irreligious men fall into this notion also, and beguile any into thinking that, as in former times the Word was used to come into each of the saints, so now he sojourned in a man, hallowing him also, and manifesting himself as he had in others [. . .]. [However,] neither was it said that when they were begotten was he had become man, nor, when they suffered that he himself suffered. (*Contra Arianos*, 3.30–31)

Jesus was not merely another prophet in whom the Word of God dwelt. "Becoming" is more than a form of "adoptionism" whereby God inspires or loves his prophets and saints. The Word became flesh such that in the "becoming," the Son of God can rightfully be said to suffer and die as a man. It is precisely the direct predication of human attributes, such as suffering, to the Son that attests to the Son actually becoming man and so existing as a man. This authentic predication guarantees our salvation—it must be truly the divine Son who actually suffers and dies in our stead and on our behalf.

Moreover, the incarnational "becoming" must be an ontological "becoming" if the Son is to exist as man and so suffer and die as man, but it cannot be an ontological "becoming" whereby the Son of God "changes into" man. Athanasius insists throughout his writings, against the Arian assumption, that "become" does not mean to "change into." He grasped that the Son of God must remain unchangeable in becoming man not only in accordance with his divine status, but also for the sake of the incarnation. If the Son of God changed in becoming man, then it would no longer be truly the perfect Son of God who now exists as man, but rather a lesser form of himself. Worse still, if the Son of God changed into man, then it would no longer be the Son of God who existed as man. What would then exist would simply be a man who once was, but no longer is, God. If any of the above where true, then the Son of God would not suffer and die as man and thus our salvation would not have been secured.

If, for Athanasius, the incarnational "becoming" does not mean either "come into" or "change into," what then does it mean? The answer lies within the very denials. The incarnational "becoming" is defined by the terminal incarnational "is." Because the Son of God "is" man, the "becoming" must express and assure both that he remains the unalterable God so that it is truly God who is man and that the humanity remains unalterably human so that the Son of God is truly man. Inherent within Athanasius's thought is the notion that "to become man," means that the Son of God "comes to exist" or "comes to be" man since in becoming man, the Son of God exists as man. That such is Athanasius's understanding is perceived in his constant non-negotiable claim that it is the Son of God who suffers and dies as man for our salvation, something he could not do if he did not actually come to exist as man.

While the Arians were scandalized at the thought of God being born, growing, hungering, thirsting, suffering, and dying, Athanasius gloried is it because he knew that, in coming to exist as man, the Son of God could be born of a woman (thus *theotokos*), hunger, thirst, suffer, and die for our salvation.

> Suffering and weeping and toiling, these things which are proper to the flesh, are ascribed to him [the Son] together with the body. If then he wept and was troubled, it was not the Word, as being the Word, who wept and was troubled, but it was proper to the flesh. If he also pleaded that "the cup might pass away," it was not the Godhead that was in terror, but this passion too was proper to the manhood. And the words "Why hast thou forsaken me?" are his, according to the explanation offered above, though he suffered nothing, for the Word was impassible. This is nonetheless declared by the evangelists, since the Lord became man and these things are done and said as from a man, that he might himself lighten these sufferings of the flesh, and free it from them. (*Contra Arianos*, 3.56; see also 2.16 and 3.26)

Athanasius unwaveringly predicates all human attributes, human actions, and human experiences, to one sole subject—the Word.[4] This is of the utmost soteriological significance. If it is the Son of God who was actually born, grew in wisdom and grace, thirsted, wept, suffered, and died, then it was the Son of God as man who won for us our salvation. The efficacy of the cross precisely resides in the Son of God offering his holy human life to the Father as a loving sacrifice on our behalf—as one truly like us. Moreover, the Father raised his Son gloriously from the dead as man so that by partaking of his risen human glory we might share in his divine eternal life. Athanasius's understanding of the incarnation is thoroughly soteriological, as we see from this moving summary:

> For he (the Son) suffered to prepare freedom from suffering for those who suffer in him. He descended that he might raise us up, he went down to corruption, that corruption might put on immortality, he became weak for us, that we might rise with power, he descended to death, that he might bestow on us immortality, and give life to the dead. Finally, he became man, that we who die as men might live again, and that death should no more reign over us. (*Festal Letter*, 10.8)

Incarnational Soteriology

Having articulated Athanasius's soteriological understanding of the incarnation, it is now possible to flesh out more fully his soteriology that flows from it. First, Athanasius sees the salvific incarnation of the Son of God as something predestined by the Father before the foundation of the world. Commenting on Ephesians 1:3–5, Athanasius observes that human beings were chosen, before they were created, to be adopted by the Father through Christ. Thus, "the Lord himself was predestined 'before the world,' inasmuch as he had a purpose, for our sakes, to take on him through the flesh all the inheritance of judgment that lay against us, and we henceforth were made sons in him" (2.76).[5] As the wise architect not only prepares

---

[4] This has come to be known as the *Communication of Idiom*, that is, that divine and human attributes are predicated on one and the same person.

Many scholars accuse Athanasius of denying a human soul in Jesus primarily because he does not mention such until late in his theological career. This is a false accusation. Throughout the whole of Athanasius's writings he insists, as we have seen, that Jesus expressed all of the human emotions and feeling common to humankind. Such emotions and feelings—hunger, fatigue, fear, suffering—implicitly and necessarily involve not only a human body but also a human mind and thus a human soul. The whole human being suffers in mental anguish and physical pain and not merely his body. For a fuller explanation of Athanasius's thought, see T. G. Weinandy, *Athanasius: A Theological Introduction* (Aldershot: Ashgate, 2007), 91–96.

[5] All citations in this section are drawn from *Contra Arianos*.

all of his materials prior to undertaking his building project, but also lays aside ample supplies for future needed repair, so the Father not only created us through his Word, but also even before creation. The Father foresaw, in the light of sin, the need and so centrally placed, from the onset of creation, his incarnate Son within the divine economy as the means of humankind's salvation.

Second, Athanasius perceives that the salvific work of the Incarnate Son must first progress within his own humanity and only then, after he himself has been made perfect and so deified, are human beings, by being conjoined to him, able to progress themselves in the process of deification. The perfect Word of God first "puts around himself an imperfect body," that, "paying the debt in our stead, he might in himself perfect what was wanting in man" (2.66). Jesus, as the "first born," must first experience the fruit of redemption and only then can humankind participate in it (2.61; cf. 2.64). The Son of God in assuming our sin-marred humanity perfects himself through his sacrificial death on the cross and glorious resurrection and in so doing allows those who believe in him to share in his own perfection.

Third, Athanasius equally understands Jesus's resurrection, following Philippians, as his perfecting "exaltation." The Son is exalted not as God, "but the exaltation is of the manhood," for he humbled himself in assuming humankind's humanity even unto death on the cross (1.41). The Son's humanity was raised up and exalted because it was not external to him, but his own (1.45). The exaltation of the Son's humanity was fully deified and so made perfect (1.42 and 45). Moreover, since all Christians die in him, so now they share in his exaltation (1.41). As the Second Adam then, the exalted and so deified incarnate Son becomes the paradigm in which all human beings can come to share in his perfected risen humanity (1.44). Where the "first man" brought death to humankind's humanity, the Son "quickened it with the blood of his own body" (2.65).

Fourth, in a similar fashion, Athanasius perceives that, in being exalted and so perfectly hallowed, the incarnate Son becomes "Lord," "in order to hallow all by the Spirit" (2.14; cf. 18). In being made fully holy in the Spirit, Athanasius argues that we can rightly be called "gods," not in the sense that we are equal to the Son by nature, but because we have become benefactors of his grace (3.19). Human beings are, therefore, "sons and gods" because they "were adopted and deified through the Word" (3.19; cf. 38). For Athanasius, the perfecting and so hallowing of Jesus through his glorious exaltation as a risen man is summed up in his notion of deification. Deification is not the changing of our human nature into something other than it is, that is, into another kind of being. Rather, deification for Athanasius is the making of humankind, through indwelling of the Holy Spirit, into what it was meant to be from the very beginning, that is, the perfect image of the Word who is the perfect image of the Father, affected by being taken into the very divine life of the Trinity. Commenting on Jesus's prayer that Christians would be one with him as he is with the Father (see John 17:21), Athanasius perceives that it is through being united to Jesus's "body" that we become one body with him and so are united to the Father himself (3.22). This "uniting" is the work of the Holy Spirit. "The Son is in the Father, as his proper Word and Radiance; but we, apart from the Spirit, are strange and distant from God, yet by the participation of the Spirit we are knit into the Godhead" (3.24). Thus the goal of creation is now achieved, that is, human beings have united to the Father through his eternal Word in the communion of the Holy Spirit.

> For since the Word is in the Father, and the Spirit is given from the Word, he wills that we should receive the Spirit, that when we receive it, thus having the Spirit of the Word which is in the Father, we too may be found, on account of the Spirit, to become one in the Word, and through him in the Father. (3.25)

Divinization, for Athanasius, is then the sharing fully in the life of the Trinity and it is this sharing in the divine life that thoroughly transforms the believer into the adopted likeness of the Son.

Three points need to be emphasized in concluding our discussion of Athanasius's incarnational soteriology. First, while the goal of humankind's salvation is in its deification, this goal, for Athanasius, is achieved only through the Son assuming a humanity like our own and through his sacrificial death on the cross reconciling us to the Father. Apart from the cross there is no deification, for deification is the fruit of the cross. Second, to become divinized, human beings must come into communion with the risen divinized humanity of the Son. Only through this union with Christ's risen humanity are believers transformed into his likeness and so share in his own divine life, which is communion with the Father. Third, what is noticeable here is that Athanasius in his later writings, unlike in *Contra Gentes* and *De Incarnatione*, gives due recognition to the Holy Spirit as the bond by which Christians are united to the Word's risen humanity, being transformed into his likeness through this union, and so coming into communion with the Father as his children. That being said, we can now turn to Athanasius's final work, his *Letters to Serapion*, where he champions the divinity of the Holy Spirit, not surprisingly, for soteriological reasons.

Pneumatological Soteriology

Once major portions of the church had accepted the *homoousion* doctrine of the Council of Nicea, the issue of the full divinity of the Holy Spirit came to the fore. Athanasius provides his fullest defense and exposition of the divinity of the Holy Spirit in his letters to Serapion, the Bishop of Thmuis. At the onset of his first *Letter to Serapion*, Athanasius espoused ten scriptural soteriological arguments demonstrating that the Holy Spirit is indeed God. All of them pertain to the Holy Spirit's intimate relationship to the Father and to the Son and so his oneness of being with them; for only if he is equal to them in divinity is he empowered, in union with them, to enact the salvific effects scripturally attributed to him.[6] Here, we are unable to treat the whole of Athanasius's Pneumatology, but focus on those arguments that are of the greatest soteriological significance.

1. The first argument is founded upon 1 Corinthians 2:11–12.

> For if, as no one knows the things of man save the spirit of man that is in him, so no one knows the things of God save the Spirit of God; would it not be evil speech to call the Spirit who is in God a creature, him who searches even the deep things of God? (1.22)[7]

As the spirit of a human being is within him, being part of his very being, and comprehending his deepest thoughts, so too the Spirit, if he is to comprehend the inner thoughts of God, must be one in being with him and so equally divine. The divine Holy Spirit dwells in believers and reveals the salvific truth of the Father's Word.

2. Within the Bible the Holy Spirit is called the Spirit of holiness and renewal.[8] Human beings are sanctified in the Spirit and so renewed in him. Since it is the Holy Spirit who sanctifies and renews all creatures and is not sanctified or renewed himself, "how can he be from among all things or pertain to those who partake of him?" As all is created through the Son, thus establishing that he is not one of the creatures, so the Holy Spirit, who sanctifies all creatures, thus establishes himself to be not one of them as well (1.23; cf. 1.22). Moreover, it is the sanctification and renewal of the Spirit that is

---

[6] I am examining only the series in his first letter. In his third letter he has a similar series, though not as complete.
[7] All citations in this section are from *Ad Serapion*.
[8] Athanasius employs Romans 1:4, 1 Corinthians 6:11, Titus 3:4–7, Psalm 104:30, and Hebrews 6:4.

the salvific fruit of the Son's redemptive work. It is the Spirit who transforms believers into the likeness of Jesus, the Son, making them children of the Father.

3. The Holy Spirit is called the "quickening Spirit" for it is by the Spirit that the Father raised Jesus from the dead, and it is that same Spirit that now dwells within believers who will raise their mortal bodies to life.[9] Again, Athanasius asks a rhetorical question: "He that does not partake of life, but who is himself partaken of and quickens the creatures, what kinship can he have with originated things?" (1.23). Only insofar as the Holy Spirit shares fully in the incorruptible divine life of the Father and the Son can he dispense that salvific incorruptible life to those who believe.

4. Athanasius returns to a point that he briefly referred to already; through the Spirit believers "become partakers of God." Christians are temples of the God because the Spirit of God dwells within them. Moreover, the unction and seal that is within Christians belong not to a creature, "but to the nature of the Son who, through the Spirit who is in him, joins us to the Father." The Spirit, abiding within believers, joins them to the very nature of the Word for the Spirit abides in the Word, and so abiding in the Word through the Spirit, Christians abide in the Father himself. Because of this salvific effect, one would be "mad to say that the Spirit has a created nature and not the nature of God" for "the Father, through the Word, in the Holy Spirit, creates and renews all things" (1.24; cf. 3.3 and 5).[10]

5. Athanasius, in the above, clearly argues for the Spirit's full divinity by elucidating the manner in which the Scriptures testify to the collaboration between the Son and the Spirit in the work of salvation within Christians. Because the Spirit is of the proper essence of the Son, he is "the image" of the Son, and not because he images the Son in a manner similar to the way the Son images the Father. "Image" pertains to his being God, a partaker of the divine "*ousia*," and not to his distinct subjective divine identity as Spirit, his *hypostasis*.[11] Nonetheless, being God as the Son is God, the Holy Spirit partakes of the Son's divine soteriological virtues.

> And so, as the Lord is Son, the Spirit is called Spirit of Sonship. Again, as the Son is wisdom and truth, the Spirit is described as Spirit of wisdom and truth. Again

---

[9] Beside Romans 8:11, Athanasius also employs John 4:14 and 7:39.
[10] Athanasius refers to 1 Corinthians 3:16–17, 1 John 4:13, 2 Peter 1:4, Psalm 104:29–30, and Titus 3:5.
[11] While Athanasius rightly wants to establish that the Holy Spirit is God as the Son is God, the use of the term "image" it is not an apt concept to employ.

the Son is the power of God and the Lord of glory, and the Spirit is called Spirit of power and glory. (1.25; cf. 4.4)

The Son being begotten of the Father is his Wisdom, Truth, Power, and Glory. Similarly, because the Holy Spirit is the Spirit of Sonship, the Son having conferred upon him all that he has received from the Father, he is the Spirit of Wisdom, Truth, Power, and Glory.

6. Athanasius returns to a point made in relation to previous arguments on behalf the Spirit's divinity, that is, that "the Holy Spirit is partaken of and does not partake." Angels and creatures are able to fall away from God, but the Holy Spirit is "always the same" and he is the one, being proper to the Word, who enables creatures to partake of what is of God and so is not a creature (1.27). Only if the Holy Spirit rightfully possesses "holiness" within his very nature as God in union with the Father and the Son, who are all holy, and so not in need of being sanctified himself, is he capable of sanctifying others.

Conclusion

By way of conclusion, a number of summary points need to be highlighted. Athanasius's incarnational soteriology is thoroughly biblical. The whole of his soteriological thought follows the biblical narrative from the beginning to the end—beginning with creation and the sinful fall of humankind, to the incarnation and the saving work of Jesus, culminating in his Second Coming in glory. Moreover, precisely because the Word holds central place within Athanasius's incarnational soteriology, the Father and the Holy Spirit assume their rightful place within his soteriology. The Father begets his Son and creates all through his Word and in so doing creates humankind in the image of Son so that it could be in living communion with himself through his Son. The Father sends forth his Son into the world so that through his humanity, he might recreate human beings in the image of his Son and so once more share in his divine life. The Son of God incarnate enacts this recreation through his death on the cross whereby he reconciles humankind to the Father. In his resurrection, human beings are able to assume their divine likeness in communion with him and so once more know the Father and share in his incorruptible divine life. The deification of human beings is the fruit of Christ's sacrificial death and glorious resurrection. While the salvific role of the Holy Spirit only finds its proper place within Athanasius's later writings, yet it does so in a mature fashion. The divine Holy

Spirit transforms human beings into the image of the Son and so makes them holy. In possessing the Holy Spirit, human beings live in Christ and so live in communion with the Father as his children. This Trinitarian and incarnational soteriology, for Athanasius, finds its completion at the end of time. At Jesus's coming in glory the saints will share fully in his resurrection possessing the fullness of his deifying Spirit and so live forever within the fullness of the Father's life and love. For Athanasius, what the Father planned from all eternity and began in creation will then find its consummation—all being united in Jesus Christ his Son, the universal Savior and definitive Lord, through the communion Holy Spirit.[12]

---

[12] For a fuller treatment of Athanasius's soteriology, see Weinandy, *Athanasius: A Theological Introduction*. See also K. Anatolios, *Athanasius: The Coherence of His Thought* (New York: Routledge, 1998); *Athanasius* (New York: Routledge, 2004); D. Brakke, *Athanasius and Asceticism* (Baltimore: The John Hopkins University Press, 1995); G. D. Dragas, *St. Athanasius of Alexandria: Original Research and New Perspective* (Rolllinsford: Orthodox Research Center, 2005); P. J. Leithart, *Athanasius* (Grand Rapids, MI: Baker Academic, 2011).

St. Gregory of Nyssa on the Dynamics of Salvation

John A. McGuckin

Introduction

The "Cappadocian Fathers" is a collective title for a group of important fourth-century theologians and ascetics who lived in eastern Asia Minor (modern Turkey near the Syrian borders). This Neo-Nicene party was that group of theologians younger than Athanasius of Alexandria, Paul of Samosata, and Eustathius of Antioch (the first generation of Nicene defenders) who prepared the theological settlements of the Second Ecumenical Council in 381.[1] They have traditionally been regarded as the "Three Cappadocians," Basil of Caesarea (330–379), Gregory of Nyssa his brother (331–395), and Gregory of Nazianzus their friend (329–390), who is more commonly known as Gregory the Theologian in Eastern Orthodoxy.[2] This chapter chiefly considers one of the most philosophically brilliant of that circle, Gregory of Nyssa. Gregory's family used its ecclesiastical and social rank energetically to advance the Nicene Christology of the *Homoousion* (the Son-Logos of God as ontologically coequal and coessential with the Father) and the unqualified divinity of the Holy Spirit. This context of a deep incarnational Christology lies behind all Cappadocian thought as its macro-context.

---

[1] J. A. McGuckin, *St. Gregory of Nazianzus: An Intellectual Biography* (New York: SVS Press, 2001), 229–369.
[2] There were other ecclesiastical leaders in this circle too such as Amphilokios of Ikonium, and less literary patrons such as Gregory the Elder of Nazianzus and Peter of Sebaste, as well as a large circle of monastic and political supporters.

Approaching the Cappadocian Doctrine of Salvation

This macro-context of incarnational Christology that we see in Gregory of Nyssa was heir to that of Origen and Athanasius. It saw the descent of the Logos into the flesh of fallen humanity as the reversal of the ontological decline of our race: a "fall" that had as its immediate effect alienation from the single divine source of life that resulted in *Ptharsia* (corruption both moral and ontological[3]) spreading out in the race, and bringing death as its result. This reversal to health (*soteria*, salvation) that the Word brought to humanity was not simply moral or theoretical, rather it reversed the ontological collapse of humanity by the process of the divine incarnation, so that the latter's power of deifying union[4] might then be effected. Athanasius had expressed it very succinctly: "He (the Logos) became Man, that Man might become god."[5]

The incarnation of the divine Lord was thus to be seen as wholly energized by the process of restoration (soteriology). The incarnation of God was the deification of humanity. This *enanthropesis*, which the Word accepted, was not a forced natural fusion of deity and humanity (a mythological conception) but rather a divine grace of the acceptance and uplift of the human race in the adoption of the human life by the Word. Similarly, the *theopoiesis* or deification the Alexandrian and Cappadocian fathers conceived of was a way of speaking about the transformation of human nature by virtue of the gift of restorative grace that the proximity of God now afforded to human ontology, or creature-hood. In other words, human nature which had once been described in terms of its alienation from God, as a tendency to ontological dissolution, was now lifted back into the divine ambit of life by the incarnation of the Logos and given back the stability of life that had originally flowed into the Race from its closeness to the creative power. The ontological rescue was thus a result of the return to divine communion provided by the advent of the Word.

The two things (ontological stabilization and return to divine communion) accordingly were one and the same *energeia* in two aspects of its mystery: moral

---

[3] The first expressed by alienation from God, the second expressed by the onset of death into humanity (not its natural condition) by virtue of that alienation from the source of its being: proximity to which was, in fact, its life-source.

[4] Athanasius and the later Alexandrian and Cappadocian fathers argue that the union-*Henosis* of Godhead and Manhood in the person-*hypostasis* of Christ had an impact on the humanity of Jesus (deified and immortalized it)—so that it could both die and not die (rise again) and pass on these things as from an archetype to the rest of redeemed humanity as a foretaste of immortality already gifted to the race through the church.

[5] Athanasius, *De Incarnatione*, 54. Irenaeus described it in terms of: "Out of his great love, he became what we are, so that we might become what he is." *Adversus Haereses.* 5. Praef.

and physical. What the Fathers were arguing, therefore, was that Creation theology and Soteriology were one and the same *mysterion*, and the descent of the Word into human life in the incarnation event was no less than a recreation of the Cosmos in the person and *energeia* of the Logos-Incarnate who was the instantiation (*hypostasis*) of the Redeemed Adam. This salvation process, which we can therefore synopsize as a sense of "deifying incarnationalism"[6] was something very concrete for these ancient authors. The doctrines of God (theology), human nature (anthropology), creation, and redemption cannot be separated or argued discretely when considering early Greek patristic approaches to "Atonement," as they came to be in later scholastic thought. Indeed, the concept of "Atonement" is excessively delimiting when one tries to capture the overall schematic of the liberative process that they wish to communicate concerning God's restoration of Humanity to divine communion, and thus life, in Christ the Savior.

Patristic "Atonement" Theory

Although this sense of "transference of divine energy" to the human race in the incarnation of the Logos sounds highly metaphysical to modern ears, its ontology is deeply personalist and morally freighted in the hands of the Fathers. The ontological restoration is ultimately a renewal of communion—a reconciliation. From the time of Origen onward, this double sense of salvation was rooted additionally in an exegesis of Paul despite the apparent "strangeness" to modern eyes of the exegetical method. The set of major analogies of atonement in Origen, Athanasius, and the Cappadocians, therefore, basically followed the diverse Pauline language of sacrificial substitution to effect reconciliation, but extended it in a metaphysically pedagogical manner (arguably what Paul also intended by his rhetoric of the spiritual *analogy* of sacrifice). This nexus of ideas rooted in Paul was conveyed by a string of correlated images that can be found in the Fathers (even when they are stressing one particular image, other ideas from the same nexus often intrude) and is reissued as an extended Pauline

---

[6] For a fuller exposition, see J. A. McGuckin, "*Soter Theos*: The Patristic and Byzantine Reappropriation of an Antique Idea," in *Salvation According to the Church Fathers*, ed. D. V. Twomey (Dublin: Four Courts Press, 2010), 33–44; also "Deification in Greek Patristic Thought: The Cappadocian Fathers' Strategic Adaptation of a Tradition," in *Partakers of the Divine Nature. The History and Development of Deification in the Christian Tradition*, ed. M. Christensen and J. Wittung (Farleigh Dickinson University Press, 2006), 95–114. An extensive and detailed treatment of the theme of deification is offered in the excellent study by N. Russell, *The Doctrine of Deification in the Greek Patristic Tradition* (Oxford, 2004).

exegesis[7] understood, in turn, as a synopsis of the "Apostolic Tradition" about redemption-salvation.

In its original matrix, the overall Pauline-Apostolic pattern can be seen as follows, touching on ten chief and closely interwoven points: (1) Christ's blood was a cleansing of sins (Eph. 1:7; Heb. 9:1–28) and (2) a humble atonement for the entire world (Heb. 2:9–10). (3) In his victory over death Christ became the leader of many kindred in (4) a (reconciled) communion (Heb. 2:14–18) which (5) brought them out into freedom from their bitter slavery to death and corruption. (6) It was a mystical and cosmically significant transactional exchange, whereby those who were assimilated to his death thereby became enfolded in the gift of his resurrection triumph and glory (2 Tim. 2:11–13). (7) Christ's atoning work on this great scale was a high-priestly activity, an offering up of prayers and tears for the sanctification and illumination of the communion of the faithful (Heb. 5:1–10). (8) It was also a cosmic victory over all the forces hostile to God (for by the cross he cast down the demonic powers and influences), and (9) a triumph that definitively changed the manner in which the High Priest's Divine Father related to the world thereafter, since it opened the gates of mercy for a new covenant through the mediation of the priestly Victor (Phil. 2:6–11; Col. 1:15–20; 2:14–15; 1 Tim. 3:16). (10) Christ's work was also seen as a moral instruction (*paideia*) that gave a supreme example of godliness to the world, and established a pattern of behavior for all disciples to scrutinize and follow (Heb. 12:1–4).

Patristic soteriology is therefore at once bigger and looser than Atonement theory as traditionally understood. Listening to what the Fathers have to say on the matter of "transformative salvation" in Christ is part of that larger package. Twentieth-century patristic theorists often attempted to force order onto the sprawling patristic images of atonement, describing various "schools" or theories (Physical Theory, Christ the Victor etc.[8]). The simple fact is that the patristic writing is organically diffuse on the central mystery of Christ's economy, and its context is generally that of encomiastic preaching. The writers used a combination of images to devolve in some sense or another from the poetic tapestry of scriptural texts about the work of Christ. To impose systematic order on this wildly vivid kerygmatic witness is often inappropriately scholastic. Even

---

[7] Hebrews is taken as a core part of the Pauline corpus, by the Alexandrian and Cappadocian Fathers.
[8] Gustav Aulén is especially notable in this regard, but equally his close reading of the Fathers was manifest in his attempt in his influential study, *Christus Victor*, to call for a wholesale and positive reevaluation of the merits of the patristic approaches which had, in his lifetime, been sidelined and scorned as poor dogmatic efforts.

so, in many instances, the "nexus" of patristic soteriological thought can be summed up as (1) a macro context of transfigurative incarnational thought, and (2) a set of exegetical examples revolving around the ten chief points found in the Pauline imagery of liberative redemption as set out above as the "apostolic synopsis."

Today it is perhaps better to approach the subject in two ways: first, to consider the works of the writers themselves individually (before lumping them as a school of thought) because while there are many common assonances, all three Cappadocians[9] demonstrate significantly different nuances in terms of God's salvation in Christ. And second, to study their ideas about salvation in terms of the concepts and imagery they actually use in situ. Indeed they apply a range of rhetorical imagery, not restricted to "Atonement" thought but ranging over ideas of liberation, purification, enlightenment, reconciliation, transfiguration, deification; as widely and diversely, in fact, as we find in the biblical writers themselves. And as they were all professional rhetoricians at the height of their skills we ought not to marshal imagery from their work as if it were some kind of rigid patristic theory.[10] Such images need not so much be cut out and listed in a collage, but rather considered in the overall flow of the writer's own systematic (a task of basic methodology that was advocated by Continental writers but often neglected by an earlier generation of English patristic scholars who tended to read texts woodenly, and very generically, before the 1970s). And so, this present chapter will proceed not so much by addressing what was the Gregorian theory of Atonement, but by asking what this very subtle theologian thought about the soteriological energy present in the church as a result of Christ's work.

Gregory of Nyssa's Sense of Salvation in Christ

The divine incarnation, and especially the understanding of the transaction of ontological power that manifests in the fabric of the human being, is for Gregory the core and central locus of human redemption. Gregory speaks of it as almost

---

[9] Not to mention their Cappadocian neighbors and enemies such as Aetios and Eunomios of Cyzikos, the radical (*heterousiast*) Arians.
[10] Poor Gregory of Nyssa is one of the worst examples of victim of this kind of superficial reading; which takes one of his incidental sermon allusions (Christ's capture of Leviathan) and wholly missing the Leviathan allusion elevates it to make him the originator of the "Fish-Hook Theory of Atonement." He would have found this hilarious, but generations of textbook readers since have taken it all too seriously.

like a massive magnetic presence of God in Christ that "draws to himself" all of humanity:

> Man was led back to the true and living God, and those who through the adoption followed the Son were not cast out or banished from their paternal inheritance. Thus, the one who had made himself the firstborn of the good creation among many brothers (Col. 1.15) drew to himself the whole of that Nature which he had shared in through the flesh that was mingled with Him.[11]

The incarnation is a uniquely bright locus of the generic presence of God in the created order: "For who, when they survey the universe, can be so simple-minded as to fail to believe that there is Divinity in everything, penetrating it, embracing it, and seated within it."[12]

This bright point, however, is effectively the radiant light of the restoration of a perfect divine-human union in Christ:

> Why then are people scandalized to hear of God's plan of Revelation when it teaches that God was born among men? This same God whom we are certain even now does not stand outside of mankind? Because although this last form of God's (incarnated) presence among us is not the same as that former presence, even so his existence among us is equally manifested in both; except that now the One who holds together in being all of Nature is transfused within our nature; just as in earlier times he was transfused throughout our nature, and this in order that by this very transfusion of the divine, our nature might itself become divine: being rescued from death in this way, and set beyond the caprice of the Antagonist. For His return from death [in the resurrection] became for our mortal race the beginning of our own return to immortal life.[13]

We shall come, in a moment, to discuss more fully Gregory's ransom theory ("Redemption" discretely understood[14]), but it is worth noting in passing that at the root of its rhetorical force is this sense that the Race has passed under the yoke of the slavery of death, as if passing from a natural (original) condition of creation into an unnatural one, and this because it became enslaved to the Deceit. Along with many of the other Fathers he means the deceit originally imposed on Adam by the Serpent (the Antagonist) and that deceit was fundamentally a confusion sown in the mind and spirit of Man about the purpose of

---

[11] *On the Three Day Interval*, ed. Geberhardt (1967), vol. 9, 305.
[12] *Catechetical Oration*, c. 25; W. Moore and H. A. Wilson (eds), *Select Writings and Letters of Gregory Bishop of Nyssa: the Nicene and Post Nicene Fathers*, vol 5 (Oxford: Parker & Co., 1893).
[13] Ibid.
[14] For the Latin word signifies "buying back" from a slave master.

his existence. From knowing he would be immortal because of his conscious union with God, he fell into a materially obsessed self-love and with the alienation of the consciousness from God came, according to the Alexandrians and the Cappadocians, an increasing captivity to materiality's logical end, namely, death. The physical restoration to life of the broken human body of the Logos was, for Gregory, the symbol of the restoration of the whole potentiality of "life in union with God" to the redeemed believer, and thus the restoration of that immortal state of which the loss of union had robbed us.

This is why Redemption theory for Gregory is fundamentally about two things: *Paideia* and Ontology—teaching Mankind their origins as immortal beings in union with the God who is the source of all being. In his hands the two things become fused as one: and in this he shows himself a faithful follower of Athanasius and Origen.

This energy of pedagogic restoration is a great victory in the battle of Christ the Pedagogue against the Deceiver of the Race. It is not only a battle for minds, hearts, and spirits, but also a cosmically scaled battle over the meaning of existence: as freedom or oppression. Commenting on the Psalms used in the Paschal Vigil, Gregory brings out the manner in which the incarnation is a War, in which Christ is the Victor who brings benefits of peace to his followers:

> Let us imitate the prophetic hills and mountains and leap for joy (Ps. 113.4) Come let us rejoice in the Lord who destroyed the power of the Enemy and for our sake set up his standard of the Cross over the very corpse of the foe. Let us raise a cry of victory, for cheers are the fitting shouts of triumph raised by victors over the vanquished. And since the enemy line has collapsed, and the very one who commanded the evil army of demons has gone, has vanished, and has been brought to nothing, then let us join in saying: The Lord is a great God (Ps 94.3) and "A great king over all the earth." (Ps. 46.3)[15]

Interpreting Psalm 68 ("Lift up your gates you princes and the King of glory shall enter in") Gregory says that here the Psalmist departs from his body in an ecstatic trance so as to see higher mysteries. He tells us that the words the "Princes" shout out are the exclamations of the angels when they see the Logos first of all descend to earth to engage in the battle of the incarnation, donning his body like a warrior putting on a suit of armor. The shouts of the same angels as they see the Logos ascending after the Passion back into the glory of heaven then follows. The great angels guard the "portal" of the gateway between heaven

---

[15] *Homily on the Holy and Saving Pascha*, Geberhardt (1967), vol. 9, 311.

and earth. They cannot recognize the Logos who descends to earth because of the armor of flesh that he has adopted. So they cry out to the earthly (guardian) angels to identify this strange Lord who now stands in their midst:

> For this reason the guardians address this enquiry to those who were leading the regal procession: "Who is this King of Glory?" And now their answer is no longer, "The mighty one strong in war," but rather: "The Lord of Hosts," He who has surpassed all in power, He who has recapitulated all things in himself (Eph. 1.10); the One who holds the first place over all, who has restored all things to the primal creation. This is the King of Glory.[16]

This passage is partly aimed at explicating an *aporia* Origen had left unresolved in his works. He had wondered what would be the method of restorative union designed by the Logos for the sake of the angelic ranks. Here Gregory slants the discussion to emphasize the manner in which acclamation of the power of God is constant in both schemes of salvation, the human and the angelic. Christ comes to liberate humanity, which has been led into death by angelic deceit. The Elder Race has led the younger race astray. The *Paideia* necessary to reverse this false seductive teaching will be a bloody and bitter one. However, the unconquerable power of the Godhead will affect it. Here we see already how the theme of "deceit" is close to Gregory's thinking, a sub-aspect of his overarching theme that the Passion qua salvation is fundamentally a Paschal Song of Victory. The deceit element belongs to his major theme of restorative *paideia*: in order to effect a change of mentality, the false views have to be addressed first.

The theme will emerge more graphically, of course, in the image of the deceit of Leviathan (the baited fish-hook). But this conception of the incarnation as a battle with the heavenly powers is more properly set in this larger context suggested by his exegesis of the Psalms and his homilies on Pascha and Ascension Day. Gregory, we need to remember, does not invent this "mythology" of the Satan-Antagonist holding real power over the affairs of the sublunary world. It is a fundamental part of Jesus's own teachings on the Kingdom of God struggling against the forces of the "Prince of this world,"[17] the "Mighty One,"[18] and it is why Jesus himself elevated exorcisms as one of the great signs of the imminent advent of the Kingdom: a structure of theology as cosmic victory that underpins all of the Gospels and much of the Pauline literature. In this context it is important,

---

[16] *Homily on the Ascension*, Geberhardt (1967), vol. 9, 325–326. The title "King of Glory" was also the traditional superscript of the painted crosses in the liturgical Passion icons of the Eastern Church.
[17] See Matthew 9.34; 12.24; John 12.31; Ephesians 2.2.
[18] See Matthew 12.29; Mark 3.27.

I think, when one encounters the image of the great fish-Leviathan, to set aside the rather "cute" concept of a fisherman landing a prize specimen, and remember that the idea is meant to convey the landing of "the Beast." Leviathan was most commonly depicted in ancient symbology as the crocodile: and its jaws were the mouth of Hell, for its grip was the power of death. The image, graphic as it is, is meant to signal to the receptive audience, above all else, Christ's victory over death and the Human Race's impotence before the swallowing jaws of mortality.

Before looking, finally, at the "baited hook" rhetoric of Gregory's more popular text the *Great Catechetical Oration*, I would like to add one further manifestation of this overarching sense of cosmic victory in the way that Gregory keeps stressing it, in the form of his noted analogy of the Cosmic Cross. This appears in several places in his opus.[19] And in both Irenaeus and Gregory, as we can abundantly see from the following text, it derives as an extended exegesis of Paul's conception of the *Pleroma* of salvation (Eph. 3.18–19): the height and depth, the length and breadth of Christ's cosmic dominion over the spiritual powers.[20] We can look at two instances of this Gregorian theology of salvation. For Gregory the *signum crucis* is marked within the essential fabric of the universe; it is not simply the vehicle of his death on Calvary. It is not merely a sign for the angelic (or demonic) powers, but all of humanity is included: the cosmic "breadth" alongside the heights and depths. For Gregory, the cross summarizes cruciform (and crucified) humanity itself; its glorious origin, its failed destiny, and its restoration. The Cosmic Cross is thus the very dynamic of salvation (*oikonomia tes soterias*).

He approaches the issue in his *Homily on the Three Day Interval* (in the tomb). Gregory begins here by noting how the death of Christ was a necessity, foretold as such by Christ himself (Luke 9:22; 24:7). This mystery, is a paradox of theology of the first order—namely, that God should die and moreover that this was a "necessary" thing—Gregory exegetes using the image of Paul as prophet of the New Age. Paul who is rapt out of the body to the Third Heaven (2 Cor. 12:2) and who has the "scales taken from his eyes" (Acts 9:18) is the only one who is

---

[19] The full list of *loci* is given by D. Balás in his study *Metousia Theou: Man's Participation in God's Perfections According to Saint Gregory of Nyssa* (Studia Anselmiana, 55) (Rome: Pontificium Institutum S. Anselmi, 1966), 150–152. Cf. fn. 53; see also D. Balás, "The Meaning of the Cross." in *The Easter Sermons of Gregory of Nyssa*, ed. A Spira & C Klock (Philadelphia, 1981), 305–318. Cf. Irenaeus's *Proof of the Apostolic Preaching* (New York: SVS Press, 1997), chapter 34.

[20] See J. A. McGuckin, "Patterns of Biblical Exegesis in the Cappadocian Fathers," in *Orthodox and Wesleyan Spirituality Vol 2*, ed. S. T. Kimborough (Biblical Theology—Papers of the Orthodox-Methodist International Theological Consultation, Crete, 2002) (New York: SVS Press, 2006).

capable of rising to be able to speak about that *Pleroma* which the cross truly signifies; a fullness of envelopment in the breadth and length and height and depth of God's energy:

> It was for a reason then, that the Apostle here (Eph. 3:18-19) discerned the shape of the Cross … He saw that this shape, divided as it was into four projections from its central crossing, signified the power and providence of the One who was made manifest upon it, and thereby penetrated into all things. This was why Paul named each of the four projection with a separate title … so as to indicate that there is nothing whatsoever in existence that is not entirely controlled by the divine being: what is above the sky, what is beneath the earth, what stretches to the edges of existence outwards in every direction. "You," Paul says, "Are the One who thus penetrates all in order to become the bond of all, comprehending all the limits within yourself."[21]

In the Cross, then, Christ becomes the "bond of all," the interlinking weave penetrating all reality and bringing all together in union in Himself. Gregory has here shown how the Pauline *en Christo* theology (of the resurrection glory) is one with the theology of the Passion; and both harmonize in a cosmic theology of reconciliation. The largest of his treatments of the cosmic cross, however, is given in the *Great Catechetical Oration*,[22] where we notice how it comes close after the "baited hook" section; in other words where that imagery serves as a preface to this. He begins his discussion noting how many regard the Christian conception of the necessary death of God as a defective theology: illegitimately juxtaposing the conception of weakness with that of supreme power. Moreover the death by crucifixion was a shameful scandal to choose as central icon of the theology of salvation. To answer this Gregory says that the death was a simple corollary of his birth: an entering into mortality. But the whole syntax of the incarnation in history was affected as an act of power not of weakness since it was meant to regenerate a dying nature by giving it the power of life (the principle of resurrection). Here Gregory exegetes the Pauline theology of the Mystical Body of Christ:

> Since, then, what the whole of our nature needed was a lifting out of death, He stretches forth a hand, as it were, to prostrate man, and stooping down to our fallen corpse He came so far within the grasp of death as to touch a state of deadness himself, and then in His own body to bestow on our nature the principle

---

[21] *On the Three Day Interval*, 299–301.
[22] Op cit., chapter 32.

of the resurrection, raising along with Himself the whole of man, as He accomplished by His power. But his own flesh which was the receptacle of the Godhead had come from no other source than the concrete lump of our nature, and it was this that was raised up in the resurrection together with the Godhead. Following from this ... the resurrection principle of this single Member of Mankind [Christ], passes through the entire human race, as if the whole of mankind was a single living entity, and it is passed on from this single Member to the whole body by virtue of the continuity and oneness of the nature.[23]

For Gregory the Cosmic Cross is especially a symbol of the interpenetration of things human and divine, which the incarnation brings about as a new condition of existence. He goes on to conclude how God employs the Cosmic Cross to reconcile all of human nature with Divine presence to demonstrate the philanthropic mercy of the Godhead on one side, and the healing divinization of the mortal race on the other:

It is the property of the Godhead to pervade all things, and to extend itself through the length and breadth of the substance of existence in every part—for nothing would continue to be if it remained not within the existent ... the Divine Being ... This is exactly what we learn from the figure of the Cross. It is divided into four parts, so that there are the projections, four in number, from the central point where the whole converges upon itself; because He Who ... was stretched upon it is He Who binds together all things into Himself, and by Himself brings to one harmonious agreement the diverse natures of actual existences.[24]

Last of all I wish to come to Gregory's soteriological analogy (not "theory," we should note by now) of the capture of Leviathan, commonly called the "Fish-hook theory." I put it last because so many seem to put it first, apparently having read nothing other than this from Gregory of Nyssa. And I put it last because its rhetorical imagery serves in the *Great Catechetical Oration* to provide a preface to the theology of the Cosmic Cross, not a replacement for it. The idea has to be seen as a smaller part of the Nyssen's more fundamental thrust of argument in his theology of salvation, that the incarnation is the core dynamic of Christ's rescue of the Race through a *paideia* of repentance toward an ascent of divinization. Only in the light of all this can we contextualize the notion of the baited hook. It was, unfortunately for Gregory's reputation as a theologian of the atonement, too exciting an image to forget. This is why he put it in a

---

[23] *Catechetical Oration*, c. 32.
[24] *Catechetical Oration*, 32. A similar argument is found in Gregory's *Contra Eunomium* 3, 39–40, Geberhardt (1967), vol. 2, 121.

text designed for a more common audience, designed to illustrate two issues. The first is that the whole discourse is a reflection on the capture of Leviathan. He does indeed talk about catching a fish, but his exegetical mind is revolving around the Great Leviathan—the biblical symbol of all that is opposed to God's ordered Kingdom, namely, all that is chaotic, sinful, and dark. The second is that this is fundamentally a crowd pleaser meant to show the utility of deceit in the cause of *paideia*. It has annoyed many people largely because of the description of God and/or Christ as being deceitful.

The first of these many annoyed readers was his own teacher of Oratory, St. Gregory the Theologian, who made a censorious rebuttal of the utility of attributing deceit to God in his *45th Oration* along with a refutation of the whole notion of "ransom paid," if this was understood in any concretely graphic way.[25] It was Origen who had first stretched the Pauline idea of Christ's ransom[26] of humanity from the power of Satan (death) as comparable to the liberation (manumission) of a slave. The idea took its original force in Paul from the fact that legally speaking, manumitted slaves were "reassigned" from the service of a human master to the service of a divine master, in one of the temples of the gods. The freedman, now a *doulos theou* (as Paul also uses the concept), could expect that his god would not call on his services in the old manner. His divine slavery was, in fact, a full liberation. Origen rhetorically pushed this image to imply that Satan had acquired rights of dominion over fallen humanity,[27] and in this Gregory Nyssa follows his lead, while Gregory Nazianzen called for a setting aside of the ransom notion, in favor of the larger-scale argument in Origen of cosmic rehabilitation (in which both Gregorys followed his lead). All three theologians find this much more useful than any reliance on a Satisfaction theory of redemption, which they consider distasteful (largely influencing the whole of later Eastern Christian redemption theology which likewise finds the Western Church's sharply focused attention on Satisfaction theory, somewhat disturbing).

---

[25] Gregory of Nazianzen regarded all three concepts of deceit of Satan, a necessary ransom paid to an oppressor who had acquired rights over humanity, and God the Father somehow requiring "satisfaction" as completely brainless approaches to divine salvation gifted to the race out of love. And he criticized his younger mentor for appearing to encourage some of those attitudes in his Catechetical Oration. He rebuked Gregory of Nyssa particular for appearing to endorse the Ransom theory: "Was a ransom paid to the Evil One? It is a monstrous thought. To pay off the Evil One?—What an outrage! Well was it to pay a ransom to God then? But we were not in bondage to God so how could that be? And who could think the Father ever would delight in the blood of His Son?"

[26] See 2 Timothy 5–6; Mark 10.45.

[27] He derived this, I think, from his close reading of the Gospels and their doctrine of the role of the "Prince of this World."

Gregory of Nyssa, however, was clearly impressed by "elements" of the Ransom Theory as a form of popular image, and set it out in several parts of his *Catechetical Oration*. He starts by noting how humanity's fall is comprised of the inability to recognize what is truly good, because of our superficiality. It is easy to deceive human beings morally, he says, and applies the old legend of the dog and its reflection to show his point:

> Under these circumstances it is a matter of risk whether we humans happen to choose the real beauty, or whether we are diverted from choosing it by some deception arising from appearances ... This is what happened, we are told in the heathen fable, to the dog which looked sideways at its reflection in the water when it was carrying food in its mouth. For it let go of the real food, and, opened its jaws wide to swallow the reflection of it, ending up still hungry.[28]

The theme of deceit is important here to explain the moral dimension of soteriology. For Origen and the Cappadocians, the fall of humanity is fundamentally a moral alienation of the human consciousness from divine communion. They have no explanation of this other than ignorance proceeding from ignorance. The Race's choice of ugliness and death in preference to beauty and life is, for them, metaphysically incomprehensible; and can only arise out of malicious deceit on the part of superior evil powers played out on a more innocent, "younger" spiritual race of mankind. They imagine the terrestrial demons as encouraging this ignorance out of despair at their own fate, and so pressing humans to choose false realities instead of moral ends, thus keeping up the state of alienation from God that results in the death of beings who were once designed for immortality. In Gregory of Nyssa, as in Origen, the pedagogic motivation of the incarnation is paramount. Christ takes pity on a race that is willing to drop the real food from its mouth in order to grasp at the reflection of it in water. As in the "heathen fable" the moral point is driven home with humor. However, we are not meant to take it all that literally. In the twenty-second chapter of the same book, however, Gregory picks up the ransom theme of Paul, concerning a lord purchasing a slave from bondage, and he applies this to the necessity of someone wishing to liberate a slave who thus needs to pay the slave price in accordance with law. This time he does ascribe quasi-legal rights to the one who holds humanity under bondage: "Since we had voluntarily bartered away our freedom, it was necessary that no arbitrary method of recovery, but one that was

---

[28] . *Great Catechetical Oration*, 21.

in harmony with justice should be devised by Him who out of his goodness had undertaken our rescue."[29]

Gregory, in the section immediately following, draws out further aspects of the analogy. Satan, who was the slave master of the human race, and kept all things in bondage to death, and moral blindness, saw Christ walking the earth and was astounded at his great power. The miracles seemed to set Jesus aside as an Archetypal spiritual Man, and he lusted after the captivity of this creature, which was more precious to him than the countless powerless souls he already dominated. He wished to make an exchange, and Christ substituted himself, as slave payment, for the entire human race:

> Now unquestionably in not one of the men who had lived in history from the beginning of the world had [Satan] been conscious of any such circumstance as he observed surrounding this One who then manifested Himself. And here the Enemy saw in Him a chance to better his position.[30] This was why he chose him as a ransom for those who had been shut up in his prison of death. But to look on the clear power of God was beyond Satan's power, and so he could see in Him only that fleshly part of the nature which through sin he had so long held in bondage. And this was why the Godhead clothed itself in flesh, namely that by looking on that part which was congenial and akin to himself, the enemy would have no fear in approaching the Supreme Power, and might think that since these acts of power appeared only gradually in more and more splendour from the miracles, he should take them as an object of desire instead of a source of fear. And so, you see how goodness was here conjoined with justice, and how wisdom was not divorced from this too.[31]

Gregory in the following section argues that once the terms of the incarnation have been established, the mingling of deity and humanity in Christ, the Devil is lulled into a false sense of security approaching Christ. Not sensing the force of the deity in him, he comes at him like a ravenous beast. His image is that of the large fish or shark that snatches at the bait, not seeing the hook until it is too late:

> In order to ensure that his ransom on our behalf might be easily accepted by the one who demanded it, He hid the Godhead under the veil of our nature, so that just as it is with a ravenous fish, the hook of the Deity might be gulped

---

[29] *Catechetical Oration*, 22.
[30] By taking possession of the spiritual powers Christ had manifested on earth.
[31] *Catechetical Oration*, 23.

down along with the bait of the flesh. For in this way, Life was brought into the House of Death and Light shone in the darkness, so that all that was diametrically opposed to light and life might vanish away.[32]

His central image here is very graphically the beast (Leviathan) taking the bait. One remembers that in symbological code, the jaws of the beast are the gates of Hell and Death. And it is this latter aspect that he sees (and intends to convey) as the dynamic of salvation. However memorable the image of the beast's capture is, then, it yields in his text to the concluding section where he speaks of the victory of light: Life is brought into the House of Death.

Aristotle had long before divided a rhetorical oration into three forms: *ethos*, *pathos*, and *logos*. They were discrete styles of presenting an argument: turning around the idea's (and the speaker's) credibility, the graphic impact the idea had as an emotional persuasion, and the quality of the arguments the concept could muster in its support. In this instance of his work, Gregory is applying the idea of enslavement and redemptive purchase with an extension of the *pathos* to include the motif of the deceit of the slave owner/the capture of the dangerous sea monster. It is subordinate, then, to the idea of victory over death in which the context is shown to be the *logos* of his doctrinal argument here. The theme of the "capturer captured" was an ancient one present in much antique literature, and it is applied here by Gregory to make a common appeal to the audience in the *Catechetical Oration*, which was itself designed to offer to preachers a straightforward guide to complex doctrines: a graphic analogy of how Christ communicated Life to the Race as the quintessential dynamic of salvation. Perhaps we have since been led aside by focusing too much on the details of the image, and imputing to him the theme of "ignoble deceitfulness" which he (explicitly) tries to avoid. This imagery would originally have been taken as a delightful joke by his ancient listeners, who loved stories of bazaar swindles (Luke 16:1–8; Mt. 13:44)!

In short, I suggest that the "beast caught on the hook" imagery is comparable to the "Lion roaring for its prey" that 1 Peter 5:8 talks about. The latter is fearsome: but not meant to be taken literally as if he was a lion. Likewise Gregory's images of the Satan tricked by getting the worst part of a bargain, as in a bazaar,[33]

---

[32] Ibid., 24.
[33] Ibid., 26. Satan gets his comeuppance: a moral lesson taught to him tricking him like a fool since he tricked humanity into death as if they were fools: "He who practised deception receives in return that very treatment, the seeds of which he had himself sown of his own free will. He who first deceived man by the bait of sensual pleasure is himself deceived by the presentment of the human form [in Christ]."

or the monster hooked in the moment of its savage attack, were meant to elicit from the ancient audience a whoop of delight: exactly what Gregory described earlier as "cries of victory suitable for those who have triumphed." But at the end of the day they are images pressed into the service of his overarching message. The incarnation of the Logos into humanity restores the lost gift of Life to the Race.

While these images of his in the *Catechetical Oration* would have pleased an antique crowd, they are not theories that bear the force of "logical" doctrine, for this would be to mistake his rhetorical *pathos* section for what follows in his *logos* section of the *Oration*. Several modern commentators have not been at all aware of this division of antique rhetorical argument and have simply added image upon image as if they were all aspects of his logical doctrine. In each instance of his use of the deceptive bait image, Gregory immediately goes on to speak of the honorableness of God's actions in the incarnation, and the manner in which his work demonstrates moral *paideia*, and ontological rescue of the race from death. He carefully follows Origen, his esteemed mentor, who set it as an exegetical axiom for all theological texts: "Nothing inappropriate to God." And so the deceit/bait imagery is subordinated to the main point of an illustration of the Victory over Death motif. This can be seen quite clearly in the peroration to this same section of his *Catechetical Oration* when Gregory sums up what he thinks he has demonstrated by his graphic images, and we see it is the theology of victorious reconciliation, nothing more: certainly not satisfaction or retribution theory:

> Thus have we demonstrated that God's goodness, wisdom, justice, power, incapability of decay, are all of them in evidence in the doctrine of this economy of Salvation in which we exist. His goodness is caught sight of in His election to save lost man; His wisdom and justice have been displayed in the method of our salvation; His power, in that though born in the likeness and fashion of a man, on the lowly level of our nature ... he nevertheless produced those powers peculiar and natural to Him. For it is the peculiar effect of light to make darkness vanish, and of life to destroy death. And since we had been led astray from the right path, and diverted from our original life, and brought under the sway of death, what is there at all unbelievable in the lesson we are taught by the Gospel mystery? For it is this: that cleansing reaches out to those who are defiled in sin, and life reaches out to the dead, and guidance to wanderers, in order that defilement may be cleansed, error corrected, and what was dead restored to life.[34]

---

[34] *Great Catechetical Oration*, 24.

In a final reference to the theme of trickery, in *Catechetical Oration* 26, Gregory shows that his master-theme has been pedagogical restitution of health (immortality and communion with God). He again reflects back here on the theme of "tricking the devil" and argues that this, like many other instances of deceitfulness, is basically an act of kindness (*philanthropia*). One might think of the many instances a parent leads a child down the right path by parental guidance somewhat akin to trickery. Gregory offers a practical illustration derived from his own practice as a part-time surgeon; arguing that the doctor often has to give a patient a bitter pill for a better end, and sugarcoat it in the process to make the recipient take the course of action beneficial to him. Surgery has to be forced on really ill people, and they hate it (pre-analgesic days); but they come to thank the doctor "eventually." He concludes:

In like manner, when, after long periods of time, the evil of our nature, which is presently confused in it and growing side by side,[35] has been expelled, and when those who are now lying in Sin have been restored to their primal state, a harmony of thanksgiving will rise up from all creation, even from those who in the process of the purgation have suffered chastisement. Such are the benefits that the great mystery of the Divine incarnation grants to us. For in those points in which He was mingled with humanity, passing as He did through all the accidents proper to human nature, such as birth, rearing, growing up, and advancing even to the taste of death, He accomplished all the results mentioned, freeing both man from evil, and healing even the introducer of evil himself. For the chastisement, however painful, of moral disease is a healing of its weakness.

In his *Homily on the Holy Pascha* Gregory likewise describes the Incarnate economy as the Lord being compared to a hero who sees a man drowning having fallen through the ice of a fast river. "And in order to save the one who was perishing as a result of the deception"[36] he boldly casts himself into the turmoil of history. He comes to save.

Conclusion

Ransom transactions, even those accomplished by a certain amount of underhanded shenanigans, have been regularly attributed to Gregory of Nyssa as a

---

[35] Matthew 13.25–30.
[36] *Homily on the Holy and Saving Pascha*, 248.

distinctive part of his soteriology, but such themes are not primary in his work. He has led his readers astray, perhaps, by some of the vivid imagery present in his most popularizing discourse, the *Great Catechetical Oration*. But even then a close reading of those passages that speak of ransoms, baiting the fish, and so forth reveal that he subordinates all of the graphic illustrations to the overarching theme that the salvation brought by Christ to the human race is a moral *paideia* that is ontologically rooted. In our separation from God, we divorced our being from the source of its life and light, thus our proximity to God. In returning us to union with God—a deifying grace Christ communicates to the Race through his own incarnate instantiation (*hypostasis*) as Redeemed Adam—Gregory argues that the Inhominated Logos recreates humanity and restores it to the original plan of its creaturely being. Namely, he restores it to immortal closeness to Deity: a *symbiosis* which the God-Man himself exemplifies, of course, as *theopoiesis* hypostatized.

The breaking down of Gregory's soteriology into discrete theories, following his rhetorical images as if they were propositional, has been a mistaken pathway of much twentieth-century patristic interpretation in regard to the Nyssen's soteriology. It has largely misunderstood both the extensive dependence of patristic thought on apostolic (exegetical) patterns (especially Paul) and has regularly confused fundamental literary structures (*pathos* with *ethos* and *logos*) in the intellectual patterns of ancient discourse. The deceit of the devil and the ransom paid to get us free are both graphic images meant to elicit the delight of familiarity from an audience. As such they belong to the modes of *pathos* and *ethos*; subordinate clauses, as it were, to exemplify what Gregory is really saying about soteriology—namely, that Christ has achieved a cosmically scaled victory over Death. This victory itself devolves (as we can see from his majority of other discourses where he does not lay on so many supportive images, presuming a more scholarly audience) into the notion that the incarnation effects an ontological change in humanity: no longer mortal but immortal by virtue of returning to the vision of God. Gregory's master theme, like that of Origen, Athanasius, and Gregory of Nazianzus before him, is that humanity, in Christ's divine incarnation, is given back the capacity for the divinizing vision of God (*theopoiesis*). It is this communion, a veritable participation in the Godhead (*Metousia Theou*), which is our life and beatitude. To it we shall ascend: an ascent that begins here on earth in our fallen condition but develops everlastingly in an *Epektasis* which is an ecstatic outreach and extension of our being's limits, driven by divine Eros. In short, this is a cosmically scaled theology of salvation that radically links moral *paideia* and ontological rescue and has a breath-taking universal scope across time and space. It is a Christ-Mysticism that is both immediately concrete and personal, as well as ecclesially collective, embracing all the noetic orders within it: angelic as well as human.

10

Anselmian Atonement

Katherine Sonderegger

Perhaps no other theologian was so honored in his day and rebuked in ours as St. Anselm of Canterbury.[1] A life led in reforming monasteries and powerful episcopal sees is hardly likely to be a placid one, and Anselm knew intimidation and exile throughout his episcopacy, as did the theologian-bishops of the early church. But even during that heavy weather, Anselm found safe harbor in the straightforward praise and admiration of his generation, friend and foe alike—for his counsel and friendship to monks, his gritty defense of the church's privilege, and above all, for his theological mastery, depth, and startling independence of mind. It is hard to say, of course, how widely read Anselm's doctrinal treatises may have been in his own day. For myself, I cannot feel persuaded that St. Thomas Aquinas had read the *Proslogion* directly, for his comments on

---

[1] As befits a Doctor of the Church, the literature on Anselm of Canterbury in enormous and growing. The student who would like to gain a foothold on this material might begin with the general biographies of Anselm: Benedicta Ward, *Anselm of Canterbury: His Life and Legacy* (London: SPCK, 2009); Sally N. Vaughn, *Archbishop Anselm, 1093–1109* (New York: Routledge, 2012); G. R. Evans, *Anselm* (Wilton, CT: Morehouse, 1989); and a series by the great medievalist R. W. Southern, *The Life of St Anselm, Archbishop of Canterbury* (London: Thomas Nelson, 1962); *St Anselm and His Biographer* (Cambridge, 1963); and *Saint Anselm: A Portrait in a Landscape* (Cambridge, 1990). Three collections of Anselm's writings will also be of help: B. Davies and G. R. Evans, eds., *Anselm of Canterbury, the Major Works* (Oxford, 1998); Anselm, *The Letters of Anselm of Canterbury*, trans. Walter Fröhlich (Cistercian Publications, 1990); Benedicta Ward, ed., *The Prayers and Meditations of St Anselm* (London: Penguin, 1973). Then, more specialized studies: Sandra Visser and Thomas Williams, *Anselm* (Oxford, 2009); B. Davies and B. Leftow, eds., *The Cambridge Companion to Anselm* (Cambridge, 2004); G. R. Evans, *Anselm and a New Generation* (Oxford, 1980); Giles E. M. Gasper and H. Kohlenberger, *Anselm and Abelard* (Toronto: Pontifical Institute of Medieval Studies, 2006); and then a series of monographs from Ashgate, a major publisher of works on Anselm: David S. Hogg, *Anselm of Canterbury: the Beauty of Theology* (2004); Giles E. M. Gasper, *Anselm of Canterbury and his Theological Inheritance* (2004); Daniel Deme, *The Christology of Anselm of Canterbury* (2003). Readers of a philosophical bent will want to examine works on the Proslogion and Monologion (the "Ontological Argument"), beginning with the justly famous collection edited by Alvin Plantinga, *The Ontological Argument, from St Anselm to Contemporary Philosophers* (London: MacMillan, 1968). The entry "Ontological Arguments" in the Stanford Encyclopedia of Philosophy by Graham Oppy will be helpful as well, including the extensive bibliography.

an Anselmian-like argument for God's necessary existence fail to observe the nuance and distinction of Anselm's own proof—a rare failing in the *Summa*. The treatise that has dominated Anselmian doctrines of atonement—*Cur Deus Homo*—may not have circulated widely in Anselm's lifetime; the historical record is uncertain. Yet, his larger notions of exchange, restoration, representation, and satisfaction appear to have influenced broad circles of theological debate in his day and for some generations after. Certainly, Thomas's own account of the atoning death of Christ bears the imprint of these larger Anselmian themes.

All of this changes in our own day. In an odd fashion, Anselm succeeds with greater theological éclat in our day than in his own: He is more widely read in our time than his, more closely studied and more securely stapled to every syllabus and every course on the Person and Work of Christ—much more in our time than in his. Yet Anselm rides this wave of theological homage at some peril. Since the nineteenth century, Anselm belongs in every discussion on Christ's atoning work, not as hero and teacher, but rather as *the* exemplar of a wrong turn in Christology. He has become the poor Doctor of the Church, the Latin theologian who can offer the very least to modern Christian reflection on the Passion and on the larger themes in Christ's redeeming work. Adolf Harnack gave voice to an entire generation of Protestant academic theologians when he described Anselm as confined to a "model"—not doctrine—of atonement, a wooden superstructure built upon the hardpan of the *Wergild*, a price levied on human injury or death.[2] Not Roman law but rather Germanic custom, the *Wergild* aimed to ward off violence and the sword by placing a value on the human head—the higher the status, the higher the tribute—exchanging conflict for a payment that in turn could pacify and restore communal ties. Such primitive exchange, Harnack warned, could hardly serve a Christian generation seeking spiritual relief from the market, not a dogmatic application of it.

Later theologians have judged Anselm's *Cur Deus Homo* more harshly still. Anselm is thought to teach a God who demands a cruel and violent end to His own Son as ruthless payment to a Divine, and abstract, justice. Anselm teaches a juridical notion of atonement, others say, that accords pride of place to vengeance, to honor, and to punishment for sin. Worse, Anselm values a God, his harshest critics charge, whose mechanism for "dealing with sin" is frankly abusive: the violent suffering of the Innocent whose absolute trust in His Father was met with terrifying silence, and the stern counsel that the Son's rejection and

---

[2] Adolf von Harnack, *The History of Dogma*, 3rd edn, trans. N. Buchanan (New York: Dover Books, 1960), Vol. V. 323–330; Vol. VI. 54–79.

pain was all for the good—the good of the whole earth. From such mixture of savagery and piety, abuse is built, they say, and even Anselm's most fervid disciple, the monk Boso, admits worries of just this kind.

A few more minor charges round out the whole. What becomes of the large covenant narrative of salvation in Anselm's foreshortened and starkly individualistic account? What makes Christ's earthly ministry—his teaching and healing and feeding and exorcism—worthy of so little attention in His saving work? Are they beneath notice? Is not Anselm's bold claim to treat the God-creature relation "*remoto Christi*" a symptom of the larger problem with the whole work—an abstract and colorless rationalism that even Anselm himself cannot maintain? Further, Anselm's account of the "debt payment" and "satisfying offer" appears dangerously Nestorian to some, as if Christ's humanity could be given the autonomous work of innocent dying, apart from the concomitant and Personal Union of the Deity. In addition, Anselm's early scholastic handling of the idea of infinity, both in the assessment of sin and in the calculus of Christ's personal worth, seems to his philosophically minded critics neither cogent nor persuasive.[3]

Well, this is quite a charge sheet. But all the same, I propose we stay the course. We need not find Anselm a bright and shining lamp to see that in *Cur Deus Homo* and in his prayers and meditations, he grasps an inalienable dimension of Christ's saving work: Christ's self-offering as remedy for sin. There is much to marvel at in Anselm's broad Doctrine of Atonement: his careful treatment of modal categories, especially in the notion of Divine and human necessity; his lovely evocation of the "fitting" and the beautiful in joining of New Covenant to Old; the breathtaking reach of his vision of Christ's saving work, from the fall of the primal angels to the great Judgment Seat of Christ in the end times; his great freedom in handling Divine honor and sovereignty; and the delicate balance of the substitutionary and representative elements in his doctrine of Christ's atoning work. All these are remarkable strengths in Anselm's theology.

So disparate are the assessments of Anselm's work—my own, and the critics', from Aulén to Harnack and theologians of our own day—that a reader may be forgiven the growing suspicion that there are two entirely different Anselms

---

[3] I have summarized with broad strokes a number of movements and texts in modern dogmatics. A sampling of these criticisms may be found in: von Harnack, *The History of Dogma*; Gustaf Aulén, *Christus Victor: A Historical Study of the Three Main Types of the Idea of Atonement*, trans. A. G. Herbert (New York: Macmillan, 1951); Timothy Gorringe, *God's Just Vengeance* (Cambridge: Cambridge University Press, 1996); J. Denny Weaver, *The Non-violent Atonement* (Grand Rapids, MI: Eerdmans, 2001); Darby Kathleen Ray, *Deceiving the Devil: Atonement, Abuse and Ransom* (Cleveland: Pilgrim Press, 1998); John McLeod Campbell, *The Nature of the Atonement and Its Relation to the Remission of Sins and Eternal Life* (London: Macmillan, 1869).

in play here. One Anselm seems the province of medievalists: the "historical Anselm" is a monastic and church theologian, a powerful prelate and passionate spiritual friend, the author of prayers and prayerful treatises that breathe the air of the cloister, redolent with psalms, deep repentance and longing, and the grace-filled arc of salvation. This Anselm draws his meditative theology from the whole of Holy Scripture, from the lives of saints and martyrs, and from the dazzling vision of the Heavenly City, alive with the light of angels and the songs of the blessed. It is an intellectually rich, humane, and inviting portrait. The other Anselm belongs to modern theological debate: the "theological Anselm" is a Christian intellect overcome by scrupulosity, calculating a burden that can only fill a sensitive conscience with despair, consumed by a logic that turns the pardon and compassion of redemption into a pitiless demand for naked justice, and entreats a God who can only be termed a prisoner of His own relentless honor. This is a portrait of a theologian hemmed in on every side by a penitential system and a notion of reparation that can peddle only a "miserable exchange"—Christ's glorious atoning victory for a gruesome calculation of penalty and satisfaction, exacted from an Innocent to save a sin-sick world.

These two portraits, the "historical" and the "theological Anselm," only diverge further when one studies the texts of Anselm closely and in their full range. Oddly, the more one corrects, it seems, the more the distortions live on. Modern theological criticism of Anselm appears to miss its real, historical object by no small distance, and yet the modern portrait survives and flourishes. And in truth, it is this modern Anselm, the "theological Anselm" of the critics, that warrants any entry in a Companion to the Atonement; the "historical Anselm" seems to have left too small a mark on his contemporaries—at least as a theologian of the Atonement—to demand such extensive examination and preservation. So an essay on Anselm for a Companion to the Atonement must look Janus-like, forward and back. The "theological Anselm" must step first on stage, as it is his "logic of Atonement" that carries weight and censure in our modern doctrinal debates. But the second Anselm, the "historical Anselm" of the medievalist, must appear by story's end, because it is only by an encounter with this fuller, richer, and humane Anselm that theology can be properly instructed by this luminous intellect and passionate lover of souls.

We begin with the heart of the "miserable exchange," the dry nub at the core of modern Anselmian atonement theory: the calculus of sin. In *Cur Deus Homo*, Anselm himself gave this chapter the ominous title, "How Heavy the Weight of Sin Is" (I.21).[4] Many moderns are offended by his relentless focus on

---

[4] All page numbers within parentheses in the chapter are from Anselm's work.

the intolerable burden of sin, and indeed his prayers give vivid testimony to a penitent heart crushed by the defilement and shame of sin.[5] But more offensive still to modern ears is the sound of the calculating machine, toting up and taking measure of sins, as if so many pounds of wheat and tare. It is the infinite weight of sin, after all, that appears to drive the hard bargain of Divine justice. Therefore, we must ask first in our exploration of the "theological Anselm" if sin be weighed and calculated at all? Is "quantity" a category fittingly applied to a Christian Doctrine of Atonement? Anselm answers confidently, yes, indeed. His reasons for doing so, however, might surprise; and instruct.

"Let us hypothesize," Anselm begins, "that those things which you [Boso] proposed you could offer in repayment for sin are not a debt which you owe, and let us see whether they can suffice as recompense [*satisfactio*] for a single sin, even so small a sin as one glance contrary to the will of God."[6] Note the neuralgic terms already in play: "repayment," "debt," "recompense" or "satisfaction," and a "calculation," "one small sin," and "a single glance away." In the previous chapter, Anselm's interlocutor, Boso, has already suggested that "penitence, a contrite and humbled heart, fasting and many kinds of bodily labor, the showing of pity through giving and forgiveness, and obedience" (II.7) could be offered as payment proportionate to the "magnitude of sin." It is these tokens of monastic contrition that Anselm proposes to weigh up against the sins of disobedient creatures. Why will these not atone for sins? Indeed, why will a Merciful God not pardon, through and even apart from these acts of contrition? The "Weight of Sin" is designed to answer these pressing and very modern-sounding questions.

Though not mentioned explicitly here in the text, Anselm appears to draw upon the Pauline notion, central to the argument of the Letter to the Romans, of the religious search for a "righteousness of one's own" (Rom. 5:19; 10:3). Anselm imagines that the contrite sinner relies implicitly upon the good or righteousness of his or her own religious life to *justify* or outweigh the evil of sin. The *calculus*, that is, belongs to the sinner; it is the fallen creature's method of "handling sin." Anselm puts it this way: "Consider, with exclusive reference to the particular sin in question, whether you can commit it in order to *secure your own redemption*" (I.21; emphasis mine). This is a theme dear to an Augustinian heart, that we secretly, or proudly, imagine we save ourselves, through our own

---

[5] See, for example, the Prayers to St Mary, in Ward, *The Prayers and Meditations of St Anselm*, 107–126.
[6] *Anselm of Canterbury: The Major Works*, ed. B. Davies and G. R. Evans, trans. Janet Fairweather (New York, Oxford University Press, 1998), 305.

works, whether in obedience to the moral law or even in acts of particular pride, in disobedience.

Anselm has his own case study in mind, but we might gain greater insight into it by considering a more homespun example from our own day. Consider speeding down the highway to rush a sick child to the hospital. We break several laws, conventional and even moral, in our headlong frenzy to the emergency room. But these, we reckon, are justified! (The law of double effect has been engineered for cases of just this kind.) We run the risk of hitting other cars and striking vulnerable pedestrians; we even take into our calculus the danger we run to the child herself. All this we balance against the great good of trained minds and hands that cure and save—save *this very one*, this child, dear to our heart. We calculate wrongdoing, that is, in most everyday decisions, and we do so in order to justify an act or an aim. Ignoring Romans 6:1, it is not foreign, not "medieval" or "pedantic," to calculate sin; indeed, we can scarcely do without it.

Quantifying sin does not simply belong to one era or one style of moral deliberation: it is not the act only of the consequentialist, say, or the confessor, weighing out the measure of penance for wrong done. Rather, calculating or quantifying wrong is the framework of the everyday moral life. Less a theory than a rule-of-thumb, weighing out sin in a rough and ready manner gives us a guide to daily practice. It is the stuff of casuistry; but much more besides. In Heaven above, it is otherwise, we may be sure; but here below we see and take up few absolutes but instead many limited evils and goods, and we must weigh them, willy-nilly, one against the other. We know how good an act or aim might be by the sin it outweighs. We know the measure of our wrongdoing, for good or ill, by the greater good we grasp or lose, if evil outstrip it. All this we might term a "negative" doctrine of sin: the evil of a particular act is weighed against the good end that outbalances it, the shadow to good's bright light.

In Anselm's own case study, his own moral counting-house, the notion of infinity makes a noisy entrance. The infinite, both Divine and creaturely, became a topic of considerable and growing fascination to the early scholastics. It now becomes salient as a measure of sin itself. Anselm asks us to consider a single act of disobedience—a glance in another direction, which would save whole worlds of living beings. Indeed, "an infinite multiplicity of universes," laid out before the viewer, could be saved from destruction by our casting our eyes upon them. Now, Anselm does not argue that the glance away is evil in itself, nor does he deny that such an act could spring from a good heart. It is critical to Anselm's entire argument that we see that he is probing our attempts and intuitions about *justification*, about good acts that outweigh the bad. We might very well consider the perishing worlds to be worth saving; just this thought, after all, makes the glance away a grave and very real temptation. Anselm does not dispute that! His point, rather, is this: the calculus we carry out as we live our moral and mortal lives cannot justify us *before Almighty God*.

We see that first in this "negative" form: the good of infinite worlds saved by our disobedience does not outweigh, Boso admits, the wrong of our rebellion, even a brief darting-away of our eyes. Now, many modern Christians find the "theological Anselm" repellant on just these grounds: how could it be a sin to disobey God should a glance save an infinite world of worlds? Our own intuition may well tell us that the infinite good of lives saved from perishing must outweigh and justify any wrong before God. It is important to see that such intuitions do not *contradict* Anselm; indeed, they *confirm* him. Anselm begins this whole section of *Cur Deus Homo* with the conviction that we are mistaken about sin: we have not taken the measure of "the great weight of sin." We frankly disbelieve that sin is serious. Many, many good deeds, we reason, justify sin and wrongdoing; and the sins we commit are much like the glance away—small, petty infractions that have to be viewed, on the whole by and large, in the light of the contrition and discipline and love we strive to carry out. We are minimizers, that is, and Anselm knows that full well. His aim throughout Book I is to show us that "we live very dangerously" (citing Boso, Book 21, 306). The "negative" assessment of sin is designed to show us that "everything that is not God," even infinite worlds of the not-God, worlds that are created good and very good, cannot outweigh or justify sin against the Holy Creator.

Now to convince the very large schools of moral creatures that do not share Boso's intuition, Anselm introduces his "positive account" of sin. We must take the measure of sin not merely by the good act that may justify it, but principally by the wrong it does a particular person. Anselm here agrees with his modern critics: sin is fundamentally a "personal matter," not a lifeless, objective "thing." Indeed, the universe itself is a personal realm: we walk always in God's sight. (Just this we quietly deny when we assume the calculation of good and evil is ours alone, a dice thrown in a shadowy and an all-too-human universe.) And this Holy God has issued an explicit command; we are not left without exact direction from a Living and Personal God. The good of infinite worlds of creatures saved does not justify or outweigh the sin of glancing away from God just because this act is against *God* and His express command. We are to weigh sin against the Person who is harmed, not against another earthly good that might arise from wrong done. And here, once again, the "theological Anselm" comes in for sharp rebuke.

What kind of savage demi-god takes offense at a creature whose glance is all for the good? Do we worship a proud tyrant who believes his own honor matters more than worlds of worlds? Surely Scripture teaches a God of mercy, who desires not the death of a sinner! Even Boso—he of the well-trained Anselmian intuitions—complains that God teaches forgiveness to all His disciples. Should He not, He supremely, forgive?[7] Go, learn what this means, "I desire mercy; not sacrifice": that is the counter-text held against the theological Anselm and his Satisfaction Theory. Here the benevolence of God comes under threat, no small risk to any proper Christian Doctrine of Atonement. We want to attend to Anselm's position with special care just here.

To sin against God is to injure His honor: Anselm is quite firm on this point. And to our modern ears all this sounds like so much feudalism, run riot in the field of doctrine. To be sure, "honor," especially as it is tied to person and office, belongs squarely in imperial, monarchial societies. But we need not reduce theological idiom to the culture out of which it springs. Indeed our very ability to learn from the doctors of the church rests on a non-reductive account of theological discourse. (Of course much more could be said here about historicism, translation, and cultural integrity.) Could we not say, in more modern idiom, that certain acts take on a measure of harm or cruelty or folly in proportion to the significance and intimacy of the person wronged? This is the second form of calculation in sin that can be expressed, mutatis mutandis, in the intuitions of a modern age. Consider the long overdue phone call to a neighbor and to one's mother. (Again, much ethical theory is subsumed here quietly about the particular and concrete in moral decision-making.) The intuition may be argued against on certain abstract principles, but it is the rare conscientious son or daughter, I would wager, who would treat the slight of a missed telephone call as "all the same" between the neighbor and the mother. Our intuitions are strongly formed, I would say, by ties of loyalty, intimacy, and obligation; and these belong to particular persons, in special relation to us, to our culture, and to our flourishing. The salience of the person—her irreplaceable significance in our lives—weighs heavily in our moral reasoning. When we object—"You did *that* to your own *mother*?"—we replicate the form of Anselm's claim that sin is principally a wrong against the Person and Honor of God.

Such a "personal calculation" remains notoriously difficult to fix. Anselm wisely refrains from offering a mechanism for weighing such loving fealty.

---

[7] See, for example, Book 1, Chapter 12, on whether it is fitting for God to forgive a sin out of mercy alone.

Rather he appeals once again to our intuitions. When we fervently admit—"we would do anything for her!"—we do not offer an enumerated list of the tasks we would undertake for the beloved, nor do we aim to express the conviction that fifteen acts of love would be far more acceptable than twelve. We intend something far more tangible, earthy, and global than all that. Our deeds carry our heart: that is closer to the calculus here. The Good who is God outweighs infinite worlds of worlds; indeed, outstrips the good of saving them.[8] God's Goodness is Infinite, then—"positively Infinite," in later scholastic terms. But unlike the negative form, the positive calculus remains ineffable. It is just who God is, what I mean by the very word "God," that He is beyond any creaturely worth. Always He is greater: from this worshipping impulse springs the Name of God evoked in the *Proslogion*, "That than which none greater can be conceived" (II).

Now, Anselm is equally firm in his conviction that God and His honor are not in truth harmed by our sins. "Nothing can be added to, or subtracted from, the honour of God, in so far as it relates to God himself," Anselm tells Boso. "For this same honour is, in relation to him, inherently incorruptible and in no way capable of change" (I.15). The language of "debt," "obligation," and "injury," then, does not in fact express a *transaction* between God and sinner, such that "recompense," "satisfaction," or "repayment" conveys a metaphysical transfer from creature to Creator. Here the Germanic convention of the *wer-gilt*, the blood-price, has distracted us from the actual metaphysical crisis and remedy Anselm has in mind. The payment we owe our Maker does not establish peace between injured parties; it does not compensate for loss or restore dignity and well-being through gifts in kind. The weight of sin, when calculated positively, comes to this: it wrongs One who exceeds infinitely an infinite universe of worlds. (This is no theological correlate to the telephone call, followed by a bouquet of flowers!) We might suspect something of a Cantor-like cardinality of infinite sets here, but I think we might borrow from another tool in Cantor's workshop. The Infinite Dignity of God stands in relation to the infinite worlds of creatures, something like the Absolute Infinity does to the transfinite numbers. They are radically incommensurate; a radical difference in kind. The metaphysical character of the God-world relation in Anselm's theology forbids any real exchange of payment or restitution. The work done in Atonement is by and for the sinner: it establishes the *sinner's* justice, not God's. Far from the Moloch who demands the blood of his children to salve his fury, the God of Anselm is the Supreme Good who rules His kingdom

---

[8] Anselm offers to Boso the consolation of a Creator remaking His lost world, an homage, perhaps, to Noah's flourishing after the great flood.

in serene and benevolent sovereignty. All that He does and all that He commands is *for* the sinner: God's Honor is "vicarious" in just this sense.

The "historical Anselm" will aid us in seeing this point more clearly. Anselm the monk and spiritual friend knew with the passion reserved for the deeply observant that God was the Source and Exemplar of all loves, earthly and celestial. In his "Prayer for Friends," Anselm lifts up his intercession for the friends he dearly needed and helped in his religious vocation:

> So love them, you source of love, by whose command and gift I love them; love them, Author and Giver of love, for your own sake, not for mine, and make them love you with all their heart, all their soul, and all their mind, so that they will and speak and do only what pleases you and is expedient for them.[9]

And not simply in invocation and intercession does Anselm stretch out his hands to a Benevolent God! In *Cur Deus Homo*, Anselm notes that "God does many good things, in all manner of ways, for the benefit of wrong-doers" (289); indeed, the "Supreme Wisdom changes [a sinner's or bad angel's] wrong desire or action into the order and beauty of the universal scheme of things" (ibid.). This "universal scheme" is the Serene Wisdom by which the whole world is ordered in beauty, preserved and directed for the flourishing and beatitude of the creatures within it. So strongly sounds this note of beauty, throughout the treatise, that we would not be far wrong to call Anselm's Doctrine of God the Doctrine of the Beautiful One.

God has created the universe, Anselm holds, in order that rational beings enjoy Him forever in the Celestial City, the Home of the Blessed. *That*, and not some abstract justice, drives the workings of Anselm's entire Doctrine of Atonement. We owe Almighty God just everything because He has made the world for Himself: the universe of angels and human beings are fashioned for a joyful eternity with their Maker. This is the majestic sweep of Anselm's vision. All the ways and works of God, from before time until the ages of ages, aim toward the Peaceable City, an ordered family of nations and angelic beings who together and in harmony praise their Creator and bless Him. Anselm is quick to note that the Creator is not bound to exalt and glorify His creatures in this way; Anselm's famed "necessity" does not spring from his Doctrine of Creation. Rather, a luminous and glorious light over-spreads his vision of the universe, a beauty born of Divine grace and rational order, that speaks of the Creator's fitting and lovely aim to gather all creatures freely to Himself. Here is where "God's

---

[9] Anselm, *Prayers and Meditations*, 212–215, ll. 77, 78; 81–87.

grace meets with praise": the universe rings out with thanksgiving as Creation gives way to Consummation, and the wedding feast begins.

Now something has gone horribly wrong with this great pilgrimage of praise. The beautiful and the harmonious has been marred, disordered, and ignored. Anselm's Doctrine of Sin, as we have seen, is a full-throated lament. But it is important to see too that the despoliation of sin stands out sharply against the luminous arc of a creation destined for glory. Anselm teaches that angelic rebellion and human sin *necessitate* a Divine restoration of order. *Cur Deus Homo* offers complex and demanding arguments about modal properties—the possible and the necessary, chiefly—and shows Anselm at his most scholastic in his worries over freedom, Divine and human. The famed "necessity of the God-man" haunts the modern reception of the "theological Anselm," so it is important to begin matters aright. The principal necessity in Anselm's Doctrine of Atonement, the motive power of the whole, lies in the Divine Being, and not in some iron-clad logic of God's *opera ad extra*. God is not necessarily a Creator; but He is necessarily Just and Good. This just *is* His Being, and Anselm will make much of this in his *Monologion*, an Augustinian treatise on the Doctrine of God. "If we are faithless, He remains faithful, for He cannot deny Himself": this verse from 2 Timothy (2:13) might well sum up Anselm's notion of Divine Necessity. Now, we should be quick to say that Anselm does not conceive of necessity as a form of coercion to which God Himself must bow down and serve. Like Augustinians of every age, Anselm affirms a form of necessity that is compatible with, indeed identical to, Divine grace and sovereignty.

> Ultimately, God does nothing under compulsion of necessity—because he is in no way forced to do, or prohibited from doing, anything ... The necessity to which I am referring is plainly nothing other than the unchangeability of God's honour, which he possesses of himself, and from no one apart from himself. (II.5)

So strongly does Anselm defend this Self-governing and sovereign necessity that he can make the startling concession: "For this reason, 'necessity' is a misnomer" (II.5). God freely binds Himself, and upholds His Bond necessarily: He cannot deny Himself.

As the Absolute Just One, God will exercise His Justice *either* as punishment *or* restoration. An important historical correction to the theological Anselm springs from seeing clearly this dilemma. Necessarily, God punishes or restores; but not each one, necessarily. It is not necessary for God to punish, and indeed Anselm believes that the extraordinary truth of the Gospel is that the Good and Just God has in fact carried out a massive restoration of the whole world, *rather than* a fiery condemnation and penalty. But the dilemma—punishment or satisfaction—remains necessary. Simple pardon of sinners does not satisfy this Divine necessity. Principally this stems from Anselm's conviction that forgiveness of sin does not repair the breach: order is not restored, and the sinner is left spoiled and defiled, like a muddy pearl, placed unwashed in a treasure chest (I.20, where he quietly comments on Mt. 20). Either arm of the dilemma realizes God's Just Nature, not equally but truly. Were God to punish sinners only, Divine Justice would be served by exacting from the rebellious what they do not freely offer. But if satisfaction is made, by sinners or by Another, Divine Justice is served by setting to rights what God intended from of old, that all creatures would reside with their Creator in glory. This is the more fitting, more beautiful, and more merciful expression of the Divine Justice, and it is the form through which God's own gracious aim for His creatures is preserved, directly and majestically.

Yet, once again, the very notion of justice, Divine and human, so central to Anselm's Doctrine of Atonement, strikes Anselm's critics as pitiless and ironclad, a poor substitute for mercy, the attribute so widely praised in our day. Two sides of this criticism might occupy our attention here. On one side is the revulsion some critics voice for the relentless press of justice, in the Divine Being and in His ways with creatures. Is God in truth a Supreme and Unremitting hammer of heretics, an Eternal Avenger? Is this the God we are to love and adore? In *God's Just Vengeance*, Timothy Gorringe traces a cruel and unstinting system of criminal justice to an Anselmian account of atonement, one that dominated English clerics and jurists during that cold season of jurisprudence in the seventeenth and eighteenth centuries. Perhaps Gorringe remonstrates with Anselm at just this point, that justice *must* be served, and it must be "retributive," tallied up and met out, in proportion to the wrong done. (As we shall see, Gorringe's own warm endorsement of restorative justice will in fact mirror the historical Anselm's theology more closely than he appears to recognize.) But is justice, meted out to sinners, foreign to modern notions of a merciful and humane society, a merciful and loving God?

The oppressed of this and every age have reason to press these questions upon us. Feminists share an interest in this matter, as do the persecuted and enslaved and immiserated in every culture. We need not take a particular position on forms of penal justice—Anselm does not—and can sit somewhat loose on the form of "proportionality" that would make justice fitting as restraint on wrongdoing. But the oppressed mirror Anselm's convictions when they insist that wrongs must be made right, and the oppressors cannot be left untouched, unchallenged, unpunished. A full theological exploration of the remarkable Truth and Reconciliation Commissions in South Africa must wait for another day, but even here we strike an Anselmian note when we recall that the truth was demanded from the oppressors in a public setting, and a restoration or repayment of wrongs done was expected; simple pardon, where no one or nothing has changed but the verdict, did not satisfy the just ends of the commissions.[10] Our intuitions of social justice, that is, rest on broad notions of *change*, of work being done to correct, to strip away, to renovate, to return. A God who is indifferent to this revolutionary demand would be a deity unmoved and uninvolved with a world of suffering and of wrong, a "High and Lofty One" who did not in truth "dwell with the lowly and poor in heart." Were justice to be a "discretionary" act of God, a happenstance that from time to time the LORD contingently enacted in a disordered realm, we creatures, those harmed and those committing harm, would rely upon a God whose Inner Reality was something other than Just—a Mystery, perhaps, or a Terrible Numinosity, but not a Necessary and Absolute Justice. Anselm teaches that such a god would be self-contradictory, a monster.

The second aspect of this central affirmation of Divine Justice concerns the very heart of Atonement Doctrine: Is it, in truth, *necessary*? Could Almighty God not simply pardon? Is this not the question pressed upon Christians by devout Jews and Muslims, by the religious of many non-Christian traditions? Is it not, in another key, the question pressed on us by Pelagius, or more properly, his followers, in the bitter controversy with Augustine over grace and good works of the Law? Could we not repair the breach between God and creature through some other means, some other offering, or some other Divine Pardon? Why this whole terrible spectacle, this tormented body, this ghastly death? We will not grasp the heart of the objection to Anselmian Atonement if we do not heed the urgency of this complaint. Anselm's critics do not simply object to the form of God's remedy—this Roman execution—but also to the very notion of necessity that is proposed to govern the entire doctrine. Such brutality is *necessary*? *This* is the bitter kernel of complaint.

It is the very idea of sin *necessitating* punishment or satisfaction—the very notion of Divine Justice as Necessary Predicate—that stands under fire here. So deep is this question in the Doctrine of Divine Attributes that John Zizioulas in his unstinting defense of Divine freedom denies that necessity

---

[10] See, for example, Desmond Tutu's careful reflections on these points in: *No Future without Forgiveness* (New York: Image Books, 2000), 47–66.

governs God in His Being, Perfections, or Works *ad extra*, in any way at all; even an Augustinian "freedom from coercion."[11] In more biblical idiom, we might ask, how can this God of Necessary Honor be the LORD God of Israel, the One who is long suffering and of great kindness? Have we not already established that the True God does not suffer harm at sinners' hands? If God and His Honor are not harmed, and sinners can be forgiven and restored, as they have been since the days of Covenant and Temple rites, why the necessity, why the death? Why not simply punish? Or more mercifully, why not punish some; forgive the rest? Why this framework of necessary Attribute, necessary remedy, at all? The Christian Doctrine of Atonement weighs in the balance here.

The world must be "set to rights," "satisfaction" made, for the salvation that is Divinely promised to be made real; that is Anselm's answer. "It is necessary," Anselm affirms in the famous chapter 6 of Book II, "that the heavenly city should have its full complement made up by members of the human race, and this cannot be the case if the recompense (*satisfactio*) of which we have spoken is not paid, which no one can pay except God, and no one ought to pay except man: it is necessary that a God-Man should pay it." To this firm summary of the argument in *Cur Deus Homo* Boso breaks out in confident cry: "Blessed be God! Now we have made a great discovery relating to the object of our search" (II.6). Can we moderns be so confident?

It may be, after following Anselm this far, that we find ourselves haunted by the possibility that the weight of sin puts us in peril before the Justice of God. The calculus about sin, our justification for it, and the offense against God that it represents may strike modern ears as an odd refrain, but one, perhaps, that can be transposed into modern dress; that, at least, has been the quiet hope of this chapter so far. But the notion of satisfaction, of making things right, may be found insuperable in modern idiom. Just here, we might say, the historical Anselm is of little help to the theological Anselm, for it is of little aid to explain the means and sweep of Anselm's Christology—his rich account of Christ's earthly ministry, his victorious battle with the devil, his free and freely obedient death, his gift of merit to penitent sinners—should modern Christians find the whole notion of repair and recompense a hollow and vain wish. It may seem odd to begin the final, and crucial, turn in Anselm's Doctrine of Atonement by such bleak questions about Atonement as

---

[11] John Zizioulas, *Being and Communion* (St Vladimir's Press, 1997), 27–66.

a whole. But it is important to see that Anselm and his contemporaries shared a fundamental optimism that we moderns strain to believe. Much present-day criticism of Anselm stems from a deep but often unvoiced conviction that this world of suffering and cruelty, of indifference and stony hearts, cannot in truth be set to rights, cannot be renovated or renewed or restored—not radically, not down to its bitter core—but must rather be endured, quietly, faithfully, soberly; for, really, there is no help for it. The objection to necessity, that is, finds its deepest springs in the denial of *possibility*: it is cruel and irrational to demand what cannot be done. The Christian appeal to forgiveness for sin, the exhortation to ever more radical discipleship, the calm and somber call to confess the pitiless sin of the world ground down into our very institutions, our ways of life, our very bones—all this eloquent examination of the modern conscience betrays a Stoic resignation about a world that cannot be repaired at its very heart. This broken world, we moderns say, must rather be accepted, and loved, all the same, we might say. No grand revolution, from our side, or from God's, it seems; no "master narrative," as we phrase this chastened realism these days; nothing "magical" or "utopian," but rather the hard work, we tell ourselves, the small steps of making peace here in our pilgrimage, soldiering on.

Anselm is of another mind altogether. It is his firm conviction that a Sinless Adam, the God-Man, has made the world right, restored and released it from the tomb. This can happen, it must happen, it has happened: that is Anselm's Doctrine of Atonement in short compass. That confident affirmation is the core of the "Satisfaction Theory of the Atonement," the breathtaking optimism that animates its entire structure and life. That this seems childishly mechanical to us moderns, frankly incredible in the face of the horrors we have seen and done in our days, and vulgarly insular in an age of religious pluralism and "protest atheism" is, for Anselm, simple confirmation of the miraculous grace of God's Atoning Work. He explains his radical hope in this way.

Human beings are destined for angelic things, he says. We cannot begin to understand the historical Anselm if we do not take our bearings from the "heavenly city" that illumines the human pathway. Contrary to much modern intuition, Anselm holds that a pronounced otherworldliness—a firm citizenship in another country, a heavenly one—alone gives us hope for the darkened world we now inhabit. The Divine promise is anchored in that heavenly or "supernatural" destiny: God, not human worthiness or ability, underwrites this audacious hope. Now, sin, in all the ways laid out above, lays an incalculable burden on this shimmering destiny. We creatures, sinners all, cannot set this terrible destructiveness and greed to rights. We know this in our bones, the hopelessness of a human-engineered salvation. And this austere honesty leads us to despair about the state and future of our world. We do not believe it can be repaired, for we at heart know all too well that we lack the resources to renew it, all the way down to its lifeless center. Just this is the force of Anselm's calculus about infinite worlds, and the infinite harm our attempt to discover a righteousness of our own can wield. In the end, we have done all this *against* our Maker, the One Helper. When sinners offer everything that is in the world, their soul and body, their livelihood and loves, they raise up before Almighty God just what has been already given, the shower of created goods that a Benevolent Creator rains down upon the earth, the just and the unjust. This is what Anselm intends when he speaks of what creatures owe and what they must pay their Maker: not a bill due but rather a self-giving, an offering of the first fruits to the Lord of the Harvest. Because it is what properly and already belongs to God, nothing can be made whole, made good, restored, or renewed for Heavenly Use in such a creaturely offer. God alone can act; God alone restore the heavenly vision. Indeed, God must, for He has freely bound Himself to just this Heavenly Jerusalem. Yet, the *world*—not God, not His Justice or Honor—must be set to rights; the creature and the creaturely realm must be changed, liberated, healed, and restored. The One who acts to do these things is rightly called Lord and Savior: He alone has done what the lost and helpless, the burdened, cannot do, but only despair of.

The Creator becomes the creature, to restore from within. This Incarnate Son is of the earth, born of Mary, His mother; He is a child of Eve, a brother to all humankind. Like us in every way but one, he owes to God all that He is and has, just as do we. Thus begins the long scholastic tradition, captured elegantly by Thomas Aquinas, that Jesus Christ in His humanity owed righteous obedience to God: He too must obey the Law, loving God above all things, and His neighbor as Himself. The life of Jesus, His earthly ministry, including His submission to the Law, plays no small role in Anselm's theology, for Jesus Christ must be understood to perfectly follow the Covenant obedience all others have rejected. Christ offers Himself as the perfect Exemplar, humble, patient, self-giving. Moreover, Jesus must be seen, in His perfect humanity, as the One who finally and fully breaks the devil's thrall. It is famous, to be sure, that Anselm rejects an older account of Atonement, in which the devil is seen to hold rightful power over human sinners, and must in some fashion, licit or no, be stripped of this overlordship. Though favored by Gustav Aulén as a "classic" Doctrine of Atonement, the sway of the devil over the cosmos, and the drama of the Divine victory over and against him, struck Anselm as illegitimate, or "mythological"—a plastic depiction of demonic vicegerency that could never be just or legitimate in the realm ruled by a Holy and Just God. Atonement is not made to Satan! That Anselm firmly insists upon. But to affirm that is not to deny the devil any part in the great work of redemption, or a share in the shabby work of human rebellion against God. No, here too Jesus Christ in His earthly ministry renews and restores from within. For He alone struggles against Satan, the Righteous against the unrighteous; He alone overthrows the tempter's power (II.11). This too is His work of obedience, His perfect sinlessness, that he overcomes temptation and remains in every trial, open, obedient to God, and victorious. The death of Christ is but one—the most perfect and definitive, to be sure, but still just one—of the acts of Self-giving that restore and remake the world from within. It is the ultimate expression of a life lived for God.

Christ's death, then, "satisfies." It recompenses for and sets to right what is wrong, terribly wrong with us, and with our kind. In close dialogue form, Anselm sets out the death of Christ to Boso as harm to the "Person of Christ," on one hand, and self-offering by this "Precious Life," on the other. Once again we are asked to measure sin and its recompense through an intuition about the Inestimable Worth of God. First, the negative calculus.

> Anselm: "If the man we have in mind were to be present, and you knew who he was, and someone were to say to you, 'If you do not kill this man, the whole of the universe will perish, and whatever is not God,' would you do it in order to preserve the whole of the rest of creation?" Boso: "I would not do it, even if an infinite number of universes were offered to me." Boso continues, "A sin which is directed at this man's person is incomparably greater than all conceivable sins which are directed elsewhere than at his person." Anselm sums up firmly: "We see therefore that no sins, no matter how immeasurably great or numerous, which are directed elsewhere than against the person of God, can be regarded as equal to the violation of the bodily life of the man whom we have in mind." Now, the positive calculus. Anselm: "Consider also that sins are as hateful as they are bad, and that that life which you have in mind is a loveable as it is good. Hence it follows that this life is more loveable than sins are hateful." And: "Do you think that something which is so great a good and so loveable can suffice to pay the debt which is owed for the sins of the whole world?" Boso: "Indeed, it is capable of paying infinitely more." So: "If then to accept death is to give one's life, just as his life outweighs all the sins of mankind, so does his acceptance of death." (II.14)

Christ's Sinless Perfection outstrips all the world's sin; it is the Pauline "how much more." His very Person just is the resource for the world's renewal that could not be found or produced or offered from within the sin-sick world. It is important to see that, for Anselm, the atoning death of Christ offers to God a good that cannot be found within the fallen realm: it is a *novum*, pure gift. What sinners cannot engineer, God provides. His very own Perfection, Divine and human, is the incomparable Good that makes good, satisfies. The death of Christ completes this Perfect Self-offering. Necessarily, this Life is laid down *freely*. Anselm is quite firm in his Johannine reading of the Passion: "No one takes my life from me; I lay it down on my own accord" (John 10:18). Only this freedom is consistent with a Perfect Offering, a Sinless Obedience. Christ alone does not owe his death as penalty to sin; He alone can lay it down as Incomparable Boon. Once again we see the Augustinian affirmation of necessity with gracious freedom: God's own Goodness binds Him freely to the cross. The cross of Christ is planted down deep into the wretched earth, healing at the very core.

Now, Anselm teaches that this free death transforms sinners who call upon the Name of the LORD. They may receive from Christ's "treasury of merit" pardon for their sins. Indeed by the end of *Cur Deus Homo*, Anselm has rung the changes on almost every "theory of atonement" modern theology has laid out for the student textbook. Christ is the Satisfaction for sin; He is the Representative of our kind, the Perfect Human; He is the Substitute, the One who can be taken and given on sinners' behalf (II.20, on Divine Mercy); He is the Victor over sin, death, and the devil; He is the Restorer of the heavenly hope; He is our Mother, "for, longing to bear children into life, [Christ] tasted of death, and by dying [He] begot them" (Prayer to St Paul, ll. 409–411). What could not be done has been done by Another. God has made right what creatures have made wrong, and the heavenly destiny of humankind is now opened, secured, healed. All this has been done beyond all measure and beyond all calculus; for the "free gift is not like the trespass."

The theological Anselm and the historical Anselm, then, meet at long last. The more closely we study Anselm, the full sweep of his thought, its ambition and rigor, the more we see the larger world into which our cramped Anselmian theories belong—their proper measure and breathing-room. Anselm may appear too confident in his own rational powers, all the same, too ready to argue, defend, and analyze what lies beyond human insight and deduction. But even here, we might give Anselm, the monk whose faith sought understanding, a chance to place even his own achievement under the measure of Eternity: "I think," Anselm concludes, "that I have now gone some little way towards a satisfactory reply to your question, although someone better than I could do it more fully, and there are more, and greater, reasons for this thing than my intellect, or any mortal intellect, can comprehend" (II.19). In the end, the Atoning Work of Christ is Mystery, even for Anselm of Canterbury; no, especially for him. In this, as in so much else, Anselm remains and proves himself a true Doctor of the Church.

11

Thomas Aquinas's Pauline Theology of the Atonement

Charles Raith II

For those even remotely aware of scholarship on Aquinas's "theory of the atonement,"[1] especially after the paradigm-setting work of Gustav Aulén,[2] the topic of Aquinas and atonement immediately conjures up the concept of "satisfaction." Aquinas is frequently (and neatly) slotted into the satisfaction theory of the atonement, often being presented as an inheritor of Anselm's theology, with this theory (and this theory alone) functioning as the guiding interpretive framework—the "heart"—of Aquinas's teaching on Christ's work of salvation.[3] The problem with this approach is not that satisfaction is unimportant in Aquinas's soteriology; it is indeed present at many central junctures in his explanation of how sinful human beings have "peace with God" through Jesus Christ (Rom. 5:1).[4] Rather, the problem is more paradigmatic: satisfaction is not

---

[1] As Richard Muller reminds us, the English origins of the word "atonement" and the surrounding debates in the seventeenth and eighteenth century around universal atonement, limited atonement, and various atonement theories render the claim that someone like Aquinas has a "theology of the atonement" somewhat anachronistic and can lead to reading later debates and developments into his theology; Richard Muller, *Calvin and the Calvinist Tradition: On the Work of Christ and the Order of Salvation* (Grand Rapids, MI: Baker Academic, 2012), 74–78; though Muller is particularly concerned with John Calvin, his caution holds true a fortiori for Aquinas.

[2] Gustaf Aulén, *Christus Victor: An Historical Study of the Three Main Types of the Idea of the Atonement*, trans. A. G. Hebert (Eugene, OR: Wipf & Stock Publishers, 2003).

[3] Philip L. Quinn, "Aquinas on Atonement," in *Trinity, Incarnation, and Atonement: Philosophical and Theological Essays*, ed. Ronald J. Feenstra and Cornelius Plantinga, Jr. (Notre Dame, IN: University of Notre Dame Press, 1989), 153; Aulén, *Christus Victor*, 93 Eleonore Stump, "Atonement according to Aquinas," in *Philosophy and the Christian Faith*, ed. Thomas Morris (Notre Dame, IN: University of Notre Dame Press, 1988), 61–91; Alister E. McGrath, *Christian Theology: An Introduction*, 3rd edn (Oxford: Blackwell, 2001), 421–422.

[4] For more on Aquinas and satisfaction and how satisfaction is understood in the Christian life, see Romanus Cessario, O. P., *The Godly Image: Christ and Salvation in Catholic Thought from Anselm to Aquinas* (Petersham, MA: St. Bede's Publications, 1990).

at the "heart" of his understanding of Christ's work of salvation; a better candidate for the "heart" (if we are safe to say there is one at all) is love (*caritas*), both God's love for us and our love for God as a participation in His love. As Aquinas crisply states, "[In loving God] lies the perfection of human salvation."[5] Aquinas's soteriology is driven by his broader vision for human participation in God's triune life of love. For Aquinas, human beings are unique among all created, non-angelic beings in that they have a "capacity" for God.[6] They are made for the ultimate end of enjoying the joy that God has in and of Himself through a graced participation in the divine life. And they obtain that happiness through the operations of knowing and loving God.[7]

Sin is all that hinders this participatory union with God through knowledge and love, and it is in this context that Aquinas presents Christ's work of salvation. For Aquinas, the *totality* of Christ's work enabling sinful human beings to participate in the divine life through knowledge and love properly corresponds to his work of atonement. For this reason, Aquinas presents us with a multifaceted account of Christ's salvific work that corresponds to the way Christ addresses the multifaceted problem of sin that hinders chartable union between God and sinful human beings. In the process, Aquinas interprets the Incarnation in ways reflecting many so-called models of the atonement: *Christus victor*, moral exemplar, recapitulation, and satisfaction, to name a few.[8] It is illuminating that even when Aquinas focuses on the Passion of Christ, where the topic of satisfaction appears most frequently, his account hinges around love, and not just God's love

---

[5] *ST* III, q. 46, a. 3; English citations of the *Summa theologiae* are taken from the Blackfriars translation. In his commentary on Galatians, Aquinas links love with freedom, stating that the state of freedom established by Christ consists in love (*caritas*), "without which a man is nothing" (*S. Ep. ad Gal.* §301).

[6] *ST* III, q. 4, a. 1, ad. 2.

[7] It is not simply the possession of knowledge and love that constitutes participatory union with God but rather the *activity* of knowing and loving God. God is pure act, and we participate in God through action; hating and loving God are things we do, not just dispositions we have. While the virtues that reside accidentally within the powers of the soul give rise to certain actions, and therefore certain virtues are needed for certain activities—the virtue of love (*caritas*) in the soul must be present (by God's grace) if the act of loving God as one's supernatural end is to occur—the virtues are not what it means to participate in God per se. It is the activity arising from the virtues that forms the essential place of participation in God. On the relationship between knowledge and love in Aquinas's theology, see Michael Sherwin, *By Knowledge and By Love: Charity and Knowledge in the Moral Theology of St. Thomas Aquinas* (Washington, DC: The Catholic University of America Press, 2005).

[8] Adam Johnson, "A Fuller Account: The Role of 'Fittingness' in Thomas Aquinas' Development of the Doctrine of the Atonement," *International Journal of Systematic Theology* 12 (2010), 303. For an account of the *Christus victor* model in Aquinas's teaching, see Jonathan Morgan, "*Christus Victor* Motifs in the Soteriology of Thomas Aquinas," *Pro Ecclesia* XXI (2012), 409–421; Hans Urs von Balthasar hints at the elements of recapitulation in Thomas's soteriology (*Theo-Drama Volume IV: The Action* [San Francisco: Ignatius Press, 1994], 390).

for us but our need to love God: "By Christ's Passion ... man knows thereby how much God loves him, and is thereby stirred to love Him in return."[9] Driving Aquinas's "theory of atonement," then, is not a doctrine of satisfaction but rather human need for love and how Christ enables a participatory oneness of the human being with God in love.

This participatory vision for Christ's work of at-one-ment that makes charitable union with God the guiding interpretive lens is for Aquinas not only Augustinian[10] but also thoroughly Pauline, and in what follows I explore a few of the Pauline pericope—Colossians 1:18–20 and Romans 3:21–26—that inform his overall soteriology. Focusing on the Pauline dimensions of Aquinas's theology is not only interesting—Aquinas's biblical commentaries are still largely unexplored territory[11]—but it brings us to the heart of Aquinas's own theological approach. The entire shape of Aquinas's interpretation of Christ's Incarnation is (in Aquinas's mind) determined by the teaching of Scripture. Leading up to and during Aquinas's day, some theologians such as Rupert of Deutz, Roger of Martson, and William of Ware had argued that Christ would have needed to become incarnate even apart from human sin.[12] But Aquinas rejects this claim and maintains that the Incarnation must be understood through the lens of human sin; no human sin means no incarnation for Aquinas.[13] Why does he hold this position? The reason is Scripture: "everywhere in the Sacred Scripture the sin of the first man is assigned as the reason of the Incarnation."[14] Thus for Aquinas if our approach to interpreting Christ's incarnation is to line up with the sole "incontrovertible proof" of Christian theology, that is, Scripture,[15] Christ's incarnation must be viewed as a remedy for human sin *and especially the sin of the first parents*,[16] which means for Aquinas that Christ's Incarnation remedies the ignorance and lovelessness of God intrinsic to fallen human existence. In

---

[9] *ST* III, q. 46, a. 3.
[10] See Michael Sherwin, "Aquinas, Augustine, and the Medieval Scholastic Crisis concerning Charity," in *Aquinas the Augustinian*, ed. Michael Dauphinais, Barry David, and Matthew Levering (Washington, DC: The Catholic University of America Press, 2007), 181–204.
[11] Noticeable progress has been made on this front in the past decade. See, for example, Christopher T. Baglow, *Modus et Forma: A New Approach to the Exegesis of Saint Thomas Aquinas with an Application to the* Lectura super Epistolam ad Ephesios (Rome: Editrice Pontificio Instituto Biblico, 2002); Matthew Levering, *Scripture and Metaphysics: Aquinas and the Renewal of Trinitarian Theology* (Oxford: Blackwell, 2004); Matthew J. Ramage, *Engaging Scripture with Benedict XVI and St. Thomas Aquinas* (Washington, DC: The Catholic University of America Press, 2013).
[12] Ilia Delio, "Revisiting the Franciscan Doctrine of Christ," *Theological Studies* 64 (2003), 7.
[13] *ST* III, q. 1, a. 3.
[14] Ibid.
[15] *ST* I, q. 1, a. 8, ad. 2.
[16] As we shall see, Aquinas's emphasis on the "sin of the first man" is important for his interpretation of Christ's atonement in Romans.

this context, as we shall see, satisfaction becomes less an objective transaction between the incarnate Son and the Father on behalf of sinful human existence and instead has in its sights the transformation of human beings into lovers of God. But if Scripture navigates Aquinas's approach, the Apostle Paul is at the helm. For Aquinas, Paul's writings "contain nearly the whole teaching of theology."[17] They are, Aquinas notes, the most frequently used writings of the New Testament in the church.[18] Aquinas evidences his unique intellectual connection to the Apostle not only in the frequency of the citations to Paul's letters in the *Summa theologiae* but also in the quality of his Pauline commentary work.[19]

While a thorough investigation into the Pauline dimensions of Aquinas's theology is still needed,[20] in what follows I provide a limited contribution to understanding Aquinas's Pauline soteriology by (1) addressing Aquinas's understanding of Pauline corpus as a whole in relation to Christ's work of atonement and (2) exploring the details of Aquinas's interpretation of Colossians 1:18–20 and Romans 3:21–26. In the process, I hope to the show the centrality of love—both God's love for us and our love for God understood as a participation in his love—in Aquinas's atonement theology.

The Pauline Corpus and the Centrality of Indwelling Grace for At-one-ment

Before delving into Aquinas's exegesis of particular Pauline passages, it is helpful to highlight how Aquinas understands Paul's corpus as a whole in relation to Christ's work of atonement. Aquinas divides the sacred scriptures into two

---

[17] *S. Ep. ad Romanos* §6.
[18] Ibid. The Psalms are the most frequently used Old Testament writings.
[19] Ceslas Spicq long ago singled out Aquinas's commentaries on St. Paul as "the maturest fruit and most perfect realization of medieval scholastic exegesis" ("Saint Thomas d'Aquin Exégète," in *Dictionnaire de Théologie Catholique*, ed. Alfred Vacant et. al. [Letouzet et Ané, 1908], 15-A, col. 695). Jean-Pierre Torrell highlights Romans in particular as being "the most fully finished and most profound that he has left us" (*Saint Thomas Aquinas*, vol. 1, *The Person and His Work*, trans. Robert Royal [Washington, DC: Catholic University Press, 1996], 200); see also Eleonore Stump, "(Aquinas') Biblical Commentary and Philosophy," in *The Cambridge Companion to Aquinas*, ed. Norman Kretzmann and Elenore Stump (Cambridge: Cambridge University Press, 1993), 260; Terence McGuckin, "Saint Thomas Aquinas and Theological Exegesis of Sacred Scripture," *New Blackfriars* 74 (1993), 206–207.
[20] For recent studies on particular Pauline commentaries, see Charles Raith II, *Aquinas and Calvin on Romans: God's Justification and Our Participation* (Oxford: Oxford University Press, 2014); Michael Dauphinais and Matthew Levering, eds., *Reading John with St. Thomas Aquinas: Theological Exegesis and Speculative Theology* (Washington, DC: The Catholic University of America Press, 2005); Baglow, *Modus et Forma*; for Aquinas's use of Paul in the *Summa theologiae*, see Matthew Levering, *Paul in the* Summa Theologiae (Washington, DC: The Catholic University America, 2014).

principal parts corresponding to the two testaments, "Old" and "New." He summarizes the content of the Old Testament in terms of "commanding"; the Old Testament is principally about various kinds of laws (i.e., public and private) that command various things (i.e., issues of equity, worship, and offices) and are commanded in various ways (i.e., as from a king, a herald, and a father), all of which work in some form or fashion to direct the one under the law to life: "All that keep it shall come to life."[21] But while the Old Testament directs one to life, it cannot impart life; it is unable to heal the broken souls of sinners who transgressed the law and find themselves at enmity with God. Said another way, the commands are unable to justify.[22] The life pointed to by the Old Testament can only be established through the indwelling of Christ's grace, which brings us to the New Testament.[23]

Aquinas summarizes the New Testament as "helping."[24] God's "helping" is God's giving of grace: "For the Law was given through Moses; grace and truth came through Jesus Christ."[25] This grace establishes at-one-ment between God and sinners by repairing the effects of sin on the soul and elevating its powers in order that sinners may participate in the divine life. Receiving grace is not the *effect* of being at one with God; rather it is what *establishes* a sinner at one with God.[26] For Aquinas, grace is an accidental quality of the soul that reorders the soul so as to participate in the divine life and have God as its supernatural end.[27] Grace does not alter the substance of the soul—the human being always remains human even with grace. Rather, grace acts in the manner of a formal cause and

---

[21] Thomas Aquinas, "Commendation of and Division of Sacred Scripture," in *Thomas Aquinas: Selected Writings*, ed. and trans. Ralph McInerny (London: Penguin Books, 1998), 5–11. This is a sermon Aquinas preached in 1256 at his inauguration as master of theology—or otherwise known as *magister in sacra pagina* (master of the sacred text).

[22] *S. Ep. ad Romanos* §212–213 (all citations of Aquinas's Pauline commentaries are taken from the Marietti edition); *ST* I–II, q. 100, a. 12.

[23] For Aquinas, those who were saved in the Old Testament are saved in the same manner as those in the New Testament, namely, through faith in Jesus Christ. The difference is that those in the Old Testament had faith in a Christ to come, while those in the New Testament have faith in a Christ that has come; see *S. Ep. ad Galatians Lectura* §112, in Galatians 2:21; *S. Ep. ad Romanos* §661, in Romans 8:3.

[24] Aquinas, "Commendation," 7.

[25] Ibid., citing John 1:17.

[26] It is not the case that Christ's work of satisfaction establishes at-one-ment between God and sinners, and grace is merely the by-product of that atoning work. Rather, Christ's work of satisfaction—which is, again, just one of many aspects of Christ's salvific activity—makes possible the reception of grace in the soul, with the reception of grace establishing at-one-ment between God and sinners.

[27] The debate surrounding the relationship between nature and grace (and the natural and supernatural) in Aquinas's thought has a long history, becoming particularly vigorous since the rise of *nouvelle théologie*; for a recent offering from a more classic Thomist viewpoint, see Steven A. Long, *Natura Pura: On the Recovery of Nature in the Doctrine of Grace* (New York: Fordham University Press, 2010).

reorders and *enhances* the powers of the soul to more deeply penetrate into truth, goodness, and beauty; that is, the soul is now able to know God and love God in a manner not possible with the ungraced soul. Yet these enhanced powers, like all powers, act in particular ways due to the habits residing in the soul; the habits inform the powers and move them to action either toward the true and good (virtues) or falsehood and evil (vices). Thus, with the infusion of grace in the soul God gives the virtues of faith, hope, and love—the "theological" virtues—that direct the enhanced powers toward their intended, supernatural end: "as man in his intellective power participates in the Divine knowledge through the virtue of faith, and in his power of will participates in the Divine love through the virtue of charity, so also in the nature of the soul does he participate in the Divine Nature, after the manner of a likeness through a certain regeneration or re-creation."[28]

For Aquinas, all grace has its source in Jesus Christ, and it comes to us and is sustained in us through his salvific activity. Thus for Aquinas the entire New Testament revolves around the grace of Jesus Christ and how Christ makes possible our reception of grace and its ongoing presence in the soul so as to be at one with God in this life, culminating in the life to come. Within the New Testament, as noted earlier, the Apostle Paul's writings hold a special place for Aquinas. For Aquinas, these writings converge on one topic: Christ's grace, which enables proper knowledge and love for God; that is, grace brings at-one-ment. For Aquinas, Paul is uniquely concerned to unpack the "power" of grace to bring about peace between God and humans beings and enable human beings to live the wayfarer life of ever-deepening oneness with God, culminating in the life of glory with God eternally.[29] Aquinas cites Romans 1:16–17 as a summary of Paul's message: "I am not ashamed of the Gospel [of grace], for it is the power of God unto salvation for everyone who believes."[30] He divides Paul's letters according to the way Paul principally expounds on grace: as it is in the Head, namely, Christ (e.g., Hebrews); as it is found in the "chief members" of his Mystical Body, namely, the prelates (e.g., 1 Timothy); and as it is in the Mystical Body itself, namely, the church (e.g., Romans).[31] The totality of Paul's teaching, therefore, according to Aquinas, expounds on the Gospel of grace by demonstrating how

---

[28] *ST* I–II, q. 110, a. 4.
[29] For Aquinas, the origin of grace is principally addressed in the Gospels, and the exercise of the virtues is principally addressed in the other New Testament letters; Aquinas, "Commendation," 11.
[30] Ibid., 12.
[31] *S. Ep. ad Romanos*, §11. Aquinas further divides the letters to the churches according to different ways the grace of Christ can be considered in the Mystical Body.

Christ's grace enables a sinner to participate in the triune life of love through the presence of grace in the soul.

Colossians 1:18–20—Atonement and the Union of Head and Members

Paul (1:20) describes the relationship between Christ and the church in Colossians 1:18 as one of "head" and "body," with this relationship being rooted in Christ reconciling "all things" by making peace through "the blood of the cross." Aquinas's framework for interpreting the head-body metaphor is how Christ's grace indwelling the members of his body—the Christian faithful— enables their mystical union with the head, Christ, through the activities of knowing and loving God. For Aquinas, when Paul describes Christ as the "beginning" (*principium*)—"he is the head of the body, the church, who is the *principium*"—and connects this beginning to his work of reconciliation, Paul is addressing Christ as the source of grace that enables sinners to be justified and participate in the divine life: "Christ is not only *principium* in grace insofar as he is a man, but all are justified through faith in Christ."[32] We must recall that justification for Aquinas is not an extrinsic declaration or imputation. Rather, justification consists of the soul being transformed by grace into a state of justness through participation in the justness of Christ.[33] Grace not only enhances the powers of the soul, but also heals the disorder in the soul caused by sin that hinders the soul from being one with God in love (*caritas*). When God forgives sin, the effect of that forgiveness is the soul's restoration or rebirth; God gives grace to the soul and infuses the virtues of faith, hope, and love so that the effects of sin are purged and we are enabled to participate in the divine life through knowing and loving God—which is nothing more than to participate in God's love for us.[34] It is important to note that merely having the virtues of faith, hope, and love is not what makes a person "at one" with God. While the presence of

---

[32] S. Ep. ad Colossenses, §48.
[33] Charles Raith II, *Aquinas and Calvin on Romans: God's Justification and Our Participation* (Oxford: Oxford University Press, 2014), chapter 1.
[34] Not all the effects of sin are purged, however, which is why the Christian continues to struggle with the flesh. The "fomes" remain, for example, which cause the sensible appetites to wander from perfect submission to reason. We are also still subject to the penalty of physical death. But we are no longer subject to the punishment of eternal damnation since the obstacle that would bring damnation—a lack of love (*caritas*) for God—has been removed; see *ST* I–II, q. 81, aa. 1–3; q. 85, a. 3.

these virtues in the soul corresponds to the soul being "justified," it is the *activities* of knowing and loving God that constitute participation. As Aquinas states, "Activity is at the root of man's life."[35] To be "at one" with God is therefore not to stand *before* God as just; rather, to be "at one" with God is for God to *live in us* and us to *live in God* through the principal virtues of wisdom and love.

Aquinas then unpacks how Christ as "head" of the church makes possible such at-one-ment. To be "head" for Aquinas is to be the source of grace. Christ himself is "full" of grace, and to be united to God is to participate in his fullness. This is how Aquinas understands Colossians 1:19: "In him the Father was well pleased that all fullness should dwell." Aquinas explains each of the terms "all," "fullness," and "dwell" with reference to the grace possessed by Christ: "all" because some have one or another gift of grace while Christ has them all; "fullness" because a person can have a gift without fully having it or fully having its power while Christ has all the gifts to the full; and "dwell" because some receive a gift for only a time (e.g., prophecy) while all gifts to the full are continually present in Christ.[36] For Aquinas, Paul then links Christ's grace with our salvation when he states, "And through him to reconcile all things unto himself" (Col. 1:20). Aquinas interprets Christ's work of reconciliation in terms of our reception of Christ's grace in the soul that enables our participatory oneness with God. Christ as a human being is the mediator between God and human beings, and thus the abundance of Christ's grace—an abundance he has by being the God-man—"overflows" from him into human beings.[37]

The overflow of Christ's grace into his members enables a "mystical union" of head and members, in which God and human beings are at one.[38] It cannot be stressed enough how central the mystical union is for Aquinas's atonement theology, for this union is what enables us to participate in Christ's work of salvation: "Grace was bestowed upon Christ, not only as an individual, but inasmuch as He is the Head of the Church, so that it might overflow into His members; and therefore Christ's works are referred to Himself and to His members ... Consequently Christ by His Passion merited salvation, not only for Himself but likewise for all His members."[39] As will become important below while addressing Christ's work of satisfaction, Aquinas makes the mystical union the key to enabling us to benefit from Christ's satisfying work: "The head and members are

---

[35] *S. Ep. ad Philippians*, §32.
[36] *S. Ep. ad Colossenses*, §50; see also *ST* III, q. 7, a. 9.
[37] *ST* III, q. 7, a. 1.
[38] See *ST* III, q. 8, a. 3, for the diverse ways human beings are united to Christ as "head."
[39] *ST* III, q. 48, a. 1.

as one mystic person; and therefore Christ's satisfaction belongs to all the faithful as being His members."[40]

When the members receive the influx of grace from the head—when the mystical union is constituted—the members are then "reconciled" to God through Christ; that is, peace is established between God and sinners (Col. 1:20).[41] What does Aquinas mean by "reconciliation"? For him, two parties are *not* reconciled, that is, they are not at peace with one another, whenever the will of one party is in conflict with the will of another. God's will for human beings is that they be ordered and order all things to him as their end; they are to cling to him in love as their eternal purpose for existing and engage temporal realities in a manner that lines up with this clinging. The problem is that human beings have desired temporal realities too strongly and have therefore willed something other than God's will, that is, human beings have "sinned" by contradicting the order of the divine governance through ordering themselves toward temporal realities over their eternal end.[42] For peace to be established between God and human beings, this sin—this disordering—must be addressed. That is, the will of human beings must be realigned according to the divine ordering so as to cleave to God in love (*caritas*) as their end.[43]

Atonement for Aquinas, then, is about aligning these wills. It is about enabling human beings to know and love God according to the order that God established for human beings. But how do these wills become aligned, which for Aquinas occurs through sinners being forgiven of their sin and "justified"? Paul addresses this when he states, "Making peace through the blood of his cross" (Col. 1:20). The blood of the cross, that is, Christ's Passion and death, enable human beings to be at one with God. Aquinas says very little regarding how Christ's cross addresses sin and establishes peace between God and human beings in his commentary on Colossians 1:18–20. What we gain from this section is the participatory dimensions of Aquinas's soteriology, namely, how Aquinas understands the head-member metaphor in terms of the influx of grace from the head to the members that constitutes the "mystical union." Atonement enables this influx of grace and the establishment of peace between

---

[40] *ST* III, q. 48, a. 3. Aquinas notes at *ST* I–II, q. 87, a. 8, that while no one can take on another's *penal* punishments, it is possible for someone to take on another's *satisfactory* punishments if the two parties are "one."

[41] See *ST* III, q. 8, a. 1, for Aquinas's exposition of Christ as "head," which addresses "order, perfection and power." It is with "power" that Aquinas claims, "He has the power of bestowing grace on all the members of the church, according to John 1:16, 'Of His Fullness we have all received.'"

[42] *ST* I–II, q. 71, aa. 1, 2, and 6.

[43] *ST* I–II, q. 87, a. 3: "Whatever sins turn man away from God, so as to destroy love (*caritas*), considered in themselves, incur a debt of eternal punishment."

God and human beings by realigning human wills with God's will through the presence of love (*caritas*) in the heart of the sinner. But it is not yet clear how all this occurs "through the cross." For this, we turn to Aquinas's commentary on Romans 3:21–26 and Romans 5:1–12.

Romans 3:21–26

Through Aquinas's commentary on Romans 3:21–26, we observe the central role that the *iustitia dei* (justice of God) plays for Aquinas in enabling sinful human beings to have peace with God and how this *iustitia* is connected to the cross of Jesus Christ. Aquinas situates 3:21–26 within Paul's larger argument for the equality between Jews and Gentiles regarding both sin and grace. In 1:18–3:20 Paul places both Jews and Gentiles equally under the guilt of sin, and then in 3:21–31 he reveals that Jews and Gentiles are also equal with regard to being in grace. Paul accomplishes the latter by expounding on the relationship between the justice of God and the law, claiming, "But the justice of God is now manifest without the law" (Rom. 3:21). Throughout Romans 1:17–3:26, Aquinas approaches the *iustitia dei* from what he considers to be two equally viable perspectives: (1) the justice by which God is just,[44] which is reflected in God keeping his promises of salvation; and (2) the justice by which God justifies human beings.[45] In Romans 3:21, Aquinas explains that the law cannot establish the justice by which God is just because God *himself* fulfills his promises of salvation.[46] Christ's grace (and not the law) justifies a person by realigning a person's will so as to be in harmony with God's will. Said another way, Christ's grace transforms a person's soul and enables a person to know and love God as his supernatural end understood as a participation in God's love for that person. And only Christ's grace—and not the law—can do this.

Aquinas then turns to discuss the *cause* of our justification at 3:24b, "through redemption." In Colossians 1:19–21, Aquinas emphasized Christ's work of "reconciliation," which consists of God and sinners being at one through having their wills aligned, with this reconciliation occurring through the "blood of the cross." Aquinas now unpacks the "blood of the cross" in terms of "redemption." Redemption makes reconciliation possible; redemption leads to human beings

---

[44] *Iustitia qua Deus iustus est.*
[45] *Iustitia qua Deus homines iustificat*; S. Ep. Romanos §102.
[46] Aquinas quotes Romans 15:8, "Christ became a servant to the circumcised to show God's truthfulness, in order to confirm the promises given to the patriarchs"; S. Ep. ad Romanos §300

submitting their minds to God in faith and their wills to God in love. Aquinas's take on redemption, then, is not simply an objective transaction that occurs *on behalf of* human beings; rather, redemption has in its sight the transformation of sinners into lovers of God.[47]

In his commentary on Romans 3:24, Aquinas is principally concerned with the slavery caused by original sin, also known as the "sin of nature" or "sin of the first parent," rather than actual sins, which are sins of the individual person that are systemic of having a nature affected by original sin. It is worth pausing to consider why Aquinas focuses on original sin rather than actual sins.[48] Aquinas's concern is to reflect on Christ's ability to overcome the disorderliness of our souls that prevents our union with the divine through love. While original sin is not as "grave" as actual sins, given that actual sins are the result of personal disordered activity but original sin is the result of the disordered activity of the first parent, the effects of original sin are greater on human nature, for actual sins spring forth from the disordering effects of original sin and further these effects. Thus, original sin is more problematic than actual sins in terms of preventing human beings from participating in God's ordering of the human being to himself in charity.[49] Also, original sin has a greater breadth to its effects than actual sins. Actual sins negatively affect the one committing the sin, but original sin impacts the entire human race.[50] For Aquinas, then, if Christ's work of at-one-ment is going to reestablish the union of God and human beings through love, there is a sense in which Christ's work vis-à-vis original sin fittingly takes precedence.

Original sin has placed human beings into multiple forms of bondage. There is bondage to the devil, who acts as a "torturer" of human beings. In sinning, the first parents consented to the devil; as punishment God justly permitted humanity to fall under the devil's servitude.[51] There is also the bondage of punishment corresponding to the guilt of original sin. This punishment consists of the removal of original justice—the initial justice given to the first parents in

---

[47] This will be of particular significance when we come to the concept of satisfaction.
[48] Note that the "Pelagian" reading of Romans is also targeted in Aquinas's interpretation.
[49] *ST* I–II, q. 83, aa.1–4.
[50] *ST* I–II, q. 82, aa. 1–4.
[51] *ST* III, q. 48, a. 4, ad. 2; q. 49, a. 2. For more on the *Christus victor* motifs in Aquinas's soteriology, see Jonathan Morgan, "*Christus Victor* Motifs in the Soteriology of Thomas Aquinas," *Pro Ecclesia* XXI (2012), 409–421. It is worth noting that Aquinas roots God's work of overcoming the devil in justice: "Although the devil assailed man unjustly, nevertheless on account of sin, man was justly left by God under the devil's bondage. And therefore it was fitting that through justice man should be delivered from the devil's bondage" (*ST* III, q. 46, a. 3, ad. 3). Notice the similarities between Aquinas's view and that of Ireneaus, who Aulén cites as a contrast to the "Latin" view. Cf. *Adv. Haer.* V., 1, 1, cited in Aulén, *Christus Victor*, 27.

grace that ordered their being to God as their supernatural end and sustained their physical existence from experiencing death—and the related punishments of a disordering of a human being's powers—the body does not submit to the soul, the lower powers do not submit to reason, and reason does not submit to God—as well as death of the body and eternal damnation of the soul.[52] In sum, original sin distorts human nature, disposing it away from God's ordering of the human being to Himself as its supernatural end, with this end being reached through the human being's charitable participation in the life of God.[53] By focusing on original sin, Aquinas is getting to the root of the problem between human beings and God, namely, the distortion hindering human love for God.

How can someone be redeemed from the slavery of sin? That is, what must take place in order to receive the transformation necessary to be rightly ordered to God in love (*caritas*) and no longer be in bondage to the devil and the guilt of sin? Aquinas claims that redemption occurs "if he [the one in bondage] makes satisfaction for sin."[54] The theme of redemption brings us to what is often considered the "heart" of Aquinas's theory of the atonement: satisfaction.[55] Using "debt" imagery, Aquinas explains that redemption occurs when someone pays the fine of the debt incurred by the debtor. But the *value* of the thing offered must equal or exceed the offense if satisfaction is to occur justly. When the thing offered does fit this requirement, the one in debt is redeemed by the payment. The redemption spoken of at 3:24b, however, explains Aquinas, involves not merely the debt of each individual person but the debt of the whole human race. This debt was incurred through the "infection" caused by the sin of the first parent.[56] Due to the universality of the infection and thus the corresponding gravity of the debt, no individual human person could offer the appropriate payment for satisfaction. Humanity needed a special help in order for satisfaction to take place. God himself had to provide the redeemer; God himself needed to be the redeemer. This was Christ, "who was immune from all sin." He was "ordained" by God to satisfy for sin.[57] And he did so through "the blood of the cross," that is, through offering himself to God in love as the sacrifice needed to redeem a fallen human race.[58] Commenting on Romans 3:25, "Whom God proposed to be a propitiation," Aquinas explains that Christ is called the *propitiation* for humanity

---

[52] *ST* I, q. 95, a. 1; I–II, q. 81, a. 1; III, q. 52, a. 5.
[53] *ST* I–II, q. 82, a. 1.
[54] *S. Ep. ad Romanos* §307.
[55] See note 3.
[56] *S. Ep. ad Romanos* §307.
[57] *S. Ep. ad Romanos* §307–308.
[58] See *ST* III, q. 46, a. 6; q. 47, a. 2, ad. 3.

because he "obtains pardon for our sins."[59] Aquinas roots Christ's propitiation in Exodus 25:17, claiming (by means of an allegorical interpretation of the passage) that the propitiatory seat placed on the ark was a figure of Christ, while the ark itself was a figure of the church.[60] It was "fitting," states Aquinas, that Christ undergo death for satisfaction, since the human race has incurred death by its sin, as stated in Genesis 2:17, "In the day that you eat of it you shall die."[61] Hence, claims Aquinas, as 1 Peter 3:18 states, "For Christ also died for sin once for all."[62] This payment reaches us "by faith" (1 Pet. 3:25), through which we are justified before God, since "even among men payment made by one man does not benefit another, unless the other considers it valid."[63] Aquinas therefore demonstrates the connection between Christ's redeeming work as the causal principle of justification, and grace as the causal principle of justification within the believer. He thus shows how the grace that justifies a sinner—that is, that reorients a sinner to God through faith, hope, and love—is at all times rooted in the salvific sacrificial work of Christ on behalf of humanity.

It is important for understanding Aquinas's view on Christ's work of redemption to keep in mind the "debt" humans have before God. For Aquinas, a person

---

[59] *S. Ep. ad Romanos* §308; cf. Ps 79:9. See also *ST* III, q. 22, a. 3, where Aquinas explains the satisfaction made by Christ in terms of His office as priest. Christ is a unique priest, claims Aquinas, in that as man, he is both priest *and* victim (*hostia*). Moreover, although it is true that Christ is priest as man and not as God, and only God can forgive sins, Christ is unique in that in Christ one and the same *hypostasis* was united with both the divine and human natures. From this, Aquinas goes on to claim, "Insofar as His human nature operated by virtue of the Divine [see *ST* III, q. 19], that sacrifice [i.e., Christ offering himself] was most efficacious for the blotting out of sins"; see also, *ST* III, q. 49, aa. 1, 3.

[60] For more on Aquinas's understanding of literal and spiritual interpretation of Scripture, see especially his *Scriptum super libros Sententiarum*, I, d. 27, q. 2, a. 1; *Quodlibet 7*, articles 14–16; *In Psalmus Davidis Expositio*, Psalmus III; *ST* q. 1, a. 10; *Lectura romana in primum Sententiarum Petri Lombardi* I, a. 4, qc. 1, ad. 3. On the way Aquinas sees Christ as fulfilling the role of temple and Torah, see Matthew Levering, *Christ's Fulfillment of Torah and Temple: Salvation according to Thomas Aquinas* (Notre Dame, IN: University of Notre Dame Press, 2002).

[61] "It is a fitting way of satisfying for another to submit oneself to the penalty deserved by that other," *ST* III, q. 50, a. 1; cf., III, q. 46, a. 3; on the effects of Christ's death for salvation, see *ST* III, q. 50, a. 6. On the role of "fittingness" in Aquinas's atonement theology, see Johnson, "A Fuller Account," 302–318.

[62] *S. Ep. ad Romanos* §309. Aquinas elsewhere explains that on account of the nature of the Incarnation, namely, that Christ's humanity was the "organ" of his divinity, "all acts and sufferings of Christ's human nature were salutary for us, considering that they flowed from the power of his divinity." Christ's death, then, by which "moral life was extinguished in him," is also the cause of "extinguishing our sins." Christ's resurrection, moreover, by which he "returns to a new life of glory," is the cause of our justification in that "we return to the new life of justice" (*S. Ep. ad Romanos* §380).

[63] *S. Ep. ad Romanos* §309. Aquinas elaborates in *ST* III, q. 49, a. 1, ad. 3; q. 50, a. 6, that by his passion and death Christ delivered us from our sins causally; he "set up the cause of our deliverance, from which all sins whatsoever, past, present or to come, could be forgiven." This established causality is likened to a medicine prepared by a doctor that can be used to heal both present and future ailments. It is through faith that this causality reaches *this* person, since the effect of Christ's propitiatory work "reaches us" by faith (*S. Ep. ad Romanos* §309).

can be in debt to another in many ways, and be redeemed from the debt in many ways. But key to redemption is that the debt and the payment must have a certain fitting relationship of value if redemption is to occur. In the context of the relationship between human beings and God, we are dealing with a love relationship between a human being and a divine being who is the human being's creator. The value of the love that ought to exist in this relationship far exceeds the value of love existing between two human beings. Human beings owe God a love far superior to the love owed to any created being by virtue of the dignity of the divine nature and the relationship of God to human beings as creator; in fact, they owe God a love that they are not able to offer by the powers of human nature alone, which is why supernatural grace in the soul is necessary for human beings to love God properly, that is, meritoriously.[64] The "debt" that human beings have incurred through sin and that must be repaid if redemption is to occur, then, is a debt of love of an exceeding valuable nature. This is why no animal sacrifice can redeem: such sacrifice is of a lesser kind of value than love, and therefore unable to redeem. Moreover, the debt is of such gravity that no human being can love God in the way that repays the love lost. Humanity, then, finds itself in a dire predicament due to being under a debt that is impossible to be repaid. It is here that Christ's love manifest in his loving endurance of the Passion is offered to God on our behalf as a fitting payment—a superabundant payment—to satisfy for the debt of love we owe to God. Aquinas notes that satisfaction occurs if one offers something to the offended that the offended loves equally or more than he detests the offense.[65] This leads Aquinas to root satisfaction in the "exceeding charity" of Christ which is offered to God on our behalf; it is of greater value than the debt of human sin.[66] The whole context of redemption and satisfaction

---

[64] Recall that even in the original state, Adam was given grace to participate in God as his supernatural end.

[65] *ST* III, q. 48, a. 3.

[66] There has been some debate surrounding the penal aspects of Aquinas's satisfaction theory; see, for example, Romanus Cessario, "Aquinas on Christian Salvation," in *Aquinas on Doctrine: A Critical Introduction*, ed. Thomas Weinandy, Daniel Keating, and John Yocum (London: T&T Clark, 2004), 124; Adonis Vidu, *Atonement, Law, and Justice: The Cross in Historical and Cultural Contexts* (Grand Rapids, MI: Baker Academic, 2014), 76; Frederick Christian Bauerschmidt, *Holy Teaching: Introducing the* Summa Theologiae *of St. Thomas Aquinas* (Grand Rapids, MI: Brazos Press, 2005), 243. While all the dimensions of the debate cannot be addressed here, I note that Aquinas does claim that "one satisfies for another's sin by taking on himself the punishment due to the sin of the other" (*ST* III, q. 14, a. 1). But this gets us to the question: what penalty does Christ undergo on our behalf? Aquinas believes that the penal aspect of Christ's work of satisfaction does not pertain to Christ taking on any spiritual suffering—he does not absorb or incur in any way the "wrath" of the Father—but rather in his passion Christ takes on the *physical* punishments due to *original sin*. Aquinas spends a great deal of time connecting Christ's bodily suffering with satisfaction by linking these sufferings to the punishment due to the human race on account of original sin: "These bodily defects, to wit, death, hunger, thirst, and the like, are the punishment of sin, which was brought into the world by Adam ... Hence it was useful for the end of the Incarnation that He should

in Aquinas's account then revolves around Christ's love. His love for the Father on our behalf removes the debt of love humanity owed God, so that Christ's love becomes the means of reestablishing the loving (charitable) union of human beings with God.

Yet we can say more regarding the centrality of love in Aquinas's account of the atonement. We must not pass over too quickly Aquinas's brief comment at Romans 3:25 that the whole redemption schema—God requiring satisfaction and Christ providing that satisfaction—is rooted in God's "ordination."[67] Behind this statement lies Aquinas's broader explanation for why God required what He did for satisfaction and the manner in which He provided for what he required: God's ordained plan of salvation works ultimately to cultivate love in the hearts of sinners.[68]

For starters, Aquinas believes that God did not have to require satisfaction for sin.[69] God is the one offended, and therefore God is able to forgive without demanding payment, just as I act permissibly when I forgive someone who offends me without demanding repayment. Moreover, God's love never changes; it is human beings that put up hindrances to participating in that love. Satisfaction, then, is not a prerequisite for God loving us, since his love never changes. Why, then, did God require satisfaction? Aquinas claims that, on the one hand, God demands satisfaction in order to show his "severity."[70] God is certainly just in demanding satisfaction (even if he did not have to demand it), and through demanding satisfaction he demonstrates the severity of his justice.[71] Yet this severity works as the backdrop for the principal reason God demanded satisfaction: in order to demonstrate his "mercy." The very satisfaction God requires God provides in Christ. For Aquinas, God's mercy is more "copiously" displayed by requiring and then providing for satisfaction than if he would have simply forgiven our debt.[72]

---

assume these penalties in our flesh and in our stead" (*ST* III, q. 14, a. 2; a. 4). Thus, there is a penal dimension to satisfaction, but it corresponds to Aquinas's belief that the physical ailments of death, hunger, thirst, and so on are the result of original sin and punishments "according to the justice of God who inflict them as punishment" (*ST* I–II, q. 85, a. 5). And since these realities are present in the passion and death of Christ, he reasons that Christ is taking on the physical punishments due to original sin. Yet this is far from the "penal substitutionary" model of atonement that will develop after Aquinas and into the Reformation era.

[67] *S. Ep. ad Romanos* §308.
[68] Aulén's claim that satisfaction "provides for the remission of the punishment due to sins but not for the taking away of the sin itself" (*Christus Victor*, 92) illustrates the depth of Aulén's failure to penetrate into the essence of Aquinas's thought on satisfaction.
[69] *ST* III, q. 49, a. 1.
[70] *ST* III, q. 47, a. 3, ad. 1.
[71] *ST* III, q. 46, a. 1, ad. 3.
[72] Ibid.

God's activity of demanding and providing satisfaction works, then, to transform the soul for the sake of love.[73] On the one hand, God's requirement of satisfaction serves to press upon the sinner the negative weight of acting contrary to love of God; it speaks to the destruction that such disordered activity has on the soul. On the other hand, God's provision for the very satisfaction he requires presses upon the human being that he is an object that *ought* to be loved. Aquinas reasons that human beings only love that which they perceive to be good; if human beings are to love God, they must perceive him as such. By showing his love for us through mercifully supplying the necessary satisfaction for our sins, we see God as a being that is good and are thus motivated to love him. This means that Christ's work of satisfaction is not just about making the necessary compensation to God for our debt; rather, the whole paradigm of God's requiring Christ's Passion as satisfactory presses upon the sinner the loveliness of God in order that love might be invoked in the human heart.[74]

Yet Aquinas goes further and argues that satisfaction itself could have been provided for in a manner other than through Christ's passion.[75] This leads to the question: why did God provide satisfaction *in this way*? Once again, Aquinas's framework for explicating satisfaction is driven by love—both God's love for us and our love for God. For Aquinas, Christ's Passion is the most fitting means of satisfaction because it best served to create love for God in the human heart; it is the most fitting way for moving human beings away from evil and toward love. First, by observing the depth of love Christ has for sinners as displayed through his willingness to suffer for their salvation, sinners might thereby be "stirred" to love him in return.[76] This reason is in line with the above observation regarding God demanding and supplying satisfaction: God presents himself as an object that *should* be loved. Second, through Christ's Passion, God doesn't just show us *that* he is loveable; he also shows us how to love him in return. In the passion, Christ sets forth an example of obedience, humility, constancy, justice, and the other virtues, all of which are part of living in the divine life.[77] Christ is a moral example to be followed, and by following it we live a life at one with God in love.[78]

---

[73] This is missed altogether in Aulén's account.
[74] Contra Aulén's claims that satisfaction is atonement worked from the side of man rather than God, Cessario notes of Aquinas's satisfaction model, "Satisfaction is not something God requires of man, or even of Jesus, as a condition for accomplishing his saving plan. Rather, it is the mean whereby God in very fact accomplishes his plan to bring all men and women into loving union with himself" (*The Godly Image*, xviii).
[75] *ST* III, q. 46, a. 2.
[76] *ST* III, q. 46, a. 3.
[77] Ibid.
[78] When such consideration is given to the reason Aquinas gives for God requiring satisfaction and the way satisfaction was provided, Aulén's bifurcation that the satisfaction theory of the atonement

From Aquinas's commentary on Romans 3:21–26, we see how the "blood of the cross" is the means by which human wills are brought back in line with the will of God (i.e., reconciliation). In willingly suffering in the flesh out of love for the Father, Christ becomes an offering more valuable to God than the debt of our sin. Through participating in Christ by grace—through being transformed by grace so as to know and love God (i.e., justification)—human beings come out from under the bondage of guilt and the debt of punishment, that is, they are redeemed. They now are rightly ordered to God in wisdom and love as their supernatural end and are able to live a life of love for God and neighbor that culminates in beatitude.

Conclusion—Setting Aside the Aulén Paradigm

The "Aulén paradigm" for understanding Aquinas's theory of the atonement is seriously lacking in its ability to capture Aquinas's multifaceted presentation of the work of Christ on behalf of sinful human beings. Not only does Aulén underappreciate the presence and function of a number of atonement "models" in Aquinas's account, but even when it comes to satisfaction Aulén fails to penetrate into the underlying *ratio* driving Aquinas's thought, namely, love (*caritas*) and not just God's love for us but our need for love for God. Though satisfaction plays an important role in Aquinas's thought, for Christ to have merely paid the Father for a debt on our behalf that releases us from the punishment of sin would not itself go far enough in addressing the heart of reconciliation for Aquinas: the human alignment of the mind and will to God through knowledge and charity. That is, Christ's work of at-one-ment corresponds to *all* that Christ has done to bring us into the wayfarer life and guide it to its culmination in glory.

---

is atonement "from below" as opposed to atonement "from above" is substantially undermined (*Christus Victor*, 82).

12

The Fury of Love: Calvin on the Atonement

Paul Dafydd Jones

This chapter presents Calvin's account of the atonement in three stages. First, I argue that Calvin's presentation is, by design, a rhetorical performance that deploys a surprisingly broad array of categories and concepts. This performance attests to Calvin's concern that "theology be a low-level flight over the reading of scripture," whereby the particulars of the biblical witness (and, to some extent, previous efforts to understand that witness) have a direct bearing on theological writing.[1] The intertextual qualities of this performance, further, show Calvin's concern to have reflection on the atonement animated and, in certain respects, unsettled by a (dis)array of images, ideas, and motifs—the goal being to prevent a precipitous theorization of Christ's saving history and, more positively, to emphasize its "unsubstitutable" character. The second stage of the chapter analyses what Calvin takes to be the most important dimensions of the atonement: the incarnation as a communication of divine blessing; Christ's voluntary obedience to the Father, under the Law; Christ's willingness to endure God's fury toward and judgment against sin; Christ offering himself as a sacrifice; and Christ's victory over sin and death. This analysis, which draws on Calvin's commentaries and the final version of the *Institutes of the Christian Religion*, demonstrates Calvin's preoccupation with the "*man* Christ Jesus" (2 Tim. 2:5, KJV): the human whose obedience-unto-death effects reconciliation between God and God's people.[2] Finally, I consider the practical upshot of Calvin's exegetical and conceptual

---

[1] Stephen Edmondson, *Calvin's Christology* (Cambridge: Cambridge University Press, 2004), 6.
[2] As this sentence suggests, the *Institutes* and the commentaries should be read alongside each other. The relationship might be described as interactive and complementary: the commentaries being microscopic exercises that gesture toward larger claims; the *Institutes* being a macroscopic statement, summative of beliefs that arise from the community's Spirit-led reading of scripture. See here, inter alia, Elsie A. McKee, "Exegesis, Theology, and Development in Calvin's *Institutes*: A Methodological Suggestion," in *Probing the Reformation: Studies in Honor of Edward. A. Dowey, Jr.*,

endeavors. I suggest that Calvin's dogmatic efforts connect with a particular vision of piety, with reflection on Christ's death being a constitutive element of believers' responses to God's redeeming activity.

While I am not uncritical of Calvin, I should acknowledge that this chapter is not merely an exercise in interpretation. It is also a gentle commendation, motivated by the belief that Calvin's views can and should enrich contemporary constructive work. Generally, because Calvin ties a central element of our "knowledge of God the redeemer" (the title of book II of the *Institutes*) to the complex textures of the Hebrew Bible and New Testament, he is able to develop a rich and multifaceted perspective on Christ's life-unto-death—a rebuke to those whose suspicion of "classical" authors is used as a pretext for disengagement, and a reminder that abstract talk about "models" or "theories" of atonement tends to degrade and stultify reflection. More particularly, I aim to show that Calvin's perspective on atonement is rather more interesting than suggested by a familiar, but overused, phrase: "penal substitution." Christ's decision to "bear our sins in his body on the cross" (1 Pet. 2:24) is not a juridical operation, undertaken by a deity whose "stern inflexibility" and "iron spirit" reflect something of Calvin's own character.[3] It is the central act in the continuing drama of God's life with us and our life with God[4]: an expression of God's righteous and lawful hostility toward sin, matched with a perfect human obedience, vicariously rendered, that enables a relationship between God and God's children that is defined by intimacy, assurance, and freedom.

The Rhetoric of Atonement

It is in chapter 12 of the second book of the *Institutes*—the hinge by which readers are moved from a disheartening report of human sinfulness to a lively exposition of divine grace—that Calvin begins to write about Christ's life and death in earnest. Creation, God's triunity, God's governance of history, the nature of humanity and its fall, the publication of the Law, and God's solicitude for

---

ed. E. A. McKee and B. G. Armstrong (Louisville, KY: WJKP, 1989), 154–174; Richard A. Muller, *The Unaccommodated Calvin: Studies in the Foundation of a Theological Tradition* (New York: Oxford University Press), 140–158; and David Gibson, *Reading the Decree: Exegesis, Election and Christology in Calvin and Barth* (London: T&T Clark, 2009), 21–25.

[3] Georgia Harkness, *John Calvin: The Man and His Ethics* (New York: Abingdon, 1931), 74 and 5. The most recent (and best) intellectual biography of Calvin is Bruce Gordon, *Calvin* (New Haven, CT: Yale University Press, 2009).

[4] This phrasing signals my indebtedness to Matthew Myer Boulton, *Life in God: John Calvin, Practical Formation, and the Future of Protestant Theology* (Grand Rapids, MI: Eerdmans, 2011).

Israel: these issues, powerfully addressed across hundreds of pages, move into the background. Calvin's concern is now the "office of Mediator," the content of which is the scripturally attested history of Jesus Christ, undertaken for our salvation at the behest of God the Father. Because Christ fulfils the demands of this office, God and God's children are put in right relationship. He, and he alone, is the "material cause ... of eternal election, and of the love which is now revealed"; he, and he alone, is the one who ensures that "the love of God is poured out"; he, and he alone, stimulates "glorious praise of such abundant grace."[5]

How does one engage a topic of such gravity? A powerful passage discloses something of Calvin's answer:

> The second requirement of our reconciliation with God was this: man, who by his disobedience had become lost, should by way of remedy counter it with his obedience, satisfy God's judgment, and pay the penalties for sin. Accordingly, our Lord came forth as true man and took the person and the name of Adam in order to take Adam's place in obeying the Father, to present our flesh as the price of satisfaction to God's righteous judgment, and in the same flesh, to pay the penalty that we had deserved. In short, since neither as God could he feel death, nor as man alone could he overcome it, he coupled human nature with divine that to atone for sin he might submit the weakness of the one to death; and that, wrestling with death by the power of the other nature, he might win victory for us ... we should especially espouse what I have just explained: our common nature with Christ is the pledge of our fellowship with the Son of God; and clothed with our flesh he vanquished death and sin together that the victory and triumph might be ours. He offered as a sacrifice the flesh that he received from us, that he might wipe out our guilt by his act of expiation and appease the Father's righteous wrath. (II.xii.3)

While elements of this passage are present in the 1536 edition of the *Institutes*,[6] in the 1559 text it introduces and epitomizes a mode of reflection—and, more specifically, a style of *writing*—that Calvin deems befitting with respect to the atonement. Precisely because Christ's life-unto-death, as the pivot around which

---

[5] *Comm. Eph.* 1:5. When quoting from the New Testament commentaries, I use *Calvin's New Testament Commentaries*, ed. David W. Torrance and T. F. Torrance, 12 vols (Reprint, Grand Rapids, MI: Eerdmans, 1959–1972). For the Hebrew Bible, I quote from *Calvin's Commentaries*, ed. The Calvin Translation Society, 22 vols (Reprint, Grand Rapids, MI: Baker, 1979). Per convention, footnotes refer to the biblical verse(s) that Calvin considers. In-text citations are from John Calvin, *Institutes of the Christian Religion* (1559), trans. Ford Lewis Battles and ed. J. T. McNeill, two vols (Louisville, KY: Westminster John Knox Press, 2006).

[6] John Calvin, *Institutes of the Christian Religion, 1536 Edition*, trans. Ford Lewis Battles (Grand Rapids, MI: Eerdmans, 1986), 51.

salvation turns, is an event of excessive meaning that "ravish[es] us with wonder," Calvin adopts a rhetoric that is conceptually diverse, richly allusive, and highly dynamic.[7] Scriptural motifs and classical allusions are gathered, juxtaposed, combined, and glossed; Calvin's disdain for "frigid speculation" (II.ii.2) is countered by a fast-moving torrent of claims.[8] An initial reference to Romans 5:19 is followed by gestures toward Anselm and Aquinas, with "satisfaction" given a juridical and financial twist; the Adam-Christ pairing, as well as the juridical-financial framework, is then reprised, albeit with the suggestion that Christ offers himself as a representative sacrifice to the Father (a variation of Rom. 12:1, perhaps). Then an allusion to Gethsemane, flanked by Pauline remarks about the "defeat" of death (1 Cor. 15:26, Col. 2:15, etc.) and a nod toward patristic depictions of Christ's victory. And finally an acclamation of believers' "adoption" (Rom. 8, Gal. 4:5, Eph. 1, etc.), which segues into a reading of Romans 3:21–26, with the key term in v. 25, *hilasterion*, understood to encompass expiation and propitiation. Calvin's aim, I think, is simultaneously to overwhelm and involve readers as they approach the principal act in the drama of salvation. "Overwhelm," in that Calvin wants readers to be newly astonished, if not disconcerted, by the depth and richness of Christ's mediating work; "involve," in the sense that "we"—the first person plural used to great effect—are not detached spectators, but a people gathered to understand the cost of our salvation and to receive the benefits that issue forth.[9]

It is not inapt, further, to say that in this passage Calvin aims to *unsettle* theological reflection. The prose shifts quickly between diverse figures and motifs, as if to dissuade readers from tarrying with any particular conceptual or doctrinal scheme; a consciously allusive style "plunges us into a network of textual relations" and the reader finds herself shuttled, quickly, between Calvin's own writing, the works of earlier thinkers, and, most importantly, the texts of the Old and New Testaments.[10] An intertextual style of writing does not signal, of course, that Calvin abandons the task of instruction in favor of an impressionistic hymn to the cross. He remains committed to the task of "preserving the

---

[7] *Comm. Gal.* 1:4.
[8] The word *frigidis*, translated by Battles as "idle," is better rendered "frigid." See Boulton, *Life in God*, 70–76.
[9] It is not only the atonement, of course, that prompts rhetoric of this kind. J. Todd Billings shows nicely that Calvin's exposition of the *duplex gratia* of justification and sanctification leads Calvin to "incorporate … forensic and transformational images of salvation" in a "theology of salvation [that] sought to be as wide-ranging as the theologies of salvation derived from the exegesis of Scripture itself." See "John Calvin's Soteriology: On the Multifaceted 'Sum' of the Gospel," *IJST* 11, no. 4 (2009), 428–447 (428 and 429).
[10] I borrow here from Graham Allen, *Intertextuality*, 2nd edn (London: Routledge, 2011), 1.

doctrine of God." He continues to delineate a coherent *summa pietatis*, through which believers *know*—cognitively, affectively, and relationally[11]—themselves to be part of Christ's body, in the Spirit, as this body receives the love of God qua Father. Notably, too, Calvin's prose is not always intertextual. For better or worse, on occasion he describes the atonement using a fairly delimited categorical set. (A good example: "God's wrath and curse always lie upon sinners until they are absolved of guilt. Since he is a righteous Judge, he does not allow his law to be broken apart from punishment, but is equipped to avenge it" [II.xvi.1].) Still, the very fact that Calvin does write intertextually, drawing on the figurative diversity of the New Testament while gesturing toward the works of earlier thinkers, demonstrates a determination to make reflection on atonement an inherently dynamic, even restless, matter. This is a posture, to draw again from literary studies, that is "against, beyond, and resistant to (mono)logic," and that seeks to rivet attention on Christ's "unsubstitutable" history.[12] Since no single conceptual scheme (juridical, sacerdotal, military, financial, etc.) can adequately describe this history, it is fitting for theological writing to draw on and move between a wide range of concepts, motifs, and figures. By so doing, the theologian is well-placed to think well about the Mediator who "possesses hidden within Himself all the treasures of the heavenly life, of blessedness and glory, which He dispenses by His Word and apportions to all who embrace the Word by faith."[13]

Jesus Christ, Mediator

Since Calvin's account of Christ's life-unto-death does not settle into the groove of a delimited conceptual scheme, the interpretative challenge is to identify the principal accents of this redescription of Christ's atoning work, and to do so in ways that do not reduce Calvin's distinctive (and, I think, coherent) perspective to a conceptually homogeneous "theory" or "model" of atonement. In the past fifty years, the best scholarship on Calvin has met this challenge. Paul van Buren places the word "substitution" at the center of his analysis, and then lends it a meaning that encompasses distinct dimensions of Christ's

---

[11] The qualification is crucial; Calvin insists that faith not be reduced to a "cold and bare knowledge," for no one "can believe except he be re-formed by the Spirit of God" (*Comm. Jn* 1:13) and adopted as a son or daughter of the Father. See also, inter alia, I.xiii.2, III.ii.19, and III.ii.36.

[12] Allen, *Intertextuality*, 44. For more on Christ's "unsubstitutability," see Hans Frei, *The Identity of Jesus Christ: The Hermeneutical Bases of Dogmatic Theology* (Philadelphia: Fortress, 1975).

[13] *Comm. Lk.* 11:27.

mediating work—obedience, condemnation, punishment, and sacrifice in particular. Robert A. Peterson discerns six "themes" in Calvin's treatment of atonement: obedience, victory, legal substitution, sacrifice, merit, and example. And, most recently, Stephen Edmondson has shown that the *munus triplex* of king, priest, and prophet permeates Calvin's exposition of Christ's person and work.[14] Explicitly or implicitly, these works challenge the idea that Calvin promotes a textbook-ready perspective ("penal substitution," *Christus victor*, etc.). None have recourse to Karl Barth's famous description of Calvin as "a waterfall, a jungle, a demon, something directly down from Himalaya, absolutely Chinese, wonderfully mythological," but there is a wholly apt sense that Calvin's account of the atonement is so rich and so far-reaching as to confound our received categories.[15]

The modest distinction of my interpretation lies in its determination to follow Calvin as he follows the arc of the gospel narratives, so as to show how different claims about Christ intertwine and cohere. I begin with Calvin's acclamation of the incarnation and his account of Christ's ministry; I turn then from Christ's ministry to his death on the cross—a furious punishment that effects an expiation of sin, and a voluntary sacrifice that is a propitiation of divine wrath; I conclude with remarks about Christ's resurrection, ascension, and session at the Father's right hand.[16] Following the "whole course of [Christ's] obedience" (II. xvi.5) in this way provides the interpretative leverage needed to come to terms with two of Calvin's lasting contributions to reflection on the atonement: the claim that God's love is routed through the horror of the cross and a strong emphasis on Christ's *human* activity as decisive for the reconciliation of God and humankind.

To begin at the beginning: for Calvin, the incarnation is God's merciful overcoming of the "distance" that separates God and sinners. This action, grounded exclusively in God's sovereign love and mercy, means that God draws near and dwells with God's people in a newly personal, intimate, and transformative way. On one level, and most obviously, the assumption of an individual human

---

[14] See Paul van Buren, *Christ in Our Place: The Substitutionary Character of Calvin's Doctrine of Reconciliation* (Reprint, Eugene, OR: Wipf & Stock, 2002); Robert A. Peterson, Sr., *Calvin and the Atonement* (Fearn, UK: Mentor, 2009); and Stephen Edmondson, *Calvin's Christology* (Cambridge: Cambridge University Press, 2004).

[15] Barth wrote these words in a letter to Eduard Thurneysen in 1922. See Eduard Thurneysen, ed., *Karl Barth—Eduard Thurneysen Briefwechsel, Band II: 1921–1930*, in *Karl Barth Gesamtausgabe*, vol. 4 (Zürich: TVZ, 1974), 80.

[16] This approach to the atonement is embraced, incidentally, by one of Calvin's distinguished descendants: see G. C. Berkouwer, *Studies in Dogmatics: The Work of Christ*, trans. Cornelius Lambregtse (Grand Rapids, MI: Eerdmans, 1965).

essence means that the Son "showed Himself openly to the world."[17] God reveals Godself to sinners in an unprecedented way, and thus begins to establish once more a genuine knowledge of God's triune being (the revelation of the Son, for Calvin, being coextensive with a revelation of the Father and Spirit).[18] On another level, this "showing" is an occasion whereby the Son's "divinity and our human nature might by mutual connection grow together (*inter se coalescerent*)" (II.xii.1).[19] Calvin's spatial framework does not rule out intimacy and transformation. On the contrary, God's condescension, in Christ, inaugurates a (divinely superintended) process whose culmination is the restoration of human nature. The "old human," defined by sin and death, is gradually overtaken by the "new human," animated by grace and led toward eternal life. Not that this process entails an "infusion" or "instilling" of grace in the way that Calvin's pseudo-Lutheran opponent, Andreas Osiander, imagined.[20] While Calvin's affirmation of the hypostatic union supports an account of the *unio mystica* that imagines God's dwelling with us to be the beginning of our journey toward God, this is a journey in which the strict distinction between creature and Creator is always upheld. Again, though, this distinction does not preclude genuine interaction between God and God's people. God's advance toward us, in Christ, enables us to approach the Father, become intimate with him, and enjoy the status of adopted sons and daughters. Calvin's remarks on Jacob's ladder (Gen. 28:12) illustrate the point: "Christ alone ... is the only Mediator who reaches from heaven down to earth: he is the medium through which the fullness of all celestial blessings flow, and through whom we, in turn, may ascend to God."[21] Because of God's condescension, human beings can participate in the divine life. We can be carried in the "flow" of love that the Son and the Spirit direct back to God the Father.[22]

---

[17] *Comm. Jn* 1:14.

[18] Calvin appeals to Gregory of Nazianzus to make his point: "I cannot think of the one without quickly being encircled by the splendor of the three; nor can I discern the three without being straightway carried back to the one" (I.xiii.17, quoting *On Holy Baptism*).

[19] This is not an isolated claim. It is reprised in III.ii.25 ("Christ is not outside us but dwells within us. Not only does he cleave to us by an indivisible bond of fellowship, but with a wonderful communion, day by day, he grows more and more into one body with us, until he becomes completely one with us") and appears at key points in the commentaries.

[20] Even prior to his controversy with Osiander, Calvin was careful on this front. A remark from 1540: "The gift of righteousness ... does not signify a quality with which God endows us ... but is the free imputation of righteousness" (*Comm. Rom.* 5:17).

[21] *Comm. Gen.* 28:12. For further remarks about Christ as the "fountain" through whom God's blessings flow see, inter alia, *Comm. Matt.* 13:12; *Comm. Jn* 5:26, 6:11, and 6:51; *Comm. Rom.* 8:9; *Comm. Heb.* 7:25; and *Comm. Col.* 1:19. Brian Gerrish offers useful remarks about the convergence of liquid and parental images; see *Grace and Gratitude: The Eucharistic Theology of John Calvin* (Reprint, Eugene, OR: Wipf & Stock, 2002), esp. 26–27, 57–62, and 132. See also Edmondson, *Calvin's Christology*, 126–129.

[22] For more on these matters, see Dennis Tamburello, *Union with Christ: John Calvin and the Mysticism of St. Bernard* (Louisville, KY: WJKP, 1994); J. Todd Billings, *Calvin, Participation, and*

For "ascent" to the Father to occur, however, sin must be overturned, and it is at this point that talk of Christ's obedience takes center-stage. Fittingly so: because "disobedience was the beginning of the Fall" (II.1.4), the restoration of human beings requires that the primordial fault be remedied, with a "Second Adam" undoing the defection of the first. A wholehearted, unstinting enactment of the Father's will, specifically, is needed to (re)establish the *right* way of being human. Yet the perfect "form" of Christ's obedience does not, in and of itself, suffice to effect atonement. The Mediator must live out a particular history, within the context of God's Law and God's relationship with Israel, that has as its exclusive goal the outworking of God's wrath against and judgment upon our sin. He must represent those whom God predestines to life *and* bear the cost, as a substitute, of their sins. This much is clear, in fact, from the outset of Jesus's life. Calvin's treatment of the genealogy of Matthew 1, populated with figures of often-dubious character, makes the point nicely:

> The Son of God might have kept his lineage free and pure of any crime or mark of shame, but as He came into the world to empty himself and taking on the form of a servant to become a worm, and no man, a reproach of men and despised of the people (Ps. 22.7), at last to undergo the accursed death of the cross, He did not refuse either this outrage in His own descent—one born from incestuous union, to be counted among his ancestors.[23]

From the beginning, "the Incarnation is ordered to the Cross as its goal."[24] Christ lives toward, and into, the future that sinners deserve.

For Calvin, an obedience to the Father directed toward death—and not just death as the cessation of physical life, but death "covered with ignominy in the sight of men" and "accursed in the sight of God"[25]—is an obedience to be *achieved*. The temptations that Christ undergoes and the agonies that he suffers in the garden of Gethsemane demonstrate the point: "sinlessness" is less a state of moral purity, more a matter of Christ committing himself, again and again, to receiving God's judgment against sin on behalf of others.[26] For sure,

---

the Gift: *The Activity of Believers in Union with Christ* (New York: Oxford University Press, 2007); Charles Partee, *The Theology of John Calvin* (Louisville, KY: Eerdmans, 2008); and, most recently, Julie Canlis, *Calvin's Ladder: A Spiritual Theology of Ascent and Ascension* (Grand Rapids, MI: Eerdmans, 2010).

[23] *Comm. Matt.* 1:3.

[24] Hans Urs von Balthasar, *Mysterium Paschale: The Mystery of Easter*, trans. Aidan Nichols (San Francisco: Ignatius, 1990), 22.

[25] *Comm. Phil.* 2:8.

[26] This is, of course, an important element of the description of Christ's obedience in the *Institutes*; see esp. II.xvi.5 and II.xvi.12. See also *Comm. Matt.* 26:36–44 and parallels.

Christ never deviates from the task set before him. He adheres wholly to the Father's will; he always accepts that his kingly, priestly, and prophetic work has as its denouement his reception of the "curse of God ... the total sum of human guilt ... the very powers of darkness."[27] Yet, as Hebrews 5:8 suggests, this is an obedience that Christ *learns*. It is obedience, routed through fear and struggle, which Christ must humanly ascertain and humanly enact. Contrary, then, to Thomas Aquinas's ingenious attempt to apportion Christ's struggles to the less rarefied regions of his human soul, and contrary to Friedrich Schleiermacher's belief that the communication of righteousness necessitates that Christ's own life be an instance of "imperturbable blessedness,"[28] Calvin shows acute interest in scriptural reports of Christ's fear, perplexity, and even confusion. These reports are not an occasion for doctrinal discomfort, much less "puzzles" to be solved; they indicate the steep cost of atonement for the incarnate Son.

What actually happens when Christ dies? How does the conclusion of his life secure right relationship between God and God's children? Certainly it is important to reckon with the juridical language of guilt, punishment, and payment at this point. Against those who understand atonement in terms of Christ offering himself to the Father in order that "punishment is averted" (cf. Anselm of Canterbury's masterpiece, *Cur Deus Homo*), Calvin insists that the cross is where punishment is exacted and "absorbed."[29] On this reckoning, the interactions with Pontius Pilate and the mode of Christ's death are not accidents of history, but finite forms that convey divine content: Christ takes on the "role of a guilty man and evildoer" in such a way that the "guilt that held us liable for punishment has been transferred" (II.xvi.5). Notice, too, how the activity of Christ and the Father converge. On the one side, Christ takes the place of those who are guilty before the Law. He substitutes himself for sinners; he accepts and bears the consequences of their chronic waywardness. On the other side, God qua Father shifts sinners' deserved punishment onto Christ, rerouting their just and accursed "future" into the singular horror of Christ's suffering and death.

---

[27] *Comm. Heb.* 5:5.
[28] Aquinas, *Summa* III.46.7 and 8; Friedrich Schleiermacher, *The Christian Faith*, ed. H. R. Mackintosh and J. S. Stewart (London: T&T Clark, 1999), 436. Schleiermacher is a little—but only a little—more receptive to the idea that Christ was, on occasion, troubled, in a sermon in Matthew 26:36–46, "The Power of Prayer in Relation to Outward Circumstances." See *Selected Sermons of Schleiermacher*, trans. Mary F. Wilson (New York: Funk & Wagnalls, n.d.), 38–51. I owe thanks to Christophe Chalamet for drawing my attention to this text.
[29] Ben Pugh, *Atonement Theories: A Way through the Maze* (Eugene, OR: Cascade, 2014), 56. Emphases removed. Anselm's perspective is echoed by later medieval authors. See, for instance, Peter Lombard, *The Sentences, Book 3: On the Incarnation of the Word*, trans. Giulio Silano (Toronto: Pontifical Institute of Mediaeval Studies, 2008), 76–77, and Thomas Aquinas, *Summa Theologiae* III.49.3.

Because of this convergence, our future becomes Christ's end, and Christ's upholding of the Law becomes our pardon. Christ, "by bearing our sins, takes them away. Although ... sin continually stays in us, yet in the judgment of God it is nothing, for as it is abolished by the grace of Christ, it is not imputed to us."[30]

It is possible, if one builds on Calvin's legal phraseology, to gloss these claims in a fairly quantitative way—as if the "weight" of guilt that Christ shoulders can be precisely measured, and the punishment delivered by the Father made precisely proportionate to the sum of the crimes committed. Yet this gloss fails to reckon sufficiently with God's *fury* toward sin. For Calvin, the cross is not so much an instance in which God's inflicts punishment according to a legal metric as it is a long-deferred exercise of righteousness: an "unleashing" of wrath that encompasses the past, present, and future of our faithless rebellion. The difference here is certainly fine—Calvin would not suppose that God's "outrage" and divine justice are unrelated, and he pointedly reminds readers that language about God's hatred of sin and sinners is an instance of "accommodation"—but it is important to register.[31] While some of Calvin's successors treated the atonement as "a matter of legal relation," Calvin's use of juridical motifs is crisscrossed with a dramatic sensibility, wherein God's hostility toward sin, previously checked by God's mercy and patience, is outworked on the cross.[32] While the cross is a just punishment, it is also an expression of holy indignation: a vehement assault, long deferred, on that which obstructs God's purposes—sin and the "curse" that is its necessary corollary.

Key moments in Calvin's Old Testament commentaries substantiate these claims. For instance: considering Genesis 6, which describes God's decision to flood the earth, Calvin writes about a "vengeance ... that [God] had hitherto deferred" and appends a somewhat menacing remark: "there will never be an end of contention, unless some unprecedented act of vengeance cuts off the occasion of it."[33] Is the "unprecedented act of vengeance" the flood? Perhaps

---

[30] *Comm. Jn* 1:29.
[31] On accommodation, see the classic article by Ford Lewis Battles, "God Was Accommodating Himself to Human Capacity," *Interpretation* 31, no. 1 (1977), 19–38. More recently, see Jon Balserak, *Divinity Compromised: A Study of Divine Accommodation in the Thought of John Calvin* (Dordrecht: Springer, 2006).
[32] So A. A. Hodge, *The Atonement* (Philadelphia: Presbyterian Board of Publication, 1867), 171. Earlier in his text, Hodge even goes so far as to measure Christ's vicarious suffering: "Christ suffered precisely that kind, degree and duration of suffering that the infinitely wise justice or the absolutely just wisdom of God determined was a full equivalent for all that was demanded of elect sinners in person—*equivalent* ... in respect to sin-expiating and justice-satisfying efficacy—and a *full equivalent* in being of equal efficacy in these respects in strict rigour of justice" (66; emphases in the original).
[33] *Comm. Gen.* 6:3.

not. When describing God's destruction of Sodom and Gomorrah (Gen. 18), Calvin notes how God moderates his punishment of sin, "sparing" human beings "until we have come to the utmost limit of impiety."[34] The implication is intriguing: humanity's infidelity is met with God's reprimand, but in a provisional and tempered way. Despite the outrage of human sin, God stays God's hand; mercifully, God opts not to punish immediately. This, in fact, is why Israel endures—and why humanity continues to play a special role in the *theatrum mundi*. Yet God does not exercise restraint when Christ dies. Embracing our guilt, Christ approaches the "dread tribunal," whose Judge is "armed with vengeance beyond understanding," and commits him to bearing the full weight of God's anger.[35] His death, then, is *more* than the (lawful) passing of a divine sentence. What transpires, in a way that is providentially decreed, yet not a matter of course, given Christ's learning of obedience, is Christ bearing "the weight of divine severity, since he was 'stricken and afflicted' by God's hand, and experienced all the signs of a wrathful and avenging God" (II.xvi.11; cf. III.iv.27).[36] Calvin differentiates, of course, between Christ's inherent purity and Christ's vicarious assumption of our guilt. Christ takes on a *substitutionary* role while maintaining his own "innocence"; he does not actually become the sin that God rejects.[37] But Calvin's depiction of divine wrath is just as acute, and just as intense, as Luther's. The cross is more than a settling of accounts. Even to talk of a "retributive view of penalty" would understate it.[38] The crucifixion is the moment at which God is given—and takes—the opportunity to lose patience, to suspend God's forbearance of sin, and to express an unrestrained holy anger. This is why Christ dies so terribly; this is why Christ descends—and, of course, is *sent*—into the depths of hell; this is why Christ suffers a death worse than death. But, again, savingly so! Precisely because Christ takes on the role of Mediator and "meets" God's anger, those who are incorporated into his body can do so without fear, and can "hide under the precious purity of our first-born brother" (III.xi.23).

---

[34] *Comm. Gen.* 18:21. See also, inter alia, *Comm. Pss.* 94:1–2, *Comm. Nah.* 1:2–3, and *Comm. Rom.* 3.25.

[35] *Comm. Matt.* 26:37. Cp. *Comm. Heb.* 5:7.

[36] The reference is to Isa. 53:5. See also II.xvi.8–12, on the *descensus*. Randall C. Zachman is good on the issue of divine wrath in *Reconsidering Calvin* (Cambridge: Cambridge University Press, 2012), see esp. 155–157.

[37] Bruce McCormack makes this point deftly with respect to 2 Corinthians 5:21. See "For Us and Our Salvation: Incarnation and Atonement in the Reformed Tradition," *The Greek Orthodox Theological Review*, 43, no. 1–4 (1993), 281–316, esp. 297.

[38] Paul S. Fiddes, *Past Event and Present Salvation: The Christian Idea of Atonement* (London: Darton, Longman & Todd, 1989), 102.

While talk about substitution, punishment, and wrath focuses attention on what God the Father does and the suffering that Christ undergoes, Calvin employs the motifs of sacrifice and satisfaction in order to describe what *Christ* does.[39] These motifs present Christ as the agent of salvation: someone who does not simply receive God's furious punishment, much less succumb to it, but whose passion is an action that dispels sin and overcomes the curse. In the *Institutes* and the commentary on Hebrews, for instance, Calvin describes the cross as an event of priestly self-offering. It is a voluntary sacrifice with propitiatory force, continuous with but superior to those offered by the ancient Israelites, rendered to God for the purpose of establishing a parental relationship between God and God's children. A typical claim:

> The priestly office belongs to Christ alone because by the sacrifice of his death he blotted out our own guilt and made satisfaction for our sins ... we or our prayers have no access to God unless Christ, as our High priest, having washed away our sins, sanctifies us and obtains for us that grace which the uncleanness of our transgressions and vices debars us. (II.xv.6)[40]

The intertwining of sacerdotal and juridical imagery is important to appreciate. God's wrathful punishment of sin and Christ's singular self-offering are two dimensions of a complex unity: the suffering that Christ undergoes, as our substitute, is coincident with a representative act of obedience, in death, as he offers himself to the Father.

The language of "washing" supplies an additional dimension of meaning. While Calvin opens the *Institutes* with a canny use of neo-Platonic language, writing about the "benefits shed like dew from heaven" that ensure we are "led to the spring itself" (I.i.1), as the text progresses it becomes clear that the "living water" (John 7.37) animating those incorporated into Christ's body is inseparable from the blood that is poured out on the cross. As well as holding together the ideas of expiation (understood, *in nuce*, as the negation of our guilt) and propitiation (understood, *in nuce*, as the placation of God), then, Calvin supposes that Christ's death, and the shedding of Christ's blood, are the means by which God's children are cleansed, nourished, and empowered to approach God qua Father. In the same moment at which Christ shields human beings from God's

---

[39] For more sacrifice in Calvin, see the useful article by George H. Kehm, "Calvin on Defilement and Sacrifice," *Interpretation* 31, no. 1 (1977), 39–52.

[40] See also, inter alia, III.iv.26; *Comm. Matt.* 1:23, 17:1, and 26:1; *Comm. Jn* 1:29; and *Comm. Rom.* 8:3. Calvin's insistence that the priestly office "belongs to Christ *alone*" correlates with his later critique of (what he took to be) the dominant Roman Catholic approach to the Eucharist.

punishing anger, he serves as the conduit by which the love of God flows toward and into those predestined to life. He pours himself out, literally, for our sake. It is not just that the love that "flows" from the Father to the Son is routed through Christ. It is also that Christ's blood, which cleans God's children (being "sprinkled" on them by the Holy Spirit), becomes the stream that, as the Son and Spirit move "back" toward the Father, carries God's people in its wake.[41]

What meaning does Calvin attach to Christ's resurrection, ascension, and session at the Father's right hand? Granted that Christ's cross is the central act of Christ's atoning history, how does Calvin think about its aftermath?

Calvin would likely be uneasy with such questions. He considers death and resurrection inseparable, for the *risen* Christ is the crucified Christ, and it is the *crucified* Christ who the Father, in the Spirit, raises from the dead.[42] Yet the questions help to show that Christ's mediating "work" takes new forms after his death. The resurrection is the preeminent demonstration of Christ's triumph, the moment when "Christ came forth from hell as Victor over death ... showed that the power of new life was in His hands," and assured those gathered into his body of their eventual resurrection.[43] The atonement cannot be reduced to an event that effects a "legal" change of status. This justifying event is also an ingredient in sanctification as growth into holiness: an occasion for those incorporated into Christ's body to embrace their being moved away from the tragic tangle of sin and death, and to *enjoy* being moved toward the flow of love and blessings that circulate between Father, Son, and Spirit. The ascension, concomitantly, ensures that God's love and blessings are transmitted to Christians in the here-and-now. Intriguingly, there is here a *re*establishment of the "distance" between heaven and earth—the "gulf" separating God and humankind being, recall, the starting point for a discussion of Christ's mediating work—but in such a way that the space between divine and human is filled with the communicative activity of Christ's Spirit, who ensures that Christ's benefits are spread far and wide. (A striking clutch of sentences: "Carried up to heaven, therefore he withdrew his bodily presence from our sight, *not* to cease to be present with believers still on their earthly pilgrimage, but to rule heaven and earth with a more immediate power. But by his ascension he fulfilled what

---

[41] For additional remarks on Christ's blood, see *Comm. Rom.* 3:24–25, *Comm. Heb.* 9 (esp. vv. 11 and 14–22), and. *Comm. Heb.* 10:19: "the blood of Christ is not corrupted by any decay but flows continually in unadulterated purity, it will suffice for us until the end of the world ... This is the continual consecration of His life that the blood of Christ is continually being shed before the face of the Father to spread over heaven and earth."

[42] So II.xvi.13.

[43] *Comm. Matt.* 26:1 (cp. II.xvi.6). See also *Comm. 2 Tim.* 2:8.

he had promised: that he would be with us even to the end of the world. As his body was raised up above all the heavens, so his power and energy were diffused and spread beyond all the bounds of heaven and earth" [II.xvi.14; my emphasis].) And Christ's session at the right hand of the Father? Continuing his work on the cross, Christ works now as "our constant advocate and intercessor" (II.xvi.16): one whose righteousness "distracts" the Father from the continuing fact of human sin.[44] The present mode of Christ's relationship with the Father, according to Calvin, guarantees our *continued* justification. Having dispatched the curse of sin and death, Christ holds the Father's attention in a new way: he advocates, constantly and actively, for those who are now being incorporated into his body.

While this narrative could be nuanced and expanded—say, by considering Calvin's remarks on God's covenant with Israel, or by examining the connection between atonement and the rituals of baptism and Eucharist[45]—it showcases the key features of Calvin's thinking about atonement and provides a necessary complement to the interpretative claims staked in this chapter's first section. While Calvin's rhetoric unsettles those who would reflect on Christ's atoning history, this unsettling is not bought at the expense of a coherent depiction of Christ's person and significance. Quite the contrary: an interpretation that follows the arc of Christ's life shows how Calvin gives the "form" of the mediating office a quite specific, if not easily theorizable, content. Because Christ is obedient unto death, bearing God's furious punishment of sin while simultaneously offering himself to the Father, those whom God favors can begin to "ascend" into new life. The Holy Spirit, for her part, communicates the benefits hid in Christ, and Christ *and* the Spirit begin to commend the elect to the Father—a commendation that is, in and of itself, an act of inclusion, such that believers participate in the "flow" of love that circulates in God's Trinitarian life.

Two points to round out this section. First, as is surely already evident, this account of atonement should give serious pause to those who would dismiss Calvin's God as tyrannical, capricious, and bent on retribution. It may be, as Karl Barth argues, that Calvin's treatment of election raises the specter of a *Deus nudus absconditus*, with God's predestining decision shrouded in a pernicious kind of mystery, anterior to and separate from the revelatory

---

[44] I use this language purposefully; Calvin himself writes that Christ "turns the Father's eyes to his own righteousness to avert his gaze from our sins" (II.xvi.16).

[45] Edmondson is instructive on the first point; see *Calvin's Christology*, esp. 40–88. Gerrish is excellent on the latter; see *Grace and Gratitude*.

and mediating work of Jesus Christ.[46] Calvin's treatment of "accommodation" compounds the concern: while the Christian presumes that her knowledge of God as creator and redeemer is reliable, God does not present Godself as God truly is, but in ways that are adjusted to human beings' finitude and sinfulness. And if that is the case, can one be fully assured of God's loving character?[47] Well, *yes*. Insofar as the faithful do not become enmeshed in dogmatic debates, but keep their attention trained on Christ's atoning death, Christian piety cannot be anything other than a delighted reception of the benefits of the redemption that Christ effects. God's judgment against sin, realized on the cross, which is coincident with Christ's obedient offering of himself to the Father on our behalf, which is in turn a genuine battle against death that has as its nadir Christ being "cast into the labyrinth of evil,"[48] this sequence of events is decisively demonstrative of God's loving determination to remove that which stands in the way of a saving relationship between God and God's children, and provides a firm bulwark against soteriological anxiety. It is, in fact, the key to Christian assurance. For those whose lives are anchored in and defined by the *unio cum Christo*, Christ's history is a "shining and remarkable proof of the divine love towards us."[49] In his death, one sees "the heart of God poured out in love," and one discovers the possibility of a life defined by gratitude, confidence, and joy.[50]

Second, Calvin's emphasis on Christ's *human* obedience as an integral element of the atonement is noteworthy. This emphasis signals Calvin's frank embrace of the dyothelitism endorsed at the Third Council of Constantinople (680–681 CE)—a clarification of the "Definition" of Chalcedon (451 CE), such that the affirmation of Christ's divinity and humanity means an affirmation of

---

[46] So Barth: "All the dubious features of Calvin's doctrine [of election] result from the basic failing that in the last analysis he separates God and Jesus Christ, thinking that that was what was in the beginning with God must be sought elsewhere than in Jesus Christ" (*Church Dogmatics* II/2, 111.

[47] Paul Helm argues that while no one can know God *in se*, the "accommodated" quality of God's revelation makes for reliable knowledge. God may adjust God's mode of expression to fallen creatures, but the faithful are not misled; they can infer who God is, eternally, from what God does. (So *Calvin's Ideas* [Oxford: Oxford University Press, 2004], esp. 11–34 and 184–208.) I am not convinced. Helm seems to neglect the quite radical ways in which God accommodates himself to us and downplays Calvin's abiding sense of God's inscrutability. The fact that many of Calvin's scholastic successors preferred to lean on the archetypal/ectypal distinction is also perhaps telling. Did not these theologians worry that Calvin's God was rather too mysterious?

[48] *Comm. Matt.* 27:46. The "labyrinth" (*labyrinthum* or *ambages*) is a recurrent image in Calvin's writing, and a central element of William J. Bouwsma's intellectual biography, *John Calvin: A Sixteenth-Century Portrait* (New York: Oxford University Press, 1988).

[49] *Comm. 1 Jn* 4:9.

[50] *Comm. Jn* 3:16.

"two natural wills and two natural operations"[51]—and a determination to prove dyothelitism's soteriological worth. For sure, Calvin does not lean on the prestige of a patristic council to make his point, even as he polemicizes against "the old heretics called 'Monothelites.'"[52] At issue here is the belief that the scripture bears witness to the centrality of Christ's human resolve to effect atonement, and Christ's human realization of the Father's will.

To this end, Calvin identifies occasions in which Christ's divine nature subdues itself, even conceals itself, in order that the human activities of obedience, struggle, suffering, and death might come to the fore. With respect to John 12:27 ("Now my soul is troubled"), Calvin notes that the Son's "divinity was hidden, did not put forth its power and, in a sense, rested, that an opportunity might be given for making expiation." Matthew 26:37 ("he began to be grieved and agitated") occasions a similar claim: "the divine power of Christ is said to have reposed as it were in concealment for a time."[53] Of course, Calvin has no doubt that Jesus Christ, as the Mediator, is fully divine and fully human.[54] That is not up for debate. Yet Calvin wants also to say that the execution of Christ's mediating office involves, at key moments, actions that are especially associable with Christ's humanity.

Whether these moves are theologically persuasive, however, is another matter. On one level, talk of the "quieting" of the divine Son's activity raises the possibility that Christ's obedience is not consistently a matter of his divine and human wills operating concurrently. Setting aside the fact that Calvin's exegesis seems strained, does not such "quieting" raise doubts about the unity of Christ's person? Stephen Edmondson responds negatively; he claims that Calvin's attribution of "a certain independence of activity or feeling to Christ in his human nature ... is an independence of will necessary to the integrity of his human nature and in no way impinges on the unity of that nature with the divine."[55] But that will not do. Dyothelite Christologies head in the direction of a degraded form of Nestorianism when the "independence" of

---

[51] "The Definition of Faith" from the Sixth Ecumenical Council, in *The Seven Ecumenical Councils*, vol. 14 of *NPNF*, second series, ed. Philip Schaff and Henry Wace (Reprint, Peabody, MA: Hendrickson, 2004), 345. Calvin would likely worry about talk of a "deified" human will, even though this is affirmed in the Sixth Ecumenical Council.

[52] *Comm. Matt.* 26:39. Cp. II.xvi.12.

[53] *Comm. Jn* 12:27 and *Comm. Matt.* 26:37. Cp. II.xvi.12.

[54] Thus Calvin's responses to Francesco Stancaro, who argued that Christ was only Mediator with respect to his humanity. See Joseph N. Tylenda, "Christ the Mediator: Calvin Versus Stancaro" and "The Controversy on Christ the Mediator: Calvin's Second Reply to Stancaro," *CTJ* 8, no. 1 (1973), 5–16 and 8, no. 2 (1973), 131–157.

[55] Edmondson, *Calvin's Christology*, 217.

Christ's human will becomes a desideratum; only when they describe a perfect and incessant coincidence of divine and human action, complemented by due awareness of differentiation—something like, to borrow from Sergius Bulgakov, "a single thread woven by two separate threads"—can they claim to make good sense of New Testament witness (and, for that matter, claim to stand in the mainstream of Christological reflection).[56] On another level, when Calvin mentions the quiescence of Christ's deity, we are returned to an issue raised by Barth: the prospect of a disconnect between God's eternal being, as Son, and the lived history of Jesus Christ. If Christ's history involves conduct not ascribable to and revelatory of the identity of God in God's second way of being, it becomes hard to say, without qualification, that "in Christ, *God* was reconciling the world to himself" (2 Cor. 5.19), and even harder to claim that our reconciliation with God is always a matter of God's merciful and gracious action. Still worse, there is the prospect of a mismatch between Calvin's powerful description of Christian assurance and Calvin's explication of the (divine) ground of this assurance. For example: when Calvin suggests that Christ's "*human nature* ... performed that obedience by which we are acquitted before God" in his commentary on Isaiah, he opens the door to the idea that the atonement is not thoroughly animated by God's love and mercy.[57] For a brief moment, God's determination to "pour out" God's heart, to communicate God's blessings in the most direct way imaginable, falls from view; what takes its place is the idea that the atonement requires Christ's human placation of God's fury against sin. And with *that* idea in play, it is no longer sufficiently clear that God's "love is operative every step along the way in the accomplishment of our redemption."[58] The claim that "God's *love* was revealed among us in this way: God sent his only Son into the world so that we might live through him" (1 John 4:9) remains at the center of Calvin's theology. That much is clear. The question is whether this claim is consistently—or only *mostly*—determinative of Calvin's account of Christ's atoning history.

---

[56] Sergius Bulgakov, *The Lamb of God*, trans. Boris Jakim (Grand Rapids, MI: Eerdmans, 2008).
[57] *Comm. Isa.* 53:11; my emphasis.
[58] McCormack, "For Us and Our Salvation," 302. I should add that this critique owes much to Bruce McCormack's incisive essay. I agree: "in the final analysis, Calvin was convinced that the grace and mercy of God is the effective ground of atonement" (ibid.). *Comm. 1 Jn* 4:9 makes this very point (so fn. 51). The problem is that, on occasion, Calvin makes a *human* satisfaction of God's righteousness the pivot around which atonement turns. And when that happens, it is no longer quite clear *who* God is: one whose justice is an expression of God's love ... or one who withholds love until justice is done?

Atonement and the Christian Life

Over the past couple of decades, English-language scholarship has become attentive to the ways in which Calvin's prose attempts to affect and shape its readers. Sometimes it is a matter of feints and nudges, as when Calvin opens the *Institutes* by appealing to a number of different constituencies—French humanists steeped in classical learning, students preparing for the ministry, and persecuted French evangelicals, for instance—as a means of garnering support for his theological program.[59] Sometimes it is a matter of doctrine being an element in the process of Christian *paideia*, that engraced "disciplinary" process whose telos is a deepened participation in the body of which Christ is the head.[60] And sometimes it is a matter of reworking patristic spirituality for a changed ecclesial context.[61]

This section considers Calvin's account of the benefits that attend Christ's saving death, and tracks the ways in which the Spirit's communication of those benefits connect with Christian piety. The intellectual disorientation induced by Calvin's rhetoric about atonement, on this reckoning, is not only complemented by an orderly dogmatic exposition. The claim that the "obedience of faith" (Rom. 1:5) is "more of the heart than of the brain, and more of the disposition than of the understanding" (III.ii.8) plays out in distinct ways with respect to the cross as it shapes the life that Christians can and should lead.

Foundational here is Calvin's already-noted belief that the cross is an occasion for assurance. Incorporated into Christ's body, the Christian understands herself to be one in whom the death to sin is underway, and one whose reception of justification, in faith, is complemented by a sanctified movement into God's ways and works. Precisely because judgment has fallen on Christ, the Christian may now enjoy her gradual envelopment in the Trinitarian economy: the approach to the Father (not God the *judge*) being animated by the Spirit and guided by a Mediator whose prophetic, priestly, and kingly activity at the Father's right hand ensures that "we are really and effectually supplied with invincible weapons to subdue the flesh."[62] Yet this "arming" does not make the crucifixion a distant memory. On the contrary, believers ought to meditate on Christ's history—a history charted in scripture, acclaimed in sermons and catechisms, and described

---

[59] So Serene Jones, *Calvin and the Rhetoric of Piety* (Louisville, KY.: WJKP, 1995).
[60] So Boulton, *Life in God*.
[61] So Canlis, *Calvin's Ladder*.
[62] *Comm. 1 Pet. 4:1*.

dogmatically in the *Institutes*—to focus their disposition, and intensify their sense of gratitude to God.

> Suppose someone is told: "If God hated you while you were still a sinner, and cast you off, as you deserved, a terrible destruction would have awaited you. But because he kept you in grace voluntarily, and of his own free favor, and did not allow you to be estranged from him voluntarily, he thus delivered you from that peril." This man then will surely experience something of what he owes to God's mercy. On the other hand, suppose he learns, as Scripture teaches, that he was estranged from God through sin, is an heir of wrath, subject to the curse of eternal death, excluded from every hope of salvation, beyond every blessing of God, the slave of Satan, captive under the yoke of sin, destined finally for a dreadful destruction and already involved in it; and at that point Christ interceded as his advocate, took upon himself and suffered the punishment that, from God's righteous judgment, threatened all sinners; that he purged with his blood those evils which had rendered sinners hateful to God; that by this expiation he made satisfaction and sacrifice duly to God the Father; that as intercessor he has appeased God's wrath; that on this foundation rests the peace of God with men; that by this bond his benevolence is maintained toward them. Will the man not then be even more moved by all those things which so vividly portray the greatness of the calamity from which he has been rescued? (II.xvi.2)

This compressed re-narration of Christ's "course of obedience" (and note, once again, Calvin's deft combination of diverse scriptural figures) makes the point: "replaying" the plotline of Christ's atoning history allows the believer to be affected, evermore deeply, by the fact of God's grace. And theological writing is a spur to this kind of "replaying." Against the anodyne description of atonement that opens the passage, Calvin supplies an expansive, unnerving depiction of sin—but then "overwrites" his remarks about our fallen condition with a *more* expansive, and somewhat breathtaking, hymn to Christ's mediatorial work.[63] The goal here is not to refine theological understanding, but to help believers understand their gradual movement to the Father as passing through the cross. Or, to put it a bit differently: while believers stand now in the bright light of the resurrection and know that Christ, seated at the Father's right hand, continues to intercede for them, their reception of Christ's benefits is enhanced by a

---

[63] This being a feature, as suggested earlier, of Calvin's *Institutes* as a whole, especially with regards to the "arc" of book II and the transition to book III. Edmondson makes the point nicely: "the introduction of sin in Book II [is] a cosmic cataclysm that will open out into inestimable blessings" (*Calvin's Christology*, 45). Edmondson also reads II.xvi.2 much as I do; see *Calvin's Christology*, 109.

meditative re-narration of Christ's atoning history. This meditative re-narration, further, reminds believers of the absolute sufficiency of Christ's saving work. Precisely because "the force and the curse of sin were slain in his flesh when he was given as a victim, upon whom the whole burden of our sins … [was] cast" (III.iv.27), feelings of doubt, anxiety, and fear—an invariable consequence of sin's continuing reality—are beaten back. Concomitantly, there is a growing sense of freedom to live with God and others, an "emancipation … through the liberality of God's work in the incarnation."[64]

More particularly, Calvin connects Christ's atoning death with the experience of mortification: a dimension of the sanctification that God effects, wherein the believer becomes sorrowfully cognizant of her ongoing sinfulness, even as the communication of Christ's benefits initiates the process of vivification. "Bearing the cross," in particular, is a public expression of the internal labor of self-denial that deepens one's sense of a blissful eschatological end: "we share Christ's sufferings in order that as he has passed from a labyrinth of all evils into heavenly glory, we may in like manner be led through various tribulations to the same glory" (III.viii.1). Not that the difficulties, woes, and pains of this life are anticipations of future punishment; that is precisely what Christ's substitutionary work has freed us from. They are, rather, "fatherly chastisements" (III.viii.6), providentially imposed to assist with the process of Christian formation: occasions for the believer to deepen her union with Christ and to ready herself for eternal life, before and with God. When faced with trouble, then, believers should not accuse God of neglect or injustice. They should view "the testing of the cross" as a means by which God "brings them into a deeper knowledge of himself" (III.viii.2) and conforms them to the image of Christ crucified.[65]

By contemporary lights, such claims are obviously worrisome. As a number of feminist and womanist scholars have shown, the counsel to suffer with Christ, to forbear with meekness, is often offered without regard for long-standing patterns of ecclesial, familial, racial, sexual, social, and economic injustice. When directed toward individuals or communities who are consistently disadvantaged by a maldistribution of power and opportunity, the counsel becomes downright perverse. Those who ought to be emboldened to protest wrongdoing are encouraged, in effect, to consider their "lot" to be divinely ordained, and to view acquiescence to suffering as a mark of holiness. Calvin himself might be a case in

---

[64] Jane Dempsey Douglass, *Women, Freedom, and Calvin* (Philadelphia: Westminster, 1985), 11.
[65] See here, further, Randall C. Zachman, "'Deny Yourself and Take up Your Cross': John Calvin on the Christian Life," *IJST* 11, no. 4 (2009), 466–482; and Ronald S. Wallace, *Calvin's Doctrine of the Christian Life* (Reprint, Wipf & Stock, 1997), esp. 43–86 and 258–266.

point: in a letter of 1559, he advises against a wife leaving her physically abusive husband, so long as the violence does not bring "imminent peril to her life," and "exhort[s] her in the name of God to bear with patience the cross which God has seen fit to place on her."[66] An occasion in which one might say *abusus non tollit usum* (abuse does not remove use)? Not really. If Calvin's thinking is so readily enlisted to support patterns of behavior that Christians ought *never* to tolerate, there is good reason to query its dogmatic legitimacy and to ask about the ways in which Calvin connects doctrine and ethical counsel.[67]

Now it can be granted that this critique is supported by contemporary insights, the likes of which Calvin did not anticipate. It may be, too, that Calvin's perspective could be reworked. Calvin's understanding of a *duplex mortis Christi similitudo* (the twofold likeness of the death of Christ), for instance, could be curtailed: the Christian is *not* expected to mirror Christ "outwardly in reproaches and troubles"; she should focus only on dying to sin.[68] Alternately, the advice to "bear one's cross" could be set within an updated frame: an exhortation to reinterpret the entirety of Christian experience in light of the *unio cum Christo*, such that the miserable prospect of our lives being ruled by an impersonal "fate"—or, perhaps worse, a deity whose punitive vengeance is *not* exhausted on the cross, but continues to affect the lives of those who are predestined to life—being countered by the belief that our postmortem life with God will, somehow, disclose the value of, and then *overcome*, instances of wordly suffering.[69] This reinterpretation would not shy away from any identification of wrongdoing, much less give it any sanction. It would view even the worst aspects of human life through the prism of sanctification and encourage believers to treat misfortune as means to receive, yet more fully, the grace that accompanies their incorporation into Christ's body. Yet neither of these options quite resolves the problem. Whether it is a matter of tying self-denial to the spiritual progress of an individual or relativizing contingent instances of injustice through reference to an eschatological

---

[66] Philip E. Hughes, ed. and trans., *The Register of the Company of Pastors of Geneva in the Time of Calvin* (Grand Rapids, MI: Eerdmans, 1966), 345; see also the exchange of letters between Calvin and an unknown women in 1552 on 193–198.

[67] Nancy Duff puts it nicely: "Feminist and womanist theologies remind the Reformed tradition of something *it already knows but is prone to forget*: if Christian doctrine serves the gospel of Jesus Christ it cannot be formulated in indifference to the human experience of suffering. Although the experience of suffering does not allow individuals or groups to dictate the content of Christian doctrine, *the very nature of the gospel demands that the voices of those who suffer be heard*" (emphasis in the original). See "Atonement and the Christian Life: Reformed Doctrine from a Feminist Perspective," *Interpretation* 53, no. 1 (1999), 21–33 (22).

[68] Wallace, *The Doctrine of the Christian Life*, 52.

[69] On this point, see Marilyn McCord Adams, *Christ and Horrors: The Coherence of Christology* (Cambridge: Cambridge University Press, 2006).

reward, the basic direction of Calvin's thought remains questionable. The cross is not clearly presented as an imperative for action. It is not treated as a call to resist wrongdoing in the here-and-now, such that Christ's "end" serves as the beginning for new modes of individual and communal life. Those of us who believe that "classic" accounts of atonement, such as Calvin's, can and should be allied with a liberationist ethic, then, have constructive work to do—insisting that Christ's suffering and death does not need to be supplemented by undignifying acts of self-degradation; circumscribing "self-denial" in ways that are not easily assimilable to the socio-sexual status quo; and imagining Christian life as a manifestation of joyous freedom, wherein the "secret energy" of Christ's death is the engine of ecclesial, political, social, and sexual transformation.[70]

Conclusion

> Not only is there this marvel, that He hath given His Son, but yet further that He hath given him in such a way, as that the Beloved One Himself should be slain! ... See, how high a price He sets upon us. If when we hated Him and were enemies, He gave the Beloved, what will He not do now, when we are reconciled by Him through grace?[71]

Calvin's account of the atonement, at least as I have presented it, might be read as an extended gloss on these sentences from John Chrysostom. There is, first of all, a determined effort to focus readers' attention on the "marvel" of the atonement. This effort is marked by Calvin's intertextual rhetoric, which deftly combines and recombines scriptural motifs and classical conceptualities, thereby scotching the idea that any single conceptual scheme suffices to describe Christ's work and pressing readers to encounter Christ's atoning history as "unsubstitutable." Yet while Calvin's writing might unsettle readers, it does not augur dogmatic unintelligibility. The *Institutes* and the commentaries train our attention on certain dimensions of the atonement—the incarnation as conduit through which

---

[70] *Comm. Gal.* 2:20. A useful starting point: Calvin here takes the important step of glossing mortification as being "dead" to the Law and "alive" to God: "Engrafted into the death of Christ, we derive a secret energy from it, as the shoot does from the root ... Having said that we are nailed to the cross along with Christ, he adds that this makes us alive."

[71] John Chrysostom, *Homilies on Ephesians* I, from *Chrysostom: Homilies on Galatians, etc.* vol. 13 NPNF, first series. Calvin was fond of Chrysostom, and even started work on a French edition of his sermons. See W. Ian P. Hazlett, "Calvin's Latin Preface to His Proposed French Edition of Chrysostom's Homilies: Translation and Commentary," in *Humanism and Reform: The Church in Europe, England, and Scotland, 1400–1643*, ed. James Kirk (Oxford: Blackwell, 1991), 129–150.

God's love is communicated, Christ's voluntary obedience to the Father, Christ's willingness to endure God's furious judgment against sin, Christ's sacrificial self-offering, and Christ's victory over sin and death—and do so in ways that show Calvin providing something *much* more interesting than supplying a "theory" of atonement. These texts also foreground two of Calvin's most distinctive dogmatic claims: that it is through the cross that God realizes God's love for God's children, and that this realization of divine love is bound up with Christ's humanity and human agency. Finally, Calvin answers Chrysostom's question as to what God does now, in light of the cross. On one level, there is Calvin's (quite laudable) proposal that piety be enriched as believers meditate on the "arc" of Christ's saving history. On another level, there is a (more questionable) suggestion that "bearing the cross" should form a key element of the believer's sanctification.

Is Calvin's account of the atonement usable today? I think so. Certainly, those who have decided that salvation can be unhooked from Christ's person, and those who have concluded that the atonement has nothing to do with the cross—I am reminded here of the young Schleiermacher's heartfelt admission: "I cannot believe that he who called himself the Son of Man was the true, eternal God; I cannot believe ... his death was a vicarious atonement"[72]—will continue to view Calvin with suspicion. Yet there is richness and sophistication in these texts that anyone interested in atonement ought to engage. At the heart of Christian faith, for Calvin, is something that would be inconceivable, were it not for its disclosure in Scripture: the cross as the Father's furious judgment against sin, through which God articulates God's love for God's children, and promises to them the riches of union with Christ.

---

[72] Quoted in Brian Gerrish, *A Prince of the Church: Schleiermacher and the Beginnings of Modern Theology* (Reprint, Eugene, OR: Wipf & Stock, 2001), 25. Schleiermacher came to think of Christ as "the true, eternal God"; he remained ambivalent about the cross as a vicarious atonement.

13

Karl Barth

Shannon Nicole Smythe

Introduction

The doctrine of the atonement is anything but ancillary within the theology of Karl Barth—quite the opposite, in fact. To begin to grasp the centrality of the doctrine in Barth's mature thought is to enter into the very heart of his theology. Like the copy of Grünewald's painting of the crucifixion hanging over Barth's desk while he worked,[1] an understanding of Barth's theology of the atonement gives a framework by which to understand the whole of his theology. For Barth, the covenant fulfilled by Jesus Christ in the atonement lies at the center of the gospel message that is received and proclaimed by the Christian community. The atonement speaks the good news of "God with us"—of how God makes peace in Jesus Christ between Godself and us. It testifies to God's historical intervening as a human and taking up our case.[2] Within Barth's mature doctrine of reconciliation, the atonement is the objective realization of humanity's justification

---

[1] In a perhaps somewhat corresponding manner, the fact of my having been a student of Bruce McCormack's continually "hangs over" my understanding of Barth's theology of the atonement. What I have written here is a result of learning from him how to understand the theology of Karl Barth. Any errors in my interpretation are, of course, my own, but any insights I have into Barth's theology of the cross are due in no small part to his teaching, writing, and advising.

[2] Atonement is, in some of Barth's opening words in CD IV/1, the "closing of the breach, gulf and abyss between God and us for which we are responsible ... Because He is God He is able not only to be God but also to be this man ... in our place and for our sake. Because He is God He has and exercises the power as this man to suffer for us the consequence of our transgression, the wrath and penalty which necessarily fall on us, and in that way to satisfy Himself in our regard. And again because He is God, He has and exercises the power as this man to be His own partner in our place, the One who in free obedience accepts the ordination of man to salvation which we resist, and in that way satisfies us, i.e., achieves that which can positively satisfy us." Karl Barth, *Church Dogmatics* [hereafter indicated by CD followed by volume number, part-volume number, and page number], 4 vols in 13 parts, edited by G. W. Bromiley and T. F. Torrance (Edinburgh: T&T Clark, 1956–1975), here citing vol. IV/1, 12–13.

in Christ. In the death of Jesus, sin and sinful humanity were annihilated in the person of Jesus Christ, thereby saving us from destruction, rescuing us from eternal separation from God, and exalting us to covenant partnership with God.

This chapter intends to offer a synthetic exposition of Barth's mature doctrine of the atonement. It will proceed in two main parts by way of a series of investigative topics intended to expose the key conceptual moves inherent in Barth's innovative, and often misunderstood, approach. In the first part, we consider Barth's first extended treatment of the doctrine in volume II/1 of the *Church Dogmatics*. Barth works with the satisfaction theory of atonement of his Reformed predecessors but improves it by grounding it within a discussion of the attributes of God. Yet it is not until his revolutionary revision to the doctrine of election in *CD* II/2 that he is really able to articulate a different kind of satisfaction theory altogether—one that does not abstract the righteousness of God from God's love as mercy. There, he makes the radical claim that God "decreed His own abandonment"[3] even as God chose mercy, grace, and life for humanity.

Continuing to trace Barth's revision to the satisfaction theory, the second part moves into Barth's mature doctrine of reconciliation in *CD* IV/1. Now working within an explicitly judicial framework, he considers how the suffering and death of the God-human Jesus Christ reconciles us to God. Consonant with the kind of revisions he made to the doctrine in *CD* II/2, Barth continues to deepen and go beyond a merely judicial approach, especially in his articulation of how sin is overcome in the atonement. The second section of this part moves briefly into *CD* IV/2, where he treats the second moment of the one divine act of atonement as the exaltation of humanity in Jesus Christ. Here, stressing the exaltation of humanity in Jesus Christ as both our coming to God and the glorious end of all God's ways in the work of atonement, Barth incorporates a central ethical element from the moral framework for the atonement. The chapter concludes by reflecting briefly on what it might mean to speak of the atonement with and after Barth given the ongoing concerns over penal substitution and judicial theories of the atonement.

Atonement and the Perfections of Divine Love

In *CD* II/1, Barth locates his initial treatment of the atonement within his exposition of the unity of God's grace and holiness and mercy and righteousness as

---

[3] Barth, *CD* II/2, 168.

perfections of God's love. This is significant in and of itself. Calvin, for example, erred precisely in his reticence to say much at all about the being and attributes of God. This meant that the doctrine of the atonement he articulated, stressing as it did the outpouring of the wrath of God on the cross, implied a contradiction in the being of God.[4] It ends up making "God's mercy the prisoner, so to speak, of His righteousness until such time as righteousness has been fully satisfied."[5] In pairing God's holiness and righteousness under the perfection of God's loving, Barth makes clear that there is no such thing as a cleavage between the grace and holiness of God, nor between God's mercy and righteousness. "The holiness of God consists in the unity of His judgment with His grace. God is holy because His grace judges and His judgment is gracious."[6] "God does not need to yield His righteousness a single inch when He is merciful. As He is merciful, He is righteous."[7]

All of this comes together most concretely in the crucifixion. It is precisely in the death of Christ that mercy reaches its goal through the execution of the righteous judgment of God.[8]

> God is the God who for the sake of His righteousness is wrathful and condemns and punishes. He is not only this, but He is also this ... The event of Good Friday embodies the divine No, which contains in itself the divine Yes and is the presupposition of it, but which must not be any the less on that account understood as a definite divine No.[9]

God's holy wrath serves the gracious purposes of God's love, and it is the mercy of God to suffer with us in our suffering even as God is righteous in creating fellowship with sinful humanity. Barth's main point is that in the event of the cross, God's righteous judgment is expressed as wrath and condemnation.

---

[4] I agree with Bruce McCormack's assessment that it is "not enough to affirm that the reconciling activity of the Son of God has its ground in the divine love if we are not then able to affirm in a coherent way that that love is operative at every step along the way in the accomplishment of our redemption." Bruce L. McCormack, *For Us and Our Salvation: Incarnation and Atonement in the Reformed Tradition*, Studies in Reformed Theology and Tradition vol. 1:2 (Princeton: Princeton Theological Seminary, 1993), 27.
[5] Ibid.
[6] Barth, *CD* II/1, 363.
[7] Barth, *CD* II/1, 383.
[8] "But the real judgment of God is alone the crucifixion of Christ, and the terror of this event is that it is the reality which all other judgments upon Israel, the world and mankind can only foreshadow or reflect ... For in the strict sense we can truly say that human sin and sinful man have comes the object of divine anger and judgment only as we look at this event." Barth, *CD* II/1, 396.
[9] Barth, *CD* II/1, 394.

"There God's condemning and punishing righteousness broke out, really smiting and piercing human sin, man as sinner, and sinful Israel."[10] In God's transcendent mercy, "the eternal God Himself in the unity with human nature" took up and suffered the wrath of God in Christ's death on the cross. In so doing, "God was true to Himself."[11] In Jesus Christ, God was "not only the God who is offended by man. He was also the man whom God threatens with death, who falls a victim to death in the face of God's judgment."[12]

Barth is guarding against any notion that in Jesus's death, we are dealing with the suffering of an innocent man that intercedes for us and somehow persuades God to relent from wrath and to be merciful to us instead. "There is no moving of God by the creature on the basis of which God can then decide on a universal amnesty. But it is God's own heart that moves in creation on the basis of His own good-pleasure. It suffers what the creature ought to suffer and could not suffer without being destroyed."[13] Barth is lifting up the love of God as the true motive force behind the death of Christ. He urges us to "see, feel and appreciate His love to us even in His anger, condemnation and punishment."[14] In working with a concept of penal substitution, Barth does not make the critical error of implying that the crucifixion somehow changed God's mind.

Yet Barth still struggled to maintain the unity of the righteousness and mercy of God's love. This is seen in his remark that God's punishing righteousness happened to Jesus in such a way that on the cross "the righteousness of God which we have offended was really revealed and satisfied."[15] "At the crucial point, he [Barth] repeated the error of the sixteenth and seventeenth-century Reformed theologians and made the death of Christ a satisfaction offered to the divine righteousness."[16] In failing to articulate how God's merciful love is operative throughout God's punishing righteousness on the cross, Barth, whether intentionally or not, seems to abstract God's righteousness, satisfied in God's atoning death, from God's love as mercy. We are left to wonder if God's mercy toward us is indeed held captive until God's righteousness is satisfied. What this might also suggest is that Barth, despite his insistence on looking to the history of Jesus Christ, still retains remnants of abstract reflection on the being of God at this point in the *Church Dogmatics*. With the development of his doctrine of election in *CD* II/2, Barth's

---

[10] Barth, *CD* II/1, 396.
[11] Barth, *CD* II/1, 402.
[12] Barth, *CD* II/1, 397.
[13] Barth, *CD* II/1, 402.
[14] Barth, *CD* II/1, 394.
[15] Barth, *CD* II/1, 396.
[16] McCormack, *For Us and Our Salvation*, 30.

dogmatic reflection becomes more consistently postmetaphysical[17] just as his language around penal substitution begins to take a backseat to his much more prominent insistence that Jesus Christ is the subject and object of election, such that the second person of the Trinity, in his divine-human unity, is the Subject of the atonement.

Election and Atonement

Barth's doctrine of the atonement in *CD* II/1 is a revised form of the modified Anselmianism[18] of his Reformed tradition. Though his characterization of penal substitution is now on a firmer foundation, having brought together the righteousness and mercy under the perfections of God's love, when he came to his discussion of the death of Jesus Christ, he did not articulate the role of God's mercy as he spoke of the satisfaction of God's righteousness. Now, however, in *CD* II/2, Barth makes explicit that it is God's love that is satisfied in the atonement. Armed with the new insight that election is "the beginning of all the ways and works of God,"[19] he stresses, "Jesus Christ is the decision of God."[20] In other words, the foundational element of Barth's revision of election is naming Jesus Christ as electing God and elect human.[21] Ultimately, this will provide him with a more solid foundation upon which to make explicit how God's wrath is an instrument of God's love.

God's self-determination to bear the name of Jesus reveals that the material content of election is the covenant of grace.[22] If Jesus Christ is both the object

---

[17] This means that Barth's theology, especially beginning with his doctrine of election, attempts to say nothing of God that cannot first be read off the history of God's self-revelation in Jesus Christ. He starts with Jesus, and there begins to speak of God. In other words, we speak of God only by beginning with the economic trinity not the immanent trinity. David Congdon explains that "classical orthodoxy is metaphysical because it presupposes what it means to speak of deity and humanity *prior* to wrestling with the particular reality of Jesus. The object of its inquiry has already been essentially defined before coming to grips with the object itself." See David W. Congdon, *The God Who Saves: A Dogmatic Sketch* (Eugene, OR: Cascade Books, 2016), 108.

[18] Whereas Anselm set up satisfaction and punishment as mutually exclusive alternatives, sixteenth- and seventeenth-century Reformed theologians followed Thomas in seeing satisfaction as occurring through punishment. "The righteous demands of God are satisfied through punishment, a punishment consisting of the death of the sinner." McCormack, *For Us and Our Salvation*, 25.

[19] Barth, *CD* II/2, 3.

[20] Barth, *CD* II/2, 7. Barth's corrective to the traditional Reformed teaching on election is centered upon making "Jesus Christ the eternal, *ontic* ground of election." McCormack, "Grace and Being: The Role of God's Gracious Election in Karl Barth's Theological Ontology," in *Orthodox and Modern: Studies in the Theology of Karl Barth* (Grand Rapids, MI: Baker Academic, 2008), 284.

[21] First, "in so far as He is *God*, we must obviously—and above all!—ascribe to Him the active determination of electing." Second, "in so far as He is *human*, the passive determination of election is also necessarily proper to Him." Barth, *CD* II/2, 103, rev.

[22] McCormack, "Grace and Being," 189.

and the subject of election, then God's decision for the incarnation has "an eternal bearing on the divine life."[23] The implication here is that God's being is constituted in the fact of God's decision to turn toward humanity in Jesus Christ in self-giving love.[24] There is "no height or depth in which God can be God in any other way."[25] The event of the incarnation, then, is the instantiation of the decree of God's eternal love.[26] As any doctrine of the atonement assumes a particular conception of God, here we see that Barth's doctrine of election, insofar as it suggests that the second person of the Trinity "assigns himself an identity bound to the concrete life of Jesus Christ,"[27] has radical consequences for understanding the being of God in the event of the atonement. The gospel message inherent in the doctrine of election is "not No but Yes ... not Yes and No, but in its substance, in the origin and scope of its utterance, it is altogether Yes."[28] The "Yes" of election is constitutive of God's being, and therefore when God in Christ deals with sinful humanity in the atonement, there is no bifurcation between the mercy and righteousness of God's love.

Barth's version of the satisfaction theory is now articulated through closer dependency on the history of God's self-revelation in Jesus Christ as witnessed to in Scripture. One example of this comes in a long fine-print section of §35.4 where Barth undertakes an exegetical study of New Testament occurrences of the Greek verb *paradounai*.[29] Barth traces various New Testament uses of the term, instances both of human and divine handing-over. He considers John 1:14 as "the original and authentic" divine *paradidōmi* and God's handing-over of Jesus in the atonement the second.

> The fact that ... the Son of God had to be delivered into the hands of sinful men has its basis in this original and authentic handing-over whose author

---

[23] Paul Dafydd Jones, "The Heart of the Matter: Karl Barth's Christological Exegesis," in *Thy Word is Truth: Barth on Scripture*, ed. George Hunsinger (Grand Rapids, MI: Eerdmans, 2012), 184.

[24] "The most basic content of the doctrine of election is a choice God makes with respect to himself. God chooses to be God only in the covenant of grace." McCormack, "The Ontological Presuppositions of Barth's Doctrine of the Atonement," in *The Glory of the Atonement: Biblical, Historical, & Practical Perspectives*, ed. Charles E. Hill and Frank A. James III (Downers Grove, IL: IVP, 2004), 359.

[25] "In the primal and basic decision in which He *wills to be* and actually *is* God, in the mystery of what *takes place* from and to all eternity within Himself, within His triune being, God is none other than the One who in His Son or Word elects Himself, and in and with Himself elects His people" (emphases in the original). Barth, *CD* II/2, 77.

[26] Barth, *CD* II/2, 76.

[27] Jones, "Barth and Anselm: God, Christ and the Atonement," *IJST* 12, no. 3 (2010), 262.

[28] Barth, *CD* II/2, 13.

[29] For more on this topic, see Shannon Smythe "The Sum of the Gospel: Barth's Intracanonical and Intertextual Interpretation of *paradidōmi*," in *Reading the Gospels with Karl Barth*, ed. Daniel Migliore (Grand Rapids, MI: Eerdmans, 2017).

and subject is God Himself or Jesus Himself, just as the fact that Jesus humbled Himself in obedience unto death, the death of the cross (Phil. 2:8), is based on the fact that primarily and decisively He had emptied Himself of that divine form and taken the form of man. The first took place for the sake of the second, and the second was the outcome and revelation of the first.[30]

Barth's reading of the incarnation and the events of Golgotha suggests that he is determined to say nothing of God's being apart from what can be read off of God's actions in history as narrated in Scripture. In this way, his reflections on the eternal life and identity of God go beyond even what he had been able to say in his treatment of the doctrine of God's being and perfections in CD II/1. Now he can draw an intentional connection between the divine "self-emptying" of the incarnation and the event of the crucifixion.

Barth's exegetical word study also demonstrates that his version of forensicism has a decidedly apocalyptic tone to it as he begins to wonder after the condition of the possibility for the handing-over of Jesus to death at the hands of the reigning political powers.[31] His investigation of a handful of *paradidōmi* passages in Matthew, Mark, and Acts (Mt. 5:24, 18:34, 4:12, 24:10; Mark 1:14; Acts 21:11, 28:17, 21:1, and 12:4) leads him to suggest that "'delivery' is the handing-over or transfer from a free or relatively free person to the confining power of those who wish him harm, from whom he must expect harm."[32] Thus what "God visited on Himself in the handing-over of His Son" is nothing less than the "true and proper handing-over of man in weakness to a strange and overwhelming and hostile authority," which he elsewhere calls both "power of Satan" and "evil powers."[33] In other words, the divine willing of Jesus suffering death came before the divine handing-over of humanity to the power of sin, which Paul thrice repeats in Romans 1:24, 26, and 28.

> Clearly the necessity and power and meaning of all delivery are established in this *first* and radical delivery, in which God, in the power of Jesus, or Jesus as the Son of God, made Himself the object of delivery. It is not permissible to

---

[30] Barth, CD II/2, 490–91.
[31] Nathan Kerr suggests that Barth's Christology follows an apocalyptic logic in that "history is what it is just insofar as *God acts*, and acts *apocalyptically*, precisely as revealed in the concrete, particular history of Jesus of Nazareth" (emphases in the original). Nathan Kerr, *Christ, History and Apocalyptic: The Politics of Christian Mission* (Eugene, OR: Cascade Books, 2009), 77.
[32] Barth, CD II/2, 481. This points, he thinks, to a technical meaning of handing-over as "to be delivered up in powerlessness to [a] strange and hostile overwhelming power. To 'hand over' is to deprive a powerful person of his freedom, so that his power is not merely damaged but is as such destroyed, and he has no option but to submit to that which is inflicted on him." Barth, CD II/2, 490.
[33] Barth, CD II/2, 494–495.

understand any other delivery except with reference to this one (without prejudice to its special meaning). All other delivery looks either to or from this. It has its reality in what happened here. It is impossible to interpret it apart from its connection with this event.[34]

With the development of a theological ontology consistent with forensic thinking, Barth is able to tie together election, incarnation, and atonement under the heading of God's eternal love. God's love is revealed in the history of the positive instance of the divine handing-over. Hence Barth suggests that the "decree of God's eternal love, in which the Father sent the Son and the Son obeyed the Father"[35] necessarily overflows in history in the divine positive *paradidōmi* in which God's will is revealed through God's willingness "to deliver Himself into the situation of impotence in face of the power by which man is overborne."[36] Applying this definition to the positive divine handing-over of Jesus in Romans 8:32 and his own self-giving for us in Galatians 2:20, Barth continues to frame Jesus's condescension and rejection in the atonement as the event of God's judging, condemning, and punishing sinful humanity.

> Before it can be positively made good, that which stands between God and us must first be removed, and removed according to justice and righteousness. The handing-over of Jesus shows how great and serious is that which must be removed. It shows that it can be removed only when God takes upon Himself its necessary condemnation and punishment, so that we may be set free for that which God wills to give us. This is what God resolved to do in the person of Jesus Christ. God *could* do it because in His omnipotence He is capable of this handing-over, because in His self-abasement—far from committing any breach against His own nature—He causes His omnipotence to conquer, and because the concealment and darkness and mire to which He gave Himself are quite unable to diminish His divinity. God acted divinely when He did this ... The mercy which He manifested was an act of His righteousness, and the righteousness which He exercised was an act of His mercy.[37]

In Barth's thinking, concepts such as divine judgment, condemnation, and punishment of sinful humanity remain necessary due to the seriousness of sin in the face of God's righteousness. They serve the purpose of removing the

---

[34] Barth, *CD* II/2, 489, rev.
[35] Barth, *CD* II/2, 491.
[36] Barth, *CD* II/2, 491.
[37] Barth, *CD* II/2, 493; emphasis in the original.

obstacle that stands between God and humanity even as God, in God's great love, is the one who removes the offending obstacle. It is nothing but God's "utter love for us" to have actually willed "his own handing-over" to this very judgment, condemnation, and punishment. Barth calls this "the offering of His freedom to His love."[38] Focusing on God's willed decision for the divine handing-over, Barth can reunite God's righteousness and mercy when speaking of the crucifixion.

Yet Barth is also forging new territory by focusing on how Christ's death, as the God-human, means the removal of the human as sinner. By following the divine handing-over clauses in the New Testament, Barth recasts divine judgment in radically dynamic terms. God's judgment, executed in the divine handing-over, destroys sin at its root. In contrast, traditional forensic accounts of the atonement might focus only on the removal of guilt, explain the atonement as the result of a divine verdict that leaves God unaffected in Godself, or maintain the event of the cross as an external transaction between God and the human Jesus, rather than an event in God. Barth, in his treatment of election, casts the atonement as an event in the divine life rooted in God's self-constituted being as a God who suffers for us because of God's great love. "That God 'gave up' His Son, that *Jesus 'gave up' Himself*"[39] for us "shows us in what sense this handing-over is the eternal will of God."[40] "So great is His *love* that He regarded it as worthy of this offering."[41] The atonement is not merely a divine verdict. "He does not merely execute judgment upon sin. He takes it upon Himself and suffers so that there can be no further question of suffering it ourselves. There can be no going behind this regulation of the order between God and the world He created."[42] Barth's historicized actualistic ontology pushes the bounds of his version of a satisfaction theory way beyond its traditional bounds.[43]

---

[38] Barth, *CD* II/2, 491.
[39] Barth, *CD* II/2, 490, rev.; emphasis in the original.
[40] Barth, *CD* II/2, 493, rev.
[41] Barth, *CD* II/2, 491, rev.; emphasis in the original.
[42] Barth, *CD* II/2, 494.
[43] "If it is truly the will of the Father to send His eternal Son, and the will of the Son to obey His eternal Father in the execution of this mission; if it is truly the will of God to give Himself to man in such seriousness and fullness that He Himself becomes what man is—flesh, a bearer of human unworthiness and incapacity—then this means that it is the will of God to deliver Himself into the situation of impotence in face of the power by which man is overborne, giving Himself not merely to the constraint of the limitation of creaturely life, but to the curse of human guilt, to the rejection of the life of man as it is ruled and determined by his sin, abandoning Himself to the utter opposite of His own divine form of existence." Barth, *CD* II/2, 491.

Atonement in Barth's Doctrine of Reconciliation

By *CD* IV/1, all of the main pieces of Barth's mature Christology are in place allowing him to be more consistent than ever. Even so, much of the material content for Barth's treatment of the atonement within his doctrine of reconciliation is already contained in the gains made by Barth's revolutionary doctrine of election. What comes together with new force in Barth's treatment of the atonement in *CD* IV/1 and 2 is first the way he is able to coherently integrate the saving nature of both the person and work of Jesus and second the fact that in the history of Jesus, the atonement is the result both of God coming to us in self-humiliation, and the restoration of true humanity in the exaltation of humanity in him.

Self-Humiliation and the Cry of Dereliction in the Triune Life

In §59.1 Barth approaches his discussion of the person of the mediator, Jesus Christ, by wondering how the meaning of the incarnation is revealed in the question of Jesus on the cross (Mark 15:34). In his determination to understand the person of Jesus Christ in light of his narrated history as witnessed in Scripture, Barth takes the cry of dereliction very seriously, yet in such a way that does not create any sort of contradiction or conflict in God. Barth's single subject Christology leads him to suggest that the passion and death of Jesus are human experiences that take place in God. While the experience that gives rise to the cry is a human experience, it points to a deeper truth that the subject of the cry is God. Nothing is held back in God's solidarity with us in Jesus. At the same time, while God makes Godself one with humanity in this cry, God does not cease to be God.

> God gives Himself, but He does not give Himself away. He does not give up being God in becoming a creature, in becoming man. He does not cease to be God. He does not come into conflict with Himself. He does not sin when in unity with the man Jesus He mingles with sinners and takes their place. And when He dies in His unity with this man, death does not gain any power over Him. He exists as God in the righteousness and the life, the obedience and the resurrection of this man. He makes His own the being of man in contradiction against Him, but He does not make common cause with it. He also makes His own the being of man under the curse of this contradiction but in order to do

away with it as He suffers it. He acts as Lord over this contradiction, even as He subject Himself to it.[44]

Barth confronts our temptation to think this is impossible for God, remarking that it simply shows that

> our concept of God is too narrow, too arbitrary, too human—far too human. Who God is and what it is to be divine is something we have to learn where God has revealed Himself and His nature, the essence of the divine. And if He has revealed Himself in Jesus Christ as the God who does this, it is not for us to be wiser than He and to say that it is in contradiction with the divine essence.[45]

Barth's doctrine of the atonement evinces a steadfast commitment to let even the words of the God-man, Jesus Christ, on the cross, tell us who God is—a God who suffers for us and in our place. At the same time, the reason Barth is trying to make sense of the suffering and death of Jesus is because he is, in fact, operating with a particular version of penal substitution, which must speak coherently about his suffering and death.

Christian faith has always had pastoral reasons to proclaim that God came and died for us; that God came and did for us, in Jesus, what we could never do for ourselves; that God alone saves us. Somewhat ironically then is the fact that classical orthodoxy has always held to a metaphysically based theological ontology, which was put in place to secure the impassibility of God. The problem with a metaphysically based theology is that it does not take as its starting point God's self-revelation in Scripture but with a more general category of being, of which God is the highest form. This will not do in Barth's mind because to end with God we must start with God. Everything depends, he says, on our acceptance of the New Testament's witness to the "one true God in Jesus Christ the Crucified."[46] This means we must accept that God's being contains "an above and a below ... that it belongs to the inner life of God that there should take place within it obedience."[47] As foreign as it may sound, Barth implores that we state firmly that God's "unity consists in the fact that in Himself He is both One who is obeyed and Another who obeys."[48] The event of the atonement, in other words, reveals the being of the triune God. The triune God takes into the divine life the human experience of suffering

---

[44] Barth, *CD* IV/1, 185.
[45] Barth, *CD* IV/1, 186.
[46] Barth, *CD* IV/1, 199.
[47] Barth, *CD* IV/1, 200–201.
[48] Barth, *CD* IV/1, 201.

and death, but does so in a way that does not compromise God's unchanging nature. The self-emptying and self-humiliation of God in the incarnation and atonement are not done apart from their basis in God's own being and inner life. "He does not do it without any correspondence to, but as the strangely logical final continuation of, the history in which He is God."[49] Barth's reasoning here, again going wildly beyond his Reformed predecessors, still fits within a forensic framework, where being is understood as a function of decision and act. God elects for Godself not only the divine being God would have but also the human experience of suffering and death God would experience in Jesus Christ. "He is in and for the world what He is in and for Himself. He is in time what He is in eternity."[50] Never before had the defenders of a judicial atonement developed a theological ontology commensurate with what they saw happening in the suffering and death of Jesus. In this way, Barth is more consistent in his development of the doctrine.

Atonement and the Overcoming of Sin

In §59.2 Barth discusses what it means that God was for us in Christ under four judicial headings. "In this passion there is legally reestablished the covenant between God and man, broken by man but kept by God. On that one day of suffering of that One there took place the comprehensive turning in the history of all creation."[51] Far from emphasizing some sort of external transaction that takes place as a result of God's divine verdict, Barth's point is that the "eternal God Himself" takes on the passion, acts as a judge, and allows himself to be judged.[52] The torture, crucifixion, and death of Jesus is God's redemptive judgment on all humanity, but it is also the conversion of the world to God because God himself suffers in the confrontation so that "eternal death" and "sin itself and as such" are annihilated.[53] Again, this indicates that Barth is using a judicial framework in a very unique way.

Barth's focus on the problem of sin, eternal death, and sinful humanity take us to the very core of his understanding of the atonement. He firmly insists that the atonement is necessary in order to deal with the disruption of the sinful humanity. "Sin, therefore, is the obstacle which has to be removed and overcome

---

[49] Barth, *CD* IV/1, 203.
[50] Barth, *CD* IV/1, 204.
[51] Barth, *CD* IV/1, 247.
[52] God "gives Himself to be the humanly acting and suffering person in this occurrence." Barth, *CD* IV/1, 246.
[53] Barth, *CD* IV/1, 247.

in the reconciliation of the world with God as its conversion to Him. But it is also the source, which has to be blocked in the atonement, of the destruction which threatens man, which already engulfs him and drags him down."[54] The sinful human faces "eternal death, death as the invincibly threatening force of dissolution."[55] Acknowledging the full reality of sin and the consequential eternal death that results, Barth states that the "very heart of the atonement is the overcoming of sin."[56] In this sense, Barth says, we can indeed speak of Jesus suffering the punishment humanity deserved. But he cautions that we must not make punishment

> a main concept as in some of the older presentations of the doctrine of atonement (especially those which follow Anselm of Canterbury), either in the sense that by His suffering our punishment we are spared from suffering it ourselves, or that in so doing He 'satisfied' or offered satisfaction to the wrath of God. The latter thought is quite foreign to the New Testament. And of the possible idea that we are spared punishment by what Jesus Christ has done for us we have to notice that the main drift of the New Testament testaments concerning the passion and death of Jesus Christ is not at all or only indirectly in this direction.[57]

Barth comes very close to getting rid of the concept of punishment altogether because it does not have strong biblical support. It comes into Christian theology from Isaiah 53, but it is referred to not at all or only indirectly in New Testament passages. For his part, he stops just shy of completely rejecting or evading the concept, reasoning that "[m]y turning from God is followed by God's annihilating turning from me."[58] In other words, the subordinated place for a concept of punishment

> derives from the decisive thing that in the suffering and death of Jesus Christ it has come to pass that in His own person He has made an end of us as sinners and therefore of sin itself by going to death as the One who took our place as sinners. In His person He has delivered up us sinners and sin itself to destruction. He has removed us sinners and sin, negated us, cancelled us out.[59]

In the end, the concept of punishment, in and of itself, is not adequate enough for understanding what God in Jesus Christ accomplished for us on the cross, nor for understanding the righteous mercy of God's holy love. Instead, removal,

---

[54] Barth, *CD* IV/1, 252–253.
[55] Barth, *CD* IV/1, 253.
[56] Barth, *CD* IV/1, 253.
[57] Barth, *CD* IV/1, 253.
[58] Barth, *CD* IV/1, 253.
[59] Barth, *CD* IV/1, 253.

destruction, negation, and cancellation of the sinner and sin are Barth's chosen terms for answering the question of what takes place in the suffering and death of Jesus. He

> caused sin to be taken and killed on the cross in His own person (as that of the one great sinner). And in that way, not by suffering our punishment as such, but in the deliverance of sinful man and sin itself to destruction ... He has ... blocked the source of our destruction ... He has saved us from destruction and rescued us from eternal death.[60]
>
> ...
>
> For the sake of this best, the worst had to happen to sinful man: not out of any desire for vengeance and retribution on the part of God, but because of the radical nature of the divine love, which could 'satisfy' itself only in the outworking of its wrath against the man of sin, only by killing him, extinguishing him, removing him. Here is the place for the doubtful concept that in the passion of Jesus Christ, in the giving up of His Son to death, God has done that which is 'satisfactory' or sufficient in the victorious fighting of sin to make this victory radical and total.[61]

The cross, therefore, is not about the satisfaction of God's wrath. In fact, God's wrath has no independent existence in and of itself. It is merely the outworking of God's holy love when it has been spurned. The wrath of God always serves the purposes of God's mercy, and mercy is always God's posture toward the world. Still working within a judicial framework, Barth now incorporates the language of "radical victory" in order to describe just how profound and total is God's work of extinguishing of sin and sinful humanity.

What Barth has done, then, not only by radicalizing but also subordinating the concepts of punishment and satisfaction, is to provide a historicized theological ontology by which the incarnation and atonement are seen to be the outworking in time of God's eternal will and therefore rooted in the holy love of God. To the extent that notions of satisfaction and punishment do retain a subordinated place in Barth's doctrine of the atonement, their intention is to point to the reality that God's love is not only so holy and righteousness that it cannot allow sin to stand and but it is also so powerfully constitutive of God's being that God wills to take sin and sinful humanity into the divine life in order to remove them once and for all.

---

[60] Barth, *CD* IV/1, 254.
[61] Barth, *CD* IV/1, 254.

Atonement and the Creation of New Humanity

We have seen how Barth's doctrine of election brings his mature Christology into sharp focus when he takes up the doctrine of atonement in *CD* IV/1. The moves made by him everywhere build upon the claim that Jesus Christ is both the electing God and the elect human. Up until now we have reflected primarily on the centrality of Jesus as the electing God, but we must not forget that Barth establishes the necessity and importance of his human action. "God Himself in person is the subject of a real human being and acting. And just because God is the Subject of it, this being and acting are real. They are a genuinely and truly human being and acting."[62]

In *CD* IV/2, we see that God's assumption of human flesh is not only an act of God's humiliation and obedience but also the exaltation of humanity. Barth's theological anthropology proclaims that true humanity is realized in the obedience of Jesus Christ. "On the one hand, the Son became incarnate by loving God and mirroring his will; on the other hand, humanity's highest good is to love and obey God."[63] In taking up "our human and sinful existence as a man He did not sin."[64] Instead, as the God-man, he overcame our sinfulness "at the deepest level."[65] "Humanity becomes the creature that rejects that which God rejects since, in Christ, humanity itself endorses and participates in God's rejection of sin."[66] On the other hand, as the elect human, he offered unbroken obedience to God and remained steadfastly faithful in doing God's will. He offers back to God the perfect response to God's initiating covenant thereby recreating humanity as the covenant partner of God.[67] Thus Jesus Christ, the

---

[62] Barth, *CD* I/2, 151. "Barth uses the category of 'history' to emphasize that Christ's human action is ingredient to the accomplishment of atonement" (Jones, "Barth and Anselm: God, Christ and the Atonement," 271).

[63] Kevin W. Hector, "Atonement," in *The Westminster Handbook to Karl Barth*, ed. Richard E. Burnett (Louisville, KY: WJK, 2013), 14.

[64] Barth, *CD* IV/2, 92.

[65] Barth, *CD* IV/2, 92. Jesus's divine and human essence "are coordinated—commonly actualized—in His work ... The one death and passion of Jesus Christ is the final depth of the self-humiliation of God and it is also, following and completing it as a human death and passion, the way which the man Jesus entered and traversed secretly from the very outset, and publicly at the last, even to the extremity of misery and need as prepared for Him, not by men, but by God Himself ... In the work of the one Jesus Christ everything is at one and the same time, but distinctly, both divine and human. It is this in such a way that it never becomes indistinguishable. Where Jesus Christ is really known, there is no place for a monistic thinking which confuses or reverses the divine and the human. Again, there can be only a historical thinking, for which each factor has its own distinctive character. The divine and human work together. But even in their common working they are not interchangeable. The divine is still above and the human below. Their relationship is one of genuine action." Barth, *CD* IV/2, 116.

[66] Jones, "Barth and Anselm: God, Christ and the Atonement," 279.

[67] Jones, "Barth and Anselm: God, Christ and the Atonement," 276.

Son of God, has, by the grace of His origin, with its "supreme necessity and power," achieved

> the exaltation of His human essence ... [t]o that harmony with the divine will, that service of the divine act, that correspondence to the divine grace, that state of thankfulness, which is the only possibility in view of the fact that this man is determined by this divine will and act and grace alone ... We may indeed say that the grace of the origin of Jesus Christ means the basic exaltation of His human freedom to its truth, i.e., to the obedience in whose exercise it is not super-human but true human freedom.[68]

In other words, Jesus Christ brings humanity into its fullness, completing God's intention for humanity, which is that we would follow after and correspond to the decisions of God in freedom and obedience, that we would be, in short, God's people.

The person and work of Jesus reveal that to be truly human is to be in right relationship with God and to exist for the sake of others in free service. That he accomplished this for us in his life and death means that the second moment of the divine act of atonement is our exaltation in him. In Barth's understanding, humanity's exaltation in Jesus did not first begin with the resurrection. The exaltation of Jesus's human nature occurred at each moment of his life and culminated in the event of the cross. "His death on the cross was and is the fulfillment of the incarnation."[69]

> In the free penitence of Jesus of Nazareth which began in Jordan when He entered on His way as Judge and was completed on the cross of Golgotha when He was judged—there took place the positive act concealed in His passion as the negative form of the divine action of reconciliation. In this penitence of His, He "fulfilled all righteousness" (Matt. 3:15). It made His day—the day of divine judgment—the great day of atonement, the day of the dawn of a new heaven and a new earth, the birthday of a new man.[70]

For Barth, then, it is not the resurrection but Jesus's death on the cross that is the birthday of new humanity. The resurrection is, instead, Jesus's transition from "himself in his life history to us in our sphere"[71] in the power of the Holy Spirit.[72]

---

[68] Barth, *CD* IV/2, 91–92.
[69] Barth, *CD* IV/2, 140.
[70] Barth, *CD* IV/1, 259.
[71] John L. Drury, *The Resurrected God: Karl Barth's Trinitarian Theology of Easter* (Minneapolis, MN: Fortress Press, 2014), 72.
[72] "The power whose operation is presupposed in the New Testament is the outgoing and receiving presence and action of the Holy Spirit." Barth, *CD* IV/2, 319.

In the resurrection he reveals himself as the true human as well as the exaltation of humanity in him. "Christ's resurrection is thus the outworking of the exaltation of humanity, as it is the means by which we come to participate in it."[73] The work of the Spirit is that of binding us to the risen Christ.[74] While we are not, in ourselves, God's faithful covenant partners, the meaning of Christ's resurrection is that the Spirit of the risen Christ empowers us to correspond to our perfected humanity in Jesus. Given the fact that Barth's forensically construed theological ontology has made being a function of decision and act, the Spirit-empowered change in our lived behavior testifies to the atonement effecting true ontological change in us.

Conclusion

This chapter highlighted the most salient features of Barth's doctrine of atonement, working to show the deep connections between Barth's doctrine of God and Christology in relationship to the atonement. We've seen how Barth correlates the *pro nobis* of the triune God with an integrated approach to the saving person and work of Jesus where the person is defined by the work. Barth's employment of a forensic framework allowed him to speak not only about what is accomplished in the atonement and how it is accomplished, but also to develop his mature Christology along the lines of a teleologically ordered divine ontology. The result is that the atonement is a central piece not only to Barth's soteriology but also to the doctrine of God, Christology, and theological anthropology.

Broadly speaking, judicial language governs Barth's most developed approach to the atonement in *CD* IV/1. His defense for adopting this particular standpoint and terminology includes its strong biblical basis, its ability to bring dogmatic clarity and distinctness and what he calls the actual importance of this way of thinking. Barth knows that the New Testament has other ways of speaking about the atonement (he mentions financial and military frameworks) and that theology can always ever only speak approximately. Yet in his mind the legal

---

[73] Drury, *The Resurrected God*, 81.
[74] "It is He who brings it about that men like all others, existing in the same limitations, can also be, and are, witnesses of Jesus Christ. It is He who brings it about that others are awakened and moved by their witness ... It is He who creates the fellowship ... It is He who opens its mouth ... It is He who directs its *kerygma*. And it is He who gives to it ... the appropriate contour and impression and form and direction ... It is He who calls them ... It is He who directs and controls their activities. It is He who gives them the power to execute them." Barth, *CD* IV/2, 319–320.

framework provides the best way to express the good news of God for us. He also insists that the judicial treatment not "be anything other than that which could and can be said in the images and categories of cultic language."[75] Thus, using broad brushstrokes, he also restates his four judicial answers to the question of *Cur Deus homo* using cultic language from the book of Hebrews.[76]

Barth's judicial language is not directed by abstract notions of justice nor is it taken from the realm of human legal spheres. Instead, it follows strictly from what took place in the history of Jesus. The chapter provided evidence of just how relentless Barth was in revising and expanding the traditional theory and judicial framework to incorporate not only other metaphors but also to weave in some of the most important contributions of other atonement theories. Furthermore, the vestiges of the classical forms of the satisfaction theory and penal substitution that remain in Barth's approach to the atonement throughout the *Church Dogmatics* stay for very clear reasons and with very careful boundaries and qualifications. Barth's commitment to the victorious grace and love of God results in his making critical correctives to the concepts of satisfaction, God's wrath, and penal substitution. Nothing remains untouched in Barth's approach.

For all these reasons, it is easy to understand why scholars debate how best to classify Barth's doctrine of atonement, or if it should even be classified, using the standard typologies. His theology permits of no quick assessments, and his doctrine of the atonement is everywhere nuanced and complex. He is at once steadfastly committed to God's self-revelation in the witness of Scripture even as he "imaginatively appropriates various theological and philosophical ideas—German idealism, Luther's depiction of a 'blessed exchange' and the *Christus victor* motif being of chief importance."[77] At the same time, it is important to recognize that many facets of Barth's approach to the atonement are wont to cause alarm in many. The very real concerns, often brought forth by feminist, womanist, and liberationist theologians, as to whether a cross-centered atonement valorizes suffering or violence or whether a harmful view of God is communicated by notions such as debt satisfaction or penal substitution, must be addressed with seriousness and sensitivity.[78] How does Barth's doctrine of the atonement speak into the context of current cultural and political issues? At first blush Barth's theology of the cross may seem to be entirely out of step with the

---

[75] Barth, *CD* IV/1, 275.
[76] Barth, *CD* IV/1, 275–283.
[77] Jones, "Barth and Anselm: God, Christ, and the Atonement," 275.
[78] See, for example, *Cross Examinations: Readings on the Meaning of the Cross Today*, ed. Marit Trelstad (Minneapolis, MN: Augsburg Fortress, 2006).

work being done by so many Christian theologians today. And yet the very real question to be pressed is how Barth's doctrine of atonement, with its treatment of the power of sin, the death of sinful humanity, the self-constituted *Deus pro nobis*, and Spirit-empowered human correspondence to our true humanity in Jesus Christ, might be harnessed to speak with and after Barth into the problems and hopes of our world today. The answers may be anything but straightforward, but Barth proves to be a worthy guide.

14

Christ's Descent into Hell

Rodney Howsare

The outer reaches of the Scylla and Charybdis that surround our topic are occupied, on the one hand, by the still somewhat mythologized view of the majority of Church Fathers that Christ descended into a hell that was neatly divided into compartments and only reached that section that held the righteous dead of the Old Testament, and, on the other, by the majority of modern scripture scholars who say that Christ's so-called descent into *hell* means nothing more than that Christ really died.[1] In addition to these irreconcilable positions, we have the renewed theological interest in the descent among twentieth-century theologians such as Karl Barth, Hans Urs von Balthasar, and Joseph Ratzinger, who don't strictly adhere to either of the above. In what follows, I shall try to give an overview of the important data (mythological background, apocalyptic and apocryphal speculations, biblical foundations, and theological interpretations) so that we might better assess where the issue stands at present. My thesis is that neither the still-too-mythological view of many of the Fathers, with their notion of a limited descent, nor the more modern "there's-nothing-to-see-here" approach does justice to that data. I will argue that the positions of Barth, Balthasar, and Ratzinger occupy something like a *tertium quid*, that while Christ's descent into the place of the dead should not be overloaded with the mythical imagery of a hero triumphantly conquering the underworld (the Bible, they will argue, is much more sober than this), it can also not be reduced to the seemingly banal observation that Christ really did die. I will also show that the positions on this

---

[1] I begin by using the generic "hell" as this is what the Apostles' Creed uses, what the Fathers use, and how the English versions of the New Testament tend to translate Hades. Later I will specify the vocabulary (Sheol, Hades, Gehenna) as needed.

question in the early church and Middle Ages are not nearly as uniform as is sometimes suggested.

Myth, Apocalyptic, and Apocrypha

In his excellent entry "Descent to the Underworld," Richard Bauckham alludes to one aspect of my thesis when he points out that "descents [into the underworld] of all these kinds and more are found, to varying extents, in the various cultures of the biblical world. The following survey will show, by contrast, how remarkably lacking they are in the biblical literature itself."[2] Whether we are talking about Mesopotamian, Egyptian, Syrian, or Greek and Roman mythology, a number of typical characteristics emerge. First, although there are accounts in which the dead are held in a particular geographical location in the cosmos (e.g., the farthest western extremity), the vast majority depicts the dead as being held in the underworld. Second, there is a recurring theme of gods descending into the netherworld to rescue one of their beloved departed. This usually involves some sort of exchange, which is a way of saying that death is not only (a necessary?) part of the order of things, but also that it can't simply be defeated.[3] Third, an inherent connection is often made between the descents and ascents into and out of the underworld and the cycle of seasons.[4] Again, we get an indication here that death is a necessary part of the cosmic order or what we might call an ontologizing of death. Fourth, across the mythical landscape there is a tendency to see the underworld as divided into regions (rooms, halls, chambers,

---

[2] Richard Bauckham, "Descent to the Underworld," in *The Anchor Bible Dictionary: Volume 2*, (New York: Doubleday, 1992), 145–146. For what follows on the mythological background for the descent of Christ I will rely heavily on Bauckham, but also on the still valuable study of J. A. MacCulloch, *The Harrowing of Hell: A Comparative Study of an Early Christian Doctrine* (Edinburgh: T&T Clark, 1930). For the apocalyptic background I will also refer to Metropolitan Hilarion Alfeyev, *Christ the Conqueror of Hell: The Descent into Hades from an Orthodox Perspective* (New York: SVS Press, 2009).

[3] In the Akkadian *Descent of Ishtar*, for instance, Inanna is rescued from the netherworld, but only after Enki fashions two strange creatures who sneak into the underworld in order to revive and retrieve her; still, she is only allowed to leave if she provides a substitute. See Bauckham, "Descent to the Underworld," 146.

[4] See, for instance, the *Homeric Hymn to Demeter* in *Hesiod, the Homeric Hymns, and Homerica*, trans. Hugh G. Evelyn-White (Loeb, 1914): "Come, my daughter; for far-seeing Zeus the loud-thunderer calls you to join the families of the gods, and has promised to give you what rights you please among the deathless gods, and has agreed that for a third part of the circling year your daughter shall go down to darkness and gloom, but for the two parts shall be with you and the other deathless gods: so has he declared it shall be and has bowed his head in token. But come, my child, obey, and be not too angry unrelentingly with the dark-clouded Son of Cronos; but rather increase forthwith for men the fruit that gives them life" (l. 459).

etc.) where different sorts of dead people experience different fates. For instance, in the Gilgamesh epic, when Enkidu's ghost is granted temporary release from the place of the dead, he visits Gilgamesh and reports that some "categories of the dead fare better than others."[5]

At this point we should pay special attention to one particular account: the Egyptian myth of Setne and his son Si-Osire. The latter, who had been in the realm of the dead, was reincarnated as the son of Setne and his wife. Before returning to the netherworld at age twelve, he and his father witnessed two funerals, one of a rich man who was buried with great pageantry, fancy burial clothing, and much mourning, and the other of a poor man who was buried without pomp or mourning. When Setne mentioned that he would prefer the fate of the rich man, Si-Osire took him on a tour of the netherworld where he showed him seven halls, containing three types of dead: those whose good deeds outweighed their bad (the poor man was here), those whose bad deeds outweighed their good (the rich man was being punished here), and those whose good deeds equaled their bad.[6] In the fragment of the myth in which only four of the halls are described, the above general description is specified accordingly: in the fourth and fifth, the dead are being punished; in the sixth there are gods and "attendants"; and in the seventh, Osiris is depicted as judging the dead.[7] Bauckham sums up the significance of this myth accordingly: "The story is of special importance, both because it is an example of the genre of conducted tours of the underworld ... and because it passed into Jewish religious folklore ... and has been claimed as the original of the parable of the rich man and Lazarus" (Luke 16: 19–31).[8]

While, as we shall see, the canonical accounts of Sheol/Hades and any possible descents there (it remains to be seen, for instance, how the infamous text in 1 Peter should be taken) are quite circumspect and sober in comparison with these various myths, the mythological elements do make their way into the Jewish and Christian imagination by way of Jewish and Christian apocalyptic traditions.

---

[5] Bauckham, "Descent to the Underworld," 146.
[6] "And it was commanded before Osiris that the burial outfit of that rich man, whom thou sawest carried forth from Memphis with great laudation, should be given to this same poor man, and that he should be taken among the noble spirits as a man of God that follows Sokaris Osiris, his place being near to the person of Osiris. (But) the great man whom thou didst see, he was taken to the Te, his evil deeds were weighed against his good deeds, and his evil deeds were found more numerous than his good deeds that he did upon earth" (Francis Llewellyn Griffith, *Stories of the High Priests of Memphis* [Oxford: Clarendon, 1900], 49).
[7] Bauckham, "Descent to the Underworld," 147. See also MacCulloch, *The Harrowing of Hell*, 9, and Griffith, *Stories of the High Priests of Memphis*, 45–50.
[8] Bauckham, "Descent to the Underworld," 147.

While even a cursory overview of this apocalyptic literature is beyond the scope of this chapter, some highlights from a couple of particularly influential works will be necessary in order to illustrate how the mythological sources get mediated to the New Testament and early church. 1 Enoch[9] merits special consideration, both because of its retrieval of numerous mythological elements, but also because of its undoubted influence on 1 Peter 3:18–4:6. Important details to be noted are: (1) the place of the dead is not in the underworld, but in the westernmost part of the world, as is the case in many ancient myths (in 2 Enoch, the tour through the realm of the dead involves seven heavens); (2) an extended commentary of sorts on Genesis 6:1–4, as well as speculation on the entire flood narrative; (3) the division of the place of the dead into four "hollow places" holding various categories of the dead; (4) Enoch's proclamation to the fallen spirits there, which really entailed his announcement of their judgment; and (5) the containment of these fallen spirits until the final judgment, when they will be cast into the fire.[10] We should draw special attention to the fact that the four hollow places will allow the mythological element of various sections in the realm of the dead to make its way into the Jewish and Christian imagination. We also get our first glimpse of one of those places being occupied by the righteous of the Old Testament, specifically, as far as Enoch goes, Abel. For instance, at 22:7, Enoch is told, "And he answered me, saying, 'This is the spirit that came forth from Abel whom Cain, his brother, slew: and he will bring accusations against him until his seed parishes from the face of the earth, and from the offspring of men his seed is destroyed." And then at 22:9, "And he answered me saying: 'These three have been made that the spirits of the dead might be separated. And yonder one was separated off for the spirits of the righteous, one in which there is a spring of pellucid water.'"

This notion of the dead already receiving some sort of punishment prior to a last judgment only escalates in later Jewish apocalyptic tales. As Bauckham puts it:

> It seems that during the first two centuries C.E. a gradual change took place in Jewish and Christian belief about the fate of the wicked after death, from the older view that the wicked are not actively punished immediately after death, but held in detention awaiting punishment at the last judgment, to the later view that the eternal punishment of the wicked begins already after death. This

---

[9] For the English translation of what follows, see *The Book of Enoch Or I Enoch: A New English Edition*, ed. Matthew Black and James C. VanderKam (Brill, 1985).

[10] For a detailed analysis of the Enoch cycle, especially in view of its influence on 1 Peter, see William Joseph Dalton, S.J., *Christ's Proclamation to the Spirits: A Study of 1 Peter 3:18–4:6* (Rome: Pontifical Biblical Institute, 1965), 163–184.

change was very important for apocalyptic descents into the underworld (where increasingly only the wicked were located).[11]

But what is interesting is that, after passing through the filter of the New Testament canonical writings, later Christian apocalyptic writings appear closer to the older view. As Georgia Frank explains:

> Unlike apocalypses with graphic punishments of the wicked dead, the dead whom Jesus visits endure no bodily torment. Instead, their suffering is temporal in nature: the misfortune of having lived before the coming of Christ into the world. And so these righteous ones remain captive in hell's dark abode until their liberation by Christ, less punished than detained. With Christ's descent, the punished would no longer be the dead so much as Death and Hades personified.[12]

And it would be a mistake to underestimate the influence of these apocalypses on the view of the descent in the later church. One more example of apocalyptic will have to suffice.

A particularly influential source for early Christians, some of whom believed it to be canonical, is the *Odes of Solomon*, likely a second-century Christian text written in either Greek or Syriac.[13] Ode 42, for instance, refers to Christ's descent into hell accordingly:

> Sheol saw me and was shattered, and Death ejected me and many with me. I have been vinegar and bitterness to it, and I went down with it as far as its depth … And I made a congregation of living among his dead; and I spoke with them by living lips; in order that my word may not be unprofitable. And those who had died ran towards me; and they cried out and said, Son of God, have pity on us. And deal with us according to your kindness, and bring us out from the bonds of darkness. And open for us the door by which we may come out to you; for we perceive that our death does not touch you. May we also be saved by you,

---

[11] Bauckham, "Descent to the Underworld," 154.

[12] Georgia Frank, "Christ's Descent to the Underworld in Ancient Ritual and Legend," in *Apocalyptic Thought in Early Christianity*, ed. Robert J. Daly, S.J. (Grand Rapids, MI: Baker Academic, 2009), 212.

[13] James H. Charlesworth writes (*The Anchor Bible Dictionary*, v. 6, 114):

> "The date of the *Odes* has caused considerable interest. H. J. Drijvers contends that they are as late as the 3d century. L. Abramowski places them in the latter half of the 2d century. B. McNeil argued that they are contemporaneous with *4 Ezra*, the *Shepherd of Hermas*, Polycarp, and Valentinus (ca. 100 C.E.). Most scholars date them sometime around the middle of the 2d century, but if they are heavily influenced by Jewish apocalyptic thought and especially the ideas in the Dead Sea Scrolls, a date long after 100 is unlikely. H. Chadwick, Emerton, Charlesworth, and many other scholars, are convinced that they must not be labeled 'gnostic,' and therefore should not be dated to the late 2d or 3d century."

> because you are our Savior. Then I heard their voice, and placed their faith in my heart. And I placed my name upon their head, because they are free and they are mine.[14]

As we can see, the dead are not so much being punished as they are being detained until they can be rescued by the mercy of Christ. It should also be noted that the Odes were an important source for the majority Patristic position (especially in the West) that Christ's descent only benefitted the "righteous dead" of the Old Covenant.[15]

Finally, mention should be made of a work of early Christian poetry (mid-second century), not least because, here, Christ's descent is more extensive. In St. Melito of Sardis's, *On Easter* we get the following:

> The Lord, when he had clothed himself with man ... arose from the dead and uttered this cry: "I am the one that destroyed death and triumphed over the enemy and trod down Hades and bound the strong one/I carried off man to the heights of heaven; I am the one," says the Christ. "Come then, all you families of men who are compounded with sins, and receive forgiveness of sins. For I am your forgiveness, I am the Pascha of salvation, I am the lamb slain for you; I am your ransom, I am your life, I am your light, I am your salvation, I am your resurrection, I am your king. I will raise you up by my right hand; I am leading you up to the heights of heaven; There I will show you the Father from ages past."[16]

Notice, in particular, the "all you families of men who are compounded with sins."

Old and New Testaments

The New Testament's Hades has its origins in the Old Testament's Sheol, which, in the LXX translation, was almost always rendered as Hades. As stated earlier, compared to the world of ancient myth, the biblical accounts both of Sheol/Hades in general, and of any descents there, are strikingly sober. In the Old Testament, Sheol is a place of "stillness, darkness, powerlessness, and inactivity. It was a land of forgetfulness where God's wonders were unknown. Since people were thought to be separated from God in Sheol, it was greatly feared by the living."[17] Consider, for instance, Psalm 6:4–5, "Turn, O Lord, save my life; deliver me for the sake of

---

[14] Ode 42, 11–20, cited in Alfeyev, *Christ the Conqueror of Hell*, 41–42.
[15] MacCulloch, *The Harrowing of Hell*, 254.
[16] Melitio of Sardis, *On Pascha and Fragments*, SC 123, 120, text and trans. ed. Stuart George Hall (Oxford, 1979), 57–59, 100–103.
[17] Robert Rainwater, *Mercer Dictionary of the Bible*, general ed., Watson E. Mills (Macon, Georgia: Mercer University Press, 1990, 91), 819.

your merciful love. For in death there is no remembrance of you; in Sheol who can give you praise" (RSV). Or, in the same vein:

> I said, in the noontide of my days I must depart; I am consigned to the gates of Sheol for the rest of my years. I said, I shall not see the Lord in the land of the living; I shall look upon man no more among the inhabitants of the world ... Behold, it was for my welfare that I had great bitterness; but you have held back my life from the pit of destruction, for you have cast all my sins behind your back. For Sheol cannot thank you, death cannot praise you; those who go down to the pit cannot hope for your faithfulness. (Isa. 38:10, 11, 17–19, RSV)

Even then, if we encounter something like a demythologization of both death and the place of the dead in the Old Testament, there is certainly not a de-theologization. The place of death is feared precisely because it is a place without fellowship, either with God or with one's fellow human beings. Death is also "theologized" insofar as it is connected with sin. In the Isaiah passage just cited, God's rescue of Hezekiah from the "pit of destruction" is directly linked to God's casting Hezekiah's sins "behind his back." This same connection—between death, sin, and loss of fellowship with God—can be seen in Job 24:19, "Drought and heat snatch away the snow waters; so does Sheol those who have sinned."

In contrast to the mythological view, the God of Israel's power extends over death and the realm of the dead. Death is not a necessary aspect of reality, nor is it a contrary but equally primal power vis-à-vis God. In Psalms (49:13–15, RSV), for instance, we hear:

> This is the fate of those who have foolish confidence, the end of those who are pleased with their portion. Like sheep they are appointed for Sheol; Death shall be their shepherd; straight to the grave they descend, and their form shall waste away; Sheol shall be their home. But God will ransom my soul from the power of Sheol, for he will receive me.

Or in Amos (9:2, RSV), "Though they dig into Sheol, from there shall my hand take them; though they climb up to heaven, from there I will bring them down." "The experience of Yahweh's power to deliver them was a step toward the belief that his sovereignty over the world of the dead would in the future be asserted in bringing the dead back to the world of the living in eschatological resurrection."[18] This will become explicit in later writings in the notion that God "leads down to Hades and brings up again" (Tob. 13: 2; cf., Wisd. 16:13).

---

[18] Bauckham, "Descent to the Underworld," 148.

Finally, are there descents into Sheol in the Old Testament? The short answer is "No," although with three caveats. First, there is the case in 1 Samuel 28:3–25 of someone being summoned from Sheol through necromancy, but this practice is consistently condemned in the Old Testament. Next, there is the reference to going down to Sheol and rising up again in reference to coming very close to death and recovering (as we saw above in the Isaiah text). And then there is the question of Psalm 24:7–10, with regard to gates being lifted up so that the "King of glory" may enter. Although almost all biblical scholars do not see this as a reference to the gates of hell,[19] it should be noted that it was often interpreted as such in both Jewish and Christian apocalyptic, as well as in the Fathers of the church. This can be seen especially in the Gospel of Nicodemus. When Christ comes to hell, Hades gives the command to "shut the hard gates of brass and put on them the bars of iron," in response to a loud voice saying, "Lift, O princes, your gates, and be ye lifted up ye doors of hell, and the King of Glory shall come in."[20]

In the New Testament things get more complicated. In his *Infinity Dwindled to Infancy*, Edward T. Oakes lists nine New Testament passages which, taken together, "not only speak of a journey to the underworld, but ... also attribute a saving, soteriological significance to that descent."[21] These passages range from hints, for instance, in Matthew's Gospel—"For as Jonah was three days and three nights in the belly of the whale, so the Son of Man will be three days and three nights in the heart of the earth" (Mt. 12:40, RSV)—which need imply no more than that Jesus died and was buried, to the more explicit verses from 1 Peter—"For Christ died for sins once for all, the righteous for the unrighteous, to bring you to God. He put to death in the body but made alive by the Spirit, through whom he also went and preached to the spirits in prison who disobeyed God long ago" (1 Pet. 3: 18–20), and "But they [sinners] will have to give account to him who is ready to judge the living and the dead. For this is the reason the gospel was preached even to those who are now dead, so that they might be judged according to men in regard to the body, but live according to God in regard to the spirit" (1 Pet. 4:5–6). It should be noted that even this latter text—when

---

[19] On this, see ibid.
[20] J. K. Elliot, ed., "The Gospel of Nicodemus," in *The Apocryphal New Testament: A Collection of Apocryphal Christian Literature in an English Translation* (Oxford: Oxford University Press, 2005), 188.
[21] Edward T. Oakes, S.J., *Infinity Dwindled to Infancy: A Catholic and Evangelical Christology* (Grand Rapids, MI: Eerdmans, 2011), 384. The texts that Oakes lists are: Matthew 12:29, 40; Acts 2:24 (Peter speaking); 1 Peter 3:18–20, 4:5–6; Romans 10:6–7, 14:8–9; Ephesians 4:7–10; Philemon 2:9–11.

taken with the former—is often not seen as evidence of a descent by contemporary New Testament scholars. For instance, regarding the verses in 1 Peter, Bauckham says, "It is now widely recognized that in 3:19 the proclamation to the spirits follows the resurrection ... while 'the spirits in prison' are most probably angels." And then, of 4:5–6: "A reference to the idea, widely attested from the beginning of the 2nd century, that Christ, after his death, preached the salvation he had achieved to the saints of the OT period, is more probable in 4:6, but on the other hand 'the dead' here may refer to those who heard the Gospel while alive, but subsequently died."[22] This minimalist interpretation, however, is very difficult to square with the almost certain influence of 1 Enoch (see above) on 1 Peter, as demonstrated by William Dalton's thorough study.[23] It should be noted, furthermore, that even biblical scholars who do not read these 1 Peter texts as supportive of a descent—for instance, Karl Gschwind[24] and Dalton—do not, for this reason, reject a theology of descent.[25]

Nevertheless, because the 1 Peter passages are so central to the discussion, I shall make a few observations, based especially on von Balthasar's careful study in *Mysterium Paschale*. First, with Oakes I agree that it is the weight of the New Testament texts (listed in note 20) as a whole that supports the traditional and creedal teaching that Christ descended into hell, although we will have to see what "hell" means in this context. In short, even if we find no support for the teaching in 1 Peter, that would not be decisive. Next, however, von Balthasar makes a number of observations regarding the 1 Peter passages that are difficult to dismiss. These observations will also give us a glimpse of the approach to the doctrine that will be argued for below. First, von Balthasar insists (against Gschwind) that we cannot make a neat separation between spiritual and physical death, so that the proclamation to the dead of 4:6 would only refer to the

---

[22] Bauckham, "Descent to the Underworld," 156.

[23] As Dalton puts it, "According to Charles, 'the influence of 1 Enoch on the New Testament has been greater than that of all the other apocryphal and pseudepigraphical books taken together.' So important was the book in early Christian times that in some circles of the Church it was regarded as divinely inspired ... Interestingly enough, it is above all in the Catholic Epistles that its direct influence is most at work. Jude not merely refers explicitly to the text of 1 Enoch ... but even cites it ... 2 Peter also depends directly from 1 Enoch in a couple of places ... Whatever view one may have about the author of 2 Peter, it is surely reasonable to suppose some common tradition between the two Petrine epistles. Without defining this further, we should at least not be astonished to find the influence of 1 Enoch also present in 1 Peter" (*Christ's Proclamation to the Spirits*, 164–165). Dalton also makes a very powerful case, based on a close textual comparison, for 1 Enoch's direct influence on these verses from 1 Peter.

[24] Die Niederfahrt Christi in die Unterwelt (Münich, 1911).

[25] As Dalton (*Christ's Proclamation to the Spirits*) points out, even many in the tradition, including Augustine and Aquinas, who did not see these texts as supporting Christ's descent into hell, nevertheless believed in Christ's descent into hell on the basis either of other texts and/or traditions coming from extra-canonical sources.

spiritually dead (an interpretation that goes back, at least, to St. Augustine). As we saw above, with reference to the Old Testament, the fear of Sheol was inseparable from the fear of sin and separation from God. A key piece of our thesis is that death is never merely a brute, "biological" fact for the Old or New Testaments. Gschwind's contention is also difficult to square with the fact that these texts in 1 Peter are almost undoubtedly a reworking of 1 Enoch, wherein Enoch's proclamation is precisely to those spirits held in Hades (the place of the dead). Finally, to say that 4:8 refers to the spiritually dead precludes any connection between this verse and 3:19, and this seems very unlikely given the context. Again, in Enoch the "spirits" to whom Enoch makes his proclamation are in the place of the *dead*. Second, "the preaching [to the dead] is an event in the world beyond [wherever that is depicted], producing there the effective fruits of Christ's suffering in the flesh." We make special note here of the distinction between the dead being judged "in the flesh like men" and being judged by Christ. Third, von Balthasar insists to "the highest degree probable" that the proclamation to the dead, in 4:6, is the same as the proclamation to the "spirits" in 3:19 (he mistakenly cites this as 3:9), and this doesn't rule out the possibility that these spirits included the "world powers of the age before the Flood, *including* those human beings whose lords they were."[26] Fourth, the entire context from 1 Peter 3:18–4:6 is based upon a contrast between two types of judgment (the disobedient of the days of Noah and those judged in the light of Christ's death and resurrection), two types of baptism (the baptism of judgment in the waters of the flood, and the baptism in Christ which saves), and two types of salvation (salvation from the temporal death caused by the flood provided by the ark, and salvation from sin and death effected by Christ). This can be seen very clearly in the following:

> In which he went and preached to the spirits in prison, who formerly did not obey, when God's patience waited in the days of Noah, during the building of the ark, in which a few, that is, eight persons, were saved through water. Baptism, which corresponds to this, now saves you, not as a removal of dirt from the body but as an appeal to God for a clear conscience, through the resurrection of Jesus Christ. (1 Pet, 3:19–21)

---

[26] Hans Urs von Balthasar, *Mysterium Paschale: The Mystery of Easter* (hereafter MP), trans. Aidan Nichols, O.P. (Grand Rapids, MI: Michigan, 1990), 158; emphasis in the original. Balthasar agrees, here, with Bo Reicke's *The Disobedient Spirits and Christian Baptism* (Copenhagen, 1946). Reicke argues that it makes no sense to see, as does Gschwind (and later Dalton), Christ's "going" (*poreutheis*) and making proclamation to the spirits as something that occurred at his ascension into heaven, when it is clear that 1 Peter is presenting Christ as the new Enoch.

That Christ's preaching here is directed only at the disobedient spirits in the days of Noah, a fact that kept Augustine from seeing this text as a support for Christ's descent into hell, can be explained in this light. That is, if a contrast is being made between the relatively few that were saved from the Flood and the many that are saved now through baptism, this might explain why the passage only mentions the disobedient spirits from Noah's time. The author would therefore only be remaining consistent with the parallel between Noah's time and the time of Christ, and not suggesting that Christ's preaching was literally only to the disobedient of that time.[27] Fifth,

> the "proclamation" in 1 Peter 3, 19 cannot be anything other than a preaching of salvation to the dead of 4, 6 ... Furthermore, one should not present this as a subjective kind of preaching, meant to move others to conversion: it is the objective announcement ... of a fact—the fact, namely, that what appeared to be definitive judgement (a "prison") on the unbelief which greeted the first sign of salvation is overcome by the grace of Christ, which has turned the sign of judgment (the Flood) into a sign of salvation (baptism), and created from the "tiny remnant" ("eight souls") who survived the great catastrophe an entire redeemed people. (1 Pet. 2, 9)[28]

In short, against Gschwind and Dalton, et al., and with von Balthasar and Reicke, et al., I see 1 Peter 3:18–4:6 as a Christian reimagining of 1 Enoch[29]—that is, Christ as the new Enoch—and therefore as supportive of the traditional doctrine of the descent. As Joachim Jeremias puts it:

> It is scarcely to be doubted that the theologoumenon of the Hades journey of Christ has as its model the myth of Enoch as just described. On the disobedient spirits in the darkest dungeon of the infernal fortress there advances once more a divine messenger with a divine message. But whereas Enoch has to announce to them the impossibility of pardon, the new message reads quite differently: it is the Good News (4, 6). Thus the doctrine of Christ's preaching in Hades gives expression to the fact that the Righteous One died for the unrighteous (3, 18); even for those who were lost and without hope, his atoning death has brought salvation.[30]

---

[27] This is the view of MacCulloch and makes good sense: "Why these only are mentioned is not clear, when all the dead are spoken of in iv. 6. They may be typical of a larger number to whom the good news was brought, or they may be mentioned in order to introduce a reference to the Flood as typical of baptismal grace" (*The Harrowing of Hell*, 60).

[28] MP, 157–159.

[29] So do Dalton (1965) and Gschwind (1911), but they don't see this as implying that Christ, too, preached in the place of the dead, at least in this text from 1 Peter.

[30] Joachim Jeremias, *Der Opfertod Jesu Christi* (Stuttgart, 1963), 8, cited in MP, 160.

The Fathers through the Reformation: An Overview

It is just this thesis of Jeremias that will prove divisive to the Fathers and Scholastics. Contrary to Alyssa Pitstick's suggestion that there is *a* traditional view on this matter,[31] not only do we find a variety of positions in the tradition, we often find inconsistencies in the same thinker. Again, in the interest of space, we will offer nothing like a sufficient overview of the Patristic, and even less so the Scholastic and Reformation, literature on the matter, but only wish to show that almost all of the issues still dividing theologians today were already contested in the early church. To the question of *whether* Christ descended to the dead the Fathers answer with a unanimous "Yes." But when we turn to the precise *nature* of that descent, things get more complicated. While it is certainly the majority view that Christ descended into a compartmentalized hell in order to pronounce his victory over death and sin, conquer the Devil and Hades, and whisk away the Old Testament saints, this position is not unanimous. This becomes especially true as other interpretations of Christ's descent begin to emerge in the Middle Ages. Because the majority position is well documented, allow me to call attention to some contrasting voices.

First, let us recall the mention already made of the influential work of Melito of Sardis mentioned earlier, which suggests that Christ's descent was more far-reaching than to the righteous dead of the Old Testament. Second, we should take note of Augustine's well-known letter to Evodius. Not only does Evodius's letter imply that there is a widespread opinion at the time (414 CE) that the 1 Peter text was a reference to Christ's descent, it also asserts that "Christ, descending, preached to them all and set them all free by His grace from darkness and suffering, that from the time of the Lord's resurrection judgment might be awaited by an empty hell?"[32] While Augustine is not prepared simply to assert that Christ emptied hell, nor to agree that 1 Peter refers to Christ's descent into hell, he does acknowledge the following: (1) that Christ indeed descended into hell; (2) that he descended beyond the bosom of Abraham (the

---

[31] Alyssa Lyra Pitstick, *Light in Darkness: Hans Urs von Balthasar and the Catholic Doctrine of Christ's Descent into Hell* (Grand Rapids, MI: Eerdmans, 2007). Even the title of the work wrongly suggests that there is something like *the* Catholic doctrine of the descent. This not only denies important developments, it also downplays the very real differences between various saints, theologians, and doctors within the church's tradition. For a trenchant critique of Pitstick's argument, see, most recently, Edward T. Oakes, "*Descensus* and Development: A Response to Recent Rejoinders," *International Journal of Systematic Theology* 13, no. 1 (January 2011), 3–24.

[32] Augustine, *Letters*, Vol. 3 (131–164), trans. Sister Wilfrid Parsons (Washington, DC: Catholic University of America Press, 1953), 381.

place of the righteous dead), otherwise "if the Holy Scripture has said that Christ after death came into that bosom of Abraham, with naming hell and its sorrows, I wonder if anyone would dare to affirm that He descended into hell"; (3) that "He was in hell, and that He granted this favor to those entangled in its sorrows."[33] He says that he is without doubt about this final assertion and that he can't figure why Christ would have even bothered descending if it were only for those in Abraham's bosom who were already in an "abode of peace and quiet."[34]

In addition to Augustine, the following Fathers believed that Christ's descent extended beyond the realm of the righteous dead of the Old Testament: Cyril of Alexandria, Origen, Ambrose, Gregory Nazianzen, among others. Gregory's position bears special mention because it includes a dimension that we will see again in the Middle Ages, specifically in Thomas Aquinas, and in recent theologians like von Balthasar, Ratzinger/Benedict, and Barth: namely, that Christ's descent into hell forms part of a double *katabasis* (twofold descent), the first being his descent into the human condition in the incarnation. In his *Oration 45*, Gregory asks: "If [Christ] descends into Hell, descend with Him. Learn to know the mysteries of Christ there also: what is the providential purpose of the twofold descent, to save all humans absolutely by his manifestation, or there, too, only them that believe?"[35] Besides the notion that Christ's descent into hell can be conceived as an extension of his descent into the human condition—a notion which Jean Daniélou says was common in early Christian literature[36]—note Gregory's question as to whether or not the descent saved everyone in hell or, like the descent into the human condition in general, only those who believed.

Thomas Aquinas in his *Exposition of the Apostles' Creed* takes this additional insight, that Christ's descent into hell is salvific in a way continuous with his descent into human nature, farther, where he offers four reasons for Christ's descent into hell. Here he states:

First, He wished to take upon Himself the entire punishment for our sin, and thus atone for its entire guilt. The punishment for the sin of man was not alone death of the body, but there was also a punishment of the soul, since the soul had its share in sin; and it was punished by being deprived of the beatific vision; and

---

[33] Ibid., 385–386.
[34] Ibid., 386.
[35] Cited in Alfeyev, *Christ the Conqueror of Hell*, 57–58.
[36] Jean Daniélou, *The Theology of Jewish Christianity*, trans. John A. Baker (London: Westminster, 1977), 233.

as yet no atonement had been offered whereby this punishment would be taken away. Therefore, before the coming of Christ all men, even the holy fathers after their death, descended into the underworld. Accordingly in order to take upon Himself most perfectly the punishment due to sinners, Christ not only suffered death, but also His soul descended to the underworld.[37]

To Gregory's note of double descent, Thomas adds the note of vicarious substitution: just as Christ took on our sinfulness and death on the cross, so he took on our descent into the underworld in his descent.

This view that Christ descended into hell, at least in part for substitutionary reasons, finds an even further deepening in two thinkers who come after Thomas. First, Nicholas of Cusa introduces something new when he suggests that Christ didn't descend into hell victorious (at least not in the straightforward sense), but in order to "undergo" the "vision of death." As Cusa puts it:

> And since the death of Christ was complete, since through his own experience he saw the death which he had freely chosen to undergo, the soul of Christ went down into the underworld, *ad inferna*, where the vision of death is ... When God raised Christ he drew him, as we read in the Acts of the Apostles, from out of the lower underworld, after delivering him from the torture of that underworld ...Christ's suffering ... was like that of the damned who cannot be damned any more. [It] ... went to the length of infernal punishment.[38]

Finally, the reformer Jean Calvin rejects the notion of Christ as harrower of hell in his *Institutes of the Christian Religion*. Instead, Calvin's sees the descent as the logical conclusion of the fact that Christ had to receive the full punishment due to sin and therefore undergo the full wrath of God. "It was expedient at the same time that [of his bodily death] for him to undergo the severity of God's vengeance, to appease his wrath and satisfy his just judgment. For this reason, he must also grapple hand to hand with the armies of hell and the dread of everlasting death."[39]

---

[37] *Expositio in Symbolum Apostolorum (The Apostles' Creed)*, ed. and Html-formatted Joseph Kenny, O.P., trans. Joseph B. Collins (New York, 1939). Available at, http://dhspriory.org/thomas/Creed.htm#5, art. 5. Part of this text was cited and brought to my attention by Oakes, "*Descensus* and Development: A Response to Recent Rejoinders," 11.

[38] *Excitationes* 10 (Basle 1565), 659, cited in von Balthasar, *Mysterium Paschale*, 170–171.

[39] Calvin, *Institutes of the Christian Religion*, ed. John T. McNeil, trans. Ford Lewis Battles (Philadelphia: Westminster Press, 1960), II.xvi.10, 515, cited in David Lauber, *Barth on the Descent into Hell: God, Atonement and the Christian Life* (Burlington, VT: Ashgate Publishing Co., 2004), 11.

Conclusion: The Descent in the Theology of Hans Urs von Balthasar

I would like now to draw some conclusions from the foregoing overview in the light of the work of "*the* theologian of the Descent into Hell."[40] I will say at the outset, however, that I think von Balthasar's retrieval and rehabilitation of this doctrine is very much in keeping with two other important twentieth-century theologians: Josef Ratzinger and Karl Barth.[41] In short, much of what follows could be said in the light of their work also.

First, we should make a distinction between what it is that the early mythology of descents into the underworld were trying to say—that is, that death for a spiritual being is a deep tragedy and mystery which cannot be spoken of sufficiently in the language of empirical experience—and the apparatus that they used to say it. In speaking of the text from 1 Peter, for instance, von Balthasar says that the mythological traits are "nothing other than the imagistic and rhetorically embellished linguistic raiment which clothes a thoroughly non-mythical body."[42] To return to a previous point, when we get to the canonical Scriptures, the mythological details of a neatly divided hell and the notion of a literal, physical descent either disappear altogether, or are reduced to a minimum. The closest we get, for instance, to a compartmentalized hell in the New Testament is in Jesus's parable of the Rich Man and Lazarus, and even there we get no more than a distinction between a realm of punishment and a realm of relative peace. Finally, Augustine is an important ally for von Balthasar in this regard in that he raises questions both about the physicality of hell—"One may reasonably ask why they say of Hades that it exists beneath earth, when it is no physical place, or why it must be called the underworld, if it is not under the earth"[43]—and about its condition before and after the descent of Christ: prior to Christ's descent, hell is the Sheol of the Old Testament and includes both the righteous and the unrighteous. "Augustine distinguishes between a lower *infernum* ... and a higher ... The two are separated by a *chaos magnum*, yet both belong equally to Hades."[44]

---

[40] Wilhelm Maas, *Gott und die Hölle: Studien zum Descensus Christi* (Einsiedeln: Johannes Verlag, 1979), 245; emphasis in the original.
[41] For the similarities between von Balthasar and Ratzinger on the theology of the descent, see Edward T. Oakes, "Pope Benedict XVI on Christ's Descent into Hell," *Nova et Vetera* 11, no. 1 (2013), 231–252, and for a comparison with Barth, see Lauber, *Barth on the Descent into Hell*.
[42] Von Balthasar, *Mysterium Paschale*, 151.
[43] From *Literal Commentary of Genesis*, cited in ibid., 163.
[44] Ibid., 162.

Second, Christ did not descend, therefore, to hell in the full-blown eschatological sense, because heaven, hell, and purgatory are Christological categories. How could anyone merit, for instance, eternal damnation without rejecting Christ? This seems to be the rather obvious meaning of Hebrews 6:4–8, for instance, where it says that "there no longer remains a sacrifice for sins," for those who deliberately sin after receiving the truth. And then in 10:26–29, after stating that the transgressing of the Law was punishable by death, the writer asks: "How much worse punishment do you think will be deserved by the man who has spurned the Son of God, and profaned the blood of the covenant by which he was sanctified, and outraged the Spirit of grace?" Augustine is again an ally here when he distinguishes between the punishment for the sin of Adam, which he calls "first death" [i.e., Hades] and the punishment of rejecting Christ, which he calls "second death [i.e., Hell]."[45]

This second point gets at the chief problem of what I have called the majority Patristic view—that Christ only descended to the righteous dead of the Old Testament—as if hell is already neatly divided into the hell of the damned and purgatory. Here is John Saward, summarizing Balthasar's position:

> Balthasar does not disagree with St Thomas' answer: the soul of Christ did not descend into Hell in the sense of the place or state of eternal punishment. He did not himself, as the Reformers imagine, become "one of the damned." The soul of Christ is an unshakeable Yes to the Father; even his Descent into Hell is an act of obedience to God. It is unthinkable that the absolutely sinless Son of God could experience the torment that only one who irrevocably says No to God can know. Nonetheless, Balthasar regards the Thomist question [whether Christ descended into the Hell of the damned] as wrongly posed. Before the coming of Christ, there was neither Hell nor Purgatory, only the single Sheol of the Old Testament, in which the souls of the Patriarchs were detained. The Hell of damnation exists only as a consequence of the Paschal Mystery.[46]

Third, however, and to go back to the Nicholas of Cusa quote above, to say that Christ did not experience damnation does not mean that Christ did not experience something unique, for who else but the very Son of God could experience the full weight of precisely what the Old Testament feared most about death: namely, loss of fellowship with God. Here Balthasar draws on Gregory

---

[45] Augustine, *City of God*, trans. Henry Bettenson (New York: Penguin Edition, 1984), XIII, 23, 537–538. Cited in ibid., 172.

[46] John Saward, *The Mysteries of March: Hans Urs von Balthasar on the Incarnation and Easter* (London: Collins, 1990), 119.

the Great's notion that Christ descended *inferno profundior* (deeper than hell) and Cusa's notion that Christ's suffering was "the greatest one could conceive."[47] Indeed, it is precisely Christ's experience of the *visio mortis* that makes possible the transition from the Sheol of the Old Testament to the New Testament's hell. Christ is willing to taste this experience so that nobody else must. Christ is our representative there as much as he is our representative on the cross. But this has a corollary: that Christ can't be there in a way that is simply different from everybody else. Just as Christ has to have a fully human nature and experience a fully human death, he must also experience the results of that death in a fully human way. This follows, for Balthasar, from the principle that what has not been assumed has not been saved. He builds here on the notion, borrowed above from Gregory Nazianzus, according to which the descent is the second *anabasis* of Christ into the human condition, and, here too, then, he must be like us in all things, except sin. In short, any preaching that is being done by Christ in hell must be the proclamation of being dead with the dead. This may seem to be in conflict with 1 Peter, but as Saward points out: "The traditional image and the Balthasarian theology can be reconciled ... when we recall that it is precisely as passively dead that Christ actively preaches. The Word sounds most resonantly ... when he lies in the silence of death."[48]

Fourth, just as in Karl Barth's theology the vicarious suffering of Christ must be kept squarely within the context of the doctrine of God, lest it appear that the Father is simply punishing Christ,[49] so in Balthasar, the theology of Christ's descent must be kept within a Trinitarian context. Christ's descent into the godforsakenness of the human condition presupposes a prior decision of love on the part of the Trinitarian persons. Indeed, it is precisely because of the Son's unique and indestructible relationship with the Father that he can enter into the fallen human condition, and even into hell, without thereby simply losing the Father. Here Balthasar wishes to steer a middle course between Calvin (cited above), who understands Christ's crucifixion and descent in a one-sidedly penal way,[50] and Karl Rahner, who sees Christ's suffering as "merely the manifestation of the superabundance of divine love," in an insufficiently dramatic/covenantal fashion.[51] In order to strike this balance, Balthasar

---

[47] Von Balthasar, *Mysterium Paschale*, 167 and 170.
[48] Saward, *The Mysteries of March*, 123.
[49] For an excellent discussion of this, see Lauber, *Barth on the Descent into Hell*, 10–21.
[50] Von Balthasar does acknowledge in *Mysterium Paschale* that Calvin conditions Christ's punishment at the hands of the Father within a prior obedience, which makes his suffering distinct from that of the damned. As Calvin puts it: "The weakness of Christ was pure of all stain, since it was enclosed within obedience to God." *Institutes* 2, 16, cited in von Balthasar, *Mysterium Paschale*, 169.
[51] Hans Urs von Balthasar, *Glory of the Lord*, VII (Edinburgh: T&T Clark, 1982), 205.

situates all distance between the Father and Son in the economy (even the descent into hell) within the undying and eternal love between the Father and the Son in the immanent Trinity. Therefore he can say that "the deepest experience [in Christ] of abandonment by God ... presupposes an equally deep experience of being united to God and of life derived from the Father."[52] But it is more than this. From all eternity the Son has the characteristic of the Lamb of God, insofar as he has always been about doing the will of his Father. Balthasar can therefore speak of a positive distance between that Father and Son—a distance made possible by the real difference between the two required for genuine love—that is, greater, because positive and more primal, than the distance between God and his creatures caused by sin. It is this positive distance of love that enables, to go back to Gregory, Christ to descend *inferno profundior*. Indeed, Balthasar will sometimes speak of death, suffering, and separation as modes of life, joy, and union:

> Earlier we spoke of death as a mode of eternal life, of suffering as a mode of joy, of separation as a mode of union. Now we have seen dereliction as a mode of eternal communion between Father and Son in the Spirit, and in conclusion we begin to see how the "economic" modes of relations b/t the Divine Persons are latent in the 'immanent' modes, without adding a foreign element to them as such. The only foreign element is sin, which is burned up within these relations—which are fire.[53]

Finally, none of this means the abrogation of the doctrine of hell or the real possibility of eternal damnation. Recall the passages from Hebrews cited above: the only truly damnable offense is the rejection of Christ's offer of reconciliation with the Father through his death, descent, and resurrection. For Balthasar this remains a real possibility. Christ's descent into hell does not mean that hell will necessarily be empty. Nevertheless:

> In Christ's death and Resurrection the bonds of death have been burst and eternity stands before us as our "reward": accordingly, the Old Covenant's this-worldly, symmetrical doctrine of retribution collapses. Now there is a fundamental *asymmetry* insofar as God's judgment has been pronounced once and for all in the Cross and Resurrection of Jesus; whatever follows can only be an effect and consequence of this event, already inherent in it.[54]

---

[52] Ibid., 216.
[53] TD V, 268.
[54] Ibid., 277.

This asymmetry means that God wills no one to end up in Hell. From now on hell can no longer be a place for those whom God has not chosen from all eternity. Now hell can only represent God's final respect for human freedom. It is here that Balthasar gives the last word to his great friend Josef Ratzinger, "Christ allots perdition to no one ... He does not pronounce that fatal verdict. It happens where a person has held aloof from him. It comes about where man clings to his isolation."[55]

---

[55] Cited in ibid., 278.

15

The Persistence of the Ransom Theory of the Atonement

Adam Kotsko

Broadly speaking, contemporary Christians' views on the meaning and purpose of the incarnation, death, and resurrection of Christ can be divided into two camps. On the one hand, there are those who insist that Christ has somehow vicariously paid the penalty for our sins, while others emphasize the idea that Christ became incarnate in order to provide us with a living example of his moral teachings. These views can be characterized as "objective" and "subjective," respectively, in the terminology of modern theologians—or as conservative and liberal in the terminology of everyday political-theological debates.

From either of these common contemporary perspectives, the patristic answer to the question of why God became human appears bizarre and foreign. While there are important differences of detail among the patristic authors, in general the Church Fathers claimed that Christ came to set us free from the devil. Often citing Paul's dictum that "you are slaves to the one you obey" (Rom. 6:16), they argued that our first parents had effectively transferred their allegiance from God to Satan by preferring the latter's advice over God's explicit command. As in human systems of slavery (or other forms of obligatory obedience, such as in political communities), Adam and Eve's descendants subsequently inherit this condition of servitude to the devil.

Faced with this situation, God could in theory seize humanity back from Satan by force. Yet the Church Fathers believed that such an act would not be in keeping with God's nature, which was utterly incompatible with any form of arbitrary violence. Instead, God chose to undermine the devil's rule over humanity from within by becoming incarnate in a human being who descended from Adam and Eve through Mary and hence was still formally subject to the devil's claim. In various ways, Christ confronted the devil until he was forced to exercise the ultimate power of a ruler over his subjects: the power to put them to death. For the Fathers, this represented a fatal overreach, insofar as the devil was tacitly claiming to have jurisdiction over God, which is impossible for any created being. This illegitimate act undermined the foundation of his entire regime, opening up a new space wherein human beings could switch their allegiance to God through Christ.

This patristic theory completely defies categorization in terms of either of the dominant contemporary views. It is not, like the conservative position, thought in the primarily "religious" terms of divine retribution, nor is it concerned primarily with personal morality, as in the liberal view. Instead of viewing the problem facing humanity through either a religious or a moral lens, it envisions our basic dilemma as an economic or political one of subjection to an oppressive master or ruler. It is neither "objective" nor "subjective," but intersubjective and social.

Further, while the dominant contemporary views focus primarily on individual transformation, the patristic account begins with the structures of power and legitimacy within which humanity lives. This feature has made it very popular among liberation theologians of many stripes, as it provides a theological language for addressing questions of systemic oppression and revolutionary change.

The patristic view was brought to the attention of modern theologians by Gustav Aulén's pathbreaking study *Christus Victor*.[1] Contrary to previous scholars who saw the patristic theory as an incoherent mythological narrative, Aulén boldly claimed not only that it belonged alongside the familiar objective and subjective theories, but also that it was in fact the normative Christian view. On the historical level, he argues, the patristic or "classical" theory is most likely the view of the New Testament authors, given that it was almost universally held by the earliest generation of Christian writers. Beyond that, it persisted in popular piety even after Anselm's more rationalistic view had eclipsed it in elite theological circles, and it made an unmistakable comeback in the biblical theology of Martin Luther.

These historical arguments are convincing as far as they go, but Aulén's theological rationale for why the patristic view is to be preferred is much less cogent.

---

[1] Gustav Aulén, *Christus Victor: An Historical Study of the Three Main Types of the Idea of the Atonement*, trans. A. G. Herbert (London: Society for Promoting Christian Knowledge, 1931). Note: Page numbers in the chapter refer to this work.

His basic argument is that the patristic theory "represents the work of Atonement or reconciliation as from first to last a work of God Himself, a *continuous* Divine work" (21; emphasis in original). By contrast, he argues that Anselm's theory is discontinuous insofar as Jesus qua human being makes an offering to God.

Aulén's rhetorical strategy here seems to be to put forth the patristic theory as even more objective than the objective theory itself. His emphasis on divine sovereignty serves to align the patristic view with the theology of the Reformation, particularly as Karl Barth and others had forcibly reclaimed it in the early years of the twentieth century. However much sense it may make rhetorically, however, his position makes no sense doctrinally. Anselm shares with the patristic writers the conviction that Jesus Christ was both fully human and fully God, such that every action he took was simultaneously divine and human. Worse, it makes no sense as an interpretation of the patristic view itself, given that Christ's human nature is every bit as essential in that theory as in Anselm's.

Thus, while "Christus Victor" is an appropriate title for the patristic theory from a certain perspective, it may be misleading insofar as it evokes Aulén's insistence on unilateral divine sovereignty. Hence in this chapter it will instead be called the "ransom theory," which highlights the theory's distinctively nonviolent means of redemption.

The goal of this chapter is to show that despite the limitations of his account, Aulén's fundamental point is sound: the ransom theory *really is* the normative account of redemption in the mainstream Christian tradition. Yet Aulén is right for the wrong reasons. His historical evidence, though broadly true, is fundamentally little more than an argument from authority, and his theological claims are one-sided at best. Over against this approach, this chapter will demonstrate that the ransom theory has concretely been normative for all subsequent accounts of redemption, providing the unavoidable framework within which they moved even when—perhaps especially when—they wanted to reject or refute the ransom theory.

The reason the ransom theory is able to play this privileged role is that it represents the most coherent response to the apocalyptic and political-theological forces that converged in the early Christian movement. Hence the discussion will begin by giving an account of those forces before turning to a more detailed examination of the theory itself, as exemplified by Gregory of Nyssa.[2] It will then show that Anselm's theory remains deeply shaped by the patristic theory, of

---

[2] Gregory of Nyssa, *An Address on Religious Instruction*, in *Christology of the Later Fathers*, ed. Edward R. Hardy (Philadelphia: Westminster, 1954).

which it could more fittingly be called a variant or mutation rather than a refutation or replacement.[3] Within a similar vein, it will also investigate the subterranean influence of the ransom theory on Christian political theology. Finally, having noted that the ransom theory is capable of taking both liberating and destructive forms, it will conclude by arguing that the truly crucial point to consider in assessing the ransom theory is not so much the role of God as the role of the devil.

Apocalyptic and Political Theology

The New Testament straightforwardly presents the devil as the ruler of this world. This is clear above all in the temptation of Christ, where Satan's offer of worldly power makes no sense unless he really has worldly power to give (Mt. 4:1–11; Luke 4:1–13). More dramatically, the author of Revelation associates contemporary Roman rulers with demonic forces and appears to anticipate a direct takeover by Satan in the near future. And throughout the Pauline epistles, there are references to expelling someone out of the community to make their way through the world as "handing that person over to Satan" (e.g., 1 Cor. 5:5).

The ransom theory of the atonement grows directly out of the New Testament authors' experience of the world as ruled by Satan. That experience in turn grows out of Jewish apocalyptic thought, which stands at the end of a long series of attempts on the part of Israelite and Jewish intellectuals as they grapple with what we would now call the "problem of evil." While they did not yet have the full conceptual apparatus of classical monotheism that underwrites most versions of that problem, the basic existential question was the same: how can we square our relationship with a good and powerful God and our experience of evil and suffering?

Deuteronomy provides an answer that will prove foundational for all further reflection in this vein: God rewards us when we obey the Torah and punishes us when we neglect it. Insofar as God both promulgates and enforces the law, the Deuteronomistic scheme leads necessarily to a theocratic ideal, and within that framework, the role of earthly leaders naturally became a site of intense theological reflection. While the Book of Deuteronomy itself envisions the possibility of a just king who serves as something like a faithful functionary for the divine ruler (17:14–20), the remainder of the Deuteronomistic history is significantly

---

[3] This recapitulates one of the core arguments of Adam Kotsko, *Politics of Redemption: The Social Logic of Salvation* (New York: T&T Clark, 2010), chapter 6.

less optimistic about the prospects for an Israelite king. In the famous passage where the Israelites demand that Samuel appoint a king, Samuel predicts that the king will oppress the people, while God repeatedly claims that the people are rejecting him as a ruler (1 Sam. 8:4–22). Subsequently, it is the relative faithfulness of the kings that determines the fate of Israel—and later Judah—in the view of the Deuteronomistic historian.

This ambivalent relationship between God and the earthly ruler is intensified in the prophetic tradition, which conceives of God's punishment for Israel's unfaithfulness as taking the form of conquest by a foreign ruler. The same ambivalence between ruler-as-functionary and ruler-as-rivalry reappears here in a more directly paradoxical form. Where the Deuteronomistic history could assess individual kings as falling into one or the other category, the prophets can often insist that the foreign kings overrunning Israel are *both*, simultaneously. For instance, God in Jeremiah can call Nebuchadnezzar "my servant" (25:9) and in practically the same breath, promise that Babylon will be overthrown for its own unjust actions.

The truly decisive turning point comes in the Maccabean period, where historical events shatter the expectations of just retribution inculcated by both the Deuteronomistic and prophetic paradigms. Under the mad king Antiochus Epiphanes, the Jewish community experienced an unprecedented and seemingly incomprehensible turn of events: they were brutally persecuted, tortured, and even killed precisely *for* being faithful to God's law. Hence the king is no longer God's unwitting servant, but his conscious and willful enemy. Yet though it stretches the Deuteronomistic-prophetic paradigm nearly to the breaking point, this newly emerging apocalyptic paradigm does not depart from it entirely. Even the king conceived as demonic plays a necessary role in God's plan, as he serves as God's final enemy, whose defeat ushers in the messianic age.

The radical evil of the earthly ruler in the apocalyptic scheme thus paradoxically leads to a more elevated cosmological status. If he is to be a rival to God, he must operate not only on the earthly political plane, but on the spiritual plane as well. Hence the rich imagery of apocalyptic literature, which produces a kind of spiritual overlay for geopolitics—above all in Daniel, whose apocalyptic portions narrate the history of world empires up to the time of Antiochus (the "little horn" of the vision).

In his seminal work *Political Theology*, Carl Schmitt grounds the titular discipline in the homology between God and the earthly sovereign.[4] While that

---

[4] Carl Schmitt, *Political Theology: Four Chapters on the Concept of Sovereignty*, trans. George Schwab (Chicago: University of Chicago Press, 2005).

parallel did perhaps hold in the early modern period on which Schmitt focuses, this historical survey shows that in the Jewish (and subsequently Christian) experience, the problem of political theology centered instead on the conflict or rivalry between God and the earthly ruler. The most relevant theological homology from the perspective of apocalyptic thought is, rather, that between the earthly ruler and God's demonic enemy.

From this perspective, we can see that it is not accidental that the leaders of the Maccabean revolt belonged precisely to the priestly class rather than to the remnants of the ruling dynasty. Within the apocalyptic worldview, at least at this stage of its development, the prospect of a "good king" is no more acceptable than the rule of a "good emperor" on the model of Cyrus. A return to the theocratic ideal is the only legitimate option once the earthly ruler becomes God's cosmic rival.

It is within this apocalyptic political-theological framework that the New Testament image of the devil as the "prince of this world" emerged. Working from within the apocalyptic paradigm, Christianity radicalizes the theo-politics of martyrdom that arose out of the experience of persecution under Antiochus, insofar as the messiah himself becomes a martyr. This unexpected turn of events raises the stakes of the apocalyptic hope for the resurrection of the dead, which the scriptural tradition first puts in the mouth of the faithful Jewish mother who witnesses her seven sons being tortured to death for refusing to violate the Torah (specifically by eating pork; cf. 2 Macc. 7).

The New Testament images and narratives I cited at the beginning of this section represent attempts to grapple with the profound tensions and paradoxes that resulted from this radicalization of the apocalyptic paradigm. It fell to the patristic writers to find some way to systematize the specifically Christian mutation of the apocalyptic outlook, which gradually crystallized in the ransom theory of the atonement. In the next session, I will present Gregory of Nyssa's account of the ransom paid the devil in his *Address on Religious Instruction* as an elaboration of that theory that is at once exemplary and tellingly exceptional.

Gregory of Nyssa as Model Ransom Theorist

Gregory of Nyssa writes at a decisive moment in Christian history. He was among the first generation of theologians to live in a Roman Empire where Christianity had not only been legalized (by means of the Edict of Milan in 313), but also provided with imperial patronage. The first ecumenical council at Nicea represented the new situation most famously in 325, but also more ominously by Constantine's use of military force against the schismatic Donatists in 316. By the time Gregory came to write his *Address on Religious Instruction*, that imperial patronage had shifted to outright imperial enforcement, beginning with the Emperor Theodosius I declaring Nicene Christianity the official religion of the empire in 380 and convening the First Council of Constantinople in 381, in which Gregory himself was involved, in order to reaffirm Nicea.

The text presents itself as a guide for catechists, with a special emphasis on winning over pagan converts with some kind of philosophical background. One could read the text as taking two initial passes at the task, using three key presuppositions. First, he is able to use commonly shared presuppositions about God to get as far as the orthodox doctrine of the Trinity (preface—§3). Second, he draws on the widely shared beliefs in a skillful designer of the universe (§5) and in the division of human nature into sensible and intellectual parts (§6) in order to get to the creation and fall. Yet in both cases Gregory comes up against a stubborn obstacle. After his first pass, he says: "Neither Greek nor Jew, perhaps, will contest the existence of God's Word and Spirit—the one depending on his common ideas, the other on the Scriptures. Both, however, will equally reject the plan by which God's Word became man, as something incredible and unbefitting to say of God" (§5). His second pass stumbles at the same place:

> One who has followed the course of our argument up to this point will probably agree with it, since we do not appear to have said anything unbefitting a right conception of God. He will not, however, take a similar view of what follows ... I refer to the human birth, the advance from infancy to manhood, the eating and drinking, the weariness, the sleep, the grief, the tears, the false accusations, the trial, the cross, the death, and the putting in the tomb. (§9)

Gregory shows a certain reluctance in attempting to overcome this severe obstacle, suggesting at one point that humans should not presume to dictate to God the method of salvation (§17) and then that the extraordinary success of Christianity should convince everyone sufficiently *that* the incarnation happened and render less urgent the attempt to understand *why* it did (§18–19).

This hesitation makes it perhaps surprising that Gregory would introduce a still further obstacle into the mix: namely, the notion of Christ as paying some kind of ransom to the devil. Whereas he had used an anthropological argument to establish the propriety of the incarnation as a way of overcoming death on behalf of all of humanity, in this section he relies primarily on political and economic imagery. Centering on the metaphor of slavery, he claims that by allowing them to be misled by the devil, the first humans were essentially selling themselves into bondage. Once such transactions are complete, "neither [those selling themselves] nor anyone else can reclaim their freedom, even when those who reduce themselves to this wretched state are nobly born" (§22)—and implicitly, the same holds for their progeny as well, insofar as Gregory believes that all of humanity is together held under the devil's tyranny.

Believing, in unison with the other patristic writers, that a violent seizure of humanity is contrary to God's persuasive nature, Gregory does note one possible nonviolent solution: "no law stands in the way of his buying back humanity's freedom, if he wants to" (§22). God must simply figure out some price to pay the devil, and the transaction can go forward. The key to finding an acceptable price can be found in the devil's own previous behavior. In Gregory's account, the devil was an angel "appointed to maintain and take charge of the region of earth," and he was present for the creation of humanity, whose exalted state sparked the devil's envy:

> In [humanity] was the divine excellence of the intelligible nature, an excellence blended with a certain ineffable power [i.e., the image of God]. In consequence that angelic power [the devil], which had been given the government of earth, took it amiss as something insufferable that, out of the nature subject to him, there should be produced a being to resemble the transcendent dignity. (§6)

Consequently the devil devised the plan to lead humanity astray and assumed lordship over them. With this history in mind, Gregory believes one can "make a reasonable guess about his wishes": "We argued at the beginning that he envied man his happiness and closed his mind to the good. He begot in himself the darkness of wickedness, and sickened with the love of power ... What, then, would he exchange for the one in his power, if not something clearly superior and better?" (§23). This superior prize is Christ, whose miraculous birth and signs of power are unparalleled in human history and who therefore seemed to the devil to be "a bargain which offered him more than he held" (§23).

The twist, however, is that since Christ is God, the devil simply *cannot* rule over Christ. By exchanging humanity for Christ, the devil winds up with nothing. The devil naturally would never agree to this, and so Christ must appear as a mere human being to prevent the devil from knowing he's getting more (and therefore less) than he bargained for. Here Gregory uses a famous fishing metaphor: "as it is with greedy fish, [the devil] swallowed the Godhead like a fishhook along with the flesh, which was the bait" (§24)—in other words, the incarnation was, from the perspective of the devil, a classic bait and switch.

Gregory initially justifies this deception with the principle that turnabout is fair play, but then goes a step further, claiming that by acting in this way, God "benefitted, not only the one who had perished, but also the very one who had brought us to ruin" (§26). A bit further on, he repeats this basic parallel: Christ "freed humanity from evil, and healed the very author of evil himself" (§26). In addition to setting all of humanity free, Christ also leverages the devil's illegitimate yet real relationship to humanity to bring about the devil's own salvation as well.

By the end of the patristic era, the main points of Gregory's scheme, which were adopted and developed by later theologians as well, had come to seem unacceptable. Their problem is not, as Gregory seems to anticipate, that it is inappropriate for God to use trickery. Rather, they object to the idea that a power other than God could come to rule over humanity in a way that is, if not strictly legitimate, at least in some sense *real*. And it is indeed initially unclear how this idea is compatible with monotheism. Gregory's account of how the devil's rule could come about is both elliptical and metaphorical, but the key to understanding it is the idea that humanity "sold itself into slavery"—that humanity in some sense consented to and acknowledged the devil's authority.

This element of acknowledgment brings Gregory's text into contact with the mainstream of modern political theory, which even in its most monarchical mode (as in the work of Hobbes) relies on the concept of the consent of the governed. In this scheme, there is a sense in which all political leaders are giving their subjects what they want, or at least enough of what they want. From this perspective, one can begin to see how a newly sinful humanity might actually accept the devil's rule more easily than God's. Most notably, many of the perceived needs of sinful humanity—for the fulfillment of greed, for the exercise of violence and dominance—could be much more easily met by someone like the devil than someone like the persuasive God of the patristic literature. Indeed, with desires warped by sin, humanity might perceive God as a heartless tyrant were he to violently overthrow the devil and begin ruling directly.

The rule of the devil is "real," then, is a fact to be reckoned with, insofar as sinful humanity and the devil somehow *fit* each other and so are allied with one another. God's strategy of subverting the devil's power from within might thus appear to be two-pronged, simultaneously undermining the devil by causing him to overreach and healing humanity in order to bring about *new* desires incompatible with the devil's rule. Such a process cannot take place all at once—once the alternative power center (in this case Christ) is established, the balance of power must slowly shift, and that is one way of reading the patristic authors' confidence that the spread of Christianity even in the face of persecution demonstrates the gospel's truth. The world is not redeemed all at once, but it is in their view approaching a critical mass. On the other hand, as Gregory says in response to those who object that the world does not seem sufficiently redeemed, "it is possible for evil to have been struck a mortal blow, and yet for life to be harassed by its vestiges" (§30).

Although they appear to be powerful now, the follower of Christ acts in confidence that the devil and his followers are essentially "dead-enders." Interestingly, however, for Gregory the devil will not simply be defeated, as in nearly all other apocalyptic literature, but will also be somehow redeemed. On this point, Gregory is essentially unique among all Christian authors regarded as orthodox, and I suspect that his ability to envision the salvation of Satan stems from his perception that Christianity was transforming the Roman empire—in other words, the apocalyptic identification of the earthly ruler and the devil allowed Gregory to read recent political events as tantamount to the devil converting to Christianity.

Even if the apocalyptic tensions had slackened in Gregory's time, then, the apocalyptic framework of the ransom theory remained determinative. Within a generation or two of imperial Christianity, however, the apocalyptic identification of the devil and the earthly rulers was no longer intelligible to most Christian theologians, leading to the critiques of the ransom theory noted above. Yet it took many centuries for a concrete alternative to emerge, and it is to that alternative that we now turn.

The Afterlife of the Ransom Theory in Anselm

Throughout the modern period, Anselm's argument in *Why God Became Human (Cur Deus Homo)* has been viewed a decisive break with the patristic understanding of the salvific nature of Christ's work, and at first glance, the contrast seems clear enough.[5] Nevertheless, Aulén and other interpreters go too far in presenting Anselm as a complete break with the patristic understanding. It is

---

[5] Anselm of Canterbury, "Why God Became Man," in *Major Works*, ed. Brian Davies and Gillian Evans (New York: Oxford University Press, 1998).

more productive to read Anselm's theory as a particular development *within* the conceptual scheme put forward by the patristic writers.

To summarize what we can draw from Gregory, taken here as a model, in the patristic theory of atonement, the unity of humanity leads to a universal and twofold bondage (to death and the devil), and Christ's redemptive act mobilizes that unity in order to undo both forms of bondage at once in a way that is "persuasive" or nonviolent in a broad sense.

Anselm retains this basic framework, most importantly the core principle of the unity of the human race. This principle comes to the fore at pivotal moments in *Why God Became Human*. For instance, discussing the fact that the first humans' sin affected the whole human race, he says:

> Now, the whole nature of the human race was inherent in its first parents; human nature was as a result entirely defeated in them with the consequence that it became sinful—with the exception of one man alone, whom God knew how to set apart from the sin of Adam, just as he knew how to create him of a virgin without the seed of a man. In just the same way, human nature would have been entirely victorious, if they had not sinned. (1.18)

In order to make up for this fault, humanity "needs to conquer the devil through the difficulty of death, and in so doing sin in no way" (1.22), but he cannot do this since "because of the man who was conquered, the whole of humanity is rotten, and, as it were, in a ferment with sin" (1.23). By the same token, the savior must come from the same race (*genus*) founded by Adam, or else "he will not have an obligation to give recompense on behalf of this race, because he will not be from it" (2.8).

The unity of the human race is not the only thing Anselm shares with the patristic authors—he also clearly embraces the notion that death is a result of sin and that Christ's work must not be carried out by fiat. The particular significance of these aspects of his scheme is, however, best understood in relation to the single greatest change that Anselm introduces: the displacement of the devil from his role as a "substantial" oppressor alongside death. I say "displacement" rather than "removal" for two reasons. First, Anselm does give the devil a role, albeit a significantly downgraded one of subjecting humanity to temptation or more general "harassment" (1.7). He is aware of the patristic view that "God, in order to set humankind free, was obliged to act against the devil by justice rather than mighty power," which he characterizes as something "we are in the habit of saying" (1.7). He rejects the patristic view, but replaces it with the idea that it is more appropriate for humanity "to defeat in return the one by whom humanity had been defeated" (2.19). Hence undercutting the devil remains a goal of Christ's work, but a distinctly subordinate one.

The second reason for calling it a "displacement" has more momentous consequences for Anselm's argument: the "slot" formerly occupied by the devil remains a part of the overall framework, to be filled by different agents at different times. Once one recognizes this, it becomes clear that Anselm follows the patristic scheme to a surprising level of detail. For instance, with the devil reduced to a supporting player at best in the drama of sin and salvation, the most obvious agent of Christ's death becomes humanity, or at least particular human beings. This creates a possible problem, as one of the earliest steps in Anselm's chain of reasoning is that any offense against God is of infinite magnitude, since God is infinite (1.13). Surely murdering God counts as an offense, so it would seem that humanity would only compound its debt through the very act that was supposed to satisfy it. To solve this problem, Anselm mobilizes the theme, found in Gregory of Nyssa, of Christ's humanity as a kind of disguise, but in this case, it serves to allow Anselm to claim that humanity's sin in killing Christ was committed in ignorance and therefore forgivable: "For no member of the human race would ever wish to kill God, at least no one would willingly wish it, and therefore those who killed him unknowingly did not fall headlong into that infinite sin with which no other sins can be compared" (2.15).

The devil's more basic role in the patristic scheme is of course that of the tyrant who has unjustly seized humanity. For Anselm, there is a sense in which humanity itself, despite the apparent paradox, can be seen as taking on this role, but he does not develop this theme in detail. Instead, the primary agent filling the devil's role is the only other meaningful agent available in Anselm's scheme: God himself. As this claim may be somewhat jarring, I should be clear. My point here is not to say that Anselm straightforwardly presents God as an oppressive ruler. Naturally the role undergoes considerable mutation when held by God rather than the devil. I also do not intend to claim that Anselm consciously cast God in a role based on the traditional role of the devil in patristic atonement theories. Instead, I would argue that the inherent logic of his subject matter leads him, once he has downgraded the devil, necessarily to place God in an analogous role.

To get at why this is, it may be helpful to think about what it would have looked like if Anselm had simply *removed* the role of the devil rather than displacing the devil from it. What would have remained was humanity's bondage to death alone as the problem that the incarnation solves—and indeed, later Eastern theology has tended toward that claim. Yet it seems obvious that there is much more going wrong in the world than the fact that people die. Violence, greed, lust for domination, and even simple callousness are historical constants that can sometimes make death seem to be a welcome relief.

The patristic theory accounted for all that in terms of the influence of the evil powers that hold humanity under subjection. Yet once God takes up the role of ruler, human sinfulness is no longer a matter of being subject (albeit initially voluntarily) to an evil power, but instead becomes a matter of being in the wrong before God, or in Anselm's terms, of being in debt to God. The inheritance of debt from one's parents is a familiar feature of many human cultures, and in fact Anselm appears to misunderstand the patristic authors as claiming that humanity owed a debt to the devil that God was in some sense obligated to repay in order to set humanity free (1.7). In rejecting this view, Anselm effectively transforms humanity's indebtedness from something that is provisionally recognized as part of the actually existing situation in which God's strategy must work into something with much greater ontological weight.

One must recall here that God's recognition of the devil's claim in the patristic theory was oriented toward undercutting all justification for that claim. By contrast, once we assume that God is in the business of exacting payment for debts incurred, then that debt must ultimately and *really* be paid: the abolition of that system of debt, parallel with the abolition of the devil's rule, is no longer an option once it is a matter of the divine nature. Further complicating the picture is the fact that debt to God is not simply a debt but, by definition, a moral failing. Hence death becomes not a future-oriented corrective or purifying measure, but a punishment. Yet a problem arises here. The Christian tradition has always maintained, virtually without exception, that moral failing can only be a matter of the individual will. The inheritance of a social or political status or even of indebtedness unwillingly or through no fault of one's own is, however regrettable, at least familiar and comprehensible. But how can one inherit the condition of being in the wrong before God unwillingly, the condition of being morally blameworthy through no fault of one's own?

That is the circle Anselm attempts to square with the doctrine of original sin. To put it briefly, Anselm follows Augustine in claiming that humans subsequent to Adam inherit a distorted will, specifically because the distortion of the male will during the sexual act introduces a distortion into the child. However questionable this may be at the biological level, this allows Anselm to square the circle insofar as moral judgment is only possible when the will is involved—since original sin is a kind of wrongness precisely *in the will*, it can rightly be regarded as a moral issue. This scheme also allows for an "out" for Christ. Since he is born of a virgin, the distorting effects of the male will are absent in his case. Consequently, Christ begins with a clean state.

Now since Christ begins and remains in a state of original justice, he does not owe any form of satisfaction, but rather only the basic obedience God demands of everyone. Despite the common understanding of Anselm's argument, he does not claim that Christ is performing a vicarious satisfaction. Instead, he draws on another ecclesiastical system that is essentially common to both East and West: a baseline of obligations for the everyday believer, coupled with opportunities to exceed the requirements and gain greater merit. Anselm even explicitly uses the example of someone taking a monastic vow, albeit couched in more general terms of "a vow about holy living" (2.5).

The problem requiring the intervention of a God-man rather than a normal sinless human being was that an offense against the infinite God is necessarily infinite, meaning that no finite human being could make satisfaction for it—but by the very same principle, the merit accrued by the infinite God-man is itself infinite. Had he been an ordinary sinful human being, Christ's death would have had no merit, but his sinless state makes his death voluntary and thus meritorious in much the same way as a monastic vow is. As a result, his death not only gives him infinite merit, but also makes him the first human being *ever* to accrue any merit for himself. Anselm then stages a scene in which God the Father offers Christ his reward and then—paralleling the patristic theme of the human flesh as a disguise—discovers that Christ is already the infinite God and can therefore receive nothing. Since someone must receive the merit, the Father allows Christ to designate humanity as the recipient. From that point forward, any human being who knows of this infinite store of merit need only call upon it to receive salvation.

It's clear that Anselm regards this as a profound relief, and indeed his praise of this elegant act of grace elicits what is perhaps the closest to an outburst of emotion that we find in Anselm's body of work: "Nevertheless, he gave his life, so precious; no, his very self; he gave his person—think of it—in all its greatness, in an act of his own, supremely great, volition" (2.18). Yet to my mind, his argument is ultimately claustrophobic and even a little terrifying. In the patristic scheme, the God of Jesus Christ was rescuing us from the devil conceived as the god of this world—an oppressive god characterized by acquisitiveness and pride. When the devil is displaced, however, does the God of Jesus Christ not become precisely the god of this world?

Anselm presents us with a God who is not motivated by his love of humanity—indeed, that theme is virtually absent from Anselm's argumentation—but by his love of honor. One might even characterize God's goal as saving face by fulfilling the original plan of the heavenly city. What's more, even after Christ's superabundant fund of merit has been established, the debt economy is not abolished. God is still fundamentally a God who exacts payment, even if his demands have been fulfilled. In short, Anselm has turned God into a being motivated by pride and something like greed, features that we more conventionally associate with the devil.

Even though Anselm set out to reject and refute the ransom theory, its conceptual framework still makes itself felt—in notably destructive ways that will be repeated and in some cases amplified in the many subsequent theories that take Anselm's argument as their starting point.

The Legacy of the Ransom Theory in Political Theology

Although the later tradition sought to downplay the role of the devil in atonement, the role of the state could not be so easily displaced. The gospel narratives are unanimous in presenting Christ's death as resulting from something like a judicial sentence (although there are significant ambiguities here, as pointed out by Giorgio Agamben),[6] carried out by the local political authorities, a historical fact that was theologically enshrined in the Nicene Creed's confession that Christ was "crucified under Pontius Pilate." Hence Christian theologians have been nearly unanimous in insisting on the necessity that Christ's specific mode of death was not accidental. Yet if it was clear *that* the cross was necessary, it was far from clear exactly *why* it was. In *On the Incarnation*, for instance, Athanasius engages in a lengthy disquisition on the reasons that Christ had to undergo a *public* death (§§21–29), ultimately concluding that Christ wanted to display his victory over death for all to see.[7] At no point, however, is the role of the state in the proceedings at all clarified.

As the bond between church and empire solidified, Christ's acceptance of a public execution under the Roman authorities came to appear not as a ploy to trick the devil into overreaching, but as a sign of Christ's endorsement and legitimation of Roman authority. Peterson's "Monotheism as a Political Problem" documents the ways in which Eusebius, Ambrose, and Orosius "bound the

---

[6] Giorgio Agamben, *Pilate and Jesus*, trans. Adam Kotsko (Stanford: Stanford University Press, 2015).
[7] Athanasius, *On the Incarnation of the Word*, trans. Archibald Robertson, in *Christology of the Later Fathers*, ed. Edward R. Hardy (Philadelphia: Westminster, 1954).

Roman Empire and Christianity together."[8] In this theological scheme, Christ is continually announcing his submission to the Roman state: by allowing himself to be enrolled in the census, by acknowledging Rome's right to tax, and finally by submitting to its legal judgment. Far from being God's apocalyptic rival, the Roman emperor has a political mission akin to Christ's spiritual mission, that of unifying all peoples into a peaceable kingdom in which the gospel can readily spread.

Just as in Anselm's theory, the overall political-theological structure of the ransom theory remains intact. In both cases, the devil is displaced from the scheme, and in both cases, God takes over the devil's role. In Anselm, God replaces the devil as humanity's spiritual captor, and here God replaces the devil as the spiritual analogue for earthly rule. This shift opens up the theological space for late medieval and early modern thinkers to assert the prerogatives of state power over against ecclesiastical claims to earthly authority. Dante's *De Monarchia* is exemplary in this regard, giving significant space to a theological argument in favor of the divine legitimation of the secular power of the Roman Empire.[9] This development reaches its end point in Hobbes's *Leviathan*, where the earthly sovereign is presented as a veritable God on earth—and in an echo of the apocalyptic identification of state and devil, the king is identified with the sea monster from Job, which the tradition of commentary had long regarded as a symbol for Satan.[10] It is as though the original apocalyptic paradigm reappears just as the Christian empire gives way to the secular state.

Conclusion

This chapter has argued that the ransom theory was an attempt to systematize the mutations of the Jewish apocalyptic political-theological paradigm arising from the Christian experience of a crucified Messiah. It has shown that once the patristic writers arrived at the solution represented by the ransom theory, its basic conceptual structure remained determinative for subsequent atonement theories and political theologies alike. Nevertheless, it has indicated that those later versions work toward conclusions directly at odds with the original intent of the ransom theory, a reversal that stems from the disidentification of the devil

---

[8] Erik Peterson, "Monotheism as a Political Problem," in *Theological Tractates*, trans. Michael J. Hollerich (Stanford: Stanford University Press, 2011), 102.
[9] Dante, *De Monarchia*, trans. and ed. Prue Shaw (New York: Cambridge University Press, 1995).
[10] Thomas Hobbes, *Leviathan* (New York: Penguin, 1982).

with the state and the consequent recruitment of God to play the devil's theological and political-theological roles. The result is an image of God that is difficult to recognize as good or loving and an idolization of the state.

Contrary to Aulén's claims, then, it is precisely *when* the ransom theory becomes "from first to last a work of God Himself, a *continuous* Divine work" that serious problems begin to arise. The decisive factor that differentiates the "classical" version of the ransom theory from its later versions is not its greater emphasis on divine sovereignty, but its identification of God as the persuasive, nonviolent opponent of earthly sovereignty.

Liberation theologians coming from many different perspectives, for instance, Leonardo Boff and Darby Ray, have recognized the promise of the original ransom theory for contemporary theological reflection.[11] The identification of earthly power structures as opposed to the divine justice understandably appeals to theological movements grounded in communities of the oppressed and marginalized. Things become more complicated, however, when we recognize that many of the more dominant theological paradigms that these theologians reject as oppressive are actually variants on the ransom theory.

The question then becomes not merely how to reclaim the early patristic heritage, but how to avoid the reversal—a reversal that, in many respects, came about precisely because of the *success* of the Christian movement. It is easy to decry the compromise made with the Roman Empire, but is it possible to maintain a purely oppositional movement indefinitely? Had the Christians somehow succeeded in overthrowing the empire altogether, would God not have become identified with whatever political structure they set up in its place, ultimately repeating the same problem? Coming at this political-theological problem from the more explicitly theological side, can we trace the root of the reversal to the very claim that earthly political authorities have a necessary theological role in the first place (even if a negative one)? Does the very element that gives the ransom theory its urgent political relevance also doom it to eventual co-optation?

---

[11] Leonardo Boff, *Passion of Christ, Passion of the World*, trans. Phillip Berryman (Maryknoll, NY: Orbis, 1987); Darby Ray, *Deceiving the Devil: Atonement, Abuse, and Ransom* (Cleveland: Pilgrim, 1998).

16

Penal Substitution

Stephen R. Holmes

The theory of penal substitution is a way of answering the question of how Jesus's death is salvific. Although the history is somewhat disputed, I will argue that it comes to prominence as a theory during the Reformation, becomes the normal and assumed way of describing the atonement among Protestants during the seventeenth and eighteenth centuries, and then fades fairly rapidly after about 1800, save among certain confessional Protestant groups. Today it is a controversial idea, insisted on as an indispensable mark of orthodoxy by some conservative evangelical groups, but derided as not just wrong but profoundly theologically dangerous by other writers. It nonetheless retains a significant place in the history and liturgy, particularly hymnody, of evangelicalism and broader Protestantism.

The Idea of Penal Substitution

Penal substitutionary atonement assumes the logic of the law court. Sin is understood as law-breaking, and so necessarily attracts a penalty, which is inevitably death. In dying on the cross, Jesus pays the penalty of death for all those who are saved, and so they are freed from their deserved punishment. God's justice is satisfied by Jesus's death.

In this brief summary, several potential problems are already visible. Most seriously, perhaps, "law" is understood as a fundamental reality, to which even God appears to be subject. Second, the logic of the law court does not typically provide for a substitute; while I might pay another's fine, I cannot serve another's prison sentence, still less exchange places with someone awaiting execution, and so the doctrine appears incoherent even in its own terms. Third, the account seems to drive an improper separation between the Father, who is pictured as concerned only for the upholding of justice, and the Son, who acts in mercy to deliver us from justice (and it appears to have no place at all for the Spirit). Fourth, the account so presented would seem to offer a merely negative righteousness: our guilt is atoned for, but there is no account of our being clothed in Jesus's righteousness. Fifth, the narrative seems to justify divine violence as an act of justice, and so to legitimize violence more generally.

I will suggest in this chapter that while many of these criticisms can fairly be leveled at many more popular accounts of penal substitution, they fail to undermine more serious theological presentations. I will also argue that the cultural plausibility of the doctrine depended on a particular understanding of criminal justice which is no longer dominant, at least in the late-modern West, and so the doctrine is potentially anachronistic.

The Plausibility of Penal Substitution: Responding to Criticisms

The five criticisms outlined above are not trivial, and suggest that there can be no theologically adequate account of the atonement in penal substitutionary terms. That said, serious presentations of the doctrine have regularly noticed the dangers and sought to escape them. Before addressing the history and present worth of the doctrine, these criticisms must be addressed, to show that there is at least some reason to believe the doctrine can be presented in a form worthy of consideration. In addressing the criticisms I will also give a positive account of the content of a serious doctrine of penal substitution.

First Criticism: Is God Subject to the Law?

Although Anselm's doctrine is not a version of penal substitution (I shall argue this in the historical section below), he offers helpful conceptual clarity for addressing the first point. Anselm's reason for asserting that God cannot simply forgive sin in *Cur Deus Homo* turns on the nature of God, and on creation's relation to God. God, being perfect in bliss and *a se*, is not of course damaged in any way by creaturely sin, but the honor creation owes to God (in Anselm's logic) is seriously damaged by sin, and so the purpose of creation is frustrated. If creation remains damaged and frustrated, then God's purposes in creating will have failed, which (Anselm believes) is unthinkable. So God must act in atonement to restore creation to what it always should have been.[1]

Borrowing this logic for an account of penal substitution, we can argue that the implacable law is not something to which God is subject, but rather an expression of God's purposes for creation. The world is to be a place of justice and joy, and where there is injustice, it must be put right and not merely passed over. The wages of sin are the necessary consequence of God intending creation to be a place of perfect justice. Now, in this account there is an assumption, of which more later, that retribution is an appropriate part of perfect justice. The logic presumes, that is, that crime necessitates punishment if justice is to be maintained. An adequate doctrine of penal substitution will need to defend this intuition, particularly as it is not now so self-evident as it might have seemed some centuries ago. With such a defense, however, the place of law in the system is not theologically improper.

Second Criticism: Can Guilt be Transferred?

In the history of penal substitution, at least three different responses are discernible to the second question raised above, concerning the transference of guilt. The first, and earliest, relies on the doctrine (central to Calvin, for instance) that union with Christ is the fundamental reality of salvation (from which flow the twin benefits of justification and sanctification).[2] The union of the believer with Christ results in "Christ-and-the-church" being a single moral agent, and so there is no transference of guilt, rather the head being held responsible for the sins of the body. This understanding was advanced by Calvin[3] and was common to the post-Reformation scholastic dogmatic systems.[4] It was still being defended in the twentieth century by so serious a theologian as Bavinck (who emphasizes covenantal headship and the divinely instituted reality of the *pactum salutis*).[5]

---

[1] This is the argument of much of the first book of *Cur Deus Homo*; see particularly I.12–25. See Stephen R. Holmes, "The Upholding of Beauty: A Reading of Anselm's *Cur Deus Homo*," *SJT* 54 (2001), 189–203, 195–197, for a summary of the argument here.
[2] Calvin makes this very clear in the course of his refutation of Osiander's notion of "essential righteousness" in *Inst.* III.xi.10; he begins his account of "the way we receive the grace of Christ" in *Inst.* III by insisting that we can only know any benefit of salvation because we are united with Christ by the Spirit. *Inst.* III.i.1.
[3] See, for example, *Inst.* III.iv.30.
[4] So (e.g.) Wollebius, *Comp. Theol. Christ.* I.xxx.xiii or Ames, *Medulla*, I.xxvii.1.
[5] Herman Bavinck, *Reformed Dogmatics III: Sin and Salvation in Christ*, trans. John Vriend (Grand Rapids, MI: Dutch Reformed Translation Society, 2006), 404–406.

Dogmatically, because on this account justification is the consequence of union with Christ, not its cause, the teaching necessitates a fairly strong doctrine of election, and a particular account of redemption. Christ's death is the basis of justification, and so is for those, and only those, who will be united with him through election. This of course was not a problem for the seventeenth-century dogmatic systems, but creates potential difficulties for later defenders of penal substitution who denied limited atonement, particularly Methodists and others in the Arminian strand of the evangelical revival. The difficulties are not insoluble, however: if we suggest faith is the basis of union with Christ, rather than election, and then work a similar argument through, the problem largely evaporates.

This strong account of union with Christ appears difficult to hold, however, in the face of conceptions of personhood as unassailable interiority that arose at the beginning of the nineteenth century.[6] If possessing an unconquerable will is intrinsic to my being a person, and so to my being morally significant, then I cannot be a shared moral agent with another, even Christ. (Although Arminianism is generally more compatible with Romantic conceptions of personhood than classical Calvinism, on this point it fares no better: the problem is the result of union with Christ—the existence of shared moral agency—not its origins in election or freely embraced faith.)

It is perhaps no surprise, then, that nineteenth-century defenders of penal substitution offered a different solution to the "transference of guilt" problem. Charles Hodge offered the most compelling account. He suggested that there are two distinct realities that, in English, are conflated in the word "guilt": one is a moral awareness of failure, and the other is a judicial liability to punishment. Hodge asserted that the former cannot be transferred between agents, but that the latter can.[7] This seems to me counterintuitive; Hodge's argument for it is essentially that in the atonement it happened, so it must be possible (which works if we are convinced that the atonement must be understood in penal substitutionary terms for some other good reason—perhaps exegesis—but otherwise is in danger of being circular).

A third way of addressing the question of transference of guilt, which is beginning to stretch the definition of penal substitution, arises out of the Arminian debates, which posed the question sharply. (My example above, of the difference

---

[6] On which, see Jan Olof Bengtsson, *The Worldview of Personalism: Origins and Early Development* (Oxford: Oxford University Press, 2006).
[7] Charles Hodge, *Systematic Theology II: Anthropology* (Grand Rapids, MI: Eerdmans, 1960), 476–477.

between a fine that can be paid by anyone and a sentence that must be served by the offender, was first offered by Faustus Socinus.[8]) On the Arminian side in the seventeenth century, the problem was generally accepted to be insoluble, and so the atonement was narrated in "governmental" terms rather than penal terms. The most famous example of this is the argument of Hugo Grotius, who asserted first that God could and did forgive sin without any need for satisfaction, but that at the same time God made a public display of displeasure at sin in the death of Jesus so as to preserve the moral order of the universe.[9]

The Genevan theologian François Turretin certainly intended to defend a (by his day) traditional penal substitutionary view, but moved at least a little in the same direction in trying to cope with this question. He suggested that it is within the competence of a judge to "relax" the precise demands of the law so that the strict demands of justice remain unmet and instead to allow some sort of vicarious equivalent punishment to answer the case.[10] Turretin defends this in part by an appeal to God's sovereignty over the law: God is not merely a judge, but the ruler who establishes laws, and so God is able to vary the laws.

There is certainly a prima facie plausibility to this analogy, and so this is an interesting account of the atonement; whether it is properly regarded as a form of penal substitution seems less clear. Certainly the clarity of the penal logic is muddled: if there is no absolute legal requirement for the penalty of death to be inflicted, then it is not clear why Jesus had to suffer such humiliation and agony, a question that any serious atonement account must answer, and that the standard doctrine of penal substitution deals with well.

Third Criticism: Trinitarian Concerns

The third criticism above was that penal substitution is sub-Trinitarian in proposing a separation between the Father and the Son, and in having no place for the Spirit. The plausibility of this criticism depends on a theology that at least leans toward a "social" doctrine of the Trinity, particularly on the supposition that the Son and the Father are capable of willing differently. If, as classical Trinitarianism universally claimed, the divine will is one and indivisible, then an assertion that the Son desires mercy whereas the Father desires only justice is already demonstrably nonsense.

---

[8] Faustus Socinus, *De Jesu Christo Servatore* (1598) III.7–10.
[9] Hugo Grotius, *Defensio Fidei Catholicae de Satisfactione Christi* (1617).
[10] Turretin, *Inst. Elenc. Theol.* XIV.x.viii–xi.

Of course, this recognition merely changes the form of the criticism: if penal substitution demands differing divine willing, then it is necessarily wrong, because the position demanded is incompatible with the doctrine of the Trinity that was asserted by those theologians who developed and defended the doctrine of penal substitution. This seems an unlikely state of affairs, but it needs to be shown to be wrong. The demonstration lies in a better account of the various intentions on display in the imagined courtroom narrative that is at the heart of the penal substitutionary account.

To say the Son desires only to save is wrong; in pursuing the particular painful and costly road to salvation that he does, the Son clearly intends to save in a way that is consistent with the upholding of justice. Similarly, the broader narrative insists that the Son is sent by the Father to save, so to portray the Father in the narrative as in some sense vengeful or bloodthirsty is clearly wrong. Father and Son (and, at least implicitly, Spirit) are united in providing salvation while simultaneously upholding justice. (The scholastic doctrine of the *pactum salutis* supports this point, but it can be held independently.[11]) As noted above, this concern for the upholding of justice is properly understood as a concern that the creation shall be what the triune God intended it to be, and so is not something to be dismissed or belittled.

These defenses can stand even if a social doctrine of the Trinity, including an account of separate divine wills, is adopted.[12] On such an account, however, with no theological pressure to find the Son's desiring to be identical to that of the Father, there will be an inevitable lingering suspicion of some difference in emphasis. Perhaps the account will portray the Son looking for mercy within the constraints of justice, whereas the Father demanding justice but accepting a merciful way of enacting it. For this sort of reason, it is both very easy to give a simplistic presentation of penal substitution if a social doctrine of the Trinity is assumed, and very difficult to construct a serious presentation.

What of the role of the Spirit? Jonathan Edwards complained that the atonement theology he had received pictured the Spirit merely as the one who applied the benefits of the atoning transaction between Father and Son,[13] which he

---

[11] On the *pactum salutis*, see John Fesko, *The Covenant of Redemption: Origins, Development, and Reception* (Gottingen: Vandenhoeck & Ruprecht, 2015).

[12] On the problems of social Trinitarianism, see Stephen R. Holmes "Three vs One? Some Problems of Social Trinitarianism," *Journal of Reformed Theology* 3 (2009), 77–89; Karen Kilby, "Perichoresis and Projection: Problems with Social Doctrines of the Trinity," *New Blackfriars* 81 (2000), 432–445; and in response Gijsbert van den Brink, "Social Trinitarianism: A Discussion of Some Recent Theological Criticisms," *International Journal of Systematic Theology* 16 (2014), 331–350.

[13] Jonathan Edwards, *Treatise on Grace and other Posthumously Published Writings*, ed. P. Helm (Cambridge: James Clarke, 1971), 68–69.

believed did undervalue the divine personhood of the Spirit. His solution was to propose that the gift given to the redeemed in the atonement was not merely Christ's righteousness, but the person of the Spirit. I am happy to accept this as a theological claim, but it once again seems to be a move beyond the logic of penal substitution; it is not a claim that can be made sense of within the logic of the law court. If we believe that penal substitution is an exhaustive account of what happens at the atonement, then, the claim of a Trinitarian, specifically pneumatological, deficit is plausible.

Fourth Criticism: A Merely Negative Righteousness

The fourth criticism addresses a similar point. It is an important Reformation principle that in the atonement we are clothed with Christ's righteousness, not merely cleansed from our own guilt.[14] This is vital because it removes any possibility of a theological account of "merit," and so undercuts the ecclesial system of indulgences and masses for the dead that were central to the protests that sparked the Reformation. Perfectly righteous by imputation, we have no need of, and there is no possibility of, supererogatory grace. Penal substitution seems to fail to teach this doctrine of imputation, however: the criminal declared guiltless because her sentence has been served is not thereby transformed into an upstanding member of society deserving of civic honors. Luther's "marvelous exchange," whereby we are granted the positive righteousness of Christ, the credit of all his obedience, as he takes our sin and guilt on himself, is not reflected in the logic of penal substitution.

I see two possible responses to this: one is to refuse the language of positive imputation, while maintaining the intent. The pure logic of penal substitution certainly removes the need for indulgences and the like, because all our transgressions are forgiven through the death of Christ. What matters is to be guiltless, not meritorious, and the atonement renders us completely guiltless. This logic works, but seems some distance from classical Reformation theology.

The other response is again to accept the problem here, but to notice that it is only a problem if penal substitution is taken to be a complete account of what is happening as Christ makes atonement for us. As with the Trinitarian deficit discussed above, if we can construct a theology of the atonement that places penal

---

[14] See, for example, Alan D. Strange, "The Imputation of the Active Obedience of Christ at the Westminster Assembly," in *Drawn into Controversie: Reformed Theological Diversity and Debates within Seventeenth-Century British Puritanism*, ed. Michael A. G. Haykin and Mark Jones (Göttingen: Vandenhoeck & Ruprecht, 2011), 194–209.

substitution as a true, but not complete, account of what is going on, the problem is soluble. (We will need to show how other aspects of the account address the deficits, of course.)

Fifth Criticism: Legitimizing Violence

Perhaps the most lasting contemporary criticism of penal substitution is that it somehow legitimizes violence. There is a graphic form of this criticism, which is relatively easy to dismiss, and a more subtle form, which is harder. Third, I will suggest, there is a cultural issue here, which will lead us into historical considerations.

The graphic form speaks of the cross as an example of child abuse: a father gratuitously inflicting suffering on his innocent child.[15] As an account of the atonement, this is very simple to reject: it simply ignores the unity of God which is the heart of Trinitarian theology. There may be more sophisticated versions which turn on social models of the trinity, but these will be adequately addressed by my comments on the supposed divide between the Father and the Son above. If Father and Son (and Spirit) are one in will, purpose, and desire, then there cannot be an abusive relationship between them.

That said, the argument might be made that, even if this is not an abusive relationship of necessity, to speak of a Father-Son relationship in these terms will inevitably legitimize domestic violence by analogy. This is a nontrivial argument, but in both directions. Its strength relies on a claimed powerful analogy, but there is (as far as I am aware) no statistical evidence for the truth of the analogy. (There is some evidence for an increased propensity for domestic violence in conservative religious families, but nothing that can be construed as relating to the atonement—conservative denominations that stress penal substitution in their doctrinal bases do not, for example, tend to record higher levels of abuse.)

The force of the argument then becomes theoretical. This is not to dismiss it: collecting empirical evidence for causal links like this is very difficult, given the profusion of other factors at play, and so theory becomes powerful. The most interesting theoretical perspective here draws on René Girard's theory of scapegoating. Girard argued for a basic repeated motif in human culture, by which the violence inherent in any society is periodically released by the creation of

---

[15] This criticism was first developed by Rita Nakashima Brock and Rebecca Ann Parker in *Proverbs of Ashes: Violence, Redemptive Suffering, and the Search for What Saves Us* (Boston: Beacon Press, 2001) — see particularly around 30–31.

a scapegoat, someone who, however innocent, is constructed as the monstrous other who is blamed for all the faults and frustrations of the society, and eventually killed in an act of mob violence. Scapegoating itself brings unity of purpose and so peace to a culture, and the violent removal of the scapegoat can bring the illusion of healing.[16]

Girard reads the New Testament as a profound subversion of this otherwise universal scapegoating mechanism, with its sustained focus on the perfect innocence of Jesus. The scapegoating myth is thus revealed for what it is: an irrational response that fails to achieve an abiding peace. Instead, the ethic of Jesus, with its emphasis on repeated forgiveness and non-retaliation, offers an alternative way to construct a society that will not repeatedly lapse into violence.

Some theologians have tried to press Girard's theory of culture into a complete account of soteriology.[17] On such a view, penal substitution appears to be a profound misreading of the atonement, glorifying the violence inflicted on Jesus as a divine act, when in fact it is the epitome of everything Jesus came to bring to an end. Penal substitution on this account legitimizes violence because it subverts and obscures the truth of the overthrow of cultural violence in the passion of Jesus, instead insisting on a mythical implacability of law to maintain the old scapegoating system, demanding the regular identification of lawbreakers who will suffer the violence of the mob and so bring temporary peace to society.

An alternative theory of culture comes from another French writer, Michel Foucault. In his *Discipline and Punish*,[18] Foucault is in part fascinated by our modern fascination with violence. He focuses in on the moment, around 1800, when Western criminal justice systems shifted their basic penal sanction from the public infliction of violence to incarceration. This move, driven by the seminal work of Beccaria,[19] is celebrated as a shift from barbarism to civilization, but Foucault demurs; Bentham's "panopticon" is as much an attempt to impose control on its inmates as any torture chamber ever was, and is proposed not because it is more "civilized" but because it promised to be more efficient. Foucault sees

---

[16] René Girard, *Violence and the Sacred*, trans. Patrick Gregory (Baltimore: John Hopkins Press, 1977); *Things Hidden since the Foundation of the World: Research Undertaken in Collaboration with Jean-Michel Oughourlian and Guy Lefort*, trans. Stephen Bann and Michael Metteer (London: Athlone, 1987); *Job: Victim of His People* (London: Athlone, 1987).

[17] See, for example, S. Mark Heim, *Saved from Sacrifice: A Theology of the Cross* (Grand Rapids, MI: Eerdmans, 2006).

[18] Michel Foucault, *Discipline and Punish: The Birth of the Prison*, trans. Alan Sheridan (London: Penguin, 1977).

[19] Cesare Beccaria, *On Crimes and Punishments*, trans. David Young (Indianapolis: Hackett, 1986). See also Marcello Maestro, *Cesare Beccaria and the Origin of Penal Reform* (Philadelphia: Temple University Press, 1973).

the prison as an attempt to impose control by mental torture, which is morally no different from an attempt to impose control by physical torture.

Foucault's theories are just as controversial as Girard's of course, but he offers a counter-narrative which, by focusing on power as the desired end rather than physical violence as the chosen means, suggests an alternative understanding to Girard's. If Foucault is right (or even just if Girard is wrong), then the proponent of penal substitution has little to fear from the complaint that the doctrine justifies violence. Foucault's theories, as I will suggest, also help us to make sense of the difficult history of the doctrine, to which I now turn.

The History of Penal Substitution

The Bible

The history of penal substitutionary theories of the atonement is controverted. Unsurprisingly, those who hold that the doctrine is a necessary component of orthodox belief find it in the Scriptures and extensively in the history of the church.[20] An examination of the textual evidence offered, however, suggests that penal substitution is being read into texts which do not demand to be read that way, and perhaps are more naturally interpreted differently. Mark 10:45 offers a classic example: "the Son of Man came not to be served, but to serve, and to give his life as a ransom for many." This is clearly a reference to the atonement, and appears to be naturally read as substitutionary, but to insist that the single word "ransom" (Gk *lutron*) implies the full logic of the law court seems hard.[21]

Another famous NT text, Romans 3:24–25, uses three technical terms in rapid succession to describe the atonement: "justified," "redemption," and "atoning sacrifice" (or "sacrifice of propitiation"). Justification is the language of the law court; the Greek word we translate "redemption," by contrast, has its roots

---

[20] For several examples, see the various treatments in Steve Jeffrey, Mike Ovey, and Andrew Sach, *Pierced for Our Transgressions: Rediscovering the Glory of Penal Substitution* (Nottingham: IVP, 2007).

[21] Older commentators tended to make the link by suggesting that the language of "serving" in the text is a deliberate echo of the fourth servant song in Isaiah 52–53, allowing the "ransom" language to be read in the light of the more directly substitutionary language of Isaiah. This proposed link to Isaiah has been seriously questioned in biblical scholarship at least since the 1950s, however. See, for example, Morna D. Hooker, *Jesus and the Servant: The Influence of the Servant Concept of Deutero-Isaiah in the New Testament* (London: SPCK, 1959), 74–79; C. K. Barrett, "The Background of Mark 10.45," in *New Testament Essays: Studies in Memory of Thomas Walter Manson*, ed. A. J. B. Higgins (Manchester: MUP, 1959), 1–18.

in the slave market, the payment of the price of manumission, setting free the captive. "Sacrifice" is clearly cultic language, referring to ritual slaughter in the temple. We might, of course, argue that the collision of these three images is best represented in penal substitutionary terms, and that argument is certainly worth attending to. Even before such an argument is advanced, however, we have already a collection of different images for atonement, none of them developed into a worked-out theory of how the death of Jesus is salvific, but each offering a helpful metaphor.

This sense of many different images of atonement, with few (if any) worked out in the sort of detail which would characterize the competing or complementary "theories of atonement" in later theology, is characteristic of the biblical material. It is open to the proponents of any of the theories to seek to demonstrate that their preferred doctrine best interprets the collected biblical data, of course, but even a successful argument of this form would be rather different from claiming a clear biblical teaching. As with the developed doctrines of Trinity or Christology, Scripture does not offer us a worked out theology of the atonement.

Confessional Documents

When we turn to the history, we might first reflect on the major confessional documents, which have a privileged place in interpreting dogmatic history. Unlike Trinity or Christology, no significant symbol of the patristic, medieval, or Reformation eras proposes any normative doctrine of atonement, and so none suggests that penal substitution is the only acceptable theory. All speak in terms that are open to a penal substitutionary reading, but none demand it. Historically, the church has neither insisted on, nor rejected, penal substitution.

This point is obvious in the ecumenical creeds, which are spare in their treatments of atonement. The Reformation documents deserve more attention. On the Lutheran side, the Augsburg Confession offers its brief account of justification in Article IV. Unsurprisingly, it focuses on the claim that justification is free and unmerited and received through faith in Christ; the only hint concerning how Christ's death saves us is in the claim that "sins [are] remitted for the sake of Christ, who has made satisfaction for our sins by his death" (my translation). This could certainly be understood in penal substitutionary terms, but hardly demands to be so understood (particularly given if "satisfaction" is heard as an echo of Anselm, who I shall discuss briefly below). The Formula of Concord, Article III, focuses on Christ's obedience, as the cause of justification (because of the particular controversies it was addressing) and so is harder to read as an example of penal substitution, but certainly does not deny the doctrine.

On the Reformed side, The Heidelberg Catechism discusses the work of Christ under the rubric of the *munus triplex* (see q. 31) and so describes the work of Christ in priestly, rather than substitutionary, terms. As "mediator" his blood "covers" my sin (q. 36); his passion is an "atoning sacrifice" (q. 37). Other imagery is also used: Christ has "purchased" us (q. 34); "taken the curse" for us (q. 39) and "overcome death" (q. 45). It asks why Jesus suffered under Pontius Pilate, and answers (with Calvin) in penal terms: "That, innocent, he might be condemned by the earthly judge and so free us from the severe judgment of God" (q. 38). Were this the only teaching of the Catechism, we might claim it insisted on penal substitution, but alongside all the other imagery we can at most claim that the text demands that we are prepared to talk about the atonement in penal terms as well as others.

The Belgic Confession offers a clearer statement of penal substitution in Article 20, but immediately follows it with a rather different account of the atonement focusing on Christ's priesthood (Art. 21). Similarly, the 1560 Scots Confession has a clear statement of penal substitution in Article VIII, but again some broader sacrificial language about the atonement in Article IX. It would be possible in either case to claim that the first doctrine interprets the second, but it is far from clear that the authors intended that reading. More naturally both documents can be read as offering penal substitution as one of a number of complementary ways of narrating the atonement.

Probably the document which is most amenable to the suggestion that penal substitution is the only orthodox way of narrating the atonement is the Second Helvetic Confession. Again, the text is not directed toward the question of how atonement happened, rather treating the standard sixteenth-century concerns of the nature of justification, the work of repentance, the relationship between law and gospel, and so on. That said, there is no doubt that its preferred imagery for the atonement is legal, although this is not exclusive (see particularly the lyrical passage in XI.15, which piles up different images, most of them focused on victory).

Individual Writers

I suggested above that many claims to find penal substitution clearly taught in Scripture work by taking imagery that is more naturally read differently, and transposing it into penal substitutionary categories and imagery; this move is also visible in most attempts to find penal substitution in the Church Fathers. There are odd passages which certainly deploy a legal metaphor, but there is no sense that this is a developed doctrine in the early church, and certainly no evidence that it was an assumed badge of orthodoxy. This situation persists through the medieval period. Indeed, the first fully worked out account of penal substitution that I can find in history is in Calvin's *Institutes* (1536–1559). Luther had certainly been developing similar ideas a couple of decades earlier, and no doubt there are important precursors among fifteenth-century medieval writers, but Calvin offers the doctrine in detail and maturity. Earlier writers again said things that could be understood in penal substitutionary terms, but never taught the idea directly.

Anselm of Canterbury deserves special mention here, as critics and proponents of penal substitution often link him with the doctrine. His remarkable treatment of the atonement is demonstrably not, however, an example of penal substitution. Most obviously, Anselm explicitly contrasts "punishment" and "satisfaction" and insists that it is inconceivable that God should punish sin (because God's intended purpose for the creation would then be thwarted), so instead satisfaction must be made. Further, Anselm's logic assumes not an implacable impersonal law, but the necessity of honor being given to personal majesty (this is what is meant by the common claim that it is "feudal"). Sin is such a serious matter for Anselm because God's majesty is infinite, and so any offense against God is of infinite gravity.

Calvin similarly appeals to culturally plausible concepts in his doctrine of the atonement, in his case the idea of a law that cannot be broken or set aside. The intervening cultural change may be illustrated by the English Magna Carta, a document that takes its stand on the idea that there are certain things even kings are not permitted to do, because there is a law beyond the good pleasure of the monarch. For Anselm, God cannot simply forgive sin without satisfaction because to do so would allow creatures to dishonor God, and so to frustrate their own being; for Calvin God cannot simply forgive sin without punishment because God has established a law for the creation, and allowing that law to be broken would again frustrate the purposes of creation. The penalty for sin is death, and God has no more ability to vary that penalty than a contemporary judge has to set aside statutory sentencing guidelines.

After Calvin, penal substitution became so widespread as to be almost ubiquitous, at least among Protestant churches. Around 1700, for example, the great dogmatic systems of Reformed and Lutherans alike taught the atonement in penal substitutionary terms without very much awareness that it had ever been taught otherwise; the same was true of the Anglican Joseph Butler's hugely influential *Analogy of Religion* from a few decades later.[22] Given this context, it is perhaps no surprise that penal substitution became a normal way of narrating the atonement for early evangelicals; it was the normal way of atonement for almost all Protestants as the eighteenth-century revivals began.

Given this virtual doctrinal hegemony in the early decades of the eighteenth century, it is surprising to find penal substitutionary understandings of the atonement widely repudiated and attacked as the nineteenth century dawned, even among evangelicals—in the United Kingdom we might note Thomas Erskine of Linlathlen,[23] Edward Irving,[24] and Henry Drummond; in the United States, Edwards's heirs in the New Divinity.[25] Of course, other evangelicals held tenaciously to penal substitutionary understandings of the atonement, but outside evangelicalism, the doctrine had few supporters left by about 1830. What happened to create so rapid a change in understanding?

The Changing Cultural Plausibility of Penal Substitution

I suggested above that theories of atonement prosper in part because they have a certain cultural plausibility; as I have already noted a very significant change in penal policy swept Europe around 1800, and rendered penal substitution far less culturally plausible than it had been before. The change is illustrated graphically in the opening pages of Foucault's *Discipline and Punish*, where a graphic newspaper account of the public torture and execution of a murderer in Paris in 1757 is placed alongside Faucher's rules for a new Parisian "House of Correction" in 1838. In the few decades between there had been a transformation in public understandings of appropriate penal sanctions, from the public infliction of violence directed toward retribution and deterrence to incarceration and a structured life intended to reform the offender.

Foucault recounts these events in order to call into question the claim that the change was progressive, or an act of civilization; his argument is challenging and controversial, which highlights the long-standing consensus that this shift

---

[22] Joseph Butler, *The Analogy of Religion to the Constitution and Course of Nature* (London: RTS, n.d.), 224–225.
[23] See, for example, Thomas Erskine, *The Unconditional Freeness of the Gospel in Three Essays* (Edinburgh: Waugh and Innes, 1828) and *The Brazen Serpent* (Edinburgh: David Douglas, 1879).
[24] See, for example, Edward Irving, *The Orthodox and Catholic Doctrine of Our Lord's Human Nature* (London: Baldwin and Craddock, 1830).
[25] For a recent defense of this tradition and extensive reference to primary sources, see Oliver D. Crisp, "Penal Non-Substitution," *Journal of Theological Studies (ns)* 59 (2008), 140–168.

was precisely civilized and progressive. The change in policy happened across Europe around the close of the eighteenth century, and followed the publication of an enormously influential Italian text that might be seen as the beginning of modern criminology, Cesare Beccaria's *On Crimes and Punishments* (1764).

The relevance of this cultural change to the cultural reception of penal substitutionary accounts of the atonement is clear enough: narrating the passion of Christ using the logic of the law court made good cultural sense in a context where flogging and public execution are normal and accepted penal sanctions; once such penalties are dismissed as backward, unenlightened, and/or barbaric, the logic of penal substitution becomes much less culturally plausible. (Gorringe's argument that changes in the doctrine of atonement influence the development of penal policy mistakes effect for cause.[26]) Foucault's critique might cause us to pause before assuming that this cultural move is simply correct, but that it has happened is undeniable, and its effect on the plausibility of penal substitution is substantial. In a history of atonement doctrine published in 1920, Grensted asserted that "amongst reputable theologians the Penal theory is now extinct."[27] A way of thinking about the atonement that was unquestioned around 1700 could be regarded as extinct not long after 1900.

Two other cultural changes that have also impacted the cultural plausibility of penal substitution deserve mention. One has already been raised in passing: penal substitution depends on a retributive account of punishment. If we assume some sort of basic moral inviolability of the human person, the infliction of punishment in response to the committing of a crime requires justification. What gives the magistrate/the state the right to impose a fine, to inflict violence, or to remove freedom? Two broad theories have dominated philosophical reflection on this question: retributive and consequentialist.[28] Put simply, consequentialist accounts claim punishment is moral because some good follows from it—perhaps deterrence; perhaps reform; perhaps merely the protection of wider society from the offender—whereas retributive accounts claim punishment is moral because it is simply deserved.

It is possible to offer a consequentialist account of a penal understanding of the atonement, no doubt—the theory of Grotius, outlined above, might be

---

[26] Timothy Gorringe, *God's Just Vengeance: Crime, Violence and the Rhetoric of Salvation* (Cambridge: CUP, 1996).
[27] L. W. Grensted, *A Short History of the Doctrine of the Atonement* (London: Longmans, Green, & Co., 1920), 306.
[28] For a good introduction to the philosophical debate, see T. Brooks, *Punishment* (London: Routledge, 2013).

an example; but penal substitution demands some form of retributive account. Christ does not accept our punishment to become a visible deterrent, or because that specifically will lead to our reformation; he "pays the price for our sins." In the philosophical literature both consequentialist and retributive accounts have been subject to serious criticism[29]; culturally, however, it seems fair to say that attempting to justify punishment on grounds of retribution in the contemporary West is difficult; the prevailing instinctive political liberalism among cultural elites does not give such arguments much space.

Finally, penal arguments of course depend for their plausibility on an acceptance that every human being is guilty of sin in the first place. As Alan Mann has pointed out,[30] this assumption lacks some cultural plausibility presently. Many people either do not instinctively regard themselves as sinners, or see what faults they do admit to as excusable because of circumstance (one widely reported successful result of counselling is that a person has "learnt to forgive themselves"). This is not of course to deny the theological truth of the universal sinfulness of humanity, but to suggest that where this truth is denied, it will be difficult to narrate the atonement in penal substitutionary terms.

The Future of Penal Substitution

Should we, then, just give up on penal substitution? This depends both on how we understand the nature of atonement doctrine, and on how we view the role of historical theology in contemporary ecclesial reflection.

The Role of Historical Theology

I have commented above fairly disparagingly on the sort of historiography that tries to find a golden thread of a single atonement theory running all through Christian history; it is just not there. Instead, we see a series of atonement theories being proposed and accepted for a time, and then fading away. Penal substitution is interesting in these terms in achieving an unusual level of dominance for a period; in earlier periods there were generally two or three major models of atonement being deployed. In the later patristic period, ransom theories

---

[29] See, for example, Ted Honderich, *Punishment: The Supposed Justifications Revisited* (London: Pluto, 2005).
[30] Alan Mann, *Atonement for a Sinless Society* (Eugene, OR: Cascade, 2015).

remained popular, but so were medicinal theories based around the ingestion of Christ's benefits through the Eucharistic elements, and physical theories that asserted the healing of human nature in the incarnation. Anselm and Abelard's theories were famously jointly popular during much of the later medieval period, and so on.

Of the accounts just mentioned, only penal substitution and moral exemplarism could find any defenders today; the others have passed into history, essentially victims of their own cultural locatedness. Physicalism makes little sense without assuming a Platonic understanding of human nature; Anselm interprets the atonement in feudal terms, and so on. Despite this, Anselm in particular is still taught regularly in relatively low-level courses on atonement theology, and is certainly still discussed regularly in scholarly work on the doctrine. This is not because Anselm offers a live option for atonement theology today, but because his arguments reveal aspects of the doctrine in ways that remain helpful.

Let us assume that, despite its contemporary confessional defenders, the criticisms of penal substitution are as devastating as Grensted (quoted in the previous section) asserted; should we then forget the doctrine? A comparison with Anselm would suggest no, or only if it has been rendered simply uninteresting; even if penal substitution were not a meaningful possibility for a contemporary theology of the atonement, we might still expect it to be interesting as a way of understanding more of the logic of the doctrine. (I will propose ways in which I believe penal substitution remains interesting in the next subsection.)

Is the situation so desperate for penal substitution, though? To answer that, we need to turn to our second issue.

The Nature of Atonement Doctrine

One of the themes that runs through this chapter is a question about the shape of a properly formulated doctrine of the atonement. Should we be seeking one theory of the atonement to defend and apply, or should we be comfortable with a multiplicity of theories? The former is the more obvious route: if (say) penal substitution is the right way to understand the atonement, then it seems clear that (say) *Christus victor* accounts are just wrong, and vice versa. In fact, however, very few theologians argue like this. Perhaps because there are at least several theories of the atonement with some biblical and theological plausibility, defenders of one model generally suggest that other models are not so much wrong as incomplete.

A defender of penal substitution, that is, will not claim that the "moral influence" theory is wrong in what it asserts—of course the believer is deeply moved by reflecting on Christ's sufferings, and no doubt that can be a motor for personal change—so much as that it is (probably profoundly) inadequate. If moral influence is all we say about the atonement, we have missed the most important and most transformative aspects of the reality of what God has done in Jesus. Many—perhaps all—of the traditional models of atonement are correct in what they affirm, but only one gets to the heart of the matter, and so is a truly adequate model. Much recent atonement theology has gone further than this, however. No one model is central, or interprets the others; instead each is a helpful parable of a fundamentally indescribable reality. There are many metaphors for the atonement, each useful and true.[31] The language of "models" of the atonement, which I have quietly appropriated in this chapter, already assumes something like this.

Clearly, if we adopt the first approach, we have two choices: penal substitution is the one right, or the one best, way of talking about the atonement, or it is simply wrong, or at best inadequate. If it is wrong/inadequate, then we should indeed give up on it. I have suggested above that there are significant problems both doctrinally (a Trinitarian weakness and potentially a concern over the imputation of Christ's righteousness) and in terms of cultural plausibility, if we consider penal substitution to be the one right way of understanding the atonement. The cultural problem seems sometimes to be taken almost as a badge of honor by contemporary proponents of penal substitution, a mark of the hatred by the world that true believers share with Christ, and of course if the doctrinal belief is correct this is a valid inference. The theological problems may be soluble, but as I suggested above significant theologians have wrestled with them unsuccessfully, and so they must be considered weighty. That said, if they can be addressed, and arguments can be adduced for regarding penal substitution as the best way of narrating the atonement, then, of course, we must not give up on it.

What reasons might there be for adopting the second approach, however? I have hinted at some already in this chapter. First, it seems true to the biblical presentations; as I noted above, in Romans 3:24–25 we find several different images for the atonement used in very quick succession; this is characteristic of

---

[31] This approach has been defended by, for example, Colin E. Gunton, *The Actuality of Atonement: A Study of Metaphor, Rationality and the Christian Tradition* (Edinburgh: T&T Clark, 1988).

the biblical material, and suggests that using multiple different models to capture the fullness of the reality of the atonement is appropriate. Second, there is a historical argument. With a few exceptions, such as Anselm's *Cur Deus Homo*, most historical accounts of the atonement use more than one image/metaphor; this was demonstrated above for several central Reformation symbols, and in passing for such writers as Turretin and Edwards; it is true of most major treatments in the tradition, however. (Even Anselm, although he develops his novel theory tenaciously, makes passing use of victory motifs and moral exemplarism.)

One more theological reason might be added. Asserting a single correct model of the atonement seems inevitably to locate the event of atonement within a particular sphere of human experience, which is at least in danger of devaluing what God has done. That is, if we assert that penal substitution is simply the right way to understand the atonement, we appear to be saying that the atonement is properly understood as a legal event, which can be listed alongside other legal events. But God's work in Christ should not be limited to just another legal event. (The same point may be made about considering the atonement as "really" a sacrifice, or about the moral example theory; Jesus's death is not just another sacrifice, or one more inspiring act of self-giving.) The alternative is to insist that the atonement is not fully explicable in any category we have available, which will at least lead us toward a "many metaphors" view. (We might try to find a middle position, accepting the inadequacy of every metaphor, but claiming that one is less inadequate than any other, and so central.)

If some sort of "many metaphors" view is correct, then a further question arises: is penal substitution a good/useful metaphor? If it is, then we should hold on to it; if not, we should discard it. What criteria might we offer for judging the worth of a metaphor in this context? Clearly we are looking for a metaphor that illuminates more than it obscures, even if it does not offer an answer to every question, and helps us to repeat faithfully biblical insights about Christ's atoning work, and has sufficient cultural purchase to be useful in the proclamation of the gospel (an atonement theology that does not aid the task of evangelization is obviously seriously deficient).

To be of lasting, rather than passing, worth we are also looking for a metaphor that illuminates some aspects of the event of atonement better than any other metaphor we have available. Anselm's account is still explored and rehearsed because it exposes something about the nature of sin and the damage sin does to creation's relationship with its creator that remains illuminating. In a similar way, I suggest, penal substitution remains of value because it reveals something about the inescapability of guilt and so about our need for atonement; at the same time, it speaks powerfully of the cost God is prepared to bear to bring salvation.

This implacable insistence that guilt cannot be hidden, and will be addressed, is important in a cultural context acutely aware of the frequency with which those in power are able to prevent their abuses from being discovered, whether in the context of occupying military forces, corporate wrongdoing in the business world, or a powerful sexual abuser. The promise of implacable, inescapable justice is of course good news for the victims/survivors of such evils, and much recent theology has emphasized this, but it is also a message of hope for the perpetrators—that they have not yet put themselves beyond the reach of God's Kingdom, that repentance remains a possibility. At the same time the emphasis on the cost of God's love, on the pain of forgiveness, is not only true to human experience—we know forgiveness hurts—but a powerful proclamation of something true and important about the atonement.

I have argued that there is good reason to hold to a "many metaphors" account of atonement theology, and that penal substitution has a place within that as a useful metaphor. I have further argued that, even if we regard it as an impossible doctrine to preach today, it is a doctrine that should remain of theological interest, because it has things to tell us about the nature of the atonement which we cannot hear so clearly anywhere else.

17

Methodological Issues in Approaching the Atonement

Oliver D. Crisp

Contemporary works on the atonement are replete with language of doctrines, theories, models, metaphors, and motifs. Yet the consensus among modern theologians is that the New Testament does not offer a single explanation of Christ's atoning work. For instance, in the middle of the twentieth century the Scottish Presbyterian theologian Donald Baillie remarked, "If we take the Christology of the New Testament at its highest we can only say that 'God was in Christ' in that great atoning sacrifice, and even that the Priest and the Victim both were none other than God. There is in the New Testament no uniformity of conception as to *how* this sacrifice brings about the reconciliation."[1] Similarly, T. F. Torrance writes, "No explanation is ever given in the New Testament, or in the Old Testament, why atonement for sin involves the blood of sacrifice."[2] Some more recent theologians have argued that the search for models and theories of atonement is itself a forlorn enterprise. Instead, we should acknowledge that Scripture offers a number of motifs or metaphors, but no single mechanism for atonement, such as one would expect in something more conceptually sophisticated, like a model or theory.[3] Still other contemporary theologians argue that

---

[1] D. M. Baillie, *God Was in Christ* (London: Faber and Faber, 1961), 188. For a catena of modern theologians that say something similar to Baillie about the lack of an explanation for atonement in the New Testament, see Michael Winter, *The Atonement* (Collegeville, MN: The Liturgical Press, 1995), 30–37.

[2] Thomas F. Torrance, *The Mediation of Christ* (Colorado Springs: Helmers and Howard, 1992 [1983]), 114.

[3] A good example of this is Colin Gunton's work, *The Actuality of Atonement* (London: T&T Clark, 1988). In his little book Michael Winter criticizes modern theologians who agree that the New Testament offers no explanation of the atonement, and yet "offer no explanation of it themselves to

the kaleidoscope of images for Christ's atonement in the New Testament should lead theologians to the conclusion that a plurality of models for atonement is mandated on the basis of Scripture. Thus, Joel Green writes:

> The hermeneutical task that occupied Paul and Peter and other New Testament writers, and Christian theologians and preachers subsequently, is located at the interface of this central affirmation of the atoning work of Christ and its contingent interpretation. This continues to be the hermeneutical task today, and this explains not only the presence of but also the mandate for multiple models of understanding and communicating the cross of Christ.[4]

Not only is there no single explanation of the atonement in the Bible; the atonement is not a theological notion whose dogmatic shape is universally agreed upon in historic Christian thought either. It has no canonical definition, no creedal statement that gives it a particular shape beyond the idea that Christ's work reconciles human beings to God. Hence, different accounts of the atonement have proliferated in historic Christianity, and constructive theologians continue that tradition today, bringing forth from their treasure stores things old and new.

This is not to say that there are no symbolic resources in the Christian tradition that might help give dogmatic shape to the atonement. Protestant confessions of the sixteenth and seventeenth centuries and the *Catechism of the Catholic Church* of the twentieth century provide some understanding of the reconciling work of Christ. But, unlike the two-natures doctrine of the ancient Christian church, the views expressed by these documents do not stem from some earlier understanding of the reconciling work of Christ that is universally agreed upon by Christians East and West, on the basis of what is found in the biblical traditions.

How should we understand the views expressed in this symbolic material? For that matter, how should we understand the views expressed by historic theologians on this topic, or the views of contemporary divines as they develop their own ways of understanding the mediatorial work of Christ? Much depends on the status of such accounts. Are they the sober truth of the matter? An

---

compensate for that omission" (*The Atonement*, 30.) While he documents many modern theologians that do appear to omit such explanation, some of the more recent work on atonement does, I think, attempt to address this issue.

[4] Joel B. Green, "Kaleidoscopic View," in *The Nature of the Atonement: Four Views*, ed. James Beilby and Paul R. Eddy (Downers Grove, IL: IVP Academic, 2006), 171. See also Mark Baker and Joel B. Green, *Recovering the Scandal of the Cross: Atonement in New Testament and Contemporary Contexts*, 2nd edn (Downers Grove, IL: InterVarsity Press, 2011 [2000]).

approximation to that truth? Merely metaphors or pictures that do not have any necessary connection to the way things actually are? In this chapter I will focus in on these methodological questions by attempting to clarify the scope of what might be called the dogmatic ambition of atonement theology. In other words, we shall consider what metaphors, motifs, doctrines, models, and theories of atonement amount to, as an important methodological concern in approaching the atonement. This involves some attempt to give an orientation to these different concepts, as well as offering some account of their interrelationship, and the way in which they function in some of the major views of the atonement.

To that end, what follows offers one way of understanding doctrines, models, theories, metaphors, and motifs as applied to Christian theology in general, and the atonement in particular. Having done that, we shall trace out the relationship between these different methodological concepts so as to provide some explanation of how they should function in approaching the atonement. A short concluding section considers the upshot of this discussion for future work on the atonement.

Approaching the Atonement

Let us begin with the notion of reconciliation at the heart of traditional notions of the work of Christ. "Atonement" (at-one-ment) is the English word that expresses this concept, and that has passed into English-language theological parlance. As the English Reformed theologian Colin Gunton once remarked, atonement "is the portmanteau word used in English to denote the reconciliation between God and the world which is at the heart of Christian teaching."[5] That seems broadly correct, although for present purposes, a more narrow working definition of atonement will be more serviceable than this—one that focuses on human beings and includes an indication of why reconciliation is needed. Thus, *the atonement is the act of reconciliation between God and fallen human beings brought about by Christ*. According to Scripture human beings are estranged from God because of sin. As Romans 3:23 puts it, "All [human beings] have sinned and fall short of the glory of God." Christ's atoning work brings about reconciliation with God by dealing with human sin, which is an obstacle to divine-human relationship. It also has outcomes other than this, for

---

[5] Colin E. Gunton, *The Actuality of Atonement: A Study of Metaphor, Rationality and the Christian Tradition* (London: T&T Clark, 1988), 2.

the atonement is not merely about the removal of obstacles to relationship with God but also about securing the goods accompanying a right relationship to God. Nevertheless, this is a fundamental concern of atonement theology, in fact, to my way of thinking, the most fundamental concern. For without atonement for sin there can be no reconciliation with God for fallen human beings. Without atonement we are all "dead in our trespasses" (Rom. 5:6; Eph. 2:5; Col. 2:13). We might say that, at a bare minimum, any theologically adequate account of the atonement must assume that the atonement is the act of reconciliation between God and fallen human beings brought about by Christ. In what follows we shall assume this way of thinking about the atonement as a point of departure. With this in mind, let us turn to consider some key terms in atonement theology.

Motifs and Metaphors

Motifs and metaphors play an important—indeed, indispensable—role in atonement theology. Biblical metaphors abound: Christ is the lamb of God who takes away the sins of the world, the shepherd who dies for his sheep, the high priest who enters the holy of holies on our behalf, and so on. Motifs are often metaphors with staying power, for they are recurring. Christ as the lamb of God, as the Pascal lamb, as the sacrificial lamb, and so on are examples of such a biblical motif, which is also metaphorical in nature. But in principle motifs may simply be recurring themes or ideas that are not necessarily or fundamentally metaphorical in nature, such as leitmotifs that appear and then recur with variations in a piece of orchestral music. In atonement theology motifs like sacrifice, substitute, satisfaction, ransom, and so on are important features of particular accounts of the reconciling work of Christ. Metaphors often provide important building blocks. Take the notion of the lamb of God being offered up as a sacrifice on our behalf. This is clearly a metaphor and a biblical motif that characterizes Christ's saving work. But it may also become (and has become) a stepping stone toward more complex ways of thinking about the work of Christ that have at their heart the notion that Christ somehow offers himself up as a vicarious sacrifice of our sins—a theological element that can be found in several different historic and contemporary accounts of the atonement such as satisfaction or penal substitution.[6]

---

[6] For instance, Richard Swinburne's penetrating account of the atonement as a sacrifice is really an updated version of a satisfaction doctrine, indebted more to Thomas Aquinas than to Anselm. See his *Responsibility and Atonement* (Oxford: Oxford University Press, 1989).

In recent theology there is a tendency to speak of different approaches to the doctrine of atonement as so many different metaphors—as if Christ's reconciling work as a ransom, a satisfaction for sin, a penal substitution, a moral example, or whatever constitutes a picture, or a representation, or a symbol that stands in for something else. Of course, these are pictures of the atonement, but (as we shall see) doctrines and models of the atonement are more than just metaphors, though they include metaphors as elements of a larger conceptual whole. Doctrine in Christian theology, as Christine Helmer reminds us, "is said to be concerned with the truth of the eternal God." It "recognizes God as its source; and like Sacred Scripture, doctrine contains the knowledge that God has revealed about [the] divine nature and about the divine perspective on self and world... Stripped of the accretions that human traditions and interpretations have added to it, doctrine is synonymous with the truth of the gospel."[7] But if that is right, then doctrines, and, by extension, models that attempt to offer some explanatory framework for making sense of the atonement, cannot be merely metaphors. For they include, in this way of thinking, irreducibly propositional components.

Getting a clearer idea of the role played by motifs and metaphors in accounts of atonement is important for another reason as well. It helps us to see whether views proposed as particular doctrines or models or "theories" of atonement actually pass muster. For instance, the ransom view of atonement has recently become a popular option for theologians that are troubled by some of the language and content of other traditional models of Christ's reconciling work, particularly satisfaction and penal substitution. But it is not clear on examination that the ransom view actually amounts to a doctrine or model of atonement. As I have argued elsewhere, it seems that it is more like a motif or metaphor, for it does not provide a clear mechanism of atonement.[8]

This is only underlined by the fact that, in recent discussion of the ransom view, the notion of *Christus victor* (Christ the victor), which had previously been regarded as a synonym for ransom, has been decoupled from it. Now there are ransom views, and then there are *Christus victor* views where Christ's victory is not regarded as part of any act that ransoms fallen human beings. Thus Denny Weaver in *The Nonviolent Atonement* can say,

> What this book calls narrative *Christus Victor* thus finally becomes a reading of the history of God's people, who make God's rule visible in the world by the

---

[7] Christine Helmer, *The End of Doctrine* (Louisville: Westminster John Knox Press, 2014), 23.
[8] See Oliver D. Crisp, "Is Ransom Enough?" *Journal of Analytic Theology* 3 (2015): 1–11, located at: http://journalofanalytictheology.com/jat/index.php/jat/article/view/jat.2015-3.141117021715a.

confrontation of injustice and by making visible in their midst the justice, peace, and freedom of the rule of God. The life, death, and resurrection of Jesus constitute the culmination of that rule of God, and also the particular point in history when God's rule is most fully present and revealed.[9]

Later he adds, "Since Jesus' mission was not to die but to make visible the reign of God, it is quite explicit that neither God nor the reign of God needs Jesus' death in the way that his death is irreducibly needed in satisfaction theory."[10] These are significant admissions, and say something about the way in which one family of metaphors to do with Christ's work being a ransom can fund distinct approaches to the doctrine of atonement. We turn to the question of doctrine next.

Doctrine

By the term *doctrine* I mean (minimally) a comprehensive account of a particular teaching about a given theological topic held by some community of Christians, or some particular denomination. So, on this way of thinking, a doctrine of the atonement is an account[11] of the atonement that has been taught by a particular group of Christians such as Baptists, Anglicans, Mennonites, Orthodox, and so on. A doctrine is a *comprehensive* account of a given teaching because it is a complete, theological whole that forms part of what we might call the conceptual fabric of the life of the particular ecclesial community. Doctrines are not normally partial, piecemeal, or ad hoc notions that are thrown together. Rather, a doctrine used in this sense is a conceptual whole that usually develops over time, often in the fires of controversy. This process of doctrinal development is ongoing, even where a doctrine has a "fixed" canonical form, for such doctrines are still the subject of dogmatic scrutiny, revision, and reassessment in light of new insights, new arguments, and, sometimes, new data.

Perhaps the preeminent example of this is the doctrine of the Trinity, which developed from an early devotion to Christ alongside Jewish monotheism into the central and defining theological doctrine of Christianity through the vituperative ecclesiastical struggle that eventually produced the Nicene Creed of

---

[9] J. Denny Weaver, *The Nonviolent Atonement*, 2nd edn (Grand Rapids, MI: Eerdmans, 2011), 84–85.
[10] Ibid., 89.
[11] Throughout this chapter I use the term "account" as a placeholder that ranges over metaphors and motifs, doctrines, and models of atonement rather like the term "attribute" in discussion of the divine nature is a placeholder and can mean "property," "predicate," and so on.

AD 381. Unlike the Trinity, the atonement is a doctrine that has no undisputed canonical shape, though it does take on particular forms in certain ecclesiastical contexts, such as the notion of vicarious satisfaction beloved of historic Presbyterians.[12] Doctrines like the Trinity that have such a canonical form are typically part of the conceptual core of the faith. For these reasons they are sometimes referred to as *dogmas*.[13] So dogmas are a particular kind of doctrine that have a definite canonical shape. All dogmas are doctrines, but not all doctrines are dogmas, for some doctrines lack a canonical shape, such as the atonement. It will be helpful for our purposes to observe this distinction. However, even if a doctrine has a canonical form—that is, is a dogma like the Trinity—which acts as a kind of theological constraint on how it is understood, this does not prevent there from being different ways of making sense of a given dogma consistent with its basic canonical shape. Thus, historic Christianity has taken the Nicene Creed as the point of departure for thinking about the Trinity. Yet today there are a number of different accounts of the Trinity consistent with the dogmatic shape of the Nicene position, yielding distinct models that (in some cases at least) are incommensurate in important respects, such as "social," "psychological," or "Latin," and "constitution" models of the Trinity.[14]

Suppose we take the atonement to be the act of reconciliation between God and fallen human beings brought about by Christ. (As I have already indicated, it is at least this sort of action even if, like Gunton, we think the scope of the reconciliation brought about by the atonement is greater than this.) As such, this characterization of atonement is far too broad to be of much theological use beyond demarcating one sort of theologically realist understanding of the atonement from non-realist ones. More would need to be said to make it theologically useful. And more would need to be said in order to generate a full-orbed account of the atonement. Specifically, in the case of the atonement, one would need to provide some kind of *mechanism* by means of which Christ's work reconciles us to God. For if a doctrine is a comprehensive teaching about the

---

[12] See *The Westminster Confession*, chapter VIII. V: "The Lord Jesus, by His perfect obedience, and sacrifice of Himself, which He through the eternal Spirit, once offered up unto God, has fully satisfied the justice of His Father; and purchased, not only reconciliation, but an everlasting inheritance in the kingdom of heaven, for those whom the Father has given unto Him."

[13] Some Protestants may baulk at this distinction between dogma and doctrine. But I think it does capture an important difference regarding those doctrines that have canonical form (i.e., some sort of settled shape agreed upon and promulgated in Catholic creeds, such as the incarnation or Trinity), and those that do not (like the atonement). It is possible for a doctrine to be at the heart of the Christian faith and yet lack a clear, canonical form. The atonement is the paradigm of this.

[14] For detailed recent essays that deal with each of these trinitarian models, see Thomas McCall and Michael C. Rea, eds. *Philosophical and Theological Essay on the Trinity* (Oxford: Oxford University Press, 2009).

atonement, it must offer some explanation—even if this falls short of a complete explanation—of *how* it is that Christ's work reconciles us to God. But, it is just here that doctrines of atonement segue to models of atonement. For it is models of atonement that take the more general doctrinal ideas about Christ's work of reconciliation, and specify a particular way in which this makes sense, in light of the data of Scripture and tradition. We shall return to this matter when considering models more directly in the next section.

It may be objected that the characterization of doctrine as *a comprehensive account of a particular teaching about a given theological topic held by some community of Christians, or some particular denomination*, is ambiguous in at least two important respects. First, it is ambiguous regarding the nature of Christian doctrine, that is, what it is that Christian doctrines like the atonement are supposed to be. Second, it is ambiguous regarding the dogmatic substance of Christian doctrine, that is, what it is that Christian doctrines like the atonement are supposed to convey. Let us consider these two sorts of ambiguity in turn.

First, the characterization of doctrine offered here is consistent with one of several ways of thinking about the nature of Christian doctrine. For instance, it is commensurate with the idea that the doctrines of Christian theology are in large measure regulative, providing a grammar for theology that may or may not correspond to some state of affairs beyond the doctrinal matrix, as post liberal theologians aver. In a similar fashion, the rules of a game such as chess regulate play but do not (necessarily) correspond to a state of affairs beyond the game. Alternatively, it could be that doctrine has more than a merely regulative function. Perhaps (as was intimated earlier in connection with Christine Helmer's work) it also has a propositional function as much historic Christianity has presumed. On this way of thinking, doctrines are statements that express concepts that are truth-apt and truth-aimed. A third option: doctrine has a largely symbolic value. Here, doctrine is, as George Lindbeck puts it, "experiential-expressivist" in nature. It functions "as non-informative and non-discursive symbols of inner feelings, attitudes, or existential orientations."[15] This third option is a much more radically subjective way of thinking about the nature of doctrine, but one that would be consistent with the idea that Christian doctrine is concerned to provide a comprehensive account of a particular teaching about a given theological topic held by some community of Christians, or some particular denomination.

---

[15] George A. Lindbeck, *The Nature of Doctrine: Religion and Theology in a Postliberal Age* (Louisville, KY: Westminster John Knox, 1984), 16.

In attempting to give an account of how different approaches to Christ's reconciling work function as Christian doctrine, it is important not to preclude certain live options at the outset. The three live options of Lindbeck's treatment of the nature of doctrine are three ways in which our working definition of doctrine could be construed,[16] though perhaps not the only three ways in which the term could be construed.[17] My own view is that doctrine is conceptual and propositional in nature, which I take to be the way in which doctrine has been understood in much, though by no means all, of the Christian tradition. But it is not a requirement of the way I have characterized doctrine here that it be understood in this way.

This brings us to the second ambiguity in the characterization of doctrine, which has to do with the material content, or substance of doctrine. I have deliberately tried to provide what seems to me to be a *dogmatically minimalist* way of framing Christian doctrine. It seems to me that such dogmatic minimalism is a theological virtue rather than a vice. Think of the Trinity once more. If any central theological concept is dogmatically minimalist in nature, the Trinity is. For in its Nicene form it provides a canonical shape and constraint on what Christians should believe about the divine nature, yet without necessarily committing the believer to a particular way of understanding key notions that comprise fundamental elements of the doctrine, such as "person" and "nature/essence." Something similar is true of the atonement—yet with the vital difference that, unlike the Trinity, the atonement has no definite canonical shape. To use our earlier distinction, it is a doctrine not a dogma.

I have said that the atonement is the act of reconciliation between God and fallen human beings brought about by Christ. I take it that this, or something very like it, is a kind of dogmatic minimum that all, or almost all, Christians can agree upon. More would need to be said to flesh this out in order to provide a comprehensive account that would constitute a doctrine of atonement. The provision of this additional material can usually be found by appealing to confessions, catechisms, and writings of theologians of particular ecclesiastical persuasions belonging to particular Christian traditions and communions. But even here the results are often dogmatically thin, and (so it seems to me)

---

[16] That is, the regulative view, the propositional view, and the subjective and symbolic view mentioned previously. These are the three live options around which Lindbeck structures his discussion of doctrine in *The Nature of Doctrine*.

[17] For instance, Helmer suggests a rather different account of doctrine that takes Lindbeck as a point of departure in *The End of Doctrine*.

deliberately so, committing adherents to what seems to be non-negotiable while leaving certain matters ambiguous or underdeveloped.

For instance, Article 31 of the Anglican *Articles of Religion* states, "The Offering of Christ once made is that perfect redemption, propitiation, and satisfaction, for all the sins of the whole world, both original and actual; and there is none other satisfaction for sin, but that alone." Here is a doctrine of atonement. It certainly expresses the notion that the atonement is the act of reconciliation between God and fallen human beings brought about by Christ. But it construes this in a particular way: as a propitiation (i.e., a way of appeasing God) and a satisfaction. These are two theologically loaded terms. Propitiation focuses our attention upon the manner in which Christ's work brings about reconciliation, and satisfaction provides us with a mechanism by means of which this goal is achieved. But this is also underdeveloped. Much more would need to be said about the role of propitiation and satisfaction, and what is meant by satisfaction in particular, in order for us to have a full-orbed account of the atonement. This requires some model of atonement, most likely, some version of the satisfaction view, or some version of penal substitution.[18] So, although the *Articles of Religion* appear to commit Anglicans to a particular range or family of views on the reconciling work of Christ (either satisfaction or penal substitution, or something very similar to these views), it is also sufficiently dogmatically thin, so to speak, as to leave open a number of issues that require further development in order to provide a full-orbed understanding of the atonement. And this is usually provided by a model of atonement.

Model

At first glance models of atonement have certain apparently paradoxical qualities. On the one hand, such models thicken up the dogmatic minimalism of atonement doctrines, "expanding" such doctrines, so to speak, so as to provide a fuller explanation of the nature of the atonement and in particular, the

---

[18] I am not conflating satisfaction and penal substitution, which are distinct models of atonement (though they are often conflated in popular presentations of these two accounts of the atonement). However, in point of fact, a number of Reformation and post-Reformation Protestant theologians speak in terms of a vicarious satisfaction although, upon examination, their views are actually species of penal substitution. So it seems that the contemporary popular conflation of satisfaction and penal substitution has some basis in the unfortunate way in which historic accounts of penal substitution are often described, by its defenders, as vicarious satisfaction. A good example of this can be found in Francis Turretin's *Institutes of Elenctic Theology*, one of the most sophisticated products of the period of Protestant Orthodoxy.

mechanism of atonement. On the other hand, models of atonement do not necessarily attempt to provide a complete or comprehensive view of Christ's reconciling work. Rather, they offer a simplified description of the complex reality that is the work of Christ, which gives particular attention to the nature of that work and its effectiveness in terms of human reconciliation with God.

This apparent tension can be resolved by distinguishing between the conceptual goals of doctrines and models of atonement, and their dogmatic function. The conceptual goal of doctrine is to provide a comprehensive account of a particular teaching about a given theological topic held by some community of Christians, or some particular denomination. But usually this is dogmatically minimalist in nature. Something can be both conceptually wide-reaching in its scope, and yet rather "thin" in the information it provides, like a map of the world. Such maps function to provide us with general information about the world, such as the shape of its continents and seas, and the political divisions of different countries. The conceptual goal of a model of atonement is more narrowly focused than a doctrine, and conceptually "thicker." It is like a road map of the United States, which is limited to one geographical region, and gives more information about that region than the map of the world does. The "dogmatic function" of a road map of the United States is also different from a map of the world in that it provides much more detailed information about how to get about the particular geographical region it represents, as well as about the size of the towns and cities of the region. In a similar way, doctrines of atonement are conceptually broad and thin, whereas models of atonement are narrower and conceptually thicker. But also like the road map, models of atonement do not give comprehensive information, but are by their very nature selective in what they convey.

Consider the notion of model utilized in much contemporary scientific literature, which has been appropriated in the science and religion literature as well. A model in this connection offers a coherent simplified description of a more complex reality. It attempts to "save the phenomena" but it does not attempt to give a complete description. As Ian Barbour puts it:

> Models and theories are abstract symbol systems, which inadequately and selectively represent particular aspects of the world for specific purposes. This view preserves the scientist's realistic intent while recognizing that models and theories are imaginative human constructs. Models, on this reading, are to be taken seriously but not literally; they are neither literal pictures nor useful fictions but limited and inadequate ways of imagining what is not observable. They make

tentative ontological claims that there are entities in the world something like those postulated in the models.[19]

This conception of models can be very helpful when attempting to provide a comprehensive picture of a particular data set that would otherwise be too complex to be rendered into a whole that is easily comprehended. (The diagram of an atom, familiar to any high school student of physics, is a good example of a model in this regard.) Applied to models of atonement, we can say this: such models are pictures of the reconciling work of Christ, its nature, and its effectiveness, which do not necessarily claim to offer a complete account of this aspect of Christ's work. Rather, they provide simplified descriptions of a particular data set that would otherwise be too complex to be rendered into a whole that is immediately comprehensible. Although not everyone working on the atonement in recent years would think of atonement models in this way, the language of much of this discussion reflects the intuition that no single approach to the atonement can hope to offer a comprehensive account of it. The attempt to make sense of the atonement in terms of models also reflects the epistemic fallibilism that can be found in much recent work on the atonement. In this context "fallibilism" is the notion that a particular belief or view—in this case, a belief about or view of the atonement—is partial, and does not (perhaps, cannot) adequately reflect the whole truth of the matter. Such beliefs or views are said to be epistemically fragile and dubitable. For these reasons they should be held tentatively.

Furthermore, Barbour's comments about models in a scientific context also indicate something else that is important to flag up in the appropriation of such language for atonement theology. This is whether models of atonement should be understood to be *realist* in nature—that is, reflecting, and expressing in some manner, even if only partially and fallibly, a mind-independent truth of the matter.

Models of atonement could be regarded as instrumentalist rather than realist, in nature. Instrumentalism in the philosophy of science is the notion that a particular scientific concept or theory is important because it has some heuristic value, and is a useful way of organizing certain data, not because it is literally true or false. Applied to theology, we can say that an instrumentalist view of models of atonement (or any other Christian doctrine) conceives of the value of such models as primarily heuristic. The question of truth-aptness, or the extent to which a given atonement model expresses or captures some facet of the

---

[19] Ian G. Barbour, *Religion and Science: Historical and Contemporary Issues* (San Francisco: HarperCollins, 1997), 115.

truth of the matter, is not salient on this view. However, lest we misunderstand instrumentalism, it is important to see that an instrumentalist view of models of atonement is consistent with there being some truth of the matter. It is just that the instrumentalist is not concerned with questions of truth as such; only with questions of use, function, and application.

Alternatively models of the atonement could be thought of in terms of theological realism. On this view, although they may only approximate the truth of the matter, atonement models are nevertheless truth-apt and aimed at truth. That is, they are aimed at the explanation or partial explanation of some truth of the matter regarding the atonement—a truth that is mind-independent.[20] The assumption in such models is that there is some truth to be had about the reconciling work of Christ. Accounts of the atonement are not just metaphor all the way down, so to speak, though they may contain metaphorical elements. Nor are they entirely socially constructed, being merely the product of human imagination. Nevertheless, even a theological realist must concede that models as applied to approaches to the atonement can only be approximations to the truth of the matter much as, in a Physics 101 textbook, the model of the atom pictured is only an approximation to the truth of the matter. It is understood that if we were able to see an atom, it would not actually look like the picture in the textbook. There is theological precedent for such reasoning to which we can appeal as well. For in a similar manner, theologians enamored of classical theism often write about the properties of God such as omnipotence or immutability, though, in point of fact, their commitment to a doctrine of divine simplicity entails the denial of any composition in God, including distinct divine properties.

In addition to instrumentalist and realist ways of thinking about models, and atonement models in particular, there are ways of thinking about the atonement, and models of the atonement, that are antirealist in nature. Such accounts decouple the doctrinal content of a given model of atonement from the ambition to give an account of this doctrine that is aimed at truth. A given doctrine or model of atonement may still be a useful fiction on this way of thinking, just as the rising of the sun or its setting are useful fictions from a human point of view. (Strictly speaking, the sun neither "rises" nor "sets," though these metaphors are deeply ingrained in the English language and shape many of the ways in which English speakers relate to our solar neighbor.) According to antirealist accounts of atonement, doctrines and models of the work of Christ are not aimed at truth.

---

[20] Or, at least, independent of any *creaturely* mind.

They are aimed at something else: eliciting within us a certain disposition or particular response. In a similar fashion, when a narrator begins speaking to an audience with the phrase "Once upon a time," we are habituated to expect what follows to be a fiction of some kind. In the right circumstances, the uttering of such a phrase elicits in us a certain disposition and a particular response. It is not the same response as would be had if the narrator had begun with the phrase, "This is an update on our breaking news story." In the latter case we expect there to be a connection between what is being said and some truth of the matter, for we expect that the reporting of current affairs at least has the ambition of being truth-aimed. We do not have the same expectation in the case of the telling of a fairy tale.

Although it is possible to approach the atonement and atonement models in an antirealist manner, it seems fairly clear that the vast majority of historic accounts of the atonement have presumed some sort of realism about the atonement. Even if the language of atonement models is not present in much of the historic discussion of this doctrine, it is, I think, fairly safe to assume that theologians attracted to the historic assumption that Christian doctrine is realist in nature will be sympathetic to the idea that some sort of chastened realism also applies to atonement models. By "chastened" realism I mean a realism that makes allowances for things like fallibilism, and social context, as well as the fact that models are, on this way of thinking, only ever approximations to the truth of the matter.[21]

It seems that metaphors are important features of models, as they are important features of doctrine. Yet they are not the whole of a doctrine any more than they are the whole of a model. When the Apostle Paul speaks of the church as a body with many parts in 1 Corinthians 11, this is not a model of the church, it is a metaphor. Such metaphors may be used to provide a model of the church as something that is, in many respects, organic, and composite, as can be found in the work of a number of historic theologians, such as the Reformed theologian

---

[21] However, some modern theological treatments of models as applied to theology have argued that they are, in fact, no more than metaphors. For example, Sally McFague writes that "a model is, in essence, a sustained and systematic metaphor." Sally McFague, *Metaphorical Theology, Models of God in Religious Language* (Philadelphia: Fortress Press, 1982), 67. However, it seems to me doubtful that models are just metaphors writ large. And, upon examination, it is not clear that McFague's position is entirely consistent on this matter. Later in her work she writes that "models are the hypotheses of structure or set of relations we project from an area we know reasonably well in order to give intelligibility to a similar structure we sense in a less-familiar area" (76). But how are "hypotheses of structure" or "sets of relations" constitutive of metaphors, given her claim that models are essentially metaphorical in nature? At the very least it seems that the reader requires some explanation of how these apparently non-metaphorical notions feature as parts of models that are supposed to be essentially metaphorical in nature.

John Williamson Nevin.[22] But this involves laying out a conceptual framework for thinking about the nature of the church that a metaphor alone cannot provide. It is just such a conceptual framework that McFague seems to be hinting at in her use of terms like "hypotheses," "structures," and "sets of relations."

Theories

What, then, of *theories* of atonement? Here, as with our account of models, we turn to consider the way in which theories function in scientific work, and apply that to theology. Like models they may offer generalized accounts of a great deal of complex information, which may be simplified using concepts independent of the data (e.g., concepts like "incarnation" or "Trinity," neither of which are to be found in the New Testament). Unlike models, theories do not necessarily correlate to facts. Theories can be used to provide an explanation of counterfactual states of affairs. For instance, one might have a theory about what would happen to a particular population if it were exposed to a deadly virus, of the form "*if* the population were exposed to this virus *then* the following state of affairs would obtain" or "*were* the population expose to this virus, then the following state of affairs *would have* obtained." Typically, theories of atonement are not counterfactual in this sense. They are not deployed in order to provide explanations of what would have happened had Jesus done something else. Instead, they are used to offer some explanation of what we should believe about what did, in fact, obtain in the case of his incarnation, life, death, and resurrection, as witnessed to by the writers of the canonical gospels. Also, a theory can itself be complex. It need not be a picture that simplifies the data. What is more, it may be used to offer a complete account of a given data set. In this respect theories may be more metaphysically ambitious in scope than models—think, for example, of Einstein's general theory of relativity in physics.

The language of "atonement theories" is now commonplace, though this is actually a development that doesn't reflect patristic, medieval, or early modern usage any more than language about "models" of atonement do.[23] Nevertheless,

---

[22] See Oliver D. Crisp, "John Williamson Nevin on the Church," in *Retrieving Doctrine: Essays in Reformed Theology* (Downers Grove, IL: IVP Academic, 2011), chapter 8.

[23] This point has been made elsewhere in the recent literature. See, for example, Adam J. Johnson, *Atonement: A Guide for the Perplexed* (London: Bloomsbury, 2015), 28. Nineteenth-century theologians like Schleiermacher, Charles Hodge, and John Miley write of "theories" of atonement, not models. (See, e.g., Friedrich Schleiermacher, *The Christian Faith*, ed. H. R. Macintosh and J. S. Stewart [Edinburgh: T&T Clark, 1999 [1830]], 460; Charles Hodge, *Systematic Theology Vol. 2* [Grand Rapids, MI: Eerdmans, 1940 [1845]], part III, chapter IX; and John Miley, *Systematic Theology Vol. II* [Peabody, MA: Hendrickson Publishers, 1989 [1893]], chapter IV.) But it seems that they mean by theories of atonement what I am calling models of atonement. The classification

I suggest that most theologians engaged in the project of providing some doctrinal explanation of the work of Christ as an atonement are attempting to give a model of atonement that they find compelling. They are not actually engaged in providing a theory of atonement. Often the model in question is offered as one, but only one, among several possible models. Some authors do go beyond this to delineate something more like theories of atonement—that is, they attempt to give not just one compelling (and approximate) picture of the work of Christ, but also reasons for thinking that the account they set forth is preferable to, or more comprehensive than, competing views. There are also those that have offered what might be called meta-models, or theories about models of atonement. That is, they hazard a theory that explains why there is a plethora of different, and apparently mutually exclusive, models of the atonement. This is how I understand the kaleidoscopic account of the atonement favored by Joel Green and Mark Baker.[24]

The Relationship between Motifs, Metaphors, Doctrines, Models, and Theories

Having set out the distinction between motifs and metaphors, doctrines, models, and theories of atonement, we may now step back and consider the theological relationship between these different notions. I have argued that the atonement is the act of reconciliation between God and fallen human beings brought about by Christ. Motifs and metaphors of atonement are elements that may compose aspects of a doctrine or model of atonement. However, they are not doctrines or models of atonement as such, any more than, say, an illustration is a sermon, or a denouement is a story. It may be that some accounts of atonement that are often thought to be doctrines or models do not, in fact, rise above motifs of metaphors for atonement, for example, many *Christus victor/* ransom views.

Doctrines and models of atonement are more than motifs or metaphors. A doctrine of atonement is a comprehensive account of the reconciling work of Christ held by some community of Christians, or some particular denomination. Such a comprehensive account will include some mechanism of atonement,

---

offered here more closely follows current language of models and theories in the current scientific literature than it does nineteenth-century theological usage.

[24] See Baker and Green, *Recovering the Scandal of the Cross*.

unlike motifs and metaphors. Doctrines are also often dogmatically minimalist in nature.

To my way of thinking, models of atonement are in one respect less comprehensive than doctrines of atonement (because of a difference in conceptual goals), though in another respect they usually offer more by way of explanation of the nature of atonement (because of a difference in dogmatic function). By definition they are attempts to give an approximation to the truth of the matter, a simplified picture of more complex data, such as can be found in Scripture, creeds, confessions, and the work of particular theologians. Still, a model, like a doctrine, provides a mechanism for atonement—it does have ambitions to give some explanation of the reconciling work of Christ, even if models do not offer complete explanations as such. It is also the case that models are often the products of individual theologians, whose particular opinions and arguments are offered up as contributions to the furtherance of our understanding of the atonement, as it is understood in particular communities, and by particular churches. So models are narrower in scope than doctrines of atonement. Classic atonement models, on this way of thinking, include satisfaction, penal substitution, the governmental view, the vicarious humanity view of John McLeod Campbell, some versions of the moral exemplar view, and, perhaps, some of the patristic accounts of atonement such as those provided by Athanasius and Irenaeus.[25]

What is more, models in atonement theology often specify more detail by way of explanation of the mechanism of atonement than some doctrines of atonement. Earlier, we saw that this was the case with the dogma of the Trinity, which has a canonical form that I have called "dogmatically minimalist." Models of the Trinity are attempts to spell out that canonical form more explicitly, offering particular ways of thinking about the doctrine that fill in the metaphysical gaps, so to speak, so as to provide a fuller or richer understanding of the nature of the Trinity. This is true of the atonement as well.

Our earlier example of the *Westminster Confession* will make the point here. Recall chapter VIII. V says, "The Lord Jesus, by His perfect obedience, and sacrifice of Himself, which He through the eternal Spirit, once offered up unto God, has fully satisfied the justice of His Father; and purchased, not only reconciliation, but an everlasting inheritance in the kingdom of heaven, for those whom the Father has given unto Him." But here, as with the Anglican *Articles of Religion*, there is a certain dogmatic minimalism at work. It is possible to construct one

---

[25] I give an account of these different views in Oliver D. Crisp, *Approaching the Atonement: Introducing the Reconciling Work of Christ* (Downers Grove, IL: IVP Academic, 2017).

of several models of the atonement on the basis of what is affirmed in this passage. Taking it as a kind of dogmatic constraint, which provides a theological framework for thinking about the atonement, a model could be provided that explained what divine justice consists in, how Christ satisfies divine justice, and how this act of satisfaction purchases everlasting life for a specific number of fallen humanity. But clearly, there is more than one way to think about each of these constituent parts of the doctrine, which would generate more than one model of atonement. For instance, how is satisfaction related to divine justice? How does Christ's work provide a satisfaction? What about Christ's work is a satisfaction? Does this include all the elements of Christ life or only his work on the cross? And so on. From this it seems clear that there is an important difference between models and doctrines, and that models are more modest in their explanatory ambitions than doctrines, but often more detailed in the metaphysical stories they provide in order to make sense of the doctrinal claims they seek to explain.

Theories of atonement are more comprehensive than either doctrines or models. Of the current accounts of the atonement, one seems to fit this category particularly well, and that is the kaleidoscopic view of Mark Baker and Joel Green. The idea here is to provide a theory about how we should think about different models of the atonement relative to one another and to the doctrine of atonement. Baker and Green do not put matters in this way. Nevertheless, on the classification offered here it would be appropriate to think of their account in these terms rather than as another model or doctrine of atonement because they claim to be offering a way of understanding all the existing models of atonement as partial metaphorical "windows" onto some larger whole. This is not so much another model, as a meta-model, or a theory about how to regard extant models of atonement, one that also takes into consideration other relevant factors like social location and epistemic purview.

The Upshot

What can be learned from this methodological reflection on some of the key terms and concepts that inform discussion about the atonement? First, such engagement helps to make clearer the theological ambition of different doctrines of atonement. Second, this sort of work raises important questions about the scope of atonement theology—what can such reflection actually achieve, theologically speaking, if there is no universally agreed upon doctrinal core to the reconciling work of Christ? Third, there is a question about how we characterize different accounts of atonement. Since the 1930s, and the work of Gustaf Aulén,[26] it has been common to classify atonement doctrines into a threefold typology. If our analysis is on target, this seems far too simplistic as a way of characterizing the differences that exist between different ways of conceiving the saving work of Christ. Not only does this flatten out the differences between particular doctrines, it distorts the nature of the differences that exist between the different historic approaches to this matter. For if some of these approaches are mere motifs or metaphors, and others doctrines or models that set out a mechanism for atonement, while still others are more like theories about atonement models, then what we have is not a typology of different doctrines of atonement. Instead, we have different levels of theological explanation regarding the atonement. Motifs and metaphors are partial pictures or windows onto the doctrine; doctrines are more complex wholes that have motifs and metaphors as constituent elements; models are more narrow, but conceptually richer attempts to provide a particular way of understanding the reconciling work of Christ; and theories about atonement models offer a way of thinking about these different doctrines relative to particular cultural and contextual hermeneutical concerns that shape the particular accounts of the work of Christ.[27]

---

[26] Gustaf Aulén, *Christus Victor: An Historical Study of the Three Main Types of the Idea of the Atonement*, trans. A. G. Herbert (London: SPCK, 1931).

[27] My thanks to Adam Johnson and James Arcadi for detailed comments on an earlier draft of this chapter that greatly improved the argument.

18

Crucified—So What? Feminist Rereadings of the Cross-Event

Arnfríður Guðmundsdóttir

The second wave of feminism, beginning in the 1960s, made a great impact in the Western part of the world and beyond, generating a consciousness regarding the widespread problem of violence against women and changing the lives of many women and their families. The feminist critique has first and foremost been directed against the sources of violence and oppression women experience within patriarchal power systems (which are based on the perception that men are superior to women, and therefore power should belong to them)—against the power of the strong ones, of those who are in control.

Within theology, the feminist critique is directed at the patriarchal bias and abuse of the Christian tradition, including within the doctrine of the person and work of Jesus Christ. Since the time of the early church, doctrines about Christ have been used to justify women's inferiority to men and to keep them in powerless situations. Women have, for example, been (and still are within large denominations) denied access to ordained ministry based on Christ's maleness. At times, the cross has been used to justify, or excuse, abusive and oppressive behavior of the powerful toward those with less power. As a clear minority among those in power, women have been the majority among victims of such abuse. Responding to abusive interpretations of the cross are those who maintain that the cross should be eliminated from the theological discourse, focusing instead on Jesus's life and his message. Others argue for a critical retrieval of the meaning and importance of the cross, while calling for a clear stop to all the abuse that continues to take place in the name of Christ.

From the beginning, Christians have used many and various models and illustrations to interpret the meaning of the cross. The Christian tradition includes multiple interpretations of the suffering and death of Jesus Christ, often strongly reflecting the historical context they emerge from. Feminist critique has emphasized the significance of the historical contexts, when it comes to interpreting the Christian message. A critical reinterpretation is called for because the Christian tradition has been formed within patriarchal societies, and consequently been heavily influenced by patriarchal values and principles.

During antiquity, the cross was commonly used to punish criminals or enemies of political authorities. Hence, at the time when Jesus Christ was crucified, the cross was an instrument of power used by those in power against the powerless. The cross was not generally accepted as a religious symbol until Roman authorities banned crucifixion after Christianity became the acknowledged religion of the Roman Empire. While the Christian community was still young and frequently persecuted by political authorities, a serious reluctance toward the cross remained prevalent among Christians. This is, for example, apparent in 1 Corinthians, where Paul encouraged his fellow sisters and brothers not to hesitate to proclaim the good news about the crucified one, "a stumbling block to Jews and foolishness to Gentiles, but to those who are the called, both Jews and Greeks, Christ the power of God and the wisdom of God" (1 Cor. 1.23–24). Because the cross indicated powerlessness to their contemporaries, Paul stressed that in Christ, the crucified one, "God chose what is weak in the world to shame the strong; God chose what is low and despised in the world, things that are not, to reduce to nothing things that are" (1 Cor. 27–28). This is why, according to Paul, the cross signifies a reversal of our expectations, based on our experience, by creating a new reality, where the weak is stronger than the strong, where life conquers death, and love is the ultimate response to evil.

The focus of this chapter will be on feminist rereadings of the cross-event. The aim is to examine what difference it makes when Christ's passion-story is interpreted in light of women's experience of suffering, particularly women who suffer "as women" (i.e., because of their sex), from domestic and/or sexual violence. A particular attention will be paid to the concept of power, and how our understanding of power, based on our daily experience, contradicts the power revealed in the suffering and death of Christ on the cross. Images of *Christa*, a female Christ on the cross, disclose this reversal of our understanding of power, and provide challenging representations of the meaning of the cross from the perspective of suffering women.

In Light of Women's Experience

By criticizing the patriarchal bias of the Christian tradition, feminist theology intends to reveal how the tradition has frequently been used against women, and to make sure such *ab*use will be stopped. A key to any feminist theology is the conviction that women and men are created in the image of God, and are therefore equal. The church has affirmed this fundamental principle by baptizing girls and boys "into Christ." Despite its practice of baptism, from early on the church has maintained the opposite in its preaching as well as its practice, affirming that men are superior to women. When the power of men over women has been justified on theological grounds, one of the basic premises of the Christian tradition has been betrayed.

Mary Daly's criticism of the patriarchal bias of the Christian tradition was a logical outcome of the second wave of feminism, and its strive toward gender equality. Daly's critique of Christian theology proved to be groundbreaking and the beginning of a new way of doing theology where women's experience is taken seriously. Having been criticized for a strong tendency to universalize the experience of white and privileged women, feminist theologians have become increasingly concerned with the danger of overlooking the diversity of women's experience.

While respecting the diversity of the "lived experience" of women, it is nevertheless important to recognized women's "shared experience," namely, the experience of living within patriarchal systems.[1] Experience of violence against women is an example of such "shared experience," "particularly intimate partner violence and sexual violence against women." In a report from the World Health Organization on violence against women, issued in November 2014, it is maintained that recent global prevalence figures indicate "that 35% of women worldwide have experienced either intimate partner violence or non-partner sexual violence in their lifetime."[2] Feminist theology seeks to respond to this "shared experience," without denying that women's experience is fundamentally shaped by their historical context.

---

[1] On the role and meaning of experience in feminist theology, see Arnfríður Guðmundsdóttir, *Meeting God on the Cross: Christ, the Cross, and the Feminist Critique* (New York: Oxford University Press, 2010), 8–14.
[2] *Violence against Women. Intimate Partner and Sexual Violence against Women*: http://www.who.int/mediacentre/factsheets/fs239/en/.

"Jesus Was a Feminist, But So What?"

Mary Daly was a true pioneer in the early days of feminist theology, and her 1973 book, *Beyond God the Father: Toward a Philosophy of Women's Liberation*, set the agenda for feminist criticism for decades to come. Daly criticized Christianity for being too focused on Jesus Christ, insisting that "Christolatry" was a real hindrance to women's liberation. To give a male human being the status of the "Second Person of the Trinity" was to Daly the same as to divinize sexual hierarchy. This is why, when responding to Leonard Swidler's famous 1971 article "Jesus Was a Feminist," she asked: "Jesus was a feminist, but so what?"[3]

Jesus's example as a "sacrificial victim" has, according to Daly, been idealized for women, who have been without power in patriarchal societies. This has proven to be harmful for women. Given the patriarchal value system of the Christian tradition, qualities of the victim, such as sacrificial love, passive acceptances of suffering, humility, and meekness, have been especially dangerous. Daly argued:

> Given the victimized situation of the female in sexist society, these "virtues" are hardly the qualities that women should be encouraged to have. Moreover, since women cannot be "good" enough to measure up to this ideal, and since all are by sexual definition alien from the male savior, this is an impossible model. Thus doomed to failure even in emulating the Victim, women are plunged more deeply into victimization.[4]

Daly dismissed the message of Jesus Christ, characterizing it as bad news for women. In order for women to break free from patriarchal oppression and to put an end to their victimization, she maintained they needed to leave Christ and Christianity behind. Despite a real diversity within the feminist theological discourse, there has been a widespread consensus among feminist theologians about the danger Daly labels as "the idealization of the sacrificial victim." The diversity becomes apparent in various outcomes of their critical rereadings of the cross-event.

The Glorification of Suffering

To exalt or glorify suffering, which Mary Daly blames Christianity for doing, has by some feminist theologians been seen as a primary force behind extensive

---

[3] Mary Daly, *Beyond God the Father: Toward a Philosophy of Women's Liberation* (Reprint. Boston: Beacon, 1985), 73.
[4] Ibid., 77.

abuse of women (and children). This is, for example, true for many authors of articles in the collection of essays titled *Christianity, Patriarchy, and Abuse: A Feminist Critique* (1989), which launched a comprehensive critique of the abusive nature of a theology of the cross in Western Christianity. In their jointly authored article "For God So Loved the World?," Joanne Carlson Brown and Rebecca Parker denounce any theology that argues that suffering is redemptive, including Jesus's suffering and death on the cross. According to Brown and Parker, the image of the crucified Christ as the savior of the world not only gives suffering a redemptive significance, but it also encourages self-sacrifice and total submission. Applying the image of the "divine child abuse," Brown and Parker compare the relationship between God the Father and the Son to the relationship between an abusive father and an abused child. Hence, they charge patriarchal Christianity of not only justifying, but also actually encouraging the abuse of women and children.[5]

In their coauthored volume *Proverbs of Ashes: Violence, Redemptive Suffering, and the Search for What Saves Us* (2001), Rita Nakashima Brock and Rebecca Ann Parker develop further the critical evaluation of the Christianity they introduced in their respective articles in *Christianity, Patriarchy, and Abuse*. Brock and Parker's book is a collection of stories, their own together with those of people they have known, either personally or encountered in their work within the church and the academic world. By applying personal testimonies to the correlation between violence and the Christian tradition, Brock and Parker seek to provide firsthand evidence in support of their demand for a critical reevaluation of Christianity. More than any other theological theme, the authors focus on the cross-event as the source of the problem, and the reason why they are searching for a "new theology," free of violence and abuse.[6]

A recurrent theme in Brock and Parker's book is the violent situation of women who believe they are to suffer "like Jesus." Brock and Parker became alarmed by what they describe as a "spiritualizing of suffering" in Christianity, through their encounters with women in violent situations, who had been told by the church to endure their sufferings. They maintain that suffering is often given a spiritual significance as God's way to "edify

---

[5] Joanne Carlson Brown and Rebecca Parker, "For God So Loved the World?" in *Christianity, Patriarchy, and Abuse: A Feminist Critique*, ed. Joanne Carlson Brown and Carole R. Bohn (New York: Pilgrim, 1989), 2.
[6] Rita Nakashima Brock and Rebecca Parker, *Proverbs of Ashes: Violence, Redemptive Suffering, and the Search for What Saves Us* (Boston: Beacon, 2001), 8.

or purify human beings."⁷ Not only does this prevent people from resisting suffering, but it renders them even more passive and acquiescent to it.⁸ They argue that the church expects women to be Christ-like, by encouraging them to remain passive and helpless in violent situations. Parker offers the testimony of a woman, named Anola Reed, whose priest told her to tolerate her husband's violence because it made her become like Christ. This woman came to Parker, hoping a woman priest would understand her problem and be able to help her:

> "I haven't talked to anyone about this for a while," she began, the smile fading, and sadness deepening in her eyes. "But I'm worried for my kids now. The problem is my husband. He beats me sometimes. Mostly he is a good man. But sometimes he becomes very angry and he hits me. He knocks me down. One time he broke my arm and I had to go to the hospital. But I didn't tell them how my arm got broken."
>
> I nodded. She took a deep breath and went on. "I went to my priest twenty years ago. I've been trying to follow his advice. The priest said I should rejoice in my sufferings because they bring me closer to Jesus. He said, 'Jesus suffered because he loved us.' He said, 'If you love Jesus, accept the beatings and bear them gladly, as Jesus bore the cross.' I've tried, but I'm not sure anymore. My husband is turning on the kids now. Tell me, is what the priest told me true?"⁹

Based on their own and other's experiences of violence and abuse, Brock and Parker called for a radical reinterpretation of the Christian message. What was needed was both a different understanding of the person and work of Jesus Christ, and a radical revision of the image of God. Instead of a theology that spiritualizes suffering, by supporting victimization and helplessness regarding the abuse, Brock and Parker called for a theology that empowers people "to affirm their own agency, to resist abuse, to take responsibility for ethical discernment, and to work for justice."¹⁰ They thought this kind of theology was supported by a model of Jesus as "a prophet who confronted injustices and risked opposition,"¹¹ and whose death was "an unjust act of violence that needed resolution."¹² Such a theology did not have to cover up Jesus's death

---

[7] Ibid., 44.
[8] Ibid., 157–158.
[9] Ibid., 20–21.
[10] Ibid., 156.
[11] Ibid., 31.
[12] Ibid., 60.

with a belief in resurrection, so as to avoid facing the horror and anguish of his death. Rather, it presented an image of God who "delights in revolutionary disobedience and spiritual protest."[13] Parker wondered what a difference such an image of God might have made to the life of the woman whose husband abused and finally killed her:

> If Anola Reed had believed in a God who supported protest, might she have protested and resisted her husband's violence, rather than accepted and endured it? If her husband didn't regard God as the divine enforcer of obedience, would he have enforced obedience from his wife with violence. Would they have had more of a chance at life?[14]

Jesus, "The Ultimate Surrogate Figure"

Delores S. Williams, the womanist theologian, agreed with theologians like Brown, Brock, and Parker, about the problematic understanding of a redemptive significance of Jesus's suffering and death. Williams wrote about African American women's experience of surrogacy (coerced or voluntary), which serves as a hermeneutical key to Williams's Christological interpretations, in her book *Sisters in the Wilderness: The Challenge of Womanist God-Talk* (1995).[15] By comparing the Christian understanding of Jesus's cross to black women's experience of surrogacy, Williams wanted to show how dangerous the idea of human salvation taking place through suffering and death really is. Jesus, "the ultimate surrogate figure," who stands in the place of a sinful humankind, she insisted, only supports the exploitation that surrogacy brings. Hence, given the social context and experience of African American women, salvation of black women cannot depend on surrogacy of any kind.

Williams states that if womanist theologians are going to take seriously black women's experience of surrogacy and oppression, they "must show that redemption of humans can have nothing to do with any kind of surrogate or substitute role Jesus was reputed to have played in a bloody act that supposedly gained

---

[13] Ibid., 31.
[14] Ibid.
[15] Williams explains: "Surrogacy has been a negative force in African-American women's lives. It has been used by both men and women of the ruling class, as well as by some black men, to keep black women in the service of other people's needs and goals." Delores Williams, *Sisters in the Wilderness: The Challenge of Womanist God-Talk* (Maryknoll, NY: Orbis, 1995), 81.

victory over sin and/or evil."[16] While Williams sees the image of the cross as an image of degradation, a clear indication of collective human sin, she wants the focus of hope to shift toward the wilderness and Jesus's act of resistance.[17] Instead of being saved by Jesus's death, black women's salvation "is assured by Jesus' life of resistance and by the survival strategies he used to help people survive the death of identity caused by their exchange of inherited cultural meanings for a new identity shaped by the gospel ethics and world view."[18] By understanding Jesus's life of resistance in the sociopolitical context of African American women, Williams insists that redemption is freed from the cross at the same time that the cross is freed from patriarchal interpretations of Jesus's death.

Jesus, "The Divine Co-Sufferer"

While women's oppression is frequently associated with abusive interpretations of the cross, a significant difference is still noticeable between involuntary and voluntary suffering and abuse. White Western women typically focus more on women's choices to serve and suffer for the sake of others. On the contrary, African American and mujerista women, as well as women in other parts of the world, are mostly concerned about women's experience of involuntary suffering and servanthood. While Delores Williams makes the distinction between involuntary and voluntary surrogacy (referring to their experience of surrogacy before and after emancipation), she nevertheless maintains that African American women are still under enormous social pressure to accept surrogacy roles. Jacquelyn Grant, another womanist theologian, argues that the history of black women in the United States shows that African American women have been the "servants of the servants." Because service has so often turned out to be "a life of suffering for those 'relegated' to that state," the following questions have been unavoidable: "Why do black women suffer so? Or even more pointedly, why does God permit the suffering of Black women? Does God condone the fact that Black women are systematically relegated to being 'servants of servants?'"[19] Grant responds to those questions with the Christological statement

---

[16] Ibid., 165.
[17] Ibid., 166,
[18] Ibid., 164.
[19] Jacquelyn Grant, "The Sin of Servanthood: And the Deliverance of Discipleship," in *A Troubling in My Soul: Womanist Perspectives on Evil and Suffering*, ed. Emilie M. Towns (Maryknoll, NY: Orbis, 1993), 200.

about Christ, the black woman," but also by the image of Jesus as "the divine co-sufferer."[20] JoAnne Marie Terrell has written about Grant's understanding of the role of Jesus Christ in the lives of African American women. She writes:

> Among womanists, Grant consistently lifts up the image of Jesus as the "divine co-sufferer." For Grant, that Jesus Christ was born, lived, struggled, and died among the poor was an affirmation that his ultimate victory is theirs to appropriate. That "Christ came and died, no less for the woman as for the man" was an affirmation of black femininity, indicating that Christ's significance lay not in Jesus' maleness but in his humanity. For Grant, the bold declaration that "Christ is a black woman" carries a step further black theologians' assertion that "Christ is black" by radicalizing black women's conceptual apparatus for imaging God.[21]

Grant's understanding of who Jesus Christ is for African American women represents a very different interpretation of Jesus's person and work, from that of Williams, but also of Brown, Parker, and Brock, the main difference being that Grant thinks it is possible that Jesus's death, and not only his life and work, brings hope to suffering women (while the others agree with Mary Daly's negative conclusion about the hopeless model of the crucified Son of God).

"Making meaning out of suffering" can for sure function both as "a seed of liberation and an opium for oppression" for women who suffer, not only because of their race and class, but also because of their gender.[22] Virginia Fabella, a Catholic theologian from the Philippines, maintains that theologians have to take into account in their work the meaningless suffering of women, caused by the injustice of their society. She explains what she means by that, by using examples of Indian women:

> In India, the theology of sacrifice thrust upon women is of no purpose. Indian women theologians tell us that their women silently bear taunts, abuse, and even battering; they sacrifice their self-esteem for the sake of family honor, subject themselves to sex determination tests, and endure the oppressive and even fatal effects of the dowry system. A woman who is raped will invariably commit suicide rather than allow her husband and family to suffer the ignominy of living with a raped woman. While we seek in Jesus' passion, death, and resurrection a meaning for our own suffering, we cannot passively submit ourselves as women

---

[20] Grant, "'Come to My Help, Lord, For I'm in Trouble': Womanist Jesus and the Mutual Struggle for Liberation," in *Reconstructing the Christ Symbol: Essays in Feminist Christology*, ed. Maryanne Stevens (New York/Mahwah: Paulist, 1993), 67.

[21] JoAnne Marie Terrell, "Our Mothers' Gardens. Rethinking Sacrifice," in *Cross Examinations: Readings on the Meaning of the Cross Today*, ed. Marit Trelstad (Minneapolis: Augsburg Fortress, 2006), 43.

[22] Chung Hyun Kyung, *Struggle to be Sun Again* (Maryknoll, NY: Orbis, 1990), 54.

to practices that are ultimately anti-life. Only that suffering endured for the sake of one's neighbor, for the sake of the kingdom, for the sake of greater life, can be redeeming and rooted in the Paschal mystery.[23]

Fabella points out how different images of Jesus bring hope to women in oppressive situations. While women, suffering from injustice and oppression, find hope in Jesus the suffering servant, who is with them in their suffering, others are encouraged by Jesus the liberator, who accompanies them in their struggle for liberation. Unfortunately, she admits, suffering women are too often only able to see the suffering or crucified one, who understands their suffering, while the liberator remains unknown to them. Fabella makes an important distinction between the passive and the active moments of Jesus's suffering. Contrary to the experience of "undergoing" passive suffering, "'doing' and 'accompanying' are acts of solidarity which constitute the other moment of Jesus' passion. How Jesus was able to stand his ground during his arrest and trial brings us to a consideration of his passion as an act of being in solidarity."[24] According to Fabella, Filipino women have been able to identify with this active side of Jesus's passion, as they have resisted the consequences of unjust and oppressive powers on behalf of their suffering sisters and brothers.

The Power of God—The Compassion of God

Experiences of suffering and evil often drive people to ask pressing questions about God, such as: Where is God when I suffer? *Who* is God in the midst of my suffering and pain? Criticism of unhelpful, even dangerous understandings of *who* God is, and *what* God's redemption stands for, has been prevalent within feminist theological literature since the early 1970s. Hence, a call for a radical reinterpretation of basic categories of Christian discourse has been prevalent. Among those categories are the basic characteristics of God, and how they are reflected in the cross of Christ.

From early on, there has been a broad consensus within the Christian tradition about an all-powerful and benevolent God. Since the time of the Enlightenment, an increasing uneasiness regarding these classical attributes has been surfacing,

---

[23] Virginia M. M. Fabella, "Christology from an Asian Woman's Perspective," in *We Dare to Dream: Doing Theology as Asian Women*, ed. Virginia M. M. Fabella and Sun Ai Lee Park (Maryknoll, NY: Orbis, 1990), 7–8.

[24] Virginia M. M. Fabella, "Asian Women and Christology," in *In God's Image* (September 1987), 15.

particularly in light of the *theodicy* question, which asks: how it is possible to hold on to God's omnipotence and perfect beneficence in the presence of evil and suffering among God's creation? Among theologians who have addressed the theodicy question is Wendy Farley, who insists on the need to reconsider our understanding of God's power. Instead of interpreting the power of God as dominion or coercion, Farley suggests that we understand God's power as *compassion*. This is "a different *kind* [emphasis in the original] of power," Farley explains, but still a real power, not simply a feeling or mood, but "the kind of power that God exercises toward the world." She continues:

> The power of the compassion is the most real thing in the world, the signature of ultimate reality, and the name that truth bears in its active aspect. If we understand this—not in our heads but in our very bones—we will talk about God differently, interpret our scriptures differently, and relate to victims and perpetrators of violence differently. Compassion vitiates neat divisions between theory and practice, transforming theology into a practice of compassion even as it demands that all practice be rooted in the wisdom that discerns compassion as the signature of reality.[25]

By interpreting power as compassion (as a form of love), Farley provides a solution to the conflict between God's power and love. In the midst of suffering, she insists, the presence of God as compassion is there as the power to resist the causes of suffering, but also in the form of consolation and courage.[26] It is indeed God's identification (the *passive* aspect of the cross), together with God's active transformation of suffering and death (the *active* aspect of the cross), that sustains a feminist theology of the cross.[27]

Building explicitly on Farley's theology of divine compassion, Elizabeth Johnson has made a significant contribution to a feminist critical retrieval of a theology of the cross. In her 1992 book *She Who Is: The Mystery of God in Feminist Theological Discourse*, Johnson describes God's active solidarity with those who suffer as an expression of God's "compassion poured out."[28] Central to her understanding of a "suffering God" is her rejection of the classical idea

---

[25] Wendy Farley, "Evil, Violence, and the Practice of Theodicy," in *Telling the Truth: Preaching about Sexual and domestic Violence*, ed. John S. McClure and Nancy J. Ramsay (Cleveland, OH: United Church Press, 1998), 15.
[26] Wendy Farley, *Tragic Vision and Divine Compassion: A Contemporary Theodicy* (Louisville, KY: Westminster/John Knox, 1990), 116–117.
[27] Guðmundsdóttir, *Meeting God on the Cross*, 142.
[28] Elizabeth Johnson, *She Who Is: The Mystery of God in Feminist Theological Discourse* (New York: Crossroad, 1992), 246.

of God's impassibility, which she thinks is both "morally intolerable"[29] and "not seriously imaginable."[30] At the same time, Johnson warns against assuming that God suffers because God cannot do otherwise.[31] To affirm God's ability to suffer is, on the contrary, to imply the notion that God, out of freedom of love, chooses to suffer with suffering people. Such a God is "the compassionate God," a God who helps by "awakening consolation, responsible human action, and hope against hope in the world marked by radical suffering and evil."[32]

Critical to Johnson's feminist interpretation of the cross of Christ (as well as her development of the symbol of a suffering God) is to renounce any view of redemption that suggests that God required Jesus's death as a payment for sin. For Johnson, such an idea is today "virtually inseparable from an underlying image of God as an angry, bloodthirsty, violent and sadistic father, reflecting the very worst kind of male behavior." On the contrary, Johnson insists that Jesus's death was an "act of violence," resulting from his message and behavior.[33] Instead of signifying a payment required for human sinfulness, Johnson describes the cross as a sign of God's identification with human beings in the midst of their suffering and pain. Using a range of metaphors drawn from women's experience, she skillfully redresses the theology of the cross in feminist terms as the cross becomes a part of "the larger mystery of pain-to-life, of that struggle for the new creation evocative of the rhythm of pregnancy, delivery, and birth so familiar to women of all times."[34] While the resurrection cannot be humanly imagined, Johnson argues that in faith it means that evil does not have the last word. Moreover, the belief in the risen Christ appears consequently as the expression of "the victory of love, both human and divine, that spins new life out of this disaster."[35]

Abusive or Abused

Criticism of any theological justification of abuse of power has played a critical role in feminist theology from the beginning. What has frequently been

---

[29] Ibid., 249.
[30] Ibid., 253.
[31] Ibid., 253–254.
[32] Ibid., 269.
[33] Johnson, "Redeeming the Name of Christ—Christology," in *Freeing Theology: The Essentials of Theology in Feminist Perspective*, ed. Catherine Mowry LaCugna (San Francisco: Harper San Francisco, 1993), 124.
[34] Johnson, *She Who Is*, 159.
[35] Johnson, "Redeeming the Name of Christ—Christology," 124.

lacking in this criticism is to make a clear distinction between *use* and *abuse* of theological arguments, between theology being *abused* or essentially *abusive*. This is particularly true of theological discourse about the cross. While abusive interpretations of the cross have been strongly criticized, the crucial distinction between an abuse of the cross, and the cross being abusive in itself, has often been ignored. I think such a distinction is necessary. It is indeed radically different to talk about something as being abused and to argue that something is abusive in itself. If the cross is not abusive in itself, as I maintain, and the abuse does not abolish the use,[36] the cross can still bring hope to women, even if it has been used against them for abusive purposes.

When theology of the cross starts glorifying (or spiritualizing) suffering per se, it is being abused. Glorification of suffering keeps people from resisting the causes of their suffering, and, furthermore, renders them acquiescent to it. When suffering is glorified, it has been made into a goal in itself, something to be sought out and endured because of its Christ-like character. Glorification of suffering must be stopped at all costs. Church communities must lead the way, by speaking out against the danger of abused theology. Churches need, for example, to stress the importance of careful and judicious readings of biblical passages, in order to resist their co-optation for abusive purposes. An example is the passage where Christ encourages his disciples to "take up their cross and follow him" (Mt. 16.24). Church communities have raised the call for action worldwide, among them the World Council of Churches (WCC), confronting the challenge of violence, including violence against women and children, by establishing a *Decade against Violence: Churches Seeking Reconciliation and Peace* (2001–2010).[37] The Lutheran World Federation (LWF) targeted the violence against women, in its document *Churches Say "No" to Violence against Women. Action Plan for the Churches* (2002). In 2013 LWF issued its *Gender Justice Policy*, where the importance of awareness raising regarding violence against women, domestic violence, and gender-based violence was emphasized. On gender-based violence as an issue of faith, it writes:

> Each act of gender-based violence injures the creation in God's image and violates the community of believers who are called to live in just relationships. Therefore, the silence needs to be broken. The church's prophetic role is to

---

[36] For important analysis of the difference between use and abuse, see Vitor Westhelle, *The Scandalous God: The Use and Abuse of the Cross* (Minneapolis: Fortress, 2006).
[37] See Margot Kässmann, *Overcoming Violence: The Challenge to the Churches in All Places* (Geneva: WCC, 1998).

provide processes for healing and safe places for victims and survivors in mutual collaboration with multiple partners in healing ministries. Holistic mission and ministry also mean that perpetrators of gender-based violence are held accountable. This implies that also men are part in gender discussions reflecting on how models of masculinities sustain violence and control.[38]

The *NoXcuses Campaign*, launched in the fall of 2014, was meant "to add a faith dimension to discussions around violence against women." The campaign was run by the World Young Women's Christian Association (YWCA), together with LWF and WCC, and the message was clear: "There are noXcuses for violence against women!"[39]

Despite strong commonalities, feminist theology is not all the same.[40] While some side with Daly's early statement of an essentially oppressive character of Christianity, others insist on the message about Christ, including his suffering and death, as a source of strength and courage for women in oppressive situations. It is critical that all these voices be heard, because they proclaim important, and often uncomfortable, truth about the praxis and preaching of the church. Feminist theologians, who rely heavily on testimony about abusive messages that are being preached and practiced by the church, are saying something of great significance. They remind the church of its utmost responsibility to listen and to take into (theological) account the experience of suffering people, when they address questions about God, the cross of Christ, and human suffering. This is particularly important since women's experiences of evil and suffering have often been ignored, or even worse, silenced, in the theological tradition, with devastating results. Likewise, feminist theologians, who have dismissed the cross as a dangerous symbol for women, must pay attention to women who want to hold on to the cross as a symbol of hope and life. Mujerista and non-Western women have been instrumental among those who see the cross as being meaningful to suffering and violated women. To not only criticize abusive interpretations of the cross, but also reject it as an abusive theological symbol in itself is to "trivialize" the theological reflection of all those women who do not agree with that conclusion.[41]

---

[38] https://www.lutheranworld.org/sites/default/files/DTPW-WICAS_Gender_Justice.pdf, 34.
[39] https://www.oikoumene.org/en/press-centre/news/there-is-no-excuse-for-violence-against-women.
[40] Serene Jones writes about "eight plays of mind" feminist theologians generally share. See *The Oxford Handbook of Feminist Theology*, ed. Mary McClintock Fulkerson and Sheila Briggs (New York: Oxford University Press, 2012), 26–29.
[41] Darby Kathleen Ray, *Deceiving the Devil: Atonement, Abuse, and Ransom* (Cleveland, OH: Pilgrim, 1998), 71–72.

The Cross as a Kenosis of Patriarchy

Even if the Christian tradition has proved to be both multilayered and androcentric, and repeatedly used against women, I do not agree with Mary Daly and others who think the abuse prevents the Christian message from being relevant in our time. Still, the importance of a hermeneutic of suspicion is a useful key, when it comes to abusive interpretations of the cross. By interpreting the cross as a symbol of the *kenosis of patriarchy*, such abuse is rejected, and instead the cross is seen as a compelling criticism of the patriarchal understanding of power and masculinity.[42]

Against abused theology of the cross, the cross has been lifted up as an important symbol of the *kenosis* of patriarchy, calling for a radical reinterpretation of our understanding of power and humanity as well as of maleness and femaleness. Elizabeth Johnson explains:

> Above all, the cross is raised as a challenge to the natural rightness of male dominating rule. The crucified Jesus embodies the exact opposite of the patriarchal ideal of the powerful man, and shows the steep price to be paid in the struggle for liberation. The cross thus stands as a poignant symbol of the "kenosis of patriarchy," the self-emptying of male dominating power in favor of the new humanity of compassionate service and mutual empowerment. On this reading Jesus' maleness is prophecy announcing the end of patriarchy, at least as divinely ordained.[43]

When the cross is understood as a symbol of kenosis of patriarchy, the self-emptying of male dominating power, the power of the cross becomes the power of love instead of the power of control. God, who we meet on the cross, is neither strong nor powerful according to the standards of patriarchy, and neither does Jesus's maleness fit the stereotypical understanding of masculinity. The female portrayal of Christ on the cross can help interpret the reversal of our expectations revealed on the cross, where the weak conquers the strong, evil is transformed into something good, and life defeats the power of death.[44]

---

[42] Johnson, *She Who Is*, 160–161.
[43] Ibid.
[44] Guðmundsdóttir, *Meeting God on the Cross*, 129–130.

Christa—A Crucified Woman

While there is a general agreement on the contextualization of Jesus's race and class, the issue of gender remains a controversial one.[45] This is why, for example, people have not found the black Jesus nearly as challenging as the female Christ. Images of a suffering woman on the cross, *Christa*-figures, have been created in order to emphasize the compassion of the crucified Christ with women who have suffered from beatings, rapes, or other abuse of power. Hence, female Christ-figures represent important examples of revised interpretations of the cross, which at the same time denounce any abuse of the symbol of the cross. The intention of the Christa-figures is not to glorify suffering or make it meaningful in itself. Still, it is acknowledged that suffering can, at times, be a necessary accompaniment to resistance against injustice and evil, as is the case in the passion of Christ.

Christa-figures have stimulated interesting discussions about contemporary interpretations of the passion story, and from time to time, they have called for strong reactions. While a female Christ-figure has been considered by some a powerful symbol of God's identification with suffering women today, others have thought it nothing less than a gross misinterpretation, even a violation of the historical event. Christa-figures have stimulated important questions about the meaning of the contextualization of the Christ-event, especially the gender-question. They have also challenged the role of gender, when it comes to interpreting the story of Jesus Christ, compared to other historical particularities, such as race and class. Hence, Christa-figures have already proved to be worthwhile dialogue partners in the Christological discourse.

One of the early female Christ figures was a bronze sculpture made by Edwina Sandys in 1974 for the *United Nations Decade for Women: Equality, Development and Peace*, from 1976 to 1985. Sandys's *Christa* "portrays a slumped female nude wearing a crown of thorns with arms outstretched depicting the cross."[46] The sculpture was originally exhibited in London in 1975, and attracted great attention of people who either admired or detested it. When the sculpture was placed at the side of the main altar in the Episcopal Cathedral of St. John the Divine in

---

[45] On this issue, see, for example, Theresa Berger, "A Female Christ Child in the Manger and a Woman on the Cross, Or: The Historicity of the Jesus Event and the Inculturation of the Gospel," *Feminist Theology II* (January 1996), 32–45.

[46] Julie Clague, "The Christa: Symbolizing My Humanity and My Pain," *Feminist Theology* 14, no. I (2005), 84–85. Available: http://fth.sagepub.com/cgi/reprint/14/1/83. See also http://www.yorku.ca/finearts/news/edwinasandys.htm and http://www.time.com/time/magazine/article/0,9171,954312,00.html.

New York City during Holy Week in April of 1984, many criticized Sandys for going too far in order to make the symbol of the cross meaningful for her contemporaries. Due to strong protest by those who disapproved of it, the sculpture was removed from the Cathedral within two weeks.[47]

Crucified Woman is another representation of a crucified female Christ. It is a sculpture, created by Almuth Lutkenhaus-Lackey, which was originally placed in the chancel of Bloor Street United Church in Toronto during Lent and Eastertide of 1979, but was later moved to the grounds of Emmanuel College in Toronto.[48] Originally, the artist did not think of the crucified woman as a religious symbol, as her intention was rather to make "a portrayal of human suffering."[49] Therefore she was hesitant about the placement in a church. She changed her mind, when she realized how many women were inspired by a female body on the cross, and it had influenced their understanding of the cross of Jesus Christ.

Lutkenhaus-Lackey's *Crucified Woman* called for no less commotion than Sandys's *Christa*. Regardless of what people thought of the figure, it was obvious that the figure had not only stimulated important theological discussions about the meaning of the suffering and death of Christ on the cross, but no less significantly had she challenged the meaning of his humanity, or what it really means to believe in a God who "became flesh." Many thought the sculpture had been able to create something new, by helping people understand core issues of their Christian faith in a new and fresh light.[50]

Margaret Argyle made an image of a female Christ in celebration of *The World Council of Churches Decade for Churches in Solidarity with Women*, from 1988 to 1998. Her image was originally displayed in a service, celebrated in the cathedral in Manchester, England, on October 24, 1993. Argyle's Christa, *Bosnian Christa*, was meant to interpret the artist's reaction to the horrible abuse of women in the former Yugoslavia, when rape was systematically used as a weapon of war, and women were systematically raped and impregnated, during the war in the early 1990s. Julie Clague describes Argyle's image in the following way:

> Despite the disturbing subject matter and explicit sexual imagery of "Bosnian Christa," the impact of the work is restful rather than aggressive. A deep black

---

[47] Ibid., 87.
[48] Ibid., 87–90. Lutkenhaus-Lackey's sculpture stimulated strong reactions, recounted in Doris Jean Dyke's book, entitled as the sculpture itself, *Crucified Woman* (Toronto, ON: The United Church Publishing House, 1991).
[49] Dyke, *Crucified Woman*, 3.
[50] Ibid., 1–9.

wool backdrop is slit in its centre to reveal a bloodred opening framed by dark red crushed velvet curtain-like lips. Standing within the opening of the vulva is an elongated cross bearing a slim, stylized naked female.[51]

The *Bosnian Christa* became instrumental in helping Argyle reconsider her own understanding of the cross of Christ. Looking at the cross from the perspective of women's suffering changed her idea of the cross as a key symbol of the Christian faith. In Argyle's own words:

> Previously I had not been able to use the cross in my work at all because I had thought it was a terribly overused symbol which had become almost meaningless to me … But the cross now has a meaning for me. It's about a God who is in the world and present wherever anyone suffers. That was an enormous revelation for me. I had never associated God with women and their suffering before.[52]

As in the case of the earlier Christa-figures, Argyle's Christa called for much attention and sometimes harsh reactions, including accusations of blasphemy. Argyle herself suggested that the negative reporting had something to do with the decision made by the General Synod the year before to ordain women to the ministerial priesthood in the Church of England.[53] Given the strong emphasis on Jesus's maleness within the Christian tradition in the past, negative reactions to the Christa-images shouldn't come as a surprise. His maleness has been used as an argument against women's ordination, by large denominations like the Roman Catholic Church, which has insisted that women cannot become Christ's representatives, because they do not share the same sex.[54]

Despite widespread and strong negative reactions, images of a female Christ have become powerful symbols of hope and healing for many women, particularly for those who have suffered from sexual or domestic violence. As such they have helped instigate the much needed feminist critique of a male-biased tradition. Female Christ-figures can continue to serve as important dialogue partners if we allow them to help us understand better the meaning of the cross-event in contexts, dominated by forces of injustice and oppression.

---

[51] Clague, "The Christa: Symbolizing My Humanity and My Pain," 97.
[52] In Clague, "Interview With Margaret Argyle," 58–60. Quoted in Clague, "The Christa: Symbolizing My Humanity and My Pain," 97.
[53] Ibid., 95.
[54] Louis Ligier, S.J., "The Question of Admitting Women to the Ministerial Priesthood," *L'Osservatore Romano*. Weekly edition in English, March 2, 1978, 5. Available: http://www.ewtn.com/library/Theology/ORDWOMEN.HTM.

Symbol of Hope

The story of the suffering and death of Jesus Christ takes up a significant part of all four Gospels. The Gospel writers, as well as other writers of the New Testament, tried to present meaningful interpretations of what happened on the cross, and why it happened. The Christian tradition includes multiple models and illustrations that have been introduced through the centuries, in order to analyze the scriptural testimonies.[55] Originally the cross was a tool of oppression, used by authorities to prove their power. The feminist critique has called attention to abusive interpretations of the cross of Christ within the Christian tradition. The cross has continued to be used by the powerful against the powerless, and such abuse of the cross has to stop! That will happen either by removing the cross from the center of our faith, or by critical rereadings of the cross-event, which take full account of the abuse. The Christian faith confesses that Christ was crucified. Christians at all time are faced with the challenge: so what?

The prerequisite to my feminist rereading of the cross-event is the conviction that the abuse of the cross does not abolish the use. While testimonies of the abuse belong to our Christian tradition, it is also true for testimonies of those who have found hope in the symbol of the cross.

In her book *Trauma and Grace: Theology in a Ruptured World*, Serene Jones examines how people who have experienced violence "come to feel and know the redeeming power of God's grace."[56] Jones asks how the church "might more effectively minister to people who live through an event of overwhelming violence and continue to suffer from its emotional, cognitive effects." The "challenge of preaching about the cross to such people," probes the following question: "How do we make theological sense of what happened on the cross in a way that speaks to the experience of traumatized victims without glorifying violence?"[57] I agree with Jones, and other feminist theologians, who have stressed the danger of "glorification" of violence or suffering. Such danger has to be avoided, by all means. To put the cross in context is also crucial, if the cross is to the make sense theologically. As it is necessary to take notice of the situation of the people who are being addressed, the context of Jesus's cross should never be overlooked. First

---

[55] For a critical evaluation of classical atonement theories, see, for example, Ray, *Deceiving the Devil: Atonement, Abuse, and Ransom.*

[56] Serene Jones, *Trauma and Grace. Theology in a Ruptured World* (Louisville, KY: Westminster John Knox Press, 2009), viii.

[57] Ibid., 85.

of all, it has to be put in the context of Jesus's life, as it is known from the Gospels, and second, it has to be considered in close connection with the resurrection.[58]

If the cross is to be a meaningful symbol of people suffering from violence and abuse, it cannot remain a symbol of passive victimization. Within the Christian tradition, Jesus has frequently been portrayed as a passive victim, of his contemporaries, his heavenly Father, or both. The life he lived, according to the Gospels, was not a life of a passive victim, but rather of active resistance against injustice, oppressive authorities, and expected social roles. Thus, Jesus ended his life on the cross because of the kind of life he lived, and not as a passive victim, who did not have the power to choose what kind of live he lived. By simply giving up his life for a good cause, Jesus becomes a martyr, and as such he doesn't necessarily bring hope to those who suffer from injustice and abuse of power. In fact, the martyr image can easily become an excuse not to stand up for oneself and resist evil forces that threaten one's well-being. This is why it is only if the one hanging on the cross is God incarnated (is God among us), and not just another martyr sacrificing his life for a good cause, that the cross of Christ brings hope into hopeless situations. A naked female body on the cross helps us understand how radical the idea of incarnation truly is. As God in flesh, "truly human," Jesus Christ gives hope by identifying with those who suffer, but also by giving them courage to stand up and resist. If God's loving nature is revealed through Jesus's life, as well as his suffering and death of Jesus on the cross, then, despite abusive interpretations of the cross, theology of the cross can truly become a theology of hope for all suffering people.

Most importantly, the story of Jesus does not end with the crucifixion. Only in light of the resurrection, on the other side of Golgotha, were the friends of Jesus able to see the cross as a symbol of life. Without the resurrection, the cross leaves us without hope. Without the resurrection, the cross remains an example of one more victim of evil; of one more person who lost her/his life for a good cause. The cross stands as a symbol of suffering and evil in our midst. But because of who God is, and because God is with us, we are able, *in retrospect*, to witness God bringing life out of death, transforming evil into something good, making the victim into a survivor. Testimonies to God's compassion poured out *pro nobis*. Evil, indeed, does not have the last word.

---

[58] Marit Trelstad has made an interesting proposal for a feminist rereading of the cross, where she suggests that the cross should be understood in the context of the biblical tradition of the covenant. See Marit Trelstad, "Putting the Cross in Context: Atonement through Covenant," in *Transformative Lutheran Theologies* (Minneapolis: Fortress Press, 2010).

Essays

19

Peter Abelard

Adam J. Johnson

Abelard was a highly contentious figure, so much so that his views on the atonement were automatically controversial, falling on largely unsympathetic ears. Bernard of Clairvaux documents his disagreement with Abelard on this topic in his *Epistle 190* to Pope Innocent (Lane, 80–105). In modern works on the atonement, Peter Abelard is thought to be the father of "exemplarism"—that theory of the atonement that attributes the efficacy of Christ's death and resurrection in the transformative power of his example—though in fact "exemplarism" was formulated largely in the Enlightenment (McGrath). The primary reason for this reputation lies in the fact that theologians (beginning with Bernard) have relied almost exclusively upon a short excerpt from Abelard's *Commentary on Romans* as the source for his view on the matter (Lane 27, 102–104; cf. Fairweather, 276–287). Given the role of "exemplarism" in twentieth-century accounts of the history of the doctrine, it is challenging to re-enter the context of his thought to understand his views as they would have been received in his day. The purpose of this chapter is to help clear the ground of exemplarist biases, to allow his thought to speak more clearly for itself.

While Abelard's work was contested from the start, scholars in recent decades have challenged this interpretation, largely through careful attention to the full text of his *Commentary on Romans*, recently translated by the late Steven R. Cartwright. Within the broader context of his *Commentary*, it is evident that Abelard's view included but far transcended an exemplarist understanding of the atonement, just as is the case with Anselm, Thomas, and so many other theologians in that time period. We will consider the genre, relevant doctrinal commitments, and Abelard's views on the atonement.

Those interested in understanding Abelard's views do well to attend to the fact that this is a *Commentary*, rather than a sustained treatise on a doctrine.

Granted, the range of genres was fluid in the twelfth century, but Abelard repeatedly breaks off these doctrinal digressions, after raising a set of questions, giving a brief answer, and then moving ahead to comment on the next passage of Paul's letter. In other words, we should not expect this to be Abelard's comprehensive or final statement on any matter, including the atonement. At the conclusion of his excerpt on the atonement (three pages of questions, and one page of answers), he writes: "But now briefly, as far as it pertains to the brevity of the exposition concerning the means of our redemption, this seems to us to suffice. If anything is missing, however, we reserve it for our more thorough treatise, *The Tropologies*," a work which has not come down to us (Abelard, 168). Discerning Abelard's view of the doctrine, therefore, should be a synthetic project, pulling together a range of insights and commitments from across his works, rather than selecting a single passage from the *Commentary*.

As it turns out, these doctrinal commitments are such that a purely exemplarist reading of Abelard is impossible. Abelard defends a doctrine of original sin: "men are begotten and born with original sin and also contract this same original sin from the first parent," which refers "more to the punishment of sin, for which, of course they are held liable to punishment" (216; cf. 208). Concerning this liability, he writes: "just as Adam transferred what was his, that is, sin, to his descendants, so [Christ transferred] what is his, namely, the grace of justification, to his [descendants]" (212). Elsewhere, he writes: "we committed sin, the penalty of which he bore," and "he swept away the penalty for sins by the price of his death, leading us into paradise, and through the demonstration of so much grace ... he drew back our souls from the will to sin and kindled the highest love of himself" (204). The strength or power of original sin is manifest in Abelard's statement that "even in the first parents I am sold with them under sin ... and taste of the fruit for which Eve longed. Behold whence we were made captives!" (259). While "exemplarist" lines of thought are present (as in every other theologian since the Apostle Paul), they take place within a broader account of Christ's saving work.

Funding this account of original sin is Abelard's view of God's righteousness (which he consistently affirms alongside God's love and mercy). Though at one point he defines righteousness as "the charity which is applicable to men of our time" (163), shortly thereafter he defines it as that "which renders to each person what is his" (169; cf. 212, 219), or "his vengeance due for individual sins" (122; cf. 125, on Abelard's alignment of vengeance, wrath, and justice). This commitment to divine righteousness plays itself out in a consistent denial of salvation by works: "we were able to sell ourselves, we cannot redeem ourselves. Innocent blood was given for us; we can free ourselves from the dominion of sin not by our own strength, but by the grace of the Redeemer" (259). Such an affirmation of our bondage and the necessity of God's saving grace in Christ further mitigates the role of exemplarism alone in Abelard's soteriology.

Hedged in by these doctrinal commitments are a set of themes regarding Christ's atoning work, which call for further study. Abelard is thoroughly trinitarian, for instance, writing that the Father is "the one who was made merciful to me just as also to other sinners through his Son, our Redeemer and Mediator" (107; cf. 117)—a problematic though interesting statement. Elsewhere, Abelard integrates the role of Judas into his account of the triune God's atonement, arguing that while Peter's teaching may have led to the salvation of some, it was Judas who "brought about the common redemption of all people": for in "one and the same act, God the Father and the Son and Judas cooperated, because the Father handed over the Son, and the Son handed over himself, and Judas handed over the Lord" (154; cf. 296. Abelard also relates the Trinity and atonement in 203–204 and 231–232).

Other themes Abelard develops include the connection of the whole life of Christ with his atoning work (230), including the implications thereof for spiritual formation, a brief allusion to the work of Christ as that of prophet, priest, and king (99), and a consistent interaction with the *Christus victor* or ransom theory (154, 164–166, 264, 277, 344, 394) which consists (just as in Anselm's *Cur Deus Homo*) in a modest affirmation while denying Satan's power as the basis for the necessity of Christ's redemptive work. Abelard also briefly considers Christ's descent into hell (307, 376), and argues for Christ's vicarious bearing of our sin, that in his assumed, passible, and mortal humanity he might bear the punishment of sin for us, by the will of the Father (265–266).

All of this argues strongly against an exclusively or even dominantly exemplarist interpretation of Abelard, at least as found in his *Commentary on Romans*. This does not mean that exemplarism is not present (though we need a constant reminder that "exemplarism" is an anachronistic term, properly emerging as a theory of the atonement only during the Enlightenment period)—for Abelard places a strong emphasis not merely on our redemption from sin, but on that for which Christ saved us, "so that when we have been kindled by so great a benefit of divine grace, true charity might fear to endure nothing for his sake," and that by Christ freeing us from the slavery of sin, he might gain "for us the true liberty of the sons of God, so that we may complete all things by his love rather than by fear" (168). It is this emphasis on the role of freedom (or consent) that plays such a profound role in his *Ethics* (cf. I.29–30), which may prove to be one of the more helpful aspects of his rich and diverse work on the atonement.

Bibliography

Abelard, *Commentary on the Epistle to the Romans*, trans. Cartwright, 2011.
Fairweather, *A Scholastic Miscellany: Anselm to Ockham*, 1956.
Lane, *Bernard of Clairvaux, Theologian of the Cross*, 2013.
McGrath, "The Moral Theory of the Atonement: An Historical and Theological Critique," *Scottish Journal of Theology* 38.2, 1985.
Quinn, "Abelard on Atonement: Nothing Unintelligible, Arbitrary, Illogical, or Immoral About It," in *Reasoned Faith*, 1993.
Weingart, *The Logic of Divine Love*, 1970.
Williams, "Sin, Grace, and Redemption," in *The Cambridge Companion to Abelard*, 2004.

Acts (Book of)

I. Howard Marshall

On the assumption that Luke and Acts are two parts of a single work on Jesus and the early church by the same author, both volumes must be considered together in discussion of any aspect of his theology. We must also ask to what extent Luke and the characters in the work share the same theology: Had Luke a theology of his own that can be distinguished from that of Peter or Paul or Jesus? Does he put his own theology on the lips of these characters? Were there developments over the historical period described? And was the theology of Luke the same as that of other early Christians (and of Jesus)?

In Luke's Gospel the violent death of Jesus is prophesied and described in much the same way as in the other Gospels: Jesus must suffer because this is a divinely imposed necessity; it is in some sense a fulfillment of Scriptural prophecy (Luke 9:22, 18:31–33). Luke's depiction of it, however, is often thought to show stronger martyrological characteristics than in the other Gospels, though all four Gospels do make some reference to the death being on behalf of sinners or for their benefit or having the character of atonement (although these motifs are found in martyrology). In Mark a crucial saying of Jesus refers to his giving of his life as a ransom for many (Mark 10:45) and at the Last Supper Jesus speaks of his blood of the covenant which is poured out for many; the repetition of the phrase "for many" links these two sayings closely together and requires that we interpret each in the light of the other. Luke's Gospel, however, has no parallel to Mark 10:45 (unless we regard Luke 22:24–30 as a replacement for it with a call to lowly service and a promise of future authority and glory). The wording of the saying at the Last Supper is also problematic in light of the omission of Luke 22:19b–20 in some textual witnesses. Certainly many scholars find it easier to produce plausible arguments in favor of the originality of the longer text and its subsequent deliberate shortening rather than to the originality of this shorter form and its subsequent expansion to harmonize it with the longer wording in the other Gospels and 1 Corinthians 11:24–25.

Nevertheless, some defenders of the shorter form of wording have argued that Luke deliberately veered away from the developing doctrine of the death of Jesus having atoning significance. They confirm this conclusion by reference to the phenomena in Acts. Here in the preaching of the gospel there is very little of the reference to the crucifixion as the means of deliverance that we find in Paul, and especially in the words of 1 Corinthians 15:3–5, where early church teaching that "Christ died for our sins according to the Scriptures" is summed up by Paul who expresses his full agreement with it.

Instead the preaching of Peter, as quoted in Acts, lays the emphasis much more on the resurrection of Jesus (which, it might be argued, has little atoning role in the Gospels); the death of Jesus is the act of wicked men, though planned and foretold by God in Scripture. Its theological significance is that by raising him from death God the Father exalts him to a heavenly throne and he is empowered to declare his victory over death and Satan, through which believers are delivered from the power of sin and death. The resurrection and exaltation of Jesus give him the divine authority to be Savior and Lord (Acts 2:22–36, 5:29–31, 13:26–37).

For upholders of this view, it is the resurrection of Jesus that is the fundamental saving event. One might even say that for Luke the significance of the death of Jesus is not much more than that it is the essential prerequisite for the act of God in resurrecting Jesus. The death of Jesus is secondary so far as soteriology is concerned. The one text that might stand out from this consensus is Acts 20:28 with its ambiguous statement about the church of God which he bought with his own blood. This has been reinterpreted to signify that Jesus had to die in order to bring about the recognition of human guilt that leads to repentance (Ehrman).

The positive value of this discussion has been to make people aware that the resurrection and lordship of Jesus are central, integral, necessary elements in bringing about salvation instead of being simply the corroboration of what took place in the crucifixion. So statements to this effect are not a theological embarrassment. Rather they are close to Paul's affirmation that the way to salvation for human beings is through belief in the resurrection of Jesus and confession of him as Lord (Rom. 10:9–13). The Lucan emphasis on this element in the preaching in Acts is thus fully in harmony with the early church.

But this does not deprive the cross of its significance in Acts any more than it does in Romans! We should not, in fact, expect any such conclusion. There is not the remotest evidence that Luke tried to go against the common mind of believers in the early church, and no convincing reason for him doing so has been offered.

With regard to alleged omissions in the Gospel it needs to be recognized that when Luke omits some material from the Gospel of Mark (which provided the central structure of his own Gospel) he generally has some equivalent for it elsewhere, whether in the Gospel or in Acts. In the case of Mark 10:45, while Luke 22:24–27 provides a partial substitute for it, this is not the only such compensatory element, and I have argued elsewhere that Acts 20:28 is intended to serve such a function. Just as in Mark 10:45 the subject ("Son of Man") lays down his life to deliver "many" by offering a ransom, so in the statement by Paul in Acts 20:28 "he" (God or possibly Christ) dies ("blood") to buy or pay for the members of the church at the cost of his life. This common structure and content suggests that Luke saw this statement as equivalent to Mark 10:45.

The statement in Acts 20:28 is thus an example of the use of Gospel material related to the Gospel saying and refers to the redemption of many to become part of the new people who are the church of "the many." The creation of a kerygmatic summary with its own distinctive vocabulary rather than simply quoting the teaching of Jesus verbatim was an early church practice. The ransom saying was evidently the basis for other such statements. A similar use of the same saying is reflected in Titus 2:14 (cf. 1 Tim. 2:6); we are able to catch glimpses of the common stock of theological motifs that Paul and Luke were able to utilize. Reconciliation and redemption in Christ are seen to be closely tied to justification and victory and forgiveness (Acts 13:38–39).

Although the use of Isaiah 53 by early Christians was minimized by M. D. Hooker, there has been something of a shift in scholarly opinion toward recognizing its presence in the New Testament. Various scholars have demonstrated beyond all doubt that Luke was strongly influenced by Isaiah in both the Gospel and Acts. The influence extends to language, structure, and theology. Acts 8:32–33 contains the longest citation of a Servant text from Isaiah 53, placed prominently well toward the front of Acts. The suggestion that it omits anything to do with atonement, and that therefore Luke was not interested in it is improbable. There is no convincing explanation of how it could have come about that Luke was in some way hostile to atonement theology. Rather, the eunuch is reading a passage which might apply to him as one who is despised and rejected by other people, but does it? He and Luke's readers might have been familiar with passages in Jeremiah that reflect the experience of the prophet himself (Jer. 11:18–20): is that also the case here? Philip's answer is unexpected: this is a prophecy about Jesus who shares the lot of eunuchs and other despised people.

The resulting conclusion is that Luke (and the early Christian preachers) did a better job of interpreting the saving event as being a complex unity embracing death and resurrection, cross and empty tomb, with the resurrection and ascension bringing about the victory and enthronement of Jesus as the Lord and source of salvation after dying at the hands of sinners but nevertheless within the plan and purpose of God. It is important to remember that even for Paul the path to salvation is through confession of Jesus as Lord; it should not surprise us that Acts says the same.

Bibliography

Anderson, *"But God Raised Him from the Dead,"* 2006.
Bock, *A Theology of Luke and Acts*, 2012.
Conzelmann, *The Theology of St. Luke*, 1960.
Ehrman, *The Orthodox Corruption of Scripture*, 1993.
Hagene, *Zeiten der Wiederherstellung*, 2003.
Marshall, "The Place of Acts 20:28 in Luke's Theology of the Cross," in *Reading Acts Today*, 2011.
Mittmann-Richert, *Der Sühnetod des Gottesknechts*, 2008.
Pervo, *Acts*, 2009.
Pokorný, *Theologie der lukanischen Schriften*, 1998.
Schnabel, *Acts*, 2012.

21

Angels

Adam J. Johnson

The intersection between angelology and the doctrine of the atonement offers an indirect route for exploring the connection between the atoning work of Christ and the broader created spectrum which experiences the effects of sin, without itself having sinned.[1] Such reflection brings balance and proportion to a doctrine which runs a strong risk of being overly anthropocentric. In this chapter, we will explore some of the benefits received by the un-fallen angels from Christ's atoning death and resurrection. While angels need no saving from sin (Heb. 2:16), the New Testament relates Christ's work to them: they are said to long to understand things pertaining to the sufferings of Christ (1 Pet. 1:12), and most significantly, God reconciled to himself all things in heaven, "making peace by the blood of his cross" (Col. 1:19–20). What might it mean for the things in heaven to experience reconciliation?

The most familiar view regarding the impact of the atonement on the angels is that of Christ's work repopulating the heavenly city. Origen influentially argued that God predetermined a definite number of rational creatures, which would be sufficient for his creative purposes (289). Drawing on this idea, Augustine writes:

> Since it was not the whole company of angels that had perished by deserting God, those who had perished should remain in perpetual perdition, while those who had persevered with God … should have the joy of knowing that their future happiness was assured. As for … humanity, since they had totally perished by reason of their sins and punishments … some of them were to be restored to fill the gap left in the company of the angels by the devil's fall. (61)

---

[1] An expanded version of this chapter appeared originally as Adam Johnson, "Where Demons Fear to Tread," *Journal of Reformed Theology* 9 (2015), 37–55, reproduced with permission.

This is the same fundamental framework employed by Bernard of Clairvaux (245–246) and Anselm, who integrated this view with the question of God's honor, in *Cur Deus Homo* (289–300). On this view:

> Christ did not die for the angels, but the redemption and liberation from evil of any human by his death benefits the angels since such a person in a sense returns into good relations with them after the enmity caused between men and the holy angels by sins, and by the redemption of men the losses caused by the fall of the angels are made good. (Augustine, 90)

Second, the work of Christ affected the angels by changing their song (compare, e.g., the song of Isa. 6 with that of Rev. 5). The work of Christ, revealing the character of God to the angels in an unprecedented manner, resulted in a corresponding change and development in the worship of the angels (Aquinas, 81). As Jonathan Edwards argues in his *Miscellanies*, "The perfections of God are manifested to all creatures, both men and angels, *by the fruits of those perfections, or God's works* ... so the glorious angels have the greatest manifestations of the glory of God by what they see ... in the death and sufferings of Christ" (197). Growth in knowledge unfettered by sin, immediately resulted in spiritual growth, which in turn naturally manifests in worship. At the sight of Christ the angels are "filled with admirations of God, ascribing praise, honour, and glory unto him for evermore; for the beholding of the mystery of the wisdom of God in Christ ... is the principal part of the blessedness of the angels in heaven, which fills them with eternal delight, and is the ground of their ascribing praise and glory unto him for evermore" (Owen, 265).

But are there limits on the extent to which they can change? The church typically asked this question under the category of the "confirmation" of the angels: the point at which the choice of the angels to love and worship God is ratified so as to be irreversible. Augustine thought that consequent to the fall of the angels, the remaining angels experienced "a sure knowledge to make them secure concerning their own everlasting stability, from which they were never to fall" (60–61; Dante, 310–311). While this view proved dominant in early and medieval theology, some Protestant theologians departed from this view, tying the confirmation of the angels to the atoning work of Christ (Turrettini, 384–385).

Calvin offers one of the boldest accounts of Christ's confirmation of the angels. Of Colossians 1:20, writing:

> It was, however, necessary that angels, also, should be made to be at peace with God, for, being creatures, they were not beyond the risk of falling, had they not been confirmed by the grace of Christ ... Farther, in that very obedience which

they render to God, there is not such absolute perfection as to give satisfaction to God in every respect, and without the need of pardon. And this beyond all doubt is what is meant by that statement in Job iv.18, *He will find iniquity in his angels* ... We must, therefore, conclude that there is not on the part of angels so much of righteousness as would suffice for their being fully joined with God. They have, therefore, need of a peace-maker, through whose grace they may wholly cleave to God. (Calvin, *Colossians*, 156; emphasis in the original)

We find in John Donne delightful exploration of this theme:

How have [the angels] any reconciliation (Col. 1:19–20)? ... They needed a confirmation; for the Angels were created in blessednesse, but not in perfect blessednesse ... But to the Angels that stood, their standing being of grace, and their confirmation being not one transient act in God done at once, but a continual succession, and emanation of daily grace, belongs to this reconciliation by Christ, because all manner of grace, and where any deficiency is to be supplied ... proceeds from the Crosse, from the Merits of Christ ... Yet the Angels might fall, if this reconciler did not sustain them. (298–299)

While the possibility of angelic iniquity, fear, or lack of perfect blessedness after the fall provides one avenue for exploring this topic, focusing attention more specifically on their response to the mystery of the incarnation provides a second. John Owen says:

By the recapitulation of all things into this one head, the manifold, various, unsearchable wisdom of God was made known unto the angels themselves. They knew not before of the design and work of God after the entrance of sin. These could not comprehend the wisdom that might repair that loss ... But hereby the manifold wisdom of God, his infinite wisdom in the treasures of it, able by various ways to attain the ends of his glory, was made known unto them. (374)

This similar to John Newton, who suggests that "there are likewise an innumerable company of *elect* or *good* angels (Rev. iii.11) who were *preserved* by sovereign grace, and are now *established* (together with believers) in Christ Jesus" (199).

A variant of this line of inquiry relates the confirmation of the angels to the work of the Holy Spirit. Basil, for instance, wrote that "the ministering spirits exist by the will of the Father, are brought into being by the work of the Son, and are perfected by the presence of the Spirit, since angels are perfected by perseverance in holiness" (62). John of Damascus similarly held that "through the Word, therefore, all the angels were created, and through the sanctification by the Holy Spirit were they brought to perfection" (19). Drawing these reflections together, we might reaffirm that the atonement of Jesus Christ is effective for the angels in that it is through his death and resurrection that they are confirmed by means of the Spirit of the risen Lord Jesus Christ, whose ministry of sanctification is the same (generally speaking) for the angels as it is for us, in that he makes the power of the atonement real and effective in us.

Our fourth line of inquiry considers the impact of Christ's atonement upon the unfallen angels as he becomes their "head," bringing order to the angelic ranks (and the whole of creation). The *Catholic Catechism* states, "Christ is the center of the angelic world. They are *his* angels … They belong to him because they were created *through* and *for* him" (86). That they were created for Christ opens the interesting possibility of a *telos* yet to be fulfilled: the idea that Christ has not always been the center of their world in the same way. Calvin inquires: "But who might reach [fallen man]? … One of the angels? They also had need of a head, through) whose bond they might cleave firmly and undividedly to their God" (Calvin, *Inst.*, 464; cf. Eph. 1:22; Col. 2:10). While in some manner Jesus has always been the head of the angels (they were created through and for him), the way in which the triune God elected himself to be head of the angels was as the incarnate Son, Jesus Christ—and therefore the angels awaited their rightful head from the time of their creation until the incarnation, passion, and ascension of Jesus.

Thinking about angels helps us to "resist the confines of our usual theological constructions of the relation between God and creatures" (Pauw, 56). And how does reflecting on the relationship between Christ's atoning death and the angels help us resist our usual theological constructions of the atonement? Reflecting on the intersection of angelology and soteriology helps cultivate our appreciation of the atonement as ordered toward creation as a whole, rather than merely an act directed at remedying the problem of human sin. That is to say, Christ's atonement is intended by God to bring to completion his treasured creation, which of course includes dealing with human sin, but reaches far beyond it, including the above ways of bringing wholeness and completion to the angelic realm.

Bibliography

Aquinas, *Commentary on Saint Paul's Epistle to the Ephesians*, trans. Lamb, 1966.
Augustine, *The Augustine Catechism*, trans. Harbert, 1999.
Basil, *On the Holy Spirit*, trans. Hildebrand, 2011.
Bernard of Clairvaux, *Bernard of Clairvaux: Selected Works*, trans. Evans, 1987.

Calvin, *The Epistle of Paul the Apostle to the Galatians, Ephesians, Philippians Colossians, Thessalonians, Timothy, Titus and Philemon*, trans. Pringle, 1979.
Calvin, *Institutes*, 1960.
Catechism of the Catholic Church, 1994.
Damascus, *Orthodox Faith*, 1995.
Dante, *The Divine Comedy*, trans. Sayers, 1955.
Donne, *The Sermons of John Donne*, 1959.
Edwards, *The Works of Jonathan Edwards*, vol. 20, 2002.
Newton, *The Works of the Rev. John Newton*, vol. 1, 1847.
Origen, *De Principiis*, in Ante Nicene Fathers of the Christian Church, 2004.
Owen, *Works*, vol. 1, 1965.
Pauw, "Where Theologians Fear to Tread," *Modern Theology* 16:1, 2000.
Turrettini, *Institutes of Elenctic Theology*, 1992.

22

The Apostolic Fathers

Harry O. Maier

The Apostolic Fathers, like the writings of the New Testament, portray Jesus's death with a spectrum of terms, concepts, and metaphors.[1] The documents sometimes use different vocabulary or more expansively interpret Jesus's death, but in general they share ideas found in the canon. Yet it should also be stated at the outset that it is surprising, given the importance of theologies of atonement in later centuries, that these writers give relatively little attention to the atoning nature of Jesus's death. Indeed, in the case of the *Didache* there is no direct reference to it or its salvific significance. Further, where these authors refer to it soteriologically, like New Testament writers, they do so without a concise explanation as to its precise mechanism. Polycarp, for example, in his *Epistle to the Philippians*, invokes atonement only once, when he refers to "our Lord Jesus Christ, who endured for our sins, facing even death [*hos hypeneinen hyper tōn hamartiōn heōs thanatou katantēsai*], whom God raised up, having loosed [*lusas*] the birth pangs of Hades [*odinas tou hadou*]" (Pol. Phil. 1:2). This evocative language places the death of Jesus in a belief Polycarp shares with his audience, but he nowhere expands on it.

The dearth of detailed atonement theology may be due to the fact that these authors could assume beliefs and cultural expectations without mentioning them and could invoke them without further explication. A red thread that runs through all the writings is the belief that suffering for another entails a reciprocal social arrangement, in which one returns honor for benefits received, and

---

[1] The Apostolic Fathers, a phrase used from the seventeenth century to describe a set of authors contemporary with New Testament writers, include Clement of Rome, Ignatius of Antioch, Hermas, Polycarp of Smyrna, Papias, as well as the anonymous authors of the *Epistle of Barnabas*, the *Didache*, the *Epistle to Diognetus*, and *2 Clement*. This volume dedicates a separate discussion to ideas of atonement found in Ignatius of Antioch.

that sacrifice is a chief means by which God and God's people relate with one another. Still, one must proceed with caution and not explain earlier texts with later concepts, or introduce them where they are absent or unspoken. Often, the same texts are patient of multiple interpretations and theological frameworks. Modern readers who come to these writers are like people who are listening in on a conversation that began before writers composed their documents and continued after they finished them. None of the Apostolic Fathers dedicates himself to the subject of "the atonement": these are occasional writings in which soteriological reference to Jesus's death takes place in a larger context of exhortation, admonition, ethical instruction, apologetic, polemic, and so on. Like New Testament writings, these texts invite us to enter narrative worlds in which reference to Jesus's death forms a part of larger persuasive strategies.

The two writings of the Apostolic Fathers that give the fullest account of the atonement are *1 Clement*, a letter to the church in Corinth attributed to Clement of Rome, and the pseudonymous *Letter of Barnabas*. *1 Clement* seeks to heal divisions that erupted in Corinth when certain church officials were replaced with other leaders. *Barnabas* is a polemical letter directed against Judaizing opponents, designed to convince a Gentile audience that it is the true inheritor of God's covenantal promises to Israel. To achieve their rhetorical aims these writers deploy Hebrew Bible notions of atonement. Clement casts the divisions in Corinth as factionalism and sedition. With the help of commonplaces drawn from political treatments of concord, he represents those responsible for conflict as transgressors who have destroyed the harmony the Corinthians once enjoyed. Clement invokes the death of Jesus as an exemplary and sacrificial death that brought salvation; the usurpers risk undermining their redemption through division. His descriptions of Jesus's death are valuable because they show the kinds of terms and concepts a writer roughly contemporary with the Synoptic Gospels as well as the deutero-Pauline writings was using to convey the religious meaning of the crucifixion. Clement acclaims the love of Christ when he refers to Jesus as the one who "gave his blood for us, and his flesh for our flesh, and his life for our lives" (49.6). Central to his rhetorical strategy is his citation of Old Testament/Hebrew Bible texts. This he does in a way more thoroughgoing than in the New Testament. In 12.1–8 he typologically exegetes Rahab's tying a scarlet cord in the window (Josh. 2:18–21). For Clement this is proof of the atoning death of Christ as redemption: Rahab shows that "it is clear that through the blood of the Lord redemption [*lutrōsis*] will come to all who believe and hope in God" (12:7). Later, in 16.3–14, he quotes the whole of the LXX Isaiah 53:1–12 as a description of the atoning sacrifice of Jesus and the exchange of his life for sinners. But for him the text also conveys another message, namely, that such a death also depicts Jesus's humility (16.1–2), an ethic the Corinthians are to imitate. He rhetorically presents the atonement to portray the Corinthian insurrectionists as proud; indeed, it is those like them who made Jesus suffer. The death of Jesus points to their continuing sin and need for forgiveness and hence the ongoing effects of Jesus's atonement as cleansing (8.4, quoting LXX Is. 1:16–20). A similar theme occurs in 21.6 where Clement describes "the Lord Jesus Christ, whose blood was given for us [*to haima hyper hēmōn*]." Later Clement makes a similar connection. In 35.12 he describes Jesus as "the high priest of our offerings, the benefactor and helper of our weakness." The language and conceptualization here echoes Hebrews 8:3, a document that may also come from Rome and be contemporary with *1 Clement*. In contrast to Hebrews, where the writer develops the notion of Christ as high priest to affirm the once and for all sacrifice of Jesus, *1 Clement* invokes it to furnish the basis for the analogy that follows in 40.5–44.6. Here Clement connects Hebrew Bible concerns that right sacrifice be made by rightly appointed priests with obedience to properly appointed Christian officials. The whole development then serves not to outline a theory of atonement but to convey the importance of church harmony and the healing of faction.

The *Epistle of Barnabas* works with a far more elaborate and complex set of Hebrew Bible texts, symbols, and traditions to represent the atonement. Here the application is at once polemical against Jews, whose covenant, pseudo-Barnabas argues, has been cancelled and given to Christians, and hortatory, that Christians live faithfully as God's newly cleansed people. Barnabas deploys a variety of atonement concepts: cleansing/purification (5.1, 8.3, 11.10), destruction of death (5.6), renewal (6.11), a means of a second creation (6.13–14), innocent suffering (5.2), atoning sacrifice (7.2–3, 8.3), scapegoat (7.7–9), and healing (13.7). He develops these concepts through extensive quotation of the Hebrew Bible and typological exegesis. The sacrifice of Isaac is a type for Jesus's sacrifice for sins (7.3); Moses's outstretched arms (Ex. 17:8–13) is a type for the cross (11.2–5); and the viewing of the lifted serpent in the wilderness (Num. 21:8–9) is symbolic of those who place their hope of new life on the cross (11.6–7). The most elaborate typology (7.1–8.7), however, centers on the scapegoat ritual of the Day of Atonement (Lev. 16:3–37, 23:26–32, 25:9; Ex. 30:10; Num. 29:7–11) and the sacrifice of a red heifer to purify water for the cleansing of impurity (Num. 19:1–10). In the case of the scapegoat, Barnabas bases his typology on details that are foreign to the biblical narrative, and parallel treatment found in in the Babylonian Talmud, especially Yoma 4a–8b. Possibly he drew them from another unknown, perhaps apocryphal, tradition. The description in Leviticus prescribes ritual actions with two goats, one driven into the wilderness (the Azazel) and the other sacrificed. Unlike the biblical account, Barnabas quotes an account that has the priest eat the intestines of the "goat that is offered at the fast of our sins" washed with vinegar for God to consume, while people fast and lament clothed with sackcloth (7.4–5). This is a type for the vinegar and gall offered Jesus when crucified (7.3). Equally different from the biblical account is his account of the Azazel goat (7.7–9), "the type of Jesus who was destined to suffer" (v. 10). Barnabas quotes a source that prescribes that scarlet wool be tied around the goat's head, and which the people spit upon and jab as it is driven into the wilderness. (The reference to scarlet wool parallels the Babylonian Talmud (Yoma 67a), which, of course, does not offer a Christological application.) The red wool represents Jesus's crucifixion—his wearing of a scarlet robe, mockery, and piercing. Barnabas similarly expands the account of the heifer sacrifice (8.1–7), where after its sacrifice the people take the ashes and tie a red piece of wool around a piece of wood and hyssop and sprinkle the people with water. He explains, "The calf is Jesus; the sinful men who offer it are those who brought him to the slaughter ... The children who sprinkle are those who preached to us the good news about the forgiveness of sins and the purification of the heart" (v. 3). These typologies function both polemically to relate the Passion narratives to Jewish rejection of Jesus and as injunctions to faithfulness as the new inheritors of God's favor. Barnabas teaches that suffering and death achieve the removal of impurity and sin, received through baptism.

Some of the Apostolic Fathers concentrate their attention on the meaning of the death of Jesus for Gentile idolaters. The author of *2 Clement* addresses an audience of former polytheists who have converted to monotheism. The anonymous *Epistle to Diognetus* is an apology addressed to persecutors. *2 Clement*, like Paul, cites "the suffering Jesus Christ endured for our sake [*heneka hēmōn*]." His suffering attests to his mercy and compassion: "he saved us ... even though he had seen in us so much deception and destruction" (1.7). The author, in a way analogous to Barnabas, likens this as a creation: "he called us when we did not exist [*hēmas ouk ontas*], and out of nothing he willed us into being [*ek mē ontos einai hēmas*]" (v. 8). The *Epistle to Diognetus* defends Christian faith with an appeal to the necessity of Jesus's death for sinners. Its author states that when punishment and death—the wages of sin, together with humankind's inability to save itself—were revealed, God in his love for the unrighteous "gave up [*apedoto*] his own Son as a ransom for us [*lutron hyper hēmōn*], the holy one for the lawless, the guiltless for the guilty, the just for the unjust, the incorruptible for the corruptible, the immortal for the mortal." The logic here is not unlike Romans 3.24-26, although there God has presented (*proetheto*) Jesus as a *hilasterion*, a term that ranges in meaning from expiation to propitiation in a possible connection with the Seat of Mercy associated with sacrificial ritual for atonement. He echoes Paul more directly when he goes on to describe Jesus's death as "the sweet exchange [*glukeias antallagēs*]" and "the incomprehensible work of God [*anexichniastou dēmiourgias*] ... that the sinfulness [*anomia*] of many should be hidden in one righteous person [*en dikaiō heni krybē*], while the righteousness [*dikaiosynē*] of one should righteous [*dikaiōsē*] many sinners [*anomous*]" (Diog. 9.2-5). The author nowhere indicates to whom the ransom is paid or why, whether as restoration, purchase, compensation, or reparation, the range of meanings the term *lutron* has in the LXX. The letter's chief aim is to affirm the love and mercy of God rather than to outline transactional mechanisms (9.6).

Finally, the *Shepherd of Hermas* (broadly classified as an Apocalypse) presents the atonement of Jesus as a strategy for exhortation and admonition. It forms a series of visions, commandments, and allegorical parables designed to convince Roman believers that they have not kept the baptismal covenant, due largely to their pursuit of wealth and business at the expense of care for the poor and virtuous conduct. Hermas refers to Jesus's death only in one passage, as the "cleansing [*katharizein*]" of sins or people (*Sim.* 5.6.2-3). Baptism as the washing away of impurity confers the benefits of Jesus' death. Hermas expects that believers, once baptized, will preserve purity through obedience to God's commands and thus win salvation (Man. 8.2-6, 12.1-6). Hermas's interest is to admonish Roman Christians to repent of their sins. He thus emphasizes obedience rather than atonement as the chief means of purity, but the former would not be possible for Hermas without the latter.

Bibliography

Aloisi, "'His Flesh for our Flesh': The Doctrine of Atonement in the Second Century," *Detroit Baptist Seminary Journal* 14, 2009.

Danker, "Bridging St. Paul and the Apostolic Fathers: A Study in Reciprocity," *Currents in Theology and Mission* 15, 1988.

Stökl Ben Ezra, *The Impact of Yom Kippur on Early Christianity: The Day of Atonement from Second Temple Judaism to the Fifth Century*, 2003.

Torrance, *The Doctrine of Grace in the Apostolic Fathers*, 1996.

23

Ascension

Andrew Burgess

The atonement God works in Christ and his ascension are often not held together, although ancient sources do so regularly, and a new interest in this matter is rising. For many modern Western theologians, the cross alone is the moment of Jesus's atoning work, and the resurrection and ascension do not add anything in this regard. Jesus's identity as ascended "High Priest" may well be acknowledged, but not as adding in any way to atonement completed on the cross. Many serious discussions of atonement lack any reflection upon Jesus's ascension.

A second broad approach is far stronger on the link between ascension and atonement via an emphasis on atonement as a function of Christ's being in the hypostatic union of human and divine natures expressed in his obedient acts, including his suffering, death, resurrection, and ascension. This approach lends itself to seeing Jesus's ascension to "God's place" as the final step in the movement of reconciling fallen creatures to the Creator and recreating humanity in union with him. In this fashion the atoning work of the Spirit is connected to the goal of creating a new humanity in union with Christ as he is active in the heavenly sphere. We might note 1 Corinthians 15 and the claim there that without Christ's resurrection we remain dead under the power of sin. Resurrection and ascension are readily understood together in this regard, so that Barth, for example, saw resurrection as two poles of one event straddling the forty days of appearances. Such understandings sit well with the patristic thought of Irenaeus, Athanasius, Gregory Nazianzen, and Cyril of Alexandria, for instance. A strong recent example can be found in T. F. Torrance (especially *The Trinitarian Faith* and *Space, Time and Resurrection*). The latter work is of particular note as a twentieth-century attempt to address Jesus's ascension.

Although he does not have a great deal of material directly connecting Jesus's saving work to his ascension and ascended state, like Barth, Torrance strongly links resurrection and ascension. Much that he has to say about resurrection and atonement (in *Space, Time and Resurrection*) should also be connected to ascension, in addition to the explicitly ascension-focused material. Indeed, reconciliation between God and humanity is not only a matter of Jesus's acts or achievements, as in the hypostatic union of divine and human natures Jesus Christ *is* intercessor and advocate (Torrance might well say that he *is* intercession and advocacy), as his very being and act are together atonement on behalf of humanity. "It is an Advocacy in which his Word and Person and Act are one and indivisible" (*The Trinitarian Faith*, 116). In William Milligan's late-nineteenth-century treatment Jesus's ascension functions to make possible his role as High Priest—it is only as ascended that Jesus has this role and function. In Torrance, although he commends Milligan's treatment, it is less clear that this is so. However, Torrance certainly sees Jesus as High Priest prior to resurrection and ascension, and thus what happens in the ascension is an ongoing fulfilment of what was always there, but offers significant encouragement to see Christ's ascended role as actively advocating and uniting believers to the life of God.

Farrow further provides an extremely significant discussion of Jesus ascended and the Church (*Ascension and Ecclesia*). There is limited reference to atonement themes as such, but Farrow is clear that union with Christ's ascended humanity is the goal of salvation, worked out largely in relation to Eucharistic participation. Irenaeus and *recapitulation* are to the fore. Recently Michael Horton has written on believers' participation in the life of Jesus ascended, especially in relation to Irenaeus and Reformed theology. Horton's essay contrasts Origin's reading of ascension—as a spiritualized movement away from embodiment—against Irenaeus and his emphasis on the ascension of Christ in his resurrection body. Horton discusses Reformed writers such as Calvin, Ursinus, and Turretin, and also John Owen, who follow Irenaeus's track and emphasize participation in Christ and the (chastened) deification involved as the goal and crown of atonement. Horton likewise shows Calvin to place significant weight on *recapitulation*: Christ's obedience as his saving work across his entire incarnate journey, centrally but not only in the removal of guilt through the cross (so *Inst*, 2.12.3, also see 4.17 and commentaries, especially on Ephesians and Colossians). Jesus's ascension is key to humans being united to God so as to share in the life that God gives, glorified with the glory of Christ's ascended humanity.

The general move here is to understand that the movement and work of atonement is not complete until Christ is ascended and that it is in the ascension that Jesus's people are united with him in "at-one-ment" with God. So Horton has it that "the atonement should be seen as a central aspect of recapitulation that is realized in the whole life and ministry of Christ from the incarnation to his return in glory" (235).

An important addition to the conversation comes from recent discussion of Jesus's ascension and atoning work as High Priest in Hebrews and further in Luke-Acts. Moffitt examines the strong emphasis in Hebrews on Jesus's self-offering as culminating in the heavenly sanctuary ("Atonement and the Logic of Resurrection"). Central to his work is the argument that in Old Testament sacrificial liturgy the death of the animal was not the culmination but a necessary step in the movement, with the offering of the "life" of the animal in the sanctuary marking the peak of atoning action. So Jesus's ascension to the Father as the "lamb who was slain" and presentation of his life as sacrifice, in the true sanctuary, mark the peak of his atoning work. Moffitt argues for a similar understanding in Luke-Acts, claiming that the well-known lack of sacrificial language in relation to the cross in these writings is explained by Luke's understanding of atonement taking place in the final movement—Christ's presentation of himself as the atoning sacrifice in the presence of the Father ("Atonement at the Right Hand").

As a counterpoint Karl Barth sounded a different note in refusing to align Jesus's humiliation and exaltation to consecutive periods of the incarnation. Barth certainly sees an exaltation in Jesus's ascension, but it is the exaltation of the "Son of Man" who is *already* exalted in being united to God in the *hypostatic union*, so that Barth sees a humiliation of the Son of God in being united to sinful human being (*CD* §59 and §64). While Barth takes the ascension seriously and it has considerable influence on his theology (Burgess), the question is whether the emphasis on concurrent humiliation and exaltation removes too much active significance from the ascension as a distinct event (for this complaint, see Farrow, *Ascension and Ecclesia*). While Barth is a theologian who emphasizes *recapitulation* as the center of atonement, does the ascension add in any way to the movement of atonement enacted from conception to cross? Torrance believed that here Barth was in error (*CD*), and Farrow is even more concerned about Barth on this point (*Ascension and Ecclesia*, 243ff). Deciding on the adequacy of Barth's theology of Christ ascended will likely turn on verdicts regarding the sufficiency of his Pneumatology, doctrine of Sanctification, and treatments of human agency.

Overall, the key question of Jesus ascended and atonement theology focuses on the all-sufficiency of the cross as atoning, or upon inclusion of the resurrection, ascension, and ongoing life of Christ in atonement, especially as believers participate in his life. Pneumatological concerns will be to the fore. Additionally this may connect strongly to Jesus's self-offering as the atoning sacrifice in the "heavenly sanctuary" as the culmination of an atoning sacrifice.

Bibliography

Barth, *CD*.
Burgess, *The Ascension in Karl Barth*, 2004.
Calvin, *Commentary on Colossians*.
Calvin, *Institutes*.
Farrow, *Ascension and Ecclesia*, 1999.
Farrow, *Ascension Theology*, 2011.
Horton, "Atonement and Ascension," in *Locating Atonement*, 2015.
Milligan, *The Ascension of Our Lord*, 1891.
Moffitt, "Atonement and the Logic of Resurrection in the Epistle to the Hebrews," *NT* Sup. 141, 2011.
Moffitt, "Atonement at the Right Hand: The Sacrificial Significance of Jesus' Exaltation in Acts," in *New Testament Studies*, 62.4, 2016.
Torrance, *Space, Time and Resurrection*, 1976.
Torrance, *The Trinitarian Faith*, 1988.

24

Augustine

David Vincent Meconi

Saint Augustine of Hippo (354–430) never composed a treatise focused solely on the meaning and mechanics of Christ's atonement. What he has to say on the nature of expiation of human sinfulness and consequent reconciliation with the Father is a theological kaleidoscope with many moving parts found in several different places. The purpose of this chapter is to show where and how to retrieve these insights, arguing that Augustine holds a threefold doctrine of atonement: (1) beginning in the identification of our own need for salvation, (2) Christ's subsequent unifying himself to each of the elect, and (3) their final deifying transformation.

Since these elements of Augustinian atonement are strewn throughout his amazing output of hundreds of doctrinal works, sermons, and letters (5.4 million words), the standard manuals canvassing the history of Christian atonement prove minimally helpful. Augustine's theory of atonement goes well beyond the overly facile "ransom theory" that Christ's death on the cross paid a debt to Satan incurred by human disobedience (*Enchiridion* [*ench.*] §41; *Expositions of the Psalms* [*en. Ps.*] 64.6; *sermon* [*s.*] 263), and it is not reducible to the cross acting as a "mouse trap" (*muscupula diaboli*; *s.* 130.2, 265D.5) by which God tricks the devil into taking the bait. While these traditional categories are certainly present in Augustine's vision of the cross and its effects on those who draw near to Christ on Calvary, no one model exhausts how Augustine thinks atonement works.

So, what exactly is a theology of atonement, and why is it a crucial tenet of Augustine's theology? Think of this doctrine as a bridge connecting two opposite extremes separated by a direly deep chasm. On one side of the chasm stands sinful humanity, self-centered, habitually concupiscent children of Adam, and far off to the other side is the crucified Christ whose loving countenance seeks to woo the sinner ever nearer. Augustine's theology of atonement thus seeks to make sense of how Christ's sacrificial life and death effect a transformation in sinners. To understand this better, let us now turn to these three moments of identification, incorporation, and transformation. *Some places for further study of basic atonement language: Confessions [conf.] 4.12.19, 10.42.67–70; s. 130, 134; Commentary on the Letter to the Galatians [ex. Gal.] 22.8; ench. §108; Homilies on the Gospel of John [Jo. eu. tr.] 3.3, 41.5, 50.2, 79.2; Homilies on the First Epistle of John 2.14; On Admonition and Grace [corrept.] 10.27–11.30.*

Identification

The first step in Augustinian atonement theory is a twofold identification: (1) fallen humans must first identify themselves as sinful (2) only by identifying the crucified Christ who has become ugly for the sake of sinners' beauty. "Christ had taken the identity of the first human being to himself … for it is by longing for him and imitating his passion that we are made new" (*en. Ps.* 37:27; Augustine, *Expositions* III/16, 166). Since such identity formation for Bishop Augustine is a matter of deep personal introspection fostered best through the silence and ritual of Christian worship, it is not surprising to find most of his theology of atoning identity in his sermons. Liturgy is where and how the truest look at ourselves can be realized. We accordingly hear our preacher challenge his congregation to let him help show them who they truly are: "You blame others, you don't look at yourself; you accuse others, you don't think about yourself; you place others before your eyes, you place yourself behind your back. When I accuse, I do the opposite. I take you from behind your back, and put you down in front of your eyes" (*s.*17.5; Augustine, *Sermons* III/1, 369). Why do people not want to face their truest selves? Because it would mean seeing our own pride and infidelities; but in denying a true examination of our souls, we inevitably eclipse God from acting in our lives as well: "So, those who won't acknowledge the Creator are proudly denying their maker, while those who deny their sickness don't acknowledge the necessity of a savior. So let us both praise the Creator for our nature, and for the flaw in it which we have inflicted on ourselves" (*s.* 156.2; Hill, *Sermons* III/5, 97).

In his goodness, God has made us human; in our sin, we have made ourselves less than human. As such, admitting our own repulsiveness is the first step in effecting the atoning work of Christ:

> First of all, you must find your deformity displeasing, and then you will receive beauty from him whom you hope to please by being beautiful. He who formed you in the beginning will reform you … If in your ugly condition you find

yourself repulsive, you are already pleasing to your beautiful bridegroom ... Begin by admitting your ugliness, the deformity of soul that results from sins and iniquity. Initiate your confession by accusing yourself of this ugliness, for as you confess you become more seemly. And who grants this to you? Who else but he who is fairer than any of humankind? (*en. Ps.* 103, *exp.* 1.4; Boulding III/19, 10–11; *s.* 301A.2)

Through this process of dual-identification, the Father uses the lowliness of his Son on the cross to attract our attention. Before the cross, we are invited to take the truest look at ourselves to see both our sinfulness and its lethal effects, but even more truly our own redemption and promise of new life.

In fact, this is how the Father persuades us (*persuadendum*) us of his love, thereby assuring us that his love is greater than our sins. Through the Son's humility on the cross, God shows us simultaneously both his care as well as our own wretchedness: the cross shows his love so we know our worth, it reveals our sins so we desist in our pride. God thus "arranged it so that the power of charity would be brought to perfection in the weakness of humility" (*On the Trinity* [*Trin.*] 4.2, 153). In holding up the bloody and mortal Christ as a mirror of our human condition, Augustine wants to show us how our own wounds are healed. In this identification he invites sinful humanity to see its own ugliness now made beautiful in Christ. Beholding the blood of the cross helps us to see the toxicity of our own concupiscence that placed Christ there. If we remain in such pride, we will never see the cross as beautiful, but if we find our own deformities displeasing, we will receive Christ's own beauty precisely there. This sort of identifying our haughtiness with Christ's lowliness leads to our incorporation into Christ. Through operative grace, the sinner stops seeking to flee and finally offers him or herself to God. Here one receives God's own self, as Christ extends his very life to make the faithful into other sons and daughters. *Some places for further study of Identity: s.* 73A; *Trin.* 4 and 13; *Faith and Creed* §4.6; *On True Religion* §16.32; *Instructing Beginners* §48.

Incorporation

God uses the experiences of our lives to draw us to himself, the way the heart is drawn by its bands of love (cf. *Jo. eu. tr.* 26.4–7). To show this, Augustine most often relies on a rich image of the "whole Christ" (*totus Christus*), his method of showing how Jesus the Head chooses to identify himself with his

Body the Church. This is an essential move in understanding Augustinian atonement because love always identifies with the beloved. That is, in his love for sinners, Christ neither glosses over the grave condition of sinners, nor simply forgives from afar. In his self-emptying, the incarnate Son becomes one with all of humanity and in this assumption of the human condition, all can see in Christ his or her own humanity. Most often this type of identification appears whenever Augustine uses various lines from Matthew 25 ("Whatever you do to the least of these, you do to me") or Acts 9:4 ("Saul, Saul, why do you persecute me?"). Inevitably, Augustine will use these two loci to depict the extension of Christ's own heavenly body into his mystical body on earth. For example, notice the casual movement from identification ("look at ourselves") to incorporation where our truest identity is the "whole Christ," head and body:

> Now, however, I wonder if we shouldn't have a look at ourselves, if we shouldn't think about his body, because he is also us (*quia et nos ipse est*). After all, if we weren't him, this wouldn't be true: *When you did it for one of the least of mine, you did it for me* (Mt 25:40). If we weren't him, this wouldn't be true: *Saul, Saul, why are you persecuting me?* (Acts 9:4). So we too are him, because we are his organs, because we are his body, because he is our head, because the whole Christ is both head and body. (s. 133.8; Hill, *Sermons* III/4, 338; s. 263A.2; *en. Ps.* 21.3, 40.6)

This incorporation of Christians into Christ is effected in the sacrifice of the Eucharist, where Augustine tells his faithful, the Body of Christ, to see their own lives on the altar: "it's the mystery meaning you that has been placed on the Lord's table; what you receive is the mystery that means you" (s. 272; Hill, *Sermons* III/7, 300; *Jo. eu. tr.* 26.13–18).

Most of Augustine's reflections on the atoning power of charity are found in his commentaries on the Gospel and Epistles of John, to which he turned in order to combat the ever-divisive Donatists. The unity which grace effects not only atones for the most dastardly of repentant sinners (something the Donatist could not allow), thereby bringing him or her back into ecclesial communion, it makes one into another Christ:

> Let us congratulate ourselves then and give thanks for having been made not only Christians but Christ. Do you understand, brothers and sisters, the grace of God upon us; do you grasp that? Be filled with wonder, rejoice and be glad; we have been made Christ. For if he is the head, and we the members, then he and we are the whole man … The fullness of Christ, then, is the head and the

members. What is that, head and members? Christ and the Church. (*Jo. eu. tr.* 21.8; Hill I/12, 379)

Atonement is an ecclesial reality for Augustine: the stress he gives is on how Christ saves his people, his body, and not just disparate individuals. The church is where and how God's people are brought out of their sinful self-centeredness and adopted into his own life. *Some places for further study of Incorporation: s.* 15, 115, 166, 337, 341; *ciu. Dei,* 10.6, 19.23; *en. Ps.* 26, *exp.* 2.2, 40.6; *Jo. eu. tr.* 108.5.

Transformation

Incorporation is inevitably transformative and that is why atonement for Augustine ultimately means deification. The oneness achieved through the incarnate Son's physical death for our spiritual death not only awakens our soul but divinizes us into new creatures—adopted children of the Father, coheirs with Christ, temples of the Holy Spirit (*ench.* §15.56). This is why Augustinian atonement is much richer than standard accounts appreciate: it bridges the heart's ultimate desire with the greatest promise God could possibly make a creature:

> We carry mortality about with us, we endure infirmity, we look forward to divinity. For God wishes not only to vivify, but also to deify us. When would human infirmity ever have dared to hope for this, unless divine truth had promised it?
> ... Still, it was not enough for our God to promise us divinity in himself, unless he also took on our infirmity. (*s.* 23B.1, Hill, *Sermons* III/11, 37)

Since justification leads to divinization, and are oftentimes synonymous in Augustine's mind, he always sets Christ's atoning work in a larger picture of our deifying transformation: God becomes human and undergoes the toxic effects of our disobedience on the cross in order to turn us into his own brothers and sisters.

While Augustine has no problem calling the elect "gods" or "other Christs," he most often draws from originally Pauline "great exchange" imagery (e.g., 2 Cor. 8:9) to describe how atonement occurs. On the cross, God exchanges his weakness for our power; his *kenosis* is humanity's *theosis*. That is why the bishop exhorts his flock to appreciate the vulnerability which first unites God to sinners, thus pointing to the weakness of the crucified one: "There you have something for your infirmity, something for your becoming perfect. Let Christ set you on your feet by that in him which is man, let him lead you forward by that in him which is God-man, let him lead you right through to that which is God" (*Jo. eu. tr.* 23.6; Hill, 410; *s.* 80, 128; *ex. Gal.* 17.7–9). This is the purpose of the Incarnation as a whole and the cross in particular; to transform the sinner into a saint.

Augustine never cowers from stressing the lowliness of Christ because only here can the lowly be transformed into godly creatures: "You were [children] of men and you have become (*estis facti*) [children] of God. He has shared with us our ills, and he is going to give us his goods" (*s.* 121.5; Hill, *Sermons* III/4, 236; *conf.* 7.18.24; *en. Ps.* 49.2, 103, *exp.* 4.1, 118.9.2). As such, Christ's death offers much more than instruction or moral improvement. The atoning work of Christ Augustine envisages may begin by justifying the sinner and removing the concupiscence he or she once so freely embraced, but it ends in the divinizing elevation of mortals into immorality, humans into divinity. *Some places for further study of Transformation: ep.* 10.2; *s.* 117.17, 192.1; *Jo. eu. tr.* 22.1; *en. Ps.* 33, *exp.* 1.6, 45.14, 102.22).

Conclusion

To see the fullness of what Augustine of Hippo is doing when he preaches or theologizes on the cross of Christ, one must keep these three factors in mind. Augustine almost always begins with an invitation to self-reflection and therein has his readers and hearers see who they are becoming in light of the love of Christ. Second comes his Christology of unity and his stress on Christ sharing the fragility of sinful humanity. Third, this incarnation lifts the wicked out of the dissolution and death their disobedience brings, and renders them into children of God. This building up of the "one Christ" (*ep. Jo.* 10.3) is ultimately the only purpose of Augustine's theology of atonement.

Bibliography

Augustine, *Expositions* 3.16, 2000.
Augustine, *On the Trinity*, 1991.
Augustine, *Sermons* 3.1, 2007.
Aulén, *Christus Victor*, 1969.

Cavadini, "Jesus's Death Is Real: An Augustinian Spirituality of the Cross," in *The Cross in Christian Tradition: From Paul to Bonaventure*, ed., Dryer, 2000.

Cavadini, "The Tree of Silly Fruit: Images of the Cross in St. Augustine," in *The Cross in Christian Tradition: From Paul to Bonaventure*, ed., Dryer, 2000.

Fairbairn, *Grace and Christology in the Early Church*, 2003.

Turner, *The Patristic Doctrine of Redemption*, 1952.

25

Gustaf Aulén

Roland Spjuth

Gustaf Aulén's book *Christus Victor* can be regarded as one of the most influential soteriological books of the twentieth century. Originally based on lectures he held at the University of Uppsala, Sweden, in the year 1930, it was published in English with certain minor revisions the year after. In this book, Aulén presents the doctrine of atonement in terms of a history of three different types that emerged in a particular sequence: in the Ancient Church views of the Christus Victor type, then views of the Latin type formulated by Anselm that became dominant then in Protestant Orthodoxy, and finally views of the subjective type proclaimed by Protestant liberalism. Aulén claimed that the Christus Victor type represented the classical (earliest) model. After the publication of Aulén's book, writings on the atonement in Protestant theology typically employed Aulén's typology in presenting differing views regarding the atonement and for promoting their own contributions.

Christus Victor was one of several books that emerged within a new theological milieu that developed early in the twentieth century. Aulén was born in 1879 in a family in which the father was a vicar in the Swedish Lutheran Church. When Aulén began his theological studies at the University of Uppsala, he encountered both a Swedish theology and a Swedish Church that he considered to be at "a historical low point." Theologians there were split between a rationalistic Lutheran Orthodoxy that had lost its attraction and a liberal theology that had compromised its faith. Aulén's theology can be seen as a part of the theology of crisis incipient at the beginning of the twentieth century, although he was not directly influenced by dialectical theology. According to him, this crisis was most obvious within soteriology. His aim in writing *Christus Victor* was to show that neither the doctrine of penal substitution nor the subjective motif of moral influence held true to the inner essence of the Christian faith. The genius of *Christus Victor* was its claim that the retrieval of earlier theological traditions would both create and open up alternatives to the conflicting positions present at the time. He viewed the notion of victory as a kind of "trumpet-call" stemming from the early church and able to lift the church from its current crisis.

Aulén maintained very strongly, however, that *Christus Victor* was not a constructive or apologetic work but was instead a rigorous scientific account of the history of doctrine. From 1913 until 1933 he was professor of systematic theology at the University of Lund in southern Sweden. Together with a colleague and friend of Aulén's in Lund, Anders Nygren (1890–1978), he developed what later was termed the Lundensian school of theology. According to both of them, theology was a strictly scientific undertaking aimed at clarifying the distinctiveness of Christianity and exposing any confusion that could arise between Christian and non-Christian motifs. They presupposed there to be a basic conception underlying any given religious system, the most important task of a scientific theology being to clarify—regarding each such system—its driving and unifying motif, type, idea, or theme (Aulén used these as equivalent notions throughout the book). Although Aulén and Nygren should not be identified with one another too closely, both of them found in their respective histories of dogma the same essential motif to be fundamental to Christian faith, that of God being a God of totally self-surrendering *agape* who through pure grace brings about and enacts human liberation from enslavement by evil powers (see, e.g.. Nygren's contemporary book *Eros and Agape*). In these terms the God of Love must thus be the sole enactor of atonement theology having to reject all conceptions of atonement that compromise this essential Christian motif.

In retrospect, one of the most curious aspects of the book is its claim to be a purely scientific theology describing *the* motif of Christianity. Yet, it was just this matter that was of fundamental importance to Aulén. This same basic idea structures his book on systematic theology, *The Faith of the Christian Church* (published in Swedish in six successive revised editions from 1923 to 1965). He argued that it provided a strictly scientific presentation of the authentic Christian Faith. There were serious problems connected with this approach, however, not simply in its lack of hermeneutical self-awareness. More seriously, it presupposed a modern idea of a religious value lying concealed beneath "the outward dress" of actual faith. It also became a dubious tool for those systematic theologians who, in endeavoring to understand earlier theologians, tended to reduce the plentitude of their soteriological images and ideas to a single motif. Thus, Aulén's description of early theologians has rightfully been criticized for its historical simplifications. Still, the most problematic effect of Aulén's methodology would appear to be that it highlighted penultimate questions but neglected the more important ones. Treatments of atonement in the tradition of Aulén have tended to discuss which motif is *the* correct interpretation of *how* God accomplishes atonement, rather than the more decisive questions of *what* atonement is and how creatures can participate in this divine action.

Shortly after the publication of *Christus Victor*, Aulén became a bishop of the Lutheran Church of Sweden (1933–1953). As bishop he was highly engaged in producing liturgical handbooks and in ecumenical affairs. Aulén was a highly committed ecumenical theologian, strongly influenced by his former teacher, the archbishop Nathan Söderblom. Yet the Lundensian school of theology also maintained that an ecumenical theology had to be based on the distinctively Christian motif of divine *agape* and according to their view Luther represented this ideal to an unsurpassable degree. A description of Luther's theology tended to become identical with describing what is distinctively Christian in general. Accordingly, *Christus Victor* is also characterized by its Lutheran perspectives. Luther can be said to have utilized the same basic theme as the Fathers "but with a greater depth of treatment." Aulén connected this "greater depth" with the contrast Luther perceived there to be between Gospel and law, that is, between God's grace and human attempts to satisfy God through their offerings, as in the medieval practice of penance.

Luther's distinction between Gospel and law also meant that God's victory over evil powers included the liberation from God's own Wrath as it is expressed through God's law. As Aulén interpreted it, the dramatic struggle here was carried out almost within the divine Being itself. In a manner closely similar to that espoused by Anselm, Luther's doctrine of atonement can be seen as assuming a conflict within God between God's curse and God's love (corresponding to Luther's idea of the hidden and the revealed God). However, Aulén perceived there to be a fundamental difference between Luther and Anselm in the sense that Luther provided no rational explanation of how God solved this inner conflict. Although Luther conceived of God's love as breaking through divine Wrath, he had no rational explanation to this riddle, but only a faith that lives on, counter to both law and reason. The combination of Aulén's rejection of any notion of human cooperation in redemption, and his notion of atonement as taking place within the Divine Being provides certain justification of Tillich's widely known complaint that Aulén's cosmic drama takes place "above man's head" (*Systematic Theology*, Vol. 2, 171).

The distinct contribution of Aulén's work, however, is that atonement is a cosmic drama, a theme which is of perpetual significance. In his theological works after his writing of *Christus Victor*, Aulén also took steps to include universal history and human cooperation in the cosmic drama. One reason for his shift toward a more positive inclusion of the human struggle within the cosmic drama of salvation was the experiences he had had during World War II. As bishop in Sweden at that time, he became much engaged in supporting the resistance to the Nazi occupation of Norway. In this struggle he came to realize that the law is not simply God's alien work in punishing sinners; it also provides a basis for joint human engagement in opposing evil.

After his retirement, Aulén moved back to Lund and began a second long period of productive writing, which lasted up to his death in 1977 at the age of ninety-eight. During this time he reflected self-critically on the Lutheran polemic against synergism, endeavoring to incorporate in a more consistent manner human activities and discipleship within the concept of redemption. In those terms, justification is not simply a proclamation of forensic imputation but rather it expresses membership in the Kingdom of God and partnership with God in God's struggle to liberate creation from all tyrants opposing it. Aulén never explicated, however, how such revisions would effect what he had maintained in his earlier conceptions of atonement.

Bibliography

Anderlonis, *The Soteriology of Gustaf Aulén*, 1988.
Aulén, *Christus Victor*, 2010.
Aulén, *The Drama and the Symbols*, 1970.
Aulén, *Eucharist and Sacrifice*, 1958.
Aulén, *The Faith of the Christian Church*, 2002.
Ferré, *Swedish Contributions to Modern Theology*, 1967.
Jonson, *Gustaf Aulén: biskop och motståndsman*, 2011.
Nygren, *Agape and Eros*, 1983.
Tillich, *Systematic Theology*, 1957.

26

Baptism

W. Travis McMaken

If there is something like a consensus position in the Christian theological tradition concerning the sacrament of baptism, it is that baptism is the sacrament of initiation that stands at the commencement of the Christian life. Metaphorically speaking, it is the doorway into the church. As such a central and ritually enacted element of Christian identity, it is no surprise that baptism should be bound up in profound and complicated ways with Christian thinking about how Jesus Christ reconciled humanity with God. Teasing out these interconnections requires that one consider how baptism relates to salvation in scripture and in the broader theological tradition.

New Testament authors deploy baptism in diverse ways aimed at various ends and this polyphony persists vis-à-vis baptism's relation to atonement. Although it is impossible to do justice to each usage, it is salutary to briefly address some of the most important passages as instances of different approaches to the question.

One such approach is to treat baptism as somehow involved in the process whereby individuals are authorized to view themselves as established in a positive relationship with God. In other words, these passages suggest that baptism is part of what "saves." For instance, Mark 16:15, "the one who believes and is baptized will be saved"; John 3:5, "no one can enter the kingdom of God without being born of water and Spirit"; Romans 6:3, "all of us who have been baptized into Christ Jesus were baptized into his death" (all biblical quotations are taken from the NRSV). Of course, none of these passages spells out in any detail precisely how or on what basis baptism contributes to one's soteriological status. Each of these passages likewise contains knotty interpretive issues. Nevertheless, they are examples of a tendency to view baptism as a productive part of the soteriological process.

Another approach is to treat baptism as the proper action taken in response to God's gracious work of reconciliation wrought in and by Jesus Christ. Perhaps the paradigmatic example here is Peter's Pentecost sermon. When the crowds ask what they should do in the face of Peter's proclamation, he answers: "Repent, and be baptized every one of you in the name of Jesus Christ so that your sins may be forgiven" (Acts 4:38). Here we see a blending with the first approach insofar as this response of baptism seems to play a role in one's forgiveness. But the accent is on the response that baptism enacts rather than on the act of baptism itself. In addition to approaching baptism as an individual's response to God, it might also be a communal response to God. Matthew 28:19 reads, "Go therefore and make disciples of all nations, baptizing them." Here the apostles, standing in for the Christian community as a whole, are commanded to perform baptism. The church's performance of baptism therefore takes on the character of obedient response.

Attending to the role of baptism in Jesus's life constitutes a third approach. The primary locus for baptism in Jesus's life is his baptism by John at the beginning of his public ministry (explicitly in Mt. 3; Mark 1; and Luke 3; implicitly in John 1). This event, and the divine attestation that accompanies it in the narratives, stands symbolically as the commencement of Jesus's saving activity. It also serves to bind Jesus more tightly to his first-century Jewish context in terms of purification rituals and messianic/apocalyptic expectation. Although this is the primary locus for baptism in Jesus's life, it also appears elsewhere. The Gospel of John speaks of Jesus baptizing (3:22), although it shortly thereafter complicates matters by asserting that it was not he but his disciples performing the baptisms (4:1–2). Either way, there is reason to think that baptism continued to play a role in Jesus's ministry. Finally, baptism appears as a symbolic mode of speech that designates the culmination of Jesus's life in the confrontation, suffering, and death that awaits him (Mark 10:38–39; Luke 12:50). Thus baptism occupies an important place in Jesus's life and work as an event at its start, an interpretation of its end, and as a continuing practice that connects them.

Finally, it is absolutely vital when reflecting on the biblical texts that discuss baptism to resist the idea that there is a single, unified biblical doctrine of baptism. In fact, there are many different views of baptism within the biblical text and "one can hardly add all the views together, call the result 'The NT Doctrine of Baptism,' and assume that one has done justice to the NT authors by doing so" (Hartman, "Baptism," 592).

While one must be sensitive to the particularities of biblical texts that address baptism, it is nonetheless necessary to integrate them within a larger theological framework in order to supply the coherence necessary for a well-regulated doctrine of baptism. Such integration has a long history and the following will touch on some of the most important moments vis-à-vis the intersection of baptism and atonement.

Baptism in the early Christian centuries was widely regarded as a spiritually significant event that cleansed one from sin and, to certain extents, from sin's effects. The Cappadocian theologians of the fourth century understood this in terms of integrative imitation and reorientation. Gregory of Nyssa made much of the point that Christians imitate Jesus's baptism in their own baptism, although they are not able to imitate his life exactly and in its entirety. Nonetheless, this imitation means that the baptized "participate in Purity; and true Purity is Deity" (Gregory, 504). Imitation, then, becomes a means of integration whereby Christians live with and for God. Baptismal imitation is integrative, however, because it reorients one's life. It is something of a spiritual reset button, providing "a kind of break in the continuity of evil" so that one "is in a measure freed from … congenital tendency to evil" (503). This reorientation frees the baptizand from undue servitude to passion and allows for the development of a life that imitates God and Christ in virtue.

Further west, Augustine developed his doctrine of baptism through controversies with the Donatists and Pelagians. With reference to the Donatists, he distinguished between the formal character of baptism as a sign (*signum*) and the soteriological effect of the reality (*res*) depicted by that sign. Baptism's mere performance does not secure its saving quality, he argued; rather, one's fellowship with the "Catholic church" (as opposed to the "Donatist church") as the sphere of the Holy Spirit's special operation provides its efficacy. With reference to the Pelagians, Augustine argued that the only way to make sense of the North African practice of infant baptism is by understanding baptism as the event wherein the baptizand receives forgiveness for the guilt of original sin. A basic soteriological assumption that drives both aspects of Augustine's engagement with baptism is that baptism is a critical element whereby the grace or salvation that Jesus Christ makes available becomes effective for the baptizand.

Thomas picks up on this basic assumption. Part of the work he thinks a sacrament performs is the conference of a certain kind of grace to the individual recipient. In the case of baptism, this is "principally" the grace that serves "as a remedy for original sin" and its associated guilt (Thomas, ST 3, q.66, a.9; 40–41). Baptism thus helps to make the soteriological jump from the salvation made possible by Jesus Christ there and then to its application to individual Christians here and now: "to every one baptized the passion of Christ is communicated for … healing" (Thomas, ST 3, q.69, a.2; 126–127). Thomas weds this strand to another train of thought latent in Augustine, namely, that baptism not only confers a certain grace upon the baptizand but also marks the baptizand with a certain character or status within the Christian community. The character imparted by baptism is permanent (*indelebilis*) and entitles one to participate in the church's other sacraments. Indeed, it is "the gateway of the sacraments" (Thomas, ST 3, q.63, a.6; 96–97).

The Protestant Reformation shifted the mechanism of exchange, which transfers the salvation achieved by and in Jesus Christ to the individual Christian, from baptism to faith. While the thinkers mentioned above all maintain a close association between baptism and faith in salvation, they also permit the corporate faith of the church to substitute for the individual's faith in a way that reformational theology does not. Martin Luther attests this subordinating of baptism to the baptizand's faith when he comments: "When faith comes, baptism is complete" (Luther, 246). Reformational theology does, however, continue reflection on the character conferred by baptism in terms of covenant. This is present in Luther but is developed more systematically by John Calvin in his defense of infant baptism: since "the children of believers are partakers in the covenant …, there is no reason why they should be barred from the sign [i.e., baptism]" (Calvin, *Inst.* 4.16.24 [1347]).

In the modern period, Karl Barth rejected the soteriological assumption that the saving work accomplished by and in Jesus Christ there and then required a transfer or application to ensure its effectiveness for the individual here and now. This saving work is always already effectual here and now. One must simply be made aware of this—which occurs for Barth in the event of Spirit baptism—and consequently undertake a new and corresponding form of life. Water baptism becomes in Barth's theology a paradigmatic moment that stands symbolically at the beginning of this life. The imitation theme previously observed in Gregory of Nyssa's theology comes to the fore again in Barth in that Christians are baptized in imitation of Christ's baptism: "As they entered on this way [i.e., the Christian life], the beginning of his way could not be of mere historical interest for them … Since His concrete act was baptism with water, it [i.e., the early Christian community] had to perform this act in the same concrete form" (Barth, *CD* 4.4, 68). Through this corresponding act, the baptizand assumes responsibility as part of the Christian community for its missionary task of proclaiming the gospel of Jesus Christ. Thomas Torrance, one of Barth's students, emphasizes once more the connection between imitation and integration by speaking of Christ's baptism as vicarious and thus as Christian baptism's "dimension of depth" (83).

Beyond these considerations of how baptism and atonement intersect in scripture and the theological tradition, the church's liturgical tradition offers a further field for fruitful reflection on these themes. Unfortunately, space does not permit a survey of that field. Suffice it to say that the liturgical tradition is very rich, encompassing all the biblical approaches and theological themes sketched above as well as many others. Sources in the bibliography below provide a helpful introduction to this liturgical tradition, especially the volumes from Bryan Spinks.

Bibliography

Augustine, "The Correction of the Donatists," in *Nicene and Post-Nicene Fathers*, 1994.

Augustine, "The Punishment and Forgiveness of Sins and the Baptism of Little Ones," in *Answer to the Pelagians*, 1997.

Barth, *Church Dogmatics*, 1956–75.

Calvin, *Institutes*, 1960.

Ferguson, *Baptism in the Early Church: History, Theology, and Liturgy in the First Five Centuries*, 2009.

Gregory of Nyssa, "The Great Catechism," in *Nicene and Post-Nicene Fathers*, 1994.

Hartman, "Baptism," in *The Anchor Bible Dictionary*, 1992.

Hartman, *"Into the Name of the Lord Jesus": Baptism in the Early Church*, 1997.

Luther, "Concerning Rebaptism: A Letter of Martin Luther to Two Pastors," in *Luther's Works, 40*, 1958.

Spinks, *Early and Medieval Rituals and Theologies of Baptism: From the New Testament to the Council of Trent*, 2006.

Spinks, *Reformation and Modern Rituals and Theologies of Baptism: From Luther to Contemporary Practices*, 2006.

Thomas. *Summa Theologiae: Baptism and Confirmation (3a. 66–72)*. Edited by James J. Cunningham. Cambridge University Press, 2006.

Thomas. *Summa Theologiae: The Sacraments (3a. 60–65)*. Edited by David Bourke. Cambridge University Press, 2006.

Torrance, "The One Baptism Common to Christ and His Church," in *Theology in Reconciliation*, 1996.

27

Bernard of Clairvaux

Anthony N. S. Lane

There is a vast body of literature on Bernard of Clairvaux. Separate volumes list works of and about Bernard published to 1890, from 1891 to 1957, and from 1957 to 1970, and since then there have been regular surveys in journals. Despite this fact, very little has been written on Bernard's doctrine of redemption. The problem in some quarters is not just a neglect of the topic but also a misapprehension of its significance. When I mentioned Bernard's teaching on the cross to one of the great medieval historians of the previous generation, he looked at me with surprise and said, "But, surely, for Bernard the cross was just a holy relic?" Nothing could be further from the truth. In my research on this topic I found 669 passages where the cross is mentioned to a greater or lesser extent. These passages present a rich theology of the work of Christ, with just one single mention of the cross as a relic (Lane).

Many historical surveys of the doctrine confine themselves to two major medieval theologians, Anselm and Abelard. The former is represented as having reduced the work of Christ to an "objective" doctrine of satisfaction, the latter as having reduced it to a "subjective" doctrine of an ethical example. This portrayal goes back to two of the key figures of nineteenth-century Liberal theology, Ritschl and Harnack. Their aim was to present Anselm and Abelard's views as alternatives, with the latter being preferable. Unfortunately too much of subsequent scholarship has accepted this portrayal. There are, however, a number of problems with it. First, it is not true that either Anselm or Abelard reduced the work of Christ to one idea only. Second, while it is true that Anselm laid considerable emphasis on the single aspect of Christ's death as a satisfaction of God's honor, in this respect he is not typical of medieval theology. Bernard's teaching contains a wide range of views, which is much more typical.

Those historical surveys of the doctrine that do mention Bernard almost all confine themselves solely to his letter-treatise on *The Errors of Abelard*. This provides just 17 of the 669 passages that I have studied. At least it does give a moderately representative picture of Bernard's teaching on this topic, unlike the roughly 2,000 words (in English translation) of Abelard's Excursus on 3:19–26 in his *Commentary on Romans*, which is the exclusive source for Abelard's teaching in the great majority of modern accounts. Unfortunately this also appears to have been the exclusive source for Bernard's knowledge of Abelard's teaching on this topic.

Of the 669 passages, some come in extended sections of teaching. Most noteworthy are his treatises *In Praise of the New Knighthood* 10:17–11:29, *Loving God* 3:7–5:15, and *The Errors of Abelard* 5:11–9:25. A number of sermons also contain extended sections of teaching, especially Sermon 1 on the Annunciation of the Lord, the Sermon on Holy Wednesday, and (more surprisingly) Sermon 1 on the Resurrection of the Lord. Here the same themes are developed as in the treatises, though in a manner suited to popular teaching and with a greater "Abelardian" emphasis on the subjective effects of the cross, albeit firmly based on the objective redemption won by Christ.

Bernard viewed Christ as the Second Adam. He saves us supremely, but not exclusively, by his cross, but he also saves us by his conception, birth, circumcision, life, descent into the underworld, resurrection, ascension, and Pentecost. As with most accounts of the work of Christ throughout history, the cross is portrayed as affecting God the Father, Satan, and ourselves. These aspects will be expounded in the following paragraphs. Bernard also, drawing upon Hebrews, portrays it as making Christ himself merciful. Generally Bernard treats the cross as central, citing 1 Corinthians 2:2 and Galatians 6:14, for example, but on five occasions he is influenced by an Origenist mysticism and atypically speaks of the cross as something to be left behind as one grows into maturity.

Bernard, no less than Abelard, saw the cross as a demonstration of God's love that evokes our response and leaves us an example to follow. Unlike modern portrayals of Abelard (though not necessarily unlike Abelard's teaching as a whole), for Bernard the reason that the cross demonstrates God's love is that it has an objective purpose.

Bernard portrays Christ as the Victor over death and death's author (Satan). His teaching on victory over Satan is confined mostly to the treatise against Abelard. How are death and Satan defeated? By the fact that Christ has dealt with our sins on the cross. For Bernard the fundamental problem is not death or Satan but the source of their power over us, which is sin. Bernard also takes up the patristic idea that Christ defeated Satan by a holy deception. The idea here is not that Satan overstepped his rights, but rather that by mistakenly causing Christ's death, Satan brings about his sacrificial death on the cross, which puts us right with God.

As we have seen, while Bernard saw Christ as the Second Adam, as a demonstration of God's love, as Victor over death and Satan, the central idea is that Christ died for our sins to put us right with God. He uses a range of biblical imagery to make this point. Bernard's writings as a whole are permeated with biblical quotation and allusion and it has been said that he spoke, wrote, and thought biblically (Dumontier, 157; Leclercq, 3:249, 4:11–33). Christ bore our sins on the cross, which is a sacrifice offered to God. Christ is the Lamb of God and saves us by his shed blood, by his wounds. He paid the price for us, paying off our debt. He bore our punishment. He is the propitiation for our sins and the cross is a satisfaction for our sins.

Among this range of imagery, is one of these ideas central for Bernard? Jean Rivière, the greatest nineteenth-century exponent of Bernard's doctrine of redemption, argued that it is penal substitution that has Bernard's preference (70). It is true that Bernard teaches penal substitution, but mistaken to suppose that this is central. At the heart of Bernard's teaching is the idea that sin has separated us from God and that Christ reconciles us to God by dealing with it. How does he do this? By offering himself as a sacrifice, by paying the price for us and paying off our debt, and by bearing our punishment. These are three different ways of stating that Christ died for us and that through his death the Father is appeased and our relationship with him is restored.

Such a view of the work of Christ has come under heavy fire since the Enlightenment, following the critique given by Faustus Socinus. Many of the objections posed today are preempted by the questions that Abelard asks in his brief Excursus, to which Bernard responds. In particular he holds together two sets of ideas that are in tension with one another. The cross was needed to propitiate God's wrath, but at the same time it is because God loves us that he gave his only Son. The Father sends the Son, who is obedient unto death, but at the same time the Son voluntarily gives himself for us. As with other areas of Christian doctrine, fidelity to biblical revelation comes not by a rational resolution but by holding ideas together in creative tension.

Bibliography

Akin, "Bernard of Clairvaux and the Atonement," in *The Church at the Dawn of the 21st Century*, 1989.

Billy, "Redemption and the Order of Love in Bernard of Clairvaux's *Sermon 20 on 'The Canticle of Canticles,'*" *Downside Review* 112, 1994.

Dumontier, *Saint Bernard et la Bible*, 1953.

Evans, "*Cur Deus Homo*: St. Bernard's Theology of the Redemption. A Contribution to the Contemporary Debate," *Studia Theologica* 36, 1982.

Lane, *Bernard of Clairvaux: Theologian of the Cross*, 2013.

Leclercq, *Recueil d'études sur saint Bernard et ses écrits*, 5 vols, 1962–1992.

Rivière, "Le dogme de la rédemption au début du moyen-âge III—Rôle de saint Bernard," *Revue des Sciences Religieuses* 13, 1933.

28

Blood

Eugene F. Rogers, Jr.

The New Testament mentions the "blood of Christ" three times as often as his "cross" and five times as often as his "death." Evangelicals argue that "blood" means "death" (Heb. 9:22), liberals that blood means "life" (Lev. 17:11, 14; Gen. 9:4; cross-cultural studies). Still the whole debate takes place in terms of "blood." Anselm "free[s the soul] from servitude" by "the blood of God" as debt-payment for insulted honor. Anselm himself connects the blood of the cross with that of the Eucharist: "Chew this, bite it, suck it, let your heart swallow it, when your mouth receives the body and blood of your Redeemer ... not otherwise than through this will you remain in Christ and Christ in you." There one accepts Christ not without faith but by accepting wine or wafer (*Human Redemption*, ll. 3, 167–171). Abelard writes that "we have been justified by the blood of Christ ... in that [he] has taken upon himself our nature and persevered therein in teaching us by word and example even unto death ... [so] that ... true charity should not now shrink from enduring anything for him" (Fairweather, 283). Blood gives Anselm and Abelard a language *in which* to disagree.

Like "the body of Christ," "the blood of Christ" orders a series connecting cosmology and community, atonement and kinship, salvation and sacrament. The human blood of Jesus is the blood of Christ; the church lives from the blood of Christ; the blood of the martyrs is the blood of Christ; the wine of the Eucharist is the blood of Christ; the believer drinks salvation in the blood of Christ; icons display the blood of Christ; and the blood of Christ is the blood of God.

Why Christ's blood instead of his body? "Body" suggests

> a bounded entity, carrying and unifying the human being. But this idea of a body as a material, bounded entity is far from self-evident ... Far from providing a smooth envelope, skin constantly receives and emits fluids [making it] impossible to determine which atom, say, is still part of the epidermis and the

intestinal lining and which is not, and which pork molecule has turned into a human molecule. Even the inside of a body is full of skins, opening up many surfaces ... We live as much in processes across and through skins as in processes "within" skins ... Despite the usefulness of the ... body as a separate, enclosed unit, ... this view is not at all obvious, and *instead needs a lot of cultural work to be upheld.* (Bildhauer, 3–6; emphasis in the original)

Although the body's *unremarked* boundary is that of skin, its *salient, defended, critical* boundary is that of blood. When something foreign penetrates the body, the skin reddens with blood. Society reacts with more or less alarm as this blood trickles or floods. So blood marks and defends society's own boundaries; we both affirm and challenge the social body in blood's terms. In thinking of bodies, social or individual, we imagine a bounded entity and hide from ourselves its entrances, exits, permeations, and vulnerabilities: blood once out gives those bounds the lie and paints their fiction red. Blood exposes, stains, and alarms a leaky body, individual or social. In Christ and the church, God takes this leaky body on.

Sometimes blood cleanses, washing "white in the blood of the Lamb" (Rev. 7:14, cf. Milgrom). Anthropologists call this blood a "detergent." Sometimes blood atones: "without the shedding of blood, there is no remission of sin" (Heb. 9:22). Sometimes blood defiles: "The city [gendered feminine] sheds blood from her midst to defile herself" (Ez. 22:3). Christian blood has worked in ambivalent—even gendered—ways. When men (Jesus, Abraham) shed blood in sacrifice, it cleanses. When women shed blood in menstruation, it once defiled. Blood marks not only society's external boundaries, but also its internal structure: gender, priesthood, sacrament, martyrdom, relics all express their power in terms of blood.

Internal and external critics of Christianity have protested for half a century that Christian blood-language is dangerous. Yes, it is dangerous, but the protest has been anthropologically naïve. Christian blood-language is not going away, but the options are not exhausted by leaving it unchanged, on the one hand, or deploring it, on the other. A third option remains: to repeat blood's language subversively, to free it from contexts of oppression or violence. This is what Jesus does founding the Last Supper: he takes a structure of violent oppression—the crucifixion—and turns it to a peaceful feast.

Bibliography

Abelard, *Commentary on Romans* in Fairweather, *Scholastic Miscellany*, 1956.
Anselm, *Meditation on Human Redemption* in Ward and Southern, eds., *Prayers and Meditations of St. Anslem; Why God Became Human* in Fairweather.

Biale, *Blood and Belief*, 2007.
Bildhauer, *Medieval Blood*, 2006.
Bynum, *Wonderful Blood*, 2007.
Douglas, *Purity and Danger*, 2002.
Milgrom, "Israel's Sanctuary," *Révue Biblique* 83, 1976.
Rogers, *Analogy of Blood*, forthcoming.
Rogers, review of Gil Anidjar, *Blood: A Critique of Christianity*, in *Syndicate: A New Forum for Theology* 2/1, 2015.

29

Bonaventure

Andrew B. Salzmann

Bonaventure (1221–1274) entered the Order of Friars Minor (Franciscans) at about the age of twenty-two, going on to become its seventh Minister General. Perhaps his greatest influence on the Franciscan order was his defense of integrating Francis of Assisi's heartfelt piety with rigorous theological reflection. As a theologian, Bonaventure—called the *Doctor Seraphicus* for his emphasis on divine charity—was deeply influenced by the "father" of Franciscan theology, Alexander of Hales, and through him twelfth-century Augustinianism. This influence is clear throughout his writings on the atoning work of Christ.

While it is only God who infuses faith, hope, and especially charity into the soul, graces by which the human heart marked by sin reaches atoning union with God (e.g., *Itin.* 4.8 [V.308]), Bonaventure asserts in a particularly important passage that this justification can also be attributed to Christ's human nature, insofar as his humanity merits that saving grace. Indeed, as Christ could not suffer in his divine nature, it must be attributed only to his humanity (*Brev.* 4.9 [V.251]). Christ's atoning work, by which all humanity is justified, extends beyond the passion alone to encompass his resurrection, "without any contradiction" between the two and in a manner which can be described using the four Aristotelian causes—material, efficient, formal, and final (III *Sent.*, d.19, a.1 q.1, concl. [III.400–402]).

The passion alone is the *material* cause of justification. As a material cause is the subject which is acted upon, Christ's passion causes justification by way of humanity earning that intervening merit which initiates atonement through the offering of satisfaction for the offense of sin against God. Though this "objective" dimension of atonement is the most prominent in Bonaventure's thought, by no means does it exhaust Christ's atoning work (Gonzalez, 374). Anselm's influence is clear: the magnitude of humanity's offense against God's infinite dignity is itself infinite; to make appropriate satisfaction for the offense therefore surpasses human ability. Bonaventure offers his own reasons why no mere human could make satisfaction (*III Sent.*, d.20., a.*unicus*, q.3 [III.422]; Gonzalez, 375). No single human life has a value proportionate to the infinite offenses of the entire human race against God. Even if one did, humanity would then (unjustly) owe that person the sort of gratitude that is proper to God alone. What is more, true satisfaction must involve restoring humanity to a condition of justice, which no human could do. Yet, Bonaventure explains, in a Trinitarian key, that God cannot allow this hopeless situation to continue. The power of God cannot allow Satan to keep possession of the human race; the wisdom of God cannot permit its greatest creatures to be corrupted; God (presumably, the kindness of God) cannot permit all of humanity to be condemned for the singular sin of Adam. The answer, then, is the meritorious work of a God-man, whose infinite life can pay the debt of sin, who can restore humanity to its lost condition, to whom all could rightly render worship.

The question of Christ's merit raises problems for Bonaventure, as his definition of condign merit—acting in charity—meant that Christ had the fullness of merit from the moment of his conception (*III Sent.*, d.18, a.1, q.2, concl. [III.383]; Gonzalez, 377). Why, then, the meritorious action of the cross? Due to the punishment deserved by sin, the penal work of satisfaction had to be a bitter experience (*III Sent.*, d.18, a.2, q.3, concl. [III.393]; *III Sent.*, d.20, a.*unicus*, q.5, concl. [III.429]). Thus, the suffering of the cross was appropriate to Christ's saving work (*III Sent.*, d.20, a. *unicus*, q.1 [III.417–418]). Though God might have saved humanity by some other means, no other way could have been as appropriate as this one, which placates God and cures human pride (*III Sent.*, d.20, a.*unicus*, q.6, concl. [III.431]).

Both Christ's passion and his resurrection are *efficient* causes of justification. As an efficient cause is an agent of change which acts upon its object, the passion of Christ justifies by way of offering a model of Christian life that provokes and excites the soul to love God, not only by the gratitude occasioned in those who contemplate Christ's death but, ultimately, by inspiring the soul itself to die to sin (III *Sent.*, d. 19, a.1 q.1, concl. [III.401]; 1 Pet. 2:21). Humanity needed a savior who would take up a flesh capable of suffering, precisely to demonstrate that sinful pride could be conquered only by a love expressed through the obedience and humility of the cross (*III Sent.*, d.15, a.1, q.1, concl. [III.330–1]; Dreyer, 197). The cross reveals the character of true love; the cross inspires or excites love. Bonaventure explains that nothing else reveals the way to virtue more clearly than the example of an agonizing death obediently endured. Nothing could more effectively invite the human heart to love God than the kindness of one who would lay down his own life (*Brev.* IV.9 [V.250]; Gonzalez, 380).

But if Bonaventure echoes Peter Abelard in explaining the value of the cross as its ability to move the soul's free will to imitate the love of Christ, a common misunderstanding of Abelard must also be avoided here: this is no merely moral theory of atonement. If love for God can be "excited" by contemplation of the crucified Jesus, by "the warm, deeply felt descriptions of the passion of Christ" so central to Bonaventure's devotional works, it is not sufficient to say that the cross merely awakens sympathetic affections in the heart. The death of any martyr could do the same (*III Sent.*, d.19, a.1, q.1, dub.1 [III.412]; Gonzalez, 380). Rather, contemplation of the cross as a model of human life "excites" a love that is given to the will by the infusion of God's own sanctifying charity. Thus Bonaventure also speaks of Christ's resurrection as an efficient cause and a model (*exemplum provocans*), which compels the Christian toward justification, for the resurrection shows the importance not just of dying to sin but also of rising to the new life of virtue. Christ's resurrection attracts souls to the justifying virtues of faith, hope, and love, and that fire of the Holy Spirit, which is charity, is called down only upon those who seek after it with desire (*Brev.* 4.10 [V.251]).

Christ's passion and resurrection are also *formal* causes of justification. As a formal cause is the essential pattern of a thing, the passion and resurrection justify by way of being the very pattern (*exemplaris regulantis*) of human existence as dying to self and rising to newness of life (III *Sent.*, d.19, a.1 q.1, concl. [III.401]). Bonaventure's Christian Platonism saw each existing thing as an expression of an ideal exemplar existing in the mind of God (*Itin.* 2.12 [V.303]; Hayes [1994] 72–73). Christ, in a sense, is the very divine idea of humanity existing in the mind of God, made flesh, revealing God's truest intention for the human race. Christ is the most adequate form of humanity, "the key that unlocks to us the meaning of all reality" (Hayes [1994] 84). Christ, the mold "which ought to shape each particular expression of human nature," bears a "paradigmatic" cross (Gonzalez, 381; Dreyer, 197). As such, Christ's exemplarity can be seen as "a form of the ancient doctrine of *recapitulatio*" (Gonzalez, 378). Related to Christ's exemplarity is his archetypal role in acting on behalf of others, as Adam had done in "bringing all into sin" (*III Sent.*, d.20, a.*unicus*, q.4, concl. [III.425–426]; Patout Burns, 297). Christ needed to have the same "grace of headship" (*gratiam capitis*) over the human race that had been Adam's. Thus, just as the Devil, in defeating the first, archetypal man, had defeated all humankind, so in being defeated by Christ, the new Adam and truer archetype, he is likewise defeated by all of humankind (*III Sent.*, d.19, a.1, q.3 [III.405]; Gonzalez, 383).

Christ's resurrection alone, however, is the *final cause* of justification. As a final cause is the final state toward which a work strives, the resurrection causes justification by way of revealing the final condition (*termini quietantis*) of humankind, "the exemplar of glory" to which the world, through humanity, will finally attain (Hayes [1994] 96). This final condition consists in an intellect full of light, a will deeply at peace, a memory of eternal duration, a body robed in luminosity, subtlety, agility, and impassability—one that obeys the soul even as the soul obeys God (*Brev.* 7.7 [V.289-290]). Bonaventure explains by analogy how it is that Christ rightly entered after only three days that resurrected state which will only later be extended to all humanity. Just as the Word had formed all things perfectly in the creation at the dawn of time, so the Incarnate Word, in its recreation through the work of the cross, could not allow the work of restoration to go forth unfinished but needed rather to allow it to reach completion (*ad perfectum*) in Himself (*Brev.* 4.10 [V.231]). If Bonaventure's systematic treatment of the resurrection as cause of justification is relatively sparse, his contemplative and mystical writings develop it at greater length (Gonzalez, 384).

Bibliography

Bracketed references refer to the volume and page number from the Quaracchi edition of Bonaventure's *Opera Omnia*.

Bonaventure, *Opera Omnia* (Quaracchi, 1882-1902), 10 volumes.

Burns, "The Concept of Satisfaction in Medieval Redemption Theory," *Theological Studies* 36:2, 1975.

Dreyer, "A Condescending God: Bonaventure's Theology of the Cross" and "Mysticism Tangible through Metaphor: Bonaventure's Spirituality of the Cross," in *The Cross in Christian Tradition: From Paul to Bonaventure*, 2000.

Gonzalez, "The Work of Christ in Saint Bonaventure's systematic Works," in *S. Bonaventura 1274-1974* vol. 4, 1973.

Hayes, *The Hidden Center: Spirituality and Speculative Christology in St. Bonaventure*, 1992.

Hayes, "Bonaventure: Mystery of the Triune God," in *The History of Franciscan Theology*, 1994.

30

Book of the Twelve

Don Collett

Prophecy and the Torah

Under the aegis of German Protestant scholarship in the late nineteenth century, a view of the prophets emerged which argued that pre-exilic prophets such as Amos, Hosea, and Micah rejected the validity of the temple cultus and its sacrificial system, as codified in the book of Leviticus. To cite but one example from the Book of the Twelve, on the basis of the implied "no" to the rhetorical question posed by Amos 5:25—"Did you bring to me sacrifices and offerings during the forty years in the wilderness, O house of Israel?"—historical critical scholars judged that Israel's prophets espoused an anti-ritualistic stance toward Israel's sacrificial cultus. In light of this alleged opposition between the Torah and the prophets, the first question to ask is whether there are two antithetical trajectories of theological thought on the atonement at work in the Torah and the prophets. Does the Twelve's prophetic witness to God's atoning forgiveness reflect an anti-liturgical or anti-ritualistic stance? The answer given will be a qualified no. This chapter suggests an alternative account of the relation between the Twelve's witness to God's atoning forgiveness and the models for atonement on offer in Israel's Torah.

According to Wellhausen, the prophets were ethical revolutionaries who rejected cultic sacrifice as a theological basis for atonement, regarding it as a fundamentally heathen or pagan basis for propitiating God's wrath. In contrast to the pagan nations surrounding them, the prophets grounded the ongoing maintenance of God's relationship with Israel in the ethical outlook and moral stance implied by monotheism. In the late exilic and post-exilic periods, however, the rise of scribal prophets and prophetic epigones who claimed the mantle of prophecy—but who were by nature priests—served to establish a connecting link between Israel's prophets and the law. The prophet Ezekiel gave rise to the archetypal example of this phenomenon when he enclosed "the soul of prophecy" in the temple and its cultus, as evidenced by the literary witness of Ezekiel 40–48. In this way, prophecy in the late exilic and post-exilic period came to be associated with the priestly model of Levitical sacrifices (Wellhausen, 421–425).

The assessment of Wellhausen's thesis vis-à-vis the Twelve calls for a brief survey of the Hebrew terminology associated with atonement in the Torah, as well as the theological models based upon this grammar. Before embarking on this survey, however, it should be noted that the prophetic outlook on the temple cultus is not be understood as the wholesale rejection of Israel's sacrificial cult, but rather as the rejection of its abuses. The prophets emphasize the need for loyalty on Israel's part, not to erase the need for sacrifices, but to teach Israel that animal sacrifices must be accompanied by steadfast love and faithfulness (Hos. 6:6). Israel is to do justice, love, kindness, and walk humbly with God (Mic. 6:6–8). Such admonitions demonstrate that the prophets were concerned with an approach to sacrifices and offerings that severed ritual from ethics, and liturgical worship from repentant forms of obedience grounded in humility. For this reason, acceptable sacrifices include the offering of unblemished animals (Mal. 1:6–14), *as well as* heartfelt sincerity (Mal. 2:1) and faithful obedience to the Lord's covenants (Mal. 2:10–16). This approach to sacrifices stands in contrast with the priestly practices of the nations surrounding Israel, which typically regarded the forgiveness of the gods as something automatically rendered by cultic sacrifice, apart from the need for personal commitment or ethical change.

Models for the Atonement in the Torah

The close relation between atonement and forgiveness is shown in the Torah (Lev. 4:20, 26, 31, 35; 5:10, 13, 16, 18; 6:7; 19:22; cf. Num. 15:25, 26, 28). These texts present readers of the Torah with a priestly model for making atonement, in that forgiveness is understood as the *effect* of an atonement enacted by Israel's priests through animal sacrifices and offerings. That forgiveness in these texts is an effect of atonement is evident from the fact that sin that has been atoned for (*kippēr*), has been forgiven (*sālaḥ*), resulting in reconciliation between God and Israel. Moreover, while this restorative effect is primarily associated with the sacrificial cultus and priesthood described in Leviticus, this is not exclusively the case in Israel's Torah. Alongside the priestly model for atonement in Leviticus is the Mosaic model found in passages such as Exodus 32–34 and Numbers 14, the latter of which operates in connection with the two pivotal moments of idolatry and rebellion in Israel's history.

In Exodus 32–34, Israel's experience of the Lord's atoning forgiveness takes place, not in the context of priestly sacrifices offered on her behalf, but in the context of Mosaic intercession. Here forgiveness is accomplished through the intercessory prayer of Moses (Exod. 32:12–14), resulting in the Lord's relenting from divine judgment and wrath (*nāḥam*). Interestingly, the LXX translators of Exodus 32:14 do not make use of the Greek verb *metanoéō* to render the Hebrew verb *nāḥam* (unlike Jon. 3:9–10), but instead translate it with the aorist passive of *hiláskomai* (to propitiate or turn away wrath). Exodus 32 also raises the possibility of Moses bearing the judicial consequences of Israel's sin in his own person (Exod. 32:32—see further below), though the narrative progress of Exodus 32–34 ultimately reveals that the Lord's character as merciful, just, and compassionate (Exod. 34:5–7) constitutes the basis for the divine "bearing" (*nāśā'*) and "relenting" (*nāḥam*) described in Exodus 32, and thus for her forgiveness.

Forgiveness as divine bearing also finds expression in the context of the Mosaic intercession, found in Numbers 14:18–20. Verse 18 invokes the Lord's character as merciful, just, and compassionate (cf. Exod. 34:6–7), while in verse 19, the Hebrew verb *sālaḥ* used to describe the forgiveness effected by priestly acts of atonement in Leviticus is used in parallel with the Hebrew verb *nāśā'*. In this way Numbers 14 also links Israel's forgiveness with a divine "bearing" of her sin that is rooted in the Lord's character and identity. Taken together, Exodus 32–34 and Numbers 14 present readers of the Torah with a Mosaic model for atonement that interprets the forgiveness accomplished by sacrifice and offering in the priestly model as the effect of Mosaic intercession rooted in the Lord's divine identity as merciful, just, and compassionate.

In sum, forgiveness in Israel's Torah may be understood as the effect of an atonement enacted by sacrifice and offering through the agency of Israel's priests, or as the effect of Mosaic intercession. In the context of priestly sacrifice in Leviticus, this forgiveness is typically described using the Hebrew term *sālaḥ*, though in the context of Mosaic intercession, the terms *nāśā'* and *nāḥam* are also used, especially in contexts that appeal to the Lord's character as the basis for his "bearing" of Israel's sins and "relenting" from wrath and judgment.

The Torah and the Twelve

Although the Hebrew verb associated with priestly acts of atonement does not appear in the Twelve (*kippēr*), verbs associated with the effects of atonement in the Torah (e.g., divine forgiving, bearing, relenting) are found in Amos 7:2–3, Hosea 1:6, 14:2–4, Micah 7:18–20, Joel 2:13, and Jonah 4:2. In Amos 7:2–3, the prophet functions in the Mosaic role of intercessor, calling upon the Lord to forgive (*sālaḥ*) and relent (*nāḥam*) in language that reflects the Mosaic model for atonement depicted in Exodus 32 and Numbers 14. The link this model establishes between forgiveness as divine sin-bearing (*nāśā'*), divine turning away from wrath, and the Lord's character as merciful also finds expression in Hosea 14:2–4 and Micah 7:18–20. Hosea 1:6 links forgiveness and the divine bearing of Israel's sin to the Lord's identity as merciful, albeit negatively, when it asserts that the absence of the Lord's mercy means that he will not "bear" or forgive Israel. Finally, the language of relenting invoked by the Mosaic model in Exodus 32:12–14 (*nāḥam*) also finds expression in the Twelve in contexts that invoke the Lord's character as merciful and compassionate (Joel 2:13, Jon. 4:2; cf. Exod. 34:6–7). Although the LXX translator of Jonah 4:2 does not make use of the aorist passive *hilásthē* to translate *nāḥam* (unlike Exod. 32:14), Jonah 3:9–10 makes it clear that the divine relenting in Jonah 4:2 involves the turning away of his wrath.

In sum, the Twelve exploits language drawn from contexts in Israel's Torah (*sālaḥ*, *nāśā'*, and *nāḥam*) to associate the atoning forgiveness effected by the priestly model in Leviticus with Mosaic intercession and the Lord's character as merciful and compassionate. The predominance of this Mosaic model for atonement in the Twelve probably stems from a theological concern to present the ministry of Israel's prophets in accordance with the paradigm the Mosaic Torah offers for construing the institution of prophecy (Deut. 18:15–22). Thus atonement in the Twelve is effected through the intercessory ministry of prophetic mediators "like unto Moses" who ultimately ground the theological reality of atoning forgiveness, not in animal sacrifices per se, but in the Lord's identity as the One who forgives by bearing Israel's sin, relenting from his wrath and judgment.

Divine Sin-Bearing and Israel

How does Israel stand related to this divine "bearing"? In Micah 7:9, the figure of Israel bears the wrath of the Lord (LXX: *orgēn kyríou*), where Israel's bearing or carrying of God's wrath is the just consequence of her sin. This demonstrates that Israel does not understand her history as "the struggle of nations against one another and against her but rather as God's dealings with her, which she willingly takes upon herself and bears (*nāśā'*) ... Only by the acknowledgement of one's own guilt and transgression is it possible to accept the wrath of God"

(Wolff, 221). The close relation between divine sin-bearing and the representative character of Israel's prophetic office is also suggested by the grammatical linkage between Micah 7:18, where the Lord "bears" Israel's iniquity, and Micah 7:9, where Israel "bears" the Lord's wrath. In terms reminiscent of the Mosaic model of prophetic intercession, the prophetic "I" of Micah 7:9 bears the judicial consequences of Israel's sin (Exod. 32:32; cf. Deut. 1:37). Yet Micah 7:9 not only speaks of the bearing of sin and its consequences, but also of sin's forgiveness. Here the judge acts as both lawyer *and* defense attorney, resulting in a redemptive transformation of the legal controversy against Israel. Thus, while the goal of the lawsuit is to execute judgment (cf. Mic. 6:2), in this context it is the execution of justice unto Israel's redemption. This is what leads to the praise expressed in Micah 7:18–20, and also explains why Israel's fall will not be the last word. Rather, her rising will follow her fall, just as her exaltation will follow her humiliation (Mic. 7:8; cf. 3:12–4:2).

What the reader of the Twelve learns from the prophetic witness to Israel's sin-bearing in Micah 7:8–20, which is also modeled upon the ministry of Moses, is that the Lord's forgiveness involves a sin-bearer, whether it be the Lord himself or Israel, and also that the act of sin-bearing is inextricably and mysteriously linked to the Lord's identity (7:18) *and* Israel's judgment (7:9). Interpreted in light of this twofold theological context, we learn that a "bearing" that ignores righteousness and justice for the sake of mercy does not enact Israel's forgiveness, but rather one that fulfills righteousness and justice. This atoning forgiveness, which stands at the center of Israel's redemption and the new creation it brings, reflects the revelation of the Lord's character and identity given in the wilderness to Israel (Exod. 34:5–7; cf. Mic. 7:18–20).

Bibliography

Barton, "The Prophets and the Cult," in *Temple and Worship in Biblical Israel*, 2005.
Boda, *A Severe Mercy*, 2009.
Childs, "Atonement, Expiation, and Forgiveness: The Old Testament Witness," in *Biblical Theology of the Old and New Testaments*, 1992.
Gese, "The Atonement," in *Essays on Biblical Theology*, 1981.
Jeremias, *Kultprophetie und Gerichtsverkündigung in der späten Königszeit*, 1970.
McKeown, "Forgiveness," in *Dictionary of the Old Testament Prophets*, 2012.
Tiemeyer, *Priestly Rites and Prophetic Rage*, 2006.
Wellhausen, *Prolegomena to the History of Ancient Israel*, 1958.
Wolff, *Micah*, 1990.

31

Rudolf Bultmann

David W. Congdon

Rudolf Bultmann is not known for his theology of the atonement, and for good reason. He says relatively little about the doctrine, and when it does come up, he is an unwavering critic. Precisely for this reason, however, he makes an important contribution to the conversation.

For Bultmann, the term *Sühne*, meaning atonement or expiation, is just one image among many in the New Testament that specifies the sacrificial nature of Jesus's death, in which forgiveness of sin is effected by the shedding of his blood. The word also appears in his writings in two other forms: *Sühnopfer* (sometimes *Sühneopfer*), meaning expiatory (or atoning) sacrifice, and *Entsühnung*, meaning expiation or remission. A broader study of atonement in Bultmann would have to examine two other words: *Erlösung* (redemption), which he associates with Gnosticism, and *Versöhnung* (reconciliation), which he associates with Pauline theology. I focus here on *Sühne* since it highlights why Bultmann is critical of the traditional atonement doctrine.

Bultmann acknowledges that Jesus's death was understood "as an atoning sacrifice [*Sühnopfer*] already in the early church-community" (*Theologie des Neuen Testaments*, 47). This is indicated especially by the tradition of the Eucharistic meal, which is closely associated with sacrificial language (144, 147), as well as the frequent talk of Jesus dying "for our sins" and "for us" (47, 84, 290). The sacrificial understanding of Jesus's death within the early church finds further support in Paul's use of ἱλαστήριον (means of expiation) in Romans 3:25, but also by the fact that such language is atypical for Paul; he appears to be using traditional Jewish-Christian language that predates him (47, 290–291). "The interpretation of Jesus's death as an *atoning sacrifice for sins*" was therefore not a view specific to Paul or to any one community of the ancient church, but was "a general-Christian idea" (84; emphasis in the original). In short, Bultmann the historian recognizes that talk of Jesus's death as an atoning or expiatory sacrifice is part of the original theology of the Christian community. That in itself, however, does not make the idea theologically normative, nor does it prevent him from arguing that, in places like the epistle of 1 John, we see evidence of redaction "in the interest of a proposition of church dogmatics, ... namely the proposition of atonement [*Entsühnung*] through the blood of Christ" ("Die kirchliche Redaktion des ersten Johannesbriefes," 391).

There are two primary reasons that Bultmann puts forward for rejecting a traditional view of the atonement: (1) a theology of divine action and (2) the hermeneutical problem. I will treat these in order.

1. An early clue to Bultmann's theology of atonement appears near the end of his 1926 book, *Jesus*, where Bultmann discusses the act of forgiveness, which is an event that cannot be seen "objectively" as part of the "world of objects." By contrast, "church tradition ... sees the event, the decisive act of salvation, in the death of Jesus or in his death and resurrection" (*Jesus*, 144). Insofar as the salvific death and resurrection of Jesus are understood in the tradition "as occurrences of history" that are objectively observable, the church is "wrong." For "all speculations and theories are false that seek to secure through proof that the death and resurrection of Jesus have the power of forgiveness for the atonement of sins [*Sündensühne*]" (144). The problem with church tradition on this point is that it binds salvation to a sacrificial logic and portrays the crucifixion as a kind of objective, causal mechanism that propitiates God. Bultmann calls this speculative or theoretical, since it interprets the significance and efficacy of Jesus's death by positing a metaphysical explanation.

Bultmann is here giving voice to his inchoate doctrine of divine revelation and action that he was still developing in light of his turn to dialectical theology in 1920. Karl Barth and Friedrich Gogarten convinced him that, given the justification of the ungodly, God has to be understood as an eschatological (i.e., "wholly other") reality that acts within the world in a way accessible to faith alone. Consequently, divine action cannot be apprehended within the "world of objects" as one cosmic force among others (144). Just as divine justification reveals our inability to secure forgiveness of sin by our own moral effort, so too it reveals our inability to secure knowledge of God through our own intellectual effort. The latter is what Bultmann has in mind when criticizing theories and proofs about the death and resurrection of Jesus. Such theories objectify Christ in a way that no longer requires an encounter with him through faith, and thus they no longer speak of the same reality. Bultmann's later theology remains consistent with the views articulated in the 1920s; however, what changes in his later work is that he gives more sophisticated attention to the problem of hermeneutics.

2. The problem of hermeneutics can be summarized as the problem of translating the kerygma from one cultural-historical situation to another. The biblical texts "speak in a foreign language with concepts from a faraway time, from a foreign world-picture." As a result, "they must be *translated*, and translation is the task of historical science" ("Ist voraussetzungslose Exegese möglich?," 145). Bultmann's hermeneutical program is an attempt to understand the message of the New Testament within a new cultural context or "world-picture" (*Weltbild*). Perhaps nowhere is the hermeneutical problem more acute than in the doctrine of Christ's atoning sacrifice on the cross, for here we face a world-picture—shaped by assumptions regarding the propitiating and expiating power of animal sacrifice—that is utterly foreign to most people today.

Bultmann is of the conviction that we are no more bound to traditional interpretations of the atonement than we are to the Hellenistic culture of first-century Palestine, not to mention the still older cultures of the Ancient Near East. The point is not that we can simply dismiss the thought-world of that time, but that we cannot pretend we share their world-picture; we need not and should not bind our theology to a foreign conceptuality. In order to do justice to the historicity of both text and reader, we need to differentiate between the New Testament talk of Jesus as a sin offering and the soteriological meaning of such talk. Conflating the two is to speak mythologically, while contextualizing the latter within a new conceptuality is to speak existentially. Bultmann thus replaces the idea of the cross as an expiating sacrifice with the idea of an "eschatological occurrence" that places one before the decision of faith ("In eigener Sache," 187).

In conclusion, Bultmann finds a traditional account of atonement or expiation problematic because talk of a sin offering bearing the sins of the people is not only a culturally relative notion, but it also objectifies and misrepresents the nature of divine action. According to Bultmann, therefore, "this then is the task of theology: to make this word of the cross understandable—not through any dogmatic theory about the vicarious atonement of Jesus Christ, but as the word that calls him who hears it to accept the cross" ("Theology for Freedom and Responsibility," 967).

Bibliography

Bultmann, "Die kirchliche Redaktion des ersten Johannesbriefes [1951]," in *Exegetica: Aufsätze zur Erforschung des Neuen Testaments*, 1967.

Bultmann, "In eigener Sache [1957]," in vol. 3 of *Glauben und Verstehen: Gesammelte Aufsätze*, 1960a.

Bultmann, "Ist voraussetzungslose Exegese möglich? [1957]," in vol. 3 of *Glauben und Verstehen: Gesammelte Aufsätze*, 1960b.

Bultmann, *Jesus*, 1983.

Bultmann, *Theologie des Neuen Testaments*, 2nd ed., 1954.

Bultmann, "Theology for Freedom and Responsibility," in *The Christian Century*, August 27, 1958.

32

John McLeod Campbell

Peter K. Stevenson

Published in 1856 *The Nature of the Atonement* is Campbell's best-known work, regarded by many as a classic contribution to Christian thinking about atonement. However, several factors have probably contributed to significant misunderstandings of his approach.

By describing his approach as "moral and spiritual" rather than "penal," Campbell left himself open to the inaccurate criticism that he was advancing a "moral influence theory" of atonement. In addition, his cumbersome style of writing can deter readers from moving beyond the famous passage about Christ offering, "*a perfect Amen in humanity to the judgment of God on the sin of man*" (*The Nature of the Atonement*, 118; emphasis in the original). Stopping here means missing ten further chapters in which Campbell develops a more complex approach to atonement.

Other critics focus on comments about Christ making "a perfect confession" of sin on the cross; arguing that such notions of "vicarious repentance" indicate an inadequate form of exemplarism. As Campbell did not use the term "vicarious repentance," such assessments are open to question. A fuller examination of the material, however, reveals a multidimensional exploration of atonement.

A failure to read Campbell's theology in the light of his ministerial career severely distorts the picture. Writing to his second son in 1886, Campbell explained that what he had "written for the press" in later years "was all present substantially very early in my preaching." A consistency of thought can indeed be detected by noting key themes in his earliest preaching at Row (1825–1831), which are not only present in sermons from his Glasgow ministry (1832–1859), but also evident in *The Nature of the Atonement* in 1856 (Stevenson, 114–151). His dramatic life and ministry supplied essential background for a more accurate picture of this theology.

Campbell's Theological Journey

Within a few years of being inducted to the parish of Row in Dumbartonshire in 1825, the young John McLeod Campbell was tried for heresy. In May 1831, the Church of Scotland found him guilty of heresy and removed from its ministry "one of the profoundest theologians in the history of Scottish theology since the Reformation of the Church of Scotland" (Torrance, T. F., 287).

Controversially, Campbell challenged prevailing Federal Calvinist orthodoxy by proclaiming that Christ had died for all, not solely for the elect. Reflection on encounters with parishioners, who had no assurance of salvation, led him back to the Bible and to the conclusion that the only reliable basis for assurance was in knowing that Christ died for all upon the cross. Such convictions about the *extent* of the atonement are assumed twenty-five years later when Campbell starts to write about the *nature* of Christ's saving work.

In both his sermons and books, Campbell affirmed that God's love is the cause, and not the consequence of the atonement. While opponents regarded his theology as a challenge to Scottish Reformed orthodoxy, Campbell was actually being loyal to the Reformation heritage. For by affirming that God did not need to be persuaded to be loving, Campbell was echoing teachers such as Calvin who stated that "the work of the atonement derives from God's love; therefore it has not established the latter" (*Inst.* II. xvi, 4).

Atonement as the Natural Development of the Incarnation

Campbell connected incarnation and suffering by describing the atonement as "the natural development of the incarnation" (19; 228). Leanne Van Dyk suggests that "as a general rule, 'natural' means an interpretation which starts from the facts of Christ's life on earth as recorded in the Scriptures rather than an interpretation which starts from an external point of inquiry such as the necessity, or possibility of the atonement" (41–42).

This means understanding the atonement in light of the biblical story of Jesus and not as the mechanical outworking of external laws of justice. Seeing it "in its own light" led Campbell to conclude that atonement should be understood in personal rather than penal terms. The incarnation of the divine Son leads naturally to atonement, because such a mediator would sympathize with both God's anger at sin and the divine desire to create a way for sinners to enter into a life of Sonship. Understanding atonement as the natural development of the incarnation means suffering, therefore, is unavoidable. In a fallen world, suffering inevitably arises when the absolute holiness of the incarnate Son comes face-to-face with human sinfulness. So "the truth is that the sufferings of Christ arose so naturally out of what He was, and the relation in which He stood to those for whose sins He suffered" (Campbell, *Nature of the Atonement*, 105–106).

The Flesh of Christ Differed Not In One Particle From Mine

In a sermon from his ministry at Row, Campbell explains the complete counsel of God, emphasizing one topic which "is the foundation of every thing [sic] else." He is referring to "the subject of our Lord's humanity—the subject of our Lord's having taken our nature, just as we have it—flesh and blood, just as it exists in you and me."

In various sermons, Campbell emphasizes that Christ assumed our "sinful, fallen nature," taking into personal subsistence with him not some "better flesh," but our "sinful flesh" (Stevenson, 152–182). At the same time, he clearly stated that the incarnate Son was sinless, overcoming temptation, "as a man" through constant dependence upon the power of the Holy Spirit. It is probable that the immediate source of such ideas was the teaching of Edward Irving, who had been teaching about Christ "taking up fallen humanity" over a number of years (182–189).

Insufficient attention has been paid to this dimension of Campbell's thought, due to an understandable lack of engagement with the Row sermons, which quickly went out of print. However, Campbell's teaching about Christ assuming fallen human nature is significant because it potentially sheds fresh light on the controversial proposal in *The Nature of the Atonement* about Christ making "a perfect confession of our sins" (118). For if the Son of God assumed our sinful, fallen nature, he would then be better able to make a meaningful confession of the sinfulness which is part of the warp and weft of human existence. Recognizing the Son's assumption of sinful, fallen human nature may not answer all the questions about Christ offering "a perfect confession," but it offers resources for responding to criticisms of Campbell's approach.

The Nature of the Atonement

Campbell's book *The Nature of the Atonement* articulates a priestly and representative theology of atonement. Trevor Hart claims that Campbell's theology, in alignment with Anselm's *Cur Deus Homo*, affirms "the necessity for the accomplishment of an objective atonement between God and man in which the divine wrath over human sin is dealt with" (331). Campbell's fourfold discussion focuses upon what he calls the *retrospective* and *prospective* dimensions of redemption (114–150).

Retrospective—Christ's Witnessing with Humanity on the Part of God

This focuses on the incarnate Son witnessing to God's truth in the midst of a fallen world. Being perfectly obedient to God in a fallen world inevitably involves suffering as perfect love encounters hatred. Campbell emphasizes that these were not punitive sufferings inflicted upon a loving Son by a vengeful Father; but the pains that God, in our nature, was bound to experience under constant pressure from human sin.

Retrospective—Christ's Dealing with God on Behalf of Humanity

This aspect of Campbell's thought attracts most debate. He detects within the writings of Jonathan Edwards a hint that an alternative way of understanding atonement might be possible.

> In contending "that sin must be punished with an infinite punishment," President Edwards says, that "God could not be just to Himself without this vindication, unless there could be such a thing as a repentance, humiliation and sorrow for this (viz. sin) proportional to the greatness of the majesty despised," for that there needs be, "either an equivalent punishment or an equivalent sorrow and repentance"—"so," he proceeds, "sin must be punished with an infinite punishment," thus assuming that the alternative of "an equivalent sorrow and repentance" was out of the question. (*The Nature of the Atonement*, 118–119)

Working with this idea unearthed from his Reformed heritage, Campbell explores the notion of Christ offering "an equivalent sorrow and repentance," which acknowledges both the full horror of sin and God's righteousness in confronting sin with the full weight of judgment.

> That oneness of mind with the Father, which towards man took the form of condemnation of sin, would in the Son's dealing with the Father in relation to our sins, take the form of a perfect confession of our sins. This confession, as to its

own nature, must have been "a perfect Amen in humanity to the judgement of God on the sin of man." (118)

For Campbell, this "perfect Amen" does not mean the Son merely offers a sincere apology to God for the sins of the world. A closer reading of his theology reveals a much more robust, objective understanding of atonement.

This controversial statement needs to be viewed through the lens of the conviction, expressed in Campbell's earliest sermons, that the Son assumed our "sinful, fallen nature." Seen from the perspective of Christ assuming our "sinful flesh" suggests that through this "perfect Amen," the incarnate Son confessed to the Father that the fallen humanity he assumed is so diseased and riddled with sin that it deserved and needed to be judged and put to death upon the cross. On this basis, James Torrance can claim that the response of the Son to the Father included a "perfect submission on our behalf to the verdict of guilty" (309).

Further support for this perspective is provided by a sermon from his ministry in Glasgow where Campbell asks:

> Now, how does Jesus receive the suffering? ... He receives it as *the righteous reward of sin*, the wages of sin which is death. He does not rebel or kick against it, therefore, but says, "Thou art righteous, O Lord, because Thou hast judged thus." And this righteousness of feeling in Christ, this willingness that transgression shall meet with its due reward, even when He himself stands in the transgressor's room, is well-pleasing in the sight of Him who loveth righteousness. (1898; emphasis in the original)

Interpreting Campbell's statement in the light of these earlier sermons uncovers an objective atonement achieved by Christ fully accepting the need for divine judgment upon sin, and enduring death upon the cross; believing that such suffering was not an arbitrary punishment, but rather the only way to destroy sin by taking it out of circulation. For "Christ receives suffering as the wise and perfect remedy approved by a tender Father, for the recovery of His children from an otherwise incurable disease" (1898).

Prospective—Christ's Witnessing for the Father to Humanity

Some atonement models concentrate so heavily on the retrospective aspect that it can be difficult to see how that past event and present experience of salvation is connected. Campbell, however, was concerned to explore not only what human beings have been saved *from* but also what they have been saved *for*. "I have said above, that the atonement is regarded as that by which God has bridged over the gulf which separated between what sin had made us, and what it was the desire of the divine love that we should become" (*The Nature of the Atonement*, 127).

Prospective—Christ's Dealing with the Father on Our Behalf

Christ's retrospective dealing with God on humanity's behalf involved offering a confession of human sinfulness; and an acknowledgment of God's righteousness in responding to sin in wrath and judgment. The corresponding dynamic within the prospective aspect of atonement consists of Christ's intercession for people to participate in eternal life.

Campbell believes that something objective has taken place, because Christ offered a perfect confession that was accepted by the Father. However they respond, the saving work accomplished by the Son and the Father has changed the status of sinful people, who now can be drawn back to God, through Christ in power of the Spirit.

Taken in isolation no single perspective yields an adequate soteriology. However, holding all four aspects together, as Campbell intended, results in a suggestive construal of the doctrine of atonement.

Bibliography

Campbell, "The Consolations of Christ; Sermon on 2 Corinthians 1:3–7," in *Fragments of Truth: Being Expositions of Passages of Scripture Chiefly from the Teaching of John McLeod Campbell, D.D.*, 1898.

Campbell, *The Nature of the Atonement*, 2nd edn, 1996.

Hart, "Anselm of Canterbury and John McLeod Campbell: Where Opposites Meet?" *Evangelical Quarterly* 62, 1990.

Stevenson, *God in Our Nature: The Incarnational Theology of John McLeod Campbell*, 2004.

Torrance, J. B., "The Contribution of McLeod Campbell to Scottish Theology," *Scottish Journal of Theology* 26, 1973.

Torrance, T. F., *Scottish Theology from John Knox to John McLeod Campbell*, 1996.

Tuttle, *John McLeod Campbell on Christian Atonement: So Rich a Soil*, 1986.

Van Dyk, *The Desire of Divine Love: John McLeod Campbell's Doctrine of the Atonement*, 1995.

33

Catherine of Siena

Adam Eitel

Caterina di Iiacopo di Benincasa (1347–1380) came of age in the plague-ravaged and politically contentious Fontebranda district of the Republic of Siena. From a young age Catherine exhibited unusual piety and independence: at fifteen, she cut off her hair in defiance of familial pressure to marry; at eighteen, she was received by the *Mantellate*, a female religious movement, under whose influence she spent three years of formation; at twenty-one, an unexpected mystical encounter catapulted her onto the public stage as a spiritual guide, political advisor, and social reformer. She died at thirty-three. Her extant works include over three hundred and eighty letters, twenty-six prayers, and a single book—the *Dialogue*—an extended conversation between God and Catherine's soul.

Catherine did not write in conventional genres of fourteenth-century faculties of theology. Her *Dialogue*, much as her letters, is built up neither by *tractationes* nor *quaestiones*, but rather by networks of metaphors designed to exhort and admonish. The images she uses to portray Christ's saving work vary in this connection according to intention and context. On several occasions Christ is described as a bridegroom who ransoms his adulteress bride—the human race—from the devil (*Letters*, 1:23; cf. 1:147). Elsewhere she styles Christ a great knight who jousts with sin and death (2:324). His blood is the key that unlocks heaven (*Dial.*, §27: 66). In one instance Christ is pictured as both doctor and wet nurse: "Adam's sin oozed with a deadly pus, but you were too weakened to drain it yourself. But when the great doctor came (my only-begotten Son) he tended that wound, drinking himself the bitter medicine you could not swallow." Catherine continues, "And he did so as the wet nurse who herself drinks the medicine the baby needs, because she is big and strong and the baby is too weak to stand the bitterness" (§14: 52).

This proliferation of disparate metaphors for Christ's saving work might suggest that Catherine espouses no formal teaching on the subject. A single passage from the *Dialogue* shows this assumption to be unwarranted. For Catherine, as for most of the Christian tradition in general, Christ's death is properly understood as a sacrifice.

> The clay of humankind was spoiled by the sin of the first man, Adam, and so all of you, as vessels made from that clay, were spoiled and unfit to hold eternal life. So to undo the corruption and death of humankind and to bring you back to the grace you had lost through sin, I, exaltedness, united myself with the baselessness of your humanity. For my divine justice demanded suffering in atonement for sin. But I cannot suffer. And you, being only human ... could not fully atone (*satisfare*) either for yourself or for others since it was committed against me, and I am infinite Goodness.
>
> Yet I really wanted to restore you, incapable as you were of making atonement for yourself. And because you were so utterly handicapped, I sent the Word, my son. I clothed him with the same nature as yours—the spoiled clay of Adam—so that he could suffer in that same nature which had sinned ... And so I satisfied both my justice and my divine mercy. For my mercy wanted to atone for your sin and make you fit to receive the good for which I had created you. Humanity, when united with divinity, was able to make atonement for the whole human race—not simply through suffering in its finite nature, that is, in the clay of Adam, but by virtue of the eternal divinity, the infinite divine nature. In the union of those two natures I received and accepted the sacrifice of my only-begotten Son's blood, steeped and kneaded with his divinity into the one bread, which the heat of my divine love held nailed to the cross. (§14: 51–52)

Catherine's smooth arrangement of lofty terms is liable to conceal the complexity of her argument, which may be summarized as follows: (1) The sin of the first human being, Adam, "spoiled" or "corrupted" human nature, rendering human beings unfit for the gift of eternal life. Sin is moreover an offense to God, "whose divine justice demanded suffering in atonement." (2) Yet, the suffering of a finite and fallen creature could not have made full atonement for sin, "since it was committed against God, who is Infinite Goodness." Rather, as Catherine later puts it, "to make satisfaction ... human nature, which had sinned and was finite, had to be united to something infinite" (§135: 278). (3) Because God is merciful, he "wanted to atone for ... sin and make human beings fit for the good for which [he] had created them." In the incarnation, God therefore made atonement possible by uniting his infinite divine nature with finite human nature.

(4) The crucifixion then actualizes this possibility: "in the union of those two natures [God] received and accepted the sacrifice of [his] only begotten Son's blood" (§14: 51–52).

Several aspects of this argument should be noted. First, Catherine's chief focus is the character of God: God redeems human beings in a manner that comports with divine justice and mercy. Second, Catherine grounds the significance of Christ's sacrificial death in his divinity. Christ "was able to make atonement for the whole human race—not simply through suffering in its finite nature ... but by virtue of the eternal divinity ..." Third, the entire argument is constructed from inherited authorities: the image of Christ's body held to the cross by divine love derives from Domenico Cavelca's *Specchio di croce*, which in turn recalls Hugh of St. Victor, *De laude charitatis* (176: 974–975). The actual substance of the argument could be traced through any number of mediate sources to Thomas Aquinas's *Summa Theologiae*, not to mention Anselm's *Cur Deus Homo*.

If Catherine's originality is found not so much in her doctrine as in her capacity for vivid expression, her complex metaphors nevertheless show theologically remarkable ingenuity. A good example can be seen in a letter addressed to Sano di Marco di Massacorno. Drawing upon Pauline legal metaphors, Catherine reminds Sano that Christ "assumed responsibility [for sin], paid our debt, and then tore up the bond" when he "assumed our humanity" and "gave up his life on the wood of the most holy cross" (*Letters*, 1:66–67). As if to complete this thought, Catherine notes that "that bond was written on nothing less than lambskin, the skin of the spotless Lamb. He inscribed us on himself and then tore up the lambskin!" This concatenation of images holds together several views that moderns have sometimes deemed incompatible: it suggests that Christ ransoms human beings from bondage to sin precisely *by* sacrificing himself on their behalf. A final example comes from the *Dialogue*, where Catherine extends this imagery to encompass a view often associated with Peter Abelard. It is from Bernard of Clairveaux, however, not Abelard, that Catherine learns to picture Christ's wounds as windows to God's own heart: "'Why, gentle spotless Lamb, since you were dead when your side was opened, did you want your heart to be pierced and parted?' He answered, 'There were plenty of reasons, but I shall tell you the chief.... I showed you this in the opening of my side. There you find my heart's secret and it shows you, more than any finite suffering could, how I love you'" (*Dial.*, §75: 138; cf. Bernard, 183: 1072). For Catherine, surely no explanation of Christ's saving work would be complete apart from this God—"mad lover" of human beings (*Dial.*, §153: 325).

Selected Bibliography

Bernard of Clairveaux, *In Cantico sermo LXI*, 4, ed. Migne.
Catherine of Siena, *Il Dialogo della Divina Provvidenza ovvero Libro della Divina Dottrina*, ed. Cavallini, 1968; trans. Noffke as *The Dialogue*, 1980.
Noffke, *The Letters of Catherine of Siena*, vols 1–4, 2000.
Raimondo da Capua, [*Legenda major*] *S. Caterina da Siena*, trans. Giuseppe Tinagli. Siena: Cantagalli, 1934; trans. George Lamb as *The Life of St. Catherine of Siena*, 1960.
Thomas Antonii de Senis "Caffarini," *Libellus de Supplemento: Legende Prolixe Virginis Beate Catherine de Senis*, ed. Cavallini and Foralosso, 1974.

34

Covenant

Jeremy R. Treat

In the grand narrative of Scripture, the refrain *forgiveness through atonement* comes within the broader covenant song of *I will be your God and you will be my people*. And yet, despite its prominence in Scripture and theology, the concept of covenant has often been overlooked in atonement theology, a trend that Michael Gorman calls "the absence of the obvious" (9). Fortunately, scholars from various traditions have begun to rediscover the need for covenant in the church's understanding of Christ's atoning work. This chapter seeks to advance the conversation by further clarifying how covenant informs the doctrine of atonement.

I understand the doctrine of atonement to be the church's understanding of the way in which Christ, through all of his work but primarily his death, has dealt with sin and its effects in order to restore the broken covenant relationship between God and sinners and thereby establish God's redemptive rule over his creation. A covenant in Scripture is a binding relationship based on obligations and sealed with an oath that makes two parties as close as family (Hahn, 168–175). How, then, do covenant and atonement relate? I offer three theses.

Covenant Is Indispensable for the Context of Atonement

Covenant provides indispensable context for atonement in at least two ways: redemptive historical, and relational. First, covenant provides redemptive historical context for atonement. Within the unfolding story of Scripture, atonement enters in at a stage where God has already bound himself to his people. The sacrificial ritual in Genesis 15 takes place in the context of God making a covenant with Abraham. The sacrificial system, the means of atonement in the Old Testament, is introduced as part of the instructions of the covenant. In the New Testament, Christ's atoning work is presented not merely as the fulfillment of general promises but rather as the culmination of God's covenants with his people and as the inauguration of the promised new covenant (Mt. 26:8; Jer. 31:31). Jesus is the mediator of this new covenant, accomplishing the forgiveness of sins through his atoning work. Covenant also provides redemptive historical context for atonement not only by showing its background and its fulfillment in Christ, but also by pointing forward to its goal. Atonement is aimed at a new covenant with a renewed people in a new creation.

Second, covenant provides relational context for atonement. Scripture is a story of overcoming the sin-induced separation between God and his people (Is. 59:2) within the broader aim of mending the breach between heaven and earth (Rev. 21:1–5). But what type of "separation" is implied in this story? The answer to this question is significant, for prescribing the remedy depends on rightly describing the ruin. The covenantal background of atonement reveals that the "separation" between God and sinners is primarily relational, which, far from ruling out the other aspects (e.g., legal, ontological, geographical), actually provides a framework for them (Horton, 10–16). If relational separation is at the heart of the problem, then at-one-ment between God and sinners will be at the heart of the solution. Yet, while Christ died to bring sinners into a relationship with their creator, it is not a generic, non-defined relationship. Rather, Christ's atoning work brings sinners into a *covenant* relationship with God, a relational bond that makes two parties as close as family. Reconciliation has always been the aim of atonement, but reconciliation in Scripture has a covenantal ring.

Before moving on, I should clarify the scope of my claim. Covenant is *an* essential aspect of the context of atonement, not *the* context by itself. My proposal is therefore much more modest than that of Gorman, for example, who offers a "comprehensive model" based on the new covenant (*The Death of the Messiah and the Birth of the New Covenant*, 19). I question whether producing new exclusive models or theories is the best approach to begin with, but granting Gorman's aim, it seems to me that covenant (and the new covenant in particular) functions in the New Testament more in the background rather than in the foreground. I see covenant, therefore, as *a* (not *the*) key theme that informs atonement. Covenant fits within a broader story of the kingdom of God coming through the Son of God for the glory of God.

Covenant Is Intrinsic to the Definition of Atonement

Covenant is not only indispensable context for atonement, it is also intrinsic to its very definition. In other words, one cannot rightly understand atonement itself apart from covenant. Jesus is the mediator of a new covenant who brings about a new binding relationship between God and his people through his multifaceted work of atonement. But how precisely does covenant inform the definition of Christ's atoning work, particularly in the various stages of Jesus's ministry? Each aspect of Christ's atoning work is essential, for, as John Webster says, "No one moment of the history can bear the weight of the whole" (41).

The concept of covenant fills Christ's life not only with meaning, but also with atoning significance. This truth shines bright upon the backdrop of the biblical story of three sons: Adam, Israel, and Jesus. Adam was created in a covenantal relationship with God (or at least a covenant-like relationship with God) and given the task of extending God's royal blessings from Eden to the ends of the earth (Gen. 1:28, 2:15; cf. Ps. 8). Adam, however, "transgressed the covenant" (Hos. 6:7) and rather than extending God's blessings, spread the curse. Israel was then called into a covenant with God and similarly commissioned to be a "kingdom of priests" (Ex. 19:6) and a "light to the nations" (Is. 49:6). Yet Israel broke the covenant as a disobedient son, and just as Adam was banished from Eden, Israel was exiled from the Promised Land. Enter Jesus. The eternal Son of God came as the last Adam (1 Cor. 15:45; Rom. 5:12–21) and faithful Israel (Mt. 4:1–11), recapitulating their histories in his own life and ministry and keeping the covenant at each point they had broken it. Jesus was not merely sinless; he was faithful. And he was not merely faithful; he was faithful to the covenant.

Covenant is essential for understanding the atoning significance of Christ's death for at least three reasons. First, Christ's death must be understood as a covenantal sacrifice, meaning that it atoned for sins and served to remind the covenant parties of the consequences for breaking the covenant, thereby calling for faithfulness. Second, in his death, Christ does not bear *any* penalty; rather, he bears the covenant curses, which include refusal of forgiveness and the bestowal of God's anger (Deut. 29:20–21). Third, and cumulatively, by bearing the curses of the covenant through his sacrificial death, Jesus ratifies the new covenant. When Jesus said, "This is my blood of the covenant" on the night before he was betrayed (Mt. 26:28), he was drawing upon Exodus 24:8 where Moses ratified the covenant made between God and Israel after the exodus by sacrificing animals and dashing blood on the people. As the old covenant was inaugurated by blood, Christ's sacrificial death seals the new covenant between God and his people (Heb. 10:15–22).

How does covenant help make sense of the atoning value of Christ's resurrection and ascension? The author of Hebrews forcefully reminds the reader that Jesus is the "mediator of a new covenant" (Heb. 9:15) and that his priesthood is not limited to his work on the cross, for "he holds his priesthood permanently, because he continues forever" (Heb. 7:23–24; O'Collins and Jones, 265). It is important, however, that the continuing priesthood of Christ, and particularly the atoning value of his offering in the heavenly sanctuary (Heb. 9:11–14), is not set against Christ's atoning accomplishment on the cross (as Socinus did). Rather, the cross and the ascension display the breadth of Christ's atoning work and demonstrate that, just as in the Old Testament sacrificial system, atonement is a process. Furthermore, it is the resurrected and ascended Christ who sends his Spirit to continue his work on earth. "*Pentecost belongs to the atonement*," says Thomas Torrance, "for the presence of the Spirit is the actualization amongst us of the new or redeemed life" (178).

We have seen that covenant is intrinsic to the definition of atonement. Christ fulfills the covenant obligations with his life, bears the covenant curses through his sacrificial death, and then resurrects and ascends as the high priest of the new covenant—all of which are part of his work of reconciling God and sinners into a covenant relationship.

Covenant Is Integrative in the Doctrine of Atonement

While we have seen what covenant *is* in relation to atonement, I will now make a proposal for what covenant can *do* in atonement theology; namely, bind together various aspects of Christ's atoning work. In other words, a covenant is about God binding himself to his people, but the concept of covenant can bind together disparate themes in atonement theology. Vanhoozer aptly summarizes the integrating power of covenant for understanding Christ's work:

> While the sundry conceptualities championed by the various atonement theories do not, strictly speaking, cohere, they are nevertheless compatible thanks to the integrative framework of the covenant—a complex, multilevel reality that combines the judicial and relational aspects of Jesus' death "for us" in a garment as seamless as the one for which the soldiers cast lots. (387)

The concept of covenant reveals the fully orbed nature of the atonement and how the various aspects of Christ's work complement one another in a comprehensive and expansive account. Covenant, therefore, has an adhesive function in atonement theology, encouraging integration and upholding coherence. The integrating power of covenant has the potential to repair many common false dichotomies that plague atonement theology and thereby demonstrate, for example, that Christ's atoning work is relational *and* juridical, individual *and* corporate, and restorative *and* retributive. Covenant is significant for both a biblically faithful understanding of Christ's work and a theologically rich account of atonement.

Bibliography

Gorman, *The Death of the Messiah and the Birth of the New Covenant*, 2014.
Hahn, *Kinship by Covenant*, 2009.
Horton, *Lord and Servant*, 2005.
Levenson, *The Death and Resurrection of the Beloved Son*, 1993.
O'Collins and Jones, *Jesus Our Priest*, 2010.
Shelton, *Cross and Covenant*, 2006.
Torrance, *Atonement*, 2009.
Treat, "Atonement and Covenant: Binding Together Aspects of Christ's Work," in *Locating Atonement: Explorations in Constructive Dogmatics*, 2015.
Vanhoozer, *The Drama of Doctrine*, 2005.
Webster, "*Rector Et Index Super Omnia Genera Doctrinarum*? The Place of the Doctrine of Justification," in *What Is Justification About?*, 2009.

35

Thomas Cranmer

Scott Harrower

Thomas Cranmer was born in 1489, and studied at Cambridge where he developed as a humanist scholar and earned a doctorate in divinity. After graduation he was a Don at Cambridge and also worked as ambassador and researcher for Henry VIII. He became the archbishop of Canterbury from 1532 and held that position until his martyrdom in 1556. As archbishop, his theological and liturgical work enshrined the biblical and patristic foundations for what is today the Anglican Communion. The immediate pressure behind this work was King Henry VIII's personal and political ambitions, including establishing himself as the sovereign of an independent Church of England. The more gradual aspect of his work stemmed from developments in religious and intellectual movements on the European continent and their reception by a number of English church leaders. The atoning work of God in Christ was one of the key theological themes along which the early English reformers coordinated their efforts to theologically reorient the church in England (Null, 21–27; MacCulloch, 617). Wide ranges of means were deployed to ensure the atonement as central to the beliefs and practices of the church. These included parliamentary statutes, forms of worship, the reintroduction of the Bible into parish life, regular preaching of select sermons, and new standards of theological beliefs. Cranmer's role in this process was crucial. In addition, his importance lies in the fact that the evolution of his own theology of the atonement (and the practices which stemmed from it) collated and preserved various strands of sixteenth-century reformist perspectives and practices to do with the atonement (McGrath, 232–241; 258–263; MacCulloch, 173–200).

Cranmer's own theology of the atonement matured over the course of his lifetime, as his theology in the middle and later phase of his life clearly broke with his late medieval scholastic training (Null, 120–133, 211–212; MacCulloch, 345–347).

Previous to his appointment as archbishop, his view on the atonement was formed under the influence of German Lutherans. This evolved in the course of his participation of the evangelical and humanist reformation under the reign of Henry VIII. During Cranmer's Henrician phase (1534–1547), he oversaw the production of works with a Lutheran theology of the atonement such as the *Ten Articles* (1536). His views are also expressed in his *Thirteen Articles, with Three Additional Articles* (1538) and in *Preface to the Great Bible* (1540). His mature theology of the atonement was Reformed, and was explicitly reflected in the theological and liturgical works and developments which he brought about during the reign of Edward VI. Cranmer never states this evolution explicitly in a dedicated tome on the atonement; rather, the implications of the atonement pervaded his works. The key elements of his mature atonement theology will be discussed below.

Homily 3, *Of the Salvation of Mankind* (1547), reveals that for Cranmer the central theological focus of the Christian faith was a forensic imputation of Christ's righteousness to the sinner (Null, 215–222). The homily provides the warrant for this gracious action by powerfully describing the problem that God's atoning work in Christ addresses. It is a problem intrinsic to human beings and its solution is sourced in God himself:

> Because all men be sinners and offenders against God, and breakers of his law and commandments, therefore can no man by his own acts, works, and deeds, seem they never so good, be justified, and made righteous before God; but every man of necessity is constrained to seek for another righteousness or justification, to be received at God's own hands, that is to say, the remission, pardon, and forgiveness of his sins and trespasses in such things as he hath offended. (Homily 3; Cranmer, 128)

The goal of Jesus's death was to enable the "remission of our sins and our justification," which is "the office of God only," and hence was an act of grace since the declaration of being justified before God "is not a thing which we render unto him" (Homily 3; Cranmer, 131).

Cranmer was also very clear on the fact that Christ's death on the cross was the sole historical basis for God's gracious forensic imputation of Christ's righteousness to the believer (Thompson, 210–214).

> But this saying, that we be justified by faith only, freely, and without works, is spoken for to take away clearly all merit of our works, as being unable to deserve our justification at God's hands; and thereby most plainly to express the weakness of man and the goodness of God, the great infirmity of ourselves and the might and power of God, the imperfectness of our own works and the most abundant grace of our Saviour Christ; and thereby wholly for to ascribe the

merit and deserving of our justification unto Christ only and his most precious bloodshedding. (Homily 3; Cranmer, 131)

The extent of the justification received is comprehensive and sufficient (Thompson, 215–217), and hence not partial or incomplete: "And this justification or righteousness, which we so receive by God's mercy and Christ's merits, embraced by faith, is taken, accepted, and allowed of God for our perfect and full justification" (Homily 3; Cranmer, 128).

Cranmer's view of God's wrath and mercy established the propitiatory nature of the atonement. For Cranmer, Jesus's death was a satisfaction, a propitiatory sacrifice in response to God's wrath at human sin (Thompson, 207–210, 213–214). Homily 3 states:

> It is our parts and duty ever to remember the great mercy of God, how that (all the world being wrapped in sin by breaking the law) God sent his only son our saviour into this world, to fulfil the law for us; and by shedding of his most precious blood to make a sacrifice and satisfaction, or (as it may be called) amends, to his Father for our sins, to assuage his wrath and indignation conceived against us for the same. (Cranmer, 128)

In addition to the penal substitutionary nature of the atonement, Cranmer grounded an exemplarist (as in an example to be followed) aspect to the suffering and death of Christ, as expressed in his Collect for the Sunday next before Easter in the 1549 Book of Common Prayer (Thompson, 217–218).

During the reign of Edward VI, Cranmer gave more robust liturgical expression to his atonement theology. For example, in *The Sacrament Act* (1547), he restored the reception of the Eucharist in both kinds to the laity, thereby distancing Edwardian sacramental atonement theology from its medieval predecessors (MacCulloch, 354–360). Cranmer's eucharistic theology, whereby the elements become the body and blood of Christ only upon reception by faith, made it clear that the sacrifice of Jesus's body was a once and for all event which was not repeated or extended by eucharistic actions or events in any way. This view was consolidated in his 1549 *Book of Common Prayer*, in which he altered the late medieval language to do with sacrifice at the Mass (Brooks, 155–160; MacCulloch, 412–415). His *A Defence of the True and Catholike Doctrine of the Sacrament* (1550) and the *Book of Common Prayer* (1552) cemented his views (MacCulloch, 506–513). These would become normative for the Church of England when they were taken up with little modification during the Elizabethan settlement and its aftermath (contra Null, 252–253).

Bibliography

Brooks, "The Theology of Thomas Cranmer," in *The Cambridge Companion to Reformation Theology*, 2004.

Cranmer, "Homily of Salvation" and "A Short Declaration of the True, Lively, and Christian Faith," in *Miscellaneous Writings and Letters of Thomas Cranmer*, 2001.

MacCulloch, *Thomas Cranmer: A Life*, 1996.

McGrath, *Iustitia Dei*, 2005.

Null, *Thomas Cranmer's Doctrine of Repentance*, 2000.

Thomson, "An Anglican Account: Thomas Cranmer on the Death of Christ," in *Christ Died for Our Sins*, ed. Stead, 2013.

36

Creation and Animals

David L. Clough

Throughout the history of the church, theories of atonement have rarely been discussed with other-than-human creatures in mind. This is surprising, given the emphasis in some New Testament texts on the cosmic scope of the reconciliation effected in Jesus Christ. The first chapter of Colossians affirms that in Christ, God "was pleased to reconcile all things (*ta panta*), whether on earth or in heaven, by making peace through the blood of his cross" (v. 20). Ephesians has a similarly broad view of the work of Christ, picturing "all things" in heaven and earth being gathered up in him (1:10). We seem, therefore, to be in need of an explanation of this lacuna in traditions of Christian atonement doctrine. Such an explanation does not seem to be far away: other New Testament texts state that Jesus Christ was "the atoning sacrifice for our sins" (1 John 2:2), "handed over handed over to death for our trespasses," and "raised for our justification" (Rom. 4:25). If these latter texts are correct and Jesus died for sins and trespasses, it seems to make little sense to say that he makes peace between things for which sins and trespasses have no relevance. Following this logic, theologians seem to have preferred to understand the Colossian and Ephesian "all things" as hyperbolic, and to construe atonement as a human-specific event. There are reasons to think, however, that this settlement is unsatisfactory. In this essay, therefore, I will explore options for a more expansive view that attends more closely to the cosmic vision of Colossians and Ephesians.

Andrew Linzey suggests that there are three options for orthodox Christian belief in relation to nonhuman animals and the atonement: (1) "animals are not capable of sin or estrangement and therefore are not able to be included in the saving work of Christ"; (2) "if they have sinned or fallen from grace it may be possible for the Son of God to become incarnate in their nature to in order to reconcile them" (Linzey, 99); (3) "by becoming incarnate in one rational species, the Son of God has *ipso facto* become the redeemer of all" (Mascall, 107). If the first or second option is correct, either nonhuman animals are not sinful or estranged and are not therefore in need of reconciliation, or they need a nonhuman incarnation for redemption. In either case, theories of atonement that treat humans exclusively are well-formulated: atonement is human-specific because the problem to which it responds is human-specific. Only if the third option is correct, that God's reconciling work in Jesus Christ is redemptive of all creatures, as the Christologies of Colossians and Ephesians suggest, do we need to rethink human-centered atonement theories.

One objection to the third option of extending the concept of atonement through the work of Jesus Christ to nonhuman creatures is that it is implausible to think that nonhuman creatures stand in need reconciliation. There are a range of ways of approaching this question, however, that indicate we need to think more broadly about the creatures for whom reconciliation is relevant. For example, the partners in the Genesis 9 covenant are repeatedly identified as Noah, his descendants, and "every living creature" of "all flesh" (vv. 10, 12, 15, 16, 17), and the later division between clean and unclean animals can plausibly be interpreted as between those that kept the covenant by eating the green plants specified for them in Genesis 1:30, and those that did not (Grumett and Muers, 73; Clough, 54–55). Transgressing or forgetting God's covenant representing the original ordering of things therefore seem modes of sin that are clearly applicable beyond the human realm. The covenant in Hosea also addresses nonhuman animals (Hos. 2:18). The judgment of God proclaimed by the prophets often falls humans and other animals together, in Jeremiah (7:20, 14:6, 21:6, 12:4), Ezekiel (14:13–21, 38:19–20), Joel (1:4–20, 2:4–7), Zephaniah (1:2–3), and Haggai (1:11). When Jonah prophesies to Nineveh, all humans and other animals fast and cover themselves with sackcloth (Jon. 3:7–8) and when God forgives Nineveh, God refers to nonhuman animals as well as humans to explain the decision to Jonah (4:11). There is therefore a broad biblical basis for thinking of the need for reconciliation going beyond the human sphere.

Another reason to judge that human beings are unique in their need for reconciliation is that many other attributes formerly considered uniquely human have been shown in studies of nonhuman animals to be more broadly shared. Crows have been observed to fashion tools to solve problems; chimpanzees are capable of empathy, morality, and politics, and of outdoing humans in numerically based memory tests; dolphins interpret grammar; parrots understand abstract properties of objects, such as color and shape; whales show cultural specificity in their behavior and communication (see discussion in Clough, 29–30 and 64–76). Given the overlap of many of these capacities with what we have understood as rationality, it is very difficult to advance a definition of rationality that distinguishes between human and nonhuman animals. Given this new knowledge of nonhuman animal capacities, it is unclear how we could retain a concept of wrongdoing and a consequent need for reconciliation that did not overlap in some way with at least some nonhuman animals. This general point is supported by specific examples, such as the account Jane Goodall gives of a history of the stealing and eating of infant chimpanzees by a particular female and her family, and the opposition and disgust manifested by other members of the troop (193–195, 206–207; Clough, 112–115).

While I judge that there is no good theological reason to restrict language of sin to human beings (Clough, 105–119), it may be that Linzey's reference to "estrangement" in his options noted above provides a category of creatures in need of reconciliation that is broader than sinfulness. Estrangement is more than innocent suffering. It is clear that both human and other-than-human creatures suffer as a result of sinful human cruelty, but such innocent victims are not thereby estranged from God. They require redemption from their suffering, certainly, but not reconciliation. Other creatures, however, could be seen in a different category. For example, Luther judges that the natures of nonhuman animals were changed by human sin to make some of them vicious and threatening (vol. 1, 76–77; vol. 2, 74). If this were the case, then wolves and lions, ordered originally to eat only green plants (Gen. 1:30), have, as a result of the Fall, departed from the way God set for them and become dependent on killing other creatures for their food. We might not in this case wish to say that wolves or lions sin in killing for food, but we might say that in this way of life they have become estranged from the God who wished them to live in peace. Wolves and lions might then be judged not as sinful, but as estranged, and so in need of reconciliation in order to participate in the renewed peaceable creaturely relations prophesied by Isaiah (11:1–9, 65:25).

This consideration of the question of whether nonhuman animals could be considered sinful, or estranged, from God suggests that Linzey's first option—that only humans require reconciliation—is not an attractive one. Sin and estrangement from God spills out beyond the human realm, and therefore humans are not the only creatures in need of reconciliation by God. The recognition of such sin or estrangement in nonhuman creatures is compatible with the second option Linzey presents, that in Jesus Christ God acted to bring reconciliation to human beings, and reconciliation of nonhuman species would require God to assume their nature in other incarnations. This is an unattractive prospect, however, for a number of reasons. First, it is as strongly at odds with the "all things" Christological visions of Colossians and Ephesians as the first option that denies the relevance of reconciliation to nonhuman creatures. On this account, Jesus Christ reconciles only one kind of thing, and some other savior is required for the rest. Second, replacing one cosmic incarnation with millions of species-specific ones seems unattractive in its complexity, and difficult conceptually, since species change over time, boundaries between them are fluid, and definitions of the boundaries between species are contested among biologists (Wilkins). The second option of God reconciling nonhuman creatures through a multitude of species-specific incarnations, therefore, does not commend itself.

While most of this discussion has been in terms of whether atonement and reconciliation relates to nonhuman animals in addition to human ones, it is important to take one step further and ask whether reconciliation is even more broadly applicable, to all creatures of God, the whole of creation. The Christological visions of Ephesians and Colossians so emphatically specify "all things" that there seems little justification for confining this work of God to animal creatures. The lack of a clear demarcation between animal and non-animal life—sponges and slime molds are borderline cases—is an additional reason to put significant theological weight on this boundary line. If "all things" are reconciled in Jesus Christ, we are better off thinking through atonement as God's reconciliation through Jesus Christ of an estranged creation, including creatures that are human animals, nonhuman animals, other living creatures such as plants and bacteria, and nonliving creatures, such as rivers, rocks, and stars. Only such a broad vision can do justice to these comprehensive and cosmic visions of God's work in Jesus Christ; to attempt to delimit the action of God to any subset of creatures seems very likely to encounter problems parallel to those we have discussed in relation to nonhuman animals. Clearly, creatures such as mountains and oceans are not in need of forgiveness of the kind of deliberate acts of rebellion that characterize the need of some humans for reconciliation, but rock falls and tsunamis remind us that these inanimate creatures are not always at peace with plant and animal life, and therefore that the peacemaking between all things effected in Jesus Christ (Col. 1:20) is needed even here.

Extending the reach of the doctrine of the atonement in this way raises a range of other doctrinal questions. If other-than-human creatures are estranged from God, as suggested above, we must reckon with a more-than-human doctrine of the Fall, rather than alternative options either that retain its application to humans alone, or discard it entirely (122–127). If Christ's reconciling work relates to those elected by God, then there are implications for the doctrine of election as well (Clough, chapter 4). If reconciliation leads to redemption, we should give consideration to more-than-human visions of the new creation and the creaturely relations that operate there (chapters 6–7). The theological reappraisals demanded within these other doctrinal loci illustrate the broad scope of fruitful theological questions provoked by attending to other-than-human animals in relation to the atonement. The alternative course of retaining a human-only account of atonement seems, in contrast, to represent an oddly constricted and over-modest vision of the atoning work of Jesus Christ.

Bibliography

Anselm, "Cur Deus Homo," in *Anselm: Basic Writings*, 2007.
Aquinas, *Summa Theologica*, trans. Fathers of the English Dominican Province, 1963.
Clough, *On Animals: I. Systematic Theology*, 2012.
Goodall, *Beyond Innocence: An Autobiography in Letters: The Later Years*, 2001.
Grumett and Muers, *Theology on the Menu: Asceticism, Meat and Christian Diet*, 2010.
Linzey, *Animal Theology*, 1994.
Luther, *Luther's Works*, ed. Lehmann and Pelikan, 1958.
Mascall, *The Christian Universe*, 1966.
Wilkins, *Defining Species: A Sourcebook from Antiquity to Today*, 2009.

37

Creeds

Ashley Cocksworth

Christianity is unique among the world religions in the doctrinal authority it locates in the creeds (Young, 1; Kelly, 163). In the early church, the creeds were written to provide the principles of faith against which orthodoxy could be tested, heresy identified, and heretics expelled. Yet the creeds "seem" to say very little about one of the central affirmations of the Christian faith: the atoning work of Christ. The creeds were nevertheless composed under the "experience" of being saved by the atoning work of Jesus Christ. Therefore, "issues of soteriological concern were always of paramount importance" in the debates that fed into the composition of the creeds (Wiles, 95).

For example, the Apostles' Creed, probably the most confessed creed, mentions Christ's death but says little about *why* Christ died. Issues traditionally related to the atonement—forgiveness of sins, resurrection of the body, and the life everlasting—are included instead under the third article. The later ecumenical creeds of 325, 381, and 451, however, do suggest that the motive of the incarnation was "for our salvation." Notice, then, that contrary to many of the dominant atonement theories the creeds place more soteriological attention on the incarnation than on the death and blood of Christ.[1] But despite that soteriological emphasis, the mechanics of how the atonement is "achieved" is not spelt out with any systematic precision. It is confessed, without elaboration, and the question of how the atonement is effected is left open. However, this "settling

---

[1] It is worth emphasizing that the creedal questioning of the "violence" that some find in the dominant atonement theories has connections with feminist, womanist, and other nonviolent conceptions of the atonement. See Denny J. Weaver, *The Nonviolent Atonement* (Grand Rapids, MI: William B. Eerdmans, 2001). It is equally worth emphasizing, however, that many of the dominant atonement theories depend on the classical Christological moves articulated in the creeds—for example, Anselm's *Cur Deus Homo* is informed exactly by the logic of Christ's fully divine and fully human nature as settled at Chalcedon in 451.

of doctrinal dispute" is not the task of the creeds (Webster, 69–83). Saying the creeds is more about providing some structure, a "grammar," as it were, to all that is said about God and therefore about God's atoning action. The creeds, in other words, provide us with "rules" and reciting the creeds help us to become more skilled at using those rules (Adams, 201–229). But what does this theological grammar entail? At least two things.

First, most creeds follow a three-part structure (with articles on the Father, Son, and Spirit) and in doing so provide a way of organizing doctrine in response to God's revelation (as Father, Son, and Spirit). The creeds, therefore, confess that thinking about the atonement means thinking *trinitarianly* about the atonement (Brümmer). This means more than simply that the atonement is a Trinitarian event (which puts pressure on the two-sidedness of much atonement theology) but that if the word "atonement" is going to gain meaning (and count, therefore, as theological) it must be shaped by the Trinitarian pattern of the creeds.

Second, and following this, the creed itself, to use Nicholas Lash's phrase, is about saying one thing more than one way: three ways, in fact. The creeds—themselves the product of argument—model ways of arguing, and some models of creedal argumentation are better than others. The Athanasian Creed, for example, presents a potentially unhelpful model of theological argumentation. The inclusion of anathemas on alternative understandings closes down rather than encourages further thought and disagreement. The Chalcedonian Definition (which affirmed and clarified the second article of the Nicene Creed), however, is a better example of holding together alternative, competing understandings of the diverse ways in which Christ's human nature and divine nature relate. The mysteries of the atoning work of Christ are just as irresolvable as the mysteries concerning the person of Christ. That the creeds are said in the context of worship, and end with "Amen" (Lash, 1–3), is further suggestive that accounts of the atonement are offered not as final, closed statements (no matter how brilliantly argued) but as prayer. Indeed, offered as prayer, theories of the atonement start to look somewhat different: prayer involves the slow realization that for all that has already been said there still remains much more to be said about the mysteries of God's atoning work.

Together these "grammatical" points help to structure one's handling of the doctrine of the atonement: it should attend to the incarnation as well as the death of Christ and it should be shaped trinitarianly. Ultimately, the mysteries of the atonement defy the ability of being grasped by a single universally accepted definition. The task of making sense and remaking sense of the atonement as described in the Bible is endless; and though the creeds remain even today, centuries after their composition, an appropriate place to start that labor of interpretation.

Bibliography

Adams, "Confessing the Faith: Reasoning in Tradition," in *The Blackwell Companion to Christian Ethics*, 2006.
Brümmer, *Atonement, Christology and the Trinity*, 2005.
Kelly, *Early Christian Doctrines*, 5th ed., 1989.
Lash, *Believing Three Ways in One God*, 2003.
Webster, "Confession and Confessions," in *Confessing God: Essays in Christian Doctrine II*, 2005.
Wiles, *The Making of Christian Doctrine*, 1975.
Young, *The Making of the Creeds*, 2010.

38

Culture

Paul Louis Metzger

This chapter seeks to assist the readers in developing their own theological cultural work with reference to the atonement. The aim is to show how atonement theory and culture can influence and benefit from critical and constructive dialogue.

Theologies of the atonement emerge in various cultural contexts. How could it be otherwise, when Jesus's atoning work took place within the common or pop cultural milieu of Jesus's day? As defined here, "*pop* culture" involves the common values, attitudes, perspectives, experiences, and images of a given age. Jesus was a Palestinian Jewish peasant, who lived in a Hellenistic cultural setting where Jewish tradition and values existed in creative and painful tension with Greco-Roman civilization. The Gospel writers' exposition of Jesus's atoning work reflects this tension. For instance, Jesus is the biblical tradition's ultimate sacrificial lamb, who is put to death on a cross—Rome's instrument of horrific torture and shame to destroy rebels—for the world in bondage to sin. Far from impotent and unjust, Jesus's resurrection reveals his power and validates his righteous life and death as the Son of Man who sacrifices himself to free a suffering world. As Mark's Gospel (10:45; ESV) puts it, "For even the Son of Man came not to be served but to serve, and to give his life as a ransom for many." In the end, Jesus's sacrificial death and resurrection expose the ultimate frailty of Rome's rule and fallible justice; Jesus liberates the world to a new order of being shaped by the power and purity of his kingdom's sacrificial love.

Much could be said about the various cultural, biblical, and theological dimensions of Jesus's atoning work. No one motif or image exhausts its beauty: the atonement is like a multifaceted jewel. Theories of Jesus's atoning work serve as refracted light, highlighting the various biblical facets of substitution, representation, liberation, and more. Penal Substitution, Satisfaction, Moral Influence, *Christus victor*, and other models have their place; however, we must account for these models' emergence in given cultural settings and how they shape those settings, including ours today.

For example, much has been made of feudal society's influence on St. Anselm's Satisfaction theory (Gunton, 89). While his twelfth-century European context does not relativize the merits of his theological endeavor, it does particularize it. Jesus's atoning work satisfies God's offended honor (resulting from his subjects' rebellion) and restores order to the world. So, too, consideration has been given to the *Christus victor* model of atonement's predominance in the early church and its waning influence in the medieval period. It has been argued that the dissipation of the conflict between the church as a persecuted minority and the empire reduced the need for placing theological emphasis on Jesus's atoning work as a cosmic battle between God and Satan's forces (Wink, 89–90). In what follows, consideration will go beyond the historical backdrop to exploration of pop cultural motifs in our day.

Benefits of Dialogue between Atonement Theory and Culture: Golgotha and *The Green Mile*

What follows is a theological cultural exposition of atonement theory against the backdrop of one of the chief genres of popular culture today—film. More specifically, attention will focus on the benefits of dialogue involving atonement themes and contemporary culture; the movie *The Green Mile* will serve as a case study (Darabont, *The Green Mile*, 1999). Each of the four points below highlights a value or benefit of such dialogue illustrated through Frank Darabont's 1999 film adaptation of Stephen King's *The Green Mile* (1999).

Playwrights, novelists, and filmmakers function as theologians and high priests of the masses. These artists may appear to reveal hidden mysteries and mediate the divine to us in theaters and living rooms. Sometimes their productions are so moving that they result in cathartic experiences and conversions to new ways of life. Our most imaginative sages often shed light on religious symbols and themes, such as Jesus's cross and atoning work. *The Green Mile* is no exception. This fantasy/drama film with elements of horror is a stunning example of how artistic mediums of pop culture can bring us into contact with the depth dimensions of life and faith, including Jesus's atonement.

The film takes place on death row at "Cold Mountain State Penitentiary." The prison's death row is called "The Green Mile" because of the green floor tiles that span the building and lead from the inmates' cells to the electric chair (usually death row is called "The Last Mile"). The narrator is the prison guard in charge of death row, Paul Edgecombe (played by Tom Hanks). One of the prisoners is an African American man named John Coffey ("J. C."; played by Michael Clarke Duncan). Coffey has been found guilty of the violent murder (and presumed rape) of angelic-looking twin girls. As the story unfolds, Edgecombe comes to the realization that Coffey is innocent, yet intimately connected with the sufferings of everyone around him. Although not exhaustive, the following account will highlight benefits of constructive dialogue involving atonement theory and cultural engagement with *The Green Mile*.

Theological Dialogue with Popular Culture May Shed Light on Existential Questions

In the film, the observer comes to the realization that Coffey has been sojourning a very long time; he identifies with people of all walks of life and suffers the dark tragedy of people's inhumane treatment of one another. He refers to himself as a wanderer. Someone gives Coffey St. Christopher's medal; St. Christopher was known as the patron saint of travelers and died a martyr (Christopher means "bearer of Christ").

Like Jesus, Coffey is a man of sorrows, lonely and familiar with suffering (Is. 53:3). He appears to be one who has no place to call home and lay his head (Mt. 8:20; Luke 9:58). He is so tired from his utter loneliness paradoxically wed to his intimate dealings with people's pain and evil that he simply wants to die. Jesus is not simply judicially our representative; he takes upon himself our suffering, as does Coffey. Jesus is present to us through the intimate, perichoretic relation of time and eternity in his person. One can never abstract Christ from Jesus, or Jesus's history from our own. For all their distinctiveness, there is unity and solidarity. Such unity and solidarity bears upon his atoning work.

A friend once remarked that he could not believe in God given the horrific evil that people endure unless God were somehow identifying with them in every time and place, not once upon a time. I believe the film makes possible theological engagement of such existential struggles and questions. As symbolized through the wandering Christ figure in *The Green Mile*, Jesus is present. He takes our human condition in all its various temporal particulars to himself in atoning for the sins of the world. His identification with us is complete.

Jesus is a time-space traveler, whose once-for-all-sufficient sacrifice is an eternal sacrificial life throughout time. So, too, he gives eternal life. He who will go to be with the murdered girls, playing with them in Paradise, also gives exceedingly long life to those he heals like Edgecombe (urinary tract infection) and a pet mouse in the prison (Mr. Jingles), which someone crushed, but which Coffey raised from the dead.

Theological Dialogue with Popular Culture May Help to Resolve Theological Puzzles

Coffey is an innocent victim. He is like a little child, ignorant of many things (he does not know much more than his name). Though big and imposing, he is meek, and afraid of the dark in strange places. Beyond this, Coffey also has the power to heal, which makes Edgecombe believe he is innocent. After healing others, he coughs, often releasing a cloud of dark spores from his mouth, likely portraying the evil he has ingested and subsequently expels. Furthermore, Coffey psychically feels the pain and evil of everyone around him. He appears horrified when coming into physical contact with fellow death row inmate "Wild Bill" Wharton, whom Coffey realizes is responsible for killing the two girls (Wharton is on death row for other crimes).

Coffey's psychic connection where he experiences humanity's sin and suffering may shed light on Paul's mysterious claim in 2 Corinthians 5:21: "For our sake he made him to be sin who knew no sin, so that in him we might become the righteousness of God" (ESV). How can Jesus become sin and remain sinless? In seeking to resolve this theological puzzle, it might prove helpful to view Jesus's solidarity with sinful humanity as involving a psychosomatic connection; perhaps this connection permeates Jesus's being; thus he remains sinless while still experiencing sin's full burden.

Like Coffey, Jesus is an innocent victim who dies as the guilty victimizer. He brings the two together in his person. The rest of us, no matter how innocent we appear, are somehow involved in evil. Rowan Williams puts it this way: "I am, willy nilly, involved in 'structural violence,' in economic, political, religious and private systems of relationship which diminish the other (and I must repeat once more that the victim in one system is liable to be the oppressor in another: the polarity runs through each individual)" (73). Jesus becomes the victim and the victimizer. He absorbs the wrong done to us and also becomes sin so that we can become God's righteousness (2 Cor. 5:21).

Theological Dialogue with Popular Culture Can Serve as Reminders of Biblical Themes

According to Scripture, only the innocent can take away and terminate sin and evil (Is. 53:5–6; John 1:29). Coffey's life and death reminds us of this truth: he brings an end to an unjust system and to unjust lives in his life and death that intersects them. Even though the system carries on, individuals like Edgecombe cannot carry on with business as usual. It is the last execution in which the chief prison guard participates.

Jesus alone can bring justice and healing. As the prototypical person wrongly judged, signifying how judicial systems have often made people like the Jews (and black men like Coffey) the sin bearers for everyone, Jesus alone can provide forgiveness and pay the debt. These systems cannot. Jesus engages mercifully, though he could wreak havoc on all concerned. He engages concretely—from within the fallen system in a relational way that is intrinsic to his merciful and just being. Jesus absorbs and defeats evil in his person: "Evil is defeated only if the injured person absorbs the evil and refuses to allow it to go any further" (Caird, 98). Far from operating as an inferior, Jesus's determination to become the innocent lamb of sacrifice confronts evil head on and eradicates injustice, as in the case of Coffey.

Theological Dialogue with Popular Culture: Practical Implications and Applications

Further to the previous point, Edgecombe realizes he is guilty for his participation in innocent Coffey's execution. For the first time in his life, he feels that he is in true danger of hell. Although he had offered to help Coffey escape and Coffey refuses to flee, even pardoning his executioner, still Edgecombe knows he is guilty of wrongdoing. At the end of the film, Edgecombe claims that his "atonement" is seeing everyone dear to him die for letting Coffey die in the electric chair. After Coffey's death, Edgecombe and other guards leave The Green Mile to work at a youth corrections institution. Perhaps they realize the mockery of a system that allows innocent people to die in place of the guilty.

The American church has often failed to recognize the prophetic connection between Jesus's cross and such symbols of execution as the lynching tree—that image of horrific oppression and trauma for many African Americans. In the African American Christian experience, the cross has often been tied to the lynching tree (Cone). Contrary to reductionist categories, Jesus is personal substitute and representative for individual sins *as well as* personal liberator from systems and institutions of oppression, providing healing in the face of trauma and victimization. There is no contradiction between these various dimensions in Jesus's person and work. It is striking that Stephen King's John Coffey character is an African American man. All too often, African American men still bear the brunt of injustice, including unjust treatment in the American judicial system bound up with mass incarceration (Alexander). Theological dialogue with culture can generate practical implications and applications, as illustrated in consideration of *The Green Mile*; the film in conversation with atonement theology sheds light on the prophetic import of the biblical witness for confronting such injustices today.

Concluding Words

The preceding discussion signifies some of the benefits of theological cultural dialogue concerning the doctrine of atonement. Just as various facets to atonement theory in culture are vast, so the benefits and values of such dialogue are multiple. Given the subject matter and context, avid practitioners, readers, and viewers will be pleased to know that theological-cultural "sequels" to the mysterious drama of salvation never end.

Bibliography

Alexander, *The New Jim Crow*, 2012.
Caird, *Principalities and Powers*, 2003.
Cone, *The Cross and the Lynching Tree*, 2011.
The Green Mile, directed by Frank Darabont, 1999.
Gunton, *The Actuality of Atonement*, 1988.
Williams, *Resurrection: Interpreting the Easter Gospel*, rev. edn, 2002.
Wink, *The Powers That Be*, 2009.

39

Cyril of Alexandria

Donald Fairbairn

As a theologian, Cyril of Alexandria is best known for his Christology (focusing on the Word as the active agent in the incarnation, the one who took humanity into his own person in order to accomplish our salvation) and for his doctrine of deification (emphasizing human participation in the Word's Sonship with the Father—we become sons by adoption through our union with the One who is Son by nature). Cyril's teaching on the atonement is much less well known, but it grows directly out of his more famous emphases and is, in the opinion of this writer, very valuable for consideration by contemporary Christians.

The basis for Cyril's atonement doctrine is the interplay of deity and humanity within the person of Christ. Cyril writes:

> The one who was the Only-Begotten as God, has become firstborn among us and among many brothers [Rom 8:29] as man, according to the incarnational union, in order that we also in him and because of him might become sons of God naturally and by grace. First, we have become sons naturally in him and in him alone, but then also by participation and grace we have ourselves become sons through him in the Spirit. (*Incarnation of the Only-Begotten* [Sources chrétiennes 97.254–256])

Here Cyril's point is that the Word who is Son by nature gives his Sonship to his own humanity, thus making humanity—*his* humanity—son by adoption. But since his humanity represents our humanity, this means that as we are united to him, we too can become sons of God by adoption. Another way that Cyril makes the same point is by writing that he who was Son by nature became himself son by grace/adoption (considered in his humanity), so that in him we might become sons by adoption as well. (See *Dialogues on the Trinity* 3, 6 [Sources chrétiennes 237.82; 246.22–24].) Here Cyril follows the traditional teaching of the Greek fathers, especially Athanasius, and some modern scholars refer to this understanding as a "physical theory" of the atonement—we are saved/deified through the very act of taking humanity into the person of the Logos when he became fleshly/physical/human (Kelly, 395). Contrary to what one might expect, however, Cyril does not concentrate exclusively on the incarnation in elaborating his understanding of the atonement. He also focuses significant attention on the death of Christ—indeed, his attention to the death of Christ is the source of two of his most significant emphases: his insistence that only if Christ were truly the Son by nature could his death be efficacious for us, and his famous assertion that the Word suffered impassibly.

Regarding the first of these emphases, Cyril frequently quotes 1 Corinthians 2:8, in which Paul asserts that if the rulers of this age had recognized Christ as Lord of glory, they would not have crucified him. Cyril argues that only the death of the Lord of glory—not the death of a mere man—could avail for our salvation. (See, e.g., *Against Those Who Are Unwilling to Call Mary the Theotokos* 17, 25 [Patristic and Ecclesiastical Texts and Translations 1.40–43, 62–63], *Explanation of the 12 Anathemas* 31 [McGuckin, *St. Cyril of Alexandria: The Christological Controversy*, 293].) Cyril explains the reason for this most fully in his commentary on John 19:16–19. He writes:

> They now lead out the author of life to die. Even this, however, was done for our sakes. By the incomprehensible power and design of God, his suffering accomplished an unexpected reversal. The passion of Christ set a snare, as it were, for the power of death, and the Lord's death was the source of renewal to incorruptibility and newness of life ... He took upon himself the punishment that the law justly assigns to sinners. (*Commentary on John*, book 12 [Ancient Christian Texts, 342])

Here we see that Cyril boldly affirms the paradox that the author of life (cf. Acts 3:15) is being put to death, and precisely because he is the author of life rather than a mere man, his death breaks the power of death and brings incorruption to humanity. In this passage, Cyril shows a strong emphasis on the atonement as a victory over the power of death, but it is important to recognize that this is not all he stresses here. The reason Christ's death can break the power of death was that it constitutes his bearing upon himself the sentence of the law against sinners. In other words, there is an element of punishment for our sins in Cyril's view of the atonement.

This aspect of his thought is even clearer as Cyril comments on John 13:31–32:

If we examine as well as we can the account of the mystery concerning him, we will see that he died not merely for himself and not strictly for his own sake, but it was for all humanity that he suffered and that he carried out both the suffering itself and the resurrection that followed. He died according to the flesh, making his own life the counter-weight to the life of all, and he who is worth everyone put together fulfilled in himself the force of the ancient curse. (*Commentary on John*, book 9 [Ancient Christian Texts, 134])

Here we see Cyril affirming a strongly sacrificial understanding of Christ's death. The statements that Christ offered his own life as a counterweight for the life of all, and that he is worth everyone put together clearly have a substitutionary ring to them. In Cyril's thought, victory over death and substitutionary sacrifice are intimately intertwined. The reason Christ's death can accomplish both of these things is that it is not the death of a mere man (nor—to use modern terminology—the death merely of the humanity of Christ) but is indeed somehow the death of the Lord of Glory, the author of life, the true Son of God. He dies "according to the flesh," in his humanity, rather than in his divine nature per se. But Cyril insists that the one who died was—and had to be—the Son himself. J. N. D. Kelly aptly summarizes: "Cyril grasped the fact, more clearly than any of his predecessors, that what enabled Christ to achieve this [substitutionary death for us] was not only His identification of Himself with sinful human nature, but the infinite worth of His Person" (399).

Cyril's bold affirmations about Christ's death raise the obvious question of how it is possible for God's Son to die and lead directly to the second of his major emphases. Contrary to some of his contemporaries and many modern writers, Cyril famously insists that the Word suffered impassibly. For example, at a crucial point in the rapprochement that brought the Nestorian controversy to a close, Cyril writes:

We all confess that the divine Logos is impassible, even though, since he himself carried out the mystery [of salvation], he is seen to attribute to himself the sufferings that occur in his own flesh. And in this way, also, the all-wise Peter speaks, "since Christ has suffered in the flesh" [1 Pet. 4:1] and not in the nature of his ineffable divinity. For in order that he might be believed to be the Savior of all, according to incarnational appropriation, he assumes, as I said, the sufferings of his own flesh. (*Letter 39* [Fathers of the Church 76.151])

Cyril envisions the Word acting in two ways at once: as God, the way he has always lived from eternity past, and as man by virtue of his having assumed humanity at the incarnation. The atonement was something that only God could accomplish, but it had to be accomplished "as man." Therefore, God the Son became man while remaining who he was as God, in order that God, acting as man, might suffer for us and accomplish our salvation.

Cyril's view of the atonement thus includes elements of "physical salvation," victory, and substitution, but his main contribution to our reflection on the atonement lies in his careful elucidation of who Christ had to be in order to accomplish what Scripture indicates he accomplished. Cyril's thought stands as an indictment of various modern views that sidestep the central paradox of God the Son making atonement as man. Some theologians consciously or unwittingly divide Christ as he hangs on the cross by insisting that it was not the deity that died; only the humanity suffered and died. Cyril would call this Nestorianism and would argue that it deprives the atonement of its efficacy. Other theologians today obviate the need for God the Son to make atonement *as man* by asserting that God is passible in his own nature. In his own day Cyril was accused of saying this, but he insisted that it was God the Son acting in his flesh, as a man, who suffered (see Gavrilyuk, chapter 6; Kim, 216–229). Indeed, if God were passible in his own nature, he would not have to become incarnate in order to die.

In summary, we may affirm that although later theologians have explained *what* Christ accomplished with far more precision than Cyril did, perhaps none have more clearly articulated the connection between what he did and who he was.

Bibliography

Gavrilyuk. *The Suffering of the Impassible God*, 2004.
Keating, *The Appropriation of Divine Life Cyril of Alexandria*, 2004.
Kelly, *Early Christian Doctrines*, 5th edn, 1977.
Kim, "Apatheia and Atonement: Cyril of Alexandria and the Contemporary Grammar of Salvation," in *Ancient Faith for the Church's Future*, 2008.
Smith, "Suffering Impassibly: Christ's Passion in Cyril of Alexandria's Soteriology," *Pro Ecclesia* 11:4, 2002.
Weinandy and Keating, eds., *The Theology of St. Cyril of Alexandria: A Critical Appreciation*, 2003.

Ecclesiology

Joseph Mangina

The precise relation between the atonement and the church is nowhere formally defined in Christian teaching. The Nicene-Constantinopolitan creed asserts that Christ lived and died "for us human beings and for our salvation," and that the Spirit's work includes the creation of "one, holy, catholic, and apostolic church." The creed does not elaborate on these claims, however, much less tell us how they are related.

Still, Christianity has always assumed a grammar whereby Christ's atoning action somehow lies at the heart of the church's life. Paul writes that the *ekklesia* was founded by the "word of the cross" (1 Cor. 1:18), the joyful announcement of Christ's dying and rising as a defeat of the powers of sin and death and the dawn of a new creation. The cross—both the historic event and the apostolic word that proclaims it—is what makes the church to be the church. We find evidence of a more specific tie between atonement and the church in the second Corinthian letter: "For our sake [God] made him to be sin who knew no sin, so that in him we might become the righteousness of God" (2 Cor. 5:21). Along with Galatians 3:13, this verse is often taken as a *locus classicus* of substitutionary, especially penal, understandings of atonement, with an accent on the salvation of individuals. Read in context, however, we can see that Paul is talking about the cross as the power that effects reconciliation within the Christian community and beyond. The "new creation" of which the apostle writes is ecclesial, social, and even cosmic in scope. It is in light of the cross as an apocalyptic, reality-constituting event that Paul can urge the fractious Corinthians to be reconciled (*katallagete!*) both to God and to each other.

A somewhat different way of picturing the atonement-church nexus may be found in Ephesians 2. Here Paul (historical questions concerning authorship are irrelevant for present purposes) links the shedding of the blood of Christ (this sacrificial language does not appear in 2 Cor.) with the overcoming of the hostility between Jew and Gentile: Christ dies so that "he might create in himself one new man in place of the two, so making peace, and might reconcile us both to God in one body through the cross." The present-tense effect of this action can be seen in the church: "So then you are no longer strangers and aliens, but you are fellow citizens with the saints and members of the household of God, built on the foundation of the apostles and prophets, Christ Jesus himself being the cornerstone, in whom the whole structure, being joined together, grows into a holy temple in the Lord." Also notable are Paul's hints in this passage concerning the Spirit, as the agent who both provides access to the Father and who builds up the church.

The exchange motif discernible in 2 Corinthians 5 continues in patristic thought. For the Fathers, Christ's death is the culmination of that "wonderful exchange" (*admirabile commercium*) whereby the Son enters fully into the human condition so that humans might partake of God's life. Christ's death is a ransom paid for sinners (to the Devil?), who, delivered from the clutches of the Evil One, now form the *ekklesia*. The church is precisely the company of the "redeemed." The cross plays a larger role in Eastern Christian soteriology and ecclesiology than is often recognized (Behr). Yet it remained for a Western Church Father, Augustine of Hippo, to bring cross and church together in a more systematic way. He does so via the concept of sacrifice. A sacrifice—so Augustine argues—is any act of compassion performed for God's sake. Christ's death is thus the unsurpassable sacrifice. But now note that it includes the church:

> It immediately follows that the whole redeemed community, that is to say, the congregation and fellowship of the saints, is offered to God as a universal sacrifice, through the great Priest who offered himself in his suffering for us—so that we might be the body of so great a head—under "the form of a servant" ... Thus the Apostle first exhorts us to offer our bodies as a living sacrifice, holy, acceptable to God, as the reasonable homage we owe him, and not to be "con-formed" to this age, but to be "re-formed" in newness of mind ... This is the sacrifice of Christians, who are "many, making up one body in Christ." This is the sacrifice which the Church continually celebrates in the sacrament of the altar, a sacrament well-known to the faithful where it is shown to the Church that she herself is offered in the offering which she presents to God. (Augustine, 380)

Christ offers, the church offers, the church is offered—these realities coexist and imply each other. The enabling doctrine here is Augustine's teaching concerning the *totus Christus* or whole Christ, comprising both the head and the members.

If you had asked Augustine, anachronistically, for his "doctrine of the atonement," he might well have pointed to the Eucharist.

The Augustinian linking of cross, church, and sacraments via the *totus Christus* became a Western Christian commonplace. It can be seen, for instance, in Aquinas's *Summa Theologiae*: "For since [Christ] is our head, then, by the Passion which he endured from love and obedience, He delivered us as His members from our sins, as by the price of His Passion" (*ST* III 49.2). Interestingly, Thomas does not think he has to choose between exemplarist, sacrificial, and redemptive understandings of atonement. The atonement is "cause" of human salvation in multiple ways. The Augustinian understanding also informs Julian of Norwich's *Showings*, where the crucified Jesus addresses Julian saying: "All the health and life of the sacraments, all the power and grace of my word, all the goodness that is ordained in holy church for you: I it am" (Bauerschmidt, 180). In Thomas and Julian we still see traces of the patristic "exchange" motif, indeed the *totus Christus* can be seen as a specification of that idea.

The Western schism of the sixteenth century may be seen in part as a prolonged debate over the relation between the atonement and the church. All parties agreed that Christ's sacrificial self-offering at Calvary lay at the heart of the church's life. But did the church, through the ministry of her priests, offer Christ to the Father, thereby in some measure repeating or imitating his sacrifice? If so, was such action soteriologically efficacious? Catholics answered yes to both questions, Protestants a resounding no. Thus, for Luther, the mass understood as sacrifice is "the greatest of all abominations" and "nothing but a terrible and abominable blasphemy" (*Luther's Works*, 36, 370, 318). The reasoning here is both Christological (the once-for-all atonement cannot be repeated) and soteriological (works do not save). The other Protestant reformers concurred—if anything, with greater vehemence than Luther.

Nevertheless, Protestantism did not entirely depart from the ancient tradition's understanding of the Eucharist as sacrifice. The Anglican Book of Common Prayer (*BCP*) is exemplary in this regard, on the one hand insisting that "we [the congregation] are unworthy, through our manifold sins, to offer unto thee any sacrifice," but on the other hand petitioning God to "mercifully to accept this our sacrifice of praise and thanksgiving"; the people also present themselves to God as "a reasonable [i.e. rational], holy, and living sacrifice" (*BCP*, Order for Holy Communion). With typical Protestant paradox, the Eucharist is a sacrifice by not being a sacrifice. Missing the irony, Trent would sternly reject the evangelical doctrine:

> If any one saith, that the sacrifice of the mass is only a sacrifice of praise and of thanksgiving; or, that it is a bare commemoration of the sacrifice consummated on the cross, but not a propitiatory sacrifice ... and that it ought not to be offered for the living and the dead for sins, pains, satisfactions, and other necessities; let him be anathema. (Council of Trent: Session 22)

Antagonisms of this sort would help to define Catholic and Protestant mentalities for generations to come.

Protestant insistence on the sole sufficiency of Christ's self-offering thus gave rise to "the doctrine of the atonement" in its modern form, although arguably this development can be traced back to scholasticism, Anselm in particular. The work of Christ is his suffering and dying *for me*; the church's role is correspondingly downplayed, if never absent entirely. For evangelical Protestants the church is the company of those whose hearts have been strangely warmed by acceptance of God's gift. For liberal Protestants, by contrast, the church is the community of those who have been drawn into Jesus's moral influence, as in Albrecht Ritschl's theology of the kingdom. Thus, evangelicals and liberals arguably adhere to an ecclesiology centered on the atonement, though in very different ways, the one stressing the divine-human aspect of reconciliation and the other the human-human aspect. Contemporary "atonement wars" between critics of Anselm (Weaver) and defenders of penal substitution (Packer) reflect these historically different emphases within Protestantism.

Befitting his radically Protestant vision, Karl Barth's most sustained reflection on ecclesiology occurs in *Church Dogmatics* 4.1–3, his doctrine of reconciliation (*Versöhnung*; the term encompasses but is broader than English "atonement"). For Barth, Christ simply *is* the event of reconciliation, while the church, along with Israel, is his witness—"the community of those whom already before all others He has made willing and ready for life under the divine verdict executed in His death and revealed in His resurrection from the dead" (*CD* IV/1, 643). The church is the community that announces the once-for-all reality of reconciliation in Christ. Only announces? Some would argue that the price Barth pays for his Christocentric actualism is a downplaying of the church as means of grace, and of the importance of individual conversion/repentance (Hinlicky, 279). Moreover, it may be asked whether Barth's account of Christ's high-priestly work is genuinely *priestly*. Does his almost exclusive reliance on judicial and revelatory categories occlude cultic understandings of atonement, and if so, what effect does this have on his ecclesiology? Does it tend to undermine a view of the church as a "royal priesthood" (1 Pet. 2:9, cf. Rev. 1:6)? To be sure, Barth is not the only evangelical thinker who invites such questions.

One of the more important intersections between atonement and ecclesiology in modern Christian thought occurs in ecumenical theology. The most profound ecumenists understood that Christian unity could be achieved only by a kind of ecclesial dying to self, a form of participation in the cross as indicated by Ephesians 2. This insight informs such great works as Michael Ramsey's *The Gospel and the Catholic Church* and Lesslie Newbigin's *The Household of God*, both of which are indebted to Barth, as well as Ephraim Radner's *The End of the Church* and *A Brutal Unity*; Radner's influence may be discerned in the manifesto *In One Body through the Cross: The Princeton Proposal for Christian Unity*. Traces of cruciform ecclesiology may also be seen in Catholic thinkers such as Hans Urs von Balthasar and Joseph Ratzinger, although they are understandably more reluctant than Protestants to speak about the church's "dying." For all their differences, the thinkers just named share a concern to set the Crucified at the center of the church's existence, to avoid triumphalism, and to highlight the church's solidarity with the suffering and lost of this world.

Roman Catholicism's thinking about the atonement continues to be shaped by the event of the Mass, where the fruits of Christ's atoning work become visible and available for the people of God. Hence Vatican II's Dogmatic Constitution on the Church, *Lumen Gentium*, moves directly from consideration of the birth of the church in the blood and water flowing from the side of the Crucified—an ancient trope in patristic thought—to the present-tense reality of the Eucharist:

> As often as the sacrifice of the cross in which Christ our Passover was sacrificed, is celebrated on the altar, the work of our redemption is carried on, and, in the sacrament of the eucharistic bread, the unity of all believers who form one body in Christ is both expressed and brought about. All men are called to this union with Christ, who is the light of the world." (*Lumen Gentium*, 3)

Some evangelicals will balk at the notion that redemption is "carried on" each time the Mass is celebrated. Yet ecumenical dialogue in recent decades has made clear that the re-presentation of Christ's once for all sacrifice is by no means to be thought of as its repetition (Hunsinger, 179–81, 317). The Eucharist is a participation in the atonement and not a replacement for it. Protestants and Catholics alike may thus affirm that all humanity is called to partake of the reconciliation effected "in one body through the cross," and provisionally visible in the life of the church.

It may be that the place where the unity of cross and church is most severely tested nowadays is in the ongoing reality of Christian martyrdom. For it is in the bodies of the martyrs that the church is most fully joined to the cross and to her Lord's sacrifice: "These are the ones coming out of the great tribulation. They have washed their robes and made them white in the blood of the Lamb" (Rev. 7:14). In this vision the church not only surveys the wondrous cross, but also enters into it with joy.

Bibliography

Aquinas, *Summa Theologica*.
Augustine, *City of God*.
Barth, *Church Dogmatics*, vol. IV.1, 1956.
Bauerschmidt, *Julian of Norwich and the Mystical Body Politic of Christ*, 2008.
Behr, *The Way to Nicea*, 2001.
Braaten and Jenson, *In One Body through the Cross*, 2003.
Hinlicky, *Beloved Community*, 2015.
Hunsinger, *The Eucharist and Ecumenism*, 2008.
Packer, *In My Place Condemned He Stood*, 2008.
Weaver, *Nonviolent Atonement*, 2001.

41

Jonathan Edwards

Garry J. Williams

Edwards did not write a treatise on the atonement, but there are comments on the subject scattered throughout his works. The most notable is the sermon series *A History of the Work of Redemption*, since it is as close as he came to the historical account of Christian doctrine that he aspired to write.[1] In the sermons Edwards rigorously presses home the pastoral applications of his doctrine. Different theological emphases cluster at different times of his ministry, but they form a broadly coherent doctrine. The diversity of his thinking should be taken as a sign of its richness, not internal disagreement (contra Holmes, 142).

Many aspects of his doctrine locate Edwards firmly in the tradition of Reformed scholasticism. He grounds the atonement in the covenant of redemption between the Father and the Son. In eternity, the Son covenanted to enter a state of humiliation to purchase the church. In time, the atonement was prophesied and prefigured in the Old Testament. Edwards understands the atonement as occurring during the period of Christ's humiliation, from his incarnation to resurrection, including his burial. Throughout this entire time, but supremely in his suffering and death, Christ acted to redeem his people by satisfying the wrath of God. He endured the furnace of wrath, suffering the arrows of avenging justice as he bore the guilt and punishment due to his people in their stead. By itself, however, this would have simply put man

---

[1] The atonement is also frequently discussed in the miscellanies (especially b, s, t, oo, 113, 161, 245, 265, 281, 306, 319, 321b, 357, 385, 398, 424, 449, 451, 452, 483, 497, 502, 621, 653, 664b, 741, 761, 764a, 772, 779, 781, 791, 798, 846, 898, 912, 1005, 1025, 1035, 1068, 1076, 1145, 1159, 1175, 1177, 1196, 1208, 1214, 1217, 1295, 1352, 1360), and in a number of other sermons and discourses (particularly *Christ's Sacrifice*, *The Threefold Work of the Holy Ghost*, *The Sacrifice of Christ Acceptable*, *Justification by Faith Alone*, *The Free and Voluntary Suffering and Death of Christ*, *The Excellency of Christ*, and *Christ's Sacrifice an Inducement to His Ministers*).

back into a probationary state like Adam, with no merit to deserve eternal life. Therefore, through his life and culminating in his death, Christ also purchased eternal life for his people by his meritorious obedience. He obeyed as a man, a Jew, and supremely as the mediator given a special work to do. Edwards thus sides with the Reformed majority on the need for Christ's obedience to be imputed to the believer.

As in most of his theology, however, Edwards also develops creative emphases and insights that expand the traditional formulations. It is important to diagnose these correctly. The prevalence of governmentalism among his successors in New England may tempt us to find novelty in any mention of God as ruler, but such an emphasis was not new. It was the isolation of governmental grounds for the atonement that marked the departure of New England from the tradition, whereas Edwards maintained both governmental and essentialist grounds. In *Misc.* 779 he finds several reasons for the necessity of satisfaction. For example, his argument from holiness as justice reveals the governmental Edwards: justice means that God maintains beautiful order. Sin itself inherently merits punishment, and God will maintain this connection. Alongside this, God's holiness absolutely considered requires that sin be punished, not to maintain order, but simply because sin is odious. Here is the essentialist Edwards: God's holiness is the "infinite opposition of his nature to sin" (18:437). If there is a distinctive element here it is not the emphasis on divine government, but the prominence of the aesthetic concern for beauty.

Whence then the exclusive governmentalism after Edwards, even in the work of his own son Jonathan Jr.? This continues to be disputed. Guelzo argues that it was simply an elaboration of Edwards's own position on original sin. When Edwards abandoned the idea that Adam's sin was imputed as the ground of depravity in his children, he broke the link between sin and punishment, thus clearing the way for Christ's death to be viewed as an affliction rather than a substitutionary punishment for imputed sin. The difficulty with this reading is that Edwards affirmed the oneness of Adam with his children, and used this to ground, not to deny, imputed sin. Atwater, who finds the New Divinity views all "utterly abhorrent" to the system of Edwards (589), has a more probable argument. While Edwards himself did not break the sin-punishment link, when the metaphysic of his treatise on original sin was rejected, the idea of imputed sin vanished and the system was left affirming that punishment comes upon us without sin. The sin-punishment link broke when it lost its underpinning in Edwards's metaphysic, clearing the way for it to be abandoned in the doctrine of the atonement.

Another wrongly identified novelty concerns the position taken by Edwards on limited atonement. While Edwards clearly affirmed the doctrine (e.g., *Misc.* t), Holmes has argued that there is a trajectory present in his theology toward a universal atonement. When Edwards writes of Christ dying for the "whole world," Holmes thinks that he holds an ontology of human being that identifies every individual as finding their true eschatological nature in Christ (akin to Karl Barth), and requires that Christ acted for all men without exception. Edwards, he asserts, could not have missed this point and so spoke of a universal aspect of the atonement (158–159). The simpler and less anachronistic explanation is that Edwards, like most advocates of limited atonement, felt the need to maintain a sense in which Christ died for the "whole world" because the Bible says this (1 John 2:2). This seems more probable than the attempt to posit a nascent Barthian anthropology in Edwards.

A real development in Edwards is his use of infinities to explain the human plight and the efficacy of Christ's work. Humanity owes God an infinite debt because of the infinite demerit of sin. The demerit is measured against the infinite greatness of God against whom sin is committed, and by the creature's infinite obligation to him. No finite human repentance could make satisfaction for sin; only the infinite God-man can help, whose divine nature was the altar on which he sanctified the gift of his life, and whose blood was the blood of God. Christ's death involved an infinite descent from the society of the Trinity. He offered himself because he had an infinite regard for the Father, and was accepted because of his infinite worth, and because the Father infinitely loves the Son. The sheer extent of the infinity *Leitmotif* in Edwards is unprecedented, but the ideas here are not new. Rudisill (114) thinks that the tradition affirms the "quantum of suffering" that Christ bore while Edwards appeals to his infinite worth, but the appeal to the person of Christ to explain the value of his work was standard Reformed fare. Indeed, like his predecessors, Edwards maintains that Christ bore the "very same" and "equivalent" punishment deserved by sinners (13:402, 14:452), while experiencing it differently from them. His experience was worse than that of the lost, because he came to it from an infinite height, and because he saw the evil of sin more clearly. Unlike the lost, he was not himself hated by God, and he did not despair of rescue as they do. The difference was thus in the person, not the extent of the punishment: Christ and the lost are like a green and a dry tree, both thrown into the same fire, but with different effects.

For Christ to bear sin and punishment he needed to be in union with sinners. Here is another area where Edwards makes distinctive contributions. On the basis of the common metaphors used, Hamilton argues convincingly that the metaphysics of identity developed in *Original Sin* may also stand behind Edwards's view of the unity of Christ and his people. This is a fruitful thought, particularly given contemporary philosophical interest in the persistence of things. It remains, however, implicit in Edwards, while the explicit focus is on the incarnation and love of Christ for his people as the basis of union. Edwards takes the idea of union by love—rooted in his theology of the Holy Spirit as the bond of love in the Godhead—to a new level. The extent of love is seen in Christ's willingness to face destruction for sinners, and it sufficed for God to look on his people "as it were as parts of him" (14:403). From the human side, faith is the "act of union" (19:158) that makes Christ and his people one. The unity of Christ and his people is such that he is not just the head of the body, but is "as the whole body," covering us all over (13:454). In a sustained analogy unpacked in exhaustive detail, Edwards compares the love of Christ to the love of a patron for his client, a love strong enough to constitute union. The analogy demonstrates the imputation involved in the atonement to be "a very rational thing" (13:359), a particular concern for Edwards against the background of Socinianism and in the context of attacks from theologians embracing Enlightenment individualism.

A further development occurs when Edwards engages in extended discussions of the ideas present in the mind of Christ as he suffered. His metaphysics told him that a clear idea of something brings it into existence in the mind. Thus he writes of the clear view that Christ had in Gethsemane of both the odiousness of sin and the dreadfulness of God's wrath. Indeed, in his suffering Christ had a unique view of the heinousness of sin as both Jews and Gentiles manifested the universal human desire to murder God. Sin and wrath: these were the two fires that tormented Christ, both hateful to his holy nature. Yet the more he saw of them, the more he desired to avoid sin himself and to rescue his people from them. His humanity was thus sanctified in the fire of the ideas of his suffering, and then in the suffering itself. Such discussion of the thoughts of Christ in Gethsemane might seem speculative, but Edwards insists that Christ's intentionality and freedom in laying down his life meant that he needed to have certain thoughts, otherwise, he acted blindly.

Unlike much contemporary evangelical theology, Edwards does not focus on the cross to the exclusion of the resurrection, making the new life of Christ nothing more than a seal on his death. Rather, the resurrection is vital as the justification of Christ, and therefore the justification of his people with him. Nor does Edwards feel the need to choose between penal and other descriptions of the work of Christ. Especially in his typological writing, he commonly describes the cross as an act of conquest in which Christ defeats Satan by using his own weapon against him: Christ is David severing Goliath's head with his own sword, Jonah swallowed by the whale but poisoning it, the ark of God captured in Dagon's temple but breaking off his head. It is as Christ's heel is struck that he crushes the serpent's head; it is by the very plan of Satan that he defeats Satan and purchases his bride.

Bibliography

Atwater, Review of *A Discourse Commemorative of the History of the Church of Christ in Yale College*, by Fisher, *BRPR*, 30:4, 1858, 585–620.

Biehl, *The Infinite Merit of Christ*, 2009.

Crisp, "The Moral Government of God: Jonathan Edwards and Joseph Bellamy on the Atonement," in *After Jonathan Edwards*, ed. Crisp and Sweeney, 2012.

Edwards, *The Works of Jonathan Edwards*, 1957–.

Guelzo, "Jonathan Edwards and the New Divinity," in *Pressing toward the Mark*, ed. Dennison and Gamble, 1986.

Hamilton, "Jonathan Edwards on the Atonement," *IJST*, 15:4, 2013.

Holmes, *God of Grace and God of Glory*, 2001.

Rudisill, *The Doctrine of the Atonement in Jonathan Edwards and His Successors*, 1971.

42

Eschatology

Graham A. Cole

Atonement has been defined in terms that include an eschatological perspective. R. W. Yarbrough writes: "'Atonement' may be defined as God's work on sinners' behalf to reconcile then to himself. It is the divine activity that confronts and resolves the problem of human sin so that people may enjoy full fellowship with God both now and in the age to come" (388). The canon of Scripture exhibits that divine activity as a saving history (*Heilsgeschichte*) with a plotline. In Aristotelian terms there is a beginning, a middle, and an end to the biblical story. In more formal literary terms Scripture exhibits the U-shape of comedy. That is to say, Scripture begins with harmony (Gen. 1–2), descends into disharmony (Gen. 3 to Rev. 19) before a higher harmony obtains (Rev. 21–22). The higher harmony is seen in the progress from the garden of God to the city of God, which incorporates features reminiscent of the Edenic paradise (cf. Gen. 2 and Rev. 22).

Eschatology relates to the story in two ways. The traditional understanding of eschatology deals with the last four things: death, judgment, heaven, and hell. This is the narrow definition of the term, and atonement and eschatology is the story of how the atoning death of Jesus impacts on the last four things with a focus on the fate of individual (individual eschatology). The broader definition of the term has to do with how the divine project unfolds from beginning to end. On this definition atonement and eschatology have to do with how the atoning death of Jesus, canonically considered, advances the divine project. The divine project is nothing less than the reclamation of creation, and thus addresses both individual and cosmic eschatology. At the center of the reclamation strategy is the cross of Christ "as the act whereby the good creation is brought back into harmony with the wise creator" (Wright, 97).

Both ideas—the cosmic and the individual—are on view in Colossians 1:19–20, where the Apostle Paul argues: "For God was pleased to have all his fullness dwell in [Christ], and through him to reconcile all things, whether things on earth or things in heaven, by making peace through his blood, shed on the cross." The reference to "blood" is significant because "blood" is so often used in the New Testament as a synecdoche for the death of Christ. In Colossians 1:22, St. Paul speaks of the Colossians themselves and how the death of Christ enables their future with God: "But now [God] has reconciled you by Christ's physical body through death to present you holy in his sight, without blemish and free from accusation." This is the hope of the gospel (Col. 1:23). Clearly for St. Paul in this letter the death of Christ needs to be understood within an eschatological frame of reference. Our task then is to consider "the subject of a Christian eschatology ... Within the framework of the *theologia crucis*—that is, when it is seen to be *eschatologia crucis*" (Hall, 212).

How then are we to understand the significance of Christ's atoning sacrifice in relation to death, judgment, heaven, and hell? In relation to sin, Hans Boersma wisely comments: "In a number of ways, then, the death of Christ as the penalty for human sin—whether a recapitulation of the exile of humanity from the garden of Eden or the exile of Israel from the promised land—serves the purposes of God's eschatological justice" (195). Sin is the great spoiler and the atoning sacrifice of Christ is central to the divine response to it. This was St. Paul's view. He wrote to the Romans: "He [Jesus] was delivered over to death for our sins and was raised to life for our justification" (Rom. 4:25). As for death, in biblical perspective it connotes separation. The archetypal story of such a death is that of the Garden of Eden. After their sin, the man and woman are separated from the garden zone and the cherubim with the flaming swords prevent reentry (Gen. 3:24). They are cut off. The idiom of being cut off from the people becomes the way capital punishment comes to be described a number of places in the Torah (e.g. Lev. 17:10). In his death Christ experienced the cutting off on behalf of others and in so doing removed its sting and victory (1 Cor. 15:54–57). The seventeenth-century puritan John Owen wrote a tome with an eloquent title that captures that sense of victory: "The Death of Death in the Death of Christ." His title refracts an important New Testament testimony. In his death, Christ tasted death for every one of us (Heb. 2:9). In relation to judgment the New Testament witness is that the grounds of devilish accusation have been removed through the sacrifice of the cross (cf. Rom. 8:33–34 and Col. 2:13–15). On the cross, Jesus experienced the God forsakenness of the world to come (Mt. 27:45–46). Penal substitutionary theories of the atonement especially consider the atonement in these terms. The propitiatory sacrifice of Christ averts the wrath of a righteous God. Calvin is emblematic of this atonement tradition. For Calvin, Christ's atoning death removes the prospect of divine wrath for the elect by satisfying divine retributive justice (Cole, 137–138). Karl Barth comes close to this view when he describes the event of the cross in terms of "The Judge Judged In Our Place" (Barth, *CD* IV/I, 273): "He [Jesus] took our place as Judge. He took our place as the judged. He was judged in our place. And he acted justly in our place."

Regarding heaven, the eschatological prospect for the individual is that where the head has gone the rest of the body will follow. Jesus thus promises the repentant thief on the other cross that he would be with Jesus in paradise (Luke 23:43). However, a caveat is in order here. The narrow definition of eschatology can leave the misleading impression, especially as expressed in some hymnody, that heaven is the end of the story, but in fact the biblical witness makes it clear that heaven is penultimate. The new heavens and the new earth are ultimate (Rev. 21–22). Christianity is not Gnosticism. Material creation is caught up in the eschatological prospect (Rom. 8:18–25). Hence we have the need for both the narrow and the broad definitions of eschatology. In relation to hell, the Pauline witness is that there is no condemnation for those in Christ and no separation for those beloved by Christ (cf. Rom. 8:12, 38–39 and 2 Thess. 1: 8–10). Whatever the ontology of hell might be, having been experienced by Christ, as the Apostles' Creed affirms, it need not be experienced by those in him.

In brief, Christ so dies that those incorporated into his humanity as member of his body (Gal. 3:27) need not experience these eschatological prospects: the second death, the judgment and hell (John 5:24), rather they are enabled to travel the path which he has trod, the one that leads to the new Jerusalem, and the new heavens and the new earth of biblical hope (cf. Heb. 2:10 and Rev. 21:1–4).

How then is the atoning sacrifice of Christ to be related to the Bible's metanarrative of salvation? The triune God is the chief actor in the canonical story that moves from creation to fall through redemption to consummation. The conflict between good and evil organizes the plot. Stephen Sykes captures the plot in a striking way: "In Christian narrative, God's world is the *setting*, the *theme* is the rescue of the fallen world and of humankind; the *plots* are the biblical narratives, from creation, election, to incarnation, crucifixion, resurrection and ascension; the *resolution* is the last judgment, heaven and hell" (14; original emphases). The great goal of the story is a creation restored to its rights, meaning nothing less than the redemption of time and space to the glory of the triune God and the welfare of creatures (Wright, 257–264). The pivotal cluster of events that begins the resolution of the plot is found in the Christ event (Sykes, 14).

Carl E. Braaten rightly suggests: "The cross and the resurrection together mark the apocalyptic turning point of history" (23).

In terms of Oscar Cullmann's famous analogy, the cross represented D-Day in the plan of God. D-Day in 1944 was arguably the turning point in the European theater of war. VE [Victory in Europe] Day came in 1945. Likewise the death of Jesus was the key event in the defeat of the devil and evil, but the dénouement is still to come. On this view the Christian lives in the in-between. In retrospect, there is the atoning death of Christ and in prospect the coming again of creation's king. This in-between period of time is variously characterized in the New Testament. St. Paul can describe it as that upon which "the end of the ages has come" (1 Cor. 10:11, NRSV) or as "the present evil age" (Gal. 1:4, NRSV). The writer to the Hebrews uses the idiom of "these last days" (Heb. 1:2, NIV). The question may be asked however, as to why God hasn't acted to bring about VE Day, as it were, before now. Evil seems so powerful still. One New Testament answer to such a question may be found in the Petrines. Both the believer and unbeliever live in the time of the divine patience (2 Pet. 3:8–9). Time has been afforded for our return to the waiting Father's house (cf. Luke 15:11–32 and 2 Pet. 3:9).

The atonement theory that comports best with an eschatological understanding of the cross broadly conceived is that of *Christus victor*. This was the theory that dominated the first millennium of Christian thought and in the twentieth century was revived in a class work of that title by the Swedish theologian Gustaf Aulén (Cole, 125–126). This view exhibits the apocalyptic imagination, which takes angels, Satan, and demons with utmost seriousness. As Carl E. Braaten provocatively suggests, "Though we say we are Christians and believe in Christ, without the apocalyptic worldview and cosmic framework, we lose sight of what Christ is for. 'The Son of God was revealed for this purpose, to destroy the works of the devil' (1 Jn. 3:8)" (15). The Book of Hebrews makes a similar claim in its own idiom: "Since the children have flesh and blood, he too shared in their humanity so that by his death he might destroy [*katargein*, "to nullify," "to render ineffective"] him who holds the power of death—that is, the devil—and free those who all their lives were held in slavery by their fear of death" (Heb. 2:14). Indeed a case may be made that the first note about atonement in the canonical text is a *Christus Victor* note, as struck in the *protoevangelium* of Genesis 3:15 (Boyd, 30). This text speaks of the defeat of the serpent but at a cost to the progeny of the woman. The New Testament does not lose sight of the primal promise as is seen when Paul writes expectantly: "The God of peace will soon crush Satan under your feet" (Rom. 16:20).

In sum, the divine project is comprehensive in scope. It addresses the plight of the groaning creation (Rom. 8:18–25), the barriers between ethnic groups (Eph. 2:14–18), and predicament of the individual (1 Tim. 1:15). The end point is shalom. Shalom is not merely the absence of strife but the fruition of relationships: a new heavens and new earth in which righteousness is at home (2 Pet. 3:13). To understand how the atoning death of Christ plays the central part in this unfolding divine quest to recover order in the creation requires an apocalyptic imagination. Such an imagination is sensitive to the dramatic and antagonistic aspects of nature and history (the contest between good and evil), and is fed in Eucharistic celebration in which Christ's death is proclaimed in the symbols of bread and wine until He comes (1 Cor. 11:26).

Bibliography

Boersma, "Eschatological Justice and the Cross: Violence and Penal Substitution," *Theology Today* 60, 2003.
Boyd, "Christus Victor View," in *The Nature of the Atonement*, ed. Beilby and Eddy, 2006.
Braaten, "The Recovery of Apocalyptic Imagination," in *The Last Things*, ed. Braaten and Jenson, 2002.
Cole, *God the Peacemaker*, 2009.
Hall, *The Cross in Our Context*, 2003.
Sykes, *The Story of Atonement*, 1997.
Wright, *Surprised by Hope*, 2008.
Yarbrough, "Atonement," in *New Dictionary of Biblical Theology*, ed. Alexander and Rosner, 2000.

Eucharist

Scott Harrower

The Eucharist, or Lord's Supper, is a Christian symbolic ritual. In and through this practice, believers affirm God's historic work in Christ as the basis for the present reality of atonement (at-one-ment) between God and his people. The Eucharist also anticipates the return of Christ, thus relating the believer to past, present, and future realities to do with the atonement. The Eucharist is essentially related to the other key Christian ritual: baptism. The Eucharist is the ongoing practice that publicly displays the logic of the initiatory sacrament of baptism and its claim to atonement through Christ's representative sacrifice. By means of the Lord's Supper, Christians corporately participate in a past event of atonement. The ontological, theological, ecumenical, and pastoral aspects of this debate are numerous and wide ranging, but discussion of these outstrips the nature of this chapter. For this reason, I will provide the biblical starting points for the theological dialogue that must be developed from them, refraining from advancing a particular theological position in the space of this chapter.

The historical basis for the Eucharist is a meal that Jesus had with his disciples shortly before he was crucified around the time of the Passover. Jesus's Last Supper and the ongoing practice of the "Lord's Supper" in the primitive church specifically drew upon Old Testament theological themes to do with the Passover and future meals in the Kingdom of God. The Old Testament themes of a Passover meal and anticipated realities to do with God's Kingship are discussed below.

The Passover meal

By actively participating in the Passover event, and recalling it at future times, the Hebrew people affirmed atonement at the center of Gods' actions toward his chosen people (Exod. 12). The essential benefits of the Passover included freedom from divine judgment against Egyptian oppression and sin on one hand, as well as the presence of God's name in the midst of the people on the other (Exod. 12:27, 34:23–27; Deut. 16:2, 5–6; 2 Chr. 35:1–19). This perpetually celebrated meal was a domestic event that functioned to establish the identity of all future generations as people who were redeemed and blessed (Foley, 30–33) by YHWH through blood sacrifice (Mic. 7:19) (Gane, 690–691). Such memorialization was set into laws about Passover in Exodus 12:43 ff., Leviticus 23:4–8, and Numbers 9 (Hartley, Atonement, day of, 54–60).

In Second Temple Judaism, the Passover feast continued as a commemoration of the Exodus event. This shared meal revolved around animal sacrifice, which affirmed fellowship with God (Bradshaw and Johnson, 7–8). Hence, participation in this event involved forgiveness and eating (Foley, 33). The meal probably involved bread as well as wine (Bradshaw and Johnson, 8) (drawing on passages such as Num. 28:24).

Anticipated Realities to do with God's Kingship

In Isaiah 25:6–8, God's kingship is on display through the bountiful banquet that awaits people from all nations. As he reigns upon Mount Zion (24:23), God hosts a banquet for all people where he displays his power through lavish food and by swallowing death (Abernethy, 34–36). Who will participate in this feast? When we step into the larger story of Isaiah, perpetual human hardness finds is match in the atoning work of the suffering servant (52:13–53:12). The servant's suffering creates an international community of "servants" who according to Isaiah 65:13 "shall eat" (Abernethy, 156–160, 198). This certainly fits more broadly with Deuteronomy's expectation of eating in the land, though this will only take place through obedience, which includes regular sacrifice and festival celebrations associated with atonement. Isaiah linked these ideas with atonement in a way that expanded on deuteronomistic theology (Abernethy, 60, 90). The deuteronomistic perspective was that life in God's promised land was in part signified and embodied by eating while being cognizant of God's redemption from Egypt (Deut. 6:10–12) (Gane, 690–691). This would be secured by obeying God's word (cf. Deut. 28), given through his servant Moses and perpetuated through "the prophet like Moses' to come" (Deut. 18:15, 18; 34:10). For Isaiah this character was the "suffering servant" whose atoning work ultimately paves the way for eating with God in his future kingdom (Isa. 40–66). In particular, this servant enables all peoples, Israel and the nations, to come to God (Isa. 49:1–7). Moreover, the servant suffers like a slaughtered lamb to provide atonement for the iniquities of the people (Isa. 53:6–7, 11–12). Hence, the prospect of bountiful eating in God's kingdom is associated with atonement via the vicarious guilt offering provided by the suffering servant (Isa. 53:10). It is only through the servant's atoning suffering that participation in the King's banquet is possible for all nations (Abernethy, 143–147, 148–160, 198).

Jesus's Life, Words and Death Merge Passover and Regular Blood Sacrifices Into a New Public Ritual

The New Testament connects strands of atonement theology with Jesus and the Eucharist in a number of ways. Perhaps the primary emphasis originates in Jesus's framing the Last Supper as a Passover meal in which sacrifice is central (Mark 14:22; Matt. 26:26). Jesus alluded to the Passover, which he understood in light of sacrifice (cf. Lev. 23; Num. 29; Deut. 13). This is consistent with his self-identification as a "ransom for many" (Mark 10:45). Hence, Jesus's ritual actions in the meal (taking, blessing, breaking, giving, exhorting imitation) were pregnant with meaning. Taking on the role and ratcheting up the significance of the Passover lamb, Jesus employed wine and bread at a Passover meal to communicate the significance of his death. He took bread to communicate the fact that his body would be offered on behalf of his people (Luke 22:19; Mt. 26:26; Mark 14:22; 1 Cor. 11:23–24). He did this by simply taking the bread, blessing it, breaking it, and saying "Take it, this is my body" (Mark 14:22), "this is my body given for you" (Luke 22:19a). Jesus also performed a parallel action, which made use of a cup to symbolize the meaning of his blood shed on the cross. He said it was of the "new convent in my blood, which is poured out for you" (Luke 22:20), "my blood of the new covenant which is poured out for many" (Mark 14:24). In Matthew's Gospel, Jesus aligns the ideas of covenant and benefit for the recipients with the mechanism of forgiveness for sin: "This is my blood of the new covenant, which is poured out for many for the forgiveness of sins" (Mt. 26:28, 1:21). The cup imagery is thus linked to two ideas: Jesus's death on the cross was a substitutionary Passover for the forgiveness of sin, as well as confirming a new covenant between God and his people. In this way, the new covenant refers to the blessed state of at-one-ment between God and people, and this is predicated upon the atoning event of Jesus's substitutionary death on the cross (Cole, 149–151).

Another prominent way that the atonement is related to the Eucharist is that Jesus is the host of a banquet for undeserving people whom Jesus has redeemed into his kingdom. Jesus's teaching on the kingdom of God was often enacted and confirmed in terms of table fellowship and banqueting. Jesus rejected table fellowship hosted by the unforgiven and the unloving (Luke 7:36–50) and not aligned with a holistic view of life with God (Luke 11:37–54). True table fellowship with Jesus was the sign of a relationship based upon his gracious and saving acceptance of those who had faith in him, such as Levi (Luke 5:27–32) and Zacchaeus (Luke 19:1–10). Likewise, the climax of the parable of the lost son is a feast (Luke 15:11–32). During his Last Supper, Jesus related redemptive and blood atonement to the concepts of the kingdom of God as a Messianic banquet (Luke 22:18, 1:53, 13:29, 14:15) or future banquet with God for people of all nations (Isa. 25:6–8) (Perrin, 496). Atonement alone is the basis for table fellowship with Jesus that also would have a future and fuller expression of the kingdom of heaven as a joyful banquet for the underserving (Mt. 8:11, 22:1–14). A central relational outcome, which the Eucharist assumes as a result of the atoning work of Christ, is the expansion of notion of covenantal inclusion to include Gentiles.

The way in which the Eucharist is a perpetual remembrance of Jesus's death underscores the uniqueness of Jesus's atoning work. Jesus commanded his disciples to emulate the Last Supper, to "do this in remembrance" of him (Luke 22:19b). After taking the bread, he gave thanks, broke it, gave it, and spoke about its symbolic meaning and exhorted his disciples to perpetually replicate such a meal (Perrin, 495–497). The elements to be ingested are bread and wine received by continual faith (John 6:4), which is accompanied by the gift of eternal life predicated upon Jesus's self-offering as an atonement (John 6:27–59). By means of ingesting the symbolic bread and wine (Mark 14:23), the disciples were (perhaps unknowingly before Pentecost) confessing the atoning significance of Jesus's death and the central role this would play in their believing communities. These ritual actions identified Jesus to the disciples who had been the way to Emmaus, and were adopted as a mark and practice of the early church (Acts 2:42, 46), even in the direst of circumstances (Acts 27:35).

Past, Future, and Present Aspects to the Lord's Supper

Throughout his ministry (including the Last Supper), Jesus established two time-indexed ways in which the Lord's Supper would relate the benefits of the atonement to his people. These are the anamnetic and proleptic aspects to the meal. On one level, Jesus set up the meal so that the gathered community would remember a past atonement which functioned as an inclusive, reconciliatory, and liberating event. Anamnesis is "remembering as if I were there," hence it is more than merely backward looking. It actively recalls this unique event signified that the atonement was foundational and could not be repeated, but rather provides the grounds for the riches that flow from it (Bradshaw and Johnson, 350–535). However, Jesus also impressed a futuristic and anticipatory sense to this memorial meal (Bradshaw and Johnson, 9, 17). He said he would not finish that Passover meal until the time of its fulfilment in his kingdom to come (Luke 22:16, 18). Hence the meal, which Jesus urged his followers to practice, was a temporal participation in a meal which has been commenced in the past and which will be fulfilled in the future (Perrin, 496). The Eucharist is therefore a time to remember the atonement and an eschatologically oriented meal which never loses sight of the coming King who will finally establish his kingdom in which the righteous belong by only grace (Bradshaw and Johnson, 354–356) (Mt. 22:1–14; Isa. 61:10).

The present aspect of the Eucharist goes beyond memorialism by way of experiencing in the present a partial incursion of the life to come (Kennedy, 236–243). Though the Christian continuation of the Last Supper as the Eucharist is not a full participation in those realities which lie at the other side of the return of Christ, Jesus offered the consumption of his flesh and blood as the means by which he would abide in his disciples and they in him (John 6:56). Hence, by the Spirit Jesus is especially present as the indwelling Lord of the Eucharistic table (Kennedy, 242). The apostle Paul had a strong view that because God through Christ was the patron of the Lord's Supper, participation in the Supper meant a real participation in the benefits of the atonement in his presence (1 Cor. 10:16–17). At the Eucharist, Jesus is especially present as the mediator of a real meal between God himself and his people. This is only possible as a result of the new covenant through Christ's atonement (1 Cor. 11:25). This is an aspect of Paul's wider theology of Christians already being raised with Christ to new life based upon the believer's participation in his death (Rom. 6:4; Eph. 2:6).

The atonement that the Eucharist celebrates is clear in Pauline theology. Paul's view of the present reality as symbolized by the Lord's Supper is immediately connected to the past historical reality to which the Lord's Supper harkens back (1 Cor. 11:26). For Paul Jesus was the ultimate Passover Lamb (cf. 1 Cor. 5:7). Hence, the event that is remembered is "Christ died for our sins in accordance with the Scriptures ... he was buried ... he was raised on the third day" (1 Cor. 15:3–4). Ecclesiastical history reveals continual efforts to theologically align the Eucharist and the atonement that Jesus enabled via his death on the cross. That there is a profound relationship between the two has rarely been in question. The issue has been how they are related to each other and in what way do they communicate the benefits of the atonement to those who ingest the elements of bread and wine by faith. For a number of theological proposals have been made throughout ecclesial history, please see the ecumenically slanted works listed below.

Bibliography

Abernethy, Andy, *The Book of Isaiah and God's Kingdom* (Downers grove, Ill: IVP, 2016).

Bradshaw and Johnson, *The Eucharistic Liturgies*, 2012.

Cole, *God the Peacemaker*, 2009.

Foley, *From Age to Age*, 2008.

Gane, "Sacrifice and Atonement," in Boda & McConville eds., *Dictionary of the Old Testament Prophets*.

Hartley, "Atonement, day of," in Alexander and Baker, eds., *Dictionary of the Old Testament Pentateuch*.

Kennedy, *Eucharistic Sacramentality in an Ecumenical Context*, 2008.

Perrin, "Last Supper," in Green et al., eds., *Dictionary of Jesus and the Gospels*.

44

Exemplarism

Adam Kotsko

Exemplarism, sometimes also called the "moral influence theory" of the atonement, refers to the view that the primary goal of Christ's saving work is to produce positive moral change in human individuals and communities. In the modern period, such theories have emerged as a major point of theological controversy, and already in late scholasticism there was significant debate surrounding the question (such as that between Abelard and Bernard of Clairvaux).

On one level, this situation may seem strange, because surely no Christian theologian would deny that Christ's work should have positive moral effects. One could even say that for much of the history of Christian thought, there was no particular need to bring forward exemplarism as a distinct theory. There could be considerable debate about the exact implications of Christ's life, death, and resurrection on humanity's standing before God, whereas the moral benefits could be taken largely for granted by all parties. Indeed, Athanasius could claim in *On the Incarnation* that it is precisely the profound moral changes brought by the spread of Christianity that prove that Christ really was the Savior and Son of God (§§48, 51).

For critics of exemplarism, however, the danger comes when such moral benefits are overemphasized, to the detriment of what might be called "objective" effects of Christ's saving work. Particularly in the wake of the Reformation, a strong emphasis on human moral striving could appear to give inadequate attention to divine sovereignty and grace, potentially returning to the "salvation by works" alleged to be taught by the Roman Catholic Church, as opposed to a Reformed "salvation by faith alone."

The perceived dichotomy between divine sovereignty and human morality grew stronger in the modern period, when some liberal Protestant theologians such as Adolf von Harnack focused on the importance of Christ's moral teachings to the near exclusion of traditional questions surrounding sin and salvation (passim). Indeed, one can say that it is only in the modern period that exemplarism becomes a "stand-alone" theory, rather than a supplement to other theories that dealt with what moderns might regard as supernatural or mythological themes.

The key influence behind this shift was Immanuel Kant, who in his *Religion within the Limits of Reason Alone* had claimed that the goal of religion is to help us attain to universal moral norms that are in principle accessible to any reasonable human being. He viewed Christianity as particularly suited to this role, claiming that Christ was a perfect embodiment of rational morality (see part two, section one).

This one-sided position prompted an equally one-sided reaction by more traditional theologians such as Karl Barth, who retrieved and radicalized the Reformers' emphasis on divine sovereignty over against liberal Protestants, whom he portrayed as advocating a return to Roman Catholic "works righteousness."

A theologian advocating a theory of Christ's work as being exclusively moral in nature faces considerable actions. First of all, the New Testament and Christian tradition are virtually unanimous in claiming cosmic significance for Christ's death. There is considerable debate about what that significance is—setting us free from the rule of Satan, paying our debt of honor to God, taking on the punishment our sin deserves, and so on—but in no case is Christ merely a moral teacher providing a particularly compelling ethical code. To the extent that Christ promotes moral transformation, it is precisely the change he has brought about on the cosmic level of the relationship between God and creation that makes such transformation possible and meaningful.

This dynamic is clearly visible in the work of Peter Abelard, who is often misleadingly put forward as the creator of the "moral influence theory." The key evidence for Abelard's view is a brief passage in his *Commentary on the Epistle to the Romans* where he responds to certain questions that are apparently inspired by Anselm's atonement theory in *Why God Became Human*. In responding to them, he deviates from Anselm's emphasis on human indebtedness and divine honor, instead claiming that God became incarnate in Christ and died on the cross so that human beings would no longer fear God, but love him (164–168). On the surface, this view may seem to contradict Anselm's, but in reality it is a variation on the theme. For Abelard, the sin of Adam and Eve had cosmic consequences, thus turning humanity into the object of God's wrath. In the crucifixion, Christ offers himself up as the vessel of this wrath, thereby putting the relationship between God and humanity on an entirely new basis. Outside of this broader framework, it is difficult to understand how a brutal crucifixion ordained by God could have done anything but increased humanity's fear (for a more detailed discussion, see Kotsko, chapter 7).

Contemporary liberation-oriented theologians are very attentive to the connection between the cosmic implications of Christ's work and the possibility of moral transformation. For James Cone, for example, Christ's position as a member of an oppressed group within the Roman Empire demonstrates God's profound solidarity with African Americans, as the most oppressed group within the modern-day American empire. His death attests to his full identification with the suffering of the oppressed, while his resurrection assures the African American community that earthly powers and their violent oppression will not have the last word (Cone, chapter 6). Rosemary Radford Ruether's emphasis is more on the example of Christ and particularly on his treatment of women as equals, which she believes should be normative for the Christian community, and yet for Ruether as well Christ's cosmic role as God incarnate serves to embolden his contemporary followers in their ongoing struggle to overcome oppression and build new communities characterized by love and justice (chapter 5).

There is another problem with the "moral influence theory" as generally understood, namely, that it fails to confront the profound strangeness of Christ's teaching and practice. Certainly there is very little in his example that coheres with what one would normally associate with everyday moral striving. As the gospels portray him, he has no fixed abode, no family, and no steady employment. His teaching is purposefully indirect and often seems to contradict our basic moral intuitions, as when he encourages his disciples to "hate" his family and abandon them in favor of Christ. In the end, he is condemned to a criminal's death, a death he seems to have anticipated and even courted. What kind of example is this?

Whatever we make of it, it is impossible to deny that it has proven to be a deeply attractive example for many throughout Christian history. In the early church, martyrs, who directly imitated Christ's faithfulness unto death, were viewed as the most exemplary Christians—and attracted many more to Christ in their turn. When the persecution ended, that mantle of exemplary actions passed on to monks, who sought to imitate Christ's radical rejection of the standards of a corrupt world, thus attracting many followers in their turn. Athanasius, who lived through the transition between the two eras, presents the hand-off very literally, as he portrays St. Antony as narrowly avoiding martyrdom before becoming the archetypal monk (§46).

In his recent study of monasticism, Giorgio Agamben reminds us that what was at stake for the monks was not a theological doctrine or an abstract moral code, but a concrete way of life. The monastic communities did not first sit down and write by-laws, but began by imitating a particularly compelling imitator of Christ. Only later, as the community grew, did the written rules become a practical necessity. Ultimately, Agamben argues, the rule grew into a quasi-legal institution that stood in the way of the original goals of the monastic movement, paving the way new solitary imitators of Christ such as St. Francis, who could gather new communities of monks eager to live the life of Christ (passim).

It is this living, radical exemplarism—more than abstract debates about the relative emphasis on divine sovereignty or human responsiveness—that has done the most to challenge the theologians and church authorities of past eras, and it should continue to challenge us today.

Bibliography

Abelard, *Commentary on the Epistle to the Romans*, trans. Cartwright, 2011.
Agamben, *The Highest Poverty*, trans. Kotsko, 2013.
Athanasius, *Life of St. Antony*.
Athanasius, *On the Incarnation*.
Cone, *God of the Oppressed*, rev. edn, 1997.
Harnack, *The Essence of Christianity*, trans. Saunders, 1903.
Kant, *Religion within the Limits of Reason Alone*.
Kotsko, *Politics of Redemption*, 2010.
Ruether, *Sexism and God-Talk*, 1993.

45

Expiation/Propitiation

Graham A. Cole

The concepts of expiation and propitiation refer to sacrifices that have different purposes. Expiation refers to a sacrifice that wipes away or covers from sight that which offends. The object of expiation is nonpersonal. Propitiation refers to a sacrifice which turns away the wrath of a person. The object of propitiation is an offended moral agent. N. T. Wright captures the difference well: "You propitiate a person who is angry; you expiate a sin, crime, or stain on your character" (476). The question is whether one or both of these notions are found in the biblical testimony. The relevant Greek terms are *hilastērion*, *hilaskomai*, and *hilasmos* which are found in four key texts. The four key New Testament texts adduced in answering the question are Romans 3:25 (*hilastērion*), Hebrews 2:17 (*hilaskomai*), 1 John 2:2 (*hilasmos*), and 1 John 4:10 (*hilasmos*). Each of these texts will be briefly considered in turn.

In Romans 3:25 Paul claims that Christ's sacrifice effects atonement. Just how exactly this is so becomes the question. Famously C. H. Dodd argued that Christ's death did so by providing expiation for sin (22–23). Dodd maintained that predicating wrath of God's character was a theological misstep, unworthy of *digno dei* (the divine dignity). Frances M. Young argues likewise that expiation and not propitiation is the biblical view and early church thinkers such as Origen thought similarly (71–80). More recently Joel B. Green and Mark D. Baker have argued similarly and controversially that a concept of the wrath of God that required both propitiation and a penal substitutionary sacrifice fails exegetically and assumes a retributive view of justice unworthy of God (Green and Baker). Leon Morris argued against Dodd's position and contended that propitiation was Paul's view and not only in Paul but in every place in the New Testament where a cognate of is found (151–176). Morris has support in recent scholarship on Romans. N. T. Wright, for example, maintains: "Paul's context here demands that the word [*hilastērion*] not only retain its sacrificial overtones (the place and means of atonement), but that it carry the note of propitiation of divine wrath—with, of course, the corollary that sins are expiated" (476). There is merit in Morris's argument with regard to Romans because the wrath of God is a motif found both before and after the text on view (cf. Rom. 1:18; 2:5, 8: 4:15; and 5:9). Divine displeasure at both Gentile and Jewish behavior seems integral to Paul's argument, especially over the first three chapters of the epistle. It is important to note that in Morris's understanding, wrath is not a celestial temper tantrum but the reaction of holy love to that which spoils. On this view wrath is not an essential attribute of God but how holiness expresses itself when meeting sin.

Significantly, the only other occurrence of *hilastērion* is found in Hebrews 9:5 where it clearly refers to the Old Testament mercy seat. The noun *hilastērion* is found some twenty-eight times in the LXX. Twenty-one of these occurrences refer to the mercy seat. The mercy seat was the place where on the Day of Atonement (*Yom Kippur*) the blood was sprinkled that enabled the holy God of Israel to live in the midst of an unholy people. Douglas Moo champions the mercy seat reading and argues that Christ becomes the "New Covenant equivalent, or antitype, to this Old Covenant 'place of atonement,' and, derivatively, to the ritual of atonement itself. This means that what was hidden in the OT sacrifice is now made public and brought from behind the veil in Christ" (232). There is much merit in the suggestion that Paul in Romans construes Jesus as the mercy seat where both the issues of wiping away human sin and the divine wrath are definitively addressed by divine design.

On view in Hebrews 2:17 is Christ as the merciful and faithful high priest who offers a sacrifice for the sins of the people. The key term here is the verb *hilaskomai*. Simon Kistemaker contends that *hilaskomai* "can communicate the sense of both propitiation and expiation and thus express a double meaning" (Kistemaker, in Hill and James III, 166). The question becomes which of the two meanings is in the foreground and which is in the background. That question can be put because expiation and propitiation can be corollaries of one another. If a sacrifice expiates sin, why is such a sacrifice needed? It is needed because of divine wrath. And if the sacrifice is propitiatory, then how does it work? It is needed because the sacrifice expiates or wipes away the sin that offends. Richard Averbeck, in a seminal article on *kpr* in the Old Testament and its resonances in the New Testament, sees both expiation and propitiation at work in Hebrews 2:17 with expiation to the fore (NIDOT 2:689–710). Given the context in Hebrews 2:17 expiate makes better sense than propitiate because sins are specifically on view.

The third and fourth texts are both found in 1 John. In 1 John 2:1–2 Jesus is presented as our advocate (*paraklēton*) with the Father and as the *hilasmos* for our sins. J. Ramsey Michael argues: "The image of Jesus as "Advocate" with the Father makes God the *object*, not the subject, of the reconciliation said to be taking place, and to that extent supports 'propitiation' as the meaning of [*hilasmos*]" (Michaels, in Hill and James III, 114; original emphasis). In relation to 1 John 2:2, Robert W. Yarbrough's argument for what he terms "expiatory propitiation" is attractive: "While Jesus' death certainly has the effect of expiating sin (wiping away its penalty), it is difficult to avoid the impression that it also propitiates (turns away the wrath of) God's promised punishment of sin and sinners whose transgressions are not atoned for on the last day" (77–80).

The final text to consider is 1 John 4:10. Again *hilasmos* is the key term. J. Ramsey Michaels argues that God is not the object of the action in this verse but the subject. God provides the *hilasmos*. He contends: "But here the initiative rests with God the Father, not with Jesus acting as Advocate on our behalf, and the accent is not placating God so much as on removing the guilt of 'our sins'" (Michaels, in Hill and James III, 115). He concludes cautiously that the usage here "supports 'expiation.'" Even Leon Morris concedes that in the case of 1 John 4:10 the case for "propitiation" is not compelling. He commends it though, since "expiation" is "less colourful" (Morris, 172)—hardly a persuasive argument.

In sum "propitiation" would be an appropriate translation of *hilastērion* in Romans 3:25 but "mercy seat" would be better; "to make expiation" is defensible for *hilaskomai* in Hebrews 2:17 but with the idea of propitiation as a corollary; "propitiation" makes sense as a translation for *hilasmos* in 1 John 2:2 with expiation as a corollary; and finally, "expiation" is a suitable translation for *hilasmos* in 1 John 4:10 with propitiation as a corollary. There is wisdom in those modern translations (such as the NRSV and NIV) that leave more open to the reader the exact interpretation of the sacrifice of God's faithful Son.

The atoning death of Christ as sacrifice addresses the problem of human sin and its entailments in the light of the divine character as holy love. The God of biblical rendering is both light (1 John 5) and love (1 John 4:8). Assumptions about the divine character and the nature of divine justice greatly affect how the key New Testament texts are read (e.g., the Dodd-Morris debate). The balance of the exegetical evidence suggests that Christ's atoning death on the cross was both expiatory and propitiatory. Which of the two notions is to the fore in a given text is a matter of placing such texts in their argumentative contexts. As Ludwig Wittgenstein has taught us the meaning of a word is its use in the language. What seems clear is that the biblical testimony affirms both ideas when it comes to the atoning work of Christ.

Bibliography

Averbeck, *kpr*, NIDOT 2:689–710.
Dodd, *The Epistle to the Romans*, 1944.
Green and Baker, *Recovering the Scandal of the Cross*, 2000.
Hill and James III, *The Glory of the Atonement*, 2004.
Moo, *Romans*, 2001.
Morris, *The Atonement: Its Meaning and Significance*, 1983.
VanGemeren, *The New International Dictionary of Old Testament Theology and Exegesis*, 1996.
Wright, *The Letter to the Romans*, 2002.
Yarbrough, *1–3 John*, 2008.
Young, *Sacrifice and the Death of Christ*, 1975.

Forgiveness

Cynthia L. Rigby

Forgiveness is a concept pivotal to Christian faith we seem to have neglected, in recent years, in favor of the doctrine of the atonement (Bash). Perhaps this is not surprising, given that everyone nods at the idea that forgiveness is essential for spiritual and communal health, while there are conflicting views about whether theories of atonement cause more harm or good. This chapter examines why some think atonement is not necessary for forgiveness, while others think forgiveness requires atonement. It ends by considering how atonement might be understood to be an essential component of forgiveness, rather than altogether unnecessary or that which makes forgiveness possible.

Forgiveness Without Atonement

Those who think atonement is unnecessary for forgiveness often point out that doctrines of atonement did not even develop, as such, until the eleventh century (with the word "atonement" itself not appearing until the fifteenth-century Tyndale Bible). Early Christian art does not dwell on the crucifixion as a symbol of redemption, but rather features images of Paradise (Brock and Parker, chapter 8). There has never been an ecumenical council that has decided on a standard of orthodoxy for atonement. By contrast, major ecclesial councils had already, by the fifth century, determined standards for reflecting on many matters considered important to faith, including that the Son is "of the same substance" as the Father (Nicea 325), God is simultaneously both one and three (Constantinople 381), and Jesus Christ is "one person in two natures" (Chalcedon 451). Further, what seemed to motivate those involved in these councils was their desire to better participate in the salvation that is the promise of the Christian Faith. The Chalcedonian Statement explicitly insists, for example, that Jesus is "fully human and fully divine ... *for our sake and the sake of our salvation.*" Given that our forebears went to great lengths to articulate what they understood to be true about Jesus's identity because they thought gaining clarity mattered to their lives, it seems reasonable to assume they would have engaged in similar kinds of explorations of atonement, if they had thought them crucial for understanding what it means for us to be forgiven before God.

The focus of our forebears seemed to be more on the story of Jesus than on any particular interpretation of his acts on our behalf. There was a clear sense that the event of God's self-emptying in Jesus Christ (Phil. 2) is saving insofar as it manifests God's love and forgiveness. Interpretations of the cross and resurrection were not likely to be extrapolated from reflection on the entirety of Jesus Christ's life. The "secret of the cross" was understood as "the secret of the incarnation ... in all its fullness," as Barth later put it (IV.2, 293).

A compelling theological argument for why forgiveness does not require atonement is that having any requirement for forgiveness would be antithetical to the nature of God, who loves us unconditionally. Proponents of this position often point out that the father in Luke 15 does not require anything of his "prodigal" son in order to receive him fully back home. So God receives us, and so we, in turn, should receive each one another. In addition, it is often argued, God's sovereign character means God is not subject to any extrinsic rules of exchange or recompense. If God wants to forgive us, then we are forgiven, because "God gets what God wants" (Bell, chapter 4). Finally, atonement theories that understand violence as necessary are seen as particularly contradictory to the character of God. Abelard is among those who argue against the idea that God would in any way be "pleased" by the death of the "innocent Son," suggesting that dealing in such a way with human sinfulness would only compound the atrocities that would then stand in need of forgiveness (283).

Forgiveness Requiring Atonement

There are many who agree God is loving and forgiving who nonetheless argue some atoning action is needed before forgiveness can take place. If God were simply to forgive, Anselm held, God's character as the perfectly righteous one would be compromised. Others point out that God is not only merciful, but also just—and justice requires there be some kind of amends for wrongdoing.

Interestingly, those who insist atoning actions are integral to the dynamics of forgiveness run the political and theological gamut, from those who hold there is a causal relationship between Jesus Christ's death on the cross and God's forgiveness of us, to those who insist reconciliation requires reparations be paid to those who have been oppressed and victimized. Those who believe the cross makes God's forgiveness of us possible point to the sacrificial system of the Old Testament as well as to the biblical teaching that "the shedding of blood" is necessary for God's forgiveness of us (Heb. 9:22). It might be necessary to ransom us from the devil, who has bound us by way of our sin. Or it might be integral to honoring God as righteous, as Anselm argued. Either way, the cross is understood not only as an essential part of Jesus Christ's life and ministry, but as the essential event that, coupled with the resurrection, makes forgiveness possible.

Those who work for reconciliation between victims and perpetrators of injustice insist that forgiveness is not only the work of the one has been harmed, but also of the one who has done the harm. Changed behaviors might be understood as forms of atonement that facilitate reconciliation. Remedying the broken relationships between blacks and whites, for example, might require intentionally sharing the same living spaces (Jennings, chapter 6) or concretizing sincere apologies by paying monetary reparations to the ancestors of former slaves (Brooks, chapter 5). Forgiveness, in these scenarios, is closely identified with mutual sharing in communal life.

Forgiveness Inviting Atonement

Some approaches to relating atonement to forgiveness reject the idea that atonement in any way *causes* forgiveness while insisting that where there is forgiveness, there will necessarily also be, atoning behaviors. This approach takes seriously the fact that Jesus's forgiving was frequently followed by the mandate to "go and sin no more," as if forgiveness should have a lasting effect on behavior. Similarly, the Lord's Prayer (Mt. 6) and the parable of the unforgiving servant (Mt. 18) both argue there is a correlation between the forgiveness extended to us and the way we treat others, suggesting that where there are no atoning behaviors forgiveness simply is not. One biblical example of what this atoning dynamic looks like is the story of Zaccheus, the tax collector, in Luke 19. What forgiveness looks like, in this story, is both Jesus's visit and the atoning work Zaccheus does in response to it, giving money to the poor and making reparations to those from whom he has stolen.

In this paradigm, the sacrificial system of the Old Testament might be understood less as effecting God's forgiveness than as human beings entering the dynamics of it by way of the rites of atonement. Similarly, the taking of the elements of the Lord's Supper might be interpreted, in part, as an act of living into the dynamics of forgiveness. The Table where the crucified Christ is remembered reconciles all who partake; to eat and drink is to step into the behavioral transformation that comes with the claim that Jesus holds nothing back from us human beings, even when we are at our worst and most violent. In the dynamics of forgiveness, the cross moves us beyond the limits of proximate justice to the possibility of actual justice, or true forgiveness (Cone).

Changed behavior on the part of those who are forgiven is so integral to the dynamics of forgiveness itself, that questions emerge where there can be no opportunities for atonement. Simon Weisenthal is distraught because he, a prisoner in a death camp, is unable to forgive a dying Nazi who asks him for absolution for killing Jews. It is too late for the Nazi to make any form of amends, and what right would he have, Weisenthal asks, to forgive on behalf of those who had been murdered? Regardless of how these questions are answered, they helpfully insist that "forgiveness" must never be treated as an abstract concept that floats somehow above the existence of history and human life. Reconciliatory acts that ground it and makes its transformative power manifest might well be considered essential acts of atonement—acts that "make one," again, those that have been separated by sins and injustices.

Bibliography

Abelard, Peter, "Exposition of the Epistle to the Romans," in *A Scholastic Miscellany*, 1956.
Barth, *CD*, vols. IV.1–IV.2, 1953–1967.
Bash, *Just Forgiveness*, 2012.
Bell, *Love Wins*, 2011.
Brock and Parker, *Saving Paradise*, 2008.
Brooks, *Atonement and Forgiveness*, 2004.
Cone, *The Cross and the Lynching Tree*, 2011.
Jennings, *The Christian Imagination*, 2011.
Jones, *Embodying Forgiveness*, 1995.
The Kairos Document, 1985.
Nussbaum, *Anger and Forgiveness*, 2016.

Sölle, *Political Theology*, 1974.
Telstad, *Cross Examinations*, 2006.
Tutu, *No Future without Forgiveness*, 1999.
Volf, *Exclusion & Embrace*, 1996.
Weisenthal, *The Sunflower*, 1969.

P. T. Forsyth

Jason A. Goroncy

P. T. Forsyth (1848–1921) was a high-Victorian Congregational minister and theologian turned Edwardian college principal (for a fuller biographical sketch, see Bradley, 13–110; Goroncy, *Hallowed Be Thy Name*, 29–93; Goroncy, *Descending on Humanity and Intervening in History*, 6–21). All of Forsyth's major theological concerns are examined *sub specie crucis*, under the aspect of the cross. This is no less true of his thinking on atonement. He insists that the development of any meaningful doctrine of the atonement calls for more than merely cataloguing biblical texts, or seeking to contain the atonement's meanings by recourse to metaphors. While metaphors may provide the requisite linguistic accoutrements for better comprehending God's atoning work, Christ did not die for a metaphor, and the relationship between human language and things as they are will always be indirect. It also calls, he believes, for situating the atonement within the frame of a universal, coherent, and moral ontology more basic and more unfailing than is its physicalist counterpart. This ontology, which is the expansion of an "eternal moral personality" in creation (*The Church, the Gospel and Society*, 19), engages human persons through the organ of the conscience, and directs creation toward the end for which God creates all things; namely, the realization of divine holiness everywhere, God's self-realization in the other. It is precisely this demand *by* God *upon* God—the sense that God owed it to God's self to self-propitiate, to self-atone, to save, and to find God's self "on a world scale amid the extremest conditions created by human sin" (*The Preaching of Jesus and the Gospel of Christ*, 299)—that necessitates God's atoning work.

Requisite to such work is that God's entire human life *must* confront and bring to naught God's antithesis—sin—lest all things, and God, be placed at risk: "Holy love must heal itself. The personality of God, being holy, must recover and assert itself in the sanctification of the whole universe, and by its own resources make itself good in its infinite harmony everywhere in and between all souls" ("The Preaching of Jesus and the Gospel of Christ," 298–299). The "must" spoken of here reaches its most rhetorically powerful articulation in Forsyth's expression, "Die sin must or God" (*The Justification of God*, 151). Plain here is that Forsyth's presentation of the atonement is characterized by a relentless theocentrism—the atonement is first and foremost God's answer to God's self, God's definitive response to the first petition of the Lord's Prayer—"hallowed be thy name." What is at stake, Forsyth claims, is the entire fabric of reality. More critically, unless God's antithesis be brought to naught, the erasing of God's own being remains a terrifying possibility. Whether this implied dualism is a provisional or ontological one is never resolved in Forsyth's writing. What is resolved is that such a situation is unmarked by permanence.

Echoes of Immanuel Kant and G. W. F. Hegel inform Forsyth's unyielding conviction that God alone can satisfy the moral order God never disturbed, and pay the cost God never incurred. This leads Forsyth to reject as false to Holy Scripture all claims of divine impassibility, and to boldly speak of the living God as "the dying God" (Forsyth, "The Pulpit and the Age," 1885, in Goroncy, *Descending on Humanity and Intervening in History*, 136) who in the holiness of the cross finds God's self. By taking this route, Forsyth avoids an unacceptable and rarely resolved schism in most Protestant theologies—the rift between Christology and theology proper. Everything that Forsyth says about the cross concerns God. There is no redemption by proxy.

Forsyth locates his staurology in the territory of moral action, weaving three traditional strands—triumph, satisfaction, and regeneration—into one comprehensive cord, convinced that their unity and atoning value lay in Christ's perfect obedience. Such obedience is replete with the moral content and fervor that characterizes the divine life. There is nothing in the Father's perfect Word that is not answering the Father in their history together with the world as it is drawn out by the Spirit. The obedience unveiled in the divine economy is an unbroken prolongation of that which marks the triune life *in tempus* and *in aeternitas*, and so constitutes Christ's whole personality as God's Son.

The cross's value, moreover, lies in it being not only the act of God performed *ab extra* upon humanity, but also in it being that act of God done *ab intra*—from the side of and within the limitations of the human situation. Here, God's voluntary self-humiliation finds a most gratifying and creative voice in Forsyth's modified kenoticism. Forsyth's chief genius on this front is twofold: first, he argues for a complementary two-act movement of *kenosis* (emptying) and *plerosis* (filling) in Christ's life. Second, he anticipates and responds to objections of the doctrine by defining *kenosis* in terms of the self-limitation or self-contraction or self-compression of the divine attributes. This idea bears witness to God's true omnipotence while underscoring Christ's moral achievement: omnipotence because God would not be truly omnipotent if God did not have "the power to limit Himself ... to bend and die" (*God the Holy Father*, 33), and a moral achievement because the nature of confession that holiness seeks must come from the side of the creature.

It is at this point that Forsyth is particularly indebted to Anselm's conviction that there is a requirement, demanded by its reconciliatory nature, that atonement also arrives "from sin's side," as it were. Given humanity's moral quagmire, however, the undoing of the effects of sustained blasphemy "from the sinner's side" remains impossible, let alone that done "on the scale of the race" as Forsyth insists is called for (*The Preaching of Jesus and the Gospel of Christ*, 108–109). Atonement therefore is, from first to last, wholly grace: "Procured grace is a contradiction in terms. The atonement did not procure grace, it flowed from grace" (*The Cruciality of the Cross*, 78). Neither is God reconciled by any third party: "God came, He did not send" (Forsyth, "The Christianity of Christ and Christ our Christianity," 1918, 263). Forsyth is not uncritical of Anselm, however. While preserving Anselm's view that for God to simply forgive would be dishonorable (Forsyth concurs with Anselm on the subject of sin's weightiness, on the *ponderis* of sin), Forsyth believes that by highlighting (feudal) honor rather than holiness, Anselm "put theology on a false track" (*The Work of Christ*, 223), sponsoring a compounding of sin rather than sin's full abrogation. Moreover, he contends that Anselm failed to appreciate the *personal* nature of Christ's sacrifice, its concern with holy obedience. Anselm's Christ acts entirely over our heads, without any real reference to the human nature wherein the benefit is to take effect and so leaves human subjects mere beneficiaries. Middle Age soteriology, Forsyth believes, required the ethical advances of Protestant orthodoxy which placed the making of satisfaction in the moral and personal realm of the conscience.

Unsurprisingly, Forsyth welcomed—with some caution—many of the nineteenth- and early-twentieth-century assaults on penal theories of the atonement, and showed some sympathy with the "new" Christologies proposed by theologians such as R. C. Moberly and J. McLeod Campbell. He does not, however, follow the fashion of rejecting wholesale the penal and substitutionary *elements* within the atonement. He wants to retain these elements for their "positive worth" while shifting away from the "*quid pro quos*" and "dubious ethics of substitution" that characterize such and which tend to vacate the action of genuine personality and vicarious moral weightiness and reduce it to an external transaction or "mere distributive equity" (Forsyth, "The Atonement in Modern Religious Thought," 67; "Sunday Schools and Modern Theology," 1887, 126; *God the Holy Father*, 4). Whether or not he wholly succeeds in this effort remains an open question. But one way that Forsyth does achieve this retention at key junctures is to rework atonement theologies old and new into the threefold cord noted earlier—triumph, satisfaction, and regeneration—which corresponds, according to Forsyth, to Christ's threefold confession of God's holiness: "The first [i.e., triumph] emphasizes the finality of our Lord's victory over the evil power or devil; the second [i.e., satisfaction], the finality of His satisfaction, expiation, or atonement presented to the holy power of God; and the third [i.e., regeneration] the finality of His sanctifying or new-creative influence on the soul of man" (*The Work of Christ*, 199). Positively, Forsyth might say, through its confession of God's holiness, the atonement reveals, establishes, and puts into historic action the changeless grace of God. Negatively, the revelation and establishment of holiness takes place through the revelation of sin's sinfulness and of sin's judgment. Creatively, the atonement constitutes out of the wreck of the old a new humanity in communion with God.

Regarding this latter object, Forsyth contends that one of the grounds for divine satisfaction is the atonement's anticipation and effect upon creatures called to share in the divine holiness. One reason for Forsyth's hesitation about penal theories is their fundamentally backward vista. Within their own terms of reference, penal models leave human beings pardoned criminals but not participants in God's new work. Conversely, cruciform justice is transformational, transforming not only human subjects but also the structures they occupy. This too is part of Christ's one work of reconciliation and not its mere sequel. Put otherwise, Holy Love does not overcome its antithesis by merely destroying it, but through the recreation of those persons for whom sin has become a way of being and the transformation of those structures that befit such. It is because judgment has a particularly teleological, liberating, and creative character to it that it is to be anticipated in hope rather than recoiled from in dread.

Finally, this raises a matter of prolonged concern to Forsyth—theodicy. Donald MacKinnon has observed, "If the cross provides a theodicy in which there is no facile extrapolation of teleological schemata, it does so at the cost of a continuing tragedy. If the atonement shows God himself profoundly engaged with human evil, it is an engagement (even when its authenticity is affirmed by Jesus' resurrection) that leaves many questions unanswered" (MacKinnon, in Hart, *Justice the True and Only Mercy*, 108). Both in light of Forsyth's most judicious and penetrating "theodicy" (presented in *The Justification of God*) and his lack of sympathy with perfunctory prognostications of teleological programs, readers of Forsyth will need to navigate the unresolved—and unresolvable—fissure in his thought between God's being fully immersed in the universe's tragedy and Forsyth's relative neglect of the enduring surd elements within the cosmos. This too is part of the mystery of the atonement.

Bibliography

Bradley, *P. T. Forsyth*, 1952.
Forsyth, P. T. "The Preaching of Jesus and the Gospel of Christ. [VII:] The Meaning of a Sinless Christ." *The Expositor 8th Series*, 25 (1923): 288–312.
Forsyth, *Sunday Schools and Modern Theology*, 1887.
Forsyth, in "The Atonement in Modern Religious Thought," 1901.
Forsyth, *The Christianity of Christ and Christ our Christianity*, 1918
Forsyth, *The Church, the Gospel and Society*, 1962.
Forsyth, *The Cruciality of the Cross*, 1909.
Forsyth, *God the Holy Father*, 1957.
Forsyth, *The Justification of God*, 1916.
Forsyth, *The Preaching of Jesus and the Gospel of Christ*, 1987.
Forsyth, *The Work of Christ*, 1910.
Goroncy, *Descending on Humanity and Intervening in History*, 2013.
Goroncy, *Hallowed Be Thy Name*, 2013.
Hart, *Justice the True and Only Mercy*, 1995.

René Girard

Adam J. Johnson

According to René Girard, society is constantly on the brink of self-destruction.[1] Our inclination to imitate others ("mimetic desire"), good and natural in and of itself (Girard, *Satan*, 15), easily mutates into envy, for the "imitation of the neighbor's desires engenders rivalry" and the rapid escalation of hostility, in which we perceive that our neighbor can possess the object of her desire (whether tangible or not) only at our own expense or loss (10). Such conflicts constantly threaten to tear society apart in a pattern of violence and revenge. Moreover, they tend to be opportunistic: at advanced stages they "are easily drawn to another scandal whose power of mimetic attraction is superior to theirs," such that one scandal is substituted for a new and more powerful and prestigious one, until finally "the most polarizing scandal remains alone on the stage ... when the whole community is mobilized against one and the same individual" (23). This process of mimetic substitution is a vital one for the survival of the community, such that the crisis of war of "*all against all*" is transformed "into a war of *all against one*" (24; emphases in the original).

At this climactic point, Satan reveals his astonishing power of "expelling himself and bringing order back into human communities" (34). At the very height of mimetic conflict, and "in order to prevent the destruction of his kingdom, Satan makes out of his disorder itself, at its highest heat, a means of expelling himself": he "persuades the entire community, which has become unanimous, that this guilt [of a single, random and indefensible victim] is real" (35). By expelling and destroying this sacrificial victim or "scapegoat," "the crowd finds itself emptied of hostility and without an enemy ... Provisionally, at least, this

---

[1] An expanded version of this chapter appeared originally as Adam Johnson, *God's Being in Reconciliation* (New York: T&T Clark, 2012).

community no longer experiences either hatred or resentment toward anyone or anything; it feels *purified* of all its tensions, or all its divisions, of everything fragmenting it" (36; emphasis in the original). Satan restores the semblance of peace to the community, so that his reign can continue. So while rivalry and conflict naturally escalate, Satan diffuses them by casting himself out, by uniting the mass against an innocent victim (or one "suitable to receive the blame for society's ills, regardless of their actual innocence" [Hunsinger, 22], because their murder will not demand an act of reprisal by another segment of that society), such that the tension of rivalry is temporarily gathered together and expelled by the community—a "sacrificial theory of social cohesion," as Hunsinger calls it (22). In this way the community "sleep[s] the sleep of the just," and Satan forestalls "the total destruction of his kingdom" (Girard, *Satan*, 37). The community, finding that the scapegoated victim actually achieved the miracle of peace, divinizes the victim and celebrates the event in the form of sacrifices, thereby "regulating a 'sacrificial crisis' that recurs periodically" (Balthasar, 303).

This cycle, while present in every culture, is likewise veiled in every culture, such that one never finds a conscious understanding or exposure of this reality. Only through exploring and reading between the lines in the poets of ancient cultures was Girard able to piece together this thesis. The exception is the Bible: though this is true to a certain extent in the Old Testament, according to Girard this mimetic cycle is explicitly and resoundingly revealed in the New Testament in the life and death of Jesus Christ. Only here do we find the perspective of the victim, and the questions: (1) is the victim in fact guilty? (2) Who will throw the first stone? And more importantly still, only in the resurrection are we confronted with the undeniable fact that Jesus was an innocent victim and that in the community which followed him the cycle of mimetic violence was not only confronted and exposed but reversed (The role of the resurrection in *I See Satan Fall Like Lightning* also suggests the development in Girard's thought. While previously it was thought that Girard's was a closed system that denied a historical resurrection, this no longer seems to be the case. Cf. Balthasar, 308; Hunsinger, 26–27; Love, 205). This is the atonement Jesus Christ accomplishes: fully casting out Satan by rendering the cycle impotent through exposure. With the irrefutable vindication of a single victim, the question is unleashed upon the world of whether each and every victim might not be innocent, such that the power of Satan's mimetic cycle collapses.

At first glance, there is much to critique in Girard's thesis. He ravages the Old Testament, admitting that much of it speaks of a God wholly unlike the Christian God (a good reading of Irenaeus would be helpful here!). His position ultimately offers no real solution to the problem of sin, for in unveiling Satan he admits that in so doing, and as Satan can no longer "expel" himself, he now unleashes himself fully (*Satan*, 185)—"these mechanisms continue in our world usually as only a trace, but occasionally they can also reappear in forms more virulent than ever and on an enormous scale" (158; Balthasar, 308; Heim, 263–264). Within atonement studies, it seems evident that Girard's position is merely a demythologized and exemplarist account of *Christus victor* in which the work of Christ amounts to little more than what it teaches or inspires in us (Hunsinger, 28). Finally, one might argue that his work ultimately stems from his literary/cultural studies (Girard, *Violence and the Sacred*), with only a thin theological veneer attached, and one focused almost exclusively on theological anthropology at that. But while these criticisms are significant, they are ultimately shallow, missing the power of Girard's thesis and touch on points which are accidental to his argument and could in principle be altered.

The key to appropriating Girard's thought lies in appreciating the limits he sets for his project: "the present book can define itself as ... an *apology* of Christianity rooted in what amounts to a Gospel-inspired breakthrough in the field of social science, not of theology" (*Satan*, 3; emphases in the original; cf. 105, 137, 141, 150). While he does occasionally make slightly bolder statements (150, 182), the gist of Girard's project lies in developing the anthropological insight of the gospel in such a way that is not at all antagonistic toward but rather inseparable from its theological point—a project he explicitly roots in the double nature of Jesus Christ (190). The question we ought to ask, given Girard's aim, is not whether he advances an account of the work of Christ which is in and of itself sufficient or orthodox, but rather whether Girard has uncovered a significant aspect of the work of Christ which belongs in a fuller account. The answer to this much more charitable question is yes, and the key, once again, has to do with anthropology.

There are a number of aspects of our sin of sin, which necessarily correspond to the aspects of Christ's reconciliation. One of these "moments" operates at the social level of reality—sin against neighbors and the reconciliation thereof. There is every reason to charitably presuppose that Girard's anthropological insight into the gospel may in fact bring some clarity to Scripture's witness to this specific moment, and in doing so, open our eyes to the other moments that relate to it. The key for future development lies in bringing this anthropological insight within the sphere of a more properly theological vision, rather than burdening Girard's contribution with the need to single-handedly offer a sufficient account of the death and resurrection of Christ (such as we see in Heim).

Bibliography

Balthasar, *Theo-Drama: Theological Dramatic Theory*, Vol. 4: The Action, 1988.
Girard, *I See Satan Fall Like Lightning*, 2001.
Girard, *Violence and the Sacred*, 1977.
Heim, *Saved from Sacrifice*, 2006.
Hunsinger, "The Politics of the Nonviolent God," in *Disruptive Grace*, 2000.
Johnson, *God's Being in Reconciliation*, 2012.
Love, "In Search of a Non-Violent Atonement Theory," in *Theology as Conversation*, 2009.

Global Theology

Mark D. Baker

Since the earliest reflection on and proclamation of the cross there has been diversity within atonement theology. In recent centuries the diversity has commonly been described in terms of three main theories of atonement: satisfaction, moral influence, and *Christus victor* (Baker and Green, 142–191). These theories were taught globally. Imagery related to each theory was proclaimed throughout the world. Generally speaking, one's ecclesial and theological location determined which atonement theology was used—not geographical or cultural location. Increased missiological attentions to contextualization and the rise of contextual theologies have changed that reality.

Previously, the critical question had been, "What is the correct theory?" Now, rather than moving from theory to proclamation, many have begun first to ask, "How are sin and alienation from God expressed and experienced in this context?" What is the salvation that is needed in this place? What does Jesus's death and resurrection deliver people *from*? Four main themes have been recognized: guilt, shame, fear, and economic oppression. Each one of these is often thought to be more pronounced in a particular region of the globe: deliverance from a burden of guilt—Western nations; deliverance from shame—Asia, North Africa; deliverance from fear—tribal peoples in Africa and other parts of the world; deliverance from economic/political oppression—identified closely with Latin American liberation theology and found in other regions as well (Muller, 15–55). General articulations of atonement theology have been written connecting the saving work of the cross to these themes, at times linking to the global region associated with the theme (Muller; Tennent, 77–134).

Although recognizing regional differences and the need for contextualized atonement theology is a helpful step, linking an atonement theology with a particular region can also mislead. First, it implies that atonement theology related to shame is applicable to Asia, but not to North America or Europe. Although salvation from shame may be a more pronounced need in Asia, it is needed in other parts of the world as well. Evidence of this need is a work of atonement theology by Alan Mann; writing for a British audience, he focuses on shame. Similarly George Prabhu articulates an atonement theology of liberation from powers oppressing the poor; he writes in India, not Latin America. Diverse atonement theologies are needed not just globally, but also locally. Second, it implies that a general contextual atonement theology about shame, fear, or liberation from oppression is sufficient. But a general atonement theology for one region cannot simply be transported and used directly in another. Prabhu's work is similar to, but differs from a Latin American liberation theology. Mann describes a different experience of shame in Great Britain than one in South Asia, and thus he articulates a different theology of liberation from shame as well.

This points to the need for developing articulations of atonement that begin with particularities of a specific context, pay attention to needs for salvation in that context and then use imagery that will facilitate proclamation in that context. Yet if context alone is the guide, atonement theology can quickly get off track. Therefore, the turn from atonement theories to context also demands a return to the Bible as theological and missiological guide. Joel Green has undertaken an in-depth study of the New Testament writings about the atonement (Baker and Green, 17–141). He highlights the diversity of atonement imagery in the New Testament, affirming the point made above that different contexts require different images. At the same time, the common themes of the whole New Testament provide the following theological and missiological guidelines—or orientation points—for articulating the meaning of Jesus's death and resurrection in new contexts (Baker and Green, 134–141; see also Flemming, 296–322).

First, atonement theology should include a focus on the human predicament. "Sin" and its effects may be articulated in a variety of ways—blindness, deafness, hard-heartedness, slavery to an evil power, enmity, and so on—but it is one of the constants in the equation of biblical thinking about the atonement. Humanity does not have the wherewithal to save itself, but needs help (salvation, redemption, deliverance, and so on) from the outside, from God.

A second guideline is to include the necessity of human response that flows out of the gracious act of God. The lives of God's people must already begin to reflect the new reality (new creation) toward which God is moving history. We are saved *from*, it is true, but we are also saved *for*. This life is modeled after the cross and has service as its basic orientation. Atonement *theology* therefore cannot be separated from *ethics*.

Between the human predicament and the imperative of human response is the divine drama, the ultimate manifestation of the love of God. This is the third orientation point: God, acting on the basis of his covenant love, on his own initiative, was at work in the cross of Christ for human salvation. Our articulation must clearly communicate the atonement as the work of God and do so in a way that does not divide the Trinity, but presents it as unified Trinitarian action.

Fourth, following the New Testament our atonement theology should not accord privileges to any one group over another. What happened on the cross was of universal significance—in the language of the day, for Jew and Gentile, for slave and free, for male and female—and its significance is not limited to humanity, but includes all creation.

Two missiological guidelines for articulating the significance of the atonement follow from the diverse New Testament witnesses. First, we must avoid the temptation simply to read the biblical authors' words and metaphors into our world. Rather, we must follow their example of drawing on images from the everyday experience of people's lives that communicate similar content in our setting. If we would be faithful to Scripture, we too must continuously seek out metaphors, new and old, that speak effectively and specifically to our various contexts. Second, our atonement proclamation should connect with, but also challenge, the intended audience. The metaphors we deploy should be at home, but never too comfortable, in our settings. That is to say, the New Testament calls us to contextualize, and to avoid over-contextualization.

To over-contextualize is to use a metaphor from the context that carries with it meaning that contradicts, overwhelms, or distorts the atonement theology articulated in the above biblical guidelines. For example, in *Cur Deus Homo* Anselm uses images and experiences from daily medieval life to illustrate the atonement. One imagines it connected well with people at that time. Yet he missteps by allowing his experience of medieval life—its logic and conventional wisdom—to have an overwhelming influence in the shaping of his model of the atonement. Anselm offers a less-than-biblical view of the cross—not because he uses terms like "vassal" or "satisfaction" that are foreign to biblical writing on the cross, but because he uses them in a way that gives the cross and the atonement a meaning at odds with the message of Scripture (Baker and Green, 151–161; Boff, 97). Penal substitution theory of atonement borrows elements of Anselm's thought, strips it of its medieval garb, and instead uses imagery borrowed from a Western courtroom. Yet, often the penal substitution theory is also over-contextualized, and a concept of justice foreign to the Bible is allowed to shape the logic of the theory (Baker and Green, 166–191). The problem of over-contextualization is not limited to Western theologies. In Africa, for instance, "ancestor" is often used effectively as a metaphor in Christological thinking and atonement proclamation. Yet Kwame Bediako, of the Akan people, critiques some uses of this metaphor as being over-contextualization. Referring to one theologian's work, Bediako states, "He does not let the biblical revelation speak sufficiently in its own terms into the Akan situation. He too easily assumes similarities between Akan and biblical worldviews, underestimating the potential for conflict, and so does not achieve real encounter" (99).

Non-contextualization, using imagery foreign to a setting, is also problematic. For instance, Japanese pastors complained to C. Norman Kraus that atonement theology explained as release from guilt using concepts from Western understandings of justice was difficult for them to comprehend (Baker and Green, 192–209). Imagery of blood sacrifice connects well in tribal contexts that practice it. In many parts of the world, however, it finds no traction at all. Biblical proclamation of the atonement will follow the biblical authors and discern whether metaphors will be understood in a given context. This does not necessarily mean abandoning all imagery, including biblical imagery, foreign to a place. Imagery from one time and place can be adapted for use in another. For instance, in her book, *Power in the Blood*, JoAnne Terrell adapts imagery of blood sacrifice to an African American context. She relates it to the blood-loss suffered by black women and men as slaves, through lynching, and during the civil rights movement. Rowan Williams, preaching a sermon in Great Britain, proclaims the cross and resurrection as victory over the devil and evil. He does not, however, simply repeat biblical language of spiritual powers of evil; rather he explains and reframes it for his audience (75–79).

This chapter will end by pointing to additional examples of atonement theology or proclamation of the atonement relating to diverse themes and contexts that the reader can study further using the bibliographic information given.

Suggested Further Reading

Liberation from shame/restoring honor: Central Asia, Jayson Georges and Mark Baker, *Ministering in Honor-Shame Cultures*, 2016, 91–114, 172–176; China, Jackson Wu, *Saving God's Face*, 2012, 193–292; Chinese American, Grace May, "The Family Table," in *Proclaiming the Scandal of the Cross*, ed. Baker, 2006, 135–144; Honduras, Mark Baker, "Freed to Be Human and Restored to Family," in *Stricken by God?*, ed. Jersak and Hardin, 2007, 288–314; Japan, C. Norman

Kraus, in Baker and Green, *Recovering the Scandal of the Cross*, 2nd edn, 2011, 192–209; Thailand, Christopher Flanders, *About Face*, 2011, especially 242–261; Great Britain, Mann, *Atonement for a "Sinless" Society*, 2005.

Blood Sacrifice imagery: Africa, David Shenk, *Justice, Reconciliation & Peace in Africa*, 1997, especially 87–104; Tanzania, Marwa Kisare, *Kisare*, 1984, 76–83; Zimbabwe, Gwinyai Muzorewa, "Salvation through the Sacrifice of God's Firstborn Son," in *Proclaiming the Scandal of the Cross*, ed. Baker, 2006, 163–171; African American, Terrell, *Power in the Blood*, 1998.

Victory over evil, spirits, and so on: Africa, Mercy Oduyoye, "Jesus Saves," in *Hearing and Knowing*, 1986, 97–108; John Mbiti, "Some African Concepts of Christology," in *Christ and the Younger Churches*, ed. Vicedom, 1972, 51–62; Marwa Kisare, *Kisare*, 1984, 76–83; China: Simon Chan, *Grassroots Asian Theology*, 2014, 91–127.

Cross-exposing and confronting human power, technological/bureaucratic efficiency, and healing wounds: Asia: Kosuke Koyama, "The Crucified Christ Challenges Human Power," in *Asian Faces of Jesus*, ed. Sugirtharajah, 1993, 149–162.

Solidarity with the poor and victory over the powers, Liberation Theology: Brazil, Leonardo Boff, *Passion of Christ, Passion of the World*, 1987; India, George Prabhu, "The Jesus of Faith," in *Spirituality of the Third World*, ed. Abraham and Mbuy-Beya, 1994, 157–162; Latin America, Carmelo Alvarez, *People of Hope, 1990*, 13–22 (includes atonement theology beyond this victory theme).

Reconciliation, freedom from guilt in postmodern North America: Chris Friesen, *Atonement in the Coffee Shop*, in *Proclaiming the Scandal of the Cross*, ed. Baker, 2006, 46–62; Kevin Vanhoozer, "The Atonement in Postmodernity," in *The Glory of the Atonement*, ed. Hill and James, 2004, 367–404.

Bibliography

Baker and Green, *Recovering the Scandal of the Cross*, 2nd edn, 2011.
Bediako, "Jesus in African Culture," in *Emerging Voices in Global Christian Theology*, 1994.
Boff, *Passion of Christ, Passion of the World*, 1987.
Flemming, *Contextualization in the New Testament*, 2005.
Muller, *Honor and Shame*, 2000.
Tennent, *Theology in the Context of World Christianity*, 2007.
Williams, *A Ray of Darkness*, 1995.

Gospel of John

Edward W. Klink III

Introduction

For a good part of the past century the concept of atonement has been strongly denied to the message and theology of the Gospel of John. Rudolf Bultmann, followed by others (Forestell), argued that the Gospel's presentation of Jesus was intended to depict him as revelation, not atonement. Even refractions of atonement, Bultmann suggests, are best taken as John "adapting himself to this common theology of the church," for "the thought of Jesus's death as an atonement for sin has no place in John" (2:53–54). Such recent minimization of the passive, sacrificial nature of the death of Jesus stands in sharp contrast to the longstanding interpretation of the Fourth Gospel. Even more, it fails to do justice to the Gospel's depiction of the reconciliatory engagement between Jesus and the world, as well as the manner in which the concept of atonement is specifically and progressively applied to the person and work of Jesus.

The Light of the World and Reconciliation

The Gospel of John introduces the story of Jesus by employing concepts that depict the cosmic nature of Christ's ministry of reconciliation. The evangelist explains that Jesus entered a world where there was a seemingly insurmountable separation between the Creator and his creation, God and the world. But it is into this context of cosmic separation that Jesus, the Creator himself (1:3), came to his creation (1:11), in order to reconcile the world to God. This return involved a battle against the forces and agents of estrangement (Klink, "Light," 78–81), described by John as darkness (in contrast to Light), flesh (in contrast to Spirit), falsehood (in contrast to Truth), and death (in contrast to Life). Jesus became all the things the world needed and had failed to be, in order to perform a ministry of reconciliation, revealing—for the first time since the Garden of Eden—the grace and truth of God the Father (1:17–18). This cosmic ministry of reconciliation is introduced and explained in the prologue of John (1:1–18), orienting the reader of the Gospel to the larger context of Jesus's ministry, as well as to the nature of these cosmic themes of estrangement, over which Jesus would become victorious.

The Gospel of John employs cosmological themes and concepts in a storied manner, depicting the reconciliatory ministry of Jesus as Light, Spirit, Truth, and Life. Each of these themes explains Jesus's engagement with the world and the nature of his reconciliation. The theme of *Light and darkness* (e.g., 1:5, 8:12; cf. 1 John 1:6–7) symbolizes the condition of the world and the cosmic battle into which Jesus waged war. The theme of *Spirit and flesh* (e.g., 1:14, 3:6, 4:24, 6:63) symbolizes the broken condition into which Christ entered and the source of his redemptive work. The theme of *Truth and falsehood* (1:17–18, 14:6, 16:13, 17:3; cf. 1 John 1:8, 2:4, 3:19) symbolizes Jesus's ministry of revelation and the true vision of reality he alone provides. Finally, the theme of *Life and death* (1:4; 5:24, 26; 6:57; 11:25–26) symbolizes the blessed existence under the saving sovereignty of God and the communion between God and humanity made possible by the one who is called "the Life" (14:6).

The prologue of John (1:1–18) is especially significant in its depiction of the larger reconciliation theme in the Gospel, intentionally echoing the opening verses of Genesis. The narrative's symbolism is given a pointed announcement in 1:5, where the narrator explains that "the Light shines in the darkness, and the darkness did not overcome/recognize it." The verb in the second clause (*katelaben*) refers either to the physical confrontation between the Light/darkness ("overcome"; NRSV, NIV, ESV), or to the misunderstanding regarding the things of God that will become so prevalent throughout the Gospel ("recognize"; KJV, NASB). The remainder of the Gospel fleshes out this introduction to the encounter between the Creator and his creation, where Christ's appearance as "the Light" is met with direct and robust confrontation by the darkness (cf. 3:19–20, 8:12, 9:5, 12:35). While the idea of "overcoming" is necessarily present (12:31), it is not merely a physical confrontation that is being referenced. The greater confrontation, the one more deeply rooted, is the spiritual encounter. The reconciliation initiated at the beginning of the Gospel by the coming of Jesus is finalized at the Gospel's end by the cross, the pinnacle act of atonement, where the Light of the World is revealed also as the Lamb of God.

The Lamb of God and Atonement

Jesus's ministry of reconciliation transitions from the cosmic themes of Light, Spirit, Truth, and Life introduced in the prologue (1:1–18) to the Lamb in the very next pericope (1:19–34), the first of arguably seven plot movements in the Gospel. The narrative reorients these cosmic concepts discussed above into a meaningful plot, directing all their energies to a developing story, which has as its goal the depiction and explanation of the death of Jesus.

1. *The Announcement of Sacrifice (1:29)*. This is the first and most important passage that explicitly connects Jesus's person and work to the concept of atonement. With the Old Testament (OT) as a certain context for John, and in light of the reference to the removal of "sin," the pronouncement in John 1:29 can only be understood as pointing to Jesus as the "Lamb of God," who reconciles the world to God; a fitting development to the prologue's description of his reconciliatory coming into the world. This title for Jesus is clearly sacrificial, especially with the inclusion of the explanatory description regarding the removal of sin. While the sacrificial title has several possible referents (e.g., the Passover lamb, the lamb of Isaiah 53, the lamb provided by God in Genesis 22, or the triumphant lamb of Revelation 5:6), it is difficult to deny that the Gospel has introduced the theme of substitutionary atonement at its very beginning. The Lamb of God is Jesus, the crucified one. Ultimately, the title ascribed to Jesus at his first appearance in the narrative proper is coterminous with his last moments of life: a Passover sacrifice (18:28, 19:36).

2. *The Mode of Mediation (2:19)*. The first mention of Passover includes Jesus's engaging in dispute in the temple with the religious authorities where he declared in no uncertain terms that his body—not the temple structure—was the true temple of God, that is, the place where God would meet with his people. John 1:14 had already made clear that Jesus constitutes the true temple of God by virtue of his incarnation. But when Jesus commands and foretells of his death ("destroy this temple") and resurrection ("I will raise it again in three days"), he declares himself to be the mode of mediation between God and humanity. The connection between Jesus's death and resurrection and the temple and its replacement associates the cross with sacrifice and expiation, especially with the OT as a context (Carson, 515).

3. *The Condition of the World (8:21)*. The prologue already described the world with the cosmic category of darkness (1:5), which the Gospel would

later reveal to be as a result of sin and death. The world was in darkness because it was plagued, stained, and enslaved to sin. Early in the Gospel the narrator explains that the work of Jesus was intended to take away "the sin of the world" (1:29). The world was so darkened by sin that it did not recognize (1:5), know (1:10), or receive (1:11) God in the person of Jesus. The narrative depicts throughout the consequences of sin, often detailing a person's condition and not their name, like the blind man (9:1–41), the lame man (5:1–15), and the Samaritan woman (4:1–42), with the last suggestive of religious illness. The Gospel of John speaks about sin in a manner that matches its discussion throughout Scripture. Sin is a condition or state of all people, and its consequence is clearly stated in John 8:21: death. Jesus is the only remedy for sin and death (5:24, 8:24, 16:9), and the nature of his entrance into the world already depicts his sacrifice. By entering into the sinful state of the world and taking on "flesh" (1:14), the incarnate body of Jesus is presented as both a corpse and a sacrifice. The Gospel does not spend much time defining sin because it assumes that the rest of the biblical story has made it clear.

4. *The Need for Liberation (8:32)*. The world is enslaved to sin and death and needs to be redeemed. Jesus declares that truth brings freedom. "Truth" in the Gospel is not only a philosophical concept but also a relational one: a true knowledge of God. The truth to be known is that Jesus is the eternal existence and the saving mission of God, the one through whom grace and "truth" came (1:17), and the authoritative expression of the Father and his love for the world. In short, the "truth" is the gospel of Jesus Christ. The term "freedom" is contrasted in John with sin (cf. 8:34), which suggests that the "freedom" about which Jesus speaks is equivalent to salvation. The truth, which centers upon the person and work of Jesus, is liberating. Again, this liberation is not philosophical or rooted in politics, but a spiritual freedom (cf. 12:31). Nor is this kind of freedom based on the original freedom of humanity that belongs to him, the authentic self of man, but a freedom that belongs entirely to God. It is the kind of liberation that can only come from a birth "from above" (3:3); it is the kind of kingdom politicking that requires the eschatological birth "from water and spirit" (3:5).

5. *The Exchange of Life (10:11)*. The liberation Jesus alone provides comes at a great cost: his life. John 10:11 clearly expresses this, when, referring to himself as the Shepherd caring for his sheep, Jesus explains that the Shepherd "lays down" his life for his sheep. The referent can only be to his

sacrificial death on the cross. This interpretation is not derived from the OT or any other source—its background can only be the cross of Christ. This is made all the more clear when it is described as being "for" (*hyper*), that is, "on behalf of," the sheep, a preposition that denotes purpose (cf. 6:51, 11:50–52). This exchange is given further explanation in John 10:18, where Jesus explains that he lays down his life (and regains it again!) by his own authority, which he received from God the Father. This is no Shepherd who falls to thieves or wolves while trying to defend his sheep; a martyr who can save his sheep but not himself. No! Death is not something this Shepherd might face; it is the very thing he must face—and willingly so. What makes this Shepherd and this act of shepherding so mysterious and remarkable is that death is the means by which he saves his sheep. For this Shepherd is not only guarding the sheep from those on the outside, but also from the sheep themselves. This Shepherd wields not a wooden staff but a wooden cross. The authority of Jesus is confirmed when the religious authorities themselves announce their plan to use Jesus's death to save all the people (11:50–52). These texts depict not merely the power of Jesus over his death and resurrection, but also how his death is an act of substitutionary atonement.

6. *The Reception of Salvation (17:26)*. The liberating, life-saving work of Jesus is obtained, according to the prologue of the Gospel, by "receiving" Jesus, that is, by "those who believe in his name" (1:12). "Believe" is a central term for John, used a total of ninety-eight times, which towers above the use of the term by other New Testament (NT) authors (even more than Paul—fifty-four times). The concept of belief makes a clear connection between knowledge and the atoning work of Jesus. The Gospel invites the reader to hear its message of the work and person of Jesus and believe (5:24), an act that requires alignment and allegiance. To receive Jesus is to hear his voice and follow him (10:16). This is expressed most clearly in Jesus's prayer for his disciples, especially John 17:26, where Jesus connects the knowledge he gave to his disciples and links it to their participation in the love of the Trinitarian God. Jesus even defines eternal life as knowledge of God through Jesus Christ (17:3). This is the vision of God mediated by the Son first announced in the prologue (1:18), a vision of not only the person of God (ultimately the Father), but also the work of God (specifically the Son). To know God is to know and participate in his life and his mission, the extension of his life to the world, a life with the Father, through Christ, and in/by the Spirit.

7. *The Passover of the New Covenant (19:31).* The date of the crucifixion is a climactic component of the Gospel's multiform depiction of the sacrificial death of Jesus. When the prologue describes Jesus as "flesh" (1:14), the Baptist declares Jesus to be "the Lamb of God" (1:29, 36), Jesus declares himself to be the replacement of the temple (2:21), and Jesus commands the eating of his flesh and drinking of his blood (6:51–56), the system of atonement rooted in the OT is being applied to his crucified body and sacrificial work. Even more, the role of the Good Shepherd (10:11), the political strategy of Caiaphas (11:51–52), the imagery of his public statement (12:4), the humiliation of the foot washing (13:10), and the prayer of consecration (17:19) cumulatively reflect the image of sacrifice. Even the narrative's account of the death of Jesus is filled with detailed allusions that directly connect the crucifixion of Jesus to the Passover and its elements: the unbroken bones of Jesus (19:33–36), the hyssop used to give Jesus a drink (19:29), and possibly even the reference to "the sixth hour" (19:14). By connecting the Passover to the death of Jesus, the Gospel transfers the theology of Passover and the Old Covenant (the lamb, the blood, the ceremony) to Jesus and the New Covenant. The entire Gospel had been aimed at the cross, the sacrificial death of Jesus—his life on behalf of the world. And fittingly, precisely on the Day of Passover, God's Lamb and firstborn Son was the offering that atoned for the sin of the world.

Conclusion

Was the evangelist adapting himself to what the church already believed, as Bultmann suggested, or was the church responding to the Gospel's message? The evidence from the Gospel suggests the latter. The entire Gospel is aiming at the cross, and the time spent on the last week of Jesus's life and ministry is by far the longest section of the narrative. For John *the* gospel is the fact that Jesus died and rose again, and the meaning of that fact: that Jesus has now accomplished the full purposes of God and fulfilled by his life and body all human persons (he is the Second Adam), all human religion (he is the fulfillment of Judaism and the true High Priest), and all human kingdoms (he is the King and Lord of God's Kingdom). The death of Jesus is the atonement for sin and the reconciliation of the world to God, the Creator renewing his creation on his terms and by his Word.

Bibliography

Bultmann, *Theology of the New Testament*, 1952–1955.
Carson, "Adumbrations of Atonement Theology in the Fourth Gospel," *JETS* 57:3, 2014.
Forestell, *The Word of the Cross*, 1974.
Frey, "Die 'theologia crucifixi' des Johannesevangeliums," in *Kreuzestheologie im Neuen Testament*, 2002.
Kim, "The Concept of Atonement in the Gospel of John," *JGRCHJ* 6, 2009.
Klink, *John*, 2016.
Klink, "Light of the World," in *Cosmology and New Testament Theology*, 2008.
Knöppler, *Die theologia crucis des Johannesevangeliums*, 1994.
Metzner, *Das Verständnis der Sünde im Johannesevangelium*, 2000.
Michaels, "Atonement in John's Gospel and Epistles," in *The Glory of the Atonement*, 2004.
Morris, "The Atonement in John's Gospel," 1988.

51

Hugo Grotius

Gert van den Brink

Grotius's view on the atonement may be found in his *De Satisfactione*, written in 1617 against Faustus Socinus's *De Servatore* (1594). In *De Servatore*, the anti-Trinitarian lawyer Socinus offers a severe critique against the Reformed doctrine of the atonement, as defended by the Reformed Genevan theologian Jacques Covet. Covet stated that because of God's justice every sin must be punished. Socinus's reply was twofold: first, God is able and willing to forgive without receiving satisfaction. Just like any creditor, he can recede from his right to demand the pecuniary debt. Second, it is impossible that one innocent person would bear the punishment of eternal death for many others. Satisfaction is therefore unnecessary and impossible.

Grotius's response against Socinus was innovative in two aspects. First, he accused Socinus of not distinguishing between God as ruler (*rector*) and as sovereign (*dominus*). As *dominus*, God could indeed forgive by receding from his right to punish; however, as a *rector* God is not a private but a public person. As such, he has the task of maintaining and establishing the order and the government of the world. From that perspective, it is necessary that God punishes sin. Being a *rector*, God cannot recede from his right to punish, but he is obliged to put that right into practice. However, according to Grotius, God decided to exercise that right against Jesus Christ by punishing Him, at the same time promising forgiveness to everyone who repents and believes. In this way, Grotius stated, we may still defend the necessary concurrence of punishment and forgiveness.

The second point of Socinus's criticism is not correct either, in Grotius's view. Grotius admitted that it is impossible that one person should bear eternal death for many others. However, it was not necessary that Christ undergo the punishment of eternal death. The Mediator ought not to undergo the same (*idem*) as what sinners are due, but only something of the same worth (*tantundem*). That the death of Christ was of the same worth as the guilt of humankind, Grotius infers from the fact that both options lead to the same result: whether sinners die in their own persons, or whether Christ dies for all, in both cases God maintains the rulership of his creation.

Grotius's view on the atonement is structured by two principles. First, Grotius distinguishes between private and public law, a distinction he used against the Socinians in order to defend the legitimacy and the necessity of the atonement. According to private law, God could (as *dominus*) decide to forgive without satisfaction, which he cannot do according to public law (as a *rector*). Second, Grotius's view on law and punishment is strikingly consequentialist: laws are just and good, if they serve the common good. They can therefore be altered, abrogated, or renewed according to what is demanded by the *bonum commune*. Also justice is, in Grotius's opinion, a functional concept. By stating that the death of Christ should be regarded as a satisfaction to justice, he meant governmental (consequentialist) justice. It is, therefore, common to call Grotius's theory the governmental theory of the atonement.

This view is on several points significantly different from the traditional Reformed view (as found in, e.g., Covet and Sybrandus Lubbertus). Seeing the law, first and foremost, as the expression of the nature and/or the will of God, the Reformed regarded it as unalterable. Justice is an essential propriety of God, constituting his moral character. The necessity of the atonement flows for them not from consequentialist but from deontological, retributive motives. How much punishment Christ had to undergo in quality and quantity was essentially determined not by governmental effects, but by the nature and will of God.

Grotius's view on the atonement had an enormous influence. Among the latitudinarian Anglicans (like Henry Hammond and Edward Stillingfleet), his view became the dominant one. Despite his Arminianism, which caused Reformed theologians to treat Grotius with some caution, his distinction of private and public law was widely accepted even in the Reformed tradition. Because of Grotius's *De Satisfactione*, many Reformed theologians distinguished between *rector* and *dominus* in their responses against Socinianism (John Owen, Andreas Essenius, etc.). The case was different with *idem* and *tantundem*. The Puritan John Owen and the Dutch lawyer Ulrich Huber were highly critical. However, other Reformed theologians accepted Grotius's distinction of *idem* and *tantundem*, particularly the Puritan Richard Baxter. Others followed him partially, such as Essenius, Melchior Leydecker, Francesco Turrettini, and Petrus van Mastricht: terminologically, they regarded the death of Christ as a payment of *tantundem*, but they gave it a deontological meaning and not a consequentialist one. Christ underwent the eternal death, because that was the necessary punishment in case of trespassing God's unalterable law. He did not, however, in all aspects suffer the *idem* of what the damned suffer in hell.

Some German theologians in the nineteenth century (A. B. Ritschl, F. C. Baur, M. Schneckenburger) claimed that Grotius's view was, in the end, not so different from that of Socinus himself. They stated that both Socinus and Grotius saw the death of Christ only as a moral cause on human beings, who, being moved by his severe sufferings, come to faith and repentance. In their view, the only difference was that in Socinus the exhortation was encouraging (people being impressed by God's great love), while in Grotius it was threatening (Christ's death as a deterrent manifestation of God's wrath). This reproof against Grotius was adopted by several neo-reformed theologians in America, such as Charles Hodge, A. A. Hodge, and B. B. Warfield, and also by the Dutch dogmatician Herman Bavinck. The criticism is, however, not correct. In Grotius's schema, the death of Christ is primarily an act of God as *rector*, in order to maintain his reign and establish his rulership. Even if nobody would ever be moved unto faith and repentance, Christ's punishment was still not in vain. Whether one finds Grotius's theory of the atonement acceptable or not depends inter alia on the question whether one accepts a consequentialist definition of punishment.

Bibliography

Bedau and Kelly, "Punishment," in *The Stanford Encyclopedia of Philosophy*, 2010.
Grotius, *Defensio fidei catholicae de satisfactione Christi adversus Faustum Socinum Senensem*, 1617.
Grotius, *Defensio fidei catholicae de satisfactione Christi adversus Faustum Socinum Senensem*, ed. Rabbie, Opera Theologica 1, 1990.
Mortimer, "Human and Divine Justice in the Works of Grotius and the Socinians," in *The Intellectual Consequences of Religious Heterodoxy, 1600–1750*, 2012.
Nellen and Rabbie, *Hugo Grotius, Theologian*, 1994.

52

Colin Gunton

Andrew C. Picard

Colin Gunton (1941–2003) was a Reformed theologian who is recognized as one of the leading figures in the retrieval of Trinitarian theology in twentieth-century Britain. Gunton's theology developed against the backdrop of the instinctive Deism that dominated mid-twentieth-century British theology. In response, he reasserted the truth of orthodox Trinitarian faith and pursued its implications for renewing Western theology and culture (Webster, 261). Working from Barth's renewed stress upon the doctrine of the Trinity, Gunton seeks to show that "in the light of the theology of the Trinity, everything looks different" (*Promise of Trinitarian Theology*, 7). Gunton explicitly develops his theology of atonement in *The Actuality of Atonement*, and in a variety of subsequent writings. However, his fullest understanding of the subject is found embedded in his later Trinitarian theology of mediation, where God redeems and perfects the project of creation through the Son and the Spirit.

The Actuality of Atonement

In *The Actuality of the Atonement*, Gunton seeks to counter the direct language demanded by Enlightenment rationality with a theory of metaphor as indirect, yet truthful, speech about God. Metaphor is language that emerges from indwelling the world in relationship and is appropriate for seeking to know the being of God from the action of God (32–36). Gunton contends that when language is seconded by the gospel, the old wineskins of meaning burst with the new reality it attempts to describe. He develops three metaphors of the atonement: victory, judgment, and sacrifice.

The metaphor of victory acknowledges that the atonement is a victory over sin, evil, and the enemy, but it also renews our understanding of the meaning of victory, namely, that it is "the kind of thing that happens when Jesus goes to the cross" (79). In the metaphor of judgment, Gunton opposes individualistic accounts of salvation that are excessively preoccupied with abstract and juridical notions of the atonement in which God appears excessively punitive. While atonement is certainly the justification of sinners, it is the Creator's desire for relationship with the creature through love. For Gunton, the metaphor of judgment is changed by the gospel so that the concept is personalized instead of being viewed as a legal process. As Barth has shown, God judges in holy love, which takes the shape of the judged judge who, having the right to judge, does not behave in the way expected of judges (Gunton, *The Actuality of Atonement*, 110). In Gunton's final metaphor of the atonement, we learn the meaning of the word "sacrifice" from the life, death, and resurrection of Jesus Christ, receiving from him the means of living our lives sacrificially. Gunton draws from Edward Irving to emphasize the importance of the full humanity and career of Jesus Christ as a sacrifice, not merely the cross. Sacrifice is revealed in the actions of the self-giving God who acts to bring humanity, and creation, back into relationship with himself by means of himself. Atonement as a sacrifice is not a transaction outside the human sphere, but a divine action within the heart of the sinful human condition (126). *The Actuality of the Atonement* is an important starting point for understanding Gunton's theology of atonement, but his more mature thought is found in his work toward a fully Trinitarian theology (Gunton, *Father, Son, and Holy Spirit*, xiii).

Atonement and the Project of Creation

The atonement in Gunton's work is an expansive doctrine that situates God's redemptive activity in the context of the whole created order, and cannot be reduced to a mere transaction between God and an individual. Gunton is concerned to ensure that balanced weighting be given to varying doctrinal foci for the sake of greater wholeness in theology. The ongoing influence of Hellenistic dualisms, which he believed persisted in the Enlightenment, resulted in imbalances in the Western theological tradition. These dualisms manifest themselves in a view of creation as a timeless whole; a docetic view of Jesus Christ; an underdeveloped pneumatology; and a loss of eschatology to protology. Gunton's doctrine of atonement takes a particular shape as he seeks to correct such imbalances. It is especially concerned with perfecting the project of creation; the Son as Mediator of creation and salvation; the Spirit as perfecting cause; and the Church as the community of reconciliation.

Perfecting the Project of Creation

Gunton believes that creation is often misconceived as a timeless whole for which atonement and eschatology are a return to an Edenic beginning. The result is a systematic imbalance that gives protology precedence over eschatology, and creates a divorce between God's timeless creating action and his temporal redemptive action (Gunton, *Father, Son, and Holy Spirit*, 138). Such timeless conceptions conceive human salvation apart from its wider context within creation, with the effect that human salvation is *from* creation instead of participation in the salvation *of* creation.

In his shift to a mature Trinitarian theology of mediation, Gunton asserts more clearly the *Selbständigkeit* (relative independence) of Creator and creation and the personal action of the Son and the Spirit who mediate the Father's presence. The creation, while dependent upon God for its ongoing existence, does not share the divine being but is given its own *created* reality—its own temporal and spatial createdness. Creation is a project that is projected in space and through time toward its eschatological perfection. This perfecting happens through the incarnate Word, in whom all things were created, and by the perfecting Spirit, who orients each created thing to its own particular end in Christ. Creation's perfection is not reached through historical processes, but is redirected to its proper *telos* in the life, death, resurrection, and ascension of Jesus Christ. The Spirit perfects creation by drawing created being into relationship with God, through Christ, in whom the created order reaches its true destiny and the at-one-ment of all things is realized and anticipated (Gunton, *The Promise of Trinitarian Theology*, 184).

The Son as Mediator of Creation and Salvation

In Gunton's thought, God comes into relationship with that which is not himself—the temporal and contingent creation—through his eternal Word. As the eternal Word *in* whom creation was established in the goodness of its temporality, *through* whom God entered time to redeem his creation from within and to whom all things are directed, Jesus Christ is the Mediator of creation and salvation. The eternally begotten Son is the Mediator of creation who was begotten within time to redeem not only humanity, but also the creation itself. Gunton emphasizes the significance of the full humanity and divinity of Jesus Christ, because it is through his recapitulation of faithful human being that humanity and creation are set free by the Lord who came to reclaim his own (Gunton, *Father, Son, and Holy Spirit*, 155). Now, as the ascended High Priest of creation, Christ offers the first fruits of redeemed humanity and creation to the Father, perfected in him by the power of the Spirit. This does not happen in a general way, but takes place as the Spirit sets the creation free to render its true being in relationship to God and all else through Christ—an anticipation of the universal redemption of the age to come (123). To be free in the biblical tradition is to be set free by the redeeming work of the Son in the power of the Spirit for relationship with God, others and God's creation (Gunton, *Act and Being*, 105).

The Spirit as Perfecting Cause

Drawing from Basil the Great, Gunton affirms the Spirit as God's eschatological perfecting cause who perfects creation by enabling it to be itself in proper relation with the Father through Jesus Christ. The Spirit directs created beings to Christ to be what God created it to be in its particularity. This is most clearly displayed within the economy in the career of Jesus Christ. Gunton draws from Irving's Spirit Christology to stress the full humanity of the Son whose sinless perfection is established and upheld by the Spirit (Gunton, *Theology through the Theologians*, 161). The Spirit is not an immanent possession of the Son, but acts as the eschatological other who establishes and maintains Jesus in his particular humanity. As a truly Jewish man, Jesus recapitulates Israel's story to be the faithful and obedient Son of the Father.

Gunton's emphasis upon the Spirit's work in perfecting creation in its createdness extends to his doctrine of election. Gunton was critical of pre-temporal doctrines of election that posit either double predestination or universal election of humanity in Christ, because they cause us to look for a nontemporal reconciliation. Both are in need of a stronger doctrine of the Spirit in which the Spirit creates, within time, the conditions of the eschatological redemption of all things (Gunton, *Becoming and Being*, 239). The universal election of humanity in Christ is worked out in time by the perfecting work of the Spirit. The Spirit completes God's electing work in time by bringing particular persons into the reconciled community, which is upheld, in right relationship to God and the creation in Christ (Gunton, *The Christian Faith*, 163–164).

The Church as Community of Reconciliation

For Gunton, the church is the eschatological community of at-one-ment who are set free *in* and *for* relationship with God and others—a school of personal being where we learn to be with, from and for one another in communion (Gunton, *Father, Son, and Holy Spirit,* 17). Life in communion is a gift of the Spirit and offers, through Christ, a sacrifice of praise to God for his wise purposes in the beginning. Gunton's metaphor of sacrifice carries the dual meaning of God's sacrificial gift of himself in Jesus Christ *and* Christ's sacrificial offering, from within the created order, of redeemed creation to the Father. The church, as the eschatological community, is drawn by the Spirit to participate in Christ's self-offering of the first fruits of liberated creation back to the Father as a sacrifice of praise. Such praise "perfects perfection" and takes the form of culture in which created being is oriented by the Spirit to its own particular end in Christ. The Spirit perfects creation by bringing all things under Christ their head and, from time to time, enables particular events to realize eschatological truth, goodness, and beauty (culture). Gunton states that culture is "that set of activities in which those made in the image of God share in the divine perfecting of that which was made in the beginning" (Gunton, "Reformation Accounts," 80). The perfecting of creation in time and in Christ gives rise to possibilities for the Church's involvement in culture-making by relating to creation in such a way that it can become what God intended it to be in relationship. As sub-creators in culture-making, the church is called to forms of faithful human action and culture which participate in offering a sacrifice of praise, in Christ by the Spirit, to the Father for his wise purposes in the beginning. According to Gunton, such an offering will often take the shape of the cross as the living of redeemed creaturely being in a fallen world is decidedly cruciform (Gunton, *The One, the Three and the Many*, 226).

Gunton's theology of atonement is deeply embedded in his wider theological project and he seldom discusses it as an independent topic. This means that, at times, he moves across the details of doctrine quickly, perhaps too quickly. It also means that Gunton's theology of atonement is one of the essential threads that contributes to the immense scope and integrative implications of his work that continues to invite conversation about the breadth and length and height and depth of the love of God in Christ.

Bibliography

Gunton, *Act and Being*, 2002.
Gunton, *The Actuality of Atonement*, 1988.
Gunton, *Becoming and Being*, 2nd edn, 2001.
Gunton, *The Christian Faith*, 2002.
Gunton, *Father, Son, and Holy Spirit: Toward a Fully Trinitarian Theology*, 2003.
Gunton, *The One, the Three and the Many*, 1993.
Gunton, *The Promise of Trinitarian Theology*, 2nd edn, 1997.
Gunton, "Reformation Accounts of the Church's Response to Human Culture," in *Public Theology in Cultural Engagement*, 2008.
Gunton, *Theology through the Theologians*, 1996.
Gunton, "Towards a Theology of Reconciliation," in *The Theology of Reconciliation*, 2003.
Gunton, *The Triune Creator*, 1998.
Harvey, *The Theology of Colin Gunton*, 2010.
Webster, "Systematic Theology after Barth: Jüngel, Jenson, and Gunton," in *The Modern Theologians*, 2005.

53

Hebrews

David M. Moffitt

The concept of atonement in Hebrews is linked to the context of the ritual activity of the high priest on Yom Kippur (Lev. 16) more explicitly and consistently than anywhere else in the New Testament. It is unsurprising, therefore, that the author's reflection on Jesus's atoning work focuses primarily on how Jesus solved two interrelated problems that separate God and humanity—sin and impurity (e.g., 1:3; 2:17; 5:1; 8:3; 10:2, 11–12). While the Levitical sacrificial system was about more than simply mitigating these problems, certain of the blood rituals, particularly those performed by the high priest in the Holy of Holies on Yom Kippur, were designed for that specific purpose (see esp. Lev. 16:15–17, 30–34; cf. Lev. 17:11). In general, the Levitical blood rituals dealt with these correlated problems—that is, effected atonement—by providing redemption and purification, which also involved removal/forgiveness of sins and ritual impurities (see esp. Sklar, 183–187). For the author of Hebrews, the preexistent heavenly Son became the human high priest, Jesus, who performed the ultimate atoning sacrifice in the heavenly Holy of Holies (9:11–12, 24; cf. 4:14; 6:19–20; 8:1–5). Jesus thereby accomplished redemption and purification, as well as forgiveness/removal of sins for God's people. These categories, broadly conceived, constitute the contours of atonement in Hebrews.

The author uses a number of different terms in relation to these categories. He speaks of Jesus as the high priest whose entry into the heavenly sanctuary obtained eternal redemption (*lutrōsis*, 9:12). Jesus's death was for (*eis*) or, perhaps better, resulted in redemption (*apolutrōsis*, 9:15) from transgressions. That Jesus's death was instrumental in the destruction of the Devil and the release (*apallassein*) of those enslaved by the fear of death (2:14–15) may also be pertinent here.

Language related to purification recurs throughout the text. In 1:3 the writer provides the first hint of the Son's high-priestly ministry by noting that the Son made purification (*katharismos*) for sins (cf. Lev. 16:30) and then sat down at God's right hand. Jesus's blood purifies (*katharizein*) both the individual conscience (9:14; cf. 10:2) and the heavenly space where he ministers (9:22–23). The author describes Jesus in 2:11 as the one who sanctifies (*ho hagiazōn*), while his brothers and sisters are those who are being sanctified (*hoi hagiazomenoi*), presumably because as their high priest his sacrificial ministry expiates (*hilaskomai*) their sins (2:17; cf. 10:11, 14, 29; 13:12). Several references to perfection deserve mention here as well, given the parallels between perfection and purification in Hebrews (cf. 9:9, 14; 10:1–2; Moffitt, "Perseverance, Purity, and Identity," 374–379). That Jesus's own perfection is not a moral category (cf. 4:15), but one related to his immortal life and ability to approach God's presence (cf. 5:8–10; Moffitt, *Atonement*, 194–214; 259–270; 301–302) indicates that the author is as concerned with concepts of ritual purity as he is with sin.

Clearly, though, Jesus's high-priestly work also results in the removal of sins. In Hebrews forgiveness is not granted by Divine fiat or legal declaration, but comes by way of Jesus's sacrificial offering taking away sin (*aphesis*, 9:22, 10:18; *athetēsis*, 9:26; *aphairein*, 10:4; *periairein*, 10:11). Thus forgiveness in Hebrews is, as in the Levitical system, closely related to purification (cf. 9:22–23; 10:4, 11–14).

According to Hebrews, Jesus accomplished atonement by making the ultimate high-priestly offering in the true tabernacle in the heavens (8:1–5; 9:11–14, 24). Just as the high priests who entered the earthly Holy of Holies once every year offered a sacrifice of blood for the purpose of effecting atonement, so Jesus had to offer something to God (8:3). The author identifies the sacrifice that Jesus offered in terms of himself (7:27; 9:25), his blood (9:12–14; 12:24; 13:12) and his body (10:10).

Among modern interpreters a strong consensus holds that in Hebrews the real content of Jesus's sacrificial offering is his death—Jesus's offered his life to God by dying. Thus, when the writer speaks of Jesus's blood, body, and self in sacrificial terms, Jesus's crucifixion is assumed to form the conceptual core that unifies these terms. In general, modern commentators conclude that the author's high-priestly Christology correlates the Son's humiliation and exaltation with the slaughter of the victim and presentation of the blood on Yom Kippur. The crucifixion is the atoning sacrifice while Jesus's exaltation is likened to the high priest's entry into the Holy of Holies. Thus the writer's appeal to the high priest's work on Yom Kippur is often taken to be part of a larger metaphor that seeks to unpack the spiritual/heavenly significance of Jesus's death (e.g., Attridge, 260–266; Eberhart, "Characteristics of Sacrificial Metaphors"; Finlan;

Isaacs; Schenck). Because Jesus's crucifixion is assumed to stand at the center of Jesus's atoning sacrifice, the majority of modern interpreters find no significant role for Jesus's resurrection in the soteriology of Hebrews, or indeed in Hebrews at all (see the survey in Moffitt, *Atonement*, 1–42).

Jesus's bodily resurrection, however, may be more central to the Christology and soteriology of Hebrews than has generally been assumed in modern interpretation (Moffitt, *Atonement*; "Blood, Life, and Atonement"). If the author envisions the resurrected Jesus ascending bodily into the heavens, then his language about Jesus's presentation of his high-priestly sacrifice (his blood, body, and self) before God in the heavenly tabernacle is not likely to be reducible to a metaphor for the crucifixion. Just as the slaughter of the victim was necessary but not sufficient for sacrificial atonement on earth—the earthly high priest had to offer blood in the Holy of Holies on Yom Kippur before atonement was effected (Lev. 16:15–16), so also Jesus had not only to die but then also to ascend into God's presence in the heavenly Holy of Holies. There he did what high priests do. He presented his offering in order to make atonement. The power of Jesus's resurrected life, by way of analogy to the power of life in the blood in the Levitical sacrificial system, effected ultimate atonement.

Such an understanding of Jesus's atoning work in Hebrews aligns well with the logic and practice of sacrifice as described in Leviticus. There sacrifice is presented as an irreducible process whose atoning effects are not directly linked with the act of slaughtering the victim (e.g., Eberhart, *Studien zur Bedeutung der Opfer im Alten Testament*; Gane; Gilders; Milgrom). Later elements in the process, in particular the manipulation of blood at the altars and burning of fat, are identified as effecting atonement. Moreover blood as life (not as a symbol for death) has the power to deal with sin and impurity, and thereby enable God and humanity to dwell together.

Bibliography

Attridge, *Hebrews*, 1989.
Bruce, *Hebrews*, 1990.
Eberhart, "Characteristics of Sacrificial Metaphors in Hebrews," in *Hebrews: Contemporary Methods, New Insights*, 2005.
Eberhart, *Studien zur Bedeutung der Opfer im Alten Testament*, 2002.
Finlan, "Spiritualization of Sacrifice in Paul and Hebrews," in *Ritual and Metaphor*, 2011.
Gane, *Cult and Character*, 2005.

Gilders, *Blood Ritual in the Hebrew Bible*, 2004.
Isaacs, *Sacred Space*, 1992.
Milgrom, *Leviticus 1–16*, 1991.
Moffitt, *Atonement and the Logic of Resurrection in the Epistle to the Hebrews*, 2011.
Moffitt, "Blood, Life, and Atonement," in *Day of Atonement*, 2012.
Moffitt, "Perseverance, Purity, and Identity: Exploring Hebrews' Eschatological Worldview, Ethics, and In-Group Bias," in *Sensitivity to Outsiders*, 2014.
Schenck, *Cosmology and Eschatology in Hebrews*, 2007.
Sklar, *Sin, Impurity, Sacrifice, Atonement*, 2005.

54

Hegel and Baur

Peter C. Hodgson

Georg Wilhelm Friedrich Hegel (1770–1831) introduced a new language and conceptuality for atonement, while Ferdinand Christian Baur (1792–1860) provided a warrant for Hegel's interpretation from the history of Christian doctrine.

The term used by Hegel is *Versöhnung*, "reconciliation." It is in fact very close to the root meaning of the word "atonement," which derives from the Middle English *at-onen*, "being at one," "being reconciled." But "atonement" has been burdened by its theological history, a history in which it has come to mean (among the principal theories) a ransom paid to the Devil, a satisfaction of a legal debt, or a substitutionary death of Christ. From Hegel's point of view, these are merely external representations of a deeper and inward truth. Hegel himself virtually ignored the history of the doctrine of atonement and instead offered his own philosophical construction.

Hegel

Hegel's interpretation is set forth principally in the third volume of his *Lectures on the Philosophy of Religion* (first published in 1832, English critical edition 1984–1987). Christianity, the topic of this volume, is "the consummate religion" because it articulates the three "elements" or "kingdoms" that constitute the triune life of God. The first element is the idea of God in and for itself (the immanent Trinity, the kingdom of the Father); the second element entails differentiation and reconciliation (the kingdom of the Son); the third element is the actualization of reconciliation in the spiritual community and the world (the kingdom of the Spirit).

Reconciliation presupposes differentiation (*Unterscheidung*). The differentiation within the divine life (a play of love with itself, the eternal Son) must have the freedom to "release" the other to exist as a free and independent being (the incarnate Son). This releasing constitutes the creation of the world. The independence of the world is not, however, autonomy: the truth of the world is its ideality, not its reality; it is something posited or created, and its destiny is to subsume its separation from God and return to its origin. Hence the second element of the divine life is "the process of the world in love by which it passes over from fall and separation into reconciliation." Humanity is implicitly good because it is created in the divine image, but the human vocation is not to remain in the condition of implicitness or natural immediacy. If it chooses to do so, to exist "according to nature," then it is evil. But passing beyond the natural condition constitutes another kind of evil, of which knowledge or cognition is the instrument. Hegel calls this second evil cleavage, rupture, disunion (*Entzweiung*); it is the consciousness of "being-for-self" in opposition to nature and to God as absolute spirit. "Cleavage" means "singularizing myself in such a way that cuts me off from the universal." Such singularization (*Vereinzelung*) is a necessary step in the process of humanization. This explains why the human condition is a tragic one, and why God must undergo the tragedy.

Hegel argues for the possibility, the necessity, and the actuality of reconciliation through Christ. The *possibility* is simply that the opposition between divinity and humanity is already implicitly overcome within the divine life, which includes otherness or difference within itself in such a way that "the finitude, the weakness, the frailty of human nature cannot harm that divine unity which forms the substance of reconciliation" (Hegel, 3:311). The *necessity* is that, while the human subject is aware of its need for reconciliation, it cannot achieve it on its own. Reconciliation must "appear" in the world, not simply for philosophical reflection but in a form accessible to the whole of humanity, the form of sensible certainty. This means it must appear in the flesh of a single human being, who is set apart from all others. This one is what humanity intrinsically is, humanity in itself and as such; there can be only one such human being. For this one, the church has used the "monstrous compound," the "God-man."

The *actuality* of reconciliation focuses on who this human being is, namely, Jesus of Nazareth or "Christ." Hegel distinguishes between nonreligious and religious perspectives. The nonreligious perspective views Christ as an ordinary human being or a teacher of humanity like Socrates. However this teacher does not share the corruption and evil inclinations of others or pursue worldly affairs.

He lives only for the truth and its proclamation. He is not merely a teacher but a prophet, a voice of God.

> It is the Son of Man who speaks thus, in whom this expression, this activity of what subsists in and for itself, is essentially the work of God – not as something suprahuman that appears in the shape of an external revelation, but rather as [God's] working in a human being, so that the divine presence is essentially identical with this human being. (Hegel, 3:320)

Thus the nonreligious history of Christ attests to the truth of the religious perspective, the witness of the Spirit to the community of faith that *God* is present in this individual. The same two perspectives apply to the death of Christ. He dies as a martyr to the truth, but his death is also the death of God. The Lutheran statement "God himself is dead" means that everything human, fragile, and finite is a moment of the divine, that "God himself is involved in this," and that what happens is a "stripping away" of the human element, an entrance into glory. God takes the tragedy of the human condition into and upon himself, thereby transforming tragedy into comedy.

Yet tragedy remains in the world, and the third element of the divine life, the kingdom of the Spirit, is concerned with how reconciliation is actualized in the midst of discord. It happens, according to Hegel, not only in the faith of individuals but also in the spiritual community, its unique intersubjectivity, its institutions, and its cultic practices. The sacrament of the Lord's Supper is the "midpoint of Christian doctrine" because through it persons receive not merely the assurance of unity with God but the actual enjoyment and partaking of it. Reconciliation must also be accomplished in the world, in a just and ethical civil life and the humanitarian state. "It is in the organization of the state that the divine has broken through into the sphere of actuality; the latter is permeated by the former, and the worldly realm is now justified in and for itself, for its foundation is the divine will, the law of right and freedom" (Hegel, 3:342, n. 250). Hegel is aware of the gap between this "eschatological" vision and the empirical states of his time, but he insists that secular history is the place where reconciliation must be realized.

Baur

Baur, professor of theology at the University of Tübingen from 1826 until his death, provides what is lacking in Hegel, a history of the Christian doctrine of reconciliation (*Die christliche Lehre von der Versöhnung in ihrer geschichtlichen Entwicklung*). This is a relatively early work, Baur's first major study in Christian doctrine, and it has serious flaws, such as the disproportionate allocation of periods, but it is rich in detail and insight. The doctrine of the reconciliation of God and humanity constitutes the midpoint of every religion but attains its true signification only in Christianity because Christian doctrine expresses the two aspects of the divine-human relationship in the form of the antithesis of sin and grace (a theme central to Friedrich Schleiermacher). The more deeply the separation (*Zwiespalt*) between finite and absolute spirit penetrates into human consciousness, the more deeply reconciliation achieves its full meaning. Reconciliation is accomplished in Christianity because the idea of the unity of the divine and the human comes to its fullest expression in the person of the God-man. This *objective* consummation of reconciliation must also be *subjectively* realized in each individual.

Baur distinguishes three moments in the concept of reconciliation, moments that involve the dialectic of objectivity and subjectivity. (1) As a divine act, reconciliation is a self-generating process within the essential nature of God, a process by which God realizes God's essential nature. From this *purely objective* standpoint, reconciliation occurs for the sake not of humanity but of God and humanity is assumed into God's own life-process. (2) As a human act—the *purely subjective* standpoint—humanity completes its reconciliation with God only within its own self-consciousness. (3) Between these two one-sided moments is a third, which emphasizes the concept of *mediation*. Reconciliation occurs by means of an external historical act that is the necessary condition of an ensuing subjective reconciliation. These three moments form the basis for the history of the development of the doctrine. Each moment is present in every period, but one moment prevails in each period.

In the first major period, which extends from the early church fathers through the late Middle Ages, reconciliation is understood principally in terms of its external historical objectivity and absolute necessity. Its fundamental concept is that of justice (*Gerechtigkeit*), with the twin aspects of guilt and punishment. The first major atonement theory is that of ransom, which is found among the Gnostics, Irenaeus, and Origen; Augustine modifies it in the Pelagian debates and John Scotus Erigena reformulates it in Neoplatonic terms. In the Middle Ages Anselm's idea of Christ's satisfaction of a debt and substitutionary atonement becomes the crowning achievement. Anselm is challenged by Abelard, refined by Bonaventure and Thomas Aquinas and rejected outright by Duns Scotus. The late-medieval debates represent the exhaustion of the purely objective idea.

The second period runs from the Reformation to the end of the eighteenth century. The Reformation and its aftermath is a period of conflict in which the element of subjectivity becomes increasingly predominant but no actual mediation occurs between objectivity and subjectivity. Baur is a master of the post-Reformation doctrinal disputes and describes in detail how Protestant scholasticism emerges on the one side, with its various modifications of the satisfaction theory, and Socinianism and Arminianism on the other side, preparing the way for the pietism and rationalism of the eighteenth century. Rationalism attains its finest expression in the philosophy of Kant, who recognizes the presence of radical evil but argues for a purely moral theory of reconciliation based on the inner law of reason (the categorical imperative).

The third period is the briefest, consisting of the early decades of the nineteenth century when Schleiermacher and Hegel make the concept of mediation central. They do so in quite different ways. While appreciative of Schleiermacher, Baur regards Hegel's speculative theology to offer the most profound insight into the meaning of reconciliation. The divine life-process is nothing other than the reconciliation or mediation of God, as absolute spirit, with himself. The idea of reconciliation attains its full reality through the intensification of the antithesis of divine and human to its ultimate point in the sin and death of the human being. This is the significance of Christ as the God-man, since through him the essential unity of the divine and the human enters into the consciousness of humanity. Objectively speaking, God, as the God-man, appears in the world, thereby revealing that God is reconciled with the world; but the main point is that reconciliation is also subjectively realized in the consciousness of human subjects, whose consciousness is the self-consciousness of God. Religion is essentially nothing other than becoming conscious of the unity of God and humanity in the midst of sin and estrangement. The "becoming conscious" is not simply a cognitive act but entails a new way of life.

Baur concludes his book by describing the breakup of the Hegelian school and laying out his own position. He says there cannot be an *absolute* actualization of the divine idea in a single individual; indeed, the tradition has recognized this truth by identifying Christ not simply with Jesus of Nazareth but with the archetypal human being, the species-concept (*Gattungsbegriff*) of humanity. The question then becomes how the idea of God-manhood is related to the historical person. The answer cannot be that of either the orthodox doctrine (the person of Christ is essentially divine) or the Ebionite fallacy (the person is essentially human). "Between the two extremes there is space enough to attribute to Jesus a value and dignity that specifically distinguishes him from all other human beings and raises him high above them" (Baur, 735). The historical person of Jesus is "none other than the one impressed by [the idea] in the most intensive manner possible, the one who consummates its reality up to the point beyond which it is not possible for it to be portrayed in a single individual" (624). Such an interpretation allows Jesus to *belong* to history and to mediate reconciliation *to* history. It also leaves the door open to recognizing the validity of other religions.

Bibliography

Baur, *Die christliche Lehre von der Versöhnung in ihrer geschichtlichen Entwicklung*, 1838.
Hegel, *Lectures on the Philosophy of Religion*, 1832, 1840, trans. Brown, Hodgson, and Stewart, 1984–1987, reprint 2007.

The Historical Books

Richard S. Briggs

The strange world of the Old Testament's "historical books" (Joshua to Esther) may seem a long way from theological concerns with atonement. In fact this observation is an extension of a more immediate and puzzling instance of "conceptual distance": that these historical books also seem somewhat removed from many of the concerns of the Pentateuch. Their contribution to wider Christian theological thought may thus helpfully take its lead from this feature of the Old Testament itself.

Most English translations render verbs using the *kpr* root as "atone/make atonement" or "expiate/make expiation," especially in priestly writings. (There remains considerable discussion of the etymology of the root, with some suggesting that its single *qal* occurrence in Gen. 6:14 points to a sense of "covering.") The verb occurs 102 times in the Old Testament, almost always in the *piel*, with the sense of "atone." Of these, 78 are in the Pentateuch, but only 6 in the historical books (1 Sam. 3:14 [the only biblical occurrence in the *hithpael*, though this does not affect our discussion]; 2 Sam. 21:3; 1 Chr. 6:34; 2 Chr. 29:34 and 30:18; Neh. 10:34). These statistics amply attest to the relative emphases of these two collections of the texts, especially since only the two Samuel occurrences are in the "former prophets"/"deuteronomistic history." While the later books of Chronicles and Nehemiah (no longer thought to be themselves all the work of one author) can draw upon Pentateuchal categories, as well as various elements of the Psalms, it is likely that the books Joshua, Judges, and Samuel represent some of the earliest literary records of Israelite history and practice. How significant is it that Israel can tell this history without reference to the core vocabulary of atonement?

Neither of the two verses in Samuel is overly specific with regards to what was understood about atonement. The first refers to the *lack* of atonement available to Eli's house. The second places on the lips of David a question (to the Gibeonites) about how atonement might be possible in light of the bloodguilt on Saul's house. Both these verses could arguably be later additions to the text, though this would be an argument dependent solely on the rarity of the vocabulary. More likely the two verses attest to a functional but not precise notion of atonement that was common neither in speech nor written record.

The language of "sacrifice" (*zebah*) in the historical books is less uncommon, particularly in 1 Samuel. In 2 Kings it is used frequently to describe sacrifices to other gods. On occasion such language seems deliberately to avoid any connotation of atonement; for example, "Let us now build an altar, not for burnt-offering, not for sacrifice" (Josh. 22:26–29). References to "the yearly sacrifice" in Samuel (1:21, 2:19, 20:6) seem based on 1 Samuel 1:3, which describes Elkanah going up "year by year" to sacrifice (though using the idiom "day by day" in Hebrew). 1 Samuel 2:29 is the only reference in these passages to "sacrifices [and offerings] that I commanded," though note Joshua 8:31, referring to an altar, commanded, "As it is written in the book of Moses." There are indeed occasional references in these books to the *olah* (whole burnt offering) and the *shelem* ("peace offering"), but the most natural reading of these terms here seems to be to basic practices of making sacrifices that are burnt and designed to bring peace, without specific reference to the Levitical framing of these sacrifices in atoning terms, or indeed without much reference to such practices having been previously commanded by Moses.

These observations lead to the standard scholarly reconstruction of the Old Testament wherein the historical books predate the legal sections of the written Pentateuch. While dating texts has never been an exact science, on this point there is much agreement. The Pentateuch thus subsequently offers theological reflection on the nature of the practices of sacrifice, even though these sacrificial practices existed long before the Pentateuch itself was written. The book of Judges offers a particularly clear test case of such an approach, since it contains no references to priests or Levites outside its concluding section (notably Jgs. 17–18), and when it does it has little to do with the Levitical priesthood of Exodus 28–29. References to priests in the books of Samuel tend to be to certain named individuals with local responsibilities (Eli and his house; Ahijah [1 Sam. 14]; Ahimelech [1 Sam. 21]), and there is no obvious notion of a continuous role for a single priesthood at the center of the narrative. The picture here is complex, but the text has little interest in describing the structure and function of priesthood (or, likewise, notions of sin), however one imagines that historical reconstruction might proceed.

Standard historicizing readings of this data tend toward one of two positions. (1) The Pentateuchal handling of these categories was available to the authors of the historical books, but their interests and agendas left them relatively uninterested in atonement and associated categories. This seems unlikely, especially given the later prominence of the Mosaic conceptualities. (2) As per the critical reconstruction noted above, the discrepancy is "explained" by reorganizing the historical order of composition, with the final written form of the Pentateuchal approach to the matter postdating that of the historical books. This is probably true, but it is not an adequate analysis of the achievement of the Old Testament canon in presenting matters this way.

After the work of Brevard Childs, scholars with theological interests may instead look for a canonical approach that assumes that there is theological meaning in the canonical arrangement. Thus while the practices of sacrifice may well predate the Pentateuch's theological account, their significance is still adequately described by that account. The Pentateuch thus offers a theological redescription of prior practices that articulates the true nature of such sacrifice.

Hence "atonement" can be an extrinsic but faithful category for reading the work of priesthood and sacrifice in the historical books. The theological implications of this approach are interesting. On the one hand, most Israelites in the period(s) of the historical books may have had little conceptual framework for explicating how God forgave sin. On the other hand, the practices of prayer, sacrifice, and devotion were widely understood, and seen to be efficacious in maintaining Israel's relationship with God. Convictions about atonement were perhaps enacted more than articulated. It is the priestly traditions that turn toward conceptual analysis.

It may be that Joshua, Samuel, and even David understand that certain actions are required of them in devotion toward God because of their understanding of who God is. The "grammar" of belief in a God who is just and holy requires sacrifice, and the performance of acts that acknowledge ways in which they sin, or fall short. If this is true, then the historical books bear witness to the reality of sin and atonement, while sitting light to any particular conceptualization of them. Here the reality of atonement lies less in language and more in human practices in response to the divine.

Typically, the Old Testament does not resolve the tension between these different blocks of text. Arguably the Pentateuch holds a certain canonical priority and has greater impact. But canonically oriented analyses seek to allow the various emphases to stand in mutually qualifying tension, resisting attempts to reduce theological complexities to single perspectives. The witness of the historical books is an alternative report alongside the work of the priestly traditions.

The Christian reader of the historical books is left with some leeway in understanding how the acts described in them are taken up in Christ's atoning work. Regarding the familiar typology of prophet-priest-king, it is the royal perspectives that come to dominate Samuel and Kings, while the books of Chronicles make a strong case for the significance of priestly activity. Again, the two variant historical traditions (the "Deuteronomistic" and the "Chronistic") are allowed to exist side by side in the canon without being resolved into one picture. 1 Samuel itself incorporates ongoing tensions over the desirability of kingship alongside more established prophetic traditions, and highlights the dangers that attend to too strong a notion of kingship.

One mediating image is that of the judge, which retains aspects of military leadership and wise ruling. The book of Judges offers a clear, if troubling, portrait of the evils let loose in the absence of appropriate ruling judgment. In such a perspective, atonement without judgment would equate to atonement without justice.

More striking is the dramatic military (even violent) imagery of the book of Joshua, with its narratives of *herem*, variously understood as "placing under the ban" or "putting to destruction" (e.g., 6:17–18 and 7). Such texts might contribute to an understanding of atonement that incorporates the violent defeat of evil, as well as dividing between what is made holy through atonement and what is thereby excluded.

The lack of precision about how these historical/narrative accounts relate to atonement and its categories results in interpreters having considerable scope for developing their understanding. Correspondingly these Old Testament books resist attempts to overdetermine a doctrine of atonement.

Bibliography

Anderson, *Sin: A History*, 2010.
Averbeck, "*kpr*," in *NIDOTTE* 2: 689–710.
Childs, *Introduction to the Old Testament as Scripture*, 1979.
Fretheim, *Deuteronomic History*, 1983.
Sklar, *Sin, Impurity, Sacrifice, Atonement*, 2005.

Ignatius of Antioch

Harry O. Maier

Ignatius, bishop of Antioch, wrote seven letters to churches in western Asia Minor and Rome, while en route as a prisoner to the capital where he was martyred in 113 CE, or perhaps later in the 130s or 140s. The letters represent the largest post-canonical collection of letters of the period and are especially important for the ways they attest to the continuing influence of Pauline soteriological understandings of Jesus's death, and how they build on them. As the other writings of the Apostolic Fathers, Ignatius's are occasional and not doctrinal treatises. He formulates his understanding of Jesus's death as a means of refuting false teachings, especially docetic Christology. Ignatius connects right confession of Jesus's suffering with obedience to the bishop, presbyters, and deacons that lead each of the churches his letters respectively address. Only those leaders who correctly teach Jesus's suffering furnish believers with true sacraments. Here in these epistles, Ignatius builds upon ideas found in the New Testament, by connecting the efficacy of baptism and the Eucharist with right beliefs about the physical birth, death, and resurrection of Jesus.

Ignatius's atonement language is bold. He speaks without qualification of "new life" that has come to believers "through the blood of God [*en haimati theou*]" (Eph. 1.1). It is also graphic: Jesus was "truly nailed in the flesh for us" (Smyrn. 1.2). Jesus's blood is a metonym: it is "incorruptible love" (Rom. 7.3) and "eternal and everlasting joy" (Phld. inscrip.). Peter and the disciples when they touched the crucified resurrected body of Jesus were "closely united with his flesh and blood" (Smyrn. 3.2). Judgment comes to those who "do not believe in the blood of Christ" (Smyrn. 6.1). For Ignatius the blood and flesh of Jesus refer to the entire physical event of the incarnation; he places equal emphasis on the physical birth and resurrection of Jesus as he does his death (Eph. 18.2; Mag. 11.1). Once Ignatius uses priestly language to refer to Jesus, but develops the metaphor in a more Johannine direction when he refers to him as "high priest" who has been entrusted "with the hidden things of God" and is "the door of the Father, through which Abraham and Isaac and Jacob and the prophets and the apostles of the church enter in" (Phld. 9.1). Where he refers specifically to the death of Jesus, he follows Paul in referring to his suffering "for us" (Tral 2.1; Smyrn 1.2—*dia hēmas/hyper hēmōn*) and "for our sins [*hyper tōn hamartiōn*]" (Smyrn. 6.2). Christians await the return of "the Eternal, the Invisible, who for our sake [*di' hēmas*] became visible; the Intangible, the Unsuffering, who for our sake [*di' hēmas*] suffered, who for our sake [*di' hēmas*] endured in every way" (Pol. 3.2). Also, like Paul, if Jesus dies "for us," it is not a substitutionary death: we die with Christ, and live in him. Again, like Paul, he also refers to participation in Jesus's resurrection as a future event: "[Jesus's] Father will ... raise us up in Christ Jesus who believe in him" (Trall. 9.2).

The language of participation is much bolder than in Paul: Ignatius celebrates the Smyrnaeans's faith "having been nailed, as it were, to the cross of the Lord Jesus Christ in both body and spirit, and firmly established in love by the blood of Christ" (Smyrn. inscrip). Ignatius greets the Philadelphians "in the blood of Jesus Christ, which is eternal and lasting joy" (Phld. inscrip.); he greets the leaders of Smyrna "in the name of Jesus Christ and in his flesh and blood, his suffering and resurrection" (Smyrn. 12.1). Believers are thus "members of his [the Father's] Son" and "have a share in God" or are "in Christ" (Eph. 4.1; Trall. 11.1; similarly, 5.1, 9.3, 10.3, 12.2, 20.1, 21.1; Magn. 1.1, 6.1, 12.1, 13.1; Rom. 2.2; Phld. 10.1; Smyrn. 3.1, 12.2; Pol. 3.1). Jesus's "life is not in us unless we voluntarily chose to die into his suffering" (Magn. 5.1; also, Eph. 3.1). Believers are to be "imitators of Jesus Christ" (Phld. 7.2). Their initiation into such a life of participation in Christ and imitation of him comes through baptism (Eph. 18.1) and is preserved through the Eucharist, which Ignatius calls "the medicine of immortality" and an "antidote we take in order not to die but to live forever in Jesus Christ" (Eph. 18.2; similarly, Smyrn. 6.2).

Such language of participation helps to make sense of Ignatius's graphic representations of himself as a martyr (e.g., Rom. 4.1–5.3) and self-depiction as a sacrifice for the Asia Minor churches. Three times he refers to himself as a ransom [*antipsychon*] for his audience (Eph. 21.1; Pol. 2.3; 6.1; see also Smyrn. 10.2; Eph. 18.1). This language bears similarities with language found in the apocryphal *4 Maccabees* (ca. 100 BCE–70 CE), a document from Antioch with which Ignatius may have been familiar, or with which he shared cultural concepts. In that account Jewish martyrs are similarly an *antipsychon* (4 Macc. 6.29, 7.21); their death is a ransom paid for the sins of their

Jewish compatriots. It is very possible that Ignatius thinks he is similarly suffering to heal disputes in Antioch, but the idea of Christian participation in and heralding of the atoning death of Jesus better explains its use with reference to the Asia Minor churches. Ignatius calls himself "a prisoner in Christ Jesus" (Trall. 1.1) and his own suffering and anticipated martyrdom is a sharing with and proclamation of Jesus's physical suffering (Magn. 5.1; Rom. 6.2; Trall. 10.1). As a consequence he calls himself "image-bearer" (Eph. inscrip.; Trall. inscrip.; Phil. inscrip.). His martyrdom thus represents a continuing affirmation of the achievements of Christ's death for believers. Ignatius uses it rhetorically to reinforce the belief in Jesus's physical death, as well as the confession that through baptism and the Eucharist believers continue to participate in and enjoy its benefits.

Bibliography

Perler, "Das vierte Makkabäerbuch, Ignatius von Antiochien und die ältesten Märtyrerberichte," *Rivista di archaeologia Cristiana* 25, 1949.
Rashdall, *The Idea of the Atonement in Christian Theology*, 1920.
Schoedel, *Ignatius of Antioch*, 1985.
Torrance, *The Doctrine of Grace in the Apostolic Fathers*, 1996.

57

Imagination

Trevor A. Hart

Our thought and speech about the atonement are necessarily imaginative. Maybe this has not struck you before, but it is true nonetheless. Actually, this is not a state of affairs peculiar to the doctrine of the atonement, but applies equally to all of our talk and ideas about God. As Thomas Aquinas pointed out in his *Summa Theologiae*, since (according to the tenets of Christian faith) the reality of God is mind-blowing and lies well beyond the ordinary range of our language, we can only get our heads (and our words) around that reality by resorting to poetic strategies—speaking and thinking in terms of analogies and metaphors, highly imaginative forms (*Summa*, 1a Q. 12–13; Hart, *Between the Image and the Word*, 13–42). And, since the atonement has to do fundamentally with the mystery of God and God's relationship to the world, what is true more widely is certainly true here too, and perhaps supremely so.

Let's be quite clear: the force of the claim I have just made about imagination has to do with the way our words and our thoughts about God and about the atonement work. It is not a claim about their ultimate origin, as though "imaginative" meant "imaginary" or even "make believe." Christian theology begins with the claim that God has given himself and his ways to be known by humans. The claim here is simply that he has done so and does so in ways that accommodate our creaturely finitude and the limitations of our thought and speech, stretching them poetically until they refer us appropriately to the reality of his character and his dispositions, intentions and actions toward us (McCormack, 431–55). This ought not to be an odd or uncomfortable suggestion for anyone familiar with Jesus's characteristic ways of communicating—through story, parable, symbol and the like—or with the wider literary character of Scripture as a whole. Whatever else may have to be said, God reveals himself by an appeal to our capacity for imagination, and by deploying a set of divinely sanctioned and sanctified images (Gunton; Hart, "Redemption and Fall," 189–206; MacIntyre).

Consideration of biblical materials relevant to the doctrine of the atonement in particular reveals a rich and at times bewildering pattern of different images or metaphors functioning in a complementary manner, each granting us a partial glimpse of some aspect of the dense and ultimately mysterious reality of God's dealings with us and our sin in such a way as to reconcile and restore us to himself. Where the New Testament is concerned we might cluster these under three distinct headings for the sake of convenience (Hart, "Redemption and Fall," 194–196).

First, there are images of *release*. Thus Christ has come "to destroy the works of the devil" (1 John 3:8), to break the hold of him who holds the power of death (Heb. 2:14), a theme reflected in gospel portrayals of Jesus's struggle with dark and demonic forces from his baptism to his crucifixion where the "prince of this world" is finally disarmed and driven out (Col. 2:15; John 12:31). The metaphor of "redemption" (*apolutrosis*) itself draws on related ideas. Just as someone sold into slavery in Israel might be redeemed or ransomed by a blood relative (see Lev. 25:47–55), so now Jesus's life, death, and resurrection bring release to captives (Luke 4:18–19), constituting a "ransom" (*lutron*) for many (Mark 10:45; 1 Tim. 2:6) which sets them free from slavery to sin (Rom. 6:6; John 8:34) and sins use of the law as a device of restraint rather than blessing (Titus 2:14; Gal. 4:4; Eph. 2:15; Col. 2:14; Heb. 9:15, and so on).

Second, there are images of *access*—namely, a new, confident, and joyful access to God for those estranged and distanced from him by sin and its consequences (Mt. 27:51; Eph. 2:18, 3:12; Heb. 10:19f.). It is here that the language of "atonement" (*hilasterion*) in its most precise and focused sense arises, referring to whatever is held to secure and facilitate this surprising access into God's presence. Here the imagery both of Israel's cult and her legal-code are variously appealed to, and sometimes seems to cross-fertilize. So, for instance, Jesus's life and death are likened variously to the covenant sacrifice (Mt. 26:28; 1 Cor. 11:25), the Passover (1 Cor. 5:7), and the sin offering (1 John 2:2). Christ purifies our nature from the ritual defilement of sin, and mediates between the most Holy God and sinful humankind (Heb. 9:11–15). Alternatively, Jesus's suffering by being immersed in a human circumstance dominated by sin is pictured as a bearing of the divine judgment on sin. So, the crucifixion is a bearing of the curse of the law (Gal. 3:13) in which Jesus was "made sin for us" (2 Cor. 5:21), and his death crucifies or circumcises and thereby does away with the sinful nature (Col. 2:11; Rom. 6:6), the wages of sin being paid in full, and the wrath of God being rightfully owned and played out (Col. 3:6; 1 Thess. 1:10).

Third, there are images of *transformation*, which picture atonement as involving the bestowal upon us of new and unimaginable blessings. So, for instance, Christ brings healing and immortality through resurrection to counteract the sickness and death contingent upon sin (1 Cor. 15:20f; 2 Tim. 1:10; John 5:24). The gift of eternal life in union with the Son of God (1 John 5:11), the enjoyment of discovering ourselves to be sons and daughters of a heavenly Father (Gal. 4:1–7), the personal indwelling of God's Spirit within us (1 Cor. 3:16), the moral fruit of the Spirit in transformed lives (Gal. 5:22f.), the eventual glorification of our humanity (1 Cor. 15:43; Eph. 2:6; Phil. 3:21), and (perhaps the most enigmatic verse in the New Testament) participation in the divine nature (2 Pet. 1:4) are all pictured as outcomes bound up with what God has done in "taking flesh" and conforming it to his own life and character in Jesus.

All of this and more besides forms part of the rich cornucopia of soteriological imagery offered to us in the apostolic writings, and provides the soil in which our own further reflections and attempts to unpack the terse summary insistence that "Christ Jesus came into the world to save sinners" must be rooted. Each image offers an imaginative handhold on the mystery of what was involved, for God and for us, when he laid hold of our sin-burdened and corrupted nature and wrestled it back (from within) into its proper created correspondence to his own character, so that it might share in his life and glory—humanity at last existing "at-one" with its Creator. They are precisely images and metaphors (albeit divinely sanctioned ones), not explanations or theories. Laid out serially as we have attempted above, they can be seen sometimes to conflict with one another even as they complement one another.

After all, a victory on the battlefield has little obviously in common with the offering of a sacrificial victim on the altar, or the bearing of a penalty prescribed by law. Yet the clash (such as it is) is merely at the level of the metaphors, none of which tells it "exactly as it was," none of which claims a stranglehold on the truth of the matter. We may safely presume that all are important, and that each has something vital to contribute to our grasp of the underlying reality, which is bigger and more mysterious than any of our attempts to reach it or circumscribe it in human terms. They thus grant us a rich language in terms of which to refer helpfully to something that is, strictly speaking, beyond human telling.

It is of the nature of images that they are suggestive of reality rather than prescriptive with regard to it, and that they thus naturally call for and encourage further acts of holy imagination rather than closing them down. The history of theological and liturgical reckoning with the atonement bears eloquent witness to this, as Christians have constantly sought new and fresh ways to capture something of that reality to which the biblical texts bear witness. One classic example of this is St Anselm's attempt to reimagine the workings of salvation in terms proper to his own feudal medieval society, as the payment by Christ of a "satisfaction" rendered due to God by the dishonor done to him in human sin (Anselm, 260–356). The greatness of Anselm's accomplishment, though, is perhaps also its greatest failure. So extensive and thoroughgoing is his account that it quickly petrifies into a "theory," a comprehensive explanation that both claims to understand too much, and in doing so neglects many of the rich and suggestive images with which Scripture furnishes us as an appropriate starting point. There is something refreshing, by comparison, about C. S. Lewis's refusal to tread any further in the direction of accounting for the power of Aslan's death at the hands of the White Witch than to refer his childlike readers to the workings of "Deep Magic" (chapters 13–15). What matters finally is not that we can get our heads around it, but that it works.

Of course, Lewis's allegorical allusion is only a bit of fiction, and we might thus suppose that it need not be taken too seriously. But, as we have seen, all treatments of the atonement have it in common with fiction that they are the products of careful theological imagining, even though the two no doubt work on different levels. We should at least reckon with the possibility, therefore, that more explicitly imaginative treatments (in literature, film, music, or wherever) may nonetheless be quite powerful in putting us in touch with aspects of that underlying reality which doctrinal imagining aspires to address in more rigorous and ordered ways. After all, in approaching the thing suggestively rather than analytically—and fusing the responses of the heart and the will with those of the head—works of fiction arguably function in a manner consonant and resonant with the literary and poetic quality and substance of Scripture itself. The motifs of a reconciling act which proceeds from a surprising love and forgiveness and which heals human brokenness, of a victory over evil which works paradoxically not by retaliation but via a nonviolent submission to death and humiliation, of the purging of evil and the redemption of goodness only through struggle, suffering, and death occur with surprising frequency in Western literature, and are explored in such mainstream movies as Roland Joffé's *The Mission* (1986), Clint Eastwood's *Gran Torino* (2008), Chris Nolan's *The Dark Knight* (2008), and numerous others. Such "secular" glimpses are no substitute for more careful theological reflection within the church of course; but their un-canonical resonances, powerfully suggestive of the underlying reality may, perhaps, grant those masses in our society not inclined toward reading theology or likely ever to be exposed to any through preaching and liturgy fleeting yet meaningful handholds on the reality of God's atoning love, and some sort of language in terms of which to respond to that when it finds them.

Bibliography

Anselm, "Why God Became Man," in *Anselm of Canterbury: The Major Works*, 2008.
Aquinas, *Summa Theologiae*, 1a Q.
Gunton, *The Actuality of Atonement*, 1988.
Hart, *Between the Image and the Word*, 2013.
Hart, "Redemption and Fall," in *The Cambridge Companion to Christian Doctrine*, 1997.
Lewis, *The Lion, the Witch and the Wardrobe*, 1950.
MacIntyre, *The Shape of Soteriology*, 1995.
McCormack, "Divine Revelation and Human Imagination: Must We Choose between the Two," *Scottish Journal of Theology* 37:4, 1984.

Imago Dei

Ryan S. Peterson

Atonement for the Image of God

Human life in the image of God, established at creation and brought to fulfillment in the new creation, requires atonement with God. Humans must know God and fellowship with God in order to carry out the task of representing God in the world.

Humanity's distrust of and rebellion against God severed humanity's creational fellowship with God. Since fellowship and knowledge are interconnected, this break in fellowship compromised human knowledge of God. Humanity's sin did not change human identity within creation—humans continue to be identified by God as the creatures intended to represent God as God's image and likeness—but sin compromised the ability for humanity to succeed in representing God faithfully.

Restoring integrity to God's creaturely image requires reconciliation. The rapprochement of God and humanity is required for humans to faithfully image God in the world. Jesus Christ reconciles God and humanity, restoring humanity's fellowship with God and reestablishing human knowledge of God. The nature and means of the reconciliation accomplished by Jesus Christ for the sake of bringing the *imago Dei* to fulfillment are expressed diversely in the Christian tradition. To illustrate this diversity, it will be helpful to consider briefly the accounts of Irenaeus, Athanasius, and John Calvin.

Irenaeus describes Adam and Eve as children when they are created, indicating that humanity was created in immaturity. God's intention was to bring humanity to maturity through fellowship and union with God. In the process, humanity would overcome sin and arrive at incorruptibility, truly enjoying the vision of God.

> Now it was necessary that man should in the first instance be created; and having been created, should receive growth; and having received growth, should be strengthened; and having been strengthened, should abound; and having abounded, should recover [from the disease of sin]; and having recovered, should be glorified; and being glorified, should see his Lord. (Irenaeus, IV.34.3)

After humanity showed itself unable to mature in the knowledge of God and conformation to God's image, the Word of God became incarnate in order to conform humanity to God's image.

> And then, again, this Word was manifested when the Word of God was made man, assimilating himself to man and man to himself, that by means of his resemblance to the Son, man might become precious to the Father. For in times long past, it was said that man was created after the image of God, but it was not yet shown; for the Word was as yet invisible, after whose image man was created. Wherefore also he did easily lose the similitude. When, however, the Word of God became flesh, he confirmed both of these: for he both showed forth the image truly, since he became himself what was his image; and he re-established the similitude after a sure manner, by assimilating man to the invisible Father through means of the visible Word. (V.16.2)

For Irenaeus, then, Jesus Christ brought human nature to perfection by bringing humanity into union with the Father. In Jesus Christ, for the first time, human nature was demonstrated truly. All who are in Christ will share in the perfection of human nature when they are raised from the dead. For Irenaeus, Jesus Christ recapitulates human nature, and since he is the perfect Word of God he brings human nature to fulfillment in the process. Jesus Christ brings atonement by becoming the last Adam and fulfilling God's permanent intention for humanity.

For Athanasius, humans at creation were allowed to share, and thereby image, God's attributes as long as they continued to contemplate God (§4). Contemplation, as Athanasius understood it, is not contrary to earthly acts; rather, contemplation orders and directs right action, and it is maintained even while doing other earthly activities. When Adam and Eve took the fruit of the tree of the knowledge of good and evil, they were drawn into contemplation of the creature rather than the Creator (Rom. 1:20–32). They looked to creation itself to give them wisdom. They were therefore consumed by interest in creation and took no notice of God. The knowledge of God was lost, and fellowship with God was lost. Therefore, the benefits of sharing in God's attributes were lost as well. Athanasius focuses attention upon the loss of immortality and incorruption. Humans cut off from God's immortality were left to be mortal creatures, and they would surely die. But God would not allow the human creature, intended to live forever in union with God, end in death. There was only one solution: "the Word of God came himself, in order that he being the Image of the Father, the human being 'in the image' might be recreated" (Athanasius, §13). Athanasius captures his vision with a beautiful metaphor:

> For as a figure painted on wood has been soiled by dirt from outside, it is necessary for him whose figure it is to come again, so that the image can be renewed on the same material ... In the same way the all-holy Son of the Father, being the Image of the Father, came to our place to renew the human being made according to himself, and to find him, as one lost, through the forgiveness of sins. (§14)

Only the Creator was fit to be the Re-Creator. Through the incarnation, the eternal Word of God forged a new union of God with humanity. Through his death and resurrection, Jesus Christ defeated human death and provided the means by which humanity once again shares in God's attributes of immortality and incorruption. Humanity represents God again, thus the realization of God's intention for creation is restored.

John Calvin argues that the true meaning of the image of God is revealed when it is seen in Jesus Christ (I.15.4). Genesis 1:26 reveals God's intention to make humanity in God's image and likeness. The narratives of Genesis 3–11 describe humanity's movement away from God. The rest of Genesis and the bulk of the Christian Scriptures aim to show how God and humanity enter into fellowship once again. Reconciliation with God is accomplished in Jesus Christ, and those united to him are a new creation, now able to fulfill the original goal for humanity revealed in Genesis 1:26. Paul picks up this language in Colossians 3:10 where he describes "the new self, which is being renewed in knowledge according to the image of its creator." In Ephesians 4:24, Paul's description is of "the new self, created according to the likeness of God in true righteousness and holiness." Because atonement is accomplished and Jesus Christ has perfected human nature, humans united to Christ are recreated by the power of the Holy Spirit to bring God's original intention for humanity to fruition. Post-Reformation Reformed theologians have perhaps maintained the closest attention to the covenantal connections between the image of God and the atonement (see, e.g., Bavinck, vol. II).

Uniting the Image of God and the Atonement

In the Christian tradition, doctrinal connection of the image of God and the atonement has at least a threefold importance. (1) It reveals that the whole Bible hangs together, from creation to new creation. As the examples above illustrate, from the perspective of the image of God the atonement is the restoration of divine and human fellowship for the sake of bringing God's creational intention to fulfillment. (2) It serves as an important vista from which to contemplate Jesus Christ's saving work. The incarnation, life, death, resurrection, and ascension of the Son of God are all atoning acts that reunite humanity to God. Jesus Christ is the image of God, establishing fellowship between God and humanity and making God known in the world. (3) It reveals that humans are restored to fellowship with God for the sake of the whole of creation. Just as God originally made humanity to represent God on the earth, making creation fruitful, so redeemed humanity's faithful action as the image and likeness of God in the world is the means by which all of creation will ultimately flourish (Rom. 8:18ff). Thus, the resurrected Lord Jesus Christ is the one in whom all creation finds fulfillment.

However, the Christian tradition has often limited the meaning of human life in the image of God to one human attribute or another (e.g., rationality or relationality). Similarly, the tradition's understanding of the atonement has at times been limited to one atonement theory or another (e.g., *Christus victor*, satisfaction, penal substitution). In both cases the doctrine of God has played too little a role in the development of doctrine.

With respect to the image of God, humans are created to representatively embody God's character in the world. Human capacities, such as human rationality and relationality, are the created means by which humans receive the knowledge of God and experience fellowship with God. These are also means by which humans commune with one another and exercise godly dominion over the other creatures. In themselves these capacities are not the image of God, although they may be considered analogous to certain divine attributes. Humans image God when their use of these capacities is conditioned by knowing and fellowshipping with God. Realization of the image of God, therefore, is the fruit of God's communication of God's own life to humanity (see Peterson). A human person's participation in imaging God is the result of being conformed to the character of God's life by the work of the Son and the Spirit. The doctrine of the image of God must be as rich and multifaceted as is human conformation to God's inexhaustible life.

With respect to the atonement, the riches of God's character are expressed differently. In every way that humanity has failed in its God-ordained task of representing God in the world, the atonement reconciles humanity to God. Since human sin violates God's character *in toto*, so the reconciliation with God effected by the atonement addresses every human vice and every human deficit (see Johnson). So, doctrinal accounts of the atonement need to be as rich and multifaceted as the ways that sin is out of concert with God's own life.

The knowledge and fellowship necessary for creaturely conformation to the life of God is promised, established, and fulfilled in Jesus Christ and through union with him. The economic work of the Son and the Spirit is itself the expression of that life in the world and the accomplishment of atonement.

As this final section suggests, the doctrine of the image of God and the doctrine of the atonement are united by the doctrine of God. God is the One in whose image humanity is created and in relationship with whom humanity must primarily be reconciled. Moreover, conformation to God's image and the reality and extent of the atonement are both determined by the contours and content of God's own life, the riches of which are inexhaustible. Unfortunately, the connection between the image of God and the atonement has not figured prominently in contemporary theology. The reason for this may be related to the difficulty that modern interpreters have had in interpreting what it means for humans to be made in the image of God and the philosophical difficulties that have plagued modern theories of the atonement. The connection between these doctrines deserves renewed attention, especially as they are fitted to the doctrine of God.

Bibliography

Athanasius, *On the Incarnation*, 2011.
Bavinck, *Reformed Dogmatics*, Vol. II, 2004.
Calvin, *Institutes of the Christian Religion*, 1960.
Irenaeus, *Against Heresies*, 1994.
Johnson, *Atonement*, 2015.
Peterson, *The* Imago Dei *as Human Identity*, 2016.

Impassibility (Divine)

Daniel Castelo

Historically and theologically, the associations made between divine impassibility and the atonement have been strained. This situation is significantly due to the dominant narratives surrounding divine impassibility and to the privileging of certain models and themes within atonement discussions. Need the relationship between impassibility and the atonement be precarious? As with so many theological matters, the answer to this question depends on a priori operative definitions and commitments that contribute collectively to the logic of particular theological narratives and trajectories. In what follows, the relationship between both themes will be considered both historically and constructively so that readers may not only derive a sense of how the discussion of the relationship has developed thus far but also imagine the shape it can take moving forward.

One must begin with the challenge of defining divine impassibility. Many scholars and writers have thought of it as a divine attribute best understood in terms of "classical theism," a conceptual conglomerate that people believe is an inheritance from the Greek metaphysical tradition in which divinity is thought of in abstract and conceptual rather than concrete and active forms such as those one finds in the Bible. The typical generalization is that divine impassibility makes more sense in terms of Aristotle's "Unmoved Mover" than the biblical portrayals of YHWH in the Old Testament or the cross of Jesus in the New Testament. An additional difficulty with divine impassibility is that it assumes a normative account of feeling, suffering, and interiority when evaluations of these have varied significantly over time. In past Western contexts, feelings and suffering were often considered as vile features of existence largely because of their variability and implied passivity in relation to agents. Assuming this vision, one would see feelings as movements of the soul that one "suffers" or "endures," as when one is "moved to anger" or "overwhelmed with sadness." Within this context, affectivity and suffering are generally depicted as unbecoming of those who exercise self-control and their rational faculties. This evaluation is in significant contrast to today's context in which oftentimes feelings are considered the most important part of human beings, both in terms of their interiority and their relationships.

Philo of Alexandria is an important exemplification of the older frameworks not only because of his general agreement with them but also in light of the significant influence he wielded upon early Christian reflection. For Philo, the realm of the pathic is vile because feelings are fleeting, inconsistent, and unreliable within human experience. If these characterizations are true of affectivity in the human realm, then they are unreliable forms of speech for the divine. For Philo, thinking of God as changing or being swayed is intolerable and coarse, so when Scripture speaks of God anthropopathically, a hermeneutically explanatory mechanism is especially needed. Commenting on the controversial mutability passages of Genesis 6 in his treatise *On the Unchangeableness of God*, Philo remarks,

> Now, some persons, when they hear the expressions which I have just cited, imagine that the living God is here giving away to anger and passion; but God is utterly inaccessible to any passion whatever. For it is the peculiar property of human weakness to be disquieted by any such feelings, but God has neither the irrational passions of the soul, nor are the parts and limits of the body in the least belonging to him. (XI)

The case of Philo helps point out long-standing concerns associated with divine impassibility. First, a significant tension at the level of language is in force. Yes, the Bible speaks of God in affective terms, but the Bible also claims God and humans to be distinctly different. Philo tended to think of this form of speech as a kind of condescension by the divine to accommodate human limits of understanding. Others have opted to consider such speech analogically. The mechanism of analogy helps one to recognize that continuity and discontinuity exist between analogues. In this sense, when someone says that God and humans suffer, a relationship can be claimed (under the single rubric of "suffering") alongside a working sense of vast difference (God is the Creator and humans are creatures so they must "suffer" in distinct ways). Whatever strategy one finds appealing, the divine impassibility debates require some account of theological language generally. Second, Philo connects God's non-corporeal self to God's impassibility. Oftentimes, affectivity is characterized as a feature of bodily existence. This link is a prominent one that was maintained throughout

Christian history (one important case being Thomas Aquinas), but one should also note that it has been questioned and reconfigured as well. Particularly in the cases of Tertullian, Gregory Thaumaturgus, and others, pathic concerns have not been strictly connected to corporeality but rather thought of in a wider sense so that God is affectivity's ultimate exemplar. At play in these matters is affectivity's theological evaluation (is it positive or negative?) and depiction (is it bodily only or in some sense psychological and/or voluntary?). Finally, one sees in Philo that divine impassibility is located within the broader rubric of divine immutability, a move that calls into question the larger issue of the content and shape of divine attribution. How is one to describe God, and what are the sources and patterns to be utilized in such endeavoring? If impassibility is a subcategory of immutability, and if immutability is itself an extension of divine simplicity, then one has imagined a very particular setting for divine attribution, one that does in fact have resonances with patterns in Greek metaphysics. And yet, one must ask at such junctures: Have Christians gone on to adopt this vision thoroughly and unqualifiedly in their God-talk? The verdict is unclear, especially as one proceeds to analyze instances on a case-by-case basis. But the source of the tension is obvious: Divine attribution within Christian theology is an internally contested affair, driven in part by a number of theological and metaphysical commitments.

As noted above, the understanding, outworking, and perpetuation of divine impassibility throughout Christian thought has been mixed, but one dominant feature at various stages in the discussions has been to interpret or reformulate the notion along Christological lines. In other words, for many Christian thinkers, divine impassibility was either inadmissible or tenable as a theological category only subsequent to an apprehension of the God-human, Jesus Christ. Many who perpetuate the standard contemporary narratives say that impassibility is unviable because it does not match what one sees in Jesus. However, others (especially ancient sources) have suggested that because of the operative requirements surrounding Jesus's life and work as displayed in the canonical gospels and remembered and proclaimed in the life of the church, one must go on to affirm divine impassibility so as to maintain a species of theological integrity. In these latter cases (ones where impassibility is Christologically cast and so redefined and appropriated in a manner distinctly different from Hellenistic approaches), the attribute is often called to exercise an apophatic function. The sensibilities culled from such activities are crucial for the active and fruitful deployment of terms aimed at highlighting the divine transcendence. For instance, Ignatius of Antioch holds that the notion of impassibility secures the Son's transcendence prior to the incarnation as well as after the resurrection so that a so-called high and low Christology is kept in one's purview. Ignatius represents an approach that defies the totalizing exhaustiveness often assumed by purveyors of the Hellenization thesis when they assume all proponents of divine impassibility from antiquity to have been "classical theists."

Where do these considerations lead in terms of the atonement? Interestingly, this question was taken up in the Anglophone world during the latter part of the nineteenth century and early part of the twentieth. At this time, writers such as A. M. Fairbairn and Douglas White made some scathing remarks about divine impassibility, registering anew the uneasiness that has often surrounded Christian usage of the term. Many of these detractors of impassibility assumed similar commitments. For instance, these individuals often considered the compassion of God as a pivotal rationale for the incarnation. God became flesh because God antecedently felt sorrow on account of the plight of the world. Therefore, the remedy that is Jesus's life and work emits out of the pain God felt upon witnessing a hurting creation. Famously illustrating the point, C. A. Dinsmore said, "There was a cross in the heart of God before there was one planted on the green hill outside of Jerusalem" (232). The kenosis of the Son, then, is intricately related to the passibility of God. Many of these detractors of impassibility also rigidly maintained an interrelationship between love and suffering so that one was unthinkable without the other. If God is love, these figures averred, then God must be passible as well. For G. A. Studdert-Kennedy and others, the heart of the Christian gospel is the claim that God is suffering love. This sensibility sets up a third point, namely, that the atonement is largely depicted as an act of God's vicarious suffering in Christ. G. B. Stevens summarized the mood when he stated, "If Christ gave his life in utmost sacrifice for men, it is because there is in the being of God himself the possibility of vicarious suffering which, so far from marring his blessedness, is one of the elements of that matchless perfection whose name is love" (446). This depiction of the atonement as vicarious suffering coincides with a rising influence of Protestant liberalism among English speakers and the devastating effects of the World Wars. These factors simply made divine impassibility unpalatable to the collective sensibilities of the age, and these judgments and tendencies have continued to be present on the contemporary scene, particularly via the influential work of Jürgen Moltmann.

From this very brief survey, one can garner a number of concerns related to the interplay between divine impassibility and the atonement. It should be clear that the dominant narratives associating divine impassibility with a process of corruption—the Hellenization of Christian speech—create a staunch determination, one that suggests that divine impassibility has no place moving forward in Christian dogmatics, especially in terms of divine attribution. Many have and continue to maintain this posture despite the availability of historical and contemporary alternatives. Also, if one assumes that the basic qualities associated with Christ's atoning work relate to a kind of vicarious sacrifice that emits from God's eternal suffering love, then this represents another kind of determination that further reinforces the irrelevance of divine impassibility for atonement discussions.

However, if these specific judgments can be particularized and suspended for the sake of accounting for other possibilities, then a fruitful interplay between both themes can ensue. For instance, if one were to attend to the function that divine impassibility has often played among its Christian espousers—a function related to securing apophatic, analogous, and transcendent features of Christian speech—then these can in turn inform and expand particular depictions of Christ's atoning work. For instance, the sensibilities forged through giving divine impassibility a more charitable reading could lead to the following questions and outlooks: In what ways is a given atonement model limited or unable to account for important claims related to the work of Christ? Interestingly, the vicarious suffering models outlined above do little by way of emphasizing the resurrection and ascension as features of Christ's atoning work, yet these are legitimate atonement themes in their own right. Furthermore, why are certain models of the atonement more appealing than others in a given context, and what does such privileging say about the shape of the theological task generally but also about the theological proclivities of a given society? An ongoing engagement with divine impassibility has a way of exposing the unwieldy sentimentalization of Christian speech that dominates many current forms of Christianity; these tendencies depict Jesus as an able "co-sufferer" to be sure but often lack focus on other themes less palatable to modern inclinations, including Jesus's lordship. And finally, does a given atonement model recognize that certain depth dimensions surrounding Christ's work exist because this work ultimately stems from an infinite, transcendent, and self-revealed mystery? An ongoing appreciation for divine impassibility has a way of registering for theological speakers that God is beyond the simple categories readily employed in God-talk. Simply put, divine impassibility can destabilize dominant atonement models by cutting to the precariousness of all theological speech, thereby opening it up to ongoing imaginative construal. This possibility is a real gift for Christian dogmatics given the ways salvation is often commodified in contexts dominated by late capitalism.

Bibliography

Castelo, *The Apathetic God*, 2009.
Dinsmore, *Atonement in Literature and Life*, 1906.
Gavrilyuk, *The Suffering of the Impassible God*, 2004.
Keating and White, *Divine Impassibility and the Mystery of Human Suffering*, 2009.
Mozley, *The Impassibility of God*, 1926.
Philo, *On the Unchangeableness of God*.
Stevens, *Christian Doctrine of Salvation*, 1905.
Weinandy, *Does God Suffer?*, 2000.

Irenaeus of Lyons

John Behr

One of the difficulties of studying a figure like Irenaeus, the late-second-century bishop of Lyons (who had known Polycarp, who in turn had known the apostle John) is simply the distance from which he speaks to us. We have become so used to the classical categories of Christian theology—the Trinity, Creation, Fall, Incarnation, Atonement, the Church, and so on—that they seem to be a given part of the Christian revelation itself. They, however, are not. The theologians of the first centuries did not work with these categories in mind. They did not think of "Incarnation" as something separate from "Atonement," or any of all of this as separate from liturgy, which yet rarely makes it into textbooks on the history of doctrine. He stands as the first voice articulating a comprehensive theological vision, the first exposition of a self-confident Orthodox Catholic standpoint, yet one whose feet, therefore, stand prior to all elements that become the standard framework of Christianity thereafter.

If we are to get back to what Irenaeus was saying, not only do we need to overcome the contrast between "satisfaction" and "physical" theories of Atonement, but we might also need to overcome the contrast between "incarnation" and "atonement"; these elements, held apart in our systematic exposition of doctrine, cohere in their genesis and always need to be thought of together. And we need to take one further step, which is to hold together creation and atonement—*together*, as two aspects of the single overarching economy of God. If we want to understand how Irenaeus views the atonement, we need to do so within his understanding of the single overarching economy of God, funded in significant part by the "rhetorical device of 'recapitulation,'" which provides "a restatement of the argument in an epitome or résumé, bringing together the whole into one conspectus, so that, while the particular details will have made little impact because of their number or apparent insignificance, the picture summarily stated as a whole will be more forceful, giving new significance to each particular detail and bringing them all together into one" (Behr, 137; cf. the Roman precedent in Quintilian, *Inst.* 6.1.1).

An example of Irenaeus's approach to these issues is found in the scriptural image used by Christ to explain his own work: the sign of Jonah. Irenaeus gives the case of Jonah, who, by God's arrangement, was swallowed up by the whale, not that he should perish, but that, having been cast out, he might be more obedient to God, and so glorify more the One who had unexpectedly saved him (*Haer.* 3.20.1). For Irenaeus, God has borne the human race, from the beginning, while the great whale swallowed it up. There is no lost golden age of primordial perfection when we might not have needed Christ. Such language sounds strange to us, accustomed to thinking of God in all-too-human, temporal terms, imagining him "before" creation, deciding what he is going to do (plan A), and responding (plan B) after we messed up. However, as Irenaeus asserts repeatedly throughout his work, theological reflection is not to start from any other (hypothetical or counterfactual) position than the one proclaimed by the apostles, in accordance with the Scriptures (*Haer.* 1.10.3). We are, he insists, to seek out the wisdom of God made manifest in the Christ preached by the apostles, the Word, Wisdom, and Power of God.

For Irenaeus, the starting point for all theological reflection (including the Fall) is the given fact of the work of Christ, his life-giving and saving death (cf. Barr, 89). So it is that in the passage we are considering Irenaeus speaks of God "arranging in advance the finding of salvation, which was accomplished by the Word through the sign of Jonah." Creation and salvation, for Irenaeus, cohere as the one economy of God, which culminates in the work of Christ, to be understood and told from this point.

According to Irenaeus, this does not mitigate human responsibility for their action of apostasy, nor the reality of the work of the devil in beguiling Adam and Eve under "the pretext of immortality" (*Haer.* 3.23.5; 4.Pref. 4). For Irenaeus, death is the result of human apostasy, turning away from the one and only Source of life, instigated by the devil. But death is also embraced within the divine economy, the way everything fits together in God's hand. When viewed from the perspective of the salvation granted by Christ through "the sign of Jonah," we can see that, as it was God himself who appointed the whale to swallow up Jonah, so also the engulfing of the human race by the great whale was "borne" by God in his arrangement, his economy, which culminates in the finding of salvation accomplished by the sign of Jonah. There is an important change of perspective involved in this, which runs through the whole of Scripture (cf.

Gen. 45:5–6; Acts 2.23). Catastrophe happens, but the same event, with further reflection, is seen to be inscribed within God's plan, his overarching economy that human beings might become fully acquainted with their total dependency upon the power of God, allowing God to work in and through them, to deploy his power in them as the recipient of all his work (*Haer.* 3.20.2). Irenaeus takes Christ's words to Paul, that his "strength is made perfect in weakness" (2 Cor. 12:9) as paradigmatic for the human race. And Jonah, a sign of both the transgressing human race and its Savior, simultaneously represents both dimensions of this economy—the engulfing of the human being, and the salvation wrought by the Word.

By starting with the work of Christ, the divinely foreseen sign of Jonah—the satisfying, atoning, and death-destroying death of Christ—Irenaeus can see *in* the tragedy and absurdity of death the Wisdom of God being deployed, playing an educational role within the divine economy. While apostasy and death are nothing less than a catastrophic victory of the devil (*Haer.* 3.18.2), the Wisdom of God is nevertheless so powerful that even this catastrophe can be encompassed within a larger, divine economy, and so be turned to good effect. The victory could only be won by the Word of God himself, but this victory over death is something that he accomplishes in no other way than by the act of death itself—the sign of Jonah—again turning the apparently catastrophic situation inside-out. From different perspectives, we can therefore discern two dimensions to the apostasy and death: catastrophic and pedagogic. Yet these are only a matter of perspective. For Irenaeus, there is but the one economy of the one God, which is unfolded in Scripture.

In *Haer.* 4.37–9, Irenaeus provides further reasons why human beings need to experience weakness and death, before being glorified by God. Responding to those who ask why God did not make human beings perfect from the beginning, Irenaeus says that only *free* creatures are capable of love and growth, to move from their created state into the transfigured immortality and incorruptibility of communion with God. Moreover, Irenaeus argues, it is only by experience of contrasts that we come to know the value of gifts (*Haer.* 4.39).

By having knowledge of both experience and opinion, and rejecting disobedience by repentance, human beings can become ever more tenacious in their obedience to God. But if human beings ever try to avoid the twofold faculty of knowledge, they forget themselves and kill their humanity (*Haer.* 4.39.1). "God therefore has borne all these things for our sake, in order that, having been instructed through all things, henceforth we may be scrupulous in all things and, having been taught how to love God in accordance with reason, to remain in his love" (*Haer.* 4.37.7; Jer. 2:19). Irenaeus thus (again) inscribes human apostasy into the unfolding of the divine economy, as with the sign of Jonah, giving it moment (see the argument from a different angle in *Haer.* 4.38).

This inscription of human apostasy within the overarching single economy of God (rather than an ad hoc "rescue mission") demonstrates the omnipotence of God: that he is not forced to react to the devil's mischief or the failings of humans. Instead, by the work of God in Christ, we can now see God's creative act from a new perspective, transforming what appeared to be negative into something positive, and integrating, or sublating, both creation and apostasy into the definitive, once-for-all, work of God in Christ in his atoning work, reconciling the human being to God.

Irenaeus is able to do this precisely because, as noted earlier, he is theologizing at that primitive moment of history, still in the immediacy of the Passion, rather than after a history of controversies and conclusions for which a systematic account is needed. The completeness with which this goes for Irenaeus is shown by one of his most dramatic statements: "Adam himself was termed by Paul 'the type of the One who was to come,' [Rom. 5:14] … For, since he who saves already existed, it was necessary that the one who would be saved should come into existence, that the One who saves should not exist in vain" (*Haer.* 3.22.3). In Adam, the Word prefigured or sketched out in advance the fullness of the human being that would be manifested in Christ. However, the One who was to come existed before Adam (as the seal does before the imprint) and so it was by him and for him that Adam came into being. So, although only appearing at the end, this One is indeed the Beginning (cf. *Haer.* 1.10.3, 4.34.4). Creation and salvation, for Irenaeus, are not distinct actions or episodes in an ongoing narrative, but are, rather, the one economy that can only be understood when the victorious lamb opens the books (Rev. 13:8; 5), so that, "unveiled" (cf. 2 Cor. 3:18), one can see how Scripture has always spoken of Christ ("Moses wrote of me," John 5:46), the one whom, according to "Moses and the Prophets had to suffer" (Luke 24:26). As the Beginning appearing at the end, Christ is indeed "the lamb slain before the foundation of the world" (Rev. 13:8).

This passage of Irenaeus also introduces another Pauline theme: the first Adam was psychical, while the last is spiritual, referring both to Genesis 2:7 and to 1 Corinthians 15:45. The apostasy did not transform an originally spiritual Adam into a merely psychical being. Through the apostasy Adam and Eve lost the "strength" of the breath of life (*Dem.* 14); they did not "lose" the Spirit. The Spirit was present with Adam and the human race in a preparatory manner, typifying the fullness which was and still is to come: "For never at any time did Adam escape the hands of God, to whom the Father speaking, said, 'Let us make the human being in our image, after our likeness'" (*Haer.* 5.1.3). Irenaeus thus understands creation and salvation, *together*, as God's skilful fashioning his creatures into the stature of the Savior. The starting point for this economy is the Savior himself, and so Irenaeus gives no space to counterfactual hypothetical questions.

The goal of the economy is the manifestation of the glory of God in a fully living human being, partaking of the life, incorruptibility, and glory of God. But how can the created become a partaker of the Uncreated, unless the Uncreated first joins himself to his creature? This necessity is decisive for Irenaeus's understanding of the economy, where "incorruptibility and immortality had become that which we also are, so that the corruptible might be swallowed up by incorruptibility and the mortal by immortality" (*Haer.* 3.19.1; cf. 1 Cor. 15:53–54; 2 Cor. 5:4; Gal. 4:5). The growth and increase that God set before the newly created being was intended to accustom that being to receive such adoption in Christ.

Yet, just as we saw two aspects to the place and role of death in human existence—as catastrophic, yet embraced within a divine pedagogy—so too Christ's work is twofold: on the one hand, it renders beings animated with a breath of life into beings vivified by the Spirit, bringing them into full communion with the incorruptibility and glory of God. The other side of Christ's work is that, as the apostatizing human race is dead "in Adam," enslaved by the devil, so Christ came to set it free (*Haer.* 3.18.6; cf. Rom. 5.19; Mt. 12.29). The liberation of the human being from the tyranny of the devil is effected by Christ, who as human fought the enemy and loosened the disobedience through obedience, and who as God set free the weak and gave salvation to his handiwork, doing so by voluntarily accepting that death which had no claim on him, so manifesting his omnipotence in weakness.

As the two dimensions of the apostasy, catastrophic and pedagogic, are but a matter of perspective, so also are the two dimensions of Christ's work of salvation. While the human being, in Adam, was inexperienced, weak, and easily led into apostasy, the human being in Christ, being strong, conquered the enemy by remaining obedient. Likewise, Adam was a psychical being, and while obedient, would have remained immortal; yet he could not have become a partaker in incorruptibility, nor have been united to the Spirit, had God not united himself to the human being in Christ. These two aspects are, of course, inseparable: the one Jesus Christ, who is, for Irenaeus, the first manifestation of the true, fully human being, realized them both.

Irenaeus has some very particular, and rich, insights into the role of death, if we view the economy of God as one overarching act. Irenaeus's theology is also centered upon God's fashioning of the human being in a very striking manner, such as viewing death, when seen in the light of the mystery of Christ, in Eucharistic terms. Going beyond a statement by Ignatius of Antioch (Rom. 4; *Haer.* 5.28.4.), Irenaeus develops a close relationship between the process that leads to the Eucharist and to the resurrection. It is by receiving the Eucharist, as the wheat and the vine receive the fecundity of the Spirit, that we are prepared—as we also make the fruits into the bread and wine. And just as the bread and wine receive the Word and so become the Body and Blood of Christ, the Eucharist, so also our bodies will receive immortality and incorruptibility from the Father (*Haer.* 5.2.3). As such, death, within the overall economy of God seen in the light of the Passion of Christ, takes on a Eucharistic dimension, alongside its educative and limiting function, and the economy as a whole can be described as the Eucharist of God.

If this transformed reality is a living human being, then it really is only first in Christ that the work of God, announced at the beginning of Genesis—"Let us make a human being in our image" (1:26)—is now complete. After preparing the world and everything in it, he says, "Let us make a human being in our image"—not as an injunction, but as an intention. It is in the voluntary self-offering of Christ upon the tree that Irenaeus sees the project of God finally completed, fulfilled. "It is finished," Christ says on the cross, in the Gospel of John, just after Pilate unwittingly says, "behold the man" (John 19:5, 30). Christ is, as Irenaeus put it, "the beginning which appears at the end" (*Haer.* 1.10.3). For God's intention—to create a human being—to be fulfilled requires not a divine fiat from God. It requires the "fiat," "let it be," "thy will be done," of one able to break the bonds of death, the tyranny of the devil, but to break this tyranny of death in no other way than by voluntarily dying, as human, so that we are all now able to give our own consent, our own fiat, to be reborn in him in baptism, taking up his cross, culminating in martyrdom, and so in this way ourselves become human.

For Irenaeus, then, the work of atonement is not simply a once-for-all act in the past. Rather, it is the one economy of the one God effected by the one Son in the one human race which encompasses both creation and salvation, embracing our apostasy and death, yet turning them inside out, in the mystery of Christ, the Wisdom of God, in which the atonement is seen as the bringing into one (at-one-ment) of God and the human being (*Haer.* 5.36.3).

Bibliography

Barr, *The Garden of Eden and Hope of Immortality*, 1992.
Behr, *Irenaeus of Lyons*, 2013.
Holsinger-Friesen, *Irenaeus and Genesis*, 2009.
Irenaeus, *De Haeresis*.
Minns, *Irenaeus*, 1994.
Osborn, *Irenaeus of Lyons*, 2001.
Steenberg, *Irenaeus on Creation*, 2008.
Wingren, *Man and the Incarnation*, 1959 (Swedish, 1947).

Letter of James

Robert W. Wall

A study of the Letter of James seems out of place in a volume dedicated to atonement theology. This is because the church has typically articulated its understanding of God's reconciliation with sinful humanity as a divine activity mediated by Jesus's messianic work on the Cross—as a sacrifice for sin, a ransom or penalty paid, a victory won, or some other kind of result that mended a sinner's broken fellowship with a loving (or perhaps angry) God.

Most of these theological descriptions, at least in the West, are indebted to Paul, whose gospel is evidently concentrated on the messianic death of Jesus as a faithful God's way of putting sinful humanity to rights. If this is true, then most would allow that the Letter of James has very little, if anything, to contribute to the church's theological agreement: James mentions Jesus only in passing (1:1, 2:1) and does not mention (or allude to) his death at all. Perhaps the reader should stop the study before even beginning for fear of spending precious time tracking an idea down a rabbit trail leading nowhere.

In pressing forward, I would suggest the reader begins the quest of atonement images in James with a broader set of assumptions. For example, at its most essential level, the biblical idea of atonement mostly concerns the mending of a covenant relationship between God and God's people fractured by sin. Sin, in this case, is any failure of a covenant community to keep its obligations pledged to God in maintaining their partnership. As such, atonement renews a broken covenant between God and God's people by whatever means or practices efficacious for doing so. Naturally, the community takes on faith that it is renewed in its friendship with God by performing those communal practices that demonstrate this spiritual reality, which are also thematic of this letter, such as rejecting "friendship with the world" (i.e., materialism), forgiveness, sharing possessions, hospitality, and defending the poor and powerless.

While narrowly applied by the Pauline witness to Jesus's death, this same idea also supplies a critical theological subtext of the entire Letter of James. The mechanism of covenant renewal in James, however, is not the community's trust in the reconciling effects of Christ's death, which is never mentioned; rather, the letter (as well as the entire sevenfold Catholic Epistles collection it introduces and frames) concentrates its faithful readers on the Lord's exemplary life as typological of God's way of salvation.

In one of the letter's most contested texts, James 2:1 asks believers whether their "acts of prejudice are consistent with the faithfulness of our glorious Lord Jesus Christ." Paul rightly insists that Jesus's faithfulness to God is the decisive metric of his messianic mission: that is, his death is expiatory precisely because God considers it an act of faithfulness to God's plan to save the world from death (Rom. 3:22; Phil. 2:5–8; 1 Tim. 2:3–6). James's single mention of Jesus also underscores the purchase of his faithfulness (τὴν πίστιν τοῦ κυρίου ἡμῶν Ἰησοῦ Χριστοῦ; James 2:1; cf. Rom. 3:22), not in reference to his death but because it exemplifies a covenant community's genuine devotion to God (cf. 1:27).

Naturally, as the community's *Lord*, Jesus sets the normative example for his followers to imitate. The piling on of titles to name the Lord Jesus in James 2:1 not only commends his faithfulness as messianic or redemptive (hence, Lord Jesus *Christ*) but also as divinely approved (hence, *glorious* Lord Jesus Christ; cf. Phil. 2:8–11). The implication of this exhortation, then, is that any act of prejudice, which favors the rich over the poor (see 1:27–2:17), not only fails Jesus but also fractures the community's covenant with God.

Significantly, read within its immediate context, God's recognition of Jesus's faithfulness (and so also God's glorification of him as Lord) is not the effect of his obedient death on the Cross, as found in the Pauline witness (e.g., Phil. 2:5–11), but in his ministry to the poor as alluded in the adumbration of echoes that rebound from the canonical Gospel's narrative (cf. 2:2–13; so Wall). In this way, Jesus personifies those practices that gain God's approval by caring for the community's most vulnerable, marginal members (1:27). The community that covenants with God and receives God's promised blessing (cf. 1:25), therefore, is "pure and undefiled" not because it is cleansed by Jesus's blood but because it willingly cares for its poor membership (cf. 1:27) in obedience to the "perfect law of liberty" (i.e., Torah; cf. 1:25; 2:12), which commands love of God (cf. 1:12) and neighbor (cf. 2:8). Sharply put, the eschatological community that is approved and blessed by God demonstrates mercy toward its poor and powerless neighbors (cf. 2:12–13).

While this quick take on the profoundly ethical idea of atonement in James seems to trade on Abelard's so-called moral influence view, James neither retreats from a robust conception of sin, nor from a realistic view of the believer's duplicity that confesses faith in God but then befriends the world when that faith is tested by various trials. In fact, what seems to characterize James's soteriology in general is the emphasis placed upon the faith community's covenant-keeping purity, which "completes" or underwrites the community's orthodox profession of allegiance to God (2:22). God doesn't befriend the believer merely because s/he "says" the right stuff—even demons can do this (2.19)! Nor is there any indication in James that a prior belief in Christ effects an inward Spirit-directed transformation that enables the faith community to live for God as never before. God befriends the believer whose loving actions toward others, freely willed, agree with the messianic standard set out by the exemplary life of Jesus (cf. 2:23). After all, much to Luther's well-known dissatisfaction, James contends that believers are justified by their (Christ-like) works, and not by professions of faith in the crucified Christ alone (cf. 2:24)!

This more ethical idea of atonement, whenever it is found detached from the church's traditional belief in the atoning death of Jesus, begs the question how James's atonement theology should then be read as an integral part of Scripture's canonical witness to God's reconciliation with sinners through Christ (Nienhuis and Wall). Most importantly, James, along with the Catholic Epistles collection it introduces, extends Scripture's apostolic witness of the messianic event and its atoning result to include the exemplary life of the historical Jesus (cf. James 2:1; 1 Pet. 2:21–25; 1 John 1:1–4; 2:4–6; Jude 17–23). This added dimension has the salutary effect of correcting the church's historic tendency of appealing to the Pauline witness alone to underwrite an undemanding gospel according to which God's atoning grace is received and applied by trusting in the merit of Christ's death alone. Moreover, James's pastoral address of believers reminds readers that God's interest in a reconciled relationship does not end once the sinner is initiated into the covenant community by grace through faith, especially since the temptation of spiritual failure threatens its covenant relationship with God (cf. James 1:13–15; 1 John 1:5–2:3). In this sense, then, James may be read as encouraging the community's continuing participation in God's reconciling grace by actively engaging in those purity practices that follow the example of Christ. By doing so, the community maintains its covenant with God and thereby the prospect of eternal life (cf. 1:12).

Further Reading

Allison, *James*, 2013.
Johnson, *The Letter of James*, 1995.
McKnight, *The Letter of James*, 2011.
Nienhuis and Wall, *Reading the Epistles of James, Peter, John & Jude*, 2013.
Wall, *Community of the Wise*, 1997.

John's Letters

Matthew D. Jensen

Introduction

Of John's three letters, only the first has any explicit material relating to the atonement. This material contributes in three ways to any doctrinal formulation of atonement: first, it identifies the death of Jesus as a *hilasmos* for sin; second, this *hilasmos* is efficient for the sins of the whole world; and third, Jesus's death is the basis for Christian ethical behavior.

Hilasmos: Expiation or Propitiation?

1 John is unique in describing the death of Jesus as a *hilasmos* (2:2; 4:10). Even though the word group is used elsewhere in the New Testament (*hilaskomai* in Luke 18:13 and Heb. 2:17; *hilasterion* in Rom. 3:25 and Heb. 9:5), only 1 John uses the noun *hilasmos*.

There is debate about how *hilasmos* should be understood, as "expiation" (Dodd; Do) or "propitiation" (Morris). Reasons proposed for translating *hilasmos* as "expiation" include: the lack of mention of wrath in the immediate context, the observation that *hilasmos* occurs as a result of God's love (4:9–10), the historical context which suggests that without knowledge of the Old Testament background *hilasmos* would be understood as expiation, and the argument that even with relevant knowledge of the Old Testament, the *hilas*—word group—does not always mean propitiation because God's wrath is not always on view in every LXX and New Testament context.

Two of these observations are cogent but neither of them prevent understanding *hilasmos* as propitiation. The reason for Christ's death being a *hilasmos* for sin is the love of God (4:9–10). However, this love does not preclude God being angry and needing to have his anger propitiated. Further, while it is true that words for wrath (*orge, thumos*) are not mentioned in the immediate context, the judgment of God is mentioned in 4:17–18 with the associated themes of fear and punishment. Morris (206) also argues that in 2:1 the reader is about to face the judgment of God since the Paraclete is located in heaven before the Father. Thus even though the nouns *orge* and *thumos* are not used, the concepts of God's anger and judgment of sin are still present.

The other arguments, which exclude the Old Testament from the background of the writer and the readers, do not hold. The writer of 1 John is steeped in Old Testament language and thought (Carson) and recent research has shown that the audience of 1 John and the opponents are most probably Jewish (Streett, Jensen). So the use of specialized language like *hilasmos* should be understood against its Old Testament background.

The first occurrence of *hilasmos* occurs in a highly structured section of 1 John where three claims and their solutions are placed in parallel (1:6–2:2). The Old Testament sacrificial system is presented as the solution to the problems of sin. Therefore, the blood of Jesus achieves fellowship with God, which purifies from sin (1:7) after confession (1:9). In this context, Jesus is described as the Paraclete before the Father and as the *hilasmos* for sin. So, when 1:6–2:2 is read as a unit against an Old Testament background, it appears that the specialized use of *hilasmos* to mean propitiation is most likely given the wealth of specialized sacrificial language in the parallel statements and its predominant usage in the Old Testament.

The Extent of Atonement (2:2)

After describing Jesus as the *hilasmos* for sin, 1 John expands the statement to describe the extent of this sacrifice. So 1 John 2:2 states Jesus is the *hilasmos* for our sins, not just ours but also for those of the whole world. This is a significant passage for any systematic theology of the atonement, as it seems at first glance to indicate that Christ's death is sufficient for all people.

However, given the nature of the Jewish audience and the intra-Jewish schism (2:19), it is better understood to be a reference to the Gentiles. The Jewish audience would have read themselves into the first personal plural pronouns leaving the whole world to refer to the Gentiles. Given the disputes about the inclusion of the Gentiles within the early church (cf. Acts 15), this verse is not about the extent of the atonement with respect to every individual. Rather, it makes the point that Jesus's death is efficient for both types of people—Jew and Gentile.

The Basis for Ethics

Finally, the death of Jesus is also appealed to in 1 John as the basis for ethical behavior. In 3:16 the readers are encouraged to lay down their lives for their brothers just as Jesus did for them (cf. John 10:11, 15). Again in 4:11, the writer commands his readers to love one another because God loved us, a love shown and defined by the death of Jesus for sin (4:9–10; cf. John 15:13).

Conclusion

John presents Jesus's death as a propitiation for sin, not just the sins of the Jewish people waiting for their Christ, but for the sins of the Gentiles too. Additionally Jesus's death also acts as the basis for ethical behavior.

Select Bibliography

Carson, "1–3 John," in *Commentary on the New Testament Use of the Old*, 2007.
Do, *Re-Thinking the Death of Jesus*, 2014.
Dodd, "Hilaskesthai, Its Cognates, Derivatives and Synonyms in the Septuagint," *JTS* 32: 352–360, 1931.
Jensen, *Affirming the Resurrection of the Incarnate Christ*, 2012.
Morris, *The Apostolic Preaching of the Cross*, 3rd ed., 1965.
Streett, *They Went Out from Us: The Identity of the Opponents in First John*, 2011.

Justification

Alan Spence

What does justification mean? It is interesting that such an apparently innocent question could lie behind one of the most divisive controversies ever to engulf the Western Church. While the debate raged, more energy, time, and printer's ink were devoted to explaining the nature, ground, and implications of justification than have probably been spent on any other single doctrinal issue. For the German reformer Martin Luther, "justification by faith" was not only the heart of the gospel. It was for him the "chief article" or measuring rod of all theological truth. At the Council of Trent, the Catholic Church responded to the Lutheran challenge to its interpretation of justification by offering a carefully reworked exposition of the dogma. Although the language used was outwardly similar to the formulations of the Protestant Churches, subtle but important differences between the confessions remained.

Some readers might be surprised that we should have an eye to the historical discussion when considering the meaning of justification. They argue that we simply need to examine the etymology of the word "justify" and seek to understand how it was used specifically in the Scriptures. Opening up the ancient debate appears as something of a red herring, or at least as an unnecessary complication of the task in hand. Nevertheless, there are lessons to be learnt from the study of historical theology. Let us consider one of them.

A major sticking point in the sixteenth-century discussion between Catholics and Protestants over the meaning of justification had to do with demarking the saving events to which the word referred. Catholics writers tended to use the term "justification" to describe the whole course of salvation. They often spoke of the divine event whereby a sinner is reconciled to God as "initial justification." But "justification" was also used by them to include the transformation of the pilgrim's life through the work of divine grace. In contrast, Protestants employed the word "justification" only with reference to the initial atoning or reconciling event. They came to describe the ongoing process of divine transformation in the believer's life as "sanctification." The notional distinction between these two closely related and theologically dependent concepts, crucial for the Protestant argument, was a logical development of Luther's differentiation between the passive and active righteousness of believers—between an alien righteousness that comes from God and their own personal righteousness brought about in them by the Holy Spirit.

The historical debate suggests that a fruitful starting point in any contemporary discussion of justification is to clarify the relation of justification to other saving events. In the context of this book it would be helpful to think through the relation between justification and what we now describe as the doctrine of atonement.

Since the 1931 publication of Gustaf Aulen's seminal work *Christus Victor*, the idea that we are able to discern both in the Bible and in subsequent Christian thought a number of quite distinct atonement theories has become widely accepted in theological circles. These are sometimes characterized by their dominant metaphor, whether it be redemption, victory, sacrifice, or justification. According to this way of looking at things, "justification" is but one of a number of paradigms that we can use to interpret the atonement. In particular, it is one that is determined by forensic terminology and is best understood in the context of a court of law. This perspective has certainly taken the sting out of the justification controversy. What sensible person today would be willing to defend a doctrine of justification with their life, as many did in an earlier age, if it is but one among many models of the imagination that help us to grasp hold of the mystery of divine salvation?

Whatever the merits of the view outlined above, it is important to recognize that it is quite a novel way of looking at things. It is, one might say, a modern theory. Words like redemption, reconciliation, salvation, and justification have, in most part, been used historically not to indicate different doctrines of atonement but to embrace the whole subject matter of divine salvation. In his *Church Dogmatics*, Karl Barth expounded the saving work of Christ under the heading "the doctrine of reconciliation," but he could just as well have called it "the doctrine of redemption." In much the same way today "the doctrine of the atonement" is an expression now widely used to refer not only to the act of making one with God but to everything that is achieved for human salvation through the life, death, and resurrection of Jesus. In short, expressions such as the doctrine of redemption, reconciliation, or justification were generally used historically as interchangeable salvation terms to include everything that is now intended by the term "atonement." The multiplicity of concepts in the Scriptures that are employed to portray Christ's redemptive ministry was not taken by theologians of an earlier age to suggest that there were equally valid, *alternate* accounts of how men and women might be reconciled to God and come to eternal glory.

Granted that terms such as redemption, salvation, atonement, reconciliation, and justification have been used historically to refer to the whole saving work of Christ, does this reflect how they are used in the Scriptures? In short, what are the saving events to which terms such as redemption and justification refer when they are employed in the Bible? How broad is their scope?

Let us consider briefly the biblical use of the concept of redemption or more particularly of the word "redeem." We know that in the Old Testament it refers to a prescribed payment that could be made to remove an obligation that stood over against a person. If a man's bull gored another man to death, he could avoid the death penalty by paying over a sum of money, a ransom price, to the family of the dead man (Ex. 21:28ff.). Jews paid a five-shekel redemption price at the Temple so that they did not have to undergo the religious obligations of the firstborn, which was now assigned to the Levites (Num. 3:42–51). However, if we look at those passages where the word "redeem" is used with reference to God's saving action, its meaning does not appear to be constricted to this technical usage. Consider the following verses:

> Therefore, say to the Israelites: "I am the LORD, and I will bring you out from under the yoke of the Egyptians. I will free you from being slaves to them, and I will *redeem* you with an outstretched arm and with mighty acts of judgment." (Ex. 6:6)
>
> "I have swept away your offences like a cloud, your sins like the morning mist. Return to me, for I have *redeemed* you." (Is. 44:2)
>
> "I will deliver this people from the power of the grave; I will *redeem* them from death. Where, O death, are your plagues? Where, O grave, is your destruction?" (Hosea 13:14)
>
> Christ *redeemed* us from the curse of the law by becoming a curse for us, for it is written: "Cursed is everyone who is hung on a pole." (Gal. 3:13)

None of these texts suggest of a price being paid or of a party to whom payment is due. There is, however, in them all an indication of divine deliverance from some sort of bondage. "Redeem" then functions in these passages as a synonym for "set free" and is used with reference to a whole range of liberating acts of God. It is of interest that the Greek Fathers got themselves into a theological tangle when they tried to interpret "redeem" according to its technical meaning.

Who, they asked, was the one to whom the ransom was paid? It could only be the devil. But why should God have to pay the devil? Satan must have earned some sort of right over humankind, thus they dug themselves into a deeper and deeper theological hole as they sought to follow the logic of the word's original use.

What about the term "justification"? To what did it refer in the Scriptures? We need to remember that in the Greek "justify" and "righteousness" belong to the same word group. This means that the relation between "justify" and "righteousness" is of the same sort as that between "redeem" and "redemption," or between "save" and "salvation." So our question becomes: to what does "righteousness" or more particularly "the righteousness of God" refer in the Scriptures when used in the context of Christ's atoning work?? Is it a precise, technical term referring to divine justice or is it a broader expression that can also indicate human salvation? Recent studies have argued that "the righteousness of God" when used with respect to salvation is a characteristic of God and refers in particular to his covenant faithfulness. It is the divine characteristic whereby God lovingly fulfils the commitment he has made to his people. But in earlier discussions, "the righteousness of God" was recognized by nearly all parties to refer to the redemptive state into which God brought a believer through his justifying action. It was considered to be an aspect of human salvation and not an attribute of God. Augustine represents this view. "Just as the righteousness of God is used in the sense of our being made righteous by His gift; and the salvation of the Lord in that we are saved by Him" (56). Furthermore, a number of biblical passages highlight this tendency in Old Testament thought to use "God's righteousness" as a synonym for "salvation" (Ps. 98:2; Is. 45:8b, 55:1–5, 56:1b, 59:17a; Mt. 6:33).

We see then that "the righteousness of God" or "the righteous acts of God," originally identified with divine justice and judgment, came in due course to refer also to God's saving act of pardon: "O Lord, in keeping with all your righteous acts, turn away your anger and your wrath from Jerusalem" (Dan. 9:16; see also Ps. 51:14; 143:1; Micah 7:9).

It is this idea of pardon or acquittal that historical theology has generally recognized as the basic meaning of the word "justify." It is pardon which brings about a new righteous order, that restores relationships, that creates the *shalom* of God. "The remission of sins is justification" (Aquinas, *ST* 1.2q.113 article 1). "To justify is therefore nothing else than to acquit from the charge of guilt, as if innocence were proved" (Calvin, *Inst.*, 3.11.3).

Now if we allow that "redeem" is used as a synonym for "set free" and "justify or make righteous" signifies the act of divine pardon or acquittal, it does not mean that we have here two ways of salvation. God liberates the believer through his act of pardon, and pardons the sinner on the grounds of Christ's redemptive action. Christ's death is redemptive because of its sacrificial or atoning nature. It is atoning in that it brings about reconciliation through an act of forgiveness. See how these closely interrelated ideas are held together in Paul's thought: "All are justified freely by his grace through the redemption that came by Christ Jesus. God presented Christ as a sacrifice of atonement, through the shedding of his blood—to be received by faith" (Rom. 3:24-25)

Paul is not here presenting a number of different perspectives on the atonement, encouraging his readers to make a choice between them, not at all. Rather, he is offering a single account of the nature of salvation by weaving together the themes of redemption, forgiveness, and sacrifice.

Whether in the controversy between Paul and the circumcision party, Augustine and Pelagius, Luther and Rome, Calvinists and Arminians, questions about the source, nature, and role of faith in relation to justification have (rightly) taken center stage. In short, the issues of faith and good works, law and grace, judgment and acquittal lead us to the heart of Paul's doctrine of justification. These are grand and complex themes that are integral to the gospel message and are more than worthy of the attention that has been given to them historically.

In conclusion, the doctrine of justification should not be considered as a subsection of a broader subject called atonement. It is, rather, a comprehensive account of how the ungodly are acquitted of their sins and find peace with God through the atoning death of Jesus as they come to believe the gospel. It might actually be more helpful to view the atonement as an aspect of the doctrine of justification.

Bibliography

Aquinas, *Summa Theologica*, trans. Fathers of the English Dominican Province, 1947.
Augustine, *On Nature and Grace*, NPNF first series, vol. 5.
Aulén, *Christus Victor*, 1978.
Calvin, *Institutes*, trans. Beveridge, 1970.
Gunton, *The Actuality of the Atonement*, 1988.
Luther, *Two Kinds of Righteousness*, in *Martin Luther: Selections from his Writings* ed. Dillenberger, 1961.

Kant

Nathan A. Jacobs

Immanuel Kant's thoughts on atonement appear in Book 2 of *Religion within the Boundaries of Mere Reason*.[1] Discerning the meaning of his remarks is not simple, for the nature and intentions of *Religion* is a point of controversy.[2] These varied interpretations converge into two camps, however, when it comes to atonement, with both recognizing the following claims.

In Book 1 of *Religion*, Kant investigates the moral disposition (*Gesinnung*) of humanity. He concludes (1) corruption is not essential to humanity but comes upon us by choice (6:18–21); (2) this choice is somehow universal and prior to all other choices (6:22, 32–33, 42–43); and (3) corruption taints our every deed (6:36–37). Kant's conclusion comes from considering that humanity is a *moral* species. This assertion offers three roads: The species is (1) morally neutral, (2) morally good, or (3) morally corrupt. Kant proves incapable of defining moral neutrality, since indifference toward the moral law is not neutrality but corruption. Therefore, the species must be either evil or good—a dichotomy Kant labels *moral rigorism* (6:20–25). Kant rejects the second option of morally good as obviously false (6:20, 32–34), so the third assertion of morally corrupt follows: this condition Kant calls "radical evil" (*radikal Böses*) (6:37).

---

[1] Citations of Kant are embedded in the chapter and refer to the German *Akademie* pagination, which can be found in the margins of *The Cambridge Edition of the Works of Immanuel Kant*.

[2] For a survey of readings (pre-2008) of Kant's *Religion*, see Chris L. Firestone and Nathan Jacobs, *In Defense of Kant's "Religion"* (Bloomington, IN: Indiana University Press, 2008), part I. Since the publication of *In Defense*, significant works on *Religion* include *Kant's Religion within the Boundaries of Mere Reason*, ed. Gordon Michalson (Cambridge: Cambridge University Press, 2014); James Dicenso, *Religion within the Boundaries of Mere Reason: A Commentary* (Cambridge: Cambridge University Press, 2012); Lawrence Pasternack, *Kant's Religion within the Boundaries of Mere Reason* (London: Routledge, 2013); Lawrence Pasternack, *Routledge Philosophy Guidebook to Kant on Religion within the Boundaries of Mere Reason* (New York: Routledge, 2014); and Stephen R. Palmquist, *Comprehensive Commentary on Kant's Religion within the Bounds of Bare Reason* (Oxford: Willy-Blackwell, 2014).

In Book 2, Kant discusses a Christ figure he names the prototype (*Urbild*) (6:60), who is the exemplar for all moral pilgrims. Redemption requires that the pilgrim undertake a radical conversion, casting off his corrupt disposition and appropriating the disposition displayed in the prototype (6:60–62). If successful, a new moral identity emerges. The convert's former self is put to death and the new self bears a disposition pleasing to God (6:61–62, 67, 74). As for atonement, Kant rejects both forensic justification and vicarious suffering. Regarding justification, Kant thinks no reasonable person can believe God would favor a sinner without him first changing his ways to win God's approval (6:116–117, 170–171). Regarding vicarious atonement, Kant identifies sin as a personal burden that cannot be transferred to another (6:72). Yet, there is a sense in which vicarious atonement is true. Because the moral convert's new identity is not the source of prior failings, this new self bears the sins of the former self. Therefore, conversion and repentance is an atoning journey in which one pleasing to God—the new self—bears the sins of one who offended God—the former self (6:73–74).

Despite agreement by scholars on the above points, there is disagreement about how best to interpret these claims. On the more traditional understanding, Kant's remarks on the fall and redemption center on the individual. Radical evil is not a universal condition, but the peculiar phenomenon that every person begins un-fallen and, prior to every other exercise of will, freely chooses to subordinate the moral law to competing incentives, thereby embracing corruption. This choice is not necessary, but it is universal (6:20–21). Kant grants that divine grace is necessary to undo this choice (6:37), since radical evil taints every deed, including those aimed at conversion (6:32–34). But Kant (1) cannot grant that God would favor someone prior to him earning such favor (6:116–117, 170–171), and (2) insists that one cannot make maxims (rules) for moral conduct based on what someone else *might* do (e.g., 6:101). Hence, the pilgrim needs grace to proceed but cannot presume it when proceeding. What, then, is the moral pilgrim to do?

Some in this camp suggest that though the convert cannot form a maxim based on God supplying grace, if conversion proves successful, the convert can conclude that grace was involved (Reardon, 106; Hare, 254–256; Michalson, 97). Others take a less mysterious approach, wherein the grace God supplies is the moral example personified in the prototype (Jesus or another symbol) (Michalson, 109; McCarthy, passim; Davidovich, 5; Ward, 62–63, 149–151). Practically speaking, however, whether grace is unseen empowerment or a divinely supplied exemplar, the result is the same: hope requires that moral pilgrims attempt a conversion in an effort to cast off their former disposition and enact a new disposition pleasing to God. The convert puts to death his former self, thereby satisfying the demands of retributive justice. The new self, by contrast, is pleasing to God, and earns a surplus of merits as he walks a road of repentance and moral progress, not for his sins, but for the sins of the former self (6:74–75) (McCarthy, 77–81; Ward, 147–149; Davidovich, 3–4; Hare, 257; Reardon, 103; Michalson, 85–92).

The second camp understands Kant to be working with a corporate vision of humanity's fall and redemption. Within this camp there is a metaphysical reading and a non-metaphysical reading. For the non-metaphysical reading, the problem of radical evil is universal among our species, and may be attributable to fallen social structures that negatively influence individuals (Wood, 31–57). But regardless of the cause, the solution to this problem requires that moral pilgrims band together in moral communities, which help counteract negative influences that turn them away from the moral law (6:97–98). As for atonement, the road that leads to forgiveness and reconciliation with God looks very much like the road described in the previous reading (Byrne, 152; Anderson-Gold, 26).

The metaphysical side of the corporate camp understands Kant's doctrine of radical evil to be about the human species. Kant's moral rigorism is a conclusion about human nature in the Aristotelian, secondary substance sense: Human nature per se is either good or evil. This does not mean that humanity is essentially evil, since *moral* entails *freedom* for Kant (6:20–21). Instead, what emerges, on this reading, is the very odd claim that human nature itself has one free choice, namely, whether to be good or evil. Hence, prior to any individual making a free choice, the essence of man must freely determine the moral disposition of the species. Whichever choice the essence makes constitutes the innate disposition of every individual (6:22, 42–43). And evidently, our species chose evil (Firestone and Jacobs, chapter 5).

Just as Kant turned to the human universal (in the medieval sense) in his doctrine of corruption, on this reading, so he turns to universals for his solution. Kant's prototype is neither Jesus per se nor a mere symbol, but an idea in the Platonic sense. The prototype is God's idea of morally perfect man, generated by the divine mind from eternity (cf. 6:60 with 28:1058–1059). This ideal substance is divine because it proceeds from God but human because it is the idea of perfect man (6:66). As such, the prototype bears the very disposition God desires, and it is this disposition that should have been emulated in the self-determination of our created species (Firestone and Jacobs, 155–172).

This view of the prototype supplies a different picture of moral hope than explored thus far. On this reading, the individual is bound by radical evil because it is as innate in him as human nature. Redemption requires the existence of something outside of his humanity in which he can participate. The prototype supplies this something. Moral conversion is an attempt to appropriate or participate in the disposition of the prototype, thereby usurping the corruption of our species (28:1058–1059). Grace, on this reading, is the provision of the prototype and his disposition (6:60–61). For without this provision, we would be irreparably bound by radical evil (Firestone and Jacobs, 170–172). In conversion, the moral pilgrim rejects the rulership of the corrupt disposition and lays hold of a new disposition from the prototype. The convert casts off the disposition that displeases God, and with it his corrupt identity, acquiring a disposition pleasing to God that brings a new identity (6:73–74) (Firestone and Jacobs, 172–173).

This reading also opens the door to the possibility that Kant advocates a form of atonement involving imputation. There is a tension in Kant's remarks on atonement. On the one hand, he says moral guilt cannot be transferred (6:72). On the other hand, he speaks of the prototype suffering on behalf of sinners and passing to them his surplus of righteousness (6:74–75). When reading the prototype as a mere symbol, this language is a picture of the road the convert must walk. If, however, the prototype is an entity, then Kant's remarks are in conflict. To what imputation of the prototype's merits refers is clear: in appropriating the prototype's disposition, one appropriates its merits (6:73–74). But what of the prototype suffering for sinners?

Distinguishing the infinite guilt of the disposition from the finite guilt of particular infractions can relieve this tension. Kant's remarks against vicarious suffering are made in reference to the former: because the disposition is the fount of every evil, its guilt is infinite (6:72). This remark is reminiscent of Leibniz's comments on hell, according to which particular sins bear finite weight but the heart from which sins perpetually flow is an infinite source of divine displeasure (6:274–79). Granting this infinite-finite distinction, Kant rejects vicarious atonement for infinite dispositional guilt. This can only be dealt with in conversion by displacing the corrupt disposition. But this does not mean that the finite guilt of particular infractions cannot be atoned for by the prototype. Kant is clear that moral converts continue to sin, for they bear two moral dispositions that are at war, even though the disposition of the prototype has the upper hand (6:82–83). Moral lapses do not bring infinite guilt, since they do not de-convert the pilgrim, but they are infractions. On the metaphysical reading, one may read Kant's talk of the prototype suffering on behalf of sinners as a description of his vicarious atonement for the finite guilt of these lapses (Firestone and Jacobs, 173–180).

Regardless of which camp is correct, Kant's views on atonement sit outside the mainstream Christian accounts. Yet one must remember that Kant insists that his role as a philosopher is different from that of the theologian. The philosopher is bound by reason alone. Kant cannot deny that God might reveal certain truths to mankind (6:169, 8:142, 28:1119), and thus cannot claim that his account of atonement exhausts all truth on the subject. It merely identifies what can be said, according to Kant, from within the boundaries of mere reason. And though revelation may not contradict reason, it certainly can add to it. Kant thus remains ever open to the possibility that more is true about atonement than he has said. But this more, if revealed, God entrusts to the theologian, not to the philosopher.

Bibliography

Anderson-Gold, *Unnecessary Evil*, 2001.
Byrne, *The Moral Interpretation of Religion*, 1998.
Davidovich, "How to Read *Religion*," *Kant-Studien* 85:1, 1994.
Firestone and Jacobs, *In Defense of Kant's "Religion,"* 2008.
Hare, "Augustine, Kant, and the Moral Gap," in *The Augustinian Tradition*, 1999.
Kant, "Religion within the Boundaries of Mere Reason," in *The Cambridge Edition of the Works of Immanuel Kant*, 1998.
Leibniz, *Die philosophischen Schriften von Gottfried Wilhelm Leibniz*, vol. 6, 1875–1890.
McCarthy, *Quest for a Philosophical Jesus*, 1986.
Michalson, *Fallen Freedom*, 2008.
Reardon, *Kant as Philosophical Theologian*, 1988.
Ward, *The Development of Kant's View of Ethics*, 1972.
Wood, "The Evil in Human Nature," in *Kant's Religion*, 2014.

Kierkegaard

Murray Rae

Commentators upon the work of Kierkegaard commonly observe that Kierkegaard's presentation of the doctrine of atonement, with its emphasis on satisfaction, is predominantly Anselmian in character, but that there is also an Abelardian strain in Kierkegaard's thought according to which Christ's death on the cross calls forth a strenuous effort to imitate Christ's "work of love." (See, e.g., Gouwens, 142–150; Barrett). Some suggest further that Kierkegaard is "in basic agreement" with Luther's penal substitution view of the atonement (e.g., Marshall, 11), but the idea that Christ endures punishment in satisfaction of the wrath of God is much less prominent than Kierkegaard's repeated emphasis on the love shown forth in the atoning death of Christ. George Pattison observes that Kierkegaard "offers a subtly different take from that of conventional atonement theory" (216). In contrast to a traditional emphasis on the satisfaction of God's righteous condemnation of sin through Christ's bearing of punishment on our behalf, "Kierkegaard allows us to see the movement culminating in Christ's death as an extension of the exchange of love seen in the icon of the sinful woman" (216). The reference here is to the woman who washed Jesus feet with her tears and anointed them with ointment (Luke 7:37–50).

Kierkegaard takes this woman's story as an exemplary instance of Christ's atoning work. Jesus proclaims that the sins of the woman are forgiven (Luke 7:48), but Kierkegaard ponders how this can be when she yet lacks the comfort of Christ's "death as the Atonement, as the pledge that sins are forgiven" (WA, 158). "In his lifetime," Kierkegaard explains, "Christ is for his contemporaries primarily the prototype, even though he is the Savior and even though his life is suffering, so that even in his lifetime he can be said to bear the sins of the world" (158). There is no suggestion here of punishment. Christ's bearing of the world's sin during his lifetime is seen to be, in the encounter with the woman who was a sinner, a matter of his taking upon himself the burden of her estrangement and setting her free from *the world's* condemnation.

A similar theme is evident in Kierkegaard's several discourses on the text of 1 Peter 4:8, "Love hides a multitude of sins." The role love plays, through Christ, is to shield the sinner from the demands of justice. "If justice then were to fly into a rage, what more does it want than the death penalty; but that penalty has been paid, and his death is your hiding place. What infinite love!" (Kierkegaard, WA, 186). In Kierkegaard's explorations of the matter, however, and as is evident in the case of the woman caught in adultery (John 8:1–11), it is often the world's "justice" that poses the threat to the sinner. Kierkegaard writes, "The world's judgment requires what belongs to the world, and this conceals from the world whatever is lacking; but love's judgment requires what belongs to love" (EUD, 76). "If there is a righteous indignation that has to be propitiated by Christ's death, a wrath that must be covered, it is precisely the (un)righteous indignation of human justice" (Pattison, 216).

There are in Kierkegaard's works occasional suggestions of a punitive divine judgment: "Thus when punitive justice here in the world or in judgement in the next seeks the place where I, a sinner, stand with all my guilt, with my many sins—it does not find me" (WA, 123), but the "justice" that demands satisfaction is commonly presented by Kierkegaard as an abstract concept, rather than being attributed directly to God. While Kierkegaard stresses the magnitude and the seriousness of human sin, he also prompts consideration of whether the compassionate justice of God is to be understood in rather less punitive terms than appear in penal substitution theories. In heaven, "the case [of our sinfulness] will now go before a more lenient judge," he writes (JP, IV/3994). It is this thought that sustains the penitent sinner who knows that forgiveness has been won through the death of Christ.

Satisfaction, as we have noted, is a prominent theme in Kierkegaard's references to the atonement, thus aligning him with Anselm, but it is the demands of love that are satisfied, rather than the demands of justice. Or, we might say, it is the demands of God's just love that are satisfied in and through the one who takes our place. Christ, the infinitely compassionate Savior, accomplishes a more comprehensive satisfaction of God's purposes than can be understood through the contractual logic of punitive justice. The "high priest of sympathy" puts himself completely in our place—not only in the place of those justly found guilty, but also in the place of those who are tempted, in the place of those who suffer, and in the place of those who endure spiritual trial. In satisfaction of the love of God, Christ places himself in our human situation, takes our place where the danger is greatest, and shields us from every threat to our lives before God (see, e.g., Kierkegaard WA, 123). Occasionally, Kierkegaard employs the language of sacrifice in this connection (e.g., WA, 159), but the emphasis is clearly upon the love of Christ shown forth in his sacrificial death. Atonement, and so also reconciliation, are accomplished in virtue of Christ's putting himself in our place, thus ensuring that in our place of sin and temptation, of suffering and spiritual trial, we are not forsaken by God.

It is with respect to the love of God shown forth in the atonement that the Abelardian strain in Kierkegaard's thought becomes apparent. Although Kierkegaard repeatedly stresses that the atonement is accomplished without any contribution from sinful human beings, the demonstration of divine love calls forth in us a striving to imitate Christ. "It is by no means man's effort which brings atonement, but it is the joy over reconciliation, over the fact that atonement has been made, it is the joy which produces an honest striving" (JP I/983). In a prayer introducing a discourse on Matthew 6:24–34 Kierkegaard writes:

> O Redeemer, by your holy suffering and death you have made satisfaction for everyone and everything; no eternal salvation either can or shall be earned—it has been earned. Yet you left your footprints, you, the holy prototype for the human race and for every individual, so that by your Atonement the saved might at every moment find the confidence and boldness to want to strive to follow you. (JFY, 147)

The atonement is most certainly for Kierkegaard an objective reality, but the atonement brings about an alteration to our human situation that becomes apparent first in the Lord's Supper through which the news of forgiveness and reconciliation is declared and received, and then, subjectively, in the response of those who strive to imitate Christ. Kierkegaard here adds an intriguing qualification whereby the Spirit is called the Atoner:

> Christ is the Atoner. This is continually in relation to the past. But at the same moment he is the Atoner for the past he is "the prototype" for the future.
> Here, alas, is the difficulty. Measured by the criterion of "imitation," the first step in my future will again make me in need of the Atoner—indeed, I cannot even make a beginning because I am stifled by anxiety.
> Then "the Spirit" is the Atoner. (JP II/1919)

Kierkegaard here attests the role of the Spirit as helper and comforter who relieves us of sin's debilitating impediment and helps us in our striving, even though what we accomplish in response to the atonement is always "shabby in relation to the ideal" (Kierkegaard, JP II/1919).

Kierkegaard's attention to the subjective element, not only in the atonement, but also in Christianity itself, is a defining characteristic of his entire corpus. In an age that had reduced Christianity to an insipid, social convention that required no alteration to the lives of those who professed to be Christian, the subjective had to be stressed; but the objective reality is indispensable. Christianity, and the atonement along with it, "exists before any Christian exists; it must exist in order for one to become a Christian" (BA, 117). There is, however, a further reason for Kierkegaard's stress upon the subjective. Only those who know their own need, Kierkegaard contends, can understand the atonement: "How could anyone sitting placidly and objectively in his study and speculating ever be able to understand the necessity of an atonement, since an atonement is necessary only in the understanding of an anguished conscience" (JP, III/2461). Commensurate with this observation, everything Kierkegaard has to say about the atonement is directed, not toward the clarification of a doctrine, but to the pastoral situation. His remarks are addressed, above all, to those who come to the Lord's Supper seeking forgiveness of their sin.

Bibliography

Barrett, "The Crucifixion: Kierkegaard's Use of the New Testament Narratives," in Barrett and Stewart, *Kierkegaard and the Bible, Tome II*, 2010.
Gouwens, *Kierkegaard as Religious Thinker*, 1996.
Kierkegaard, *The Book on Adler*, 1998.
Kierkegaard, *Eighteen Upbuilding Discourses*, 1990.
Kierkegaard, *For Self Examination* and *Judge for Yourself!*, 1990.
Kierkegaard, *Søren Kierkegaard's Journals and Papers*, 7 vols, 1967–1978.
Kierkegaard, *Without Authority*, 1997.
Marshall, *Kierkegaard for the Church*, 2013.
Pattison, *Kierkegaard and the Quest for Unambiguous Life*, 2013.

Kingdom of God

Cynthia L. Rigby

How do different theories of the atoning work of Jesus Christ shape different understandings of the character and coming of the Kingdom of God (also sometimes known as the "kin-dom" or the "reign" of God)? Here, we consider how envisioning God's kingdom in relation to the whole of Jesus Christ's person and work makes it possible for human agents to participate with God in bringing the kingdom "to earth as it is in heaven." We will give special attention to a key term—"*kairos*"—explaining how Jesus Christ gifts us with the opportunity and responsibility to perceive, discern, and act in accordance with God's reign.

Atonement Theories and the Coming of the Kingdom

How we understand the character of the Kingdom of God is shaped, profoundly, by whatever atonement theory we have in play when we consider it. According to Matthew 28:18, Jesus Christ has been given by God "all authority" in heaven and on earth. Given this, Christian believers have always understood who he is, what he has done, and what he promises, expects, and desires to lie at the heart of the divine reign.

Christus Victor. When Christ is understood to redeem us, as Luther puts it, by "crushing ... those tyrants" who are "the devil, death, and sin" (Aulén, 105), the Kingdom of God is seen as a place of victory both for him and for all who revere him as King. With *Christus victor* atonement theory in play, this world is seen as a "battleground" between evil and good; between "principalities and powers" that are trying to undermine the reign of God and Spirit-filled forces that are committed to being strong and courageous until final victory is secured.

Christians who have *Christus victor* in play often explain misfortunes, failures, and the sins that keep them from enjoying the benefits of God's reign as temporary, if challenging, setbacks that require them to stay strong and continue "fighting the good fight." They know someday all the battling will be over, and God's reign will be realized in all of its fullness.

While all who imagine the Kingdom of God by way of *Christus victor* think inhabitants of the Kingdom are at war with an enemy, there are various understandings of who the enemy is. Luther is among those who understand the war to be against supernatural powers and our own personal sinfulness. Gutiérrez and King insist that the battle of the Kingdom is against all forces that perpetuate injustices, reminding us that the liberation of the bodies of the poor and disenfranchised is a trademark of God's rule. Another and related approach to thinking about the battle faced identifies the "enemy" not with particular persons, but with institutions or systems that encourage resistance to the will of the sovereign God. These goad us to serve worldly gods, promising benefits by way of their idolatrous powers (Wink).

The Kingdom of God, seen through the lens of *Christus victor*, is a sure thing that will certainly one day be fully realized because it is grounded in the reality of Jesus Christ's victory over sin and death—his resurrection from the dead. Yet in this world that is not our home, Christians hold, we are encouraged to continue courageously battling until the sure victory in Christ is fulfilled in time.

Moral Exemplar. When the lens through which the Kingdom of God is perceived is more attuned to the atonement theory of Abelard, the agenda is not focused on battling warring powers but on learning, growth, and sanctification. Jesus Christ is our teacher who shows us where to look for the seeds of the Kingdom of God that are in our midst. As we faithfully follow this one who so perfectly models what it is to love, we too are able to love, to serve, and to keep God's commandments. God's righteousness becomes manifest in this world, and God's Kingdom gains strength and influence (Rauschenbusch). As Christ represents Christians, his loving, righteous life compels their participation; so Christians represent those outside of the church, bearing witness to the fact that human beings can help precipitate the reign of God by caring for the weak and correcting injustices (Sölle).

While those more drawn to the *Christus victor* model of atonement might conceptualize the coming of the Kingdom as abrupt and dramatic, subscribers to the *moral exemplar* theory understand the formation of the kingdom to be a long process. Signs that progress is being made serve as incentive to continue the work.

Substitution. An understanding of the Kingdom of God that is influenced by certain aspects of Anselm's thinking attends more to the cross than to the life of Jesus. The emphasis on Christ taking the place of sinners, when dying on the cross, extends beyond Christ's death to touch surrounding human lives. A tendency toward passivity might be noted, a tendency to "wait on God" to bring the Kingdom without fighting for it or working toward it, ourselves.

A benefit of a substitutionary outlook—one that can actually contribute to human beings taking active places in relation to what God is doing in the world—can be seen when substitutionary atonement is understood to apply very narrowly, that is, only to the sins that incapacitate us. Any "replacing" done by Christ would be only in order to make it possible for us to have a place in relation to the rest of our lives. Barth explains it this way: the judge is "judged in our place" (IV.1) in order "to free us to engage in better, and happier, and more fruitful activities" than our own self-judgment (IV.2, 234). The cross, in this way, becomes a symbol of Christian hope (Moltmann).

The activities Christians are now free to engage in are the work of the kingdom of God. This kingdom is not realized progressively, or by way of battle, when the lens of substitutionary atonement is in place. Rather, the idea that Jesus Christ has solely and completely paid the price for our sin suggests, as a corollary, that God's Kingdom is already complete, and that we simply need to synchronize our lives and the life of the world with what already is. So Christians are commanded to act faithfully, as those who have been ensured a place, out of gratitude for what God has done on their behalf.

Glimpsing God's Kingdom: The Kairos Moment

Regardless of what atonement theory is in play, Christians are keenly aware of a disparity between the Kingdom of God and the world of our day-to-day lives. Perhaps this is why Jesus invites the disciples to issue an imperative to God, demanding, "Thy Kingdom Come!" It is also why the imperative is followed by "thy will be done." This chapter has considered three ways human beings may participate in the work of God's kingdom: they may join in the battle, model their lives after Christ's, or live into the forgiveness that allows them to live abundant lives. It is important to note, however, that each of these approaches to doing the will of God that contributes to the coming of the Kingdom pivots on the person of Jesus Christ. It is because the Jesus who redeems them is the very heart of the Kingdom, Christians testify, that they are able both to recognize the reign of God and move to participate in it. It is because Jesus is the victor, the example, and the one who took away our sins that those who know him are able to see the reign of God even when and where it is far from obvious.

Charles Sheldon told a story, over a century ago, about a community of people who asked themselves the question "What Would Jesus Do?" before every action they took, and then followed through, accordingly. The community was transformed. Allan Boesak today argues, similarly, that Jesus is the "true revolutionary" who leads us to experience "*kairos*" moments to which we should be ready to respond. "Kairos moments" are instances when Christians glimpse the Kingdom of God on earth. These moments call us, Boesak argues, to discern and decide whether there is an immediate, and perhaps fleeting, opportunity to do something that helps advance God's reign. This might mean joining in battle alongside the one who is already the victor, or showing love to a beloved one who appears to be unlovely, or resisting self-loathing in favor of accepting that forgiveness which allows us to celebrate and enjoy God's good gifts. In any of these cases, the Christian focus should be to take full advantage of God's atoning work in Christ in ways that close the gap between the actualities of our day-to-day lives and the realities true to the Kingdom of God.

Bibliography

Aulén, *Christus Victor*, 1975.
Barth, *CD* IV.
Boesak, *Dare We Speak of Hope?*, 2014.
Boesak, *The Kairos Document*, 1985.
Gutiérrez, *The God of Life*, 1991.
King Jr., *Strength to Love*, 2010.
Moltmann, *The Trinity and the Kingdom*, 1993.
Rauschenbusch, *A Theology for the Social Gospel*, 1917.
Sheldon, *In His Steps*, 1896.
Sölle, *On Earth as in Heaven*, 1993.
Wink, *Engaging the Powers*, 1992.

Liberation Theology

Jules A. Martinez Olivieri

The precise semantic range of the theological concept of "atonement" does not have an equivalent in theological Spanish or Portuguese. In order to refer to the salvific work of Christ, Latin American theologians hold the metaphors of salvation in dialogical relation with words such as *redención, expiación, salvación,* and *liberación*.

Liberation theology (henceforth, LT) uses the adjective "liberation" not as a topic added to doctrinal discourse, but rather as a way of orienting and shaping Christian theology in its diverse dimensions. LT is better conceived as a theological movement, a mode of doing theology with the flexibility to include multiple ecclesial traditions (Roman Catholic and Protestant) around key motifs: soteriology, the primacy of Christian praxis as the first act of theology, and a methodological option that seeks the perspective of the impoverished and marginalized as a *locus theologicus* (C. Boff, 10–13). Moreover, adjectival use of "liberation" when modifying "theology" has become a way to refer to a range of contextual theologies that elaborate theological discourse in light of challenges faced in different regions of the world. Hence, there is a plurality of theologies of liberation inspired by Latin American liberation theology. Some of them concentrate on responding to globalized economic oppression, ethnocentrism, racism, gender and sexual violence, and colonialism.

A main point of discussion in LT is the *nature* of Christ's salvific work. If humanity needs salvation, from what do we need to be saved? Liberation Christology conceives salvation as freedom from personal and collective sin. Gustavo Gutierrez, one of the early vanguards in LT, views sin as not only a relational break with God and neighbor, but as a "historical reality" that distorts human praxis and is an obstacle to human flourishing. Sin encompasses a metaphysical, historical, and personal reality of rebellion. Accordingly, if sin is an intra-historical reality, then salvation should be experience in history.

Liberation Christology delves into Jesus's salvific significance by attending to the meaning of his "life-acts." That is to say, one must interpret the cross and resurrection in light of the proclamation of the arrival of God's kingdom. Furthermore, the proper recipients of this proclamation, as evidenced in the synoptic gospels, are the victims of poverty and oppression induced by sinful religious and political systems (Sobrino, 67). Therefore, the salvation proclaimed by the Messiah is an immanent eschatological reality. To follow Jesus and his work is to seek after his cause and his concrete praxis.

The meaning of Jesus's death is inseparably tied to the historical causes of the crucifixion. LT opts for a methodological retrieval of the humanity and concrete history of Jesus, a Christology "from below," in order to approach the question: "Why was he killed?" The death of Jesus was a political execution, a consequence of the prophetic and political nature of his message. Jesus was in conflict with religious and imperial authorities, accused of conspiring to destroy the temple (Mark 14:58), of being blasphemer (Mark 14:64), and claiming the royal title of King of the Jews (Mark 15:2). These accusations evidence the intensity of the conflict created by Jesus's political and economic teaching and praxis. These elements are vistas into the kind of liberation Jesus communicates through all his acts. Jesus's radical humanizing of the impoverished masses—women, children, and religiously marginalized groups posed a threat to temple theology and Roman politics. Jesus died the way he died because his teachings destabilized oppressive religious, political, and economic systems. This historical *datum* is indispensable for soteriology because it provides the narrative content and hermeneutical key for many liberation theologians' concepts of salvation.

The meaning of Jesus's death is necessarily transcendent, for the death of Jesus is not the death of an ordinary human being, but the death of one whose life is identified with God's life (Sobrino, 220). As such the cross is God's definitive expression of love, a credible love offered for suffering humans. Liberation theology is aware that the New Testament has multiple social, political, and religious metaphors that frame one's understanding of the cross. Feminist liberation theologians have identified the detrimental effects on women by the ideological use of concepts like the atonement, for the purpose of legitimizing the suffering of women as analogous to Jesus's own trials. But the explanatory power of concepts such as redemption, sacrifice, substitution, and reconciliation find their power in the Messiah's example. That is, Jesus is the "sufferer" par excellence; he is the "sacrifice" that ends all sacrifices (Tamez, *The Amnesty*, 58). Jesus is the *persona salutis* who, in filial obedience to God is driven as the spirited Messiah, succumbs to death, and gives his life for others. Jesus confronts death for the sake of sinners, providing hope for women and men through the power of sacrificial love.

Liberation from structural manifestations of sin depends upon the dialectic of his cross and resurrection—the vindication of the victims in the resurrection of the crucified Messiah. Jesus is powerfully representative of both the ideal human and the victims that long for God's justice (Sobrino, 229). Jon Sobrino, the principal Christologist in Latin America, interprets God's suffering on the cross as good news, for in God's immanence in the cross Jesus took upon himself the mechanisms that negate life and overcame the patterns of death in history. The redemptive value of Jesus's death is not causally efficacious for humanity. Instead, the efficacy of the cross pertains to its symbolic power "in the form of an exemplary cause more than of an efficient cause" (230). Accordingly, the construal of salvation as liberation refers to the present aspects of God's work that advance social and personal justice, thus reframing life for the most vulnerable as a gift shared by everyone. Subjectively, the experience of liberation includes faith, awareness of communion with God, hope for a new world, and so on. Objectively, liberation encompasses the public witness of the transformation of the human *habitus* and *actus*, where men and women are not only accepted by God the Father through the Son, but are made free (from oppression) with the Spirit, and given the opportunity to live life as co-participants of God's liberating acts. These are the visible and historical signs of the in-breaking of God's reign.

The cross is a victory over the dehumanizing powers of death and violence; an atonement, an event of reconciliation with God and neighbor. Liberationist elaborations on the significance of the cross treat it with attention to its historical reasons, while elaborations of the metaphysical or transcendent consequences of Jesus's redemptive work are modest. Still, the crucifixion of Jesus communicates that the God of love is with us in suffering. God has determined to be on the side of the victims, for they are the main recipients of Jesus's acts. The community of faith is called to be a people that find God in solidarity with their cause. God shows his love preferentially by revealing the Gospel and siding with those who are condemned by the world. The cross and the resurrection delegitimize ideologies of injustice, and as doctrinal discourse, also function as hermeneutical lenses for interpretation. For in the cross we "know" that God is close to us in our experiences of hopelessness; the victims of sin are vindicated, and the struggles for justice are the will of God.

The history of the crucified is the unraveling of sin and liberation from it. The solidarity offered by Jesus is the solidarity of God. In the new gospel logic, the marginalized become the subjects of that reign and are the first citizens of God's kingdom. What Jesus requires of the recipients of his Gospel is faithfulness. The poor who receive the good news find themselves in a privileged situation.

Jesus's liberations concern the poor, the sick, the demon-oppressed—all signs that God's rule has arrived. Sin is a force that distorts human praxis, and Christ's saving action is materially experienced. In this way LT declares that Jesus saves from sin. There is a broad cosmic affirmation that God's salvation includes the complete recreation of humanity and creation (Rom. 14:7), but the modes of salvific actions presented in the ministry of Jesus are concrete expressions—that is, temporal liberations that anticipate the nature of eschatological salvation, while creating a historically visible community. This community is the recipient of communion, peace, and justice (Gonzalez, 160).

Bibliography

Boff, C., "The Method of Theology of Liberation," in *Systematic Theology: Perspectives from Liberation Theology*, 1996.
Boff, L., *Passion of Christ, Passion of the World*, 1987.
Gonzalez, *The Gospel of Faith and Justice*, 2005.
Pixley, *La resurrección de Jesús, el Cristo*, 1997.
Sobrino, *Jesus the Liberator*, 1994.
Tamez, *The Amnesty of Grace*, 1993.
Tamez, "Latin American Christology in the Light of New Theological Actors," in *Voices from the Third World* 22.2, 1999.

Peter Lombard

G. R. Evans

Peter Lombard (1095–1160), scholastic theologian of the twelfth century, was originally born in Novara and later settled in Lombard. Though he and his family had little money, Lombard allied himself with patrons such as St. Bernard, allowing him to study at Bologna and the cathedral school in Rheims. However, it was in Paris that he settled as a teacher of theology at Notre Dame and was later made bishop of Paris in 1159 shortly before his death.

In step with other theologians in his day, Lombard often lectured on the Pauline Epistles, versions of which survive to this day. However, his most pivotal work, *Sentences*, completed in the mid-1150s brought him to the world stage throughout the Middle Ages. This work is a compilation of "opinions" (*sententiae*) of earlier Christian writers, especially those of Augustine. In both his lectures on the Pauline Epistles and in *Sentences*, Lombard explores the role of the atonement.

Peter Lombard's first exploration of the atonement comes in his lectures on Romans, primarily in the passage with the modern verse reference to Romans 5:8–10 and its assertions that "while we were still sinners, Christ died for us and we are now 'justified by his blood' and 'saved from God's wrath through him'" (NIV). The commentaries—which seem to survive in more than one version—are believed to be earlier than the composition of the *Sentences*. When Lombard gave the lectures on which they are based, he believed the Devil possessed rights, but was also influenced by Anselm of Canterbury's alternative account in the *Cur Deus Homo* which dispenses altogether with the rights of the Devil. Reflecting on Romans 5:8–10, Peter Lombard accepts that an omnipotent God could have found other ways to rescue mankind, but he argues that the one he chose, atonement and salvation through the death and resurrection of Christ on the cross, was the most fitting (*conveniens*, a favorite term of Anselm's). Lombard believed

God's choice of the atonement gave people a story to contemplate, thus rescuing them from despair and giving them hope. He also held the belief at that time that the Devil's power is real, but it is not a matter of, nor does it stem from, his having any right: God simply tolerated this "power" for a time. Lombard accepts the Anselmian argument that only a God-man was both able to die and thus offer the necessary sacrifice and to do so in a way God would be bound to accept since it was the gift of his Son.

In the *Sentences*, Peter Lombard addresses a series of questions about the atonement in Book II, beginning at Distinction 18.v. What, he asks, is the "cause of the death and Passion of Christ" (*Causa mortis et passionis Christi*)? "Why did he will to suffer and die, when his virtues alone would have sufficed? He did it for you not for himself. How did he do it for me? His passion and death might be a 'form' and a 'cause' for you: a form (example or model) of virtue and humility; a cause of glory and freedom." This, in broad terms is the Abelardian answer.

In Distinction 19.i, Lombard addresses technical questions that had been engaging many theologians in an active debate for the past half century. How did Christ through his death redeem us from the Devil and sin? Christ's death justifies us when love is awakened in our hearts. In Distinction 19.ii he moves on to the question why God had to become man and die (*Cur deus homo et mortuus*). Unless it was a man who rescued mankind, it would not have been just to snatch us from the Devil, but rather theft. Christ through the atonement instead redeems mankind from both temporal and eternal punishment in a holy and just manner.

In Distinction 20.ii, Lombard asks how and if Christ could have freed us in any other way. As God is omnipotent, it appears that he could have chosen another way, but he specifically and intentionally chose Christ's atonement. Lombard later borrows Hugh of St. Victor's scenario (*De Sacramentis* I.viii.4) in his Distinction 20.iv of the lawsuit involving God, man, and Devil, which he reproduces in detail. In Distinction 20.vi, he touches on another current debate, as to how far the Jews are to be blamed for crucifying Christ.

In the *Sentences*, Lombard still accepts the theory of the Devil's rights up to a point, but he is also apparently persuaded by Peter Abelard's arguments (shared in part by Bernard of Clairvaux) about the way Christ's incarnation and crucifixion work in the individual to bring about a change of heart. This however does not resolve the problem of the need to free mankind from the guilt of original sin and the punishment it deserves. It remains a puzzle for theologians that human beings continue to sin despite the atonement which has been made for them. A solution seemed to lie in the idea that through making a difference in the human soul, through conversion, baptism, and penance, the threat of punishment receded as the soul opened itself to feel the love of Christ. It is here that Lombard differs from Anselm—Anselm argues that Christ's merits are simply imputed to human beings, yet Lombard suggests that there is a real change, something more than merit being merely "counted" to the believer.

Who was to blame for the act of crucifying Christ? This was a topic of some contemporary interest because of the claim that the Jews were responsible. No, says Lombard, Christ freely gave himself up to suffering and death so God is responsible and there is no need to think in terms of blame. This was an act of ultimate generosity. In God's eyes, what was effective for redemption was Christ's sheer merit, his perfection as a man. Essentially we are "cleansed" and freed from the situation in which we formerly lay because of the Devil's seduction of Adam and Eve.

From Controversialist to Authority

The work of Peter Lombard sparked controversy during a time when the views expressed in these two surviving works and others in the course of his teaching over the years gave offense in some quarters. Pope Alexander III condemned him in a letter of 1170 to the Papal Legate in France, William of Champagne, archbishop of Sens. The pope reminds him that he had "enjoined" him in person to summon all his suffragans to make a joint "renunciation" of the "vicious doctrine" of Peter Lombard, who had allegedly said that Christ "is nothing" as a man (*non est aliquid*). They are to ensure that masters teaching in Paris do not associate themselves with this view or mislead their students. Peter Lombard was listed among the "four Labyrinths of France" by one critic, Walter of St. Victor (d.c.1180), who called him a "nihilianist," claiming that he taught that Christ's humanity was "nothing." Joachim of Fiore attacked him as a heretic. By the time of the Fourth Lateran Council of 1215, Joachim was himself being condemned as a heretic while Canon 2 of the Council moved to uphold Peter Lombard's teaching: "So we condemn and disapprove the book or treatise which Abbot Joachim published against Master Peter Lombard about the Trinity".

After this difficult beginning, and beyond his own lifetime, Lombard's reputation and that of his *Sentences* rose, and for the remaining medieval centuries, the *Sentences* became the standard textbook of theology in the universities—which emerged soon after his death as formal "institutions" of higher education. The success of the book depended partly on its achievement in creating a resource in which a student could find all the key questions of systematic theology marshalled in a reasonably systematic way. It in fact formed an early *summa theologiae*. Peter Lombard posed the questions, quoted the views (*sententiae*) of authorities, and often left the resolution open, so that masters and students could use it almost like the *Sic et Non* of Peter Abelard as a training manual in the skills of disputation.

Reading

Baltzer, *Die Sentenzen des Petrus Lombardus*, Leipzig, 1902; Scientia-Verlag, 1987.
Colish, *Peter Lombard*, 1994.
de Clerck, "Droits du démon et necessité de la rédemption: Les écoles d'Abélard et de Pierre Lombard," *RTAM* 14, 1947.
Glorieux, "Le *Contra quatuor labyrinthos Franciae de Gauthier de Saint-Victor*: Édition critique," *Archives d'histoire littéraire et doctrinale du moyen-âge* 19, 1952.
Landgraf, *Einführung in die Geschichte der theologischen Literatur der Frühscholastik unter dem Gesichtspunkte der Schulenbildung*, 1948.
Lombard, *Commentaries on the Pauline Epistles*, PL 191.
Lombard, *Sententiae Spicilegium Bonaventurianum* (Rome, 1971 and 1981), 2 vols.
Rosemann, *Peter Lombard*, 2004.

Martin Luther

Robert A. Kolb

Medieval popular piety had presented the young Martin Luther with various images of the suffering Christ, including the "Man of Sorrows" (in German literally, "Man of Pain," *Schmerzensmann*) who shared human suffering and died to help clear the way to God's grace (Hamm, 391–445). Luther's university instructors, who were educated by the late-fifteenth-century theologian Gabriel Biel, placed those images in the framework of a mixture of "Anselmian" and "Abelardian" explanations of how Christ aided sinners in obtaining God's grace. His agonizing sufferings and bloody death paid the price Luther owed God. If this sinner did his best (*facere quod in se est*) in following Christ's example, and thus merited that grace, it would provide sufficient aid to empower him to follow that example sufficiently well to gain admission to heaven. That would happen only after the temporal punishments attached to his sin, for which Christ had not died, were worked off with the satisfactions prescribed in penance, either on earth or in purgatory (Oberman, 131–145, 261–280).

Luther broke the medieval mold into which biblical teaching on the atonement of sinners through Christ's work had been poured. As his evangelical insights matured in the late 1510s, a new way of defining what it means to be Christian formed in his mind. He abandoned the medieval perception that, although God's grace preceded any human effort, it was human effort which sealed the contract for eternal life between sinners and God. Particularly, the performance of sacred works and religious activities was able to win God's favor. In that system of defining the Christian faith, both the popular use of Anselm's theory, labeled "vicarious satisfaction" by modern scholars, and Abelard's, the "moral example theory/motif," had enabled human performance of God's law to play a critical role in determining whether God's grace became effective in the sinner's life. Luther rewrote the script of salvation around his conviction that, as

Paul had written, "Christ was handed over to death for our trespasses and was raised for our justification" (Rom. 4:25).

Often in Christian history the need to defend specific expressions of biblical teaching has served as the catalyst for the sharper development of dogmatic teaching. During the Reformation, the atonement itself did not become a focal point of controversy, and so the polemic did not hone the Wittenberg reformer's formulations on this doctrine. Nonetheless, Luther's understanding of Christ's atoning work fifteen hundred years earlier served as the necessary foundation for his doctrine of justification and the Holy Spirit's restoration of the righteousness of sinners in God's sight in the sixteenth century. Apart from the atonement, Luther had no teaching on the restoration of righteousness before God. Almost always he discussed Christ's atoning work in order to proclaim justification to his contemporaries. Furthermore, Luther tried to avoid the speculative flights of fancy that had graced scholastic theology, for it had failed to provide him comfort when confronted by his own failure to "fear, love, and trust in God above all else" (*BSELK*, 862; *BC*, 351). He regarded attempts to explain precisely how God's action in Christ functions as foolhardy and presumptuous. The mechanics of salvation lie beyond the reach of the human imagination. That meant, however, that when he referred to Christ's work in the first century—his incarnation, obedience to the law, suffering, death, resurrection, and ascension to God the Father's right hand of power and glory—he often wove such references into his doctrine of justification through the faith in Christ and his work bestowed in the sixteenth century by the work of the Holy Spirit.

Gustaf Aulén's classic investigation of "atonement motifs" argued that Luther's focus in teaching the atonement fell on the ancient emphasis depicting Christ as the Victor over all the believer's enemies and that the Wittenberg reformer largely (though not completely) abandoned the terminology expressing a "vicarious satisfaction" (101–122). In reaction to Aulén, Ian Siggins observed that Luther did not teach a "coherent explanatory discourse about how the atonement works," but instead his sermons "abound in the motifs which figure in the historic atonement theories—patristic classic, dramatic, or Western, Latin, and penal; objective or subjective" (109; Arnold, 283–285). Indeed, Luther clearly did embrace elements of the language used in the so-called Anselmic motif of "vicarious satisfaction," but as Lauri Haikola notes, Luther

> did not need to divide the single act of reconciliation into two parts: one an act of reconciliation directed toward God and the other an act of redemption against the powers of destruction (sin, death, wrath, the devil) ... Reconciliation

and the battle for liberation are of one piece. Where one stops and the other begins cannot be defined. Neither the concept of satisfaction nor the concept of battle in and of itself offer a satisfactory expression of this battle for reconciliation. The satisfaction of the law, along with the demand of [God's] righteousness for punishment, flows together with the aspect of battle. (Haikola, 120, 122–123; cf. Peters, 122–139)

Aulén's criticism of "vicarious satisfaction" may have led him to underestimate the importance of Christ's human nature in the atonement because the divine nature fits more easily into his "Christus Victor" motif. Luther's firm commitment to Chalcedonian Christology, which was closely related to his understanding of the atonement, led him to presume that it was, at least in some sense, "necessary" for the Savior from sin to be both God and a thoroughly human creature. That this God-man kept the law of God perfectly was self-evident and taken for granted. That he suffered at the hands of sinners (Luke 24:7) rather than dying as the tower of Siloam fell also dramatically confronted the fallen nature of humanity. For Luther, Christ's saving work embraced his incarnation, obedience, and suffering as the indispensable and essential presupposition of his death "for our trespasses" and his resurrection "for our restoration to righteousness" (Rom. 4:25)—with the ascension to the Father's right hand as the inevitable completion of the narrative of his time on earth. But Christ's death, which took away human sin, and his resurrection, which restored the dead sinner to life and peace with God (Rom. 4:25), claimed central place in Luther's proclamation of the justification of sinners (Kolb, 39–60). Romans 4:25 prefaces Christ's dealing with the death that Adam exchanged for life and Jesus traded back (Rom. 5:12–21; cf. Luther's sermon on John 19, 1528: WA28:349,30–351,35; LW69:230–231), and Paul demonstrates how the delivery of that gift of life takes place for believers in Romans 6. Romans 4:25, along with John 1:29, occurs at key points in his presentation of God's plan for rescuing and transforming sinners.

After lecturing on the Psalms in 1513–1515, Luther began expositing Romans in the winter semester of 1515–1516. On verse 4:25, he told his students that Christ died "for our offenses," "that they might be destroyed and put to death," and "for our justification," "that it might be established and brought to completion" (WA56:48,15–17; LW25:42). His schooling addressed what he had learned from his scholastic teachers, but it also demonstrated that he was edging away from their understanding of Christ's saving work as he developed his definition of justification as taking place solely on the basis of God's grace and through trust in Christ (as well as the Holy Spirit's actual delivery of the benefits of Christ's death and resurrection through his recreative Word).

> The death of Christ is the death of sin, and his resurrection is the life of righteousness, for through his death he made satisfaction for sin and through his resurrection he delivers righteousness to us. Thus, his death does not merely signify but also accomplishes the remission of sins as an all-sufficient satisfaction. His resurrection is not only the sacrament of our justification, but it effects this righteousness in us, if we believe in it. The resurrection is its cause. (WA56:296,17–23; LW25:284)

He found the concept useful in his preaching. A sermon on Romans 4:25 from late 1516 spoke of God's "alien work"—the work he does not like to do—as that which "is necessary to identify people as sinners, unrighteous, liars, miserable, foolish, lost"; in other words, it is "the suffering of Christ and sufferings in Christ, the crucifixion of the old man and the mortification of the old Adam." He continued, "God's proper work, however, is the resurrection of Christ, justification in the Spirit, and the vivification of the new creature" (WA1:112,24–113,10; LW51:19).

God had constituted this plan before the creation of the world. The Old Testament prophets gave witness to the coming Messiah who would die and rise again. Isaiah 53 served Luther as a key attestation of this point. His lectures on the chapter in 1529 identified 52:13 as the beginning of the passage regarding God's servant, who is a "minister of God's Word, an apostle, and an ambassador." From the beginning it is clear that this servant will "prosper," that is, triumph. "This matter will be imposed on him in a way to make his task seem entirely impossible, but he will deal with it so successfully that he will accomplish it without force and harm ... wisely and without commotion" (WA31,2:428,18–429, 9; LW17:215–216). What he accomplished, the rescue of sinners and their restoration as God's children, took place because "the law demands that everyone die for his own sins." But the gospel shows that "Christ suffered for our sake contrary to law, justice, and custom." His was a substitutionary death, which repeated the Levitical sacrifice. The law is not the path to the restoration of righteousness. Only the intervention of Christ can accomplish that (WA31,2:431,13–434,17; LW17:220–224).

To clarify how Christ's death under the law's accusation of sinners functions, Luther turned to an analogy which had served him for over a decade, the "joyous exchange" (*fröhlicher Wechsel*), which he developed out of the medieval monastic-mystical tradition but conformed to his own theology. Lecturing on

Psalm 22:1 in 1522, Luther explained Christ's use of the verse on the cross; "God is life, light, wisdom, truth, righteousness, goodness, power, joy, glory, peace, blessedness and all good. I have been abandoned by God in death, darkness, foolishness, deception, sin, wickedness, weakness, sadness, confusion, disorder, despair, condemnation, and every kind of evil." This abandonment placed him who had come to be under the law (Gal. 4:4) under God's wrath in order to deliver sinners from that wrath and eternal death (WA5:602,13–606,28).

Originally, Luther's use of the concept of this joyous exchange found expression in the analogy of the union of bride and bridegroom, which under Germanic common law provided a full, complete sharing of possessions by the two marriage partners. This analogy also served his sharp rejection of mystical thinking that saw salvation as absorption of the inferior material creature into the spiritual divine since the "union" of husband and wife enriches and enhances the distinct identity of each partner (Freedom of a Christian: WA 7:54, 31–55, 36; LW 31:351–352). Perhaps Luther's most dramatic application of the "joyous exchange" came in his lectures on Galatians in 1531, where he named Christ "the greatest thief, murderer, adulterer, robber, desecrator, blasphemer, etc. there has ever been anywhere in the world." As such, Luther observed, Christ

> is not acting in his own Person now. Now he is not the Son of God born of the Virgin. But he is a sinner, who has and bears the sins of Paul, the former blasphemer, persecutor, and assaulter; of Peter, who denied Christ; of David, who was an adulterer and a murderer, and who caused the Gentiles to blaspheme the Lord's name. (WA40,1:433, 26–31; LW26:277)

Luther had God the Father say to Christ, "Be Peter the denier; Paul the persecutor, blasphemer, and assaulter; David the adulterer; the sinner who ate the apple in Paradise; the thief on the cross. In short, be the person of all people, the one who has committed the sins of all people." The Father's design: "See to it that you pay and make satisfaction for these sins." Thus, the law assaulted and killed Christ (WA40,1:437,23–27,438,12–13; LW26:280; cf. WA40,1:433,33,434, 12; LW26:277). This satisfaction was not a buy-out or pay-off but execution. The law collected the wages of sin: finding Christ among thieves, "it condemned and executed him as a thief" (WA40,1:434,19–20; LW26:278).

The lecture on Isaiah featured instead the grafting of one plant into another as the metaphor for the "joyous exchange" of the sinner's sin for Christ's righteousness: "He has carried our iniquities" (Isa. 53:5–7) elicited this dialogue with Satan, when the Tempter comes to suggest that the sinner is carrying his own sins: "You must say, 'I see my sin in Christ, therefore my sin is not mine but belongs to someone else.' ... He possesses them. This is the grafting of the wild olive [cf. Rom. 11:17–24] into the olive tree" (WA31,2:433,35–434,17, LW17:223–224). In this exchange the sinner's sin becomes Christ's possession, and his peace becomes the possession of the sinner (WA31,2:435,8–25; LW17:224–225). Clearly, in these lectures the inevitable application "for you" or "for us" appears: proclamation of the atoning work of Christ in the first century necessarily led to its application to sixteenth-century hearers and readers (WA31,2:432,14–30; LW17:221).

Luther recognized that Isaiah's suffering servant not only suffered cruel death. The one "cut off from the land of the living," whose grave was with the wicked, would "see his offspring and prolong his days" (53:8–11). "Note the two contradictory statements: someone dying yet enduring forever." "You now have a person suffering and a description of his death and resurrection. Now Isaiah describes the fruit of [the servant's] passion. This is his fruit, that he will have his future kingdom" (WA31,2:435,26–436,30; LW17:227; WA31,2:438; LW17:225–228).

Luther's blend of elements of Aulén's "Christus victor" and "vicarious satisfaction" images employed the language of payment and satisfaction more frequently than Aulén suggested. In a sermon on Matthew 2 (1522) Luther stated that

> divine righteousness had to be satisfied, sin paid for, and death overcome with righteousness. Therefore, it was Saint Paul's practice, when he preached God's grace in Christ, to refer at the same time to his suffering and blood, so that he might show how all good things have been given to us through Christ, but not without his unspeakable merit and cost. (WA10,1:720,3–6; LW 76:132)

An undated sermon published in 1544 described the sinner's debt and Christ's payment of it through his suffering and death arises out of Mark 10:45 (WA52:679,31–680,34). Luther's catechetical instruction and his exposition of biblical texts in university lectures also reveal his use of this concept of payment. In his *Small Catechism,* Luther summarized what children need to know before all else. Reviewing the second article of the Apostles Creed, he taught children that Christ "had redeemed me, a lost and condemned person, acquired (*erworben*) and freed me from all sins, from death, and from the power of the devil, not with gold or silver but with his holy precious blood and his innocent suffering death." "*Erworben*" is usually translated as "purchased," a meaning it often has, but with the underlying implication of acquiring possession. This is reinforced as Luther continued with the goal of Christ's atoning work: "that I may belong to him, living under him in his kingdom, and serve him" on the basis of his resurrection and his living and ruling forever (*BSELK* 872; *BC* 355).

This close connection between the satisfaction of the law's demand for the death of the sinner with liberation from sin, and the restoration of righteousness in the resurrection became clear in Luther's explanation of the Creed's second article in his *Large Catechism*. Its model sermon on the redemption of sinners focused on Christ's victory over sin, death, and Satan. There, redemption or rescue from captivity and condemnation is Luther's theme. "Before this I ... was captive under the power of the devil. I was condemned to death and entangled in sin and blindness." Satan, sin, death, and all misfortune had dominated the sinner's life.

> Those tyrants and jailers have now been routed, and their place has been taken by Jesus Christ, the Lord of life, righteousness, and every good and blessing. He has snatched us, poor lost creatures, from the jaws of hell, won us, liberated us, and restored us to the Father's favor and grace. As his own possession he has taken us under his protection and shelter, in order that he may rule us.

Indeed, he "made satisfaction for me and paid what I owed," but that was not a ransom comparable to payment with silver or gold (1 Pet. 1:18–19) but instead, with blood, with death. Christ's death led to his resurrection in which he swallowed up and gobbled down death (*BSELK* 1054–1058; *BC* 434–435), another of his rich array of images and metaphors depicting the atonement.

Luther's sermons on 1 Corinthians 15 (1533) proclaiming Christ's atonement for sinners clearly presupposed his understanding of sin and death, anchoring the need for atonement in human sin. On 15:56–57, the Wittenberg reformer observed, "Saint Paul now calls sin death's spear or weapon as though he were to say, 'If it were not for sin, death would surely have to desist from slaying....' Sinners squirm and die when sin's accusation confronts them, saying 'Alas! What did you do! How you angered God!'" Despair and terror over sin drives some to sudden death or suicide. Sin's power to terrify and kill comes from God's law.

> The Man Jesus Christ has come and has assumed and borne our sin and death, which we had justly deserved, and that he now steps forth in our behalf, confronts the law, sin, and death. He says, "I am of the same flesh and blood; these are my brothers and sisters. What they did, I did; and I paid for it. Law, if you want to condemn them, condemn me. Sin, if you want to bite and kill them, bite me. Death, if you want to consume and devour, devour me." ...Therefore, he also calls himself a sinner in Scripture. (Ps. 41:4, 69:9)

However,

> through the very event by which they expected to exterminate him and to win the victory he emerged again and said to the law, sin, and death, "Do you not

know that I am your Lord and God? What right do you have to accuse and to slay your lord? Therefore you shall do this no more; but, rather, I will accuse and condemn you and dispatch you so completely that you will henceforth have no claim on anyone who believes in me. For what I did, I did for their sake." … In this way we have a complete victory in Christ, now spiritually by faith but later also physically and visibly. (WA36:688,37-696,16, LW28:208-213)

Christ's victory as the second half of his atoning work naturally emerged prominently in his Easter preaching as well as his lectures to students. To them Luther affirmed Christ's "victory over the law, sin, our flesh, the world, the devil, death, hell, and all evils"—a rather complete catalog of the enemies of the believer—as the basis of the sinner's restoration to righteousness in God's sight. "Even though these tyrants, our enemies, accuse and terrify us, they cannot drive us into despair or condemn us. For Christ, whom God the Father raised from the dead, is victor over them, and he is our righteousness" (WA40,1;65,10-18; LW26:21-22). The lectures on Galatians also highlighted Luther's motif of Christ's magnificent duel with Satan, which attained atonement through victory over the Evil One and every evil. Christ's

> victory is a victory over the Law, sin, our flesh, the world, the devil, death, hell, and all evils; and this victory of his he has given to us. Even though these tyrants, our enemies, accuse us and terrify us, they cannot drive us into despair or condemn us. For Christ, whom God the Father raised from the dead, is Victor over them, and he is our righteousness. (WA40,1:65,12-17; LW26:21-22; WA40,1:439,17-27; WA26:281; Rieske-Braun, 66-100)

In 1544 the account of Christ's resurrection in Mark 16 served as Luther's Easter text. He emphasized the parallel nature of God's original creation in Genesis 1 and recreation on the basis of Christ's atoning work. God's original work of creation had "gotten moldy, obsolete, obscured, so that we could hardly recognize it as creation. Now there is a new day, a new beginning. Christ has renewed us, polished us up, made us new—yes, even us! That is a joyous proclamation of God's mercy, which he began and completed in his dear Son" (WA49:353,25-31). On Christ's cross he completed everything—eternal life and righteousness. "He drowned and lynched death, sin, and hell and broke them to pieces—all of them disappeared. There they all are hanging on the gallows in the bright sun, condemned, accursed." Luther summarized the battle that had ended in Christ's victory with a reference to Colossians 2:15 with its comparison of the resurrection to a Roman parade of triumph, which put the conquered powers on public display in a spectacle of shame (WA49:353,33-354,31). This victory becomes complete on Pentecost when the Holy Spirit brings God's people to faith, giving them life and righteousness, even though it may not seem visible in the midst of a sinful world (WA49:355,32–357,25). As he moved toward the completion of his sermon, he emphasized: "Christ died for me, that the sin in me should be dead and that righteousness might be alive in me again," Luther created several brief dialogs to drive home his point. The law addressed fallen human nature, "You have sinned, you belong to the devil," to which that nature must agree. Luther urged this nature to open its eyes to the gospel and listen: Christ is not to be found among the dead. He has devoured and strangled the law, the devil, and death. The sinner should look all three in eye and say, "Don't you know that the man who is named Christ has chomped you down? He has strangled you. He chewed you up again and today has risen from the dead. The battle is over" (WA49:357,30–37).

Simple, without elaborate explanation, Luther's proclamation of Christ's atonement confessed God's mysterious plan of salvation through the complete destruction of the sinner's identity through Christ's death and his burial of sinners in his tomb, and the raising up of new creatures through his resurrection for the life of trust that follows in his footsteps. Integrated into the reformer's doctrine of justification by faith, atonement and justification stand inseparable at the heart of this theology.

Bibliography

Arnold, "Luther on Christ's Person and Work," in *The Oxford Handbook of Martin Luther's Theology*, 2014.
Aulén, *Christus Victor*, 1969.
The Book of Concord, ed. Kolb and Wengert, 2000.
Dingel, ed. *Die Bekenntnisschriften der Evangelisch-Lutherischen Kirche*, 1992.
Haikola, *Studien zu Luther und zum Luthertum*, 1958.
Hamm, *Religiosität im späten Mittelalter*, 2011.
Kolb, "Resurrection and Justification. Luther's Use of Romans 4,25," *Lutherjahrbuch* 78, 2011.
Luther, *Die Bekenntnisschriften der evangelisch-lutherischen Kirche*, 11th ed., 1992.
Luther, *Luther's Works*, 1958–1986.
Luther, *Martin Luthers Werke*, 1883–1993.
Oberman, *The Harvest of Medieval Theology*, 1967.
Peters, *Kommentar zu Luthers Katechismen, Band 2*, 1991.
Rieske-Braun, *Duellum mirabile*, 1999.
Siggins, *Martin Luther's Doctrine of Christ*, 1970.

Major Prophets

Mark S. Gignilliat

A theological engagement with the prophets necessitates close attention to the words of the text *and* to the subject matter of Holy Scripture: the two are insoluble. All the achievements of modern criticism notwithstanding, the relationship between Scripture's verbal character and its theological subject matter strains under the governing assumptions of modern criticism. While Old Testament exegetes by and large resist the unrestrained imposition of Christian categories onto the Old Testament's literal sense, some theological effort is necessary for making substantial and organic connections between the testaments on matters of central, theological importance. The atonement is undoubtedly one of these topics.

The Major Prophets—Isaiah, Jeremiah, and Ezekiel—offer no tightly packaged "doctrine of the atonement." Such a claim comes as no surprise because the whole of the Christian Bible offers no tightly packaged doctrine of anything. The hard and patient task of Christian theology is an attentive listening to the polyphonic voices of Scripture in search of a complex yet unified understanding of the doctrine under investigation. Karl Barth reminds us that theology is not a repeating of what the apostles and prophets said but an attendance to "what we should say on the basis of what the apostles and prophets said" (*CD* I/1, 16). In this case, the church has long wrestled with what to say about the atonement on the basis of what the apostles and prophets have said.

This chapter aims at providing exegetical and interpretive questions for the Major Prophets as an initial step toward first-order theological reflection. Put in negative terms, it is not a comprehensive overview of the Major Prophets on the atonement. Rather, it is an aid to research for students trying to frame good exegetical questions in their reading of Isaiah, Jeremiah, and Ezekiel.

To gain purchase on these questions, several focal points will come under consideration. First, what are the particular terms that come within the lexical field of God's reconciliation of sinners to himself? Second, because there is a danger in confusing words with concepts, the conceptual matters in need of inquiry will be addressed. For example, the means of forgiveness within the prophets are multivalent and speak to the multifaceted nature of atonement in the prophets. Finally, our attention will focus on Isaiah 53 and the scholarly discussion of "place-taking" (*Stellvertretung*). Does a Christian notion of vicarious nature of the atonement have Old Testament warrant? Again, no promises of comprehensiveness are on offer, but these three subject-headings may help students to make initial step in pursuit of their own research.

Two of the more significant lexical matters relating to atonement are the various forms of *kōpēr*, the lexeme associated with atonement, and verbs within the lexical field of forgiveness, namely, *nāśā' 'āwōn*, *sālaḥ*, and, again, *kippēr* (verbal form of *kōpēr*). The basic meaning of *kōpēr* is contested. Though most often translated simply as "atone," the term's etymology betrays easy solutions. The term's unresolved(able) status trades on whether *kōpēr* in its basic sense means to cover or to wipe. Our attention will return to this lexical conundrum in the next section. The term *kōpēr* does not appear very often in the prophets. Its presence in Leviticus is replete and there is no shortage of debate regarding the connotative effect of this term, for example, does *kōpēr* relate to expiation or propitiation? The cultic context of *kōpēr* is the Day of Atonement (*Yom Kippur*) in Leviticus 16 where the holiness and purity of the temple and people are in view (Nidotte, *ad loc*). The cultic atonement rituals associated with various sacrifices (burnt, sin, and cereal) appear in Ezekiel 43:18–27 and 45:15–17. Zimmerli clarifies the import of these priestly atoning rituals: "Thus, in the context of the consecration of the altar in Ezekiel 43 it is a question not only of a sanctifying of what was previously profane, but of a removal of the sinful substance which is contrary to God and which clings to the altar which has been man-made of earthly material" (433).

Two texts in particular come into view with *kōpēr* in the Major Prophets: Isaiah 6:7 and Ezekiel 16:63. The former scene is the atonement of Isaiah's sins by means of the burning coals placed on his lips by the seraphim. One particular facet of this text remains elusive, namely, why the placing of hot coals on Isaiah's lips has its atoning effect. Readers of Isaiah are left wondering at this point. What is clear, however, is Isaiah's need for atonement and the atoning effect of the hot coals to remove or wash away his iniquity. No atonement ritual takes place; no *μ¦‰¹ºâ* (sin offering) is offered. Atonement takes place by means of this act. The atoning effect of the hot coals raises an issue we will encounter more fully in the next section. One has within the Old Testament a forgiveness theology—God can forgive sins from his great mercy apart from any ritual—and a priestly theology that attaches atonement to the ritual acts of sacrifice. Isaiah's scene relates, even if tangentially, to the former and not the latter. God can forgive sins at his good pleasure and apart from ritual expiatory acts (cf. Hosea 6:1).

Ezekiel 16 follows one aspect of Isaiah's use of *kōpēr*. God acts unilaterally to forgive sins. But Ezekiel diverges from Isaiah's use in a significant way. Isaiah is conscious of his sinful state and desperate need before the atoning act takes place. Repentance leads, in this case, to atonement. In Ezekiel, however, the unilateral atonement of the people's sin takes place apart from their conscious recognition of sin. The atoning act of forgiveness leads to the knowledge of their sin and shame. Paul's admonition that God's kindness is intended to lead to repentance (Rom. 2:4) shares Ezekiel's outlook. Atonement as forgiveness is the immediate cause for remembering and acknowledging covenant infidelity. Humility remains the final outcome.

Investigation into the use of *kōpēr* would need to expand its semantic scope to include *nāśā' 'āwōn* and *sālaḥ*. Both terms relate specifically to the forgiveness of sins. The former is of particular importance because the "bearing away" of sin (*'āwōn, μα‰‰¹⁰, peša'*), most often translated simply as "forgive(ness)," may provide insight into sin's nature—sin and punishment bound together in one term—and why forgiveness of sin demands its carrying or bearing off. The term may refer to "carrying a burden" and "removing a burden." Sin, according to this lexical construal, is a burden to be borne or lifted off. The prophet Ezekiel's "bearing" of the weight of sin in his prophetic act of lying on his side signals this notion of sin as a weight (Ez. 4:4–6). The vicarious activity of Isaiah's servant entails the "bearing" of sin's burden and its effectual "lifting off" (Isa. 53:12). In this respect, the "bearing" of sin involves its "taking away" (Koole, 341–342).

Sālaḥ is not as frequent a term for forgiveness as *nāśā' 'āwōn*. Still, it falls within the purview of the subject matter. Of particular importance is the sole predication of Yahweh with this verb. Yahweh alone offers *sālaḥ*. While the ritual activity of the priest may effectuate atonement (*kōpēr*; Lev 4:31), *sālaḥ* is the lone activity of Yahweh (TLOT, vol. 2, 798). The promise of a new covenant in Jeremiah's Book of Consolation has the forgiveness of sins as a central future promise (Jer. 31:31–34).

Identifying the linguistic field for atonement/forgiveness in the prophets starts a conversation. It does not end one. Anthony Thiselton understands the limits of lexical study in his own engagement with the Greek term *hilasterion* (the Greek term associated semantically with *kōpēr*). He claims that the contested meaning of the term can be adjudicated "only within the appropriate horizons of understanding, not by lexicography alone" (Thiselton, 332). In other words, identifying and explaining words lexically does not always lead to a clear connotative or denotative end nor does it suffice for a full view of the subject matter.

By way of illustration, does *kōpēr* have as its basic meaning to wipe or to cover? Sorting this etymological matter out is not straightforward or, for that matter, likely. Even if the thorny lexical issues can be determined, the next move toward understanding what the term signifies given its particular use across large swaths of texts presents its own challenges. This lexical situation is not necessarily bleak. But its reality points to the fact that one must navigate a broader path of inquiry than the lexical and denotative alone. Within the context of this particular investigation, atonement within the prophets must reach beyond lexical matters to include broader conceptual and thematic matters pertaining to the subject, for example, restoration after exile and beyond (Isa. 40–42, 60–61).

A thorny problem for Old Testament interpretation remains sorting out the diachronic and synchronic aspects of the text. The different theologies, say, between the priestly tradition which links atonement to cultic ritual and the prophets where the religious abuses of ritual are highlighted along with God's unilateral initiative to forgive apart from ritual means, are not easily negotiated along diachronic lines of inquiry. From a religious-historical perspective, imaginative and reasoned socio/religious historical projections may account for these differences. But the fact that they are embedded in texts Christians and Jews understand as Sacred Scripture remains a matter for canonical and hermeneutical reflection.

Another matter of some consequence that follows from the above is the different understanding of forgiveness flowing from sacrifice/atonement and from vicarious representation. Hermann Spieckermann, for example, takes umbrage with Hartmut Gese and Bernd Janowski's mingling of vicarious representation and atonement. For Spieckermann, God accepts the blood of the sacrificial animal as life, the life that had been forfeited by sin and ritual impurity. "On the part of the offering, the blood is a gift due only to God, which, by granting atonement, he allocates anew as life to the one offering sacrifice. This has nothing to do with vicarious representation" (Feldmeier and Spieckermann, 314–315). The blood of the sacrifice is deemed by God as the means for replenishing the life depleted by the guilt of the one bringing the sacrifice. The sacrifice itself is not necessarily a place-taker for the guilty. The life is in the blood and reckoned so by God's own initiative.

The relationship between vicarious representation and sacrifice/atonement remains a disputed matter in the interpretation of Isaiah 53. Suffice it to say at this point, the notion of atonement via sacrifice and vicarious representation may have been distinguishable theological concepts at some point in the diachronic history of the Old Testament's compositional history. Nevertheless, they remain related to each other canonically because both have their source in divine grace with the "common objective of removing guilt and enabling life" (Feldmeier and Spieckermann, 315). The tradents of the biblical material did not see these various conceptualities of atonement/forgiveness in competition, the one with the other.

The three conceptualities of atonement via sacrifice, vicarious representation, and unilateral, divine forgiveness relate to each other on a common plane, and this despite their very real differences. This common plane is their source in God himself as one who initiates the reconciliation and purification of sinners to himself for the sake of continued fellowship and participation between God and humanity. God's gracious initiative toward humanity is rooted in God's own character to be a God for us. Yahweh is a judging self. Nevertheless, even his judgment has as its *telos* the reconciliation of sinners (Ez. 16). As Spieckermann claims, "Forgiveness is his *opus proprium*, judgment an *opus alienum*" (Feldmeier and Spieckermann, 316). The prophets may not offer a one-dimensional theory of atonement. What they do offer through various avenues to a complex subject-matter is a portrait of Israel's God whose basic character is toward mercy, even in his severity. Moreover, Israel's God takes the initiative in restoring the broken fellowship with humanity by various means: ritual sacrifice, vicarious representation, and unilateral forgiveness.

A text that demands particular attention is Isaiah 53. Few texts in the prophets are as influential and contested as this one. Questions pertaining to the identity of the servant figure, clarifying the "we" voice of the text, and the numerous textual difficulties contained therein result in an enormous amount of literature on this text. Again, comprehensive is not the aim here but a pointing finger in the right direction regarding Isaiah 53's material role in a Christian doctrine of the atonement.

Barth raises the question about penal substitution and whether it is a legitimate understanding of Jesus's atoning work. In short, did Jesus suffer our punishment for us? He is quick to note that the New Testament does not put this foot forward in its account of Jesus's atoning work. "But," he adds, "it cannot be completely rejected or evaded on this account." Barth's rationale for his none-too-quick dismissal of penal substitution is Isaiah 53's material role in a

Christian account of atonement. "If Jesus Christ has followed our way as sinners to the end to which it leads, in outer darkness, then we can say with that passage [Isaiah 53] from the Old Testament that He has suffered this punishment of ours" (Barth, *CD* IV/1, 253). Barth does not understand penal substitution as *the* all-encompassing theory of atonement. But what is of crucial hermeneutical importance is to note his insistence on the pressure Isaiah 53 puts on a Christian doctrine of atonement.

Of particular importance in this discussion is the notion of "place-taking" (German: *Stellvertretung*). Though many elements of this text remain obscure, what readers observe is the place-taking of the righteous Servant. Moreover, the effect of the Servant's suffering in the place of others is the making righteous of "the many" (Isa. 53:10–12). Contextually speaking, "the many" has within its purview the "many nations" of Isaiah 52:15. The scope of the servant's "place-taking" spills over the borders of Israel to the nations at large who themselves will benefit from the expunging of their guilt by the Servant's self-offering. The very obscurity of Isaiah 53's prehistory and its minimal impact intertextually on the expanding prophetic tradition makes the text all the more mysterious. It is as if the text is waiting for a referent.

Bernd Janowski has perhaps given the most sustained attention to the concept of "place-taking" (*Stellvertretung*) in the Old Testament (48–74). For Janowski, the lexical field of *nātan tahat* (given in place of/for), *sabāl*, or *nāśā'* (to bear) help clarify the character of "place-taking." He concludes, "It always means that one person, by some action or suffering, takes the 'place' of others who are not willing or able to take it up themselves" (43–53). Isaiah 53 is a signal text for the redemptive effects of a guiltless figure "taking the place" of the guilty.

Janowski addresses head on Kant's insistence that the place-taking of the guilty by the guiltless is nonsensical. The very nature of guilt, according to Kant, renders it nontransferable. But for Janowski, a text like Isaiah 53 provides fertile ground for the exploration of counterfactual evidence against Kant's basic premise. The net result of Janowski's reading is his understanding that the "we" voice throughout this text—Who has believed *our* message? 53:1—are those who recognize their own guilt in retrospect as the guilt born by the Servant's vicarious suffering "in their place."

In conclusion, atonement in the prophets is a theological concept whose borders expand within the prophets to include multiple lexical and conceptual spheres. As observed, lexical work pertaining to atonement and forgiveness is a first step but not a final one. Broader horizons of understanding are necessary to come to terms with sin, sin's nature, forgiveness, and the means toward reconciliation.

A few matters hover near the center of this conversation. First, Yahweh makes the initiative toward his people to make atonement/forgiveness possible and actual. Whether this is through sacrificial means (Ez. 43–44), vicarious sin-bearing (Isa. 53), or unilateral forgiveness (Ez. 16:63), Yahweh's proclivity toward mercy and reconciliation manifests itself throughout the prophets. Even Yahweh's acts of judgment come from the wrath of his love whose end is mercy. Second, the recognition of sin and necessity for repentance either leads to atonement/forgiveness (in the majority of cases) or is the result of atonement (Ez. 16:63). Atonement has as its chief aim the restoration of the fellowship between God and humanity torn asunder by sin. This restoration necessitates the knowledge of one's sinful state and a returning to the fellowship once abandoned. The prophets, like the whole of the Christian Bible, present the reconciliation of sinners with God by means of multiple metaphors and descriptions. This complex presentation of God's atoning work should not surprise readers of Scripture given the enormity of the subject matter.

Bibliography

Anderson, *Sin: A History*, 2009.

Childs, *Isaiah*, 2000.

Feldmeier and Spieckermann, *God of the Living*, 2011.

Greenberg, *Ezekiel 1–20*, 1983.

Gunton, *The Actuality of the Atonement*, 1988.

Janowski, "He Bore Our Sins: Isaiah 53 and the Drama of Taking Another's Place," in *The Suffering Servant*, 2004.

Janowski, *Stellvertretung*, 1997.

Koole, *Isaiah III, Vol. 2/Isaiah 49–55*, 1998.

Spieckermann, "The Conception and Prehistory of the Idea of Vicarious Suffering in the Old Testament," in *The Suffering Servant*, 2004.

Thiselton, *The Hermeneutics of Doctrine*, 2007.

Zimmerli, *Ezekiel 2*, 1983.

Matthew and Mark

Jonathan T. Pennington

It is not an accident that atonement has always been a central and foundational element of orthodox Christianity, even if it has been understood in a variety of ways. It is not an accident because the central and foundational documents of Christianity, the Gospels (or better, the singular fourfold Gospel book), put great emphasis on the sacrificial death of Jesus. In this, the Gospels are in continuity with the Old Testament's theme of cultic sacrifice for sin (cf. Leviticus) as well as the rest of the New Testament's theological instruction about the death and resurrection of Christ and its atoning value.

The Gospels serve as the keystone of the archway into Holy Scripture (Pennington). They consummate the story and teaching of the Jewish Scriptures and serve as the fount for the theological understanding and reflection in the Epistles. We should not be surprised, then, to find an important thread of continuity from the Old Testament through the Gospels and into the Epistles' teaching, all of which emphasize the atonement, now consummated and completed in Jesus the Christ.

In this chapter we will examine the meaning and function of the idea of the atonement in the first two Gospels, Matthew and Mark. Because there is so much overlap in content between Matthew and Mark, we will begin with Mark's account and subsequently comment on any additional elements regarding atonement found in Matthew.

Atonement in the Gospel According to Mark

It has long been noted that in many ways Mark's Gospel account reads like a Passion narrative with an extended introduction. This means that the clear focus of the Second Gospel is Jesus's suffering and death (what is called his "Passion"). Everything else in Mark points and leads up to the final week of Jesus's life, and when the story gets to that point it slows down to a snail's pace, giving the sense of how important and weighty these events are. This emphasis on the Passion is true of the other Gospels as well, but it is perhaps more keenly felt in Mark because of the breakneck speed and pace and urgency of his whole account—demons are cast out, storms are stilled, food is miraculously multiplied, all in a matter of paragraphs. This makes the radical change in pace at Jesus's last week all the more noticeable and felt. Whatever else we might say about Mark's purpose in writing, he sees the suffering and death of Jesus as of great importance among the many other important aspects of Jesus's coming in to the world. This does not explain what atonement means in Mark, but it inclines the reader to recognize that there is something very significant about Jesus's suffering and death that Mark wants his readers to understand. This then pushes us to consider what he might mean by this emphasis.

To answer this question with regards to atonement we must consider two matters: (1) the matrix of context in which Mark is thinking and writing; and (2) his own statements about the meaning of the atonement.

Mark's Matrix

The historical and canonical matrix in which Mark was written is clearly that of the Old Testament/Jewish Scriptures and the history and story of Israel (Hays). The stories about Jesus (both historically and canonically) do not come to us in a vacuum. Jesus was a Jew, living within the Old Covenant and the ancient (even in his day) story of Israel. Therefore, to understand the significance of who he was and what he did we must refer to the story of Israel as found in the Jewish Scriptures and the historical context of Second Temple Judaism during Jesus's day. When we do so, intentional links between Jesus's life, suffering, and death and the Old Testament emerge. The Old Testament in story and citation is constantly evoked and used as the explanatory mechanism (matrix) for what is happening in and through Jesus. The great emphasis that the Old Testament (and Old Covenant) put on the necessity of sacrificial, atoning death is both affirmed and brought to its completion by the Gospels' emphasis on this aspect of the coming of the Son of God into the world.

One obvious and immediate connection is how Jesus exemplifies the role of the Suffering Servant of Isaiah 53. While this complex and rich prophetic passage communicates many things, one clear theme is the idea of "place-taking" and forgiveness/healing granted through the suffering of God's Servant (Isa. 53:4–6). While the Gospel of Mark and the other Gospels do not explicitly offer Isaiah 53 as the way to interpret Jesus's Passion, they do so more powerfully and subtly by letting the savvy reader see that the description of this lowly, despised man of suffering in Isaiah matches precisely how Jesus is depicted. From the earliest days of Christian theology this is in fact how the Church understands it as well. In other words, the idea of a self-sacrificing Servant of God who will atone for his people's sins is built into the expectation and hope of the Old Testament prophets' vision (Bellinger and Farmer), and appropriated by the Gospel writers as such.

But even earlier than the prophets, God's foundational covenant with his chosen people Israel was based on a sin-sacrificial system that God himself instituted. With the Exodus God rescued his people from slavery in Egypt and made a covenant with them in the wilderness. This covenant included many and varied details on how God's people were meant to live in proper relationship to him and to each other. At the core of much of this covenantal instruction is the idea of sacrifice for atonement, including the most solemn holy day of the Jewish calendar, Yom Kippur or the Day of the Atonement (Lev. 16).

These ideas of a necessary sacrifice for sin and the hope of a substitution are the air that every Jewish person breathed and they form the natural background and worldview of the first-century Judaism into which Jesus came and from which Mark the Evangelist writes.

Mark's Witness

One does not have to read very far into Mark's Gospel to see this Jewish matrix and hope appear. The first character in the story, John the Baptist, preaches this message: a baptism of repentance for the forgiveness of sins (1:4), which Jesus reiterates as a call to repent and believe (1:15). This emphasis on the need to repent for sin and obtain forgiveness is directly connected to Jesus's coming. This raises the issue of why Jesus came and also evokes the idea of blood sacrifice so prevalent in the covenant.

This dominant theme of forgiveness of sins continues from the beginning as the story unfolds, with explicit high points such as Mark 2:1–12, where Jesus emphasizes his authority to forgive sins (2:10). Indeed, the overlapping ideas of forgiveness of sins and healing of diseases that is found in Isaiah 53 explains the same dual theme that Mark depicts, with Jesus healing many people and offering to them forgiveness. One might even say that the stories of Mark 1:21–3:6 interweave the instructions of Leviticus with the healings of Isaiah 53, showing Jesus as the culmination of both.

Jesus continues to heal various people (5:1–42, 6:53–56, 7:24–37, 8:22–26, 9:14–29, 10:46–52), perform many miracles that testify to his divine nature (4:35–41, 6:30–52, 8:1–10, 9:1–13), as well as teach people about the nature of God's coming kingdom (3:22–4:34, 7:1–23, 9:33–10:31). Peppered purposefully throughout this developing story is Jesus's threefold passion prediction (8:31, 9:30–32, 10:32–34). These important passages serve as a lodestar orienting all that Jesus is doing and saying toward his impending suffering, death, and resurrection. So far in the story there has been no explicit teaching on atonement, even though the emphasis on healing and forgiveness through death is prevalent (Bolt).

This changes in Mark 10:45 with Jesus's famous "ransom logion"—"The Son of Man came not to be served but to serve, and to give his life as a ransom for many" (ESV). Here Mark gives us the first explicit teaching on Jesus's purpose and the effect of his life, death, and resurrection: It is place-taking, a giving of himself in the place of others, reminiscent strongly of the same theme already observed in Isaiah 53 (Edwards). It is no accident that this ransom atonement saying occurs at the beginning of the last week of Jesus's life. In Mark 11 Jesus will enter Jerusalem and proceed directly to the great place of atonement, the Temple, where he performs a prophetic symbolic cursing of its distorted practices, culminating with another statement about the forgiveness of sins (11:12–25).

Jesus's Passion Week activities come to a climactic moment on the last night before his arrest, with the celebration of the Last Supper with his disciples (14:12–25). This event contains the fullest implicit and explicit theological explanation of Jesus's death and resurrection found in the Gospel. Implicitly, it is significant that Jesus's last supper and death are tied to the Passover, which was the great event celebrating God's salvation through blood sacrifice (Ex. 12). Jesus's death, then, is inextricably linked to God rescuing or ransoming his people through the blood sacrifice of an unblemished lamb, sparing the first-born of each household. Explicitly, the atonement is explained through the words Jesus uses to interpret this last supper. The broken bread represents his broken body; the poured-out blood represents his spilled blood; the partaking of both of these is partaking in a new covenant that is forward-looking to the restoration of the kingdom (14:22–25). In this, combined with the earlier ransom saying (10:45), Mark presents his understanding that Jesus came, lived, died, and rose again as a place-taker, providing the forgiveness of sins, offering a new covenant, and orienting his people toward the coming kingdom. Mark's record of the actual events following this Last Supper fill the rest of his account, with many details about Jesus's suffering, crucifixion, and resurrection. In these the theme of Jesus as the recipient of God's wrath is alluded to with references to the cup Jesus must drink, the noon-time darkness at his crucifixion, and his cry of dereliction. Each of these deepens the idea of Jesus as the great place-taker, with him experiencing the wrath of God instead of his followers (McKnight).

Additional Aspects of Atonement in the Gospel According to Matthew

Regardless of the exact historical and literary relationship of the Gospel of Matthew to the Gospel of Mark, it is clear that Matthew shares the same material and vision of Mark while adding further theological reflection, including on the meaning of the atonement.

The biggest way in which the atonement theology of Matthew matches that of Mark is in their shared focus on Jesus's Passion, death, and resurrection. This four-Gospel emphasis does much to explain why the Epistles, which are occasional and more specific in their teaching, also highlight this aspect of the gospel message. Jesus's death (and resurrection) as atoning, as place-taking and resulting in a new, reconciled relationship with God, is a non-negotiable element in the understanding of the New Testament's witness.

Beyond this, Matthew also shares with Mark the two main Gospel texts that explain the atonement, the ransom saying (Mark 10:45; Mt. 20:28) and the words of the Last Supper (Mark 14:22–25; Mt. 26:26–29). In the case of the former, the context and wording is identical. In the case of the former, the content and wording matches almost exactly with the exception of a crucial additional line in Matthew (14:28): "This is my blood of the covenant, which is poured out for many *for the forgiveness of sins.*"

This additional phrase in no way contradicts or corrects Mark's shorter version. Matthew's additional phrase provides an explicit clarification and emphasis on the understanding of what Jesus's broken body and spilled blood will do—secure forgiveness of sins, which is the great effect of the atonement.

This extra phrase "for the forgiveness of sins" serves not only as a clarifier within the Last Supper account, but also functions as a matching bookend to the same point already made at the beginning of Matthew's Gospel. In the earliest moments of Matthew, the angel of the Lord appeared to Joseph, directing him to name the child "Jesus," which in Greek is the same name as "Joshua," which means "the Lord saves." The reason why the child should be given this special name is "because he will save his people from their sins" (Mt. 1:21). Thus, here in the first story of the First Gospel the reason for Jesus's coming into the world is described as "saving his people from their sins." The way God has instituted the forgiveness of sins is only through atoning sacrifice, precisely what Jesus is going to offer in ultimate form in himself. On the last night of his life he reiterates this truth in the words of the Last Supper.

Conclusion

Human nature is prone to imbalance and oversimplification, and the history of Christian theology is no exception. While it would be too narrow of a reading to say that the singular point of Matthew and Mark is to present Jesus as an atoning sacrifice, a careful reading of the Gospels shows this is at least a central focal point. There are many other goals that the Gospel writers apparently had: to explain Jesus's nature as human and divine; to tie Jesus's life to the history of Israel; to show that Jesus is bringing about God's kingdom; to cast vision for how to be in the world as Jesus's disciples, and so on. So it is overly reductionistic to read the Gospels as merely filling in the backstory to the Epistles' great emphasis on Jesus's saving and atoning sacrifice; they do far more than this. Nonetheless, the Gospels, including Matthew and Mark, do make clear that at the core of Jesus's coming into the world was to "give his life as a ransom for many," "saving his people from their sins." In biblical language this means providing an atonement that reconciles humanity with its God.

Select Bibliography

Bellinger and Farmer, *Jesus and the Suffering Servant*, 1998.
Bolt, *The Cross from a Distance*, 2004.

Edwards, *The Ransom Logion in Mark and Matthew*, 2012.
Hays, "The Canonical Matrix of the Gospels," in *The Cambridge Companion to the Gospels*, 2006.
McKnight, *Jesus and His Death*, 2005.
Pennington, *Reading the Gospels Wisely*, 2012.
Tidball, Hilborn, and Thacker, *The Atonement Debate*, 2008.

Ministry

Andrew Root

When it comes to the practice of ministry, discussions of atonement have become particularly confused. If ministry is the participation in divine action deep within the human experience, then it feels as if many classic atonement theories have significant disconnect. The existential depth of the human experience in Anselm's theory is dry and brittle next to the heat of God's atoning work, yet, Abelard's atonement theory seems to lose the otherness and potency of God's atoning work, giving us no vision for divine action that can do anything other than compassionately share in others' experience.

Those in ministry have often (maybe tacitly) felt stuck between these two weighty atonement perspectives, leading them to believe that understandings of atonement are academic and have little to do with the day-to-day practice of ministry. How might we understand experience in light of the atonement, giving us a way of thinking of the atonement for the sake of ministry? To answer these questions, we turn to the work of Eberhard Jüngel, who helps us hold together the cosmic action of God to atone for us, and the depth of our concrete and lived human experience.

For atonement to hold together divine action and human experience, while creating a space for ministry, we can follow Jüngel by exploring atonement within an existential framework, imagining atonement/justification as the articulation of the depth and contradiction of human existence. *Justification is God's coming to humanity to minister to us within our lived experiences of impossibility.* When we are careless in our formulation, atonement/justification takes on an overly legal framework, minimizing the living and life-giving nature of the justice which is the lived experience of God and those who are in God. Jüngel pushes justification from a merely legal framework into an existential one, allowing for atonement/justification to thrust us into the lived experience of God's unique justice. Justification is thus a lived and concrete perspective that looks for divine action in and through and within our many experiences of death, brokenness, and impossibility. This existential frame for atonement/justification frees it from potentially stale doctrine, making it the hermeneutic of divine action and the very shape of God's ministry.

This may lead some to scratch their heads, for it may seem that to move atonement/justification off the platform of the legal and onto the stage of the existential locks it into a perspective outside of revelation itself and into some opaque philosophy. Rather, it is the legal perspective that runs the risk of being an artificial philosophical conception, adopting Platonic and Aristotelian notions of perfection. The existential justification perspective Jüngel employs is animated by revelation itself, because it claims justification as the very shape of God's ministry; but again justification as existential/experiential and not as legal.

The existential/experiential dynamic of justification runs so deeply that it is bound in creation itself. Justification is not animated solely by human offense, but rests at the core of God's own being, forged as the shape of God's ministry to concrete human beings, as those bound to God through nothingness. Jüngel creatively binds justification with creation *ex nihilo*, asserting that justification and creation, so often standing in opposition within theological systems, are fused. For Jüngel to understand creation (as God's ministry) is to see it through the concrete experience of justification. Atonement is the fullness of God's ministry of coming to humanity through *ex nihilo*.

Justification is the continuation of God's coming through *ex nihilo*, with the culmination found in the turning of death into life, by God's Word (Jesus), which creates *ex nihilo*, and perishes *in nihilo*, so that through the perishing, through the nothingness, we might be born into new possibility (1 Pet. 3:18; cf. Jüngel, *Theological Essays I*, 113). This is God's very ministry, to *speak* possibility out of nothingness, starting in creation and culminating in the atoning work of justification. It is to create being from nonbeing, in and through God's giving of God's own being through becoming in the Word. Justification then is God's act to go into nothingness in our being (justification) or in the universe (creation) to bring forth justified existence out of nothingness. This going into nothingness is ministry that brings forth new possibility. It is then this ministry that enters death for the sake of new life that is atoning.

Nothingness stands as the opposition to God's ministry; it threatens the creation for which God unveils Godself to minister. Nothingness can threaten creation because God choses to create and act continually within creation as *possibility*, as a minister who brings the event of God's Word, and not as a hard deity of *actuality* that imposes a will outside the being of God's very self. *Nothingness can threaten God's creation because God chooses to be with creation as minister and not as static force* (Zizioulas).

But while this nothingness stands as a threat to all that is, leaving wives without husbands and children without fathers, nothingness cannot impose itself on God (Jüngel, *Justification*, 112). Rather, this nothingness has become the doorway into which God breaks as event (revelation). God's act is an act of possibility, and this possibility is seen only against the backdrop of nothingness. It is out of nothingness (*ex nihilo*) that God ministers. The nothingness is bound to God, by God acting, ministering through it, by God bringing possibility *out* of nothingness. The confession of creation *ex nihilo* is the claim that God's ministry is God's being as becoming out of nothing, that acts through nothingness itself.

So while God's Word stands over and against nothingness, the unbinding creativity of God's Word makes nothingness serve God, using it as the doorway into the possibility of God's act. For this act of God to remain always a possibility, it must come out of nothingness, therefore out of impossibility. The Word always speaks of possibility as it is the Word spoken over the void of nothingness that creates (Gen. 1:1–6), the Word spoken of the possibility of a dead womb that brings forth the promise (Gen. 21), the Word spoken of the possibility of an old man leading a people from slavery (Ex. 12), and the Word spoken as the possibility that a poor nobody virgin might bear the Word itself (Luke 1:30). God's ministry is always the Word of possibility. Possibility appears as an event next to, in, and through nothingness. Possibility can only shine with the force of a million suns against the backdrop of nothingness.

Nothingness, as in the beginning, is the stage set for divine action to come to human experience. Justification reinstates that nothingness, that death and sin, must serve God by becoming the location (the concrete place) of God's ministry, the space where nothingness is turned into something and turned into the all-new possibility of sharing in God's being as the becoming of ministry.

The cross stands arm in arm with creation *ex nihilo*, they are *the* two profound acts of God's ministry to give Godself to humanity through nothingness. In creation, God gives God's Word to the nothingness so that the possibility of creation might spring forth. And the Word, Jesus, perishes into nothingness, descending into the demonic nothingness that sin freed to exist outside the ministry of God, outside the creative Word itself. So in perishing, the Word descends into death to envelope it *again*, to bind nothingness once more to the creative Word, to make nothingness again serve the ministry of God. As it was in the beginning, as the Word created *ex nihilo*, as the ministry of God came out of nothingness, so in the cross, God as the Word itself goes into nothingness, atoning for us. God's ministry is framed by the twin movements of creation *ex nihilo* and cross *in nihilo*.

Now that the Word has both come out of and come into nothingness, nothingness is surrounded (in resurrection); it is forced again to serve God, by being as it was in the beginning, the stage of eternity breaking into time, the location of God's giving of Godself in ministry of justifying and atoning love. This is the depth of atonement because it happens at the ontological level, stretching to the existential state of our own being. As God gives God's being to create being out of nothingness, now in the cross God gives God's being again so that the estranged being of humanity might again share in God's own being (Athanasius, see *On Incarnation*). We are atoned and justified through the cross, for the cross turns our nothingness into possibility, our deaths into life.

God's ministry is to love creation, welcoming the creature to share in God's very being, but to share in it through nothingness (again at the ontological level, which is often missed when the minister leans on an Abelardian perspective). We share in God by being ministered to by God, by God coming to us *ex nihilo* and *in nihilo*. Atonement is not a result of God's just anger for being wronged; it is the fullness of God's cosmic ministry.

The cross is central because through the perishing Jesus, who is the eternal creative Word, nothingness itself is turned into life in the resurrection. Because this Jesus is the Word, and this Word is crucified, perishing (nothingness) is turned into possibility, and nothingness is again taken up in the creative act of God's ministry.

The resurrection turns perishing into possibility; *it makes concrete lived experiences of perishing the location of God's ministry*; the human experience of perishing becomes the locale to explore the breaking in of the divine into the human. Nothingness is transformed from the place of God's absence, to the place of God's presence through absence; this is atonement in ministerial frame. God's ministry is fulfilled in Jesus's death and resurrection (Jüngel, *Theological Essays I*, 109), for God's ministry, the place where the divine and human encounter each other, is shown to be the place where perishing turns into possibility—by the act of the Word itself.

So now where God should *not* be found, in death, God *is* found. God should not be found in a morgue, but he is. Jüngel says, "The death of God, in that it defines the being of God, changes death. In the event of God's death, God allows death to define his being, and thereby disposes of death. In the event of God's death, death is ordained to become a divine phenomenon" (quoted in Webster *Eberhard Jüngel*, 84). The concrete and lived places of God's absence are the very places where ministry begins, for it is in these places of nothingness that the creative Word moves, bringing new possibility. Jüngel states, "The cross reveals not just the fact that God is creator, but also the pattern or mode of God's creative activity" (DeHart, 122).

Human ministry that follows the atoning ministry of God seeks to attend to the places where God should not be found. When we speak of *the experience* of God's absence, when we attend to impossibility, when we invite those bearing impossibility to articulate their impossibilities, we trust again in the possibility of God's coming to us as minister. When such impossibilities are spoken they become shared. When nothingness is shared, ministry occurs; the divine shares in the human and new possibility spills forth with the chorus of new life.

We participate in God's being by taking God's form of ministry, by being ministers. But as ministers, our concrete actions are directed not toward the actualities we can create (big churches and powerful programs), but the call to share in concrete persons' experiences of nothingness (in their homelessness, in their hunger, in their nakedness [Mt. 25], their experience of the death of a loved one). We invite them to speak of nothingness, trusting that when the event of spoken nothingness is shared, the practice of ministry is so ignited that it connects the eternal with time.

We are justified to participate in God's being by joining God's ministry, to witness to God's turning of perishing into possibility, death into life. We are freed to be ministered to by God through our nothingness and therefore to minister to others through their own nothingness. When we share in the nothingness of the creation, participating in others' lives, we share in the divine act to turn what is broken and dead into new life.

The human minister participates in God by participating in the life of her neighbor, by being a minister; but this participation is not in itself a human act that can create an actuality. Atonement/justification claims the impotence of all human action, even human ministry. Rather, this human action, even as ministry, can *only* share in nothingness, proclaiming in its shared concrete humanity that the possibility of God's *own* act is on its way. In the love of one to another, in a love that seeks only the possibility of the other, the divine moves in and through us. We can join it because shared nothingness is not a work toward an actuality, but a *prayer* for God's being to come as a new possibility. Human ministry is deep sharing in the life of our neighbor, not as a work, but as a prayer for God's possibility to come in and through our shared nothingness.

Bibliography

Athanasius, *On Incarnation*
DeHart, *Beyond the Necessary God*, 1999.
Jüngel, *Justification*, 2001.
Jüngel, *Theological Essays I*, 1989.
Root, *Christopraxis*, 2014.
Webster, *Eberhard Jüngel*, 1986.
Zizioulas, "Created and Uncreated," in *Communion and Otherness*, 2007.

The Missions of the Divine Persons

Adonis Vidu

Atonement is the work of one who was sent. "But when the fullness of time had come, God sent forth his Son, born of a woman, born under the law, to redeem those who were under the law, so that we might receive adoption as sons. And because you are sons, God has sent the Spirit of his Son into your hearts, crying, 'Abba! Father!'" (Gal. 4:4–6). To claim that the reconciling work of Christ is the work of one sent from the Father is not a mere platitude. It is theologically interesting in that it presents a dogmatically appropriate approach to the work of Christ. This chapter will explore what contribution an approach through the doctrine of the missions of the divine persons might make to the doctrine of the atonement.

Scripture leaves us in no doubt that Jesus is one who comes as one sent from the Father (John 3:16–17; cf. John 5:37; 8:16; 14:26; 16:7, 17). However, even as sent from the Father, Christ makes the Father available to us: "Whoever receives me, receives not me but him who sent me." (Mark 9:37) The theme of the inseparability of Father and Son is replete in John. "Whoever has seen me has seen the Father" (John 14:9), Jesus proclaims in response to Philip's request to see the Father. Not only is the Father received through the sent Son, but the Spirit is as well, the promise of the Father, sent by the sent Son (Luke 24:49).

The Western theological tradition regarded the theme of "mission" as theologically significant, even central. In its earliest phases, the theme provided a focus for the debates over the divinity and equality of the Son with the Father. Arians and others readily appealed to these mission-texts as demonstrating the inferiority and subordination of the Son to the Father. In response, pro-Nicene theologians sought to demonstrate the coherence of the respective missions of the Son and the Spirit with their equality with the Father and full divinity.

Augustine applies an exacting Christological hermeneutic of the two natures to show that the Son's being sent implies no inferiority to the Father (Augustine, Bk. IV, chapter 5). Simultaneously, however, his being sent does reveal something of the eternal identity of the Son, namely, his proceeding from the Father as Word (Augustine, Bk. IV, chapter 5). So the mission reveals to us something about the very procession of the Son, a theme to be exploited later by Aquinas.

A second dimension of mission developed by Augustine is the claim that the one sent does not begin to exist where he wasn't before. Here Augustine is correlating the biblical language with the divine attributes of preexistence, omnipresence, and immensity. Appealing to John 1:10, he says about the Son, "where he was sent he already was" (Augustine, Bk. II, chapter 2).

Finally, Augustine seeks to correlate the notion of the sending with his other central insight about the inseparability of external Trinitarian works (*opera ad extra*). He argues that while the persons are acting inseparably in the production of created effects (e.g., the voice from heaven, the dove, the human nature of Jesus Christ), nevertheless the distinct persons are manifested distinctly through these created effects (Augustine, Bk. IV, chapter 5).

Aquinas develops the Augustinian legacy in a number of significant ways (Q.43). Space permits only highlighting some of these directions. First, Aquinas develops the Augustinian point that the missions reveal the processions. He defines a mission as a procession to which a created effect is added. While this created effect is produced by the whole Trinity, it nonetheless reveals and mediates communion with distinct Trinitarian persons. Second, Aquinas reiterates the two dimensions already noted by Augustine: the person sent does not arrive at a place where he was not previously present; and the person sent does not leave its place of origin, as it were. Together these aspects consolidate the fundamental insight that the mission of the divine persons are simply an extension of the Trinitarian life to the creature.

Precisely in this consists the soteriological significance of the divine missions. Gilles Emery is right to claim that "the doctrine of salvation *is* the doctrine of the missions of the Son and of the Holy Spirit ... This approach shows well that salvation resides in the Trinity itself, because the missions bear in themselves the eternal mystery of the divine persons, the mystery of the Son begotten by the Father and the mystery of the Holy Spirit who proceeds" (193).

Unpacking this claim, and approaching the doctrine of the atonement through the missions of the Son and the Holy Spirit, as explained above, has a number of implications.

First, the historical actions of the man Jesus Christ need to be placed in the context of his mission as the sent Son. In an Augustinian/Thomistic framework this would mean that these actions are precisely the actions of God, the very presence of God among us. John Webster refers to the history of Christ's actions as "commissioned history," pointing out that it is only soteriologically significant if seen as the action of God in Jesus Christ. Christ has no human works as such, he claims: "There is no such one; there is only the human Jesus whose coming is the descent to us of the 'very majesty of God'" (Webster, 157).

This raises, second, the issue of the instrumentality of Christ's human works in relation to the divine action. The doctrine of divine missions holds, as Bernard Lonergan has explained at some length, that the human actions of Jesus are not causal conditions or constitutive causes, but consequent conditions of the divine action (439, 441, 443). If the actions of Jesus are always enhypostatic actions of the Logos, and further if this Logos' actions are inseparable from the actions of the Father and the Spirit, it follows that the historical and economic works of Christ cannot be conditions of the ultimate divine action. This undercuts claims that the incarnate Son enables divine forgiveness, or any other divine action, from the human side, as it were (Vidu).

Barth brings about this point in stressing that the power of the saving work of Christ is rooted in his divinity: "The presupposition of the atonement is a single, self-sufficient, independent work of God in itself" (*CD* IV/1, 49). The instrumentality of Christ's actions is not causal in relation to God, but consequent upon God's eternal decision to save. As such, "God does not need reconciliation with men, but men need reconciliation with Him" (*CD* IV/1, 74). The manner in which he accomplishes this is through his very presence. While Barth does not self-consciously employ the terminology of missions, the result is identical: "It means that in being present and active in the world in Christ, God takes part in its history. He does not affirm or participate in its culpable nature, its enmity against Himself, but He does take it upon Himself, making His own the situation in which it has fallen" (*CD* IV/1, 75). In not so many words, Barth gives voice to the fundamental insight of an approach through the missions: Jesus Christ is soteriologically significant primarily because he is the manifestation of God among us. Christ saves primarily in that he extends to us his filiation (by adoption) and his mutual love with the Father (by the pouring out of their common love. Cf. Rom 5:5). If the economic works of the Son are causal conditions for anything, it must be something on the human side, not the divine side.

From this vantage point there seems to be a prioritization of the person of Christ as the God-man over his work, such that his work is a function of his person, rather than the other way around. This need not imply any neglect of the human dimensions of his work (e.g., his human will, obedience, sacrifice, etc.), but it stresses their proper logical ordering as consequent conditions of the prior "decree" of salvation (see Barth on the priority of the Covenant, of election, etc.). This need not imply an abandonment of satisfaction or penal substitution models, although it will deny that either Christ's sacrifice or his penal death are necessary precursors to divine forgiveness.

A third area of the significance of an approach through missions relates to the inseparability of the missions of the Son and the Spirit. Although not without opposition, this tradition stresses that the three persons act inseparably in the economy to produce effects together. It becomes then problematic to so individuate Trinitarian action that certain effects are ascribed to just one of the divine persons. This will result in a critique of the artificial dichotomy between objective and subjective soteriology, between the work of the Son and the work of the Spirit, between justification and sanctification. While these distinctions are still useful, they will acquire a new significance in light of the stress on the fundamental unity of God's saving missions.

In closing, a number of objections and loose ends need to be pointed out. First, the historical tethering of the doctrine of missions to the doctrine of inseparable operations is being undone in certain quarters, usually on the background of a suspicion about the latter doctrine. On the traditional framework, missions are not separate actions in their own right, but dimensions of the one inseparable work of the Trinity. The divine persons give themselves to us in and through their created effects (created grace, the human nature of Jesus Christ, tongues of fire, etc.). When decoupled from the doctrine of inseparable operations, missions are no longer "particular aspects of broader divine operations" (Holmes, 73), but action tokens in their own right. Proponents of such an approach will insist that it preserves the individuation and identifiability of the distinct persons through their missions (Rahner, 343–346; LaCugna, 99). Critics, on the other hand, fear that it compromises divine transcendence, unity, and simplicity (Marshall, "The Unity of the Triune God," 1–32; Ormerod, 125–141). Moreover, it raises issues about the unity of the two missions and thus the link between the particular and historical work of Christ and the work of the Spirit, to which some wish to ascribe more autonomy (Johnson; Marshall, "What Does the Spirit Have to Do?").

Second, as hinted above, an approach through the missions runs counter to much modern Christology, with the latter's almost exclusive concentration on the human history of Jesus. The challenge of a missional doctrine of the atonement is to resist a docetist relapse, without, however, compromising divine self-sufficiency and prevenience (Dalferth). Such a tension is readily to be seen in Barth and his followers, especially in the so-called Trinity and election controversy.

The doctrine of the mission of the divine persons invites us to reconsider anew the historical activity of God in ways that are consistent with his Trinitarian nature. This task includes reconsidering the historical reconciling work of Christ as the Trinitarian action of the free God.

Bibliography

Aquinas, *Summa Theologica*, 1981.
Augustine, *The Trinity*, trans. Hill, 2015.
Barth, *Church Dogmatics*, 1956.
Dalferth, *Crucified and Resurrected*, 2015.
Emery, *The Trinity*, 2011.
Holmes, "Trinitarian Action and Inseparable Operations," in *Advancing Trinitarian Theology*, 2014.
Johnson, *Rethinking the Trinity and Religious Pluralism*, 2011.
LaCugna, *God for Us*, 1991.
Lonergan, *The Triune God*, 2007.
Marshall, "The Unity of the Triune God: Reviving an Ancient Question," *The Thomist* 74, 2010.
Marshall, "What Does the Spirit Have to Do?," in *Reading John with St. Thomas Aquinas*, 2010.
Ormerod, *The Trinity*, 2005.
Rahner, "Some Implications of the Scholastic Concept of Uncreated Grace," *Theological Investigations I*, 1965.
Rahner, *The Trinity*, 1970.
Vidu, "Trinity, the Cross, and Necessity," forthcoming in *Irish Theological Quarterly*.
Webster, *God without Measure. Volume 1*, 2016.

Jürgen Moltmann

Matthias Grebe

We can observe three major influences on Jürgen Moltmann's particular understanding of the atonement (Bauckham, 149). The first is the dialectical method of interpreting the cross and resurrection. This is based on the work of the philosopher Georg Wilhelm Friedrich Hegel and the theologian Hans-Joachim Iwand, and became the underlying principle of Moltmann's Trinitarian doctrine of atonement. The second major influence on his atonement theology is his own biblical exegesis, which Moltmann takes as the grounding norm of his systematic outworking. Here he was strongly influenced by his teachers at Göttingen, Ernst Käsemann (in New Testament) and Gerhard von Rad (Old Testament). Third, Moltmann's eschatological perspective of the Kingdom of God and the ethical implications for the mission of the church provided his overarching theological perspective. Otto Weber and the Dutch theologians Arnold Albert van Ruler and Johannes Christiaan Hoekendijk, and the latter notion, by Ernst Wolf and the work of Dietrich Bonhoeffer, influenced his eschatology.

The following study of Moltmann's understanding of the saving work of Christ examines his doctrine of the atonement as it appears in *The Crucified God* (particularly chapter 4 *The Historical Trial of Jesus* and chapter 6 *The "Crucified God"*).

For Moltmann, the history of Jesus of Nazareth and his crucifixion represent the very foundation of theology. In *The Crucified God*, he writes that Jesus's death on the cross is the "*centre* of all Christian theology. It is not only the theme of theology, but it is in effect the entry to its problems and answers on earth. All Christian statements about God, about creation, about sin and death have their focal point in the crucified Christ" (210; emphasis in the original). Moltmann describes Lutheran Christology and soteriology in the sense of a *theologia crucis*, which highlights the dialectic between cross and resurrection from a theodical point of view. He therefore considers the cross from the perspective of God's love, suffering, and solidarity, asking "How can a God of love be justified before a suffering humanity?" "The cross of the Son," Moltmann maintains, "divides God from God to the utmost degree of enmity and distinction. The resurrection of the Son abandoned by God unites God with God in the most intimate fellowship" (154f). Thus the center of theology occupies both *the cross of the risen Christ* and the *resurrection of the crucified Christ* (210).

Bauckham summarizes this dialectic as follows: "The cross and the resurrection are taken to represent opposites: death and life, the absence of God and the presence of God. Yet the crucified and risen Jesus is the same Jesus in this total contradiction" (149). The contradiction of cross and resurrection correspond, according to Moltmann, to the reality in the *here and now* and the promises of God of the *not yet*.

On the cross, we see Jesus's love for the world in his completely identifying himself with the fallen human condition and the state of the world in all its negativity, dying a godforsaken death in solidarity with the godforsaken, and becoming a fellow-suffer with those who suffer. Moltmann states, however, "though they are godless, they are not godforsaken, precisely because God has abandoned his own Son and has delivered him up for them" (251). He understands the verb "deliver up" ($\pi\alpha\rho\alpha\delta\iota\delta\acute{o}\nu\alpha\iota$—Rom. 1:18f., 8:31f., and Gal. 2:20) in a negative sense and interprets Pauline atonement theology in light of verses such as 2 Corinthians 5:21 and Galatians 3:13, which he places alongside the *kenosis* of the Son as described in the Christ-hymn in Philippians 2. Together, these prompt his conclusion that when the *Logos* was incarnate in the man Jesus of Nazareth, he not only entered into the finitude and godforsakenness of humanity, but was also delivered up by God to die the violent death of a criminal on the cross. Moltmann therefore contends that Jesus's "death was not a 'fine death,' as he died as somebody rejected by his God" (148) and abandoned by his disciples.

The torment that Jesus experiences on the cross is expressed by his cry of dereliction, a cry with which (according to Moltmann) every theology needs to come to terms. It is, he maintains, the abandonment by the Father, the ultimate rejection by God, "which separates the Son from the Father [and] is something which takes place within God himself; it is *stasis* within God—'God against God'" (154). In viewing Jesus as abandoned and forsaken by God, Moltmann constructs a Trinitarian theology of the cross, an event between the Father and the incarnate Son. It is in their deepest separation that Father and Son are united in the perichoretic saving work of the world through the bond of love, the Holy Spirit. Their love for each other bridges the gap in their separation and is the foundation of the Trinitarian relational community of the divine persons. In this way, Moltmann incorporates this experience of abandonment and suffering into the life of the Godhead itself.

Since Jesus was raised from the dead, his risen life represents something of a contradiction to the cross. Moltmann sees the resurrection as the first fruits of God's promise of a new creation, mediating the salvific presence of God to the "godless and godforsaken." In the love between Father and Son, the Spirit opens up a hopeful future and creates new life, thereby giving hope to a world of plight, transforming it into the Kingdom of God. It is God's eschatological action, showing that the Kingdom of God will bring about a different and better world, without evil, suffering, and death; a world in which God's presence will be dwelling in all things. Thus the central theme of *The Crucified God* is God's "suffering" love and his all-embracing solidarity with those who suffer. In this way, not only does Moltmann's doctrine of the atonement alter the traditional doctrine of divine impassibility and mutability, as he sees that God both affects and is affected by the world, but his understanding of a social Trinity also allows him to observe a reciprocal relationship between God and world. In this, God and world do not dissolve into one, but rather, there is a real interaction between the two.

Ultimately, Jürgen Moltmann's theology of the cross rests on a strong theology of abandonment. We have seen that according to Moltmann, the cross was an event between "God and God," which reveals God's own suffering and solidarity with the godforsaken. However, a closer look reveals some apparent internal contradictions or logical incoherencies in Moltmann's view. Although he seeks to offer a Trinitarian account of the atonement, seeing the Spirit as the "link in the separation" between Father and Son, some of Moltmann's statements regarding separation remain puzzling. He writes, "It was a deep division in God himself, in so far as God abandoned God and contradicted himself, and at the same time a unity in God, in so far as God was at one with God and corresponded to himself" (253). Here, Moltmann seeks simultaneously to express both sides of a contradiction: he maintains that the Son is abandoned on the cross (Father and the Son are divided to the upmost degree) but at the same time, he is at pains to highlight the unity between Father and Son in the atoning work (the Father's own activity and suffering in the dying Jesus). And yet what he is expressing is exactly that; a contradiction, which raises questions that Moltmann fails to answer. Either the Father and Son are separated on the cross, or the Spirit, which would necessarily indicate that they are not separated and the Son is not abandoned, unites them.

However, the very idea of God being against God, of one person of the Trinity being abandoned by the other, is itself problematic for many. Does the Father really abandon his own Son, an innocent sufferer? And if so, how can this Father also come to represent love and a reason for hope to the godforsaken?

What is lacking in Moltmann's atonement theology of identification with the godless is a biblical understanding of the rejection of sin by the Trinitarian God. He describes something of a metaphysical separation between Father and Son, but does not handle the biblical account of the condemnation of sin on the cross in light of the cultic and substitutionary atonement, and the reconciliation achieved. As I argue elsewhere (Grebe), the cross cannot and should not be seen as an event in which "God is against God," the Son abandoned by the Father. Instead, by highlighting that the Father works *in*, *through*, and *with* the Son in the perichoretic unity and power of the Spirit, toward the reconciliation of the world, we not only arrive at a fuller Trinitarian theology, but also shed new light on the atonement. When seen from this perspective, the cross does not display "God against God" but instead "God against sin and evil," in this way revealing God's action of love toward humanity "for us and for our salvation."

Bibliography

Bauckham, "Jürgen Moltmann," in *The Modern Theologians*, 2005.
Grebe, *Election, Atonement, and the Holy Spirit*, 2014.
Moltmann, *The Crucified God*, 1974.

Munus Triplex

Adam J. Johnson

The doctrine of the *munus triplex* (Christ's threefold mediatorial office as prophet, priest, and king) is a traditional schema for understanding the person and work of Jesus Christ, as the one who fulfilled in his person and work those offices distinguished by anointing with oil in the Old Testament. Found in many popular and academic works today, the doctrine remains a significant conceptual tool by means of which to account for the unity of the doctrine of the work of Christ.[1]

One form of the current interest in this conceptual scheme revolves around the way that the unified diversity inherent within the tripartite *office* of Christ suggests a tripartite *work* of Christ. It thus unifies what are often thought to be the three main aspects of Christ's atoning work: his substitutionary sacrifice, his defeat of Satan, and the example he provides us. For example, Robert Sherman argues that "theology should recognize a certain correspondence and mutual support between the three persons of the Trinity, the threefold office of Christ, and the three commonly recognized models of his atoning work," offering what is to date one of the more detailed biblical accounts of the relationship between the *munus triplex* and the doctrine of the atonement (xx). While his thesis concerning the doctrine of the Trinity is problematic, many are sympathetic when it comes to using this scheme to unify their account of Christ's atoning work, for the unified diversity proper to the threefold office would seem to bear promising fruit for integrating the diverse aspects of Christ's work (cf. Torrance; Van Dyk; Wainwright; and Williams).

---

[1] An expanded version of this chapter appeared originally as Adam Johnson, "Munus Triplex and Atonement," *SJT* 65:2, 2012, 159–173, © Cambridge University Press 2012, reproduced with permission.

Karl Barth may be one of the most aggressive developers of the role of the *munus triplex* within his theology (and with him, T. F. Torrance), organizing much of his *Church Dogmatics*, volume 4, around this scheme. But even though he is eager to show that in retrospect his constructive project aligns with the traditional view, he does not rely upon the *munus triplex* for the material or formal content of his doctrine of reconciliation in the *Church Dogmatics* (Johnson).

While there is much to appreciate in this line of thought, particularly the way that it draws on the Old Testament for its understanding of the work of Christ (Pannenberg, 224), it is also prone to significant weaknesses. One should heed Karl Barth's warning that "the particular danger of dogmatics is to think schematically" (*CD* IV/2, 7), for this is precisely the great temptation attending the use of the *munus triplex* schema: to take a helpful conceptual device and use it as a comprehensive or sufficient account of the unity of Christ's work. Consequently, the schema takes on a life of its own, threatening to divorce itself from the resources and constraints offered by the biblical witness and to operate with an increasingly ambiguous understanding of the key concepts involved.

My concern with contemporary uses of the *munus triplex*, despite its elegance and usefulness (particularly for integrating the theocratic aspects of Israel into Christ's work), is that this framework is simply too constricting to be of abiding service to the church in offering sufficient conceptual unity to Christ's saving work. To put the point more positively, it is a significant though insufficient aid to the church's understanding, and must be complemented by other approaches to the work of Christ.

The limitations of this scheme are directly related to its greatest strength. For as Schleiermacher notes, the *munus triplex* "make[s] clear the relation of the Kingdom of heaven to this earthly theocracy [of Israel]" by representing Christ "as uniting all these three offices in Himself" (439–440). Clearly this is a tremendous benefit, offering the church great resources for understanding the person and work of Christ in light of the Old Testament, and rendering the latter more fruitful in the preaching of the church.

However, before drawing upon the *munus triplex* to create a comprehensive account of the unity of Christ's work, we must consider how the theocratic offices of Israel are related to Israel as a whole. Do they subsume its other elements within themselves, such as the marriage relationship, poets, shepherds, and the role of kinsman redeemer? While many of these offices, roles, vocations, and relationships can and do overlap, are they not distinct, each possessing its own unique significance within the history and vocation of Israel? What is to prevent us from expanding beyond the constraints of the *munus triplex*, to consider

Jesus Christ in such ways as the bridegroom, wise man, servant, shepherd, and kinsman-redeemer, in addition to his role of priest, king, and prophet?

A second question lies close on the heels of the first: while Jesus fulfilled in his person and work the vocation of Israel (including its theocratic offices), is this a sufficient framework from which to understand Christ's work? If so, then what do we make of the host of concepts employed throughout the New Testament to explain Christ's work (such as a ransom, seeking that which is lost, defeat of Satan, propitiation/expiation, justification of God, justification of sinners, Passover, redemption, reconciliation, and payment of our debt, to name but a few)? While some of these relate more closely than others to the Old Testament offices of priest, king, and prophet, does integrating them under this rubric strengthen and invigorate the New Testament concepts, or do some of them become weaker and less poignant in the process? While this remains an open question, it is clear that we must allow the integration of the *munus triplex* with these concepts to be an exegetically driven conclusion rather than a presupposition, in order to ensure that we allow each of these concepts to play their own distinct role in contributing to our understanding of the work of Christ.

With these reflections in place, we do well to return to Calvin—the one largely responsible for the prominence of the *munus triplex* in the past half-millennium. As Robert Peterson notes, "Calvin uses six biblical themes of the atonement to describe the saving work of the Mediator" (61). Leaving to the side the precise nature of these themes and the question of whether they ought to be revised or expanded, this point is significant because Calvin used the *munus triplex* as one part of a full account of Christ's work rather than a sufficient conceptual scheme by means of which to unify the whole. In other words, the *munus triplex* is an important though limited conceptual device rooted in Scripture to account for certain aspects of Christ's work, particularly as it relates to the Old Testament theocracy.

What might this mean for the use of the *munus triplex* in the church's teaching ministry? First and foremost, the church should use this schema as a way of integrating the person and work of Jesus Christ, the Messiah or anointed one of Israel, with the history of that people and particularly its offices of prophet, priest, and king. Such a line of thought opens up a host of interconnections, tensions, and questions between the Old and New Testament which are of great value to its teaching ministry. Second, we should be cautious in our use of this schema lest it take on a life of its own and outstrip the biblical foundation upon which it rests—for Calvin and Barth would agree that while the *munus triplex* is valuable, in and of itself it does not sufficiently explain the work of Christ.

Finally, integrating these two points, we should use the *munus triplex* as an impetus for understanding and employing other dimensions of the people and history of Israel which Jesus takes up and fulfills in himself, as the representative of Israel. For if the *munus triplex* is significant but insufficient, this motivates our appropriation of further aspects of the person and work of Christ by means of which to give a fuller account.

Bibliography

Barth, *Church Dogmatics*, Vols 4.1–3, 1958–1962.
Calvin, *Institutes*, 1960.
Johnson, "Munus Triplex and Atonement," *SJT* 65:2, 2012.
Pannenberg, *Jesus—God and Man*, 2002.
Peterson, *Calvin and the Atonement*, 2008.
Schleiermacher, *The Christian Faith*, 1968.
Sherman, *King, Priest and Prophet*, 2004.
Torrance, *Atonement*, 2009
Van Dyk, "The Three Offices of Christ," *Catalyst* 25:2, 1999.
Wainwright, *For Our Salvation*, 1997.
Williams, "Towards a Unified Theory of the Atonement," in *The Atonement Debate*, 2008.

John Owen

Kelly M. Kapic

John Owen (1616–1683) was an English Puritan involved in various spheres (pastoral, political, vice chancellor of Oxford University, etc.), but he is best known for his distinctive theological contributions, compiled in an authoritative twenty-four-volume nineteenth-century collection of his *Works*. Here he showed particular attentiveness to dogmatic topics such as the Trinity, Christology, Pneumatology, and Perseverance, as well as exegetical engagement (e.g., a seven-volume commentary on Hebrews) and pastoral reflections, all of which inform his writings.

Owen's lasting and most significant contribution to the theology of the atonement came in 1647 when he penned his second major work, *The Death of Death in the Death of Christ*. Exegetically and philosophically layered, it appeared in the form of a disputation after "seven-years' [of] serious inquiry." The work considers the relationship between the nature and extent of the atonement of Christ. Specifically, Owen attempts to clarify specifically what Christians mean when they confess a penal substitutionary view of the atonement: that Christ died *for us and in our place*. Simply put, if Christ's death was a substitution, then the question naturally arises: for who, exactly, was Christ's death a substitute? For *all* or only for *some* in the world? With this question we enter into one of the most heated atonement debates in mid-seventeenth-century England and also Owen's most controversial and memorable arguments pertaining to the issue.

The *Death of Death* was principally written as a polemic directed at Arminians like Thomas More espousing *universal* or *conditional redemption*; namely, that Christ elected to die for all humans without exception, and that his death made it *possible* for anyone to be saved. Owen understood the distinctive appeal of this position, for its advocates unambiguously intended to elevate the "glory of God ... his goodness and kindness towards men abundantly manifested in this enlargement of [the atonement's] extent" (To the Reader …). But Owen was concerned about a glaring lacuna: it made the death of Christ potentially ineffective, because this meant it was possible that none would respond. It made salvation a possibility rather than an actuality. How could both the sufficiency of God's redemptive act in Christ for the *whole world* and the *particularity* of the salvation of *God's elect* coexist peaceably? In answer, Owen retrieved a key distinction from medieval scholastics: "That Christ died for all in respect of the sufficiency of the ransom he paid, but not in respect of the efficacy of its application" (Book IV, chapter 1). From this, Owen's memorable quip can easily be found: Christ's death was sufficient for all but efficient only for some.

In a sense, the death of Christ had to be sufficient for all, so reasons Owen, because the person of Christ—the Son of God—is of infinite value, worth, and majesty; furthermore, in his death the Son of God bore the whole wrath of God. In this, he followed the lead of the Canons of Dort, which similarly stated that the death of Christ is "of infinite worth and value, abundantly sufficient to expiate the sins of the whole world" (chapter 2, article 3). It was a perfect sacrifice. As such, *in itself* the death of Christ is perfectly sufficient for all.

But, of course, the death of Christ is not an event that stands *by itself* or *in itself*—it stands as the culmination of the whole redemptive history of God's particular action in creation, electing Israel, and electing himself to be Israel for all humankind; it stands at the end of a long host of decrees through which God's specific plan unveils itself.

Owen is unwilling to consider the crucifixion of Christ apart from the economic Trinitarian drama of salvation history. In other words, though his sacrifice is *hypothetically* or *intrinsically* sufficient for all due to its infinite worth, it is *actually* or *extrinsically* sufficient only for some according to the definite will and intention of God the Father. And though the Father *could* have intended to apply the sufficiency of Christ's death to all (hypothetical sufficiency), he actually applied it definitely to the elect and not to all (actual sufficiency or *efficiency*). "It was in itself of infinite value and sufficiency to have been made a price to have bought and purchased all and every man in the world. That it did formally become a price for any is solely to be ascribed to the purpose of God, intending their purchase and redemption by it" (Book IV, chapter 1). Thus, Owen's atonement theology finds its roots in an important theological disjunction between the *actuality* of God's redemptive-historical action from Israel to Christ and the *possibility* of God's redemptive action viewed abstractly or ahistorically. Owen decidedly sided with the actuality of the atonement.

To the "Universalists," as Owen dubbed them, his distinction was tantamount to denying the gospel, which was meant to be *freely* offered to all humans, without exception. For if God's redemptive action was *actually* sufficient for the elect alone, then God's grace appears to be severely limited: Christ died not to save all humans, but only some humans. Owen's oft-quoted response has turned into a famous dilemma:

> God imposed his wrath due unto, and Christ underwent the pains of hell for, either
>
> (A) all the sins of all people, or
> (B) all the sins of some people, or
> (C) some sins of all people. (Book I, chapter 3)

If (C), then the cross was ineffective and humans still have sins to answer for before God. If (A), then all humans are freed from their sins. However the universalism of (A) was unpalatable even to Arminians who took refuge in the idea that it was due to human unbelief, not the limited extent of the death of Christ itself that accounted for the salvation of some and not others. Owen could have none of this, because he viewed unbelief as a sin. And if it is a sin, then surely Christ died for it. If it is not a sin, then it is not something in need of punishment. The only real option for Owen was option (B): Christ died for all the sins of some people.

In plain language, what Owen shows with this syllogistic dilemma is that all atonement theologies, if they're honest, recognize that they limit the atonement in some way: if not in extent (as Owen's theology does), then in effectiveness. For, though the option that Christ died for all the sins of all humans looks appealing, it subtly denies that God's salvation overcomes at least one sin: unbelief. And if it cannot overcome that sin, if it is indeed a sin, then the atonement of Christ is efficaciously limited: God's will is, in the end, confounded and undermined by the will of humans.

Owen expressed great confidence that his arguments were cogent and sound and that the only viable option for Christian thinkers was to accept a limited, or better, *particular* atonement. "Altogether hopeless of success I am not; but fully resolved that I shall not live to see a solid answer given unto it" (To the Reader...).

But Owen's atonement theology comprised more than just strictly logical arguments. To properly orient Owen's conclusions, one must read them in light of his strongly held Trinitarian assumptions. In a later work written in 1650 entitled *Of The Death of Christ*, he clearly lays out the Trinitarian logic of his earlier work, *The Death of Death*: "My aim was, to hold out the whole work of redemption, as flowing from the love of the Father, dispensed in the blood of the Son, and made effectual by the application of the Spirit of grace" (chapter 1). Thus, the death of Christ unifies the saving work of God: the Father, out of his love, sends the Son who willingly dies on behalf of those whom the Father has entrusted to him, and the Spirit of Christ then moves to bring life to those who were born dead in their sin, that they might be born again. Without the Spirit they will not respond, and without the Father drawing them, they will not come to Christ. And without Christ's death on their behalf, they remain in their sin, even the sin of unbelief. Jesus's death, according to Owen, was meant to bring about not merely the possibility, but the actual salvation of God's people. One cannot have Christ wanting his death to save everyone, but have the Father reluctant about such a redemptive move. Nor can you have Christ dying for everyone, but the Spirit of Life hesitant to apply the saving work of the atonement to all for whom Christ died. Therefore, he concludes, his death, while sufficient for all in a sense, is truly efficient only for the elect. To conclude otherwise, Owen worries, is to risk a rift in the Trinity.

Many contemporary Reformed theologians, represented by the prolific J. I. Packer, agree with Owen's assessment: limited atonement or particular redemption is the "theology of the Bible viewed from the perspective of the Bible" (5). Carl Trueman also observes a strong biblical bent in Owen, since his theological presupposition is to ground the work of Christ within the context of the covenant of redemption. For Trueman, Owen is being supremely faithful to the story of God's electing action in Israel and then in Jesus Christ. Trueman also notes that Owen's atonement perspective in *The Death of Death* depends on the presupposition that the necessity of Christ's death is based on God's decreed will, rather than his essence. This is a position he would later repudiate in his *Dissertation on Divine Justice* in 1653, when his audience changed from Arminians to Socinians. In fact, in this later work he agreed with an Arminian position that he had earlier lambasted in *The Death of Death*: that Christ's sacrifice was necessary according to the character of God's essential justice. In this respect, Owen moved from voluntarism to intellectualism, retracting his earlier emphasis in *The Death of Death* that made God's redemptive action dependent on his *will*. But Christologically, Owen's later writing served to compound his earlier insight that what is important in the death of Christ is the *history* of God's electing action in the *actual* person of Jesus Christ who, standing at the center of the drama of redemption, actually and effectively saves people, not a hypothetical atonement that purely makes salvation possible.

Other scholars, however, offer a different appraisal. Alan Clifford indicts Owen with greatly distorting Calvin's theology by allowing an Aristotelian means-end logic to get in the way of Scriptural evidence: "Owen pleaded for the 'infallible efficacy' of the atonement at the expense of the significant textual data" (97). It should be recognized, however, that while Clifford makes it seem as though John Owen alone was appropriating Aristotelian logic in his theology, that is a bit misleading, for just as commonly one finds someone like the eclectic Richard Baxter (who strongly disagrees with Owen's atonement views; Trueman, *Claims*) making heavy use of a scholastic methodology dependent on the Philosopher's categories.

More recently, Graham Cole cautions theologians from absolutely precluding the possibility that God may have had more than one design or intention with respect to the cross. As Martin Foord has recently argued, it should be recognized that while other Reformed theologians were able to speak both of (1) God desiring all people to be saved, though (2) in the end not all would be saved, Owen greatly struggled with this paradoxical tension (283–295). Scholars such as these would ask Owen to account more fully for the mysterious reality in Scripture, which appears to offer Christ's death for all even if in the end only the elect are saved by his blood. In any case, Owen's atonement contributions should not too quickly be dismissed since his Trinitarian instincts, his careful logic, and his exegetical explorations can serve to remind readers of the ineffable majesty of salvation that is secured only by the death of Jesus Christ.

Bibliography

Blacketer, "Definite Atonement in Historical Perspective," in *The Glory of the Atonement*, 2004.

Clifford, *Atonement and Justification*, 1990.

Cole, *God the Peacemaker*, 2009.

Foord, "John Owen's Gospel Offer: Well-Meant or Not?," in *The Ashgate Research Companion to John Owen's Theology*, 2012.

Kapic, *Communion with God*, 2007.

Kapic and Jones, *The Ashgate Research Companion to John Owen's Theology*, 2012.

Moore, *English Hypothetical Universalism*, 2007.

Owen, *The Death of Death in the Death of Christ, Of The Death of Christ*, and *A Dissertation on Divine Justice* in *The Works of John Owen*, Vol. 10, 1967.

Packer, "Introduction," in *The Death of Death in the Death of Christ*, reprinted from *The Works of John Owen*, Banner of Truth and Trust, 1959.

Thomas, *The Extent of the Atonement*, 2006.
Trueman, "Atonement and the Covenant of Redemption," in *From Heaven He Came and Sought Her*, 2013.
Trueman, *The Claims of Truth*, 1998.
Trueman, "John Owen's Dissertation on Divine Justice," in *Calvin Theological Journal* 33, 1998.

Wolfhart Pannenberg

Kent Eilers

In one of Wolfhart Pannenberg's (1928–) earliest published sermons he remarked, "Since the beginning of Christianity the sign of the Cross has been the sign by which Christians are recognized ... Jesus' mission by the wisdom of God was not his own protection, but his self-abandonment" (*Gegenwart*, 176–177). Years later and after several intervening attempts, Pannenberg formulated a doctrine of atonement that no less heralded the self-abandonment of the Son. It also more clearly detailed the theological frame within which the entirety of Christ's self-giving can be viewed as an action of the triune God.

Pannenberg's mature doctrine of atonement is developed in the three volumes of *Systematic Theology* (*ST1–3*). He there locates the doctrine within an account of God's faithfulness to heal and restore creation. In the structure of Pannenberg's dogmatics, God's reconciling acts are meant to be seen and understood as an open process that he describes as the anticipation, actualization, and completion of reconciliation. Reconciliation with God is not a punctiliar divine act. Rather, it includes the entire process of renewing broken fellowship initiated in the Christ-event (anticipation), carried forward through the work of the Holy Spirit (actualization), and finally completed in the eschatological arrival of the kingdom of God at history's end (completion).

Atonement is part of the *anticipation* of reconciliation that encompasses the incarnation of the Son, expiation for sin through his death (the removal of offense, guilt, and consequences), and his resurrection and his ascension to the Father. Christ's death overcomes the misery of our estrangement and mediates salvation, the restoration of peace and fellowship with God (*ST2*, 397–410). While reconciliation is anticipated in these events, Christ's death and resurrection point ahead to its *actualization* in human recipients and finally its *completion* in the eschatological coming of God's kingdom. Through Christ's crucifixion and resurrection, God "showed himself to be the Victor over sin and death in reconciliation of the world," but only in the form of *anticipation* "can we say that the reconciliation of the world has already taken place." Through the church's proclamation "the event of reconciliation that has its origin and center in the death of Jesus Christ still goes forward" (*ST2*, 412–413; *ST3*, 641–642). For Pannenberg, treating reconciliation within this dogmatic frame most effectively portrays it as "opened up for us" and in need of completion through the Spirit's reconciling activity in the church's proclamation.

As the doctrine of atonement is developed in *ST*, Pannenberg departs significantly from his earlier formulation in *Jesus, God and Man* (*JGM*). He does so in order to more plainly represent God's action in Jesus's human history and specifically his path to the cross. In *JGM*, Pannenberg presented Christ's death as a tragedy that befell Jesus, and he was criticized for this because it gave no clear account of God's agency in the event itself. Pannenberg subsequently said he would "supplement" his interpretation of Christ's crucifixion with a discussion of "the action of God in the cross of Jesus" ("Afterword," 305; "Teilhabe am Kreuz," 31), but he never revised that aspect of *JGM*. Instead, he later wrote in the afterword to the fifth German edition (1976) that his largely "from below" approach to the atonement would need to be supplemented with a corresponding move "from above." Doing so, however, would only be possible "within the context of the doctrine of God and thus within the overall framework of a comprehensive dogmatics" (*JGM*, 406).

The uncertainty seen in Pannenberg's faltering early attempts to account for God's agency in the Christ-event is a signal of his still-developing Trinitarianism. During this period, it seems Pannenberg was unsure how to proceed along his preferred methodological lines while still making "God's action in Jesus' history ... thematic as God's action" (*JGM*, 406). In the years following *JGM*, the maturing of Pannenberg's Trinitarianism is glimpsed in several essays as he established the contours of his doctrine of God and soon thereafter began composing his dogmatics ("Christologie und Theologie"; "Der Gott der Geschichte"; "Theology of the Cross").

In the material in *ST* specifically related to atonement, Pannenberg counterbalances his earlier focus on Jesus's historicity by emphasizing the actions of each member of the Godhead. Doing so reveals a Trinitarian pattern basic to Pannenberg's theology: the actions of the divine persons in time (economic Trinity) are to be understood with recourse to the relationships of eternal mutual self-distinction within the Godhead (immanent Trinity). The eternal relations are mirrored and thus *revealed* in the life of Jesus and his acceptance of death on the cross (*ST1*, 432, 447; *ST2*, 324–325; Eilers, 38–47).

The Father: Taking 2 Corinthians 5:18–21 and Romans 5:10 as points of departure, Pannenberg argues that the death of Jesus involved *not* finally the actions of his Roman executioners or Jewish judges but the work of the Father. Echoing Romans 8:32, Pannenberg describes the Father's agency as "gifting" his Son to the world (*ST2*, 438, n. 117). His involvement in the crucifixion was an extension of his providential care for creation: "Through all the baseness, cowardice, and brutality" of the crucifixion "God the Father was at work in this event" (*ST2*, 438).

The Son: Pannenberg portrays the Son's obedience as intimate cooperation with the Father's sending (Rom. 5:19; Phil. 2:8; Heb. 5:8–10). The Father and Son act cooperatively, but both act. Their actions should be understood as the "same thing in different ways" (*ST2*, 439). The Son was an active, willing participant and not a mere object of the Father's will. Clearly departing from his position in *JGM* (see above), Pannenberg argues that the cross may appear to have befallen Jesus, but the actions of the Son can be found where Jesus seemed passive. While Jesus did not set himself toward the cross, "nothing unforeseen or unplanned can happen to the Son of God" (*ST2*, 442). The pressing question for Pannenberg, then, is how the cooperative agency of the divine persons is understood from the perspective of Jesus's historicity. Pannenberg's earlier position emphasized Jesus's historicity to the near exclusion of divine involvement in the Cross, so how would his mature formulation in *ST* "preserve and integrate" the action of the Son of God with Jesus's genuine *human* history (Wenz, 195)?

Toward a solution, Pannenberg interprets Jesus's life in terms of two histories: the human history of Jesus available to historical research and the history of the Son present in Jesus. If only the former is kept in view, one easily falls into the mistakes of *JGM*. The second must be viewed together with the first in order to approach Jesus's genuine human history "on the solid basis of the reality of the eternal son of God present in Jesus" (*ST2*, 441). Pannenberg reasons, "Naturally the Son of God incarnate in Jesus acts through his human activity, but his action embraces the distinction between human activity and the fate of Jesus. The earthly activities thus have contexts other than those that appear on a purely historical approach" (*ST2*, 446; also 442). Jesus's crucifixion was an act of self-offering on the part of the incarnate Son of God at work in Jesus's genuine human history.

The Spirit: The Spirit's agency remains largely implicit in Pannenberg's doctrine of atonement, except for his action that raised Christ from the dead (*ST1*, 314). Four features of Pannenberg's dogmatics may account for this. First, Pannenberg conceives God's reconciling movement as a unified Trinitarian act including both the reconciliation event (incarnation, crucifixion and resurrection, ascension) and its "actualization" in human recipients by the Spirit (*ST2*, 442–443, 449–454). Pannenberg may not have felt the urgency of demarcating the Spirit's agency in Christ's passion because he sought to integrate it into a unified, Trinitarian account of reconciliation. Second, the Spirit's presence is implicitly affirmed in the crucifixion because Pannenberg's doctrine of creation emphasizes the Spirit as the life-giving principle to which all creatures, including Jesus, owe life, movement, and activity (*ST1*, 315, 373, 414; *ST2*, 76, 136, 190). Third, the Spirit was Jesus's empowering presence for the work of self-offering because Pannenberg names the Spirit as "the mode of God's presence in Jesus as he was of God's presence in the prophets" (*ST2*, 266–267).

Within Pannenberg's theological vision, the crucifixion is a stunning demonstration that God expresses and thereby *reveals* his faithfulness to creation as cruciform love. Divine faithfulness expresses the consistency between God's life as it exists in the eternal relations of the Godhead (*in se*), and that which is manifested through God's reconciling action toward alienated creation (*ad extra*). The faithfulness of God revealed through his acts of salvation discloses what has always and forever been true for his own life (*ST1*, 444; Eilers, 9–11, 38–57, 63–70). Said differently, the eternal faithfulness of the divine persons is the backdrop *upon which* and the source *from which* we understand the faithfulness of God as demonstrated through his reconciling acts. For Pannenberg, that God is faithful and acts faithfully through his saving acts is a reality that proceeds from God's life in himself: "the mutual faithfulness of the Son to the Father and the Father to the Son" (*ST2*, 53). The Trinitarian backdrop for the atonement is simply and significantly that God is *faithful to save.*

Bibliography

Eilers, *Faithful to Save*, 2011.
Pannenberg, "Afterword," in *The Theology of Wolfhart Pannenberg*, 1973.
Pannenberg, "Christologie und Theologie," *KuD* 21, 1975.
Pannenberg, "Das Kreuz Jesu und das des Christen," in *Gegenwart Gottes*, 1973.
Pannenberg, "Der Gott der Geschichte," *KuD* 23, 1977.
Pannenberg, *Jesus—God and Man*, 2nd edn, 1977.
Pannenberg, *Systematic Theology*, 1991–1998.
Pannenberg, "Teilhabe am Kreuz," in *Das Wort vom Kreuz heute gesagt*, 1973.
Pannenberg, "A Theology of the Cross," *Word and World* 8:2, 1988.
Wenz, *Wolfhart Pannenbergs Systematische Theologie*, 2003.

The Apostle Paul

Timothy G. Gombis

Introduction

Paul has much to say about the atonement, employing a wide range of metaphors, and much has been written about Paul on the atonement. While many inquiries involve the pursuit of "Paul's theology," all we have are Paul's letters—contingent expressions of Paul's convictions about the gospel of Jesus Christ. And in many of his letters, Paul was attempting to resolve communal conflicts. It is in precisely these contexts that we find his most strategic discussions of the atonement. In this chapter, then, I will argue that Paul's fundamental conviction regarding the death of Christ is that it is the means whereby God brings into being the new creation people of God. I will discuss how Paul relates the death of Christ to the creation of a single people made up of Jewish and non-Jewish Christians (representing all ethnicities) from three Pauline texts well known for their strategic statements on the meaning of Christ's atonement—Galatians 2:15–21; Romans 3:21–31; and Ephesians 2:11–22. I will then argue that for Paul, Christian churches in their new practices that are generative of ever-stronger unity must embody God's work of bringing into being the new creation people of God. In his rebuke of the Corinthians for their corrupted practices involving the Lord's Supper, Paul relates the proper practice of eating the love feast in terms of the embodiment and proclamation of the Lord's death (1 Cor. 11:26).

Galatians 2:15–21

In Galatians 2:11–14, Paul recounts for his Galatian audience his confrontation of Peter in Antioch. The Church in Antioch where Paul and Barnabas ministered was made up of Jews and non-Jews who ate their meals together. This practice would have struck Peter. While he could affirm in theory that all ethnicities are united in God's singular people, Jews and non-Jews did not eat together in Jerusalem, since there were no Gentiles in that church. Peter, however, initially participated in this practice (Gal. 2:12) when he visited Antioch. When other Jewish Christians from the Jerusalem church came to Antioch, however, Peter was intimidated and no longer ate with the Gentile believers. In Paul's view this was a fundamental affront to "the truth of the gospel" (v. 14).

In vv. 15–21, Paul elucidates the theological logic of the unity of the people of God for his Galatian audience, relaying what he likely told Peter in Antioch. In verses 15–16, he states basic gospel principles, agreed-upon by Peter and perhaps even the Jewish teachers causing the crisis in Galatia. Beginning by playing on Jewish assumptions about the status of non-Jews, he notes that even though Peter and he are "Jews by nature and not Gentile sinners," they have been justified before God on the very same basis as non-Jews—by faith. This is because no one is justified before God "from works of law." This expression, "works of law," is at the heart of a number of contemporary debates, but it is clear that Paul equates being "from works of law" (v. 16) with Jewish identity (v. 15). A person's Jewish identity has no relevance at all with regard to justification before God since justification is only through the faithfulness of Jesus Christ. Jews and non-Jews are justified on the very same basis before God (vv. 15–16).

For Paul, the fact that all humanity—Jews and non-Jews—is justified before God on the same basis indicates that all those in Christ must share a common table. This new family embodies their family relation by participation in the common meal. This is the point being contested, however, by Peter in Antioch and the Jewish Christian teachers in Galatia, who are claiming that the Gentile believers in Galatia must be circumcised to participate in the people of God: they must convert to being Jewish in order to be Christian. The Jewish Christians in Antioch and Galatia are convinced that they cannot fellowship with non-Jewish Christians without sinning.

Paul exposes the logic at work here in v. 17. Is it really the case that Christ has become a "minister of sin" by uniting Jews and non-Jews in justification and making them one new family that eats at one table?

In vv. 18–20, Paul describes how this is not so. First, in v. 18, in a remarkably cryptic statement, he notes, "If I rebuild what I once destroyed, I demonstrate myself to be a transgressor." He is saying that if he (along with other Jewish-Christians like Peter) recognizes the universal character of the people of God and fellowships with non-Jewish Christians, but then also claim that only Jews can be among the people of God and may only fellowship with fellow Jews, he becomes worse than a sinner. He becomes a transgressor. He is claiming that one must be *within the Law's bounds*, withdrawing from Gentiles, while also recognizing the gospel's call to fellowship with Gentiles in Christ.

Second, in vv. 19–20, Paul describes how his (and Peter's) identification with the death of Christ has solved the problem in v. 18. Through the Law's mechanism of requiring the death of transgressors, they have died to the Law's requirement to remain within its requirement to avoid fellowship with gentiles. Paul has been crucified with Christ (v. 20) and has been raised to new life so that he might enter into the new creation reality which is made up of all those in Christ, Jew and non-Jew.

Paul's arguments, while not easy to trace, are for the unity of the people of God. All those in Christ belong to one another and Jewish Christians who are free enter the full enjoyment of relationships among believers of any and every ethnicity.

This argument leads to the climactic statement in v. 21. Here, Paul connects the creation of the one people of God directly to the death of Christ. He does not nullify the grace of God. His gospel, rather, is the full articulation of it, and the singular united people of God are the embodiment of it. The "righteousness" (*dikaiosunē*) of which he speaks has direct reference to the discussion of "justification" (*dikaioutai*) in v. 16. Participation in the justified people of God does not come through an act of conversion to a Jewish identity. That is, it does not come about "through the law." If it did, then Christ died for reason. This is the fundamental thrust of Paul's point here: Jesus's death created the justified people of God, made up of those who are "of the works of the law" (i.e., Jewish) and those who are of other ethnic identities. Christ died to create the new people of God. Paul is strongly implying here that to claim that some other means create the people of God, which is what his opponents in Galatia are doing, is to claim that it was pointless for Christ to die.

Romans 3:21–31

Just as the previous passage functions as the "theological heart" of Galatians, Romans 3:21–31 plays this role in Paul's argument to the church in Rome: just as Galatians 2:15–21 leads up to the climactic statement of the death of Christ and its relation to the creation of God's new people in v. 21, this pivotal text revolves around the statement in Romans 3:25 of Christ's death to this same new creation reality.

Paul argues that God's saving program is being worked out without reference to the Law (Rom. 3:21). Just as in Galatians, Paul is referring to the conflict between Jewish and non-Jewish Christians in the Roman church(es). Two distinct groups are seeking to gain an advantage over the other. Paul claims that God is setting people right without any reference to their ethnic identity. On the contrary, "the righteousness of God through the faithfulness of Jesus Christ" is "for *all* who believe" (v. 21). Paul's repeated use of "all" throughout the first two chapters of Romans emphasizes that *everyone* in the Roman fellowships stands in need of God's salvation and is equally welcome among God's people. No one has any advantage, "for there is no distinction" between Jews and gentiles (v. 22), "since all have sinned and fall short of the glory of God" (v. 23).

Jews and non-Jews in Christ have been justified "by his grace as a gift" (v. 24) because both groups stand in equal need of salvation. It is at this point that Paul introduces the means whereby God has accomplished this salvation in Christ Jesus, making explicit reference to "his blood" in v. 25, an obvious reference to his death. While many analyses of Christ's atoning work have focused on the mechanics of the atonement in vv. 24–26, the larger point Paul makes in this section is that Christ's atoning work has direct reference to creating a unified people of God. Grammatically, the major point of vv. 23–26 is the initial statement of this paragraph in v. 23—that *all* have sinned, each member of the Roman Christian community, and not just the Jewish Christians or the non-Jewish Christians. And his point in vv. 24–26 is that they have all been justified by grace as a gift, though this entire paragraph is subordinate to v. 23, beginning as it does with the participle *dikaioumenoi* in v. 24. Though the paragraph makes strategic theological points, it is subordinate to the statement in v. 23 so that the next point Paul makes begins in v. 27.

The upshot of the grammatical structure of this passage is that vv. 22–23 stress that God's saving program is being worked out without reference to ethnic identity. And this point is going to be reemphasized and extended in vv. 27–31, where Paul turns to argue that the character of God's saving program ought to eliminate posturing and agitating for prominence in the Roman church community (i.e., "boasting"). The death of Christ, then, in this strategic passage in Romans—the heart of the letter—has direct reference to the creation and ongoing unified life of the multiethnic people of God.

Ephesians 2:11–22

This passage is an elaboration of Paul's statement in Ephesians 1:19–23, where God demonstrates his power by raising Jesus from the dead and seating him victoriously as cosmic Lord over all powers that pervert God's good creation and which currently work to hold creation and humanity in slavery to death through transgressions and sins. God has broken their hold over creation and has signaled that their final future defeat is certain. In two subsequent portions of text—vv. 1–10 and vv. 11–21—Paul discusses how God is making manifest Christ's triumph.

In vv. 1–10, God's triumph is demonstrated in snatching his people from the grip of Satan, who held them in bondage to death through transgressions and sins. God has acted powerfully, however, to free his people from slavery to death, to give them life, and to transform them so that they no longer "walk" in death (v. 2), but in the "newness of life" (v. 10).

In addition to freeing humanity from death, Paul describes in vv. 11–22 that God is manifesting his triumph in Christ by reuniting a formerly divided humanity. In vv. 11–12, Paul depicts how the powers inimical to God's rule have divided humanity, setting ethnic groups against each other. Paul writes from a Jewish perspective, so he points to how the covenantal sign of their relationship with God had been turned into a racial label of derision toward non-Jews. Outsiders were called "the uncircumcision"—that is, the "unacceptable," "the outsiders," "sinners," "Gentile dogs." Israel, becoming like other nations and thereby failing to fulfill its commission to be a light to the nations, had cut off the nations from access to the grace of God. They turned their status as God's chosen people into a mark of pride, working against the redemptive purposes of God for the world.

Paul locates the source of this international animosity in the Law (v. 15). But it wasn't the Mosaic Law itself that was the problem, just as distinctions between races and ethnicities are goods in themselves. The Law had distinguished between Israel and the nations for the redemption of the nations. But this distinction was hijacked by the hostile cosmic powers and turned into a source of conflict. Intended for good in the plan of God, the Law had become an accomplice in further enslaving the cosmos.

The death of Christ has direct reference to healing this ethnic breach, not only that between Jew and non-Jew in Christ, but to all tribal, racial, and ethnic conflicts (v. 13). In his death, he took upon himself racial hatred and division and broke down the dividing wall between Jews and Gentiles so that both groups could become one in Christ (vv. 14–15). All those who are in Christ have their life by the Spirit and exist in the realm of new creation in which Christ is our peace.

Having put to death the enmity through the cross of Christ (v. 16), God has made his one new people into the new temple of God in Christ by the Spirit. To celebrate the triumph of God, the people of God no longer gather at the temple, but gather as the temple (vv. 19–22). This temple ideology, found throughout

Ephesians, is strategic for Paul's argument throughout 1 Corinthians, to which we will turn presently. For both of these letters, the church stands as a monument to the atoning work of God in Christ, for it depends on this work for its very existence. In 1 Corinthians, Paul's burden is to note that a new mode of life must characterize this new people who make up this new temple, or the triumphant work of God will not be made manifest.

1 Corinthians 11:17–34

Thus far we have seen that in Paul's most strategic expressions of the atonement, he is speaking about how God brings into being his new creation people through the death of Christ. In 1 Corinthians 11:17–34, he discusses the church's improper practice of the Lord's Supper in terms of the death of Christ.

He writes this letter mainly to rebuke the Corinthians because they have split up in to factions (1 Cor. 1:10–11). He exhorts them to be unified because of their new corporate identity as God's temple, his dwelling place on earth, and warns them of the consequences of offending the Spirit of God who dwells among them (1 Cor. 3:16–17). God is powerfully working to unite them, and anyone who is an agent of division is subject to the judgment of God. These sobering words shape Paul's rebuke regarding the Lord's Supper in 1 Corinthians 11:17–34.

In 1 Corinthians 11:17–22, Paul informs the Corinthians that their practice of the Lord's Supper is a sham. It is not the Lord's Supper at all (v. 20) because they eat it while factions exist (v. 19) and their eating reflects the corrupted Corinthian social codes. The rich bring their good food and wine and eat with their social equals while they exclude the poor. Then, when they are satisfied to the point of being drunk they admit the poor church members, but by then the food is gone and many remain hungry. The way they eat the meal reinforces the sinful social realities that God overcame in Christ.

This is unthinkable to Paul, who reminds them of what he taught them previously (vv. 23–26). The important point comes in v. 26 where he states, "As often as you eat this bread and drink the cup, you proclaim the Lord's death until he comes." The eating of the meal *is itself* the proclamation of the Lord's death. But this is only the case if the wealthier members bring more than they need and the poor are treated with dignity and welcomed to share in the Lord's bountiful blessings along with their siblings in God's new family. Eating in this manner is the social embodiment of a radically new people created by the death and resurrection of Jesus Christ.

The Lord's Supper as a social practice informs what Paul means by eating and drinking "unworthily" (v. 27). If they gather to celebrate the Lord's Supper, but do so by neglecting the poor and needy, or by secretly fostering factions, God will judge them. Such behavior amounts to an attempt to destroy the temple of God that he has established in Christ and is building by his Spirit. It is opposition to God and can only result in judgment.

Conclusion

Paul employs a variety of metaphors to speak of the atoning work of God in Christ throughout his letters. This chapter has focused on what God achieved in the atonement, however, and that is the bringing into being of his new creation people. In Christ, God has freed humanity from bondage and has united all people by the Spirit through the death and resurrection of Jesus Christ. This new reality must have a social embodiment through new practices of mutual sharing and the enjoyment of relationships characterized by self-giving love and service. This is the only way that God's triumph in Christ is demonstrated visibly and actually, to both human and cosmic audiences.

Select Bibliography

Beker, *Paul the Apostle*, 1980.
Dunn, *The Theology of Paul the Apostle*, 1998.
Gombis, *The Drama of Ephesians*, 2010.
Gorman, *The Death of the Messiah and the Birth of the New Covenant*, 2014.
Gorman, *Inhabiting the Cruciform God*, 2009.
Longenecker, *The Triumph of Abraham's God*, 1998.
Matera, *God's Saving Grace*, 2012.
Tannehill, *Dying and Rising with Christ*, 1967.

Pentateuch

T. Desmond Alexander

This chapter approaches the Pentateuch in its final received form: a carefully crafted story that involves a plot, presenting a predicament and the process toward resolving it. The plot at the heart of Genesis to Deuteronomy concerns the restoration of the deeply fractured relationship between God and humanity. This story begins by describing how God and humanity become alienated. As it develops, we witness a partial restoration of this broken relationship when God comes to reside among the Israelites, in a dwelling that is aptly named the "tent of meeting" (Ex. 27:21). With its distinctive plot, the Pentateuch as a whole is undoubtedly a story about atonement, interpreting the word "atonement" as meaning "at one-ment" or "to be united"—corresponding with the mediaeval Latin term *adunamentum*, meaning "unity."

To appreciate how the Pentateuch contributes to a fuller understanding of atonement in Christian theology it is important to understand something of the unique relationship that existed between God and humanity before they were alienated from one another. According to the opening chapters of Genesis, God created human beings and set them apart from all other creatures by giving them authority to rule over the earth as his vice-regents (Gen. 1:26–28). In addition, they were given a priestly or holy status, which enabled them to meet with God face-to-face. Appointed by God as his priestly vice-regents, they were commissioned to create a global community among whom God would dwell.

Unfortunately, Adam and Eve betray God through disobeying him when tempted by a malevolent serpent, and this results in their expulsion from the Garden of Eden (Gen. 3:22–24). Excluded from God's presence, they no longer govern as God's representatives on the earth, and the task of guarding the garden is taken from Adam and delegated to cherubim (Gen. 3:24). By way of punishment Adam and Eve come under the domain of death and no longer have access to the tree of life. The consequences of humanity's alienation from God are tragically illustrated through various episodes recorded in Genesis 4–11. By graphically recording the depravity of people and their violent impact upon the earth and all its creatures, these chapters underscore the extent to which human beings are alienated from God.

Against this background, Genesis 12–50 narrates the initial stages of the process by which God will repair this broken relationship. The patriarchs receive divine promises that offer hope, not merely for their biological descendants, but for all the families of the earth. These promises will ultimately find their fulfillment in a royal descendant of Abraham through whom all the nations of the earth will be blessed. While God's promises to the patriarchs are not fulfilled within the Pentateuch, the plot of the Pentateuch establishes the trajectories by which this process will come to fulfillment.

Moving beyond Genesis, the book of Exodus begins with Abraham's descendants living in the land of Egypt: Exodus 1:7 records that "the Israelites were fruitful and prolific; they multiplied and grew exceedingly strong, so that the land was filled with them" (NRSV). This brief description recalls Genesis 1:28, implying that the Israelites are living according to God's creation mandate. However, this state of affairs provokes a hostile reaction from the Egyptian pharaoh, who embarks on a campaign of subjugation and genocide. This sets the scene for the story that unfolds. Exodus begins by introducing a pharaoh, who is the antithesis of God, compelling the Israelites to build store cities (*arei miskenot*; Ex. 1:11), but concludes with them building a dwelling place (*mishkan*; Ex. 25:9) for Yahweh, who has acted to bring the Israelites closer to him. Exodus highlights Yahweh's role in transforming the experience of the Israelites, but in doing so the narrative underlines that this transformation also involves a process of atonement.

While the book of Exodus is often perceived as a story that focuses on the theme of the divine liberation of people from slavery, there is considerably more to the book than this. At the heart of Exodus is the theme of atonement as the Israelites are united with God in a unique relationship. Importantly, the Exodus narrative shed significant light on the multifaceted nature of the process by which God and humanity are reunited.

The plot of Exodus involves the rescue of the Israelites from the clutch of a despotic Egyptian pharaoh, who is portrayed as defiantly opposing God. Exodus alludes to God redeeming the Israelites, using the Hebrew verb *ga'al* (Ex. 6:6, 15:13). Here the emphasis is upon God's role as a kinsman redeemer, who comes to right a wrong. Yet, this type of redemption by itself is insufficient to restore the broken relationship between God and humanity. For this to occur, there are two related events that play a central role in uniting God and the Israelites: the Passover in Egypt and the sealing of the covenant at Mount Sinai.

Although it is not always recognized, the Passover is a key component for understanding atonement in the Pentateuch. Through this ritual the firstborn male Israelites come into a unique relationship with God by being consecrated or made holy. As God states: "On the day that I struck down all the firstborn in the land of Egypt, I consecrated for my own all the firstborn in Israel, both of man and of beast. They shall be mine: I am the LORD" (Num. 3:13, ESV; cf. Num. 8:17–18). As these words indicate, the Passover brings the firstborn males into a special relationship with God. Significantly, the divine consecration of the firstborn males depends upon the sacrifices offered on the evening of the first Passover. Through these sacrifices the Israelite firstborn males are rescued from death. Regarding this, two observations are worthy of note. First, on this occasion, the Israelite firstborn males are threatened with death. Previously, God always distinguished between the Israelites and the Egyptians when he afflicted Egypt with terrible "signs and wonders." The death threat to the firstborn Israelite males recalls that all humanity is under the dominion of death as a consequence of Adam and Eve's betrayal of God in the Garden of Eden. Second, from the accompanying instructions it seems likely that the firstborn males are viewed as having been ransomed from death. The concept of "ransom" is highlighted in Exodus 13:13–15, using the verb *paqad* (cf. Ex. 34:20). At a later stage a further process of ransom occurs when the Levites become substitutes for all firstborn males (Num. 3:41–51). Indirectly, the Passover explains why the Levites have a holier status than other Israelites, a status that is reflected in their close association with the tabernacle. Consequently, at one level, the Passover prepares people for serving God at his sanctuary.

Apart from ransoming the firstborn male Israelites from death, the Passover ritual incorporates other functions that are associated with atonement. The sacrificial blood is used for purification (Ex. 12:7, 22). Special instructions are also given concerning the eating of the sacrificial meat (Ex. 12:8–10). Its consumption is associated with sanctification or being made holy.

The concepts of ransom, purification, and sanctification are all bound together in the Passover ritual (Alexander, 201–208). These same concepts reappear together as the Exodus story unfolds, especially at the sealing of the Sinai covenant (Ex. 24:1–11) and the consecration of the Aaronic priests (Ex. 29:1–37; Lev. 8:1–36; cf. Davies, 119–124). Through each of these events, selected individuals are given a holy status that enables them to move closer to God. As these corresponding rituals reveal, the process of restoring the broken relationship between God and humanity includes not only the giving of a ransom, but also purification, leading to sanctification.

Following their rescue from Egypt, the Israelites come to Mount Sinai where they enter into a "covenant" relationship with God. The sealing of the covenant relationship between God and the Israelites involves the construction of an altar and the presenting of both whole burnt and peace offerings. Sacrificial blood is also sprinkled on the altar and on the people. While the text of Exodus 24 does not explain the significance of this ritual, it may be assumed that the sacrifices atone for the Israelites' sin by ransoming them from death and purifying them from the defilement of sin (see later). After the covenant ritual, some of the Israelite leaders ascend the mountain and feast in God's presence. The ritual that has just occurred has clearly sanctified those who ascend the mountain. To underscore the significance of this occasion, the narrator notes that they saw God and lived (Ex. 24:10–11).

Taken together, and noting their common features, the Passover and the sealing of the covenant are central to the process by which the Israelites become God's holy nation. These events unite God and the Israelites, achieving atonement. The establishment of the covenant relationship at Mount Sinai grants the Israelites the possibility of becoming a royal priesthood (Ex. 19:6), restoring to the people the status enjoyed by Adam and Eve prior to their rebellion against God in the Garden of Eden.

To complete the process of "atonement" or "uniting" described in Exodus, God instructs the Israelites to construct a portable sanctuary, so that he may reside among the people. This sanctuary is designated in two ways. First, it is called a "dwelling-place" (*mishkan*), underscoring its function as a residence for God. The golden table and lampstand, in particular, draw attention to the tent's use as a royal abode. Second, it is designated a "tent of meeting" (*ohel mo'ed*), highlighting its role as the location where human beings may encounter God. This function is especially important in the light of the overall plot of the Pentateuchal story, for Exodus concludes with the Lord coming to dwell in the midst of the Israelites, an event that marks an important step toward the restoration of the broken relationship between God and humanity. To signal this, aspects of the tabernacle resemble the Garden of Eden, recalling the harmonious environment that existed prior to Adam and Eve's disobedience (cf. Averbeck, "Tabernacle," 816–818).

While the story of Exodus centers on the reconciliation of God with the Israelites, this process has limitations. The "uniting" is not fully achieved for barriers still exist, preventing the people from fully encountering God. Even Moses, the principle human figure in this "atonement" story, is prohibited from seeing God's face (Ex. 33:20). Moreover, the people's tendency to disobey God is underlined by the incident involving the "golden calf." Additionally, Mount Sinai is merely a temporary destination; the goal of the people's journey is the land of Canaan. As Exodus 15:17 underlines, God will "plant" the people on his mountain, that is, the place where he will dwell and where his sanctuary will be established. Exodus anticipates further developments, especially in the light of the earlier divine promises to the patriarchs.

In the light of these factors, it is noteworthy that the portable sanctuary is deliberately portrayed as resembling Mount Sinai. "The tabernacle became the medium through which the Lord in his true presence travelled from the mountain of God (Sinai) to accompany and guide Israel from there to the Promised Land. The tabernacle was, therefore, a sort of movable Sinai" (Averbeck, "Tabernacle," 824). And as Childs observes, "The role of the tabernacle ... was to extend the Sinai experience by means of a permanent, cultic institution" (175). The tabernacle both recalled and perpetuated the Israelites' experience at Mount Sinai, where they were first enabled to come closer to God.

If the events at Sinai provide the basis for the ongoing ritual associated with the sanctuary, then it is noteworthy that the concept of atonement lies at the very heart of the "tent of meeting." It is associated with both the atonement cover (*kapporet*) and the gold and bronze altars that are positioned before the entrances to the Holy of Holies and Holy Place respectively. Although actual sacrifices are not offered on the golden incense altar, it is fashioned to resemble the larger bronze altar, and the offering up of incense coincides with the morning and evening burnt offerings. Through the daily rituals that are performed before the *kapporet* and on the two altars, atonement is made to maintain the covenant relationship between God and the Israelites. These cultic rituals perpetuate the covenant-making ceremony that initiated the special relationship at Mount Sinai.

While the book of Exodus concludes on a positive note with God in all his glory coming to dwell among the Israelites, the people remain prone to sin. As implied by the atonement rituals in Exodus, human sin has two negative outcomes. "Sin may be conceived as an objective defilement, a form of pollution that infects the sinner and the people and places with which the sinner might come in contact.... Alternatively, sin may be understood in more personal terms as an insult or offense to divine power" (Attridge, 71). Together these aspects of sin distance the sinner from God.

By defiling whatever is holy, sin desecrates the divine realm, and justifiably provokes God to anger. Against this background, the book of Leviticus sets out measures that are intended to address the impact of human sin, especially given God's close proximity to the Israelites. For this reason the opening chapters of Leviticus list different types of sacrifices that are designed to atone for the sins of the Israelites in a variety of ways (Alexander, 249–259).

The centrality of the concept of atonement for the Hebrew sacrificial system is reflected in the frequent use in Leviticus of the verb *kipper*, which is often translated "to make atonement" (cf. Lev. 1:4). Recent discussion of the meaning of *kipper* has highlighted how the verb "refers to 'ransom-purification': that which rescues the sinful and impure from the wrath of the Lord (ransom), and cleanses their sin and impurity (purification)" (Sklar, *Leviticus*, 53; cf. Sklar, *Sin, Impurity, Sacrifice, Atonement*; Gane). This understanding of *kipper* corresponds closely with the elements that comprise atonement rituals. The two elements of "ransom" and "purification" undoubtedly figure in the Passover, and probably also in the sealing of the covenant, as well as with the consecration of the priests.

A recurring element in the atonement rituals described in Exodus is the use of blood; it is placed on the doorframes of the Israelite homes (Ex. 12:7), sprinkled on the altar and the people (Ex. 24:6–8), and put of the bodies of the Aaronic priests (Ex. 29:20–21; Lev. 8:23). Blood also plays an important role in the various rituals associated with the tabernacle. From all of these examples, it is apparent that the animal's blood, which represents its life, is used (1) to ransom from death the person whose actions have angered God and (2) to cleanse both people and sacred objects from the defilement caused by sin. In Leviticus a consistent picture emerges: sacrificial blood both purifies (see Lev. 8:15, 16:19) and ransoms (see Lev. 17:11).

The significance of atonement rituals for maintaining unity between God and the Israelites is underlined in the book of Leviticus by the importance attached to the Day of Atonement (Lev. 16). The high priest is required to undertake annually a special ritual that will both cleanse the most holy objects of the tabernacle from defilement and remove from the people all their sins. These actions are designed to ensure harmony between God and the Israelites, eliminating those negative elements that would create a barrier between them. As Averbeck (כפר, 704) observes, "The Day of Atonement was, in essence, an annual decontamination and re-inauguration of the tabernacle system for the nation, both the priests and the people alike." To confirm that the sins of the nation have been removed from them, the Day of Atonement ritual includes the release of a scapegoat. A similar type of action, involving the release of a bird, is used in the cleansing rituals for a person with a defiling skin disease (Lev. 14:2-7) and a house with a defiling mold (Lev. 14:48-52). In the case of the scapegoat it seems likely that the sending away of the people's sins involves conveying them to a hostile power, Azazel, that is associated with the source of evil (Lev. 16:8, 10, 26).

The picture of atonement derived from Exodus and Leviticus continues into Numbers and to a lesser extent into Deuteronomy. Particular attention is given to the role of the high priest as the one who mediates between offenders and God. Thus, Aaron uses fire from the altar to burn incense to atone for the sins of Israelites when they grumble against Moses and Aaron in the wake of the rebellion instigated by Korah, Dathan, and Abiram (Num. 16:46-47). A further act of atonement is undertaken by Phinehas, the grandson of Aaron, when the Israelites commit idolatry by worshipping Baal of Peor (Num. 25:1-13). The mediating role of the high priest is also mentioned in connection with the cities of refuge. When the high priest died (of natural causes), his death had atoning consequences. As Wenham observes, "The atoning work of the high priest culminated in his death. This purged the land of the bloodguilt associated with violent death and allowed those convicted of manslaughter to leave the cities of refuge and return home (Num. 35.28, 32)" (54). While the emphasis in Deuteronomy is primarily upon preventing activities that will defile the land, designated "abominations" (Deut. 7:25; 13:14; 14:3; 17:1, 4; 18:12; 22:5; 23:18; 24:4; 25:16; 27:15), Deuteronomy 21:1-9 describes how atonement is to be undertaken in the case of an unsolved homicide in order to prevent the people being held accountable for the shedding of innocent blood.

The concept of atonement in the Pentateuch cannot easily be reduced to a few simple ideas. It permeates the whole, at both macro and micro levels. A remarkable convergence occurs between the story of the Pentateuch and the cultic rituals that shaped temple worship for the ancient Israelites and their descendants. The Pentateuch tells a story about achieving "atonement," records instructions for maintaining "atonement," and, as an unfinished story, anticipates the coming of a greater "atonement."

Bibliography

Alexander, *From Paradise to the Promised Land*, 2012.
Attridge, "Pollution, Sin, Atonement, Salvation," in *Ancient Religions*, 2007.
Averbeck, כפר, NIDOTTE 2, 1996.
Averbeck, "Tabernacle," in *Dictionary of the Old Testament: Pentateuch*, 2003.

Childs, *Introduction to the Old Testament as Scripture*, 1979.
Davies, *A Royal Priesthood*, 2004.
Gane, *Cult and Character*, 2005.
Sklar, *Leviticus*, 2013.
Sklar, *Sin, Impurity, Sacrifice, Atonement*, 2005.
Wenham, *Numbers*, 1981.

1–2 Peter

David R. Nienhuis

Apart from Jesus himself, no one looms larger in the gospel narrative than the apostle Peter. Simon Peter was remembered in earliest Christianity as the chief of the apostles and the "rock" on whom the church itself would be built (Mt. 16:18). While it may seem disconcerting at first that a figure of such prominence should have only two relatively short letters passed down in his name (here read together, following canonical cues), in fact these two combined offer up as thorough a rendering of the apostolic rule of faith—including its witness to the atonement—as can be found anywhere else in the New Testament (NT).

As is generally the case with the NT witness, Peter's letters are not interested in espousing an abstract theory of the atonement. Rather, the letters relate a *faith-shaping story* of what God has accomplished in and through Christ for the reconciliation of the world. This grand narrative reaches all the way back to the foundation of the cosmos (1 Pet. 1:20) and forward to the final judgment (2 Pet. 3:10) in order to establish an alternative pattern of existence for those whose lives are caught up in its redemptive vision.

Central to that story is the atoning work of God accomplished in and through the person of Christ. In 1 Peter, God is the Creator of all things (2:13; 4:19), Judge of all people (1:17; 2:23; 4:5), and thus the One who foreknows everything that happens in the world (1:2, 20). While God is of course the Father of Jesus Christ (1:3), 1 Peter is focused especially on the implications of apprehending this God as the faithful and trustworthy Father of Christians everywhere (1:2, 17). This God is the primary Actor in the universe whose Agent, Jesus, has been sent into the world as both atonement for sin and as pattern for Christian participation in God's reconciling work.

Three passages in 1 Peter stand out in prominence. The first, 1:18–21, describes Jesus as a pure and unblemished sacrificial lamb whose blood "ransomed" believers from the "futile ways" of their ancestors. While the high cost of the payment is prominent here, there is no interest in who is paid off in the exchange; the focus is entirely on the effect of the liberating act in the life of the believer. The reference to Jesus's blood recalls the purifying atonement sacrifice (e.g., Lev. 4:1–6:7), and identifying Jesus as a pure and unblemished lamb recalls the Passover sacrifice (Exod. 12), which celebrates the deliverance of God's people from Egypt. Combined, the two images describe Jesus's death as a sacrificial act of cleansing and liberation which sets believers free to place their faith and hope in God (1:21).

The second major passage focuses on the purpose of that cleansing liberation. Here the focus is the suffering servant of Isaiah 53 (an image that is surprisingly absent from the Pauline witness) whose obedient death effected a powerful atonement for sin. Strikingly, Christ's death is here described explicitly in exemplary terms: "For to this you have been called, because Christ also suffered for you, leaving you an example, so that you should follow in his steps" (2:21). The grace of God's redemption in Christ is not simply a covering for sin, but is decidedly vocational: "He himself bore our sins in his body on the cross, so that, free from sins, we might live for righteousness" (2:24). As the larger context of this passage makes clear (2:11–4:2), believers participate in God's saving work by imitating Christ when suffering harassment and abuse for their distinctively Christian lifestyle. In living "for righteousness" among people who live in service to other masters (i.e. political leaders, bosses, or spouses), Christians witness to an alternative kingdom ordered according to the politics of grace, truth, and mutual love (1:22; 2:1).

The third passage (3:17–4:2) both supports and extends this train of thought. On the one hand, "Christ also suffered for sins once for all, the righteous for the unrighteous, in order to bring you to God" (3:18). Christ's suffering for sin is the non-repeatable atoning act which brought us to God; the righteous suffering of believers has the secondary effect of drawing unrighteous others to the healing liberation God provides. On the other hand, this final passage extends 1 Peter's witness into new territory, for it is not only Christ's sacrificial death that effects atonement. No, his resurrection and ascension to God's right hand is a demonstration of his victory over all that opposes God's will. Since "angels, authorities, and powers" have all been made subject to him (3:22), believers can entrust themselves to their faithful Creator (4:19) knowing that Jesus is ruling all things to bring history to its appointed end. Believers should therefore arm themselves with the intention to suffer as Christ did, resisting sin so as to live their lives "no longer by human desires but by the will of God" (4:1–2).

But how, practically speaking, are believers to appropriate this faith-forming hopefulness in their lives? How—and perhaps even why—should they take up the difficult calling to resist unrighteousness and suffer as Christ suffered? 2 Peter extends the teaching of 1 Peter by reminding believers (1:12; 3:1) that the Christ who liberated them from bondage to sin has provided them with all they need to appropriate that victory into their lives. Indeed, they must do so, for the Lord who rescued them is coming again to judge the world and purge it of all ungodliness to complete God's atoning work (3:7–13).

The crucial element is the need for believers to adhere to the distinctive witness to Christ provided by his authorized apostles (1:4, 12–21; 3:1–2). As it turns out, Christ is preached by a variety of interpreters, and not all of them offer a faithful portrait. Some minimize the damaging effects of sin on individuals and communities; others do not believe that vice can be resisted and virtue attained; still others do not believe that God intervenes in history at all and downplay or even deny God's coming judgment. Authentic apostolic tradition insists on all of these. Indeed, those who do not follow this rule of faith are "ineffective and unfruitful in the knowledge of our Lord Jesus Christ" (1:8) and are "forgetful of the cleansing of past sins" (1:9). No, the "call and election" of Christ must be "confirmed" by the appropriate response of a faith-filled life (1:10), for only in this way will entry into Christ's kingdom be provided (1:11).

Combined, 1 and 2 Peter offer substantial witness to the social aspects of God's atoning work in Christ. While the scripture provides a variety of images to describe the atonement, no depiction may be reduced to a cosmic exchange in the heavenly realm that has no direct this-world effect on human life and relationships. Indeed, 1 and 2 Peter witness to an ethical, participatory atonement. The work of Christ is inseparable from the work God is accomplishing in Christ's followers. One is constitutive, the other consecutive, but both are inextricably linked in the eternal plan of God to restore creation.

Bibliography

Achtemeier, *1 Peter*, 1996.
Elliott, *1 Peter*, 2000.
Feldmeier, *The First Letter of Peter*, 2008.
Green, *1 Peter*, 2007.
Nienhuis and Wall, *Reading the Epistles of James, Peter, John and Jude as Scripture*, 2013.
Senior and Harrington, *1 Peter, Jude and 2 Peter*, 2003.
Watson and Callan, *First and Second Peter*, 2012.

Politics

Peter J. Leithart

Recent studies of the atonement emphasize its political aspects. Timothy Gorringe argues that Anselm's "satisfaction" theory lends itself to a political order founded on violent retribution (xx), and pacifist theologians inspired by René Girard charge that classic atonement theologies perpetuate the dynamics of sacred violence the gospel is designed to expose and unravel (*Violence and the Sacred*; *The Scapegoat*). John Milbank stresses that the atonement comes to expression as a new form of communal life (*The Word Made Strange*, 145–169; *Being Reconciled*, 94–104). New Testament scholars have brought out the ecclesiological dimensions of Jesus's ministry (McKnight) by attending to the integration of Jesus's death and resurrection with his ministry of healing, teaching, and gathering disciples. Developing a "new covenant" model of atonement, Michael Gorman argues that traditional atonement theories often treat proximate ends like forgiveness, justification, or individual holiness as the ultimate end of Jesus's saving work. For Jesus and the New Testament writers, the ultimate goal was to give birth to the new covenant, a new order of life and worship that constitutes a new people. A new covenant model unites political and religious concerns.

Though given more emphasis in recent years, political concerns are not absent from earlier treatments of the atonement. What Aulén described as the "classic" theory of the atonement construed the death of Christ as an act of deliverance from dominating powers. Even when these powers are viewed as spiritual realities, they influence political life (cf. Yoder, 134–161; Berkhof). Thomas Aquinas's treatment of the Passion (*ST* III, 46–49) combines elements of various atonement theories, but the logic of the whole depends on the union of the Head and Body: Jesus acts for us because of His union with His people (III, 48, 1). Though Thomas does not work out an explicit ecclesiology, the atonement saves because Christ's life extends to the faithful through the institutions and practices of the Christian church. Indeed, Thomas's theory might even be characterized as a covenant theory, an explanation of how Jesus's death achieves the transition from the Old Law to the New.

Contemporary political theories of the atonement are often linked with critiques of the violence of satisfaction theory. One of the weaknesses these critiques is a truncated understanding of sacrifice. In Scripture, sacrifice involves more than violent death. Rites of sacrifice move through death into transfiguration and union with God. Sacrifice is as much about resurrection and *theosis* as it is about sacred killing. A more accurate grasp of the politics of the atonement awaits more careful attention to the specifics of biblical sacrifice.

Patristic sources offer considerable assistance in this project. In his classic treatment of true sacrifice in *de Civitatis Dei 10*, Augustine combines a general theory of sacrifice with an account of the sacrifice of Jesus and the formation of the city of God. Sacrifice is any act that aims at the end of holy society with God (*sacrificium est omne opus, quo agitur, ut sancta societate inhaereamus Deo*, 10.6). True sacrifice takes the form of humility, contrition, mercy, and love, insofar as such acts and dispositions unite us in society with God and with one another. On the cross, Jesus offered this true sacrifice, and as the church receives the sacrifice of Christ in the Eucharist, she becomes a communal sacrifice participating in the one sacrifice of Christ. Christ's death not only forms the *civitas Dei*, but impels the citizens of that city toward sacrificial actions that unite it with God. Caught up in the sacrifice of Christ, the church is the one body, a city of justice: *Hoc est sacrificium Christianorum: Multi unum corpus in Christo* (10.6).

Putting these various contemporary and historical elements together, we might offer a sketch of a constructive theory of the politics of atonement. Though in quite different ways, both Girard and N. T. Wright have explained the "crucifiability" of Jesus by attending to the dynamics of the gospel narrative, rather than by constructing a theoretical framework from other sources (cf. Jenson, 128–130). From that angle, it is apparent that Jesus's entire life-history is a "theory" of atonement. The atonement begins with Jesus's formation of a renewed Israel within Israel, centered on Himself as the true Israel. His risky path of renewal inevitably puts Him on a collision course with the religious elites of first-century Judaism, and they conspire with Romans to crucify Him. Yet the Father to whom Jesus was faithful vindicates Him by raising Him from the dead, and in vindicating Jesus the Father gives his stamp of approval to the way of life inaugurated in a seminal form by Jesus and His disciples. Loyal to the resurrected Christ, the disciples continue to follow the Way he inaugurated, forming communities of new covenant life throughout the Eastern Mediterranean and beyond.

This account might become a merely exemplarist theory unless it is also fundamentally pneumatological. Kevin Vanhoozer helpfully describes sacrifice in terms of gift, arguing that the atonement is the gift of Christ that elicits from the Father the counter-gift of the Spirit, who is the bond of unity in a new human polity. Political and pneumatological treatments of the atonement need to work in tandem. The One who empowers the church's new way of life is the Spirit who empowered the life of Jesus Himself. By securing the gift of the Spirit, Jesus's death, resurrection, and ascension of Christ ensures that a redeemed human polity will take form on earth.

The Spirit comes as the Spirit of the Crucified, so that the power of the resurrection is the extension of the power of the cross into the daily lives of disciples. Filled with and molded by the Spirit of Christ, the disciples relive the life and death of Jesus repeatedly, taking their cross daily to follow Him. As they do, they "fill up what is lacking in the sufferings of Christ" (Col. 1:24). The Father vindicates them as he vindicated Jesus, raising the church again and again from the dead as the Spirit turns enemies of the Way into new disciples.

Many of the traditional elements of atonement theology can be integrated into this framework. Christ's death is for the forgiveness of sins, making it possible for God to be present among and in his people by the Spirit. Christ's death and resurrection justifies because that event is the Father's delivering verdict that vindicates Christ in the Spirit. Christ's death delivers from the domination of spiritual powers by unleashing the power of the Spirit. Jesus's death expresses the love of God, calling sinners to respond with love. By condemning sin in the flesh of Jesus, God announces His Lordship over all things. As Gorman has pointed out, all of these elements of atonement have their place in a larger framework that emphasizes Jesus's death and resurrection as the birth of a new covenant people of God.

To make this more concrete, we can highlight the political potency of martyrdom. According to Paul Kahn, Christian martyrs exposed the weakness and impotence of Roman power (78–84). The more the Romans killed fearless martyrs, the less fearsome their killing became. The sheer existence of the body of Christ as an independent polity within the Roman world posed a challenge to the totalizing pretense of Rome. Simply by forming the church, the atonement disturbs the political status quo. But the formation of a *martyr* church poses a more fundamental challenge still, not only to Roman politics but to every political order whose ultimate foundation is violence and the fear of death. A community conformed to the dying and living of Jesus, witnessing with the courage of the Spirit in the face of death, is the most powerful political expression of the atonement.

Bibliography

Aulén, *Christus Victor*, 2003.
Berkhof, *Christ and the Powers*, 1977.
Girard, *The Scapegoat*, 1989.
Girard, *Violence and the Sacred*, 1979.
Gorman, *The Death of the Messiah and the Birth of the New Covenant*, 2014.
Gorringe, *God's Just Vengeance*, 1996.
Jenson, *Theology as Revisionary Metaphysics*, 2014.
Kahn, *Putting Liberalism in Its Place*, 2008.
McKnight, *A Community Called Atonement*, 2007.
Milbank, *Being Reconciled*, 2003.
Milbank, *The Word Made Strange*, 1997.
Vanhoozer, "The Atonement in Postmodernity," in *The Glory of the Atonement*, 2004.
Wright, *Jesus and the Victory of God*, 1997.
Yoder, *The Politics of Jesus*, 1994.

Post-Reformation Dogmatics

Brannon Ellis

Introduction

Nothing was more hotly debated at the famed Synod of Dort (1618–1619) than the death of Christ. Although the nature of predestination was at the heart of the Arminian controversy, Reformed theologians from around Europe also offered a range of ripostes to the Arminian gauntlet thrown down eight years earlier over the purpose and effects of Christ's atoning sacrifice. Arminius's followers had asserted—appealing to biblical statements like John 3:16, 1 Timothy 2:4, 1 Timothy 4:10, and 1 John 2:2—that Christ "died for all men and for every man, so that he has obtained for them all, by his death on the cross, redemption and the forgiveness of sins," though these benefits come to final fruition only for those who choose to embrace God's grace (Schaff, 3.546). The Synod roundly rejected this and related Arminian claims as inimical to the true meaning of Scripture and the Reformed faith. But contrary to the popular modern picture of a classical Reformed consensus on the meaning of the "L" in TULIP—so-called limited atonement—the nuances of the views espoused at this international synod were nearly as varied as the delegations themselves (cf. *Acta synodi nationalis ... Dordrechti habitae*; on TULIP, see Muller, 58–62).

The delegation from Emden, for example, argued so strongly against the Remonstrant position that they expressed doubt about whether Christians had a necessary obligation to preach the gospel indiscriminately to all people. They even suggested that no one is able to truly say, "Christ died for me," except those who already know themselves to be regenerate through bearing the fruits of the Spirit (*Acta synodi*, 2.118–126). At the opposite end of the spectrum, some among the British and the Bremenese insisted that in a very real sense Christ died for the sins of the whole world, each and all, if they but believe. Though only God's freely chosen elect are given such faith to receive him for salvation, the good news of redemption is for all (*Acta synodi*, 2.78–83 for the British; 2.103–108 for Martinius). During one heated exchange, Franciscus Gomarus, who had been Arminius's chief opponent, challenged the Bremen theologian Matthias Martinius to a duel, and, after the day's session ended with prayers, challenged him again!

During and after the era of Dort, the heart of the controversy surrounding the atonement was the relation between God's eternally purposed *intention* in Christ's satisfaction for sin, its *accomplishment* by Christ in time, and its *application* by Christ and the Spirit toward the ultimate fruition of the divine work of rescuing sinners. Do any or all these aspects of Christ's satisfaction pertain to every human being indiscriminately, or only to the elect? Though sophisticated Reformed approaches to the intent and extent of the atonement predated Arminius by several decades, Arminius's equally sophisticated challenge sharpened and clarified them. These sharpened approaches can be called, broadly, particularism and hypothetical universalism.

Two Distinctive Reformed Responses to Arminius

Arminianism: Universal Redemption and Potential Application

For Arminius, Christ's atoning death satisfied God's justice for the entire human race, obtaining redemption and the forgiveness of sins for all. Yet not all enjoy this salvation; God only brings it to ultimate fruition among those whom he foresees will embrace by faith the grace universally available to humanity through Christ's atoning work. In this way of reasoning about God's saving purposes, the elect are not brought to faith through Christ's redemption (as in the typical Reformed view); rather, the redeemed and believing are brought into election. This means for Arminius that Christ's satisfaction *provides for* the salvation of all people through faith and repentance, but it does not also *secure* the faith and repentance required for the salvation of any particular person. This is how we should reconcile the Bible's claims about God's general desire to save with the reality that many are lost (*The Works of James Arminius*, 3.346; see also 89–90). For Arminius and the Remonstrants, then, the scope of satisfaction's saving intent and the scope of its accomplishment are universal, yet these *are not coextensive with its application*. God's intent for, and Christ's accomplishment of, atonement are restricted in their saving effectiveness because of persistent human unbelief.

Reformed Particularism: Definite Redemption and Definite Application

Particularism represents the clear majority in international Reformed thinking on the atonement, certainly after Dort. For particularists, God specifically intends, and Christ specifically accomplishes, satisfaction for the sins only of those who have been eternally chosen for salvation. Particularists argued that God's saving purpose is not conditioned by (foreknowledge of) any creaturely response; its motives lie entirely in God's sheer good pleasure and free mercy—not *on account of* faith, but *unto* faith. The atonement's application or fruition depends entirely upon God (Turretin, 456–457, 467–472, 669–675).

For Reformed particularists, then, the scope of satisfaction's intent, accomplishment, and application *are entirely coextensive* (cf. *Formula Consensus Helvetica*). Bible passages identifying God's universal compassion, while true, must be understood in light of these other biblical and theological truths—God's redeeming love for "all" and the "world" cannot be exhaustive of every individual, since God does not in fact save every individual.

Hypothetical Universalism: General Redemption and Definite Application

Despite the widespread supremacy of particularism, hypothetical universalism was an influential—and, in the British Isles, relatively common—alternative approach to understanding the atonement among the post-Reformation Reformed. In its Canons (Articles 3–8) the Synod had endorsed—in substance, if not verbatim—the medieval theologian Peter Lombard's influential maxim that Christ's satisfaction was "sufficient for all, efficient for the elect." Most of the Reformed interpreted this to mean that the redeeming power and dignity of Christ's death are of infinite *value*, but their redemptive *intent* is focused entirely and exclusively on the elect (Muller, chapter 3). Hypothetical universalists interpreted this universal sufficiency to mean, as Moïse Amyraut later interpreted the Canons, that Christ's "intention was to die for all men in respect of the sufficiency of his satisfaction, but for the elect only in respect of its quickening and saving virtue and efficacy" (Armstrong, 92–93).

In this approach, there is extensiveness or comprehensiveness belonging to Christ's atoning work that means its redemptive import truly belongs to all humanity. James Ussher, for example, grounded the universal sufficiency of Christ's satisfaction in the incarnation, in which he participates in the lot of every human being and through which he both renders God "placable" toward humanity as such, and purchases for all people a stake or "interest" in his redeeming work (Ussher, 555; Snoddy, 63–65). Hypothetical universalism is not hypothetical in the sense that it is merely theoretical, but *conditional* as it pertains to actual salvation. Christ's redemption relates to all and is offered indiscriminately; if all would believe, then all would be saved.

Hypothetical universalists thus suspected their particularist colleagues of overreaction in recoiling from Arminian "Semipelagianism" (Snoddy, 63 and 56–57; Baxter, 301). If the non-elect have no part of Christ's redemptive work *in any sense*, can preachers genuinely command those who may be reprobate to repent and believe the gospel, or urge them to take hold of a salvation in Christ that was never for them to begin with?

Just as there was variety among particularists as to what definite atonement entailed, some hypothetical universalists explained this twofold intentionality for Christ's death in a distinctly stronger sense than others. Amyraut, for example, was censured by a national French synod for claiming that Christ died for all human beings "equally." He could even speak of a "conditional predestination" applying to all humanity as rendered savable through Christ's redemption (Armstrong, 93–94), though he agreed to avoid such language after his censure. Unlike many of his peers, Amyraut seemed to say that the divergence between sufficiency and efficacy identifies a divergence *within* God's saving purposes, which is at the root of the complexity we see in the saving effectiveness of what Christ accomplishes and the Spirit applies.

Nonetheless, for Reformed hypothetical universalists of all stripes, God's very real love for all people, Christ's general redemption, and the indiscriminate offer of salvation on condition of faith are not coextensive with God's (or Christ's) ultimate salvific intent. Like particularists, hypothetical universalists affirmed that God intends the satisfaction accomplished by Christ to effectually bring to repentance and faith those whom God in his good pleasure has freely chosen to save from deserved condemnation (*Acta synodi*, 2.80–81; cf. Davenant, "Dissertation"). This balance, hypothetical universalists argued, does justice to the contested biblical statements about God's love for "all" and "the world" while upholding the effectiveness of God's purposes in salvation.

Approaching Atonement: Post-Reformation Reformed Theological Distinctives

The common themes that arise in theological formulation and in criticism of Arminianism from particularists and hypothetical universalists are illuminating for tracing the theological convictions shared across the broad mainstream of post-Reformation Reformed approaches to the doctrine of the atonement. I want to highlight two interrelated themes as especially theologically significant.

The Freedom and Consistency of God's Purposes and Acts

A constant refrain of Reformed orthodoxy is that the good pleasure of God—an immanent motive unqualified and unconditioned by anything other than or in addition to himself—must be the only ground of God's redemptive purpose and action if salvation is to be thoroughly and consistently monergistic. God's grace finds its basis wholly within his inscrutable yet good and wise character and will (Turretin, 350–372). Yet in post-Reformation Reformed reasoning about the atonement, we see two distinctive ways of unpacking this shared commitment to the unconditional grace of God in salvation. The choice can be posed this way: In the formation and execution of God's wholly free saving purposes are the person and work of the incarnate Son determined and circumscribed by the decree of election, or is the salvation of the elect only part of the scope of Christ's work (albeit the chief part)? Gomarus challenged Martinius to a duel over precisely this question (Thomas, 142–145).

While this is a significant (and arguably unresolved) question for historic Reformed theology, on both sides we nevertheless find a Reformed emphasis on the unity of God's *free* immanent purposes and their *full* actualization in the economy. For the post-Reformation Reformed, it was theologically inappropriate to posit any unrealized or frustrated intention, any ultimately impeded will, in God.

The Coherence Between Christ's Work and its Fruits

The unity between God's immanent decree and economic acts further entails that God's purposes in Christ's satisfaction will be completely realized, since the fruition of these purposes *is not determined* by those who receive its benefits—either by being actualized (through foreseen faith), or by being thwarted (through ultimately resisting the gracious working of the Spirit) (Thomas, 145). Just as the electing purposes of the Trinity must never be separated from the accomplished work of the incarnate Son, so the intention of Christ's satisfaction should never be decoupled from its fruition by his Spirit. This is true even for hypothetical universalists who allow a broad scope to Christ's redemptive work on behalf of all people, since the benefits Christ procures and the Spirit bestows on the non-elect are genuinely good and loving but, in God's purposes, ultimately non-saving.

Conclusion

It is crucial for a proper perspective on the disagreement among the Reformed that the debates between particularists and hypothetical universalists, while sometimes heated as at Dort, were entirely intramural. In contrast to Reformed condemnation of Arminianism as a dangerous departure from faithful teaching, hypothetical universalism—even of the Amyraldian variety—was never officially deemed outside the bounds of the Reformed confessions. The Canons of Dort and later the Westminster Confession of Faith (1647) were composed with the participation of a few (albeit influential) advocates of hypothetical universalism, and formulated to avoid explicitly disallowing this view. Even Francis Turretin, who helped draft the *Formula Consensus Helvetica* (1675), a Swiss particularist document containing a strong criticism of hypothetical universalism, referred to advocates of the view as "our ministers" (Turretin, 457). The *Formula*'s fate is in some ways redolent of the murky results of the increasingly elaborate and diverse Reformed expressions of the significance of the atonement. The *Formula* was never widely enforced outside a few Swiss cantons, and gradually fell into obscurity as the careful biblical and theological concerns of post-Reformation confessional orthodoxies gave way within European academies and churches to the Enlightenment and its much more ambivalent stance toward such seemingly parochial matters.

Bibliography

Acta synodi nationalis ... Dordrechti habitae, 1620.
Arminius, *The Works of James Arminius*, vol. 3, 1853.
Armstrong, *Calvinism and the Amyraut Heresy*, 2004.

Baxter, *Universal Redemption of Mankind, by the Lord Jesus Christ*, 1694.
Canons of Dort, online at http://www.crcna.org/welcome/beliefs/confessions/canons-dort.
Davenant, "A Dissertation on the Death of Christ," in *An Exposition of the Epistle of St. Paul to the Colossians*, vol. 2, 1832.
Klauber, "Helvetic Formula Consensus (1675): An Introduction and Translation," *Trinity Journal* 11:1, 1990.
Muller, *Calvin and the Reformed Tradition*, 2012.
Owen, *The Death of Death in the Death of Christ*, 1845.
Schaff, *The Creeds of Christendom with a History and Critical Notes*, 4th edn, 1977.
Snoddy, *The Soteriology of James Ussher*, 2014.
Thomas, *The Extent of the Atonement*, 1997.
Turretin, *Institutes of Elenctic Theology*, 1994.
Ussher, *The True Intent and Extent of Christ's Death and Satisfaction upon the Cross*, in *Works*, ed. Elrington, vol. 12, 1847.

Prayer

Ashley Cocksworth

Prayer and the atonement are (surprisingly, perhaps) complexly interwoven. There was prayer on the cross, of course, when Christ vicariously "confessed" the sins of creation as the great high priest and intercessor (cf. Luke 23:24; Forsyth). The metaphor of a cultic "sacrifice," and other atonement terminology, when applied to the death of Christ makes little sense apart from the liturgy of the Jewish tradition (Barker, chapter 3). Prayer, like the atonement, is more mysterious than mechanical. And the atonement brings about the very conditions for one to pray (or better, to be prayed "in") and on that basis to partake in the divine liturgy (Barth). Indeed, prayer is all about being united in Christ's ongoing intercessions with the Father (Rom. 8.34). It is about the covenant union between God and humanity—a union that is the direct result of Christ's atoning and mediating work. As F. W. Dillistone writes, "Prayer ... [is] supremely the meeting-place of heaven and earth," where sins are forgiven and relations healed (292).

The relation between prayer and the atonement can be seen in Jesus's earthly, as well as heavenly, ministry. The first signs of Jesus's Messianic ministry include the casting out of a demon, the healing at Peter's house, the cleansing of the leper and the forgiving of the sins of the paralytic. In each case, there is an association of "the rite of healing" (Barker), prayer, and the effecting of atonement (hence the reference to Is. 53 in the story of the healing of Peter's mother-in-law and the curing of "all who were sick" in Mt. 8). Jesus's earthly ministry of reconciliation and healing, which is accompanied by prayer throughout, therefore can be seen to prefigure in complex ways (cf. Mark 2:1–12) that which was to come in Golgotha's supreme ministry of reconciliation climactically expressed in the prayer on the cross: "Father, forgive them." And just as Christ "carried" our burdens in and through prayer into the presence of God in perfect intercession "through the eternal Spirit" (Heb. 9:14), we are commanded likewise to follow his example and take on the burden of others in our own hearts and carry them into the presence of God; or better, our intercession is a sharing in the ascended Christ's ongoing intercession at the right hand of the Father. According to P. T. Forsyth, who perhaps saw the connections between prayer and the atonement more than most, "the intercession of Christ in heaven is the continuity and consummation of His supreme work on earth. To share it is the meaning of praying in the Spirit" (23). Viewed this way, the atonement and prayer can be seen to depend on the same Christological logic of mediation and representation (cf. John 17): because we cannot pray as we ought, our prayer depends on Christ's mediation and because we cannot atone for our sins, our atonement with God depends on Christ's mediation and vicarious action (Redding). In both, Christ's priestly work does not occlude the possibility of human participation, but founds and grounds it.

In addition to the Christological connections between prayer and the atonement, prayer is also intrinsic to the development and transmission of this doctrine and other doctrines. In a seminal essay on the development of Christian doctrine, Maurice Wiles draws out the "close interrelation" doctrine and prayer once shared (*The Making of Christian Doctrine*, 62). Although the "integrity" of prayer and doctrine has somewhat fallen out of fashion in much of modern theological discourse (McIntosh), in the early Church prayer practices often took primacy over doctrine and acted as vehicles for doctrinal development. Praying to God through Jesus Christ held a theo-logic that led to doctrinal formulations about Christ's two natures, for example. But as well as driving doctrine, practices of prayer and worship transmitted "to the next generation" important doctrinal concepts (Wiles, *The Making of Christian Doctrine*, 63), just as they continue to do today through hymns, worship songs, and liturgical texts.

One of the ablest examples of what a "close integration" of prayer and the doctrine of the atonement looks like can be found in Anselm of Canterbury (1033–1109). Anselm was first and foremost a monk and therefore a person of prayer. Alongside his more doctrinally orientated work, such as *Cur Deus Homo*, lies his significant contribution to the Christian spiritual traditions. He authored a series of extremely popular prayers and meditations that were famed for their rhetorical flair and theological dare. So popular were his prayers that they attracted multiple imitations and have been credited for bringing about a "transformation" in the prayer habits of medieval piety and still remain influential in the liturgical tradition (Southern, 99–106). Throughout his *Prayers and Meditations*, Anselm can be seen exploring a number of atonement-related issues

(Hogg, 34–35). But the prayer-doctrine relation reaches its fullest expression in his late and great "Meditation on Human Redemption" (Anselm, 230–237).

In her commentary on the prayers, Benedicta Ward rightly commends the "Meditation on Human Redemption" as "the greatest of all the meditations, and shows how Anselm himself prayed his theology till there was no difference between theology and prayer" (77). The prayed version of his doctrine of the atonement contains intricate doctrinal work that carries all the hallmarks of a distinctively Anselmic approach to the atonement. We find Anselm praying about the rejection of ransom theories ("clearly God owes nothing to the devil"), the need for the restoration of divine honor, an acute awareness of the profundity of sin ("a huge leaden weight hung round your neck, dragging you downward") that makes the honor a debt which humanity must but cannot pay ("human nature alone could not do this"), a two natures Christology, a crucicentric soteriology, and a commitment to the logic of satisfaction. The "Meditation on Human Redemption" is Anselm's theology of the atonement *in nuce*. But it is also more than vintage Anselm dressed up in prayer clothing: taking the meditation seriously presents new perspectives on what Anselm is up to in his atonement theology.

For example, a key aspect of the Anselmian transformation of prayer habits was that his authored prayers were not to be said in the company of others but alone, in one's inner chamber. The theological effect of this relocation is suggestive: "the sinner stands alone before God," contemplating one's own salvation (Southern, 100). In addressing the "Christian soul," the Meditation therefore complicates the dominant readings of Anselm that assume his theology of the atonement is too objective to be subjectively relevant. With the psalmody as his model, there is an increasingly experiential concern in the *Prayers and Meditations*: one's mind is stirred in the prayers to see God face-to-face. In his "Prayer to Christ," for example, Anselm imagines himself at the foot of the cross:

> Would that I with happy Joseph
> might have taken down my Lord from the cross,
> wrapped him in spiced grave-clothes
> and laid him in the tomb. (93–99)

What unfolds here, as Anselm reconstructs the Passion as a historical scene to be played out before the soul, is a meditation on the example of Christ. Given the sharp contrasts that are often drawn between Anselm and the young Abelard, the arch proponent of the so-called "exemplarist approach," this is an odd sort of thing for Anselm to be doing. A reconsideration of Anselm's atonement theology via his devotional writings, I propose, helps to dismantle some of the caricatures that keep Abelard and Anselm apart: Anselm (like Abelard) has lots to say about love ("admit me to the inner room of your love") and Anselm (like Abelard) has lots to say about the soul contemplating the story of Christ's life as the model of perfect and obedient response to God ("chew this, bite it, suck it, let your heart swallow it"). For the Anselm of the *Prayers and Meditations*, atonement can be seen to be happening in the slow spiritual digestion of the truth of Christ's example through which the pray-er is conformed to Christ's likeness. There, alone in the inner chamber before God, the idea that the atonement is an exclusively objective transaction would be far from the pray-er's mind. For the Anselm of the *Prayers and Meditations*, the atonement is objective in the sense that it is accomplished for all by God in the history of the world ("Christ did all this") but at the same time it is subjective in the sense that it brings about the changed conditions within us for us to respond appropriately (in prayer) to the atoning event and participate in its ongoing effects. As Wiles argues, "in spirituality the two are most effectively combined" (81).

The "Meditation on Human Redemption" is not therefore just doctrinal information about the atonement presented as first-order discourse. Anselm's point is subtler, and indeed more radical: the impartation of the knowledge of Christ's atoning action is for nothing less than the transformation of the pray-er. The result of that transformation is revealed, somewhat paradoxically, in the very act of praying the prayer. Indeed, knowing quite what to do in response to God's atoning work in Christ is always a source of anxiety, as it was for Anselm: "I owe you more than my whole self." In the "Meditation on Human Redemption," the ethical response is quite clear: it is prayer and the pursuit of holiness. In prayer the soul is lifted up in praise and thanksgiving—knowledge about the atonement becomes praise (Gunton, 200–203). And in prayer we follow Christ's example and take up our own crosses in active participation with God's ongoing mission in the world.

Bibliography

Anselm, *The Prayers and Meditations of St Anselm*, trans. Ward, 1976.
Barker, *The Great High Priest*, 2003.
Barth, *The Christian Life: Church Dogmatics IV/4—Lecture Fragments*, 1981.
Cocksworth, *Karl Barth on Prayer*, 2015.
Dillistone, *The Christian Understanding of Atonement*, 1984.

Forsyth, *The Soul of Prayer*, 2nd edn, 1949 and *The Work of Christ*, 1910.
Gunton, *The Actuality of Atonement*, 2004.
Hogg, *Anselm of Canterbury*, 2004.
McIntosh, *Mystical Theology*, 1998.
Redding, *Prayer and the Priesthood of Christ in the Reformed Tradition*, 2003.
Southern, *St Anselm*, 1990.
Ward, "Introduction," in *The Prayers and Meditations of St Anselm*, 1976.
Wiles, *The Making of Christian Doctrine*, 1975.
Wiles, *The Remaking of Christian Doctrine*, 1974.

84

The Problem of Evil

Matthias Grebe

The *Problem of Evil* is undoubtedly one of the most perplexing topics in Christian theology and one of the strongest charges leveled against theism. Located at the intersection between theology and philosophy, it is often posed as part of the "tri-lemma" of theodicy (Lactantius, in *De Ira Dei*, attributes this formulation to Epicurus): why, if God is all-loving, all-powerful, and all-knowing, is there evil and suffering in the world? A related conundrum concerns the origin of evil, *unde malum*? According to the opening line of the Apostles' Creed, God is not only omnipotent but also the creator of all things. Is not the logical conclusion of this that God must also be the author of evil? And if not, then why, in light of God's omnipotence and loving fatherhood, is there so *much* evil in the world? Can God only be either good or almighty? Or can the apparent contradiction between the coexistence of evil in the world and God's omnibenevolence, omnipotence, and omniscience be resolved?

Over the centuries, various Christian thinkers have tried to resolve this theodical "tri-lemma" by offering alternatives to the common understanding either of God or of the nature of evil. One way of solving the problem of evil is to redefine or to alter the attributes ascribed to the biblical God. God's omnibenevolence, while not wholly undisputed, is an essential part of the traditional Christian doctrine of God and therefore has not been the focus of these alterations. Instead, it is God's omnipotence that has been the focus of redefinition attempts; many modern theologians and philosophers of religion (Mackie, 150–176) have viewed the concept as logically incoherent or impossible. In modern religious thought, an all-powerful and apathetic God has increasingly been replaced with a "suffering God" who *is* or rather *has* limited God-self for the sake of humanity.

Today, many theologians and philosophers consider the prevailing problem of evil to be a fundamental impediment to belief in the existence of a God who exhibits all three attributes, and only a few have argued that such a deity can coexist alongside evil in a plausible manner (Plantinga, 54f). Others argue that we ought to acknowledge that we are faced with questions we cannot answer (Kilby, 13–29; Surin; Tilley).

Doctrinally, evil occupies an important role in a theological "system," and this role might be said to reveal much about the particular theology of atonement within this system. The biblical picture "incorporates evil into its picture of God and his activity" (Davies, 444), and highlights that "the ultimate solution of the problem of evil must lie in the fact that the God who created the world is also the God who has redeemed it" (Richardson, 193). The creator himself is *Christ the Victor*, who has conquered sin and evil by his own suffering and atoning death on the cross, and has achieved the gift of eternal life for the many. Yet the doctrine the atonement not only highlights the defeat of evil but also brings to attention the world's brokenness, and stirs us to compassion, to fight evil and suffering according to the Pauline maxim (Rom. 12:21). This kind of pastoral theodicy speaks of evil not simply theoretically, but as something to be overcome practically.

However, two key questions remain: first, if God is the perfect maker, creating the world and finding that it was "very good" (Gen. 1:31), how could he allow his creatures to become the origin of evil, or allow evil to enter and spoil creation? And second, if Christ has disarmed the powers and authorities, and triumphed over them by the cross and his atonement (Col. 2:15), why then do "horrendous evils" (Adams, 203) and suffering remain in this world?

The Old Testament does not define "evil" as such, nor does it give a clear explanation of its origin. It does, however, speak about its existence throughout its narrative. Evil occurs in creation, distorting and corrupting its divine purpose. Although the Bible offers no definite answer regarding the origins of natural evil or disasters, "in the first two chapters of the book of Job, a figure referred to as 'the Satan' has the power to inflict hardship. And, some Christians have urged, naturally occurring evil can be traced to free, malevolent, non-human agency" (Davies, 446). Moral evil, on the other hand, is often traced back to the Genesis story of the Fall.

The word "evil" occurs for the first time in the Genesis narrative in chapter 2, which describes the "tree (עץ) of the knowledge (תעדה) of good (בוט) and evil (ערו)" (Gen. 2:9), from which Adam and Eve are prohibited to eat by God's direct command. The essential meaning of the root עער (evil) "can be seen in its frequent juxtaposition with the root "טוב" (good) as parallel to "life" and "death" (see Deut. 30:15), and, indirectly, "blessing" and "curse" (Deut. 30:19; Livingston, 2.854–856). In this way the verb from the root עער denotes an activity that is contrary to the will of God, standing in opposition to the good acts of God and righteous people (see 1 John 3:12). Furthermore, the Hebrew word "תעד" (knowledge, as in the Tree of Knowledge), which derives from the root "ערי" (knowing) and occurs in the Fall narrative of Genesis 2–3, expresses both the intimacy between husband and wife (Gen. 4:1) as well as a personal "knowing of God." In particular, it means to love and obey God, since the verb "*yd*" (to know) never signifies purely intellectual knowing, but rather an "experiencing," a "becoming acquainted with" (von Rad, 81, 89). Then, in Genesis 3, we read about Adam and Eve's temptation and how evil comes to dwell within humanity through their free decision. The serpent explicitly denies God's warning that a penalty will be inflicted and appeals to human curiosity, persuading them that the results of eating this fruit will be positively desirable, thereby deceiving Adam and Eve, promising them that they can be like God "γινώσκοντες καλὸν (good) καὶ πονηρόν (evil)" (LXX, Gen. 3:5), "an extension of human existence beyond the limits set for it by God at creation" (von Rad, 89). The question of obedience is raised and the possibility of disobedience suddenly exists for the first time. What is apparent is that evil does not derive from God, but from the outside, albeit from an evil force within the created order.

Throughout history however, several thinkers have claimed that evil does not exist, has no "being" or "substance," and is therefore either not "real" (the word "evil" simply denoting the absence of good), or is already "defeated" and "conquered" through the atoning work of Christ on the cross, who came not to explain evil but to defeat it (Augustine, *Confessions*, chapter 7; Augustine, *Enchiridion*, chapter 3; Barth, CD §50). If this is the case, they argue, and evil is merely "non-being," then it also represents our perception of *privatio boni*, an imperfection in a good thing (like a hole in a wall or blindness as the privation of sight). Within this understanding of evil, they continue, it is possible to argue for the existence of a benevolent, omnipotent, and omniscient God who is not the author of evil. Ultimately, they contend that this solution means that there is no *problem* of evil at all.

Augustine's *privatio boni* argument, though logically coherent on its own terms, rests on the premise that every actual entity is good (*omnis natura bonum est*) and that evil does not exist in *itself*, but is instead insubstantial and only a "parasitic" aspect of another entity. Thus, as long as a "thing is being corrupted, there is good in it of which it is being deprived" because "not even the corruption remains, for it is nothing in itself, having no subsistent being in which to exist" (Augustine, *Enchiridion*, chapter IV.12). He concludes that a human sinner is a "good entity in so far as he is a man, evil in so far as he is wicked" (chapter IV.13).

This prompts the question of whether Augustine's view of *privatio boni* ignores or downplays the seriousness of evil. Is sickness simply the privation of health, as he would have it (Augustine, *Enchiridion*, chapter III.11)? While the latter premise—that sin and evil need a "mode in which to exist" or a "host" in which to dwell—is consistent with the biblical witness, the idea that something good remains in humanity even when it is corrupted nevertheless seems to be contrary to Jesus's teaching of the corrupting influence of the leaven in the dough (Mt. 13:33, 16:6–12; Mark 8:15; and Luke 12:1, 13:21). This "natural image for evil" (Barrett, 127) is a theme that is also picked up by Paul (1 Cor. 5:6 and Gal. 5:9), who knows that while he has the desire to do good (καλὸν—a blameless state of being, the fruit of being in relation with God who is pure ἀγαθός), nothing good (ἀγαθός or *bonum*) lives within or comes out of his sinful body (Rom. 7:18); instead he continues to do evil (κακός), that which he does not want to do (Rom. 7:19). Furthermore, in the New Testament the devil is identified as ὁ πονηρὸς—evil personified (Mt. 13:19; John 17:15; Eph. 6:16; 2 Thess. 3:2; 1 John 2:13 and 3:12)—who, along with the evil spirits, controls the world (1 John 5:19).

Knowing God, therefore, means being in relationship with goodness, which brings about good deeds, whereas knowing evil brings about evil. As Jesus says in Luke 6:45: "The good (ἀγαθὸς—referring to God) man brings good things out of the good stored up in his heart, and the evil (πονηρὸς—referring to the devil) man brings evil things out of the evil stored up in his heart." Therefore, disobeying God and turning against his command as Adam and Eve did in the Garden represents the rupture of the personal and intimate relationship with him. By eating the fruit, they did gain the new knowledge that the serpent promised, but it was a fatal and death-bringing knowledge of evil, an intimate "knowing evil" they had not experienced before. It was this experience of evil that brought about a personal relationship with the Evil One (see 1 John 3:10).

Consequently, in biblical terms, evil must be seen as an anti-relational force, contrary to the life-giving relationship with God. Key here is the separation from God, the alienation between God and humanity through "knowing evil." It is not that God did not want Adam and Eve to possess a knowledge that would change their being into a godlike one, but rather that God gave them complete security and wanted to protect them from the harm of knowing evil. Adam and Eve's disobedience negatively affected their relationship with God, who in his nature is goodness (ἀγαθός), and their intimate knowledge of evil caused them to become slaves in bondage to evil.

Augustine's view of the privation of good has impacted the Church's teaching on sin, evil, and the atonement. However, it might be argued that according to the New Testament, there is nothing good within fallen humanity *outside* of Christ. Christ's atoning work on the cross does not simply "fix" a corrupted humanity or "fill" a lack of goodness. What Christ's death on the cross achieves is the creation of a completely "new creation" (2 Cor. 5:17), by *cancelling* the old slavish existence (Rom. 6:6) under the bondage of evil and *crucifying* it (Gal. 2:20). On the cross the "principalities and powers" (Col. 2:15) are conquered. As the writer of Hebrews states in 2:14: "by his death he might destroy him who holds the power of death—that is, the devil," the "personification of all that is evil" (Arnold, 1078). John claims that Christ came to "destroy the devil's work" (1 John 3:8), and Paul explains that he does so by *destroying* evil's host (Col. 2:11–15) creating a new humanity and hiding it in the new Adam, Christ (Col. 3:3). In this way, he gathers his people into a new community (Arnold, 1079). The atonement (at-one-ment) is therefore the reestablishment of the covenantal relationship between God and humanity, which was previously destroyed by sin and evil (Wright, 36). In Christ's death, evil is conquered once and for all (as seen in the resurrection) and humanity is brought from the power of darkness into God's light (Col. 1:12–13; 1 Pet. 2:9), in intimate relationship with the triune God, her creator, sustainer, and redeemer. This new, post-resurrection relationship is, in fact, more intimate than that experienced between God and humanity pre-fall (Barth, *CD* IV/1, 13, 34).

However, the process that thus far only occurs in the human spirit—the renewal of our inward being (Rom. 7:22; Eph. 3:16)—is the Spirit's downpayment on the promise of the resurrection of the body of the new creation (Rom. 8:11; 2 Cor. 1:22 and 5:5). Consequently, although evil and sin are conquered and disarmed on the cross "in Christ," they continue to exist in the "here and now" in our "bodies of death" (Rom. 7:25). Though the Christian mind is renewed day by day, the body is still waiting to be fully transformed into a spiritual resurrection body without suffering and corruption by evil (see 1 Cor. 15:42–46).

The basis for victory over evil in everyday life is, first, continuous prayer in faith, as expressed in the seventh and final petition of the Lord's Prayer: "deliver us from evil" (Mt. 6:13). It is a prayer both for the Christian as well as for others to turn from "darkness to light, and from the power of Satan to God" (Acts 26:18). Second, victory is also found in the sacraments—in baptism and in the celebration of the Eucharist, "which repeats the meal that Jesus gave as his own interpretation of his death" (Wright, 59), bringing about divine love, healing, and forgiveness, and serving as a constant reminder to the Church of Jesus's death as a healing reality within a broken world. The individual Christian is commanded to follow in the footsteps of Christ and endure her own suffering, showing solidarity to others who suffer, since Christ's suffering on the cross contains both an invitation to eternal life as well as a summons to ethical living in the "here and now." The Spirit in the "here and now" enables her to "fight the good fight" (1 Tim. 6:12) and therefore Christians are told *not* to "imitate what is evil" (3 John 11) but to "hate what is evil [and] cling to what is good" (Rom. 12:9). The Christian is the one who lives day by day by the atoning power, who "in Christ" cannot be overcome by evil (by repaying evil with evil). Instead, the Christian herself overcomes evil with good (Rom. 12:21) in the face of suffering. The result is a life dwelt in God's mercy and goodness, and a transformation into a messenger of the atoning work of Christ (2 Cor. 4:7–11).

Bibliography

Adams, *Horrendous Evils and the Goodness of God*, 1999.
Arnold, "Satan, Devil," in *Dictionary of the Later New Testament & Its Development*, 1997.
Augustine, *Confessions*.
Augustine, *Enchiridion*.
Barrett, *The First Epistle to the Corinthians*, 1968.
Barth, *Church Dogmatics*.
Davies, "Evil" in *Encyclopedia of Christianity*, 2005.
Kilby, "Evil and the Limits of Theology," in *New Blackfriars* 84, 2003.
Livingston, "עור," *TWOT*.
Mackie, *The Miracle of Theism*, 1982.
Plantinga, *God, Freedom, and Evil*, 1989.
Richardson, "The Problem of Evil," in *A New Dictionary of Christian Theology*, 1983.
Surin, *Theology and the Problem of Evil*, 2004.
Tilley, *The Evils of Theodicy*, 1991.
von Rad, *Genesis*, 1979.
Wright, "Results: Atonement and the Problem of Evil," in *Evil and the Justice of God*, 2006.

Reconciliation

Thomas Andrew Bennett

To explain the logic behind sacrifice in the Old Testament, John Goldingay uses the example of a bouquet of flowers transferred from husband to wife (3–20). There are many occasions for such a gesture, for example, her birthday or a spontaneous display of affection, but one—apology—might be said to capture both the logic of Christian atonement and the reconciliation it brings. Fractured relationships are part and parcel of the human experience; atonement and reconciliation are therefore socially and culturally conditioned processes by which relationships are returned to a harmonious state. In the case of flowers—and, as Goldingay might add, cultic sacrifice—the offending party offers a signifying token to the offended. The token represents many things: a change of heart, sincerity of feeling, affection, and a desire to refrain from the offending behavior in the future. The husband chooses this gift, flowers, and these flowers (as opposed to some other kind) because he knows his wife. He knows what she likes, what she wants. Receiving the gift is itself a signifying act. By accepting flowers, the wife acknowledges his wrongdoing and sets it aside, no longer giving it any place in ongoing marital relations. What is done is done; now husband and wife can move forward again, together.

Goldingay's example is especially apropos as it highlights the close psychological connection between atonement and reconciliation, demonstrating clearly how the two function as an organic unity. In Christian theological ethics, therefore, a restored right relation between individuals, communities, and even whole societies is the natural outworking of *imitatio Christi*. Miroslav Volf articulates the point with special attention to the divine gift, the divine token: "As God does not abandon the godless to their evil but gives the divine self for them in order to receive them into divine communion through atonement, so also should we—whoever our enemies and whoever we may be" (23). Far from being an exemplarist account—though it is surely that as well—Volf implies that reconciliation with God means being drawn somehow into the very divine life, a life that is then marked by communion between parties once far off. Atonement and reconciliation are intimately connected; the first leads to and is bound up with the second.

According to Volf's statement, however, Goldingay's flower-giving example is dis-analogous to the real ontology of Christian atonement in three important ways. First, Volf notes that if there are any preexisting relations between human beings and God, they are not harmonious but hostile. Volf is no doubt thinking with the Apostle Paul who, in Romans 5:6–11 describes the human condition as "weak." We are "sinners," God's "enemies" and yet, in the midst of this, Paul thinks, God reconciles himself to us anyway in the death of our Lord Jesus Christ. Second, God's gift to humanity is not something outside of God's own self. Unlike flowers or a scapegoat, which are bought or raised, God reconciles us in an egregious act of self-abandonment and does so for the sake of complete communion. Last, marriage involves individuals and interpersonal relationships whereas the triune God already knows communion in the divine life and reconciles not only individual persons, but families, communities, and peoples. It is instructive that "our enemies" are often not just individuals, but rival institutions, classes, and countries. So, while Old Testament sacrifice captures the logic of atonement-bound-up-with-reconciliation, Christian ethical practice must go beyond the confines of maintaining right relations with one's friends and family. In fact, it must penetrate every level of human individual and corporate relationships, having as the end goal the consummation of all things in the peaceful, joyous communion of the divine life. In this it is to imitate God's reconciliation with us by including enemies among those to be reconciled, by generating reconciliation out of willing self-abandonment, and by transcending merely the personal sphere, taking place between communities, churches, institutions, polities, and even the creation itself.

Taking up something of this theme, John Milbank suggests, "The Incarnation and the hypostatic descent of the Spirit inaugurated on earth a counter-polity exercising a counter-sovereignty, nourished by sovereign victimhood" (105). Since divine life itself has been united to humanity and taken up special residence in a particular community, that community establishes a sort of beachhead of reconciliation—which is to say that the church is the location within which ultimate reconciliation begins. We say "begins" because of course reconciliation can and should take place between, for example, warring states, but, as Milbank is quick to point out, that sort of reconciliation depends on the "usual conditions of human rule" like the "division of powers between sovereign and executive, the exclusionist logic of inside/outside, and government by emergency and exception" (105). Neither Milbank nor we would suggest that the church somehow avoids these all too human tendencies in practice. Likening complete reconciliation to light, Milbank regards the presence of the Spirit as "inaugurat[ing] an altogether different possibility: it opens a narrow chink of light, allowing, albeit inchoately, a certain counter-movement of advance and of progress for the few (intensely) and the many (dispersedly) towards the source of this light" (105). Here Milbank acknowledges the ontological truth of the Spirit's presence in the church without ignoring what is by experience plain, that reconciliation between parties is rare, messy, and never quite free from the subtle corruption of sin.

The nod to the few—by which Milbank means "Christians"—and the many—that is, the world outside the church—alerts us to the nature of reconciliation that takes place in the secular sphere. It is derivative and, if we might exclude the pejorative aspect of the term, parasitic. In some respects it is the church's mission to practice reconciliation within and without in order that she might expose the world to the One from whence it comes. *Lumen Gentium*, the dogmatic statement on ecclesiology produced by Vatican II, echoes this theological conviction in paragraphs fifteen and sixteen, suggesting that the Spirit dispenses charismatic gifts, redemption, and reconciliation outside the Roman Catholic Church as a "preparation for the Gospel" (16) and that the Spirit's reconciling work "links" and "relates" non-Catholics and non-Christians to the Roman Catholic Church in real ways. From the perspective of the ecumenist, reconciliation thus washes out from the divine life like a tide to the church—to individual Christians, local bodies, and to the church catholic—spilling out further into the world, and from there flowing back in from world to church, and, ultimately, to communion with the divine life.

What, then, does reconciliation look like practically? Hans Boersma links the church's reconciling activities to the concept of hospitality, wherein whatever the church does, be it preaching the gospel, baptizing, partaking in Eucharist, practicing confession and penance, or participating in the sufferings that accompany a cruciform life, all is done to overcome the real boundaries that separate people from God and one another in order to offer a genuine, hospitable welcome (205–234). Boersma appears to be drawing thematically on the categories of exclusion and embrace expounded by Miroslav Volf. Reconciliation must take boundaries seriously. Boundaries are not just real; they are necessary for communal identity and cohesion. At the same time, however, they are not impermeable. The church's practices create the conceptual and relational space in which the other may be welcomed without being either forced (true hospitality, like true embrace must be engaged in freely) or assimilated (true hospitality respects personal/communal integrity) (Boersma, 205–234). Reconciliation in the church is therefore characterized by freedom and nonviolence. Jürgen Moltmann writes of Christian freedom in this way:

> Anyone who experiences God and a "deification" (*theosis*) … is freed from all the godless ties of this world, and is nobody's slave. He lives in the free space of God's creative possibilities, and partakes of them. But for that very reason he also participates in the complex web of relationships through which the Creator loves everything he has created and preserves its life. Freedom is not merely sovereignty. It is communication too, life in the communicative relationships out of which life begins and in which life comes alive. (121)

This freedom is clearly not the libertarian "freedom to" though it is noncoercive. Instead, it is manifestly a "freedom for." It is a freedom, in fact, that is known by creative, spacious, communicative *relations*. When the church practices reconciliation properly, the free Christian finds herself embedded in a "complex web of relationships" in which "life comes alive." Moltmann's vision of reconciled life therefore bears something of the mark of Aristotle's *eudaimonia*, that is, human flourishing. What begins as divine-human relations restored finds its fullest human expression in vibrant, joyous relations with all that the Creator has lovingly created.

Reconciliation has a long and storied history in the church. The gospels narrate an earthly ministry of Jesus replete with restoring outcasts to community and establishing social relations with the unwanted (Luke 19:1–10). Paul claims that "there is no longer Greek and Jew, circumcised and uncircumcised, barbarian, Scythian, slave and free; but Christ is all and in all" (Col. 3:11). James warns Christians against favoring the rich over the poor in the churches (Jas 2:1–5) as the poor of the world have been chosen by God to be "rich in faith." More recently, the Truth and Reconciliation Commission (TCR) in South Africa promoted racial reconciliation in a country torn apart by divisions of race and class. Perhaps these "narrow chinks of light," as Milbank calls them, have shown that far from abandoning her, the Spirit still calls the church to cleave to reconciliation. It would seem that she does, however inchoately. Remarking on the TCR, Bishop Desmond Tutu writes:

> We were frequently bowled over by the magnanimity, the nobility, and generosity of spirit of those who by rights should have been bristling with resentment and anger and who should have been claiming their pound of flesh but

were doing nothing of the sort. They awed us by their willingness to forgive the perpetrators of some of the most gruesome atrocities, and even on occasion to embrace publicly those who had visited so much suffering on them. (4)

Bibliography

Boersma, *Violence, Hospitality, and the Cross*, 2004.
Goldingay, "Old Testament Sacrifice and the Death of Christ," in *Atonement Today*, 1995.
Milbank, *Being Reconciled*, 2003.
Moltmann, *The Spirit of Life*, 1992.
Tutu, "The Magnanimity of Reconciliation," in *I Have Called You Friends*, 2006.
Volf, *Exclusion and Embrace*, 1996.

Revelation (Book of)

Joseph Mangina

The book of Revelation is a work awash in blood. The most famous reference to blood undoubtedly occurs in chapter 7, with its great roll-call of the 144,000 sealed (the church, understood as the messianic Israel) followed by John's vision of a "great multitude that no one could number" standing before the throne and praising God. The Seer's angelic guide asks: "Who are these, clothed in white robes, and from where have they come?" When John admits his ignorance, the angel declares: "These are the ones coming out of the great tribulation. They have washed their robes and made them white in the blood of the Lamb." There follows a description of the 144,000 sealed as enjoying eternal rest, after God has "[wiped] away every tear from their eyes."

The phrase "being washed in the blood of the Lamb" offers a good point of departure for a discussion of atonement in Revelation. As commonly used, the expression assumes a picture whereby the innocent Christ takes on the sinner's guilt, so that he or she may assume Christ's purity and goodness. The reader may explore the logic of substitutionary or exchange-like models of atonement in many articles throughout the present work. With respect to Revelation, the question is whether the book supports any such account whatsoever. There are good reasons for doubting whether this is so:

1. The human plight as understood in Revelation is not individual guilt, but oppression by anti-god powers (e.g., Satan, the two beasts, the whore of Babylon).
2. Unlike Paul in passages like 2 Corinthians 5:21, Revelation never uses the language of exchange or reconciliation between enemies, much less of Christ's "becoming sin" as in Galatians 3:13. The verb *katallageō* and its cognates are notably absent.

3. As far as conceptions of penal substitution specifically are concerned, these find precious little support in Revelation. At 12:10, it is said that Satan accuses "our brothers" day and night before God. But in the verse immediately preceding Satan is described as a source of deception (12:9, cf. 20:10). We must assume, then, that the accusations he brings against the brethren are false.
4. In the passage we have just been considering, it is not said that the redeemed themselves are washed in the Lamb's blood, but that they *wash their robes* in that blood. Their role is active rather than passive. The reference is therefore to the martyrdom of the (symbolic) 144,000 rather than to their receiving Christ's benefits achieved at the cross. Stated differently, what we see here is a soteriology of identification with Christ as example, rather than a soteriology of Christ's vicarious suffering on behalf of the guilty.

The arguments just rehearsed are weighty. They count strongly against any easy identification of Revelation's views on atonement with those of Paul or the author to the Hebrews, much less to later patristic or Anselmic theories. Nevertheless, this is not the final word to be said on the subject. Atonement is absent in the book only if we construe the term narrowly. Understood more broadly as the event in which God—through Jesus's death—overcomes the forces of evil and restores creation to himself, atonement is everywhere present in the Apocalypse, and may even be said to constitute its major theme. The famous dualisms of the book are a function of the opposition between God and the forces of evil. If the penultimate moment in the drama is the defeat of these forces ("Babylon the great is fallen!" 18:2), its real climax is the marriage of the Lamb and his Bride narrated in chapter 21. The New Jerusalem represents the human and political aspect of a wider cosmic reconciliation, in which all creatures acknowledge God as Lord in a kingdom of peace; hence, a true at-one-ment. Recognition of this universalizing aspect of the book would go a long way toward overcoming the unfortunate stereotype of Revelation as a work marked by violence, exclusion, and sectarian fanaticism (Ellul; Boring; Bauckham).

None of this occurs, however, apart from the shedding of blood, specifically that of the Lamb. This portmanteau image alludes first of all to the Passover Lamb, related to the theme of eschatological exodus that runs throughout Revelation (Bauckham). But it also suggests the whole sacrificial system of Israel. Like other biblical authors the Seer has no theory of cultic sacrifice, but simply assumes that it "works," insofar as "the life of the flesh is in the blood" (Lev. 17:11). The shedding of the Lamb's blood is the act of sacrifice par excellence, making possible the achievement of all God's purposes. Thus the elders (representing Israel/the church) and the four living creatures (representing creation) hymn the Lamb singing:

> Worthy are you to take the scroll
> and to open its seals,
> for you were slain, and by your blood you ransomed people for God
> from every tribe and language and people and nation,
> and you have made them a kingdom and priests to our God,
> and they shall reign on the earth. (Rev. 5:9–10)

As this passage shows, the shedding of blood is not an end in itself, but has a theopolitical *telos*. Christ's death summons a community into being. The church as depicted in Revelation has an undeniably military aspect. They are the Messiah's army, sent out to do battle against the forces of evil. In this respect the book may be said to underwrite a *Christus victor* understanding of atonement (cf. 5:5). Just as the Lamb's victory is won by suffering and death, in the same manner the victory of his followers is won. As noted earlier, they "wash their robes and make them white in the blood of the Lamb." They bear witness (*martyria*) by becoming martyrs. The most powerful parabolic display of this occurs in chapter 11, where the story of the two witnesses is a figure of Jesus's own prophetic existence, death, and resurrection. It is the only passage in Revelation that employs the verb "crucify" (11:8). The city in this parable is Jerusalem, Rome, and all cities where the gospel story is thus told and performed (Minear; Mangina).

The themes of witness, prophecy, and truth telling are pervasive in the Apocalypse. In this respect the book supports René Girard's understanding of the cross as exposure of the demonic mechanisms of violence at work in human society. While the public humiliation, death, and vindication of the two witnesses ends with the destruction of a tenth of the city, "the rest" (i.e., the majority) of the astonished population repents and gives glory to God. The blood of the martyrs is the seed not just of the church, but also of mission. Yet Revelation is too deeply grounded in the Old Testament to sustain Girard's or other contemporary critiques of sacrifice per se (Girard; Weaver). While the cross, considered as a human act of murder, is clearly an evil, Revelation's perspective on it is primarily that of a divinely and eternally ordained act of justice. The Lamb is slaughtered, "from the foundation of the world" (13:13; the point is valid even if eternity is only predicated of the Lamb's book of life, as in some readings). It should be noted that the reason

John and other New Testament authors can risk this sort of thinking is their conviction that Jesus is not just a human "victim" but the eternal Son of God. Revelation's high doctrine of the person of Christ is integral to its conception of his work (Bauckham). In the book's liturgical scenes, he is clearly the object of worship (5:13, 7:10, 22:1–3). It may well be that the proliferation of both atonement theories and of their criticism in modernity is the result of a loss of this foundational conviction, grounded in the New Testament and articulated dogmatically at Nicea and Chalcedon.

Viewed on this broad canvas, Revelation may thus be seen as a kind of cosmic *theologia crucis*, in which God's primordial commitment to his creation is triumphant in the face of radical evil. Christ's death is sacrifice, victory, and act of truth telling. It is participated in the life of the church, and issues in "the healing of the nations" (22:2). The vision is no less comprehensive than Paul's, though articulated in the mode of theopoetic drama rather than via dialectic and concept.

Bibliography

Bauckham, *The Theology of the Book of Revelation*, 1993.
Boring, *Revelation*, 1989.
Ellul, *Apocalypse*, 1977.
Girard, *The Scapegoat*, 1986.
Mangina, *Revelation*, 2010.
Minear, *I Saw a New Earth*, 1968.
Weaver, *The Nonviolent Atonement*, 2nd edn, 2011.

Albrecht Ritschl

Matthew J. Aragon Bruce

Albrecht Ritschl (1822–89) was the dominant theologian in Germany in the latter third of the nineteenth century. However, the theological movements of the early twentieth century roundly rejected his work and that of the school that formed around him. Though Ritschl is little studied today, there has been a series of reappraisals over the past few decades. Ritschl is increasingly considered in his own right and recognized for the profound influence he had on the very figures and movements that rejected him.

Ritschl's most influential doctrinal work is his three-volume *Die christliche Lehre von der Rechtfertigung und Versöhnung* (*Christian Doctrine of Justification and Reconciliation*), Volume I covers the history of doctrine, Volume II the biblical material, and Volume III contains Ritschl's constructive dogmatics.[1] Volume I begins with a discussion of terms; Ritschl elects the term *Versöhnung* (reconciliation) as best grasping Christ's work of "atonement" over, for example, *Erlösung* (redemption) (*RuV* I^1, 4f.; *Unterricht*, §§34–54).[2] He does so, among other reasons, to highlight "erroneous" doctrines from the tradition. Ritschl rejected the patristic "ransom" theory completely and was staunchly critical of later "legal" and "penal" theories that view Christ's death as a propitiation of God, for example, the "satisfaction" of either divine honor or divine righteousness/justice.

---

[1] Cited as *RuV*, with a Roman numeral for the volume and with superscript numbers to indicate the edition.

[2] See *RuV* I^1, 4f. In the third and final edition this terminological discussion is deleted, though elements of it remain scattered throughout the first chapter. See also, Ritschl, *Unterricht*, §§34–54, "reconciliation" is the sole descriptor for Christ's work, even "justification" (*Rechtfertigung*) becomes subsidiary.

Ritschl completely brackets out Patristic atonement theories because he judges the Patristic doctrine of sin to be a "mechanical subordination to the devil" and contends that the Father's "idea of redemption is completely indifferent to the concept of human will" (*RuV* I³, 17). For Ritschl, the idea that human beings are under the dominion of the devil is a misleading "metaphor" for it depicts God in a manner that contradicts the character of divine justice. In sum the idea that God deceived Satan into forfeiting his dominion over human beings is, for Ritschl, detrimental to a correct concept of God. Second, the Patristic model removes human moral responsibility for sin as it makes human beings merely passive agents, goods exchanged in the transaction. Third, the ransom theory makes Christ's death the sole cause of redemption, neglecting Christ's active obedience (his life and passion) and the resurrection.

His treatment of the history of the doctrine thus begins with Anselm and Abelard. In these two diverse twelfth-century figures, Ritschl perceives a soteriological shift from an emphasis on the relationship between God and the devil to that between God and human beings. For Ritschl, this shift comes to fruition in the Reformation, Luther in particular, in the principle that "one recognizes the essence of God and Christ only in their value for us" (*RuV* III⁴, 202).

However, Ritschl judges this shift to have derailed with the Protestant Scholastics, who deduce the righteousness of God by means of "rational presuppositions," but ground the knowledge of the forgiveness of sins in revelation (*RuV* III⁴, 257). The problem with this for Ritschl is that this implies that justice is essential to the divine being, while forgiveness is not. Ritschl faults scholastic orthodoxy for "its neglect of the question of which end God has, or can have, in common with the human race" (*RuV* III⁴, 257). According to Ritschl, the doctrine of God common to scholastic orthodoxy, be it medieval or Protestant, depicts divine action *ad extra*, God's creation of the world and provision of salvation for humanity, as accidental to the divine being:

> The self-purpose of God lies in an incomparable manner beyond the purpose of the world. Therefore, the creation of the world, even if explained by the love of God, is still only inferred from the arbitrary will of God. Moreover, God's revelation in Christianity appears just as arbitrary; and even if it leads man to the vision of God, this transcendental purpose extends so far beyond the nature of man that it is just as disproportionate to human being as God's purpose is disproportionate to the world created by him. (*RuV* III⁴, 258)

Ritschl judges traditional dogma to be infected with a theological voluntarism that makes Christ's work for human salvation the whimsical undertakings of a capricious deity. Ritschl counters that the creation of the world and particularly the relationship between God and humanity, namely, God's provision of salvation, belongs to the divine essence.

Thus, despite its title, Ritschl's three-volume *magnum opus* is in fact a doctrine of God. According to Ritschl, God's eternal end and highest good is the formation of the "Kingdom of God," that is, a community of human beings motivated by love of God and neighbor (*Unterricht*, §5, a). This community is the result of the love that God is, and it is actualized by the revelation of divine love in Jesus Christ (*Unterricht*, §6).

In *RuV* II, Ritschl argues that there is an evolution of understanding within Scripture itself such that God's love gains priority over God's holiness (*RuV* II^4, 89–102). Ritschl contends that the prophets give increasing attention to God's patience and long-suffering such that the wrath of God, which is wrapped up with earlier notions of holiness, is restrained and eventually set aside (*RuV* II^4, 137–138). Turning to the New Testament, Ritschl argues that the community that follows Jesus receives a more complete revelation of God's personality:

> The name of God as Father, which Jesus makes effective for the community of his disciples by recognizing them as sons of God because of their association with himself, has in this general application no other content than the *creative loving will*, which the community of the perfected revelation erects as its objective, directed to the Kingdom of God. (*RuV* II^4, 97; emphasis in the original)

This perfected revelation of God as creative loving will leads Ritschl, in *RuV* III, to revise the idea of divine wrath found in scholastic orthodoxy, such that divine wrath is directed not at sinners but rather against resistance to God's loving will:

> According to the authority of Scripture, neither the idea of the wrath of God as a metastasis of divine love, nor the relating of it to sin in general is justified (Vol. II, 129, 137); according to the authority of the New Testament, wrath signifies the resolution of God to destroy those men who set themselves definitely against the redemption and the final end of the kingdom of God (Vol. II, 154). (*RuV* III^4, 306)

On this understanding of wrath and sin, there is no need for God's honor or justice to be satisfied, no need for an exchange or sacrifice. What then does Christ do for the sake of sinners? What is the purpose of his death?

> Christ's death has the value of a covenant-offering and universal sin-offering, not because his opponents put him to death, but because in his obedience he

consented to this fate as the conclusion of his distinctive vocation determined by God's foreordination ... his death is effective as a sacrifice to justify the forgiveness of sin for his community or for its consummation of the new covenant with God only insofar as Jesus is united with the self-giving or priestly self-determination which his vocational activities fulfill. (*Unterricht*, §50)

Reconciliation then is made effective by Christ's "faithful obedience" to his vocation. His obedience maintains the fellowship of love between the Father and himself and human beings are brought into the same fellowship through him and his obedience. Thus, for Ritschl, Christ's death does not satisfy divine honor or justice; rather Christ died because he was faithful to his mission for the establishment of the Kingdom of God on which the Father sent him:

Precisely with this intent [of bringing human beings into fellowship with God] he has assumed, with patience and surrender to God's will, increased sufferings and death as the proof of his community with God ... in this manner, he has accomplished everything that could prove the originality of his community with God and the general possibility of a similar community ... as the royal priest of God, he has represented the community for the purpose of its perfect establishment. (*Unterricht*, §51)

Bibliography

Works by Ritschl

RuV I[1]: *Die christliche Lehre von der Rechtfertigung und Versöhnung* I: *Die Geschichte der Lehre*, 1st edn. Bonn: Adolph Marcus, 1870.

ET: *A Critical History of the Christian Doctrine of Justification and Reconciliation*. Translated by John S. Black. Edinburgh: Edmonston and Douglass, 1872.

RuV I[3]: *Die christliche Lehre von der Rechtfertigung und Versöhnung* I: *Die Geschichte der Lehre*, 3rd edn. Bonn: Adolph Marcus, 1870.

RuV II[4]: *Die christliche Lehre von der Rechtfertigung und Versöhnung* II: *Der biblische Stoff der Lehre*, 4th edn. Bonn: Marcus und Weber Verlag, 1900.

RuV III[4]: *Die christliche Lehre von der Rechtfertigung und Versöhnung* III: *Die positive Entwicklung der Lehre*, 4th edn. Bonn: Adolph Marcus, 1895.

ET: *The Christian Doctrine of Justification and Reconciliation: The Positive Development of the Doctrine*. Translated by H. R. Mackintosh and A. B. Macaulay. Edinburgh: T&T Clark, 1900.

Utterricht: *Unterricht in der Christlichen Religion: Studienausgabe nach der 1. Auflage von 1875 nebst den Abweichungen der 2. und 3. Auflage*. Edited by Christine Axt-Piscalar. Tübingen: Mohr Siebeck, 2002.

ET of the 3rd edn: "Instruction of the Christian Religion," in *Three Essays*. Translated by Philip Hefner. Philadelphia: Fortress Press, 1972.

Secondary Sources

Chalamet, "Reassessing Albrecht Ritschl's Theology: A Survey of Recent Literature," *Religion Compass* 2:4, 2008.

Martin Ohst, "Entre Bauer et Harnack: Albrecht Ritschl, théoricien de l'histoire des dogmes," in Albrecht Ritschl, ed. P. Gisel et al. Geneva: Labor et Fides, 1991.

Salvation in Christ Alone

Veli-Matti Kärkkäinen

Of all the challenges facing constructive theology of atonement and Christology, probably none outdoes religious pluralism and interreligious diversity. Among the many reasons, let me highlight only two here: first, unlike in past centuries (even when, of course, religions existed side by side), the interreligious situation has intensified in a manner unknown in history. Second, until now most theological work has utilized only Christian sources. As a result, so far there are hardly any comprehensive Christian statements on atonement that also engage widely religious pluralism and other religions (for such an attempt, see Kärkkäinen, *Christ and Reconciliation*).

When engaging religious plurality (the existence of different faiths) and pluralisms (various types of ideologies to negotiate plurality), two closely related theological disciplines aid Christian theology: theology of religions and comparative theology. While the former seeks to assess theologically the meaning and value of other religions, as well as consider the relationship of Christianity to other religions, the latter delves into detailed, limited comparisons between two or more faith traditions concerning a particular topic (Kärkkäinen, *An Introduction to the Theology of Religions*).

Although in theology (and philosophy) of religions there are wide debates about the meaning of *pluralism*, let it suffice to distinguish three kinds of pluralisms (Knitter, *Introducing Theologies of Religions*). The first type denies real differences among religions and hence believes that all religions are equally salvific: following an Enlightenment epistemology, this is best exemplified by Hick. The second type insists on real differences among salvific visions and seeks to honor them—in keeping with a postmodern love for diversity (Heim). Yet another form of pluralism seeks to push doctrinal considerations to the margins and focus merely on the liberative power of religious collaboration; in that template, Jesus's work becomes merely an asset to eco-socio-political improvement (Knitter, *Jesus and the Other Names*).

This short statement on forms of pluralisms already indicates that even within the Christian tradition there are widely differing views of how to best account for religious diversity; when nonpluralistic traditions are engaged, even more diverse theologies of atonement and Christ appear. As with any other doctrinal topic, views of atonement are deeply interconnected with other doctrines, particularly incarnation and resurrection (Kärkkäinen, *Christ and Reconciliation*, chapter 9). We can divide them into two camps (following Knitter, *Introducing Theologies of Religions*). The most traditional one can be called the "Replacement Model," also known as exclusivism (or particularism). It acknowledges differing interpretations of salvation among religions but insists on the normativity of Christ's work. This model has two versions. Without necessarily denying the presence of salvific elements in other religious traditions, the "Partial Replacement" model believes that only through the acceptance in faith of the benefits of Christ's atoning work may salvation be secured. The "Total Replacement" model strongly agrees with the absolute normativity of Christ's work but tends to be more skeptical about the presence of salvific insights among living faiths (for historical developments, see Kärkkäinen, *An Introduction to the Theology of Religions*, part 3).

Another important nonpluralistic option is that of the contemporary Roman Catholic "Fulfillment Model." Authoritatively stated at the Vatican II Council (1962–1965) and building on the important theological work of Rahner, Küng, and others, it teaches that while Christ is the only way of salvation, persons in other religions who have not heard the gospel may still be saved because of the universal effects of Christ's atoning work. Two conditions are set for the reception of salvific benefits, namely, that one follows sincerely the teachings of one's faith tradition and seeks to pursue ethical virtues as best as one can; these are not merits but rather indications of an incipient, "anonymous" faith that finds its fulfillment only in Christian faith. This view is also called "inclusivism," as in it many people among other faiths may be included in salvation. At the same time, it rejects pluralism as it holds up the normativity of Christ as the only Savior (Dupuis).

Hand in hand with theology of religions discourse, Christian theology of atonement should engage the interpretations of other religions concerning (1) their understandings of salvation and (2) interpretations of Christ's work. As examples of how to conduct this kind of work, let us consider two specific traditions: Muslim and Hindu. Two excellent recent publications contain basic sources for such work (Baker; Baker and Gregg; for actual comparative theological work in atonement and Christology in relation to Jewish, Hindu, and Buddhist traditions, see Kärkkäinen, *Christ and Reconciliation*, chapters 10 and 15).

Unknown to many Christian theologians, Jesus plays an important role in Islam. In addition to about one hundred references to Jesus (and his mother, Mary) in the Qur'an, the extensive *Hadith* literature contains numerous references (Leirvik). Not surprisingly, in the rich exchange between Christian theologians and Muslims for several centuries after the rise of Islam (e.g., John of Damascus), debates about the incarnation and the cross took central roles. Not a divine figure (any more than the Prophet himself), although a Teacher, Miracle-worker, and the highest Prophet second only to Muhammad himself, in the main Islamic interpretation, Jesus is not believed to have died on the cross. Rather, God took him up to heaven in order to return at the eschaton. Hence, Islamic theology considers the NT interpretations of Jesus's suffering, death, and resurrection simply false. Similarly, Islam rejects the Chalcedonian teaching on Christ's incarnation as God-Man.

In Islam salvation is not based on the atoning death of Jesus or of anyone else. Indeed, saving merit cannot be transferred to others. Rather, salvation is a matter of absolute submission (*islam*) to Allah. That is not to deny the gracious and merciful nature of Allah (consider that all but one chapter in the Qur'an begins with praise to Merciful God); it is rather to emphasize human responsibility. Nor is there any doctrine of original sin and the Fall similar to Christian tradition (although the Qur'an contains no less than three "Fall" narratives of Adam).

These radical differences have to be weighed and assessed vis-à-vis Christian theology of atonement. At the same time, there is room for common affirmations as both traditions take as authoritative Israel's Scriptures and Abrahamic legacy.

Unlike with Islam, only in the nineteenth century did mutual dialogue begin with Hindus. That soon led to the rise of wide interest in the role and meaning of Jesus and his work particularly among the advocates of the Neo-Hindu Renaissance (Thomas). Not only did they greatly honor Jesus's teachings and care for others, but many were also comfortable in calling him divine; that divinity, however, is "relative" in light of Christian understanding, and it refuses to consider any kind of atoning meaning of Jesus's history. Nor are Hindus willing to grant the once-for-all interpretation of Jesus's incarnation. Theirs is a different idea of what "incarnation" might mean.

In this respect, the most relevant comparative counterparts for Christological topics among innumerable Hindu movements are theistic traditions such as Vaishanavism (followers of the Vishnu deity and her local variations). Particularly fertile soil for comparison is the dominant popular devotional (*bhakti*) theism, based on *Bhagavad-Gita*, the "Bible" of the common folks. An important part of the Vishnu cult is the belief in *avataras*, divine "incarnations" (often numbered as ten), among whom the darling of the faithful is *Krishna* (Johnston). Importantly, these *avataras* appear when "unrighteousness" (*adharma*) is at its peak. While the *avataras* are not necessarily historical figures such as Jesus, and their death(s) are not regarded as in anyway salvific, *bhakti* spirituality considers the devotees' love and dedication for them as the way of salvation. Not surprisingly, however, the Chalcedonian claim to incarnation and atonement hardly makes much sense in this spirituality.

As noted, religious plurality and ideologies of pluralisms pose the greatest challenges to Christian theology in general and theology of atonement in particular. To negotiate constructive Christian doctrine in this kind of environment entails not only a thorough knowledge of the nuances of Christian doctrines but also familiarity with the philosophical and religious undercurrents of types of pluralisms, and—hopefully—knowledge of other faith traditions' teachings.

Bibliography

Baker, *Jesus in the World's Faiths*, 2008.
Baker and Gregg, *Jesus Beyond Christianity*, 2010.
Dupuis, *Toward a Christian Theology of Religious Pluralism*, 1997.
Heim, *Salvations*, 1995.
Hick, *The Metaphor of God Incarnate*, 1993.
Johnston, *Baby Krishna, Infant Christ*, 2011.
Kärkkäinen, *Christ and Reconciliation*, 2013.
Kärkkäinen, *An Introduction to the Theology of Religions*, 2003.
Knitter, *Introducing Theologies of Religions*, 2002.
Knitter, *Jesus and the Other Names*, 1996.
Leirvik, *Images of Jesus Christ in Islam*, 2010.
Thomas, *The Acknowledged Christ of the Indian Renaissance*, 1969.

89

Sanctification

Ben Rhodes

Sanctification deals with being made holy. It is derived from the Latin *sanctus*, which translates the New Testament Greek *hagiasmos*. Behind the Greek is the Hebrew *kadosh*, which broadly means separate or set apart. In Scripture, holiness is distinctive: this separation operates in both negative and positive senses. Negatively, holy people or objects are distinguished from the profane or unholy. Positively, holy people and objects are set apart for a unique purpose—they are consecrated. Moreover, holiness is teleological: the negative distinction is made for the sake of the positive purpose. Theologically, to be made holy is to be separated from one's un-holiness or profane surroundings and set into right relationship with the holy God.

Therefore, the biblical meaning of sanctification is always defined by reference to God's holy character. Only God is holy (Exod. 15:11; 1 Sam. 2:2; Is. 40:25). But God also calls His people to be holy as He is holy (Lev. 11:44–45, 19:2) and is faithful to make them holy (Lev. 20:8, 21:8). The God who is utterly unique, transcendently holy, and singularly righteous calls his graciously chosen people into a relationship characterized by an obedient lifestyle which witnesses to this holiness. In Exodus, God declares that Israel is his people before giving the gift of the law (Exod. 20:2) and all of the following imperatives about the ark, tabernacle, priestly garments, and various rules flow from that prior indicative of election. The law is designed to keep Israel holy so that—among other things—God may dwell among His people without destroying them, which is why Exodus culminates with God taking up residence in the tabernacle, despite Israel's sin (Exod. 40:34). The history of the covenant displays both Israel's pervasive failure to remain holy, bringing shame to God's holy name among the nations, and God's jealous fidelity to repeatedly rescue (recorded in shocking terms by Hosea). The sequence in Isaiah is representative: the seraphim cry

"Holy, holy, holy is the Lord of hosts, and the whole earth is full of his glory" (Is. 6:3), but Isaiah's sin must be atoned for prior to his prophecy (Is. 6:5–8). The yearning for an end to such temporary restorative measures is powerfully presented in Ezekiel's penultimate prophecy of God's miraculous gift of a new heart of flesh and dry bones resurrected by the Spirit (Ezek. 36–40), all for the sake of God's holy name. The book climaxes in a vision of redemption that focuses on God establishing a new temple, resettling the tribes on their land, and naming the restored city Jehovah Shammah, "The Lord is there" (Ezek. 48:35).

Jesus Christ, who is Immanuel, "God with us" (Mt. 1:23), is the fulfillment of Ezekiel's vision (John 2; Rev. 21). Jesus is the true Israelite who perfectly fulfills the covenant law in his life and work, culminating in the redemptive act of atonement, which justifies all humanity, Jew and Gentile alike, who respond to the prevenient grace of God. A recurring element of Jesus's conflict in the Gospels is over the locus of holiness. In startling contrast to the carefully constructed Pharisaical hedges around the law, Jesus exemplifies contagious holiness through preaching the kingdom to the unclean and marginalized, healing people afflicted by sickness and what we now call disabilities, and restoring sinners to right relationship with God.

At Pentecost, amid the echoes of the resurrection of Jesus Christ, the church is born in the fire of the Holy Spirit and called to follow Jesus's pattern of surprising and sacrificial love within an uncomprehending world. Throughout the book of Acts, the church is depicted as a people struggling to discern the scope of the astonishing work of the Holy Spirit as they hammer out what it means to be holy amid the deep cultural conflict of God gathering Gentiles into His kingdom apart from strict observation of the law (Rom. 9–11). Yet the order of the Christian life remains consistent with the Old Testament: abundantly life-giving imperatives to holiness flow out of the prior gracious indicative of salvation (Eph. 2:8–10). Christians are described as a holy people: a status that is given, not earned (1 Pet. 1:13–21). But this holiness needs to be enacted, which requires discernment. That is why so much of the New Testament deals with concrete ethical struggles. To take one example: Paul reminds the Corinthian church that sex with prostitutes is wrong because they are the temple of the Holy Spirit, and what Christians do with their bodies matters (1 Cor. 6:19). Christians were originally known as followers of the Way (Acts 9:2, 24:14), and the church is the community of those learning to walk this Way: we might say that sanctification is the gait of Christians. Having been justified in Christ, the church must learn how to live out of that accomplished reality, pilgrims set on the way of increasing conformity to Christ, sanctified in the power of the Holy Spirit, as adopted children of the Father.

This compact Trinitarian summary of the arc of Scripture vis-à-vis sanctification needs to be complicated by an important exegetical point. Sanctification (*hagiasmos* and cognates) is deployed in a consistent way in the New Testament. Jesus Christ is our sanctification (1 Cor. 1:30) which means that Christians are already sanctified in him (1 Cor. 1:2): sanctification is just as "past-tense" as justification. (For an exhaustive demonstration of this point, often called positional or definitive sanctification, see Peterson, 136–137.) In Christ, we have been made holy—see the work of P. T. Forsyth for a powerful treatment of why the crucifixion is incomprehensible without reference to the holiness of God. But what does this mean in our daily lives?

At the risk of oversimplification, it is possible to narrate the history of the church as a series of disagreements about the nature and scope of holiness. There is a nearly constant ebb and flow of movements of reform, when individuals and communities rediscover the possibility of holiness within the life of ordinary Christianity. Consider the rise of monastic movements after the peace and comfort brought by Constantine's political recognition of Christianity, a pattern repeated throughout various political upheavals and ensuing settlements. The Great Schism between what we now call the Roman Catholic Church and the Byzantine (or Greek Orthodox) Church was a contentious and complicated affair, but theological debates about the Holy Spirit and ecclesiastical authority ran (and still run) amid political and cultural conflict. In the West, the Protestant Reformation may be the most well-known fight about holiness in the church (indulgences are ultimately a debate about how God makes His people holy), but it was preceded by conciliar movements, mendicant orders like the Dominicans and Franciscans, and other currents of reform that attempted to provide space for the pursuit of holiness within the established church. Pietist and other holiness movements (the term is telling) emphasized the need for the Christian life to be different from the surrounding culture of the church. There have always been calls for personal and communal holiness within the church, for a more authentic Christian life that imitates Jesus, for a church that embodies holiness which is distinctive and attractive. But this historical observation may simply evade the theological question of what it means to be made holy in Christ.

Karl Barth took it to mean that justification, sanctification, and vocation are three aspects of one reconciliation, perfectly accomplished in the person of Jesus Christ, and strongly resisted all attempts to speak of progress in the Christian life (*CD* IV). Barth's powerful emphasis on Jesus Christ as the Lord who is never under our control is exemplary. While Barth's insistence that the Holy Spirit constantly confronts us is profound, it needs to be balanced with the biblical testimony that the Holy Spirit is also truly given, even if never placidly possessed (1 Cor. 12). Barth loved to note that God's omnicausality is not the same as God's sole causality, which means that human beings are never more truly agents than when liberated by power of the Spirit to live in freedom (Gal. 5:1). God is not an agent like humans are, and the exercise of divine/human agency is not competitive (Webster, *Barth's Moral Theology*, 8–9).

While it is exegetically precise to speak of sanctification as definitive, or once-for-all, Scripture also speaks of growth in holiness, of the Christian life producing fruits which are discernably different over time (2 Cor. 3:18, Eph. 4:13–15). In this sense, sanctification is progressive. Here it is interesting to note how popular protestant Christianity often speaks of a three-part *ordo salutis* (order of salvation) of justification, sanctification, and glorification that neatly maps onto our temporal experience. Justification refers to the past tense of reconciliation, wholly accomplished by the atoning act of Christ (Rom. 5:1). Glorification refers to the future, when death and sin will be no more in the new heaven and new earth (Rev. 21:1–5). Sanctification is then the middle term, the here-and-now activity of working out our salvation in fear and trembling (Phil. 2:12–13), the place where we can properly speak of the Christian's contribution to holiness, the proper domain of ethical concerns, and the right location for moral reflection.

However, such growth in holiness is not a simple linear increase. The consistent testimony of the saints—a term which the New Testament applies to all Christians, even those errant Corinthians, not solely to superheroes of the faith—is that the more we progress in conformity to Christ, the more we come to realize the extent of our sin. Luther's insight about *simul peccator et sanctus* (simultaneously saint and sinner) may be phrased with typically brutal directness in his commentary on Galatians, but this dialectic rings true to human experience (68). However, as is often the case, Calvin refines Luther's powerful proclamation into something more nuanced and responsible to the entirety of Scripture. For Calvin, sanctification has two aspects: mortification and vivification (3.3.8–9). To be made holy, we must die. Sin cannot be tolerated, and for our sake, it must be fully cut out, root and branch. That is why Jesus speaks of taking up our cross daily and following him (Luke 9:23). But the cross is not the end: resurrection is a new beginning, and in Jesus Christ we are a new creation (2 Cor. 5:17), quickened to life by the outpouring of the Holy Spirit (Rom. 8:10–11). The Christian life has a baptismal pattern, and this double aspect of sanctification has been recently articulated with particular clarity by John Webster in his *Holiness*. Again, such an understanding of sanctification is teleological: put to death for the sake of being made alive.

Atonement is evocative. What atonement evokes is holiness. Christian holiness is entirely derivative, always dependent on the prior and generative holiness of God, but it is nonetheless real. As finite creatures, we can and should grow in holiness. Consider Galatians 5. After rebuking the Galatians for submitting to the slavery from which they had been freed by substituting law for the gospel, Paul concludes by saying that Christ has set us free for freedom; not for licentious self-indulgence in the flesh, but for service in love. The Christian life is necessarily an active walking by the Spirit. A long list of specific works of the flesh provokes a powerful "No!" from Paul, because they have been crucified by Christ (5:19–21). By contrast, "the fruit of the Spirit is love, joy, peace, patience, kindness, goodness, faithfulness, gentleness and self-control; against such things is no law" (5:22–23). In a deliberate rhetorical inversion, Paul summarizes this lifestyle of bearing one another's burdens as the law of Christ (Gal. 6:2). The normative command is open-ended, intended to be a liberating imperative that is the opposite of an exhortation tamely resting in the Christian's pocket: a resounding "Yes!" now meant to call us onward and upward into newly creative acts of love. Rightly understood, this frees us from anxious self-obsession, from a constantly shifting moral calculus, or endless analysis of our subjective felt experience of faith. Christians are all holy, made truly so in the perfect atoning work of Jesus Christ. From that position of security we are liberated to love in the sanctifying love of the Holy Spirit.

Bibliography

Barth, *Church Dogmatics* IV.2, 1958.
Barton, *Holiness: Past and Present*, 2003.
Berkouwer, *Faith and Sanctification*, 1952.
Calvin, *Institutes of the Christian Religion*, 1960.
Forsyth, *The Cruciality of the Cross*, 1909.
Kapic, *Sanctification*, 2014.
Luther, *Lectures on Galatians*, 1964.
Peterson, *Possessed by God*, 1995.
Ryle, *Holiness*, 1879.
Webster, *Barth's Moral Theology*, 1998.
Webster, *Holiness*, 2003.

Friedrich Schleiermacher

Justin Stratis

When Friedrich Schleiermacher was eighteen years old, he sent a letter to his father in which he expressed misgivings about certain Christian doctrines in the light of his emerging modern sensibilities. In this letter, Schleiermacher wrote:

> I cannot believe that [Christ's] death was a substitutionary atonement because he never expressly said so, and because I cannot believe that it was necessary. For it would be impossible for God to desire the eternal punishment of those whom he had obviously not created perfect, but for the pursuit of perfection, since they are not [yet] perfect. (*KGA*, V.1)

As Schleiermacher's theology matured, reaching its zenith in *The Christian Faith* (first edition, 1821–1822; revised edition, 1831–1832), these early soteriological intuitions remained intact, even as they were developed more systematically. The key point is that humanity must be "perfected" rather than punished. Understanding Schleiermacher's theology of atonement therefore requires grasping his anthropology, specifically in the context of his doctrine of creation, and how all of this relates to his doctrine of God as revealed in the incarnation.

Like many of his era, Schleiermacher conceived the transcendental task of philosophy as that of relating God (*theos*), the world (*cosmos*), and the self (*ego*). For him, this task begins when we as individuals become aware of our constituency in a vast "system of nature," at once intuiting our particularity in that system, as well as recognizing the whole of the system represented in our own self-consciousness. The younger Schleiermacher once called the dawning of this awareness "the natal hour of ... religion," for only when we grasp the whole of the world in our individual consciousness can we awaken to the dependence of this whole upon an active reality that lies beyond its boundaries (*On Religion*, 32). In various contexts, Schleiermacher calls this reality "God," and, because this reality is by definition extra-mundane, it can only be "known" indirectly as the "Whence" of the so-called feeling of absolute dependence (*The Christian Faith* [hereafter *CF*], § 4.4.).

In *CF*, Schleiermacher corroborates this scheme with reference to the specifically Christian self-consciousness of sin and grace. In particular, he aims to highlight how Christian utterances emerge from the feeling of being redeemed through the historical figure, Jesus of Nazareth. For Schleiermacher, what makes Jesus fit for this task is not the fact that he represents a literal in-breaking of the divine into the mundane (for this would violate the feeling of absolute dependence), but the fact that, in Jesus, the divinely ordained *telos* of human nature is graciously fulfilled. Unlike us, Jesus lived fully out of his absolute dependence, that is, out of his consciousness of God, and because of this, he was able to experience the entire world, including its more sinister elements, never as a hindrance to this God-consciousness, but only as an occasion for its full expression. Thus, it is Jesus's lifelong "sinless perfection" that is the real significance of incarnation: the fully active reality of God manifest as a "continual living presence" in Jesus's historical life (*CF* § 96.3).

Outside of Christ's appearance, Schleiermacher insists, there would be no reason to expect a progression of human consciousness from an imperfect to a full and perfected consciousness of God. This is because human consciousness is socially embedded. Sin, which Schleiermacher defines as any action that is not determined by consciousness of God, is pervasive in human existence, and, naturally speaking, there is no escape from the influence of humanity's sinful activity. Jesus, however, living completely from his God-consciousness and hence "without sin," introduces a new element into the social fabric of human existence. His appearance in history is, therefore, in a certain sense, "supernatural" (*CF* § 89.4; Sherman, 187). As people encountered Jesus (e.g., the first disciples), his uniquely potent consciousness of God was communicated to them, such that they too could begin living in the light of the divine activity. This is precisely what Schleiermacher calls "redemption"—the opening of a new way of life beyond the curse of sin, in fellowship with Jesus of Nazareth. Nevertheless, the question remains: *how* did the historical features of Jesus's unique life actually facilitate this redemption? In other words, the question of atonement.

Schleiermacher insists that in order for Jesus's life to open up the possibility of humanity's perfection, it was necessary that he demonstrate the full potency of his God-consciousness in the face of all opposition. To put the matter in biblical terms, the Redeemer must be "tempted in every way as we are," yet remain "without sin" (Heb. 4:15). Jesus's death on the cross therefore differs in kind from his life only in that it represents the ultimate potential disturbance to his "blessedness." Jesus's ability to remain faithful to his vocation as the second Adam even in the face of death proves once and for all that redemption may truly be found in him (Pannenberg, 166). Or, as Horst Stephan puts it, for Schleiermacher, "the blessedness of Christ emerges … in its full depth in that it never once is overcome by the fullness of suffering" (51).

The cross is therefore a moment of supreme revelation, but only in the sense of a real, historical "proof" of Christ's "blessedness." This "proof" does not simply convince Jesus's followers of his identity as the Redeemer, however, but rather serves to draw them into his blessed existence. Christ's death was not, therefore, the catalyst for a kind of heavenly transaction between God and humanity (something Schleiermacher repeatedly criticizes as a "magical" view of the atonement), but rather it was, along with the entirety of Christ's life, the occasion for the founding of a real and concretely historical redeemed community. As Schleiermacher puts it:

> The activity of Christ in founding the new corporate life could really emerge in its perfect fullness … only if it yielded to no opposition, not even to that which succeeded in destroying His person. Here, accordingly, the perfection does not lie properly and immediately in the suffering itself, but only in His giving of Himself to it. (*CF* § 101.4)

Schleiermacher's perspective on history as a crucible for humanity's perfection, facilitated ultimately by the work of Jesus Christ as the "second Adam," has led some to characterize his view as "Irenaean" (Hick, 255–241). There is some truth to this, though Schleiermacher's real contribution has more to do with the attention he pays to the *communication* of Christ's work specifically through the medium of history. While Schleiermacher may be guilty of relying too greatly on the present phenomenon of redemption to interpret the founding event of redemption, his concern to locate the outworking of God's redemptive will somehow *in* and not simply above or even *toward* history surely foregrounds an element of the gospel that theologians ought not to neglect (Nimmo, 187–199; Hector, 86–94).

Nevertheless, many have struggled and will struggle with his account of Christ's death on the cross. Indeed, Schleiermacher's entire theory of redemption depends on Christ's God-consciousness remaining radically imperturbable—even at the point of death. Hence, for instance, he regards the cry of dereliction as historically salvageable only if the whole of Psalm 22 is implied; otherwise, he states, "I cannot think of this saying as an expression of Christ's self-consciousness" (Schleiermacher, *The Life of Jesus*, 423). The implication that the "Christ-like" response to suffering would be to refuse to accept the evil one faces as a hindrance to God-consciousness can seem profoundly unsatisfying given the horrific events that have taken place since Schleiermacher's death in 1834 (Blackwell, 64–75). The traditional Christian belief in some kind of divine solidarity with the human condition (whether or not this implies anything like divine passibility) must likely be addressed if Schleiermacher's doctrine of redemption is to gain purchase in the modern theological imagination.

Bibliography

Blackwell, "Schleiermacher's Sermon at Nathanael's Grave," *Journal of Religion* 57:1, 1977.

Hector, *Theology without Metaphysics*, 2011.

Hick, *Evil and the God of Love*, 1966.

Nimmo, "The Mediation of Redemption in Schleiermacher's *Glaubenslehre*," *IJST* 5:2, 2003.

Pannenberg, "A Theology of the Cross," *Word & World* 8:2, 1988.

Schleiermacher, *The Christian Faith*, 1928.

Schleiermacher, *Kritische Gesamtausgabe*, V.1, 1985.

Schleiermacher, *The Life of Jesus*, 1975.

Schleiermacher, *On Religion: Speeches to Its Cultured Despisers*, 1996.

Sherman, *The Shift to Modernity*, 2005.

Stephan, *Die Lehre Schleiermachers von der Erlösung*, 1901.

John Duns Scotus

Thomas M. Ward

The two most important concepts in Duns Scotus's (1265/6-1308) theology of the Atonement are satisfaction and merit. Just what these amount to and how they function in his theory are heavily conditioned by two more general commitments: voluntarism, which includes the claim that nearly all of God's relations with the created order are contingent; and his formulation of the Franciscan Thesis, which holds that fixing the sin problem is not the primary purpose of God's Incarnation in Christ and that if Adam hadn't sinned God would have become incarnate anyway.

Voluntarism is usually taken to imply that God could have issued or could issue alternative commandments. Since a commandment essentially involves an act of will, if God could not command otherwise than He has commanded, his willing would have been determined by something (in some sense) "outside" his will, such as a realm of objective moral facts together with God's understanding of these facts. Duns Scotus is undoubtedly a voluntarist, but the degree and range of his voluntarism is still a matter of scholarly debate (Wolter, 1-30; Williams, 162-181; Ingham, 173-216).

Voluntarism is relevant to the theology of the Atonement due to its implications for those aspects of the Atonement that bear on God himself as a moral agent. Two examples of these aspects are: whether God is obligated to provide a means for saving sinners and, given that he did decide to do so, whether he could have saved sinners in some other way. Voluntarists maintain that all of God's dealings with the world of creatures are contingent: he doesn't have to create, he doesn't have to sustain, he doesn't have to save, and if he does save, he could do it in a variety of ways. The precise modal character of these claims is well-captured by the familiar distinction between God's *absolute* and *ordained* power. God's absolute power extends to whatever is logically possible, whereas his ordained power ranges over those actions that are consistent with the general plan God has ordained for the world (Scotus, *Ordinatio* I.44, in Wolter, 254–261). Given God's plan to save sinners through Christ's death, Christ must die for sinners; but the *must* is completely conditioned by God's prior, free, decision to save sinners through Christ's death. Each and every one of God's plans is up to God in the sense that he could have justly planned otherwise (Scotus, *Ordinatio* I.44, in Wolter, 254–261). God has just one moral obligation: to love himself above all things. God couldn't establish a law inconsistent with this first practical truth, either for himself or for any creature, even with respect to his absolute power. So the preservation of divine justice depends on his continually loving himself above all things, and continually willing whatever this *logically entails* (*Scotus Ordinatio* IV.46, in Wolter, 238–254).

Scotus offers the most forceful (but not the first) medieval expression of the so-called Franciscan Thesis (Horan, 374–391). Scotus held that the Incarnation was not part of the divine response to sin. Rather, it was predestined, logically prior to God's foreknowledge of Adam's sin, as the crowning achievement of creation itself, that the Son should be united with human nature and rule the cosmos as its native King. God intends Incarnation, therefore, primarily as the way to *glorify* Christ and his subjects and only secondarily to *redeem* Christ's subjects (Scotus, *Ordinatio* III.7.3 [Vatican ed. IX:284–291]; Adams, 174–187).

As Adams has put it, "Not only is sin not a *sine qua non* of Incarnation; for Scotus, Incarnation is not a *sine qua non* for solving the sin-problem, either" (Adams, 183). Scotus furnishes a long list of alternative possible ways in which God could have taken care of the sin problem, including: not requiring satisfaction for sins at all, allowing an angel or a mere human to make satisfaction, or allowing Christ to make satisfaction in some way other than the cross (Scotus, *Lectura* III.20.un [Vatican ed. XXI:39–55]). Some have thought Scotus's position entails that *any* finite good could be accepted as meritorious for redemption. (Grensted, 161; von Harnack, 459). The list of alternatives is not idle scholastic speculation; it's meant to emphasize the logical independence of Incarnation and redemption (Adams, 184).

Arguably, Scotus agrees with his tradition that Christ makes satisfaction for sins and earns merit (Patout Burns, 285–304; Langston, 227–241; Cross, 129–132; Rosato, 411–441). Satisfaction is the voluntary return of equivalent for equivalent, whereas merit is the assignation of a reward to an act (Scotus, *Ordinatio* IV.15.1 [Vatican ed. XIII:59–75]; Cross, 129–132).

Rosato has argued that Scotus adopts two Bonaventurian concepts of satisfaction. Bonaventure had distinguished between satisfaction *pro iniuria*, which involves offering some good equivalent to the injury God suffers through Adam's sin, and satisfaction *pro damno*, which involves offering some good equivalent to the loss God suffers through Adam's sin (Bonaventure, III Sent. 20.1.3 [Quaracchi ed 3:423a]). Christ makes satisfaction *pro iniuria* inasmuch as God's injury was dishonor and Christ's sacrifice honors God more than Adam's sin dishonor's Him. Christ makes satisfaction *pro damno* inasmuch as God's loss was humanity itself and Christ's sacrifice restores humanity to God. Christ's sacrifice restores humanity to God precisely by meriting the graces we need to return to God. Rosato nevertheless makes a good case for the presence of each of these concepts in Scotus's texts, and for the dominance in his texts of satisfaction *pro damno* over satisfaction *pro iniuria*. Scotus endorses satisfaction *pro iniuria* inasmuch as his argument against Anselm's thesis that satisfaction requires returning to God something greater than the whole of creation *presupposes* that satisfaction involves paying a debt owed to God (Scotus, *Lectura* III.20.un.31 [Vatican ed. XXI:49]). The difference between Anselm and Scotus on this issue is simply that the former thinks the debt is infinite and therefore its payment must be infinite, while the latter thinks the debt is finite and therefore its payment can be merely finite (ibid.; Rosato, 442). Christ makes satisfaction *pro damno* inasmuch as his motivation for his sacrifice involved providing the means by which humans could escape from their sin and be united with God (Scotus, *Lectura* III.20.un.37–38 [Vatican ed. XXI:51]; Rosato, 441–442). But making satisfaction in this way is accomplished precisely by meriting the graces we need to escape from sin and be united with God (Scotus, *Lectura* III.20.un.24–26 [Vatican ed. XXI:34–35]; Rosato, 442).

Scotus's concept of merit has two well-known features: first, all merit is conventional; second, Christ's merit is intrinsically finite. The conventionality of merit follows from Scotus's voluntarism. If merit were not conventional then some creature's being what it is (meritorious by nature) would compel God to accept it as such on pain of misvaluing things (which He cannot do because he is infinitely good and infinitely intelligent). Instead, Scotus thinks that it is up to God to decide what to count as meritorious (Scotus, *Lectura* III.19.un [Vatican ed. XXI:25–38]). The argument for the finitude of Christ's merit is straightforward: God cannot merit anything, since by his nature he has necessarily every perfection He is capable of having; so Christ with respect to his divine nature cannot merit anything. Humans can earn merit, but merit follows and is proportionate to an act, any human act is finite, and therefore any merit following on a human act is finite. So Christ with respect to his human nature can (and does) earn merit, but this merit is finite (Scotus, *Lectura* III.19.un [Vatican ed. XXI:25–38]). Some have labeled this aspect of Scotus's theory Nestorian (Grensted, 159; Aspenson, 144).

Yang has argued compellingly that Scotus thinks that Christ's merits are both infinitely sufficient and intrinsically finite. Like his predecessors and peers, Scotus thinks only the elect will benefit from Christ's merit (and therefore it has only finite efficacy), despite the fact that it is sufficient to benefit all (Yang, 421–440). For Scotus, any act of sin is intrinsically finite and therefore, with respect to any one sin, the merit that wins remission of that sin need only be merely finite. Scotus raises an objection to his own view, namely, that if the universe were sempiternal such that there were an infinitely growing number of sinners, then while each act of sin would be intrinsically finite, the sum of the infinite sins committed by an infinite number of people would be intrinsically infinite by addition. He considers the hypothetical scenario valid for the sake of argument, so he is compelled to offer an account of how Christ's finite merit can overcome an intrinsically infinite evil. Scotus reasons that even though Christ's merits are intrinsically finite because they are merited on account of Christ's human nature, it is open to God to count them as of intrinsically infinite value because they are actions of an infinitely lovable *person*—the Second Person of the Trinity—subsisting in divine and human natures (Scotus, *Ordinatio* III.19.un.7 [Wadding ed. VII.1:417–418). Thus, while any number of creatures might have earned finite merit to the same degree as Christ, Christ merits can be counted as of infinite value because they are merits accruing to a divine person.

Bibliography

Adams, *Christ and Horrors*, 2006.
Aspenson, "Anselmian Satisfaction, Duns Scotus and the Debt of Sin," *Modern Schoolman* 73, 1996.
Bonaventure, *Opera Omnia*, 10 vols, 1882–1902.
Cross, *Duns Scotus*, 1999.
Grensted, *A Short History of the Doctrine of the Atonement*, 1962.
Horan, "How Original Was Scotus on the Incarnation? Reconsidering the History of the Absolute Primacy of Christ in Light of Robert Grosseteste," *The Heythrop Journal* 52, 2011.
Ingham, "Letting Scotus Speak for Himself," *Medieval Philosophy and Theology* 10:2, 2001.
Langston, "Scotus's Departure from Anselm's Theory of the Atonement," *Recherche de théologie ancienne et médiévale* 50, 1983.

Patout Burns, "The Concept of Satisfaction in Medieval Redemption Theory," *Theological Studies* 36:2, 1975.
Rosato, "The Interpretation of Anselm's Teaching on Christ's Satisfaction in the Franciscan Tradition from Alexander of Hales to Duns Scotus," *Franciscan Studies* 71, 2013.
Scotus, *Opera Omnia*, 12 vols, ed. Luke Wadding, 1639.
Scotus, *Opera Omnia*, 18 vols, ed. Scotistic Commission, 1950.
Von Harnack, *Lehrbuch der Dogmengeschichte*, 3 vols, 1890.
Williams, "The Unmitigated Scotus," *Archiv für Geschichte der Philosophie* 80, 1998.
Wolter, *Duns Scotus on the Will & Morality*, 1986.
Yang, "Scotus's Voluntarist Approach to the Atonement Reconsidered," *Scottish Journal of Theology* 62, 2009.

Sin

Adam Neder

Introduction

While Christ's work of salvation includes more than his victory over sin, that is a central aspect of it: "Here is a trustworthy saying that deserves full acceptance: Christ Jesus came into the world to save sinners" (1 Tim. 1:15). Any framework for thinking about the atonement is faced with a series of basic questions related to sin. What is sin and what are its consequences? How exactly does Jesus Christ overcome sin? What is it about Christ's person that qualifies him to accomplish this work? And how do those for whom he accomplished it come to share in it? A doctrine of the atonement cannot be persuasive if it fails to answer these questions, and the answers offered would only be compelling to the extent that they come to terms with and illuminate the widest amount of Scriptural testimony to this event.

Sin's Essence

Sin is neither caused by God nor intrinsic to human beings as such. God created human beings as good, established relationship with them, and blessed them. Sin is a disruption and distortion of this original relationship. Rather than responding to the grace, mercy, and benevolent guidance of God with gratitude and obedience, sin is the decision to live against God rather than with him. Scripture describes sin with a wide range of images—idolatry, lawlessness, unbelief, and so on. Yet in all its forms, sin is action that contradicts the will of God. Sin is doing something other than what God wants. To sin is to respond to God in the wrong way—to contradict him rather than to conform to him. Thus all sin is essentially enmity against God: "Against you, you only, have I sinned and done what is evil in your sight; so you are right in your verdict and justified when you judge" (Ps. 51:4).

Sin's Consequences

Sin has existential, social, and forensic consequences.

Sin infects every domain of life. Rather than being characterized by wholeness, love, and peace, sin distorts the sinner's relation to God, other people, the self, and the rest of creation. Cut off from the source of their life in God, sinful human beings become subject to ignorance and death: "The mind governed by the flesh is death, but the mind governed by the Spirit is life and peace. The mind governed by the flesh is hostile to God; it does not submit to God's law, nor can it do so" (Rom. 8:6–7). Rather than being oriented outward in freedom and love for God and others, human beings become dominated by ignorance and selfish desire. As sin becomes habitual, it hardens and confuses the sinner. The more one sins, the more enslaved to sin one becomes.

The repercussions of this process spill into society. Personal sin breeds societal disorder. Sin distorts the political and economic structures that shape and direct social life. Instead of contributing to human flourishing, social systems become oppressive and exploitative. Rather than resisting such systems, sinners become complicit in them and make them worse. Moral and intellectual vices multiply and become normative. Sinners and societies become incapable of healing themselves or even perceiving their true condition (Rom. 1:18–32).

The chaos that sin introduces into life leaves sinners guilty before God and subject to divine judgment: "But I tell you that anyone who is angry with a brother or sister will be subject to judgment. Again, anyone who says to a brother or sister, 'Raca,' is answerable to the court. And anyone who says, 'You fool!' will be in danger of the fire of hell" (Mt. 5:22).

Christ's Victory over Sin

Jesus Christ accomplishes atonement through his life, death, resurrection, and ascension. His person and work—his prophetic, priestly, and kingly offices—are a unity. To be understood correctly, they must be envisioned as relating to each other as an indivisible whole. Within this broad framework, Scripture's testimony to Christ's victory over sin has its center of gravity in the cross: "Christ died for our sins" (1 Cor. 15:3). In the power of the Spirit and in perfect obedience to his Father, Jesus Christ's life of sinless humility culminated in the cross by which he healed the wounds caused by sin (1 Pet. 2:24).

The Holy One of Israel displays his wrath against sin throughout Scripture, and on the cross this same God surrenders himself to this judgment. Jesus Christ experienced the condemnation that sinners deserve and died the death of a guilty criminal. He was made "to be sin" (2 Cor. 5:21) and became "a curse" (Gal. 3:13). He was crucified for the sake of sinners, "the righteous for the unrighteous" (1 Pet. 3:18). He "bore our sins in his body on the tree" (1 Pet. 2:24). He willingly drank the "cup" of God's judgment (Mt. 26:39) and was "forsaken" (Mt. 27:46) by the very God who "presented the Son as a sacrifice of atonement through the shedding of his blood" (Rom. 3:25). This latter claim eliminates the possibility that the cross somehow changed the Father's basic attitude toward humanity. The cross is an act of divine love in which God overcame sin by taking into himself the human experience of death in Godforsakenness. Jesus Christ's abandonment by his Father (an event that does not occur between two independent subjects and therefore is without analogy on the human plane) does not introduce division or contradiction into the divine being, since the cross is the historical outworking of God's gracious eternal decision to be God with and for humanity. In fact, in his self-humiliation, suffering, and death, the unity, mystery, and majesty of the living God are on full display.

Knowledge of Sin

As in Christ we encounter the full revelation of God, in him we likewise perceive sin with maximal clarity. The perversity and enormity of sin only become visible when seen against the glorious light of God's reconciling love. Knowledge of sin is not merely a general awareness of guilt or disorder; it is inseparably related to God's revelation of himself in Christ. Only as God suffers and is crucified for the sake of his enemies, and only as this event is perceived in faith, does sin come fully into view.

Thus knowledge of sin is an essential element of human self-understanding. Yet this knowledge is included within the even more fundamental truth that Jesus Christ's death and resurrection include everyone: "He is the atoning sacrifice not only for our sins, but also for the sins of the whole world" (1 John 2:2). In his death sinful humanity was judged and put to death—"One has died for all; therefore all have died" (2 Cor. 5:14)—and in his resurrection a new humanity has been established. The reconciliation of the world to God in Christ is an objective reality: "God was pleased to have all his fullness dwell in him, and through him to reconcile to himself all things, whether things on earth or things in heaven, by making peace through his blood, shed on the cross" (Col. 1:19–20). Yet God gives this gift so that it will be received in faith, and therefore the gift includes within itself the task and command that everyone become who he or she already is in Christ. In other words, the objective reconciliation that Christ accomplished for us and for our salvation is teleologially ordered toward our grateful and obedient acknowledgment of this fact. In the deepest sense, the most fully human thing a person can do is to believe in Christ and respond to his call to discipleship. The additional fact that people often contradict their identity in Christ and embrace the sinful patterns of life that he defeated (and thus run the risk of living in absurd eternal opposition to God) does not mean that sinners have the power to recreate human nature. Christ alone determines what it is to be human. He is the mirror of true humanity and the revelation of God's will for every person. Thus the cross and resurrection reveal that while sin is more real and powerful than sinners could have imagined, it is not more real and powerful than God's grace.

Further Reading

Aquinas, Thomas, *Summa Theologiae.*
Augustine, *The Enchiridion on Faith, Hope, and Charity.*
Barth, Karl. *Church Dogmatics*, vol. IV, 1956.
Breaking Bad (TV Series).
Fairlie, *The Seven Deadly Sins Today*, 1979.
Kierkegaard, *The Concept of Anxiety* and *The Sickness Unto Death.*
McFarland, *In Adam's Fall*, 2010.
Evagrius Ponticus, *The Praktikos*, 1972.

Socinus

Alan W. Gomes

Faustus Socinus (1539–1604), an Italian émigré to Poland, became the leading theologian of the so-called Minor Reformed Church, also known as the Polish Brethren. They are more commonly designated Socinians and Unitarians, labels fastened on them by their opponents (for a historical overview, see: Wilbur; Williams, 978–989). Socinus, whose collected works fill two large folio volumes, entered the lists against orthodox Catholic and Protestants theologians alike, engaging in wide-ranging disputes on such topics as the Trinity, the deity of Christ, original sin, predestination, and Christ's work on the cross.

Concerning the doctrine of Christ's satisfaction for sin, the topic of this chapter, Socinus produced what is arguably the most trenchant critique of it ever written in his magisterial work, *De Jesu Christo Servatore* (*Concerning Jesus Christ the Savior*; hereafter *DS*). It began as an oral dialog between Socinus and Jacques Couet (Covetus), a Parisian Reformed minister who was sojourning in Basle at the same time Socinus was temporarily residing there. Charles Beard well summarized the historic significance of the treatise when he described *De Servatore* as "a book in which is to be found every rational and moral argument since directed against the theory of satisfaction" (277).

The prevailing opinion among historians is that *DS* is primarily a *negative*, polemical work against the orthodox doctrine of satisfaction or penal substitution, particularly as enunciated in orthodox Protestantism. L. W. Grensted described Socinus's theory as a kind of "solvent" that breaks down the penal doctrine, noting that the positive aspects of his theory "are of less importance historically than the negative criticism of which he was a master" (Grensted, 289). It is true that Socinus's negative claims have garnered the most attention, both by friend and by foe. Yet, it would be shortsighted to see the treatise as mere denial. To understand properly Socinus's view of Christ's work, it is necessary to situate it in the context of Socinus's positive theology generally, viewed specifically through the lens of his systemic controlling principles.

Socinus himself has neatly summarized for us the matter of his theological controlling principles. As I have argued elsewhere (Gomes, "Some Observations," 49–71), the center of Socinus's theology is the attainment of eternal life through the keeping of God's commandments, as revealed specifically to us through Christ, God's unique, revelatory emissary. For example, the first two sentences of Socinus's *Summa* contain in microcosm the center of gravity for his theological system: "The Christian religion is the heavenly doctrine, teaching the true way of attaining eternal life. Moreover, this way is nothing other than to obey God, according to those things which he commands us through our Lord Jesus Christ" (Heb. 5:9; Socinus, *Summa Religionis Christianae* in *BFP* 1.281). This stands in contrast to other proposed "centers" for his thought, including the oft-repeated conventional wisdom that the system of Socinus is a species of rationalism, whether pure or a hybrid mixture of rationalism and supernaturalism. (For a discussion of works postulating a rationalistic bent in the theology of Faustus, see Gomes, "Some Observations," 56–58.) The truth is, Socinus's system has a *moral* center, and Socinus examines the necessity and importance of any given doctrine in terms of how it conduces to obedience to God's commandments, which obedience in turn leads to eternal life. Thus, the doctrine of the reward of immortality, attained through obeying the divine precepts revealed by Christ, provides the point of departure for evaluating his entire system.

We are therefore not surprised when we read the following affirmative thesis at the very beginning of *DS*: Christ is our Savior because he has announced to us the way of eternal salvation (*DS*, 1.1.2), and we obtain this salvation by imitating him (*DS*, 1.3.1). Jesus demonstrated his faithfulness in keeping God's commandments by his willingness to die for them. And when God raised him from the dead as a result of this faithfulness, Jesus himself received the reward from God that he promised to his followers if they, too, obeyed as he did. As Socinus observes in *De auctoritate Sacrae Scripturae*, it is in Christianity alone that the one who conveys the saving precepts to others first of all kept them himself. Thus, he can teach not only by words but also by his very example (Socinus, in *BFP*, 1.272). And as for the attainment of the promises attached to keeping those precepts, Jesus plainly and manifestly attained the very promises that he preached to others.

It is to safeguard these core principles that Socinus takes aim at the interrelated Protestant doctrines of justification by faith alone and Christ's satisfaction on the cross. As Socinus sees it, the doctrine of justification by faith alone directly opposes his own view that works are necessary for salvation. Speaking of the hamartiology of the "Evangelicals" (*Evangelici*), Socinus himself notes "this difference from us, who affirm that good works are the cause (*causam*) *sine qua non* of our salvation" (*Epitome*, 2372–2373). As to Luther's notion that the justified believer is *simul justus et peccator* (at the same time righteous and a sinner), Socinus will have none of it.

Accordingly, it should not be difficult to see why Socinus would recoil at the orthodox doctrine of satisfaction, given the systemic connection it sustains to the doctrine of justification. In as much as the death of Christ makes satisfaction for our own disobedience, it becomes difficult for Socinus to see in what sense our obedience can be necessary for salvation. In view of the foregoing, Socinus's motivation to launch a frontal assault against the penal theory of the atonement is clear.

Socinus's arguments generally fall into four categories: theological (in the strict sense of theology proper), exegetical/scriptural, logical, and moral. Socinus bases his theological objections primarily on his view of God's nature and attributes. He draws exegetical/scriptural arguments primarily from direct biblical citations, which, in Socinus's thinking, cut against the satisfaction theory. Socinus's logical criticisms are intended to show the irrationality and impossibility of the orthodox position. Finally, the moral objections attack the doctrine on the ground that it entails actions by God or men that run contrary to the reasonable principles of morality, generally accepted by all. In actual practice one finds considerable interpenetration between these categories; while the boundaries of demarcation are not always absolute, these formal distinctions do provide a useful basis for classification and analysis.

First, Socinus's *theology* proper involves three essential points, which inform directly his view of forgiveness: (1) God, as *dominus*, is above all compulsion. He may forgive or not forgive sin as he sees fit. (2) Socinus views sin according to the analogy of a pecuniary debt. God may, as any other creditor, freely remit the debt without further condition. (3) God's penal justice, wrath, and mercy are not habitual properties "residing in God," but are only "momentary alternating acts" (Ritschl, 300). Consequently, God's immutable holiness does not constrain him to punish sin, as the penal theory requires.

Second, underlying Socinus's *exegesis* of key atonement texts are the following ideas and principles: (1) When the Scriptures speak of "redemption," they do so metaphorically. Redemption is simply a metaphor for liberation, without implying the payment of a literal price. (2) When the Scriptures say that Christ died "for" our sins, the preposition "for" (Greek: *anti, huper*; Latin: *pro*) should not be understood as indicating substitution or exchange. Rather, it should be taken as meaning "for the advantage or benefit of." (3) Passages that teach "free forgiveness" directly confute the orthodox doctrine of satisfaction. For example, Socinus makes much of the parable of the king in Matthew 18:23–35, in which the king forgives without receiving any satisfaction and commands his servants to do the same, in imitation of him.

Third, Socinus argued against the *rationality* of the doctrine of satisfaction on several heads: (1) Satisfaction and remission are purely contradictory notions. That is, if a debt is paid then the debt no longer exists and there is nothing to remit. Even if someone other than the original debtor should step up to pay the debt in place of the debtor (as in the penal theory), this would still not constitute a remission of the debt but rather the simple transfer of that debt from one person to another. (2) Even if satisfaction through a substitute were somehow possible, a single death could only substitute for a single individual. (3) Since Christ suffered for a finite time he could not pay an eternal debt. (4) If one argues that Christ's deity lends the death infinite worth, then God should not have subjected Christ to so much distress, for even the smallest suffering would have infinite value. (5) Again, one cannot invoke Christ's alleged deity, since the Godhead is impassible and therefore incapable of participating in the suffering.

Fourth, Socinus rejects the doctrine of penal substitution as patently *immoral*. Specifically, he rejects the notion that an innocent person can be punished in place of a guilty person on the following grounds: (1) It is an obvious, direct moral intuition, drawn from "the light of reason [*rationis lumen*], which is God's gift," that the innocent should not be punished in place of the guilty (*DS*, 3.3.252–253). (2) "The consistent customs and significant consensus of all nations and all ages" demonstrate that "the bodily punishment which one person owes neither can nor should be paid by another person" (*DS*, 3.3.252–253). (3) The Bible has clearly declared, most especially in Ezekiel 18, that punishing the innocent in place of the guilty is abominable. (4) Civil and criminal law must not be confused. While "monetary penalties related to defaulting on a debt can be endured by one person in place of another" (as in a civil matter), death or corporal punishment (*mors sive corporis vexatio*), being criminal penalties, are an altogether different matter; these cannot be vicariously endured (*DS*, 3.3.251).

Bibliography

Beard, *The Reformation of the Sixteenth Century*, 1980.
Gomes, "De Jesu Christo Servatore: Faustus Socinus on the Satisfaction of Christ," *Westminster Theological Journal* 55, 1993.

Gomes, "Faustus Socinus and John Calvin on the Merits of Christ," *Reformation and Renaissance Review* 12:2–3, 2010.
Gomes, "Some Observations on the Theological Method of Faustus Socinus (1539–1604)," *Westminster Theological Journal* 70, 2008.
Grensted, *A Short History of the Doctrine of the Atonement*, 1920.
Ritschl, *A Critical History of the Doctrine of Reconciliation*, 1872.
Socinus, *Epitome colloquii Racoviae habiti anno 1601* (ed. Szczucki and Tazbir; critical Latin text printed in Warsaw, 1966).
Socinus, *Summa Religionis Christianae*, vol. 1 of Bibliotheca Fratrum Polonorum quos Unitarios vocant. 1, 2, Amsterdam, 1668.
Wilbur, *A History of Unitarianism*, vol. 1, *Socinianism and its Antecedents*, 1945.
Williams, *The Radical Reformation*, 3rd edn, 2000.

Hugh of St. Victor

G. R. Evans

Hugh of St. Victor (ca. 1096–1141) chose to become a regular canon early in life. He joined the community where he had been educated, the Priory of St. Pancras in Saxony, a district where local warfare made life dangerous. Hugh's uncle, the bishop of Blankenburg, suggested he move to Paris and join the young community of St. Victor present within the city. St. Victor was a house of Augustinian canons founded in 1208, as a result of William of Champeaux's decision to withdraw from the ruthless battles of the open schools in Paris. The bishop knew it well, having received his own education at St. Victor. Hugh made the move sometime between 1115 and 1120 and stayed there for the remainder of his life.

Canons differed from monks in that they had a role in society as priests. Cathedral canons "regular" (living under a Rule) could be used in a diocese where there was a shortage of parish priests, for example. Therefore, a higher level of education was needed than was essential for monks. Since at least the time of Charlemagne there had been an expectation that cathedrals would ensure a good standard of education among their canons and the same expectation seems to have emerged in the twelfth century when various new orders of canons appeared, such as the Premonstratensians. St Victor proved outstanding as a center of education, offering teaching in the liberal arts and theology.

Hugh's main discussion of the atonement occurs in his treatise *De sacramentis Christianae fidei*. The title should not be translated as "On the sacraments of the Christian faith," as the term *sacramentum* did not yet carry the technical meaning it had later. A better rendering of this title might be "On the mysteries of the Christian faith." It forms a comprehensive encyclopedia of essentials designed to be accessible to the general reader of its day. It is not a work of cutting-edge theology; it does, however, introduce the student to the debates of the time and suggest a position to be taken. The atonement is a topic of central importance as he divides all he has to say about the work of God into the "work of creation" and the "work of restoration" (*opus creationis; opus restaurationis*).

Book I, 8, covers the atonement. Hugh, ever the patient teacher, begins by explaining the consequences of the first sin of Adam—the punishments that followed, bodily mortality, and unbridled lust and ignorance could have led the whole of humanity to an eternity in hell, but God postponed this ultimate judgment. It was God's intention that humanity should be saved. Therefore, a time of waiting was arranged (I.8.i).

Hugh goes on to explain how things stood when it was time to put things right. He uses the metaphor of a lawsuit. There are three parties to this trial, "man, God and the Devil." The Devil is accused and convicted of having kidnapped mankind, and thus "injured" the rights of God, to whom man belonged. He did this by fraud and then held onto mankind by force. Humanity is also convicted of having injured God because Adam disobeyed his instruction not to eat the apple and handed himself to a rival, Satan, thus depriving God of his rightful service. This last notion gets its force from the social structure of feudal northern Europe, where a man expected to be "the man of" a lord, and to owe him service, its exact character depending on the social status of the individual. The Devil had also injured mankind, as first he made man false promises and then he did man harm (I.8.iii).

This metaphor created the paradoxical conclusion that the Devil has control of man unjustly, but man is held in his control quite justly because he consented to it. What could be done? Mankind needed an Advocate. The only possible advocate was God but God was justly still angry with man because of his sin. The first necessity was that God should be placated. Then man could go to court with the Devil with his divine Advocate. But what could man offer God that would please him, when man was so sinful and unworthy? God could not simply accept this unworthy offering and say it would do, because the rescue of mankind had to be reasonable in order to be just. The answer was for God as an act of mercy to provide man with a Man who could make a worthy offering. This was Jesus, the Son of God made flesh (I.8.iii). God was placated by the birth of Christ. These last steps in the argument owe a good deal to the *Cur Deus Homo* of Anselm of Canterbury.

There remained one more necessary step—to make the necessary satisfaction, for the Lord's honor demanded it. Here again is an echo of feudal thinking and a clear echo of the argument of the *Cur Deus Homo* of Anselm of Canterbury. Punishment had to be exacted, but if Jesus willingly accepted that punishment on behalf of his fellow men, God's honor would be satisfied. When he did so, his death made satisfaction.

So what was the outcome of the litigation? God's judgment of the Devil took place at the beginning of the world, the Crucifixion resolved man's case against the Devil, and the Devil no longer has any rights over man. The judgment in God's case against man will be known on the Day of Judgment.

Bibliography

Coolman, *The Theology of Hugh of St. Victor*, 2010.
Dillard, *Foundation and Restoration in Hugh of St. Victor's* De sacramentis, 2014.
Harkins, *Reading and the Work of Restoration*, 2009.
Hugh of St. Victor, *De sacramentis Christianae Fidei*, PL 176.
Hugh of St. Victor, *On the Sacraments of the Christian Faith*, 1951.
Rorem, *Hugh of St. Victor*, 2009.

Substitution and Representation

Jeannine Michele Graham

Though concepts of substitution and representation have fueled discussions about atonement for ages, they have recently become a focal point of renewed controversy. Emerging from the controversy are three distinct categories around which disagreements often cluster.

Substitution, particularly construed in its penal form, has been a lightning rod attracting vigorous objections. Traditionally understood, penal substitution depicts Jesus's atoning work as involving the following components: Jesus (1) interposing himself as the God-ordained sin-bearer; (2) bearing the sins of the world upon himself on the Cross; (3) absorbing the wrath of God rightly levied against human sinners; (4) suffering punishment as humanity's substitute—the innocent taking the place of the guilty—to spare humanity from wrath; thus enabling reconciliation between God and all those who accept Jesus's self-sacrifice in their stead (Belousek, 85, 173).

Fundamental to this view is the premise that punishment is a necessary response that must be rendered by a holy God toward sinners in order to satisfy justice: God's righteous reaction to and rejection of evil in all its forms—an intolerable affront to God's just character and loving will for creation. Integral to penal substitution is the "instead of" (*hyper*) implication embodied in the notion of Jesus as Substitute. Instead of guilty sinners reaping their just desserts, Jesus intervenes to bear the penalty of death in their place.

Numerous objections have been raised against this atonement theory. Critics charge that penal substitution is itself inherently unjust. How can an innocent party suffer penal consequences in place of the guilty, resulting in the latter getting off scot free? How can one person's guilt be transferred to another? Any foisting of responsibility for another's wrongdoing upon an innocent third party, excusing the guilty party from being accountable for their own misdeeds, encourages irresponsibility and denigrates human integrity. Closely related to that is the charge that such a view drives a wedge between members of the Trinity who appear to act independently with different agendas, setting mercy at odds with holiness. While many penal substitution advocates would strongly deny any notion of Jesus appeasing the Father via sacrifice, nonetheless critics charge that penal views encourage the unsavory impression voiced by one Bible study speaker that "Jesus really came to save us from God" (Baker and Green, 182).

Moreover, the portrayal of salvation as the end product of a vengeful God punishing his obedient Son in place of sinners so as to satisfy the demands of justice has evoked vigorous contemporary protests of "cosmic child abuse": God killing his Son in order to liberate others (Gathercole, 24). The idea of a sovereign God so seemingly constrained by a law external to himself that his hands are tied, so to speak, from pardoning sinners until vengeance has been inflicted on a compliant, sinless "whipping boy" seems not only unpalatable but logically unviable. Some critics maintain it is a short step from that formulation to legitimizing violence, fostering a culture of abuse and victimization. This has aroused vigorous critiques from feminist voices as well as spawning a spate of books exploring alternative nonviolent atonement theories (Weaver; Jersak and Hardin). Furthermore, critics claim penal substitutionary notions construe justice purely in retributive terms (Belousek, 130). Such a perspective depicts God violating his own ethics of peace and love as embodied and taught by Jesus, thus privileging retributive justice over restorative justice—a biblically dubious move. Finally, critics fault penal substitute proponents for so emphasizing Jesus's penal death that the resurrection seems inconsequential. Rebuttals to the above critiques likewise abound (Phillips, 205–225; McCormack in Hill and James, 363–366; Jeffery, Ovey, and Sach, 205–328; Gathercole, 23–28).

As an alternative to penal substitution, numerous scholars have gravitated to the concept of representation. Hofius voices a distinction between construing Jesus's role as *exclusive place-taking*, wherein Jesus's death is a substitutionary offering made *instead* of us, and (what he deems more favorably) *inclusive place-taking*, where Jesus's life and death as our Representative is offered on our behalf in a way that *includes* us (Hofius, 163–188). Dorothee Sölle vigorously excoriates the notion of substitution as eminently dehumanizing. If Jesus's acts as Substitute are rendered instead of sinners, human beings are ousted and thus devalued as inconsequential. On the other hand, Jesus as Representative upholds the dignity of individuals as irreplaceably significant. Rather than permanently replacing human beings, Jesus acts for persons as temporary placeholder like a good teacher rendering needed assistance and granting human beings time to mature so they may eventually take over full responsibility for their own lives, no longer needing representation by another (Sölle, *Christ as Representative*).

A further variation of Christ's atoning work as representation rallies around the idea of Christ identifying with humankind in his suffering and death rather than dying a unique death in our place. Even the Day of Atonement (Lev. 16) is seen through this lens: rather than interpreting the atoning ritual as a transferring of sins upon a sacrificial goat, who is then slaughtered in place of guilty sinners, this view interprets the high priest's laying of hands upon the animal primarily as a vicarious act of identification between animal and humans (Shelton, 53–56). The slain animal's blood, taken by the priest into the Holy of Holies, symbolically takes the people with it before God. The animal does not displace those offering it, sparing them from judgment; rather, the people come to God *through* the judgment of death en route to being retrieved from death, cleansed from the stain of sin, and reconciled with God (Gathercole, 32–36).

Construing Jesus as Representative rather than Substitute has prompted some to speak of his atoning work as an "interchange" between God and sinners (M. Hooker, quoted in Gathercole, 38–42). It is not that Jesus suffered and died so they don't have to but, that in Christ they *did* suffer and die; they were included in his suffering and death. Paul's assertion in 2 Corinthians 5:14–21 ("when Christ died, all died") is taken as further evidence of Christ's representative capacity in so identifying with sinners that his death was not *instead* of them but *included* them; all died *with* him. It is more than a simple straightforward exchange, as if Jesus swaps places with his people so as to die in place of them while they are spared. Rather, he goes to the place where they are and then takes them from there to salvation. United with him in his death, sinners pass out of death into resurrection life with him. They become righteous *in him*, participating in his righteousness, which he graciously shares with them (Belousek, 289).

In contrast to views of Christ's atoning work as either substitutionary or representative terms, a third approach combines the two. Rather than being mutually exclusive concepts, they are treated as indispensably complementary (Gathercole, 14, 109–113; Torrance, lxxv). Christ as Substitute champions the notion that the human condition is so dire a Savior is needed to do for sinners what they cannot do for themselves: rescuing them from the clutches of sin and death and recreating them in the ontological depths of their being so they are liberated to live according to God's good, creative design. This approach expresses a legitimate *exclusive place-taking* in that the Triune God undertook to fix the situation personally by entering into dysfunctional, alienated human flesh exclusively through the one person of Jesus in order to vanquish human corruption, exemplifying the biblical theme of the One for the many.

Such substitution is not confined to his death alone but is what T. F. Torrance calls "radical substitution" encompassing the entirety of his life as well (Torrance, lxvi). Here, relational, covenantal language is more apt to be utilized by proponents of this approach than legal, forensic terms (Torrance, 1–24; Vanhoozer, quoted in Baker and Green, 186–189). Even the judicial terminology present in Barth's fourfold affirmation of substitution (*CD* IV/1, 211–283)—Jesus took our place as Judge, as the judged, as judgment enacted in our place and as acting justly—is worked out within the context of Jesus's elective identity and covenantal mission. Barth's covenantal formulation provided grist for the mill of my own fourfold rendition of Jesus's atoning mission as follows: the One for the many (exclusive), the many in the One (inclusive), the many displaced by the One (preclusive), and the many replaced by the One (conclusive) (Graham, 203–220).

Christ's representative role is likewise radical—a double movement of grace as he both represents (as fully divine) God reaching out to humankind to set all things right and also represents (as fully human) faithful response to God rendered in human flesh. From birth to death the Incarnate Son of God lived a life of obedience, perfectly fulfilling the covenant relationship from both sides: as faithful covenant partner of God in loving, trusting dependence on God the Father while at the same time fulfilling from the divine side his covenantal commitment as God-with-us to save and to bless. All this was done not for himself alone but in place of sinners and on their behalf within his humanity, replacing chronic human infidelity with his uncompromising faithfulness, in order to repair human brokenness with his wholeness.

In this configuration Jesus as Representative Substitute is seen both as *exclusive place-taker* in the sense of acting in place of sinful humanity while in another nuanced sense also as *inclusive place-taker* by acting on their behalf in a way that includes them. As the Electing-Creator-Word through whom all was created, he has an ontological link with all of creation, including all humanity. Thus, when he assumed human flesh through the incarnation, his humanity paradoxically could also vicariously include and represent that of all persons.

Within this third Representative/Substitutionary approach, there are variations of thought about how to understand the contours of his substitutionary death. Some argue along traditional penal lines that Jesus's death was salvific because it absorbed God's wrath justly deserved by sinners whose place he took on the Cross. Others, averse to terminology suggestive of God punishing Jesus, temper the language by speaking of Jesus bearing the penalty of sin or God's judgment (Marshall, 41). The crucifixion of Jesus was "not by God's design to satisfy God's demands, but by human design to satisfy human demands ... *humanity* is 'estranged' from and 'hostile' toward God and needing to be reconciled to God, not the other way around" (Belousek 113, 139; emphasis in the original). Seen in this light, Jesus bore human hostility toward God (Baker and Green, 81), "absorbing the effects of the deadly results of sin" (Shelton, 193) into the very life of God. Still others, not finding any penal connotations hermeneutically compelling, conceptualize divine wrath not in terms of a direct infliction of vengeance upon sinners but in the sense of Romans 1:24–28 that God "gave them over" to the natural consequences of their sins (Baker and Green, 77; Belousek, 215–219, 364). As one writer puts it, "Wrath is not some sort of vengeful decree that consigns humanity to the vindictive judgment of an angry God. It is the 'eschatological symbol for the work of love that allows its objects to choose self-destruction'" (Dunning, quoted in Shelton, 221). Similarly expressed, it is "the rock of judgement upon which the sinner who refuses the divine love shatters himself or herself" (Torrance, 189).

The question of human participation is a perennial concern in atonement discussions. Advocates of the necessity to hold substitution and representation together contend that the Gospel of grace accords space both for divine grace and human participation. Both poles are vital, though carefully qualified. First, there is the need for divine intervention to "recreate" human nature through Jesus's incarnational entering into human guilt from within. The Incarnate Christ accomplished this "not simply by wearing our flesh, but ... by penetrating into the very heart of our evil, and within the sinful conditions of our flesh" (Torrance, 126–127). In so doing, he substituted his own righteous response to God at every stage of human existence for the sorry plight of human waywardness, thus *doing for and apart from human beings* what only the Incarnate Creator-Word could do. Yet this must be accomplished in such a way that truly *includes* humans as those ontologically represented in him. What has been done for and apart from persons as *passive participants* included in Christ then becomes the life-giving basis on which persons are awakened to faith. Once awakened, they are united to Christ by the Spirit and summoned to flourish as *active participants* in a life of daily union and communion with God. The net effect is the creative fleshing out through the particularities of their personalities and life context the reality of who they have already been recreated to be in Christ.

Substitution, representation, or a combination of the two? The common quest for biblical validation for each position often flushes out hermeneutical complexities not easily resolved. I have little doubt that a core atonement text like Galatians 2:20 could generate a prism of varied interpretations which might well be claimed as conducive to each of the above three positions. Perhaps that is an apt place at which to conclude—humbly attesting to an enigmatic mystery embedded in atoning grace which both embraces us with liberating promise and entices us toward further, deeper inquiry:

> *I have been crucified with Christ. It is no longer I who live but Christ who lives in me. And the life I now live in the flesh I live by faith in the Son of God who loved me and gave himself for me.* (Gal. 2:20)

Bibliography

Baker and Green, *Recovering the Scandal of the Cross*, 2011.
Belousek, *Atonement, Justice, and Peace*, 2012.
Gathercole, *Defending Substitution*, 2015.
Graham, *Representation and Substitution in the Atonement Theologies of Dorothee Sölle, Macquarrie, and Karl Barth*, 2005.
Hill and James, *The Glory of Atonement*, 2004.
Hofius, "The Fourth Servant Song in the New Testament Letters," in *The Suffering Servant. Isaiah 53 in Jewish and Christian Sources*, 2004.
Jeffery, Ovey, and Sach, *Pierced for Our Transgressions*, 2007.
Jersak and Hardin, *Stricken by God?*, 2007.
Marshall, *Aspects of the Atonement*, 2007.
Phillips, *Precious Blood*, 2009.
Shelton, *Cross and Covenant*, 2006.
Sölle, *Christ as Representative*, 1967.
Torrance, *Atonement*, 2009.
Weaver, *The Nonviolent Atonement*, 2001.

Supra/infralapsarianism

Edwin Chr. van Driel

What motivates God to become incarnate? Scripture says the Son was sent "so that the world might be saved through him" (John 3:17, NRSV), and usually this is construed to mean that the incarnation embodies God's mission to rescue us from sin. But is that all there is to it, or could it be said that what is given us in the incarnate One, according to the same Scriptures, is much richer in divine presence and friendship than what was needed to counter sin? And if that is the case, what might motivate the superabundance of this gift? This is the issue at stake in the debate between infralapsarian and supralapsarian Christology. Infralapsarian Christology holds that the incarnation is contingent upon sin. To put it in terms of a classical conceptual framework in the ordering of divine intentions, God wants to become incarnate only after (*infra*) God wills to allow for sin (*lapsus*, fall). In contrast, supralapsarian Christology posits that the incarnation is not solely motivated by sin and that God has reasons to become human that are deeper or prior (*supra*) than God's will to allow the fall. In saying that the incarnation is not contingent upon sin, the supralapsarian does not deny that in the incarnation God also deals with the sin problem. Rather, she says (with the writer of Colossians) that he through whom and for whom all things have been created, and who therefore is before all things, is now also the one through whom God reconciles all things, the firstborn from the dead and the head of the church, "so that he might come to have first place in everything" (Col. 1:18, NRSV). It is because he is central to creation and eschatological consummation that the incarnate One is also central to reconciliation.

In the context of this volume, the question is whether a supralapsarian account of the incarnation also shapes one's understanding of *how* Christ deals with the sin problem; that is, whether what one believes about God's supralapsarian intentions shapes one's account of God's infralapsarian dealings. Very little research has been done on the correlation between supralapsarian Christological arguments and particular models of atonement and so this should be a promising area to explore.

To map this territory, it may be best to start with the contrasting accounts of two medieval theologians, Anselm of Canterbury (1033–1109) and John Duns Scotus (1266–1308). Anselm's *Cur Deus Homo* contains an argument meant to show that the only way in which God could deal with the sin problem was through incarnation. All other possible avenues are, in the light of the perfection of God's character, said to be dead-end streets. What is not always taken into account, however, is that Anselm's book was actually meant to contribute to a contemporary ongoing debate between Jewish and Christian Medieval theologians about the incarnation in which the Jewish rabbis had argued that the incarnation was derogatory of the dignity of God (Southern, 198–202). How could it be that God, "that-than-which-a-greater-cannot-be-thought," would engage in this humiliating act of "descending into a human's womb, born of a woman, growing up nurtured on milk and human food" (*Cur Deus Homo* I.3)? This line of argument had hit home and, motivated Anselm to show that given the circumstances God could not have done otherwise—there was no other way to solve the problem of sin (cf. *Cur Deus Homo* I.1). It is exactly here that supralapsarians take a different route. They differ from Anselm in that they do not accept the premise of his conversation partners. Rather than seeing the incarnation as a humiliating act that God only engages in if no other possibility is open, supralapsarians see the condescending love that is embodied in the babe of Bethlehem as the ultimate expression of the very heart of God's character. It is here that we see what God's perfection actually looks like.

An example of this supralapsarian approach is the one put forth by the medieval theologian John Duns Scotus (1266–1308). Scotus embraces an Anselmian understanding of the atonement, but he rewrites Anselm's proposal in a supralapsarian key. For Scotus the heart of the incarnation is love. In a theological reflection on the Pauline notion that everything is created "for him," for Christ (Col. 1:18), Scotus argues that the decision to become incarnate, that is, the decision to unite Godself with a human nature, logically precedes all other divine intentions. God wants to love and God wants to share this love, and therefore, God decides to become incarnate. Next God decides to create all other things, humans and all creation, as the friends and accompaniments of the incarnate One (cf. McElrath). But God also decides that, once humanity has rejected this love and turned against God, it is through the incarnate One that God will make payment for sin and draw us back again in reconciliation.

Scotus agrees to Anselm's analysis of the cross as a form of satisfactory payment. He however disagrees with Anselm on two points. First, he argues that Anselm makes a mistake by conceptualizing the weight of sin, and therefore the weight of the needed payment, as immeasurable. No finite being can commit a sin of infinite weight, even against the infinitely worthy God; therefore, the payment does not have to be infinite. But, then, of course, we also do not need someone with infinite resources to supply the payment, and that means that a simple creature would do. Why then, is it God incarnate who supplies the payment? Here Scotus draws on the divine motivation he detected *supra* God's intent to allow for sin. Just as God does not *have* to give Godself to creation in incarnation but *chooses* to do so out of love, similarly God does not have to step forward to make the payment for sin, but because of love decides to do so. Second, while the incarnate One could have made the payment by a simple act of intense love—as Scotus argues, what is needed to outweigh an act of disobedience is simply an act of obedience that is of greater intensity than its negative counterpart—he chooses to bring about atonement by an ultimate act of intense love, the giving of himself unto death. "And therefore he preferred to do it in this way, I believe: to draw us to a greater love to himself." (Unfortunately, Scotus's Latin texts on the atonement have not yet been translated. For a summary and text references, see Cross, 129–132.)

The comparison between Anselm and Scotus illustrates that what one believes about God's character and supralapsarian intentions does indeed have the potential of shaping one's account of God's infralapsarian dealings. That insight, combined with Anselm's roadmap, can be used to further chart different understandings of the atonement. Anselm's decision to mark off "just forgiveness" and "punishment" as dead-end streets was motivated by his understanding of God's character and supralapsarian relating to the world. Given God's perfection, God could not "just forgive"; and given God's eschatological intentions for the world, atonement could not be brought about by punishment. Once one perceives differently of God's character and ultimate intentions, one may conceive of these different atoning acts more positively. Both the notion of "punishment" and "just forgiveness" have prominent representatives in Western theology, and among these we can in turn distinguish between theologians with Christologically infralapsarian and supralapsarian intuitions. John Calvin, who like Anselm is Christologically an infralapsarian, walked down a path Anselm had rejected as a dead-end street and understood the cross in terms of wrath and punishment. Driving him were exactly his intuitions about the nature of God. A perfect God cannot allow God's law to be broken, he argued, and therefore, even if God wants to be gracious, God has to punish: "Since he is a righteous judge, he does not allow his law to be broken without punishment" (*Institutiones*, II.XVI.2). In his conception of things *infra*, after the Fall, Calvin ends up in a different place than Anselm because he started in a different place in his conception of things *supra*, before, the Fall. Calvin's twentieth-century heir Karl Barth, in turn, rethought Calvin's account in Christologically supralapsarian terms. Covenant precedes creation, argued Barth, and covenant is Christologically filled: we are created in the context of God's decision to be a "God for us," to be Jesus Christ. "In and by themselves" human beings will however always live against this covenantal identity. Therefore, to be "a God for others," to be Jesus Christ, will have to involve an act of atonement, to be the one who also carries the wrath meant for sinners. (For an analysis of Barth's supralapsarian Christology, see Van Driel, 63–124.) Like with Calvin, Barth's understanding of matters infralapsarian, after the Fall, is shaped by his conception of matters supralapsarian—God's covenantal relating to what is not God. Finally, a similar pattern can be detected with regard to the third way God could conceivably deal with sin, by "just forgiving." Anselm had rejected this possibility because it would be incongruent with the character of the best possible person to "just forgive," and thereby, according to Anselm, to ignore sin. John Howard Yoder holds differently, exactly because he construes the divine character differently. The core of God's being is *agape*, self-giving love, Yoder argues, and confronted with sin such love responds with a self-sacrificing absorption of human rejection and sin. Such is the way of the cross: rather than it being conditioned by a divine need for payment or punishment, Jesus's suffering is the result of human rejection of God's self-giving love appearing in their midst. Christ's willingness to undergo such rejection is the ultimate expression of God's forgiving *agape* (Yoder, 303–313). Kathryn Tanner offers a related account from a Christologically supralapsarian perspective: human beings were created to participate in God through God's incarnational union with us, and the cross is an *expression* of God's desire to unite us to Godself, even in the face of sin and death, not a *condition* thereof (Tanner).

Having mapped these different accounts, I wish to offer three observations to stimulate further research. First, as my mapping illustrates, there is indeed a correlation between theological accounts of things *supra*, before, and things *infra*, after God's intent to allow for sin. This is true of both supralapsarian and infralapsarian Christologies. This correlation does not rest on one's account of divine motives for the incarnation, but rather on one's understanding of God's character and of God's relating to that which is not God. How one conceives of these latter two issues shapes both one's account of the reasons for the incarnation as well as one's understanding of God's dealing with sin. Second, "infralapsarian" and "supralapsarian" Christology are names for families of theological theories. Just as there is more than one infralapsarian account of the atonement, so there is also more than one kind of supralapsarian Christology. Each supralapsarian account carries within it a unique understanding of what happened on the cross. And third, while I mapped things here according to the three approaches to atonement as identified in Anselm's *Cur Deus Homo*, a careful analysis of the different infralapsarian and supralapsarian Christologies invites a corresponding mapping along a completely different set of coordinates. Some arguments regarding the atonement start from the perceived character of God and deduct from there the most fitting way for such God to deal with the sin problem (thus Anselm, and partly Calvin). Others start with the particular events of Jesus's life and induct from there what these events tell us about God's contingent motivation. Likewise, some arguments for supralapsarian Christology start with the nature of God and present the incarnation as a necessary implication of God's character; other accounts start from the narrative of Scripture, and argue that what is given to us in these particular events is simply too rich to be understood in an infralapsarian framework (for a mapping of supralapsarian arguments, see van Driel). In other words, both supralapsarian and infralapsarian Christologies can be divided again in deductive and inductive approaches. It is because of all of this that any analysis of the relationship between atonement, infralapsarianism, and supralapsarianism itself ought to proceed inductively.

Bibliography

Anselm, *Cur Deus Homo* and *Proslogion*.
Calvin, *Institutiones*.
Cross, *Duns Scotus*, 1999.
McElrath, *Franciscan Christology*, 1980.
Southern, *Saint Anselm*, 1990.
Tanner, *Christ the Key*, 2011.
Yoder, *Preface to Theology*, 2002.
Van Driel, *Incarnation Anyway*, 2008.

Theological Interpretation of Scripture

Scott R. Swain

In what follows we will consider three major issues that confront theological interpretation of Scripture in addressing the doctrine of atonement, namely, the identity of the God who reconciles sinners, the task of integrating the Bible's diverse teaching on atonement, and the relationship between readers and biblical teaching on atonement. In so doing, we will also consider some of the different tendencies Christian theology has exhibited in treating these three interpretive issues.

A primary question for interpreting biblical teaching on atonement is: Who is the God who reconciles sinners to himself through the cross of Jesus Christ? Different interpretations of God's identity inform and are informed by different interpretations of biblical atonement teaching. Classical Christian theologians followed two "Mosaic maxims" in interpreting the identity of God. On the one hand, scriptural teaching that "God is not man" (Num. 23:19) led interpreters to deny that creaturely characteristics such as temporality, changeability, and passibility apply when it comes to God's identity. On the other hand, scriptural teaching regarding the creation of human beings in the "likeness" of God (Gen. 1:26), along with the Bible's broader propensity toward anthropomorphism (e.g., Deut. 8:5), led interpreters to acknowledge that certain perfections which characterize creatures (e.g., intelligence, will, power, etc.) exist preeminently in God (Gavrilyuk, 43).

The classical interpretation of God's identity informed interpretation of biblical atonement teaching in a variety of ways. Given God's unchangeable perfection, the biblical story of reconciliation was not read as a story of divine self-realization but rather as a story of divine philanthropy toward creatures (Irenaeus, 4.11.2, 4.14.1–2). The supreme manifestation of divine philanthropy for these interpreters was the self-sacrifice of the Son of God on the cross

(McGuckin, 387), an event that became the subject of great interpretive controversy in the fourth century as theologians, such as Cyril of Alexandria and Nestorius, debated the significance of the claim that the Son of God, impassible by nature, suffered the pain of crucifixion as a human being for us and our salvation (Gavrilyuk, chapter 6; McGuckin, 184). The classical interpretation of God also informed debates about whether divine perfection "necessitated" the crucifixion of the Son of God incarnate or whether his crucifixion was only a "fitting" display of divine perfection (Aquinas, *Compendium*, §§ 226–227; Aquinas, *Summa*, IIIa, q 46, art. 2–3; IIIa, q 46, art. 6, ad 6; Johnson, 302–318). In the theology of John Owen, we see an example where pressure arising from the exegesis of various biblical texts leads to a shift from a "fittingness" view of the relationship between divine justice and Christ's death to a "necessitarian" view (Owen, vol. 10; Trueman, 87–103).

Contemporary theology, in many instances, has not followed the classical interpretation of God's identity. Accordingly, it has reconceived the relationship between God and the work of reconciliation. Following largely upon Hegelian influences, many theologians have sought to interpret God's identity by means of historicized metaphysical concepts as well as by idealist categories of human subjectivity (Küng; Jüngel, 63–100). According to these theologians, faithful biblical interpretation demands use of such concepts and categories. For example, Jürgen Moltmann argues that divine impassibility cannot be sustained in light of Jesus's cry of dereliction on the cross, while Robert Jenson contends that divine timelessness must be jettisoned in light of divine self-involvement in the temporally enacted stories of Israel and Jesus (Moltmann; Jenson, *Systematic Theology*, vol. 1). Indeed, according to Jenson, the work of reconciliation occurs within God (Jenson, "Reconciliation in God," chapter 8). Other contemporary theologians, however, have not followed this trajectory, arguing that traditional doctrines such as divine simplicity and the eternal processions have an important role to play in atonement theology (Webster, Holmes, Davidson and Rae).

Modern historical theology has occupied itself with identifying and describing various "models" of atonement. There is some warrant for this approach insofar as Anselm's theology of atonement works according to an identifiably different logic than does Abelard's. This approach has proven unhelpful to the extent that it has sought to explain various "models" purely in terms of their various historical-contextual provenances (e.g., medieval systems of honor, etc.) to the exclusion of their biblical-interpretive origins (von Balthasar, vol. 4). The Bible's vast array of metaphors, motifs, and historical moments requires integration in any atonement theology that would claim the Bible as its theological source and norm. The challenges here are many.

The Bible portrays the meaning of God's reconciling work through of a variety of metaphors and images, which are in turn integrally related to biblical metaphors for sin and its consequences (Anderson). Christ's atoning work is described with language associated with the righteousness of the divine judge, the purity and holiness of the sacrificial cult, and the ransom and liberation of slaves from the slave market. Atonement is also described in types and images drawn from the Old Testament's depiction of Israel's history, especially God's great act of deliverance in the Exodus. The question for theological interpretation concerns whether and how these diverse metaphors and figures may be reconciled within one coherent account of atonement. Competing theologies of atonement may be measured by the extent to which they are able to incorporate the breadth of biblical teaching on this topic (Blocher, 72–76).

Along with this variety of metaphors, theological interpretation seeks to account for the relationship between various biblical motifs associated with God's reconciling work. This facet of theological interpretation is particularly important because many debates in atonement theology (e.g., questions about the "extent" of the atonement) cannot be resolved simply through recourse to different texts where God's reconciling work is in view but only when a broader constellation of biblical themes such as Trinity, union with Christ, and covenant representation is considered (Gibson, chapter 13).

Finally, theological interpretation of atonement requires us to relate God's reconciling work to the various moments in Jesus's life and ministry. Certainly, Jesus's crucifixion is central in this regard, given its prominence in the apostolic writings. However, Jesus's incarnation, resurrection, ascension, and heavenly session must also be integrated within a theologically responsible account of atonement (Torrance, chapter 5; Moffitt). Neglect of these Christological moments in the biblical story line inevitably results in an impoverished atonement theology.

The last issue concerns the relationship between text and reader in theological interpretation of Scripture. Interpreting biblical teaching about God's reconciling work inevitably requires that we make theological judgments, first, regarding the (potential) conflict that lies between divine revelation and human reason and, second, regarding the possibility of translating biblical atonement teaching across various historical and political cultures.

In Theses 19–21 of his *Heidelberg Disputation*, Martin Luther proclaims a stark antithesis between God's self-revelation in the cross and the perceptual capacities of fallen human reason. According to Luther, a "theologian of glory" is someone "who looks upon the invisible things of God as though they were clearly perceptible in those things which have actually happened," whereas a "theologian of the cross" is someone who, by virtue of divine grace, "comprehends the visible and manifest things of God ... through suffering and the cross." The former sort of person "calls evil good and good evil." The latter sort of person "calls the thing what it actually is" (43–44). Later in the modern era, and in notable contrast to Luther's perspective, Socinians and other rationalist thinkers offer a much different understanding of the relationship between natural reason and biblical atonement teaching. According to these theologians, the notion of one person being punished in place of another is offensive to reason. Consequently, if theology is to retain its status as a rational discipline, it must find another way of interpreting biblical teaching about Christ's suffering.

Another issue requiring theological judgment concerns the translatability of biblical atonement teaching across various cultural horizons. Here judgments must be made not only about whether Ancient Near Eastern imagery of sacrifice and atonement can be communicated to inhabitants of cultures far removed from Ancient Near Eastern sensibilities (Baker and Green). Judgments must also be made about the extent to which this imagery can be appropriated in political cultures that seek to promote justice for historically marginalized persons. Is it possible to say, "there is something saving about the cross" while also saying "there is nothing saving about suffering, death, or victimhood, in and of itself" (Tanner, 261)?

The preceding discussion demonstrates the complex hermeneutical relationship that exists between theology and biblical interpretation when it comes to thinking about atonement. How one views God and humanity shapes and is shaped by how one relates to biblical teaching about God's work of reconciliation. This should not surprise us from a theological perspective because theology is intrinsically self-involving. Indeed, according to Christian theology, interpretation of biblical atonement teaching is itself a moment in the history in which God is reconciling sinful creatures to himself. It is a response, in one way or another, to the summons: "be reconciled to God" (2 Cor. 5:20).

Bibliography

Anderson, *Sin: A History*, 2009.
Aquinas, *Compendium of Theology*, 2009.

Aquinas, *Summa Theologica*, trans. Fathers of the English Dominican Province, 1948.
Baker and Green, *Recovering the Scandal of the Cross*, 2000.
Barth, *Church Dogmatics*, vol. 4.1, 1988.
Blocher, "Atonement," in *Dictionary of Theological Interpretation of Scripture*, 2005.
Cyril of Alexandria, "Scholia on the Incarnation of the Only Begotten," 12, in John McGuckin, *Saint Cyril of Alexandria and the Christological Controversy*, 2004.
Davidson and Rae, *God of Salvation*, 2011.
Gavrilyuk, *The Suffering of the Impassible God*, 2004.
Gibson, "The Glorious, Indivisible, Trinitarian Work of God in Christ: Definite Atonement in Paul's Theology of Salvation," in *From Heaven He Came and Sought Her*, 2013.
Irenaeus, *Against Heresies*.
Jenson, "Reconciliation in God," in *The Theology of Reconciliation*, 2003.
Jenson, *Systematic Theology*, 1997.
Johnson, "A Fuller Account: The Role of 'Fittingness' in Thomas Aquinas' Development of the Doctrine of the Atonement," *IJST* 3, 2010.
Jüngel, *God as the Mystery of the World*, 1983.
Küng, *The Incarnation of God*, 1987.
Luther, "Heidelberg Disputation," in *Martin Luther's Basic Theological Writings*, ed. Lull, 1989.
McGuckin, *Saint Cyril of Alexandria*, 2010.
Moffitt, *Atonement and the Logic of Resurrection in the Epistle to the Hebrews*, 2011.
Moltmann, *The Crucified God*, 1993.
Owen, *The Death of Death in the Death of Christ* and *A Dissertation on Divine Justice*, in *The Works of John Owen*, vol. 10, 1967.
Tanner, *Christ the Key*, 2010.
Torrance, *The Trinitarian Faith*, 1995.
Trueman, "John Owen's *Dissertation on Divine Justice*: An Exercise in Christocentric Scholasticism," *CTJ* 33, 1998.
von Balthasar, *Theo-Drama*, vol. 4: *The Action*, 1994.

Union with Christ

Mark A. Garcia

Atonement refers to God's act in dealing with the guilt and corruption of human sin. Classical Christian theology has affirmed both the full scope of the remedy for a uniquely human need, as well as the exclusive role of Christ as the one in whom atonement is realized. But how are these two affirmations related? How is the atonement, accomplished in Christ, good news to sinners who are *not* Christ? Christian theology has long wrestled with the most fulsome and faithful ways to articulate the relationship between Christ and sinners in the context of atonement.

How we answer this question reveals much of what we understand the atonement itself to be. While much might be said, our answer must include at least one essential Christian conviction, namely, that the atonement is good news for sinners only if God's action in Christ did not take place remotely, apart from us. It is good news only if it has taken place in true relation to us. As classical atonement theology has rightly insisted, this "in true relation to us" entails the notions of "for us," "on our behalf," and "in our stead," yet is reducible to none of these expressions exclusively. Rather, they are meaningful because of a reality more fundamental than any one of these terms, yet which is at work in all of them: union with Christ. The "in Christ" reality, effected by the Holy Spirit, renders the Word of God's work in Christ good news to those who are otherwise "far off" and in abject need of reconciliation and redemption.

In Scripture, the act and benefits of atonement are regularly framed in terms of what has taken place for us "in Christ." The decisive rupture between the old world (with its enervating, corrupting dynamics) and the new world (with its energizing, healing dynamics) is a rupture that took place in Christ's death and resurrection (2 Cor. 5:17). This was the turning of the ages, and atonement language is regularly used to disclose the nature of this hinge: it is a movement in history from wrath to grace, alienation to reconciliation, hostility to peace, death to life (Rom. 5:10–11; 2 Cor. 5:18–20; Eph. 2:16; Col. 1:20–22). In Christ the "hinge of history" is our own transition: the wrath of God has been turned away from sinners (1 Thess. 1:10, 5:9) and we are ransomed from slavery or a death sentence (Mark 10:45). In Christ death has lost its hold on us (Rom. 6:23), and the evil flesh has been "crucified" (Gal. 5:19–21; 24).

This vocabulary should not be glossed over. The vivid biblical language that our evil flesh has been "crucified"—rather than simply removed or defeated—pulls the believer into the historical reality of Christ in the most concrete way possible, signaling the deep bond between the person and work of Christ and the believer. The only meaningful sense in which the crucifixion of Christ in history can also be in truth the crucifixion of the evil flesh of his people is if our union with Christ lies at the heart of the atonement as God's action. Similarly, any attempt to articulate a thoroughgoing Christian theology of atonement must account for the Apostle's movement of thought from what God has done "in Christ" to, second and consequently, Christ as the "source" of our life *insofar as* he was "made" by the Father *our* righteousness, sanctification, and redemption (1 Cor. 1:30)—all terms with atonement significance.

To appreciate the importance of union with Christ in this setting, one need only note how the history of atonement in theology is, in a sense, a history of investigation into what has taken place in Christ *in relation to* the human need for atonement. From early interest in the cosmological effects of atonement, to medieval and Reformation focus upon matters of honor and guilt, to modern explorations of atonement and justice, union with Christ has figured prominently in this history of reflection. One influential, traditional framework distinguishes the work of Christ with its own internal structure (the *historia salutis*, the accomplishment of redemption in history) from the work of the Holy Spirit in ordering salvation in Christ (the *ordo salutis*, the theo-logic at work in the application of that redemption by the Spirit). Especially but not only within the Reformed tradition, the "connecting reality" for Christ and sinners, or for the *historia* and *ordo salutis*, is union with Christ (Garcia; Muller, 202–243). As a result, this union is centrally important for explicating the atonement itself in its nature, design, and effects, as well as the saving reality that it has secured. Theologians from across the vast scope of the Christian tradition have continued to insist in recent years that union with Christ is not a topic limited to salvation or the application of redemption, but is key to understanding its accomplishment as well. As the twentieth-century theologian John Murray once put it, "Union with Christ is really the central truth of the whole doctrine of salvation not only in its application but also in its once-for-all accomplishment in the finished work of Christ" (161).

Finely tracing the theological reach of union and atonement, however, is more challenging and has occasioned great debate, yet certain points can be established without controversy. First, and in a way expressive of its centrality, union with Christ occupies what we may term a specifically "prepositional" role in the theology of atonement. In the substance of the theology of Christ "for" believers, of believers pardoned and healed "because of," "on account of," "by," "in," or "with" Christ, it is the reality of union with Christ which accounts for the prepositions at the heart of the atonement as good news. Indeed, thus understood, union with Christ is the connective tissue binding the varied aspects of Christ as atoning sacrifice to the varied ways in which we have need of him and benefit from what has been done in him.

Second, Christ and union are woven together in the theological preconditions for traditional atonement vocabulary. The atonement language of representation, identification, association, and substitution are conventional and in each case bears an eminently biblical motif or concern. But they are meaningful only because of something they capture about the various ways union with Christ is the eschatological space in which Christ and the sinner meet redemptively (Leithart, 115–135). The believer's union with Christ, while not itself a model of atonement as such, in fact contextualizes each of these terms and the models to which they belong.

Third, and most importantly, the "prepositional," interwoven function of union with Christ in atonement theology is itself anchored in the most important facet of the atonement: the identity of Jesus Christ, the incarnate Son. It is important, however, that one account for the whole Christ, not a part of him, in order to properly configure the Christ in whom atonement is accomplished to those who receive his benefits. The biblical and theological density of Christ, union, and atonement is not limited to the Christ of two natures merely, even as this has proven to be a contentious connection to specify. It is at least true that Christ, in the union of his person as the God-man, precipitates the reconciliation of God and humankind. The incarnation, as an event, enfleshes God's loving, sacrificial determination to reconcile himself to his creatures, and establishes the necessary ontological as well as covenantal context for atonement and its application.

Yet it is also insufficient to trace Christ only in terms of the "days of his flesh" among his brethren—in Michael Welker's words, "at the beginning: the stable, at the end: the gallows" (19). Rather, it must be the Christ of the Scriptural canon in its wholeness, the "Lord Jesus Christ" of Israel's and the Church's earliest and continuing confession, the one who is the *scopus* of all of history and is living now in continuous exercise of his still-priestly love. At work in the prepositions, and thus in the various ways union with Christ relates to the atonement, is One who is at the same time, canonically, the Son of God, incarnate God, true Man, Passover Lamb, the embodiment of Israel, Husband, and sacred space. This fullness of the identity of Jesus is elemental to union with Christ and the atonement, for it clarifies how Christ can address sin and death in their full, multifaceted scope.

Crucial here is the realism of the union, which alone can properly account for the meaningfulness of the atoning work of Christ in history to sinners of any age. Affiliation and similarity will not do; sympathy and affinity are insufficient. To deploy the Pauline language, it is not enough that we died to sin like Christ; we *have died* to sin in and with Christ (Col. 2:9–3:4). Union with Christ is thus indispensable for the realism of the Gospel in its lived expression: we have died with Christ, we live in him.

Related to this conviction, while atonement theory has sometimes gravitated toward one or another of at least three facets of human sin—guilt, defilement, and estrangement—in fact elect humanity falls and rises in wholeness. The three are inseparable for the sinner's redemption for they are held together in Christ himself. The realism of the believer's union with Christ is rooted in the realism of Jesus's corporate identity: he is not a private individual but the embodied second and last Adam, and true Israel. This particular yet vast scope of his identity determines the scope of meaning for being "in Christ." Jesus bears the guilt of sin not merely as one Israelite among others but as the embodiment of *guilty* Israel. But he is also the *defiled* Israel, and the *estranged* Israel, and in his atoning work the grand reversal takes place "for us" from guilt to innocence, defilement to purity, alienation to communion.

Union with Christ also has noteworthy consequences for how we think of the various atonement models in theology. Teachers of atonement theory often speak of how the various models of atonement are not necessarily competing ones but may be seen, at least in some respects, as complementary. Union with the Christ confessed by the Church—Son of God, Israel in the flesh, Husband, and so forth—illumines ways this may be so. Christ as "substitute" is key to biblical and historic atonement theory, and brings us close to the realism of union with Christ (Gathercole). Yet, it is hardly alone in this. In a specifically Easter cast on the atonement, believers participate in the identity of Christ as victor over sin, death, and the devil, the *Christus victor* concern. Nevertheless, Christ's beloved not only partake of the benefits of that conquest but participate in it themselves, as it is the victory of Christ that is worked out in our engagement with the faces of the Enemy within and without. This lived participation in the victory of Christ belongs to the reality of union with Christ in his resurrection, a union that is the dynamic of Christian struggle and perseverance in the Spirit (Rom. 6:9–11; Eph. 6:10–18).

In an analogous way, Christ as "satisfaction" connects specifically to the church's status as forgiven or just *in Christ*. Yet again, the "moral example" or "influence" theory accents a truth easily missed in accounts of the Gospel: *in Christ*, who is not only the revelation of the Law of God but its faithful embodiment in the fullness of self-sacrificial love, believers are conformed to that same faithfulness by the Spirit (Rom. 8:3–4).

Last, despite an eminent history of fruitful reflection, union with Christ awaits still further development in relation to the atonement. As one example, a robustly biblical understanding of union and the atonement requires attention to Christ not only as, say, Passover Lamb, but also as sacred space. The Johannine theology of Christ as the embodied dwelling place of Israel's God, the one in whom God "tabernacles" among us (John 1:14; Torrance, 60), pulls together the identity of Christ with the rich cultic tradition of sacred space. This holds not only for the Johannine writings but for the Apostles Paul and Peter as well (Eph. 2:18–22, 5:25–27; 1 Pet. 2:4–9). In further work on atonement and union with Christ, it may prove useful to devote more attention to this feature of biblical teaching. Especially with a view to the marital image of the union of Christ and his church, one might explore the movement from defilement to purity in the Levitical woman of Leviticus 12 and 15—herself a homology of sacred space—and in the women made whole or healed in recognizably spousal terms by Jesus in the Gospels (Whitekettle, 31–45; McWhirter).

In this and other ways, Christian theology will undoubtedly continue to discover the interplay of union with Christ and the atonement as a deep well of rich, nourishing truth.

Bibliography

Garcia, *Life in Christ*, 2008.
Gathercole, *Defending Substitution*, 2015.
Leithart, "'We Saw His Glory': Implications of the Sanctuary Christology in John's Gospel," in *Christology Ancient & Modern*, 2013.

McWhirter, *The Bridegroom Messiah and the People of God*, 2006.
Muller, *Calvin and the Reformed Tradition*, 2012.
Murray, *Redemption Accomplished and Applied*, 1955.
Torrance, *Incarnation*, 2008.
Welker, *God the Revealed*, 2013.
Whitekettle, "Leviticus 15:18 Reconsidered: Chiasm, Spatial Structure and the Body," *JSOT* 49, 1991.

Universalism

Tom Greggs

Universalism is a minority position within the Christian faith, holding that the sovereign loving will of God is ultimately irresistible and that salvation is ultimately extended to all humanity. In this way, universalism combines the Ariminian position that God *wills* the salvation of all people with the Calvinist position that God's sovereign will *cannot be resisted*: it is the belief in the omnipotence of divine love (see Robinson). Universalism might be thought of as a contrasting position to both separationism and annihilationism. Separationism contends that there will be an ultimate and irreversible eschatological separation of the damned from the saved. Separationists disagree over the extent or number of those who are saved, but draw on apocalyptic imagery of the New Testament to claim that there will be a final division of humanity, and that there will be some (whether the majority or minority) who will be lost. Annihilationists (who sometimes describe their position as "conditional immortality") hold that while God will save the elect or those who choose to accept God's gift of salvation, those who are not elect or do not exercise their free will in accepting God's salvation simply do not live in the afterlife: immortality is a gift only given to the saved, and the lost simply perish rather than enduring an eternity of perdition in hell as immortality is only something humans possess in potential and as it is given by God in grace (see Wenham).

We might think of there being two primary forms of universalism: non-particularist and particularist. Non-particularist (or pluralist) universalism is the position that no one faith has any overview of God's ways with the world, and that each faith (theistic or non-theistic) has equal access to the divine will. This position holds that there is nothing particular or exclusive to the Christian faith or Christian revelation that gives it a unique status or singular access to salvation: all religions (construed in the broadest terms) give equal access to the

Ultimate Reality, and all peoples on their various paths will find their way to that Ultimate Reality: even if through a long purgatorial process, there will be none who will escape salvation. The particular difficulties that exist with this position (as opposed to any general opposition to universalism) are twofold. On the one hand, non-particularist universalism does not account for why *Christianity qua* a particular religion might offer a Universalist account of salvation: it is (self-consciously) not particularist enough and does not emerge from Christian revelation. On the other hand, non-particularist universalism, in addressing universal salvation as an issue, construes the very question and problem from a Christian perspective: non-particularist universalism is too particularist since *salvation* is a particularly Christian concern.

Particularist (or specifically Christian) universalism seeks to make the case for universal salvation on the basis of the central tenets of the Christian faith. The case for universal salvation in this instance stems from the revelation present in the life of Christ and the Christian scriptures of God's ultimate loving and forgiving will. As Trevor Hart describes it, this position arises from the belief that since it is God's nature to love, this must be God's most basic relationship to all creation, and that the good of all creation must be God's final will. Furthermore, the gospel itself seems to indicate a rejection of the idea that some are more deserving of God's grace and salvation than others, and the Bible points to the completeness of Christ's saving work and the reality that the sovereign majesty of God's will must prevail and be consistent with his nature (see Hart, 15f.). It is this form of particularist universalism that might be thought to represent a more specifically *Christian* account of universal salvation and that might be considered to reflect more accurately the long tradition of Christian universalism (for an account of this history, see MacDonald).

In its particularist form, Christian universalism emphasizes the objective nature of salvation in Christ. Salvation is something completed by God in grace through the life, death, and resurrection of Jesus Christ according to God's sovereign purposes. The variety of responses to this act of God cannot condition God into saving or damning individuals or groups: the response cannot undo the act of God. The cue for this perspective stems from aspects of the Pauline corpus. While Matthew and Revelation seem to have separationist tenors (at least on the surface), Paul's thought seems more universalistic in scope and hopefulness. It seems to suggest at points that there is nothing that can separate humanity from God's saving and redeeming work: we might see this, for example, in Ephesians 1:10, Colossians 1:19–20, Philippians 2:9–11, and 1 Corinthians 15. Certainly, there are also other passages in Paul that seem to suggest a final judgment or separation, but at least as an image, there exists in his work some suggestion of an ultimate universal hope; this might not be able to be systematized into one singular propositional approach, but it is nevertheless present (Boring, 291f.). Indeed, universalists have argued that it is a question of which image is given precedence: do we read the texts which suggest a universal salvation in light of those which are separationist or vice versa? Or, in terms of our understanding of the divine attributes, do we understand the love of God in light of the judgment of God, or vice versa?

Opting for the latter position, various theologians have taught universal salvation as at least a possibility throughout the history of Christian thought (see MacDonald, Parry and Partridge). Indeed, it is important to note that the church has never branded universalism as a heresy. The Council of 553, which anathematized several of teachings, stated that *apokatastasis* was an anathema in conjunction to immaterial and pantheistic understandings of eschatology and in conjunction with a belief in preexistent souls; universalism was not condemned in and of itself. Although condemned in the fifth ecumenical council, Origen (in some sense the father of systematic theology) taught universalism at least as a speculative possibility (see Greggs). Traces of the idea can also be found in the likes of Gregory of Nyssa (see Ludlow) in the Patristic era (as well as some of the teachings of the Desert Fathers), Julian of Norwich from Medieval times, the Cambridge Platonists, and Friedrich Schleiermacher (see MacDonald). The twentieth century, with increased secularization in Western Europe and an increased awareness of the existence of other faiths through mass international migration and travel, saw an increased interest in the idea of universalism and further new and creative expressions of it from such notable theologians as Karl Barth (see Greggs), Hans Urs von Balthasar, Karl Rahner (see Ludlow), J. A. T. Robinson, and Jürgen Moltmann.

Universal salvation provides a helpful tool within systematic theology for ensuring that the will of God is not separated from the love of God. Furthermore, the emphasis that it brings with it on the objective nature of God's work of salvation helps to answer difficult questions about what constitutes a saving faith (especially in light of issues relating to human anthropology and the state of faith at any particular moment in relation to the moment of death), or why God would choose to save some and not others, or what happens to those who have not heard the gospel or who are raised in non-Christian contexts. Separationists who oppose universalism point, however, to what they see as the majority of the scriptural witness and the mainstream perspective that there is an ultimate separation of saved from the lost. They claim the importance of this, furthermore, on the basis of God's freedom (such that God cannot be bound to save), the significance of human freedom (such that humans can reject God's ultimate purposes), and the significance of choices and the life of faith in the here and now (such that decisions and actions now have eternal consequences). More recent accounts of universal salvation have sought to answer these concerns by pointing particularly to the activity of the Holy Spirit in God's work of salvation: while salvation is objectively a free act of God the Son, it is related subjectively to the believer in the present in such a way that the life of faith and human freedom are of central significance (see Greggs).

Bibliography

Boring, "The Language of Universal Salvation in Paul," JBL 105.2, 1986.
Greggs , *Barth, Origen, and Universal Salvation*, 2009.
Hart, "Universalism: Two Distinct Types," 1992.
Ludlow, *Universal Salvation*, 2000.
MacDonald, "*All Shall be Well*," 2011.
Robinson, *In the End, God*, 1950.
Wenham, "The Case for Conditional Immortality," 1992.

100

Violence

Adam J. Johnson

Divine violence is an indirect though valid way of accessing the doctrine of the atonement. Violence is an indirect mode of accessing the doctrine, in that violence is not one of the governing categories of thought employed to explore the meaning of Jesus's death and resurrection in the history of the church, and other doctrines play a more significant role than divine violence in shaping our understanding of Christ's atonement, such as the doctrines of the Trinity, Christology, divine love, and justice. In other words, approaching the doctrine from the standpoint of violence must be done very carefully, for in and of itself the topic of violence does not naturally lead us to those core doctrines and commitments which decisively shape the doctrine of the atonement.

However, the topic of divine violence is not alien to the doctrine of the atonement, and is therefore a valid standpoint from which to explore Christ's saving work and its implications for contemporary theology—a standpoint increasingly common in the doctrine since the horrors of the Holocaust. The key to navigating these discussions well lies in attending to doctrinal proportion and balance, allowing the role of violence to be a helpful and constructive one within the broader matrix of Christian doctrine, rather than a superficial critique which fails to touch the substantial issues at play in the doctrine.

Critiques of divine violence within traditional accounts of Christ's work have abounded in recent years (cf. Weaver, Trelstad), providing a great deal of energy for both doctrinal retrenchment and development. The fundamental critique, nuanced in a number of (theological, philosophical, cultural, and other) ways, runs as follows: traditional theories of the atonement either legitimate violence, or too easily do so, and therefore should be critiqued and adapted or discarded. At the heart of this critique lies a vision of the incarnate Son making atonement by bearing the wrath, anger, or violence of the Father. The suffering of the innocent one placates or in some way affects the Father, so that we sinners no longer need be punished. Such a theological vision either naturally or all too easily slips into the innocent being encouraged to suffer (for their own sake or that of others) the violence and abuse of others after the pattern of Christ, such as a wife suffering the abuse of her husband for the sake of protecting her children.

Such critiques are rooted in suffering and are to be honored as profound pastoral invitations to revisit Christian dogma and its proclamation. Beneath their poignant and economic expressions lie a nexus of theological issues regarding Christ's atonement, including the nature of (divine) violence, wrath, sin, and evil, the Trinity and Christology, and imputation, and an accompanying set of profound personal and ecclesial questions regarding sin, violence, and reconciliation. While it is tempting to affirm that the incarnation was the act of our loving God, which we violently rejected (thus safeguarding God by confining violence to the human sphere), the overall shape of the doctrine of the atonement, and the nature of God's opposition to sin, call for a deeper and more theologically rooted answer to this question.

The Bible knows of violence: the minor prophets offer a continual critique of violence (Hos. 12:1; Joel 3:19; Ob. 1:10; Jon. 3:8), and the Psalms say of the Lord: "the one who loves violence His soul hates" (Ps. 11:5). This same God, of course, is responsible for what appears to be indiscriminate slaughter, such as we see in the story of Noah, the Exodus, and the possession of the land of Israel. Much the same is anticipated in the New Testament, arguably, as seen in the prophecies of Revelation (15–16, 19–20). Is God a violent God? A question immediately attending such passages is whether there is a meaningful distinction within what we broadly call violence, breaking down into evil and reprehensible forms of violence, and other acts and intentions which share common features with such violence, but in fact have more to do with appropriate and just responses to evil (such as a doctor scrubbing infection from a wound, causing a great deal of pain, without any violence intended to her patient). While the omnipotent God occasionally acts forcefully toward his creation, he does so justly, and without the will to cause harm and suffering. In other words, God is not violent, does not seek to cause harm and pain as goods or ends in and of themselves, but good, just, and loving. For an entry into such questions, see Boersma's work on the interweaving of violence and hospitality, and Kotsko's rejoinder, and the distinction between "willing" and "intending" in Lombardo. A fuller answer moves beyond definitions and arguments regarding the nature of violence, integrates such matters with a broad doctrinal synthesis such as we sketch here.

Much of this discussion hinges upon the doctrine of the Trinity. Essential to traditional accounts of the cross, this was an event in the life of the one God: willed by the Father and experienced by the incarnate Son in the power of the Holy Spirit. To what extent, then, does this imply the Father exercising violence toward the Son? The more one adopts a heterodox tri-theistic account of the Trinity, in which the Father and the Son are different personalities, with their own motives, experiences, and thought processes, the more pressing (and ultimately fatal) this question becomes. On the other hand, the more one emphasizes a monotheistic account in which Father, Son, and Holy Spirit are not three persons, but three modes of being of the fully personal God (Barth, von Balthasar), the less weight this objection carries—for God is then, at most, pouring out his wrath upon himself as the one God, rather than the Father doing so toward a Son as might happen within a human family (Johnson, McCormack). Social-Trinitarians (such as Moltmann and many essays in Trelstad) are slightly more vulnerable to weaknesses of tri-theistic accounts, but inasmuch as they affirm the oneness of God, contain the resources to rebut most critiques of divine violence within the atonement. The majority of contemporary critiques unfortunately fail to interact exclusively with orthodox Trinitarian accounts of God in relation to the atonement, instead loosely referring to "preaching" and what one hears in "the pews."

Two further factors are vital here: Christology and some form of the doctrine of imputation. Regarding the former, it is not the case that the Father is related to the eternal Son as such (the *logos asarkos*) on the cross, for the Father is relating to the incarnate Son—who is the Son, but the Son in a certain mode of existence, living out life under the conditions of humanity as the man Jesus. But not any humanity, and this is where imputation, or something like it, takes center stage. In other words, the immanent Trinity is fully enacted, fully revealed, on the cross—but revealed and enacted in the workings of the economic Trinity: what we see is the relation of the Father to the Son, in and through the relationship of the Father to his incarnate Son, Jesus, bearing in himself the plight of the human condition.

Traditional theories of the atonement emphasizing the relationship of the Father and incarnate Son on the cross employ an essential move clearly distinguishing this from any other human experience: on the cross, Jesus is in some form bearing the sin of humanity. Though this has been developed in many different ways throughout the history of the church, the key point is the affirmation that in the cross we see the Father relating to his Son—but not as this relationship takes place in heaven. On the cross, the Father relates to the incarnate Son as the incarnate one bearing our sin, thus making impossible any human analogue to the innocent submitting to the abuse of those in power after the pattern of Jesus Christ. On the cross, we see the Father relating to the Son in an entirely new way: the Father relating to the sin-bearer, and relating to him as such.

To be sure, Jesus is never merely the sin-bearer. He is this, but only as the eternal Son of the Father, and for this reason his relationship to the Father on the cross is a complex one, in keeping with a Chalcedonian affirmation of his being one person in two natures. On the one hand, therefore, it is entirely appropriate to speak in terms of the loving relationship between Father and Son, which allows for no violence, no distance, no separation—for these two, in the unity of the Holy Spirit, are the eternal triune God. But on the other hand, this fundamental and underlying reality takes upon itself a new mode expression, in the Son taking upon himself the sin of humankind, such that the love shared by Trinity now appears under a fundamentally different guise.

And this is where the doctrine wrath plays its vital role. Just as a good doctor will cause great pain to a patient in order to reset a dislocated shoulder, God wisely enacts his love in different ways, depending on the needs and condition of the beloved. And it is here that the biblical and traditionally held doctrine of God's wrath (Murray) plays its salutary role, for wrath is the entirely good and appropriate mode of love in relation to sin and the sinner (Wynne). Not that love becomes wrath, or ceases to be love—wrath is the move of God's love in relation to sin—a powerful repulsion, indignation and accompanying desire to destroy and do away with any perversion affecting, compromising, and corrupting the beloved, but all the while a movement of divine love, and therefore a longing for the comprehensive well-being of the beloved.

At play, then, is a double intentionality on the part of God: an eternal and undiminished love of the Father for the Son, and temporal and condition "will of the Lord to bruise him" (Is. 53:10). How can God will both of these things, without succumbing to an intra-Trinitarian violence which brings ontic separation and intolerable moral problems into the heart of God's own life and therefore the Christian faith at large? How can God both be the loving and good God he is, and yet relate to us sinners as the kind of God he is, without diminution or change? Only a robust doctrine of the Trinity, accompanied by a real bearing of our sin on the part of Christ, allows for the ongoing love of the Father for the Son to take the temporary (but real) form of wrath as an appropriate and effective response to the problem of our sin—an act which does not bring sinful violence into the life of God, or establish a pattern of embracing abuse as an unqualified good in the Christian life, for this is an effective and unique act of love on the part of the undivided God for us and for our salvation, to deal with the problem of sin within the resources of the triune life.

To sum up, in the doctrine of the atonement we bear witness to an utterly unique act, rooted in the efficacious vicarious bearing of sin changing the mode of relating within the triune God, allowing God to confront the problem of sin within himself as an intra-Trinitarian problem (the Father relating to the sin-bearing incarnate Son in the power of the Holy Spirit), rather than addressing the problem of sin more distantly, by God relating to sin in his creation. The atonement of Jesus Christ is God's chosen and effective way of God taking the problem of sin and evil into his own life, that we in turn might be freed in him to find salvation in Christ: God makes our sin his own, that being freed from sin, he might make us his own as well. The Trinitarian and sin-bearing dynamics of this event reshape all the fundamental features of the cross, such that this is no longer an instance of divine violence which in any way corresponds to the kinds of sinful violence which raises the question in the first place: the abusive violence of parents toward children, and other forms of gratuitous and perverse violence in our fallen communities.

But we must not leave behind the pastoral question with which we began: how to relate to violence? Briefly, the atonement sets the stage for unconditional opposition to violence, rooted in the life, ministry, and power of Jesus Christ, eschewing violence per se as a strategy for ending violence, similarly eschewing individuals attempting perverse and misguided imitation of the work of Christ by attempting to bear or suffer the sin of others to pacify or appease perpetrators. Rather, God's atoning work in Jesus calls the church as a whole to be a people committed to the ministry of reconciliation (2 Cor. 5:18), supporting victims of abuse and holding perpetrators accountable, equipping the church to suffer where necessary, but never merely a task of the individual alone, never as a good or end in itself—for the vicarious suffering of Christ was a unique and unrepeatable event rooted in the life of God and Jesus's bearing of our sin, an event to which we can and must witness, but never seek to repeat.

Such an emphasis on reconciliation will move us in at least two directions. First, it leads the church and its members toward embracing the way of suffering and the cross, for the work of reconciliation is a way of pain and loss. The life of the Christian is a life of martyrdom, of witness: oft bloodless, sometimes not—but the love to which we are called is a way of suffering and self-sacrifice. To be sure, it is this in the power of the Holy Spirit and in anticipation of our resurrection at the Second Coming of our Lord, and therefore not a defeatist, pessimistic, or complacent embracing of suffering as a good—but the way of cross it remains, and therefore a way of real, though effective, suffering. Second, God's atoning work in Jesus demands that the church face its own sin, as a prerequisite to reconciliation with others. It therefore invites and demands that we repent and seek reconciliation with those whose sufferings we have ignored, tolerated, or caused (Cone).

Bibliography

Barth, *Church Dogmatics*, 1936–1977 (esp. vols *I/1* and *IV/1*).
Boersma, *Violence, Hospitality and the Cross*, 2004.
Cone, *The Cross and the Lynching Tree*, 2011.
Johnson, *Atonement*, 2015.
Kotsko, *The Politics of Redemption*, 2010.
McCormack, "The Ontological Presuppositions of Barth's Doctrine of the Atonement," in *The Glory of the Atonement*, 2004.
Moltmann, *Crucified God*, 1993.
Murray, *Reclaiming Divine Wrath*, 2011.
Trelstad, *Cross Examinations*, 2006.
von Balthasar, *Theo-Drama*, vol. 4: The Action, 1988.
Weaver, *The Nonviolent Atonement*, 2001.
Wynne, *Wrath among the Perfections of God's Life*, 2010.

Wesleyan Theologies

Thomas H. McCall

Earnest proclamation of the meaning of the cross of Christ and the empty tomb was at the heart of the Methodist revivals, and deepening reflection on this meaning was an integral part of the development of Wesleyan theology. A brief survey of this literature shows both remarkable continuity in some senses and considerable and important disagreement in other areas.

John Wesley and the Doctrine of the Atonement in Early Methodism

It is safe to conclude that no doctrine was more important to John Wesley than the doctrine of the atonement. The precise nature of this atonement is not hard to discern for him. While it is clear that Wesley holds that Christ's atoning work in his death and resurrection indeed does set an empowering example for us and brings us victory over our final enemy, it is also unmistakably clear that Wesley's primary way of understanding the atonement is in terms of "penal substitution" (Collins, 84; Maddox, 104–105). The wrath of God is a fearsome reality, and without the work of Christ we can only tremble before it. However because of Christ's atoning work on our behalf, we can be justified fully and freely. Indeed, the nature of the atonement as penal substitution enables a proper understanding of the victory and example: "the voluntary passion of our Lord appeased the Father's wrath, obtained pardon and acceptance for us, and, consequently, dissolved the dominion and power which Satan had over us through our sins" (Maddox, 98). Adhering closely to the *Book of Common Prayer*, and drawing from such texts as Philippians 2:8 and 2 Corinthians 5:19–21, Wesley insists that

Christ offered a "full, perfect, and sufficient sacrifice, oblation, and satisfaction" for our sins (Collins, 80–81).

The Atonement in Early-Nineteenth-Century Methodist Theology

Wesley's theological inheritance is received, guarded, and passed on by his successors. Richard Watson's *Theological Institutes* (1823–1829), which was a very influential textbook in the systematization of Wesleyan theology, argues that the atonement must be considered in light of the holiness, righteousness, justice, benevolence, and wisdom of God, as well as grounded in biblical teaching about sacrifice. Watson insists that the death of Christ provides for propitiation and expiation, and he likewise argues that it is necessary for the salvation of sinners (274–275). In accordance with Scripture, Christ makes "satisfaction" for our sins (314–315), and he does so as our willing substitute (324–325).

Thomas N. Ralston argues similarly to Wesley in his work *Elements of Divinity* (1847). He argues forcefully (against "Socinians, Arians, Unitarians" and "infidels") that these two points are essential to the doctrine of the atonement: first, "that he died *for us* as a proper *substitute*—in our *room* and *stead*," and second, "that his death was *propitiatory*—a proper *expiation*, or *atonement*, for our sins" (225; emphases in the original). The death of Christ was both "vicarious" and "propitiatory," and Ralston argues that such texts as Isaiah 53 demonstrate beyond reasonable doubt that Christ's work is both *penal* and *substitutionary*. He also argues, however, that we cannot reasonably understand the penalty borne by Christ as *exactly* the same as that which is deserved by sinners; clearly, he insists, it was different in both kind (Christ does not suffer as one who is damned and without hope of redemption) and degree (Christ does not suffer *eternal* punishment). Such sentiments may also be found in other major theologians of the early to mid-nineteenth century Methodist movement (e.g., Luther Lee and Samuel Wakefield).

The Atonement in Later-Nineteenth-Century Methodist Theology

Tendencies in Methodist theology toward more traditional accounts (including penal substitution) continue into the later part of the century, as do those that tend toward governmental theories (with roots in the Remonstrant Hugo Grotius and prevalent in nineteenth-century American theology more generally). This divide can be seen in the theologies of John Miley and William Burt Pope. Miley strongly criticizes "Calvinist" doctrines of the nature of the atonement, and he offers a stout defense of a governmental theory. "The vicarious sufferings of Christ," he says, "are an atonement for sin as a conditional substitute for penalty, fulfilling, on the forgiveness of sin, the obligation of justice and the office of penalty in moral government" (68). Pope, on the other hand, articulates and defends a view much closer to that of Wesley himself (263–316).

The Twentieth Century and Beyond

Methodist and Wesleyan theologians continued to wrestle with their theological inheritance—and, indeed, with the meaning of Christ's death—into the twentieth century. Olin A. Curtis (1905) reflects at length on Christ's cry of dereliction, and he proposes a "racial theory" according to which Christ pays the "precise racial penalty for human sin" and so "expressed God's hatred of sin as to render possible the immediate foundation and gradual formation of a new race" (329). H. Orton Wiley (1952) defends a doctrine with strongly governmental themes while also insisting on the reality of both propitiation and expiation (217–300).

More recent work by Wesleyan theologians shows considerable continuity with these trends. H. Ray Dunning (1988) begins by making repeating Wiley's arguments against penal substitution; he then goes on to follow Wesley (and many other theologians, including John Calvin) in viewing Christ's work in "Prophetic," "Priestly," and "Kingly" roles (with a special emphasis on *Christus victor*; Dunning, 362–394). J. Kenneth Grider (1994) sharply criticizes what he calls "Satisfaction," "Moral Influence," and "Punishment" theories. In place of such ill-begotten conceptions, he defends "the Governmental Theory," which he defines as "the view that Christ suffered for us so that the Holy Father could forgive us and still govern us justly" (330). Thomas C. Oden represents a significant departure from these trends and a return to themes more common in Wesley and the broader Christian (and especially Anglican) tradition; notably, he holds to a more comprehensive account that includes penal substitution.

The Extent of the Atonement in Wesleyan Theology

Despite differences of substance and emphasis, however, Wesleyan theologians have been utterly convinced of both the necessity and sufficiency of Christ's atonement—we are desperate and hopeless without it, and we are redeemed and transformed by it. Moreover, Wesleyan theologians are united in their insistence upon the "universality" of atonement. Historically, they do not mean that all sinners in fact will be redeemed and saved. But they do mean that God truly desires for the salvation of all sinners, and they are convinced that Christ's work was both intended for the benefit of all and indeed that the benefits of his work are available to all.

Bibliography

Collins, *The Scripture Way of Salvation*, 1997.
Curtis, *The Christian Faith*, 1905.
Dunning, *Grace, Faith, and Holiness*, 1988.
Grider, *A Wesleyan-Holiness Theology*, 1994.
Maddox, *Responsible Grace*, 1994.
Miley, *Systematic Theology*, 1892.
Pope, *A Compendium of Christian Theology*, 1875.
Ralston, *Elements of Divinity*, 1847.
Watson, *Theological Institutes*, 1926.
Wesley, *Explanatory Notes on the New Testament* (Col. 1:14), cited in Maddox, *Responsible Grace*, 1994.
Wiley, *Christian Theology*, 1952.

Wisdom Books (Old Testament)

Craig G. Bartholomew

Theologically, atonement is concerned with what is achieved through the death of Christ. Generally theologians do not quickly reach for Old Testament (OT) wisdom as an important source for understanding it. Calvin, for example, uses the threefold office of Christ as prophet, priest, and king to explore the life and work of Christ (1, 2, XV). Notably missing from this is Christ as wisdom.

OT wisdom, as the central background to Christ as wisdom, is a contested domain, and thus it is necessary that we have a unified sense of its theology to discern its relationship to the New Testament (NT), and to the doctrine of the atonement (Ford and Stanton). Proverbs is the foundational OT wisdom book, and in it we see that wisdom: is an attribute of God (Prov. 8:22–31); the means through which God created the world (Prov. 3:19–20) so that his wisdom is built into the fabric of creation and cries out to be heard by humans in all areas of life (Prov. 1:20–21); needed by humans in every area of life to flourish in the creation (Prov. 3:13–18); finds its starting point and foundation in the fear of Yahweh (Prov. 1:7, etc.); is the opposite of folly, an ever present reality in a fallen world (see Prov. 9). Wisdom is thus not just about wise activities, but about how these fit within God's order for creation and the *eros* that directs our lives.

In the NT Christ is clearly presented as Wisdom incarnate, but the question remains, does his being wisdom relate to his work of atonement? 1 Corinthians 1:18–31 is a rich source for this question, and we will use it as our way in to this discussion. In 1 Corinthians 1:23–24, the cross, which is central to this passage as it is to Paul's theology as a whole, is directly connected to the wisdom of God. There is a play in this passage on the true nature of "wisdom," and God's wisdom manifested in "Christ crucified" is contrasted with the wisdom of the world and the wisdom of the Greeks. The cross shames these wisdoms by revealing true wisdom in Christ, and above all in the cross. How does the cross reveal true wisdom?

1 Corinthians 1:30 begins with a reminder that "he [God] is the source of your life in Christ Jesus" and in verse 32, a reason for this is given, in order that any boasting be boasting *in the Lord*. Here Paul expresses an insight that is central to OT wisdom and to the cross, namely, the contingency of creation (Bartholomew 114–115); it is not autonomous but utterly dependent on God, so that true wisdom always positions the human as a creature before the creator, with all the glory directed toward God. How much more so, Paul might say, in the light of the cross. Folly is a major theme in OT wisdom and in 1 Corinthians 1:18–31, in the sense that the cross exposes the folly of the world.

In Genesis 3 we find the wisdom motif of the tree of the knowledge of good and evil, a symbol of the quest for human autonomy (Wenham). Paul refers to "the wisdom of the world" and to Jews demanding signs and Greeks seeking wisdom. Paul, as a highly educated man, would have been well aware of the autonomy of reason at work in Greek philosophy. "Jews already had access to 'wisdom' in the scriptures, but required *signs* to locate their situation within the promised purposes of salvation history" (Thiselton, 170; emphasis in the original). The resurrection was *the* sign of the turning point in the cosmos but it did not fit with "the Jews'" preconceived categories, and thus similarly backs into human autonomy. At its roots folly is a quest for human autonomy and the cross exposes such folly by revealing humankind's sinfulness and the way back to God through the cross.

Among the three major OT wisdom books of Proverbs, Job, and Ecclesiastes, it is Ecclesiastes which most directly exposes the folly of an epistemology based on reason, observation, and experience apart from starting with the fear of the Lord. In masterly fashion the narrator shows us this through taking us with Qohelet on his journey in quest of meaning, only to find that what he thought was "wisdom" landed him in the hands of Dame Folly (Bartholomew; cf. Eccl. 7:23–29). This is precisely the reversal we find in 1 Corinthians 1. What is taken to be wisdom turns out to be folly, and this is supremely exposed in the cross. Wisdom thus alerts us to *atonement as exposure of folly*.

Clearly wisdom is a key motif in this section of 1 Corinthians but is the link much stronger, especially when Paul says Christ "became for us *wisdom from God*"? The four qualities of wisdom, righteousness, sanctification, and redemption belong together, and *both characterize Christ and are imparted by Christ*. Just as Barth insists that *what real humanness consists in* appears only in the perfect "real man" Jesus Christ, so here Paul redefines *what real wisdom consists in*, namely (in Moltmann's language), *The Way of Jesus Christ*, as exhibited and made effective in God's own action in Christ on the cross. (Thiselton, 191–192; emphases in the original)

A question often posed is whether or not Paul consciously identifies Christ with Lady Wisdom in Proverbs 8:22–31 and Wisdom 7:22–8:1. Dunn thinks not and argues that Paul probably takes up wisdom language from the Corinthians with their elitist spirituality. He finds no indication that *the Corinthians* thought of wisdom as active in creation (177). Clearly Paul is engaging contextually with the Corinthians thought world, but his Christology of wisdom is formed by far more than their spirituality, and not least by the OT.

Modern scientific certainty may sometimes need to be sacrificed for the richness of an intertextual reading and 1 Corinthians 1 is one of those places. If Paul's use of "wisdom" is primarily shaped by the OT wisdom tradition, then such phrases as "the wisdom of God" (vv. 21, 24), and "wisdom from God," need to be read in the light of OT—and inter-testamental—wisdom. We cannot be sure whether in 1 Corinthians 1 Paul had texts like Proverbs 8:22–31 in mind or Job 28, but it is certainly possible, and in my view likely.

Texts such as Proverbs 8 confirm that wisdom is far more than negative; it also shows one how to live according to the grain of creation. Christ shows us true humanity and through his atoning death provides the way for believers to become wise, that is, fully human. In 1 Corinthians 1:21, Paul says that God decided to "*save* those who believe." Wisdom is deeply rooted in a theology of creation and should inform our anthropology and thus our view of salvation at this point. Salvation involves wisdom, that is, a recovery of our full humanity.

OT wisdom is remarkable in its comprehensive range across all dimensions of human life and thus in its insight into the nature of full humanity. The Proverbs 31 valiant woman is a wonderful example of this. In Proverbs 31:30, she is described as "a woman who fears the Lord." Proverbs, unlike so many moderns, knows no sacred-secular divide, and the point of this climax to the book of Proverbs is that wisdom manifests itself in all areas of life, ranging from family life and homemaking, to crafts, importing food, buying a field and planting a vineyard, selling merchandise, charitable work, teaching wisdom, and so on. It is such a comprehensive recovery of human life in all its dimensions that the atonement achieves, when Christ becomes to us "wisdom from God."

There are many other ways in which OT wisdom is connected with atonement. Atonement is clearly about suffering and while the NT does not directly relate Job's sufferings to those of Christ, Cranfield is surely right when he asserts, "In all this the Book of Job is, surely in its own special way an eloquent witness to Jesus Christ" (196). Barth is *the* theologian who has developed the idea of Job as a type of Christ most fully (Barth, CD IV/3.1, 368–478).

Furthermore, Hebrews is a magisterial treatment of atonement and one of the passages the author expounds is Proverbs 3:11–12 (cf. Heb. 12:5–6) in relation to the appropriate response to Christ's atonement. This serves as reminder that this side of the return of Christ suffering remains a reality in the Christian life, so that wisdom books like Job and Ecclesiastes will remain indispensable for those who partake of the atonement, and wish to live such suffering wisely.

The creational, comprehensive dimension of wisdom alerts us to the scope of the atonement. At what is Christ's atoning work directed? Clearly it saves those who believe. But does it do more than this? In 1 Corinthians 1:21, the "wisdom" of God is set against "the world." Κοσμος has more than one meaning in the NT and here it refers to human life in opposition to God. But "the world" is also God's good creation and in both Old and New Testaments, God's redemptive purposes are always with a view to recovering his purposes for all his creation. Indeed, just as wisdom is comprehensive, so too is atonement. Bavinck notes the unity of Christ's work: "Scripture views the entire life and work of Christ as a single whole and never makes a dichotomy between an obedience of life ... and an obedience of death ... It is one single work that the Father assigned to him and that he finished in his death" (378). Similarly, in terms of the scope of the atonement, Bavinck comments:

> The whole re-creation, as it will be completed in the new heaven and the new earth, is the fruit of the work of Christ ... The whole person of Christ, in both his active and his passive obedience, is the complete guarantee for the entire redemption that God in his grace grants to individual persons, to humanity, and to the world. (380)

We have used 1 Corinthians 1 to open up the relationship between OT wisdom and the atonement. 1 Corinthians invites this treatment with its significant wisdom vocabulary in Chapter 1 (Inkelaar), and is demonstrably useful for this purpose. While it cannot and should not be argued that wisdom is the primary background for understanding atonement, it certainly is an important and neglected one.

Bibliography

Barth, *CD* IV/3.1, 1961.
Bartholomew, *Ecclesiastes*, 2009.
Bartholomew and O'Dowd, *Old Testament Wisdom*, 2011.
Bavinck, *Reformed Dogmatics*, vol. 3, 2006.
Calvin, *Institutes*, trans. Battles, 1960.
Cranfield, *The Bible and the Christian Life*, 1985.
Dunn, *Christology in the Making*, 1980.
Ford and Stanton, *Reading Texts, Seeking Wisdom*, 2003.
Inkelaar, *The Conflict Over Wisdom*, 2011.
Murphy, *The Tree of Life*, 2002.
Thiselton, *The First Epistle to the Corinthians*, 2000.
Wenham, *Genesis 1–15*, 1987.

Wrath

Jeremy J. Wynne

Within Christian dogmatics, "the wrath of God" names the perfection in which God is set against all sin and rebellion, not in the sense of an irrational fuming, but always as God's determination *not* to lose in his creation the good that belongs to him. Accounts of God's wrath often proceed book-by-book, gathering up the several terms within the biblical lexicon, such as *aph* (e.g., Is. 5:25) and *orgē* (e.g., 1 Thess. 2:16), which cluster around the general concept. The approach is useful; but as with all divine character descriptions, what demands closest attention is the *particular* way in which wrath belongs *to the living God*. What follows is a suggestion of the most important theological judgments at work in describing this facet of God's life.

Derivation

Modern theology offers several possibilities for grounding the concept. In one place it is distilled from an experience of ultimate reality as *tremendum*, a force more akin to stored-up electricity than moral guide; in others it is postulated as a requirement of practical reason or framed by the categories of modern analytic psychology. What these approaches share is a noetic movement that runs from below to above. Even traditional attempts to generate a suitable concept of divine anger from the creaturely one can fall into this category. One thinks of perfect being theologies, which either raise language to an unworldly excellence (*via eminentiae*), or remove from it finitude's poverty (*via negationis*).

If these approaches are dissatisfying, it is because they fail to establish whether a concept, once rendered, actually belongs to the Lord himself. And in this failure, they leave themselves wide open to Feuerbach's critique—which states they have merely smuggled in self-reflection under the guise of claims about the transcendent God. One option for redressing this weakness is to root the analogous use of "wrath" in the narrative of Holy Scripture rather than in human experience. In this way, it is God himself who would critique, fill, and baptize the concept, and so render it serviceable for theological reflection.

Ordering Wrath and Love

It is an unavoidable question for the theology and proclamation of the church whether one should give priority to God's wrath or God's love when turning to matters of atonement. The first route presents God's holy standard and just displeasure with sinners as the chief obstacle to covenant life. Sometimes this is commended as itself the more intuitive order, as though laying out the problem would better prepare sinners to receive the solution. However, if it is God's disposition toward creatures that must be changed by the cross of Christ, the approach fails. Not only is the logic viciously circular—for if Jesus alone "turns God around" toward creatures, then the motive behind his mission is rendered inexplicable (cf. John 1:16–18)—but it also moves well outside an orthodox understanding of the Trinity.

The second route, by contrast, refuses to paint God's wrath as itself the problem. Instead, the obstacle to covenant life is located decisively on the side of *a sinful world* that must be reconciled to God (2 Cor. 5:19; Rom. 5:8–10). John Calvin shows that he belongs resolutely within this broader, Western tradition when he points to the "wondrous and divine" manner in which God could both "hate what we had made, and love what he had made" (*Inst.* II.xv.4). Such accounts are notable because they take the important phrase "sacrifice of atonement" (*hilastērion*) in its most direct, biblical, and grammatical sense, as an act in which the triune God disposes of sin. Of course, this interpretive decision—often articulated as one for expiation and against propitiation—does not ameliorate the fact that God detests evil (e.g., Hab. 1:13). It underscores the utter incommensurability between the two, but it does so only within the context of a severe work in which God maintains his claim upon sinners, treating them as sons and daughters.

A Centered Work

It is a mysterious feature of God's wrath that he is *not* compelled to act within any rigid time frame. In the overflowing love and characteristic freedom of his life, God chooses a particular time and place to deal justly with all human sin (cf. Rom. 3:25; Heb. 9:12). The very shape of this salvific history presses one to consider that wrath too has a center—in the cross of Jesus. Because this is the place and time in which "the infinite weight and meaning of suffering and death has been borne," not only is God's justice finally vindicated, but, as Barth writes, all other experiences of divine judgment must appear to us in its light as mere tokens (*CD* II/1, 395; cf. 393–406). Jesus's death, in other words, establishes for Christian theology the concrete difference between physical and psychological suffering, on the one hand, and the judgment of God-abandonment, on the other.

Wrath's Moral Intelligibility

Related to this is the notion that wrath does not proceed with an immanent necessity but by a confrontation of the divine word and law, which, unlike human anger, always produce what is right (Jam. 3:17). A coherent concept of wrath-as-judgment, if it is to be such, requires the presence and activity of the Judge himself (Ps. 51:4). It is God alone who will "devise a truthful response to the offense," and thus show that judgment is a matter of "purposive action, not a blind consequence or an instinctive reaction" (O'Donovan, 113).

Certain mechanistic accounts of divine wrath break down at precisely this point. These theories—one recalls here Klaus Koch's pithy summary, "the deed is the seed"—regard wrath as a feature of creation, not as a mode of God's own being or action. Within a closed economy, one argues, all human moral activity inevitably elicits a fitting response. The proposal is appealing not least because of the tight coordination of cause and effect, and its application to the moral life. That move seems cleanly to dispose of the so-called problem of evil. Yet the consequences for a biblical concept of divine freedom are devastating. Mechanistic theories not only overplay the distinction between primary and secondary causality, but, most significantly, they undermine the pivotal difference within the gospel between the wrath *one elicits* and the blessing that is *graciously given*.

Understanding Incarnation and Wrath

Certain physical atonement theories, especially in the modern period, have only tolerated God's wrath as a correlate of final judgment. Others have dismissed it altogether as poetic excess. Schleiermacher's understanding of the incarnation, for example, excludes the possibility that God's presence *as angry* might contribute to the growth of one's God-consciousness. Nor, he argues, could it add to dogmatics any positive content not already contained in the preparatory experience of God's preventative justice (*CF* §84.3).

Attention to physical theories in general, however, suggests these conclusions constitute the exception rather than the rule. Athanasius's own classical theory focuses upon incarnation and resurrection as the heart of atonement. Yet in his exposition he makes continual reference to the God-ordained connection between condemnation and death. And while, notably, the relationship between these two and guilt is left undeveloped, still the threat of "fire at the Day of Judgment" remains that *from which* God's people are being saved (e.g., *De Inc*, §§10, 21, 37, 57). In the same way that darkness is dispersed by light and illness driven out by medicine, so too salvation includes God's opposition to the radical enmity of his creatures. Before the Immortal God, sinners can only fold and fail (Luke 5:8).

A Thick Concept of Love

At its heart the cross of Christ presents the clearest testimony to love's nature—divine, infinitely costly, and worthy. Certain revisionist theologies today have extended this as an argument for a deep division between love and wrath within God's own life (e.g., *Stricken by God?*). It is ingredient to the passion narratives, it is argued, that as the human propensity for blood lust and scapegoating is uncovered as utterly *unjust*, so too one's understanding of God must be freed from the excrescences of a pagan view of angry deity.

But it is instructive that certain early theologians passionately disagreed. Foremost among them, Lactantius argued that it was precisely a thick concept of love, one which included God's anger—not that it rules God like a tempest, but that he rules over it—which fundamentally distinguished the Christian doctrine of God from those of the pagans (*De ira Dei*, §21). When genuine love is confronted with unrighteousness, it not only can be but also *must be* angry. The truth published in the cross of Christ, then, is more complicated than it first appears. In and with the message of God's love, the cross announces there is no future in God's kingdom for those who broker deals with evil and, by means of their lies, make room for it to flourish. God has excluded them as such. And attempts to moderate this opposition by invoking the passive resistance of "a message" run aground on the biblical insistence that, in its effect, God's Word is "no less lethal than the violence of the literal sword" (Volf, 296; cf. Rev. 19:15; Heb. 4:12).

As life in the West becomes increasingly reflective of the pre-Christendom of its first few centuries, it may be that this more biblical view of God's victorious love, precisely because it is neither sentimental nor bourgeois, will be recognized in increasingly powerful ways as an answer to the cry of the faithful, "How long, O Lord?" (e.g., Ps. 13).

Bibliography

Holmes, "The Attributes of God," in *Oxford Handbook of Systematic Theology*, 2007.
Lane, "Wrath of God as an Aspect of the Love of God," in *Nothing Great, Nothing Better*, 2001.
O'Donovan, *The Ways of Judgment*, 2008.
Volf, *Exclusion and Embrace*, 1996.
Weinandy, *Does God Suffer?*, 2000.
Wynne, *Wrath among the Perfections of God's Life*, 2010.

Contributors

T. Desmond Alexander. Senior Lecturer in Biblical Studies, Union Theological College.

Mark D. Baker. Professor of Mission and Theology, Fresno Pacific Biblical Seminary.

Craig G. Bartholomew. Professor of Philosophy and Religion & Theology, H. Evan Runner Chair, Redeemer University College.

John Behr. Dean, Rector, Director of the Master of Theology Program, Professor of Patristics, St. Vladimir's Orthodox Theological Seminary.

Thomas Andrew Bennett. Affiliate Assistant Professor of Systematic Theology, Fuller Theological Seminary.

Richard S. Briggs. Lecturer in Old Testament, Director of Biblical Studies, Cranmer Hall, St. John's College, Durham University.

Matthew J. Aragon Bruce. Guest Assistant Professor of Theology, Wheaton College.

Andrew Burgess. Dean, Bishopdale Theological College, Nelson, New Zealand.

Daniel Castelo. Professor of Dogmatic and Constructive Theology, Seattle Pacific University.

Stephen B. Chapman. Associate Professor of Old Testament, Duke Divinity School, Duke University.

David L. Clough. Professor of Theological Ethics, Department of Theology and Religious Studies, University of Chester.

Ashley Cocksworth. Tutor in Systematic Theology, The Queen's Foundation for Ecumenical Theological Education, Birmingham.

Graham A. Cole. Dean, Trinity Evangelical Divinity School; Professor of Biblical and Systematic Theology, Trinity Evangelical Divinity School, Trinity International University.

Don Collett. Assistant Professor of Old Testament, Trinity School for Ministry.

David W. Congdon. Acquisitions Editor, University Press of Kansas.

Oliver D. Crisp. Professor of Systematic Theology, School of Theology, Fuller Theological Seminary.

Ivor J. Davidson. Honorary Professor, School of Divinity, History and Philosophy, University of Aberdeen.

Kent Eilers. Associate Professor of Theology, Huntington University.

Adam Eitel. Assistant Professor of Ethics, Yale Divinity School, Yale University.

Brannon Ellis. Publisher, Lexham Press.

G. R. Evans. Lecturer in History, Cambridge University. Research Reader in Theology, British Academy.

Donald Fairbairn. Robert E. Cooley Professor of Early Christianity, Gordon-Conwell Theological Seminary.

Mark A. Garcia. President and Fellow in Scripture and Theology, Greystone Theological Institute.

Mark S. Gignilliat. Professor of Divinity Old Testament, Beeson Divinity School, Samford University.

Timothy G. Gombis. Associate Professor of New Testament, Grand Rapids Theological Seminary, Cornerstone University.

Alan W. Gomes. Professor of Systematic and Historical Theology, Talbot School of Theology, Biola University.

Jason A. Goroncy. Senior Lecturer in Systematic Theology, Whitley College, University of Divinity.

Jeanine Michele Graham. Associate Professor of Religious Studies, College of Christian Studies, George Fox University.

Matthias Grebe. Post-Doctoral Researcher, Evangelisch-Theologische Fakultät, Rheinische Friedrich-Wilhelms-Universität Bonn.

Joel B. Green. Provost, Dean of the School of Theology, Professor of New Testament Interpretation, School of Theology, Fuller Theological Seminary.

Tom Greggs. The Marischal Chair of Divinity, King's College, University of Aberdeen.

Arnfríður Guðmundsdóttir. Professor of Systematic Theology, University of Iceland.

Scott Harrower. Lecturer in Christian Thought, Ridley College.

Trevor A. Hart. Rector, Saint Andrew's Episcopal Church, St Andrews. Honorary Professor of Divinity, University of St Andrews.

Peter C. Hodgson. Charles G. Finney Professor of Theology, Emeritus, Vanderbilt University.

Christopher R. J. Holmes. Associate Professor in Systematic Theology, Department of Theology and Religion, University of Otago.

Stephen R. Holmes. Lecturer in Systematic Theology, St. Mary's College, The School of Divinity at University of St. Andrews.

Rodney Howsare. Professor of Theology, DeSales University.

Nathan A. Jacobs. Visiting Scholar and Lecturer of Philosophy, University of Kentucky.

Matthew D. Jensen. Department of Hebrew, Biblical and Jewish Studies, The University of Sydney.

Adam J. Johnson. Associate Professor of Theology, Torrey Honors Institute, Biola University.

Paul Dafydd Jones. Associate Professor, Department of Religious Studies, University of Virginia.

Kelly M. Kapic. Professor of Theological Studies, Covenant College.

Veli-Matti Kärkkäinen. Professor of Systematic Theology, School of Theology, Fuller Theological Seminary.

Edward W. Klink III. Senior Pastor, Hope Evangelical Free Church, Roscoe, Illinois.

Robert A. Kolb. Professor Emeritus, International Research Emeritus Professor for Institute for Mission Studies, Concordia Seminary.

Adam Kotsko. Assistant Professor of Humanities, Shimer College.

Anthony N. S. Lane. Professor of Historical Theology, London School of Theology.

Peter J. Leithart. President, Theopolis Institute. Adjunct Senior Fellow of Theology, New Saint Andrews College.

Harry O. Maier. Professor of New Testament and Early Christian Studies, Vancouver School of Theology.

Joseph Mangina. Professor of Systematic Theology, Wycliffe College.

I. Howard Marshall. Emeritus Professor of New Testament Exegesis, University of Aberdeen.

Jules A. Martinez Olivieri. Assistant Professor of Theology, Seminario Teológico de Puerto Rico.

Thomas H. McCall. Director of Carl F. Henry Center for Theological Understanding, Professor of Biblical and Systematic Theology, Trinity Evangelical Divinity School.

John A. McGuckin. Ane Marie and Bent Emil Nielsen Professor in Late Antique and Byzantine Christian History, Professor of Byzantine Christian Studies, Columbia University; member of Oxford University's Faculty of Theology and Religious Studies.

W. Travis McMaken. Associate Professor of Religion and Chair of the Interdisciplinary Studies Program, Lindenwood University.

David Vincent Meconi. Assistant Professor of Early Christianity, Saint Louis University.

Paul Louis Metzger. Professor of Christian Theology and Theology of Culture, Multnomah University. Director of New Wine, New Wineskins.

David M. Moffitt. Senior Lecturer in New Testament Studies, University of St. Andrews.

Paul D. Molnar. Professor of Systematic Theology, Theology and Religious Studies, St. John's University.

Adam Neder. Professor and Bruner-Welch Chair in Theology, Whitworth University.

David R. Nienhuis. Associate Professor of New Testament Studies, Seattle Pacific University.

Jonathan T. Pennington. Associate Professor of New Testament Interpretation, Director of Research Doctoral Studies, The Southern Baptist Theological Seminary.

Ryan S. Peterson. Assistant Professor of Theology, Talbot School of Theology, Biola University.

Andrew C. Picard. Lecturer in Systematic and Applied Theology, Carey Baptist College.

Murray Rae. Professor of Theology, Department of Theology and Religion, University of Otago.

Charles Raith II. Assistant Professor of Religion and Philosophy, John Brown University.

Ben Rhodes. Resident Research Scholar, Christian Institute on Disability, Joni and Friends International Disability Center.

Cynthia L. Rigby. W.C. Brown Professor of Theology, Austin Presbyterian Theological Seminary.

Eugene F. Rogers, Jr. Professor of Religious Studies, University of North Carolina at Greensboro.

Andrew Root. Associate Professor, Carrie Olson Baalson Chair of Youth and Family Ministry, Luther Seminary.

Andrew B. Salzmann. Assistant Professor, Department of Theology, Benedictine College.

Fred Sanders. Professor, Torrey Honors Institute, Biola University.

Shannon Nicole Smythe. Assistant Professor of Theological Studies, Seattle Pacific University.

Katherine Sonderegger. William Meade Chair in Systematic Theology, Virginia Theological Seminary.

Alan Spence. United Reformed Church.

Roland Spjuth. Associate Professor and Teacher of Systematic Theology, Örebro School of Theology, Sweden.

Peter K. Stevenson. Principal, South Wales Baptist College; Honorary Lecturer, Cardiff University.

Justin Stratis. Director of Post Graduate Research, Tutor in Christian Doctrine, Trinity College Bristol.

Scott R. Swain. Professor of Systematic Theology and Academic Dean, Reformed Theological Seminary, Orlando Campus.

Jeremy R. Treat. Pastor for Preaching and Vision, Reality LA.

Gert van den Brink. Evangelische Theologische Faculteit, Leuven.

Edwin Chr. van Driel. Bicentennial Directors' Associate Professor of Theology, Pittsburgh Theological Seminary.

Adonis Vidu. Associate Professor of Theology, Gordon-Conwell Theological Seminary.

Robert W. Wall. Paul T. Walls Professor of Scripture and Wesleyan Studies, Seattle Pacific University.

Thomas M. Ward. Assistant Professor of Philosophy, Loyola Marymount University.

Thomas G. Weinandy. O.F.M., Cap. International Theological Commission.

Gary J. Williams. Director, the John Owen Centre for Theological Study, London Theological Seminary. Visiting Professor, Historical Theology, Westminster Theological Seminary.

Jeremy J. Wynne. Assistant Professor, and Director of Graduate Studies in Theology, Whitworth University.

Author/Person Index

Abelard, Peter 10, 12, 357–60, 399, 400, 403–4, 409, 429, 485–6, 488, 494, 496, 540, 579, 602, 610, 612, 639, 703, 704, 724, 776
Adams, Marilyn McCord 15, 233, 448–9, 708, 712, 744, 746
Agamben, Giorgio 291, 488
Alexander, T. Desmond 677–83
Alexander of Hale 407
Alexander, Michelle 456
Alfeyev, Hilarion 258, 262, 269
Alighieri, Dante 292, 366
Allen, Graham 216–17
Ambrose 269
Ames, William 297
Amyraut, Moïse 695
Anatolios, Khaled 154
Anderson, Gary 99, 777–8
Anderson-Gold, Sharon 493, 595
Anselm of Canterbury 7, 12, 16, 175–93, 241, 249, 254, 279, 286–91, 292, 296–7, 307, 311, 313, 318, 357, 359, 366, 391, 399, 403–4, 407, 424, 429, 447, 452, 486, 494–5, 501, 511, 540, 554–5, 598, 603, 609, 611, 639, 689, 702–4, 724, 760, 770, 773, 776
Aquinas, Thomas 9, 16, 48, 85, 89, 91, 93, 175–6, 195–211, 221, 269, 270, 272, 318, 357, 366, 395, 429, 463, 466, 540, 551, 555, 565, 588, 589, 646, 649, 689, 690, 698, 776, 778, 779
Arcadi, James 333
Argyle, Margaret 351–2
Aristotle 407–10, 473, 563, 716
Arminius 698
Armstrong, Brian 695, 698
Arnold, Matthieu 614, 621, 711–12
Aspenson, Steven Scott 746
Athanasius 4, 7, 9, 11, 14, 50, 69, 71, 135–54, 156–7, 290, 331, 377, 458, 485, 488, 557–9, 561, 642, 644
Athenagoras 74

Attridge, Harold 534, 535, 681
Augustine 266–9, 271, 272, 365–6, 381–7, 395, 462–3, 466, 540, 588–9, 609, 646, 649, 690, 709, 710–12
Aulén, Gustaf 2, 12, 17, 158, 177, 195, 210, 278–9, 293, 333, 389–92, 476, 586, 589, 601, 604, 615, 618, 621, 689, 692
Averbeck, Richard 490, 492, 680, 681, 682, 683

Baab, Otto J. 96
Baan, Stephen 303
Baglow, Christopher T. 197–8
Baillie, Donald 315
Baker, John A. 269
Baker, Mark D. 5, 12, 116, 316, 329, 332, 489, 492, 509–13, 732, 764, 766, 767–8, 778–9
Balás, David 163
Balserak, Jon 222
Barbour, Ian 325, 326
Barker, Margaret 701, 704, 730
Barr, James 570, 575
Barrett, Lee 597, 600, 712
Barrett, C. K. 304
Barth, Karl 6–7, 34, 39, 71, 77–92, 226–7, 237–55, 257, 269, 271, 273, 279, 377, 379, 380, 396, 418, 464–6, 469, 475, 486, 494, 496, 527, 586, 603–4, 627–8, 647, 648–9, 656, 657, 658, 701, 704, 712, 735, 737, 766, 772, 779, 789, 803–5, 809
Bartholomew, Craig 801–5
Basil of Caesarea 367
Basil the Great 530
Bash, Anthony 493, 496
Battles, Ford Lewis 222, 270
Bauckham, Richard 258–9, 261, 263, 265, 651, 652, 654, 720, 722
Bauerschmidt, Frederick Christian 208, 463, 466
Baur, F. C. 525, 537–42
Bavinck, Herman 297, 525, 559, 561, 804–5

Baxter, Richard 524, 663, 696, 699
Beale, G. K 3
Beard, Charles 753, 756
Beccaria, Cesare 303, 309
Bediako, Kwame 512-13
Behr, John 4, 23-4, 462, 466, 569-75
Beilby, James 316
Bellinger William 633, 636
Belousek, Darrin W. 15, 763-5, 767-8
Bengtsson, Jan Olof 298
Bennett, Thomas 713-17
Berger, Theresa 350
Berkhof, Hendrikus 689, 692
Berkouwer, G. C. 218
Bernard of Clairvaux 357, 366, 399-402, 429, 430, 485, 609-10
Berryman, Phillip 293
Biel, Gabriel 613
Bigger, Stephen 109
Bildhauer, Bettina 404-5
Billings, J. Todd 51
Black, Matthew 260
Blackwell, Albert 742
Blocher, Henri 777, 779
Boda, Mark J. 128
Boersma, Hans 5, 12, 16, 474, 715-17, 792, 796
Boesak, Allan 604
Boff, Leonardo 293, 511, 513, 605, 608
Bolt, Peter 634, 636
Bonaventure 407-10, 540, 744, 745-6
Bonhoeffer, Dietrich 651
Boring, M. Eugene 720, 722, 789, 790
Borowski, Oded 109
Boulton, Matthew Myer 214, 230
Bouwsma, William J. 227
Boyd, Gregory A. 16, 476, 477
Blowers, Paul M. 50
Braaten, Carl E. 476-7
Bradley, William 499, 502
Brakke, David 154
Briggs, Richard 543-6
Briggs, Sheila 348
Brock, Rita Nakashima 302, 339, 340, 343, 493, 496
Brondos, David A. 104, 112
Brooks, Thom 309, 495, 496
Brown, Joanne Carlson 339, 343
Bruce, Matthew J. Aragon 723-7

Brümmer, Vincent 448-9
Bulgakov, Sergius 229
Bultmann, Rudolf 417-20, 515, 520-1
Burgess, Andrew R. 4, 13, 377-80
Burnett, Richard E. 251
Butler, Joseph 308
Byrne, Peter 593, 595

Caird, G. B. 455-6
Calvelca, Domenico 429
Calvin, John 16, 49, 50, 53, 102, 213-35, 270, 273, 297, 306-7, 366, 368, 378, 380, 396, 422, 475, 557, 559, 561, 588, 589, 657, 658, 663, 736, 737, 770, 773, 799, 801, 805, 808
Campbell, John McLeod 7, 13, 51, 177, 331, 421-6, 501
Canlis, Julie 220, 230
Carson, D. A. 517, 521, 582-3
Cartwright, Steven R. 357
Castelo, Daniel 563-8
Catherine of Siena 427-30
Cessario, Romanus 195, 208, 210
Chapman, Stephen B. 95-113
Charlemagne 759
Charlesworth, James H. 261
Childs, Brevard S. 107, 545-6, 681, 684
Christensen, Michael J. 13
Chrysostom, John 234
Clague, Julie 350-2
Clement of Rome 372
Clifford, Alan 663
Clough, David L. 7, 53, 109, 441-5
Cocksworth, Ashley 447-9, 701-5
Cole, Graham 473-7, 489-92, 663
Collett, Don 411-15
Collins, Joseph B. 270, 797-8, 800
Colyer, Elmer M. 76
Cone, James 455-6, 487, 488, 496, 796
Congar, Yves 93
Congdon, David 241, 417-20
Cook, Albert 117
Cosgrove, Charles H. 112
Couet, Jacques 757
Covet, Jacques 523-4
Cranfield, C.E.B 804-5
Cranmer, Thomas 437-40
Crisp, Oliver 15, 308, 315-33
Cross, Richard 744, 746, 770, 773

Cullmann, Oscar 476
Curtis, Olin A. 799–800
Cyril of Alexandria 377, 457–60, 776, 779

Dalferth, Ingolf 649
Dalton, William Joseph 260, 265–6, 267
Daly, Mary 337–8, 343, 348–9
Daly, Robert J. 261
Daniélou, Jean 269
Darabont, Frank 452, 456
Dauphinas, Matthew 198
Davenant, John 696, 699
Davidovich, Adina 592–3, 595
Davidson, Ivor J. 35–56, 776, 779
Davies, B. 175, 708, 712
Davis, Stephen T. 15
DeHart, Paul 643–4
Deme, Daniel 12, 175
Dempsey, Michael T. 55
deSilva, David A. 104
Dicenso, James 591
Dillistone, F. W. 701, 704
Dinsmore, C. A. 566
Do T. 581, 583
Dodd, C. H. 97–8, 104, 489, 491–2, 581, 583
Donne, John xi, 367
Douglass, Jane Dempsey 232
Dragas, G. D. 154
Dreyer, Elizabeth 408
Driver, John 116
Drummond, Henry 308
Drury, John L. 252–3
Duff, Nancy 233
Dumontier, P. 401–2
Dunn, James 803, 805
Dunnill, John 131
Dunning, H. Ray 767, 799–800
Dupuis, Jacques 730, 732
Dyke, Doris Jean 351

Eastwood, Clint 554
Eberhard, Christian A. 99
Eberhart, Timothy 534–5
Eco, Umberto 118
Eddy, Paul 316
Edmondson, Stephen 50, 213, 219, 226, 228, 231
Edward VI 438–9

Edwards, J. Christopher 634, 637
Edwards, Jonathan 300, 313, 366, 424, 467–71
Edwards Jr., Jonathan 468
Ehrman, Bart D. 362
Eilers, Kent 665–8
Einstein, Albert 329
Eitel, Adam 427–30
Elliot, J. K. 264
Ellis, Brannon 693–9
Ellul, Jacques 720, 722
Emery, Gilles 646, 649
Epicurus 707
Erigena, John Scotus 540
Erskine, Thomas 308
Essenius, Andreas 524
Eugenio, Dick O. 76
Evans, Gill. 175, 609–12, 759–61
Evelyn-White, Hugh G. 258

Fabel, Virginia 343
Fabella, Virginia M. M. 344
Fairbairn, A. M. 566
Fairbairn, Donald 457–60
Fairweather, Eugene R. 357, 403
Farley, Wendy 345
Farmer, William 633, 636
Farrow, Douglas 4, 13, 378–80
Feder, Yitzhaq 100
Feenstra, Ronald Jay 15
Feldmeier, Reinhard 626–7, 629
Fesko, John 300
Feuerbach, Ludwig 16, 807
Fiddes, Paul 96, 103, 111, 223
Finlan, Stephen 13, 534
Firestone, Chris 591, 593–5
Flemming, Dean 510, 513
Foord, Martin 663
Ford, David 801, 805
Forestell, J. Terence 515, 521
Forsyth, P. T. 7, 499–503, 701–2, 705, 735, 737
Foucault, Michel 303–4, 308, 309
Francis of Assisi 407, 488
Frank, Georgia 261
Fretheim, Terence E. 96
Füglister, Notker 100, 105
Fulkerson, Mary McClintock 348
Fuller, Reginald H. 121

Gammie, John G. 101
Gane, Roy E. 99, 535–6, 682, 683
Garcia, Mark A. 681–6
Gasper, Giles E. M. 175
Gathercole, Simon 103, 764, 768, 784–5
Gavrilyuk, Paul 775–6, 779
Gerrish, Brian 219, 235
Gese, Hartmut 102, 112, 626
Gibson, David 5, 214, 777, 779
Gibson, Jonathan 5
Gignilliat, Mark 623–9
Gilders, William K. 99–100, 535–6
Girard, René 302–4, 505–8, 689, 690, 692, 722
Gogarten, Friedrich 418
Goldingay, John 100, 713, 717
Gomarus 697
Gombis, Timothy 669–75
Gomes, Alan W. 753–7
Gonzalez, Antonio 608
Gonzalez, Justo Luis 408–10
Goodall, Jane 443, 445
Gordon, Bruce 214
Gorman, Frank H. 107, 111, 431
Gorman, Michael J. 3, 13, 112, 432, 435, 689, 691, 692
Gormarus, Franciscus 694
Goroncy, Jason 499–503
Gorringe, Timothy 177, 186, 309, 689, 692
Gouwens, David 597, 600
Graham, Gordon 12
Graham, Jeannine Michele 763–8
Grant, Jacquelyn 342
Grebe, Matthias 651–4, 707–12
Green, Joel B. 5, 12, 115–34, 316, 329, 332, 489, 492, 509–11, 513, 764, 766–8, 778, 779
Greenberg, Moshe 105
Gregg, Stephen 730, 732
Greggs, Tom 787–90
Gregory of Nazianzus 45, 219, 269, 270, 273–4, 377
Gregory of Nyssa 155–73, 279, 282–6, 287, 288, 395, 396, 397, 789
Gregory, Patrick 303
Grensted, L. W. 309, 311, 744, 746, 757
Grider, J. Kenneth 799–800
Griffith, Francis Llewellyn 259
Griffiths, Paul J. 54

Grotius, Hugo 299, 309, 523–5, 799
Grumett, David 109, 442, 445
Gschwind, Karl 265–7
Gunton, Colin E. 5, 312, 315, 317, 321, 452, 456, 527–32, 551, 555, 704–5
Guðmundsdóttir, Arnfríður 337, 345, 349
Gutiérrez, Gustavo 602, 604–5

Hahn, Scott 431, 435
Haikola, Lauri 614–15, 621
Hall, Douglas John 474, 477
Hamilton, S. Mark 469, 471
Hamm, Berndt 613, 621
Hammond, Henry 524
Hardin, Michael 5, 764, 768
Hardy, Edward 279, 291
Hare, John 592–3, 595
Harkness, Georgia 214
Harrower, Scott 437, 479–84
Hart, Trevor 423, 426, 551–5, 788, 790
Hartman, Lars 394, 397, 397
Hayes, John H. 99, 106–7, 410
Haykin, Michael A. G. 301
Hays, Richard 632, 637
Hazlett, Ian P. 234
Hebert, A. G. 2
Hector, Kevin W. 251
Hegel, G. W. F. 500, 537–42, 651, 776
Heider, George C. 119
Heim, S. Mark 15, 303, 507, 508, 729, 732
Helm, Paul 300
Helmer, Christine 319, 322–3
Hengel, Martin 104
Henry VIII 437–8
Herbert, A. G. 278, 333
Herbert, George xi
Hick, John 729, 732, 741–2
Higgins, A. J. B. 304
Hilborn, David 16
Hill, Charles E. 16, 491–2, 764, 768
Hinlicky, Paul 464, 466
Hobbes, Thomas 285, 292
Hodge, A. A. 222, 525
Hodge, Charles 16, 298, 329, 525
Hodgson, Peter 537–42
Hoekendijk, Johannes Christiaan 651
Hofius, Otfried 133
Hogg, David S. 12, 175, 703, 705
Hollerich, Micahael J. 292

Holmes, Christopher R. J. 77–93
Holmes, Stephen R. 2, 14, 16, 295–314, 467, 469, 471, 648, 649
Honderich, Ted 310
Hooker, Morna D. 129, 131, 304, 363, 765
Horan, Daniel 744, 746
Horton, Michael 12, 13, 378, 432
Hughes, Philip E. 233
Howsare, Rodney 257–75
Huber, Ulrich 524
Hugh of St. Victor 429, 610, 759–61
Humphreys, Fisher 106
Hunsinger, George 89, 465, 466, 506–8

Ignatius of Antioch 371, 547–9, 565–6, 574
Ingham, Mary Beth 743, 746
Inkelaar, Harm-Jan 804–5
Irenaeus 12, 14, 50, 163, 331, 378, 506, 540, 557–8, 561, 569–75, 775, 779
Irving, Edward 308, 423, 528, 530
Isaacs, Marie 532, 536
Iwand, Hans-Joachim 651

Jacobs, Nathan 591–5
James, Frank A. 16, 764, 768
Janowski, Bernd 177, 626, 628–9
Jeffrey, Steve 304, 764, 768
Jennings, Willie James 495–6
Jensen, Matthew 581–3, 582–3
Jenson, Robert 25, 55, 103, 690, 692, 776, 779
Jeremias, Joachim 121, 267, 268
Jersak, Brad 5, 102, 764, 768
Joachim of Fiore 611
Joffé, Roland 554
John of the Cross xi
John of Damascus 367, 731
Johnson, Adam 1–17, 20–2, 196, 329, 333, 365–9, 505–8, 561, 655–8, 776, 779, 791–6
Johnson, Elizabeth 345–6, 349
Johnson, Keith 648, 649
Johnston Largen, Kristin 732
Jones, Mark 301
Jones, Michael 434, 435
Jones, Paul Dafydd 213–35, 242, 251, 254
Jones, Serene 230, 348, 353
Judas 359
Julian of Norwich xi, 463, 789

Jüngel, Eberhard 639, 642, 644, 776, 779

Kahn, Paul 691–2
Kant, Immanuel 16, 486, 488, 500, 541, 591–5, 628
Kapic, Kelly M. 47, 659–63
Kärkkäinen, Veli-Matti 729–32, 732
Karris, Robert J. 123
Käsemann, Ernst 126, 651
Kässmann, Margot 347
Kehm, George H. 224
Kelly, J. N. D 447, 449, 458–60
Kenny, Joseph 270
Kerr, Nathan 243
Keynes, Milton 39
Kharlamov, Vladimir 13
Kierkegaard, Søren 597–600
Kilby, Karen 300, 708, 712
Kilpatrick, G. D. 121
Kim, Paul 460
King, Stephen 452, 456
Kistemaker, Simon 490
Kiuchi, Nobuyoshi 99, 100
Kleven, Terence J. 111
Klink III, Edward W. 515–21
Knitter, Paul 729–30, 732
Koch, Klaus 110, 111, 809
Kohlenberger, H. 175
Kolb, Robert 613–21
Kotsko, Adam 12, 15, 277–93, 487, 488, 792, 796
Kraus, C. Norman 512
Küng, Hans 776, 779
Kyung, Chung Hyun 343

Lactantius 707, 810
LaCugna, Catherine 648, 649
Lane, Anthony N.S. 357, 399–402
Langston, Douglas 744, 746
Lash, Nicholas 448, 449
Lauber, David 14, 270–1, 273
Leclercq, Jean 401–2
Lee, Kye Won 76
Lee, Luther 798
Leftow, B. 175
Leibniz, Gottfried 594–5
Leirvik, Oddbjørn 731–2
Leithart, Peter J. 154, 689–92
Levering, Matthew 197–8, 207

Levine, Baruch A. 101
Lewis, Alan E. 14
Lewis, C. S. 11, 554–5
Leydecker, Melchior 524
Ligier Louis 352
Lindars, Barnabas 131
Lindbeck, George 322–3
Linzey, Andrew 441, 443, 445
Livingston, James 709, 712
Lombard, Peter 221, 609–12, 695
Lombardo, Nicholas E. 4, 16, 792
Lonerganm Bernard 647
Long, Steven A. 199
Love, Gregory 506, 508
Lovegrove, Deryck W. 13
Lubbertus, Covet 524
Ludlow, Morwenna 789–90
Luther, Martin 278, 391, 396, 463, 579, 585–6, 589, 601–2, 613–21, 724, 736, 737, 777, 779
Lutkenhaus-Lackey, Almuth 351

Maas, Wilhelm 271
Maas, F. 100, 103
Macaskill, Grant 51
MacCulloch, J. A. 258–9, 262, 267
MacDonald, Gregory 788, 789, 790
Mackie, J. L. 707, 712
MacKinnon, Donald 502
MacIntyre, John 552, 555
Maddox, Randy L. 797, 800
Maestro, Marcello 303
Maier, Harry O. 371–5, 547–9
Mangina, Joseph 461–6, 719–22
Mann, Alan 310, 510
Marshall, Bruce 648, 649
Marshall, Christopher 113
Marshall, I. Howard 361–4, 767, 768
Martinez Olivieri, Jules 605–8
Martinius, Matthias 694, 697
Mascall, E. L. 442
Maximus the Confessor 50
McCall, Thomas 2, 14, 16, 321, 797–800
McCarthy, Vincent 592–3, 595
McCormack, Bruce L. 2, 14, 55, 223, 229, 237, 239–42, 551, 555, 764, 793, 796
McElrath, Damian 770, 773
McFague, Sally 328, 329
McFarland, Ian A. 47

McGrath, Alister E. 10, 195, 357
McGuckin, John A. 155–73, 198, 458, 776, 779
McIntosh, Mark 702, 705
McIntyre, John 2, 12
McKee, Elise 213
McKnight, Scot 2, 12, 116, 635, 637, 689, 692
McMaken, W. Travis 393–7
McNeil, John T. 270
McWhirter, Jocelyn 785–6
Meconi, David 381–7
Melito of Sardis 262, 268
Metteer, Michael 303
Metzger, Paul 451
Michael, J. Ramsey 491
Michalson, Gordon 591–3, 595
Migliore, Daniel L. 12
Milbank, John 689, 692, 714–15, 717
Miley, John 329, 799–800
Milgrom, Jacob 96, 98–100, 103–5, 535–6
Milligan, William 378, 380
Mills, Watson E. 262
Minear, Paul 721–2
Moberly, R. C. 501
Moffitt, David M. 13, 107, 112, 379, 380, 533–6, 777, 779
Molnar, Paul 55, 57–76
Moltmann, Jürgen 28, 566, 603–4, 651–4, 716, 717, 776, 779, 789, 803
Moo, Douglas 490
More, Thomas 659
Morgan, Jonathan 109, 205
Morris, Leon 97, 101, 113, 489, 491–2, 581–3
Moser, Paul 15
Muers, Rachel 109, 442, 445
Muller, Richard 195, 214, 509, 513, 693, 695, 699, 782, 786
Murray, John 782, 786, 794

Neder, Adam 749–52
Nestorius 459, 460, 776
Nevin, Williamson 329
Newbigin, Lesslie 465
Newton, John 367
Nicholas of Cusa 270, 272–3
Nicole, Emile 101
Nicole, Roger R. 97, 104, 106

Nienhuis, David 579–80, 685–7
Nimmo, Paul 741–2
Nolan, Christopher 554
Nygren, Anders 390, 392

Oakes, Edward T. 29, 264, 268, 270–1
Oberman, Heiko 613, 621
O'Collins, Gerald 96, 106, 434, 435
Oden, Thomas C. 799
O'Donovan, Oliver 809, 811
Oppy, Graham 175
Origen 157, 269, 365, 378, 400, 489, 540, 789
Ormerod, Neil 648–9
Osborn, Eric 49
Ovey, Mike 304, 764, 768
Owen, John 366–7, 378, 474, 524, 659–63, 776, 779

Packer, J. I. 98, 464, 466, 662–3
Palmquist, Stephen 591
Pannenberg, Wolfhart 656, 658, 664–8, 741–2
Parker, Rebecca Ann 302, 339–40, 343, 493, 496
Parry, Robin 779
Partee, Charles 220
Partridge, Christopher 789
Pasternack, Lawrence 591
Patout Burns, J. 744, 747
Pattison, George 598, 600
Pauw, Amy 368
Pelagius 589
Pennington, Jonathan 631–7
Peters, Albrecht 615, 621
Peterson, David 103, 735, 737
Peterson, Erik 291–2
Peterson, Robert A. 218, 657–8
Peterson, Ryan 557–61
Philips, Richard 764, 768
Philo of Alexandria 564, 568
Picard, Andrew 527–32
Pitstick, Alyssa Lyra 14, 268
Plantinga, Alvin 175, 708, 712
Plantinga, Cornelius 15
Polycarp 371, 569
Pope Alexander II 611
Pope Innocent 357
Pope, William Burt 30–4, 799–800

Prabhu, George 510
Pugh, Ben 221

Quinn, Philip 12, 195, 360
Quintilian 570

Radner, Ephraim 465
Rae, Murray 597–600, 776, 779
Rahner, Karl 33–4, 273, 648–9, 730, 789
Rainey, Anson F. 103
Rainwater, Robert 262
Raith II, Charles 195–211
Ralston, Thomas N. 798, 800
Ramage, Matthew 197
Ramsey, Michael 465
Ratzinger, Josef 257, 269, 271, 275, 465
Rauschenbusch, Walter 602, 604
Ray, Darby Kathleen 15, 17, 177, 293, 348, 353
Rea, Michael C. 321
Reardon, Timothy W. 119, 592–3, 595
Redding, Graham 702, 705
Reicke, Bo 266
Rendtorff, Rolf 100
Reventlow, Henning Graf 111
Rhodes, Ben 733–7
Richardson, Robert 708, 712
Rigby, Cynthia 493–7, 601–4
Ritschl, Albrecht 399, 464, 525, 723–7, 755, 757
Rivière, Jean 401–2
Robertson, Archibald 291
Robinson, J. A. T. 789–90
Rogers Jr., Eugene F. 403–5
Root, Andrew 639–44
Rosato, Andrew 744–5, 747
Rudisill, Dorus Paul 469, 471
Ruether, Rosemary Radford 487
Russell, Norman 50, 157

Sach, Andrew 304, 764, 768
Saint Anthony 487
Salzmann, Andrew 407–10
Sanders, Fred 15, 19–34
Sano di Marco di Massacorno 429
Sandys, Edwina 350–1
Saward, John 272–3
Schaff, Philip 693, 699
Schenck, Ken 535–6

Schleiermacher, Friedrich 7, 221, 235, 329, 540–1, 656, 658, 739–42, 789, 809
Schmid, Hans Heinrich 110
Schmiechen, Peter 14
Schmitt, Carl 281–2
Schneckenburger, Matthias 525
Scotus, John Duns 540, 743–7, 770
Seybold, Klaus 105
Shaw, Prue 292
Sheldon, Charles 604
Shelton, R. Larry 3, 765, 767–8
Sheridan, Alan 303
Sherman, Robert 2, 12, 50, 655, 658, 740
Sherwin, Michael 196–7
Sklar, Jay 13, 533, 536, 682, 684
Smythe, Shannon Nicole 242
Snoddy, Richard 696, 699
Sobrino, Jon 606–8
Socinus, Faustus 16, 299, 401, 434, 523, 525, 753–7
Socrates 538
Söderblom, Nathan 391
Sokolowski, Robert 20
Sölle, Dorothee 602, 604, 764, 768
Sonderegger, Katherine 12, 175–93
Soskic, Janet Martin 5
Southern, R.W. 175, 702–3, 705, 770, 773
Southgate, Christopher 111
Spence, Alan 585–9
Spicq, Ceslas 198
Spickermann, Hermann 626–7, 629
Spinks, Bryan 397
Spjuth, Roland 389–92
Stanton, Graham N. 122, 801, 805
Stephan, Horst 741–2
Stevens, G. B. 566, 568
Stevenson, Peter 421–6
Stillingfleet, Edward 524
Strange, Alan D. 301
Stratis, Justin 739–42
Streett, Daniel 582–3
Strobel, August 122
Studdert-Kennedy, G. A. 566
Stump, Eleonore 15, 195, 198
Surin, Kenneth 708, 712
Swain, Scott 25, 775–9
Swidler, Leonard 338
Swinburne, Richard 318
Sykes, Stephen 475, 477

Tamburello, Dennis 219
Tamez, Elsa 606, 608
Tanner, Kathryn 15, 39, 771, 773, 778–9
Taylor, Vincent 115–17
Tennent, Timothy 509, 513
Terrell, JoAnne Marie 343, 512
Tertullian 565
Thacker, Justin 16
Thaumaturgus, Gregory 565
Thielman, Frank S. 104
Thiselton, Anthony 626, 629, 802, 803, 805
Thomas, G. Michael 697
Thomas, M. M. 731–2
Thurneysen, Eduard 218
Tidball, Derek 16
Tilley, Terrence 708, 712
Tillich, Paul 391, 392
Torrance, James B. 50, 425, 426
Torrance, Thomas F. 12–13, 39, 57, 58, 59, 60–76, 84, 89, 237, 315, 377, 378, 379, 380, 396–7, 422, 426, 434–5, 655, 656, 658, 765–8, 777, 779, 785
Torrell, Jean-Pierre 198
Travis, Stephen H. 110, 113
Treat, Jeremy 431–5
Trelstad, Marit 5, 13, 254, 354, 791, 793, 796
Trueman, Carl 663, 664, 776, 779
Turner, Denys 89
Turner, Max 124
Turretin, Francis 16, 299, 313, 324, 366, 378, 524, 695, 697–9
Tutu, Desmond 716–17
Tylenda, Joseph N. 228

Ursinus 378
Ussher, James 696, 699

van Buren, Paul 218
van den Brink, Gert 300, 523–5
VanderKam, James C. 260
van Driel, Edwin Chr. 23, 55, 769–73
Van Dyk, Leanne 13, 422, 426, 655, 658
Vanhoozer, Kevin 434–5, 691–2, 766
van Mastricht, Petrus 524
Vaughn, Sally N. 175
Vidu, Adonis 208, 647, 649
Viladesau, Richard 15
Visser, Sandra 175

Volf, Miroslav 713–15, 717
von Balthasar, Hans Urs 14, 23, 29, 32, 257, 266, 269, 270, 271–5, 465, 506–8, 776, 779, 789, 793, 796
von Harnack, Adolf 176–7, 399, 485, 488, 744, 747
von Rad, Gerhard 110, 651, 709, 712
Vriend, John 297

Wadding, Luke 746
Wainwright, Geoffrey 655, 658
Wakefield, Samuel 798
Walker, Robert T. 39
Wall, Robert 577–80
Wallace, Ronald S. 233
Walter of St. Victor 611
Waltke, Bruce K. 107
Walton, Steve 121
Ward, Benedicta 175, 703, 705
Ward, Keith 592–3, 595
Ward, Thomas 743–7
Warfield, B. B. 525
Watson, Richard 798, 800
Weaver, J. Denny 5, 15, 17, 113, 177, 319, 320, 447, 464, 466, 721–2, 764, 768, 791, 796
Weber, Otto 651
Webster, John B. 1, 10, 14, 25–7, 42, 433, 448–9, 527, 532, 642, 644, 647, 649, 736, 737, 776
Weinandy, Thomas G. 46, 135–54
Weingart, Richard E. 12, 360
Weisenthal, Simon 496, 497
Welker, Michael 783, 786
Wellhausen, Julius 411–12, 415
Wenham, Gordon J. 101–2, 104–5, 107, 683–4, 787, 790, 802, 805
Wenz, Gunther 667–8
Wesley, John 797–800
Westhelle, Vitor 347

Whale, J. S. 107
White, Douglas 566
Whitekettle, Richard 785–6
Wilbur, Earl Morse 753, 757
Wiles, Maurice F. 447, 449, 702, 704–5
Wiley, H. Orton 799–800
Wilken, Robert L. 50
Wilkins, John S. 444–5
William of Champagne 611
William of Champeaux 759
Williams, David 655, 658
Williams, Delores S. 341
Williams, Garry 467–71
Williams, George 753, 767
Williams, Rowan 454, 456, 512–13
Williams, Thomas 12, 175, 360, 743, 747
Wink, Walter 452, 456, 602, 604
Winter, Michael 315
Wittgenstein, Ludwig 491
Wittung, Jeffery A. 13
Wolff, Hans Walter 415
Wollebius, Johannes 297
Wolter, Alan 743–4, 747
Wolterstorff, Nicholas 28–9
Wood, Allen 593, 595
Wright, Christopher J. H. 96, 99, 105
Wright, David P. 102
Wright, N. T. 129, 473, 475, 477, 489, 492, 690, 692, 711–12
Wynne, Jeremy 794, 796, 807–11

Yang, Eric T. 15, 746–7
Yarbrough, O. Larry 15, 473, 477, 491–2
Yoder, John Howard 689, 692, 772–3
Young, David 303
Young, Frances M. 13, 15, 447, 449, 489, 492

Zachman, Randall C. 223, 232
Zizioulas, John 188, 641, 644

Scripture Index

Genesis
1	620
1–2	473
1.1–6	641
1.5	516
1.26	559, 574, 775
1.26–28	677
1.28	433, 678
1.30	442, 443
1.31	4, 708
2	473, 708
2–3	709
2.7	572
2.9	708
2.15	433
2.17	207
3	473, 709, 802
3.5	709
3.15	476
3.22–24	677
3.24	474, 677
3–11	559
4–11	678
4.1	709
4.10	111
6	222, 564
6.1–4	260
6.3	222
6.14	543
8.20–21	103
8.21	104
9	442
9.4	403
9.5	108
9.5–6	111
9.8–17	108, 442
12–50	678
15	431
18	223
18.21	223
18.25	111
21	641
22	124, 130, 517
28.12	219
32.20	97
45.5–6	571
50.20	110

Exodus
1.7	678
1.11	678
1.21	686
6.6	118, 132, 587, 678
9.9	108
12	132, 480, 634, 641, 686
12.7	679, 682
12.8–10	679
12.13	124
12.22	124, 679
12.27	480
12.37–38	108
12.43	480
12.46	124
13.11–16	108
13.13–15	679
14.21	110
15.11	733
15.13	132, 678
15.17	681
16.13	118
19.6	433, 680
20.2	733
20.10	108
21.28	587
21.28–32	108
23.11–12	108
24	680
24.1–8	131
24.1–11	679
24.6–8	682
24.8	118, 433
24.10–11	680
25.9	678
25.17	207

27.21	677	8.14–15	106
29.1–37	679	8.15	682
29.20–21	682	8.23	682
29.40–41	106	10.6	104
30.10	373	11.44–45	733
30.16	100, 106	12	785
32	413, 414	12.6–8	106
32–34	412, 413	14.1–9	106
32.9–10	127	14.1–32	103
32.32	413	14.2–7	682
32.12–14	413, 414	14.3	103
32.14	127, 413, 414	14.18	106
32.32	415	14.20	106
33.20	681	14.26–29	106
34.5–7	413, 415	14.48–52	683
34.6	127	15	785
34.6–7	413, 414	15.5–12	106
34.20	679	16	103, 125, 128, 131, 132, 533, 624, 633, 682, 765
34.23–27	480		
40.34	733	16.3–37	373
		16.8	683
Leviticus		16.10	106, 683
book	112, 411, 412, 631	16.15–16	535
1.4	103, 682	16.16	106, 125
1.9	104	16.16–20	106
1.13	104	16.19	682
1.17	104	16.20	103
2.1–16	106	16.21	102
2.2	104	16.22	103
2.9	104	16.24	103
2.12	104	16.24–25	99
3.5	104	16.26	683
3.16	104	16.30	534
4.1–6.7	128, 132, 686	17.3–4	111
4.20	99, 412	17.8–13	373
4.26	99, 100, 412	17.10	474
4.31	99, 104, 412, 625	17.11	100, 104, 403, 682, 720
4.35	99, 412	17.14	403
5.6	100	19.2	733
5.10	99, 412	19.22	412
5.11–13	99, 106	20.8	733
5.13	99, 412	20.9	111
5.14–6.7	107	20.11–12	111
5.16	412	20.16	111
5.18	412	20.27	111
6.7	412	20.15–16	108
6.14–23	106	21.8	733
6.24–7.10	128, 132	23	130, 481
7.1–6	107	23.13	104
8.1–36	679	23.26–32	373

24.4–8	480	17.12	105
25.6–7	108	17.14–20	280
25.9	125, 373	18.12	683
25.47–55	552	18.15	480
26.28	104	18.15–22	414
26.31	104	18.18	480
		21.1–9	106, 683
Numbers		22.1–4	108
3.13	679	22.5	683
3.41–51	587, 679	22.6–7	108
8.17–18	679	23.15–16	108
9	480	23.18	683
14	413, 414	24.4	683
14.18	127, 413	25.16	683
14.18–20	413	27.15	683
14.19	413	28	480
15.25	412	29.20–21	433
15.26	412	30.15	709
15.28	412	30.19	709
15.30–31	106	32.34–43	111
16.46	106	34.10	480
16.46–48	105, 683		
19.1–10	373	**Joshua**	
21.8–9	373	Book	543, 546
23.19	775	2.18–21	372
25.1–5	104	2.19	111
25.1–13	683	7.22–26	104
28.24	480	8.31	544
29	481	22.26–29	544
29.7–11	373		
35.28	683	**Judges**	
35.32	683	Book	543, 544, 546
35.33	111	17–18	544
Deuteronomy		**1 Samuel**	
Book	280	Book	544
5.14	108	1.3	544
6.10–12	480	1.21	544
7.8	132	2.2	733
7.25	683	2.19	544
8.5	775	2.29	544
13	122, 481	3.14	106, 543
13.14	683	6.4	97
14	412	7.6	106
16	130	8.4–22	281
16.2	480	15.22	107
16.5–6	480	20.6	544
17	122	21	544
17.1	683	25.9	281
17.4	683	25.38	110

26.17–20	106	22.1	617
28.3–25	264	22.7	220
		24.7–10	264
2 Samuel		36.6	108
1.16	111	40.6	107
3.39	111	46.3	161
16.7–8	111	50.10–11	108
21.1	111	51	97
21.3	543	51.4	750, 809
24.21	105	51.14	588
		51.17	107
1 Kings		68	161
2.31–33	111	72.3	110
2.36–37	111	78.38	104
8.31–32	111	94.1–2	223
8.46	97	94.3	161
		96.1	2
2 Kings		98.2	588
Book	544	104.29–30	152
		104.30	151
1 Chronicles		110	24, 120
6.34	543	113.4	161
		143.1	588
2 Chronicles		145.8–16	108
29.34	543	148.7–10	108
30.18	543		
35.1–19	480	**Proverbs**	
		1.20–21	801
Nehemiah		3.11–12	804
Book	543	3.13–18	801
4.5	100	3.19–20	801
10:34	543	8.22–31	801, 803
		9	801
Job		15.25	110
Book	292	16.14	97
1.5	103	17	801
4.18	367	20.9	97
24.19	263	25.21–22	111
28	803	26.27	110
40:15	108	28.10	110
		31	803
Psalms		31.30	803
[book]	198		
6.4–5	262	**Ecclesiastes**	
7.14–16	110	3.19–21	108
8	433	7.20	97
11.5	792	7.23–29	802
13	811		
16	120	**Isaiah**	
22	24, 741	[book]	229

1.10–17	108	53.11–12	481
1.16–20	373	53.12	123, 625
2.1–4	109	55.1–5	588
5.25	807	56.1	588
6	366	59.2	432
6.3	734	59.17	588
6.5–8	734	60–61	626
6.6–7	106	61.10	483
6.7	624	61.11	110
10.5–6	110	65.13	480
11	263	65.25	109, 443
11.1–9	443		
11.6–9	109	**Jeremiah**	
17–19	263	2.19	572
24.23	480	3.25	3
25.6–8	480, 482	7.9–11	108
38.10	263	7.20	108, 442
40–42	626	11.18–20	363
40–66	480	12.4	442
40.25	733	14.6	442
42.1	123	18.23	100, 104
43.1	132	21.6	442
44.2	587	29.11	112
45.8	110, 588	31.31	432
46.8–11	112	31.31–34	118, 120, 625
48.18	110		
49.1–7	480	**Ezekiel**	
49.6	122, 433	Book	411
52–53	304	4.4–6	625
52.13	616	14.13–21	442
52.13–53.12	123, 480	16	625, 627
52.15	628	16.63	624, 629
53	24, 96, 104, 133, 249, 363, 517, 616, 624, 627, 628, 633, 634, 686, 701, 797	18.10–13	111
		22.3	404
		33.4	111
		36–40	734
53.1	628	38.19–20	442
53.1–12	372	40–48	412
53.3	453	43	624
53.4–10	52	43–44	629
53.4–6	633	43.18–27	624
53.5	223	45.15–17	624
53.5–6	455	48.35	734
53.5–7	617		
53.6–7	480	**Daniel**	
53.7	123	9.16	588
53.7–8	123	9.24	96
53.10	481, 794		
53.10–12	628	**Hosea**	
53.11	123	Book	411

1.6	413, 414	7.18	415
2.18	442	7.18–20	413, 414, 415
2.20	108	7.19	480
4.1–3	111		
6.1	625	**Nahum**	
6.6	107, 412	1.2–3	223
6.7	433		
10.12–13	110	**Habakkuk**	
12.1	792	1.2–3	223
13.14	587		
14.2–4	413, 414	**Zephaniah**	
		1.13	808
Joel			
1.4–20	442	**Haggai**	
2.4–7	442	1.11	442
2.13	413, 414		
2.23	110	**Zechariah**	
2.28–32	120	5.5–11	103
3.19	792	9.9–11	118
Amos		**Malachi**	
Book	411	1.6–14	412
2.6–12	3	2.1	412
4.4–5	108	2.10–16	412
5.24	110		
5.25	411	**Matthew**	
7.2–3	413	1	220
9.2	263	1.3	220
		1.21	36, 481, 636
Obadiah		1.23	734
1.10	792	2	618
1.15	111	3	394
		4.1–11	280, 433
Jonah		4.1–13	280
Book	442	4.12	243
3.5–8	108	5.22	760
3.7–8	442	5.24	243
3.8	792	6	495
3.9–10	413, 414	6.13	711
4.2	413, 414	6.24–34	599
4.11	442	6.33	588
		7.1–2	110
Micah		8	701
Book	411	8.11	482
3.12–4.2	415	8.20	453
6.2	415	9.34	162
6.6–8	107, 412	11.27	43
7.8	415	12.24	162
7.8–20	415	12.29	162, 573
7.9	414, 415, 588	12.40	264

13.12	219	8.1–10	634
13.19	710	8.15	710
13.25–30	171	8.22–26	634
13.33	710	8.31	112, 117, 634
13.44	169	9.1–13	634
14.28	635	9.14–29	634
16.6–12	710	9.30–32	634
16.18	685	9.31	117
16.21	112	9.33–10.31	634
16.24	347	9.37	645
18	495	10.32–34	117, 634
18.34	243	10.38–39	394
20	186	10.45	51, 117, 166, 304, 361, 363 451, 481, 552, 618, 634, 635, 782
20.28	117, 635		
22.1–14	482, 483		
25	643	10.46–52	634
25.40	384	11.12–25	634
26.8	432	14.12–25	634
26.26	481	14.22	481
26.26–29	117, 635	14.22–25	635
26.28	433, 481	14.23	482
26.36–44	220	14.24	117, 481
26.36–46	221	14.58	606
26.37	223, 228	14.64	606
26.39	751	15.2	606
26.52	110	15.34	246
27.45–46	474	16	620
27.46	751	16.5	393
27.51	552		
28.18	601	**Luke**	
28.19	394	Book	119
		1.30	641
Mark		1.52	482
1	394	2.1–13	120
1.4	633	2.32	122
1.14	243	3	394
1.15	633	4.18	122
1.21–3.6	634	4.18–19	552
2.1–12	60, 633, 701	5.8	810
2.10	634	5.17–26	61
3.1–6	117	5.27–32	482
3.15	252	6.45	710
3.22–4.34	634	7.36–50	482
3.27	162	9.22	112, 163, 361
4.35–41	634	9.23	736
5.1–42	634	9.58	453
6.30–52	634	11.37–54	482
6.53–56	634	12.1	710
7.1–23	634	12.50	394
7.24–37	634	13.21	710

13.29	482	1.29	124, 132, 222, 455, 517, 518, 520
14.15	482		
15	494	1.36	124, 132, 520
15.11–32	476, 482	2	734
16.1–8	169	2.2	125
16.19–31	259	2.19	88, 517
18.13	581	2.21	520
18.31–33	362	2.53–54	515
19	495	3.3	518
19.1–10	482, 716	3.5	393, 518
22.16	483	3.6	516
22.18	482, 483	3.14–15	124
22.19	482	3.16	124, 693
22.19–20	117, 121, 361, 481	3.16–17	123, 645
22.24–27	363	3.17	769
22.24–30	361	3.19–20	516
22.39–46	112	3.22	394
22.41–42	112	3.34	85
23.2	122	4.1–2	394
23.5	122	4.1–42	518
23.9	123	4.9	229
23.14	122	4.14	152
23.24	701	4.24	516
23.34	113	5.1–15	518
23.35	123	5.24	475, 516, 518, 519, 553
23.43	475	5.26	87, 219, 516
23.47	123	5.37	645
24.7	163	5.46	572
24.10	243	6	124
24.26	122, 572	6.4	482
24.49	645	6.11	219
		6.27–59	482
John		6.50–51	52
1	394	6.51	219, 518
1.1–18	516, 517	6.51–56	520
1.3	7, 515	6.56	483
1.4	516	6.57	516
1.5	516, 517, 518	6.63	516
1.10	518, 646	7.27	91
1.11	515, 518	7.37	224
1.12	519	7.39	152
1.13	217	8.1–11	598
1.14	35, 219, 242, 516, 517, 518, 520, 785	8.12	516
		8.16	645
1.16	203	8.21	517, 518
1.16–18	808	8.24	518
1.17	199, 518	8.28	124
1.17–18	516	8.29	47
1.18	43, 519	8.32	518
1.19–34	517	8.34	518, 552

9	124	19.30	52, 574
9.5	516	19.31	520
9.1–41	518	19.31–37	124
10.11	518, 520, 583	19.33–36	520
10.11–18	124	19.35	124
10.15	583	19.36	517
10.16	519	20.22	84, 90
10.17–18	52	20.19–23	84
10.18	192, 519		
11.25	65	**Acts**	
11.25–26	516	1.4	88
11.42	91	2	90, 120
11.50–52	519, 520	2.22–36	362
12.4	520	2.23	52, 112, 571
12.27	228	2.33	4
12.31	162, 516, 518, 552	2.42	482
12.32–33	124	2.46	482
12.33	124	3.13–14	123
12.35	516	3.14–15	45
13.10	520	3.18	112
13.31–32	458–459	4.38	394
14.1–11	124	5.29–31	362
14.6	67, 516	5.31	120
14.9	645	7.60	113
14.18	86	8.32–33	123, 363
14.26	645	9.2	734
15.13	583	9.4	384
15.26	89, 91	9.18	163
16.7	645	10.43	120
16.9	518	12.4	243
16.13	516	13.26–37	362
16.14	89, 90	13.38–39	363
16.17	645	15	582
17	66, 702	17.30	3
17.3	516, 519	17.32	61
17.6	31	20.28	52, 121, 122, 362, 363
17.13	92	21.1	243
17.15	710	21.11	243
17.19	520	24.14	734
17.21	150	26.18	711
17.26	82, 85, 88, 519	26.25	61
18.28	124, 517	26.52	113
18.32	124	27.35	482
19	615	28.17	243
19.5	574		
19.14	124, 520	**Romans**	
19.15	48	[book]	200
19.16–19	458	1.4	41, 151
19.17	124	1.5	230
19.29	124, 520	1.16–17	126, 200

1.17–3.26	204	6.4	483
1.18	127, 490, 652	6.6	552, 711
1.18–23	127	6.9	785
1.18–32	3, 750	6.16	277
1.18–3.20	127, 128, 204	6.23	782
1.24	243	7.18	710
1.24–28	767	7.19	710
1.26	243	7.22	711
1.28	243	7.25	711
2.4	625	8	85, 216
2.5	127, 490	8.3	46, 49, 52, 128, 199
2.8	490	8.3–4	785
3	128	8.6–7	750
3.5	127	8.9	79, 87, 219
3.21	127	8.9–11	93, 736
3.21–23	127	8.11	152, 711
3.21–26	126, 128, 197, 204, 204–211 216	8.12	475
		8.14–17	66
		8.18	559
3.21–31	204, 671–672	8.18–25	475, 477
3.21–4.25	126	8.19–22	3, 109
3.22	578	8.22	3
3.23	128, 317	8.29	66
3.24–25	304, 589	8.31	652
3.24–26	375	8.32	52, 64, 130, 244, 667
3.25–26	52	8.33–34	474
3.25	127, 128, 216, 417, 489, 491, 581, 751, 809	8.34	701
		8.38–39	475
3.26	125	9–11	734
4	574	10.3	179
4.15	490	10.6–7	264
4.25	52, 441, 474, 614, 615, 616	10.9–13	362
		11.15	130
5.1	195, 736	12.1	216
5.1–11	134	12.9	712
5.1–12	204	12.19	111
5.5	647	12.21	708, 712
5.6	318	14.7	608
5.6–11	714	14.8–9	264
5.8–10	609, 808	15.8	204
5.9	128, 490	15.26	216
5.10	667	16.16	130
5.10–11	130, 782	16.20	476
5.12	3		
5.12–21	49, 433, 615	**1 Corinthians**	
5.14	572	[book]	336
5.17	219	1	803, 804
5.19	179, 573, 667	1.2	735
6	615	1.10–11	674
6.3	393	1.18	51, 461

1.18–31	801, 802	3.17	85, 92
1.21	56, 803, 804	3.18	572, 736
1.23	51	4.7–11	712
1.23–24	336, 801	5	462
1.24	56, 803	5.4	573
1.27–28	336	5.5	711
1.30	735, 782, 801	5.6	37
2.2	400	5.7	552
2.8	458	5.10	110
2.11–12	151	5.14	129, 752
3.16	553	5.14–21	765
3.16–17	152, 674	5.14–6.2	129
5.1–13	128	5.15	129
5.5	280	5.16–17	129
5.6	710	5.17	134, 711, 736, 781
5.7	128, 130, 132, 483	5.18	795
5.19	21	5.18–21	130, 667, 782
6.11	151	5.19	40, 128, 134, 229, 808
6.19	734	5.19–21	797
6.20	121	5.20	129, 778
7.11	130	5.21	46, 128, 223, 454, 461,
7.23	121		552, 652, 719, 751
10.11	476	6.1–2	129
10.16	112	6.11–13	129
10.16–17	483	7.2	129
11	328	8.9	385
11.17–34	118, 674–675	11.25	552
11.23–25	117, 481	12.2	163
11.24–25	362		
11.25	483	**Galatians**	
11.26	476, 483, 669	[book]	196
12	735	1.4	52, 216, 476
15	377, 619, 788	2.12	670
15.3	51, 52, 751	2.15–21	669–671
15.3–4	483	2.20	52, 244, 652, 711, 768
15.3–5	362	2.21	199
15.14–15	63	3.10–14	129
15.20	130, 553	3.11	129
15.23	130	3.13	51, 129, 461, 552, 587,
15.42–46	711		652, 719, 751
15.42–50	54	3.14	129
15.43	553	3.26–29	129, 130
15.45	433, 572	3.27	475
15.53–54	573	4.1–7	553
15.54–57	474	4.4	43, 44, 86, 552, 617
15.56–57	619	4.4–6	645
		4.5	216, 573
2 Corinthians		4.6	79
Book	462	5	737
1.22	711	5.1	735

5.9	710	2.5–8	578
5.19–21	737, 782	2.5–11	113, 578
5.22	553	2.6–11	158
5.22–23	737	2.8	44, 220, 243, 797
5.24	782	2.7–8	41
6.2	737	2.8	667
6.7–8	110	2.8–11	578, 788
6.14	400	2.12–13	736
		3.21	553

Ephesians

Book	442, 444	**Colossians**	
1	216	Book	442, 444
1.3–6	7	1	441
1.5	215	1.10	441
1.7	128, 158	1.12–13	711
1.10	49, 53, 109, 162, 788	1.15	160
1.13–14	7	1.15–20	109, 133, 158
1.14	121	1.16	3, 53
1.19–23	672	1.16–17	7
1.22	368	1.16–20	2
2	461, 465	1.17	44
2.2	162	1.18	769
2.5	318	1.18–20	197, 201–204, 474
2.6	37, 483, 553	1.19	53, 219
2.8–10	734	1.19–20	365, 367, 752, 788
2.11–22	672–674	1.20	42, 52, 128, 130, 366, 441 444
2.13	52, 128		
2.14–18	130, 477		
2.14	36	1.20–22	782
2.15	552	1.22	52, 130, 474
2.16	130, 782	1.23	474
2.18	552	1.24	691
2.18–22	785	2.8–11	578
3.9	43	2.9	44
3.12	552	2.9–3.4	784
3.16	711	2.10	368
3.18–19	163, 164	2.11	552
4.4	559	2.11–15	711
4.7–10	264	2.12	37
4.13–15	736	2.13	318
5.2	52	2.13–15	474
5.25	52	2.14	552
5.25–27	785	2.14–15	158
6.10–18	785	2.15	216, 552, 620, 708, 711
6.12	3	3.1	37
6.16	710	3.3	711
		3.6	553
Philippians		3.10	559
2	494, 652	3.11	716

1 Thessalonians

1.10	553, 782
2.16	807
5.9	782
5.10	52

2 Thessalonians

1.8–10	475
3.2	710

1 Timothy

[book]	200
1.15	477, 749
2.4	693
3.16	35, 158
2.3–6	578
2.5	36
2.6	52, 363, 552
4.10	693
6.12	712

2 Timothy

1.10	35, 553
2.5	213
2.11–13	158
2.13	185
5–6	166

Titus

2.14	363, 552
3.4–7	151
3.5	152

Philemon

book	130
2.9–11	264

Hebrews

book	112, 130, 133, 254, 379, 400
1.2	476
1.2–3	43
1.3	87, 533
2.9	41, 474
2.9–10	158
2.10	3, 475
2.11	44, 45, 534
2.14	476, 552, 711
2.14–15	131, 553
2.14–18	158
2.16	365
2.17	489, 490, 491, 533, 534, 581
3.2	48
3.37	100
4.12	811
4.14	533
4.15	17, 44, 46, 534, 740
5.1	533
5.1–10	158
5.5	221
5.7	44, 48
5.7–10	47, 667
5.8	221
5.8–10	534
5.9	754
6.4	151
6.4–8	272
6.19–20	533
7	107, 108
7.23–24	434
7.25	37, 219
7.26–27	46
7.27	534
8.1–5	533, 534
8.3	373
8.3	533, 534
9.1–28	158
9.5	490, 581
9.9	534
9.11–12	533
9.11–14	434, 534
9.11–15	552
9.12	533, 809
9.12–14	534
9.13–14	101
9.14	49, 534, 702
9.15	434, 533, 553
9.19–21	131
9.22	106, 107, 403, 404, 495, 534
9.22–23	534
9.24	37, 533, 534
9.25	534
9.25–28	131
9.26	534
10.1–2	534
10.2	533, 534

10.4	102, 534	1.18	132
10.5–10	47	1.19	49, 132
10.10	52, 131, 534	1.18–19	52, 132, 619
10.11	534	1.18–21	685
10.12	131	1.20	685
10.14	131, 534	1.22	686
10.15–22	434	2.1	686
10.18	534	2.4–9	785
10.19	552	2.5	8
10.26–29	272	2.9	267, 464, 711
10.29	534	2.9–10	121
11–12	533	2.11–4.2	686
11–14	534	2.12	132
12.1–4	158	2.13	685
12.5–6	804	2.15	132
12.24	534	2.19–20	132
13.12	534	2.20	132
17.11–13	105	2.21	686
18	108	2.21–25	132, 579
19	107	2.22–23	133
		2.23	685
James		2.23–24	113
1.1	577	2.24	52, 132, 214, 686, 751
1.12	578, 579	2.25	133
1.13–15	579	3.1–2	132
1.25	578	3.16–17	132
1.27	578	3.17–4.2	686
1.27–2.17	578	3.18	52, 132, 207, 640, 686, 751
2.1	577, 578, 579		
2.1–5	716	3.18–20	264
2.2–13	578	3.18–22	132
2.8	578	3.18–4.6	260, 267
2.12	578	3.19	265, 266, 267
2.12–13	578	3.19–21	266
2.19	579	3.22	686
2.22	579	3.25	207
2.23	579	4.1	132, 459
2.24	579	4.1–2	132, 686
3.17	809	4.5	685
		4.5–6	264
1 Peter		4.6	265, 267
book	130, 260, 265, 268, 271	4.8	266, 598
1.2	132, 685	4.12–19	132
1.3	66, 685	4.13–14	132
1.4	553	4.13–16	132
1.11	132	4.19	685, 686
1.12	365	5.1	132
1.13–21	734	5.8	169
1.17	685	5.10	132

2 Peter

Book	265
1.4	50, 66, 152, 687
1.8–11	687
1.12–21	687
1.21	687
2.1	121
3.1	687
3.1–2	687
3.7–13	687
3.8–9	476
3.9	476
3.10	685
3.13	477
3.14	54

1 John

Book	491, 581, 582
1.1–2	44
1.1–4	579
1.5–2.2	125
1.5–2.3	579
1.6–7	516
1.6–2.2	582
1.7	52
1.8	516
2.1	582
2.1–2	491
2.2	441, 469, 489, 491, 552, 581, 582, 693, 751
2.4	516
2.4–6	579
2.13	710
2.19	582
3.2	56
3.5	46
3.8	476, 552, 711
3.10	710
3.12	709, 710
3.16	583
3.19	516
4.2	44
4.8	491
4.9–10	581, 582, 583
4.10	489, 491, 581
4.11	583
4.13	152
4.17–18	582
5	491

5.6–8	125
5.11	553
5.19	710

2 John

7	44

3 John

11	712

Jude

17–23	579

Revelation

1.6	464
3.11	367
5	125, 366, 572
5.5	721
5.6	53, 517
5.9	52
5.9–10	721
5.12	2
5.13	722
5.14	572
7	719
7.10	722
7.14	404, 466
10.4	102
11.8	721
12.9	720
12.10	720
13.8	56, 572
13.13	721
15–16	792
18.2	720
19	473
19–20	792
19.15	811
20.10	720
21	720, 734
21–22	473, 475
21.1–5	432, 475, 722, 736
22	473

Tobit

13.2	263

Wisdom of Solomon

7.22–8.1	803

16.13	263	6.29	104
		17.21–22	104
2 Maccabees		18.4	104
7	282		
7.38	104	**1 Enoch**	
		Book	265, 266, 267
4 Maccabees		22.7	260
1.11	104	22.9	260

Subject Index

abandon 617, 653–4
　abandonment 751
　self-abandonment 665
Abelardian 597, 599, 610, 613, 642
Abraham 404
abusive 176, 335, 346–9, 792, 794–5
　child abuse 302, 339, 764
accommodation 222, 551
adoption 457
advocate 491, 760
aesthetics 54
affiliation 784
agape 772
alienation 677–8
allegiance 277
Amyraldian 698
analogy 564, 617
anamnesis 482
ancestor 512
angels 1, 7, 161, 177, 365–9, 434, 686, 744
　angelic 162–3, 173, 719
　non-angelic 196
anger 489, 577, 582, 619, 642, 682, 716, 750, 760, 791, 810
anglican communion 437
animal 7, 53, 108–9, 379, 419, 441–3, 682
annihilationism 787
Anselmian 597, 610, 613–14, 720
anthropology 507, 739, 789
　theological anthropology 507
anthropomorphism 775
anthropopathic 564
apocalyptic 258–62, 280–2, 286, 394, 461
apokatastasis 789
Apostolic Fathers 547
Aristotelian 593, 640, 663
Arminian 589, 659, 661, 787, 798
　Arminianism 524, 541, 662, 698
　Arminius 693, 694
art 15
Articles of Religion 324, 331

ascension 4, 7, 13, 35, 62–3, 74, 120, 225, 400, 434, 475, 529, 535, 560, 567, 614–15, 665, 668, 680, 686, 691, 702, 750, 777
aseity 20, 34, 82
assumption 223
　assumed 429
　son assuming fallen nature 425
atonement
　at-one-ment 4, 35
　day of 125, 131, 252, 765
　ethical 687
　extent of 5, 422, 582–3, 659, 694, 777
　governmental theory 524
　images of 158
　limited 298, 469, 662
　magical view of 741
　models of 133, 217, 316, 324–9, 776, 784
　physical theories of 809
　theories of 5, 8–10, 158, 214, 217, 305, 310, 317, 329–30, 447, 451, 474, 493–4, 509, 510, 560, 561, 603, 685, 689, 690, 722, 724, 784, 791
　universal 469
authority 285
Azazel 374, 683

Babylonian Talmud 373, 374
baptism 226, 266, 393–7, 479, 547–9, 633, 711, 715, 736
　spirit baptism 396
bearing 413–14, 458
　of the curse 552
　one another's burdens 737
　sins 419, 597, 617, 793, 794, 795
beatific vision 269
beauty 184, 382–3, 451, 468
behavior
　atoning 495
benevolent 344, 798
Bhagavad-Gita 732

birth of Jesus, as atoning 760
blessedness 741
blood 101, 106–7, 111, 117, 121, 132, 231, 306, 359, 372, 383, 401, 403–5, 417, 418, 427, 439, 441, 461, 466, 469, 474, 480–1, 495, 512–13, 533, 548, 552, 578, 582, 609, 618, 626, 633, 635, 672, 679, 682–3, 685, 719, 720, 721, 751–2, 765, 810
    Of God 547
Book of Common Prayer 439, 463, 797
border 468
bore 686
    bore our sins 751
bride 471
bridegroom 427, 657

calvinists 589, 787
Cambridge Platonists 789
canon 316, 371, 473
    canonical 475, 578, 626, 632
    canons of Dort 660
Cappadocian Fathers 155, 157, 159, 395
Catechism of the Catholic Church 316, 368
causes
    four causes 407–10
    primary and secondary causality 809
Celestial City 184
Chalcedon 44, 49, 226, 447, 493, 615, 722, 731–2, 794
    Chalcedonian Definition 448
    Chalcedonian Statement 494
changeability 775
Christ
    Christocentric actualism 464
    earthly ministry 177
    person and work of 36, 39, 176
    Remoto Christi 177
    union with 62, 297–9, 781–6
Christa 336, 350–2
Christology 20, 36, 90, 91
    two natures Christology 703
Christus victor 2, 16, 196, 254, 278, 319, 330, 359, 389, 452, 476, 507, 509, 560, 601, 615, 618, 721, 784
Church 121, 529, 531, 569, 656, 666, 672, 674, 685, 690, 715, 719, 721, 734, 769, 795
cleansing 158, 373, 375, 404, 686, 687, 701

cleansed 611, 765
cleanses 682
communication 741
communion 157–8
community 579, 608
compassion 462, 598, 708
    compassionate 413
compulsion 755
conceptual scheme 217
condescension 41, 244
confession 421, 423–4, 426, 701, 715
confirmation 366
consecrated 733
consequentalist 524, 525
constantine 735
contextualization 509
contrition 179
cosmos 3, 50, 53, 84, 95–6, 109, 112, 116, 134, 158, 161, 163, 164, 166, 172, 173, 190, 258, 281, 391–2, 403, 418, 441, 444, 452, 461, 486, 487, 515–17, 608, 639, 672–3, 675, 685, 687, 720, 722, 739, 744, 782, 802, 804
    cosmic cross 163, 164, 165
Council
    Council of 553, 789
    Council of Nicea 722
    Council of Trent 464, 585
    Fourth Lateran Council of 1215 611
Covenant 6, 13, 43–4, 50, 51, 96, 112, 117–18, 121, 125–6, 128, 131, 158, 177, 190, 237, 238, 248, 251, 253, 273, 297, 354, 361, 372–3, 375, 396, 412, 431–5, 442, 467, 483, 511, 520, 552, 578, 635, 648, 662, 673, 679, 680–2, 689, 690, 701, 711, 725, 726, 733, 766, 772, 777, 783
creation 6, 14, 21, 25–7, 53, 73, 86, 89, 95–6, 106, 110, 111, 112, 113, 129, 134–6, 150, 160, 185, 214, 248, 283, 296, 297, 307, 368, 373, 410, 431, 441–5, 461, 473, 475, 477, 486, 499, 510–11, 516, 520, 528, 529, 530–1, 557–60, 569, 572, 608, 620, 640–2, 651, 653, 665, 668–9, 671, 672–5, 678, 687, 701, 708, 711, 720, 722, 724, 736, 739, 750, 760, 763, 766, 769, 770, 772, 788, 795, 802, 804, 809
created 365

creator 515, 685
  doctrine of 184
  new 83
creature 677, 775
Creed 316, 447-9
  Apostles' Creed 475, 618-19, 707
  Athanasian Creed 448
  Chalcedon 493, 494
  Constantinople 493
  Nicene Creed 448, 493
criminology 309
cross 4
  cosmic cross 163-5
cry of dereliction 635, 652, 776
culture 182, 308-11, 419, 451-6, 531, 777-8
cup 635
curse 51, 459, 587, 709, 740, 751
Cyril of Alexandria 269

Dame Folly 802
D-Day 476
death 142
debt 206-7, 288, 289, 291, 401, 403, 408, 429, 455, 469, 540, 703, 745
  is finite 745
  is infinite 745
deceit 166, 169, 170-1
  deception 400
  deceived 724
defilement 680-2, 784
deification 145-6, 149-50, 156, 159, 172, 228, 378, 381, 385, 457, 458, 553, 716
  deifying incarnationalism 157
Deism 62, 527
demons 7, 136, 161, 163, 167, 579, 641, 701
  demonic forces 277-93
descent 156
  into hell 14, 52, 223, 257-75, 359
  into the underworld 400
desecrates 682
devil 131, 144, 158, 171, 190-1, 268, 277-93, 409, 427, 462, 476, 495, 502, 512, 533, 537, 552, 570-4, 588, 601, 609, 610-11, 614, 618, 620-1, 710-11, 724, 760, 761, 784
  antagonist 160
  Deceiver of the Race 161
  Prince of this world 162, 552

Satan 162, 166, 168-9, 231, 243, 277-93, 359, 362, 381, 400-1, 408, 452, 470, 471, 486, 505, 506, 507, 513, 617, 619-20, 655, 657, 673, 708, 719-20, 724, 760
diastasis 29
dignity 407
dilemma 39, 139
displacement 288
  of the devil 287
divine
  action 418
  attributes 3, 6-8, 14, 21, 31, 32, 558, 560, 565, 567, 725, 789
  character 772
  divine immutability 565
  divine impassibility 563-8
  election 6
  governance 203
  image 538
  justice 186-7, 332
  origins 6
  pardon 187
  perfections 42
  power 681
  simplicity 327, 565, 776
  sorrow 566
  transcendence 565
  violence 5, 15, 38
divinization 13, 150, 165, 172, 386
docetic 528, 547
  docetism 649
doctor 427
doctrine 320-4, 330-2
  of God 1-3, 19, 21, 38, 42, 86, 133, 217, 239, 243, 344, 494, 524, 561, 666, 724, 725, 733, 739
dogmatics
  post-Reformation 693-9
dominicans 735
donatists 283, 384, 395
dualism 63, 720
duel 694, 697
dythelitism 227, 228

Easter 63, 75
Ebionite fallacy 541
ecclesiology 14, 461-6
economy 20, 33, 87

economic 697
economic oppression 509
ecumenists 465
Egypt 480
election 3, 43, 56, 87, 239, 240ff., 244, 298, 367, 475, 530, 648, 649, 697, 766
  elect 385, 422, 475, 660, 694, 695, 696, 745, 784
enanthropesis 156
encomiastic preaching 158
enhypostasia 48
enhypostatic 647
enlightenment 2, 9, 159, 344, 357, 359, 401, 470, 527, 528, 698, 729
envy 284
epistemology 802
eschatology 139, 145, 272, 418, 419, 469, 473–7, 483, 528, 530, 531, 539, 578, 608, 651, 665, 720, 767, 770, 783, 787, 789
  cosmic 473
  individual 473
estrangement 443, 665, 784
eternal
  life 758
  processions 776
  punishment 798
eternal processions 22
ethnic 672
  ethnicities 669–71, 673
ethics 54, 510, 583, 713
  ethical 714, 734, 736
Eucharist 226, 378, 403, 418, 439, 463, 465, 477, 479–84, 547–9, 574, 712, 715
eudaimonia 716
evil 137, 593, 707–12, 742, 763, 792
  evil powers 390, 391
  problem of 707–12
evolution 111
exaltation 534
example 158, 218, 277, 400, 655, 720, 758, 797
exchange 128, 158, 178, 258, 284, 372, 385, 463, 494, 615, 617, 686, 719, 724, 725, 755
  blessed exchange 254
exclusivism 730
expiatory 112, 128, 578
  expiation 216, 218, 231, 375, 417, 419, 489–92, 502, 581, 605, 657, 665, 798, 799

exemplar 190
exemplarism 357, 421, 484–8, 579, 592, 613, 686
exemplarist 2, 12, 439, 463, 691, 703, 714
exemplary 372
  moral 196, 313, 602
exemplifies 132
exile 96, 474, 626
existential 750
  existential framework 639–40
ex nihilo 640–2
Exodus 118, 124, 132, 633, 777, 792
exorcism 119

factions 674
faithful 577, 685, 689, 726, 733
  faithfulness 83, 126, 128, 131–2, 433, 531, 578, 608, 668, 670, 672, 737, 758, 766
  faithfully 557
faith seeking understanding 1
fall 54
  fallen humanity 156
fear 509
feeling of absolute dependence 740
felix culpa 54
fellowship 482, 560, 582, 629, 670
feminist 14, 186, 254, 335–54, 764
  theology 232–4
feudalism 182
filiation 647
Filioque 79
firstborn 679
fitness 140
fitting 39, 42, 177, 186, 205, 207, 208, 210, 217, 280, 285, 428, 558, 609, 776, 809
force 277
foreknowledge 695, 744
  foreknows 685
foreordination 726
forensic 60, 109, 243, 244, 253, 438, 586, 592, 750, 766
forgiveness 186, 201, 262, 296, 307, 314, 395, 411–14, 417, 418, 431, 438, 480–1, 493–7, 501, 523, 554, 589, 598, 600, 626, 627, 628, 629, 633, 634, 635, 636, 647, 689, 691, 694, 712, 717, 724, 726, 755, 756, 770, 785, 788, 799
  forgave 545

forgiven 597, 701
forgiving 772
Formula Consensus Helvetica 698
forsaken 599, 751
foundation of the world 42
Franciscans 735
    Franciscan Thesis 743–4
free 571, 573, 587, 610, 649, 661, 709
    freedom 137, 232, 275, 284–5, 470, 518, 538, 539, 593, 716, 736, 737, 749, 790, 808
    free will 409
    voluntarily 401
fury 222, 228

genocide 678
German idealism 254
Gethsemane 470
gift 667, 708, 713
glory 31, 578, 617, 744, 802
    glorification 353, 553, 736
    glorified 558
Gnosticism 475
god
    abandonment by 274, 809
    anger 422, 433
    apathetic 707
    as moral agent 743
    as ruler 523
    attributes of 238, 588, 724, 755
    blood of 547
    character of 770, 771–2, 775, 807
    dignity of 183
    division of 652
    doctrine of 1–3, 19, 21, 38, 42, 86, 133, 217, 239, 243, 344, 494, 524, 561, 666, 724, 725, 733, 739
    essence of 662
    god-consciousness 741
    god forsakenness 273, 474, 652, 653, 654, 751
    god's death 642
    god's own character 627
    good pleasure of 697
    holiness of 737
    image of 136, 137, 142, 145, 150, 153
    is pure act 196
    kingdom of 432, 479, 481, 601–4, 606, 726
    knowledge of 67–71
    lamb of 274, 401
    living God 807
    nature of 755
    power of 438
    self-realization of 499
    stasis within 652
    suffering 707
    union of 205
    voluntary self-humiliation 500
    will of 662
Golgatha 252, 701
Goliath 471
Good Friday 239
Gospel of John 515–21
governmental 299
    governmentalism 468
    theory of the atonement 524, 799
grace 185, 189, 199, 214, 407, 457, 485, 501, 518, 579, 585, 594, 613, 615, 627, 686, 697, 740, 749, 752, 766, 767, 778, 782, 787, 804
    gracious 510, 731, 772
grammar 448, 461, 545
guilt 3, 221, 223, 301, 313, 374, 378, 395, 414, 425, 455, 467, 481, 509, 511, 513, 524, 540, 594, 598, 610, 626, 627, 665, 719–20, 750, 763, 767, 781–2, 784, 810

habit 750
harmony 682, 713
headship 368, 409
healing 373, 383, 455, 513, 673, 686, 689, 701, 712, 722, 734, 750–1, 781
heavenly powers 3
Hebrews 533–5
Hegelian 28
Heilsgeschichte 473
hell 225, 257–75, 455, 473, 474, 525, 594, 619–20, 750, 760
    descent into 14, 52, 223, 257–75, 359
    Hades 257–75, 371
    Sheol 257–75
Heresy 1, 447
Hermeneutics 418, 419
    Hermeneutical 626
Hilasmos 491, 581
Hilastērion 489, 490, 491, 581
Hinduism 731
History 17, 39–40, 58, 82–3, 250, 667
    Historicism 30

Holocaust 791
Holy 249, 250, 528, 679, 733, 763
   Holiness 153, 239, 367, 423, 468, 499, 501–2, 559, 689, 704, 725, 737, 755, 764, 777–8, 798
   Holiness of God 737
   Holy God 733
   Holy of Holies 533–5
   Holy Saturday 54
   Unholy 733
   Holy Spirit 14, 36, 48–9, 56–7, 59, 60, 62–3, 67–8, 77–93, 116, 120, 129, 135, 149, 151–4, 155, 226, 229, 252–3, 264, 272, 296, 300, 367, 368, 377, 385, 395, 409, 423, 434, 457, 461, 470, 500, 516, 517, 527, 529–31, 537, 539, 553, 559–60, 572, 573, 574, 579, 586, 599, 601, 614, 616, 621, 645, 646, 652, 653, 654, 665, 666–8, 673, 675, 691, 696, 698, 702, 711, 714–15, 734, 736, 737, 750–1, 781–2, 785, 790, 793, 795
   Spirit baptism 396
honor 176, 177, 182ff, 291, 307, 343, 403, 452, 486, 495, 512, 554, 703, 723, 725, 726, 745, 776, 782
   dishonor 745
hope 354, 603, 653, 678
hospitality 29, 120, 715
human responsiveness 488
humiliation 80, 140, 379, 415, 424, 467, 520, 534, 554, 721, 770
   self-humiliation 751
humility 40, 373, 383, 408, 412, 690

identification 102, 381–3, 459, 654, 720, 765, 783
image 213, 313, 401, 427, 429, 451, 511, 552, 553, 619, 687, 749, 777, 778
   Bearer 549
   Cup imagery 481
   Divine image 538
   Imago dei 557–61
   Patterns 130, 132
imagination 551–5, 586, 614, 742
   imagining 639
imitation 548
immanent 697
immortal 161
   immortality 548, 559, 570, 571, 573

immutability 65, 327
   divine immutability 565
impassibility 28, 247, 346, 410, 458, 459, 500, 653, 776
   divine impassibility 563–8
impeccability 48
imputation 60–1, 201, 222, 312, 392, 438, 468, 470, 594, 792–3
incarnation 37–8, 45, 55–6, 67, 143
   incarnation anyway 743
incorporation 382–5
   incorporated 475
incorruption 139–44, 152, 183, 374, 458, 559
   incorruptibility 557, 573
   incorruptibility of communion 571
indulgences 735
infinity 177, 469
in nihilo 640, 642
integrative imitation 395
intellectualism 662
intercession 87, 413, 701–2
   intercessor 414
interchange 129, 765
intersubjective 278
Irenaean 741
Islam 731

James, letter of 577–80
Jesus
   assumption of fallen human nature 423
   corporate identity of 784
   life history 690
John, letters of 581–3
Jonah
   sign of 570–2
joy 184
judge 546, 685, 687, 777
judgment 215, 227, 229, 231, 235, 244, 266, 413, 415, 424, 425, 473, 474, 527, 552, 582, 587, 598, 627, 629, 750–1, 767, 789, 809
   final judgment 685
judicial 248
jurisdiction 278
   juridical 435
just 374, 413, 744, 760, 792, 809
justice 28–9, 109, 111, 129, 133, 176, 296, 297, 299–300, 321, 412, 422, 428–9,

451, 455, 468, 474, 475, 487, 489, 496, 502, 512, 523, 524, 546, 588, 593, 598, 607–8, 639, 640, 662, 694, 723, 724–6, 755, 763, 791, 810
  criminal 303
  justified 579, 670, 734
  justify 588, 609, 642, 726
  original 205, 290
  restorative 764
justification 180, 207, 237, 358, 391, 392, 407–8, 418, 438, 439, 441, 470, 474, 528, 585–9, 592, 614, 616, 621, 639, 648, 657, 671, 689, 735, 755, 758

katabasis 269
kenosis 349, 385, 500, 566
kingdom 505, 506, 537, 618, 634–5, 656, 665, 687, 720–1, 725, 734, 810
kinsman redeemer 656, 678
kipper 682
knowledge 138, 214
Kōpēr 626
kpr 543
Krishna 732

Lamb 125, 132, 262, 379, 429, 455, 466, 480, 516, 517, 520, 572, 634, 686, 719, 720, 721
  Lamb of God 274, 401
  Passover lamb 784
  Sacrificial 451, 685
Last Supper 121, 404, 634, 635, 636
law 295, 297, 299, 307, 617, 619, 670, 671, 673, 734, 744
  civil 756
  criminal 756
  private and public law 524
  public law 524
legal 429, 432, 537, 639, 640, 723, 766
  Legal declaration 534
Letter of Barnabas 372
liberal arts 759
liberation 159, 234, 451–2, 487, 518, 531, 602, 615, 619, 678, 755, 777
  liberates 588
  liberating 686
  liberation theology 278, 510, 513, 605–8
  liberationist theologians 254, 293
  liberator 456

likeness 775
literature 17
liturgy 15, 554, 569, 701
Logos
  asarkos 55, 793
  incarnadus 55
Lord
  Lordship 567
  Lord's Prayer 495, 500, 711
  Lord's Supper 496, 539, 600, 669, 674, 675
love 42, 52, 56, 66, 76, 79, 85, 88, 138, 140, 196–7, 209–10, 218, 235, 238–9, 242, 244, 249–50, 273, 290, 293, 358, 374, 375, 400–1, 408–9, 412, 422, 424, 428, 429, 470, 487, 494, 502, 511, 528, 532, 538, 554, 566–7, 571–2, 577–8, 581, 582, 597–9, 606–7, 611, 614, 642, 647, 652, 654, 662, 668, 675, 686, 690–1, 696, 698, 704, 709, 716, 725–6, 732, 734, 737, 744, 749, 767, 770, 785, 787–8, 789, 791, 794, 808, 810
Luke 361
Lundensian school of theology 390
Lutheran World Federation 347
Lynch 620
  Lynching tree 455

majesty 647
Mark 641–37
marriage 617, 720
martyr 121, 403, 409, 487, 519, 539, 548, 721
  martyrdom 282, 361, 404, 465, 549, 574, 691, 720, 795
Matthew 631–7
mediator 131, 138, 215, 217, 219, 225, 226, 228, 246, 306, 316, 422, 432, 433, 434, 468, 523, 529, 530, 657, 683
  mediated 577
  mediates 552
  mediation 517, 527, 540, 541, 702
  mediating 701
  mediatorial 655
medicine 548
memorialism 483
Mercy 133, 186, 218, 238, 240, 249, 250, 296, 299, 358, 374, 375, 400, 413, 414,

428, 429, 439, 455, 494, 578, 620, 695, 712, 731, 749, 755, 760, 764
merit 367, 407–8, 439, 468, 611, 613, 618, 690, 731, 743, 744–5, 762
  condign 408
Messiah 1, 2, 3, 122, 125, 606, 607, 616, 657, 721
  Messianic 394, 577–9, 701, 719
metaphor 5, 37, 112, 130, 134, 285, 305, 307, 312–15, 317–20, 327–8, 330–2, 371, 393, 427, 428–9, 469, 499, 511–12, 527, 528, 531, 534, 548, 551–3, 558, 606, 617, 619, 629, 669, 675, 701, 724, 755, 760, 776, 777
metaphysics 247, 418, 470, 565, 586, 605
  metaphysical 563, 593, 607, 654, 776
mimetic
  cycle 506
  desire 505
ministry 639–44, 689
missions 645–9
  missiology 509
  missiological 511
model 176, 330–2, 381, 452, 567, 655
modernism 19
modern theology 27, 36
monastic 290, 735
  vow 290
monotheism 285, 320, 374, 411
  monotheistic 793
monothelites 228
moral 38, 277, 386, 500
  example 210, 313, 319, 613, 785
  exemplarism 196, 313, 331, 602
  influence 312, 421, 485, 487, 509, 579, 799
  instruction 158
  morality 591, 593, 760
  order 299
  theory 238, 409, 541
mortification 232, 234, 736
mother 192
motif 318–20, 330–2, 390, 463
Mount Sinai 679
Muhammad 731
mujerista 348
munus triplex 218, 221, 230, 306, 359, 546, 655–8, 750, 799, 801
mutability 653

mysticism xi
  mystical 427, 616, 617
myth 37, 70, 71, 258–62, 419, 486

Nazi 392
necessary 39, 42, 185–7ff, 248, 299, 361, 424, 523, 525, 540, 551, 610, 615, 809
  necessitarian 776
  necessitated 776
Nestorianism 228, 746
Nicene-Constantinopolitan Creed 78, 320, 321, 461
Noah 442, 792
nothingness 640–1, 643

obey 758
  obedient 686, 704, 752
  obedience 131, 214–15, 218, 220, 223, 227, 237, 243, 246, 251, 290, 401, 408, 412, 468, 500, 614–15, 648, 709, 710, 724–6, 751, 766, 804
objective 400, 407, 418, 485, 540, 541, 607, 614, 648, 704, 790
  transaction 704
  understanding 425
oblation 798
offering 760
Old Testament
  Wisdom books 801–5
omnibenevolence 707
omnicausality 738
omnipotence 327, 344, 501, 572, 573, 609–10, 707, 792
omnipresence 646
omniscience 707
ontology 136, 137, 156, 161, 170, 172, 173, 244, 245, 247, 248, 250, 253, 289, 432, 469, 475, 479, 499–500, 642, 766, 767, 783
  deontological 524
  personalist 157
opera ad extra 646
order 185
ordo salutis 736

pacifist 689
pactum salutis 297, 300
paideia 161, 162, 170, 172–3, 230
pantheistic 789

Paraclete 582
Partakers 152
participation 50, 62, 172, 196–7, 201, 206, 211, 230, 378, 395, 457, 480–1, 483, 529, 531, 548, 549, 579, 601, 604, 627, 639, 643, 670, 671, 685, 686, 687, 696, 702, 704, 715, 767, 772, 785
particularism 694, 695, 730
 particularists 698
passibility 775
passover 59, 124, 479, 481, 483, 517, 520, 552, 634, 657, 679, 682, 686
 passover lamb 784
pastoral 600
patience 476, 737
Paul, the Apostle 361–2, 669–75
peace 303, 720
pedagogic 167
Pelagian 395, 540
penal 208–9, 408, 421, 422, 501, 502, 614, 723, 798
 substitution 2, 16, 95, 97–106, 107, 214, 238, 240, 241, 247, 254, 295–314, 324, 389, 401, 439, 452, 461, 489, 511, 560, 627, 628, 648, 659, 720, 756, 757, 763, 766, 797, 799
penalty 127, 140–1, 207, 215, 277, 358, 433, 474, 491, 553, 577, 598, 709, 767, 799
penance 391, 611, 613
Pentateuch 543, 677–83
Pentecost 84, 86, 394, 400, 434, 621, 734
perichoresis 6, 19
 perichoretic 652, 654
personhood 298
Peter 359, 361–2, 394
philanthropy 775
philosophy 17
physical
 salvation 460
 theories of the atonement 569
Pietist 735
piety 230
placable 696
placated 760, 792
place-taking 628, 633–5
 exclusive 764–6
 inclusive 764, 766
platonic 641

platonism
 Christian 409
pluralism
 religious pluralism 729
pneumatology 20, 379, 528, 659, 691
poetry xi
 poetic 551, 554
politics 54, 689–92
 geopolitics 281
 political plane 281
 political power 243
 political theology 280–2
pollution 681
possibility 189
postmetaphysical 241
power 237, 278, 335–6, 458, 513, 617
 absolute 744
 absolute and ordained 743
 of God 438, 570
 powers 461
prayer 97, 118, 120, 150, 158, 184, 413, 448, 520, 545, 599, 643, 701–5
 Lord's Prayer 495, 500, 711
predestination 757
 predestined 744
preexistence 646
preexistent souls 789
premonstratensians 759
Priest 207, 423
 High Priest 377, 378, 379, 530, 533–4, 548, 701
 Priesthood 434, 545
 Priestly 464, 547
profane 733
promise 678, 681
prophecy 721
Prophet
 Major prophets 623–9
 Prophetic 456
propitiation 95, 97–106, 128, 206–7, 216, 218, 224, 304, 324, 375, 401, 411, 413, 418–19, 439, 475, 489–92, 499, 581, 582, 598, 657, 723, 798, 799, 808
protology 139–40, 145, 528, 529
prototype 592, 593, 594
providence 117, 269, 667
Psychically 454
psychosomatic 454
Ptharsia 156

punishment 176, 185–7, 201, 218, 221, 224, 231, 244, 249–50, 260, 280, 281, 289, 295, 299, 358, 359, 374, 401, 408, 458, 467–9, 474, 486, 491, 523, 525, 540, 582, 597, 610, 611, 613, 615, 739, 756, 760, 763, 766, 770, 772, 778, 792, 799
  penal 203
  punitive 424, 528, 598
  substitutionary 468
purgatory 613
  purgation 101
purity 719
  impurity 533, 626, 682
  purification 132, 159, 373, 394, 395, 533, 534, 627, 679–80, 682
  purified 506
  purifies 534, 552, 582
  purifying 680, 686

Qoholet 802

raised 558, 614
  from the dead 758
ransom 117–18, 166, 168, 262, 304, 318, 319, 361, 363, 374, 375, 427, 451, 462, 481, 495, 537, 540, 548, 552, 577, 587, 588, 634, 635, 636, 657, 660, 679, 680, 682, 686, 703, 721, 723, 777, 782
rationality 443
  rationalism 758
realism 784
recapitulation 3, 49, 196, 378, 433, 474, 530, 558, 569, 690
  Recapitilatio 409
reconciliation 64–6, 96, 129, 133, 159, 170, 203–4, 713–17
recreation 60
redemption 204–5
  conditional redemption 659
  universal redemption 659
reformed scholasticism 467
religious
  diversity 730
  religious pluralism 729
remission 756
remonstrant 693, 694
repentance 424
representation 44, 65, 112, 128, 129, 131, 133, 176, 177, 192, 216, 319, 352, 423, 452, 456, 479, 559, 560, 607, 626, 627, 702, 763–8, 777, 783
  representative 658, 677, 733
  representing 557
responsibility 140, 724, 731
resurrection 4, 6–8, 13, 35, 41, 54, 57–76, 84, 86, 116, 120, 123, 126, 129, 133, 141–4, 149, 153, 160, 207, 218, 225, 246, 252–3, 262, 277, 320, 343, 354, 357, 362, 364, 377–8, 400, 409–10, 418, 434, 439, 451, 464, 467, 470, 475, 485, 487, 494, 502, 506, 507, 509–10, 512, 519, 528, 529, 535, 547, 548, 552–3, 559–60, 565, 567, 574, 586, 602, 606–7, 609, 614–16, 618–19, 631, 634–5, 642, 651–2, 665, 668, 674–5, 686, 689, 690, 691, 711, 721, 724, 730, 731, 734, 750, 752, 764, 777, 781, 785, 788, 791, 795, 802, 810
retribution 278, 297, 309, 310, 689
  Retributive 435, 593
reunited 678
revelation 32–3, 71, 85, 160, 219, 240, 254, 367, 418, 448, 451, 502, 515, 569, 641, 668, 724, 725, 741, 751–2, 777, 785
  book of 719–22
  revealing 516
revelatory 758
revolution 278
rhetoric 159, 169, 170, 213, 216, 226, 230, 279, 372–3, 500, 549, 569, 737
righteous 127–8, 214–15, 226, 238–9, 244, 249, 252, 264, 296, 301, 312, 358, 375, 415, 424, 438, 439, 454, 461, 486, 494–5, 559, 586, 588, 594, 597, 602, 614–15, 617–21, 628, 671–2, 686, 709, 723–4, 751, 763, 765, 767, 771, 777, 782, 798, 802
  Unrighteousness 732
rights 401, 760, 761
rulership 525
risen 20

sacrament 403, 404, 479, 547, 711
sacred space 785
sacrifice 95, 97, 107, 113, 115, 125, 127, 128–9, 131, 133, 141–2, 149, 207–8, 213, 216, 218, 224, 231, 235, 304–6,

313, 315, 318, 343, 372, 373, 375, 379, 382, 401, 411–12, 417–19, 428–9, 431, 433, 439, 441, 454, 459, 462–3, 465, 466, 474, 479, 480, 481, 489, 490, 495, 501, 506, 512–13, 517, 520, 527, 528, 531, 533–5, 544, 545, 548, 552–3, 566, 567, 577, 582, 586, 589, 599, 606, 610, 626, 627, 631, 632, 633, 636, 648, 655, 662, 679, 682, 686, 690, 701, 713–14, 722, 725–6, 734, 745, 751, 763, 765, 777–8, 798, 808
- eternal sacrifice 454
- living sacrifice 462
- sacrificial lamb 451
- sacrificial system 13, 98–101, 720
- self-sacrifice 775, 795
- universal sacrifice 462

salvation
- by Christ alone 729–32
- by works 358
- of the devil 285–6

sanctification 133, 232, 235, 379, 499, 502, 534, 552, 586, 648, 679–80, 733–7, 782, 802
- as definitive 736

sanctuary 680, 681

satisfaction 2, 50, 65, 95, 106, 166, 170, 176–93, 195–7, 199, 208–10, 215–16, 224, 231, 237–41, 245, 249, 250, 254, 288, 290, 307, 318–19, 321, 324, 332, 391, 401, 407–8, 428, 439, 452, 464, 467, 468–9, 475, 500, 502, 509, 511, 523, 537, 540–1, 554, 560, 569, 597–8, 613–19, 648, 684, 689, 690, 695–8, 703, 723, 726, 743–4, 755, 756, 761, 767, 785, 798–9
- *Pro damno* 745
- *Pro iniuria* 744, 745
- satisfactory 770
- satisfied 694, 725
- satisfying 571, 593

scapegoat 103, 125, 131, 302–3, 373, 505–6, 524, 682–3, 714, 810

schema 656–7

science 54, 71, 74, 389, 419, 507
- scientific 803

scripture
- theological interpretation of 775–9

Second Adam 400, 401, 741
self
- abandonment 665
- emptying 243
- giving 66
- humiliation 246, 751
- offering 667
- realization of God 499
- revealing 20, 254
- sacrifice 775, 795

Semipelagianism 696
separation 794
- separationism 787
separation 432, 474
servant 657
severity 627
shalom 477, 588
shame 3, 164, 451, 509, 510, 512
simul Justus et peccator 755
sin 8, 20, 52, 749–52
- assumption of 85
- bearer 763, 794
- bearing of 401
- doctrine of 185
- incarnate Son as sinless 423
- original 47, 205, 206, 289, 358, 395, 468, 470, 610, 731, 757
- personal and collective 605
- sinless 46, 47

slavery 205–6, 277, 552, 672–3, 678, 711, 737, 782
- Slaves 711, 716, 777

social 278, 750
- social realities 674

Socinianism 470, 541
- Socinian 524, 662, 778, 798

sociology 17
solidarity 454, 652–3, 712
sovereign 714, 787
- sovereignty 177, 185, 297, 299, 485, 486, 488, 494, 523, 716

spirit 540–1
Stellvertretung 102, 628
subjective 540–1, 600, 607, 614, 648, 704, 790
subjugation 678
submission 1, 11, 65, 339, 425, 554, 731, 794
subordination 89

substitution 50, 65, 123, 129, 133, 168, 177, 192, 217, 218, 220–1, 224, 232, 258, 318, 451, 456, 459, 460, 474, 481, 501, 505, 519, 537, 540, 548, 598, 603, 616, 633, 654, 655, 679, 719, 739, 755–6, 763–8, 783, 797–9
   penal 2, 16, 95, 97–106, 107, 214, 238, 240, 241, 247, 254, 295–314, 324, 389, 401, 439, 452, 461, 489, 511, 560, 627, 628, 648, 659, 720, 756, 757, 763, 766, 797, 799
   radical 766
substitutionary punishment 468
suffer 28, 51, 59, 132, 147, 248, 254, 319, 339, 343, 347–8, 353, 373–4, 377, 394, 407, 422–4, 428, 451, 453, 458–60, 487, 547–9, 554, 563, 567, 592, 594, 606–7, 613–16, 618, 628, 634, 652–3, 686, 708, 712, 717, 720–1, 751, 772, 776, 778, 792, 795, 799, 804, 809
   cry of dereliction 51, 147, 246
   long-suffering 725
   substitute 341
   suffering God 707
   suffering Servant 122–3, 480, 627–9, 686
   unsuffering 548
sufficiency/efficacy 660, 662
   actually sufficient 660
   hypothetically sufficient 660
supra/infralapsarianism 769–73
surrogate 341–2
symbol 319, 322, 477, 479, 594, 607
sympathy 784
   sympathize 422
Synod of Dort 693, 694, 695, 698
systematic oppression 278

tabernacle 681, 733
temporality 775
temptation 220, 599
testimony 143
theism
   classical theism 563
theocentrism 500
theocracy 656–7
theodicy 280, 345, 502, 651
theo-logic 702
theological anthropology 251, 253
theopaschism 28

theory 170, 172, 315, 330–2, 418, 451, 537, 553–4, 586, 597, 601, 639, 773
   classical 389
   dialectical 418
   fish-hook 162–3, 165, 168–70, 172, 284–5
   governmental theory of the atonement 524, 799
   Latin 389
   moral influence 312, 421, 485, 487, 509, 579, 799
   penal theories atonement 501
   physical 458
   racial 799
   ransom 167, 277–93, 381, 724
   retribution 170
   subjective 389
   theoretical 696
   theorization 213
theologia crucis 474, 651, 722
theology
   global 509–13
   Wesleyan theologies 797–800
theopoetic 722
theōsis 13, 50, 385, 690, 716
theotokos 458
threefold office 50
timelessness 776
transaction 183, 248, 284, 741
transfer 183, 221, 358, 396, 592, 594, 713, 731, 763
   transference 36
   of guilt 297, 298
transfiguration 159, 690
transformation 382, 385–6, 553
translation 419
trickery 285
trinity 1–4, 6–7, 14, 17, 19–34, 41–2, 48, 52, 66, 77, 82–3, 85–6, 89, 93, 150, 153, 196, 214, 219, 225, 229, 241–2, 247, 273–4, 283, 299–302, 305, 312, 320–1, 323, 329, 359, 368, 408, 426, 448, 469, 475, 511, 519, 523, 527–32, 537, 560, 569, 607, 611, 645–6, 648–9, 652–5, 659–60, 661–3, 665–7, 691, 698, 711, 714, 735, 746, 751, 757, 764–5, 777, 791–4, 808
   economic 33, 89, 241, 666, 793
   immanent 89, 91, 241, 274, 666, 793

inner life of 82, 85
social Trinity 653
tri-theistic 793
tri-unity 31
trustworthy 685
truth 686
  Truth and Reconciliation Commissions 187, 716
tower of Siloam 615
TULIP 693
Tyndale Bible 493
typology 470

unbelief 661
unclean 734
union 141, 161, 553, 558-9, 689, 690
  consubstantial 66
  of God 205
  with God 557
  homoousion 145, 155
  hypostatic 66-7, 377, 378, 379
  unidication 677
  uniting 680
  unity 470, 672, 691
universalism 422, 787-90
  hypothetical 694-6, 698
  non-particularist 787
  particularist 787
  universalists 661
universality 800

Vatican II 465, 715, 730
vengeance 222
verdict 425
vicarious 49, 101-3, 112, 214, 223, 235, 277, 290, 299, 318, 359, 419, 481, 566, 567, 592, 594, 613-15, 618, 626-8, 701-2, 720, 756, 765, 795, 798-9
  vicarious humanity 331
  vicarious repentance 421
vice-regent 677
  priestly vice-regent 677
victim 338, 443, 454, 495, 506, 714
  victimhood 778
  victimization 340
victory 50, 158, 170, 213, 218, 235, 364, 458, 460, 474, 513, 527, 528, 553-4, 571, 577, 586, 601, 620, 686, 687, 711, 722, 749, 797
  victor 192, 225, 401, 666, 708
  victorious 516, 672
vindication 132, 721
violent 111, 117, 176, 233, 254, 277, 279, 284-5, 289, 296, 302-4, 335, 337, 346-7, 352-3, 404, 447, 494, 505, 546, 607, 678, 683, 689, 690, 691, 720, 721, 791-6, 811
  nonviolent 52, 287, 554, 764
  structural violence 454
virgin 140, 146
virtues 196, 201
Vishnu 732
vivification 736
vocation 726, 741
voluntarism 662, 724, 743, 745

Westminster Confession 321, 331, 698
whale 570
will
  alignment of 203
wisdom 184, 366, 367, 558, 570, 571, 574, 617, 665, 697, 794, 798
  Lady Wisdom 803
  Wisdom books 801-5
witness 721
World Health Organization 337
womanist 14, 254
  theology 232-4
  theologian 341
worship 1, 3, 11, 22, 30, 33, 38, 53, 99, 100, 102, 107, 116, 118, 182, 366, 382, 408, 437, 448, 531, 683, 689
wrath 98, 104-5, 127-8, 132, 218, 222-4, 231, 239-40, 249, 254, 358, 391, 401, 411, 413-14, 424, 439, 467, 470, 475, 486, 489, 490, 525, 553, 581-2, 588, 597-8, 609, 629, 635, 660, 682, 702, 725, 751, 755, 763, 766-7, 782, 791-2, 794, 797, 807-11

Yom Kippur 490, 523, 535, 617, 633
Young Women's Christian Association 348

www.ingramcontent.com/pod-product-compliance
Lightning Source LLC
Chambersburg PA
CBHW061946300426
44117CB00010B/1240